LEEDS UNITED

THE COMPLETE RECORD

LEEDS UNITED

THE COMPLETE RECORD

MARTIN JARRED MALCOLM MACDONALD

DB PUBLISHING

First published in Great Britain in 2012 by The Derby Books Publishing Company Limited, 3 The Parker Centre, Derby, DE21 4SZ.

ISBN 978-1-78091-031-4
Printed and bound by OzGraf, Poland.

Contents

Acknowledgements

IT IS impossible to put together a book of this nature without the help of other individuals and organisations. We want to publicly acknowledge their help.

Starting close to home, at Elland Road, Head of Media Paul Dews and Museum Curator Helen Castle have been crucial in making contacts and giving us access to previously unseen archive material.

Endless hours have been spent at many libraries, most notably Leeds City Library and the National Newspaper Library at Colindale, London. We are grateful to staff at both sites for their assistance.

The help of the *Yorkshire Evening Post*'s former Leeds United reporter Don Warters, who also had a stint as the club's media officer, has been invaluable.

Much of the original material was sourced at the old Football League headquarters where the archives were kept in a basement at Lytham St Annes. At the FA HQ, top man David Barber dealt with everything we asked of him.

Help from players, past and present, and their relatives, have included Jim Bullions, Tom Hindle, Bob Kane, Aubrey Powell, John Short, Jimmy Speirs, Bert Sproston, Willis Walker and George Wilson.

We are also indebted to Ross and Neil Pullan for information on former United chairman Ernest Pullan which had eluded us for months.

Dozens of statisticians and authors from other clubs have also helped to unravel a particular knotty problem. Among their number are Tim Carder, Denis Clareborough, Paul Clayton, Jim Creasy, Garth Dykes, Chris Elton, Terry Frost, Bob Goodwin, Barry J. Hugman, Mike Jay, Colin S. Jeffrey, Paul Joannou, Andrew Kirkham, Douglas Lamming, Gerald Mortimer, Gordon M. Readyhough, Roy Shoesmith, Dave Smith, Ray Spiller (who established the Association of Football Statisticians in 1978), Richard Sutcliffe, Keith Warsop, Joe Waters, Richard Wells, Alex Wilson and Trevor Clydesdale, whose help in pinpointing the correct Robert Montgomery who died in World War Two is much appreciated. There are bound to be others whose names have slipped through the net, to those, please accept our apologies.

Many pictures have been kindly obtained from the archives of *The Press*, York, and many of the photographs of the more recent era have been supplied by freelance Ian Harber, who has been firing away from the touchlines at Elland Road for many years for the *Morley Observer and Advertiser*.

Ian is a fan of the club, and other supporters like him have also played their part in helping produce this book, none more so than Mick Hewitt, well known for his pre-season tour organisational skills. He has a vast amount of Leeds United memorabilia and provided rare pre-war programme covers for this book and passed on statistical details for rechecking. To unearth Mick's Leeds United gems email him at HEWITTPROG@aol.com or visit his eBay shop.

Another Leeds fan, Terry Ruane, who works in the newspaper industry, volunteered to proofread for us – an offer we gladly accepted.

Finally, the hours we have put in compiling this book means we have not seen as much of our loved ones as we probably should have. It's one thing being a football widow on match days, but virtually every day for the last few months is beyond the call of duty. To our wives, Jenny Jarred and Isobel Macdonald, we salute your patience and understanding.

This book is dedicated to Gary Speed (1969–2011)

INTRODUCTION

IT IS 16 years since we last compiled *Leeds United A Complete Record*. In that period the club has been on a roller-coaster ride from the high of the memorable Champions League run to the low of relegation to the third tier of English football. What lies in store for the club in the future is anyone's guess.

Since the fourth edition of the *Complete Record* came out in 1996 there have been huge technological advances, both in research and production of books like these.

When we did the first *Complete Record* in 1986 the text was bashed out on a typewriter and the seasonal statistics were originally pen and ink on A4 paper. The next editions were done by using a word processor and this one on a laptop with the stats done on home computer spreadsheets.

Systems used by the publisher to store the information have also changed so compatibility issues meant that we have more or less started from scratch. We revisited the old material and did unearth the occasional error which have been rectified in this edition.

The advent of the internet has been an enormous aid to research, but the hard slog of ploughing through miles of microfilm and page after page of newspapers at libraries throughout the country remains the bread and butter approach for the researcher. Many hundreds of hours have been spent collating information, including checking through the Football League's own records.

Before 1925, the League kept no attendance records and before that date we have had to rely on those widely reported in newspapers of the time. It should be said that even different editions of the same newspaper could disagree on the number of people watching a particular game. The same applies to teams and scorers where goals were sometimes 'rushed through in a scrimmage'.

Wartime games sometimes proved difficult and for a handful of matches we have had to piece together United's team, although there has been no doubt over the actual 11 who turned out, simply that some educated guesswork has very occasionally been needed to identify their actual positions.

With the advent of players being allocated individual numbers, the numbering of the players has been continued in the familiar 1–11 format in order to give readers and future historians a concept of the starting 11 and substitutes, let alone positions played.

We are happy that what follows is as accurate as anyone is ever likely to get and the areas of doubt, both for Leeds United and Leeds City, are minute compared with the overall content of the book.

As we brought out *The Who's Who of Leeds United* only four years ago, we have opted not to carry a section in this book on every player to have appeared in first-class competitive football for each club. Instead, we have broadened the *Complete Record's* content with the inclusion of a section on players who died on active service in World

War One and Two, testimonial games, United in pre-season tournaments and a section on kits, badges and logos.

There is one other subtle change. Previous books were called *A Complete Record* – this is *The Complete Record*. We hope the content is worthy of the name.

Rather like being a Leeds United supporter, it has been a long hard slog at times. But we hope, like following Leeds, it is something rewarding and enjoyable. We hope you enjoy delving into the pages and recall all the club's peaks and troughs.

Happy reading.

Martin Jarred

Malcolm Macdonald

2012

The Leeds City Story

FOOTBALL was a late starter in the city of Leeds, where the game of rugby was the dominant force in the late 19th century and early efforts to form a soccer base met with little success.

On Boxing Day 1877, administrators of the dribbling code from Sheffield, where soccer was extremely popular, took two teams, umpires and goalposts to Holbeck Recreation Ground in an attempt to convert the people of Leeds to their game. The experiment, although apparently well received, had no lasting impact.

During the 1880s, a Leeds Association Football Club was formed and played for several seasons, including matches against Blackburn Rovers and Preston North End, but the club failed to loosen the tight grip which rugby had on the city's sporting public.

Although soccer was beginning to flourish in many parts of the country, the West Yorkshire area in general, and Leeds in particular, did not really take to the game on an organised basis until 1894. On 22 February that year, another club called Leeds AFC was formed at a meeting at the Cardigan Arms. Four days later, the West Yorkshire League was founded.

Leeds enjoyed a successful first season, winning the new league by eight points. They played at a ground in Harehills Lane, Roundhay, before moving to Headingley, next door to the famous cricket arena, where they shared the ground with Leeds Rugby Club.

A further move took Leeds AFC to the Meanwood ground but they soon returned to Headingley – and were quickly in trouble. Directors of the Leeds Cricket, Football and Athletic Club, which owned the Headingley ground, decided to abandon soccer unless Leeds AFC bowed to an ultimatum.

The soccer club, now members of the Yorkshire League, had struggled to attract large attendances and were told to come up with a scheme which would enable them to meet their expenses from gate receipts. At the club's annual meeting on 22 June 1898, only three people turned up to discuss the problem and the soccer section effectively collapsed.

Rugby's popularity, especially the Northern Union – forerunner of today's Rugby League – looked unshakable in Leeds, yet, across the other side of the city, one club more than any other was seen as soccer's standard bearer – Hunslet FC.

Hunslet had been formed in October 1889, by men working in the city's steelworks. Nicknamed 'The Twinklers', Hunslet indeed shone brightly, winning the West Yorkshire Cup four times and reaching the FA Amateur Cup quarter-finals twice, including a famous victory over the all-powerful Old Etonians.

With the West Yorkshire League maintaining its progress, more local teams sprang up and Hunslet, though regarded as the city's premier club, had difficulty in finding a ground of their own.

In 1895, they left the Wellington Ground in Low Road to move to the Laburnum Ground, off Dewsbury Road, before switching to Parkside where they shared facilities with Hunslet Rugby Club. Hunslet FC were always under pressure to move again and eventually they went under, shortly after the turn of the century, to deliver another blow to the local soccer fraternity.

Undaunted, the Hunslet committee and supporters decided that the city of Leeds could support a League club and out of that conviction came the birth of Leeds City FC. Even then, the new club, like its predecessors, had no permanent playing base.

Before gaining Football League status the newly formed Leeds City spent the 1904–05 season in the West Yorkshire League. Their first competitive game was at Scatcherd Lane, Morley, the current home of Morley RUFC, on 1 September. By all accounts, City were fortunate to escape with a 2–2 draw.

Reports in the Leeds-based newspapers were scratchy with no named scorers. It was a similar story with the *Morley Observer*, although it did state that City's opening goal came after about 20 minutes. The Leeds side included Eggington, Trearney and Tennant, a trio of ex-Hunslet players, Tim Taylor (Rothwell) and Parkinson (Beeston Hill).

City's early home games were played at Hunslet, on the Wellington Ground in Low Road, before the move to Elland Road in mid-October.

West Yorkshire League fixtures were treated with little respect after City decided to arrange a series of friendly games against Football League opponents midway through the season. Several West Yorkshire League games were called off as City entertained established clubs like Sheffield United, Preston North End and Derby County – matches that pulled in bigger crowds than the League games. Fans turned up in big numbers for the Derby game, many to see the star of the era, Steve Bloomer, the England international. However, Bloomer had a leg injury and did not play, although he did act as linesman.

Sometimes the friendlies and the League fixtures were played on the same day with a weaker City 'reserve' team fulfilling the League games. Because Elland Road was used to host many of the friendlies, City often waived ground advantage in the League and ended up playing more games away than at home.

Inevitably, a backlog of League fixtures developed and in a frantic effort to catch up, City sometimes played two League games a day, but at the end of the season they had still failed to complete their 26-match programme. Indeed, only five of the 14 competing clubs managed to fulfil all their fixtures, including Bradford City Reserves, who finished champions with 43 points.

Leeds City finished 11th, but had successfully laid the foundations on which to build their case for Football League status.

City's West Yorkshire League record

P	W	D	L	F	A	Pts
24	7	7	10	33	47	21

Many players were invited to play for City, but very few were kept on for the following campaign. Some famous names did appear for City in the more high-profile friendlies including former England internationals Fred Spiksley and Tom Morren.

Spiksley, who also played for City in a few West Yorkshire League matches, had scored a remarkable 131 goals in 126 games for Gainsborough Trinity and exactly 100 in 12 years with Sheffield Wednesday.

Capped seven times by England, he arrived at Leeds after a handful of games with Glossop, and even at the age of 34 showed the Elland Road public he was still a classy performer. He did not stay long, later turning out for Watford before coaching several sides on the continent, including the Swedish national team in 1911.

Sunderland-born Morren, a centre-half, had scored on his only England appearance – a 3–2 win against Ireland in Belfast in 1898. An amateur, he played 160 times for Sheffield United, but, like Spiksley, was at the end of his playing career when he turned out for City.

Experimental teams were fielded, the public response was generally good, and the problem of a new home was solved when Holbeck Rugby Club disbanded after losing a promotion Play-off against St Helens which would have put them in the First Division of the Northern Union.

Holbeck had used a ground at Elland Road and in October 1904, Leeds City FC became its new tenants.

Leeds was the biggest city in England without a premier soccer club but the new City officials were confident that they would gain admission to the Football League, bearing in mind that the League was anxious to extend its sphere of influence.

In April 1905 the first Leeds City limited company was floated with capital of 10,000 £1 shares. Three men held the majority of those shares: Local clothier Norris Hepworth, who became the club's first chairman; Ralph Younger, landlord of the Old Peacock Hotel close to the Elland Road ground; and A.W. Pullin, better known as 'Old Ebor', a *Yorkshire Evening Post* sports journalist. On 5 June, the club was officially formed into a limited liability company.

Gilbert Gillies, then manager of Chesterfield, was tempted to Elland Road as secretary-manager of Leeds City and when the Football League extended its Second Division to 20 clubs, the Leeds outfit polled most votes – 25 – to gain election along with Chelsea, Hull City, Clapton Orient and Stockport County.

City, clad in blue and gold, kicked-off their Football League career on 2 September 1905 with a 1–0 defeat at Bradford City in front of 15,000 fans, while the reserves entertained Nottingham Forest Reserves in a Midland League fixture at Elland Road.

The following week, 6,802 went through the Elland Road turnstiles to see West Bromwich Albion beat City 2–0 and two days later only 3,000 turned up to see Tom Drain score both goals in City's 2–2 with Lincoln for a hard-earned first Football League point.

City, nicknamed the Peacocks after the neighbouring pub, had plenty to cheer the following Saturday, 16 September, when Harry Singleton netted the only goal at Leicester Fosse to give City their first League win.

The Leeds public responded to the improvement in results and the next home game, a 3–1 win over Hull City, attracted a crowd of 13,654 as two goals from Welsh star Dickie Morris, City's first international player, and one from Fred Hargraves sealed City's first League victory at Elland Road where they only lost twice more that season.

City made a highly satisfactory entrance to League soccer, finishing sixth in Division Two.

David 'Soldier' Wilson, who died during the game against Burnley on 27 October 1906.

More significant was the effect the new League club was having on the attendances at Headingley where Leeds RL's average gate nosedived from 9,022 to 5,632 in Leeds City's first season. At last rugby's monopoly was broken as soccer attracted new supporters.

One of the bright lights of that maiden campaign had been the contribution of David 'Soldier' Wilson, who had netted 13 goals in 15 games after joining City from Hull for £120 in December 1905. A native of Hebburn in the North East, he had previously played for Dundee and Hearts after service in the Boer War – hence his nickname 'Soldier'.

He had failed to find the net as Leeds made a poor start to their second season and the Elland Roaders were stunned when the 23-year-old died at the home game against Burnley on 27 October 1906.

After about an hour of a hard physical battle, Wilson left the pitch complaining of chest pains. As play continued, Wilson was examined by Dr Taylor, of New Wortley, who strongly advised the player not to return to action. But as news filtered through that two Leeds men, Harry Singleton and John Lavery, were hobbling with injuries, Wilson demanded to go back on the field.

Despite objections from club officials, he trotted slowly on to the pitch but it was soon clear that he would not finish the game and came off again.

As Wilson made his was down the tunnel to the Leeds dressing room, he collapsed and was carried to the treatment room where efforts were made to revive him. It was a vain battle and Wilson, of Catherine Grove, Beeston, lost his fight for life.

The proceeds of an Elland Road friendly against Hull City in 19 November, were donated to Wilson's widow. The 3–3 draw was watched by 3,000 spectators.

In a curious footnote to the sad affair, the Football League rapped City's knuckles. According to a League minute of 5 November 1906, 'The secretary was instructed to write to the Leeds City chairman and point out that the word "transferred" opposite D. Wilson's name in the result sheet, for the match in which Wilson played and was injured, and his death took place before the close of the game, was uncalled for and entirely out of place, as this was a national calamity.'

City slumped to 10th place in 1906–07, largely due to poor away form, although the season did mark the emergence of the club's most notable player, centre-forward Billy McLeod, who signed from Lincoln City to fill the void left by the unfortunate Wilson.

However, City did finish 1905–06 with the first piece of silverware to find its way to Elland Road – the West Riding Challenge Cup – won by City Reserves by beating Kippax Parish Church with a couple of goals by Alf Harwood in the Final.

Despite McLeod's goals and the skills of winger Fred Croot, who provided crosses for many of McLeod's goals, City made little impact in either Division Two or the FA Cup, although they still attracted good attendances.

A crowd of 24,000 saw this 1–0 win against West Brom at Elland Road on 28 September 1907 courtesy of a Billy McLeod goal.

By 1910, a club called Leeds United – no relation to today's club – had been formed and was based in Kirkstall. The club played in the Yorkshire Combination League but soon folded.

Running a Football League club meant severe financial strain on the Leeds City board and in September 1910 shareholders were asked to take up debentures worth £4,000 which, together with £8,000 guaranteed by some directors, would secure the club's liabilities and provide much needed working capital. The shareholders formed a committee to liaise with the directors on financial matters.

During this time Frank Scott-Walford had taken over as secretary-manager from Gillies but the new man's policy of recruiting Irish players because of cash constraints at Leeds was unsuccessful.

Former Brighton boss Scott-Walford probably knew that all his Emerald Isle recruits would not make the grade in a higher class of football and tried to make them feel at home as much as possible. At the start of the 1910–11 season, the manager kitted out the team in green jerseys and supplied green flags to mark the centre line.

Although the likes of Mick Foley, Billy Gillespie, Joe Enright, Joe Moran and Tom Mulholland were fairly successful, a lot of their Irish colleagues didn't make the grade at Elland Road and in 1912, Scott-Walford quit due to failing health and the pressures of trying to cope with the club's increasing cash problems. His resignation came after City were forced to apply for re-election after a terrible season, finishing second bottom.

Cigarette card depicting Leeds City's colours of 1906–07.

Dickie Joynes was among a host of players who followed manager Frank Scott-Walford from Brighton to Leeds.

City reached another low ebb when the bank announced that it was going to call in the club's £7,000 overdraft, a move which would effectively put City out of business. Norris Hepworth poured in more cash and appointed Tom Coombes as Receiver. Coombes was to run City's affairs for the next three years as the club lurched from one financial crisis to another.

The extent of Hepworth's generosity was revealed at a public meeting at the Grand Central Hotel in April 1912. The club's major benefactor, Hepworth, had spent the then huge sum of £15,000 on trying to keep City afloat.

An extraordinary general meeting at the Salem Hall, called to try to sort out the whole miserable mess, revealed that total liabilities were £15,782, total losses since the club's formation were £11,321 and assets stood at £7,084. The meeting agreed that the company should be wound up and that Coombes should run the club.

At one stage, Leeds Cricket, Football and Athletic Club offered to take over Leeds City FC and use Headingley to stage soccer – quite ironic considering the demise of Leeds AFC – but the proposal came to nought. By this time, Headingley had already staged two FA Amateur Cup Finals while Elland Road had hosted an FA Cup semi-final between Barnsley and Everton in March 1910.

Into this monetary minefield stepped City's new manager, Herbert Chapman, who had achieved much at his previous club, Northampton Town. Chapman campaigned vigorously to keep City in the League and on 4 June, they were re-elected with 33 votes. Lincoln City (27 votes) replaced Gainsborough Trinity, who managed only nine votes.

The 1912–13 season began with renewed optimism and Chapman's team made a useful start, but in October the club found themselves in hot water with the Football League. During his team-building that summer, Chapman had signed three newcomers – goalkeeper Billy Scott, George Law and Evelyn Lintott – agreeing to pay them the full year's wage of £208 to the end of the following April. But two months had already elapsed since the end of their previous contracts. In effect, the players were getting more than the permitted wage of £4 per week.

Goalkeeper Billy Scott, one of City's stars.

Aston Villa had fallen foul of the League for the same offence and when their case came to light, City realised they had unwittingly breached the rules and reported themselves. The League were swift to act and City were fined £125 plus expenses and the players were ordered to return the excess payments. They also praised Chapman for his honesty and, perversely, warned him about his future conduct.

Despite this brush with authority, Chapman proved an inspirational manager and City finished sixth in his first season, with the mercurial McLeod netting 27 of City's 70 League goals. To cap a fine campaign, City even reported a £400 profit.

The capture of Bradford City's 1911 FA Cup winning captain Jimmy Speirs was a major coup and helped take City to within two points of promotion in 1913–14. The Peacocks form at Elland Road was outstanding and established a club League record by thrashing Nottingham Forest 8–0.

Record season ticket sales of £2,000 saw large crowds roll up to see the amateur international star Ivan Sharpe's wing-craft create goals for the deadly McLeod, while goalkeeper Tony Hogg proved an exciting discovery.

The club looked in good shape and in August 1914, a syndicate of Leeds sportsmen, headed by Joseph Connor, president of the West Riding FA, announced it had offered to run the club. Its offer of a £1,000 payment and an annual rent of £250 for Elland Road was accepted by receiver Coombes.

With the financial mess sorted, City were confident of promotion in 1914–15 after their exploits the previous season, but the optimism was not justified as City struggled to recover from losing their opening four games and finished in 15th place in the final season before the League closed down for World War One.

The campaign also saw City up before football's authorities once again.

Jimmy Speirs, a major capture from neighbours Bradford City.

Mick Foley, Arthur Price, Jimmy Speirs and Billy McLeod training outside Elland Road before City's FA Cup tie at Gainsborough in January 1914. McLeod scored in City's 4–2 win.

City could not immediately pay Fulham their full share of the gate from their meeting on Christmas Day, so the London club took swift retribution by withholding money from the return game at Craven Cottage on Boxing Day.

At an FA inquiry the following February, City said there had been a tram strike on Christmas Day and many supporters arrived at Elland Road late and there were no police to stop them rushing into the ground, so City had to take admission money on account. The inquiry ordered Fulham to pay the £20 4s 5d owed to City from the Boxing Day gate, plus three guineas expenses. City got away with a verbal warning.

The Football League Management Committee agreed that some form of competition should be played to keep the game alive during the war. The outcome was the setting up of regional competitions, to cut costs and travelling difficulties, followed by a two month League competition.

There was to be no promotion or relegation and players would all play as amateurs, for expenses only – something that was to lead to the demise of Leeds City.

The wartime competitions saw City field a mixture of their own players and guests, including some star names of the era like Tottenham's Fred 'Fanny' Walden, who had played for Chapman at Northampton and tried, unsuccessfully, to sign him for Leeds.

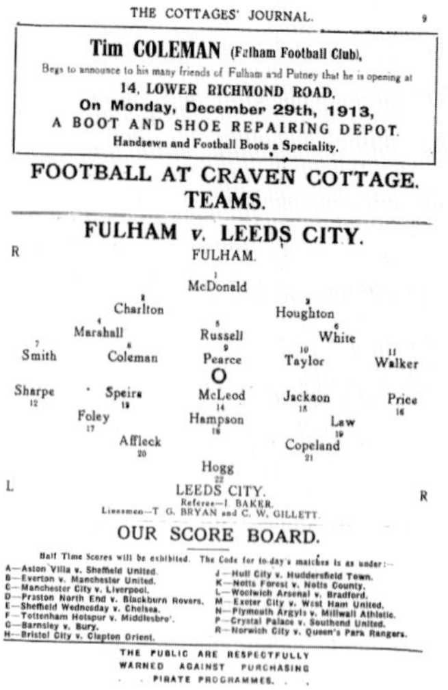
THE COTTAGES' JOURNAL. 9

Tim COLEMAN (Fulham Football Club),
Begs to announce to his many friends of Fulham and Putney that he is opening at
14, LOWER RICHMOND ROAD,
On Monday, December 29th, 1913,
A BOOT AND SHOE REPAIRING DEPOT.
Handsewn and Football Boots a Speciality.

FOOTBALL AT CRAVEN COTTAGE.
TEAMS.

FULHAM v. LEEDS CITY.

R FULHAM.

1 McDonald
2 Charlton 3 Houghton
4 Marshall 5 Russell 6 White
7 Smith 8 Coleman 9 Pearce 10 Taylor 11 Walker

O

Sharpe 12 Speirs 13 McLeod 14 Jackson 15 Price 16
Foley 17 Hampson 18 Law 19
Affleck 20 Copeland 21
Hogg 22

L LEEDS CITY. R
Referee—J. BAKER.
Linesmen—T. G. BRYAN and C. W. GILLETT.

OUR SCORE BOARD.

Half Time Scores will be exhibited. The Code for to-day's matches is as under:—
A—Aston Villa v. Sheffield United.
B—Everton v. Manchester United.
C—Manchester City v. Liverpool.
D—Preston North End v. Blackburn Rovers.
E—Sheffield Wednesday v. Chelsea.
F—Tottenham Hotspur v. Middlesbro'.
G—Barnsley v. Bury.
H—Bristol City v. Clapton Orient.
J—Hull City v. Huddersfield Town.
K—Notts Forest v. Notts County.
L—Woolwich Arsenal v. Bradford.
M—Exeter City v. West Ham United.
N—Plymouth Argyle v. Millwall Athletic.
P—Crystal Palace v. Southend United.
R—Norwich City v. Queen's Park Rangers.

THE PUBLIC ARE RESPECTFULLY WARNED AGAINST PURCHASING PIRATE PROGRAMMES.

The programme line ups for City's game at Fulham on Boxing Day 1914 which sparked an FA inquiry.

Leeds were in the Midland Section and finished 14th in 1915–16 and won it in 1916–17. The star performers were Arthur Price, a regular City player before the outbreak of hostilities, future England inside forward Clem Stephenson, a guest from Aston Villa, and Notts County's Jack Peart, who netted 25 goals in 29 appearances.

By this time Chapman was helping the war effort in his capacity as a senior manager at the Barnbow munitions factory, east of Leeds. With only one in three Saturdays off, Chapman knew he could not devote sufficient time to City, so asked Connor to promote assistant manager George Cripps to manager. In fact, Connor, the chairman, looked after team matters, while Cripps did the paperwork.

Once again Leeds won the Midland Section in 1917–18 and went head-to-head with Stoke, champions of the Lancashire Section, in what were regarded as Unofficial Championship matches. Both games attracted attendances of 15,000 with the combined receipts of £913 going towards the National Footballers' War Fund.

Goals by Peart and Newcastle winger Billy Hibbert saw City win 2–0 at Elland Road. In the rematch at Stoke, Leeds

LEAGUE CHAMPIONSHIP CUP.

LEEDS CITY v. STOKE.

Interesting Game at Elland Road.

VICTORY FOR MIDLAND SECTION CHAMPIONS.

Potters' Hard Fight.

LEEDS CITY 2
STOKE 0

The Potters were late in arriving at Leeds this afternoon to meet the City, despite the fact that they left home shortly afer nine o'clock. There was an enthusiastic crowd in waiting, and the gate receipts, as is generally known, are to be devoted to the National Footballers' War Fund. Both Leeds and Stoke are the respective champions of the Midland and Lancashire sections, and to-day's match was one of the two to be played to decide which club's name should be inscribed on the League trophy.

The Potters had a formidable side out, and a welcome face in the team was Arthur Bridgett, who was looking very fit.

Leeds were unable to play Stephenson, who had joined the Army, but Hibbert, the Newcastle United player, was included at outside left. Goodwin, who assisted Rochdale at Stoke last week, also appeared in the forward line. The team was looked upon as an exceedingly strong one.

The following were the teams:

Stoke.		Leeds City.
Peers	Goal	T. Hampson
Milne	Right Back	Millership
Twemlow	Left Back	W. Hampson
Jones	Right Half-back	Hewison
Parker	Centre Half-back	Sherwin
Turner	Left Half-back	Lamph
Harrison	Outside Right	Goodwin
Whittingham	Inside Right	Cawley
Howell	Centre	Peart
Herbert	Inside Left	Price
Bridgett	Outside Left	Hibbert

Referee, Mr. J. A. Palmer, Notts.

THE GAME.

Stoke kicked off and Howell gave out to Bridgett who lost the ball into touch. Play continued in the home territory for a time, and Whittingham was neatly dispossessed by Sherwin.

The ball was given out to the left where Milne failed to beat Price. The inside man immediately gave to Peart, who went right through and shot behind with a fast drive.

The Potters at once reasserted themselves, but robust tackling by Sherwin checked the visitors' forwards. Clever play by the home forwards led to a determined attack on the Stoke goal, and it brought in its train

A Good Goal.

The ball was swung out to Goodwin, and he got in a perfect centre, which was headed against the crossbar. Receiving from the rebound a defender got it out to his left, but Goodwin was in waiting and again centred. The ball travelled right to the head of Hibbert, who was close in, and Peers was well beaten.

The City were then seen in some clever movements, but the visitors halves, having warmed to their work, held the opposing forwards much better. Play was not long before it was in the home territory and Howell taking up a forward pass was going strong. Millership came to meet him, but the forward beat him. He could not proceed further, so he sent the ball out to Harrison.

It was a weak pass, and W. Hampson and Whittingham came into collision as they went together for the ball and both were injured, which caused a prolonged stoppage.

Following the resumption Hibbert did some delightful work on the wing, but Parker headed out his centre and the ball was as smartly given out to Bridgett. He took the ball to the goal line before centring, and then Harrison went very near, his shot being diverted for a corner.

The ball was accurately placed from the flag, but was headed away. Whittingham received, and giving the ball out to Harrison, the latter smartly returned it.

The inside right snapped up the pass brilliantly and shot, Millership getting his head in the way of a certain goal.

Peart Scores.

When the visitors were driven back Peart was given possession, and he burst through for goal. Milne might have cleared, but Peart carried the ball before him and finished with a fast drive that found the net.

The visitors were next in the picture, and on two occasions the ball was got into goal. The danger, however, was successfully coped with. Another fine movement on the part of the City led to Cawley obtaining possession, and he brought Peers to his knees with a fine ground shot.

The game was proceeding at a fast pace, and Whittingham was going through when he was fouled in front of goal, just outside the penalty area. From the free-kick the same forward shot, the ball cannoning and veering off one of the defenders, who had assisted to pack the goal.

Hibbert next started a fine forward movement. He gave to Howell at the right moment and the latter put Whittingham into possession. Harrison was at once sent away, but he

How City's Championship triumph hit the headlines.

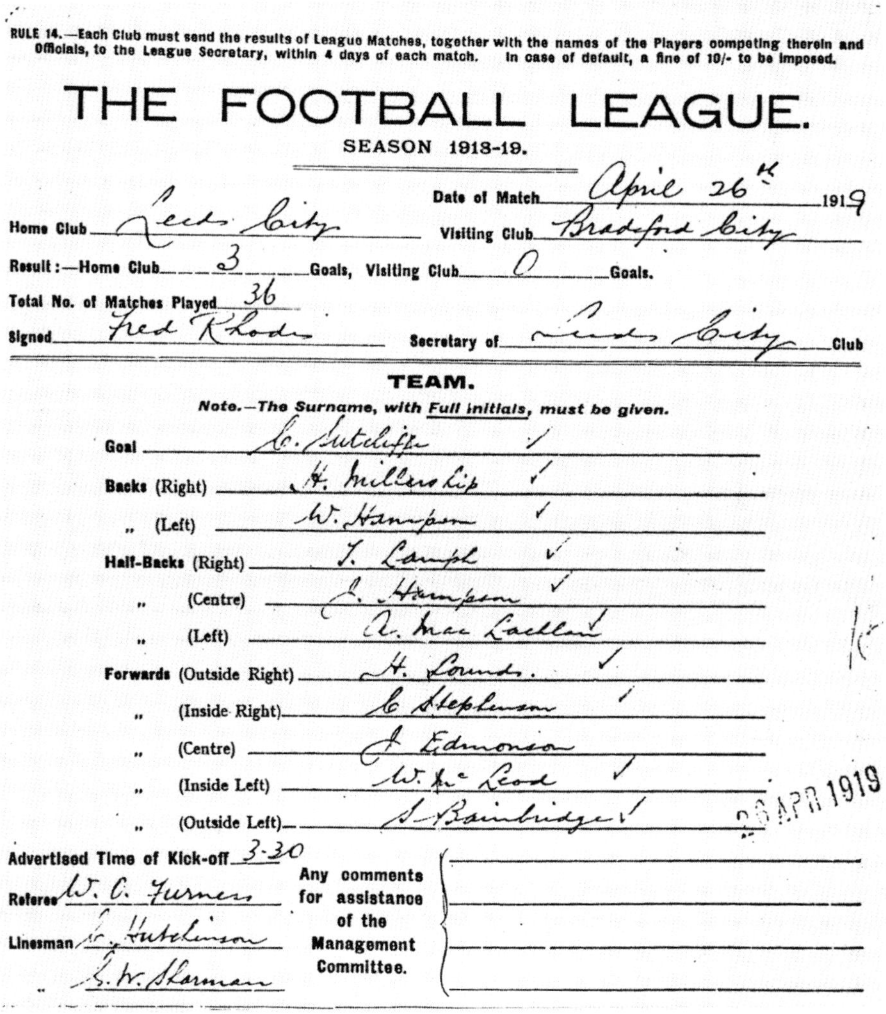

RULE 14.—Each Club must send the results of League Matches, together with the names of the Players competing therein and Officials, to the League Secretary, within 4 days of each match.   In case of default, a fine of 10/- to be imposed.

THE FOOTBALL LEAGUE.

SEASON 1918-19.

Date of Match _April 26ᵗʰ_ 1919

Home Club _Leeds City_   Visiting Club _Bradford City_

Result :—Home Club ____3____ Goals, Visiting Club ____0____ Goals.

Total No. of Matches Played _36_

Signed _Fred Rhodes_   Secretary of _Leeds City_ Club

TEAM.
Note.—The Surname, with Full Initials, must be given.

Goal	_C. Sutcliffe_ ✓
Backs (Right)	_H. Millership_ ✓
„ (Left)	_W. Hampson_ ✓
Half-Backs (Right)	_T. Lamph_ ✓
„ (Centre)	_E. Hampson_ ✓
„ (Left)	_A. Mac Lachlan_
Forwards (Outside Right)	_H. Lounds_ ✓
„ (Inside Right)	_C. Stephenson_ ✓
„ (Centre)	_J. Edmonson_
„ (Inside Left)	_W. Mc Leod_ ✓
„ (Outside Left)	_S. Bainbridge_ ✓

Advertised Time of Kick-off _3-30_

Referee _W. C. Furness_

Linesman _G. Hutchinson_

„ _G. W. Sharman_

Any comments for assistance of the Management Committee.

26 APR 1919

The official team sheet from the final wartime game, a 3–0 win over Bradford City.

had Bob Hewison carried off but the 10 men conceded only one goal, a penalty, to win 2–1 on aggregate. Although never recognised in official records, it meant Leeds City were the League champions.

It was unquestionably the highlight of City's wartime years but trouble was lurking round the corner for the club as football got itself back to normality.

Guest player Jack Peart, who scored plenty of goals in wartime.

The Leeds City Scandal

WORLD War One was finally over and Leeds City were preparing to restart League action when the club was rocked by sensational allegations concerning illegal payments to wartime guest players.

The charges were brought by a former City full-back, Charlie Copeland, after he fell out with the club over a pay rise.

The practice of paying wartime guests other than normal expenses was widespread, but once Copeland raised the issue with the soccer authorities in July 1919, neither the Football Association nor the Football League could turn a blind eye to it.

Yet Copeland was just one character in the intricate story of City's decline, and ultimate collapse, which was played out behind closed doors in a string of private meetings.

Copeland's allegations and all the backroom bickering were not made public until City were punished by the soccer overlords. Only then, thanks to a series of revealing interviews and letters in the *Yorkshire Evening Post* were the shocked Leeds public informed of what had been going on behind the scenes.

George Cripps – At the centre of the storm.

Frank and startling details of secret showdowns worthy of any blockbusting soap opera were released on the unsuspecting public in cold, hard print.

City's problems essentially began when secretary-manager Herbert Chapman went to the Barnbow munitions factory in east Leeds in a managerial capacity to help the war effort. He recommended his assistant at Elland Road, George Cripps, a schoolteacher, to take charge of City's secretarial work, leaving chairman Joseph Connor and director Mr J.C. Whiteman in charge of team selection.

It soon became apparent that there was a personality clash, as Connor did not feel Cripps was up to the job and accused him of incompetence. Matters came to a head when Connor, who was also president of the West Riding Football Association, threatened to resign unless something was done because, he claimed, the club's books were in a mess. So in 1917, City brought in an accountant's clerk to take care of the bookkeeping, while Cripps, whose own health was breaking down, was placed in charge of the team and correspondence.

Charlie Copeland – Threatened to blow the whistle.

The friction continued during the 1917–18 season and things reached such a critical stage, because of both the war and lack of money, that the directors seriously thought about closing the club down rather than risk the dwindling amount of cash they had left. Only the intervention of Football League chairman John McKenna, who persuaded the Leeds board to press on, prevented City from grinding to a halt.

The atmosphere at Elland Road remained sour as Cripps proved as unpopular with the players as he did with some members of the board. Before one wartime trip to Nottingham, for a Midland Section game, City skipper John Hampson sent a letter to the directors stating that if Cripps travelled with the team then they would go on strike. Connor stepped in to persuade Hampson that striking would be suicidal for the club and the players abandoned the idea.

Skipper John Hampson – Threatened a players' strike.

When Chapman returned to Elland Road in 1918, it seemed as though ailing City's troubles would finally end. But it was only the start of their problems.

Cripps was pushed aside to his old role of assistant. Disenchanted, he was quick to respond, claiming he would sue for wrongful dismissal and promptly contacted his solicitor, James Bromley, a former City director.

According to Connor, Cripps made a claim for £400 and told his solicitor that the board had paid improper expenses to players during the war.

Bromley was quickly in touch with the board and in January 1919, a deal was thrashed out between Cripps and the board. The terms of the settlement included a clause that Cripps should hand over all documents relating to the club, including his private cheque book, pass book and letters to and from various players, to Connor and Whiteman in the city-centre office of the club solicitor, Alderman William Clarke, in South Parade.

Alderman Clarke, who became Sir William in 1927, sealed the papers and evidence – incriminating or otherwise – in a strongbox so they could be kept secure under lock and key.

Connor said that Cripps gave a written undertaking not to disclose any of the club's affairs and that Bromley gave his word of honour that he would not reveal his knowledge of the documents. The price of Cripps' silence was £55 – well short of the £400 he had originally sought.

Bromley's version, however, did not match the story given to the local newspapers by Connor.

According to Bromley, he handed over a parcel of documents given to him by Cripps to be held in trust by Alderman Clarke and not to be parted with without the consent of Connor and himself.

One of the conditions of the handing over of the parcel was that the City directors make a £50 donation to Leeds Infirmary. Bromley said that he later asked for a receipt for the donation but was told by Alderman Clarke that Connor declined to discuss the affairs of Leeds City with him.

At that point it seemed stalemate had been reached, but it was not long before City's dirty laundry was being hung out to dry.

As City began to assemble their playing staff ready for the 1919–20 season, the first post-war League campaign, the renewal of Charlie Copeland's contract was considered. Before the war, Copeland received £3 a week with a £1 weekly increase when he played in the first team. The board had now offered Copeland £3 10s (£3.50) for playing in the reserves, and considerably more if he played for the first team, or they would release him on a free transfer.

Disgruntled Copeland demanded £6 a week and rocked the club by stating that if he did not get the cash, then he would report City to the Football Association and the Football League for making illegal payments to players during the war. City's directors felt they were being blackmailed. At the risk of forcing Copeland's hand they ignored his demands and gave him a free transfer to Coventry.

Copeland, who had got hold of certain documents, or at least knew of their contents, carried out his threat in July 1919 and told the authorities of the alleged irregularities.

He later denied passing on the information, but the City directors suspected that Bromley, who happened to be Copeland's solicitor, could have supplied the critical information which now exploded around their ears.

In Copeland's defence, Bromley said that the player served Leeds City throughout the war on the promise that his wages would be increased when regulations allowed. In 1918, the Football League allowed a 50 per cent increase in wages and accordingly, Copeland asked for his increase, but was only offered £3 10s for 39 weeks and no summer wages so, in effect, his wages were going down.

Copeland said that a request to meet the board and discuss the issue was refused, so he placed the matter in the hands of his solicitor, Bromley.

Armed with the information about the allegations, the Football Association and the Football League set up a joint inquiry which was to trigger off City's downfall.

The commission was chaired by FA chairman J.C. Clegg, and City were summoned to Manchester on 26 September 1919 to answer the charges. City were represented by Alderman Clarke, who was asked to present the club's books before the inquiry.

The commission, which included a dozen members of the Football Association and the Football League, as well as members of the international selection committee, were stunned when City replied that it was not in their power to do so. Immediately, the inquiry ordered City to produce the documents by 6 October or face the consequences.

Despite all the wrangling, City had made a solid start to their new campaign and not even the players could have guessed what was in store as they set off to play Wolverhampton two days before the deadline. Because of a rail strike the team went to Molineux by charabanc and won 4–2, with ace marksman Billy McLeod netting a hat-trick. On the way home, the City coach gave several stranded people a lift back to the North and among them was none other than Charlie Copeland.

League chairman John McKenna.

The trip to Wolves was to be City's last game. The inquiry's deadline arrived, but still there was no sign of the City documents, so the following Saturday's fixture against South Shields was suspended and after a meeting of the inquiry team at the Russell Hotel in London, City were expelled from the Football League and disbanded.

The League chairman John McKenna announced: 'The authorities of the game intend to keep it absolutely clean. We will have no nonsense. The football stable must be cleansed and further breakages of the law regarding payments will be dealt with in such a severe manner that I now give warning that clubs and players must not expect the slightest leniency.'

An FA order formally closed the club, leaving City supporters numb with disbelief, the unfortunate players out of a job and City officials to face further punishment.

Although there had been no concrete evidence of the alleged illegal payments, City's silence – whether to protect themselves or a misguided move to shield players – was akin to putting a noose around their necks.

Not even the personal intervention of the Lord Mayor of Leeds, Alderman Joseph Henry, who offered to take over the club from the directors, could persuade the inquiry to reconsider and League football came to a halt in Leeds after just eight games of the 1919–20 season.

Five City officials were banned for life – Connor, Whiteman, fellow directors Mr S. Glover and Mr G. Sykes, and, rather surprisingly, manager-secretary Herbert Chapman. The board promptly resigned, but Chapman earned a reprieve after evidence was later given that he was working at the munitions factory when the illegal payments were supposed to have been made.

Connor complained that City were not given a fair hearing by the inquiry and Alderman Henry also believed that Burslem Port Vale – the club who had replaced City in the Football League – had brought undue pressure to bear on the inquiry team, in an effort to get City thrown out, so they could take their place.

Port Vale inherited City's playing record of Played 8, Won 4, Drawn 2, Lost 2, Goals For 17, Goals Against 10, Points 10. They completed City's remaining fixtures and finished in 13th place.

Bob Hewison, a guest player with City during the war, was asked by the inquiry to act as secretary during the winding up of the club, a job he tackled while recovering from a

Bob Hewison – Named acting secretary during City's winding up.

broken leg sustained in 1918–19. Also helping to sort out the tattered remnants of the club were Alderman Henry and Leeds accountant W.H. Platts.

Hewison later became Bristol City's manager and became embroiled in another illegal payments scandal. On 15 October 1938, another joint Football League and FA inquiry into payments made to amateur players fined Bristol City 100 guineas and suspended Hewison until the end of the season.

Biggest victims of the Leeds closure were the players. The Football League promised to pay their wages until they could get fixed up with new clubs and the best way to find them new employers was considered to be by auction.

Arrangements were made for a unique sale of footballing flesh at the Metropole Hotel in Leeds city centre on 17 October when representatives from 30 League clubs turned up to haggle over prices they should pay for their acquisitions.

It was a humiliating experience for the players as they were sold off along with the club's nets, goalposts, boots, kit and physiotherapy equipment. The entire squad fetched less than £10,150 with fees fixed at between £1,250 and £100 after would-be purchasers complained that the original prices were set too high.

The League, who organised the sale, said that no player should be made to join any club he did not want to but, with the players anxious to get back into work as quickly as possible, the clubs held the whip hand.

Goalkeeper Willis Walker said, shortly before he died in his 100th year in 1991: 'It was a sad day because we had a fairly good side. There was Billy McLeod – a great finisher – George Law, George Affleck, John Hampson, Arthur Price, Tommy Lamph and others. It was a great shame for the city of Leeds.'

Walker, from Gosforth, near Newcastle, was lodging with a policeman in Beeston and made his way to the city centre and prepared for the auction.

Willis Walker – Recalled the day of the auction.

THE LEEDS CITY TEAM "GOING, GOING, GONE!"

FOUR TRANSFERS OF £1,000 EACH.

PLAYERS' NEW HOMES.

ALLOWED TO CHOOSE FROM THE

How the auction made headline news in the *Leeds Mercury*.

'We went to the Metropole,' he recalled. 'It was during the day. I think the bids were put into sealed envelopes and we were sold to the highest bidder.'

Walker, who also played cricket for Nottinghamshire, was bought by South Shields for £800 but continued to live in the Leeds area.

He said: 'After Leeds United were formed I trained with them. Leeds were very good to me and I was happy there. United had the same trainer as City – Dick Murrell.'

Walker also had a spot for Herbert Chapman, the City manager who later achieved football immortality with Huddersfield and Arsenal, saying: 'He was a lovely man and a great manager for the players.'

It must have been heartbreaking for Chapman to see these men go under the hammer:
George Affleck (£500 to Grimsby Town)
Billy Ashurst (£500 to Lincoln City)
Simpson Bainbridge (£1,000 to Preston North End)
Francis Chipperfield (£100 to Sheffield Wednesday)

Harold Millership went to Rotherham County for £1,000.

Arthur Price was snapped up by Sheffield Wednesday for £750.

Walter Cook (to Castleford Town)
William Crowther (to Lincoln City)
John Edmondson (£800 to Sheffield Wednesday)
Ernest Goodwin (£250 to Manchester City)
John Hampson (£1,000 to Aston Villa)
Billy 'Pop' Hopkins (£600 to South Shields)
Billy Kirton (£500 to Aston Villa)
Tommy Lamph (to Manchester City)
Fred Linfoot (£250 to Lincoln City)
Herbert Lounds (£250 to Rotherham County)
Billy McLeod (£1,250 to Notts County)
Harold Millership (£1,000 to Rotherham County)
Billy Pease (to Northampton Town)
Arthur Price (£750 to Sheffield Wednesday)
George Stephenson (£250 to Aston Villa)
Arthur Wainwright (£200 to Grimsby Town)
Willis Walker (£800 to South Shields)
Robert Wilkes (to South Shields)

For Kirton, recently converted from full-back to the front line, it proved a memorable move as he finished the season scoring Aston Villa's FA Cup Final winner against Huddersfield Town.

Kirton, Ashurst, Pease and Stephenson all went on to play for England and Millership was capped by Wales.

Looking back on the entire shabby episode some years later, John McKenna revealed he had some sympathy with the plight in which Leeds City found themselves trapped.

'Perhaps others have escaped being found guilty of malpractices but if they are found out now we shall not stand on ceremony or sentiment', he said.

Although the last rites had been uttered over the corpse of Leeds City, moves were already being made to breathe life into a new club with a new name – Leeds United.

The Leeds United Story

ONLY hours after the famous Leeds City auction, more than 1,000 of the club's shocked supporters turned up at the Salem Hall to try to salvage something from a disastrous day.

Leeds solicitor Alf Masser was elected to chair the meeting and a proposal that a professional club be formed was unanimously carried and a supporters' club formed. It was agreed that a seven-man committee should run the club. It comprised Masser, Joe Henry junior (son of the Lord Mayor of Leeds who had worked so hard to save City), Mark Barker, Robert E.H. Ramsden, Charles Snape and former players Dick Ray and Charles Morgan.

Things gained momentum when the new club, called Leeds United, was invited to join the Midland League where they took over the place vacated by Leeds City Reserves. Yorkshire Amateurs, who now occupied Elland Road, graciously offered to make way for the newly formed United.

Dick Ray was appointed manager and the committee chipped in with money to help meet the club's expenses. Advertisements asking for players were placed in the *Athletic News* and local newspapers.

All this activity was watched with great interest by Huddersfield Town's wealthy chairman, Hilton Crowther. Disillusioned by the lack of support in Huddersfield, where the sports-loving public preferred to watch the local rugby team at Fartown rather than the Terriers, Crowther offered to take his team 'lock, stock and barrel' to play at Leeds.

Crowther proposed that Second Division Huddersfield would play all their remaining fixtures that season at Elland Road. His idea won the blessing of the Huddersfield players, and talks were opened with the United committee. Part of the debate centred on whether the club should be called Leeds United or Leeds Trinity. The Football League studied the proposals and gave Town until 31 December to find £25,000 to pay-off Crowther or move its operation to Elland Road.

Faced with the prospect of losing their town's soccer team, Huddersfield supporters stirred themselves and got behind the Terriers whose playing fortunes began to improve. Attendances had increased at Huddersfield's Leeds Road ground but only £8,000 had been raised to pay off Crowther. Complicated legal problems also dogged the proposals and as Town continued to improve and their support swelled, the scheme eventually fell through.

Crowther, however, decided that his future still lay at Elland Road. He loaned United £35,000, to be repaid when Leeds won promotion to Division One, and gave the new club his full backing. He wasted no time in bringing Barnsley's successful manager, Arthur Fairclough, to Leeds and on 26 February 1920, Ray stepped down to become Fairclough's assistant.

Dick Murrell was recruited as trainer and Albert Stead as assistant trainer and groundsman. Crowther, now chairman of the Leeds United board, was supported by fellow directors Alf Masser, Mark Barker, Kaye Aspinall and William Platts.

While all this important work was going on behind the scenes, United had actually got down to playing some football.

After their formation they were invited by the Midland League secretary, M.J. Nicholson, to enter the Midland League – a lifeline the new club were quick to seize.

Leeds United were voted into the Midland League on 31 October, effectively taking the place vacated by Leeds City Reserves.

Just a couple of weeks after being accepted, United played their first-ever game, a friendly against Yorkshire Amateurs, with whom they shared Elland Road that season. After the demise of Leeds City, Amateurs rented the ground. Played in an Elland Road snowstorm, the new United side triumphed 5–2.

The week after the opening game, United began their belated Midland League campaign with a goalless home draw against Barnsley Reserves in front of an estimated 3,000 fans.

Sometimes, friendlies were played on the same day as the League fixtures, with United fielding their weaker team to fulfil their Midland League obligations. Dozens of trialists got a run out with the new club after advertisements were placed in the Athletic News and local newspapers for players. Manager Dick Ray and his successor Arthur Fairclough certainly had their hands full keeping track of them all but United completed all their Midland League fixtures and prepared their case to rejoin the elite.

On 31 May 1920 Leeds United were elected to the Football League. They polled 31 votes and stepped into the Second Division along with Cardiff City, who won 23 votes.

There was a touch of irony when the 1920–21 fixtures were published and United found their first-ever Football League match would be at Port Vale, the club who took over Leeds City's fixtures after their expulsion. United made little impact that season, particularly in attack, and their 10 away goals remain the worst tally in the club's history. Luckily, they had a strong defence with skipper Jim Baker and full-back Bert Duffield outstanding; and over

Tom Jennings in action against Aston Villa

Billy Down and his defenders deal with a West Ham attack in the FA Cup in 1924.

the next few years they were to be supplemented by Ernie Hart, who was destined to play for England.

United finished 14th in their first League season. Thereafter, they consolidated their position and by 1923–24 had brought together a blend of players good enough to win the Second Division title with 54 points. In attack, United now had the formidable trio of Jack Swan, Percy Whipp and Joe Richmond with winger Joe Harris their main supplier. United made a great start to the season with only two defeats in a 17-match sequence which included seven successive wins.

Adjustment to the demands of First Division football did not come easily and United finished 18th in their first season in the top flight. Strengthened by new men Tom Jennings and Willis Edwards, only a 4–1 home win against Spurs in the final match of 1925–26 ensured Leeds' safety as they limped to 19th place.

It proved third time unlucky for United in 1926–27, although they lost out only after a quite remarkable season. Tom Jennings ran riot with 35 League goals and overall United's tally was a club best of 69 – yet they were relegated with only 30 points. It must be said, however, that goals were plentiful around this time as defences were still coming to terms with the new offside law introduced the previous season.

United returned to Division One at the first attempt. Dick Ray had taken over as manager from Arthur Fairclough and again the emphasis was on attack. Jennings and Russell Wainscoat were joined up front by young Charlie Keetley and Jock White, a Scottish international signed from Hearts for £5,000. All four hit double figures as United set yet another club record with 98 League goals. They finished runners-up behind Manchester City who compounded Leeds' atrocious FA Cup record by beating them in that season's third round.

Pre-war reproduction cartoon of the Leeds squad.

Back in Division One, United reached respectability despite a late-season slump when they picked up only one point out of a possible 12.

In 1929–30, Ray's men finished fifth – the club's best position before the Revie days – thanks to a major improvement in defence where the experienced Edwards and Hart had been joined by full-back Jack Milburn, one of three brothers who were to serve the club with great distinction. There was now genuine belief in the United camp that they could mount a serious title challenge, yet they inexplicably slid into Division Two.

The defence became unreliable and the attack blew hot and cold, capable of brilliance in one match and infuriating inaccuracy the next. The team went into their final match needing to beat Derby County by at least a two-goal margin – praying that Blackpool lost at Maine Road.

United obtained their immediate objective with a 3–1 victory, but Blackpool fought back from behind to snatch a late draw and win the point which sent Leeds tumbling into the Second Division. The Seasiders had escaped despite a staggering total of 125 goals against, the highest total conceded by any club that managed to stay up. To compound United's anguish they could look back to their 7–3 win at Bloomfield Road that season – the only time Leeds have ever scored seven League goals away from home.

Once more United bounced back at the first time of asking. Some of the old guard like Jennings and Wainscoat had moved on and Leeds' strength now lay in their brilliant half-back line of Edwards, Hart and Wilf Copping. United came second, two points behind Wolves, but could have finished with the same number of points as the champions had they not lost their final game, at home to Port Vale, who had to win to avoid relegation.

A 15-match unbeaten run early in 1931–32 guaranteed a promising return to Division One, followed by 14 games without defeat in 1932–33 and a respectable mid-table showing in 1933–34.

Billy Hampson succeeded Ray as manager and immediately opted for experience with men like Albert McInroy in goal and George Brown in attack, both former England internationals. No great improvement was forthcoming, however, and in 1936–37 the drop was narrowly avoided. Pitiful away form – only three points won on opponents' grounds – put Leeds in danger and they hauled themselves to safety only after the signing of the burly South African centre-forward, Gordon Hodgson, from Aston Villa.

Hodgson, a former Liverpool and England star, scored many of the goals which put Leeds up among the title challengers early the following season, but a dismal run beginning in February dashed their Championship dreams. United also made a good start to the last full season before World War Two. In November 1938 they held third spot. Again they ran out of steam and slipped to a mid-table position.

When the League programme resumed for 1946–47, United relied on many of the men who had served them in the late-1930s but it soon became obvious that they were well past their best. United gained only 18 points – the equal lowest First Division total until Stoke's woeful 1984–85 season – and Leeds' final 17 fixtures brought 15 defeats and two draws. Only one point was secured away from home all season.

Predictably, rock-bottom United also struggled in Division Two, despite the appointment of Willis Edwards as manager. Again, Leeds suffered from travel sickness with only one away victory as they escaped relegation to the Third Division North by only two points.

To add to United's problems they had recorded financial losses for three successive seasons. New manager Major Frank Buckley boldly predicted better things and introduced a large number of young players, including a giant Welsh teenager called

DAILY GRAPHIC FOOTBALL UNIT GOES TO . . .

Bolton W. v. Leeds United

These exclusive pictures by cameraman John Pilkington bring highlights of the thrilling Cup replay at Burnden Park. Soccer writer Richard Walton sums up the game.

To-day the Unit will be at Hull City v. Stockport County.

MILBURN FREE KICK

EXTRA-TIME GOAL THAT WON GAME

After five minutes of extra time Leeds ended Bolton's Cup hopes. From a Milburn free-kick Browning headed down to the feet of Dudley and the inside-left hit the underside of the cross-bar.

CENTRE FROM IGGLEDEN

CENTRE FROM WILLIAMS

LEEDS GO AHEAD IN TWO MINUTES

An early breakaway by Leeds—and a goal in front. Cochrane dashed through on the right and made a long cross pass to left-winger Williams, whose centre was nodded home by Dudley.

ANOTHER SHOCK FOR BOLTON—2 DOWN

After only three minutes of the second half Leeds were two up. A centre from Iggleden was headed past Hanson by Browning.

INSIDE FORWARDS WERE MATCH-WINNERS

BAD luck followed Bolton Wanderers home yesterday and after being foiled of victory in their first meeting with Leeds United a goal in extra time put them out of the Cup in the replay at Burnden Park.

Constantly on the attack their forwards did everything but put the ball in the net. In contrast, the Leeds line, moving well together throughout, made far fewer raids yet scored three goals to Bolton's two.

Credit goes to both sides for a brilliant game in appalling conditions. Ice patches, miniature lakes and a greasy ball were handicaps quickly mastered.

Leeds owe their victory to inside men Dudley and Iggleden, who replaced McMorran. Bolton's weakness was here, for Moir and Bradley never made full use of their wingers' passes.

Before the players had really got the feel of the underfoot conditions Leeds were a goal up. Cochrane raced down the right wing, swung the ball across to the left where Williams made ground and centred for Dudley to head in.

It was a shock, but Bolton took it calmly and settled down to constructive attacking, in which Langton and Lofthouse were prominent. Time and again they harassed the Leeds defence, in which Charles, the 18-year-old centre half, was always doing the right thing at the right time.

Shots from Langton and Lofthouse were saved by Searson, but it was McShane, on the right wing, who missed the easiest chance to equalise from only six yards out and Leeds held their lead to the interval.

Three minutes after the restart Leeds went further ahead when Browning headed in a grand centre from Iggleden. Hanson must take some of the blame, for I thought he should have gone out to meet the pass.

Bolton two down, but still they attacked, and Lofthouse was playing a great game. Then came his reward. Following a neat solo run he put the ball through on the right for McShane to rush in and beat Searson.

Lofthouse rewarded

There were occasional breakaways by the Leeds forwards, but Bolton were hitting back all the time, and the persistent Lofthouse crowned a grand afternoon's work by putting Bolton level. Milburn, the Leeds left back, missed his kick and the ball went to McShane, who slipped it to Lofthouse, and with a left foot drive the centre-forward shot under Searson's outstretched body.

Further Bolton pressure was repelled, and then came extra-time, which brought another quick Leeds goal and victory.

A free-kick taken by Milburn just inside the Bolton half was headed down by Browning, and Dudley, with a drop shot, hit the underside of the cross-bar, leaving Hanson helpless.

Try as they may in the closing minutes Bolton just couldn't score, and so they went out fighting after a great show by both sides, and one that will remain long in the memories of the 29,440 present.

A FULL-BACK MISSED HIS KICK—A GOAL

When Milburn missed his kick the ball went to McShane, who slipped it to Lofthouse and the Bolton leader, with a great left-foot drive, put the ball in the net under the body of Searson, whose desperate dive was too late. This was Bolton's equalising goal, and a just reward to Lofthouse, their best forward.

How the *Daily Graphic* reported the 1950 Bolton Cup tie.

John Charles. But the team hit a new low with an embarrassing 3–1 home defeat by Newport County in the FA Cup.

United's Cup record was about the worst of any side in the top two divisions and they had failed to get beyond the fifth round since the club's formation. That changed in 1949–50 as United began to show signs of improvement. A magnificent fourth round replay win at First Division Bolton caught the mood and huge crowds poured into Elland Road to see Buckley's boys. Victory over Cardiff took them to the quarter-finals for the first time and they came desperately close to grabbing a replay at mighty Arsenal.

Goalkeeper Jack Scott is unable to stop Tottenham's Les Bennett netting the FA Cup replay winner in 1954.

As the Cup run gathered momentum, so United's League form improved dramatically and the highlight of the campaign was a dazzling show at Elland Road which ended Tottenham's 22-game unbeaten run. With the brilliant Charles in commanding form, United finished fifth and were highly fancied for promotion the following season.

Yet, although Leeds had the likes of Tommy Burden, Grenville Hair, George Meek and Ray Iggleden at their disposal, they continually missed out on promotion. Even when Charles smashed the club scoring record with 42 goals in 1953–54, United flattered to deceive and finished 10th.

Major Buckley had failed in his ambition to lead United back to Division One but in 1955–56, under the stewardship of Raich Carter, Leeds United returned to the top flight – the fourth time they had won promotion in a leap year.

With Charles in magnificent form in attack, young Jack Charlton improving at centre-half, and Harold Brook and Albert Nightingale proving key inside men, United owed their success to their form at Elland Road.

Their home record was stretched to 34 games without defeat until Blackburn Rovers popped up with a surprise win in March. United then unleashed a late run of six successive victories to come up on the rails and pinch promotion behind Sheffield Wednesday.

Charles continued his brilliance in the First Division but when he moved to the Italian giants Juventus for a British record fee in April 1957, United's fortunes began to wane.

The 1958–59 season was one of great change. Carter was surprisingly sacked, chief coach Bill Lambton was appointed in his place but lasted only a matter of months, and then Jack Taylor stepped into the hot seat. All this managerial chopping and changing had a profound effect on the team and in 1960 United were relegated again.

John Charles shakes hands with his brother Mel, skipper of Swansea in 1956.

Taylor had a big clear-out that summer but United looked a very ordinary Second Division side when the directors appointed Don Revie as player-manager in March 1961 – a move which was ultimately to change the entire course of Leeds United's history. United were £100,000 in debt and Revie, like his immediate predecessors, found that he needed all his skills to keep United on an even keel. His first full season in charge saw them flirt with relegation to Division Three and only a 3–0 win at Newcastle in the final game of 1961–62 guaranteed them safety.

John Charles nets against Sunderland in his final Leeds appearance before joining Juventus.

Revie had decided to build a young side around the veteran Scottish international inside-forward, Bobby Collins. Rookies like Norman Hunter, Paul Reaney, Gary Sprake and the tigerish Billy Bremner all shone as United managed fifth place and got past the FA Cup third round for the first time in a decade.

United kicked-off 1963–64 later than the rest when their first match of the season, at Northampton, was postponed due to a championship cricket match being staged at the County Ground. But they wasted no time in catching up and new winger Johnny Giles, from Manchester United, proved the vital piece of Revie's promotion-winning jigsaw. They reached the new year with a run of 13 wins in 15 matches and the arrival of centre-forward Alan Peacock helped the drive towards the title.

Promotion was assured after victory at Swansea, the Championship captured with a 2–0 win at Charlton in the final game of the season. United remained unbeaten at Elland Road and had lost only three games away from home, both club records, as was their final points tally of 63.

Revie's men based their achievements on a cast-iron defence, sheer hard work and ultra-efficiency. The same formula was used to take the First Division by storm in 1964–65 when the hitherto impossible dream of a League and Cup double lingered on until the dying moments of a dramatic season.

United were a physically hard, no-nonsense team and their style of play took them to the top of Division One for the first time in the club's history when they won 2–1 at home to Sunderland. United had extended their unbeaten League and Cup run to 25 games when they were beaten at home by their nearest rivals, Manchester United, on 17 April – a defeat which eventually cost them the title.

Ian St John's header flashes into the Leeds net in the 1965 FA Cup Final against Leeds.

United gained revenge by winning their FA Cup semi-final against the Reds at the second time of asking with a dramatic 88th-minute header from Bremner. The fiery little Scot was also on target at Wembley against Liverpool, but United lost 2–1 after extra-time. It had been a memorable but cruelly frustrating season for Leeds – something to which they were to grow accustomed over the next 10 years.

Armed with a new seven-year contract, Revie led his men on their first European quest and they turned in some brave performances in a Fairs Cup competition marred by violence on the field. With midfield general Bobby Collins ruled out with a broken thigh sustained in Turin, in United's first-ever European match, the Peacocks were involved in a bruising battle against Valencia.

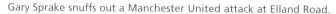

Gary Sprake snuffs out a Manchester United attack at Elland Road.

Mick Jones, in the blue shirt, rams home the goal against Ferencvaros that won United the Fairs Cup.

Police were called onto the pitch as fighting erupted, referee Leo Horn sent off three players – Jack Charlton and two Spaniards – and took both teams to the dressing rooms for an 11-minute cooling-off period. Fears of a blood bath in Spain did not materialise and United turned in a magnificent display to win with a Mike O'Grady goal.

Újpest Dózsa were swept aside in the quarter-finals but although United won the toss for choice of ground advantage in their semi-final play-off against Real Zaragoza, the Spaniards made a breathtaking start with three goals in 13 minutes to clinch a place in the Final.

In the League, United maintained the high standards they had set the previous year, finishing runners-up again, this time six points behind champions, Liverpool.

The 1966–67 season saw United faced with a crippling injury list, but the emergence of players like Peter Lorimer, Eddie Gray and Paul Madeley, saw them to fourth place and another season of European competition.

In the FA Cup, United lost their Villa Park semi-final against Chelsea in controversial fashion, and there was further disappointment in the Fairs Cup. United enjoyed a slice of luck when they won their fourth-round match against Bologna on the toss of a coloured disc, and there was no questioning their right to a Final place when a Rod Belfitt hat-trick killed off Kilmarnock. Against Dinamo Zagreb, however, United lacked the guile and penetration to break the Yugoslavians' tough defence and they lost 2–0 on aggregate.

In 1967–68, United played no less than 66 competitive games and at last won some tangible reward for their labours when a series of steady performances saw them through to the Football League Cup Final against Arsenal. The only goal of a disappointing game came from United's attacking left-back, Terry Cooper, and it gave Leeds United their first major trophy. One month later, despite having £100,000 centre-forward Mick Jones in their side, United failed to puncture Everton's defence in the FA Cup semi-final and a second Wembley appearance that season disappeared when John Morrissey scored a penalty for the Blues.

United, now with several fully fledged internationals in their ranks, were again on the fringe of the title race, finishing fourth, and in Europe they powered their way to the Fairs Cup Final, beating Scottish opposition, Hibernian, Rangers and Dundee en route. The Final, against the Hungarian outfit, Ferencváros, was held over until the following season when a magnificent defensive display in Budapest meant that Jones' goal at Elland Road had been enough to win the trophy.

After coming near to the League Championship so many times, United landed the prize in 1968–69 when they stormed through their League programme. Only two games were lost – at Maine Road and Turf Moor – and their 67 points was a record, most of them the result of a 28-match unbeaten run. A draw with closest rivals, Liverpool, at Anfield on 28 April gave them the title; two days later, a Johnny Giles goal swept them to the new points record.

Surprise defeats in the FA Cup and the League Cup, and defeat by Újpest Dózsa in the Fairs Cup, had cleared the way for United to concentrate on the League Championship.

Revie strengthened his already powerful squad by signing the clinically efficient goalscoring talents of Leicester City's Allan Clarke in summer 1969. Clarke made his mark as United set off on a season which was to see them make a serious bid for what would have been a unique treble.

In the League, Leeds stretched their unbeaten run to 34 matches, breaking Burnley's 48-year-old record. United's feat was eventually surpassed by Nottingham Forest who, in 1978, extended it to 42 matches without defeat. The Premieer League record was set by Arsenal (49 games) from May 2003 to October 2004.

Everton, the side which finally ended Leeds' own great run, also proved to be the team who pipped them for the Championship. By Easter, the strain of a long season had finally caught up with Leeds and a surprise win by Southampton at Elland Road helped Everton to the top of the table. On Easter Monday, United practically conceded defeat by fielding an entire reserve side at Derby who won 4–1. The move cost United a £5,000 FA fine, Leeds fans reckoning it was pretty harsh for a club which had played 63 competitive fixtures that season.

Revie was anxious to spare his first-team's energy because they were still in contention for the European Cup and FA Cup. Leeds had blazed a trail to the semi-final, including a 10–0 thrashing of Lyn Oslo, and were favourites to beat Celtic and reach the Final. The Scots, however, inspired by Jimmy Johnstone won 1–0 at Leeds, and played brilliantly to win 2–1 at Hampden Park to end United's challenge.

The FA Cup now remained as the Peacocks' last chance of a trophy. After three energy-sapping semi-final battles against Manchester United, Leeds outplayed Chelsea for long

Champions for the first time. Back row, left to right: Don Revie (manager), Paul Reaney, Norman Hunter, Rod Belfitt, Eddie Gray. Middle row: Mike O'Grady, Jack Charlton, Gary Sprake, David Harvey, Mick Jones, Paul Madeley. Front row: Allan Clarke, Terry Cooper, Terry Hibbitt, Billy Bremner, Johnny Giles, Mick Bates.

periods on a heavy Wembley pitch but were held to a draw. In the replay at Old Trafford, United again had much of the territorial advantage but lost in extra-time.

Further disappointments followed in 1970–71 when United were again runners-up with 64 points, the most ever accumulated by a side finishing second under the two-points-for-a-win system. Arsenal pipped them with a fabulous late run which took the Gunners to the double.

Leeds, sensationally knocked out of the FA Cup by Colchester United, led the Championship race until a controversial home defeat at the hands of relegation-haunted West Brom. Arsenal assumed the lead and even though United beat them in the penultimate match of the season, the Gunners took the title with a last-gasp goal against North London rivals, Spurs.

But Leeds did not finish the season empty-handed. For the second time they won the Fairs Cup, beating Juventus on the away-goals rule.

United had battled long and hard to rid themselves of the image of a dour side and, in 1971–72, they finally achieved more widespread appreciation with a series of breathtaking home performances. Forced to play their first four home games of the season on neutral grounds because of crowd trouble, they returned to Elland Road with a vengeance, dropping only two points in their remaining 17 home matches. Better away form and playing the first four home games at Elland Road would have surely ensured them the Championship.

A string of fine FA Cup displays took Leeds to Wembley and the Centenary Final against Arsenal. United broke their Wembley duck with a 1–0 win thanks to Allan Clarke's diving header. That gave them the Cup for the first time, but there was little time for celebrations

Princess Margaret meets the Leeds squad before the 1970 FA Cup Final.

as, 48 hours later, Revie took his team to Wolverhampton in search of the League and Cup double. But Leeds failed at this last hurdle and so did Liverpool who were at Highbury the same night, leaving Derby County as champions for the first time and Leeds runners-up for the fifth time in eight seasons.

Billy Bremner lifts the Fairs Cup trophy aloft after the Final against Juventus.

The FA Cup is finally in the hands of Leeds United and Billy Bremner.

Twelve months later, United were back at Wembley in a bid to retain the FA Cup. Outside Wearside there were few prepared to back against them but Second Division Sunderland gave a great display to cause one of the biggest Cup Final upsets of all time.

Eleven days later United's disappointment doubled when a scratch Leeds side went down to AC Milan by the only goal of the European Cup-Winners' Cup Final. In the League, Leeds were hindered by long-term injuries to Terry Cooper and Eddie Gray, and they did well to maintain their title challenge until they lost to the ultimate champions, Liverpool, towards the end of April.

Fittingly, Revie's last season at Elland Road ended with the club recapturing the Championship. United began 1973–74 in blistering style with seven consecutive wins. They were untouchable and by Boxing Day had built up a nine-point lead. A temporary slump cast doubts over what had been a relentless pursuit of the title, but they recovered and were confirmed as champions without kicking a ball when nearest rivals, Liverpool, lost a midweek game at Anfield, against Arsenal.

United went into their final game, at Queen's Park Rangers, as champions and thousands of Leeds supporters poured into the capital to see United finish in style with a 1–0 win in front of Loftus Road's biggest-ever crowd.

In the FA Cup, United inexplicably lost a fifth-round replay at Elland Road against Bristol City, and in Europe they fielded sides with a fair sprinkling of reserves, yet did enough to eliminate Scottish challengers, Hibernian, after a penalty shoot-out, before falling to Vitoria Setubal of Portugal.

With Revie installed as England's new manager, the colourful Brian Clough took over at Elland Road, only to be dismissed within weeks amid allegations of 'player-power'. It was left to the quietly mannered Jimmy Armfield to guide Leeds to a mid-table position after a dire start to the season.

United were generally below par in the League, struggled to beat non-League Wimbledon in the FA Cup, and were sent reeling out of the League Cup by lowly Chester, yet they gave some splendid performances in the European Cup. Two classic performances against Anderlecht clinched a semi-final meeting with Spanish giants Barcelona.

Taking a 2–1 lead to the vast Nou Camp stadium, United went further ahead on aggregate through Peter Lorimer, then defended stoutly after centre-half Gordon McQueen

Brian Clough did not last long in the Elland Road dugout.

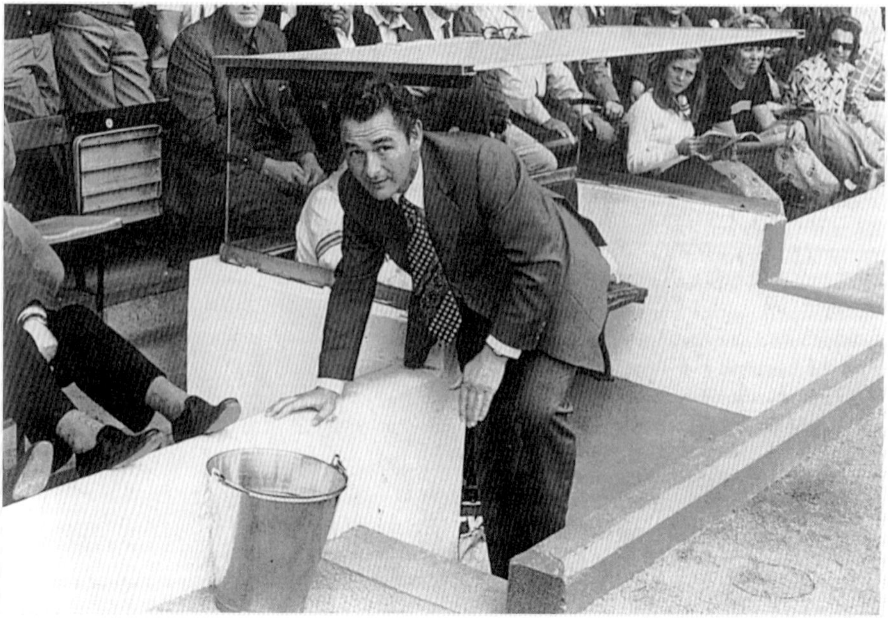

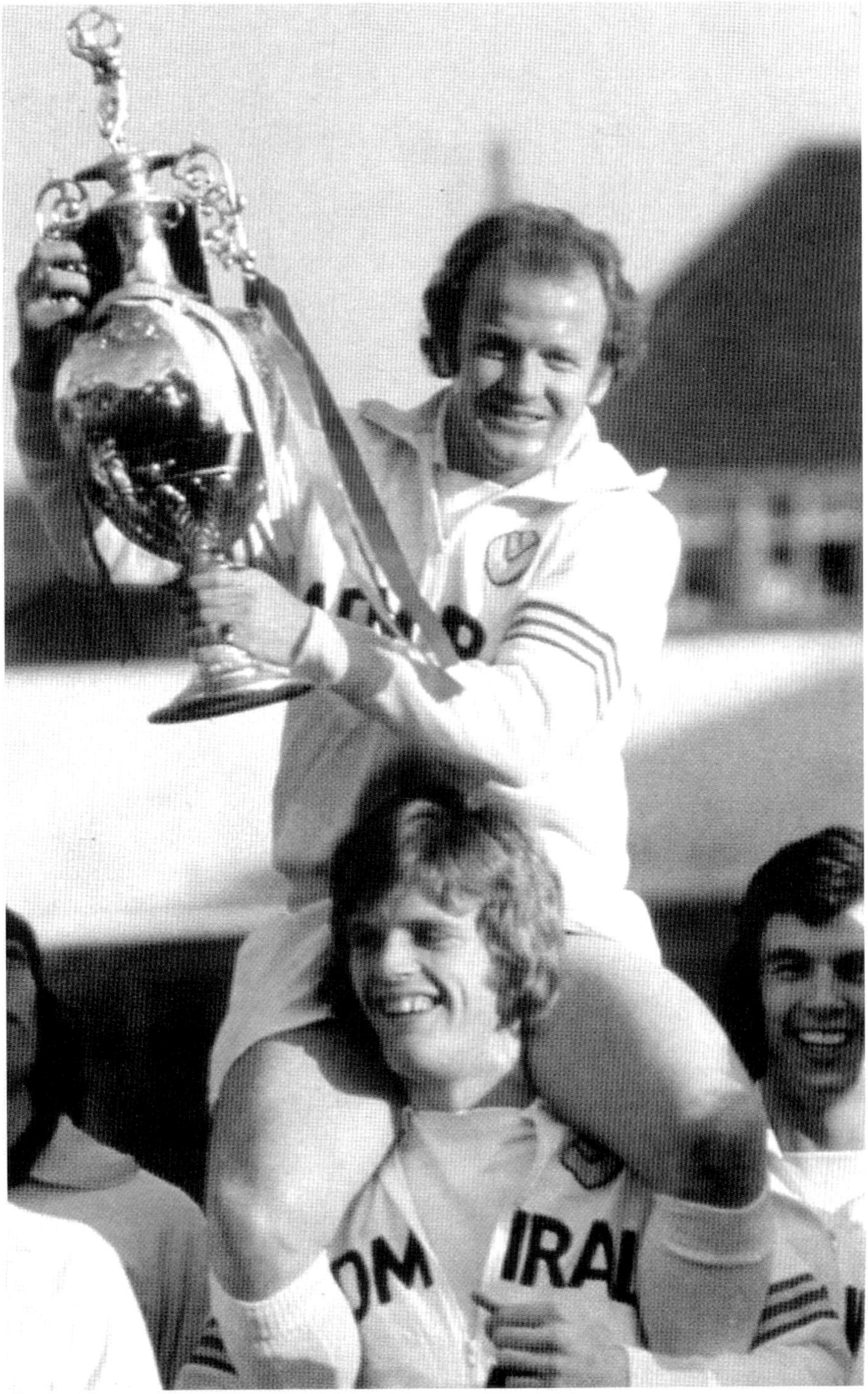

Gordon McQueen gives Billy Bremner and the League Championship Trophy a lift.

had been sent off. Barcelona pulled a goal back but 'keeper David Stewart played magnificently and Leeds earned a place in the European Cup Final. Everything went wrong for Leeds in Paris where Bayern Munich scored twice on the break after United had controlled most of the match. To make matters worse, a section of Leeds' so-called supporters ran riot.

Manager Armfield, now assisted by coach Don Howe, carefully rebuilt Revie's marvellous Leeds team. United finished a creditable fifth in 1975–76, although they lost to inferior opposition in both FA and Football League Cups.

The following season, Leeds played some fine football to reach the FA Cup semi-finals but were outgunned by Manchester United at Hillsborough where two early defensive lapses cost Armfield's men dearly.

In 1977–78, Leeds again had the scent of Wembley in their nostrils, this time through the League Cup, but Brian Clough extracted revenge for his dismissal three years earlier, taking his Nottingham Forest side through against Leeds in the semi-finals.

Crowd trouble in the FA Cup match against Manchester City led to a ban on ties at Elland Road.

Impatient for success, Leeds relieved Armfield of his duties and after Jock Stein's brief spell in charge, appointed Jimmy Adamson as the new manager. Adamson made a useful start, taking United back into Europe after they finished fifth in the League. There was, however, bitter disappointment when Leeds allowed Southampton to come back from 2–0 down to 2–2 in the first leg of the League Cup semi-final. The Saints won 1–0 at The Dell to go through on aggregate.

United's promise failed to materialise and the following season they finished mid-table, crashed out of the FA Cup in the third round, and made little impact in Europe. Worst of all was a humiliating 7–0 League Cup defeat at Highbury. Attendances at Elland Road slumped dramatically and demonstrations were mounted for Adamson's dismissal. In September 1980, the beleaguered Leeds boss lost his job.

New manager Allan Clarke tightened the defence as Leeds climbed to middle-of-the-table respectability. He paid West Brom £930,000 for winger Peter Barnes and there was the promise of better things on the Elland Road horizon. But Barnes and other investments failed to pay off for United, who found goalscoring a continual problem.

Veteran striker Frank Worthington did almost enough to ensure safety, but even when United came from behind to beat Brighton in an emotion-charged penultimate game at Elland Road, Leeds still needed a point from their final game, at West Brom, to stay up. They lost 2–0 and, to make matters worse, serious crowd disorder led to an FA inquiry. Clarke paid the price for failure and was replaced by Eddie Gray, who became player-manager.

United began their first Division Two campaign for 19 years well enough, but a loss of form in November prompted Gray to introduce a brood of promising youngsters. Leeds were back in the pack of clubs tucked in behind the leaders, but failure to win any of their last seven matches ruined any chance of a quick return to the First Division.

Relegation inevitably affected attendances and in an effort to cut their losses, Leeds sold expensive players who earned big money, for relatively small sums. Yet during 1982–83, United lost £1.5 million and were £2 million in debt.

The season had also seen the club's image blighted by crowd trouble at Grimsby, Chelsea and Derby, and during the home game against Newcastle. Such was United's predicament that chairman Manny Cussins warned that a heavy FA fine could force the club to call in the Receiver.

Gray's youth policy stemmed the tide and a profit of £196,000 was recorded, although his young team were eliminated from the FA Cup by Allan Clarke's Third Division Scunthorpe, and put out of the Milk Cup by the rapidly improving Oxford United. Perhaps Leeds' lowest ebb had already been reached when Chester City, the team that had knocked them out of the Milk Cup in 1974–75, and who were now bottom of Division Four, won a first-leg tie at Elland Road.

In 1984–85, United showed some signs of improvement and a splendid late run gave them a flicker of hope for promotion until defeat in the final game, at Birmingham when both sets of fans ran riot, dashed their First Division dreams.

A young man died at St Andrew's during the trouble – the game was played on the same day as the Valley Parade fire disaster and United were later fined £5,000 for their fans' part in the affair. Moreover, it was ruled that all Leeds' 1985–86 matches must be all-ticket. There had been crowd violence involving Leeds followers at Oxford, Barnsley and Huddersfield in 1984–85 and there was genuine talk of closing the club down to avoid further trouble.

After a mediocre start to 1985–86, Gray was sacked and Billy Bremner appointed in his place, but United slipped closer still to the relegation zone before a frustrating season ended in safety, although the team's defensive record gave the fans real cause for concern.

In his first full season in charge, Bremner came within minutes of steering United to a famous double – promotion to Division One and a place in the FA Cup Final.

The 1986–87 season saw the introduction of the end-of-season Play-offs and United finished fourth to enter the sudden-death showdown.

Skipper Ian Snodin was sold to Everton midway through the season, for a United record of £840,000, and the cash used to strengthen the Leeds side. In the opening round of the Play-offs, United squeezed past Oldham to set up a dramatic finale with Charlton Athletic, who were fighting for their First Division lives.

United lost 1–0 in London but won the return leg at Elland Road by the same score to force a final game on a neutral ground, St Andrew's, Birmingham. Leeds snatched the lead in extra-time and clung on until seven minutes from the end when two goals in quick succession preserved the Valiants' First Division status and dashed United's promotion dreams.

That bitter disappointment came nearly two months after United's brave FA Cup adventure came to an equally dramatic end.

In the third round they were paired with GM Vauxhall Conference side, Telford United, but the police ruled that Telford's Buck's Head ground could not stage the match. A section of United's 'fans' had rioted in a League game at Bradford City earlier in the season – the first game at which an existing ticket-only system had been lifted by the authorities and the police feared that it would be virtually impossible to police a game at Telford, given United's huge following.

Although the all-ticket scheme had been restored by the FA, the Telford game was switched to The Hawthorns, home of West Bromwich Albion, and kicked-off at noon on a Sunday, on a snow-covered pitch in front of a huge police presence.

FA Cup football on Sunday was something United were to get used to in their bid to reach Wembley. After beating the Telford minnows 2–1, they put out Swindon Town, by the same score, also on a Sunday.

Saturday afternoon Cup football returned in the fifth round when a partisan Elland Road crowd saw United knock out First Division Queen's Park Rangers with an excellent performance.

In another high-noon Sunday kick-off in the sixth round, Leeds won 2–0 at Wigan to clinch a place in the semi-finals against First Division Coventry City.

Again, the tie – United's first major semi-final since 1977 – was switched to a Sunday and a thrilling see-saw encounter finally tipped Coventry's way, 3–2, in a game which was watched by millions live on television.

United's exploits meant the Peacocks were installed as hot promotion favourites for 1987–88, but they struggled to recapture the high standards they had set the previous season and were never really in the promotion hunt.

When United began the 1988–89 campaign in disappointing style, Bremner, whose contract had been extended in 1987, was sacked in October 1988 and replaced by Howard Wilkinson, manager of Yorkshire rivals Sheffield Wednesday.

Leeds were 21st in Division Two when Wilkinson took charge, but by mid-February he had lifted them to sixth position without making any major signings.

Then, having fought their way into contention for a place in the end-of-season promotion Play-offs, they fell away badly in the closing weeks of the season and hopes of First Division football were dashed for another year.

Before the transfer deadline, Wilkinson swooped to recruit two big-money signings. Scottish international midfielder Gordon Strachan came from Manchester United for £300,000 and England Under-21 defender Chris Fairclough from Spurs for £500,000.

Wilkinson continued his team-building during the summer. The biggest surprise was the £600,000 signing of 'hard man' midfielder Vinnie Jones from Wimbledon. Another expensive purchase was former Bradford City striker John Hendrie, who went to Elland Road from Newcastle United for £600,000.

Other new faces were veteran Mickey Thomas, the former Welsh international midfielder who has played for a host of League clubs, and Watford's 31-year-old Northern Ireland international centre-half John McClelland, who joined Leeds for £150,000. Two full-backs, both of whom went to Leeds on free-transfers, were Jim Beglin, who could not regain his place in Liverpool's side after breaking a leg two years earlier, and 21-year-old Chris O'Donnell from Ipswich Town. In July, former Sheffield Wednesday full-back Mel Sterland joined Leeds from Glasgow Rangers for £650,000.

Howard Wilkinson had thus shown Leeds United supporters that he was acutely aware of the need to strengthen the playing staff in order to mount another challenge for First Division football. United's fans, therefore, looked forward to the new season with great expectations.

Wilkinson's gamble paid off as big-spending Leeds swept to the top of the table in December and hung on to take the title on goal-difference from Yorkshire rivals, Sheffield United, with a club record 85 points.

The Championship was sealed on the final day of the season when Leeds won 1–0 at Bournemouth, thanks to a goal from Lee Chapman, the £400,000 striker, who proved to be the final piece of Wilkinson's promotion jigsaw when he signed from Nottingham Forest in January.

But United's promotion celebrations were marred when ticketless hooligans fought running battles with police after unsuccessfully trying to gain entry to Bournemouth's tiny Dean Court ground.

Dorset police bitterly criticised the Football League for failing to switch the fixture, which was held on a Bank Holiday weekend. There were calls from various quarters to strip United of the title, but it is difficult to see what more Leeds could have done to prevent trouble.

Promotion meant United were back in the First Division after eight long seasons and the fans flocked to Elland Road to cheer their heroes every step of the way. The average attendance topped 28,000 at Elland Road as the big time returned to Leeds. This, coupled with the return to the First Division, prompted a doubling of season-ticket charges for 1990–91 with a promise of even more ambitious signings. The club record signing of goalkeeper John Lukic in May indicated that the promise was to be kept and there was further transfer activity with the signings of West Brom's former England Under-21 defender, Chris Whyte, for an estimated £600,000 and Leicester City's £1 million-rated star Gary McAllister, a Scottish international who was in his country's World Cup squad for Italy, although he did not play.

Summer departures included John Hendrie, who linked up with Iain Baird at Middlesbrough in a £550,000 move. But that was overshadowed by the exit of fans' favourite Vinnie Jones, just a few weeks after the start of the season. Jones, unable to gain a regular place since the arrival of McAllister, joined up with his old Wimbledon boss, Dave Bassett, at Sheffield United in a £650,000 deal.

Lee Chapman in aerial combat with Arsenal's Steve Bould.

It didn't take long for Leeds to adapt to life at the top and they were being tipped as dark horses for the title until a 3–0 defeat at Liverpool on New Year's Day. Eventually Wilkinson's men finished fourth and launched a three-pronged attack on the Cup front.

Leeds reached the Football League Cup semi-finals before losing out to Manchester United, slugged it out in four epic FA Cup games with Arsenal in the fourth round before giving second best to the Gunners and lost the Northern Area Final of the Zenith Data Systems Cup to Everton, 6–4 on aggregate.

It had been a tremendous season with Chapman finishing with 31 goals and taking his career tally beyond the 200 mark in senior football. Leeds-born David Batty also had a campaign to remember, his sparkling midfield displays earning him full England honours.

Gary Speed also established himself on the international scene with Wales, while veteran Gordon Strachan not only regained his place in Scotland's team but was appointed skipper by Andy Roxburgh and was voted Footballer of the Year, following in the footsteps of Bobby Collins, Jack Charlton and Billy Bremner.

They were individual successes, but team glory was just around the corner, thanks to a bit of fine tuning by Wilkinson.

The first season back in Division One had seen Leeds lose £2.5 million to add to the £3 million loss from the Division Two Championship-winning campaign, but the Leeds board had anticipated the loss and handed Wilkinson more cash to push his team to the pinnacle of English football.

In came Southampton's exciting young striker Rod Wallace for £1.6 million, Chelsea's England left-back Tony Dorigo for £1.3 million, Steve Hodge, another England man, arrived from Nottingham Forest for £900,000 while Wilkinson raided his old club, Sheffield Wednesday, for a couple of reserves, Jon Newsome and David Wetherall for a combined fee of £275,000.

Interest reached fever pitch with the Leeds public and United raked in a staggering £3.5 million in season ticket sales. The 1991–92 title soon developed into a two-horse race between the two Uniteds of Leeds and Manchester. A superb 4–1 win at Aston Villa took Leeds to the top in November and the following month soccer fans were licking their lips at the prospect of three titanic clashes between Leeds and Manchester United at Elland Road – in the League, FA Cup and Football League Cup.

League honours were shared thanks to a late Sterland penalty that gave Wilkinson's men a 1–1 draw, but Alex Ferguson's Red Devils won 3–1 in the League Cup and 1–0 in the FA Cup. These Cup setbacks may have worked in Leeds' favour as far as the title race was concerned. While their cross-Pennine rivals became embroiled in a fixture tangle, Leeds were able to focus on the Championship. As the finish line grew nearer, Leeds had the points in the bag, but Manchester had matches in hand.

Wilkinson added momentum to his side by signing French star Eric Cantona from Nimes from under the noses of his old club Sheffield Wednesday. Cantona helped Leeds' drive towards the tape while surprise defeats for Manchester United meant that Leeds would take the title if they won their last two matches.

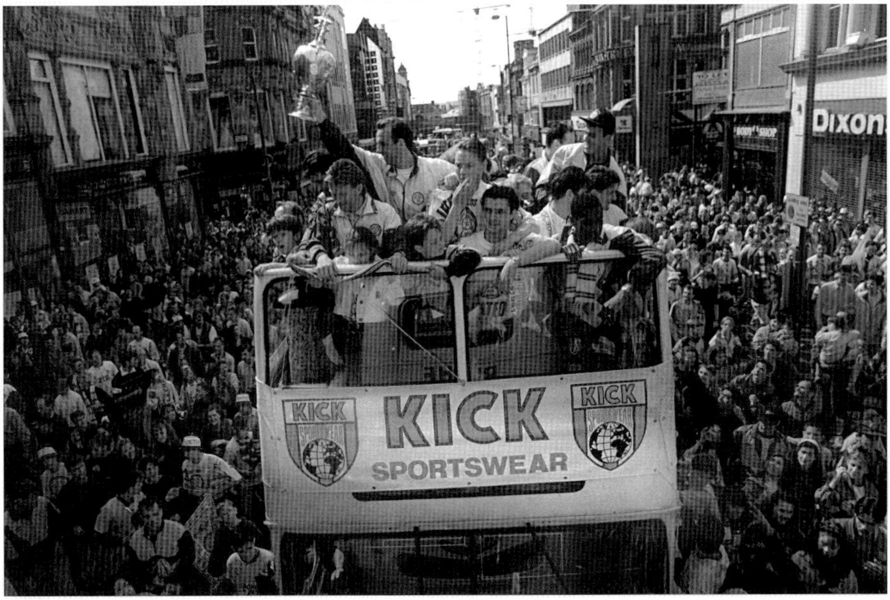

The streets of Leeds were thronged for United's open top bus tour with the Championship Trophy.

In fact, the race didn't go down to the wire. In the penultimate match of the season, Leeds won 3–2 at Sheffield United, and hours later Manchester United lost 2–0 at Liverpool – the title went to Elland Road for the first time in 18 years.

Wilkinson, named Manager of the Year, now set his sights on European Cup glory but the 1992–93 season was to go horribly wrong for his champions.

With David Rocastle signed from Arsenal for £2 million and former player Scott Sellars returning from Blackburn for £800,000, United's squad, with a fully fit Cantona available, looked stronger than ever.

Cantona's hat-trick in a 4–3 Charity Shield success at Wembley confirmed his cult status, but United spluttered badly in the League, failing to win a single away match in the new-look Premier League, and flirted dangerously with relegation before scrambling to safety.

Early exits at the hands of Watford and Arsenal soon ended any interest in the FA Cup or League Cup and the biggest prize of them all, the European Cup, also slipped from United's grasp.

Only an error by the Stuttgart management over the foreign players ruling gave United another chance to beat the Germans, which they did, gloriously, in Barcelona. That set up the 'Battle of Britain' against Rangers with the victors going through to the money-spinning Euro-Leagues, forerunner of today's Champions League. Leeds grabbed an early lead at Ibrox through Gary McAllister, but lost 2–1 and were beaten by the same scoreline at Elland Road.

Behind the scenes, a rift between Cantona and Wilkinson was growing and eventually the player joined Manchester United in a shock £1.2 million deal. The move angered Leeds fans, who watched in disbelief as the Frenchman inspired the Red Devils to a stack of silverware.

Wilkinson went back to the drawing board for the start of 1993–94. Chris Whyte joined Birmingham City and Lee Chapman went to Portsmouth, the latter's place in attack going to £2.7 million Brian Deane from Sheffield United. Other departures during the season included Hodge to QPR and Rocastle to Manchester City in a swap deal which saw David White move to Leeds from Maine Road.

But the biggest shock was the selling of David Batty to Blackburn Rovers for £2.7 million in October 1993 – a deal for which the Leeds board came in for considerable criticism. Despite all the upheaval, Wilkinson got his team back on track and they did well to finish fifth, losing only two of their last 15 League games.

He cleverly blooded several members of the squad which had won the FA Youth Cup the previous season, but the biggest success was Gary Kelly. The 18-year-old forward, converted to right-back in pre-season games, was thrown in at the deep end for the opening match at Manchester City and finished the season an ever-present and a member of the Republic of Ireland World Cup squad.

South African pair Lucas Radebe and Philomen Masinga were added in the summer but the big capture was former England midfielder Carlton Palmer from Sheffield Wednesday for £2.6 million.

Midway through the season there were two important developments. Gordon Strachan, around whom Wilkinson had built the second great era in the club's history, opted to join Coventry City as number two to Ron Atkinson, whom he was earmarked to succeed as manager. As one hero departed, another arrived in the shape of Tony Yeboah, the Ghanaian striker from Eintracht Frankfurt, who had a tremendous scoring pedigree in German football.

He rattled in a dozen goals in only 16 Premiership starts and triggered a great late sprint which saw United lose just two League games in the New Year to finish fifth and earn a place in the UEFA Cup.

Fittingly, it was Yeboah who announced United's return to Europe in spectacular fashion when he scored a stunning hat-trick as Leeds won 3–0 in Monaco.

The second leg was lost 1–0 and in the next round Dutch masters PSV Eindhoven thrashed United 8–3 over two legs. But it was in domestic Cup competitions in which United made their mark as they struggled to find any consistency in the Premiership. Thanks to some spirited away performances in the Coca-Cola Cup, they reached the Final of the competition for the first time since winning it in 1968. But their return to Wembley was a sour one as they crashed 3–0 to Aston Villa – just four days after losing by the same score at Liverpool in an FA Cup sixth-round replay.

With dreams of a Cup double in tatters, United fell apart in the final months of the season, suffering a club record equalling seven successive League defeats, a new mark being avoided with a draw at Coventry in the final game of the season.

Many fans, disillusioned at the way United had failed to capitalise on their Championship triumph of 1991–92 called for Wilkinson's head. But the board, who were considering offers for the club, stood by him and after the European Championships, United were sold to media group Caspian, who reportedly gave Wilkinson £12 million to spend on rebuilding the side so it was capable of mounting another title challenge.

The summer of 1996 saw classy midfielder Gary McAllister join Strachan at Coventry and goalkeeper John Lukic, approaching the veteran stage, returned to Arsenal, while Gary Speed was sold to Everton for £3.5 million. In came Crystal Palace's Nigel Martyn, for whom Leeds paid a British record £2.25 million for a goalkeeper, Manchester United winger Lee Sharpe for £4.5 million, young dynamic Charlton midfielder Lee Bowyer, who became Britain's most expensive teenager at £2.6 million, and legendary Liverpool goalscorer Ian Rush.

It seemed a good blend, but after a spluttering start Leeds crashed 4–0 at home to an Eric Cantona-inspired Manchester United in September and the axe fell on Wilkinson.

He was replaced by former Arsenal boss George Graham whose first job was to plug a leaking defence. Avoiding defeat, rather than winning, appeared to be the priority, even to the extent of deploying goal-machine Rush on the right-side of midfield. United kept 23 clean sheets in all competitions but managed a meagre 28 Premiership goals.

A frustrated Yeboah, suffering from a lack of full fitness and service from midfield, ended his love affair with the Leeds supporters when he tore off his shirt and threw it at the dugout when substituted by Graham in a 1–0 defeat at Tottenham in April. He never played for United again and Leeds finished a dull season in 11th place.

The biggest cheer was provided by a crop of talented youngsters under the wing of youth coach Paul Hart. Players like Paul Robinson, Harry Kewell and Jonathan Woodgate all played their part in winning the FA Youth Cup for the second time in four years, beating Crystal Palace 3–1 on aggregate in the Final.

Hart left for Nottingham Forest in the summer while Graham moved out Tony Dorigo to Italian side Torino, Carlton Palmer (£1 million to Southampton), Brian Deane (£1.25 million, Sheffield United) and Rush to Newcastle, while Yeboah and misfiring Swedish striker Tomas Brolin joined Hamburg and Parma respectively.

The question United fans posed was – who is going to score goals? The answer came in the shape of Jimmy Floyd Hasselbaink, a £2 million capture from Portuguese side Boavista.

He finished the season with 22 goals as the previous season's dour tactics were replaced by flair football with several dazzling team displays, notable against Derby where Leeds won 5–0. The Rams were also on the receiving end of one of the greatest comebacks ever seen at Elland Road. Trailing 3–0 after 33 minutes, Leeds powered back to win 4–3 with emerging midfield talent Bowyer netting a last-minute winner.

United finished the season in fifth place to net a berth in the UEFA Cup. In addition to Hasselbaink's goals and Bowyer's drive, the emergence of exciting Australian winger Harry Kewell, the defensive excellence of Radebe, potential of uncle and nephew Gary Kelly and Ian Harte at full-back and solidity of Martyn in goal were major plus points.

Brighter times were ahead for Leeds, particularly as a young group of reserve players won the Pontins League – 61 years after winning the old Central League for the first time.

However, it all could have ended in disaster on the night of 30 March 1998. United were due to fly home after a 3–0 defeat at West Ham when an engine exploded and caught fire on take-off at Stansted Airport, forcing pilot John Hackett to make a crash landing. His actions and those of Graham's assistant, David O'Leary, who coolly helped evacuate the aircraft, undoubtedly averted a major disaster as the travelling party escaped with minor injuries.

United didn't exactly get off to a flying start in 1998–99 as rumours were circulating in newspapers that Tottenham wanted Graham to replace Christian Gross as manager.

After several weeks speculation, Graham was installed as manager at White Hart Lane, leaving United chairman Peter Ridsdale to find a replacement. Initially, he turned to Leicester City's boss Martin O'Neill, but the Foxes board fended off United's interest, and eventually picked a man from within – coach O'Leary.

Ironically, O'Neill's Leicester won 1–0 at Elland Road in O'Leary's first game in temporary command and despite elimination by Roma in the UEFA Cup, United soon clicked into gear with O'Leary installed as manager on a two-and-a-half year contract with Eddie Gray as his assistant.

The new boss was not afraid to give some of his star youngsters a crack at the Premiership. In only his second game in charge, Jonathan Woodgate and Stephen McPhail made their debuts in a 1–1 draw at Nottingham Forest and local teenager Alan Smith made a sensational start, coming off the bench at Anfield to score with his first touch after 79 minutes to trigger an amazing 3–1 against Liverpool, Hasselbaink netting two late goals.

O'Leary called his squad 'my babies' and recruited a minder to look after them in the shape of returning hero David Batty, 30, who rejoined the club from Newcastle for £4.4 million. However, on his second Leeds debut Batty sustained a rib injury and missed much of the rest of the season.

O'Leary's Leeds played a thrilling brand of football, winning seven successive Premiership games between mid-February and April to finish fourth and regain a slot in the UEFA Cup.

The Leeds revolution was recognised beyond the borders of Yorkshire. Nineteen-year-old Woodgate made his England debut, Kewell was third in the PFA Young Player Award, while Hasselbaink's 18 Premiership goals made him a coveted striker. Rather than stick with Leeds, Hasselbaink put in a transfer request – which was rejected – and threatened to go on strike if he was not allowed to leave.

Eventually, United took £12 million from Atletico Madrid and the money went towards recruiting England Under-21 international Michael Bridges from Sunderland for £5.6 million, Charlton full-back Danny Mills (£4.3 million), Chelsea centre-back Michael Duberry (£4.5 million), speedy Coventry striker Darren Huckerby (£4 million) and Norwegian Under-21 midfielder Eirik Bakke (£1.75 million).

On the way out were David Wetherall, Gunnar Halle and Lee Sharpe, who all joined Bradford City, while £750,000 was received for striker Clyde Wijnhard, Bruno Ribeiro went to Sheffield United for £500,000 and reserve forward Derek Lilley was off-loaded to Oxford.

Amid all the building for the future, United were able to take time out on the opening day of the season to honour a legend with the unveiling of the Billy Bremner statue on the corner of Elland Road and Stadium Way.

The dynamic Scottish hero, who died in December 1997, aged 54, was the driving force on the pitch during the Don Revie era and his 9ft high bronze statue has become a focal point for many United fans.

O'Leary's free-flowing side were certainly focused as they entered the new Millennium jostling with old rivals Manchester United for the Premiership leadership.

O'Leary, anxious to maintain momentum, persuaded chairman Peter Ridsdale to get the chequebook out again to add Blackburn winger Jason Wilcox to his squad for £3 million.

But the Whites' League form was just starting to waver in the spring when the club was rocked to its foundations when two fans, Christopher Loftus and Kevin Speight, were stabbed to death just before United's UEFA Cup semi-final against Galatasaray in Turkey. United had stormed through the early stages of the competition, seeing off Partizan Belgrade, Lokomotiv Moscow, Spartak Moscow, Roma and Slavia Prague to set up a two-leg meeting with Galatasaray whose fans had a fearsome reputation.

United expected an intimidating atmosphere at the Ali Sami Yen Stadium, darkly dubbed as 'Hell'. But nothing could prepare the club or its fans for the horror that was about to unfold.

Jonathan Woodgate shuts out the Spurs attack in United's 1–0 win in February 2000.
Picture: Ian Harber, *Morley Observer and Advertiser*.

Before the game in Istanbul the two Leeds fans lost their lives after being stabbed in the city centre. United had to make a quick decision but chairman Ridsdale, left in a no-win situation, opted to go ahead with the game.

'I believe it was the only decision that could be taken' he said.

Relations between the two clubs became further strained when no minute's silence was held and the Galatasaray players didn't wear black armbands as a mark of respect to the dead supporters. As United players bonded together in a circle just before the kick-off, the Leeds fans on the terraces turned their backs on the field in memory of their two dead friends.

A shell-shocked Leeds lost 2–0 but the result did not seem to matter. Back in Yorkshire there was a tidal wave of emotion as the new Billy Bremner statue and the Elland Road gates turned into a floral shrine to honour the murdered men.

With the second leg still to be played, it was clearly a volatile situation and Leeds were given the right to prevent Galatasaray fans from attending the return leg. The Turks were not happy with that and felt that if United could not guarantee their safety then the game should be switched to a neutral venue.

United responded by saying that they would consider withdrawing from the competition if the game was switched to a ground other than Elland Road. The war of words ended when the Turkish champions were allowed to take a limited number of visiting dignitaries to Leeds with Galatasaray announcing that 11 members of an anti-terrorist squad would be accompanying them.

On a highly charged and emotional night, Leeds were held 2–2 with PFA Young Player of the Year Kewell sent off – quickly followed by the Turks' Emre Belozoglu.

At least United had avoided a seventh successive defeat and managed to pick up the shattered pieces of their season to remain unbeaten in their final five Premiership matches.

Leeds needed to match Liverpool's last-day result to finish third behind champions Manchester United and Arsenal to claim a Champions League spot in Europe the following

A minute's silence is held before the UEFA Cup semi-final second leg against Galatasaray at Elland Road. Picture: Ian Harber, *Morley Observer and Advertiser*.

season. Leeds wrapped up their campaign with a 0–0 draw at West Ham, Liverpool lost 1–0 at Bradford where United old boy David Wetherall scored the winner. It was the final twist in an astonishing season.

O'Leary tweaked his squad in the summer with a spending spree of £18 million for Celtic striker Mark Viduka (£6 million), French midfielder Olivier Dacourt (£7.2 million) from Lens and £4.2 million for Liverpool's versatile Dominic Matteo. Departures included former skipper David Hopkin to Bradford City, Alfe-Inge Haaland (Manchester City) and Martin Hiden (SV Saltzburg) but spending far outweighed the money generated by player sales.

Victory over TSV 1860 Munich guaranteed Leeds £10 million in the group stages of the Champions League but no one gave them a prayer when they were drawn with Barcelona, AC Milan and Turkish outfit Besiktas. A 4–0 opening game thrashing at Barcelona did nothing to dispel that view, but they roared back to beat AC Milan, crush Besiktas 6–0, draw in Turkey and picked up another point against Barca at Elland Road.

United needed a point in Milan to qualify to the next stage as runners-up and did it, Matteo's goal earning a 1–1 draw in an unforgettable night in the San Siro.

Leeds were on a roll and more highly priced stars arrived at Elland Road to join the bandwagon – West Ham's Rio Ferdinand for £18 million – a world record for a defender – and Inter Milan striker Robbie Keane, whose initial loan spell was turned into a £12 million move.

The sales of Huckerby to Manchester City for £3.5 million and young Welsh midfielder Matthew Jones to Leicester for £3.2 million did shave something off the bank balance, but few people, particularly Leeds fans, really questioned where the money was coming from. The assumption was that the club has generated the money via their Champions League run.

Leeds continued to power their way through Europe, losing at home to Real Madrid, they won in Rome against Lazio then gained back-to-back victories against Anderlecht to reach the quarter-finals with two group games to play. The spectacular 4–1 win in Belgium was achieved without Woodgate and midfield fulcrum Lee Bowyer who were in the midst of a high-profile case at Hull Crown Court.

That hearing collapsed in March 2000 as the jury were considering their verdicts and a retrial was ordered by the judge.

Woodgate, Bowyer and reserve team striker Tony Hackworth and two friends of Woodgate, had denied attacking a student after a night out in Leeds, while Michael Duberry had pleaded not guilty to perverting the course of justice.

Hackworth was soon cleared and moved on to Notts County, Woodgate and Duberry were both on the injured list but Bowyer, despite not being able to train because of the case, was in quite brilliant form and was named the club's Player of the Year.

Deportivo la Coruna were overcome 3–2 on aggregate as United booked a Champions League semi-final against another Spanish side, Valencia. That proved a step too far as they were held 0–0 in the biggest game at Elland Road for years before crashing 3–0 in the return leg to see their European dream ended.

On the domestic front, poor form in December and January ended their title hopes and although eight of the last nine Premiership games were won, they finished fourth in 2000–01 and missed out on another crack at the cash-rich Champions League. Although

United supporters didn't know it at the time, the failure to make Europe's top table was to have a savage effect of the club's finances.

After a good start to the new season, United lost their way as the Bowyer-Woodgate trial resumed. After hearing evidence for nine weeks, Bowyer was found not guilty of affray and causing grievous bodily harm and Duberry was cleared of perverting the course of justice. Woodgate was found guilty of affray and sentenced to 100 hours community service but was acquitted of the more serious charge of GBH.

A friend of Woodgate's, Paul Clifford, was found guilty on both charges and sentenced to prison for six years while another of Woodgate's pals, Neale Caveney received the same outcome as Woodgate.

Meanwhile, the Elland Road chequebook had come out again with United swooping for Liverpool goal machine Robbie Fowler (£11 million) and Derby midfielder Seth Johnson (£7 million). Although the Whites, badly hit by injuries, did climb to the Premiership summit in mid-season, they lacked the cohesion they had shown in recent seasons, confirmed by a shock FA Cup exit at Cardiff on New Year's Day. That triggered a run of 10 games without a win which included being eliminated from the UEFA Cup by PSV Eindhoven in the quarter-finals.

They finished fifth to qualify for the UEFA Cup again, but the general feeling was, as goalkeeper Nigel Martyn, Ferdinand, Mills and Fowler headed off to the 2002 World Cup with England, that United had under-achieved.

Relations between O'Leary and his chairman were reportedly strained by the publication of the manager's book about the 2000–01 season, *Leeds United On Trial*, a title that did not go down too well in the dressing room given the Bowyer-Woodgate court case.

Clearly something behind the scenes was not right and news of a financial crisis started to trickle out of Elland Road. O'Leary, who had spent about £100 million in three years, becoming the first casualty when he was sacked by Ridsdale during the World Cup tournament.

With the transfer market now in a slump and players' wages through the roof, the club's failure to make the Champions League for the second year running left United unable to recoup its outlay.

It emerged that the board had borrowed about £60 million, budgeting for a decent run in the Champions League, a strategy which had seriously backfired.

It was clear that some players would have to be sold with star names like Viduka, Kewell, Bowyer and Ferdinand linked with other clubs in the press.

Eleven days after O'Leary's departure, Terry Venables was installed as Leeds United's boss. His first priority was to persuade Bowyer, who had turned down a five-year deal and put himself on the transfer list after a spat with Ridsdale, to stay. The midfielder had talks with Liverpool but the deal collapsed and Bowyer returned to Elland Road.

However, when Manchester United came in with a £30 million bid for Ferdinand it was an offer Ridsdale could not refuse. The England defender was followed out of Elland Road by Keane, sold to Spurs for a £7 million – a £5 million loss on the player.

Within a month of arriving at Leeds, Venables had lost two big names and found himself restricted to modest buys like Paul Okon, the Australia captain, and midfielder Nick Barmby, who was recruited from Liverpool.

However, United's debts continued to rise, fuelled by sky-high wages and payments for many of its players, who had effectively been bought on a lease-back basis from a company headed by former Manchester City player Ray Ranson. It was a piece of business which hung like a financial millstone round Leeds' neck.

Although the opening two games were won, the 2002–03 season slowly began to unravel and was compounded by losing to Division One side Sheffield United in both domestic Cups.

Player departures continued as Bowyer went to West Ham for a mere £100,000, Fowler headed to Manchester City for £3 million, Dacourt joined Roma on loan with a view to a permanent move and Woodgate was sold without Venables' knowledge to Newcastle for £9 million. That created a rift between the manager and his chairman that could not be healed and a few weeks after the Woodgate sale Venables departed after eight months in charge.

Former Manchester City and Sunderland boss Peter Reid was appointed on 21 March until the end of the season with a simple brief – keep Leeds in the Premiership.

Although United still had quality players on its books, it was clearly not a happy ship and had sunk towards the relegation zone. Reid did what was required, a 6–1 win at Charlton in only his second game in charge boosting morale. However, safety was not guaranteed until the penultimate game of the season when a Viduka-inspired Leeds won 3–2 at Arsenal.

By this time Ridsdale had quit as chairman as pressure from shareholders on the way the club's finances had been handled reached breaking point.

New chairman, Professor John McKenzie, an academic who studied at the London School of Economics, rewarded Reid with a permanent deal but made it clear that he'd have to wheel and deal in the bargain basement.

That was not surprising after the interim finance figures for the second half of 2002 which showed the club lost £17.2 million before tax, while the total net debt to the end of the year was £78.9 million.

Those figures included £5.7 million in compensation pay-outs to O'Leary and Venables, £500,000 a year on Fowler's wages while he was playing for Manchester City, £70,000 a year for private jets for directors and senior management and, farcically, £20 a month on goldfish for Ridsdale's office. No wonder Whites' fans were angry.

While the conveyor belt out of Elland Road continued with Kewell going to Liverpool in the summer for £5 million, Reid had to reshape the squad with free transfers and loan signings.

Many of the new men were from abroad and not up to Premiership standard so it was not surprising that United were soon embroiled in a relegation battle – one that Reid would not see through as he was relieved of his duties after a 6–1 thrashing at Portsmouth.

Throughout all the chaos of the previous three years, loyal Eddie Gray had acted as assistant to O'Leary, Venables and Reid and he took over the huge task of trying to keep the club up.

With players uncertain if they would get paid from one month to another, morale was low and despite his best efforts, Gray, the only man to manage Leeds twice, could not conjure up a miracle. Relegation was effectively confirmed by a 4–1 loss at Bolton in early May.

McKenzie had already stood down as chairman, his position taken briefly by chief executive Trevor Birch who negotiated the sale of the club to the Yorkshire Consortium headed by Gerald Krasner – a deal which staved off the threat of administration – on 19 January 2004.

Relegation inevitably spelled the end of the Leeds careers of the remaining top players still at the club as the board desperately sought to reduce the club's £40 million wage bill.

Controversially, popular striker Alan Smith, regarded as Leeds United's poster-boy, joined bitter rivals Manchester United for £6 million, Viduka and rising star James Milner headed for Newcastle for £4.5 million and £3.6 million respectively, talented goalkeeper Paul Robinson went to Tottenham for £1.5 million, Stephen McPhail joined Barnsley, Nick Barmby went to Hull, Dominic Matteo to Blackburn and Danny Mills was snapped up on a free transfer by Manchester City.

Coach Kevin Blackwell stepped up to become manager and virtually had to start from scratch as only a handful of senior pros were retained along with home-grown youngsters Frazer Richardson, Aaron Lennon, Matthew Kilgallon, Simon Walton and goalkeeper Scott Carson, who found himself acting as number two to the experienced Neil Sullivan, who was recruited from Chelsea.

Defender Paul Butler, signed from Wolves, took the captain's armband while other newcomers included Jermaine Wright (Ipswich), Clarke Carlisle (QPR) and Danny Pugh who came as part of the deal that took Smith to Old Trafford.

Most of Blackwell's signings were free transfers as Leeds, who fielded seven debutants in their opening Championship game, a 1–0 win against Derby, were still in dire financial straits.

For several weeks it looked as though Leeds would not make it to the end of the season. The consortium had reduced the club's debt from £103 million to below £25 million with a string of cut-backs but were running out of ways to find money and were pushed to the brink of liquidation in December when the club defaulted on a £1.2 million tax bill.

Goalkeeper Scott Carson was sold to Liverpool for £750,000 to keep the club afloat, but after several bids for the club failed to materialise, it seemed just a matter of time before United went out of business.

Then, with disaster looming, Ken Bates, the former Chelsea chairman, stepped in and after five days of negotiations took over the club in January 2005 to save it from possible closure as outstanding major bills and salaries were paid.

Expectations had been low among fans and a final mid-table position was seen as a triumph for Blackwell, the highlight of the season was a 6–1 home win against QPR which saw Brian Deane, in his second spell with the club, score four times to join a select band of Leeds forwards to achieve the feat.

In the summer Blackwell, who finally had some money at his disposal, strengthened his wafer-thin squad. Teenage wing star Aaron Lennon went to Tottenham for £1 million but striker Rob Hulse's loan move from West Brom became a permanent deal. Also among the new faces were Robbie Blake, who came from Birmingham for £800,000, while Richard Cresswell and Eddie Lewis were reunited with former Preston teammate David Healy, who signed the previous season. Midfielder Jonathan Douglas arrived from Blackburn and fellow Eire international Liam Miller was secured on a long-term loan from Manchester United.

The new-look team put in some creditable performances and a 2–1 win at Crystal Palace took United to within six points of second-placed Sheffield United with a game in hand. Blackwell was rewarded with a three-year extension to his contract but United only won one of their last ten games and limped into the Play-offs.

After being held 1–1 by Preston at Elland Road, the Whites claimed a place in the final at Cardiff's Millennium Stadium by winning at Deepdale.

However, the 2–0 victory came at a cost with Cresswell and full-back Stephen Crainey, sent off. Leeds simply didn't turn up in the Final and were outplayed by a Watford side managed by former Leeds coach Aidy Boothroyd.

Despite the 3–0 defeat in Wales, United looked forward to 2006–07 with greater optimism but seven games into the season Blackwell was axed after a 3–0 home defeat to Sunderland with the Whites anchored in 22nd place.

Assistant manager John Carver took temporary charge but results did not improve and on 24 October Swindon manager Dennis Wise was unveiled as Leeds' new boss. Bates knew Wise well from his Chelsea days and was godfather to the former England midfielder's son and the appointment had long been rumoured in the press.

Wise wanted more steel and togetherness but his squad could not match his demands. He relied heavily on the loan market for players and was unable to pull United away from the drop zone.

Jonathan Douglas is tackled by Watford's Matthew Spring, a former Leeds player, in the Championship Play-off at Cardiff's Millennium Stadium. Picture: Ian Harber, *Morley Observer and Advertiser*.

It's the end of the road for United's Premiership dreams as Watford's easy win leaves them crestfallen. Picture: Ian Harber, *Morley Observer and Advertiser*.

The crunch came in the penultimate game of the season – at home to Ipswich. Leeds needed to beat the Tractor Boys and rely on Hull losing at Cardiff to have any realistic chance of staying up. A late Ipswich equaliser prompted a 15-minute pitch invasion by Leeds fans, who were aware the Tigers were winning 1–0 in Wales.

The game at Elland Road eventually finished 1–1 and a 2–0 defeat at Derby the following week condemned Leeds to relegation to the third tier of English football for the first time in their proud history.

Relegation spelled further financial disaster for the club and on 7 May 2007 – on the eve of the game at Derby – United went in to administration owing more than £35 million to various creditors. As part of the administration process United were docked 10 points – irrelevant given their hopeless position in the Championship table. The only alternative to administration was liquidation as the tax man had told Leeds if it did not pay £6 million it owed to the Revenue by 25 June they would be finished.

The administrators sold the club to Leeds United Football Club Ltd, a limited company comprising Bates, chief executive Shaun Harvey and Mark Taylor, a director of the club.

However, the revenue challenged the new ownership and the club was put up for sale by the administrators, KPMG.

In administration, the club were able to put together a Company Voluntary Agreement (CVA) to enable it to settle debts at a discounted rate. The procedure required the agreement of three-quarters of the voting creditors. A CVA is the only mechanism for a club to exit administration if it wishes to retain its League membership.

During the summer there were long protracted financial twists and turns. Bates wanted to pay non-football creditors 1p out of every pound and that meant HMRC would receive £69,000 of the £6.86 million it was owed.

There were rival bidders for the club, but KPMG went with the Bates offer after it just managed to receive the required numerical support from creditors.

The Bates takeover could only be blocked by a formal legal challenge within 28 days of KPMG's decision and would remain in administration for that period.

The Revenue, unhappy at its share, waited until the last moment, 4pm on 3 July, to put through the paperwork to mount an objection to the CVA after talks between them and Bates during the month failed to find a solution.

Bates was furious that the Inland Revenue were to appeal as it had been offered several concessions, including an increase to about 7p in the pound.

It was announced that the hearing would take place on 3 September, even though the new season was scheduled to start on 11 August. KPMG responded instantly by putting the club up for sale with a deadline of 5pm on Monday 9 July.

Four bids were lodged with KPMG, including ones by property entrepreneur Simon Morris, a consortium put together by Don Revie's son, Duncan, and Simon Franks, chairman of Redbus.

Eventually it was announced that Bates' offer had been successful and he had retained ownership of the club. He said: 'Now we've got a clean start and a clean sheet of paper. It's a big club...and we can take it forward.'

But there was another chapter in the saga.

United needed to regain the League Share that was required for the club to start life in League One.

The Football League's board, chaired by Lord Malwhinney, had been expected to give United's CVA the green light in early June but put off a decision until mid-July when it said it needed further documentation and assurances about the sale of the club until it would transfer the club's Football League share to the new company.

The League pointed out that there was nothing to stop United starting a new playing season while in administration and suggested reconstituting the CVA – a move rejected by KPMG because the Inland Revenue would not budge from its stance.

With the season just days away, the clock was ticking on United's future but the Football League accepted there were 'exceptional circumstances' in the case and agreed the transfer of the share to Leeds United 2007 Ltd. However, the sting in the tail was that it should be subject to a 15-point deduction from the start of the new season.

United appealed against the points penalty but were in a no-win situation. The other 71 League chairmen sat as judge and jury on the decision despite the obvious conflict of interest and not surprisingly upheld the League's sanction by a huge majority.

Bates and the fans were furious – their chances of going back up at the first attempt seemed to be in tatters.

At least Wise, unable to sign players while the muddy financial waters were being stirred throughout the summer, was finally able to get players to put pen to paper.

At the end of August, the Inland Revenue finally dropped its legal challenge to the CVA but Bates vowed to get the points decision overturned and asked the FA to review the case. Eventually, the issue was referred to an independent tribunal chaired by former High Court judge Sir Philip Otton.

United argued that the Football League did not have the power to impose the points punishment, that they had acted unfairly and unreasonably and that the chances of a CVA were dashed by the conflicting demands of the Football Creditors rule and Inland Revenue's refusal to be flexible with payments.

On 1 May 2008 the panel rejected Leeds' appeal, but also criticised the League's Insolvency Policy and appeals procedures, although that was little comfort for Bates and United's fans.

The whole off-the-field affair seemed to galvanise the club. Wise's hastily assembled team nicked a last-gasp 2–1 win at Tranmere on the opening day of the 2007–08 season and went on to equal a club record by winning their opening seven games in League One to wipe out their 15-point deduction.

Despite the points handicap, United were storming up the table with the main source of goals being Jermaine Beckford, a Blackwell signing from non-League Wealdstone. After just 13 games they were only six points from top spot, but momentum was lost when assistant manager Gus Poyet left to become Tottenham's assistant manager.

United no longer looked invincible, results became inconsistent, including an FA Cup defeat at home to Hereford. Then, out of the blue, Wise quit Leeds on 28 January to join Premiership outfit Newcastle in a consultancy capacity.

Bates quickly installed former Leeds hero Gary McAllister as manager with a simple brief – get promotion. McAllister instilled a passing style in his teams and gradually they regained some form, losing only once in their last ten games to secure a Play-off spot.

Having done the hard bit, Leeds looked down and out when they trailed 2–0 at Elland Road to Carlisle in the Play-off semi-final first leg. But an injury-time goal by Dougie Freedman, on loan from Crystal Palace, gave Leeds impetus and they won the return 2–0 with both goals coming from Leeds-born midfielder Jonny Howson, the clinching goal coming right at the death.

But as on so many occasions, United failed at the final hurdle, losing 1–0 at Wembley to Doncaster Rovers, who would have won by a bigger margin but for an inspired first-half display by United's Danish goalkeeper Casper Ankergren.

United were installed as hot favourites to go up the following season and after a shaky start moved up to second place in early November with a 1–0 win at Cheltenham where the winner came from new Argentinean striker Luciano Becchio, who was forging a formidable partnership with the predatory Beckford. There was even good news on the financial front with the announcement of a £4.5 million profit for the 14-month period up to 28 June 2008.

But United's defence were shipping too many goals and five successive defeats before Christmas – including being knocked out of the FA Cup by non-League Histon – spelled the end for McAllister, who had not been afraid to give young players like coveted midfielder Fabian Delph an opportunity to shine.

The job of reviving United's fortunes fell to Simon Grayson, a squad player from the Howard Wilkinson era, who had made a big impression in charge at Blackpool. Although United's away form was patchy they were strong at Elland Road and eased into a Play-off position of fourth by the end of the regular season. A 1–0 first-leg loss at Millwall didn't

Jonny Howson cracks in a shot in the League One Play-off Final against Doncaster Rovers at Wembley... but the 1–0 defeat proved too much to bear for a shattered Paul Huntington. Pictures: Ian Harber, *Morley Observer and Advertiser*.

seem any cause for alarm for a side who had won their last 11 home games, but Beckford failed to add to his seasonal haul of 34 when he missed a penalty and although Becchio put United ahead, Millwall snatched an equaliser to go through to Wembley.

The Beckford-Becchio combination quickly clicked into action in 2009–10 as Grayson's men – minus the talented Delph who had joined Aston Villa – won their opening six League games. Leeds were unbeaten in their opening 12

Max Gradel sees red against Bristol Rovers, but star striker Jermaine Beckford nets the winning goal as Leeds come from behind to clinch promotion to the Championship. Pictures: Ian Harber, *Morley Observer and Advertiser*.

League One matches before losing to their nemesis, Millwall. United recovered from that defeat at the New Den by reeling off another string of results to be eight points clear at the top as they entered a new decade.

The first game in January saw the Whites head to Old Trafford in the FA Cup where they pulled off a stunning 1–0 win against Premiership giants Manchester United in front of almost 75,000 fans and a TV audience of millions thanks to a Beckford strike. Beckford also netted twice in the fourth round at Tottenham, including a last-gasp equaliser from the spot but Leeds lost the replay at Elland Road.

Despite the Cup heroics, there was an alarming dip in League form and defeat at eventual champions Norwich at the end of March saw the Whites slide out of the automatic promotion places. However, they stirred themselves and went into the final game of the season at home to mid-table Bristol Rovers knowing victory would secure a place back in the Championship.

Like many things in United's recent history it proved to be anything but straightforward. Max Gradel was sent off early on and 10-man Leeds fell behind before Howson stepped off the bench to equalise and moments later Beckford, inevitably, scored what proved to be the winner.

It was the star striker's final game for Leeds before joining Everton, but Leeds received no fee as he was out of contract although the decision to not sell him earlier was vindicated by promotion.

Most observers expected a season of consolidation in the Championship, but an impressive 2–0 home win against leaders QPR in mid-December moved them up to second spot. That was a rare clean sheet as United's brand of attacking football won many admirers – and some expansive scorelines, none more so than the 6–4 defeat to Preston at Elland Road.

After taking Arsenal to a replay in the FA Cup, Grayson's men lacked consistency and a poor run during April saw them having to settle for seventh place.

Just before the end of the season United announced that chairman Bates had bought the club from previous owners FSF Ltd.

The question of who owned the club had repeatedly been aired by *The Guardian* newspaper and the complex issue was looked into by the Football League.

The *Yorkshire Post* had reported on 12 February 2010: 'Football League chiefs last night confirmed that Leeds United's owners have passed its fit and proper persons test. Elland Road officials were contacted by the League last year to clear up the mystery of who is in ultimate charge of the League One club.

'FSF, a company registered in the Cayman Islands, own United but their shareholders are anonymous. United chairman Ken Bates is understood to be FSF's UK representative, but, as he revealed in a sworn affidavit to a Jersey court last May, he does not have any shares in the company.

'The League are now satisfied Leeds comply with all regulations, though supporters remain in the dark as to who owns the club due to no details being made public.

'A League spokesman said: "The Football League has concluded its inquiries regarding Leeds United's Fit and Proper Persons Test documentation and has addressed the issues raised with the club. Following further information from Leeds, the League is now satisfied that the club is compliant with Football League regulations in this area".'

Those clouds of uncertainty were blown away at the end of 2010–11 but before the start of the following season midfielder Bradley Johnson went to Norwich, goalkeeper Kasper Schmeichel left for Championship rivals Leicester and Gradel, the Player of the Season, moved to French club St Etienne.

Schmeichel was replaced by Preston's Andy Lonergan and experienced midfielder Michael Brown arrived from Portsmouth.

The Billy Bremner statue is transformed into a shrine after the shock death of former Leeds title winner Gary Speed.

Three of the club's younger players, defenders Tom Lees, Aidan White and midfield man Adam Clayton, who had all benefitted from loan spells at other clubs the previous season, became regulars during the course of 2011–12.

But United struggled to find any consistency and endured a torrid time at Elland Road where they were on the end of some crushing defeats, including a 5–0 thumping by Blackpool. A week after selling skipper Jonny Howson to Norwich, Leeds crashed 4–1 at home to Birmingham City, whose tall Serbian striker Nicola Zigic scored all the Blues' goals. That signalled the finish of Simon Grayson's tenure as manager as United slipped further away from a Play-off position.

While Grayson soon got fixed up with neighbours Huddersfield Town, chairman Ken Bates appointed veteran promotion specialist Neil Warnock as the new Leeds United boss after youth coach Neil Redfearn held the reins for a couple of weeks.

Warnock had gained seven promotions in his career, the most recent being in 2011 as Queen's Park Rangers swept to the Championship title.

But he could not work an instant miracle, despite making United a much more compact unit on their travels. Homesickness continued to be a problem and on Tuesday 20 March, Nottingham Forest became the first opposition team to score seven goals at Elland Road in a humiliating 7–3 defeat for the Whites, winger Garath McLeary emulating Zigic's feat with four goals.

United, whose cause had not been helped by a plethora of red cards, went into their final game of the season against Leicester needing to avoid defeat otherwise they would rack up a record 11 League losses in a season, the previous worst being in the nightmare 1946–47 relegation season. In a match which mirrored Leeds' home form, the Foxes won with virtually the last kick of the match.

There were also tragic losses off the pitch. Gary Speed, a member of the 1991–92 Championship winning team was found hanged at home, club president Lord Harewood had died shortly before the start of the season and long-serving groundsman John Reynolds, 75, passed away in April.

Warnock wasted no time in clearing the decks. Two players had their contracts cancelled before the end of the season, loan players were sent back to their clubs, six were transfer-listed, including midfielder Clayton, and five others, at the end of their contracts, were released.

His first signing was centre-half Jason Pearce from relegated Portsmouth in a £500,000 deal.

However, further recruitment was put on hold after United confirmed it was in talks with a potential investor which would secure the club's long-term future.

The Elland Road Story

TODAY'S Elland Road stadium, with its impressive facilities, is a lasting monument to Leeds United's triumphant years under Don Revie and Howard Wilkinson and is a far cry from the open grass field of Victorian times.

Current United chairman Ken Bates has put in to place changes that provided the club with an all-year-round income stream including creating a museum, two function rooms and 24 corporate hospitality boxes in the East Stand.

Before the turn of the century the stadium land, nestling at the foot of Beeston Hill on the main road to the neighbouring town of Elland, was owned by Bentley's Brewery. It was known as the Old Peacock Ground, named after a local pub standing opposite the playing field. It was from the pub that the club took its nickname of the Peacocks, after being known as the Citizens during the days of Leeds City.

The Old Peacock Ground was brought by Holbeck Rugby Club, for £1,100 in 1897, on condition that it remained a football ground for at least seven years and that the catering rights should be held by Bentley's. Despite problems of getting sufficient labour, Holbeck were able to build a new stand ready for the following season. Rugby was immensely popular in the West Riding, but it was not long before the ground, now known as Elland Road, hosted its first competitive soccer match.

On 23 April 1898, local soccer administrators were delighted when 3,400 people turned up to see Hunslet, forerunners of Leeds City, beat Harrogate 1–0 in the West Yorkshire Cup Final at Elland Road.

Soccer became a regular attraction at the ground during the 1902–03 season when Leeds League soccer side, Leeds Woodville, shared the ground with Holbeck. But it was not until Leeds City were formed that soccer really took root at Elland Road.

Holbeck became defunct in 1904 and put the ground on the market. The men behind Leeds City were anxious to have a ground good enough to support any future application to join the Football League and saw Elland Road as their ideal home. City officials gave instructions to sign the lease on 13 October 1904, for an annual rent of £75 with an option to buy for no more than £5,000 the following March. When the lease was finally signed, in November, the purchase figure was reduced to £4,500.

Two days after giving the all-clear to sign the lease, Leeds City played their first game on the Elland Road turf. City officials were determined to make it a red-letter day in the club's history. The 3,000 crowd were entertained by a local boys match and a band, before Leeds City were beaten 2–0 by Hull City in a friendly.

After the sale went through, Leeds City directors set about improving the ground as the club prepared to move from the West Yorkshire League to the Football League. In August 1905, work began on an ambitious reconstruction scheme which ended with a £1,050 covered stand for 5,000 people being erected on the west side of the ground.

SATURDAY, MARCH 26th, 1910.
LEEDS CITY
A.F.C.
SEASON 1909-10.
Members of the Football Association. The Football League. West Yorkshire Association, and Midland League.
OFFICIAL PROGRAMME
PRICE ONE PENNY.
EMPIRE
AT 7 AND AT 9
TO-NIGHT.

A programme from the controversial FA Cup semi-final staged at Elland Road between Everton and Barnsley in 1910. Neither club felt the Leeds ground was up to standard for such a big match.

As soccer grabbed the imagination of the local footballing public, Elland Road pulled in some big early crowds – a 22,000-plus gate, bringing in receipts of £487, was recorded for the local derby with Bradford City on 30 December 1905.

Expansion continued in February 1906 as City bought 3,961 square yards of land on the Churwell and Geldard Road side of the ground, for £420, from the Monk's Bridge Iron Company.

Soccer's administrators were anxious to reward the effort that had been made in gaining a foothold in rugby-dominated West Yorkshire and selected Elland Road as the venue for an England trial match in 1906 and an amateur international against Ireland in 1909.

But the Football Association clearly acted in haste by choosing Elland Road for the 1910 FA Cup semi-final between Barnsley and Everton. It turned out to be a disaster because the ground was not big enough to cope with the thousands of fans who poured into Leeds to see the big game. Although an estimated 36,000 got inside the ground, many could hardly see the pitch and thousands more were locked outside.

The gates were closed even before many of the excursion trains and coaches from Liverpool arrived in the city. Well before kick-off, thousands of disappointed spectators were forced to scramble up Beeston Hill or perch precariously on neighbouring rooftops to get a fleeting glimpse of the action.

The *Athletic News* reported: 'It is clear that the Association and the clubs concerned lost considerably by allotting the match to a small ground constructed for Second Division football not for events of national importance'.

Not surprisingly it was another 20 years before an improved Elland Road was to host another FA Cup semi-final.

Financially, Leeds City had always found it hard to make ends meet and when the club fell into the hands of the Receiver in 1912, the Leeds Cricket, Football and Athletic Club offered to take over City's affairs and use Headingley as the soccer ground. On 14 August 1914, however, a Leeds syndicate of sportsmen announced that they had offered to run City, guaranteeing to put down £1,000 and pay an annual ground rent of £250 to stay at Elland Road.

Despite the constant financial problem, manager Herbert Chapman was anxious to brighten the image of the ground and even arranged for a new flag to be flown from the masthead outside the main stand.

As World War One raged across Europe, Elland Road contributed to the war effort by being used for Army drilling shooting practice.

After City disbanded, the future of Elland Road hung in the balance. There was even a scheme dreamed up in October 1919 to make use of the rich clay deposits below the top soil of pitch and turn it into a brickyard – even today there is a deep well sunk in the corner of the Don Revie Stand and West Stand. But Elland Road was spared such an ignominious fate when local club Yorkshire Amateurs, played several games there before newly formed Leeds United moved in.

During the 1920s, more changes were made, including covering the Elland Road terrace with a wooden barrel-shape roof which became known as the Scratching Shed. Along the whole length of the pitch on the Lowfields Road side was a stand built on a bank of terracing and opposite the Scratching Shed stood a huge open Spion Kop terrace which got its name, like many other Kops in England, after the hill in South Africa which 322 British soldiers lost their lives during the Boer War.

The Football Association now considered the ground good enough to stage more England trial games although, on 19 February 1923, one had to be called off because the pitch was covered by six inches of snow.

Football had really gripped the imagination of the Leeds public and a record 33,722 crowd witnessed the club's first game in Division One when United drew 1–1 with Sunderland on the opening day of the 1924–25 season.

Leeds United are in the big time. Fans queue at Elland Road ahead of United's first game in Division One – a 1–1 draw with Sunderland which attracted a record 33,722 crowd.

The West Stand in the 1930s with the barrel roofed Scratching Shed in the background.

Rugby briefly returned to the ground when Elland Road hosted the 1938 Rugby Championship Final between Leeds and Hunslet in front of a massive 54,112 crowd. However, even that figure failed to beat the official 56,796 attendance when United and Arsenal fought out a goalless draw on 27 December 1932 – a figure which remained a record at Elland Road for many years.

When neighbours Huddersfield Town's main stand was destroyed by fire in April 1950, the Town played Easter Saturday and Easter Tuesday fixtures at Elland Road, against Derby County and Newcastle United – the latter before a crowd 37,700. United repeated the good neighbours act in 1985 when Bradford City played three home games at Leeds because Valley Parade was still closed after the tragic fire which swept through Bradford's main stand. Two months after the Valley Parade horror, the 1966 World Cup Final teams from England and West Germany met in a rematch at Elland Road and raised £46,000 for the Fire Disaster Fund. England won 6–4.

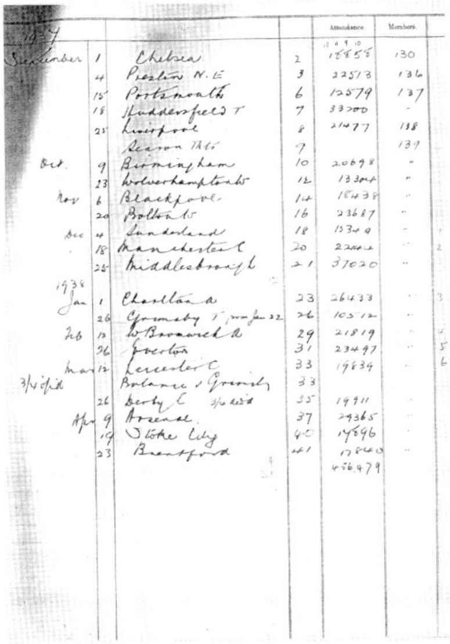

Leeds United's entry for 1936–37 in the Football League attendance log book.

Foreign Secretary Sir Anthony Eden (right), in the company of the Lord Mayor of Leeds, Alderman Willie Withy, on a morale-boosting wartime visit to Elland Road in 1941 where he addressed 10,000 people.

United can also testify to the destruction that fire can leave its wake. During the early hours of Tuesday, 18 September 1956 a blaze swept through the West Stand with such ferocity that large sections of the pitch were scorched by the heat.

Fish and chip shop proprietor Arnold Price, whose premises were opposite the main gates, dashed barefoot and pyjama-clad to raise the alarm. But the fire spread so rapidly that the stand roof had already collapsed into the seating area before the fire brigade arrived.

With damage estimated at £100,000, United lost not only the stand, but all the club's kit, records, physiotherapy equipment, dressing-rooms, offices, directors'-rooms and press-box, leaving a charred skeleton of twisted, smouldering metal.

As the players helped clear up the rubble and wreckage during the week, it was clear that it would be impossible to salvage the 2,500-seater stand and, after a five-hour board meeting, the directors decided to launch an appeal to build a new stand with assistance from Leeds City Council.

For manager Raich Carter there was the more immediate problem of preparing for Saturday's home game with Aston Villa. The fire struck just as United had made a fine start to their return to the First Division and Carter was determined that the Villa match should go ahead as scheduled, in an effort to consolidate their position in the table.

He immediately ordered 40 pairs of boots for his players, giving them strict instructions that they should be worn as much as possible to break them in before the game. United's injured players were treated in the home of former trainer Arthur Campey, who had set up in private practice.

Before...the charred skeleton of the West Stand after the devastating 1956 fire.

The fire-ravaged stand was cordoned-off and the Leeds and Villa players, together with the match officials, changed in the dressing-rooms of the Whitehall Printeries sports ground in Lowfields Road before boarding a coach which took them the short distance to the ground where they picked their way through the burnt-out shell of the stand to reach the pitch.

United's determination to play the game paid off. They won 1–0 with a John Charles goal and after the game not a single United player reported any blisters.

The public appeal raised £60,000 and at the start of the following season, the new £180,000 West Stand was unveiled. Tickets for the 4,000 seats cost 7s 6d each per game in those days and in front of the seated area was a large paddock capable of holding 6,000 standing spectators – although this was eventually replaced with seats in the successful 1970s. The new West Stand was christened in style with a 2–1 victory over Leicester City on 31 August 1957.

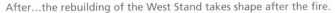

After...the rebuilding of the West Stand takes shape after the fire.

An aerial shot of Elland Road from 1963 with the ground on the right and the old greyhound stadium further up the road.

Two years later another fire hit Elland Road – also in the West Stand – but club secretary Cyril Williamson and several directors became fire-fighters to snuff out another potential disaster. After a home defeat by Preston Reserves in a Central League game, the small crowd were wandering home when flames were spotted in the stand behind the directors' box. Williamson and members of the board ran from the club's offices, armed themselves with hoses and put out the fire, thought to have been started by a carelessly dropped cigarette, before much damage could be done.

The West Stand was an impressive structure but the stadium really started to take shape when Don Revie steered United through their golden era. Cash poured into United's coffers as massive crowds turned up to see his successful teams and a lot of the money was pumped back into ground improvements.

It was during the Revie era that the attendance record at Elland Road was set – although the price had to be paid. After forcing a draw at Sunderland in the fifth round of the FA Cup, United brought the Rokerites to Elland Road for a thrilling battle, fought out in front of a record crowd of 57,892 on 15 March 1967.

Only three sides of Elland Road were open when Dundee visited in the 1968 Fairs Cup semi-final. There was an eerie atmosphere as the game was played in front of a yawning gap where the old Spion Kop had stood. The massive mound was replaced by a new covered terraced Kop.

Fascia of the West Stand which was a familiar sight for decades until the main entrance was redeveloped.

There had not been sufficient time to make the replay all-ticket and at 7.07pm the gates were shut, locking thousands outside. Inside, the crowd – about 5,000 more than the usual all-ticket limit – were packed like sardines. During the game one of the steel and concrete crush barriers on Lowfields Road gave way under the pressure and amid the panic about 1,000 spectators poured onto the pitch, as police and ambulancemen moved in to tend the injured.

The match was held up as 32 people were ferried to hospital, but luckily no one was seriously hurt. Some people had also taken their lives into their hands by scrambling on top of the Scratching Shed roof to see the game which, after extra-time, ended 1–1.

With money in the bank, United's directors embarked on a massive improvement scheme to create a stadium worthy of the great sides Revie had assembled. At the end of April 1968, the huge banked terracing of the Spion Kop was stripped away in six days to make way for a new roofed Kop, also known as the Geldard End, costing £250,000. During the clearance work United entertained Dundee in a semi-final second-leg game in the Inter-Cities Fairs Cup. There was the unusual sight of the Kop behind the goal a vast sealed-off gaping emptiness. When the new Kop was completed, United had about 60ft of space spare behind the goal, so it was turfed and the pitch moved 30ft towards the Kop.

A further £200,000 was spent in 1970 in the corner linking the Kop and the West Stand and £200,000 was outlayed on the corner of Lowfields Road and the Kop.

Improvements continued in 1974 when the old Scratching Shed was dismantled and replaced by the impressive £500,000 South Stand on Elland Road itself. It held 3,500 seats, with a standing paddock at the front capable of holding a further 4,000 fans. But as United's performances on the pitch began to wane, so the building around it ceased. Plans to link the South Stand with Lowfields Road were scrapped because of lack of cash.

Although major construction stopped, cosmetic improvements continued. The South Stand was later made all-seater, and 16 executive boxes added at the top, each one complete with TV set, refrigerator and luxury seating, all linked to a box-holders' executive lounge and restaurant.

Other alterations and additions to the Elland Road scene during the late 1970s and early 1980s continued, including the installation of an 81ft by 5ft electronic scoreboard in the Kop.

For a time in the 1970s Elland Road floodlights were the highest in Europe.

Commercially the club took a major step forward on 30 September 1972, when the Leeds United Sports and Souvenir Shop, to which a well-stocked programme shop was later added, opened.

Hooliganism was to blight the club for many years, and there was a pitch invasion during United's crucial 2–1 home defeat against West Bromwich Albion on 17 April 1971, when referee Ray Tinkler was jostled by irate Leeds fans after allowing the visitors a goal which looked well offside.

Although United became the first club in the country to install a police compound to hold arrested thugs at the ground – in the extension below the link between the Kop and West Stand – crowd trouble continued. The West Brom incident saw United banned from playing at Elland Road for the first four games of the 1971–72 season, playing two games at Huddersfield, one at Hull and another at Sheffield Wednesday during their 'home' exile.

But the lesson was not heeded by the troublemakers. As United were knocked out of the FA Cup by Manchester City at Elland Road in 1978, mounted police went on the pitch and there was a 20-minute delay as missiles were cleared and hooligans arrested. United were banned from staging FA Cup home games for the next three seasons and when United came out of the hat first against West Brom in the fourth round the following year, the 'home' game had to be played at The Hawthorns. The ban was later lifted.

More missiles were thrown during Manchester City's League visit on 29 September 1979, so a section of the South Stand – from where objects were hurled – was closed for a period. Later in the same season the Kop was closed for two matches after more objects were thrown on the pitch against Nottingham Forest. The FA meted out the same punishment after Leeds and Newcastle players were taken off the pitch on 30 October 1982, when ball bearings were thrown.

During the two-match Kop closure in 1982 it was reckoned that United actually benefitted financially because fans watched the next two home games from the more expensive seated area.

Over the years Elland Road has seen some memorable European nights under its floodlights as teams built by Revie, Wilkinson and O'Leary tackled a succession of the best teams that the continent could provide.

Floodlit football first came to Elland Road on 9 November 1953, when Hibernian provided the opposition for the big switch-on of the £7,000 lights – said to be the most expensive in the country at the time. The game pulled in 31,500 spectators who saw two goals apiece from John Charles and manager Raich Carter as Leeds beat the Scottish side 4–1. It was the first of several Monday night games against teams from north of the border and in successive weeks, Dundee and Falkirk were the visitors to Elland Road.

Three new floodlights were put up in 1973 and a fourth, in the south-east corner, was erected four years later. At 260ft, the diamond-shaped lights were the highest in Europe, with 55 lamps on each pylon.

Record receipts at Elland Road, which stood for over a decade, were established on 10 April 1980, when the FA Cup semi-final replay between West Ham United and Everton brought in £146,483. Fifteen years later a new financial benchmark was set when the Everton v Spurs FA Cup semi-final produced receipts of just over £1 million. The biggest European crowd at Leeds was achieved when Rangers were the visitors for the Fairs Cup quarter-final in 1968 when 50,498 fans were shoe-horned into the ground.

The first leg of the Rangers tie at Ibrox was covered by closed circuit TV and watched by 22,000 supporters at Elland Road. Television cameras were regular visitors to Elland Road during the Revie heyday, but the first match to be screened entirely live was on 4 January 1985, when FA Cup holders Everton began their defence with a convincing 2–0 win against Second Division Leeds. Coincidentally, the first visit by BBC *Match of the Day* cameras, on 20 March 1965, was also for a Leeds-Everton game. Leeds won the First Division match 4–1.

For many years the pitch was a churned-up muddy morass and in November 1969, United considered installing experimental pitch cover made of treated nylon but the idea was later scrapped. The pitch was reseeded in the summer of 1970 making it one of the best in the country after United had called in experts from the Sports Turf Research Institute at Bingley.

Undersoil heating was later installed in an effort to keep the pitch in prime condition during the bitter West Yorkshire winter thus reducing the number of games which had to be called off. Before the advent of the undersoil heating the pitch, was protected in winter by tons of straw and burning braziers.

Nothing, however, could save United the embarrassment of losing a youth international game to a local working mens' club pitch in 1964. On 14 March that year the England-Wales match scheduled for Elland Road, was switched to the city's East End Park WMC ground after United's pitch was waterlogged.

In the big freeze of 1963, Leeds experimented with de-icing pellets which successfully cleared part of a rock-hard surface but the club decided against using them over the whole pitch. To obtain much-needed match practice, Leeds played a Saturday morning friendly against Bradford at Elland Road dog-track They drew 2–2 with the Park Avenue club on a snow-covered pitch. The clubs' reserve teams also met in similar fashion.

Superstitious Revie was convinced that the bad luck his team seemed to suffer stemmed from a curse laid on the ground long before football had been played there, so in 1971 he called in a gypsy to lift that curse.

The pitch had improved so much that rugby league was able to make a permanent return to Elland Road when New Hunslet's home at the nearby greyhound stadium was demolished. Apart from staging New Hunslet's games, Elland Road also became venue for several key rugby league games.

Two other sports to make their presence felt at Elland Road have been American Football and Gaelic Football. The Leeds Cougars, members of the British American Football League, switched from their base at Bramley Rugby League Club's McLaren Field to Elland Road in May 1986. However, they moved off the following year because extra work needed doing on the pitch. A Gaelic Football match between Dublin and Mayo, organised by the Yorkshire County Board of the Gaelic Athletic Association, was played at Elland Road in 1987.

The ground has even staged live rock concerts with music fans flocking to Elland Road to see the band Queen in 1982, U2 five years later, the United-supporting local band Kaiser Chiefs in 2008 and Rod Stewart in June 2011. Two weeks after U2's performance, Elland Road hosted a three-day Jehovah's Witnesses Convention which attracted 15,000 people.

Boxing has also been held at Elland Road with Bradford's Frank Grant beating Herol 'Bomber' Graham and Henry Wharton (York) outpointing Fidel Castro Smith (Sheffield) in British title fights in 1991.

Exciting new plans to develop Elland Road and its surroundings as a major sporting complex were revealed in a major deal between United and Leeds City Council in the summer of 1985. United sold the ground to the council for £2.5 million and, in return, the council granted the club a 125-year lease and unveiled ambitious plans to improve the stadium and neighbouring sporting facilities.

In 1987 outline plans were designed by a Newcastle-based firm of architects and put forward by Baltic Consortium and W.H. White, developers. The estimated costs varied between £50 million and £75 million. The scheme included replacing the old 1920s Lowfields Road stand with a new 7,500-seater stand, with a 2,000-seater indoor sports arena at the other side of the stand.

Plans for the stadium complex also included a shopping centre, ice rink, cricket hall, cinema, nightclub, café, restaurant, water park, leisure centre and shops. Other innovations included provision for a railway halt for visiting supporters, and an open-air car park on three levels.

Although that actual scheme did not get off the ground, it was not long before the Lowfields Road Stand was to provide an impressive new landmark on the city's skyline.

The 1988–89 season was totally overshadowed by the Hillsborough disaster which eventually claimed the lives of 96 people at the Liverpool-Nottingham Forest FA Cup semi-final. Inevitably, ground safety came under review and the Lord Justice Taylor Report pointed the way to all-seater stadia and big reductions in ground capacities.

United cut the Elland Road capacity of 40,176 at the start of the 1989–90 season by 8,782, to comply with the interim Taylor Report, with the Kop bearing the brunt of virtually all of the reduction. With United blazing a trail at the top of Division Two, huge crowds turned up at Elland Road and a restriction of 1,500 was put on visiting supporters to enable Leeds to house their own fans, even though it meant a loss of revenue to the home club.

Midway through the season, managing director Bill Fotherby announced that Elland Road could become all-seater and that a new Lowfields Road Stand, costing between £6 million to £10 million, would be built. Within days of United celebrating their 1991–92 League title success, the bulldozers moved in to demolish the old ageing Lowfields Road stand to make way for the £5.5 million East Stand – much of the cost coming via a successful bond scheme introduced by the club.

By January 1993, it was sufficiently completed for part of the upper section to be opened for the first time. The whole stand was ready, on schedule, for the start of the 1993–94 season. However, United's floodlights, once the tallest in Europe, were removed and new lighting installed on the facia of the stand itself. Its 51-metre cantilever roof is believed to have been the largest in the world at the time, beating a stand in Seattle, USA, by two and a half metres.

The 17,000 capacity stand housed 10,000 in the lower tier and 7,000 in the upper tier, making it one of the largest in Britain. As a result of the work, Elland Road's capacity shot up to 43,000 from 30,937, but soon dropped to 39,457 after the installation of seats in the

An aerial view of Elland Road from the 1990s.

Kop. The East Stand was fully operational for the first time when Leeds beat West Ham 1–0 with a Gary Speed goal on 17 August 1993.

The next phase of making Elland Road all-seater began in summer 1994 when 7,000 seats were installed in the Geldard End Kop at a cost of £1.1 million – around £400,000 coming from the Football Trust. Fans stood on the Kop for the last time on 3 May 1994 to witness a 2–2 draw with Sheffield Wednesday but the following season it was renamed the Revie Stand and opened by Elsie Revie, widow of the late Don Revie, and the club's president, the Earl of Harewood. Ten year later, after the death of the legendary John Charles, the West Stand was renamed the John Charles Stand in honour of the brilliant Welsh star.

The changing rooms are housed below the West Stand, which boasts many corporate, banqueting and media facilities, the directors' box and a conference centre which was opened in April 1992.

The Leeds board had promised to make Elland Road one of the finest stadiums in the country and had delivered the goods.

When England was allocated the 1996 European Championships, Elland Road was named as one of the host grounds after rigorous inspections by UEFA officials.

As a trial run, England played a full international against Sweden at Elland Road on 8 June 1995 and 32,008 fans saw England hit back with two late goals to force a 3–3 draw. It was the first full England international held in England outside Wembley since a 1–1 draw with Poland at Goodison Park on 5 January 1966.

No Leeds player appeared but Harrogate-born John Scales (Tottenham) who was a United junior under Eddie Gray came on as a substitute.

Two months earlier, Elland Road had staged its eighth FA Cup semi-final when Everton beat Tottenham 4–1 in front of a 38,226 crowd which paid ground receipts of just over £1 million. In Group B of the 1996 European Championships, Elland Road staged the Spain v Bulgaria, France v Spain and Romania v Spain games.

Plans for a £11.3 million improvement to the West and South Stands, which would have brought the capacity up to around 45,000, were mooted in December 1997. The scheme would have included a 15,000-seater indoor arena at the rear of the West Stand and would have been home to basketball, ice hockey, pop concerts and other entertainment events. A new ice hockey team was named – the Leeds Lasers – but the whole project never got off the ground.

In 1998, United regained the ownership of Elland Road when the new owners Leeds Sporting PLC agreed to pay £10 million to buy back the stadium from Leeds City Council. Club chairman Peter Ridsdale wrote to all 18,500 season ticket holders and shareholders about the future of the ground complex in August 2001. He argued that the club needed a better stadium to remain competitive at the top of the Premiership and it was a clear choice of upgrading Elland Road or moving to a new site. The board said it would be possible to build the new ground at no extra cost to shareholders as it could be funded by the sale of Elland Road and sponsorship naming rights.

After the moving option was approved, Ridsdale announced the club would switch to a new 50,000-seater stadium on the south side of the A1-M1 link road near Temple Newsam in time for the 2004–05 season. However, the grand plans never came to fruition as a decline in playing fortunes, coupled with a financial crisis, meant the money was simply not there to fund the scheme. Ridsdale quit in March 2003 and the following year Elland Road was sold on a 25-year lease deal – with a buyback clause – to raise cash to help pay off a loan to Jack Petchey, an Aston Villa shareholder and former Watford chairman.

It emerged on 27 December 2006 that the stadium had been sold to the Teak Trading Corportation Ltd, based in the British Virgin Islands, about 15 months before.

Further redevelopment of Elland Road came when the South Stand was refurbished and closed for the first few games of the 2006–07 season while work was completed. Concrete columns and alcoves were boxed in to give the stand a more modern exterior; an overhaul of the kitchen concourse area, a new mezzanine-level office area, a total modernisation of the corporate facilities above and a new restaurant called Billy's Bar, named after former United hero Billy Bremner.

The revered skipper of the Don Revie era died in December 1997, aged 54, and had his ashes scattered on the Elland Road pitch. The club commissioned Leeds-born sculptress Frances Seigelman to make a statute of the great man and the nine-foot high bronze image outside the south-east corner of the ground was unveiled on 7 August 1999 and remains a focal point for many United fans.

When Ken Bates became chairman he knew it was important for the club to generate much more money from sources other than gate receipts. Ideas on the drawing board to develop Elland Road included two hotels, a shopping centre, restaurant, health club, new megastore, museum and tourist centre. In October 2008 the club released its plans for redevelopment behind the East Stand – a 350-room hotel at the south-east corner of the

The iconic Billy Bremner statue and the East Stand.

stadium, a covered arcade containing shops, bars, and restaurants; extended and improved facilities for business conferences and events, a new megastore, office block and nightclub. Shortly afterwards, it was announced that the city council would not be building the proposed Leeds Arena on land adjacent to the ground that is owned by the council, but instead would be built in the city centre.

Leeds was chosen as a host city as part of England's 2018 World Cup bid but the country's failure to land the tournament meant Elland Road would have to wait longer to stage World Cup football. Had the bid been successful and Elland Road chosen as a World cup venue, the ground capacity would have been increased to more than 50,000 by reconstructing the John Charles Stand and adding a tier to the Don Revie Stand.

At the end of 2009, chairman Bates spoke about plans to increase the capacity of the South Stand by up to 3,000. This would be achieved by removing the executive boxes and replacing them with seating.

The club launched the Leeds United Members Club during Bates' era and at the end of the 2010–11 season had 39,643 members.

The old Conference and Exhibition Centre on Low Fields Road was knocked down in 2010 and replaced by the Centenary Pavilion, which was double the size of the previous facility and can accommodate up to 3,000 members on matchdays as well as being used for other events on non-matchdays. As a result, the Howard's Way bar – named in honour of Howard Wilkinson – became the more upmarket Howard's Restaurant, based in the John Charles Stand.

During the 2011 close season, the East Stand Upper was redeveloped with a new extended concourse and 20 new executive boxes as part of phase one which also includes provision for a club museum. Once phase one is completed, building of the arcade, hotel and new megastore will begin as part of the five other phases. But when the first phase is finished Elland Road's capacity will be reduced by just over 1,500 to 37,900.

The start of the 2011–12 season saw away fans relocated from the South Stand corner with the East Stand to the south end of the John Charles Stand.

The Elland Road pitch measures approximately 115 yards long by 74 yards wide, with run-off space on each side. The under-soil heating system consists of 59 miles of piping and it is rare these days for United to lose a home game to bad weather.

Older parts of the stadium were used in the 2009 film *The Damned United*, which was based on Brian Clough's ill-fated 44-day reign in 1974 and more recently, Elland Road, was used to represent Wembley Stadium for the Oscar-winning 2010 film, *The King's Speech.*

Although Elland Road was earmarked as one of the possible stadia for England's failed 2018 World Cup bid, it is one of the venues shortlisted to host games in the 2015 Rugby Union World Cup.

At the end of April 2012 the club submitted an application to Leeds City Council for a gaming complex. If successful, the casino will form part of the redevelopment of the John Charles Stand which would lead to an overall increase in the stadium's capacity.

The casino, which would be run by specialists, not the club, covers 2,500sq metres over two floors. The redevelopment of the John Charles Stand would see a new upper tier and executive boxes.

The plan is for the casino scheme to help boost United's non-matchday income and enable the club to invest in the team.

The new imposing frontage to the East Stand which houses the club museum.

Welcome home...The plaque at the foot of the Don Revie statue which was unveiled by members of the 1972 FA Cup winning team, on Saturday 5 May 2012 – 40 years after United's only FA Cup success.

Pleased to meet you...a fan admires the Don Revie statue which was unveiled on on Lowfields Road.

That is for the future, but the club also looked to the past when celebrating the 40th anniversary of Leeds' only FA Cup success with the unveiling of the Don Revie statue on Lowfields Road.

Hundreds of fundraising events, masterminded by fan Jim Cadman, enabled the 8ft statue, created by Barnsley sculptor Graham Ibbeson to be commissioned. The statue, sited opposite the East Stand entrance, was unveiled by players from the 1972 FA Cup winning team and watched by members of the Revie family and hundreds of fans.

International Matches at Elland Road

Five full international matches have been played at Elland Road, plus England trial games, Under-23 and Under-21 fixtures and amateur internationals.

FULL INTERNATIONALS

8 June 1995

Umbro Cup

England 3 *(Sheringham 44, Platt 88, Anderton 89)*

Sweden 3 *(Mild 11, 37, K. Andersson 46)*

Elland Road had been selected as one of the stadia for Euro '96, so this Umbro Cup game was a trial run for the organisers.

The construction of the new 17,000 £5.5 million East Stand had helped Leeds to become one of the hosts for the Championships.

The game was the first full England international held outside Wembley since a 1–1 draw with Poland at Goodison Park on 5 January 1966.

England were outplayed by the Swedes for large parts of the game but rescued a draw with late goals by David Platt and Darren Anderton. England had beaten Japan 2–1 in their opening game but lost 2–1 to tournament winners Brazil in the final game at Wembley.

Former Leeds junior John Scales and future United player Nick Barmby got on as subs, while Teddy Lucic, a future loanee, played for Sweden.

England: Tim Flowers (Blackburn Rovers), Warren Barton (Newcastle United), Colin Cooper (Nottingham Forest), Gary Pallister (Manchester United) [sub John Scales (Tottenham Hotspur) 80 mins], Graeme Le Saux (Blackburn Rovers), Darren Anderton (Tottenham Hotspur), David Platt (Sampdoria), John Barnes (Liverpool) [sub Paul Gascoigne (Lazio) 63 mins], Peter Beardsley (Newcastle United) [sub Nick Barmby (Tottenham Hotspur) 63 mins], Teddy Sheringham (Tottenham Hotspur), Alan Shearer (Blackburn Rovers)

Manager: Terry Venables

Sweden: Thomas Ravelli (IFK Gothenburg), Gary Sundren (AIK Stockholm), Pontus Kamark (IFK Gothenburg), Joachim Bjorklund (IFK Gotheburg), Teddy Lucic (Vasta Frolunda), Niclas Alexandersson (Halmstads), Hakan Mild (Servette), Magus Erlingmark (IFK Gothenburg) [sub Ola Andersson (AIK Stockholm) 88 mins], Niklas Gudmundsson (Halmstads), Kennet Andersson (Caen) [sub Dick Lidman (AIK Stockholm) 84 mins], Henrik Larsson (Feyenoord)

Manager: Tommy Svensson

Referee: Leslie Mottram (Scotland)

Attendance: 32,008

9 June 1996

European Championship Finals, Group B

Bulgaria 1 *(Stoitchkov 65 pen)*

Spain 1 *(Alfonso 74)*

This game opened Group B with Romania taking on France in Newcastle the following day. All the action came in an explosive second half in which Bulgaria's star striker Hristo Stoichkov was outstanding.

He had already gone close several times before putting his team ahead from the spot after strike partner Emil Kostadinov had been fouled. Seven minutes later defender Petar Houbtchev was sent off and shortly afterwards substitute Alfonso Perez flicked in the equaliser.

More drama followed as Antonio Pizzi was sent off on 75 minutes for hacking down Radostin Kishishev, who was to have two loan spells with Leeds a decade later.

Bulgaria: Borislav Mihaylov (Reading), Radostin Kishishev (Neftochemik Burgas), Petar Houbtchev (SV Hamburg), Trifon Ivanov (Rapid Vienna), Ilian Kiriakov (Aberdeen) [sub Tzanko Tzvetanov (Waldhof Mannheim) 72 mins], Yordan Letchkov (SV Hamburg), Zlatko Yankov (KFC Uerdingen), Krassimir Balakov (VfB Stuttgart), Emil Kostadinov (Bayern Munich) [sub Ivailo Iordanov (Sporting Lisbon) 73 mins], Hristo Stoichkov (Parma), Luboslav Penev (Real Madrid) [sub Daniel Borimov (1860 Munich) 78 mins]

Manager: Dimitar Penev

Spain: Andoni Zubizaretta (Valencia), Alberto Belsue (Real Zaragosa), Rafael Alkorta (Real Madrid), Aberlardo Fernandez (Barcelona), Barjuan Sergi (Barcelona), Jose Luis Perez Caminero (Atletico Madrid) [sub Donato Gama (Deportivo La Coruna) 82 mins], Guillermo Amor (Barcelona) [sub Alfonso Perez (Real Betis) 72 mins], Fernando Hierro (Real Madrid), Luis Enrique (Real Madrid), Julen Guerrero (Athletic Bilbao) [sub Jose Emilio Amavisca (Real Madrid) 51 mins], Juan Antonio Pizzi (CD Tenerife)
Manager: Javier Clemente
Referee: Piero Ceccarini (Italy)
Attendance: 26,006

15 June 1996
European Championship Finals, Group B
France 1 *(Djorkaeff 48)*
Spain 1 *(Caminero 85)*
Two of the tournament's heavyweights went head-to-head protecting long unbeaten runs – France 24 matches and Spain 17.

In a low-key cautious affair in front of the group's largest attendance, the Spanish came within five minutes of seeing their record ended. Yuri Djorkaeff, whose father Jean played against England in the 1966 World Cup, shot France ahead just after half-time. Near the end Julio Salina laid the ball back for Jose Luis Caminero to knock in the point-saver.

France went on to beat Romania 3–1 and top the group.
France: Bernard Lama (Paris St Germain), Jocelyn Angloma (Torino) [sub Alain Roche (Paris St Germain) 65 mins], Laurent Blanc (Auxerre), Marcel Desailly (AC Milan), Bixente Lizarazu (Bordeaux), Christian Karembeu (Sampdoria), Didier Deschamps (Juventus), Vincent Guerin (Paris St Germain) [sub Lilian Thuram (Monaco) 81 mins], Youri Djorkaeff (Paris St Germain), Zinedine Zidane (Bordeaux), Patrice Loko (Paris St Germain) [sub Christophe Dugarry (Bordeaux) 74 mins]
Manager: Aime Jacquet
Spain: Andoni Zubizaretta (Valencia), Jorge Otero (Valencia) [sub Francisco Kiko (Atletico Madrid) 59 mins], Juan Manuel Lopez (Atletico Madrid), Aberlardo Fernandez (Barcelona), Sergi Barjuan (Barcelona), Rafael Alkorta (Real Madrid), Fernando Hierro (Real Madrid), Jose Emilio Amavisca (Real Madrid), Luis Enrique (Real Madrid) [sub Javier Manjarin (Deportivo La Coruna) 55 mins], Jose Luis Perez Caminero (Atletico Madrid), Alfonso Perez (Real Betis) [sub Julio Salinas (Sporting Gijon) 83 mins]
Manager: Javier Clemente
Referee: Vadim Zhuk (Bulgaria)
Attendance: 35,626

18 June 1996
European Championship Finals, Group B
Romania 1 *(Radiciou 29)*
Spain 2 *(Manjarin 11, Amor 84)*

Substitute Guillermo Amor headed a late goal to book Spain's place in the quarter-finals, but there was a hint of controversy about it.

Romania defender Daniel Prodan was lying injured in the area, playing Sergi Barjuan onside and the Barcelona man's cross was touched back by Alfonso Perez for Amor to score.

Javier Manjarin had given Spain an early lead but Gheorghe Hagi, winning his 100th cap, fashioned the equaliser for Florin Radiciou, but it was Spain who marched on to a quarter-final showdown with Terry Venables' England.

Romania: Florin Prunea (Dinamo Bucharest), Anton Dobos (Steaua Bucharest), Daniel Prodan (Steaua Bucharest) [sub Ioan Lupescu (Bayer Leverkusen) 86 mins], Tibor Selymes (Cercle Bruges), Dan Petrescu (Chelsea), Ovidiu Stinga (UD Salamanca), Gheorghe Popescu (Barcelona), Gheorghe Hagi (Barcelona), Constantin Galaca (Steaua Bucharest), Florin Radiciou (Espanyol) [sub Ion Vladoiu (Steaua Bucharest) 77 mins], Adrian Ilie (Steaua Bucharest) [sub Dorinel Munteanu (Cologne) 66 mins]

Manager: Angel Iordanescu

Spain: Andoni Zubizaretta (Valencia), Juan Manuel Lopez (Atletico Madrid), Aberlardo Fernandez (Barcelona) [sub Guillermo Amor (Barcelona) 64 mins], Rafael Alkorta (Real Madrid), Sergi Barjuan (Barcelona), Miguel Nadal (Barcelona), Fernando Hierro (Real Madrid), Javier Manjarin (Deportivo La Coruna), Fransico Kiko (Atletico Madrid) Jose Emilio Amavisca (Real Madrid) [sub Julen Guerrero (Athletic Bilbao) 72 mins], Juan Antonio Pizzi (CD Tenerife) [sub Alfonso Perez (Real Betis) 57 mins]

Manager: Javier Clemente

Referee: Ahmet Cakar (Turkey)

Attendance: 32,719

27 March 2002

Friendly International

England 1 *(Fowler 63)*

Italy 2 *(Montella 67, 90 pen)*

This was a big night for footballers' spotting anoraks. No less than 41 players featured on the Elland Road turf as two of Europe's big guns met in a pre-World Cup friendly.

Sven-Göran Eriksson changed his entire England team, while his opposite number Giovanni Trappatoni made eight substitutions.

As a spectacle it was a poor game but Leeds' recently acquired goal-poacher Robbie Fowler gave England the lead but Italy were level soon afterwards through Vincent Montella, who scored a last-minute penalty winner after Massimo Maccarone was brought down by David James. Maccarone played – and scored – in the 1–1 Under-21 meeting between the two countries at Valley Parade the previous night.

England: Nigel Martyn (Leeds United) [sub David James (West Ham United) HT], Danny Mills (Leeds United) [sub Phil Neville (Manchester United) HT], Sol Campbell (Arsenal) [sub Ledley King (Tottenham Hotspur) HT], Gareth Southgate (Middlesbrough) [sub Ugo Ehiogu (Middlesbrough) HT], Wayne Bridge (Southampton) [sub Gary Neville (Manchester United) 87 mins], David Beckham (Manchester United) [sub Danny Murphy (Liverpool) HT], Frank Lampard (Chelsea) [sub Joe Cole (West Ham United) HT], Nicky Butt (Manchester United)

[sub Owen Hargreaves (Bayern Munich) HT], Trevor Sinclair (West Ham United) [sub Teddy Sheringham (Tottenham Hotspur) 70 mins], Emile Heskey (Liverpool) [sub Robbie Fowler (Leeds United) HT], Michael Owen (Liverpool) [sub Darius Vassell (Aston Villa) HT]
Manager: Sven-Göran Eriksson
Italy: Gianluigi Buffon (Juventus), Gianluca Zambrotta (Juventus), Fabio Cannavaro (Parma), Alessandro Nesta (Lazio) [sub Daniele Adani (Fiorentina) 82 mins], Marco Materazzi (Inter Milan) [sub Mark Iuliano (Juventus) 57 mins], Christian Panucci (Roma) [sub Francesco Coco (Barcelona) 74 mins], Christiano Zanetti (Inter Milan) [sub Demetrio Albertini (AC Milan) 57 mins], Roberto Di Baggio (Inter Milan) [sub Gennaro Gattuso (AC Milan) 57 mins], Marco Delvecchio (Roma) [sub Massimo Maccarone (Empoli) 74 mins], Francesco Totti (Roma) [sub Vincent Montella (Roma) HT], Christiano Doni (Atalanta) [sub Damiano Tomassi (Roma) HT]
Manager: Giovanni Trapattoni
Referee: Herbert Fandel (Germany)
Attendance: 36,635

ENGLAND TRIALS

22 January 1906
The North 0
The South 2 *(Day 75, Woodward 78)*
Despite fielding the first £1,000 footballer, Middlesbrough's Alf Common, The North came off second best to The South.

Several of the South's gentleman players were drawn from the amateur ranks including cricketers Stan Harris (Surrey, Gloucestershire and Sussex), Gilbert Vassell (Somerset) and Sammy Day (Kent).

Of the 22 players on view at Elland Road, ten went on to play in the following month's 5–0 win against Ireland in Belfast.
The North: Nat Robinson (Birmingham), Bob Crompton (Blackburn Rovers), Tommy Rodway (Preston North End), Ben Warren (Derby County), Colin Veitch (Newcastle United), Jimmy Bradley (Liverpool), Dickie Bond (Preston North End), Alf Common (Middlesbrough), Arthur Brown (Sheffield United), Joe Bache (Aston Villa), Albert Gosnell (Newcastle United)
The South: James Ashcroft (Woolwich Arsenal), Archie Cross (Woolwich Arsenal), Tom Riley (Brentford), Pat Collins (Fulham), Walter Bull (Tottenham Hotspur), Kelly Houlker (Southampton), Gilbert Vassall (Old Carthusians), Sammy Day (Old Malvernians), Vivian Woodward (Tottenham Hotspur), Stanley Harris (Old Westminsters), Gordon Wright (Cambridge University)
Referee: E. Case (Birkenhead)
Attendance: 7,000

19 February 1923
England v The North
Cancelled because of snow

21 January 1924
The North 5 *(Jack 35, 38, Stephenson 2, Bradford 43, Seymour 50)*
The South 1 *(Haines 85)*
Northern clubs dominated the 1923–24 First Division and their strength was reflected in this comfortable victory against the amateurs of the South.

Star of the show was inside-forward Clem Stephenson of Huddersfield Town, who went on to win the title. His performance earned him his sole England cap the following month when Wales pulled off a shock 2–1 win at Ewood Park, Blackburn. None of the South trialists appeared in that match. Stephenson had played regularly for Leeds City during World War One.

The FA reallocated the game to Elland Road after the previous year's fixture was snowed off. The low crowd is attributed to a rail strike and incessant drizzle.
The North: Ronnie Sewell (Blackburn Rovers), Warney Cresswell (Sunderland), Sam Wadsworth (Huddersfield Town), Fred Kean (Sheffield Wednesday), James Seddon (Bolton Wanderers), Percy Barton (Birmingham), Sam Cheddzoy (Everton), David Jack (Bolton Wanderers), Joe Bradford (Birmingham), Clem Stephenson (Huddersfield Town), George Seymour (Newcastle United)
The South: Ben Howard Baker (Corinthians), Tom Parker (Southampton), Alfred Bower (Corinthians), Bert Smith (Tottenham Hotspur), Claude Ashton (Corinthians), Tommy Meehan (Chelsea), Dr Jimmy Paterson (Arsenal), Stanley Earle (Clapton), Willie Haines (Portsmouth), Jack Elkes (Tottenham Hotspur), Jackie Hegan (Corinthians)
Referee: E. Farrar (Leeds)
Attendance: 4,496

UNDER-23 INTERNATIONALS

9 November 1961
England 7 *(Byrne 15, 70, F. Hill 18, 53, Farmer 40, S. Hill 74, Harris 86)*
Israel 1 *(Levi 8)*
England fell behind to an early goal by Shlomo Levi but overran the Israelis.

They peppered Hapoel Tel Aviv goalkeeper Yaacov Hodorov to make it 3–1 at half-time and put four past his replacement, Yair Nosowski in the second half.

Of the England players, the peerless Bobby Moore went on to skipper England to their 1966 World Cup triumph.

England manager Walter Winterbottom watched the game, having presided over the Football League side which lost to the Italian League 2–0 at Old Trafford the previous night.
England: Gordon West (Blackpool), Joe Kirkup (West Ham United), Bobby Moore (West Ham United), Brian Labone (Everton), Gordon Jones (Middlesbrough), Alan Deakin (Aston Villa), Steve Hill (Blackpool), Johnny Byrne (Crystal Palace), Ted Farmer (Wolverhampton Wanderers), Freddie Hill (Bolton Wanderers), Gordon Harris (Burnley)
Manager: Walter Winterbottom
Israel: Yaacob Hodorov (Hapoel Tel Aviv) [sub Yair Nosowski (Hapoel Kfar-Saba) HT], Eliezer Aharonov (Maccabi Petah-Tikva) [sub Yaacob Grundman (Bnei-Yehuda Tel-Aviv)

38], Zvi Tendler (Hapoel Haifa), Shalom Peterburg (Hapoel Petah-Tikva), Amatsia Levkovih (Hapoel Tel Aviv), Gidon Tish (Hapoel Tel Aviv), Avraham Menchel (Maccabi Haifa), Nahum Stelmach (Hapoel Petah-Tikva), Rehavia Rosenboim (Hapoel Tel Aviv), Shlomo Levy (Hapoel Haifa), ReuvenYang (Hapoel Haifa)
Manager: Gyula Mandi
Referee: Menahem Askenazi (Israel)
Attendance: 12,419

7 April 1965
England 0
Czechoslovakia 0
Alf Ramsey didn't get many clues for the World Cup as the Young Lions drew a blank with Czechoslovakia in front of a poor Elland Road attendance.

The best player, Alan Ball, was making his fourth Under-23 appearance, and the only one of the team to play in the following year's glorious victory against West Germany.

Mick Jones, of course, was later to join Leeds for £100,000 while Martin Chivers came close to a last-minute winner.
England: Bill Glazier (Coventry City), Len Badger (Sheffield United), Tommy Smith (Liverpool), Vic Mobley (Sheffield Wednesday), Bobby Thomson (Wolverhampton Wanderers), Henry Newton (Nottingham Forest), Bert Murray (Chelsea), Martin Chivers (Southampton), Mick Jones (Sheffield United), Alan Ball (Blackpool), George Armstrong (Arsenal)
Manager: Alf Ramsey
Czechoslovakia: Alexandr Vencel (Slovan Bratislava), Miroslav Camarada (Dukla Prague), Vladimir Taborsky (Sparta Prague), Vaclav Migas (Dukla Slany), Karel Knesl (Dukla Prague), Ivan Hrdlicka (Slovan Bratislava), Frantisek Vesely (Slavia Prague), Stanislav Strunc (Sparta Plzen), Eduard Gaborik (Slovan Bratislava), Miroslav Rodr (Dukla Prague), Dusan Kabat (Dukla Prague)
Manager: Jira Vaclav
Referee: Henri Faucheux (France)
Attendance: 8,533

UNDER-21 INTERNATIONAL

European Championship, Group 6
7 October 2005
England 1 *(Cole 18)*
Austria 2 *(Janko 56, 76)*
Marko Janko's second half double proved extremely damaging to England's hopes of reaching the European Championship finals in Portugal.

They missed the chance to go top of the group, which was won by Germany, leaving second-placed England to go in to a Play-off with France which they lost on aggregate.

The England side included three former Leeds players – Scott Carson, James Milner and Aaron Lennon – who all went on to win full international honours.

England: Scott Carson (Liverpool), Steven Taylor (Newcastle United), Leighton Baines (Wigan Athletic), Michael Dawson (Tottenham Hotspur), Anton Ferdinand (West Ham United) [sub Ryan Taylor (Wigan Athletic) 71 mins], Tom Huddlestone (Tottenham Hotspur), James Milner (Newcastle United), Tom Soares (Crystal Palace) [sub Luke Moore (Aston Villa) 61 mins], Carlton Cole (Chelsea) [sub Cameron Jerome (Cardiff City) 87 mins], Jerome Thomas (Charlton Athletic), Aaron Lennon (Tottenham Hotspur)
Manager: Peter Taylor
Austria: Ramazan Ozcan (Austria Lustenau), Mario Sonnleitner (Grazer AK), Dennis Mimm (Wacker Innsbruck), Markus Berger (SV Ried), Alexander Pollhuber (Red Bull Saltzburg), Florian Metz (Austria Vienna), Besian Idrizaj (Liverpool) [sub Philipp Weissenberger (SC Schwanestadt) 67 mins], Gyorgy Garics (Rapid Vienna), Zlatko Junzovic (Grazer AK), Andreas Holzl (Wacker Innsbruck), Marco Janko (SV Saltzburg) [sub Lukas Mossner (SV Mattersburg) 90 mins]
Manager: Willibald Rutternsteiner
Referee: Joeni Van de Velde (Belgium)
Attendance: 28,030

AMATEUR INTERNATIONALS

20 November 1909
England 4 *(Owen 2, Woodward 44, J. Wright og 75, Jordan 88)*
Ireland 4 *(Robertson 5, 82, McDonnell 15, Hooper 20)*
This was the first full international match staged at Elland Road – and turned out to be a real thriller.

Ireland had not beaten England at football at either professional or amateur level but came mighty close at Leeds, leading 3–1 with 15 minutes remaining. They were denied by West Brom's Billy Jordan, who equalised just before the end. Oxford University graduate Jordan had been ordained into the church two years earlier.

Receipts for the match were £198 1s 3d.

England: R.G. Brebner (Darlington), W.S. Corbett (Birmingham), A.E. Scother (Oxford City), F. Fayers (Watford), F.W. Chapman (South Nottingham), J.E. Olley (Clapton), A. Berry (Fulham), V.J. Woodward (Chelmsford), W.C. Jordan (West Bromwich Albion), A.S. Owen (Leicester Fosse), E.W. Williams (Portsmouth)
Ireland: F. McKee (Cliftonville), P. McCann (Belfast Celtic), P.J. Thunder (Bohemians), J. Wright (Cliftonville), D. Martin (Cliftonville), L. Donnelly (Distillery), J. Wright (Distillery), J. Robertson (Cliftonville), J. McDonnell (Bohemians), Dr W.F. Hooper (Bohemians), F. Thompson (Cliftonville)
Referee: A.A. Jackson (Scotland)
Attendance: 8,000

16 March 1929
England 3 *(Ashton 28, Kail 67, 85)*
Scotland 1 *(Gates og 51)*

Scotland included eight players from Glasgow club Queen's Park in their line up but they were no match for the individual skill and strength of the England players.

Edgar Kail, who won three full England caps, was a thorn in the Scots' side and richly deserved his two goals. Chartered accountant Claude Ashton, also capped by the full England side, scored the opener.

On the same day Scotland's rugby union players beat England 12–6 at Murrayfield to retain the Calcutta Cup.

England: Ben Howard Baker (Corinthians), F.J. Gregory (Millwall), E.H. Gates (London Corinthians), C.E. Glenister (Navy), A.H. Chadder (Corinthians), J.G. Knight (Casuals), L. Morrish (Dulwich Hamlet), E. Kail (Dulwich Hamlet), C.T. Ashton (Corinthians), A.G. Doggart (Corinthians), K.E. Hogan (Army)

Scotland: R.L. Small (St Bernards), W.O. Walker (Queen's Park), W. Wiseman (Queen's Park), J. McDonald (Queen's Park), R. Gillespie (Queen's Park), W.S. King (Queen's Park), I. McDonald (Murrayfield Amateurs), W.S. Chalmers (Queen's Park), D. McLelland (Queen's Park), J.R. Russell (Edinburgh University), W.G. Nicholson (Queen's Park)

Referee: G.D. Nunnery (Shropshire)

Attendance: 15,571

26 March 1958

England 1 *(Bradley 6)*

France 1 *(Christobal pen 24)*

England's scorer, schoolteacher Warren Bradley, was signed for Manchester United by Matt Busby after the Munich Air Disaster. A small, tough little winger, he went on to win three full England caps to add to the 11 he won as an amateur.

Only a brilliant display by goalkeeper Mike Pinner enabled England to escape with a draw. A solicitor, he played for Pegasus, whose players were graduates drawn from the universities of Oxford and Cambridge. Pinner played 52 times for the England amateur team.

England: M.J. Pinner (Pegasus), J. Dougall (Pegasus), J.H. Valentine (Loughborough College), R. Vowells (Corinthians Casuals), S. Prince (Walthamstow Avenue), H. Dodkins (Ilford), W. Bradley (Bishop Auckland), D. Bumpstead (Tooting and Mitcham), G. Mortimore (Woking), G. Hamm (Woking), A.M. Peel (Sheffield University)

France: R. Cesaire (VS Quevilly), B. Rodzik (Stade de Rheims), F. Phillipe (AS Brest), M. Christobal (St Etienne), G. Lelong (VS Quevilly), R. Monnet (Olympic Lyonaisse), R. Hauser (FC Mulhouse), M. Mouchel (AS Cherbourg), J.L. Bettenfield (AAJ Sainte Fountaine), J. Buron (Dieppe), M. Longle (SCO Angers)

Referee: H. Anderson (Denmark)

Attendance: 6,000

FA AMATEUR CUP FINAL

4 April 1914

Bishop Auckland 1 *(Kirby 55)*

Northern Nomads 0

Bishop Auckland became the first side to win the Amateur Cup three times thanks to Fred Kirby's 55th minute winner.

Barlow missed a penalty for Nomads quarter of an hour from the end as the Bishops deservedly recaptured the trophy which they won in 1896 and 1900.

The cup was presented by the Lord Mayor of Leeds, James Bedford.

Bishop Auckland: E.J. North, T. Roe, C.J. Rudd, F. Hopper, A.M. Spence, T. Maddison, A. Appleby, D. Douglass, F. Kirby, T. Spence, T. Lunson

Northern Nomads: H. Peever, C. Barlow, H.N. Cunliffe, R. Gotobed, T.C. Porter, M. McKinnon, M.D. Davies, H. Douglass, A. Cruse, L.L. Boardman, G.O. Salt

Referee: A. Warner (Nottingham)

Attendance: 5,294

FA CUP SEMI-FINALS

26 March 1910

Barnsley 0

Everton 0

The FA came in for plenty of criticism after selecting Elland Road to host such a large game.

Elland Road simply could not cope with thousands of fans locked out and many of those inside having a poor view.

Playing for Barnsley was Ernie Gadsby, whose son, Ken, was to play for Leeds, while Billy Scott, who joined City in 1912, kept a clean sheet for Everton.

Barnsley won the replay 3–0 at Old Trafford but lost the final, also after a reply, to Newcastle.

Barnsley: Fred Mearns, Dickie Downs, Harry Ness, Bob Glendenning, Tommy Boyle, George Utley, Wilf Bartop, Ernie Gadsby, George Lilcrop, Harry Tufnell, Tom Forman

Everton: Billy Scott, John Maconnachie, Bob Clifford, Harry Makepeace, Jack Taylor, Val Harris, George Barlow, Sandy Young, Bert Freeman, Walter White, Jack Sharp

Referee: H.S. Bamlett (Gateshead)

Attendance: 36,000

22 March 1930

Arsenal 2 *(Jack 70, Bastin 84)*

Hull City 2 *(Howieson 15, Duncan 30)*

Former Leeds City boss Herbert Chapman had hoped to return to Elland Road in triumph with his outstanding Arsenal side. But they were held by battling Hull City, who were struggling in the lower reaches of Division Two.

Amazingly, the Tigers, who were relegated to the Third Division North that season, led 2–0 but Arsenal battled back to scrape a replay at Villa Park, which they won 1–0 with a David Jack goal.

Arsenal's Alf Baker was the brother of Leeds skipper Jim Baker and centre-forward Jack Lambert had been an Elland Road player as a youngster. Lambert was one of the marksmen as the Gunners beat Huddersfield 2–0 in the Final.

Arsenal: Dan Lewis, Tom Parker, Eddie Hapgood, Alf Baker, Bill Seddon, Charlie Jones, Joe Hume, David Jack, Jack Lambert, Alex James, Cliff Bastin
Hull City: Fred Gibson, George Goldsmith, Matt Bell, James Walsh, John Childs, William Gowdy, Stan Alexander, Ronald Starling, Paddy Mills, Jimmy Howieson, Dally Duncan.
Referee: A.H. Kingscott (Long Eaton)
Attendance: 47,549

14 March 1931
Birmingham 2 *(Curtis 31, 87)*
Sunderland 0
Two goals from left winger Ernie Curtis settled this tie – although some sources credit one of his goals to Sunderland goalkeeper Bob Middleton.

For some reason the Rokerites came out a full 10 minutes before the scheduled kick-off and were hanging around in the cold. They were skippered by Jock MacDougall, who joined Leeds in 1934. Birmingham lost the Final 2–1 to West Brom.
Birmingham: Harry Hibbs, George Liddell, Ned Barkas, Jimmy Cringan, George Morrall, Alec Leslie, George Briggs, Johnny Crosbie, Joe Bradford, Jack Firth, Ernie Curtis.
Sunderland: Bob Middleton, Bill Murray, Harold Shaw, Alex Hastings, Jock McDougall, Arthur Andrews, Billy Eden, Joe Devine, Bobby Gurney, James Leonard, Jimmy Connor
Referee: A.E. Fogg (Bolton)
Attendance: 43,572

16 March 1935
West Bromwich Albion 1 *(W.G. Richardson 60)*
Bolton Wanderers 1 *(Walton 12)*
This was the first drawn FA Cup semi-final since Arsenal and Hull drew 2–2 five years earlier – a game also played at Elland Road.

Bolton's Harry Goslin guested for Leeds during the war and was killed on active service in Italy in 1943.

There were two players in the Albion side called William Richardson. The centre-forward – and scorer against Bolton – took the initials 'W.G.' to distinguish himself from his centre-half colleague. The 'G' stood for Ginger. There were two George Taylors in the Bolton team, one a left-half, the other, George Thomas Taylor, a winger.

West Brom won the replay 2–0 at Stoke but lost a thrilling Final, 4–2 to Sheffield Wednesday.
West Bromwich Albion: Harold Pearson, George Shaw, Bert Trentham, James Murphy, Bill Richardson, Jimmy Edwards, Arthur Gale, Joe Carter, Billy G. Richardson, Teddy Sandford, Walter Boyes
Bolton Wanderers: Bob Jones, Bob Smith, Alex Finney, Harry Goslin, Jack Atkinson, George Taylor, George Thomas Taylor, George Eastham, George Walton, Ray Westwood, Willie Cook
Referee: R. Bowie (Northumberland)
Attendance: 49,605

29 March 1947
Charlton Athletic 4 *(Dawson 18, Welsh 40, 44, Hurst 50)*
Newcastle United 0
Don Welsh netted twice as Charlton romped home in the mud against Second Division side Newcastle to secure a second successive Wembley appearance.

The Magpies' goalkeeper Tom Swinburne, was the father of Trevor Swinburne, who played for Leeds in the 1980s.

Charlton went on to lift the Cup by beating Burnley at Wembley. The Valiants right-back Ted Croker later became FA secretary and chief executive.

Charlton Athletic: Sam Bartram, Ted Croker, Jack Shreeve, Bert Johnson, Harold Phipps, Charlie Revell, Gordon Hurst, Tommy Dawson, Bill Robinson, Don Welsh, Chris Duffy
Newcastle United: Tom Swinburne, Bobby Cowell, Bobby Corbett, Joe Harvey, Frank Brennan, Doug Wright, Jackie Milburn, Roy Bentley, George Stobbart, Len Shackleton, Tommy Pearson
Attendance: 47,978

2 April 1952
Newcastle United 2 *(G. Robledo 56, Mitchell pen 85)*
Blackburn Rovers 1 *(Quigley 78)*
Holders Newcastle clinched a second successive Wembley appearance at the expense of battling Blackburn. The Geordies clinched a dramatic victory with a late Bobby Mitchell left-foot penalty after Eddie Crossan handled in the area.

In the Final they beat Arsenal 1–0 to retain the trophy – the first team to do so since Blackburn 60 years earlier.

Blackburn inside-forward Albert Nightingale joined Leeds for £10,000 seven months after his semi-final appearance.

Newcastle United: Ronnie Simpson, Bobby Cowell, Alf McMichael, Joe Harvey, Frank Brennan, Ted Robledo, Tommy Walker, Bill Foulkes, Jackie Milburn, George Robledo, Bobby Mitchell
Blackburn Rovers: Reg Elvey, David Gray, Bill Eckersley, Jackie Campbell, Willie Kelly, Ronnie Clayton, Alec Glover, Eddie Crossan, Eddie Quigley, Albert Nightingale, John Wharton
Referee: J.E. Leafe (Nottingham)
Attendance: 54,066

18 March 1961
Sheffield United 0
Leicester City 0
This was the seventh FA Cup semi-final staged at Elland Road – and the fourth draw.

Leicester were probably the happier as injured winger Gordon Wills was a virtual passenger at the end of a deadly dull game.

It took two replays after the Elland Road stalemate before Leicester reached Wembley where they lost to Tottenham.

Sheffield United: Alan Hodgkinson, Cec Coldwell, Graham Shaw, Barry Richardson, Joe Shaw, Gerry Summers, Billy Hodgson, Billy Russell, Derek Pace, Keith Kettleborough, Ronnie Simpson
Leicester City: Gordon Banks, Len Chalmers, Richie Norman, Frank McLintock, John King, Colin Appleton, Howard Riley, Jimmy Walsh, Ken Leek, Ken Keyworth, Gordon Wills
Referee: J. Finney (Hereford)
Attendance: 52,095

16 April 1980
Replay
Everton 1 *(Latchford 115)*
West Ham United 2 *(Devonshire 94, Lampard 118)*
Everton's Brian Kidd, later to coach Leeds, missed this replay as he was sent off in the 1–1 draw in the first match at Villa Park.

All the goals in the exciting replay came in extra-time, Frank Lampard heading a 118th minute winner for Second Division West Ham who beat Arsenal in the Final.

Imre Varadi, part of United's 1989–90 Division Two title-winning squad came on as a substitute for Everton.
Everton: Martin Hodge, John Gidman, John Bailey, Billy Wright, Mick Lyons, Kevin Ratcliffe, Andy King (Imre Varadi), Peter Eastoe, Bob Latchford, Asa Hartford, Trevor Ross
West Ham United: Phil Parkes, Frank Lampard, Paul Brush, Ray Stewart, Billy Bonds, Alan Devonshire, Paul Allen, Stuart Pearson, David Cross, Trevor Brooking, Geoff Pike
Referee: C.N. Seel (Chester)
Attendance: 40,720

9 April 1995
Everton 4 *(Jackson 35, Stuart 55, Amokachi 82, 90)*
Tottenham Hotspur 1 *(Klinsmann pen 63)*
Everton pulled off a bit of a surprise by thumping Tottenham who boasted Footballer of the Year Jurgen Klinsmann, the German goal machine, in their ranks.

Nigerian striker Daniel Amokachi came off the bench to score twice late on for the Blues, who beat Manchester United 1–0 in the Final.

On the losing Spurs side was Nick Barmby, later to join Leeds.
Everton: Neville Southall, Matthew Jackson, Gary Ablett, Joe Parkinson, Dave Watson, David Unsworth, Anders Limpar (Daniel Amokachi), Barry Horne, Graham Stuart, Paul Rideout (Duncan Ferguson), Andy Hincliffe
Tottenham Hotspur: Ian Walker, Dean Austin, Stuart Nethercott (Ronnie Rosenthal), Gica Popescu, Colin Calderwood, Gary Mabbutt, Darren Anderton, Nick Barmby, Jurgen Klinsmann, Teddy Sheringham, David Howells
Referee: R. Hart (Darlington)
Attendance: 38,226

WARTIME REPRESENTATIVE GAMES

13 December 1941

FA XI 2 *(D. Compton pen, Rowley)*

RAF XI 2 *(Dodds, Smith)*

United full-back Les Goldberg was in good company for this game which raised £800 in gate receipts for the RAF Benevolent Fund.

A former England Schools player, he was alongside some of the best known players of the immediate post-war era including Wilf Mannion, Joe Mercer, Jack Rowley and Jimmy Hagan.

Goldberg, who joined Reading after the war and changed his name by deed poll to Gaunt, did not look out of place in a thrilling match which featured a penalty save by FA goalie Hesford. Another FA team member, Ken Willingham, joined United after the war.

FA XI: Bob Hesford (Huddersfield Town), Les Goldberg (Leeds United), Andy Beattie (Preston North End), Ken Willingham (Huddersfield Town), Alf Young (Huddersfield Town), Joe Mercer (Everton), Ralph Birkett (Newcastle United), Wilf Mannion (Middlesbrough), Jack Rowley (Manchester United), Jimmy Hagan (Sheffield United), Dennis Compton (Arsenal)

RAF: George Marks (Arsenal), Bert Turner (Charlton), Eddie Hapgood (Arsenal), Frank Soo (Chelsea), Tommy Jones (Everton), George Paterson (Celtic), Alf Kirchen (Arsenal), Trevor Smith (Crystal Palace), Jock Dodds (Blackpool), Les Jones (Arsenal), Billy Wrigglesworth (Manchester United)

Attendance: 13,000

21 February 1941

Northern Command 1 *(Robinson)*

Scottish Command 1 *(Hamilton)*

This game, in aid of Army Welfare funds, featured United players Aubrey Powell and Tom Holley in the Northern Command line up.

Twelve internationals were on show and put on a slick display of football. Hamilton's header five minutes after half-time put the Scots ahead, but Robinson levelled for the Northern boys after a clever dribble.

Northern Command: Jack Harkness (Heart of Midlothian), Eric Westwood (Manchester City), Andy Beattie (Preston North End), Jock Kirton (Stoke City), Tom Holley (Leeds United), Jimmy McInnes (Liverpool), Aubrey Powell (Leeds United), Jack Balmer (Liverpool), Freddie Steele (Stoke City), Jackie Robinson (Sheffield Wednesday), Walter Boyes (Everton)

Scottish Command: John Lynch (Dundee), Jimmy Carabine (Third Lanark), Alex Winning (Clyde), Matt Busby (Liverpool), Austin Collier (Third Lanark), Harry Betmead (Grimsby Town), Robert Campbell (Falkirk), Tommy Walker (Heart of Midlothian), George Hamilton (Heart of Midlothian), Andy McCall (Aberdeen), Joe Johnstone (Motherwell)

Attendance: 8,500

26 December 1942
Army 3 *(Wescott [2], Hagan)*
RAF 1 *(Dodds)*
Some of the stars of this inter-Services game went on to have great managerial success.

Bill Shankly, Cliff Britton, Stan Cullis, Joe Mercer and Raich Carter, who was in charge at Leeds, all made their mark with a variety of clubs.

The Boxing Day game attracted a healthy crowd to Elland Road and among the highlights was a penalty save by Frank Swift from Jock Dodds.

Army: Frank Swift (Manchester City), Jimmy Carabine (Third Lanark), Leslie Compton (Arsenal), Cliff Britton (Everton), Stan Cullis (Wolverhampton Wanderers), Joe Mercer (Everton), Ralph Birkett (Newcastle United), Jimmy Hagan (Sheffield United), Denis Westcott (Wolverhampton Wanderers), Gordon Bremner (Arsenal), Dennis Compton (Arsenal)

RAF: George Marks (Arsenal), Bill Shankly (Preston North End), Billy Hughes (Birmingham City), Frank Soo (Preston North End), Bernard Joy (Arsenal), George Paterson (Celtic), Stanley Matthews (Stoke City), Raich Carter (Sunderland), Jock Dodds (Blackpool), Bobby Brown (Charlton Athletic), Alf Kirchen (Arsenal)

Referee: H. Berry (Huddersfield)
Attendance: 20,000

Rugby League Internationals at Elland Road

Many games of rugby league have been staged at Elland Road which was used by the RFL for various Cup Finals and semi-finals. Hunslet Hawks shared the ground with Leeds United in the mid 1980s after their home, the nearby greyhound stadium, had been demolished. Leeds Rhinos have also played several games at Elland Road, including the 1988 Yorkshire Cup Final win against Castleford and four World Club Challenge matches. They beat Canterbury Bulldogs in 2005 and edged out Melbourne Storm three years later. In 2009 the Loiners lost to Manly Sea Eagles and the following year were beaten by Melbourne Storm.

Considerably larger crowds, though, were attracted by the following international matches, which included New Zealand's shock 24–0 victory against Australia in the 2005 Tri-Nations final.

9 November 1985	Great Britain 6	New Zealand 6	Att: 22,209
8 November 1985	Great Britain 4	Australia 34	Att: 30,808
10 November 1990	Great Britain 0	Australia 14	Att: 32,500
20 November 1994	Great Britain 4	Australia 23	Att: 39,468
16 November 1997	Great Britain 20	Australia 37	Att: 39,337
27 November 2004	Great Britain 4	Australia 44	Att: 39,120
26 November 2005	Australia 0	New Zealand 24	Att: 26,534
14 November 2009	Great Britain 16	Australia 46	Att: 31,042
19 November 2011	England 8	Australia 30	Att: 34,174

Footnote: South Africa's rugby union Springboks also played at Elland Road when 14,471 saw them beat The North 19–3 in a representative game on 10 November 1992.

International Speedway at Elland Road

Leeds Lions speedway team raced at Fullerton Park, Elland Road, between 1928 and 1938 and were Northern League champions in 1929. Fullerton Park was for many years the Leeds United training ground opposite the main stadium and is now used as a car park. Two international speedway meetings have been held at Fullerton Park.

12 July 1930	Unofficial Test match	England 29	Australia 13
13 August 1938	Division Two international	England 30	Dominions 77

Leeds Kits, Badges and Shirt Sponsors

LEEDS UNITED's famous all-white strip is known throughout the world. It is well documented that Don Revie changed the colours from old gold and blue to all white to reflect his admiration of the brilliant Real Madrid. But that is only half the story. Further research, prompted by several knowledgeable fans and writers, has proved that Leeds were kitted out in white the season before Revie took charge.

United, under the management of Jack Taylor, kicked off the 1960–61 season in their usual gold and blue shirts, white shorts with blue and gold stripe and blue and gold socks. On Saturday 17 September nine games into the Division Two season they trotted out at Elland Road against Middlesbrough wearing white shirts with a blue and gold V-neck and white shorts with blue and gold stripe. Newspaper photographs, although in black and white, in the local press clearly show the new kit in the 4–4 draw with Boro.

Taylor's men continued to wear the new strip unless the opposition wore white shorts, in which case United went back to the blue and gold colours. Curiously, though, every home programmes after the Middlesbrough match that season refers to Leeds wearing blue shirts and old gold collars, although that could have been an oversight on the programme template. Pictures in the programme also show players wearing both versions of the kit.

Colin S. Jeffrey, author of *Twelve At The Top*, which covers the club from 1963 to 1975, said: 'Why, under Jack Taylor, did Leeds United change to a basically white strip? I am not sure, but my personal theory is that United's blue and gold shirts and socks didn't stand out well under floodlights. Fifty years ago floodlights, and especially those at Elland Road, were not up to present day standard.'

Revie took over six months after the Middlesbrough game and in summer 1961 asked the board to have the club's colours officially changed to all white and they agreed.

Gone was the blue and gold trim of the previous season – Leeds were now in pristine all white, just like Real Madrid, even down to the round collar, unlike the V-neck that was in common use at the time. The switch by Taylor and Revie was quite a leap from the club's tradition.

Leeds City had entered the Football League in 1905 and the first widely published picture of the squad shows them in stripes, which were blue and white, with dark shorts and socks. The following season they were kitted out in a uniform of dark blue shirts with old gold trim, white shorts and blue socks, plus the important addition of a badge which was effectively the city of Leeds coat of arms.

Above the Latin motto '*Pro Rege et Lege*' – 'For King and the law' are three owls taken from the coat of arms of Sir John Saville, who was the first alderman of Leeds, and a fleece symbolising the city's connection with the wool trade.

The arrival of the ostentatious Frank Scott-Walford as manager in 1908 saw the introduction of an equally flamboyant strip with an old gold pinstripe incorporated on the blue shirt. The following year the stripe colours were swapped with gold becoming the predominant colour.

Although replica shirts were light years away, Scott-Walford, who doubled as club secretary, had no qualms about changing the colours for a third successive season. This time it was even more revolutionary.

Because of a lack of cash he signed up several cheaper players from Ireland and had the idea of kitting them out in green shirts to make them feel more at home. For the opening game of the season against Blackpool on 3 September 1910 he even had green flags dotted around the pitch.

It was back to stripes for 1911–12 but after City had to apply for re-election Herbert Chapman succeeded Scott-Walford and he, too, had a penchant for kit changes. In 1913–14 the blue shirts sported a large gold band round the chest and the following season the band became a chevron from the shoulder. City appear to have stuck with this version until the club's demise in 1919.

United went back to basics on their election to the Football League the following year, adopting blue and white stripes. It was a similar outfit to neighbours Huddersfield Town – not surprising as United chairman Hilton Crowther had previously been at the helm of the Terriers.

Although shorts and sock colours changed from season to season and plain blue shirts were used for some games, blue and white stripes remained the predominant outfit until 1934 when the city crest badge reappeared for the first time since the Leeds City days.

A new kit of blue and gold halved shirts, white shorts and blue socks with gold tops got its first public airing on 22 September when Liverpool won 3–0 at Elland Road.

Former Leeds City boss Herbert Chapman had long been an advocate of shirt numbering, but it was not given the thumbs up by the Football League until 1939 – four years after his death.

At this time United were playing in blue and old gold halved shirts and continued to play on a variation on the theme for several years. After World War Two, United were relegated and continued to struggle in the Second Division but were still able to appoint one of the biggest names in football, Major Frank Buckley, as manager in 1948.

He was always known as a man who would 'think outside the box'

The Leeds United badge from the 1950s.

The owl badge, 1964.

and was convinced a contributing factor to poor performances was that the halved shirts made it hard for his players to pick each other out. He promptly organised a practice match with one team in the usual colours and the other in plain shirts.

Chairman Sam Bolton and director Percy Woodward looked on from the touchline and were persuaded by Buckley to fork out for a new strip of old gold shirts, blue sleeves and collars, white shorts and black, blue and gold hooped socks.

This was the norm, apart from a switch to black shorts in 1950, until 1955 when there was a change to blue shirts with old gold collars and white shorts – a kit not dissimilar to the one originally worn by Leeds City.

The colours remained more or less the same until the Taylor-Revie switch to all white in the early 1960s and since then the changes have been less about colour but more about logos and sponsors.

The city of Leeds arms badge vanished when the all-white strip was adopted, but a new badge appeared in 1964 – an owl on a perch within a dark blue circle. For many fans it seemed to say Sheffield Wednesday rather than Leeds United and was even more curious as Revie, known to be superstitious, detested birds.

Gradually, clubs introduced away strips with Leeds usually adopting blue shirts with old gold shorts and socks. Later it became all blue, and sometimes, all red, before finally opting for all yellow.

The owl badge flew off in May 1971 when a scripted LUFC logo appeared on United's shirts for the first time in the Fairs Cup Final victory against Juventus but that was just the start.

The 1971–72 season saw a huge image change for United with Revie hiring the sports and comic artist Paul Trevellion. The man who had worked on Roy of the Rovers and You Are The Ref for *Shoot* magazine created the Super Leeds brand.

On the field, United were putting the 'Dirty Leeds' tag to rest and Trevellion's PR ensured the campaign to remodel the club gained momentum.

Pre-match warm-ups, which saw the players, kitted out in tracksuits adorning their names, put through various co-ordinated routines by trainer Les Cocker, were revolutionary. Balls were kicked into the

The LUFC logo of 1971.

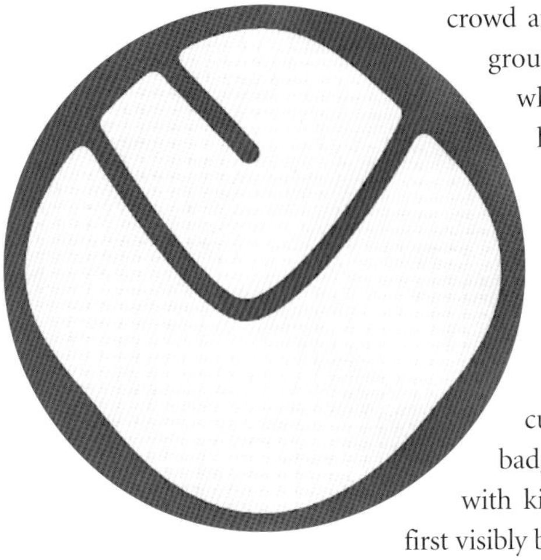

crowd and an orchestrated wave to all sides of the ground were all part of the pre-match ritual, while numbered blue stocking tags were handed out to adoring fans after the final whistle.

In this period Leeds served up some outstanding football for *Match of the Day* television viewers who lapped up the Super Leeds concept.

In 1973, United latched on to the current culture with the introduction of the LU smiley badge which shared billing on the white shirt with kit manufacturer Admiral as Leeds wore the first visibly branded kit in Division One.

Revie and Admiral had seen the potential of the replica kit market and Revie repeated the ploy when he took over as England manager in 1974 – although was widely criticised for it.

Other manufacturers quickly followed suit as club shops started to fill their shelves with replica shirts for which ardent fans were prepared to pay good money.

Although United's kit remained all white, there were subtle changes to cuffs, collars and sleeves as well as variations to the Smiley badge. After a season a replica shirt was out of date and there were plenty of supporters willing to buy a new one each year.

United switched from Admiral back to their former kit makers, Umbro, in 1981 and adopted a new badge – a logo of a peacock on a ball.

The Peacocks is the original nickname of the club but is nothing to do with the team's colours. It comes from the Old and New Peacock pubs which were close to the Elland Road ground.

Top: The 1973 LU smiley badge.
Middle: The peacock badge from 1981.
Bottom: The Yorkshire rose from 1984.

The current badge adopted in 1998.

The peacock badge lasted until 1984, when a football at the heart of a Yorkshire rose with the club name was adopted. By this time the badge was playing second fiddle to the logo of the shirt sponsor.

Top flight clubs were battling with broadcasting authorities to put a commercial sponsors' name on their shirts and Liverpool became the first club to do it when Hitachi was emblazoned across their chests in 1979.

Three years later, newly relegated Leeds, in desperate need of cash, unveiled their first sponsor, Pudsey electrical firm R.F. Winder who had RFW plastered on the Leeds shirt.

A succession of sponsors and subtle uses of old gold and blue followed until a five-year deal was struck in 1986 with Leeds-based clothiers, the Burton Group. The main man behind the contract was Peter Ridsdale, managing director of Burton's Top Man chain. He joined the board at Elland Road in 1987 and it was in the Top Man kit that Leeds won the Division Two title in 1990.

For the 1991–92 Championship-winning season, the *Yorkshire Evening Post* could be read everywhere Leeds played before Admiral Sportswear returned to the fold after penning a five-year deal worth millions.

The Admiral contract had not run its full length after a dispute between club and sponsor and the Thistle Hotels chain became sponsors until 1995.

Squad numbering and players' names on the back of their shirts came into being in 1993 and the following year United broke away from the norm with their away kit by playing in dark blue and green stripes because the previous away shirt of blue and old gold stripes had produced several colour clashes. It didn't last long and was used for the last time in February 1996 because the players said it was too dark they could not identify their teammates.

Since 1984 the badge had been a popular combination of a football inside a rose but 1995–96 season saw the return of the scripted LUFC on a crew-neck shirt. That lasted a year before reverting back to the football and rose which was replaced with the current shield-style badge in 1998.

It was reportedly designed by Ridsdale, who wanted to give the club a more global image, and certainly got plenty of exposure as United stormed to the semi-finals of the Champions League in the new millennium.

Since then there have been several different sponsors and tweaks to the traditional all-white home kit, with the more major changes reserved for away strips.

SHIRT SPONSORS

1981–82	RFW
1982–83	RFW
1983–84	Systime
1984–85	WGK
1985–86	Lion Cabinets
1986–87	Burton
1987–88	Burton
1988–89	Burton
1989–90	Top Man
1990–91	Top Man
1991–92	*Yorkshire Evening Post*
1992–93	Admiral Sportswear
1993–94	Thistle Hotels
1994–95	Thistle Hotels
1995–96	Packard Bell
1996–97	Packard Bell
1997–98	Packard Bell
1998–99	Packard Bell
1999–2000	Packard Bell
2000–01	Strongbow
2001–02	Strongbow
2002–03	Strongbow
2003–04	Whyte and Mackay
2004–05	Whyte and Mackay
2005–06	Whyte and Mackay
2006–07	Bet 24
2007–08	Red Kite
2008–09	Net Flights.com
2009–10	Net Flights.com
2010–11	Net Flights.com
2011–12	Enterprise Insurance

There was a dark blue shirt with yellow and white pinstripes which is not particularly fondly remembered as is went hand-in-hand with relegation in 2003–04 when performances were enough to turn fans to the product of sponsors Whyte and Mackay – whisky.

United's spectacular decline in the post-Champions League era was possibly best summed up in pre-season 2007. With the club in administration, and its very future hanging by a thread, several friendlies were played wearing kit boasting no sponsor at all.

Italian supplier Macron clinched a four-year deal to produce the Leeds shirts and in 2008 Terry Fisher and former Leeds star Trevor Cherry, who had once expressed an interest in buying the club, signed up as sponsors for three years with their online travel agency, Netflights.com after United's deal with another party fell through.

It became something of a tradition for the club to use the final home game of a season to play in the kit for the following campaign to give fans an early sight of what to expect.

However, the 2011–12 ensemble was kept under wraps until it was officially launched in mid-July and the idea was that it reflected the kit worn by the 1991–92 Division One title-winning squad.

However, the biggest surprise came a few days later when the away strip was launched. It was a break from tradition with essentially an all-black outfit with a green pin-stripe on the shirt with a lime green fluorescent trim.

At the end of 2011–12, United announced that sponsors Enterprise Insurance had extended their agreement for a further two years.

Fifty Memorable Matches

Match 1
Saturday 29 November 1913

Division Two

Leeds City 8 *(Price [2], McLeod [4], Hampson, Speirs)*
Nottingham Forest 0

Optimism was the watchword among City supporters at the start of 1913–14, as England amateur international winger Ivan Sharpe and rugged Northampton centre-half John Hampson were persuaded to join the Elland Road staff. Interest in the club's progress had increased to such an extent that £2,000 worth of season tickets were sold before the season started. Ace marksman Billy McLeod began in prime goalscoring form and enhanced his reputation with a sharp-shooting display against lowly Nottingham Forest as City scored their biggest-ever win.

Inside-right Arthur Price was switched to inside-left and had a sparkling game, scoring two goals and creating another in the opening half-hour. Forest 'keeper John Hanna did well to block an early Price pile-driver, but the alert McLeod followed up the rebound to score. Price then rattled in the second and third to put City in an impregnable position by half-time against a Forest side who had lost winger Fred Banks to injury.

The floodgates opened early in the second half when Hampson headed in a Sharpe corner. McLeod added the fifth and, after Mick Foley missed a penalty, Scottish international Jimmy Speirs netted the sixth, before McLeod completed the rout with two more goals to leave 10-man Forest floundering.

The *Leeds Mercury* football correspondent 'JRB' enthused: 'City forwards were a brilliant lot, who displayed fire and resolution in their attack. They were supported by a trio of

City's ace marksman Billy McLeod, who netted four times in the 1913 rout of Nottingham Forest.

halves who did their work excellently, while Copeland and Affleck were a puissant pair of backs.'

The emphatic victory, played out before 14,000 fans who paid £370 for the privilege, pushed City into third place in Division Two and left struggling Forest anchored firmly at the bottom of the table.

Leeds City: Hogg, Copeland, Affleck, Law, J. Hampson, Foley, Bainbridge, Speirs, McLeod, Price, Sharpe

Nottingham Forest: Hanna, Dudley, Gibson, Armstrong, Mercer, Needham, Firth, Bell, Jones, Derrick, Banks

Referee: J. Butterfield (London)

Attendance: 14,000

Match 2
Saturday 26 April 1924

DIVISION TWO

Leeds United 1 *(Coates 87)*
Nelson 0

Thousands of supporters poured onto the Elland Road pitch at the final whistle to celebrate the victory which brought First Division football to the city of Leeds for the first time.

Working on a shoe-string budget, the management team of Arthur Fairclough and Bill Norman had skilfully pieced together the squad which won the 1923–24 Second Division title.

With Nelson struggling near the foot of the table, United's fans expected to be swept into Division One on a tidal wave of goals, but the floodgates never opened.

For much of the first half United's defence were left chasing shadows as the lively Nelson forwards pushed the ball around with considerable poise and skill. Just before the interval United came desperately close to falling behind as dependable full-back Bert Duffield headed off the line with goalkeeper Billy Down beaten.

Fired by some choice words from Fairclough during the break, Leeds came out and gradually grew in confidence. The

Walter Coates, whose goal clinched United's first promotion in 1924.

Yorkshire Post reported: 'By sweeping passes, the Nelson goal was often in jeopardy, but good approach play was missed by faulty shooting from scoreable positions.'

Time ticked away, but the vital goal continued to elude United's front men. Then, with three minutes left, Joe Harris took a corner on the left and floated it over the packed penalty area to Walter Coates, who steadied himself before firing in the goal which sent United up to the First Division.

The fans stayed on at the end to celebrate with the players, hear speeches of congratulation and appeals for financial help – even in times of glory United's cash problems were never far away.

Leeds United: Down, Duffield, Menzies, Baker, Hart, Smith, Coates, Whipp, Richmond, Swan, Harris

Nelson: Abbot, Liley, Rigg, Newnes, Braidwood, Wilson, Hood, Wolstenholme, Edleston, McCulloch, Humphries

Referee: A.F. Kirby (Lostock Hall)

Attendance: 20,000

Match 3

Saturday 14 January 1933

FA CUP THIRD ROUND

Newcastle United 0

Leeds United 3 *(Hydes 25, 27, 79)*

FA Cup kings Newcastle, who had swept to success against Arsenal at Wembley seven months earlier, were expected to see off Leeds with little trouble in their first defence of the Cup. The previous month had seen newly promoted Leeds crash 3–1 at St James' Park and there had been little in their recent form to suggest they could gain any reward from their third-round tie.

Leeds were soon under the hammer as Newcastle made their traditional thundering start. But with inside-left Billy Furness setting up some clever counter-attacks, Leeds took

How the *Leeds Mercury* reported United's 1933 FA Cup Final triumph at Newcastle. The newspaper cutting shows Magpies goalkeeper Mick Burns saving from Charlie Keetley.

THE LEEDS MERCURY, MONDAY, JANUARY 16, 1933.
How Leeds United Humbled the Cup-Holders :
Other Pictures in Page 4.

control and made the most of their possession by stunning the Cup holders with two goals from Arthur Hydes in three minutes midway through the first half.

With a two-goal lead under their belts, Leeds, responding to the intelligent promptings of Furness, played some superbly controlled football. Wingers Tom Cochrane and Johnny Mahon beat their opponents at will while the Newcastle attacks floundered on the redoubtable half-back line of Willis Edwards, Ernie Hart and Wilf Copping.

A third goal duly arrived in the 79th minute when a brilliant feint by Furness put Cochrane down the wing and his cross was met by Hydes who completed a memorable hat-trick.

Said the *Yorkshire Post*: 'Furness, for all-round cleverness and the tremendous amount of work he did was an outstanding figure. But the whole Leeds line was in wonderful form with ball-control and combination of a high order. Only a super display by Michael Burns prevented Leeds from piling up more goals, as Furness continued his brilliant scheming and the wingers Cochrane and Mahon ran the Newcastle defence ragged.'

Newcastle United: Burns, Nelson, Fairhurst, Bell, Betton, Murray, Cape, Boyd, Allen, McMenemy, Dryden

Leeds United: Potts, G. Milburn, J. Milburn, Edwards, Hart, Copping, Mahon, Hydes, Keetley, Furness, Cochrane

Referee: E. Pinkston (Warrington)

Attendance: 47,554

Match 4
Saturday 7 April 1934

Division One

Leeds United 8 *(Duggan 28, 51, Mahon 33, 44, Furness 35, 46, Firth 62, 78)*
Leicester City 0

For much of their 1933–34 First Division campaign United had to cope without injured star, right-half Willis Edwards. An experienced England international, Edwards had been out of action for three months before returning to Elland Road for a mid-table clash with FA Cup semi-finalists Leicester City.

The presence of Edwards inspired those around him as United turned in their best performance of the season to bury luckless Leicester under a landslide of goals. Billy Furness was in top form and winger Johnny Mahon provided a string of chances as the Leeds forwards peppered Sandy McLaren in the City goal.

Willis Edwards, whose return to the Leeds ranks inspired the team to crush Leicester 8–0 – the biggest League win in United's history.

The *Yorkshire Post* reported: 'Taking complete command, Leeds launched almost continual offensives to expose the mediocrity of the Leicester wing-halves, and the backs' unsteadiness. McLaren had a thankless task in goal. The shrewd scheming of Furness and the dashing wing play of Mahon were features of the Leeds attack. Leicester struggled gamely and sportingly after the interval but were outplayed to an astonishing degree.'

Goals by Mahon (2), Furness and Irish international Harry Duggan gave Leeds a four-goal lead at half-time, which they doubled with further efforts by Furness, Duggan and Joe Firth (2), to complete an unusual feat of four men scoring two goals for the same side in one match. It all added up to United's biggest League win in history.

Ironically, United's leading scorer that season, Arthur Hydes, did not play and missed out on the goal feast.

Leicester must have been sick of the sight of Elland Road in the 1930s. Four and a half years after the 8–0 demolition they were thrashed 8–2 with Gordon Hodgson netting five times to set a new record for a Leeds player. The Foxes' cause on that occasion was not helped when luckless goalkeeper McLaren, tore tendons in an instep in the first half, and 10-man Leicester were swamped.

Leeds United: Moore, G. Milburn, J. Milburn, Edwards, Hart, Copping, Mahon, Firth, Duggan, Furness, Cochrane

Leicester City: McLaren, Jones, Wood, Smith, Sharman, Ritchie, Maw, Paterson, Gardner, Lochhead, Liddle

Referee: T.J. Botham (Walsall)

Attendance: 11,871

Match 5

28 April 1956

DIVISION TWO

Hull City 1 *(Martin 13)*
Leeds United 4 *(Charles 6, pen 62; Brook 78, 80)*

Anxious for First Division action, United's multi-talented John Charles once asked for a transfer sending the Leeds directors scurrying behind locked doors to discuss his request.

They rejected Charles' plea and told him the best way to get into the top flight was by playing for United.

Equally brilliant as centre-half or centre-forward, Charles took the advice to heart. Manager Raich Carter switched him from defence to attack during the 1955–56 season and United's fortunes immediately began to rise, taking them to the brink of promotion, needing just one point from their final match.

That game was at Hull, scene of so many triumphs for Carter, who had been idolised during his days at Boothferry Park both as player and manager.

Manager Raich Carter pours out the champagne after the win at Hull in 1956 clinched promotion to the First Division.

United clinched promotion with a big win, and it was that man Charles who sent them on their way with a thunderous left-foot shot in the sixth minute. Hull, already relegated, fought hard and drew level in the 13th minute when Tommy Martin knocked in a David Fraser pass.

The tension in United's play snapped in the 62nd minute when little George Meek was brought down and Charles smashed in the penalty, his 29th goal of the season. Leeds took command with some beautiful football and Harold Brook added further goals in the 78th and 80th minutes after Meek had created the openings.

Now the awesome power of the mighty Charles could be unleashed in football's toughest arena – the First Division of the Football League.

Hull City: Fisher, Harrison, Jenson, Davidson, Berry, Bullass, Stephens, Martin, Bradbury, Clarke, Fraser

Leeds United: Wood, Dunn, Hair, Ripley, Charlton, Kerfoot, Meek, Charles, Brook, Nightingale, Overfield

Referee: T.J. Wood (Bury)

Attendance: 31,123

Match 6

Saturday 28 April 1962

Division Two

Newcastle United 0

Leeds United 3 *(Johanneson 37, McAdams 65, Keith og 75)*

During the early part of 1961–62 United, under new manager Don Revie, looked to have booked a one-way ticket to Division Three. His side seemed unable to shake the nasty habit of giving away sloppy goals and they looked certainties for relegation until a late-season run of eight games without defeat gave them some breathing space.

On the last Saturday of the season United travelled to St James' Park, Newcastle, still needing a precious point which would keep them up and send Bristol Rovers to the Third Division along with Brighton.

Albert Johanneson proved too hot to handle as he scored twice and set up another in the vital 3–0 win at Newcastle in 1962.

Facing a stiff Tyneside wind, Leeds controlled the ball skilfully on a hard surface and made a mockery of their lowly League placing. In pint-sized Bobby Collins, a vastly experienced player whom Revie had recruited from Everton, Leeds had a natural leader in midfield; defender Willie Bell played his heart out in the unaccustomed role of inside-forward; and South African winger Albert Johanneson ran the Magpies ragged with his blistering speed and delicate ball control.

Scottish youngster Billy Bremner, whose performances attracted scouts from bigger clubs to Elland Road, came close to scoring early on, but after 37 minutes Johanneson smashed the ball in off the crossbar from Billy McAdams' cross. McAdams, a big, strong Irishman, then hit a post with a header but had better luck in the 65th minute when he rose to head in Johanneson's centre after goalkeeper Dave Hollins fumbled.

Ten minutes later Leeds' passage to safety was guaranteed when Bremner knocked the ball into the box and it was deflected into the net by the Magpies' right-back Bobby Keith.

Newcastle United: Hollins, Keith, Clish, Wright, Thompson, Turner, Day, Kerray, Thomas, Allchurch, Fell

Leeds United: Younger, Hair, Mason, Goodwin, Charlton, Smith, Bremner, Collins, McAdams, Bell, Johanneson

Referee: Jack Kelly (Chorley)

Attendance: 21,708

Match 7

Saturday 11 April 1964

DIVISION TWO

Swansea Town 0

Leeds United 3 *(Peacock 15, 19; Giles 34)*

Victory at the Vetch Field would be enough to recapture the First Division status United lost in 1960 – and they achieved their target with a spectacular success.

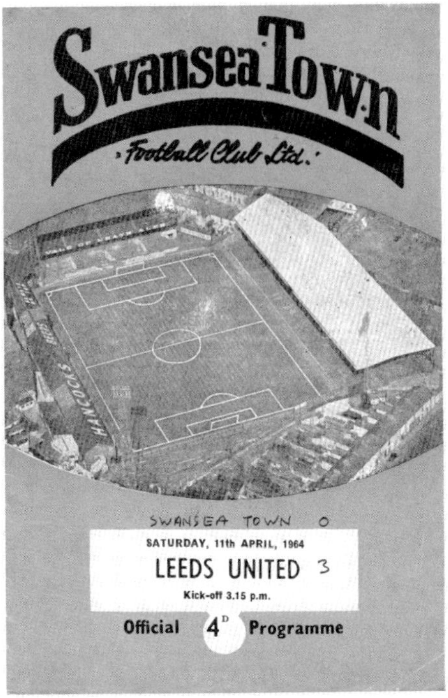

Alan Peacock, a two-goal marksman in the promotion-clinching game at Swansea.

Manager Don Revie, who had welded together a strong squad, created a major surprise by giving 19-year-old Terry Cooper his League debut on the left wing in place of the injured Albert Johanneson. Cooper, destined to become an international star of the 1970s after moving to full-back, supplied the 15th-minute pass which centre-forward Alan Peacock gleefully hammered in to set United on their way to victory.

Peacock, a £53,000 signing from Middlesbrough in February, added more weight to United's end-of-season promotion push, and struck again four minutes later after Johnny Giles flicked on a Bobby Collins corner. United, oozing confidence, were in full flow and a third goal came in the 34th minute when Cooper's corner was rifled in by Republic of Ireland international Giles via defender Roy Evans.

Revie, a superstitious character, had banned the purchase of champagne before the game just in case United were beaten, so after the match Leeds players and officials scoured Swansea's pubs to hunt down bottles of bubbly for the train journey back to Yorkshire.

In their remaining games United drew with Plymouth at Elland Road, then won 2–0 at Charlton, with a couple more Peacock goals, to wrap up the Second Division title and embark on a golden era.

Swansea Town: Dwyer, R. Evans, Hughes, Johnson, Purcell, Williams, Jones, Draper, Thomas, McLaughlin, B. Evans

Leeds United: Sprake, Reaney, Bell, Bremner, Charlton, Hunter, Giles, Weston, Peacock, Collins, Cooper

Referee: Norman Matthews (Bicester)
Attendance: 14,321

Match 8
Saturday 1 May 1965

FA Cup Final

Leeds United 1 *(Bremner 101)*
Liverpool 2 *(Hunt 93, St John 111)*
(after extra-time)

Only five days after the League Championship was snatched from under their noses, United's players strode out at Wembley for their first-ever FA Cup Final appearance.

Leeds were charging towards an unexpected League and Cup double on their return to Division One but a 3–3 draw at bottom club Birmingham on the Monday preceding the final ended their title dreams. On the same night Manchester United beat Arsenal at Old Trafford to lift the crown.

Don Revie now had to pick his men up for the club's first appearance in the shadow of the famous Twin Towers. They had booked their place by coming through the club's first semi-final in the competition with a last-gasp goal from Billy Bremner – a superb twisting header with 90 seconds remaining on the clock – in the replay against Manchester United at the City Ground, Nottingham, and now faced the mighty Liverpool, Championship winners the previous season.

Prospects of a close contest were good, but Leeds froze, leaving the more experienced Liverpool to dominate midfield. United's 34-year-old veteran, Bobby Collins, struggled on a sodden surface and was unable to bring wingmen Giles and Johanneson into the game.

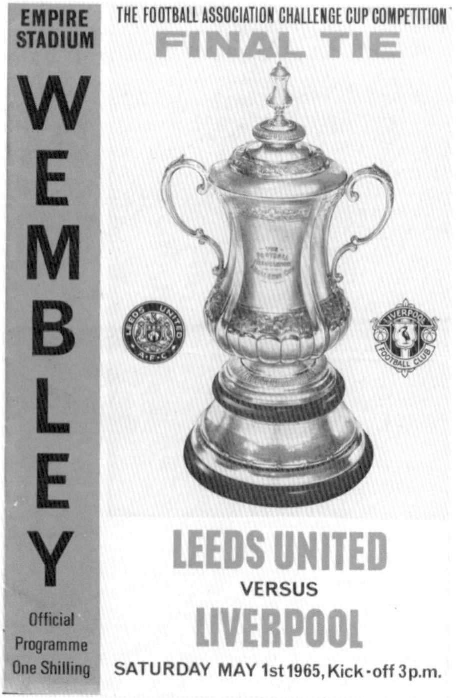

United toiled under strong pressure and only a series of fine saves by Gary Sprake enabled the game to go into extra-time for the first time since 1947.

The best soccer was telescoped into the extra period. Only three minutes had gone when full-back Gerry Byrne, who played for 85 minutes of the game with a broken collarbone, crossed the ball for Roger Hunt to dive in and head Liverpool into the lead. United, however, snatched an equaliser eight minutes later when firebrand Bremner unleashed a shot which ripped into the Liverpool net.

With nine minutes remaining United found themselves behind again – and this time there was no way back. Ian Callaghan's superb cross eluded the

Little and large – fellow Scots Bobby Collins (right) and Ron Yeats, the Liverpool skipper, shake hands before the start of the 1965 FA Cup Final.

United defence and Ian St John smacked in the header which took the FA Cup to Anfield for the first time.

Having missed the League title by 0.686 of a goal and the FA Cup in extra-time it had been double heartbreak for Leeds, a situation they would learn to live with during the next decade.

Leeds United: Sprake, Reaney, Bell, Bremner, Charlton, Hunter, Giles, Storrie, Peacock, Collins, Johanneson

Liverpool: Lawrence, Lawler, Byrne, Strong, Yeats, Stevenson, Callaghan, Hunt, St John, Smith, Thompson

Referee: Bill Clements (West Bromwich)

Attendance: 100,000

Match 9
Wednesday 29 September 1965

INTER-CITIES FAIRS CUP FIRST ROUND

FIRST LEG

Leeds United 2 *(Bremner 25, Peacock 48)*
Torino 1 *(Orlando 78)*

Despite missing out on the 1965 League and Cup double, United's consolation was a place in Europe for the first time in the club's history.

In the first round of the Inter Cities Fairs Cup they were paired with Italian side Torino and Don Revie was quick to make his managerial mark. Five minutes before the kick-off he announced five numerical changes in the United attack to confuse the opposition.

In fact, despite wearing number seven, Alan Peacock occupied his usual centre-forward's role, Johnny Giles played on the right wing with Cooper on the left, leaving Bobby Collins and teenager Peter Lorimer as inside-forwards.

Alan Peacock steams in to head United 2–0 up in their first European tie against Torino at Elland Road in 1965.

The puzzled Italian defenders soon found themselves under pressure as Leeds piled forward and were rewarded when Billy Bremner sent in a dipping shot which goalkeeper Lido Vieri could only tip into his own net on 25 minutes. Three minutes after half-time Peacock nodded in the second and Leeds looked to be coasting.

But 12 minutes from time Alberto Orlando pulled one back after a lightning counter-attack – a priceless strike as away goals counted double in the competition.

Leeds drew 0–0 in Italy and went on to reach the semi-finals where they lost to Spanish side Real Zaragoza in an extra game after the sides were locked at 2–2 on aggregate after two tense tussles.

Leeds United: Sprake, Reaney, Madeley, Bremner, Charlton, Hunter, Peacock, Collins, Cooper, Lorimer, Giles

Torino: Vieri, Poletti, Fossati, Rosato, Pula, Bolchi, Simioni, Pestrin, Orlando, Ferretti, Schultz

Referee: Michel Kitabdjian (France)

Attendance: 33,852

Match 10

Wednesday 15 March 1967

FA CUP FIFTH ROUND REPLAY

Leeds United 1 *(Giles 38)*
Sunderland 1 *(O'Hare 37)*
(after extra-time)

The biggest-ever crowd to squeeze into Elland Road – 57,896 – saw arch-rivals United and Sunderland slug out another draw in this FA Cup fifth-round replay.

The clubs had been promoted together in 1964 and matches between the two were not for the faint-hearted. That was certainly the case during the 1–1 draw in the first match at Roker Park, but the replay saw most of the action off the pitch.

Thousands of supporters were locked out when the turnstiles shut 23 minutes before the kick-off with some fans, desperate to see the action, scrambling on to the Scratching Shed roof.

Leeds had been unable to make the match all-ticket because of the time factor and it was only 10 minutes into the game that a 10ft crush barrier at the corner of Lowfields Road and the Scratching Shed collapsed. Fans, many shocked and dazed, suffering from crush injuries, spilled beyond the perimeter track and onto the pitch for safety.

United were involved in three titanic FA Cup ties with Sunderland in 1967. Here Jack Charlton, a scorer in the first match, puts the Rokerites defence under pressure.

Referee Ray Tinkler halted the match and a fleet of ambulances took 18 people to Leeds General Infirmary as United chairman Harry Reynolds appealed for calm on the public address system. After 15 minutes, United officials, police and Tinkler agreed that the match could continue with hundreds of people squatting near the touchlines.

United fell behind when Scottish forward John O'Hare, later to join Leeds in Brian Clough's brief reign, fired home. But Leeds were level within a minute, winning a free-kick on the edge of the box which Billy Bremner tapped to Johnny Giles, who sent a low shot scorching past goalkeeper Jim Montgomery.

After that, defences were on top and even extra-time could not determine a victor so the tie moved to Boothferry Park, home of Hull City, whre Leeds won a stormy clash with a controversial Giles penalty.

But it was soon United's turn to find out that the Cup fates can deal a cruel hand as a last-minute Peter Lorimer effort in the semi-final against Chelsea at Villa Park was controversially ruled out by referee Ken Burns and the Londoners held on to a 1–0 victory to face Tottenham at Wembley.

Leeds United: Sprake, Reaney, Bell, Bremner, Charlton, Hunter, Lorimer, Belfitt, Greenhoff, Giles, Johanneson (Cooper 45)
Sunderland: Montgomery, Irwin, Harvey, Todd, Kinnell, Baxter, Gauden, O'Hare, Martin, Herd, Mulhall
Referee: Ray Tinkler (Boston)
Attendance: 57,896

Match 11
Wednesday 6 September 1967

INTER-CITIES FAIRS CUP FINAL SECOND LEG

Leeds United 0
Dynamo Zagreb 0

Leeds, now an established First Division outfit, were rapidly making a name for themselves in Europe.

After reaching the Fairs Cup semi-finals in their maiden season, they went one better by reaching the 1966–67 two-leg Final where they met Yugoslavian side Dynamo Zagreb.

An injury-hit United trailed 2–0 to goals by Marijan Cercek and Krasnadar Rora after the first leg, a deficit which they attempted to overhaul at Elland Road seven days later after a modest start to the Division One campaign had seen them win just one of their opening four games.

Chairman Albert Morris congratulates Dynamo Zagreb on their Fairs Cup success.

Goalscoring had been an early season problem and it continued against Zagreb as United totally dominated possession but could find no way through a blanket 10-man defence.

Jack Charlton added his height to the attack on several occasions, Jimmy Greenhoff went close with a header and both Charlton and Rod Belfitt had attempts disallowed. Charlton had another effort cleared off the line, a goal-bound attempt by Billy Bremner was cleared from under the bar and goalkeeper Zlatko Skoric pulled off several acrobatic saves. Indeed, it was the visitors who came closest to extending their advantage when a lightning counterattack ended with Daniel Piric rattling Gary Sprake's bar with a tremendous shot.

FIFA president Sir Stanley Rous presented the trophy to Zagreb – the first Yugoslavian side to win the competition – leaving United with the consolation of collecting record receipts of £20,177 from the game.

Leeds United: Sprake, Bell, Cooper, Bremner, Charlton, Hunter, Reaney, Belfitt, Greenhoff, Giles, O'Grady

Dynamo Zagreb: Skoric Grancanin, Brnic, Belin, Ramljak, Blaskovic, Cercek, Piric, Zambata, Gucmirtl, Rora

Referee: Antonio Sbardella (Italy)

Attendance: 35,604

Match 12

Saturday 7 October 1967

Division One

Leeds United 7 *(Johanneson 5, Greenhoff 11, Charlton 14, Lorimer 35, Gray 60, Hinton og 80, Bremner 82)*

Chelsea 0

On the eve of Chelsea's Division One game at Elland Road, their manager Tommy Docherty quit for 'personal reasons' within hours of being suspended by the FA over incidents on the London club's tour of Bermuda. Now the time was ripe for Leeds to take quick revenge against a shocked Chelsea team for that controversial FA Cup semi-final defeat five months earlier.

Although the wise-cracking Docherty had hit the headlines, it was another Scot under impending suspension, Billy Bremner, who overshadowed events on

Billy Bremner nets with a spectacular overhead kick to complete the 7–0 rout of Chelsea in 1967.

the pitch. The fiery Leeds skipper was making his last appearance for United before starting a 28-day ban for being sent off against Fulham in September and was at his impish best as Leeds turned on a superb attacking display.

Eric Stanger of the *Yorkshire Post* reported: 'Bremner teased and tormented them with his astonishing dexterity of foot and his remarkable sense of balance so that he could turn and twist on the proverbial sixpence.'

It was Bremner's spectacular Brazilian-style bicycle kick eight minutes from time which crowned a five-star Leeds performance.

Speedy winger Albert Johanneson, recalled to the side, opened the scoring and the rest came, in order, from Jimmy Greenhoff, Jack Charlton, Peter Lorimer, Eddie Gray, Marvin Hinton (own-goal) and the ubiquitous Bremner. Apart from the quality of Bremner's spectacular overhead kick, the goal earned a place in the record books – it was the first match in the Football League in which seven different players had scored for one side.

One name missing from the scoresheet was centre-forward Mick Jones, a recent £100,000 buy from Sheffield United to add firepower to the attack. He left the field injured late on in through the game and was replaced by substitute Terry Hibbitt.

Leeds United: Sprake, Reaney, Madeley, Bremner, Charlton, Hunter, Greenhoff, Lorimer, Jones (Hibbitt 81), Gray, Johanneson

Chelsea: Bonetti, Thompson, Hinton, Harris, Butler, Hollins, Boyle, Cooke, Osgood, Baldwin, McCreadie

Referee: Ken Dagnall (Bolton)

Attendance: 40,460

Match 13
Saturday 2 March 1968

FOOTBALL LEAGUE CUP FINAL

Arsenal 0
Leeds United 1 *(Cooper 17)*

At last, a dream came true for Leeds United – and in the case of Terry Cooper, literally true. For three successive nights before the League Cup Final against Arsenal at Wembley, the left-back dreamed he would score the winning goal. After 17 minutes of a hard-fought game he did just that.

Eddie Gray curled in a wicked corner which Arsenal centre-forward George Graham headed away from under the crossbar to the edge of the penalty area where Cooper moved up to smash a terrific knee-high volley into the Arsenal net. Having snatched a precious lead, United concentrated on the art of defence and Arsenal simply didn't have the know-

Jack Charlton and Paul Madeley in aerial action in the 1968 Football League Cup Final against Arsenal. The Gunners' number-nine is George Graham, a future Arsenal and Leeds manager.

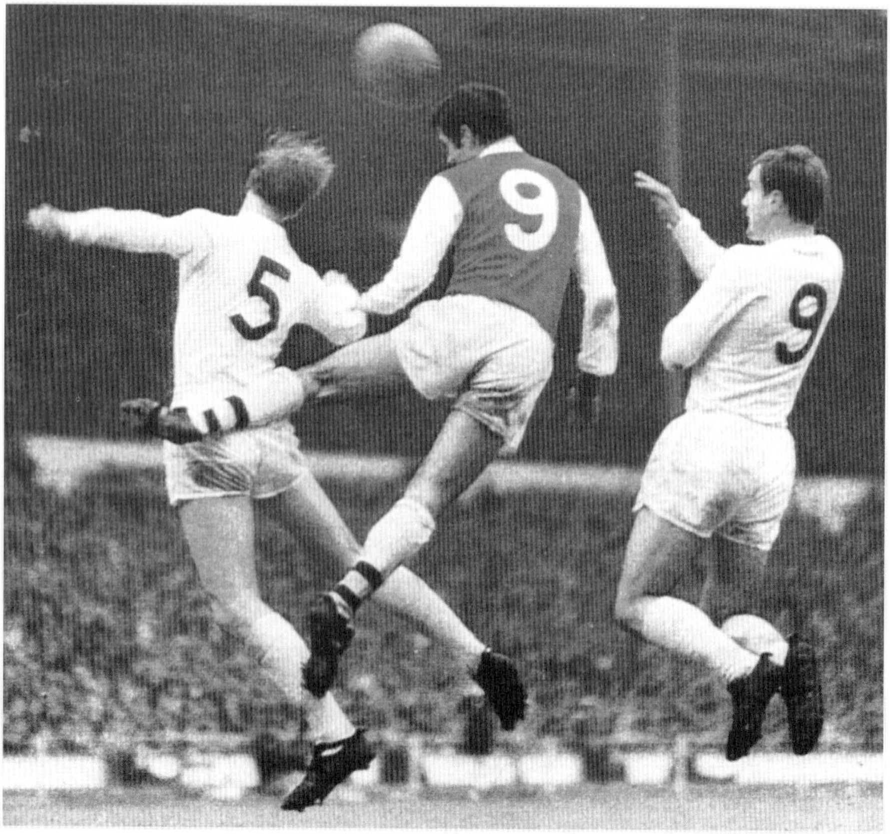

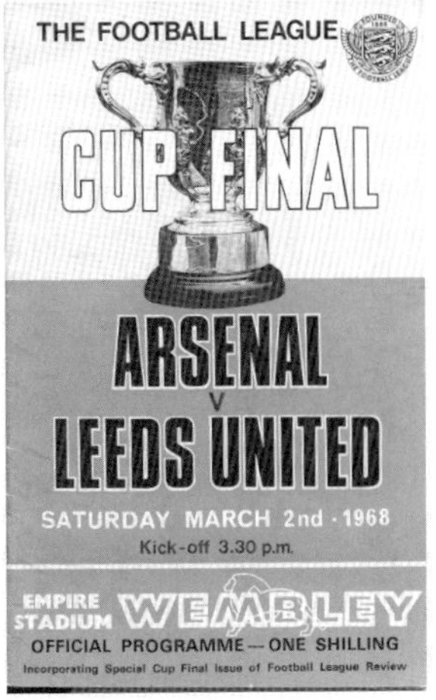

how to find a way past the likes of Paul Reaney, Norman Hunter and Jack Charlton.

Gary Sprake's only serious save of the match came when he turned a John Radford shot around a post late in the game. United, who had the versatile Paul Madeley at centre-forward in place of the Cup-tied Mick Jones, also found goal chances scarce and were content to play a game of containment.

Although the match was disappointing as a spectacle, Leeds had conquered a psychological barrier to win the first trophy in the club's history.

Thousands of United supporters welcomed home their heroes as the League Cup was displayed on the steps of Leeds Town Hall. So often United had tripped at the final hurdle because their play had been riddled with anxiety, but now they had finally cast off the mantle of also-rans and were ready to make more room for trophies in the Elland Road boardroom.

Arsenal: Furnell, Storey, McNab, McLintock, Simpson, Ure, Radford, Jenkins (Neill 75), Graham, Sammels, Armstrong

Leeds United: Sprake, Reaney, Cooper, Bremner, Charlton, Hunter, Greenhoff, Lorimer, Madeley, Giles, Gray (Belfitt 75)

Referee: Les Hamer (Horwich)

Attendance: 97,887

Match 14
Wednesday 7 August 1968

INTER-CITIES FAIRS CUP FINAL FIRST LEG

Leeds United 1 *(Jones 41)*
Ferencváros 0

AFTER battling through to their second successive Fairs Cup Final, this time United were intent on getting their name inscribed on the trophy.

Ferencváros coach Dr Karoly Lahat sent his powerful team out at Elland Road with the classic European battle orders to defend in depth and counter attack at speed. His men, who played in all white, obeyed his instructions to the letter, breaking United's rhythm with their on-the-edge tackling in a disjointed game of 45 free-kicks, and hitting back with swift breaks.

After Istvan Szoke squandered an opportunity after a rare error by Jack Charlton, United, sporting

United, playing at home in unfamiliar blue shirts and gold shorts, put pressure on the Ferencváros defence in the Fairs Cup Final at Elland Road.

unfamiliar blue shirts and gold shorts, let an even easier chance go begging moments later when goalkeeper Istvan Geczi mishit a free-kick straight to Mick Jones near the edge of the penalty area. Jones quickly slipped the ball inside to Peter Lorimer but the Scot's shot was well-saved by the grateful Geczi.

Lorimer made amends before the interval by swinging in a corner for Charlton to nod the ball down to Jones who bundled the ball over the line, leaving the Hungarians complaining that the Leeds centre-half had impeded the goalkeeper.

The visitors responded with some controlled football which saw Florian Albert go close before Gary Sprake pulled off the save of the match with a twisting leap to prevent Gyula Rakosi equalising.

Club officials hoped to have banked big money from the evening match, but televised live in the middle of the annual Leeds holidays, it attracted just 25,268 spectators.

Jimmy Greenhoff, who came on for Johnny Giles, was uniquely transferred in the middle of a Cup Final, moving to Stoke before the second leg was played.

Leeds United: Sprake, Reaney, Cooper, Bremner, Charlton, Hunter, Lorimer, Madeley, Jones (Belfitt 70), Giles (Greenhoff 65), Gray

Ferencváros: Geczi, Novak, Pancsics, Havasi, Juhasz, Szucs, Szoke, Varga, Albert, Rakosi, Fenyvesi (Branikovits 65)

Referee: Rudolf Scheuber (Switzerland)

Attendance: 25,268

Match 15
Wednesday 11 September 1968

INTER-CITIES FAIRS CUP FINAL SECOND LEG

Ferencváros 0
Leeds United 0

On a night of immense tension, United were subjected to their most rigorous European examination in the white-hot atmosphere of the Nep Stadium, before emerging heroically to become the first British winners of the Inter-Cities Fairs Cup.

A human barrier of white shirts was strung around the penalty area to keep the Magyars at bay for virtually the entire 90 minutes. Ferencváros hopes of quickly wiping out United's slender advantage soon evaporated as the Leeds defence gave one of its greatest displays by throttling every promising attack the Hungarians could mount.

After 20 minutes it looked as though Gyula Rakosi must score, but Cooper produced an acrobatic overhead clearance on the line to keep United's advantage. When the Hungarians did find a way through United's 10-man defence, Sprake stood up extremely well to a barrage of testing shots and centres, pulling off one world-class save from Istvan Szoke which helped sap the home team's spirit.

A delighted United squad with the Fairs Cup after their Ferencváros shutout in Hungary.

United attacks were rare, but they almost snatched a goal in the 33rd minute when winger Mike O'Grady chipped in a free-kick which Mick Jones headed powerfully against the crossbar.

Leeds did not need that extra goal, but it would have gone a long way to soothing manager Don Revie's nerves, as he disclosed at the end of the game: 'When we got into those final few minutes my heart nearly stopped beating. As the final whistle drew nearer every minute seemed like an hour.'

Just as Dynamo Zagreb had frustrated Leeds the previous season, so United, learning quickly, had suffocated Ferencváros into submission to earn their first tangible reward in Europe.

Ferencváros: Geczi, Pancsics, Havasi, Juhasz, Szucs, Szoke (Karaba 60), Varga, Albert, Rakosi, Katona, Novak

Leeds United: Sprake, Reaney, Cooper, Bremner, Charlton, Hunter, O'Grady, Lorimer, Jones, Madeley, Hibbitt (Bates 62)

Referee: Gerhard Schulenberg (West Germany)

Attendance: 76,000

Match 16

Monday 28 April 1969

Division One

Liverpool 0
Leeds United 0

United strode into the Anfield arena on the threshold of their greatest achievement – the 1968–69 League Championship. Only the power of nearest challengers Liverpool could deprive United of the vital point which would land the coveted crown.

The atmosphere appeared to crackle with anticipation as two football giants clashed on a Monday evening in April. The game quickly fell into the expected pattern with Liverpool throwing men forward frantically as Leeds relied upon the superb defence which had served them so valiantly throughout the season.

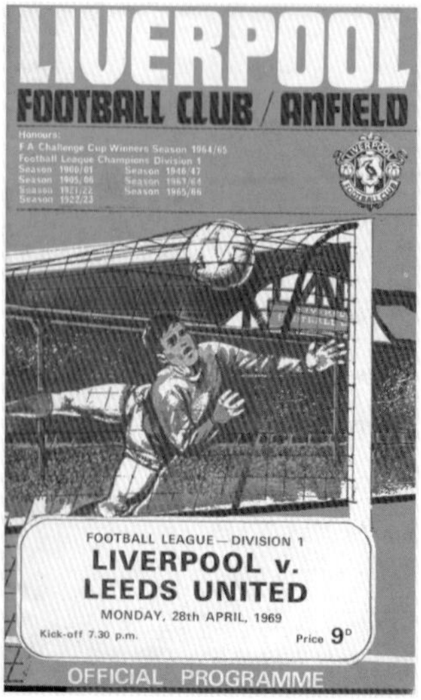

In a game of blurring speed, United, with Jack Charlton and Norman Hunter magnificent in the heart of the defence, denied Liverpool time and space. Such was United's efficiency that Gary Sprake had only one shot to deal with in the first half – an ambitious 35-yard drive by Ian Callaghan, to which United responded with a deflected Billy Bremner shot which almost beat the scrambling Tommy Lawrence.

One goal looked as though it might settle the game and the Merseysiders should have snatched it in the 35th

Jack Charlton (left), Paul Reaney and Gary Sprake celebrate at the end of the record-breaking 1968–69 title-winning season.

minute when young striker Alun Evans wasted a good chance, but United closed ranks again. Callaghan forced Sprake into action in the 62nd minute with a curling shot and United had one more scare when Evans hooked a shot wide late in the game. Leeds fans howled for referee Arthur Dimond to blow the final whistle, yet with the last moments melting away seemingly in slow motion United's players remained calm amid the cauldron of noise.

At the end of the game, the Liverpool fans on the Kop boomed 'Champions, Champions' as they saluted their triumphant rivals.

Two nights later at Elland Road the new champions beat Nottingham Forest with a Johnny Giles goal to finish the season having beaten or equalled nine club records – most points (67), most home points (39), most wins (27), most home wins (18), fewest defeats (two, both away, another record), unbeaten at home, 26 goals conceded with only nine at home.

Legendary Liverpool boss Bill Shankly offers Jack Charlton and Billy Bremner his congratulations after United's first title success.

Liverpool: Lawrence, Lawler, Strong, Smith, Yeats, Hughes, Callaghan, Graham, Evans, St John, Thompson
Leeds United: Sprake, Reaney, Cooper, Bremner, Charlton, Hunter, O'Grady, Madeley, Jones, Giles, Gray
Referee: Arthur Dimond (Harlow)
Attendance: 53,750

Match 17
Wednesday 17 September 1969

EUROPEAN CUP FIRST ROUND FIRST LEG

Leeds United 10 *(O'Grady 1, Jones 3, 9, 69, Clarke 19, 47, Giles 34, 51, Bremner 65, 88)*
Lyn Oslo 0

No club made a more dramatic entry into the European Cup than United, who turned in a blockbusting performance to demolish the Norwegian champions and set up a new club record score.

With four seasons of Fairs Cup experience behind them, Leeds were rated one of the best prepared and equipped teams to carry the English flag in Europe's premier club competition, but no one was ready for the landslide which was to bury Lyn's team of students, teachers and clerks.

Lyn, who reached the quarter-finals of the European Cup-winners' Cup the previous season, were on the rack from the start. Just 35 seconds after the kick-off United swept into attack and the transfer-listed Mike O'Grady drove in a left-foot shot for what was the quickest goal in European Cup history at that time.

Lyn Oslo goalkeeper Sven Olsen thwarts Mick Jones in spectacular fashion but could not prevent United running up their record score of 10–0 in their European Cup meeting.

Three minutes later Mick Jones powered in a header, then hooked a shot in for the third after nine minutes. Goals continued to fly past goalkeeper Sven Olsen, who had only arrived at the ground 35 minutes before kick-off.

The rout continued with goals from Allan Clarke after 19 minutes; Johnny Giles, 34th minute; Clarke, 47th minute; Giles, 51st minute; Jones (hat-trick), 61st minute, Billy Bremner completed the annihilation with goals in the 65th and 88th minutes, to equal the best-ever score by a British club in Europe.

United scored a further six goals without reply in Oslo to sink the Norwegians. For the poor amateurs of Lyn the misery dragged on and at the end of their season they were relegated.

Leeds United: Sprake, Reaney, Cooper, Bremner, Charlton, Hunter, Madeley, Clarke, Jones, Giles (Bates 55), O'Grady

Lyn Oslo: S. Olsen, Rodvang, Ostvold, Morisbak, Kolle, Gulden, Boerrehaug, Christopherson, Berg, O. Olsen (Hovden 45), Austnes

Referee: Bohimil Smejkal (Czechoslovakia)

Attendance: 25,979

Match 18

Saturday 11 April 1970

FA Cup Final

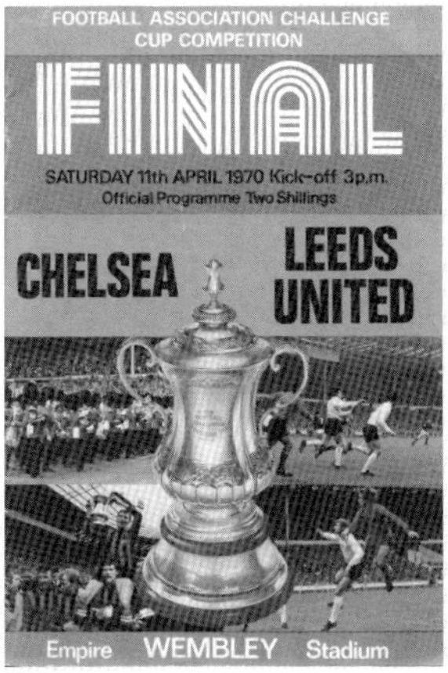

Chelsea 2 *(Houseman 41, Hutchinson 86)*

Leeds United 2 *(Charlton 21, Jones 83)*

(after extra-time)

United entered the FA Cup final against Chelsea looking like a side who had run out of gas.

Ten days before the big Wembley showdown United were beaten 1–0 at home by Celtic in the European Cup semi-final first leg and on the same night the League title was transferred from Elland Road to Goodison Park as Everton defeated West Brom 2–0.

Three energy-sapping FA Cup semi-finals against Manchester United – settled by a lone Billy Bremner goal at Bolton's Burnden Park – had added to Leeds' punishing schedule. It didn't help that the Final was about a month earlier than normal to enable England to prepare for the defence of the World Cup in Mexico.

Yet somehow Don Revie's men – minus broken-leg victim Paul Reaney – dug deep into their reserves of energy to produce football of the highest quality against Chelsea, but still failed to return to Yorkshire with the FA Cup.

Wembley looked more like Blackpool beach with masses of sand spread over the pitch in an effort to patch up the

Wembley's heavy pitch took its toll on both United and Chelsea players in the 1970 FA Cup Final. Here Gary Sprake relieves cramp in the legs of David Webb who was given the run-around by the sparkling Eddie Gray.

damage caused when the stadium hosted the recent Horse of the Year Show. The dreadful pitch contributed to United's opener after 21 minutes when Eddie Gray's corner from the right at the tunnel end was headed down towards goal by Jack Charlton, but the ball didn't bounce, tricking two defenders on the line and rolled gently into the goal.

As half-time approached, another freak goal brought Chelsea level as Peter Houseman's hit-and-hope long range effort didn't seem to have the power to beat Gary Sprake, who misjudged the ball and allowed it to slither under his body.

Determined Leeds pushed forward and man of the match Gray rattled the bar with a tremendous shot near the end before United scored the goal they thought would lift the Cup. An Allan Clarke header hit the post in the 83rd minute and Mick Jones was on hand to smack in the rebound.

The trophy looked destined for Elland Road for the first time in the Whites' history but, three minutes later, the usually solid Leeds defence was caught out at a free-kick when Ian Hutchinson headed in the second equaliser from John Hollins' cross.

With the game going into extra-time, and producing no further score, the draw – the first ever in a Wembley FA Cup Final – had extended United's marathon season still further.

Chelsea: Bonetti, Webb, McCreadie, Hollins, Dempsey, Harris (Hinton 90), Baldwin, Houseman, Osgood, Hutchinson, Cooke
Leeds United: Sprake, Madeley, Cooper, Bremner, Charlton, Hunter, Lorimer, Clarke, Jones, Giles, Gray
Referee: Eric Jennings (Stourbridge)
Attendance: 100,000

Match 19
Wednesday 15 April 1970

EUROPEAN CUP SEMI-FINAL SECOND LEG

Glasgow Celtic 2 *(Hughes 47, Murdoch 53)*
Leeds United 1 *(Bremner 14)*

Just four days after a two hours hard slog on an energy-sapping Wembley surface, Leeds attempted to overhaul Celtic for a place in the European Cup Final.

To cater for the tremendous demand for tickets, the tie was switched from Celtic Park to Hampden with around 135,000 fans crammed in to make it the biggest attendance of any European Cup tie.

A Jimmy Johnstone-inspired Celtic had won the first 'Battle of Britain' 1–0 a fortnight earlier at Elland Road with a George Connelly goal and the Scots were soon piling on the

Gary Sprake bravely dives at the feet of Celtic's John Hughes at Hampden Park.

Despite treatment from Les Cocker, Gary Sprake was stretchered off as United's European Cup dreams fell apart.

pressure in a cauldron of noise. But with 14 minutes on the clock, Billy Bremner reduced the vast crowd to near silence with a fierce right-foot shot which flew past Evan Williams.

But it proved a false dawn as Celtic, the first British winners of the competition in 1967, poured forward in waves and the inevitable goal arrived two minutes after half-time when John Hughes flung himself at Bertie Auld's cross and flicked the ball beyond Gary Sprake's reach. United's hopes evaporated in the white-hot atmosphere when the heroic Sprake was carried off after a collision with Hughes.

The first time the Welshman's replacement David Harvey touched the ball was to pick it out of the net. Jimmy Johnstone, turning on his magical skills, fed Bobby Murdoch whose 15-yard drive flashed past Harvey to seal the Hoops victory and wrap up a 3–1 aggregate score.

Celtic went on to lose to Dutch side Feyenoord in the Final, while Leeds had a little unresolved business with Chelsea before they could pull off their boots and put their feet up.

Glasgow Celtic: Williams, Hay, Gemmell, Murdoch, McNeill, Brogan, Johnstone, Connelly, Hughes, Auld, Lennox

Leeds United: Sprake (Harvey 51), Madeley, Cooper, Bremner, Charlton, Hunter, Lorimer (Bates 71), Clarke, Jones, Giles, Gray

Referee: Gerhard Schulenberg (West Germany)

Attendance: 136,505 (some reports state 135,826)

Match 20
Wednesday 29 April 1970

FA CUP FINAL REPLAY

Chelsea 2 *(Osgood 78, Webb 104)*
Leeds United 1 *(Jones 35)*
(after extra-time)

United's rematch with Chelsea at Old Trafford was the last throw of the dice for Don Revie's men to finish with something to show for their season's Herculean efforts.

The replay was a much more physical match than the Wembley encounter and once again Leeds looked the classier side.

In between some bone-jarring challenges from both sides, Leeds nosed in front with a superb 35th minute goal. Allan Clarke beat three men in a mazy midfield run before

The 1969–70 treble-chasing United squad that finished a superb campaign agonisingly short. Back row, left to right: Allan Clarke, Gary Sprake, David Harvey, Norman Hunter, Jack Charlton. Middle row: Terry Yorath, Eddie Gray, Rod Belfitt, Paul Madeley, Mick Jones, Peter Lorimer. Front row: Mick Bates, Johnny Giles, Terry Cooper, Billy Bremner, Terry Hibbitt.

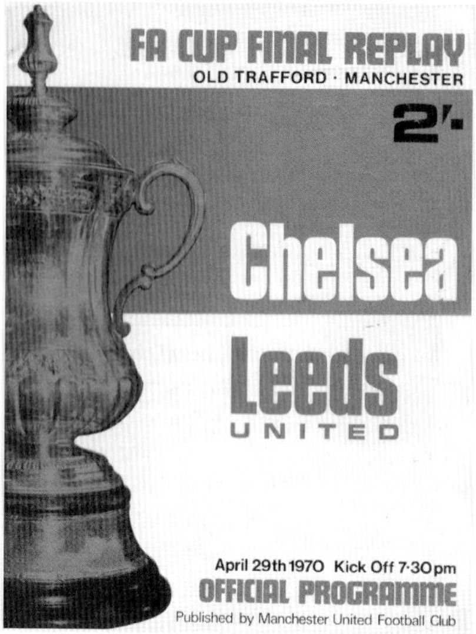

sending Mick Jones past Eddie McCreadie and John Dempsey for the centre-forward to shoot a brilliant goal.

Although the tackling became fiercer, Leeds seemed to be moving relentlessly towards victory when the London side illustrated their capacity for survival. Twelve minutes from time, Charlie Cooke clipped the perfect ball into the penalty area for Peter Osgood to torpedo a fine header past David Harvey and force extra-time.

The thunderous action continued with United still looking the better side, but, for the first time in 224 minutes of a sizzling final, Chelsea moved in front.

Ian Hutchinson wound up one of his famous long throws, Dempsey flicked the ball on, and David Webb, who had been given the runaround by Eddie Gray at Wembley, climbed to nod home from close-range at the far post.

United hammered away at the Blues in the final minutes but Chelsea clung on frantically to wrest the Cup from United's grasp and leave them empty handed from an arduous 62-game campaign.

Chelsea: Bonetti, Harris, McCreadie, Hollins, Dempsey, Webb, Baldwin, Cooke, Osgood (Hinton 116), Hutchinson, Houseman

Leeds United: Harvey, Madeley, Cooper, Bremner, Charlton, Hunter, Lorimer, Clarke, Jones, Giles, Gray

Referee: Eric Jennings (Stourbridge)

Attendance: 62,078

Match 21

Saturday 13 February 1971

FA CUP FIFTH ROUND

Colchester United 3 *(Crawford 18, 24, Simmons 55)*

Leeds United 2 *(Hunter 60, Giles 73)*

This date will go down as one of the blackest days in Leeds' history as Fourth Division minnows Colchester United pulled off one of the greatest FA Cup shocks by knocking out star-studded United.

Leeds, without Billy Bremner and Eddie Gray, never looked comfortable on the compact Layer Road ground against opponents who fought for every ball.

Former Ipswich and England man Ray Crawford rolled back the years to set the U's on their way to a famous win when Gary Sprake missed a free-kick from the left and the 34-year-old centre-forward headed in unopposed.

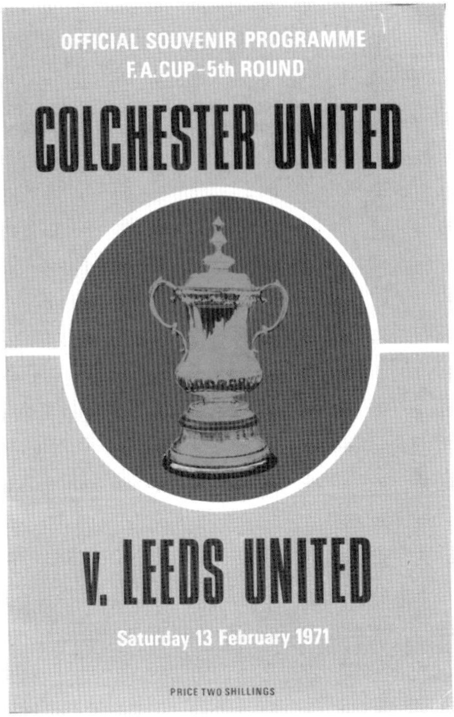

Minutes later Crawford rose above Paul Reaney to win an aerial duel and, as Sprake raced out to smother the danger, the Colchester man recovered to prod the ball over the line via an upright.

Leeds' defence, a rock on which they had built a lead in the Division One title race, crumbled again after half-time when Dave Simmons netted the third home goal after another mix-up between Reaney and Sprake.

It was simply embarrassing, but after an hour Norman Hunter threw Leeds a lifeline by heading in a corner, then with 17 minutes remaining Johnny Giles pulled another goal back to give the visitors hope of salvaging a reply. They almost got it too, only a brilliant save by Graham Smith seeing the Essex side to an astonishing victory. Leeds had done too little, too late.

In November 2008, Leeds, then in the third tier of English football, lost to non-League opposition for the first time when they were knocked out of the FA Cup by Histon, but that was a mild shock compared to events at Layer Road 37 years earlier.

Colchester United: Smith, Cram, Hall, Gilchrist, Garvey, Kurila, Lewis, Simmons, Mahon, Crawford, Gibbs

Leeds United: Sprake, Reaney, Cooper, Bates, Charlton, Hunter, Lorimer, Clarke, Jones, Giles, Madeley

Referee: Danny Lyden (Birmingham)

Attendance: 16,000

Stress is clearly etched on the faces of Jack Charlton and Mick Jones as United suffered one of the biggest FA Cup shocks of all time at the hands of Colchester in full view of BBC *Match of the Day* cameras.

Match 22
Friday 28 May 1971

EUROPEAN FAIRS CUP FINAL FIRST LEG

Juventus 2 *(Madeley 42, Bates 77)*
Leeds United 2 *(Bettega 27, Capello 55)*

Torrential rain washed out the first attempt to play the first leg of the 1971 Fairs Cup Final in Turin.

Referee Lauren van Ravens had little option but to abandon the game after 53 minutes as huge pools of water made play impossible. Two days later battle commenced in the Stadio Comunale with Juventus, the club which had once lured John Charles away from Leeds, the favourites with the bookmakers. The Italians looked a good bet early on when their multi-million lira forward line swept into action with a swift breakaway move from their own half. West German international Helmut Haller won possession and the ball was moved on by Pietro Anastasi and Roberto Causio for Roberto Bettega to finish clinically.

United responded with a lengthy spell of pressure in which both Jack Charlton and Johnny Giles went close before the equaliser came three minutes before the break. Peter Lorimer found Paul Madeley who cracked in a 35-yard shot which brushed defender

Mick Jones makes a splash as he tries to play a pass in the abandoned Fairs Cup Final game against Juventus in Turin.

Sandro Salvadore before entering the net. It was United's first goal in Italy, but within 12 minutes they were behind again to a superb 20-yard goal by future England manager Fabio Capello.

An unlikely hero emerged from United's ranks to snatch a second leveller – substitute Mick Bates. Bates, one for the talented reserves on the fringe of a first-team place, was thrown into the action after an injury to Mick Jones. Terry Cooper overlapped on the left and his cross was mispunched by Massimo Piloni to the feet of Bates, who calmly beat defender Gianpietro Marchetti and drove the ball in from close-range for a priceless goal.

Juventus: Piloni, Spinosi, Marchetti, Furino, Morini, Salvadore, Haller, Causio, Anastasi (Novellini 73), Capello, Bettega

Leeds United: Sprake, Reaney, Cooper, Bremner, Charlton, Hunter, Lorimer, Clarke, Jones (Bates 73), Giles, Madeley

Referee: Lauren van Ravens (Holland)

Attendance: 45,000

Match 23
Thursday, 3 June 1971

EUROPEAN FAIRS CUP FINAL SECOND LEG

Leeds United 1 *(Clarke 12)*
Juventus 1 *(Anastasi 19)*

With both sides playing out an action-packed 90 minutes, the outcome of the second leg of the 1971 Fairs Cup Final was in doubt right up to the final whistle.

Elland Road fans believed their side could end their luckless run and clinch the trophy for the second time – optimism which seemed justified after only 12 minutes when the razor-sharp Allan Clarke whipped around like a spinning-top to crack a loose ball past Roberto Tancredi for a brilliant goal.

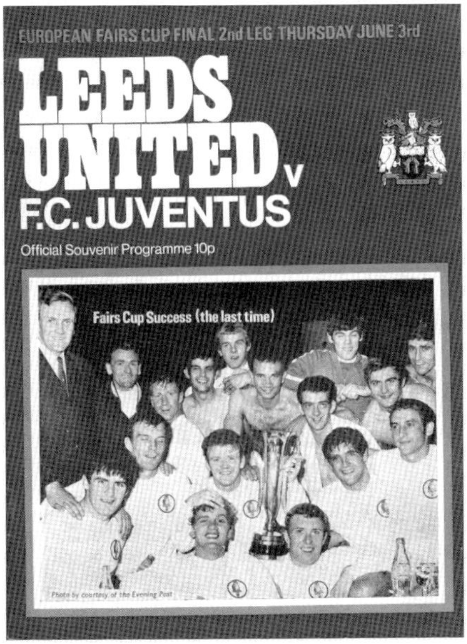

The celebrations lasted only seven minutes. A rare loose ball from Paul Madeley was picked up in midfield and fed to the quicksilver Pietro Anastasi, who justified his £440,000 price-tag drawing Gary Sprake off his line and calmly slipping the ball past him for the equaliser.

The match finely balanced, Leeds carried the extra threats of Johnny Giles and overlapping full-back Terry Cooper.

Barry Foster of the *Yorkshire Post* said: 'Giles gave the Italians plenty of problems

Captain Billy Bremner is hoisted aloft as United, wearing the shirts of the vanquished Juventus, celebrate their 1971 Fairs Cup success.

from midfield and it was from his prompting that most of Leeds' attacking play developed. Juventus never really mastered the adventurous left-wing play of Cooper...one lost count of the number of times the Leeds full-back was brought down in full flight.'

The action continued to bubble and boil. Sandro Salvadore was booked for yet another foul on Cooper, Madeley left the field with a cut above an eye and Tancredi, recalled in place of Massimo Piloni, made an athletic stop to keep out a Mick Jones header.

With away goals now counting double, United were content to play out time as Juventus failed to make any impression in attack as the game wore on. Juventus coach Cestimir Vycpalek was naturally disappointed. His side had not lost a game, yet still failed to lift the trophy. On the other hand, United, who had lost in the second round at Dynamo Dresden but squeezed through on the away-goals rule, had finally enjoyed some luck.

Leeds United: Sprake, Reaney, Cooper, Bremner, Charlton, Hunter, Lorimer, Clarke, Jones, Giles, Madeley (Bates 56)
Juventus: Tancredi, Spinosi, Marchetti, Furino, Morini, Salvadore, Haller, Causio, Anastasi, Capello, Bettega
Referee: Rudi Glockner (East Germany)
Attendance: 42,483

Match 24
Saturday 19 February 1972

DIVISION ONE

Leeds United 5 *(Jones 47, 59, 65; Clarke 54, Lorimer 74)*
Manchester United 1 *(Burns 57)*

Since gaining promotion in 1964, Don Revie had always regarded Manchester United as the yardstick by which to measure his own team's progress.

In the mid-1960s, the men from Old Trafford held the upper hand, but the balance of power tilted east of the Pennines after the three block busting FA Cup semi-final matches in 1970 and this match confirmed that Leeds had overhauled their arch rivals as a soccer super-power.

With Mick Jones back after a bout of flu to renew his lethal striking partnership with Allan Clarke, Leeds tore the visiting defence to shreds with some stunning attacking play.

Amazingly there was no score at half-time despite Jones (twice) and Jack Charlton going close, but it took only two minutes after the break for Revie's boys to unlock the Manchester defence.

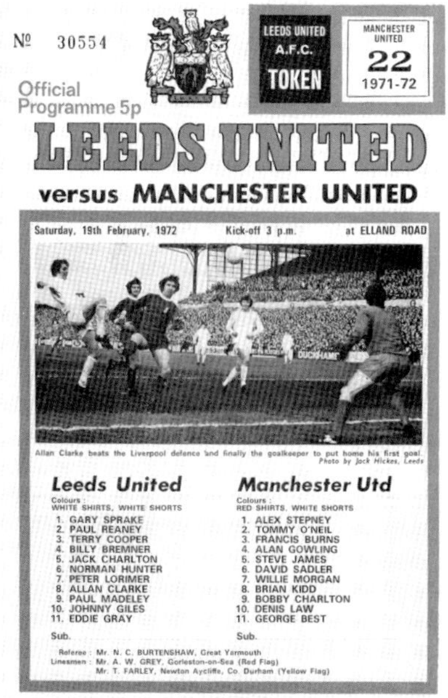

Eddie Gray, tantalising and tormenting on the wing, saw his shot pushed onto a post but Jones was on hand to nudge the ball over the line.

Seven minutes later, Leeds produced another sweeping attack which saw Peter Lorimer's cross find Jones, whose shot was deftly flicked in by Clarke.

Leeds were pouring forward at every opportunity and even when Francis Burns pulled a goal back in the 57th minute, Leeds hit back instantly when Jones got on the end of Billy Bremner's cross to head into the ground and over Alex Stepney.

Jones completed his hat-trick six minutes later when he prodded the ball over the line after more excellent approach work by Gray and Lorimer.

Mick Jones never gave defences a rest as Manchester United discovered when he netted a hat-trick in the 5–1 mauling of the men from Old Trafford in 1972.

Man-of-the-match Jones then turned provider, whipping in a cross which Lorimer thrashed into the roof of the net to complete a five-goal storm in 27 minutes.

The victory had taken United's points tally to 450 since returning to the First Division seven and a half years earlier and must rank as one of the sweetest in the club's history, particularly as the opposition had been sitting on top of the table only a few weeks earlier.

Leeds United: Sprake, Madeley, Cooper, Bremner, Charlton, Hunter, Lorimer, Clarke, Jones, Giles, Gray

Manchester United: Stepney, O'Neil, Dunne, Burns, James, Sadler, Morgan, Kidd (Mcllroy 67), Charlton, Gowling, Best

Referee: Norman Burtenshaw (Great Yarmouth)

Attendance: 45,394

Match 25
Saturday 4 March 1972

DIVISION ONE

Leeds United 7 *(Clarke 37, 60; Lorimer 42, 64, 68; Charlton 73, Jones 78)*
Southampton 0

United's critics had often branded them dour, defensive and downright dull in their quest for success, but in 1971–72 Leeds set the First Division alight with dazzling, fluent football that won thousands of new friends.

Emphasis was placed on attack and Leeds produced the sort of soccer that had the back pages of national newspapers dubbing them 'Super Leeds' and drawing comparisons with the legendary Real Madrid. Such acclaim gained credence in the eyes of millions of television viewers who tuned in to see BBC's *Match of the Day* cameras capture the action at Elland Road. One of the televised games was against Southampton in the midst of United's purple patch when they delighted the viewing public with a scintillating performance.

None of the goals were particularly spectacular, but each one followed great sweeping movements around the pitch, which had the crowd roaring 'Ole' each time the ball was passed from one Leeds player to another.

United's magnificent seven came like this: 37th minute brilliant inter-play between Mick Jones and

Allan Clarke, far right, slides in one of United's seven goals in the dismantling of Southampton at a rapturous Elland Road.

Eddie Gray opened up the defence for Allan Clarke to crack in an angled drive; 42nd minute, Peter Lorimer drove Gray's superb through-pass beyond the luckless Eric Martin; 60th minute, Clarke's footwork took him round a defender before slotting in the third; 64th minute Lorimer hit the fourth; 68th minute, Lorimer intercepted a misjudged Roger Fry back-pass to complete his hat-trick; 73 minutes, Jack Charlton arrived in the penalty area to head Norman Hunter's cross; 78th minute, Jones celebrated his 300 League game by forcing the ball in from close range after Lorimer headed down a left wing Gray centre.

Leeds United: Sprake, Reaney, Madeley, Bremner, Charlton Hunter, Lorimer, Clarke, Jones, Giles, Gray

Southampton: Martin, McCarthy, Fry, Stokes, Gabriel, Steel, Paine (Byrne 75), Channon, Davies, O'Neill, Jenkins

Referee: Dennis Corbett (Wolverhampton)

Attendance: 34,275

Match 26

Saturday 6 May 1972

FA CUP FINAL

Arsenal 0

Leeds United 1 *(Clarke 52)*

At about 4.10pm on the first Saturday in May 1972, the forehead of slim striker Allan Clarke arrowed the ball past Geoff Barnett's desperate dive and into the Arsenal net to take the FA Cup to Leeds for the first time.

The game began sensationally when full-back Bob McNab was cautioned in the first minute – the first player to be booked in a Wembley Final – and was later joined by Norman Hunter, Billy Bremner and Charlie George, although it was never a physical game.

After taking the lead, United opened up with some fine attacking moves with Clarke, who had rattled the crossbar with a first-half header, a constant menace and Bremner and Johnny Giles controlling the midfield.

Arsenal were restricted to a handful of chances – Paul Reaney kicked an Alan Ball shot off the line, David Harvey pulled off a fine twisting save to keep out a deflected Frank McLintock shot and in the 75th minute Charlie George's shot hit the crossbar – but these were isolated incidents in a game mastered by Leeds.

United were dealt a painful blow in the last minute when Mick Jones dislocated an elbow and he was still receiving treatment when his colleagues climbed to the Royal box to receive their Centenary Final winners' medals from the Queen.

The most famous goal in Leeds United's history. Geoff Barnett's despairing dive cannot prevent a header from Allan Clarke (hidden) from winning the 1972 FA Cup which they celebrated in time-honoured fashion.

Norman Hunter made a return journey after collecting the bandaged Jones and led him up the steps in a touching scene as Wembley was awash in a sea of white, old gold and blue.

Arsenal: Barnett, Rice, McNab, Storey, McLintock, Simpson, Armstrong, Ball, George, Radford (Kennedy 73), Graham

Leeds United: Harvey, Reaney, Madeley, Bremner, Charlton, Hunter, Lorimer, Clarke, Jones, Giles, Gray

Referee: David Smith (Gloucester)

Attendance: 100,000

Match 27

Monday 8 May 1972

Division One

Wolverhampton Wanderers 2 *(Munro 42, Dougan 65)*
Leeds United 1 *(Bremner 68)*

With the FA Cup already in the bag, half of Yorkshire seemed to follow United from Wembley to Molineux for another historic night as Leeds went in search of the coveted League and Cup double. They needed at least a draw in this, their final match for the season, to lift the title.

United didn't even celebrate their FA Cup triumph because the Football League had ruled they had to play this vital game on the following Monday night because of international and European fixture congestion.

Despite missing key players, Leeds drove forward and claimed that goalkeeper Phil Parkes had brought down Allan Clarke, and that full-back Bernard Shaw handled shots from Clarke and Peter Lorimer in the penalty box, but referee Bill Gow ignored their pleas.

It was Wolves, with little but pride to play for, who seized the initiative three minutes before half-time when United failed to clear a corner and Francis Munro cracked an angled drive past David Harvey.

United looked desperately for the equaliser, but the home side increased their lead with a fine goal after an hour when John Richards' pass opened up the heart of the United defence for striker Derek Dougan to run through and finish superbly.

Within minutes United's double hopes were rekindled when Billy Bremner scurried on to Paul Madeley's long pass to thump the ball in from close range.

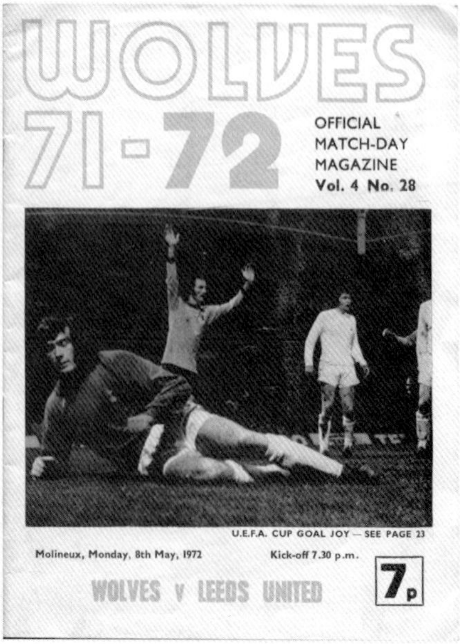

Billy Bremner celebrates his goal at Wolves, but the double eluded United's clutches.

The frantic pace continued and United came desperately close to snatching the crucial equaliser at the end when Welsh international Terry Yorath, substitute for the injured Clarke, flicked the ball over the head of Wolves 'keeper Phil Parkes, only to see defender Gerry Taylor emerge from nowhere and head off the line.

Wolves clung on to deny Leeds their glory and on the same night another of the title challengers, Liverpool, failed to beat Arsenal at Highbury, leaving Derby County, whose players were on holiday, champions for the first time in their history.

Wolverhampton Wanderers: Parkes, Shaw, Taylor, Hegan, Munro, McAlle, McCalliog, Hibbitt, Richards, Dougan, Wagstaffe

Leeds United: Harvey, Reaney, Madeley, Bremner, Charlton, Hunter, Lorimer, Clarke (Yorath 66), Bates, Giles, Gray

Referee: Bill Gow (Swansea)

Attendance: 53,379

Match 28

Saturday 5 May 1973

FA Cup Final

Leeds United 0

Sunderland 1 *(Porterfield 31)*

As United came clattering down in the 1973 FA Cup Final, the thud could be heard from John O'Groats to Land's End. Second Division Sunderland completely ripped up the form book to pull off one of the biggest upsets in a Wembley Final.

Sunderland had reached Wembley with a refreshing brand of football and, after weathering an early flurry of United attacks, began to play to their full potential. The Sunderland defence, centre-half Dave Watson in particular, closed down quickly on the off-form Allan Clarke, Mick Jones and Eddie Gray, and pieced together some promising moves of their own.

A third of the match had gone when diminutive midfield man Bobby Kerr put in a cunning lob which David Harvey was forced to tip away for a corner. Billy Hughes curled the kick in from the right, beyond United's defensive cover, where Ian Porterfield cushioned the ball on his thigh before crashing in a superb knee-high, right-foot volley for the goal which was to win the Cup.

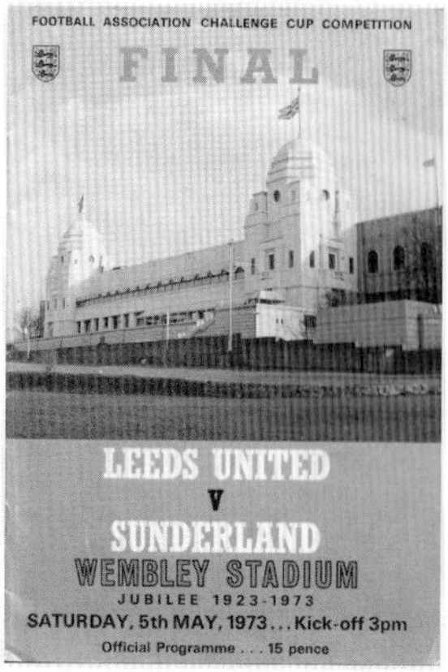

Yet the game is often remembered for the save that enabled the Wearsiders to hang on to the Cup rather than for the goal that won it. Midway through the second half Trevor Cherry linked up with the attack and put in a diving header which goalkeeper Jim Montgomery did well to parry. The ball ran loose to Peter Lorimer who hit the ball hard and true from close range, only for Montgomery to twist in the air and fling out his arms to tip the ball on to the underside of the bar for an amazing double save.

United, featuring in their third FA Cup Final in four years, were visibly shocked by Montgomery's gravity-defying effort and, although they belatedly pushed forward, anything less than victory would have been harsh on underdogs Sunderland.

Leeds United: Harvey, Reaney, Cherry, Bremner, Madeley, Hunter, Lorimer, Clarke, Jones, Giles, Gray (Yorath 77)
Sunderland: Montgomery, Malone, Guthrie, Horswill, Watson, Pitt, Kerr, Porterfield, Halom, Hughes, Tueart
Referee: Ken Burns (Stourbridge)
Attendance: 100,000

The ball is heading for the back of the United net as Ian Porterfield volleys Sunderland ahead in the 1973 FA Cup Final.

Match 29
Wednesday 16 May 1973

EUROPEAN CUP-WINNERS' CUP FINAL

AC Milan 1 *(Chiarugi 4)*
Leeds United 0

With the Wembley defeat by Sunderland still dogging them, rumours that Don Revie was to leave the club, the suspensions of Allan Clarke and Billy Bremner and an injury to Johnny Giles, it was a deflated and depleted Leeds United who prepared to contest the European Cup-winners' Cup Final in Salonika against the might of AC Milan.

Thunder and heavy rain greeted the teams as they stepped out into the new Kaftatzoglio Stadium in northern Greece. It was to prove an appropriate backcloth for an infamous match.

After only four minutes, the referee curiously penalised Paul Madeley for an infringement and Luciano Chiarugi saw his free-kick clip a United defender and brush one of his own forwards before hitting the base of a post and going in.

Once in front, the Italians retreated to their own penalty area and did not appear to mind how they stopped Leeds as referee Christos Michas ignored a succession of fouls, much to the anger of both the Leeds and Greek supporters in the crowd. Mick Jones and

Luciano Chiarugi lashes in AC Milan's goal in the scandalous 1973 European Cup-Winners' Cup Final in Salonika.

Peter Lorimer were both flattened in the penalty area, a Paul Reaney cross was blatantly handled by Romeo Benetti and a host of shots and headers all went desperately close.

United's frustration finally boiled over minutes from the end when Norman Hunter was hacked down from behind by Gianni Rivera and retaliated. In the confused mêlèe which followed, Hunter and one of the Italians, Roberto Sogliano, were ordered off.

Referee Christos Michas was later suspended by UEFA and his own Greek FA amid suspicions that United had been stitched up, but the European football authorities stopped short of a full investigation into the match and the result stood.

AC Milan: Vecchi, Sabadini, Zignoli, Anquilletti, Turone, Rosato (Dolci 59), Sogliano, Benetti, Bigon, Rivera, Chiarugi

Leeds United: Harvey, Reaney, Cherry, Bates, Yorath, Hunter, Lorimer, Jordan, Jones, F. Gray (McQueen 54), Madeley

Referee: Christos Michas (Greece)

Attendance: 45,000

Match 30

Wednesday 9 April 1975

EUROPEAN CUP SEMI-FINAL

Leeds United 2 *(Bremner 10, Clarke 78)*

Barcelona 1 *(Asensi 65)*

Dutch masters Johann Cruyff and Johann Neeskens were brought down to earth at a packed Elland Road as United edged closer to their first European Cup Final.

The pair had played in Holland's World Cup Final side beaten 2–1 by West Germany the previous year and were regarded as among the best midfield players on the planet. But it was Scottish skipper Billy Bremner and his partner Johnny Giles who controlled this nerve-tingling match, United's 60th game of the season.

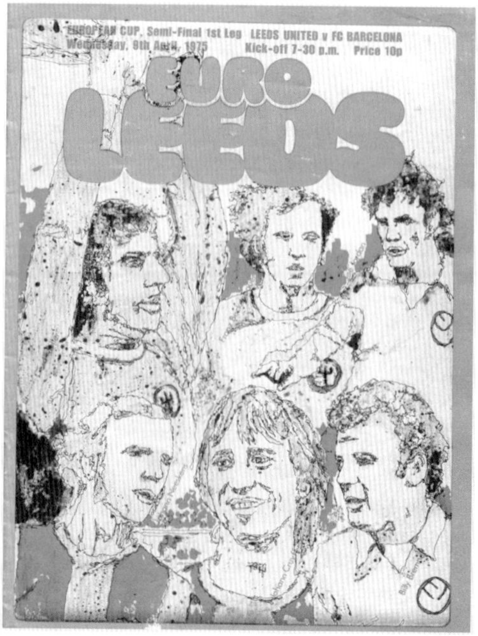

It was Bremner who gave Leeds a flying start with a goal after only nine minutes. Giles played the ball up to Joe Jordan, whose header found Bremner in space. He took a few strides forward before driving the ball past Salvador Sadurni with an angled shot to become the first player to score against the Spanish side in the competition that season.

Billy Bremner seemed to specialise in scoring semi-final goals – this time he shoots United ahead against Barcelona in the 1975 European Cup semi-final at Elland Road.

Leeds knew they would probably need a two-goal lead to take to the vast Nou Camp Stadium and headers by Allan Clarke and Gordon McQueen went close to give them that cushion.

With Paul Madeley keeping Cruyff quiet, the Spaniards were largely on the defensive but did produce some dangerous counter-attacks – and it was from one of these that they grabbed an equaliser.

In the 66th minute Cruyff slid the ball through to Juan Carlos Heredia, who was checked on the edge of the area by Paul Reaney, although Leeds were unhappy at the award of the free-kick against their full-back. Cruyff stood over the ball, bided his time and rolled it sideways for Juan Manuel Asensi to crack his shot unerringly beyond David Stewart.

It was a hammer blow for United, but 12 minutes later they regained the lead. Reaney surged down the right wing and crossed for Joe Jordan to head down in the box where Clarke, six yards out, lashed in his 21st goal of the season.

United pushed hard for a third goal but with Barcelona killing time at every opportunity, they had to settle for a 2–1 lead to take to Spain.

In the second leg, Peter Lorimer's early goal gave United much-needed breathing space and, despite having McQueen sent off, they hung on for a 1–1 draw and a 3–2 aggregate win to reach their first European Cup Final.

Leeds United: Stewart, Reaney, F. Gray, Bremner, McQueen, Madeley, Yorath, Clarke, Jordan, Giles, E. Gray

Barcelona: Sadurni, Costas (Rife 65), Marinho, Gallego, De La Cruz, Neeskens (Juan Carlos 78), Rexach, Migueli, Cruyff, Asensi, Heredia

Referee: Vital Loraux (Belgium)

Attendance: 50,393

Match 31
Wednesday 28 May 1975

EUROPEAN CUP FINAL

Bayern Munich 2 *(Roth 71, Muller 81)*
Leeds United 0

United reached new heights when they lifted the 1973–74 League Championship, producing a brand of football which earned them another shot at the European Cup. This time they bettered their semi-final appearance in 1970.

This latest European venture was undertaken without the guidance of Don Revie, who was by now England manager. Leeds' experienced squad were now led by the calm and influential Jimmy Armfield, who nursed the club through a difficult period after Revie's departure and Brian Clough's 44 days at Elland Road. Armfield extracted some excellent displays from his side during their route to the Final.

In Paris, luck deserted United in their hour of need. Playing well in the first half, they had two penalty appeals rejected and the game turned around dramatically in a matter of minutes midway through the second half. Peter Lorimer thundered a 66th-minute volley past Sepp Maier, only to have the effort disallowed because skipper Billy Bremner had strayed offside, although Leeds claimed that he was not interfering with play.

Both the mood and complexion of the match altered minutes later as Danish star Conny Torstensson slipped a neat through ball to Franz Roth who clipped it past the advancing Stewart. Seven minutes later

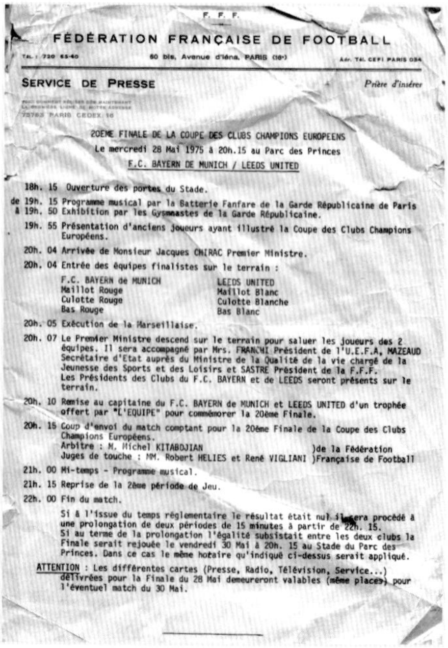

F. F. F.

FÉDÉRATION FRANÇAISE DE FOOTBALL

TÉL : 720 65-40 60 bis, Avenue d'Iéna, PARIS (16e) Adr. Tél. CEFI PARIS 034

SERVICE DE PRESSE *Prière d'insérer*

75783 PARIS CEDEX 16

20EME FINALE DE LA COUPE DES CLUBS CHAMPIONS EUROPEENS
Le mercredi 28 Mai 1975 à 20h.15 au Parc des Princes
F.C. BAYERN DE MUNICH / LEEDS UNITED

18h. 15 Ouverture des portes du Stade.

de 19h. 15 Programme musical par la Batterie Fanfare de la Garde Républicaine de Paris
à 19h. 50 Exhibition par les Gysmnastes de la Garde Républicaine.

19h. 55 Présentation d'anciens joueurs ayant illustré la Coupe des Clubs Champions Européens.

20h. 04 Arrivée de Monsieur Jacques CHIRAC Premier Ministre.

20h. 04 Entrée des équipes finalistes sur le terrain :

F.C. BAYERN de MUNICH	LEEDS UNITED
Maillot Rouge	Maillot Blanc
Culotte Rouge	Culotte Blanche
Bas Rouge	Bas Blanc

20h. 05 Exécution de la Marseillaise.

20h. 07 Le Premier Ministre descend sur le terrain pour saluer les joueurs des 2 équipes. Il sera accompagné par Mrs. FRANCHI Président de l'U.E.F.A, MAZEAUD Secrétaire d'Etat auprès du Ministre de la Qualité de la vie chargé de la Jeunesse des Sports et des Loisirs et SASTRE Président de la F.F.F.
Les Présidents des Clubs du F.C. BAYERN et de LEEDS seront présents sur le terrain.

20h. 10 Remise au capitaine du F.C. BAYERN de MUNICH et LEEDS UNITED d'un trophée offert par "L'EQUIPE" pour commémorer la 20ème Finale.

20h. 15 Coup d'envoi du match comptant pour la 20ème Finale de la Coupe des Clubs Champions Européens.
Arbitre : M. Michel KITABDJIAN)de la Fédération
Juges de touche : MM. Robert HELIES et René VIGLIANI)Française de Football

21h. 00 Mi-temps - Programme musical.

21h. 15 Reprise de la 2ème période de Jeu.

22h. 00 Fin du match.

Si à l'issue du temps réglementaire le résultat était nul il sera procédé à une prolongation de deux périodes de 15 minutes à partir de 22h. 15.
Si au terme de la prolongation l'égalité subsistait entre les deux clubs la Finale serait rejouée le vendredi 30 Mai à 20h. 15 au Stade du Parc des Princes. Dans ce cas le même horaire qu'indiqué ci-dessus serait appliqué.

ATTENTION : Les différentes cartes (Presse, Radio, Télévision, Service...) délivrées pour la Finale du 28 Mai demeureront valables (même places) pour l'éventuel match du 30 Mai.

Timetable of the biggest game in United's history given to the press by the French Football Federation.

Peter Lorimer's volley flies past Bayern Munich goalkeeper Sepp Maier into the net.

Billy Bremner can't believe Lorimer's strike was not allowed to stand.

Jupp Kapellmann cut the ball back from the byline for goal-poacher Gerhard Muller to steal in front of Paul Madeley, playing at centre-half for the suspended Gordon McQueen, and turn the ball in at the near post.

To complete a night of disaster for United, hordes of their supporters rioted inside and outside the ground – actions which cost Leeds a ban from European competition.

Bayern Munich: Maier, Durnberger, Andersson (Weiss 5), Schwarzenbeck, Beckenbauer, Roth, Torstensson, Zobel, Muller, Hoeness (Wunder 42), Kapellmann

Leeds United: Stewart, Reaney, F. Gray, Bremner, Madeley, Hunter, Lorimer, Clarke, Jordan, Giles, Yorath (E. Gray 79)

Referee: Marcel Kitabdjian (France)

Attendance: 48,374

Match 32
Sunday 12 April 1987

FA Cup semi-final

Coventry City 3 *(Gynn 68, Houchen 78, Bennett 99)*
Leeds United 2 *(Rennie 14, Edwards 83)*
(after extra-time)

United's first appearance in a major semi-final for 10 years produced a tremendous duel in the Sunday sunshine with the eventual FA Cup winners, Coventry City, at Hillsborough, Sheffield.

The game, televised live, kicked-off 15 minutes late because an estimated 6,000 fans were still waiting to get into the ground at 12.15pm, the scheduled starting time. The match proved well worth the wait.

Second Division United, who had eliminated Telford United, Swindon Town, Queen's Park Rangers and Wigan Athletic, made a blistering start, going a goal up after 14 minutes when David Rennie headed in Micky Adams' corner-kick. Only two brilliant saves by Coventry 'keeper Steve Ogrizovic prevented United from taking complete control and gradually the Sky Blues began to create chances.

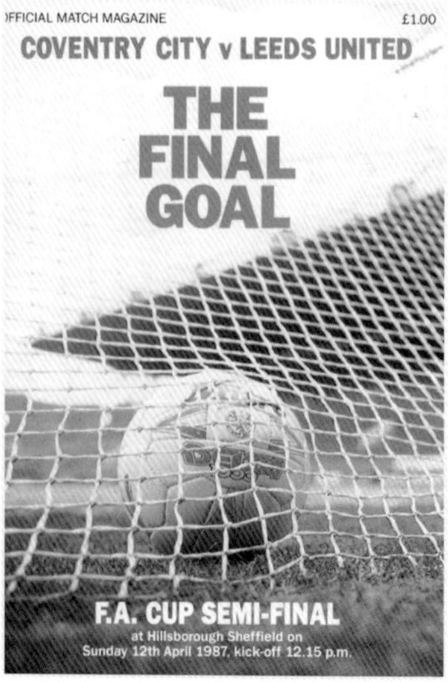

With only 22 minutes between United and a Wembley appearance the Leeds heroes were coping fairly easily with the Coventry attack when United skipper Brendan Ormsby made the error which was to tip the game City's way.

Instead of hoofing a misdirected through ball clear he opted to guide it over the dead-ball line but was robbed by the persistent David Bennett whose cross was cracked in from 12 yards by substitute Micky Gynn.

Ian Baird, who never took any prisoners, slides in to tackle Nick Pickering during the 1986 FA Cup semi-final against Coventry at Hillsborough.

Ten minutes later the United defence was opened up again and Keith Houchen rounded Mervyn Day in style to give City the lead. A pulsating match reached fever pitch seven minutes from normal time when substitute Keith Edwards headed in United's equaliser from Andy Ritchie's cross.

The pace inevitably dropped in the extra period, but it was Coventry, of the First Division, who made most of the running and won the game in the 99th minute when Bennett shot home from close range after Day blocked a Houchen effort with his legs. United fought hard and it needed another marvellous Ogrizovic save to deny Edwards a late equaliser.

Underdogs Leeds, who were also chasing promotion, had acquitted themselves superbly and their much-maligned supporters also made it a trouble-free game to remember, on a day when the club won back much of its self respect.

Coventry City: Ogrizovic, Borrows, Downs, McGrath, Kilcline, Peake, Bennett, Phillips, Regis, Houchen, Pickering (Gynn 61)

Leeds United: Day, Aspin, Adams, Stiles (Haddock 82), Ashurst, Ormsby, Ritchie, Sheridan, Pearson (Edwards 82), Baird, Rennie

Referee: Roger Milford (Bristol)

Attendance: 51,372

Match 33
Friday 29 May 1987

First Division Play-off replay

Charlton 2 *(Shirtliff 113, 118)*
Leeds United 1 *(Sheridan 99)*
(after extra-time)

The newly-adopted Play-offs in 1987 may not have produced the flowing football that United had displayed in the Hillsborough semi-final but the games were truly dramatic.

Derby and Portsmouth were promoted from Division Two, leaving Charlton, who finished fourth from bottom in Division One above Aston Villa, Manchester City and Leicester, to scrap it out with Division Two sides Oldham, Leeds, who finished fifth, and Ipswich.

Leeds substitute Keith Edwards scored the only goal of the Play-off semi against Oldham at Elland Road and looked to be going out when they trailed 2–0 in the return until super-sub Edwards scored straight from the restart with a minute left. United hung on in extra-time on the

A vast banking of United fans look on in disbelief as Peter Shirtliff heads Charlton's winner in the Play-off Final replay at St Andrew's, Birmingham.

away goals count double ruling to the Play-off Final against Charlton, who had seen off Ipswich.

A dour game in London saw United sunk by a late goal from Jim Melrose, later to join Leeds, but United reversed the scoreline to force a replay when skipper Brendan Ormsby got the final touch from rookie striker Bob Taylor.

The final game of a long, hard, season took place at St Andrew's, home of Birmingham City, where Leeds fans vastly outnumbered their Charlton counterparts.

A nerve-shredding night was once again settled by late goals. John Sheridan, who had an outstanding season in midfield, gave United the lead in the first period of extra-time with a superb curling free-kick. A return to the top flight was in touching distance.

But United, who had lost defensive lynchpin Ormsby injured in normal time, could not hang on and were shattered when Peter Shirtliff equalised on 113 minutes. Promotion looked as though it would be settled by penalties but amazingly defender Shirtliff scored again five minutes later to kill United's promotion dream for another season.

Leeds United: Day, Aspin, McDonald, Aizlewood, Ashurst, Ormsby (Edwards 45), Stiles, Sheridan, Pearson, Baird, Adams

Charlton Athletic: Bolder, Humphrey, Reid, Peake, Shirtliff, Miller, Gritt, Lee, Melrose (Stuart 96), Walsh, Crooks

Referee: Allan Gunn (Burgess Hill, Sussex)

Attendance: 18,000

Match 34

Monday 16 April 1990

Division Two

Leeds United 4 *(Strachan 18, pen 82; Chapman 74, Speed 89)*
Sheffield United 0

Yorkshire's Championship-chasing duo clashed head on in front of the biggest Second Division crowd of the season in the white-hot atmosphere of Elland Road on Easter Monday.

Pundits reckoned that the outcome of the battle would be crucial in the race for the title – and so it proved as Leeds strengthened their grip at the top of the table with an emphatic victory.

After a tense opening, Leeds skipper Gordon Strachan gave his side the lead after 18 minutes, from close range after Chris Kamara's shot had been blocked on the line by Paul Stancliffe.

Leeds continued to dominate but had to wait until 16 minutes from the end to kill off the

Gordon Strachan, who netted twice in the pivotal Easter victory against title rivals Sheffield United.

Blades. Gary Speed powered down the left and his fierce, low centre was turned in at the far post by Lee Chapman.

Leeds began to turn on the style and in the 82nd minute went 3–0 up when Bobby Davison blocked Simon Tracey's clearance and was fouled by the young 'keeper as he scampered after the rebound. Ice-cool Strachan stepped up to chip the penalty wide of Tracey.

To seal a great afternoon for Leeds, Kamara broke up a last-minute Sheffield attack and sent Speed on a long run towards goal. The Welsh youngster drew Tracey before driving a diagonal shot into the net.

Leeds eventually went on to clinch the Championship, with a club record 85 points. In the penultimate game, Strachan's late strike beat Leicester at Elland Road and the title was clinched on goal-difference from the Blades at Bournemouth with a Chapman header sealing a return to Division One after an absence of eight years.

Leeds United: Day, Sterland, Beglin, Jones, Fairclough, McClelland, Strachan, Kamara, Chapman, Davison (Shutt 83), Speed

Sheffield United: Tracey, Hill, Barnes, Booker, Stancliffe, Morris, Webster, Gannon (Wood 62), Whitehurst (Agana 52), Deane, Bryson

Referee: Allan Gunn (South Chailey, Sussex)

Attendance: 32,727

Match 35
Saturday 25 August 1990

DIVISION ONE

Everton 2 *(Nevin 67, Ebbrell 76)*
Leeds United 3 *(Fairclough 6, Speed 44, Varadi 60)*

Leeds returned to English football's top table with a brilliant 3–2 victory at Everton, who had finished sixth in Division One the previous campaign.

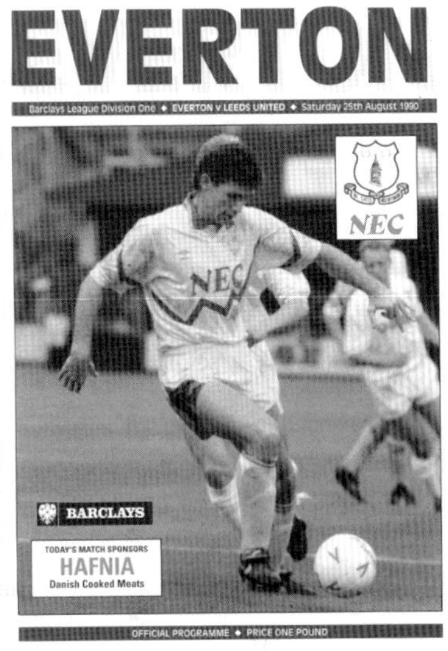

United were quickly into their stride and their vast following were roaring with delight after just six minutes when Chris Fairclough headed in David Batty's long throw.

Leeds continued to knock the ball about with style but had a couple of escapes when a Dave Watson header hit the bar and Neil McDonald missed a penalty after a handball by Fairclough. However, United continued to pose the greater threat and it was no surprise when Gary Speed slid in the second with half-time approaching.

To the astonishment of the Goodison Park crowd Everton's Welsh international goalkeeper

Imre Varadi (centre) celebrates his goal as United marked their return to the First Division in 1990 with an eye-catching 3–2 win at Everton.

Neville Southall refused to go with his teammates to the dressing rooms at half-time. Instead he sat disconsolate at the foot of a goalpost throughout the interval. But the sit-in did little to turn the tide as Everton old boy Imre Varadi put United 3–0 up on the hour with a smart finish.

However, the introduction of substitute Kevin Sheedy gave the Blues fresh impetus and goals by Pat Nevin and John Ebbrell left Howard Wilkinson's team facing a tricky final 15 minutes. But goalkeeper John Lukic, re-signed from Arsenal for £1 million, made some great saves as United, who also fielded debutants Chris Whyte and Gary McAllister, another £1 million man, deservedly hung on for maximum points.

It was a result that signalled that Leeds were back in the big time and that chairman Leslie Silver's decision to back Wilkinson financially would prove a winner.

Everton: Southall, McDonald, Hinchcliffe, Keown, Watson, Milligan, Nevin, McCall (Sheedy 61), Sharp, Newell, Ebbrell

Leeds United: Lukic, Sterland, Snodin, Batty, Fairclough, Whyte, Strachan, Varadi (Kamara 81), Chapman, McAllister, Speed (Haddock 81)

Referee: Keren Barratt (Coventry)

Attendance: 34,412

Match 36

Sunday 12 January 1992

Division One

Sheffield Wednesday 1 *(Sheridan 42)*

Leeds United 6 *(Chapman 8, 43, 66; Dorigo 34, Whitlow 68, Wallace 86)*

After such an impressive return to the First Division, United were tipped as title contenders by several pundits, particularly as the side had been strengthened by the arrival of England left-back Tony Dorigo from Chelsea and England Under-21 forward Rod Wallace from Southampton.

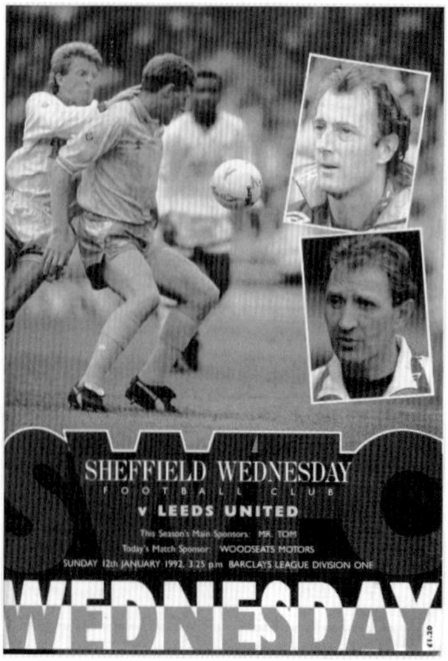

The 1991–92 Championship race was developing into a two-horse affair between the Uniteds of Leeds and Manchester. The men from Old Trafford struck a psychological blow four days before the League game at Hillsborough by knocking Leeds out of the Rumbelows Cup.

But Leeds, despite the absence of inspirational skipper Gordon Strachan (injured) and David Batty (suspended), stormed back to the top of the First Division with a blistering attacking display televised live. Leeds were regulars on satellite television, a great display of attacking football in a 4–1 triumph at Aston Villa being one highlight – but the Hillsborough super-show was to top that.

Lee Chapman wheels away in triumph after scoring one of his hat-trick goals in the 6–1 win at Sheffield Wednesday which took United to the top of Division One.

Wednesday had not lost at home for 14 matches, but Howard Wilkinson, back at Hillsborough for the first time since leaving the Owls to manage United, had a glorious return. To rub salt into Sheffield's wounds, the scoring feast was spearheaded by another Wednesday old boy, Lee Chapman, who netted the first hat-trick on away soil by a United player in 12 years.

It took Chapman just eight minutes to open his account, forcing home Chris Fairclough's headed knock down. After that, United took total control with Rod Wallace and Tony Dorigo creating havoc down the left. It was no surprise when Dorigo thumped home a 25-yard free-kick on the half-hour to increase United's lead, but Wednesday briefly crept into the game via a controversial penalty. Gordon Watson went down spectacularly in the box and referee Philip Don pointed to the spot. Up stepped former Leeds player John Sheridan, whose spot-kick was touched on to a post but came back for him to net the rebound.

Leeds were in no mood to feel sorry for themselves and before the interval Chapman headed in Gary Speed's superb left-wing cross to restore United's two-goal cushion. Chapman completed his hat-trick when he nodded in from close range after a Speed header came back off the bar.

Two minutes later a towering header by substitute Mike Whitlow made it 5–1. Leeds were in an irresistible mood and Wallace wrapped up the scoring near the end when he cut through the Wednesday defence and clipped the ball past Chris Woods.

It was United's best away victory since their 7–3 thumping of Blackpool 56 years earlier, and although Leeds were knocked out of the FA Cup by Manchester United the week after their Hillsborough triumph, they were in pole position in the race for the Championship.

Sheffield Wednesday: Woods, Nilsson, King, Palmer, Pearson (Harkes 45), Anderson, Watson, Sheridan, Bart-Williams, Jemson, Worthington (Williams 84)

Leeds United: Lukic, Sterland, Dorigo, Hodge (Davison 81), Fairclough, Whyte, Shutt (Whitlow 62), Wallace, Chapman, McAllister, Speed

Referee: Philip Don (Middlesex)

Attendance: 32,228

Match 37

Sunday 26 April 1992

Division One

Sheffield United 2 *(Cork 28, Chapman og 70)*

Leeds United 3 *(Wallace 44, Newsome 65, Gayle og 77)*

Champagne corks were popping after a truly extraordinary Sunday which ended with the League Championship returning to Elland Road for the first time since 1973–74.

Leeds kicked off at midday at Bramall Lane, knowing that victory would mean that Manchester United could not afford to lose their game at Liverpool later that afternoon, or the crown would almost certainly go to Howard Wilkinson's team. On a windswept afternoon, a bizarre match unfolded before the eyes of a 32,000 crowd swelled by a huge following from up the M1.

Leeds were clearly nervous and had several uneasy moments in defence before veteran striker Alan Cork gobbled up a half-chance after 28 minutes to put the Blades in front. Leeds came more into the game as the interval approached and they levelled on the stroke of half-time with a freak goal. A stretched Sheffield defence tried to hack the ball out of their area, but the clearance struck Gary Speed and bounced off Rod Wallace and into the net. Blades' goalkeeper Mel Rees was injured in the mayhem and spent the whole of the second half in some discomfort.

Sheffield-born Jon Newsome powered in a header from Gary McAllister's 65th-minute cross which the injured Rees was unable to reach. But Leeds' lead lasted only a few minutes as the Blades drew level with another strange goal when prolific Leeds marksman Lee Chapman turned a cross-shot from John Pemberton, later to join Leeds, into his own net.

But there was yet another twist in this strange game which was settled 13 minutes from the end. Blades' skipper Brian Gayle, struggling to clear in the blustery wind, miscued the ball high back into his own area. As Wallace and substitute Eric Cantona, sensing an

John Newsome is all smiles after his header put United 2–1 up in their extraordinary victory at Bramall Lane. Just a few hours later they were crowned 1991–92 League champions.

opening, moved into pressure the home defence, Gayle could only head the ball over Rees, who had come out of his goal to try to clear the danger, for the winner.

Three hours later Manchester United kicked-off at Liverpool needing at least a draw to keep their title hopes alive, but goals by Ian Rush and Mark Walters condemned them to a 2–0 defeat and Leeds were League champions for the first time in 18 years. The following Saturday, Leeds completed their League programme with a 1–0 home win against Norwich City, courtesy of a great Wallace solo goal after the Championship trophy was presented to skipper Gordon Strachan.

Sheffield United: Rees, Pemberton, Barnes (Bryson 76), Gannon, Gayle, Beesley, Hodges, Rogers, Cork (Whitehouse 79), Deane, Bradshaw

Leeds United: Lukic, Newsome, Dorigo, Batty, Fairclough, Whyte, Strachan (Shutt 45), Wallace, Chapman, McAllister (Cantona 76), Speed

Referee: George Courtney (Spennymoor, Co. Durham)

Attendance: 32,000

Match 38

Saturday 8 August 1992

FA Charity Shield

Leeds United 4 *(Cantona 26, 78, 87; Dorigo 44)*

Liverpool 3 *(Rush 35, Saunders 66, Strachan og 89)*

To help Leeds in their push for the 1991–92 Championship, manager Howard Wilkinson had snatched charismatic Frenchman Eric Cantona from under the noses of his old club Sheffield Wednesday.

Although used sparingly in the thrilling run-in, Cantona's class was obvious and, despite his reputation for being difficult to handle, he was seen as a key factor in United's title defence and European Cup campaign.

Cries of 'Ooh-aah, Cantona', were echoing around Wembley after his hat-trick clinched a marvellous Charity Shield victory over Liverpool a week before the start of the season.

It was the first time, other than the Mercantile Credit appearance in the mid-1980s, that Leeds had played beneath the famous Twin Towers since 1974 when Liverpool beat them in a penalty shootout after the game, overshadowed by the dismissals of Billy Bremner and Kevin Keegan, finished 1–1.

Revenge was sweet for Leeds in a match full of attacking soccer. Liverpool played with only three outright defenders and United revelled in the extra space and up front had the match-winner in Cantona.

He fired Leeds into a 26th-minute lead with a shot that deflected past Bruce Grobbelaar off David Burrows, but the Reds were soon level when Ronnie Rosenthal's cross to the far post was headed in by Ian Rush.

United recaptured the lead just before the break with another deflected goal. This time Tony Dorigo

Hat-trick hero Eric Cantona rises above Mark Wright to score in the 1992 Charity Shield at Wembley.

saw his left-foot shot clip Rosenthal before going in. Leeds looked dangerous in attack, but suspect in defence, and Liverpool equalised in the second half with a well-placed snap shot from Dean Saunders.

However, United finished the stronger in the hot sun and Cantona blasted them back in front 13 minutes from the end with an excellent goal. Pulling away from his marker, he took the ball on his chest and drilled a fierce angled drive into the net.

The game was made safe three minutes from time when Grobbelaar misjudged a cross and Cantona headed in his hat-trick goal. Wilkinson, who opted not to play midfielder David Rocastle, the £2 million summer purchase from Arsenal, had sent on veteran Gordon Strachan, who scored an own-goal with virtually his first touch as the ball got stuck between his feet when he defended a corner on the right-hand post and saw the ball trickle over the line.

But there was no denying Cantona his Wembley glory and there was a nice touch at the end when skipper Gary McAllister invited Strachan to lift the Charity Shield and show it to United's delighted fans. It was only the second time Leeds had lifted the trophy, having previously won it in 1969.

Leeds United: Lukic, Newsome (Strachan 84), Dorigo, Batty, Fairclough, Whyte, Cantona, Wallace, Chapman (Hodge 79), McAllister, Speed

Liverpool: Grobbelaar, Tanner, Burrows, Marsh (Hutchison 73), Whelan, Wright, Saunders, Stewart, Rush, Rosenthal (Kozma 83), Walters

Referee: David Elleray (Harrow, Middlesex)

Attendance: 61,291

Match 39

Wednesday 30 September 1992

EUROPEAN CHAMPIONS CUP FIRST ROUND FIRST LEG

Leeds United 4 *(Speed 18, McAllister pen 38, Cantona 66, Chapman 80)*

VfB Stuttgart 1 *(Buck 33)*

European Cup football returned to Elland Road for the first time since 1975 and in quite extraordinary fashion, too, as United came close to pulling off one of the greatest comebacks in the competition's illustrious history.

Leeds trailed 3–0 from the first leg in Stuttgart and hardly anyone gave them a prayer of overturning the deficit against the German champions.

But United were really pumped-up for action and a glance at the team sheet showed manager Howard Wilkinson's intentions with attacking midfielder Scott Sellars playing at right-back. And when Gary Speed volleyed home from close range early on, the impossible seemed possible.

United were committed to all-out attack and went close to stretching their lead several times before Stuttgart struck a hammer blow on 34 minutes when Andreas Buck cut in from the right to fire in their equaliser.

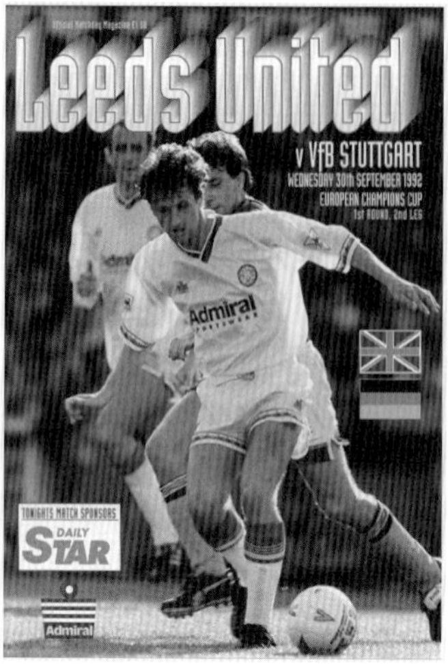

Within four minutes, though, United's faint hopes were lifted by a Gary McAllister penalty. And when Eric Cantona rattled the ball home from close range in 66 minutes, the great escape was on again.

The 20,457 crowd sounded more like 50,000 as Leeds stormed forward and the roof nearly blew off Elland Road when Lee Chapman's close-range header made it 4–1 on the night and 4–4 overall with 10 minutes remaining. Panic-stricken Stuttgart sent on Adrian Knup and Jovo Simakic for striker Fritz Walter and midfield man Maurizio Gaudino to shore up their wilting defence. The Germans just held out, but Leeds won enormous praise for their courageous display which was laced with lashings of skill and determination.

The following day it transpired that Stuttgart had broken UEFA rules by using Swiss international Knup, which meant they had fielded too many foreign players during the game. The match was declared void, and Leeds awarded a 3–0 victory and the teams ordered to play-off in Barcelona for the right to go through to the next round and meet Scottish champions Rangers.

Nine days after that extraordinary night at Elland Road, United triumphed 2–1 in a near-deserted Nou Camp Stadium with substitute Carl Shutt, on the eve of his 31st birthday, netting the winner near the end.

Leeds United: Lukic, Sellars, Dorigo, Batty, Fairclough, Whyte, Strachan, Cantona, Chapman, McAllister, Speed

VfB Stuttgart: Immel, Schafer, Frontzeck, Dubajic, Struntz, Buchwald, Buck, Sverisson, Walter (Knup 80), Gaudino (Simakic 83), Kogel

Referee: Kim Milton Neilson (Denmark)

Attendance: 20,457

Gary McAllister converts from the penalty spot to give United hope in their dramatic Champions Cup battle with German side Stuttgart.

Match 40
Tuesday 12 September 1995

UEFA Cup first round first leg

AS Monaco 0
Leeds United 3 *(Yeboah 2, 65, 81)*

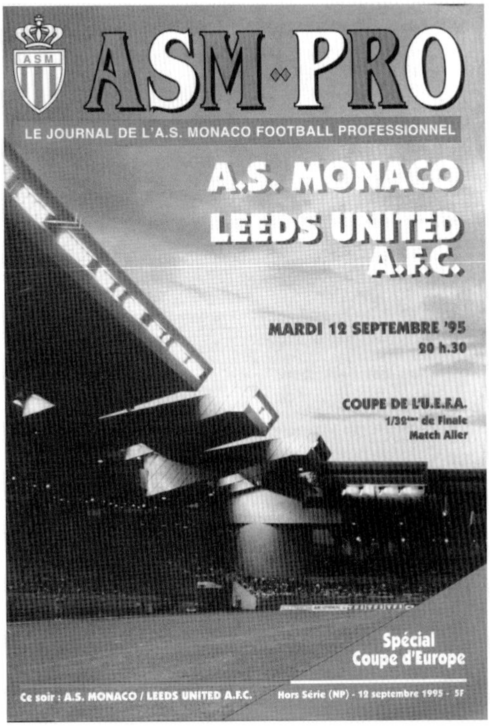

United fans had a new goal hero to cheer in Tony Yeboah, who scored a stunning hat-trick in Monaco to continue his sizzling start with Leeds.

Snapped up the previous January from Eintracht Frankfurt in Germany, the Ghanian star's goals had helped United put together a great late run to clinch a place in Europe.

The draw was not kind to United, pairing them with star-studded French champions Monaco, the previous season's European Cup semi-finalists, but they were simply brushed aside by Yeboah's superb finishing.

It took the star of Africa only three minutes to open the scoring when Monaco goalkeeper Fabien Piveteau collided with his central defender Lillian Thuram, dropped the ball and the alert Yeboah hooked it over his head into the empty net.

Monaco had plenty of possession, but United's defence was in a determined mood and the French side, driven forward by Belgian midfield star Enzo Schifo, were unable to carve out too many chances.

Then Yeboah brought Leeds fans in the Stade Louis II to their feet with a stunning second goal. Receiving Gary McAllister's throw-in from the left, he turned superbly beyond his marker to create the space to curl a magnificent shot beyond the reach of Marc Delaroche, who had come on for the injured Piveteau at half-time.

Ten minutes from the end there was more misery for Delaroche when he was involved in a sickening collision with defender Basile Boli as the cunning Yeboah lobbed in his hat-trick goal.

Delaroche and Boli were both stretchered off after receiving prolonged attention and Monaco brought on outfield player Claude Puel for the final minutes.

Yeboah, who scored another stunning treble in United's 4–2 Premiership win at Wimbledon 11 days later, was hailed by manager Wilkinson.

Tony Yeboah scored many dazzling goals for United and this tumbling volley was the first of his treble in Monaco.

'Words can't describe Tony Yeboah nor his importance to the team' purred the Leeds boss. 'He's always been able to score straightforward goals, but increasingly he is scoring more difficult ones. That was a great result for us.'

Unfortunately, United lost the home leg 1–0 and were outclassed by Dutch side PSV Eindhoven 8–3 on aggregate in the next round, so a European campaign which began so brightly was soon extinguished.

AS Monaco: Piveteau (45 Delaroche, 81 Puel), Valery, Di Meco, Boli, Thuram, Dumas, Dos Santos, Legwinski (Henry 69), Anderson, Schifo, Wreh

Leeds United: Lukic, Kelly, Pemberton, Wetherall, Dorigo (Beesley 45), Whelan, McAllister, Palmer, Speed, Deane, Yeboah.

Referee: Jose Maria Garcia-Aranda Encinar (Spain)

Attendance: 12,500

Match 41

Saturday 8 November 1997

PREMIERSHIP

Leeds United 4 *(Wallace 37, Kewell 44, Hasselbaink pen 82, Bowyer 90)*

Derby County 3 *(Sturridge 4, 11; Asanovic pen 33)*

Goals had initially been in short supply when George Graham replaced Howard Wilkinson as manager five games into the 1996–97 season.

United scraped together just 23 goals in the remaining 33 Division One games that season as Graham went about instilling defensive discipline into his squad which finished mid-table.

The arrival of Dutch striker Jimmy Floyd Hasselbaink from Portugal saw Graham gradually loosen the shackles, but the Leeds boss was devastated by United's shambolic start against Derby in which they were 3–0 down inside 33 minutes. Two uncharacteristic errors by England goalkeeper Nigel Martyn silenced the home crowd. With the game only four minutes old a poor back header by David Robertson saw Martyn at full stretch as he grabbed the ball from under his bar only to spill the ball for Dean Sturridge to prod the ball home. The Derby striker netted again minutes later when he charged down Martyn's poor clearance.

It got worse. Robertson brought down Sturridge in the box and Aljosa Asanovic fired the Rams 3–0 up. Shell-shocked United, for whom Alan Maybury was making his home debut, looked dead and buried.

They were given a lifeline when Rod Wallace diverted a Bruno Ribeiro shot past Mart Poom and the revival grew in momentum when the highly talented 19-year-old Harry Kewell scored with a stunning left-foot volley.

Leeds dominated the second period through the promptings of substitute Lee Bowyer but it was not until the arrival of fellow sub Hasselbaink that they were able to break Derby down again as a frantic match was coming to an end. The striker had only been on the pitch a few minutes when he coolly netted the equaliser from the spot after Christian Dailly's handball and with seconds remaining, Hasselbaink cut the ball back for Bowyer, running full-tilt towards the Kop, to drill the ball, low and hard into Poom's

Lee Bowyer, who netted United's last-gasp winner in the amazing comeback against Derby. Picture: Ian Harber, *Morley Observer and Advertiser*.

bottom right-hand corner. Elland Road exploded with delight as it had witnessed a quite stunning comeback.

A much-improved Leeds finished the season in fifth place with the other main highlight being a spectacular 5–0 win at Derby in March.

Leeds United: Martyn, Maybury (Bowyer 45), Wetherall, Radebe, Robertson, Kelly, Haaland, Hopkin (Hasslebaink 77), Ribeiro, Wallace, Kewell

Derby County: Poom, Dailly, Laursen, Carbon (Kozluk 52), Rowett, D. Powell (Hunt 85), Carsley, C. Powell, Asanovic (Trollope 83), Sturridge, Baiano

Referee: Neale Barry (Scunthorpe)

Attendance: 33,572

Match 42

Saturday 4 November 2000

PREMIERSHIP

Leeds United 4 *(Viduka 24, 47, 73, 75)*

Liverpool 3 *(Hyypia 2, Ziege 18, Smicer 61)*

Millions of television viewers witnessed a superb exhibition of finishing skills by Mark Viduka as never-say-die United finally overcame old rivals Liverpool.

The Aussie striker netted all four Leeds goals in a fantastic match as David O'Leary's emerging side once more showed a great capacity to entertain with style.

The Reds had a good recent record at Elland Road, one of their most famous victories being a 5–4 spectacular in 1991, when Leeds, 4–0 down after 27 minutes, came within a whisker of a point thanks to Lee Chapman's hat-trick.

Another Liverpool masterclass looked on the cards for Sky viewers when Sami Hyypia headed in with only two minutes on the clock. Injury-hit Leeds had only named four subs instead of the permitted five and one of them, Danny Hay, was thrust into the action early on when Jonathan Woodgate went off with a pulled thigh muscle. No sooner had the New Zealand international taken his place at the heart of the United defence then Christian Ziege headed the men from Anfield 2–0 up.

Liverpool could have easily have had more goals before Viduka clipped a shot

Mark Viduka, sweeps round the Liverpool defence to complete his hat-trick. Picture: Ian Harber, *Morley Observer and Advertiser*.

over the advancing Sander Westerveld and the visitors were made to pay their profligacy shortly after half-time when former Celtic man Viduka powerfully headed in the equaliser from Gary Kelly's cross.

Both sides spurned chances to go in front before the Merseysiders regained the lead just beyond the hour when Vladimir Smicer fired in his first goal of the season.

But O'Leary's Leeds had bags of spirit and summer signing Viduka latched on to Olivier Dacourt's pass, shimmied past a couple of defenders and struck home his hat-trick goal with 18 minutes left.

At 3–3 there was still a sting in the tail of a match laden with attacking intent when Viduka gently chipped in his fourth goal to put United ahead for the first time – a lead they didn't surrender as they moved up to eighth place in the Premiership.

Viduka's four-goal feat has since been matched by Alan Smith (v Hapoel Tel Aviv) and Brian Deane (6–1 v QPR) but the Australian hit-man's achievement remains the stand-out achievement.

Leeds United: Robinson, Kelly, Harte, Woodgate (Hay 16), Matteo, Bowyer, Bakke, Dacourt, Burns, Smith, Viduka

Liverpool: Westerveld, Carragher, Ziege, Babbel, Hyypia, Smicer, Murphy (Fowler 67), McAllister (Gerrard 68), Hamman, Berger (Barmby 74), Heskey

Referee: David Elleray (Harrow, Middlesex)

Attendance: 40,055

Match 43
Wednesday 8 November 2000

UEFA Champions League Group F Match 6

AC Milan 1 *(Serginho 68)*
Leeds United 1 *(Matteo 44)*

By finishing fourth in the Premiership, United qualified for the money-spinning Champions League and won their qualifying round battle with German side 1860 Munich.

That put United into the group stages where they were pitted against Catalan superstars Barcelona, Italian giants AC Milan and Besiktas. After an understrength Leeds were demolished 4–0 in their opening game against Barcelona, no one gave them a prayer of progressing in the competition.

Yet David O'Leary's emerging side went in to the final group game in the San Siro Stadium knowing a point would put them through to the second phase and six more high-profile games against the cream of the continent.

Four days after Mark Viduka's one-man demolition of Liverpool, more than 7,000 fans travelled to Italy to witness another historic night in Leeds United's history.

Leeds went about their business with no fear against a side which had already guaranteed qualification but midway through the first half Gary Kelly was adjudged to have handled in the box. Andrei Shevchenko's spot-kick came back off a post and United cashed in on their escape. Just before half-time Lee Bowyer's perfectly delivered corner was met by Dominic Matteo who sent a thumping header into the AC net. It was a goal which Leeds fans still sing about today.

A win would, amazingly, have left United top of the group but a fine solo goal by Brazilian ace Serginho set up a tense final 22 minutes as defeat would see Barcelona, who were thumping Besiktas 5–0, take the second qualification spot on goal difference.

But with Lucas Radebe and goalkeeper Paul Robinson outstanding, Leeds stood firm and

Dominic Matteo's header in the San Siro Stadium earned United the point they needed to go into the second stage of the European Champions League.

after the final whistle the Leeds party went back out on the pitch to celebrate with the massed ranks of Whites' fans for a 30-minute sing-song of terrace favourites.

AC Milan: Dida, Helveg, Maldini, Roque Junior, Chamot, Gattuso, Albertini, Leonardo (Boban 54), Serginho, Shevchenko, Bierhoff

Leeds United: Robinson, Kelly, Harte, Radebe, Mills, Bowyer, Dacourt, Bakke, Matteo, Smith, Viduka

Referee: Kim Milton Nielsen (Denmark)

Attendance: 52,289

Match 44

Wednesday 4 April 2001

UEFA CHAMPIONS LEAGUE

QUARTER-FINAL FIRST LEG

Leeds United 3 *(Harte 26, Smith 51, Ferdinand 66)*

Deportivo 0

United continued to defy the bookies' odds in the second instalment of their Champions League odyssey.

They began phase two in Group D with a home defeat against Real Madrid, bounced back to beat Lazio in Rome, then did the double over Belgian side Anderlecht to ease into the quarter-finals with two games to spare.

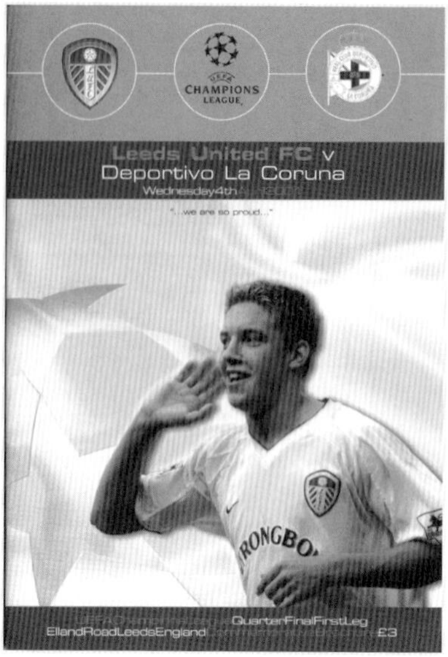

The draw for the last eight pitched Leeds against Spanish side Deportivo, whose midfielder Victor branded United 'the weakest team left in the competition'.

Those words were rammed down his throat by a rampant Leeds who earned a 3–0 first leg cushion to take to Coruna as Victor, left on the bench, must have winced as the Elland Road faithful proudly boomed out '3–0 to the weakest team'.

The Spaniards were overwhelmed by the Whites' pace and power on a wet and windy Yorkshire night. Deadball specialist Ian Harte fired Leeds ahead with a trademark free-kick and just six minutes into the second half, Alan Smith got on the end of a perfect Harte centre to head home his 15th goal of the season.

It was not long before free-flowing United bagged a third, big-money signing Rio Ferdinand, captaining the side for the first time, crowned an outstanding display by crashing in a header for his first goal in Leeds colours.

In the return, United rode their luck in the Riazor Stadium, but a 2–0 defeat was not enough to prevent them going through to the semi-finals where they were held 0–0 at

Alan Smith wheels away in delight after putting United 2–0 against Deportivo. Picture: Ian Harber, *Morley Observer and Advertiser*.

home by Valencia and were well-beaten, 3–0, in the second leg. The European dream was over, but it had been a fantastic journey.

Leeds United: Martyn, Mills, Harte, Matteo, Ferdinand, Bowyer, Batty, Dacourt, Kewell (Wilcox 84), Smith, Viduka

Deportivo: Molina, Pablo, Romero, Naybet, Scaloni (Tristran 71), Cessar, Duscher (Valeron 54), Emerson, Djalminha, Fran (Pandiani 71), Makaay

Referee: Gilles Veissiere (France)

Attendance: 35,508

Match 45

Saturday 19 November 2005

FOOTBALL LEAGUE CHAMPIONSHIP

Southampton 3 *(Pahars 27, Quashie 35, pen 45)*

Leeds United 4 *(Butler 71, Blake 77, Healy pen 84, Miller 86)*

United went into financial meltdown after failing to qualify for the 2001–02 Champions League.

Star names were sold off and relegation to the Championship followed in 2004. Manager Kevin Blackwell hastily assembled a squad that took United to 14th and the following campaign they were genuine promotion contenders.

When they went to mid-table Southampton on 19 November 2005, United were well-

Even the Leeds players don't seem to believe what they have just done as they celebrate their amazing comeback at Southampton.

placed in fifth spot, but by 4.30pm they were staring certain defeat squarely in the face. Leeds had been utterly abject and totally outplayed by the Saints who cruised into a 3–0 interval lead courtesy of Marian Pahars and a couple from midfielder Nigel Quashie, his second coming from the penalty spot after a handball by Daniel Harding. Leeds looked dead and buried as Southampton's players high-fived their way off the pitch.

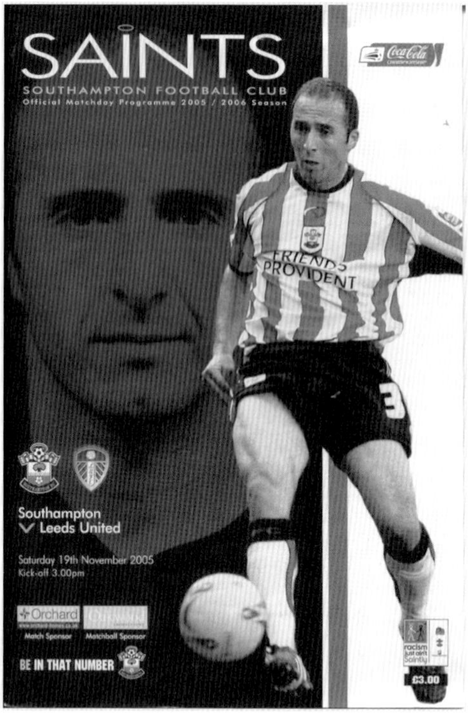

Home boss Harry Redknapp made three changes at the interval – future Leeds manager Dennis Wise among those substituted – and although Southampton, unbeaten at home, didn't hit the heights of the first half, were well in control.

It was the introduction of Northern Ireland international striker David Healy with just over 20 minutes to go which triggered United's amazing comeback. It was not long before skipper Paul Butler headed what most thought would be a Leeds consolation on 71 minutes, prompting a tongue-in-cheek 'We are going to win 4–3' from the travelling fans.

Healy then set up the second for Robbie Blake, who swivelled and shot past goalkeeper Antti Niemi. With 13 minutes remaining, United sensed they could get something out of the game while Southampton visibly wilted as the Whites grabbed the game by the throat. On 84 minutes, Danny Higginbotham handled David Healy's shot and the ice-cool Healy despatched the penalty.

Most sides would have settled for a point, but United had the momentum and immediately poured forward in search of a winner which took just 120 seconds to come after the penalty drama. Rob Hulse laid the ball perfectly into the path of Sunderland loan man Liam Miller, making only his second appearance in a Leeds shirt, and the Republic of Ireland international sent the ball whistling into the Southampton net.

Four goals in 15 incredible minutes. The 3,000 Leeds fans in St Mary's Stadium were bouncing around in delirium after witnessing an 'I was there' game which ranks as one of the most amazing feats in the club's history.

Southampton: Niemi, Delap, Lundekvam (Fuller 45), Svensson, Higginbotham, Oakley, Wise (McCann 45), Quashie, Pahars (Hajto 45), Walcott, Ormerod

Leeds United: Sullivan, Kelly, Butler, Kilgallon, Harding, Richardson (Healy 67), Derry, Miller, Lewis, Hulse, Bakke

Referee: Iain Williamson (Berkshire)

Attendance: 30,173

Match 46
Monday 8 May 2006

FOOTBALL LEAGUE CHAMPIONSHIP PLAY-OFF SECOND LEG

Preston North End 0
Leeds United 2 *(Hulse 56, Richardson 61)*

Spluttering United went into the Play-offs against Preston out of form – just one win in 10. The end-of-season collapse blew any chance of automatic promotion and many Leeds fans were not exactly confident they could get up via the Play-offs.

That view was confirmed by a 1–1 first leg draw with Preston at Elland Road, a result which prompted manager Billy Davies to declare it was 'job done' for his men, after all they had beaten Leeds 2–0 at Deepdale just eight days earlier in the final game of the regular season.

However, the Whites combined steel and skill to defy the odds to claim a place in the showpiece Final at the Millennium Stadium in Cardiff – although victory came at a cost.

Both sides traded tackle-for-tackle in a bruising encounter and an extended 34-minute half-time break because of floodlight failure seemed to work in United's favour. They bossed the early stages of the second period and Rob Hulse nodded them in front from a corner as Preston's marking plan fell apart. Five minutes later,

Rob Hulse wins an aerial tussle during the 2–0 Play-off win at Preston which earned the Whites a place in the 2006 Final at the Millennium Stadium, Cardiff.

Frazer Richardson, a big success in a surprise advanced role on the right, popped up to make it 2–0 to stun North End.

Leeds were in control but with 22 minutes remaining, Stephen Crainey was sent off after a foul on David Nugent drew a second yellow card. United's tactics were simple – keep Preston out. As the clock ticked on, Richard Cresswell replaced the outstanding Hulse, but the pumped-up substitute managed to get himself booked twice and red-carded in the final minute, leaving Leeds to see out added time with only nine men.

At the death, Preston's Tyrone Mears had an effort ruled out for offside and Leeds were able to celebrate a famous hard-fought victory to set up the chance to get back to the Premiership.

However, without Crainey and Cresswell in Cardiff, a disjointed United never got going against Watford, managed by former Leeds coach Aidie Boothroyd, and slid meekly to a 3–0 defeat in sharp contrast to the display of spirit at Deepdale.

Preston North End: Nash, Alexander, Mears, O'Neil, Davis, Mawene, Ormerod (Whaley 10), McKenna, Dichio, Nugent, Stewart (Agyemang 45)

Leeds United: Sullivan, Kelly, Crainey, Derry, Kilgallon, Gregan, Douglas, Richardson, Hulse (Cresswell 79), Miller, Lewis (Stone 87)

Referee: Mick Thorpe (Suffolk) *Attendance:* 20,383

Match 47

Saturday 11 August 2007

Coca-Cola League One

Tranmere Rovers 1 *(Greenacre 22)*

Leeds United 2 *(Heath 55, Kandol 89)*

After the Millenium Stadium disaster against Watford, United lost their way and Kevin Blackwell was axed eight games into the 2006–07 season.

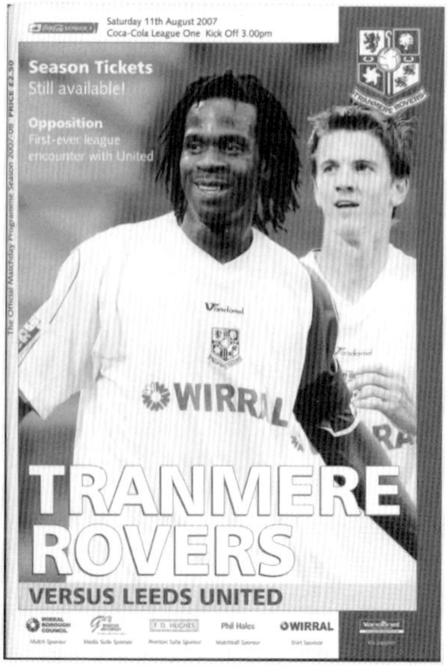

Chairman Ken Bates appointed Dennis Wise with whom he had worked closely during his days at Stamford Bridge, but the former England midfielder and his assistant, Gus Poyet, were unable to turn a struggling squad's season round. After relegation to the third tier of English football for the first time in the club's history was confirmed, cash-strapped United went into administration and were docked 10 points.

Worse was to follow, a further 15 points were removed before the start of the League One season after more than 50 Football League clubs voted for the deduction. The Football League had

Delighted boss Dennis Wise hails Tresor Kandol for his late winner at Tranmere on the opening day of the 2007–08 season.

said United had not followed the rules on entering administration – a charge United vehemently contested.

There was genuine concern that United would go into liquidation but the League finally readmitted Leeds at 6.30pm on Friday 3 August – just eight days before they were due to kick-off at Tranmere.

Because of a wage cap, several players had already left the club, so Wise and Poyet had little time to put together a squad capable of tackling the rigours of League One. That certainly showed in the first half at Prenton Park as Chris Greenacre's goal gave Tranmere a deserved lead.

But the treatment United had received off the pitch had created an 'us against them' siege mentality and Leeds dug deep to turn the game around. First, Matt Heath got round the back of the Tranmere defence to head in Alan Thompson's 55th minute free-kick, then, with a minute remaining Tresor Kandol stooped to head in the winner.

There were delirious scenes at the final whistle and the players and staff held an impromptu huddle on the pitch. It was a ritual which was to become commonplace as United rapidly moved into plus points by winning their first seven League games – a feat only achieved at Leeds by Don Revie's magnificent squad.

Tranmere Rovers: Coyne, Stockdale, Chorley, Goodison, Cansdell-Sheriff, Shuker (Curran 83), Jennings, McClaren, Davies, Zola, Greenacre (Taylor 81)

Leeds United: Ankergren, Richardson, Heath, Marques, Lewis, Weston (Flo 76), Hughes, Thompson, Westlake, Kandol, Beckford (Howson 90)

Referee: Lee Mason (Lancashire)

Attendance: 11,008

Match 48

Thursday 15 May 2008

Coca-Cola League One Play-off Second Leg

Carlisle United 0

Leeds United 2 *(Howson 10, 90)*

But for the 15-point deduction imposed by the Football League, Leeds would have secured automatic promotion to the Championship in 2007–08.

Instead they found themselves in the Play-offs after another topsy-turvey season. After a storming start to the season, Gus Poyet left for Tottenham and Wise left in January to take up a position with Premiership side Newcastle United with Leeds struggling to find their best form. Former United midfield ace Gary McAllister took charge and got the Whites back on course for a Play-off spot.

Hopes of making the final at Wembley were severely dented when goals by Danny Graham and Marc Bridge-Wilkinson put Carlisle in control at Elland Road until Dougie Freedman, on loan from Crystal Palace, scored with virtually the last kick of the game to give Leeds a lifeline.

It was a lifeline seized three days later by Morley-born midfielder Johnny Howson, who brought the aggregate scores level at 2–2 with an early strike at Brunton Park.

A disbelieving Jonny Howson has just fired United into the 2008 Play-off Final at Wembley after his last-minute winner at Carlisle.

Leeds, unchanged from the first leg, were sharper all round than the Cumbrians and as the game wore on became increasingly dominant but chances came and went. The closest came when Bradley Johnson unluckily saw his header clip the outside of an upright and it seemed the match was destined for extra-time.

Referee Alan Wiley had just signalled there would be just one minute of added on-time when Leeds built another attack. Howson, just six days before his 21st birthday, collected a lay-off from Freedman, shifted the ball into space and shot low into the bottom corner via the inside of the post past goalkeeper Kieran Westwood to send ecstatic Leeds to Wembley.

Against all the odds United were just 90 minutes away from the Championship, but, as so often in the past, they failed on the big stage, losing 1–0 to Yorkshire rivals Doncaster Rovers in the big London showpiece.

Carlisle United: Westwood, Raven, Horwood, G. Smith, Livesey, Murphy, Dobie, Bridge-Wilkinson, Graham, Hackney, Lumsdon

Leeds United: Ankergren, Richardson, Johnson, Kilkenny, Michalik, Huntington, Prutton, Howson, Beckford, Freedman, Douglas

Referee: Alan Wiley (Staffordshire) *Attendance:* 12,873

Match 49

Sunday 3 January 2010

FA CUP THIRD ROUND

Manchester United 0

Leeds United 1 *(Beckford 19)*

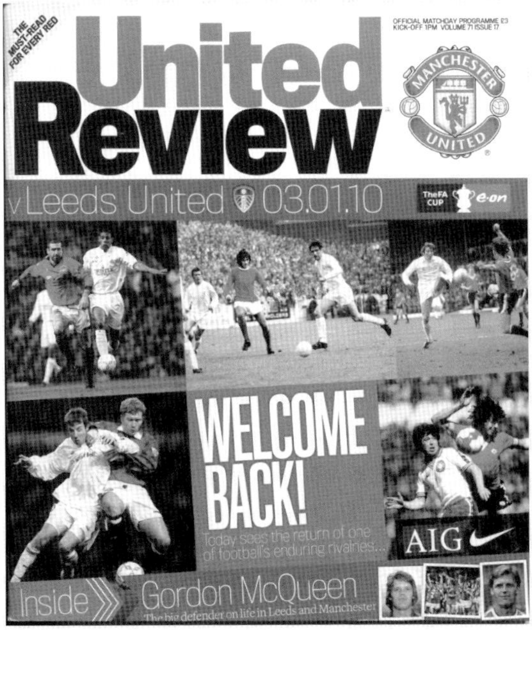

Of all Leeds' victories in the club's long and illustrious history, the stunning FA Cup triumph at Old Trafford will rank as one of the sweetest.

Once fierce rivals, the clubs were poles apart in playing stature in 2010. Although Simon Grayson had steered Leeds to the top of League One they were 43 League positions below Sir Alex Ferguson's multi-million pound side when the third-round draw was made. The Red Devils were Premiership champions and the Whites had needed two games to get past non-League Kettering Town to set up a big live televised pay-day.

Manchester United fans look on as Jermaine Beckford pulls off a famous FA Cup giant-killing act at Old Trafford.

Old Trafford had long been a graveyard for Leeds but almost 9,000 fans made the trip across the Pennines, although even the most optimistic of them could not believe the events which unfolded.

The visitors, relishing the big-game atmosphere, were sharp in the tackle and crisp in their passing straight from the first whistle. They showed no fear and sent their army of fans ballistic 19 minutes in when Richard Naylor broke up a home attack, Johnny Howson launched a superb long pass towards Jermaine Beckford. The striker's first touch was not the best, but his speed took him away from marker Wes Brown and with a flick of his left foot rolled the ball between the England man and goalkeeper Tomasz Kuszczak. Time seemed to stand still as the ball slowly crossed the line in front of a stunned Stretford End.

It should have been 2–0 minutes later but Luciano Becchio missed with a headed opportunity he had been burying all season.

A classic Cup tie unfolded as the home side upped the tempo with Wayne Rooney beating Casper Ankergren but Jason Crowe emerged to scramble the ball off the line. Leeds, with Naylor and Patrick Kisnorbo outstanding in defence, stood firm against increasing pressure and after the Reds missed decent chances to level, Grayson's men seemed to get a second wind as Beckford shaved a post with one effort and substitute Robert Snodgrass curled a free-kick on to the junction of the woodwork.

The Whites survived some late goalmouth scrambles but deservedly clung on to their first win at Old Trafford since Brian Flynn's late winner there in 1981.

In the next round, a Beckford double – including a late, late, penalty – earned a great draw at Tottenham, but Spurs won the replay 3–1.

Manchester United: Kuszczak, Neville, Brown, Evans, Da Silva, Welbeck (Valencia 58), Anderson (Owen 69), Obertan (Giggs 58), Gibson, Rooney, Berbatov

Leeds United: Ankergren, Crowe, Naylor, Kisnorbo, Hughes (White 90), Howson (Snodgrass 77), Kilkenny, Doyle, Johnson, Becchio (Michalik 89), Beckford

Referee: Chris Foy (Merseyside)

Attendance: 74,526

Match 50
Saturday 8 May 2010

Coca-Cola League One

Leeds United 2 *(Howson 59, Beckford 63)*
Bristol Rovers 1 *(Duffy 48)*

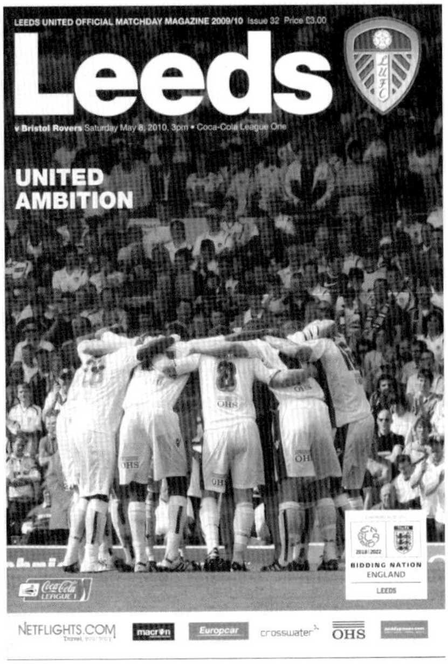

United finally clinched automatic promotion from League One with the final, gripping episode in the 2009–10 Elland Road soap opera.

Since the turn of the year the Whites had blown an eight-point lead at the top and more trouble unfolded against lowly Bristol Rovers in front of a feverish near-40,000 Elland Road crowd.

A man and a goal down with barely more than half an hour of the season remaining, United dug deep and somehow emerged 2–1 victors against Bristol Rovers.

At one stage or another rivals Millwall, Swindon and Charlton – all occupied that second promotion spot behind champions Norwich on a roller-coaster afternoon.

But come the final whistle it was the Whites, backed by a wall of noise, who crawled over the finishing line into the Championship, sparking a mass pitch invasion.

Leeds went into the game knowing victory over the Pirates would achieve their objective but a moment of madness by Max Gradel turned the game on its head. He clashed with left-back Daniel Jones after 35 minutes and received a straight red card from referee Graham Salisbury. Gradel lost it, refusing to go and had to be man-handled away by teammates Jermaine Beckford and Michael Doyle.

United's task became even harder shortly after half-time when, the home defence failed to deal with a cross and Jo Kuffour was able to knock it back for Darryl Duffy to apply the finishing touch.

Leeds fans were starting to work out Play-off permutations when substitute Jonny Howson made an instant impact curling a fine shot from the edge of the box past goalkeeper Mikkel Andersen. The equaliser gave Leeds belief and the deafening volume levels went through the roof four minutes later when Andersen made a hash of a throw out and the ball was returned to the box by Bradley Johnson for predator-in-chief Beckford to score the winner with his 31st goal of the season.

Despite their numerical advantage, Rovers rarely threatened with Leeds going close to a third goal when Leigh Bromby's header struck a post.

Goal machine Jermaine Beckford celebrates his winner against Bristol Rovers for ten-man United as they finally clinched promotion to the Championship on the final day of the 2009–10 season. Picture: Ian Harber, *Morley Observer and Advertiser*.

How fitting, and inevitable, that it was Beckford, captain for the day in the absence of the injured Richard Naylor, that got the crucial goal in what was his last game before joining Premiership side Everton after 85 goals in 130 starts in a Leeds shirt.

Leeds United: Higgs, Hughes, Collins, Bromby, Lowry (Howson 54), Gradel, Doyle, Kilkenny, Johnson, Becchio (Watt 87), Beckford (Snodgrass 90)

Bristol Rovers: Andersen, Regan, Coles, Anthony, Jones, Reece (Williams 72), Lines, Campbell, Hughes, Duffy (Richardson 79), Kuffour

Referee: Graham Salisbury (Lancashire)

Attendance: 38,234

LEEDS STARS

AFFLECK George

Full-back
Born: Auchendinney, Midlothian, 1 July 1888
Career: Penicuik. LEEDS CITY June 1909. Grimsby Town October 1919. Coach in Rotterdam July 1925.

George provided 10 years service at Elland Road, making nearly 200 appearances. He was always one of the first names on the team sheet, even when Irish defender Alec Creighton joined Leeds, Affleck switched from left-back to right-back with ease. George's game was built on positional play rather than speed and turned in a high level of consistent performances. At the age of 31 he was forced to leave City when the club was disbanded and he was sold in the historic auction in October 1919 to Grimsby Town for £500, joining the Mariners with colleague Arthur Wainwright. George stayed at Grimsby for six years, before going to Holland to take up a coaching appointment with a club in Rotterdam.

ASPIN Neil

Right-back/centre-half
Born: Gateshead, 12 April 1965
Career: Durham County Schools and England Schools trials. LEEDS UNITED October 1982. Port Vale £200,000 July 1989. Darlington free July 1999. Hartlepool January 2001. Harrogate Town player-coach June 2001, manager February 2005. FC Halifax Town manager April 2009.

Neil was just 16 and preparing to face Doncaster juniors in the Northern Intermediate League on the morning of 20 February 1982 when he was told by manager Allan Clarke about a dramatic change of plan. The youngster was handed his senior debut against Ipswich at Elland Road. With Kenny Burns suspended, Trevor Cherry, Brian Greenhoff and Neil Firm injured, Clarke kept his plans under wraps until shortly before the match. Aspin never gave less than 100 per cent for Leeds, even postponing his wedding as the date clashed with the 1987 FA Cup semi-final. After more than 200 games for the Whites he joined Port Vale, becoming a rock in the heart of the Valiants' defence. Hero-worshipped by the Vale faithful, he was a member of their side which beat

Stockport 2–1 in the Autoglass Trophy Final in 1993. However, hopes of a Wembley double evaporated a few weeks later when Vale lost 3–0 in the First Division Play-off Final to West Brom. Promotion was gained the following season and Neil was awarded a testimonial at Vale Park – a match which featured singer and huge Vale fan Robbie Williams. After spells at Darlington and Hartlepool, Neil hooked up with Harrogate Town, being appointed manager by one-time Leeds chairman Bill Fotherby who was in charge. He later steered FC Halifax Town to successive promotions up to Blue Square North.

BAIRD Ian John

Forward

Born: Rotherham, 1 April 1964

Career: Bitterne Saints. St Mary's College, Southampton. Southampton, Hampshire and England Schools. Southampton apprentice July 1980, professional April 1982. Cardiff City loan November 1983. Newcastle United loan December 1984. LEEDS UNITED £75,000 March 1985. Portsmouth £285,000 June 1987. LEEDS UNITED £185,000 February 1988. Middlesbrough £500,000 January 1990. Hearts £400,000 July 1991. Bristol City £295,000 July 1993. Plymouth Argyle summer 1995. Brighton £35,000 July 1996. Southampton youth academy manager 1996–97. Salisbury Town December 1997. Instant-Dict (Hong Kong) manager 1998. Hong Kong national coach 1999. Farnborough Town August 2000–May 2001. Stevenage Borough coach. Havant and Waterlooville manager November 2004. Eastleigh manager October 2007.

Fiery striker Ian never shirked a challenge in his two spells at Leeds – often getting himself into trouble with referees. His robust style endeared him to the Elland Road faithful who boomed 'Bairdy's going to get you' when they smelled blood in the air. But he was more than a battering ram, piling in half a century of League goals for the Whites and there were always clubs queuing up for his services. An England Schools international, he had arrived from Southampton but returned to Hampshire to play for newly promoted Portsmouth. The fee was set by an FA Tribunal at £285,000 but hard-up Pompey sold him back to Leeds nine months later for £100,000 less. His second Elland Road spell was less successful and eventually he lost his place to Lee Chapman. United netted a handsome profit when he moved on to Middlesbrough where he scored twice in Boro's 4–1 win over Newcastle on the final Saturday of the season. That result kept Boro up and helped Leeds beat off the challenge of the Magpies, enabling Ian to collect a Second Division Championship medal, even though he was no longer a Leeds player. He had a successful time with Joe Jordan's Hearts and his goals for Brighton played a big part in keeping them in the Football League in 1996–97. He's a familiar figure on the non-League scene on the south coast and is now in charge of Blue Square South side Eastleigh and runs his own vehicle leasing company, IBMH.

BAKER James William

Centre-half
Born: Basford Green, Staffordshire, 15 November 1891
Died: Leeds, 13 December 1966
Career: Ilkeston Town. Derby County. Portsmouth 1911–12. Hartlepools United 1912. Huddersfield Town May 1914. LEEDS UNITED May 1920. Nelson June 1926. Colne Valley.

Jim was a major figure at Elland Road, skippering United to promotion in 1923–24 and later becoming a director at the club. Arthur Fairclough was appointed Leeds manager in February 1920, and three months later went back to his old club, Huddersfield, to sign Baker. It was a cute bit of business as Baker became a cornerstone of the new United club. Although small for a central defender, he was an inspirational leader, whose tigerish tackling quickly made him a favourite with the fans, who dubbed him 'T'owd War Hoss'. Jim played 149 consecutive League and Cup games as United's skipper. His last appearance a 1–1 home draw against Everton on 6 March 1926 was his 200th League game in a Leeds shirt. He was 34 when he joined Nelson but always kept close links with Leeds, running the Smyth's Arms in Whitehall Road, then the Mexborough Arms in Chapeltown. He scouted for the club and served on the board from 1959 to 1961.

BATES Michael John

Midfield
Born: Doncaster, 19 September 1947
Career: LEEDS UNITED apprentice, signing September 1964. Walsall £25,000 June 1976. Bradford City £20,000 June 1978. Doncaster Rovers June 1980. Bentley Victoria.

Midfielder Mick showed immense loyalty to United during Don Revie's golden era. He often used to fill in when Billy Bremner and Johnny Giles were unavailable and several clubs, notably Southampton with a

£100,000 bid, tried to lure him from Elland Road. Mick, a Yorkshire Schools player, who trialled for England, stayed at Leeds 12 years and was a vital cog in the footballing machine which Revie had pieced together. The personal high point for Mick was a goal in the 2–2 draw with Juventus in the first leg of the 1971 Inter-Cities Fairs Cup which proved priceless as United went on to lift the trophy on away goals. He lost a couple of years to injuries before moving on to the lower divisions. At non-League Bentley, he played alongside old Leeds teammate Rod Belfitt and ran his own insurance business.

BATTY David

Midfield

Born: Leeds, 2 December 1968

Allerton Grange School, Leeds and West Yorkshire Schools. Tingley Athletic. LEEDS UNITED from trainee August 1987. Blackburn Rovers £2.75 million September 1993. Newcastle United £3.75 million March 1996. LEEDS UNITED £4.4 million December 1998–May 2004.

Local hero David was idolised by the Leeds fans in his two spells with the club. A superb ball-winner and passer, he became an established central midfield player with England under Graham Taylor after a series of magnificent displays for United. He made his debut at 18 against Swindon in November 1987 and rapidly achieved international status at Under-21 level. He progressed during United's 1989–90 Second Division Championship campaign to win England B honours and won the first of his 42 senior caps against the USSR. His midfield partnership with Gordon Strachan, Gary McAllister and Gary Speed was at the heart of United's 1991–92 Division One title success. But the United faithful were stunned by his shock £2.75 million move to Blackburn Rovers. It proved a highly successful switch for David

and he finished the season as Rovers' player of the year and the following campaign collected a Premiership Championship medal. A £4.5 million move took him to Newcastle and he featured in the 1998 World Cup, missing the crucial spot-kick against Argentina which saw England eliminated in a penalty shoot-out. Life came full circle and he re-joined Leeds in December that year as a 30-year-old. He sustained a rib injury on his second Leeds debut against Coventry which ruled him out for 15 games. He then needed pain-killers for a heart problem which was brought on by the injury. When fit he proved an inspiration to the younger members of David O'Leary's burgeoning team but an Achilles problem ruled him out for over a year. He bounced back to prime form in 2001–02 as United slid into financial decline and he retired at the end of the 2003–04 relegation season. David is one of United's modern-day legends and was under par in only a handful of his 350-plus games in a Leeds shirt – the only thing missing from his armoury was goal-power.

Picture: Ian Harber, *Morley Observer and Advertiser.*

BECCHIO Luciano Hector

Forward

Born: Cordoba, Argentina, 29 December 1983

Career: Boca Juniors (Argentina) 2002. Real Mallorca (Spain) 2003. Ciudad Murcia (Spain) loan 2004. Terrassa (Spain) 2005. Meridia (Spain) July 2007. LEEDS UNITED July 2008.

South American powerhouse Luciano was a tremendous foil for prolific scorer Jermaine Beckford with his immense workrate earning the respect of the Elland Road faithful. Born in Argentina, he played for Boca Juniors' youth sides before trying his luck in Europe, becoming a well-known lower-league marksman in Spanish football over a number of years. Leeds boss Gary McAllister gave him a trial in pre-season game in 2008 and quickly snapped him up. Luciano's appetite for work, strength and power in the air, combined with Beckford's finishing ensured Leeds got plenty of goals, Luciano contributing 19 and 17 goals in their two full seasons together. Many expected Luciano's goal tally to drop, but he stepped up to the Championship with aplomb, finishing with 20 goals in all competitions in 2010–11, although he finished the campaign prematurely because of a hamstring injury. In December 2010, he signed a new three-and-a-half year deal with the Whites for whom he had scored more than 60 goals by the end of 2011–12.

BECKFORD Jermaine Paul

Forward

Born: Ealing, London, 9 December 1983

Career: Wealdstone 2003. Uxbridge loan. LEEDS UNITED £45,000 March 2006. Carlisle United loan October–November 2006. Scunthorpe United loan January 2007. Everton free May 2010. Leicester City £2.5 million August 2011.

Hot property Jermaine was a surprise capture from Ryman League side Wealdstone where he had scored 35 goals in 40 appearances. United beat the likes of Chelsea, Crystal Palace and Watford for the RAC windscreen fitter's signature and quickly gave him a taste of Championship action from the subs' bench. He was loaned out to gain more experience and found scoring form at Scunthorpe as the Iron won promotion to the Championship, passing United on the way up. The following campaign he was

Picture: Ian Harber, *Morley Observer and Advertiser.*

named United's Player of the Season after scoring 20 League goals, earning the honour again 12 months later after netting 32 goals in all competitions. The goals continued to flow in 2009–10 including the winner at Old Trafford as the Whites sensationally knocked Manchester United out of the FA Cup. Fittingly, he netted the goal against Bristol Rovers on the final day of the season which clinched promotion to the Championship. Top flight clubs were continually checking on the goalscoring phenomenon and Jermaine did request a transfer just before the Manchester United game but later withdrew it to help Leeds win promotion. Leeds accepted that the player, who scored 85 goals in 152 appearances, would move on at the end of the campaign without the club receiving a fee. He joined Everton in May 2010 and after his debut season in the Premiership was sounded out by the Jamaican international side. He moved to Leicester for £2.5 million just hours before the 2011 summer transfer window closed.

BELL William John

Left-back

Born: Johnstone, Lanarkshire, 3 September 1937

Career: Neilston Juniors. Queen's Park 1957. LEEDS UNITED July 1960. Leicester City £45,000 September 1967. Brighton and Hove Albion July 1969. Birmingham City coach May 1970, manager September 1975–September 1977. Lincoln City manager October 1977–October 1978.

Willie was converted by Don Revie from a run-of-the-mill centre-half into a quality international left-back. He completed an engineering apprenticeship while with Queen's Park and won two Scottish amateur caps before signing as a professional with United. After an initial struggle he proved a reliable left-back as United won the Second Division title and

also played in the 1965 FA Cup Final defeat against Liverpool at Wembley. The following year he earned two Scottish caps against Portugal and Brazil. The emergence of Terry Cooper saw Willie move on to Leicester after nearly 250 games for Leeds. He completed his playing career at Brighton before becoming coach at Birmingham under old Leeds teammate Freddie Goodwin, who has been his manager at Brighton. When Goodwin was dismissed in 1975, Willie was installed as manager at St Andrew's where he remained for two years. After a 10-month spell as Lincoln manager he went to the United States to join a religious group in Colorado called the Campus Crusade for Christ. He coached at Liberty Baptist College, Lynchburg, Virginia, receiving an honorary doctorate of humanities before returning to England in 2001 to set up the Within The Walls organisation, which provides spiritual guidance for prison inmates. An ordained minister, he returned to live in South Carolina where he visits prisons throughout the state.

BOWYER Lee David

Midfield
Born: Canning Town, London, 3 January 1977
Career: Charlton Athletic from trainee April 1994. LEEDS UNITED £2.6 million July 1996. West Ham United £100,000 January 2003. Newcastle United free July 2003. West Ham United July £250,000 2006. Birmingham City free January 2009. Ipswich Town free July 2011.

Lee was rarely out of the headlines during his seven and a half years with United. He became the country's most expensive teenager when he was signed by Howard Wilkinson from Charlton in summer 1996. He arrived with a reputation of being a firebrand and did little to shake off that tag. He scored on his debut at Derby and quickly became a driving force in midfield with bags of energy, plenty of skill and a thirst for victory. His biting tackles and fiery temperament landed him in plenty of trouble on the pitch, but his performances saw him skipper England Under-21s. But his international career was put on hold by the FA as Bowyer became embroiled in a protracted court case after being charged with attacking a student in Leeds city centre. Rather than collapse in the glare of the media spotlight, Lee's performances, particularly in Europe, went from strength to strength. Eventually, he was found not guilty of actual bodily harm, but was then transfer-listed after a disagreement with chairman Peter Ridsdale over his contract. Although the issue was resolved and he finally earned his sole England cap against Portugal, he never consistently hit his best form and was allowed to leave for West Ham for a cut-price £100,000 in January 2003. In between periods of injury, he slowly began to look like the old Bowyer, being sent off three times for Newcastle in 2004–05, including a well-publicised dust-up involving teammate Kieron Dyer. Although he continued to accrue yellow cards, he was always a player in demand and won a League Cup winners medal in 2011 with Birmingham City.

BREMNER William 'Billy' John

Midfield
Born: Stirling, Stirlingshire, 9 December 1942
Died: Doncaster, 7 December 1997
Career: St Modan's High School, Stirling. Gowanhill Juniors. LEEDS UNITED December 1959. Hull City £30,000 September 1976. Doncaster Rovers manager November 1978. LEEDS UNITED manager October 1985–September 1988. Doncaster Rovers manager July 1989–November 1991.

Legend Billy was the driving force behind Don Revie's great United sides. At his peak he was one of the world's greatest midfield players and possessed an almost telepathic understanding with clubmate Johnny Giles. Billy's marvellous range of passing, eye for goal, endless depths of energy and an iron will to win makes him a Leeds legend. Arsenal, Chelsea and Celtic all gave him trials as a kid but the straight forward manner of Leeds chairman Harry Reynolds impressed young Bremner, who was one of the stars of the Scottish Boys team. Billy made his senior debut for United as a 17-year-old in a 3–1 win at Chelsea on 23 January 1960. He played on the right wing that day with former England international Don Revie as his inside partner – a combination which was to thrive as manager and captain in future years. Despite Billy's eye-catching start, Leeds were relegated and his continued homesickness prompted him to request a transfer. Hibernian offered £25,000 for the flame-haired tiger, but United wanted a minimum of £30,000 so the young Scot was obliged to stay. By this time, Revie was installed as manager and within a couple of seasons turned the club round with Billy a key player in the squad which won the Second Division title in 1964. The following year United missed the Championship on goal difference and lost to Liverpool in extra time in the FA Cup Final, but for Billy there was the compensation of the first of his 54 Scottish caps. The Revie machine was up and running with Billy in the engine room before becoming the club's most successful

skipper, leading United to two League Championships, an FA Cup Final win, two Inter-Cities Fairs Cup triumphs and the League Cup. He won the 1970 Footballer of the Year award and went on to lead the Scots in the 1974 World Cup but his international career ended prematurely after a 1–0 European Championship victory over Denmark in September 1975 when he was one of five players banned for life by the Scottish FA for an alleged nightclub brawl. It was the second high-profile incident involving Billy in just over a year. After Revie left to take up the England job, Billy was sent off with Kevin Keegan in the FA Charity Shield at Wembley on 10 August 1974. Both players were hit with a £500 fine and banned until the end of September. By the time Bremner returned to action – after suspension and injury – the Leeds board had sacked Clough. But Billy's return saw an upturn in United's fortunes and under Jimmy Armfield reached the European Cup Final. The 2–0 defeat to Bayern Munich was to be a watershed in United's history and after one more full season at Leeds Billy moved on after 587 League appearances to join Hull City. He then entered management with Doncaster Rovers, winning a couple of promotions before being tempted back to Elland Road as manager in October 1985 (see Leeds managers). The football world was stunned when Billy died of pneumonia on 7 December 1997, just two days short of his 55th birthday. But his legend lives on at Elland Road in the form of a statue created by Frances Siegelman and unveiled outside the ground on 9 August 1999.

BROMAGE Henry 'Harry'

Goalkeeper
Born: Derby, 17 May 1879
Died: Derby, June 1954
Career: Derby Constitutional. Derby County October 1898. Burton United 1901.

LEEDS CITY August 1905. Doncaster Rovers 1911. Bentley Colliery cs 1913.

The son of a Derbyshire brickmaker, Harry played more games in goal than any other City player, making his debut in the club's first game in the Football League. He was a member of a well-known footballing family from Derby and made his debut for his home-town team on Boxing Day 1899 against Glossop. After a two-year spell at Burton, where he combined playing with working as a brickburner, he joined Leeds as a professional and lived in Morley Street, Beeston, close to Elland Road, before eventually moving to Doncaster where his brother, Billy, a former winger with Sheffield United and Gainsborough was captain. Harry's uncle, Enos, also played in goal for Derby, while Enos junior, Harry's brother, also had a spell with the Rams.

BROOK Harold

Forward

Born: Sheffield, 15 October 1921

Died: Sheffield, November 1998

Career: Sheffield Schools. Woodburn Alliance. Hallam. Fulwood. Sheffield United September 1940, turning professional in 1943. LEEDS UNITED £600 July 1954. Lincoln City March 1958–May 1958. Sheffield FC coach.

Veteran forward Harold scored nearly half a century of goals for United and led the Division Two promotion-winning attack of 1955–56. Leeds spent £600 on the 33-year-old former Sheffield United skipper and it proved money well spent. The Blades thought his best days were gone after 89 goals in 229 League appearances, but his departure from Bramall Lane was premature as he was as sharp as a tack at Leeds. He marked the club's return to the First Division with a 21-minute hat-trick against Everton on the opening day of the 1956–57 season but moved on during the

following campaign to finish his career at Lincoln. He later ran a newsagent's shop in Meadowcroft, Sheffield, and had a stint coaching Sheffield FC.

BROWNE Robert James

Wing-half
Born: Londonderry, Northern Ireland, 9 February 1932
Died: 1994
Career: Maleven. Clooney Rovers. Derry City. LEEDS UNITED £1,500 October 1935. Watford (Wartime guest). York City August 1947. Thorne Colliery player-manager 1949. Halifax Town coach 1954, caretaker manager October–November 1954.

Former Leeds City, Sheffield United and Irish international star Billy Gillespie did much to further Bobby's career. Initially Bobby combined his job as a joiner with

part-time football in Ireland, where he played under Gillespie's management at Derry City. He caught the eye when the Irish League beat the Football League 2–1 at Blackpool in September 1935 and joined United the following month. He won six Northern Ireland caps during his time at Elland Road before a wartime posting took him back to Ulster. An Army PT Staff Sergeant, Bobby guested for Watford when he was stationed at Colchester.

BROWNING Leonard James

Centre-forward
Born: Leeds, 30 March 1928
Died: Leeds, 27 September 2008
Career: Quarry Brae and Leeds Secondary Modern Schools. England Youth Clubs. Headingley Rangers. LEEDS UNITED August 1946. Sheffield United £12,000 November 1951. East End Park.

Len established a reputation of being a teenage whizz-kid when he joined the United ranks. The Leeds-born youngster had represented England Youth Clubs against Wales and against the Air Training Corps at Wembley before joining United's nursery side, Headingley Rangers. Len's stock continued to rise with a hat-trick in the reserves shortly before his League debut as an 18-year-old – a 5–0 defeat at Charlton on 25 September 1946. It was almost two years before Len's name was back on the senior team sheet. But with plenty of Central League experience under his belt he showed he had learned well and was leading scorer in 1948–49 and 1950–51. His height made him an aerial threat, but he showed good groundwork too and it was a bit of a surprise when he was sold to Sheffield United with whom he won a Second Division Championship medal in 1952–53. Tuberculosis cut short his League career in October 1953 at the age of 25, but Len did play amateur Yorkshire League football before a broken

leg forced him to call it a day. He and his wife, Mollie, were also excellent table tennis players, both representing the Leeds Victoria club. Outside football Len worked as a technician at All Saints' College, Horsforth, and assisted United in their video analysis of matches.

BURDEN Thomas David

Wing-half
Born: Andover, Hampshire, 21 February 1924
Died: Taunton, Somerset, October 2001
Career: Somerset County Boys. Wolverhampton Wanderers August 1941. Chester November 1945. LEEDS UNITED July 1948. Bristol City £1,500, plus £500 a year for three years, October 1954.

Natural leader Tommy skippered United for four seasons in the early 1950s. The West Country boy was recommended to Wolves manager Major Frank Buckley by his headmaster and was only 16 when he played for Wolves in wartime. Tommy served with the Rifle Brigade and Royal

Fusiliers, he was wounded in the D Day landings, but went on to complete a physical training course at Loughborough College. He had been playing for Chester when Major Buckley, now installed at Elland Road, persuaded him to come to Leeds even though Tommy was still based in Somerset. Despite the geographical difficulties, his commitment to United never wavered until the travelling finally took its toll after more than 250 games in a United shirt. He asked to move nearer home and went with United's blessing to Bristol City where he won a Third Division South Championship medal in 1955. He continued to give City sterling service before retiring in 1960 and later worked as a senior executive with Clark's Shoes in Street, Somerset.

CHAPMAN Lee Roy

Forward

Born: Lincoln, 5 December 1959

Career: Stoke Schools. Stoke City junior June 1976, professional June 1978. Plymouth Argyle loan December 1978. Arsenal £500,000 August 1982. Sunderland £200,000 December 1983. Sheffield Wednesday £100,000 August 1984. Niort (France) £350,000 June 1988. Nottingham Forest £350,000 October 1988. LEEDS UNITED £400,000 January 1990. Portsmouth £250,000 August 1993. West Ham United £250,000 September 1993. Southend United loan January 1995. Ipswich Town £70,000 January 1995. LEEDS UNITED loan January 1996. Swansea City free /non contract March–May 1996. Stroemgodset (Norway) July 1996–December 1996.

Big, blond and brave, Lee headed United back in the top flight with the only goal at Bournemouth which clinched the 1990 Second Division title. He had arrived in January that year from Sheffield Wednesday to link up with former boss

Howard Wilkinson. Lee took over from the popular Ian Baird and added impetus to United's promotion push. He was adept at feeding off some great crosses from the right from overlapping full-back Mel Sterland and his goal tally continued to mount. Two goals against his old club, Nottingham Forest, in the final game of 1990–91 took his seasonal tally to 31 – the best in Division One – and his career total to 200. Lee was never the quickest player around but led the line like an old fashioned centre-forward. He scored 80 times for Leeds, and struck up an excellent partnership with Rod Wallace. Brian Deane's arrival at Elland Road signalled Lee's departure to Portsmouth and the start of a succession of short spells at various clubs. He popped up at Elland Road again on loan in January 1996, at the age of 37, when Wilkinson found himself short of strikers but was sent off on his second Leeds debut against West Ham. Lee kicked off his career at Stoke, netting a hat-trick for the Potters in a 3–1 win at Leeds in February 1981. England Under-21 honours and a big-money move to Arsenal followed, but it was not until he joined Wilkinson at Wednesday that he hit scoring form with 69 goals in 149 appearances. That rich vein continued at Forest after a short spell in France. Lee played in both Forest's League Cup and Zenith Data Systems Cup Final wins at Wembley. The son of Roy Chapman, the former Aston Villa and Port Vale player, Lee is married to actress Leslie Ash and after retiring from football in 1996 entered the wine bar and restaurant business in London.

CHARLES William John

Centre-half/Centre-forward
Born: Cwmbwrla, Swansea, 27 December 1931
Died: Wakefield, 21 February 2004
Career: Cwymdu Junior School, Manselton Senior School, Swansea. Swansea Boys. Swansea Town groundstaff. LEEDS UNITED January 1949. Juventus £65,000 May 1957. LEEDS UNITED £53,000 August 1962. Roma £70,000 October 1962. Cardiff City £25,000 August 1963. Hereford United player-manager 1966–71. Merthyr Tydfil manager. Swansea City youth coach 1973.

Many regard the legendary John Charles as United's greatest-ever player – a player in a relatively modest Leeds team who made a massive impact. He was on the groundstaff of his hometown club Swansea when United's scout in South Wales, Jack Pickard, alerted United manager Major Frank Buckley about the talented teenager. Pickard persuaded John and his Swansea teammates, Bobby Hennings and Harry Griffiths, to go for trials at Leeds. His two mates returned to Swansea but John was taken on. As he grew John was switched to centre-half and got his senior chance in a friendly against Queen of the South as a 17-year-old towards the end of the 1949–50 season. He kept his place for the final two League games of the season – after that there was no turning back. Charles was awesome in the air, powerful in the tackle, had a vast array of passes and could thump the ball as hard as anyone. In 1950 he became Wales' youngest international at 18 years 71 days when he won the first of his 38 caps. By this time John was doing his National Service with the 12th Lancers and skippered his side to victory in the 1952 Army Cup. He was still playing for Leeds – but in a new role as centre-forward – although he missed a big portion of the 1951–52 season because of knee surgery. The following campaign Major Buckley started with John in defence before finally settling to use him at number nine with devastating effect. John smashed in 26 goals in 28 League games as a forward, including hat-tricks against Hull and Brentford. In that period he scored 10 successive goals without any of his teammates getting on the scoresheet – no wonder Leeds were dubbed 'Charles United'. In 1953–54 he was unstoppable

with a club record 42 League goals in a season, yet United only finished 10th in the Second Division. John, who was on the maximum wage of £15 a week, was hankering to play in the First Division, but a transfer request was turned down and was used to plug a leaky defence in 1954–55 as United rose to fourth place. The emergence of Jack Charlton the following season enabled United to deploy their star asset up front again. He didn't disappoint and United grabbed promotion on a tidal wave of John's goals. He scored almost a goal-a-game in his first season in the top flight – that and a string of superb displays for Wales prompted Italian giants Juventus to make a British record bid of £65,000 for Big John. It was an offer the Leeds board could not afford to turn down and John, at the peak of his powers, became a massive star in Italian football.

He led Wales to the quarter-finals of the World Cup in 1958 when he was also named Italian Footballer of the Year. Even rough-house Italian tactics failed to ruffle John, who was dubbed Il Gigante Buono – the Gentle Giant. After five years, 108 Juventus goals, three Italian Championships and two Italian Cup medals, John returned to Leeds. He was not the same player, so United banked a £17,000 profit as he went back to Serie A with Roma after only 11 matches. He then played in defence for Cardiff and prolonged his career as player-manager at Southern League Hereford where he scored 130 goals in 243 appearances before retiring just before his 40th birthday. John then ran a pub, a toy shop and a clothes shop before hitting financial problems. In 1988 United organised a joint testimonial for John and Bobby Collins – two players hero-worshipped by United's faithful. John, never sent off or even booked in his career, was from strong sporting stock. His son, Terry is a former Cardiff and Wales B rugby union forward, brother Mel played for Swansea, Arsenal and Wales and nephew Jeremy (Swansea, QPR and Oxford) also played for Wales. True sportsman John died, aged 73, in 2004 and after his funeral at Leeds Parish Church, the procession headed to Elland Road where thousands of fans gathered inside the ground to pay their final goodbye to a genuine hero.

CHARLTON John 'Jack'

Centre-half
Born: Ashington, Northumberland, 8 May 1935
Career: Hurst Park Modern School, Ashington. East Northumberland Schools. Ashington YMCA. Ashington Welfare. LEEDS UNITED amateur 1950, professional May 1952. Middlesbrough manager May 1973–April 1977. Sheffield Wednesday manager October 1977–May 1983. Newcastle United manager June 1984–August 1985. Middlesbrough caretaker manager March 1984. Republic of Ireland manager February 1986–January 1996.

World Cup winner 'Big Jack' is the daddy of them all at Elland Road. He made more than 770 first team appearances – 629 of them in the League – for the club in 21 years. It is a long-playing record that is likely to stand forever. Jack may not have been the most elegant footballer but developed from a run-of-the-mill centre-half into one of the world's best defenders. Brother Bobby hit more headlines with Manchester United and England, but Jack forged a much longer career in football, following his playing days with success at club and international level as a manager. Jack's uncles, George, Jim and Jack Milburn, all starred with United and it was Jim who recommended the skinny teenager to Leeds. After completing his National Service with the Royal Horse

Guards he gradually cemented his place and in October 1957 represented the Football League against the League of Ireland. He had a spell as captain, but gave up the job because of his suspicion of coming out of the tunnel last. It was only when Don Revie took over as player-manager that Jack's game really started to develop. As Leeds moved into the top flight, Jack maintained his consistency, proving an excellent tackler, was near unbeatable in the air and perfected the tactic of standing in front of the goalkeeper at Leeds corners. He weighed in 70 League goals – the vast majority with his head and Jack won his first cap at the age of 29 in a 2–2 draw against Scotland when brother Bobby was in the team. The brothers played key roles in England's 1966 World Cup triumph. In total, Jack won 35 full caps, represented the Football League six times and was named Footballer of the Year in 1967. Jack featured in all United's early successes under Revie – the League Cup, first League title and Fairs Cup

honours before winning an FA Cup winners' medal in 1972, two days before his 37th birthday. The following year he was named Middlesbrough manager and was named Manager of the Year in his first season as Boro powered to the Second Division title by a record points margin. He stood down in 1977 and took over at struggling Sheffield Wednesday and guided them to promotion to Division Two. After a brief stint as caretaker manager back at Middlesbrough, he took over as boss at Newcastle United but quit after a season after being booed during a pre-season friendly in 1985. The following year he was appointed manager of the Republic of Ireland international team and pulled off a famous 1–0 win over England in June 1988. He led Eire to the 1990 World Cup quarter-finals and into round two of the USA Finals four years later. A hero in the Emerald Isle, he earned the Freedom of Dublin and retired in January 1996 after the Irish just failed to qualify for that year's European Championships in England. There is a lifesize statue of Jack at Cork Airport and he has been inducted in to England's Hall of Fame.

CHERRY Trevor John

Defender/midfielder
Born: Huddersfield, 23 February 1948
Career: Newsham County Secondary Modern School, Huddersfield. Huddersfield YMCA. Huddersfield Town July 1965. LEEDS UNITED £100,000 June 1972. Bradford City player-manager December 1982–January 1987, retiring as a player cs 1985.

When Trevor joined Don Revie's multi-talented squad he was the only non-international first-teamer. By the time he moved on 10 years later he had won 27 England caps and had the honour of captaining his country. Trevor had formed an excellent defensive partnership with

Roy Ellam at Huddersfield and led the Terriers from left-half when they won the Second Division title in 1970. Two years later United shelled out £100,000 for Trevor's services and he proved highly versatile in a number of defensive roles and was also an adept anchor man in midfield. In his second season he won a League Championship medal and as Trevor became a Leeds regular, England appearances followed over a four-year period, his first cap coming against Wales in 1976 at the age of 28. As Revie's famous squad broke up, Trevor was appointed skipper and also captained England against Australia in 1980. After United slipped into Division Two Trevor joined Bradford City as player-manager and led them into Division Two. Trevor was in charge during City's spell in receivership and at the time of the horrific Valley Parade fire disaster. Shortly after City moved back into their revamped £3.6 million modern stadium Trevor was surprisingly sacked. Since then he has been a director of a sports promotions firm, does local radio work, has been an associate director at Huddersfield Town and is a regular visitor to Elland Road.

CLARKE Allan John

Forward

Born: Short Heath, near Willenhall, Staffordshire, 31 July 1946

Career: Birmingham Schools. South East Staffordshire Boys. Walsall apprentice 1961, professional August 1963. Fulham £35,000 March 1966. Leicester City £150,000 June 1968. LEEDS UNITED £165,000 July 1969. Barnsley player-manager May 1978. LEEDS UNITED manager October 1980–June 1982. Scunthorpe United manager February 1983–August 1984. Barnsley manager July 1985–November 1989. Lincoln City manager June–November 1990.

'Sniffer' Clarke ferreted out scores of important goals for United – including the one which won the 1972 FA Cup, a stunning diving header. His nose for goals brought him 110 League goals in 270 starts and weighed in with 43 goals in other competitions in a Leeds shirt. Allan was a

deadly penalty box predator and his partnership with Mick Jones was one of the most fruitful in the club's history. Allan came from a footballing family – brothers Wayne, Frank, Derek and Kelvin all played League football. He first started knocking in goals for Walsall to earn a move to First Division Fulham where he netted 45 goals in 85 League games. The slimline striker headed to Leicester for a record fee for both clubs and stayed at Filbert Street a year and was man of the match in their 1–0 FA Cup Final defeat against Manchester City in 1969. The following month Leeds paid out a British record fee to take him to Elland Road where he quickly clicked into scoring action. Already an England Under-23 cap and Football League representative, he was elevated to full international status in the 1970 World Cup, scoring the only goal of the game – a penalty – against Czechoslovakia on his debut. He finished with 19 caps and 10 goals and was the spearhead as United won the FA Cup, 1974 League Championship and the 1971 Fairs Cup. He continued to find the net as player-manager at Barnsley, steering the Tykes to promotion from Division Four in his first season. With Leeds in free fall during Jimmy Adamson's ill-fated reign, the Whites appointed Allan as boss, but the move didn't work out (see Leeds managers). After quitting the game, he worked for a company selling industrial flue extractors to construction firms and is a regular visitor to Elland Road.

COCHRANE David Andrew

Outside-right
Born: Portadown, Northern Ireland, 14 August 1920
Died: Leeds, June 2000
Career: Portadown. LEEDS UNITED £2,000 August 1937–October 1950. Portadown. Shamrock Rovers, Linfield, Shamrock Rovers (Wartime).

Teenage starlet David, one of Northern Ireland's youngest-ever professionals, was the first Leeds winger to win full international honours. Diminutive Dave was a box-of-tricks winger with blistering speed in the mould of his father, who had played as an inside-right for Linfield. Cochrane junior was playing in Portadown's reserve team at 15 and turned professional five days after his 16th birthday. He was still only 17 when he scored 14 Irish League and Cup goals in 13 games, but it was a stunning display in Portadown's Gold Cup semi-final replay with Derry City which prompted United to sign him. Dave was gradually eased into the first team, but that did not stop the Irish selectors from giving him his full debut against England at Old Trafford when he was only 18 years and three months old. What looked like being a long and productive international career did not materialise as the war left him with just a dozen caps. During hostilities he returned to Ireland and played as a guest for Portadown, Shamrock Rovers and Linfield, winning an Irish Cup winners medal with the latter in 1945. He went back to Elland Road after the war and turned out a string of consistent displays on the right wing for four seasons before retiring in October 1950.

COCHRANE Thomas

Outside-left
Born: Newcastle upon Tyne, 7 October 1908
Died: Cleveland, March 1976
Career: St Peter's Albion. Hull City (trials). Sheffield Wednesday (trials). LEEDS UNITED August 1928. Middlesbrough £2,500 October 1936. Bradford Park Avenue £1,100 May 1939.

Patience proved a virtue for both Tom and United's fans as he took time to win over the Elland Road faithful. He was signed from Tyneside League club St Peter's Albion by Dick Ray, who first spotted Tom in trials matches with Sheffield Wednesday and Hull City when he was Doncaster's manager. After taking charge at Leeds, Ray remembered Tom's displays in those trials and persuaded him to sign pro at Elland Road. He had a bit of a rough start as the supporters preferred to see the popular Tom Mitchell flying down the left wing and the new player's inconsistent early form led to some barracking from the terraces. But Ray stuck by his man and was rewarded with more than 250 games in eight years. Tom's partnership with Billy Furness was one of the vital components of United's Division Two promotion success in 1932. He later had three good years with Middlesbrough, scoring four goals in a 6–1 rout of Manchester City at Maine Road in March 1938.

COLLINS Robert Young

Inside-forward
Born: Govanhill, Glasgow, 16 February 1931
Career: Polmadie Street School and Calder Street Schools, Glasgow. Polmadie Hawthorns. Pollok Juniors. Celtic August 1948. Everton £25,000 September 1958. LEEDS UNITED £25,000 March 1962. Bury February 1967. Morton August 1969 after trial. Ringwood City (Melbourne) player-coach August 1971. Hakoah (Sydney) player-coach October 1971. Wilhelmina (Melbourne) player-coach. Oldham Athletic player-coach October 1972. Shamrock Rovers loan April 1972. Oldham Athletic assistant manager April 1973. Huddersfield

Town manager July 1974–December 1975. LEEDS UNITED coach July 1976. Hull City coach July 1977, manager (after two weeks as caretaker manager) October 1977–February 1978. Blackpool coach March–May 1978. Barnsley coach October 1980, caretaker manager February 1984, manager June 1984–July 1985. Guiseley manager September 1987–September 1988.

Small in stature, but a huge figure in Elland Road's history, Bobby was the midfield rock on which Don Revie built the Leeds United dynasty. United, then a struggling Second Division club, paid Everton £25,000 for the 31-year-old former Scottish international. It seemed a curious piece of business all round – a large fee for a player seemingly past his best and prepared to drop out of the top level to join a moribund club. But Bobby, a former Celtic great, reeled off a series of superb displays of midfield arts and crafts while Revie skilfully slotted in his array of talent around his little talisman. Bobby skippered Leeds to the Second Division title in 1963–64 and was voted Footballer of the Year in 1965. He was recalled to the Scottish national team after an absence of six years and added three more caps to the 38 he had won with Celtic and Everton. His great revival was brought to a shattering halt when he broke a thigh bone in the second leg of United's first-ever European tie against Torino. Bobby managed a comeback before leaving on a free transfer to Bury and embarking on a football journey which took him to Australia and Ireland before several coaching and managerial jobs in the Yorkshire area. Bobby, an apprentice cobbler, was dubbed 'The Wee Barra' at Celtic where he won a Scottish Cup winners medal in 1951, scored a hat-trick of penalties against Aberdeen in 1953 and was an integral part of the Hoops squad which did the double in 1954 and enjoyed League Cup glory in 1957 and 1958. His international debut came against Wales in October 1950 and was in the squad that reached the 1958 World Cup Finals. He proved a class act at Goodison, but it was only when he joined Leeds that commentators truly recognised his influence in English football. After his Elland Road days he helped Bury to promotion in 1968 and was 42 when he made his final League appearance. Despite his greatness as a player he could not transfer his skills to management,

although was always in demand as a coach. He eventually left the game to work in the wholesale fashion business and then worked as a chauffer at Leeds University garage. Still revered at Elland Road, where he was a regular visitor, he and John Charles shared a testimonial in April 1988.

COOPER Terence

Left-back

Born: Brotherton, near Castleford, 12 July 1944

Career: Brotherton School. Wath Wanderers. Wolverhampton Wanders trial. Ferrybridge Amateurs 1960. LEEDS UNITED apprentice May 1961, professional July 1962. Middlesbrough £50,000 March 1975. Bristol City £20,000 July 1978. Bristol Rovers player-coach August 1979, manager April 1980–October 1981. Doncaster Rovers November 1981. Bristol City player-manager May 1982–March 1988. Exeter City May 1988. Birmingham City manager August 1991–November 1993. Exeter City manager January 1994–June 1995. Southampton assistant manager and overseas scout.

Terry brought a new dimension to the role of full-back. In addition to his defensive duties he became a masterly exponent of the art of the attacking overlap – providing another option on the left for Don Revie. The sight of Terry in his white boots dribbling down the left flank became one of the most feared sights in football and at his pomp was regarded as one of the world's best players. He had started at Leeds as a pacy left-winger and made his debut with a clutch of other up-and-coming young players in a famous 3–0 win at Swansea towards the end of the 1963–64 season. Terry was converted to left-back and although he regularly supplemented the Leeds attack, his goals were relatively rare, but did score against Arsenal in the 1968 League Cup Final at Wembley to give

United their first major trophy. Two years later he won the first of his 20 England caps and played in the 1970 World Cup. Terry broke a leg at Stoke in 1972 but fought his way back to fitness and even earned an England recall from Revie in November 1974, although he limped off early on – his last performance on the international stage. The following March Terry's 14-year association with United ended and he joined Middlesbrough. At Bristol City he linked up with Norman Hunter, and then took up coaching before entering management, taking the Ashton Gate club to victory in the 1986 Freight Rover Trophy. He made his final League appearance as a 40-year-old and became the country's first player-director. Terry lost his job in March 1988 when he was replaced by his assistant, another Leeds legend, Joe Jordan. Terry, who also played local amateur football bounced back as manager of Exeter, steering the Grecians to the Fourth Division title in 1989–90. After a stint at Birmingham City, where he was also a director, he returned to manage Exeter but ill health forced him to quit. He re-entered the game as assistant to Graeme Souness at Southampton and later was based in Tenerife as the Saints' foreign scout. His son Mark, who played at Bristol City, Exeter, Birmingham, Fulham, Huddersfield (loan) and Wycombe, also managed Conference outfits Tamworth and Kettering before a brief spell as boss at Peterborough. He led Darlington to FA Trophy glory at Wembley in 2011 but was dismissed a few months later. In January 2012 he was appointed caretaker manager at Kettering.

COPPING Wilfred

Half-back
Born: Barnsley, 17 August 1909
Died: Southend, June 1980
Career: Houghton Council School, Dearne Valley Old Boys. Middlecliffe Rovers. LEEDS UNITED March 1929. Arsenal £6,000 June 1934. LEEDS UNITED March 1939–42. Royal Beerschot (Antwerp) and Belgian national team coach. Southend United trainer cs 1946. Bristol City trainer July 1954. Coventry City trainer November 1956–May 1959.

Rock-hard Wilf was the 'Iron Man' of England inter-war football. His reputation went before him as an uncompromising half-back who struck fear into opponents before he even set foot on the pitch. Legend has it that he once broke his nose in a League game, reset it himself, and played on. He added to his menacing aura by rarely shaving before a match and the stubble round his Desperate Dan chin. Wilf was an astute passer of the ball, possessed a torpedo of a throw-in and was an ever-present in his first season at Elland Road. He became an integral part of the United team which boasted an all-England half-back line of Willis Edwards, Ernie Hart and Wilf. It took a £6,000 transfer to Arsenal to prise Wilf away from Leeds in June 1934. Arsenal were the big guns of the First Division and Wilf won two League Championship medals and an FA Cup winners' medal with the Highbury team before returning to Elland Road just before the war. Wilf won 20 England caps – seven of them with United, the first coming in May 1933 against Italy – and also represented the Football League twice. During the war he played a handful of games for Leeds when on leave from the Army in which he served as a Company Sergeant-Major Instructor in North Africa. He was trainer to the Army XI in Dusseldorf in 1945 and when based in Belgium had a stint training the national team and Antwerp club Royal Beerschot. Wilf settled in Southend and worked at Ford's car plant in Dagenham. A keen wireless enthusiast, he later lived at Prittlewell, near Southend.

CROOT Frederick Richard

Right-winger
Born: Little Harrowden, near Rushden, Northamptonshire, 30 November 1885
Died: Rushden, Northamptonshire, 5 July 1955
Career: Wellingborough. Sheffield United 1905. LEEDS CITY May 1907. Clydebank 1919.

Fred Croot, son of a breadmaker, was one of the most consistent of all City players, scoring 38 League goals in 213 appearances. He first caught Sheffield United's eye when playing for Wellingborough in the Southern League. Fred made his Division One debut in a 4–1 defeat at Nottingham Forest but didn't quite cut it with the Blades. However, he settled well at Elland Road where he was a trusted penalty taker – scoring 15 spot-kicks in all, including two in a game at Barnsley in April 1912.

CUBBERLEY Stanley Morris

Wing-half
Born: Edmonton, London, September 18 July 1882
Died: Patricroft, Barton upon Irwell, Lancashire, 15 June 1933
5ft 8in, 11st 3lb (1906)
Career: Cheshunt & Cliftonville 1902. LEEDS CITY May 1906. Swansea Town cs 1913. Manchester United £50 May 1914.

Stan, a London carpenter, was a versatile type who made his debut in a nightmare 5–0 defeat at West Brom, but kept his place and scored on his home debut against Lincoln. All three of his City goals in seven years at Elland Road came in that first season. He eventually settled at left-half for a long spell and was settled in Leeds, living at Holbeck, close to Elland Road, with his Leeds-born wife. Eventually, he was transferred to Swansea, who were then in the Southern League. He left Wales with teammate Arthur Allman for Manchester United but didn't play in the senior team. At the time of his death he was a motor mechanic. Stan's brother, Archie, was an inside-forward with Tottenham Hotspur.

CURRIE Anthony William

Midfield
Born: Edgware, London 1 January 1950

Career: Childs Hill Junior School. Whitefield Secondary Modern School, Cricklewood. Hendon Boys. Queen's Park Rangers amateur November 1964. Chelsea youth team. Watford May 1967. Sheffield United £26,500 May 1967. LEEDS UNITED £240,000 June 1976. Queen's Park Rangers £400,000 August 1979. Toronto Nationals (Canada) £60,000 May–June 1983. Chesham United August 1983. Southend United September 1983. Chesham United November 1983. Torquay United non-contract March 1984. Dunstable Town. Hendon. Goole Town player-coach September 1987. Sheffield United football in the community officer February 1988.

Flamboyant Tony was one of the greatest entertainers ever seen at Elland Road. After the departure of Billy Bremner and Johnny Giles, Leeds boss Jimmy Armfield turned the skills of Currie to fill the vacuum. Tony actually played a handful of games with Bremner before forging his own midfield partnership with Bryan Flynn. Tony had a wonderful range of passing, intricate ball skills and a booming shot, winning 11 of his 17 England caps while at Elland Road.

He gained England youth honours with Watford before joining Sheffield United where he was worshipped by the fans. He played for the Football League and England Under-23s before winning his first full cap in 1972 against Northern Ireland. Leeds were constantly trying to get Tony to Elland Road and he eventually moved up the M1 after a successful £240,00 bid. He added consistency to his game at Leeds but after three years with the Whites returned to his native London because his wife was unsettled. He helped QPR to the 1982 FA Cup Final against Tottenham. Eventually he rejoined Sheffield United as their full-time football in the community officer. His nephew, Darren, played more than 400 Football League games including spells with Shrewsbury, Barnet, Wycombe and Ipswich.

DAY Mervyn Richard

Goalkeeper

Born: Chelmsford, Essex, 26 June 1955

Career: King Edward VI Grammar School, Chelmsford. Chelmsford and Essex Schools. West Ham United apprentice July 1971, professional March 1973. Leyton Orient £100,000 July 1979. Aston Villa £25,000 May 1983. LEEDS UNITED £30,000 February 1985. Coventry City loan March 1991 loan. Luton Town loan March 1992. Sheffield United loan May 1992. Carlisle United free player-coach July 1993, manager February 1996–September 1997. Everton goalkeeping coach 1997. Charlton Athletic first team coaching May 1998 then assistant manager to June 2006. West Ham United assistant manager December 2006–September 2008. LEEDS UNITED chief scout July 2010.

Leeds have had some outstanding goalkeepers over the years and Mervyn fits in that category. He made a rapid climb to the top at his first club, West Ham, holding

down a first team place as a teenager. He won an FA Cup winners' medal when he was just turned 20 in 1975 and was named Young Footballer of the Year the same year. He featured in the Hammers side beaten by Anderlecht in the European Cup-Winners' Cup the following year and won a clutch of Youth and Under-23 caps. Mervyn lost form, triggering a move to Leyton Orient where he won a place on the bench for England B against New Zealand but that full cap, which looked such a certainty in his teens, eluded him. Eddie Gray brought him to Leeds and it proved a smart piece of business. Cool, calm and collected, Mervyn was unspectacular in his work but highly reliable. He passed his 600th League appearance on his way to a Second Division Championship medal in 1989–90 but John Lukic's £1 million return saw Mervyn pushed to the sidelines. He spent his last season at Elland Road helping with coaching and joined Carlisle as player-coach. The Cumbrians stormed to the Division Three title in 1994–95 and were beaten 1–0 by a sudden death goal by Birmingham City in the Auto Windscreens Final at Wembley the same season. Day stepped up as manager but could not stop Carlisle falling back into Division Three. However, the following year Mervyn got them back up again and steered the club to Auto Windscreens glory at Wembley in a penalty shootout against Colchester. Within a month of the new season he was controversially sacked by Michael Knighton and after a time as goalkeeping coach at Everton joined his old West Ham teammate Alan Curbishley as coach at Charlton. He later became assistant manager and spent eight years at the Valley. In summer 2010 he rejoined the Elland Road payroll as chief scout.

DEANE Brian Christopher

Forward

Born: Leeds, 7 February 1968

Career: LEEDS CITY Boys. LEEDS UNITED youth team 1984. Doncaster Rovers apprentice December 1985. Sheffield United £30,000 July 1988. LEEDS UNITED £2.9 million July 1993. Sheffield United £1.5 million July 1997. Benfica (Portugal) £1 million January 1998. Middlesbrough £3 million October 1998. Leicester City £150,000 November 2001. West Ham United free October 2003. LEEDS UNITED free July 2004. Sunderland free March 2005. Perth Glory (Australia) July 2005. Sheffield United December 2005 cs 2006.

Although a club record signing when he arrived at Elland Road for £2.7 million, Brian had played for Leeds' youth team in 1984 after starring with Leeds City Boys. He was not taken on, but joined Doncaster Rovers as an apprentice instead. A traditional target-man striker, his powerful displays saw him elevated to Sheffield United where he struck up a devastating partnership with Tony Agana, netting 46 goals between them as the Blades earned promotion to Division Two. He was top scorer the following season when the

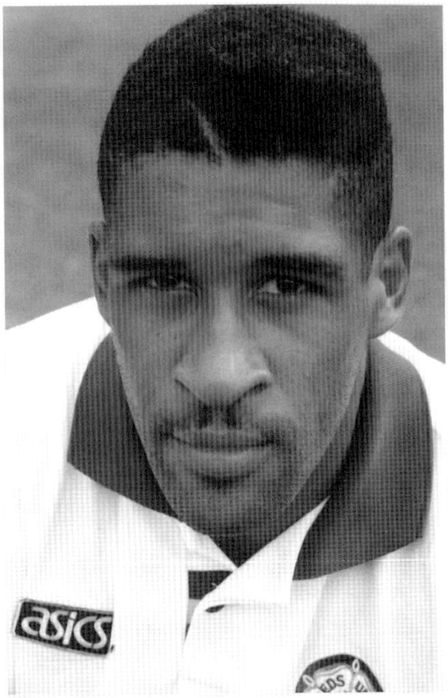

Blades finished runners-up to Leeds in the Division Two Championship and went on the England tour of Australasia, earning two caps against New Zealand. A third followed against Spain to add to his three B international caps. It was only when Tony Yeboah arrived that he really got a new lease of life at Leeds, playing on the left side of the attack. He rejoined the Blades and played for several other clubs before returning to Elland Road at the age of 37 after Leeds' relegation from the Premiership. He enjoyed a great personal highlight in 2004–05, scoring four times in the 6–1 home win against QPR before joining Sunderland.

DORIGO Anthony Robert

Left-back
Born: Melbourne, Australia, 31 December 1965
5ft 10in, 10st 10lb (1996)
Career: Birmingham Schools. Aston Villa apprentice 1981, professional January 1982. Chelsea £475,000 July 1987. Leeds United £1.3 million May 1991. Torino (Italy) June 1997. Derby County October 1998. Stoke City June 2000–June 2001.

Class act Tony was United's left-back and the club's player of the year in the 1991–92 Championship season. He probably ranks as United's best post-war left-back after Terry Cooper with his instant control, acceleration and magic wand of a left-foot marking him out as a player of international standard. Born in Australia of Italian parents, Tony got his first break at Aston Villa where he won seven England Under-21 caps and England B honours before a big money move took him to Chelsea where he was elevated to full England status. He helped the Blues win the Second Division Championship in 1988–89, was a member of England's 1990 World Cup squad and scored the winning goal in Chelsea's Zenith Data Systems Final victory over Middlesbrough at Wembley. He made a scoring return to Wembley with Leeds in the 4–3 victory over Liverpool in the 1992 Charity Shield success against

Liverpool. Nine of his 15 England caps were won at Leeds where his last couple of seasons were blighted by injury. He spent a year in Italy with Torino and returned to England as a full-back sweeper with Derby and Stoke. He then entered business with a vehicle leasing firm, a property development company in Portugal a lifestyle management company for footballers and a spot of television punditry.

DUFFIELD Albert

Right-back
Born: Owston Ferry, Lincolnshire, 3 March 1894
Died: Beeston, Leeds, 27 September 1981
Career: Gainsborough Trinity. Castleford Town. LEEDS UNITED July 1920. Bradford Park Avenue November 1925–May 1928.

An ever-present in United's first Football League season, Bert was one of the club's unsung heroes in the Peacocks' early years. He had made his name in the Midland League with Gainsborough Trinity and

Castleford Town, once scoring four goals as a stand-in centre-forward for the latter against Notts County Reserves. But United were impressed by his defensive work and signed him from Cas and were rewarded with 203 League appearances and barely a bad performance. Bert, who had served as a bombardier in France during World War One when he was wounded, helped United to their first promotion to Division One when his displays with full-back partner Jimmy Frew were a key factor. He moved on to Bradford PA before retiring after the end of Avenue's 1927–28 Division Three North Championship season. Bert then went into the pub business before working as a greengrocer near the Elland Road Greyhound Stadium and then ran a poultry farm near Goole, where he also coached Rawcliffe.

DUGGAN Henry Anthony

Outside-right
Born: Dublin, 8 June 1903
Died: Leeds, September 1968
Career: Richmond United. LEEDS UNITED May 1925. Newport County £1,500 October 1936–40.

Apprentice stonemason Harry chiselled out an excellent career with United in the inter-war years. The young Dubliner took up the trade after leaving school and played part-time with junior club Richmond United, scoring 49 goals in 1924–25. Leeds signed the talented 19-year-old and was groomed as Bobby Turnbull's understudy. In 10 years at Elland Road Harry scored 45 League goals in 187 games, captaining the 1932 promotion side. Right-winger Harry's work was rewarded with eight caps for Northern Ireland and four for the Republic between 1926 and 1935. He made his Eire debut against Italy B in April 1927 and his first NI game was a 3–0 defeat at the hands of England in October 1929.

Harry skippered Newport County to the Third Division South title in 1938–39 and during World War Two he was an ARP warden before returning to Leeds to work for a firm of glass merchants.

DUNN James

Right-back
Born: Rutherglen, 23 October 1922
Died: Leeds, 24 January 2005
Career: Rutherglen Glencairn. LEEDS UNITED June 1947. Darlington July 1959. Scarborough 1960.

Jimmy was 'Mr Consistency' and unlucky not to win a full Scotland cap. In 11 years at Elland Road he barely put a foot wrong and, although he was often tipped for full honours was ignored by the Scottish selectors. He served with the Royal Marines in World War Two – even though he could not swim – and played in the Services Cup Final at Home Park, Plymouth. Jimmy then took a labouring job and played for Scottish junior club Rutherglen Glencairn. Several clubs were on his trail and although Arbroath were favourites to sign him, they were pipped by Leeds. He became a permanent fixture at

right-back, including four seasons when he was ever-present and would play a major role in United's 1955–56 promotion season. He left for Darlington but a knee injury cut short his career and after a handful of Midland League games with Scarborough in 1960–61 called it a day because of knee trouble. He lived close to Elland Road and was a regular visitor to matches and worked as a milkman, a driver's mate and for the Post Office before retiring in 1987.

EDWARDS Willis

Half-back
Born: Newton, near Alfreton, Derbyshire, 28 April 1903
Died: Leeds, 27 September 1988
Career: Newton Rangers, Chesterfield £10 1922. LEEDS UNITED £1,500 March 1925–46, assistant trainer 1946, manager April 1947–April 1948, reverting to assistant trainer until 1960.

Willis is one of the Elland Road all-time greats with a 35-year association with the club which he served as a player, manager and trainer. His marvellous career, which stretched into World War Two saw him

play 444 times for Leeds and 16 times for England, five as captain. Although quite short for a wing-half, he had supreme heading skills, wonderful ball control and a wide range of crisp passing. As a teenager Willis was working in the mines of Derbyshire and starring for his local club Newton Rangers when he was offered a trial by Blackburn. However, Chesterfield, much closer to his home, intercepted Willis as he was about to go to the Lancashire club and he joined the Spireites on a wage of 30 shillings (£1.50) a week. On 1 March 1926 Willis won the first of his England caps – a 3–1 defeat against Wales – at the age of 22. He was the best wing-half of his day, even keeping his place in the national team when United were relegated. Willis also represented the Football League 11 times and continued to play for United in emergencies during World War Two. He became assistant to trainer Bob Roxburgh with responsibility for the Reserves and in April 1947 replaced Billy Hampson as manager after a disastrous season (see Leeds managers). He later worked briefly in a jam factory until his retirement.

FAIRCLOUGH Courtney 'Chris' Huw

Central-defender
Born: Nottingham, 12 April 1964
Career: Parkhead Academicals. Nottingham Forest apprentice June 1980, professional October 1981. Tottenham Hotspur £385,000 June 1987. LEEDS UNITED loan March 1989, £500,000 April 1989. Bolton Wanderers £500,000 July 1995. Notts County free July 1998. York City loan March 1999, retired February 2001. Nottingham Forest youth coach cs 2001, then assistant first-team coach until June 2011.

Chris was one of the stars of the 1991–92 Championship winning side, forming a

superb central defensive barrier with Chris Whyte. He arrived from Spurs, initially on loan, and made his debut on the same day as Gordon Strachan – a 1–0 home win against Portsmouth on 25 March, 1989. A deal was hammered out with Tottenham at the end of the season and Chris was United's Player of the Year in the Second Division title-winning side. He was also deployed as a defensive midfielder after David Batty's departure to Blackburn before his six years at Elland Road came to an end when he signed for Premiership newcomers Bolton. Although christened Courtney, he was always known as Chris and after retiring through injury at his last club, York, became a youth coach at Nottingham Forest, his first club. It was at Forest where he had won the first of his seven England Under-21 caps in 1985 and played for England B against Malta in October 1987 when at Spurs. He was a member of Forest's backroom staff for 10 years, leaving after manager Billy Davies was dismissed in 2011.

FLYNN Brian

Midfield

Born: Port Talbot, Neath, 12 October 1955

Career: Sandfields Comprehensive School, Neath and Wales Schools. Afon Lido. Burnley apprentice, 1970 professional October 1972. LEEDS UNITED £175,000 November 1977. Burnley loan March 1982, £60,000 November 1982. Cardiff City £15,000 November 1984. Doncaster Rovers November 1985. Bury July 1986. Limerick player-coach January 1987, Doncaster Rovers August 1987. Burnley Football in the Community Officer. Wrexham February 1988, caretaker manager October 1989, appointed manager November 1989–October 2001. Swansea City manager September 2002–April 2004. Wales Under-21 and youth coach December 2004. Wales caretaker manager September–December 2010.

Little Brian may have been small in stature at a shade over five foot three inches, but the midfielder had a huge appetite for work. His partnership with Tony Currie was among the best of the post-Revie era with busy Brian the fetcher and carrier for his skilful sidekick. Capped 66 times for Wales, Brian won half of them with Leeds and the other half at Burnley, who signed him as a youngster. The Welsh youth and Under-23 international was never a great goalscorer at Turf Moor and netted his first Wales goal in only his third appearance against Scotland before he had opened his account for the Clarets. After Burnley's relegation to Division Two, Brian became a Leeds player and made over 150 League appearances with his accurate, incisive passing and non-stop running making him popular with the fans. He returned to Burnley in 1982 and played out the twilight of his career at a variety of clubs, his last appearance coming at Wrexham as a 37-year-old player-manager. He steered the North Wales side to a famous FA Cup victory over League champions Arsenal and was in charge at the Racecourse Ground for more than 10 years – Wrexham's longest serving boss. He's since managed Swansea and the Welsh Under-21 side and had a spell as caretaker manager of the full national side until the appointment of another former Leeds favourite, Gary Speed.

FOLEY Michael
Wing-half
Born: Dublin, Ireland, 1892
Career: Shelbourne. LEEDS CITY May 1910. Shelbourne 1920.
Mick 'Boxer' Foley is regarded as one of the most successful of City's many Irish imports. He started out as a bits and pieces player at Elland Road but settled down as a commanding left-half. He also turned out for the club in World War One, returning to Shelbourne after hostilities ceased. Back in the Emerald Isle he became a big-name player, winning an Irish Cup medal in his first season back with the Shels. He represented the League of Ireland five times between 1924 and 1927 and captained Ireland in their first-ever international match – a 3–0 defeat by Italy in Turin on 21 March 1926. It was Mick's only full international appearance and also in the team were two other ex-City men, Bob Fullam and John Joe Flood, the latter never making the Leeds first team.

FORREST John Robert
Inside-forward
Born: Rossington, near Doncaster, 13 May 1931
Died: Weymouth, Dorset, 3 May 2005
Career: Rossington Modern School. Rossington Youth Club. Rossington Colliery. Retford Town. LEEDS UNITED £500

December 1952. Notts County February 1957. Weymouth July 1962.
Bobby was a bargain signing from Midland League club Retford Town, whom he had joined almost by accident. He went to Retford with a friend to see a game and the two youngsters were asked to play. Bobby did well and signed just before Christmas 1952. His non-stop running made him popular at Elland Road and he scored on

his home debut – a 2–0 victory over Everton on 11 April 1953. He didn't feature in any of the first 12 games of the following season but returned with a bang, scoring a hat-trick in a 3–3 draw against Bristol Rovers. It was still not enough to nail a regular place and he moved on to Notts County whom he skippered to promotion to Division Three in 1959–60.

FURNESS William Isaac

Inside-left
Born: New Washington, Co. Durham, 8 June 1909
Died: Norwich, Norfolk, 29 August 1980
Career: Washington Colliery. Usworth Colliery. LEEDS UNITED £50 August 1928. Norwich City £2,700 June 1937–47 then assistant trainer, trainer and physiotherapist.

Billy represents one of United's best buys of all time. He was plucked from non-League football and developed into an England player. A busy and skilful inside-forward, former colliery clerk Billy quickly stamped his mark at Leeds where he formed a dangerous left-sided partnership with his Geordie pal, Tom Cochrane. As United won promotion to Division One in 1931–32, Billy had a golden autumn, scoring in eight successive League games. His consistent brilliance earned Billy his only cap against Italy in Rome in May 1933 when he was still only 23. He went on to score 62 goals in 243 League appearances for Leeds before joining Norwich, against whom he had fractured a collar bone in a FA Cup defeat in 1935, for a big fee. He did well at Norwich and settled in the Norfolk city, qualifying as a coach for the County FA in 1939 and went into business as an electrical masseur. Billy became physiotherapist and trainer at Carrow Road until retiring in June 1970.

GIBSON Archibald

Right-half
Born: Dailly, near Girvan, 30 December 1933
Career: Girvan High School. Coylston Juveniles. LEEDS UNITED May 1951. Scunthorpe United July 1960. Barnsley September 1964.

Archie was working as an apprentice joiner and playing for Ayrshire junior club Coylston Juveniles when he first came to United's attention. His outstanding performance in a Scottish Juvenile Cup semi-final at Falkirk sealed his move to Elland Road where his tackling and non-stop running served Leeds well. During his National Service with the RASC, Archie was based at Catterick in North Yorkshire and played for Northern Command. Initially an inside-forward, he was switched to a more defensive wing-half role with great success and spent the best part of five years as a United regular, moving on after relegation in 1960.

GILES Michael John

Midfield

Born: Cabra, Dublin, 6 January 1940

Career: Brunswick Street School, Dublin. St Colombus FC. Dublin and Republic of Ireland Schools. Dublin City (later Munster Victoria). The Leprechauns. Stella Maris. Home Farm. Manchester United amateur July 1956, professional November 1957. LEEDS UNITED £33,000 August 1963. West Bromwich Albion £48,000 player-manager June 1975–May 1977. Shamrock Rovers player-manager and executive director July 1977–February 1983. Philadelphia Fury (USA) January–June 1978. Vancouver Whitecaps (Canada) coach November 1980–December 1983. West Bromwich Albion manager February 1984–September 1985. Republic of Ireland player-manager October 1973–April 1980.

No Leeds player has passed a football better than Johnny. He could coax the ball any length, pace and angle to a teammate during his time in the midfield cockpit with Billy Bremner. The brilliant Irishman was a £33,000 steal from Manchester United, where he had recovered from a broken leg in his early days at Old Trafford to feature on the right wing in the 1963 FA

Cup Final victory over Leicester City – his final competitive game for the Red Devils. He was persuaded by Don Revie to drop down a division and that started off a 12-year love affair with Leeds as he succeeded Bobby Colins as the midfield string-puller alongside the driving force of Bremner. Johnny figured in all United's triumphs of the Revie glory years. When he played in the 1973 FA Cup Final against Sunderland, Johnny equalled the pre-war mark of Arsenal and Huddersfield forward Joe Hulme of appearing in five Finals. Allied to his acute football brain was a degree of steel and mental toughness, making him the complete midfielder. He also weighed in with 88 League goals for Leeds – many coming from the penalty spot. Johnny's last game in a Leeds shirt was the ill-fated European Cup Final against Bayern Munich. He had earlier been recommended by Revie to succeed him as manager. But the Leeds board opted for Brian Clough and Johnny was to go on to West Brom as player-manager, steering the

Baggies back to the First Division in his first season. Johnny is hailed as one of Ireland's all-time greats with 60 caps in a 19-year career, many of them as player-manager. He became his country's youngest international at the time when he made his debut against Sweden aged 18 years 361 days, scoring Ireland's opening goal in a 3–2 win in Dublin. He is the brother-in-law of World Cup winner Nobby Stiles, with whom he played at Old Trafford, and uncle of former Leeds player John Stiles. Johnny's father, Dicky, and son, Michael, also played for Shamrock. A well-respected newspaper columnist in Ireland, he is also a popular TV pundit, particularly when analysing the Irish national side.

GRAHAM Arthur

Left-winger
Born: Castlemilk, Glasgow, 26 October 1952
Career: Cambuslang Rangers. Aberdeen 1969–70. LEEDS UNITED £125,000 July 1977. Manchester United £45,000 August 1983. Bradford City June 1985, reserve and junior coach February 1987, caretaker manager January–February 1989, assistant manager and first-team coach February 1990. Halifax Town coach. LEEDS UNITED Academy coach.

Arthur was one of Jimmy Armfield's best-ever buys for Leeds. Fast and direct, he was a creator and scorer of goals. Arthur shot to prominence as a 17-year-old when he won a Scottish Cup medal with Aberdeen in 1970 in a 3–1 win over Celtic after playing just four Scottish League matches. The Will o' the Wisp winger was soon scaling the international ladder with youth and Under-23 appearances followed by the first of his 10 full Scottish caps. He also represented the Scottish League and won a Scottish League Cup winners' medal with the Dons before arriving at Elland Road. He scored hat-tricks against Valetta in the UEFA Cup, Wolves and Birmingham City

– the latter coming in six minutes at St Andrew's in 1978. After United were relegated he stayed on for one more season before a surprise move to Manchester United. Arthur joined Trevor Cherry at Bradford City and took up coaching at Valley Parade, where he also worked under Terry Yorath. He then coached at Halifax, where he had a physiotherapy business, and worked at the Leeds Academy at Thorp Arch. Arthur's brothers were also footballers. Tommy played for Motherwell, Aston Villa, Barnsley, Halifax Town, Doncaster Rovers and Scarborough, Jimmy turned out for Bradford City and Rochdale and David had games with Queen's Park.

GRAY Edwin 'Eddie'

Left-winger/Left-back
Born: Holyrood, Glasgow, 17 January 1948
Career: Glasgow and Scotland Schools. LEEDS UNITED amateur 1962, professional January 1965, player-manager May 1984–October 1985, retiring as a player May 1984. Whitby Town November 1985. Middlesbrough cs 1986 reserve and youth

team coach, Rochdale manager December 1986. Hull City manager June 1988–May 1989. Whitby Town manager September 1989–May 1990. LEEDS UNITED coaching staff March 1995, assistant manager May 2003, manager November 2003–May 2004, takes up a consultancy role.

Worshipped as a player and respected as a manager, Eddie's association with United spans more than 30 years. Eddie scored on his debut as a 17-year-old in a 3–0 win over Sheffield Wednesday on New Year's Day 1966. His career took off rapidly with two Under-23 caps, followed, in 1969, with his full Scottish debut against England. The following year he scored one of the greatest solo goals ever seen at Elland road with a series of drag-backs, feints and ball trickery scattering a series of Burnley defenders before firing home from just inside the box. The following week he gave a Man of the Match performance at Wembley in the drawn FA Cup Final at Wembley. Eddie could send his marker the wrong way simply by dropping one of his hunched shoulders, making to go one way and dribbling off in the opposite direction. The football world was at Eddie's feet but a series of bad injuries restricted him to just a dozen full Scottish internationals and he seemed bound for the departure gate when Brian Clough arrived for his torrid 44 days in charge. Clough's successor, Jimmy Armfield, helped get Eddie back to full fitness by arranging for him to assist with coaching the junior players. Eddie made a triumphant comeback in January 1975 and continued to sparkle on the left flank even though United were no longer the power that saw Eddie win League Championship, FA Cup, League Cup and Fairs Cup medals. His career was prolonged at left-back and continued in that role when he took over as player-manager following Allan Clarke's sacking in July 1982 – the first of two spells in charge of the club (see Managers section). Despite injury, he notched more than 550 appearances for Leeds, was never booked or sent off and was made an MBE in 1985. His son, Stuart, has played for Celtic, Morton, Reading and Rushden and son Nick was also on Leeds' books. Eddie played alongside brother Frank many times at Leeds and is also uncle to Frank's son, Andy. He was a Leeds United matchday analyst for Radio Leeds before joining the club's official radio station, Yorkshire Radio.

GRAY Francis Tierney

Left-back/Midfield

Born: Castlemilk, Glasgow, 27 October 1954

Career: Glasgow Schools. LEEDS UNITED apprentice May 1970, professional November 1971. Nottingham Forest £475,000 July 1979. LEEDS UNITED £300,000 May 1981. Sunderland £100,000 July 1985. Darlington player-coach cs 1989, retiring as a player 1991, then manager June 1991–February 1992. Blackburn Rovers and Sheffield Wednesday scout. Harrogate Town manager December 1993–June 1994. Al

Mananmah (Bahrain) manager June 1994–97. Southampton academy coach. Farnborough Town manager May 2005. Grays Athletic manager May 2006–October 2006. Woking manager May 2007–April 2008. Basingstoke Town manager May 2008–February 2010.

Frank followed elder brother Eddie on the path from Glasgow to Leeds and international stardom. Although not as skilful as Eddie, he won 32 caps for Scotland and did gain a European Cup winners medal with Nottingham Forest. Frank trained with Celtic as a kid and was a ball-boy at Parkhead but signed for United who beat off about 30 clubs for his signature. Frank emulated Eddie by scoring on his full debut – a 4–0 thumping of Crystal Palace on 21 April 1973. He starred in five Under-23 games and was equally at home on the left-side of midfield or at left-back but it was not until he joined Brian Clough's Nottingham Forest that he hit peak form, playing in the 1980 Forest side which beat Hamburg in the European Cup Final and Barcelona in the European Super Cup. Frank had cost Forest a record fee but after two seasons at the City Ground, he returned to Leeds for four more years, playing under his elder brother's management. Frank figured in the 1982 World Cup in Spain, but after topping 400 appearances for Leeds moved on to Sunderland where he won a Third Division Championship medal. He then helped Darlington to the Conference Championship in 1990 before moving into non-League management. His son, Andy, a Scottish international began his career at Leeds and has since played for a host of clubs including Nottingham Forest, Sunderland, Charlton, Burnley and Barnsley.

GREENHOFF James

Forward

Born: Barnsley, 19 June 1946

Career: Barnsley and Yorkshire Schools. LEEDS UNITED apprentice June 1961, professional August 1963. Birmingham City £70,000 August 1968. Stoke City £100,000 August 1969. Manchester United £120,000 November 1976. Crewe Alexandra December 1980. Toronto Blizzard (Canada) player-coach March 1981. Port Vale August 1981. Rochdale player-manager March 1983–March 1984. Port Vale coach March 1984, assistant manager April–May 1984.

Jimmy had the unusual experience of being transferred in the middle of a Cup Final. He had played in the first leg of the Fairs Cup Final in August 1968 when he came on as a sub against Ferencvaros, but by the time the return leg came around Jimmy was a Birmingham player. The blond-haired forward, who was in the Barnsley side which won the 1961 English Schools Trophy, was a highly rated member of the Elland Road squad, who scored valuable goals at home and abroad. He continued the trend at St Andrew's, scoring 11 times in his first 10 games, including four against Fulham when he also missed a penalty. Such stats earned

him an England Under-23 call-up and a further move to Stoke with whom he won a League Cup medal in 1972, four years after gaining one with Leeds. He was called up by Don Revie for the England squad, but pulled out because of club commitments and didn't get another chance to add to his England B and Football League representative honours. He joined Manchester United, aged 30, and scored the FA Cup Final winner against Liverpool in 1977. Jimmy had a brief stab at management and coaching before setting up his own insurance business in the Stoke area. Brother of Brian Greenhoff, they both played for Leeds and Manchester United, but never together.

HADDOCK Peter Murray

Defender/Midfield

Born: Newcastle upon Tyne, 9 December 1961

Career: Cramlington High School. South Northumberland Boys. Cramlington Juniors. Newcastle United apprentice June 1978, professional December 1979. Dunedin City (New Zealand) loan cs 1985. Burnley loan March–April 1986. LEEDS UNITED £45,000 July 1986–July 1992.

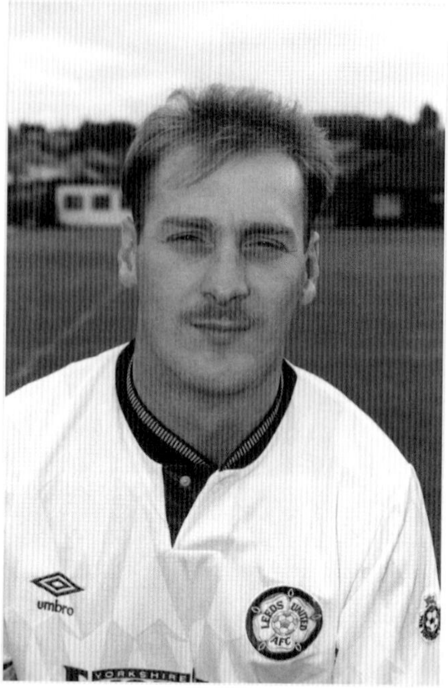

Peter was an undervalued member of the Leeds squad during the 1990 Second Division title success. 'Fish' took time to win over the fans after his move from Newcastle, but an ability to play in a variety of positions saw him pass the century mark in League games for Leeds. He looked most at home in central defence but a knee injury sustained in the League Cup semi-final second leg against Manchester United ended his career. His League debut for Newcastle as a 19-year-old came in dramatic circumstances. The Geordies' regular left-back was taken ill in London as the squad prepared for their game at QPR and Peter had to be rushed down to the capital on the morning of the game to fill in. After giving up the game through injury he sold insurance, ran a bakery, was a postman and worked as a courier.

HAIR Kenneth Grenville Arthur

Left-back
Born: Burton on Trent, Staffordshire, 16 November 1931
Died: Bradford, 7 March 1968
Career: Burton Technical High School. Newhall United. LEEDS UNITED November 1948. Wellington Town player-manager May 1964. Bradford City trainer February 1967, manager January 1968.

Had Grenville been with a more fashionable club in the 1950s then he could have been a contender for an England cap. He was a wonderful Leeds servant, notching up 443 League games after being signed from Burton and District League club Newhall United. A schools' athletics champion, Grenville also excelled at tennis and basketball, was super-fit, sharp in the tackle and a great distributor of the ball. He did his National Service alongside John Charles with the 12th Royal Lancers at Barnard Castle in North Yorkshire when they won the Northern Command trophy. A fine club ambassador, he gained FA recognition on tours to the West Indies in 1955, Nigeria and Ghana in 1958 and New Zealand in 1960. After learning the ropes as player-manager at Wellington Town he was trainer at Bradford City before taking over as boss at Valley Parade in 1968. Grenville was only in the hot-seat a matter of weeks when he collapsed and died, aged just 36, while supervising a City training session.

HARRIS Carl Stephen

Outside-right
Born: Neath, 3 November 1956
Career: Hengwert Primary and Cwrtsart Secondary Schools. Neath and Wales Schools. Britton Ferry. Burnley trial. LEEDS UNITED November 1973. Charlton Athletic £100,000 July 1982. Bury December 1985. Swansea City and Cardiff City trials July 1987, Airdrie trials August 1987. Rochdale January 1988. Exeter City December 1988. Britton Ferry player-manager 1992, later general manager to 1994.

Persistence paid off in United's pursuit of teenager Carl. The 16-year-old had been rejected by Burnley but Leeds took him on although within days he became homesick

and returned home to Wales to work in a factory. United persuaded the blazing fast winger to return and he zipped through the youth and Under-23 ranks and made his Leeds debut in the European Cup against Ujpest Doza in 1974. His League debut came five months later when he scored after coming on in a 2–1 home win over Ipswich. Eleven months later Carl won the first of his 24 caps but despite being a fairly regular performer for his country, he spent a lot of time on the subs' bench for Leeds. United's top scorer in 1980–81, he was transferred to Charlton after Leeds were relegated the following season. His patchy form with the London club was not helped by injuries, he was released and had a trial back at Leeds but was not re-signed. After football he ran a removals business in Neath.

HARRIS Joshua 'Joe'

Outside-left
Born: Glasgow, 5 November 1891
Died: Leeds, summer 1966

Career: Vale of Clyde. Ashfield. Burnley September 1910. Bristol City cs 1912. LEEDS UNITED July 1922. Fulham October 1925–28.

Joe was a mainstay of the 1923–24 Division Two Championship-winning side, providing loads of goals for Jack Swan and Joe Richmond from the left flank. An ever-present in United's first-ever Division One campaign, he spent three productive years at Elland Road. A product of Scottish junior football, Joe had made more than 200 appearances for Bristol City and played a lot of Army representative football. At Bristol he was suspended for a year and fined £50 for being paid while on amateur terms – but that did not stop the Robins from awarding him a £600 benefit before his move to Leeds. Joe's brother, Neil, played for Newcastle United and Scotland and nephew John played for Chelsea and later managed Sheffield United.

HART Ernest Arthur

Centre-half
Born: Overseal, Staffordshire, 3 January 1902
Died: Adwick le Street, near Doncaster, 21 July 1954
Career: Overseal School. Overseal Juniors. Woodlands Wesleyans. LEEDS UNITED cs 1920. Mansfield Town £350 August 1936–March 1937. Tunbridge Wells Rangers manager July 1938.

Ernie was one of United's all-time greats in the inter-war years, winning eight England caps. The solidly built former miner was signed by Arthur Fairclough from Doncaster junior club Woodlands Wesleyans shortly after United's formation. Some storming displays in the reserves saw Ernie quickly elevated to the first team at the age of 19. He spent 16 years at Elland Road, amassing 472 League and Cup appearances, many as captain. Hard but fair he was a better

passer than many of his defensive peers. A member of United's 1924 Second Division Championship-winning side, he was also in the promotion teams of 1928 and 1932. Ernie twice represented the Football League and toured South Africa with the FA in 1929. Ernie's cap tally could have been greater but for a lengthy ban after being sent off in the 1933 West Riding Cup Final against Huddersfield. He served a month's suspension, lost £32 in wages and was axed by the FA from the England tour to Italy and Switzerland.

HART Paul Anthony

Centre-half

Born: Golborne, near Manchester, 4 May 1953

Career: Manchester Boys. Stockport County apprentice June 1969, professional September 1970. Blackpool £25,000 June 1973. LEEDS UNITED £300,000 March 1978. Nottingham Forest May 1983. Sheffield Wednesday August 1985. Birmingham City December 1986. Notts County £15,000 player-coach June 1987. Chesterfield manager November 1988–January 1991. Grantham 1991. Nottingham Forest coach June 1991. Sheffield Wednesday coach 1994. LEEDS UNITED youth coach, acting as caretaker manager September 1996. Nottingham Forest coach and Youth Academy Director, manager July 2001–February 2004. Barnsley manager March 2004–March 2005. Rushden & Diamonds manager May–October 2006. Portsmouth director of youth operations March 2007, caretaker manager February 2009, manager July 2009–November 2009. Queen's Park Rangers manager December 2009–January 2010. Crystal Palace March 2010–May 2010. Swindon Town manager March 2011–April 2011. Charlton Athletic academy director June 2011.

When Gordon McQueen moved to Manchester United, Leeds brought in big Paul to fill his boots at centre-half. Although his early days were bedevilled by errors he settled in the core of the Leeds defence to become an excellent, powerful

stopper tipped for England honours. Paul, son of Manchester City inside-forward Johnny Hart, had an excellent club career but his only game at Birmingham saw him break a leg. Paul built a reputation as a fine coach and returned to Leeds to run the Youth Academy at Thorp Arch, enjoying a superb first year as his youngsters won the FA Youth Cup for the first time in the club's history. He even held the managerial fort for a few days after Howard Wilkinson left United, and although Paul's name was linked with managerial vacancies at Leeds, he didn't get the call. He's since managed a number of clubs, often called in to stave off the threat of relegation and work on a limited budget.

HARTE Ian Patrick

Left-back
Born: Drogheda, Ireland, 31 August 1977
Career: St Kevin's Boys, Drogheda. LEEDS UNITED apprentice, then professional December 1995. Levante (Spain) July 2004. Sunderland August 2007. Blackpool December 2008–February 2009. Carlisle United March 2009. Reading £100,000 August 2010.

When 18-year-old Ian came on for his Leeds debut in the Coca-Cola Cup against Reading in 1996 it completed an amazing family double as his uncle, Gary Kelly, himself only 21, was already on the pitch. In summer 1996 Ian earned his first full cap against Croatia yet the homesick Irish lad had been on the verge of leaving Leeds two months into his two-year apprenticeship. He stuck it out at Leeds and after playing in a variety of positions for the juniors and reserves settled in at left-back. Although not the quickest, he had great attacking flair and a left-foot capable of switching play in an instant. Once established in the Leeds side he became an adept free-kick and penalty scorer – something he was able to translate to international level. Ian figured for

the Republic in the 1998 and 2002 World Cup Finals. As Leeds went into decline after their Champions' League adventure, his form dipped and a move became inevitable, joining newly promoted Spanish outfit Levante. He later linked up with former Eire teammate Roy Keane at Sunderland before good spells with Carlisle and Reading where he showed he had not lost any of his deadball skills.

HARVEY David

Goalkeeper
Born: Leeds, 7 February 1948
Career: Foxwood and Seacroft Grange Schools, Leeds. LEEDS UNITED February 1965. Vancouver Whitecaps (Canada) £40,000 March 1979. Drogheda 1980–81. Vancouver Whitecaps (Canada) March 1980. LEEDS UNITED March 1983. Partick Thistle loan February 1985. Bradford City February 1985. Whitby Town player-manager May 1985–cs 1986. Harrogate Town 1987. Carlisle United non-contract 1987–88.

One of United's most popular goalkeepers, David served a long apprenticeship in the shadow of Gary Sprake. He worked in a shoe factory then joined his home club as a professional and made about 200 Central League appearances before Don Revie finally gave him a regular first-team place in 1971–72. He kept goal as United lifted the 1972 FA Cup and later in the year won the first of his 16 Scottish caps, qualifying because his father was born north of the border. A bad car accident in February 1975 saw him temporarily lose his place to David Stewart and he missed out on a European Cup Final appearance. After playing in Canada, David returned to Leeds in March 1983 as a 35-year-old and took over from the unsettled John Lukic. David went on to total 350 League games in his two spells with the Whites – a fine tally considering how many reserve games he played. He also packed a pretty powerful shot in training, but missed the penalty which saw United lose the 1974 Charity Shield to Liverpool in a shoot-out at Wembley. David had a variety of occupations including running a pub, delivering fruit and vegetables to hotels, being a postman and, finally, moving to a farmhouse and smallholding on the island of Sanday in the Orkneys.

HIRD Kevin

Full-back/midfield

Born: Colne, Lancashire, 11 February 1952

Career: Lord Street School, Colne. Blackburn Rovers, apprentice October 1970, professional February 1973. LEEDS UNITED £357,000 March 1979. Burnley free July 1984–May 1986. Colne Dynamoes cs 1986. Barnoldswick Town September 1991, Kelbrook. Blackburn Rovers academy coaching staff.

United paid a British record fee for a full-back when they signed Kevin from Blackburn. He was one of Jimmy Adamson's better buys, but the manager never seemed able to decide where to play him. Kevin's attacking instincts saw him thrust on the right wing where his mazy dribbling skills and long range shooting came in to play. Dubbed 'Jasper' by the fans because of his likeness to comedian Jasper Carrott, enigmatic Kevin never gave anything less than 100 per cent. He took on the responsibility of penalty taking and scored several spectacular goals, before dropping into Division Three with Burnley where he scored 21 League and

Cup goals from midfield in 1984–85 even though the Clarets were relegated. A cash crisis at Turf Moor saw Kevin's contract terminated and so he played local football while working for a timber merchants. Since then he has run his own soccer school in the Pendle area and coached at Blackburn's Centre of Excellence.

HODGSON Gordon

Centre-forward
Born: Johannesburg, South Africa, 16 April 1904
Died: Stoke, 14 June 1951
Career: Benoni (South Africa). Rustenburg (South Africa) 1921. Pretorian (South Africa) 1922–23. Transvaal (South Africa) 1924–25. Liverpool November 1925. Aston Villa £3,000 January 1936. LEEDS UNITED £1,500 March 1937, youth coach 1942. Hartlepools United and York City (Wartime guest). Port Vale manager October 1946–June 1951.

South African boilermaker Gordon was a powerhouse centre-forward with a fantastic scoring record in England. He joined Leeds when he was just a month short of his 34th birthday and remains the only United player to score five goals in a game – against Leicester City on 1 October 1938. In 86 League and Cup matches for Leeds he netted 51 goals and continued to lead the line during the war before going on to coach the club's younger players. Gordon shot to prominence on the South African national team's 1925 tour of England. Liverpool signed him and he banged in 233 goals in 258 League games for the Reds. Such stats brought him three England caps, four England Amateur appearances and three representative games for the Football League. Gordon arrived at Leeds after a short spell at Aston Villa and moved on from Elland Road to manage Port Vale and was still in office when he died of cancer, aged 47. An accomplished cricketer, Gordon was also a fast bowler with Lancashire CCC.

HOLLEY Tom

Centre-half
Born: Sunderland, 15 November 1913
Died: Leeds, 1992
6ft 2in, 13st (1938)
Career: Wolverhampton Boys. Sunderland. Barnsley September 1932. LEEDS UNITED £3,750 July 1936–cs 1949. Fulham (Wartime guest).

Big Tom came from excellent footballing stock. His dad, George, was a free-scoring inside-forward with Sunderland, winning 10 England caps. Tom was destined to follow in George's stud prints, starring for Wolverhampton Boys while he father was trainer at Molineux. George's beloved Sunderland signed Tom as a youngster, but he didn't make the first team. However, he established himself as a teak-tough centre-half with Barnsley and succeeded Bob Kane as United's stopper. He captained United and was an outstanding clubman, making 164 League appearances and 104 more in wartime. Tom saw active service in India and, together with George Ainsley,

was in an FA party who went to coach in Norway in summer 1946. He remained at Leeds a further three years before entering journalism and was a football writer for the *Yorkshire Evening Post* and the *Sunday People* before retiring to live in Majorca.

Picture: Ian Harber, *Morley Observer and Advertiser*.

HOWSON Jonathan

Midfield

Born: Morley, Leeds, 21 May 1988

Career: Morley Victoria Primary and Bruntcliffe High Schools. Churwell Lions. Leeds United School of Excellence. LEEDS UNITED from trainee July 2006. Norwich City £2 million January 2012.

One of the few shafts of light in the gloomy 2006–07 campaign was the emergence of local teenager Jonathan. He had signed a three-year deal under Kevin Blackwell in September, but didn't make his debut until he was 18 when Dennis Wise gave him his chance in the 0–0 home draw with Hull just before Christmas. He scored the last-gasp goal at Carlisle which took United to Wembley for the League One Play-offs and also came off the bench to net the equaliser against Bristol Rovers as United dramatically clinched promotion on the final day of the 2009–10 season. He gained England Under-21 honours that summer and went on to captain Leeds, developing into a midfield player of quality, prompting a £2 million move to the Premiership with Norwich City in January 2012.

HUNTER Norman

Defender

Born: Eighton Banks, Co. Durham, 24 October 1943

Career: Birtley Secondary Modern School. Birtley Juniors. Chester-le-Street. LEEDS UNITED apprentice November 1960, professional April 1961. Bristol City October 1976. Barnsley player-coach June 1979, manager September 1980–February 1984. West Bromwich Albion assistant manager. Rotherham United manager June 1985–December 1987. LEEDS UNITED coaching staff February 1988–October 1988. Bradford City assistant manager February 1989–February 1990.

Norman was one of the toughest competitors to pull on a Leeds shirt. The former electrical fitter certainly made the sparks fly with his tackling, prompting the popular phrase 'Norman Bites Yer Legs'. But that reputation overshadowed the fact that he was an outstanding player. He didn't look back after making his debut as a teenager in a 2–0 win at Swansea on 5 September 1962 and went on to be a bedrock of the Don Revie era. Norman was remarkably consistent, playing in five ever-present seasons during 14 years at Elland Road and featured in all United's League and Cup triumphs from 1965 to 1975, finishing with two League titles, FA Cup and League Cup winners' medals, two Fairs Cup winners medals and a Second Division Championship medal. The first Professional Footballers' Association Player of the Year, in 1973, Norman won three England Under-23 caps and 28 at senior level and would have won many more but for the presence of England captain Bobby Moore. Norman was the first England player to be capped as a substitute when he came on against West Germany in September 1966. He also represented the Football League six times before his glorious reign at Leeds ended in October 1976 when he joined Bristol City. He then worked as a player-coach under Allan Clarke at Barnsley, taking over the hot seat when Clarke became Leeds boss. Norman took the Tykes into Division Two, had a variety of managerial and assistant roles, as well as a spell back at Leeds on the coaching staff. He retired in 1983 and ran a couple of sports shops, sold life insurance and became a summariser on BBC Radio Leeds in 1993.

HYDES Arthur

Forward
Born: Barnsley, 24 November 1910
Died: Barnsley, June 1990
Career: Central School, Barnsley amateur 1928. Southport trial May 1929. Ardsley Recreation. LEEDS UNITED May 1930. Newport County May 1938. York City, Exeter City, Nottingham Forest, Barnsley and Bradford City (Wartime guest), Exeter City February 1946.

Former toffee factory worker Arthur gave defences a sticky time during his eight years at Leeds. After arriving from amateurs Ardsley, the spiky-haired forward fired in a stack on goals in the reserves and scored United's goal in a 3–1

defeat at Blackburn when he made his debut as a 19-year-old. Aggressive and speedy, he was United's top scorer for three successive seasons from 1933 to 1936. His finest game came in the FA Cup third round when his hat-trick at Newcastle gave Leeds a sparkling 3–0 win. Injuries left Arthur on the sidelines for a spell and he moved on to Newport where he was a leading light in the County side which won the 1938–39 Division Three South title.

IGGLEDEN Horatio 'Ray'

Inside-forward
Born: Hull, 17 March 1925
Died: Hull, 17 December 2003
6ft, 11st 10lb (1951)
Career: Constable Street Old Boys, Hull. Leicester City amateur July 1941, professional March 1942. Grimsby Town (Wartime guest). LEEDS UNITED player-exchange December 1948. Exeter City July 1955. Goole Town cs 1956.

Former Royal Marine Ray arrived at Elland Road from Leicester in an exchange deal with Ken Chisholm. United were certainly happy with their part of the bargain as Ray's partnership with winger Harold Williams was highly effective. Ray, a

former Hull dock worker, was United's top scorer in 1951–52 and grabbed a memorable hat-trick against his old club, Leicester, in January 1954. Strong in the air and the possessor of a powerful shot, he scored exactly half a century of goals for Leeds.

JENNINGS Thomas Hamilton Oliver

Centre-forward
Born: Strathaven, Lanarkshire, 8 March 1925
Died: Johnstone, Renfrewshire, 2 July 1973
Career: Strathaven Academy. Cadzow St Annes. Tottenham Hotspur trials. Raith Rovers January 1921. LEEDS UNITED March 1925. Chester June 1931. Bangor City manager. Third Lanark manager December 1934–39.

Tom held United's scoring records before John Charles burst on the scene. The Scot banged in 112 League goals for United with a seasonal best of 35 in 1926–27 when he netted three successive hat-tricks – a feat equalled only by West Brom's Gilbert

Allsop in 1939 and Liverpool's Jack Balmer in 1947. Despite Tom's deadly marksmanship, United were relegated that season. Tom continued to score at a rapid rate and would have added to his tally but was laid low by bouts of blood poisoning. It was surprising that he did not get the nod from the Scottish selectors, although he played in a trial, scoring for the Anglo-Scots in a 1–1 draw with the Home Scots in March 1928. As a youngster he won a Scottish Juvenile Cup winners' medal with Cadzow St Annes, but was rejected by Spurs after trials. Tom joined Raith, where his brother Charlie also played, and was a member of the Rovers team shipwrecked on route to the Canary Islands. After Leeds, Tom had a productive season with Chester before having a go at management.

JOHANNESON Albert Louis

Outside-left

Born: Johannesburg, South Africa, 13 March 1940

Died: Leeds, 29 September 1995

Career: Germiston Coloured School, Germiston Callies (South Africa). LEEDS UNITED trial January 1961, signing April 1961. York City July 1970–cs 1971.

Flying winger Albert was a twinkling star in the early days of the Revie era whose life ended in well-documented tragedy.

Nicknamed 'Hurry, Hurry' in his native South Africa, he was recommended to Leeds by a school teacher and arrived in Yorkshire at the height of winter 1961 but soon warmed to the task. The United staff were soon purring in admiration at his dazzling ball skills and blistering speed. Albert forced his way into the first team and was leading scorer when United swept to the 1964 Division Two title. The following year he became the first coloured player to feature in an FA Cup Final at Wembley when Leeds lost to Liverpool. Gradually, the emergence of Eddie Gray – and Albert's increasing reliance on alcohol – saw him nudged to the fringes of the action. The 'Black Flash', as Leeds fans called him, had a season at York before moving back to South Africa for a spell of coaching. He returned to Leeds where, unable to beat the bottle, he lost his personal battle and was found dead, aged 55, in his high-rise flat in Leeds in 1995, but for United fans the abiding memory of Albert will be of his explosive runs down the left wing. His nephew, Carl, became the British featherweight boxing champion.

JONES Michael David

Centre-forward

Born: Worksop, Nottinghamshire, 24 April 1945

Career: Priory Primary School, Worksop. Worksop Boys. Rotherham Boys. Dinnington Miners' Welfare. Sheffield United November 1962. LEEDS UNITED £100,000 September 1967–October 1975.

Three England caps, only one of them as a Leeds player, were scant reward for all the effort Mick put into the game. His partnership with Allan Clarke was a deadly formation with Mick's power, aggression and aerial power being the perfect foil for Clarke's rapier-like finishing skills. Mick excelled as a kid, once scoring 14 goals in a school game and was working in a cycle

factory when he joined Sheffield United. He won nine England Under-23 international caps and played twice for the full national team in May 1965, but was then discarded. Two years later he became Leeds' first £100,000 purchase and featured in the Whites' major triumphs of the period – two League Championship medals, two Fairs Cup winners' medals. He was one of the heroes of the FA Cup Final victory over Arsenal when he laid on the winner for Clarke. In the dying minutes he damaged a shoulder and had to be led up to the Royal Box with his arm in a sling by Norman Hunter to receive his winners' medal. Mick's form earned him an England recall against Holland but he wasn't required again after the 0–0 draw. After United's second title success he suffered a serious knee injury which brought a premature end to his career. He then had his own shop selling sportswear before running a market stall with his son selling sports clothing.

JORDAN Joseph

Centre-forward

Born: Carluke, Lanarkshire, 15 December 1951

Career: St Aidan's School, Wishaw. Blantyre Victoria. West Bromwich Albion trials. Greenock Morton October 1968. LEEDS UNITED £15,000 October 1970. Manchester United £350,000 January 1978. AC Milan (Italy) £325,000 July 1981. Verona (Italy) 1983. Southampton £100,000 August 1984. Bristol City February 1987, assistant player-manager November 1987, manager March 1988–June 1990. Heart of Midlothian manager September 1990–May 1993. Celtic assistant manager June 1993. Stoke City manager November 1993–September 1994. Bristol City manager November 1994–March 1997. Northern Ireland assistant manager 1998–2000. Huddersfield Town assistant manager and coach December 2000–May 2002. Southampton coach. Portsmouth coach, caretaker manager November 2004 and December 2005. Tottenham Hotspur first-team coach December 2008.

Joe was a superb successor to Mick Jones as leader of the United attack. An 18-year-old recruit from Morton on the recommendation of old Leeds favourite Bobby Collins, who was manager of the Greenock club, Joe gave up his job in an architect's office to be a pro footballer. Strong and brave, he was an unselfish and inspirational leader. His toothless grin earned him the nickname 'Jaws' and his development continued apace with his first Scottish cap in 1973. The following year he became a national hero when his goal against Czechoslovakia took Scotland to the World Cup Finals. Joe, who won 52 full caps and one at Under-23 level, collected a League Championship medal and played in the 1975 European Cup Final with Leeds before a record fee of £350,000 took him to Manchester United. He entered management with Bristol City, taking over from former Leeds teammate Terry Cooper and took the Robins to the Littlewood Cup semi-finals in 1989 and promotion from the Third Division the following year. Inducted into Scotland's Hall of Fame in 2005, he became a respected manager and coach.

KEETLEY Charles Frederick

Centre-forward
Born: Derby, 10 March 1906
Died: Derby, final quarter, 1979
Career: Alvaston & Boulton. LEEDS UNITED July 1927. Bradford City October 1934. Reading June 1935.

Former Rolls-Royce foundry worker Charlie was the youngest of a set of Derby brothers who played League football between the wars. Nine of his 10 brothers played for the same Victoria Ironworks team, but Charlie was at Alvaston & Boulton, where he hammered in 80 goals in 1926–27, triggering a move to Elland Road. He learned a lot from Tom Jennings and put it to good use in the reserves,

scoring seven goals in a Central League game against Bolton. Charlie, nicknamed Wag, made a scoring debut in Division Two and finished the 1927–28 promotion season with 18 goals from only 16 starts. He topped the club's scoring charts for three successive years and was reserve for the Football League against the Irish League in September 1932. He later returned to foundry life and also ran pubs in Derby and Chellaston. Of his brothers, Frank, Harold, Joe and Tom all played for Doncaster. Frank also aided Derby, while Albert played for Burton United, Jack assisted Hull City and Arthur was on Tottenham's books.

KELLY Gary Oliver

Right-back
Born: Drogheda, Ireland, 9 July 1974
Career: Home Farm. LEEDS UNITED July 1991–May 2007

From struggling reserve team front man to World Cup full-back – that was Gary's remarkable rise in 1993–94. The youngest of a family of 13, he was signed from Dublin club Home Farm. He was pitched into first-team action as a 17-year-old substitute winger in a League Cup tie against Scunthorpe, having only had 15

minutes of reserve team football under his belt. Apart from brief sub appearances, he did not re-emerge until the start of the 1993–94 season when Howard Wilkinson fielded him at right-back on the opening day at Manchester City. Gary's blinding speed and tenacity making him a daunting opponent for any winger and he matured so rapidly that within months Jack Charlton took him to the 1994 World Cup Finals. Gary netted in a 2–0 Irish win in Germany before opening his Leeds account but the one-club man, a rarity in the modern game, went on to top 500 games – even though he missed all of the 1998–99 season with shin splints. The holder of 52 Irish caps, Gary gained a deserved club testimonial against Celtic at Elland Road and donated the proceeds to build a cancer hospice, which he later opened, in his homeland after the disease had claimed the life of his sister. He often played in the same Leeds team as his nephew, Ian Harte.

KERFOOT Eric

Wing-half
Born: Ashton-under-Lyne, near Manchester, 31 July 1924
Died: 4 March 1980, Tameside, near Manchester
Career: Stalybridge Celtic. LEEDS UNITED December 1949. Chesterfield July 1959.

Eric took to Second Division football like a duck to water after joining from non-League football. He was 25 when he turned pro, having built an excellent reputation at Stalybridge. Leeds bid £3,000 for Eric – £1,000 more than Bradford City – and he proved a snip. After just one Central League game he made his full debut and became one of United's most consistent players, featuring in four ever-present seasons, including the 1955–56 promotion campaign. He had a spell as skipper before moving to Chesterfield where he was among 23 professionals released in summer 1960 after a poor season. He later ran a pub in Dukinfield.

KEWELL Harold

Forward/winger
Born: Smithfield, Sydney, Australia, 22 September 1978
Career: Smithfield Public School, Sydney. New South Wales Soccer Academy. LEEDS UNITED December 1995. Liverpool £5 million July 2003. Galatasaray (Turkey) July 2008–June 2011. Melbourne Victory August 2011.

Howard Wilkinson pulled off a masterstroke when he snapped up young Aussie Harry from the New South Wales Soccer Academy just before Christmas 1995. The youngster broke into the Leeds senior side as a left wing-back and was an integral part of the United side which won the 1997 Youth Cup. He made his international debut against Chile after just two Premiership appearances and his career took off after he switched to an attacking role. Instant control, dribbling skills at speed and fierce shooting marked him out as a star on the rise. His sensational form saw him named PFA Player of the Year in 2000 and he continued to sparkle in United's Champions League and UEFA Cup campaigns. But as Leeds went into decline the Wizard of Oz's form dipped – partly as a result of injuries – and he left the club in acrimonious circumstances with a row over his agent's cut of his transfer fee to Liverpool. He continued to battle against injuries at Anfield but won 2005

Picture: Ian Harber, *Morley Observer and Advertiser*.

Champions League Cup and 2006 FA Cup winners medals despite limping off in both games. His move from Liverpool to Galatasaray angered some Leeds fans as he had been at United when two Whites' fans were stabbed to death before the UEFA Cup semi-final against Galatasaray in Istanbul in 2000. The best player to come out of Australia, Harry played in the 2006 and 2010 World Cup Finals. He is married to actress and television presenter Sheree Murphy.

LORIMER Peter Patrick

Forward/midfield
Born: Broughty Ferry, Dundee, 14 December 1946
Career: Eastern and Stobswell Schools. Dundee Schools. Broughty YMCA. LEEDS UNITED amateur May 1962, professional December 1963. Cape Town City (South Africa) guest cs 1969. Toronto Blizzard (Canada) £25,000 March 1979. York City September 1979. Vancouver Whitecaps player-manager March 1980. LEEDS UNITED December 1983. Whitby Town December 1985. Hapoel Haifa (Israel) player-coach.

Peter's sledgehammer shooting terrorised defences for the best part of 20 years. He is the only player to have scored more than 200 goals for Leeds and is also the club's youngest debutant. Don Revie was in such a hurry to sign the Scottish teenager that he was stopped for speeding on his way north of the border. But Revie beat off a stack of other clubs to sign the young goal machine who had scored 176 goals in a season for his school team. Peter was just 15 years, 289 days old when he made his debut against Southampton in a Second Division game on 29 September 1962 and the Scottish Schools international won amateur caps on a tour of Kenya before turning pro on his 17th birthday. Peter was largely used on the right flank but his

ability to cut in and take a pot at goal spelled trouble for opposition defences as his shot had been measured at a staggering 90 miles an hour. Goals and domestic honours flowed in equal measure while Peter's return of 21 full caps and two at Under-23 level should have been greater. He did enjoy a fine World Cup in 1974 and, after a spell in Canada and a season at York, he rejoined United in December 1983. He was 37 at the time and older than his manager, Eddie Gray, but played a key role in midfield helping to nurture a talented crop of players. Peter overtook John Charles' goalscoring record in that second coming at Elland Road before being moved on by Gray's replacement, Billy Bremner. He later became mine host at the Commercial pub in Leeds and became a United board member in March 2004.

LUKIC Jovan 'John'

Goalkeeper
Born: Chesterfield, 11 December 1960
Career: Old Hall Junior and Newbold Green Secondary schools. Chesterfield and

Derbyshire Schools. LEEDS UNITED December 1978. Arsenal July 1983 £125,000. LEEDS UNITED £1 million May 1990. Arsenal July 1996–2001, coaching staff.

John topped 400 appearances for Leeds in two spells with the club. He learned his trade at Elland Road under David Harvey and when he broke into the League side at Brighton in October 1979 went on to make a club record 146 successive League games. His run ended when he asked for a transfer and was promptly dropped. Arsenal took him to Highbury where he won a 1988–89 Championship medal and a 1987 League Cup winners' medal. John won youth and Under-21 honours, but didn't gain a full cap. Howard Wilkinson brought John back to Leeds and was rewarded as his goalkeeper had a magnificent season when United won the League title in 1991–92. He then went back to Arsenal, retiring in 2001 and spent some time as the Gunners' goalkeeping coach.

McALLISTER Gary

Midfield

Born: Motherwell, 25 December 1964

Career: Fir Park Boys' Club. Motherwell 1981. Leicester City £250,000 August 1985. LEEDS UNITED £1 million July 1990. Coventry City £3 million July 1996, Liverpool free July 2000. Coventry City free player-manager April 2002–January 2004. LEEDS UNITED manager January 2008–December 2008. Middlesbrough first-team coach May 2010. Aston Villa assistant manager September 2010–June 2011.

Playmaker Gary was an articulate and intelligent figure in six seasons at Elland Road. After United won the Second Division, Howard Wilkinson invested £1 million in the rising Leicester City star to add to the midfield mix with Gordon Strachan, David Batty and Gary Speed. The international quartet were at the hub of some superb football as United pipped arch rivals Manchester United to the 1991–92 Championship. Gary's wonderful range of passing and long range shooting stamped him as one of Europe's best creative midfielders. He captained his country and won the vast majority of his 57 caps as a Leeds player. He had arrived from Leicester

after rejecting a £1.15 million move to Nottingham Forest because he was unimpressed by Brian Clough's blunt approach. Forest's loss was United's gain. He later had two spells at Coventry – the second as player-manager, with a highly successful time at Liverpool in the autumn of his career, winning the FA Cup, League Cup, UEFA Cup and European Super Cup in 2001. He was made an MBE the same year. He later rejoined Leeds as manager (see Managers section) for a brief spell.

McCABE James Joseph

Half-back
Born: Draperstown, near Derry, 17 September 1918
Died: Teesside, July 1989
Career: Billingham Synthonia Juniors. South Bank East End. Middlesbrough May 1937. LEEDS UNITED £10,000 and player-exchange March 1948. Peterborough May 1954.

Jim could fill a variety of positions but his best displays were at wing-half. He missed

a huge slice of his career to the war when he served with the Green Howards in France and the Middle East. He arrived from Middlesbrough with goalkeeper John Hodgson going in the opposite direction. Within months of arriving at Leeds, Jim won the first of six Irish caps and topped 150 appearances before moving to Peterborough.

McLEOD William

Centre-forward
Born: Hebburn, Co. Durham June 1887
Died: Newcastle upon Tyne second quarter 1939
Career: Hebburn Argyle. Peebles Rovers. Lincoln City £25 June 1906. LEEDS CITY £350 November 1906. Bradford City loan World War One, Notts County £1,250 October 1919. Doncaster Rovers cs 1921.

Billy was the undisputed king of City, holding both club goals and appearances records. He netted 177 times in 301 games and was City's top scorer for a remarkable nine consecutive seasons. Equally remarkable was the English selectors' failure to award him a full cap. Born of

Scottish parents he hailed from the North East town of Hebburn making his first big football impression with border club Peebles Rovers. Lincoln secretary-manager Jack Strawson bought Billy for £25 and stuck him straight in the first team. He scored in a 4–2 win on the opening day of the 1906–07 season and netted in both drawn games with Leeds City. Just 13 games and eight goals into the campaign, Lincoln netted a handsome profit as Gilbert Gillies persuaded the City directors to break the bank to get McLeod. It was a huge gamble on a 21-year-old but one that paid off handsomely. Billy had explosive shooting powers and bordered on the heroic when it came to getting his head on crosses. Goals flowed with his five-goal haul in a 6–2 win at Hull on 16 January 1915 being a highlight. Leeds newspapers campaigned to get Billy honoured at international level, but the nearest he got was as a non-playing reserve for a 2–0 win over Wales in Cardiff in 1914. He also suffered the same fate when the Football League played the Scottish League that year. He played a few City games in the war but most of the time was working at a Bradford engineering factory. He returned to Elland Road in peace-time and showed he had lost none of his old goalscoring magic. Fittingly he scored a hat-trick in City's final game at Wolves before being auctioned off with the rest of the squad. Not surprisingly Billy had the highest price on his head and went to Notts County for £1,250. His goal return at Meadow Lane was modest as the Magpies were relegated and the old Leeds hero, now 34, dropped in to the Midland League with Doncaster.

McQUEEN Gordon

Centre-half

Born: Kilburnie, Ayrshire, 26 June 1952

Career: Largs Thistle. Liverpool trials. Glasgow Rangers trials. St Mirren 1970. LEEDS UNITED £30,000 September 1972. Manchester United £495,000 February 1978. Seiko (Hong Kong) player-coach August 1985. Airdrie manager June 1987–May 1989. St Mirren coach June 1989. Middlesbrough reserve team coach July 1994, first-team coach 1999–June 2001, assistant scout April 2008.

Big Gordon succeeded the incomparable Jack Charlton in the Leeds number-five shirt. He was pretty raw when he arrived, but by the time he moved on to Manchester United for a then British record fee of £495,000 he was the finished article. Virtually unbeatable in the air, he was a massive presence in the heart of the Leeds defence where he weighed in a decent goal return from set-pieces. A cornerstone of the 1973–74 title success, he missed the following season's European Cup Final against Bayern Munich after being sent off in the semi-final at Barcelona. A bad Achilles tendon injury

caused him to miss much of the following season and his exit was on the cards after a bout of fisticuffs with goalkeeper David Harvey in an FA Cup tie against Manchester City at Elland Road. He soon followed Joe Jordan to Manchester United and was on the winning side in the 1983 FA Cup Final against Brighton. Gordon's father, Tom, was a goalkeeper with Hibernian, Berwick Rangers, East Fife and Accrington Stanley and Gordon was a 'keeper at school. Gordon was diagnosed with cancer of the larynx in October 2011.

MADELEY Paul Edward

Utility player
Born: Leeds, 20 September 1944
Career: Cross Flatts Park, Parkside Secondary and Leeds Schools. Middleton Parkside Youth. Farsley Celtic. LEEDS UNITED May 1962–May 1980.

Play-anywhere star Paul figured in every outfield position in a glittering 18-year career at Elland Road. The England Schools international worked in an insurance broker's office and played for

amateur side Farsley Celtic. Originally groomed as Jack Charlton's successor, the 'Rolls Royce' smoothly fitted into any position he was asked to fill by Don Revie. Ignored at Under-23 level, he did play for the Football League and toured Canada with an FA squad. He was omitted from the original 1970 World Cup squad for Mexico but when teammate Paul Reaney missed out with a broken leg, Paul was called-up but opted not to go. The following year he did win the first of his 24 caps and featured for his country at right-back, left-back, centre-half and midfield. In Leeds squads noted for their tough outlook, Paul was booked just twice in over 700 appearances in which he figured in all the major successes of the Revie years, scoring in the Fairs Cup Final against Juventus in Italy. In later seasons he was deployed solely as a defender, retiring in 1980 and kept an interest in the successful family home decor business. His elder brother, John, had a spell as chairman of Halifax Town.

MARTYN Anthony Nigel

Goalkeeper
Born: Bethel, near St Austell, Cornwall, 11 August 1966
Career: Cornwall Schools. Heavy Transport. Bugle. St Blazey. Bristol Rovers August 1987. Crystal Palace £1 million November 1989. LEEDS UNITED £2.25 million July 1996. Everton £500,000 September 2003–August 2006. Bradford City goalkeeping coach March 2007.

Nigel, the most expensive goalkeeper in United's history, was full value for his £2.25 million fee. Wonderfully consistent, he commanded his area with calm assurance, could produce breath-taking saves and had a superb sense of positioning. Twenty of his 23 England caps were won during his seven years at Elland Road and he also played for England B six

times and the Under-21s on 11 occasions. Nigel worked in a plastics factory and for a coal merchant when he played for St Blazey in the South-Western League. He was Britain's first £1 million goalie when he moved to Crystal Palace from Bristol Rovers and topped 300 games for the Selhurst Park side, winning promotions and playing in the 1990 FA Cup Final. He lost his place to Paul Robinson in 2001–02 and didn't play a senior game that season but enjoyed a renaissance at Everton where he took his career total to more than 800 matches before retiring due to injury.

MATTEO Dominic

Defender/midfield
Born: Dumfries, 28 April 1974
Career: Liverpool associate schoolboy September 1989, trainee June 1990, professional May 1992. Sunderland loan March 1995. LEEDS UNITED £4.75 million August 2000. Blackburn Rovers June 2004. Stoke City January 2007–May 2009.

Dom proved an inspirational leader in four roller-coaster years with United. He scored one of the most famous goals in the club's history when his header at AC Milan

secured a 1–1 draw which sent the Whites into the second phase of the Champions League. He went on to top a century of appearances for Leeds before moving on to Blackburn after relegation in 2004. Dom learned his trade at Liverpool where he won England B, Under-21 and Youth honours and was called into the senior squad by Glenn Hoddle but didn't figure at full international level. That could have worked in his favour when he was at Leeds as he became eligible for Scotland and figured in six games for the country of his birth. He called time on his international career because of injuries and didn't have too much luck with full fitness while at Blackburn or Stoke. Popular at Elland Road, he does some work behind the scenes for the club, is a noted after dinner speaker and is studying for his official coaching badges.

MEEK George

Winger
Born: Glasgow, 15 February 1934
Career: Thorniewood United. Hamilton Academicals 1951. LEEDS UNITED £500 August 1952. Walsall loan January 1954.

Leicester City £7,000 August 1960. Walsall July 1961. Dudley Town March 1965. Rushall Olympic cs 1965. Stourbridge Town.
Nippy little winger George fell just short of 200 appearances with United. Happy on either flank, he was good value for the £500 paid in two annual instalments to Hamilton Academicals. He did his National Service with the Royal Armoured Corps at Aldershot, spending time on loan at Walsall, and played for the Army against a Scottish XI at Ibrox in January 1955. On his return to Elland Road he played a key role in promotion to Division One in 1956. After a short spell at Leicester, twinkle-toes George served Walsall with some distinction and had an extended career in non-League football, working as a postman in Walsall.

MENZIES William John

Left-back
Born: Bucksburn, near Aberdeen, 10 July 1901

Died: Wharfedale, 3 January 1970
Career: Mugiemoss. LEEDS UNITED March 1922. Goole Town September 1933–34.
Bill was one of the unsung heroes of United's early history. He arrived on a month's trial from Scottish club Mugiemoss and after a fine debut went on to help United into Division One for the first time in their history. He first played for the senior side on a 2–2 Christmas Day draw at Oldham in 1923 and was virtually unchallenged for the left-back slot for the next six years. He relied on skill, rather than brawn, to clear his lines and after more than 250 games made his final appearance for the club in the last game of the 1931–32 promotion season. He later became a coach with the West Riding FA.

MILBURN George William

Right-back
Born: Ashington, Northumberland, 24 June 1910

Died: Chesterfield, Derbyshire, 24 June 1980
Career: Ashington. LEEDS UNITED March 1928. Chesterfield May 1937, assistant manager 1947. LEEDS UNITED and Yeovil Town (Wartime guest).

George was one of three full-back brothers who served United with great distinction. He started as a centre-half with his native Ashington but was converted to right-back and quickly dropped into the consistent groove which was a family hallmark. George partnered older brother Jack regularly – they were both ever-present in 1932–33 – until the emergence of Bert Sproston. George didn't moan about his demotion and went on to captain United to their only Central League Championship in 1936–37 before joining Chesterfield. When with the Spireites, George linked up with another brother, Stan, who became one of the few players to score a hat-trick of penalties, achieving the feat in a 4–2 victory over Sheffield Wednesday on 7 June 1947. George retired the same year and became Chesterfield's assistant manager.

MILBURN John 'Jack'

Left-back
Born: Ashington, Northumberland, 18 March 1908
Died: Leeds, 21 August 1979
Career: Spen Black and White. LEEDS UNITED November 1928. Norwich City £2,000 February 1939. Bolton Wanderers, LEEDS UNITED, Bradford City and Darlington (Wartime guest). Bradford City player-coach October 1946, player-manager January 1947–July 1948, then assistant manager until May 1949.

Jack was the oldest of the Milburn clan to represent Leeds and was as tough as old boots. He gave up a life in the North East coalfields to turn pro with United and started at Elland Road as a right-back but generally played on the left when he partnered brother George. Jack was a fierce tackler, master of the shoulder charge and possessed a thumping kick. He established himself as top-drawer penalty-taker, belting home a club record nine spot kicks

in 1935–36. Jack was rarely out of the side for 10 years in which he enjoyed three ever-present seasons on his way to 400-plus appearances. He also played for Leeds during the war, quickly recovering from a broken leg sustained against Barnsley in August 1943. At his peak Jack was touted for international honours and did go with England to Czechoslovakia and Hungary in 1934, but didn't get a game. He was married to United goalkeeper Jimmy Potts' sister, Isobella.

MILBURN James 'Jim'

Full-back
Born: Ashington, Northumberland, 21 September 1919
Died: Wakefield, January 1985
Career: Ashington. LEEDS UNITED November 1935. Bradford Park Avenue June 1952.

'Iron Man' Jim was the youngest of the famous Milburn full-backs. Like George, he was signed from Ashington, but there was to be no easy path to the first team. Although Jim was signed in November 1935 he didn't make a senior appearance until the final match of the aborted 1939–40 season – a 1–0 home defeat against Sheffield United. Jim had to wait another seven years for his next League game. After playing 52 wartime games with the club and seeing service in India before being wounded in Belgium, Jim, who also served with the Civil Defence, picked up the threads of his football career. He made up for lost time with a series of stirring displays and even had a run out at centre-forward when United were short of goals. After 208 League appearances he left for Bradford Park Avenue, severing a 24-year link between the three Milburns and United. However, the family ties were continued by their nephew, Jack Charlton, who was recommended to the club by Jim. For good measure, the Milburns' cousin, Jackie Milburn, was a legendary forward at Newcastle.

Picture: Ian Harber, *Morley Observer and Advertiser*.

MILLS Daniel John

Right-back
Born: Norwich, Norfolk, 18 May 1977
Career: Norwich City trainee, then professional November 1994. Charlton Athletic £350,000 March 1998. LEEDS UNITED £4.37 million July 1999. Middlesbrough loan August 2003. Manchester City free July 2004–July 2009. Hull City loan September–November 2006. Charlton Athletic August 2007. Derby County loan January 2008–February 2008.

Marauding full-back Danny peaked during his three seasons at Leeds. He had already won half a dozen Under-21 England caps with Charlton when a big money move took him to Elland Road. His development continued apace with Leeds, adding more Under-21 appearances before breaking into the full England set-up. After starring for Leeds at home and in Europe, Danny had an outstanding 2002 World Cup and won 19 full caps in all, the last few while on a season's loan at Middlesbrough as United had to offload their big earning stars. He won a Carling Cup winners' medal while at Boro in 2004. He announced his retirement in August 2009 and is a patron of the Association for Spina Bifida and Hydrocephaus, a condition from which his son, Archie, died in 2002. In 2010 he competed in the Brighton marathon in a wheelchair to raise money for ASBAH and the National Association of Disabled Supporters.

MITCHELL Thomas Morris

Outside-left
Born: Spennymoor, Co. Durham, 30 September 1899
Died: York, 22 November 1984
Career: Parkside United. Tudhoe United. Spennymoor United. Blyth Spartans. Newcastle United £100 May 1920. LEEDS UNITED £785 November 1926. York City September 1931–May 1933, manager March 1937–February 1950. Norway FA coach 1945. Yorkshire Schools coach.

Tom was one of United's most popular players of the inter-war years. The flying winger didn't play much football at school but was persuaded by mates to play for Durham area junior club Parkside United and when he was 21 was on Newcastle's

books. Mainly a reserve at St James' Park, he did win FA XI representative honours in 1924, but opted to join Leeds. That proved a wise decision, being an ever-present in the 1926–27 promotion season when his skill and speed delighted the crowds until he left for York in 1931, going on to manage the Minstermen. He coached in Norway for several summers and was stationed there briefly with the RAF in the war. He quit York in 1950 and set up a sports shop in the city – he had previously run one in Newcastle – later becoming a director of the Bootham Crescent club and ran a pub in Leeds.

NIGHTINGALE Albert

Inside-forward
Born: Thryberg, near Rotherham, 10 November 1923
Died: Liverpool, 26 February 2006
Career: Thurcroft. Sheffield United June 1941. Grimsby Town, Doncaster Rovers and Rotherham United (Wartime guest).

Huddersfield Town March 1948. Blackburn Rovers £12,000 October 1951. LEEDS UNITED October £10,000 1952.

Dashing inside-forward Albert put the fun into football. He had a sense of humour on the field and a great rapport with the fans at Leeds, who finally got their man at the third time of asking. United were twice beaten to his signature by Huddersfield and Blackburn, but a £10,000 bid secured his services from Rovers in October 1952. Albert marked his Leeds debut with a goal in a 2–1 defeat at one of his old clubs, Sheffield United. With his jet-black moustache and slicked back hair he was an instantly recognisable figure who made stamina sagging runs and his surges into the box won plenty of penalties. He was a great foil for John Charles and fell just short of half a century of Leeds goals – a landmark he would surely have reached but for a bad knee injury on the opening day of the 1956–57 season against Everton which proved his final League game. He then became a greenkeeper. His nephew, Lol Morgan, played for Huddersfield, Rotherham and Darlington.

O'GRADY Michael

Winger
Born: Leeds, 11 October 1942
Career: Corpus Christi School, Leeds. Huddersfield Town October 1959. LEEDS UNITED £30,000 October 1965. Wolverhampton Wanderers £80,000 September 1969. Birmingham City loan February 1972. Rotherham United November 1972–May 1974.

Mike was one that slipped through United's fingers as a kid. Although he was Leeds-born, it was at West Riding neighbours Huddersfield with whom he made his name, winning three England Under-23 caps. That proved the springboard for a full England cap, scoring twice in Belfast in October 1962 – and was promptly

dropped. Don Revie forked out £30,000 to take him back to his home-town club and although he didn't have the best of luck with injuries, he did make another England appearance, scoring again in a 5–0 win over France. He won a Fairs Cup winners' medal, a League Championship medal and scored one of the quickest goals in the club's history when he netted after 35 seconds in the 10–0 European Cup rout against Lyn Oslo. Within a few days of that quick-fire goal, transfer-listed Mike, who also represented the Football League three times, was on his way to Wolves.

OVERFIELD John

Winger

Born: Leeds, 14 May 1932

Career: Victoria Road School, Leeds. Ashley Road Methodists. Yorkshire Amateurs. Sheffield United trial. Bolton Wanderers trial. LEEDS UNITED May 1953. Sunderland £11,500 August 1960. Peterborough United February 1963. Bradford City July 1964–May 1965.

Tall, slimline winger Jack was nearly taken from under United's noses as a youngster. He trialled at both Sheffield United and

Bolton before the Leeds-born youngster joined the Elland Road set-up from Yorkshire League football. During his National Service he played in several RAF representative matches and on demob settled into United's 1955–56 promotion-winning side. He marked United's return to Division One with a goal against Everton after just two minutes of the new season in United's 5–1 victory. He played in every game in that campaign but the Everton goal was his only strike. He totalled 20 goals in 159 League appearances for United.

PEYTON Noel

Inside-forward

Born: Dublin, Ireland, 4 December 1935

Career: East Wall. Shamrock Rovers 1953. LEEDS UNITED £5,000 January 1958. York City £4,000 July 1963. Barnstaple Town

player-manager May 1965. St Patrick's Athletic.

Republic of Ireland schemer Noel clocked up a century of appearances for United. Speedy and skilful, he won five of his six full caps at Elland Road and a string of domestic honours with Shamrock including a Championship medal in 1957, and an FAI Cup winners medal the previous year. By the time he joined Leeds he had already turned out five times for the League of Ireland representative side and made his full international debut in a famous victory over West Germany.

POTTS James Forster

Goalkeeper

Born: Morpeth, Northumberland, 22 January 1904

Died: Northumberland, October 1986

Career: Blyth Spartans. Ashington Colliery. LEEDS UNITED February 1926. Port Vale May 1934–cs 1936.

The North-East has always been a rich seam of football talent for United and goalkeeper Jimmy fitted into that category. A brother-in-law of the famous Milburn clan, Jimmy worked as a coal hewer at Ashington before turning professional

with Leeds and made his debut in a 3–1 defeat at Huddersfield just two days after joining the Elland Road club. Athletic and powerful, he dominated his area for the best part of eight seasons, making him the best of United's 'keepers of the inter-war years. He was 35 when he moved to Port Vale where he missed just two games in two seasons before retiring.

POWELL Aubrey

Inside-forward

Born: Cynlais, near Pontardawe, 19 April 1918

Died: Methley, near Leeds, 27 January 2009

Career: Cwm Wanderers. Swansea Town amateur 1933 LEEDS UNITED November 1935. Everton £10,000 July 1948. Birmingham City £7,000 August 1950. Wellington Town August 1951–52.

Aubrey defied doctors' diagnosis to make a stirring comeback from a broken leg. After the fracture in United's game at Preston on 20 March 1937 he was told he would never play again but battled back to form a

highly effective partnership with David Cochrane until the outbreak of the war. Aubrey played 126 times for Leeds in wartime games and won his first official Welsh cap in October 1946. During the war he served in Belgium. A mazy dribbler, Aubrey, a compact little player, could pack a punch with his shooting but hard-up United sold him to Everton. After finishing his football days he worked as a confectionary rep in Leeds.

RADEBE Lucas Valeriu

Defender

Born: Soweto, Johannesburg, South Africa, 12 April 1969

Career: Bophuthatswana (South Africa). ICL Birds (South Africa). Kaiser Chiefs (South Africa) April 1990. LEEDS UNITED £250,000 August 1994–July 2005.

Versatile South African star Lucas is one of the most popular Leeds players of the post-Revie era. He was a marvellous ambassador for the club during his 11-years at Elland Road. He arrived with countryman Phil Masinga for £250,000 in summer 1994 – a gamble made by Howard Wilkinson which paid big dividends. Early injuries meant Lucas took time to find his best position but in 1996 he had settled as a defender and won an African Nations Cup winners' medal. A superb tackler and reader of the game he grew in stature both at Leeds and at home, making 70 appearances for his

country, many of them as skipper. 'The Chief', one of 14 children, played in the 1998 and 2002 World Cup Finals, and maintained a high level of performance in his 200 League games despite suffering from a succession of injuries in his last few seasons with Leeds. Originally a goalkeeper at junior club level in South Africa, he also pulled on the goalkeeping jersey during a couple of matches for United after injury to John Lukic and a red card for Mark Beeney. His testimonial attracted 38,000 to Elland Road and it was typical of the smiling Lucas that he shared the money raised between charities in Great Britain and Africa.

REANEY Paul

Right-back

Born: Fulham, London, 22 October 1944

Career: Cross Green School, Leeds. Middleton Parkside Juniors. LEEDS UNITED from groundstaff October 1961. Bradford City June 1978. Newcastle United (Australia) 1980.

Only Jack Charlton and Billy Bremner have played more games for Leeds than Paul. He was only a few weeks old when his family left London for Leeds where he attended Cross Green School and was an apprentice motor mechanic when he joined the United groundstaff in 1961.

Originally a winger, 'Speedy' Reaney made the number-two shirt his own, winning heaps of medals during his 17 years with the club. He was one of the best man-markers in the game and could also supplement the attack and provide pin-point crosses for the likes of Allan Clarke and Mick Jones. Three England caps and five at Under-23 level seem a poor reward for such a consistent performer. A broken leg at West Ham towards the end of the 1969–70 season forced Paul out of England's World Cup squad but he made a full recovery to give United further sterling service before moving on to Bradford City. He had a spell Down Under with New South Wales club Newcastle United and was named Australia's Player of the Year before returning to Yorkshire to run coaching courses at schools and holiday camps.

RITCHIE Andrew Timothy

Forward

Born: Manchester, 28 November 1960

Career: Moseley Grammar School and Stockport Schools. Whitside. Manchester United associate schoolboy October 1975, apprentice September 1977, professional December 1977. Brighton and Hove Albion £500,000 October 1980. LEEDS UNITED player-exchange March 1983. Oldham Athletic £50,000 August 1987. Scarborough player-coach August 1995. Oldham Athletic February 1997, player-manager May 1998, retired as a player July 2001. LEEDS UNITED Academy director October 2001–2003 Barnsley Academy manager April 2003, first-team coach March 2004, manager March 2005–November 2006. Huddersfield Town manager April 2007–April 2008.

Leeds suffered against Andy when he scored a hat-trick for Manchester United in March 1979. He won eight England Schools caps under skipper Brendan Ormsby and looked set for a lengthy career at Old Trafford after 13 goals in just 26 League starts but was surprisingly sold to Brighton where he won an England Under-21 cap against Poland. A swap deal with Terry Connor saw Andy arrive at Elland Road where he ran his socks off for the Whites' cause. 'Stitch' once scored six goals in a reserve game against Grimsby and netted 40 times in the League before his time at Leeds ended in a dispute over his contract. He was on a week-to-week contract before transferring to Oldham where he helped the Latics reach the League Cup Final and the old Second division title in 1991. He later returned to Boundary Park as player-manager, making his last appearance as a 40-year-old. Andy also guided Barnsley to promotion to the Championship via the Play-offs in 2006.

ROBINSON Paul William

Goalkeeper
Born: Beverley, 15 October 1979
Career: LEEDS UNITED from trainee May 1997. Tottenham Hotspur May 2004 £1.5 million. Blackburn Rovers July 2008 £3.5 million.

The promise shown by FA Youth Cup winner Paul bore rich fruit at Elland Road. He patiently bided his time, warming the bench as understudy to the excellent Nigel Martyn who sustained a rib injury against Roma which allowed agile Paul a run in the team. He showed that the number-one spot would be in safe hands with his superb reflexes saving the team many times. He also played his part in United's thrilling run to the Champions League semi-finals and won 11 Under-21 caps. After eventually taking over from Martyn on a regular basis, Paul won the first four of his full caps as a substitute and became England's first choice after joining Tottenham following United's relegation from the Premiership. A member of the Euro 2004 squad, he played in all England's games in the 2006 World Cup. He announced his retirement from international football in August 2010, having played 41 times for England. He is the only Leeds goalkeeper to score for the club in a first class game, his header from a stoppage time corner sending a League Cup tie against Swindon on 23 September 2003 into extra time, United eventually winning on penalties. He also scored for Spurs in 2007 with an 80-yard free-kick which bounced over the head of Watford 'keeper Ben Foster.

SCOTT John Alfred

Goalkeeper
Born: Crosby, near Whitehaven, 18 July 1928
Career: Crosby. Workington. LEEDS UNITED May 1950. Workington cs 1956.

Goalkeeper John was an ever-present in

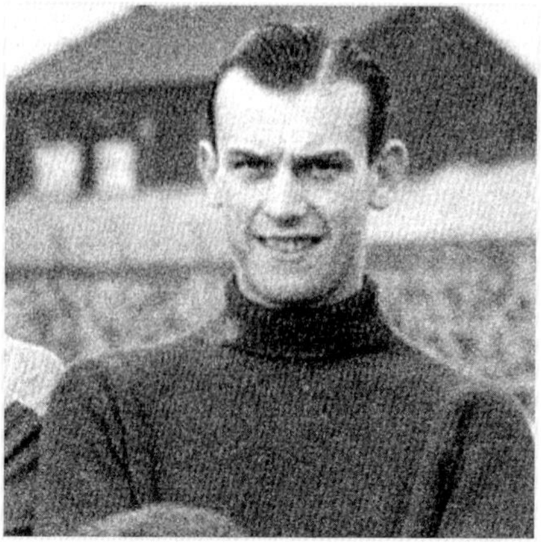

the 1952–53 season. A former blacksmith at Birkby Colliery in Cumberland, he was a fairly late starter in football. He didn't play much at school, but was bitten by the soccer bug when some pals asked him to go in goal for a kick-about. He was playing in the North Eastern League with Workington when he was invited to Hull for trials by Major Frank Buckley. John was not taken on but when the Major became Leeds boss, John joined the Elland Road roster. A noted golfer, he returned to Cumberland in summer 1956 and captained the county at golf.

SEARSON Harold Vincent

Goalkeeper
Born: Mansfield, 3 June 1924
Career: High Oakham, Mansfield and Nottinghamshire Schools. Bilsthorpe Colliery 1941. Sheffield Wednesday amateur 1942, professional August 1946. Mansfield Town June 1947. LEEDS UNITED £2,000 January 1949. York City November 1952. Corby Town cs 1954.

Harry contested the goalkeeping slot with John Scott before moving on to neighbours York. 'Polly' served with the Fleet Air Arm in India before becoming a footballer. He had a safe pair of hands and would pluck crosses out of the air with the greatest of ease before thumping the ball deep downfield. One of the few post-war players to play on his wedding day, Harry, a noted club cricketer, was football coach to Hunslet Boys' Club during his time at Elland Road.

SHERIDAN John Joseph

Midfield
Born: Stretford, Manchester, 1 October 1964
Career: St Mary's School, Manchester. Manchester City schoolboy. LEEDS UNITED March 1982. Nottingham Forest £650,000 August 1989. Sheffield Wednesday £500,000 November 1989. Birmingham City loan February 1996. Bolton Wanderers £180,000 November 1996. Doncaster Rovers cs 1998. Oldham Athletic October 1998, caretaker manager December 2003, assistant

manager March 2004, manager June 2006–March 2009. Chesterfield manager June 2009.

Teenage Manchester City discard John became a star performer with United. Within six months of arriving from Maine Road he stamped his authority on the Leeds midfield with a wonderful array of passing. He recovered from a broken leg at Barnsley in October 1983 to figure in over 250 games for the Whites. He played for the Republic of Ireland, through parental qualification, at all levels, making his senior debut in March 1988 against Romania and was in Jack Charlton's 1990 and 1994 World Cup squads, finishing with 34 caps. He spent three awkward months under Brian Clough at Nottingham Forest, where he didn't get a League game, before going to Sheffield Wednesday. John scored the only goal in the 1991 League Cup Final when the Owls beat Manchester United and won a First Division Championship with Bolton in 1997. He finished his playing career with Oldham at the age of 39 and later became boss of the Latics and Chesterfield with former Leeds striker Tommy Wright as his assistant. He took them to victory at Wembley in March 2012 with a 2–0 win over Swindon in the Johnstone's Paint Trophy. His brother, Darren, started on Leeds' books before playing for Barnsley.

SHERWIN Harry

Right-half

Born: Walsall, 11 October 1893

Died: Leeds, 8 January 1953

Career: Walsall Schools. Darlaston. Sunderland December 1913. Sunderland Rovers guest 1915–16. LEEDS CITY (Wartime guest) 1916–18. LEEDS UNITED May 1921. Barnsley March 1925. LEEDS UNITED assistant trainer June 1926. Bradford City trainer 1936.

Hard-nut Harry was a key component of the half-back line which provided the base

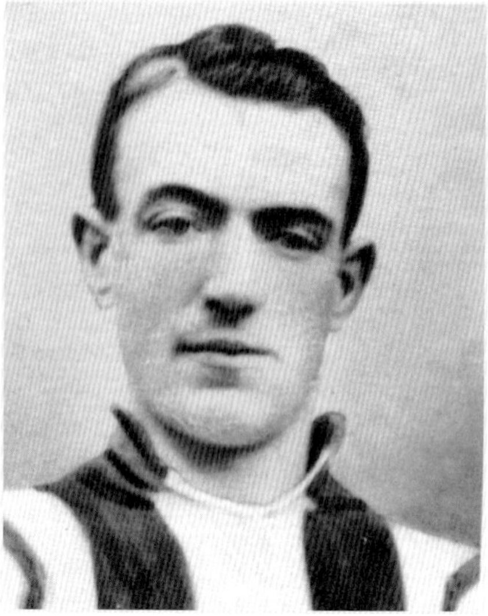

for United's 1923–24 Division Two Championship success. The son of a master chimney sweep, fierce-tackling Harry was certainly not afraid to clean-up opposition forwards. He played alongside Ernie Hart and Jim Baker for United and made 91 wartime appearances for Leeds City, including as an ever-present 1917–18 before returning to parent club Sunderland. After more than a century of United games he had just over a year at Barnsley before returning to Elland Road as assistant trainer. Harry also played against Wales in 1907 in England's first schoolboy international.

SMITH Alan

Forward

Born: Rothwell, near Leeds, 28 October 1980

Career: LEEDS UNITED trainee, then professional March 1998. Manchester United £7 million May 2004. Newcastle United £6 million August 2007. MK Dons loan January 2012.

Leeds fans were genuinely shocked when cult hero Alan joined arch-enemy Manchester United. His love-affair with the Whites ended in tears after relegation in 2004 and many supporters could not stomach his choice of new club. But there was never any doubting his commitment to Leeds' cause from the moment he burst on the scene in November 1998. After an England Under-18 tour to the Middle East was called off Alan found himself on the bench at Anfield, coming on to score with his first touch to cement a famous 3–1 win over Liverpool. The following week he came on to score on his home debut – a 4–1 win over Charlton – and his career was up and running. His aggressive style didn't give defenders a moment's peace and also earned him plenty of red cards. Fiery Alan won 10 Under-21 caps and won the first of his 17 full caps as a sub in a 4–0 win over Mexico at Derby in May 2001. Alan also had a spell on the right-side of midfield and although his goal output dipped he still netted 56 Leeds goals – including all four in a UEFA Cup victory over Hapoel Tel Aviv. After his £7 million transfer he soon won over sceptics at Old Trafford, but his career took a turn for the worse when he badly fractured an ankle against Liverpool in an FA Cup tie and after

Picture: Ian Harber, *Morley Observer and Advertiser*.

battling back to fitness found himself down the Red Devils' pecking order and moved on to Newcastle where he continued to have injury problems.

SNODGRASS Robert

Midfield/forward

Born: Glasgow, 7 September 1987

Career: Livingston from juniors July 2003. Stirling Albion loan January 2007. LEEDS UNITED July 2008.

One of the best moves by Gary McAllister during his short tenure in charge was to sign Scottish Under-21 international Robert on a free transfer. Signed from Livingston, Robert turned down a trial with Barcelona early in his career after being spotted in the 2006 Under-19 European Championships. He also rejected the chance to join Blackburn before turning professional. A superb ball carrier, he made an instant impact with United, scoring several stunning free-kicks and providing a string of assists for Jermaine Beckford and Luciano Becchio.

A member of the 2010 League One promotion side, he won his first full cap for Scotland as a substitute against Northern Ireland on 9 February 2011. He was appointed Leeds' captain in February 2012 by new manager Neil Warnock.

SNODIN Glynn

Full-back/midfield

Born: Rotherham, 14 February 1960

Career: Doncaster Rovers apprentice, then professional October 1977. Sheffield Wednesday £135,000 June 1985. LEEDS UNITED £150,000 July 1987. Oldham Athletic loan August 1991. Rotherham United loan February 1992. Hearts March 1992–May 1993. Barnsley July 1993. Carlisle United June 1995, retiring to become chief scout. Gainsborough Trinity 1995–96. Scarborough youth team manager June 1997. Doncaster Rovers coach 1998–2000. Charlton Athletic reserve team manager 2001. Southampton coach March 2006, then assistant manager. Northern Ireland assistant manager June 2007. West Ham United coach June 2007–September 2008. LEEDS UNITED first-team coach February 2009. Huddersfield Town first-team coach February 2012.

Glynn followed his brother Ian to Leeds – but the siblings didn't play in the same United side. The pair were developed by Doncaster where Glynn started as a 16-year-old. He played 300 times for Rovers, many of them alongside Ian, before the partnership split with Ian heading to Leeds in May 1985 and Glynn joining Sheffield Wednesday the following month. Two years later Glynn arrived at Elland Road where he played at full-back and in midfield. He knocked in some spectacular goals for Leeds, but glandular fever, a viral illness and injury meant he endured a stop-start time at Elland Road. He later became a respected coach – steering Charlton's reserves to regular title success before becoming a highly regarded coach with Southampton and West Ham while assisting ex-Leeds man Nigel Worthington on a part-time basis with Northern Ireland. He returned to Leeds to assist Simon Grayson in 2009.

SPEED Gary Andrew

Midfield

Born: Mancot, Flintshire, 8 September 1969

Died: Huntington, Cheshire, 27 November 2011

Career: Hawarden Grammar School. Blue Star. LEEDS UNITED trainee April 1986, professional June 1988. Everton £3.5 million July 1996. Newcastle United £5.5 million February 1998. Bolton Wanderers £750,000 July 2004, first-team coach May–October 2007. Sheffield United loan January 2008, player-coach then manager August 2010. Wales manager December 2010.

Gary made a massive contribution to United's success under the guidance of Howard Wilkinson and became one of the most respected players in the Premiership. He played for Manchester City's nursery

side Blue Star before being snapped up by Leeds. He got his first-team chance after scoring in 12 consecutive Northern Intermediate League games and didn't look back, making his mark in the 1990 promotion campaign. He provided the balance on the left-hand side of midfield, was ever-present in United's first season back in the top flight and missed just one game as United lifted the 1992 title. A complete all-rounder, whose ability in the air was an added bonus to his skill on the ground, he totalled 85 caps – just seven short of Neville Southall's Welsh record. United rejected a big bid from Everton in March 1996 but the Blues came back three months later with a deal that saw Gary join the club he supported as a boy. He left Goodison under a cloud but went on to give sterling service to Newcastle and Bolton, becoming the first player to break through the 400 and 500 appearance barriers in the Premiership. He was appointed the Welsh national team manager in December 2010. The football world was stunned when he was found hanged at his home on 27 November 2011. At Leeds' next home game, his fellow midfielders from the 1991–92 title winning side Gary McAllister, David Batty and Gordon Strachan laid a wreath in the Elland Road centre circle before the 2–0 win against Millwall.

SPRAKE Gareth

Goalkeeper

Born: Winch Wen, near Swansea, 3 April 1945

Career: Llansamlet School and Swansea Schools. Cwn Youth. LEEDS UNITED apprentice June 1960, professional May 1962. Birmingham City £100,000 October 1973–December 1975.

Gary made a flying start to his Leeds career – literally. He made his debut as a 16-year-old apprentice in dramatic circumstances when number one Tommy Younger had fallen ill on the eve of United's game at Southampton on 17 March 1962. Gary didn't get to know he was needed until five hours before kick-off when he was still in his digs in Leeds. He was whisked to Hampshire via taxi and plane from Manchester and got there for the kick-off

which was delayed by 15 minutes. United lost 4–1 but had unearthed a star in Gary who became first choice the following season. He became Wales' youngest-ever goalkeeper at 18 years 7 months and 17 days when he faced Scotland in November 1963. He won 37 Welsh caps, 32 of them as a Leeds player, plus five at Under-23 level. He was acrobatic and athletic, turning in one of his best performances in the 0–0 draw in Budapest which enabled United to beat Ferencvaros 1–0 on aggregate to lift the Fairs Cup. An ever-present in United's 1968–69 Championship-winning side, well-built Gary made more appearances than any other Leeds 'keeper with over 500 appearances. Much has been made in some quarters about his lack of concentration and mistakes – particularly the day he threw the ball into his own net at Liverpool in November 1966 – but they can't disguise the fact that he was an outstanding goalkeeper capable of pulling off impossible saves. After losing his place to David Harvey he moved on to Birmingham, but had to retire through illness. He's since suffered from heart problems which led to a couple of bypass operations and he retired in 1988 from his job as training officer for Solihull Council.

SPROSTON Bert

Right-back
Born: Elworth, near Sandbach, 22 June 1914
Died: Bolton, 27 January 2000
Career: Sandbach Ramblers. Huddersfield Town trials. LEEDS UNITED May 1933. Tottenham Hotspur £9,500 June 1938. Manchester City £9,500 December 1938. Aldershot, Wrexham, Port Vale and Millwall (Wartime guest). Ashton United August 1950. Bolton Wanderers trainer and scout July 1951.

Bert was a class-act at full-back and one of United's stars of the 1930s. After being rejected by Huddersfield as a kid, he played for non-League Sandbach from whom he joined Leeds as a 17-year-old. He didn't take long to get in the first team and won his first England cap in 1936 against Wales. By the time he was sold to Spurs for a near-record £9,500 he had represented his country eight times. He didn't settle in London and returned North to play for Manchester City six months later. He made an unusual debut for City, travelling up with the Tottenham party on Friday, completing his transfer that night, and turned out against his old team the following day. He won a Second Division Championship medal in 1946–47 to add to his 11 England caps, two wartime international appearances and Football League representative honours.

STEPHENSON Joseph Eric

Inside-left
Born: Bexleyheath, Kent, 4 September 1914
Died: Burma, 8 September 1944
Career: Tom Hood School, Leytonstone. Leeds Schools. Outwood Stormcocks. Harrogate 1931. LEEDS UNITED amateur January 1933, professional September 1934–September 1944.

England international Eric was tragically cut down in his prime while serving with the Gurkha Rifles in Burma. His parents moved to Leeds when he was a youngster and United picked him up from Harrogate, where his talent emerged in the Northern League. A creator, rather than taker of goals, he quickly rose through the ranks after turning pro and had a sparkling 1937–38 season, topped by a hat-trick in a 4–3 home win against Sunderland. Towards the end of the campaign Eric was rewarded with his England debut against Scotland and also played in a 7–0 win against Ireland in November 1938. He turned out for United in a couple of wartime seasons and the club played Celtic in a benefit game for his widow in 1946–47. Eric's younger brother also died in the war.

STERLAND Melvyn

Right-back
Born: Sheffield, 1 October 1961
Career: Waltheof School, Sheffield. Sheffield Wednesday apprentice June 1978, professional October 1979. Glasgow Rangers £800,000 March 1989. LEEDS UNITED £600,000 July 1989. Boston United player-manager cs 1994–May 1996. Denaby United. Stalybridge Celtic manager December 1997–May 1998. Hallam.

Buccaneering right-back Mel was a huge hit when he linked up with his old mentor Howard Wilkinson at Leeds. He had worked with Wilko at Sheffield Wednesday, whom he joined from school, and was immensely popular at Hillsborough. Owls fans dubbed him 'Zico' – a nickname which was transferred to Elland Road. Mel had played a key role in Wednesday's promotion to Division One in 1984 before a brief spell at Rangers where he won a Scottish League Championship medal. He opted to work for Wilkinson

again and provided United with tremendous thrust down the right flank, delivering pin-point crosses and long throw-ins for Lee Chapman to pile in the goals as well as booming in several efforts himself – many with thunderous free-kicks. Mel was a key component as Leeds stormed to the First and Second Division titles before injuries forced him to quit. Mel was capped once against Saudi Arabia and seven times by the Under-21s – all as a Wednesday player.

STORRIE James

Centre-forward

Born: Kirkintilloch, Lanarkshire, 31 March 1940

Career: Kilsyth Rangers. Airdrie December 1957. LEEDS UNITED £15,650 June 1962. Aberdeen February 1967. Rotherham United December 1967. Portsmouth December 1969. Aldershot loan February 1972. St Mirren player-coach October 1972. Waterlooville player-manager. Airdrie coach. St Johnstone manager 1976–78.

Jim's goals helped United establish themselves as a force to be reckoned with on their return to Division One in 1965. He had been a prolific marksman north of the border with Airdrie and commanded a decent fee when Don Revie signed him in summer 1962. He marked his debut with the winning goal at Stoke on the opening day on the new campaign and finished it with 25 goals. As Leeds gained momentum, he was top scorer as they finished runners-up on their return to the top flight, but after losing his place he went to Aberdeen and featured in the 1967 Scottish Cup Final, missing a penalty as the Dons lost 2–0 to Celtic.

STRACHAN Gordon David

Midfield

Born: Edinburgh, 9 February 1957

Career: Craigroyston and Edinburgh Schools. Dundee October 1971. Aberdeen £50,000 November 1977. Manchester United £500,000 August 1984. LEEDS UNITED £300,000 March 1989. Coventry

City March 1995, player-manager November 1996–June 1997, then manager to September 2001. Southampton manager October 2001–February 2004. Glasgow Celtic manager May 2005–May 2009. Middlesbrough manager October 2009–October 2010.

Gordon proved the catalyst which helped revive the Leeds glory days in the early 1990s. Howard Wilkinson pulled off a masterstroke when he signed the 32-year-old Scottish international from Manchester United. A revitalised Gordon was named skipper and was at the hub of the Leeds revival, lifting both the Second and First Division Championships and earned a recall to the national team despite being in the autumn of his career. Voted Footballer of the Year in 1991, he was supremely fit, physically and mentally, helped by a much publicised diet of seaweed pills and bananas. Blessed with supreme skill and stamina, his midfield combination with Gary McAllister, David Batty and Gary Speed will rank as one of the best-ever seen at Elland Road. Gordon could dribble, shoot with power, deliver free-kicks and corners to the inch and always seemed to play with a touch of cheek and fun. Copper-haired Gordon, made an OBE in New Year 1993, was strongly tipped to replace Wilkinson as boss, but he actually went on to extend his illustrious playing career at Coventry, where he also had his first taste of management. Gordon hung up his boots in June 1997 with 50 caps to his credit and a string of medals and honours with Aberdeen and Manchester United to add to his successes at Elland Road. A key figure in Scotland's 1982 and 1986 World Cup campaigns, he was Scottish Player of the Year in 1980. As a manager, he led Celtic to three successive Scottish League titles from 2006. His son, Gavin, a former Leeds YTS player, played for Gordon at Highfield Road.

SULLIVAN Neil

Goalkeeper

Born: Sutton, near Croydon, London, 24 February 1970.

Career: Wimbledon from trainee July 1988. Crystal Palace loan May 1992. Tottenham Hotspur June 2000. Chelsea August 2003. LEEDS UNITED August 2003. Doncaster Rovers loans November 2006 and February–April 2007, signing June 2007.

Neil, Chelsea's third-choice 'keeper, was one of the best of the free transfers picked up by Kevin Blackwell. He was a fine last line of defence for the two seasons immediately after relegation from the Premiership. An excellent shot-stopper, he saved four penalties in an ever-present 2004–05 campaign and even earned a recall to the Scotland national squad, but didn't add to his 27 caps. Prior to his arrival in Yorkshire he had spent all his time with London clubs, doing particularly well at Wimbledon for whom he played more than 200 times. Shortly after leaving Leeds he appeared in Doncaster's Johnstone's Paint Trophy Final-winning team at the Millennium Stadium, Cardiff, where he had suffered Play-off heartbreak the previous year with United. He was also in the Rovers side which beat Leeds in the League One Play-off Final at Wembley in 2008.

SWAN Jack

Forward
Born: Easington, Co. Durham, 10 July 1893
Died: Hendon, January 1990
Career: Seaham Harbour. Huddersfield Town October 1919. LEEDS UNITED November 1921. Watford £1,000 September 1925. Queen's Park Rangers £300 February 1927. Thames July 1928. Lovells Athletic October 1929.

Jack was United's top scorer in the 1923–24 Second Division Championship-winning campaign, averaging a goal every other game from 36 starts. Many of them were missile-like shots from his trusty left foot which brought him exactly 50 goals in Leeds colours. He first shot to prominence at neighbouring Huddersfield and playing in the 1920 FA Cup Final side which lost to Aston Villa. After losing his place in the Terriers' team to England international Clem Stephenson, who had guested for United in World War One, Jack was

transferred to Leeds. He went AWOL while at Elland Road and received a club suspension, suffering a similar fate at his next club, Watford. For a decade before his death he was the longest living FA Cup finalist.

TOWNSLEY Thomas

Centre-half/Right-back
Born: Reddingmuirhead, near Polmont, Stirlingshire, 28 April 1898
Died: Peterhead, Aberdeenshire, 10 April 1976
Career: Laurieston Villa. Cowie Wanderers. Falkirk August 1919. LEEDS UNITED £5,000 December 1925. Falkirk October 1951–June 1933. Bo'ness cs 1933. Peterhead player-coach September 1934, manager 1945, then groundsman until 1953.

Tom, the son of a coal miner, was a magnificent servant for Leeds, missing only four games in his three and a half seasons at Elland Road after making his debut in a 2–2 home draw with Burnley on

Christmas Day 1925. He was successfully converted from centre-half to right-back, a move that had a dual purpose – allowing the emerging Ernie Hart to take the central defensive role while Tom plugged the problematic right-back slot. Tom was a highly mobile defender and while at Falkirk played once for Scotland against Wales in October 1925 and turned out for the Scottish League XI four times. He had a second spell with Falkirk before becoming a special constable during World War Two in Peterhead where he ran a tobacconists' shop. He became Peterhead's manager for many years.

TURNBULL Robert

Outside-right
Born: South Bank, Middlesbrough, 17 December 1895
Died: Middlesbrough, 19 March 1952
Career: South Bank East End. Bradford Park Avenue January 1918. LEEDS UNITED May 1925. Rhyl September 1932–33. Smith's Dock.

United's fans were enraptured by Bobby's dazzling skills for six seasons. The right-winger gave many a full-back a sleepless night with his rapid footwork which brought him 45 goals in 204 League appearances in United colours. He began with amateur side South Bank East End and looked destined to join Middlesbrough. However, Boro missed out on his signature in unusual circumstances. Bradford Park Avenue arrived in Middlesbrough to play a benefit game for the relatives of Boro full-back Donald McLeod, who died in World War One. Avenue were a man short and Turnbull was persuaded to turn out for them, gave a brilliant display and was signed by Bradford straight after the match. He scored five times on his wartime debut for Avenue against Barnsley on New Year's Day 1918. He was capped against Ireland the following year and toured South Africa with an FA squad in 1920. After retiring from football he returned to Teesside to work for steel firm Dorman Long & Company.

TWOMEY James Francis

Goalkeeper
Born: Newry, Northern Ireland, 13 April 1914
Died: Leeds, 9 November 1984
Career: Newry Town. LEEDS UNITED December 1937. Halifax Town August 1949, later trainer-coach.

Jim had the curious honour of winning his first Irish cap while still a reserve at Leeds. As a youngster he was a skilful boxer and Gaelic footballer, but opted to pursue a soccer career and made his debut for Newry Town when he was only 15. He played twice for the Irish League and it was a brilliant display against the Football League at Blackpool in October 1937 that triggered the rush to sign him. Leeds boss Billy Hampson won the race and Jim gave up his job as a woodworking machinist to join United's payroll. Jim started life in Leeds reserves before making the breakthrough in March 1938. He played at Blackpool in a Central League game on the 12th, kept a clean sheet against Wales on his international debut on the 16th and made his Leeds senior debut three days later – also at Blackpool. Although he returned to his home town of Newry in the war, he returned to Leeds when peacetime football resumed and settled in the city. After finishing at Halifax Town he did some scouting for United and did a great deal of charity work for the Leeds United ex-Players Association.

VIDUKA Mark Anthony

Striker
Born: Melbourne, Australia, 9 October 1975
Career: Melbourne Knights (Australia) 1993. NK Croatia Zagreb (Croatia) 1995. Glasgow Celtic December 1998. LEEDS UNITED £6 million July 2000. Middlesbrough £4.5 million July 2004. Newcastle United free June 2007–May 2009.

Multi-talented Mark had all the weapons at his disposal to be a top class striker – sublime skill, heading prowess, power and no lack of pace for a big man. It brought him 72 goals in four years at Elland Road. The 'Duke' was unstoppable on his day as Liverpool found out on 4 November 2000 when he scored all United's goals as Leeds fought back from 2–1 down to win 4–3 at Elland Road. However, there were times when he looked disinterested and tended to score his goals in batches – his late flurry of 13 goals in the final 10 games of the 2002–03 staving off Premiership relegation for a year. Of Croatian and Ukranian descent, Mark was so good with Melbourne Knights that they named a stand after him. After three years with

Picture: Ian Harber, *Morley Observer and Advertiser*.

Zagreb he showcased his talents at Celtic before David O'Leary signed him for Leeds. After United's relegation from the top flight Mark was inevitably sold and teamed up with Jimmy-Floyd Hasslebaink in Middlesbrough's attack, helping Boro lift the League Cup and reach the 2006 UEFA Cup Final. He also skippered Australia in the 2006 World Cup Finals, 12 years after winning his first cap.

WAINSCOAT William Russell

Inside-left
Born: East Retford, Nottinghamshire, 28 July 1898
Died: Worthing, Sussex, July 1967
Career: Maltby Main. Barnsley March 1920. Middlesbrough £4,000 December 1923. LEEDS UNITED £2,000 March 1925. Hull City October 1931–34.

Russell reached his peak in his six years at Elland Road, winning an England cap against Scotland in April 1929. A classic inside-forward, he allied speed to slick passing and sharp-shooting to net 87 goals in 215 League games in United colours. He made a dream debut with his first League club, Barnsley, scoring a debut hat-trick against Fulham on 6 March 1920. He also scored on his Middlesbrough debut but after the Ayresome Park side were relegated he joined Leeds to stay in the First Division. The national selectors quickly sat up and took notice, taking Russell on the 1926 FA tour of Canada where he scored five in a game against Thunder Bay. Despite sustaining a broken nose and a triple fracture of an arm at Leeds, Russell's performances were rarely short of excellent. Aged 33, he joined Hull, helping the Tigers to the 1933 Third Division North title before retiring the following year. He then held a variety of jobs, including that of railway clerk, licensee, ran a shoe shop, confectioner's and drapery store. Russell was also a

splendid cricketer, turning out for Barnsley in the Yorkshire Council.

WALLACE Rodney Seymour

Forward
Born: Lewisham, London, 2 October 1969
Career: Southampton apprentice July 1986, professional April 1988. LEEDS UNITED £1.6 million June 1991. Glasgow Rangers July 1998. Bolton Wanderers September 2001. Gillingham August 2002–May 2004. Kingstonian Under-18s assistant manager January 2008. Molesey 2010. Epsom & Ewell reserve team coach October 2010.

Hot Rod, twin of Ray and brother of Danny, had pace to burn. The little forward's darting runs were the perfect complement to the raw power of Lee Chapman as the striking duo enjoyed a magnificent 1991–92 League Championship season. In September 1992 he was called up for an England trip to Spain, but injury prevented him from going. Rod won 11 Under-21 caps at Southampton and played a couple of times for England B but missed out on that elusive senior appearance. A thrilling individual player, his BBC 'Goal of the Season' against Tottenham in April 1994 ranks as one of the best solo goals ever seen at Elland Road, dribbling past a swathe of defenders in a long mazy run before curling home a wonderful shot from just inside the penalty area. After 66 Leeds first team goals Rod had great success in Scotland with Rangers.

WETHERALL David

Central defender

Born: Sheffield, 14 March 1971

Career: Sheffield Boys. Middlewood Rovers. Sheffield Wednesday July 1989. LEEDS UNITED £125,000 July 1991. Bradford City £1.4 million July 1999, player to May 2008, caretaker manager November 2003 and February 2007, reserve team manager cs 2008, reserve team and youth manager cs 2009, assistant manager February 2011. Football League head of youth development June 2011.

Chemistry student David had all the elements of a top class defender as a youngster – skills recognised by Howard Wilkinson when he was manager at Sheffield Wednesday. The England Schools captain joined the Owls, played three times for England Under-19s and played for the British Universities side which won a bronze medal in the World student Games at Sheffield. After Wilko took over at Leeds he raided his old club for David and Jon Newsome. David improved in leaps and bounds, peaking in the mid-1990s with a series of committed, powerful displays. Bradford paid a record fee to take him to Valley Parade where he was appointed to skipper and had a 12-year association with the club. He played more than 300 games for the Bantams and served them in a variety of coaching and managerial roles.

WHIPP Percy Leonard

Inside-forward
Born: Gorbals, Glasgow, 28 June 1893
Died: Ealing, London, final quarter 1962
Career: West London Old Boys. Ton Pentre cs 1920. Clapton Orient May 1921. Sunderland £500 May 1922. LEEDS UNITED £750 November 1922. Clapton Orient June 1927. Brentford May 1929. Swindon Town May 1930. Bath City August 1931.

Percy quickly repaid a chunk of the large transfer fee paid to Sunderland when he scored a United debut hat-trick against West Ham on 4 November 1922 and finished the season as top scorer. That was the start of five years at Leeds in which his clever play and decent goal return from inside-forward earned him the nickname 'The Arch General'. A member of the 1923–24 promotion side, he moved to Orient for a second spell after the arrival at Elland Road of Scottish international John White. Percy was a big financial gamble which had paid off, having made just one appearance at Sunderland where he was understudy to the great Charles Buchan. Although born in Glasgow, Percy, the son of a master mariner, was raised in London and first attracted interest among clubs in the capital with a man of the match display for a Hammersmith League XI against Fulham reserves. However, before the London clubs made their move, Percy went to Wales to turn pro with Ton Pentre, returning to London the following year for his first spell with Orient.

WHITE John

Inside-forward
Born: Coatbridge, Lanarkshire, 27 August 1897
Died: February 1986
Career: Bedley Juniors. Clyde 1914–15.

Albion Rovers 1920. Hearts £2,700 May 1922. LEEDS UNITED £5,600 February 1927. Hearts £2,350 August 1930. Margate 1934. Leith Athletic.

John became one of the most expensive footballers of his day when he joined Leeds from Hearts for £5,600. It was also a pretty profound statement by the United directors who were determined to stay in Division One. John arrived too late to save Arthur Fairclough's team from relegation but he prospered in Dick Ray's promotion side the following season when he missed just one game and top scored with 21 goals after the Leeds board rejected a £6,000 bid from Sheffield United midway through the campaign. John repaid their faith with some outstanding performances before rejoining Hearts at the age of 33. He had been a legend at Tynecastle where he was top scorer for five years running, netting 102 goals, including four in a game in three successive matches in 1925–26. He was Scotland's top scorer in 1922–23 and surprisingly only played three times for his country – once while at Albion Rovers and the other two at Hearts. He was one of four brothers to play professionally, one of the siblings being another Hearts hero, Willie White. John was brother-in-law of Andy Anderson, who also played for Hearts and Scotland.

WHYTE Christopher Anderson

Central-defender

Born: Islington, London, 2 September 1961

Career: Highbury Grove, Islington and Inner London Schools. Arsenal trainee August 1977, professional September 1978. Crystal Palace loan August 1984. Los Angeles Lazers (USA) cs 1986. West Bromwich Albion August 1988. LEEDS UNITED £400,000 June 1990. Birmingham City £250,000 August 1993. Coventry City loan December 1995. Charlton Athletic March 1996. Detroit Neon (USA) cs 1996. Leyton Orient January

1997. Oxford United February 1997. Rushden & Diamonds August 1997. Raleigh Capital Express (USA). Harlow Town November 1999. HyPS (Finland) 2000.

Dependable Chris played a key role in establishing Leeds back in the big time after the Second Division Championship was lifted in 1990. Chris' spell at Elland Road was the best of his career, showing great skills for a defender who was schooled at Arsenal. Although he won four England Under-21 caps when he was at Highbury, he found it hard to get in the Gunners' first team where future Leeds boss David O'Leary was the lynchpin in central defence. Chris was a rock-solid investment by Leeds but as he approached his mid-30s he found his place under threat from the likes of David Wetherall and Jon Newsome. He moved on to Birmingham where he won another Second Division title medal in 1995 and the following season played against Leeds in the Coca-Cola Cup semi-final, scoring an own-goal winner for United in the first leg.

WILLIAMS Harold

Winger

Born: Briton Ferry, Neath, 17 June 1924

Career: Bryn Hyfrd. Briton Ferry Athletic 1935–38. Swansea Town trials. Belfast Celtic and Cliftonville (Wartime guest). Briton Ferry Athletic 1946. Newport County November 1946. LEEDS UNITED £12,000 June 1949. Newport County March 1957. Bradford Park Avenue £750 July 1957, retiring December 1957.

Little Harold stood 5ft 4in in his size five boots but played like a Colossus on the wing for United. The flying milkman had been Leeds' tormentor-in-chief as minnows Newport County pulled off a stunning 3–1 FA Cup win at Elland Road in 1949. Harold had been up in the early hours of the morning on his milk round before skimming the cream of United's defence in the afternoon. Major Frank Buckley was determined to sign Harold, who had served on Royal Navy destroyer escorts in the Atlantic during the war, and finally got his man that summer. Leeds paid out a sizable fee, plus defender Roly Depear, to get the twice-capped Welsh international. Harold, who could play on either wing, was a fantastic dribbler with a quick turn of foot and a thumping shot. He won a couple more Welsh caps as a Leeds player, against Northern Ireland and Scotland, before breaking a leg against Everton in 1952. He bounced back to full fitness and contributed to United's 1956 promotion season before returning to Newport with 211 Leeds League games to his name. After football he kept a pub near Elland Road and later at Gildersome before retiring in 1986.

WOOD Royden

Goalkeeper

Born: Wallasey, Merseyside, 16 October 1930

Career: St George's School, Wallasey. Harrowby. New Brighton amateur. Clitheroe. LEEDS UNITED May 1952–cs 1959.

In the mid-1950s, Roy was a permanent fixture in goal for Leeds. He arrived from Lancashire Combination club Clitheroe

and proved a worthy successor to John Scott. Ever-present for two successive seasons (1955–56 and 1956–57), he missed only one game in 1957–58. All his 196 League games were as a United player and after being transfer-listed in 1959 he decided to retire and become a betting shop manager. Roy was also a member of the PFA management committee which negotiated the abolition of the maximum wage for players. Roy was a good all-round athlete who excelled at football and hockey and was regarded as one of the best wicketkeepers in the Leeds and District Cricket League during his time at Elland Road.

WOODGATE Jonathan Simon

Central defender
Born: Middlesbrough, 22 January 1980
Career: LEEDS UNITED trainee, then professional May 1997. Newcastle United £9 million January 2003. Real Madrid (Spain) £13.4 million August 2004. Middlesbrough loan August 2006, then £7 million April 2007. Tottenham Hotspur £7 million January 2008. Stoke City July 2011.

High-quality defender Jonathan emerged from United's FA Youth Cup-winning ranks to become a full England international. David O'Leary, himself a great centre-half, recognised Jonathan's talent and immediately promoted him to the first team after taking over the managerial reins from George Graham. A series of superb displays, marked by perfectly timed tackles, power in the air and all-round speed saw him win his first England cap at the age of 19 after his first season. A great career beckoned, but his football world came crashing down when he and Lee Bowyer were charged with causing actual bodily harm to a student following an incident in Leeds city centre – a charge they denied. Jonathan did not play during the protracted high-profile

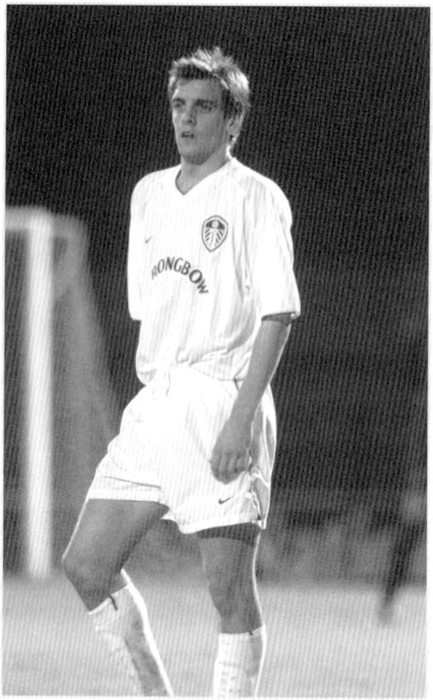

court case during which he was suspended by England. He was acquitted of the charge but found guilty of affray. He was also injured during this spell but did force his way back into the Leeds team and completed 100 League starts before the cash-strapped Whites sold him to Newcastle. He suffered badly from a succession of injuries with the Magpies, who netted a huge profit when he went to Real Madrid. More injury troubles saw him miss an entire La Liga season and his long-waited Real debut against Bilbao was a disaster as Jonathan scored an own-goal and was sent off. He did manage to establish himself in Spain and a loan move to his home town club, Middlesbrough, saw him hit peak form and an England recall. In 2008–09 he scored the winning goal for Spurs in the League Cup Final but injuries plagued his career at White Hart Lane and he moved to Stoke in 2011 on a pay-as-you play basis.

YEBOAH Anthony

Striker
Born: Kumasi, Ghana, 6 June 1966
Career: Kotoko Babies (Ghana). Omnibus Services Authority (Ghana). Neoplan Stars (Ghana). Kumasi Corner Stones (Ghana). Okwawu United (Ghana). Saarbrucken (Germany) 1988. Eintracht Frankfurt (Germany). LEEDS UNITED £3.4 million January 1995. Hamburg SV (Germany) £1 million September 1997. Al Hittad (Qatar) 2001–02.

Few strikers have made such a hard-hitting impact at Elland Road than African star Tony. He was a relatively unknown quality outside the Bundesliga where he had twice topped the scoring charts as he piled in 68 goals in 123 games. United broke their club transfer record to pay Eintracht Frankfurt £3.4 million for the Ghana star. He soon picked up the pace with Leeds, his 13 goals from 16 starts, including a hat-trick against Ipswich, speeding Leeds to a UEFA Cup place in 1996. Tony did not disappoint in Europe either, his spectacular hat-trick in Monte Carlo destroying Monaco, while the Premiership treble he notched at Wimbledon included a blistering volley. But topping the lot was the match-winning volley that sank Liverpool at Elland Road, voted by Leeds fans as United's greatest ever goal. Leeds had found a player of genuine star quality, but injuries, many sustained on international duty, saw the goals dry up. Tony's relationship with new manager George Graham deteriorated and the player burned his bridges when he threw his shirt at the bench and went straight down the tunnel as he was taken off by Graham in a 1–0 defeat at Tottenham in March 1997. He didn't pull on a Leeds first-team jersey again and despite 32 goals from just 61 starts returned to Germany, seeing out his playing days in Qatar before opening a hotel in Ghana, where he is a sporting icon, having scored 26 goals in 59 games for his country.

YORATH Terence Charles

Midfield
Born: Cardiff, 27 March 1950
Career: Cardiff and Wales Schools. LEEDS UNITED apprentice, then professional April 1967. Coventry City £125,000 August 1976. Tottenham Hotspur £265,000 August 1979. Vancouver Whitecaps (Canada) February 1981. Bradford City December 1982. Swansea City player-manager July 1986–February 1989, retiring as a player in 1987. Wales manager July 1988–December 1993. Bradford City manager February 1989. Swansea City manager March 1990. Cardiff City manager August 1994–March 1995. Lebanon manager 1995–97. Sheffield Wednesday coach cs 2000, manager October 2001–October 2002. Huddersfield Town assistant manager 2003–December 2006. Margate director of football June 2008, manager November 2008–September 2009.

If it wasn't for the longevity of Billy Bremner and Johnny Giles, tenacious midfielder Terry would have notched up more than his 200 appearance for Leeds. He was more noted at school as a rugby

union scrum-half, having trials for Cardiff Schools, but he settled down at the round ball game, playing for Cardiff and Wales Boys before joining the Elland Road groundstaff after turning down the two Bristol clubs and his native Cardiff. He had to wait patiently in the reserves and had only one senior game under his belt when he won his first full international cap in 1969 against Italy. A real ball-winning midfielder, he was a key component in the 1974 title-winning squad when Giles was out injured. Terry figured in the 1975 European Cup Final but his rugged skills were not always appreciated by United fans. He had a spell as captain under Jimmy Armfield and his leadership qualities blossomed at Coventry before joining the likes of Ossie Ardiles, Ricardo Villa and Glenn Hoddle in the Tottenham engine room. Of Terry's 59 full caps – 42 of them as skipper – the first 28 were won as a Leeds player. He then entered coaching and management, improving the fortunes of both Wales, whom he took to the brink of the 1994 World Cup Finals, and Lebanon, who rose 60 places in FIFA's world rankings under his stewardship. Terry's son, Daniel, tragically collapsed and died, aged 15, shortly before he was due to join United as an apprentice. One of his daughters, television sports presenter Gabby Logan, represented Wales at rhythmic gymnastics at the 1990 Commonwealth Games.

LEEDS MANAGERS

Leeds City
Gilbert Gillies 1905–08
Frank Scott-Walford 1908–12
Herbert Chapman 1912–19

Leeds United
Arthur Fairclough 1920–27
Dick Ray 1927–35
Billy Hampson 1935–47
Willis Edwards 1947–48
Frank Buckley 1948–53
Raich Carter 1953–58
Bill Lambton 1958–59
Jack Taylor 1959–61
Don Revie 1961–74
Brian Clough 1974
Jimmy Armfield 1974–78
Jock Stein 1978
Jimmy Adamson 1978–80
Allan Clarke 1980–82
Eddie Gray 1982–85
Billy Bremner 1985–88
Howard Wilkinson 1988–96
George Graham 1996–98
David O'Leary 1998–2002
Terry Venables 2002–03
Peter Reid 2003
Eddie Gray (caretaker) 2003–04
Kevin Blackwell 2004–06
Dennis Wise 2006–08
Gary McAllister 2008
Simon Grayson 2008 –12
Neil Warnock 2012 – to date

Gilbert Gillies 1906–08

There were more than 100 applicants for the post of manager of Leeds City when it was advertised. The man selected for the job was Gilbert Gillies, a journalist, who became the club's first-ever manager on 16 March 1905. He was given a three-year contract worth £156 a year.

As secretary-manager of Chesterfield, he played a key role in getting the Spireites elected to the Football League in 1899.

City came top of the voting when they were elected to the League and in his three years consolidated the club as a solid Second Division outfit.

Together with trainer George Swift, a former Loughborough left-back and Football League representative, Gillies attracted forwards of the calibre of Billy McLeod and Fred Croot.

Gillies, born at Glassary, Argyllshire, on 15 September 1869, was a superb organiser but felt he had under-achieved at Leeds. When his contract expired it was not immediately renewed and he took the manager's job at Bradford where he remained until February 1911. A former Football League referee, he was out of football by 1914 and running a hotel in Matlock, later becoming a licensed victualler. He died in Sheffield on 8 October 1957, aged 87.

Frank Scott-Walford 1908–12

Exactly three years after Gillies' appointment, City offered the job to Frank Scott-Walford, manager of a Southern League side.

Born in Perry Barr, Birmingham, in 1868, he was an amateur goalkeeper on Tottenham's books before joining Isthmian League club London Caledonians.

A forward thinker, he formed the Enfield and District League and became a Southern League referee.

Scott-Walford became Brighton's manager in March 1905 but soon found himself in hot water, approaching players of other clubs before their contracts had expired. He was suspended from management from 16 April until 1 August.

That ban did not deter City's directors who opened talks with Brighton to negotiate his release as he still had two years of his contract with the Sussex club to run. Brighton announced on 26 March 1908 that he would be leaving as soon as a replacement could be found.

Scott-Walford brought a posse of Brighton players with him – Jimmy Burnett, Davie Dougal, Dickie Joynes, Tom Rodger and Willie McDonald – but none made a lasting impression.

He then switched his attention to Ireland, bringing the likes of Joe Enright and Joe Moran across the water.

Many of the Irish acquisitions failed to make the grade and with little money to buy new players City began to struggle and were forced to apply for re-election at the end of the 1911–12 season, prompting Scott-Walford to quit.

He was manager at Coventry from 1913 to 1915 then dipped out of first class football and worked as a mechanical engineer. He died in Croydon on 27 June 1935.

Herbert Chapman 1912–19

Had Herbert Chapman remained with Leeds after the illegal payments scandal which led to City's expulsion from the Football League then the club could have gone on to great things. That theory was based on the staggering success he had

later at Arsenal and Huddersfield, setting both clubs on the road to a hat-trick of League Championships.

The son of a coal-miner from Kiveton Park, Sheffield, Chapman was born on 19 January 1878. He was a nomadic inside-forward who played for Kiveton Park, Ashton North End, Stalybridge, Rochdale, Grimsby, Swindon, Sheppey United and Worksop between 1897 and 1901 as he followed his career as a mining engineer.

Chapman did turn professional with Northampton Town, Notts County and Tottenham and it was in his second spell at Northampton that their directors recognised his tactical appreciation of the game and made him manager in 1907.

He steered Northampton to the 1909 Southern League title and was unveiled as manager-secretary of Leeds City in May 1912.

He successfully canvassed for City's re-election to the League and came within two points of clinching promotion in his first season in charge.

Receipts and profits were up and the directors were impressed with Chapman's ability to instill team spirit by getting players to speak their minds in team talks.

An innovator, he even had the top of his desk painted like a football pitch so he could explain his tactics to players and saw cricket and golf as ways of keeping his men trim in the summer months.

During the war Chapman worked at a munitions factory and although he returned to the club in 1918 he was suspended as investigations took place into illegal payments to wartime players.

Chapman quit on 16 December 1919 claiming he had been harshly dealt with by the FA Commission because he was not in office when the payments were allegedly made.

He became manager of an oil and coke firm in Selby and only after his appeal was upheld did he move back into management. He joined Huddersfield in September 1921 and won the 1922 FA Cup and the Division One title in 1924 and 1925.

Arsenal lured him to London in June 1925 and he repeated his success – guiding the Gunners to the League Championship in 1931 and 1933 and the FA Cup in 1930.

Chapman is also credited with introducing the 'stopper' centre-half to the game.

At the height of his managerial powers he was on a scouting mission when he caught pneumonia and died on 6 January 1934 – 12 days short of his 65th birthday.

Arthur Fairclough 1920–27

Division Two champions 1923–24

The directors of the newly formed Leeds United appointed former Huddersfield boss Arthur Fairclough as manager on 26 February 1920.

He was seen as the ideal man to rebuild the club after the dismissal of Leeds City from the Football League.

Fairclough named former City player Dick Ray as his assistant and the pair scoured the country looking for football talent as the new Leeds club, in effect, had to be started from scratch following the auction of the Leeds City players.

Fairclough, born in Redbrook, Barnsley, on 1 March 1873, had an outstanding football pedigree. He had to give up as a player with a Barnsley junior side in 1892 through ill-health, but four years later was elected to Barnsley's committee, becoming club secretary at Oakwell as Barnsley entered the Football League in 1898.

He quit the post three years later to concentrate on other business matters but returned to football in July 1902 when he

was elected to the Sheffield FA and returned to Barnsley in 1904 as manager-secretary.

Fairclough took the unfancied Tykes to the 1910 FA Cup Final which they lost to Newcastle after a replay, but two years later the South Yorkshire side were back in the final, this time beating West Brom 1–0 in a replay.

Fairclough, who was also a Football League referee, loved the game, his weekly wage of £2 being less than his club trainer and most of his players.

In April 1912 he moved to Huddersfield Town and laid down the base for Herbert Chapman to take the Terriers to outstanding success.

When Huddersfield chairman J. Hilton Crowther switched his allegiance to Leeds, Fairclough followed him to Elland Road, resigning as secretary-manager at Huddersfield just before Christmas 1919.

It was a big gamble, but Fairclough and Ray got United up and running and after Ray left to manage Doncaster, Fairclough brought in Dick Norman, the Blackpool boss, as his assistant.

Fairclough and Norman had worked in tandem at Barnsley and quickly made their mark at Leeds, steering the Peacocks into Division One for the first time in 1923–24.

Top names like Willis Edwards, Russell Wainscoat, Tom Jennings and Bobby Turnbull were brought in, but United found it tough going in the top flight and Fairclough quit after relegation in 1926–27.

He returned to Barnsley on 12 May 1929 as manager-secretary but resigned a year later. He became a Barnsley director in 1935, while Norman, his assistant at Leeds, went on to manager Hartlepools.

Fairclough, an important figure in United's history, died in Sheffield on 18 March 1948.

Dick Ray 1927–35

Division Two promotion 1927–28, 1931–32

Dick Ray served Leeds as a player, captain, committee man, secretary and manager.

Born in Newcastle-under-Lyme on 4 February 1896, Ray began his career in Macclesfield in 1893, joining Burslem Port Vale the following year, then Manchester City, Stockport County and Chesterfield before signing for Leeds City for the club's inaugural season in the Football League.

A solid left-back, he captained City in 1908, retiring in 1912. After City were expelled from the League, he was on the original committee which was formed to help get United started, running the Midland League side on a slimline budget before Arthur Fairclough was brought in.

He worked under Fairclough before becoming manager at Doncaster Rovers during their election to the Northern Section of the Third Division.

On Fairclough's resignation, Ray was appointed manager-secretary at Elland Road, responsible for both team selection and playing policy.

He developed the likes of Bert Sproston, Bill Furness, Eric Stephenson, Wilf Copping, Arthur Hydes, Tom Cochrane and the Milburn brothers – George and Jimmy – in his eight years at the helm.

Ray took United back into Division One in 1928 and two years later achieved fifth place – their highest since being formed.

They were relegated the following season, but the directors stood by Ray and were rewarded with immediate promotion.

Ray was appointed the first-ever team manager of a Football League XI as they drew 2–2 at Ibrox against the Scottish League in February 1934, receiving a gold medal for the honour.

On 5 March 1935 he decided he had taken Leeds as far as he could and quit his £1,000 a year job and the following month was installed as Bradford City's boss. He stayed at Valley Parade until the axe fell in February 1938.

After a spell scouting for Millwall, Ray ran a garage business in Leeds and also had an interest in billiards salons in the city.

Ray, who was also a fine cricketer with Bradford League club Laisterdyke, served in the RASC in World War One.

An outstanding servant at Elland Road, he died in St James' Hospital, Leeds, on 28 December 1952.

Billy Hampson 1935–47

Central League champions 1936–37

United's directors kept their early managerial appointments 'in house'.

Replacing Dick Ray was another Leeds City old boy, Billy Hampson, who was a regular guest for the club during World War One.

Born in Radcliffe on 26 August 1882, Hampson was a late developer as a player, figuring for Rochdale, Bury and Norwich before securing a £1,250 move to Newcastle in January 1914.

When St James' Park closed during the war, Hampson had a lengthy guest spell at Leeds before rejoining the Magpies and belatedly winning a first team place. At 41 years and eight months he became the

oldest FA Cup finalist when Newcastle beat Aston Villa in 1924.

He then played for South Shields from September 1927 to March 1930 before entering management at Carlisle where he is credited with discovering Bill Shankly. After a spell in charge at Ashington he took the job at Elland Road, consolidating their status as a solid First division side.

Trips to Ireland to sign Jim Twomey, David Cochrane and Bobby Browne all paid dividends, while he continued to strengthen his pool of players with a blend of experience and youth. That helped the reserves win the Central League title for the first and only time in the club's history in 1936–37 but World War Two prevented many of those younger players reaching full football maturity.

Perhaps reflecting on his own longevity as a player, Hampson stood by his loyal squad when peacetime football returned, but age had caught up with several key players and United suffered their worst-ever season in 1946–47, finishing bottom of Division One with only six wins.

Hampson stepped down and was made chief scout but only held the post for eight months and later worked as a coach for the Northumberland Schools FA.

Hampson, who died on 23 February 1966, at Congleton, Cheshire, had two footballing brothers Tom (West Ham) and Walker (Charlton).

Willis Edwards 1947–48

Leeds legend Willis Edwards took over from Hampson in April 1947 as their nightmare campaign was drawing to a close.

The former England hero had been assistant to trainer Bob Roxburgh with prime responsibility for the Central League side immediately after the war.

Edwards faced a massive task as he overhauled an aging squad. Although he improved fitness and lowered the age of the team, the 1947–48 season was mainly one of struggle. United dabbled with relegation for a while before finishing 18th and the decision was taken to move him back to assistant trainer in April 1948 after 12 months in charge.

Edwards remained on the backroom staff for well over a decade, expanding his association with the club to 35 years.

He died, aged 85, in Leeds on 27 September 1988, having spent the last years of his working life employed in a jam factory.

Frank Buckley 1948–53

United were at a low ebb when new go-ahead chairman Sam Bolton named one of the best-known people in football – Major Frank Buckley – as the new manager.

Bolton, a motor haulage contractor, had trials with Leeds City as a youngster and rose from United fan to director in 1945. Three years on, he chose the 64-year-old Buckley to revive the club's fortunes. The charismatic Buckley had a forceful style of management and was regarded as an innovator.

Born in Urmston, Manchester, on 9 November 1883, he played at centre-half for Aston Villa, Brighton, Manchester United, Manchester City, Birmingham, Derby County and Bradford City, winning an England cap against Ireland in 1914.

He had fought in the Boer War and in World War One joined the 17th Middlesex Regiment, reaching the rank of Major in 1916, commanding the Footballers' Battalion, which was made up of soccer professionals.

His first managerial job was with Norwich City before they joined the Football League. After a stint as a commercial traveller he was appointed boss at Blackpool in October 1923 and in summer 1927 stepped up to run Wolves.

At Molineux he developed a fine youth policy and took the Wanderers from the lower reaches of Division Two to Division One runners-up and an FA Cup Final.

In February 1944 he broke a contract for life to join Notts County for £4,000 and within hours of his resignation at Meadow Lane in January 1946, he took charge at Hull from where he joined Leeds.

Life at Elland Road was never dull with the Major around.

In an attempt to improve his squad's balance and mobility, he introduced dance sessions on the pitch where players paired up to strut their stuff to the music coming over the public address system.

A mechanical kicking machine was installed to improve heading, trapping, volleying and goal-kicking. To prove his own fitness he did press-ups and high-kicking tricks in the dressing room, much to the embarrassment of some of the less nimble senior players.

At Wolves he had created a sensation by treating his players with monkey-gland extract to sharpen their thinking and re-introduced a more advance form of the tonic at Leeds, although no one could say if it worked.

Despite all these high-profile innovations, United continued to struggle and an embarrassing FA Cup third round home defeat against Newport put Buckley under pressure. He didn't flinch and despite criticism for selling internationals Con Martin and Aubrey Powell, pinned his faith in youth.

Gradually United's fortunes turned. In 1950 Buckley took them to the FA Cup sixth round for the first time in their history and had unearthed a world star in Welsh teenager John Charles.

Buckley switched Charles between defence and attack, but despite the giant Welshman's massive influence, United continually missed out on promotion. At least Buckley managed to hold on to Charles as clubs were constantly knocking at United's door.

In April 1953 the Major felt as though he had taken Leeds as far as he could and, at the age of 70, became Walsall's manager, bowing out of the game two years later.

Buckley died, aged 84, on 22 December 1964 in Walsall.

Raich Carter 1953–58

Division Two promotion 1955–56

Just as he had done at Hull five years earlier, former England inside-forward Raich Carter took over the manager's post at Leeds from Frank Buckley.

The former apprentice engineer won 13 full England caps and was dubbed the 'silver-haired maestro' as his supreme passing ability saw him dictate matches.

Horatio Stratton Carter was born in Sunderland on 21 December 1913, and played international schoolboy football before joining his hometown club as an amateur in 1930.

He sparkled for the Rokerites and Derby County, becoming the only player either side of World War Two to win FA Cup winners' medals and skippered Sunderland to the First Division title.

The master tactician transferred his on-field knowledge to management at Hull where he was appointed player-manager in 1948 when Buckley moved on to Leeds.

Carter ended his playing career with 218 goals in 451 games and soon made an impact at Boothferry Park, buying and selling fellow England star Don Revie, and took the Tigers to the Division Three North title in 1949.

He resigned in September 1951 to run a sweet shop in Hull but was lured out of retirement by the Tigers as they faced relegation.

He later moved to Ireland where he took Cork Athletic to the 1953 FA of Ireland Cup Final.

At Leeds he built the team around the brilliance of John Charles and finally ended United's nine stagnant seasons by taking the club into the First Division in 1956 – clinching promotion with victory at Boothferry Park.

Pressure continued to mount on the Leeds board to sell Charles and they finally gave in when Italian giants Juventus made a £65,000 offer that was too good to be true.

Charles was irreplaceable and predictably United had a fight on to stay up and slipped to 17th in 1957–58. Less predictable was the decision to dispense with Carter's services after his five-year contract came up for renewal at the end of the campaign.

Carter, who claimed that he was only given half the Charles cash to buy players, was appointed manager of Mansfield Town in February 1960 and got them promoted from Division Four before being appointed Middlesbrough's boss, staying at Ayresome Park for just over three years.

He left football in February 1966 and later became manager of a sports section at a department store in Hull.

Carter, who also played cricket for Derbyshire and Durham, died in Hull on 9 October 1994.

Bill Lambton 1958–59

After having some relatively big names at the helm, United opted for a lower-profile man to be their fifth post-war manager – Bill Lambton.

Although he was only in office for three months, he is credited with bringing Don Revie to Elland Road.

Born in Nottingham on 2 December 1914, Lambton was a goalkeeper with Nottingham Forest, Exeter and Doncaster, before concentrating on coaching.

A fitness fanatic, Lambton helped keep British amateur boxers in trim while he was coaching in Denmark.

On his return to England he coached Scunthorpe United and among his unorthodox training methods were trampolining sessions aimed at keeping players fit and supple.

Lambton was 43 when Carter appointed him trainer coach at Leeds in November 1957, taking over from the venerable Bob Roxburgh, who had been trainer since the mid-1930s.

As Carter departed, Lambton was installed as caretaker-manager before being officially handed control on 9 December 1958.

Lambton's training methods did not always win the directors' approval and he quit after only three months.

However, by that time he had signed Revie from Sunderland and appointed him skipper after Irish international Wilbur Cush gave up the team's leadership.

Lambton's next managerial appointment was even shorter than his tenure at Leeds. In April 1959 he spent just three days in charge at Scunthorpe, although his appointment had only been verbal.

He was later in office at Chester (November 1961–July 1963).

Lambton died at his home in Sherwood, Nottingham, on 16 September 1976, aged 61.

Jack Taylor 1959–61

United were in a state of flux after Lambton's departure and the managerial picture became no clearer as the Peacocks sought his successor.

Arthur Turner, the Headington United manager and former Birmingham boss, was red-hot favourite and the United programme even announced his imminent arrival. However, he was persuaded to stay at Headington where, as Oxford United, he helped them gain admission to the Football League.

Out of the confusion, Barnsley-born Jack Taylor, the QPR chief, was appointed Leeds manager in May 1959. Taylor had played for Frank Buckley at Wolves in the 1930s and later turned out for Norwich. His first stab at management came at Southern League club Weymouth and in June 1952 replaced former Leeds forward Dave Mangall as manager at QPR.

For nine years he did a steady job with Rangers and the Leeds board thought he would be just the man to steady the ship at Elland Road after what had been a fairly unstable period.

But within a year United were relegated and with Taylor unable to shore up a shaky defence and making little headway to regain their top flight status, Taylor resigned on 13 March 1961.

He still had a year of his £2,000-per-annum contract to run and drifted out of football. Taylor died in Barnsley on 22 February 1978, one week after his 64th birthday.

Don Revie 1961–74

Division Two champions 1963–64. FA Cup winners 1972, FA Cup finalists 1965, 1970 and 1973. FL Cup winners 1968. Fairs Cup semi-finalists 1966. Fairs Cup finalists 1967. Fairs Cup winners 1968 and 1971. Division One champions 1968–69 and 1973–74. Charity Shield winners 1969. European Cup semi-finalists 1970. European Cup-Winners' Cup finalists 1973

'The Don' was the man who made Leeds United. Before he took over, the club had little to shout about in terms of success but he elevated them to one of the best in the world.

Four days after Jack Taylor's resignation Revie was appointed player-manager. Both Chester and Bournemouth had inquired about Revie's availability and director Harry Reynolds, soon to be chairman, had already drafted a letter to the Cherries singing Revie's praises.

When he re-read the letter, Reynolds realised Revie was just the man to take charge at Elland Road, tore up the letter, and persuaded the other directors to agree to the former England man's appointment.

It was a turning point in United's history.

Born in Middlesbrough on 10 July 1927, Revie began his career with Leicester in 1944 and featured in four major transfer deals totalling almost £80,000 – a record at the time. Hull paid Leicester £20,000 for Revie in November 1949; Manchester City £25,000 in October 1951; Sunderland £22,000 in November 1956 and Leeds £12,000 in November 1958.

A clever inside-right, Revie won six England caps, was Footballer of the Year in 1955 and won an FA Cup winners' medal with Manchester City the following year.

He based his innovative 'Revie Plan' of the deep-lying centre-forward on tactics formulated by the outstanding Hungarian national team in the mid-1950s and observers tipped him for a managerial future.

He was still just a player though when he made his Leeds debut in a 3–2 win over Newcastle on 29 November 1958. He was appointed skipper but after a string of poor results Freddie Goodwin took over the captaincy.

Revie's first brief was to avoid relegation which he achieved thanks to a 3–0 win at Newcastle on the final day of the 1961–62 season.

He patiently nurtured the youth policy introduced by Lambton and Taylor, giving debuts to teenagers like Gary Sprake, Paul Reaney and Norman Hunter.

His signing of veteran Scottish international Bobby Collins was inspired and the crop of kids learned quickly from the midfield master. It was also Revie that finally got the best out of Jack Charlton, who had been an inconsistent performer previously, and ensured that the inspirational Billy Bremner stayed at Leeds to lead his flourishing team.

Leeds stormed to the 1964 Division Two title and soon made their mark in Division One, winning two League titles, the FA Cup, Football League Cup and Fairs Cup twice under Revie's guidance. On top of that were a string of heart-breaking near misses.

Some critics felt Revie, who wore a lucky blue suit on matchdays and had a string of other superstitions, was over cautious, but the football his men produced in the final few seasons at Leeds was fantastic.

Revie assembled an outstanding backroom staff – trainer Les Cocker, the former Accrington and Stockport player; coach Syd Owen, the ex-Luton and England centre-half, and assistant manager Maurice Lindley, who spent 17 years as an Everton player.

United's style of play in Revie's early days was tough and uncompromising, but the criticism they received bonded his squad together. He was the club's father figure and his 'family' had an unquenchable thirst for victory.

He was able to keep his squad happy even though most of the reserves would have walked into virtually any other first team in the country.

Not all Revie's glory boys were home-grown. He was also astute in the transfer market with the bargain Johnny Giles later joined by big-money signings Allan Clarke and Mick Jones.

Revie was Manager of the Year in 1969, 1970 and 1972 and was awarded the OBE in January 1970.

After United lost the 1973 FA Cup Final to Sunderland, Revie looked set to join Everton, but he opted to stay at Elland Road.

With two more Scottish snips in the squad, Joe Jordan and Gordon McQueen,

Leeds rewarded Revie with a second title in 1974 with some magnificent football.

At the end of that superb season he severed his 13-year link with Leeds to become England's manager and plot a path to the 1978 World Cup Finals.

Revie, though, could not recapture the club atmosphere at national level, with his constant chopping and changing producing mixed results and dull performances.

In July 1977 he quit to take a lucrative job as coach to the United Arab Emirates on a tax-free contract reputed to be worth £60,000 a year.

Revie took a huge amount of flak from the Football Association, who suspected he was negotiating his escape route to the Middle East while still in charge of the England team, suspended the ex-Leeds boss from working in England until he was willing to face a charge of bringing the game into disrepute.

Revie later won a High Court case against the FA and was granted an injunction quashing the ban. However, it was a victory with a hollow ring as Justice Cantley criticised aspects of Revie's character.

There were also allegations in newspapers concerning Leeds matches when he was in charge at Elland Road.

While his stock at home was low, Revie was hailed a success by the UAE in his three years as coach. He took over club side Al Nasr in May 1980 and in August 1984 was appointed manager of Cairo club Al Al, but returned to Britain before Christmas.

Revie didn't work in full-time football again, but his court victory enabled him to take up a brief consultancy at Elland Road.

Whatever his standing nationally, his place in United's folklore is guaranteed. A road near the Leeds ground was named after him, the new all-seater Geldard End Kop was renamed the Revie Stand in 1994 and a statue of him unveiled at the ground at the end of the 2011–12 season.

Indeed, many of the ground improvements at Leeds were down to Revie's great success with the Whites.

His influence in the game continued after his retirement with Terry Cooper, Jack Charlton, Norman Hunter, Johnny Giles, Trevor Cherry, Terry Yorath, Joe Jordan, Billy Bremner, Eddie Gray and Allan Clarke all making their mark in management – the last three each filling Revie's old seat at Leeds.

In 1988 Revie revealed he was suffering from motor neurone disease, the incurable killer illness confining Revie to a wheelchair.

He did manage to revisit Elland Road in April 1988 at a joint testimonial game for John Charles and Bobby Collins but died on 26 May 1989 at Murrayfield Hospital, Edinburgh.

Brian Clough 1974

On his departure from Elland Road, Don Revie advised the Leeds board that Johnny Giles would make an excellent manager.

It was advice that went unheeded as the directors surprised the football world by appointing Brian Clough, a fierce critic of Revie and United's style of play.

While Maurice Lindley remained in temporary charge, the Leeds directors were talking to Clough, who was then in charge at Brighton.

The Leeds squad was ageing and Clough, who had been a major managerial success at Derby, was seen as the man tough enough to do the job.

Like Revie, he hailed from Middlesbrough where he was born on 21 March 1935. Cloughie piled in the goals for Boro and neighbours Sunderland, winning two

England caps in 1960 before injury ended his playing days with 251 League goals in 274 games.

As a young manager he impressed at Hartlepools and revived the fortunes of Derby, steering them to the Championship in 1971–72 with his assistant Peter Taylor.

Clough's outspoken comments on television and in newspapers prickled the Derby board and after a row at the Baseball Ground he joined Brighton on a five-year deal with Taylor.

Leeds had to fork out a huge sum in compensation to the Seagulls for Clough, although Taylor remained at the Goldstone Ground.

Clough arrived at Elland Road with trainer Jimmy Gordon, but without Taylor he seemed isolated from the players – many of whom he had blasted in the past.

Derby players John O'Hare and John McGovern came in with the mercurial Duncan McKenzie as Clough set about his changes.

But early results – not helped by the suspension of skipper Billy Bremner after his red card in Clough's first game in charge in the Charity Shield at Wembley – were poor.

Rumours soon eked out that the dressing room was unhappy and in a remarkable U-turn Clough was sacked after just 44 days in office.

Chairman Manny Cussins said the decision was made for the good of the club while Clough commented: 'I think it is a very sad day for Leeds and for football.'

Newspapers were rife with talk of player power, forcing the Leeds squad to issue a statement denying they had forced Clough out.

The suspended Bremner, assistant manager Lindley and chief coach Owen picked the side for the next game at Burnley – two days after Clough's exit. None of Clough's signings were in the squad.

Clough received £20,000 in compensation and emerged in January 1975, reunited with Taylor, as manager of Nottingham Forest.

Forest were transformed from a mundane outfit into double European champions as Clough and Taylor worked their magic. O'Hare and McGovern shared in their triumphs, leaving Leeds fans to contemplate what might have been.

Old Big 'Ead was consistently the people's choice to manage England, but the call never came, with many suspecting the FA would not be able to handle him.

Bombastic and charming in equal measure, Brian Clough, OBE, retired in May 1993 after Forest's relegation from the Premiership. After battling with a drink problem he died of stomach cancer on 20 September 2004, having had a liver transplant the previous year,

His son, Nigel, played at Forest, Liverpool and Nottingham Forest, and entered management with Burton Albion before following in his father's footsteps by taking over at Derby.

Jimmy Armfield 1974–78

European Cup finalists 1975

After the Clough debacle, Leeds needed the proverbial 'safe pair of hands' and found them in former England right-back Jimmy Armfield.

'Gentleman Jim' played a record 568 League games for his home-town club Blackpool where he was born on 21 September 1935. He was capped 43 times by England and captained his country.

A calm, quiet, pipe-smoking unassuming man, Armfield was 38 and relatively inexperienced on the managerial front. In his first post he steered Bolton to the Third Division title in 1973.

The Leeds board took their time appointing Armfield, allowing Lindley to temporarily fill the void once more. When he did take charge, Leeds were already out of the title race so Armfield opted to make few changes and gave priority to the European Cup. For the old stars in the squad it would be their last crack at the continent's top prize and they rose to the occasion, rolling back the years with some outstanding displays.

Within a few months Armfield had achieved what Revie couldn't – to take Leeds to the European Cup Final. They lost to Bayern Munich in Paris, prompting United's hooligan faction to riot triggering a European ban of fours years. Armfield's reasoned arguments at the club's appeal saw the suspension cut to two years.

Armfield went about the task of replacing Revie's aging aces, bringing in talent like Tony Currie, Brian Flynn, Ray Hankin and Arthur Graham.

His patient team-building saw Leeds reach the 1977 FA Cup semi-final and the League Cup semi-final the following year. But he was not given time to finish the job and the impatient board dismissed him at the end of the 1977–78 season.

He has not worked in football management since, but became a newspaper reporter and radio summariser. He also worked as a consultant for the FA and was instrumental in the appointment of Terry Venables as national coach in 1994 and Glenn Hoddle's appointment two years later.

Awarded the OBE in 2000, he revealed seven years later, that he had throat cancer but responded well to treatment and continues to work for radio.

Jock Stein 1978

Just one game into the 1978–79 season United installed former Celtic supremo Jock Stein as manager.

A big friend and old adversary of Don Revie, the Scot was a legend at Celtic Park becoming the first boss in Britain to win the European Cup.

He jumped at the chance to move to Elland Road on 21 August 1978 on a three-year contract reputed to be worth £85,000.

But, although taking the post, he didn't sign that contract and within weeks had replaced under-fire Scotland boss Ally McLeod as national team boss.

Stein had spent 44 days in charge at Elland Road – the same span as Clough – and left United in mid-table.

Big Jock took Scotland to the 1982 Word Cup finals in Spain and guided them to the brink of the Mexico finals four years later.

But in the pandemonium which followed a tense draw in Cardiff on 10 September 1985 – essential to Scotland's World Cup progress – Stein collapsed and died, aged 62.

Scotland, and football in general, mourned the passing of one of Britain's greatest managers.

Born in Lanarkshire on 5 October 1922, Stein was a part-timer with Albion Rovers before turning pro at 27. He returned to his old job as a miner, this time in the South Wales coalfield, and played centre-half for Llanelli before joining Celtic in 1951.

As a player he led Celtic to their first Scottish League and Cup double in 40 years in 1954 before quitting the following year.

He remained at Celtic as a coach until 1960 when he moved to Dunfermline, taking them to victory in the 1961 Scottish Cup Final before joining Celtic in 1965 and enjoyed an unprecedented run of success. He won 10 League titles – nine in a row – eight Scottish cups, six League Cups and that European Cup.

Awarded the CBE in 1970, Stein was out of the game for 10 months after a serious car accident in July 1975, followed by a heart attack and series of major operations.

When he was 55 he was given the less taxing job of general manager of the Hoops, who were paving the way for Billy McNeill to take over. It was not a role he relished and took the chance to join Leeds.

Jimmy Adamson 1978–80

Maurice Lindley once more filled the caretaker role picking the side for three weeks before Jimmy Adamson was appointed to the Elland Road hot seat.

Adamson, who was once offered the England manager's job, took over at Leeds in October 1978 for what proved to be a stormy couple of years.

Born in Ashington on 4 April 1929, Adamson turned professional with Burnley on New Year's Day 1947 and went on to become one of the Clarets' all-time greats. Although never capped at full level, he skippered the Turf Moor outfit to the 1960 League Championship and two years later was named Footballer of the Year and was included in the World Cup Finals squad for Chile, doubling up as assistant to Walter Winterbottom.

When Winterbottom later resigned, Adamson rejected an offer to take charge because he felt he lacked the necessary managerial experience and the position was filled by Alf Ramsey.

Adamson took a coaching role at Burnley and six years later was appointed manager, steering the Lancashire club back to the top division in 1973.

Continually forced to sell his young star names, he quit in January 1976. In May, he spent a fortnight with Sparta Rotterdam, but failed to settle in Holland. Within a few months he took command at struggling Sunderland but could not prevent them dropping into Division Two.

Leeds were at a crossroads when Adamson joined them and it seemed as though he had them on the right path when United finished fifth – the best position since Don Revie's departure – a place in Europe and a League Cup semi-final place.

But that early promise did not materialise. Top scorer John Hawley, talented stars Tony Currie and Frank Gray, were sold and their replacements were unsuccessful.

The likes of Alan Curtis, Wayne Entwistle and Brian Greenhoff all failed to make a lasting impact, leaving United fans impatient and angry.

A fan base that demanded the sort of success they had enjoyed under Revie demonstrated after a dire performance against Coventry in March 1980, in front of the lowest crowd at Elland Road for 17 years. Mounted police broke up the demo but Adamson survived until the end of the season.

The start of the next campaign was poor and pressure continued to mount on Adamson, who appealed for fans to stay calm as fans' protests were sapping the squad's confidence. But in September 1980, Adamson bowed to the inevitable and quit, slipping out of full-time football. He died, aged 82, on 8 November 2011.

Allan Clarke 1980–82

As player-manager of Barnsley, former Leeds striker Allan Clarke had made a big impression in South Yorkshire.

The Elland Road directors turned to Clarke to revive Leeds' fortunes, appointing him on 16 September 1980.

Confident and ambitious, Clarke declared he was a winner as a player and wanted to be a winner as a manager.

He had a big job on his hands with United one place from the bottom of Division One. Circumstances demanded

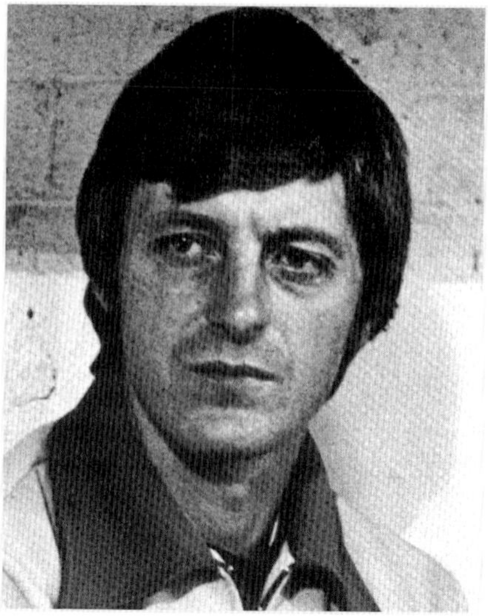

he concentrate on defensive work and his tactics worked as Leeds finished the season in ninth place despite scoring only 39 League goals.

To boost the attack he spent £930,000 on West Brom winger Peter Barnes in summer 1981, but it didn't have the desired effect. Leeds only managed 39 goals again, but the defence was not as tight and United lost their Division One status for the first time since 1964.

Clarke and his assistant, Martin Wilkinson, paid the price for relegation with their jobs. The pair re-emerged at Third Division Scunthorpe, who knocked Leeds out of the FA Cup the following season.

In July 1985 Clarke took over a second time at Barnsley, succeeding another Leeds old boy, Bobby Collins. He stayed at Oakwell until midway through the 1989–90 season and then had a five-month spell as Lincoln boss before leaving full-time football.

Eddie Gray 1982–85

Relegated Leeds were strapped for cash and the board opted to name popular winger Eddie Gray as player-manager in July 1982.

He had served United for nearly two decades and although he had no managerial experience had impressed with the way he had coached the juniors during one of his lengthy spells of injury.

With virtually no money available, Gray relied heavily on blooding a batch of talented youngsters like John Sheridan, Denis Irwin, Scott Sellars and Tommy Wright. He brought back old favourite Peter Lorimer as skipper and the tactics worked as United played some attractive stuff. He had a skilful, enthusiastic squad but they were out-muscled by more experienced opponents.

They were promotion candidates for three successive seasons but never quite

made the breakthrough. United made a bad start to 1985–86 but when a run of just one defeat in eight games seemed to have turned the corner, 38-year-old Gray and his assistant Jimmy Lumsden were sacked. The axe ended Gray's 22 years with the club on a 6–2 vote by the board.

Although Leeds were 14th the decision didn't go down too well with supporters and one of the directors, Brian Woodward, a former United reserve, resigned in protest.

Lorimer handed in a statement to the board condemning the timing and handling of Gray's dismissal on the eve of United's home game against Middlesbrough but the board did not budge.

Coach Peter Gunby was put in temporary charge and a Lorimer penalty won the game against Boro. But Leeds fans chanted in support of Gray during the game and called for chairman Leslie Silver to go.

Gray, typically, showed no bitterness, and later joined former teammate David Harvey as a player for non-League Whitby Town, to where Lorimer also moved.

After a spell as Middlesbrough's reserve and youth-team coach, Gray was appointed manager at Rochdale in December 1986 then had a year as boss at Hull before returning to Whitby as manager in September 1989.

Billy Bremner 1985–88

Billy Bremner, the heartbeat of Don Revie's superb squad, became the third successive former United player to take the helm at Elland Road.

After finishing his magnificent playing career with Hull City, Bremner took over as manager at Doncaster Rovers, a club where cash was in short supply.

Rovers had been limping along in Division Four for several years but that changed with Bremner's appointment in November 1978.

Within two years he got Rovers promoted only to be relegated immediately after a run of crippling injuries. Undeterred, Bremner got Doncaster back up the following season.

The Leeds board saw the old warrior as the man to lead United back to the top flight but, after taking over from Gray, United struggled to 14th place.

The following season Bremner almost cracked it as Leeds came close to double glory. They came within ten minutes of gaining promotion to Division One, only to fall at the final hurdle in a Play-off replay with Charlton at Birmingham, going down 2–1 late in extra time to a couple of late goals.

That shattering experience came after an FA Cup semi-final defeat – also in extra-time – at the hands of Coventry in a thrilling game.

United were installed as favourites to go up the following year and Bremner was rewarded with an extension to his contract.

However, United, after looking well placed at the turn of the year, had to be content with seventh place in 1987–88.

Poor results at the beginning of the next campaign saw Bremner axed in September. Although he was the man who blooded future England star David Batty, too many of Bremner's signings from the lower divisions failed to pay off at Elland Road.

Coach Peter Gunby took temporary command while United searched for a replacement for Bremner, who returned to Doncaster as manager in July 1989, a post he held until he resigned in November 1991. It proved to be his last job in football.

Although out of the full-time game Bremner kept tabs on affairs at his beloved Elland Road and Leeds fans were stunned when news filtered through of Bremner's death on 7 December 1997.

He succumbed to pneumonia at Doncaster Royal Infirmary, just two days short of his 55th birthday.

Howard Wilkinson 1988–96

Division Two champions 1989–90, Division One champions 1991–92, FA Charity Shield winners 1992, FA Youth Cup winners 1993, FL Cup finalists 1996

Leeds may have been struggling on the pitch in the early 1980s, but their pulling power remained undiminished.

Although he was with First Division Sheffield Wednesday, Howard Wilkinson had no qualms about dropping a division to join Leeds.

Lack of spending power at Hillsborough had frustrated Wilkinson, who felt he could not take the Owls any further without a cash injection for players.

Up the M1 at Elland Road, Leeds were a sleeping giant and Wilkinson told the United board that they could take 'route one' back to the top flight if they were prepared to back him with big transfer funds.

The Leeds directors took the gamble and on 10 October 1988 Wilkinson became United's eighth manager in 14 years.

His credentials were unchallenged. Born in Sheffield on 13 November 1943, Wilkinson had an unspectacular career as a winger with Wednesday, Brighton and Boston United, entering management with the latter when they were a non-League outfit.

Wilkinson gained a degree in physical education at Sheffield United, taught for a couple of years in Sheffield and managed the England semi-professional side before his burgeoning managerial career gained greater exposure in 1982.

An FA regional coach, he was working at Notts County when he succeeded Jimmy Sirrell as manager in 1982, replacing Jack Charlton at Wednesday the following summer.

In his first season Wilkinson got the Owls back into Division One and kept them in the top half of the table for several seasons with fifth place in 1986–87 being the high point.

His first job at Leeds was to improve the squad's fitness with the help of assistant Mick Hennigan and staff were quickly impressed by the new manager's attention to detail and organisational skills.

Leeds finished in mid-table before the board sanctioned the promised spending spree in summer 1989. In came Mel Sterland, John Hendrie, Vinnie Jones, joining defender Chris Fairclough and inspirational veteran midfielder Gordon Strachan, who were recruited in March.

His expensively assembled squad, which was laced with home grown talent like David Batty and Gary Speed, was given that extra promotion push by the arrival of goal-grabber Lee Chapman in January 1990. It was Chapman's header at

Bournemouth which clinched the title with 85 points on goal difference from Sheffield United.

Crowds poured back to Elland Road and the Whites finished fourth in their return to the First Division with Gary McAllister replacing Jones in midfield.

Leeds won huge praise for their brand of football but it got even better the following season – the last before the advent of the Premiership. Sergeant Wilko's warriors were involved in a terrific scrap before pipping Manchester United for the title – Leeds's third Championship crown.

But Leeds suffered a reaction in the following campaign, failing to win an away game in the League in 1992–93 and suffered early exits from Europe and the domestic cups.

Fans' favourite Eric Cantona was sold to Manchester United and popular local ace David Batty moved on to Blackburn.

Wilkinson, who was chairman of the Managers' Association, reshaped his side which finished fifth in 1993–94 and signed a new deal to keep him at Elland Road until the end of the century.

However, fans were unhappy at the lack of progress and when United were outplayed 3–0 in the League Cup Final, Wilkinson was booed off the Wembley pitch by a section of supporters.

The strong youth policy he put in place which nurtured the likes of Harry Kewell was just starting to bear fruition and the club won the Youth Cup for the first time in 1993.

After two successive fifth places, United looked back on track but after the resignation of Leslie Silver as chairman, Wilkinson's position was less secure.

A poor start to 1996–97, capped by a 4–0 home reverse against old rivals Manchester United saw Wilkinson ousted.

In addition to introducing young players like Kewell, Gary Kelly and Ian Harte, Wilkinson had also recruited some excellent players in Nigel Martyn, Tony Dorigo, Lee Bowyer, Tony Yeboah and Rod Wallace leaving the new manager with material to work with.

Given his excellent record, Wilkinson didn't have to wait long for employment. He was hired as the FA's technical director and managed the England side for a friendly against France on a caretaker basis in 1999 after the sacking of Glenn Hoddle.

Wilko had a relatively unsuccessful spell as Under-21 manager until June 2001, but did oversee the full national team again – a 0–0 World Cup qualifying draw with Finland – after Hoddle's successor, Kevin Keegan resigned.

In 2002, he returned to club management with Sunderland, with Steve Cotterill as his assistant, but it didn't work out and the Black Cats, anchored at the foot of the Premiership, sacked the pair in March 2003.

After two months as coach with Chinese club Shanghai Shenua, Wilkinson had a short stint as Leicester City's coach before returning to Notts County as a non-executive director. He also helped out with coaching at Meadow Lane until leaving the club in September 2007. The chairman of the League Managers' Association, he became technical advisor to Sheffield Wednesday in January 2009, taking over as interim chairman in May 2010 until the arrival of Milan Mandaric.

George Graham 1996–98

FA Youth Cup winners 1997

The Leeds directors, always seemingly able to spring a surprise whoever was on the board, brought George Graham out of exile in an effort to restore United's fortunes.

The Scot, who had fantastic success at Arsenal, had been dismissed by the Gunners

in February 1995 after a bung scandal. It was alleged that he had taken £425,000 in illegal payments from Norwegian agent Rune Hauge to sign John Jensen and Pal Lydersen while manager at Highbury. On top of his sacking he was banned from football for a year by the FA.

Despite that dark cloud hanging over him, Graham had an impressive CV.

Born in Bargeddie, Lanarkshire, on 30 November 1944, he won 12 caps for Scotland but his club career was all in England. Nicknamed 'Stroller', he was a cultured midfielder who served Aston Villa, Chelsea, Arsenal, Manchester United, Portsmouth and Crystal Palace before entering coaching with the latter.

A stint as QPR coach followed before being appointed manager of Millwall, with whom he earned promotion to the old Second Division.

In May 1986 he became Arsenal boss and the silverware soon started to roll in with two League Championships, an FA Cup, two League Cups and the European Cup Winners Cup over an eight-year period.

It was that record which Leeds' directors hoped could be transferred to Elland Road.

Graham got right back to basics and that meant concentrating on defence to start with. United scraped together just 28 goals in 1996–97 but still finished comfortably in mid-table.

Graham removed the shackles the following season and they finished fifth, gaining UEFA Cup qualification.

Things were looking up, but his two-year spell came to an end when it became clear Graham could not resist the overtures of managerless Tottenham with his hankering to return to London. Although Graham had signed a three-and-a-half year contract with United the previous December, he could not resist returning to the capital.

Ironically, Graham's last Premiership game in charge of Leeds was a 3–3 draw at Spurs.

Just months later Tottenham lifted the League Cup, but Graham was never popular with the White Hart Lane faithful because of his links with north London rivals Arsenal. His Tottenham tenure was ended in March 2001 and he has not worked in management since.

David O'Leary 1998–2002

UEFA Cup semi-finalists 2000, Champions League semi-finalists 2001

Initially, Leeds wanted Leicester City's Martin O'Neill as Graham's replacement, but he eventually opted to stay in the East Midlands.

Once O'Neill was out of the equation the obvious choice was David O'Leary, a former Irish international born at Stoke Newington on 2 April 1958.

A legendary centre-half at Arsenal, he had been signed by Wilkinson but only played a dozen starts for Leeds before taking up coaching at Elland Road. He worked as Graham's assistant but when it became clear he was not following Graham to Tottenham, he was given the Leeds job.

Despite his wealth of playing knowledge at domestic and international level, 41-year-old O'Leary had no managerial experience.

He was officially installed as manager on 25 October 1998 on a two-and-a-half year contract with Eddie Gray, who had returned to the club as a coach, as his assistant.

The pair were like a breath of fresh air as youngsters like Alan Smith and Jonathan Woodgate were given their chance to shine.

With Jimmy Floyd Hasselbaink pumping in the goals, Leeds were playing an exciting brand of football and finished fourth to qualify for the UEFA Cup.

With Harry Kewell the star of the team, United shook off the £13 million exit of Hasselbaink to Atletico Madrid by signing Sunderland striker Michael Bridges who netted 19 Premiership goals in 1999–2000.

Ten successive wins in all competitions was completed with a 2–1 victory at Watford on 3 October which sent Leeds to the top of the table.

O'Leary's young guns won unanimous praise for their exciting brand of attacking football. But the thrilling campaign hit the buffers in spring as United's form dipped and the club was plunged into mourning when fans Christopher Loftus and Kevin Speight were stabbed to death just before the UEFA Cup semi-final against Galatasaray in Istanbul.

United lost 2–0 in Turkey and were held 2–2 on an emotional night at Elland Road but got themselves together to remain undefeated in their last five Premiership games to finish third and claim a Champions League spot the following season.

Chairman Peter Ridsdale and his board splashed the cash in preparation for 2000–01 with Celtic striker Mark Viduka (£6 million), Lens midfielder Olivier Dacourt (£7.2 million) and Liverpool's versatile Dominic Matteo (£4.2 million) the big signings, who were joined a few months later by West Ham's international Rio Ferdinand for £18 million, a world record for a defender, and Inter Milan striker Robbie Keane (£12 million).

United had to go through the qualification stages for the Champions League and few gave them much hope of getting beyond the first stage, but they enjoyed a fantastic campaign – despite the on-going Lee Bowyer and Jonathan Woodgate court case – reaching the semi-finals before being knocked out by Valencia.

However, they didn't do as well in the Premiership and had to settle for UEFA Cup qualification. But the spending continued as Liverpool goal ace Robbie Fowler (£11 million) and Derby midfielder Seth Johnson (£7 million) were added to O'Leary's growing squad.

On New Year's Day 2002, United were top of the Premiership, but they nosedived in the second half of the season, finishing sixth.

By this time relations between O'Leary and Ridsdale were reported to be strained when the manager brought out a book *Leeds United On Trial*, a title that did not go down too well in the dressing room given the Bowyer-Woodgate court case.

O'Leary's failure to get United back into the Champions League also started to bite financially. Players had to be sold before new ones could be bought.

It emerged that Ridsdale had borrowed £60 million as he budgeted for a decent run in the Champions League. O'Leary had spent nearly £100 million on players in less than five years – he had generated good income from transfers and gate receipts too – and had kept Leeds in the top six of the Premiership.

While Leeds fans braced themselves for the exit of several star players, some were surprised that O'Leary was the first departure in June 2002.

After being linked with several posts, O'Leary returned to management with Aston Villa in June 2003 but he could not work the magic that he had provided during his early years at Leeds and left by mutual consent in July 2006. He landed a lucrative deal to manage Dubai-based Al-Ahli in the United Arab Emirates in July 2010 but was sacked ten months later.

Terry Venables 2002–03

Celtic's Martin O'Neill was once again linked with the Leeds post, but it was former England chief Terry Venables who accepted the challenge of leading United.

Born in Dagenham on 6 January 1943, he was seen as the experienced head that could alleviate matters on the field as the Leeds board tried to extricate the club from their perilous financial position.

Within a month Leeds, with their multi-million pound debt rising, sold Rio Ferdinand to Manchester United for £30 million. On the other hand, Venables was restricted to modest buys as the depth of United's financial troubles, thought to amount to £80 million, became clear.

More sales followed as the relationship between Venables and chairman Peter Ridsdale became increasingly strained. The sale of Jonathon Woodgate to Newcastle United without Venables' knowledge proved the final straw and with the club sliding towards relegation, Venables was sacked in March 2003 after eight months in charge.

He later assisted Steve McClaren in the England set-up, but the pair were axed two days after England failed to qualify for the 2008 European Championships.

Venables, the 59-year-old former Chelsea and Tottenham international had taken England to the semi-finals of Euro '96 and had learned his managerial trade with Crystal Palace and QPR, taking both clubs to Division Two titles.

In May 1984, Venables went to Barcelona and 'El Tel' took the Catalan club to the League title in his first season, followed by a European Cup final appearance.

He returned to London to manage Tottenham and guided them to the FA Cup in 1991 – 24 years after playing in a Spurs Cup final-winning side.

In January 1994 Venables, highly regarded as a coach, landed the England post despite his business dealings coming under scrutiny.

After Euro '96, which England hosted, Venables took Australia to the brink of their first appearance of the World Cup Finals, only to lose to Iran in a Play-off.

Next stop was a short one as chairman of Portsmouth, returning to management in March 1998, leaving the following January when Palace went into administration.

Two years later he was appointed Middlesbrough coach and assistant to Bryan Robson, but the pair left in June 2001, Venables re-emerging 12 months later with Leeds.

Peter Reid
2003

Leeds were in danger of relegation when Peter Reid was appointed to replace Terry Venables on 21 March 2003 until the end of the season.

Reid, the former Manchester City and Sunderland boss, stuck to his brief and United secured their Premiership status with a 3–2 win at Arsenal in the penultimate game of the season,

By this time Peter Ridsdale had stood down as chairman and Professor John McKenzie, an academic who studied at the London School of Economics, was at the helm. He had a sharp financial brain – the result being that Reid had to get free

transfers or loan signings in the summer as he reshaped a squad that was losing more of its star names, including Harry Kewell to Liverpool.

Many of the long-term loans were from abroad and simply not up to life in the Premiership and after a 6–1 thrashing at Portsmouth in November the board showed him the door, having survived less time than Venables.

Before the end of the season Reid was installed as manager at Coventry but left the club by mutual consent in January 2005. In September 2008 he became Thailand's national manager, stepping down to become assistant manager at Stoke a year later. He left that role in June 2010 to take charge at Plymouth Argyle, departing Home Park in September 2011. He then took charge of Indian side Kolkata Camelians for the inaugural Bengali Premier League in 2012.

Reid, who was in charge when Sunderland were promoted to the Premiership as champions in 1996, had more success as a player than a manager. After leaving Bolton he won two League Championship medals and an FA Cup winners medal with Everton and was Footballer of the Year in 1985. Born at Huyton on 20 June 1956, he played for England 13 times.

Eddie Gray
2003–04

Throughout all the chaos of the previous three years one man was constant at the club – Eddie Gray.

He had been assistant to O'Leary, Venables and Reid and became the first man to manage Leeds twice, following his efforts in the 1980s.

It was a near-impossible task with Leeds rooted to the bottom of the table and morale even lower with players never

quite certain if they were going to be paid from one month to another.

Most of the loan players were jettisoned, but Gray could not prevent the inevitable and relegation was effectively confirmed by a 4–1 defeat at Bolton in early May.

By this time United had more new faces in the boardroom with insolvency expert Gerald Krasner, who headed a takeover by local businessmen, in the chair.

Gray left at the end of the season as Leeds sold off all their top players – Mark Viduka, Alan Smith, goalkeeper Paul Robinson among them – to stave off the very real threat of liquidation.

He was given a football consultancy role at Elland Road, then worked as a matchday analyst for BBC Radio Leeds, a role he has done for Yorkshire Radio since 2008.

Kevin Blackwell 2004–06

Championship Play-off finalists 2006

It would take a brave man to step into the wreckage of free-falling Leeds United but, Kevin Blackwell took on 'Mission Impossible'.

Against a backdrop of no funds and few players, Blackwell, a former assistant to Neil Warnock at Sheffield United, took up the challenge.

He had been drafted in as coach by Peter Reid and was a relatively low-profile figure compared with many of the club's post-Revie managers.

A goalkeeper with Barnet and Boston United, he played under Warnock at Scarborough and followed the manager to Notts County, Torquay, Huddersfield and Plymouth, doubling up as a coach at the latter two clubs.

He was goalkeeping coach at Bury under Warnock and became assistant manager at Bramall Lane when his mentor took over as manager in December 1999.

At Leeds he pieced together a team of free transfers and trialists, old experienced pros with a sprinkling of younger players.

Although fans feared the club could be relegated a second successive season, Blackwell halted the slide on the field and

given the circumstances, 14th place was as good as could be expected.

Midway through the season 73-year-old Ken Bates, the former Chelsea supremo, completed his takeover of the club from Gerald Krasner.

Having stabilised the club on the pitch, Blackwell was given financial support by Bates, bringing in strikers Rob Hulse, David Healy, Richard Cresswell and Robbie Blake. United's strong home record and solid performances on opposition soil lifted them to third place by the end of February.

Blackwell was rewarded with a new contract but performances tailed off and although United reached the Play-off Final at Cardiff they were thumped 3–0 by Watford, managed by a former Leeds coach, Adie Boothroyd. Blackwell's assistant, Sam Ellis, didn't have his contract renewed in the summer, John Carver, who had replaced Boothroyd as coach, moving up to assistant.

A poor start to the next campaign saw Leeds gain just seven points from seven games and Blackwell was shown the door.

Carver filled in for a handful of games but a dire 5–1 defeat at Luton ended his prospects of landing the job on a permanent basis.

In November 2006 Blackwell announced he was suing Leeds for wrongful dismissal after it was confirmed he was sacked for gross misconduct for press comments about the club's finances.

He returned to management with Carver as his number two, in March 2007 with cash-strapped Luton, where he had been born on 21 December 1958. With the club in administration, he left in January 2008 and was appointed boss at Sheffield United, where his second in command was Sam Ellis, his former assistant at Leeds. Two years after leading Leeds to the Championship Play-offs, he did the same with the Blades, who lost 1–0 to Burnley in the Final. He left the Blades by mutual consent in August 2010.

Dennis Wise 2006–08

It was little surprise that Dennis Wise became United's next manager. He was close to chairman Ken Bates since their days at Chelsea where Wise spent 11 years.

He and assistant Gus Poyet both arrived from Swindon where in the four months they worked in tandem had taken the Robins to second spot in League One.

They watched Leeds crash 3–1 at home to Southend in the League Cup on 24 October 2006 – the Whites' side being selected by reserve team coach David Geddis.

Wise was quick to make changes, rooting out older players but with finances remaining a problem results were hard to gain.

Relegation was confirmed in the final home game of the season against Ipswich – a 1–1 draw – and Leeds slumped to the third tier of English football for the first time in their history.

United announced they were going into administration before the Derby game and were given a ten-point deduction, ensuring they finished bottom.

Worse was to follow as Leeds were deducted 15 points from the start of the League One campaign. Throughout the summer there had been a long-running battle to sort out United's future before Bates regained full control of the club. However, the League imposed the 15-point deduction as they believed United had not followed rules on clubs entering administration – a sanction Leeds hotly contested.

The club's future was secured just before the start of the new season and Wise was unable to sign any new players until the issue was resolved.

Rather than crumble, the points loss bonded the team, management, fans and directors together and Wise's side made a blazing start to the season, winning their opening seven games.

Poyet moved back to his old club, Tottenham, as assistant manager and his role at Leeds was taken by Dave Bassett, Wise's former boss at Wimbledon. Having seen United power up the table despite their points handicap, Wise surprisingly left Elland Road in January 2008 to become executive director (football) at Newcastle United – a role he left in April 2009 when Alan Shearer was appointed caretaker-manager.

Although born in Kensington on 16 December 1966, Wise was on Southampton's books as a teenager, but made his breakthrough at Wimbledon where he was part of the 'Crazy Gang' that beat Liverpool in the 1988 FA Cup Final. He won plenty of honours while at Chelsea, including 21 England caps, and was a combative midfield player.

Sacked by his next club Leicester, after a pre-season incident in Finland, Wise returned to London with Millwall, becoming player-manager in 2003. The following year he guided the Lions to the FA Cup Final but after falling out with the chairman left Millwall and reverted to playing with short spells at Southampton and Coventry followed by his appointment as Swindon boss in May 2006.

Gary McAllister 2008

2008 League One Play-off finalists

After Dennis Wise's surprise exit, chairman Ken Bates acted swiftly to install former skipper Gary McAllister as manager of the Whites on a contract until the end of the season. It was a bold move as McAllister had been out of management since leaving Coventry City four years earlier.

The former Scottish international midfielder, a member of the last United side to lift the Championship, had a simple brief – get promotion.

He took over with Leeds wobbling in sixth place after their sensational start to

the season. After technical director Gwyn Williams presided over a 1–0 loss at Southend, McAllister and his assistant, Steve Staunton, the former Liverpool and Republic of Ireland star took charge but didn't record a win until the fifth attempt.

After that McAllister got United back on track with just a couple of defeats in a dozen games and was offered a rolling 12-month contract.

Automatic promotion was beyond United but they did secure a Play-off spot but were in deep trouble as they trailed 2–0 at home to Carlisle at Elland Road before loan signing Dougie Freedman netted a late, late goal. That gave Leeds the impetus to win 2–0 at Brunton Park and a first Wembley Final appearance since the 1996 League Cup Final.

But big favourites Leeds were outplayed by Doncaster Rovers and lost 1–0, missing out on an immediate return to the Championship.

McAllister recruited the likes of Luciano Becchio and Robert Snodgrass in the summer and his side played some attractive passing football but lacked toughness. After a run of five successive defeats, including the club's first loss to a non-League team, Histon, in the FA Cup, McAllister was sacked on 21 December 2008.

Since then he turned down the chance to join the Scottish international coaching staff before being appointed first-team coach at Middlesbrough by Gordon Strachan, his former Leeds teammate.

In September 2010 he agreed to become assistant manager at Aston Villa to his former Liverpool boss Gerard Houllier. McAllister took charge of some Villa games after Houllier was taken ill and when the Frenchman was replaced by Birmingham boss Alex McCleish in June 2011, McAllister found himself out of a job.

Simon Grayson 2008–12

2010 League One promotion

Having axed one former player as manager, United turned to another to replace him.

While Gary McAllister was a stellar name at Elland Road, the same could not be said of Simon Grayson, who managed just a handful of Leeds games before carving out a fine career with the likes of Leicester City, Aston Villa, Blackburn and Blackpool.

Defender Grayson made just two League appearances for United but was to have a far greater impact as a manager. He retired from playing in 2006 and after a spell as caretaker manager with the Tangerines was handed the job at Bloomfield Road on a permanent basis and secured promotion to the Championship in spectacular fashion in 2007 when Blackpool beat Yeovil 2–0 at Wembley – a club record 10th successive victory.

That sequence was extended by two more victories at the start of the new campaign and he went on to steer the Lancashire side to their highest Football League finish since 1971–72.

Blackpool refused permission for Leeds to speak to Grayson, so he resigned and was named United's boss. Blackpool initially turned down his resignation but the parties eventually settled their differences with Blackpool receiving an undisclosed fee.

Leeds were in mid-table but he quickly got them back on track with his squad winning 11 consecutive home games to match the record set by Don Revie 41 years earlier. However, promotion was a step too far as they lost 2–1 on aggregate to Millwall in the Play-off semi-finals.

The following season saw Grayson's Leeds begin in powerful form in League One, but a spectacular 1–0 FA Cup third round win at Manchester United, followed by a draw in the next round against

another big Premiership side, Tottenham, seemed to distract the squad from the main aim: promotion to League One.

Gradually they regrouped to finish runners-up to Norwich by coming from behind at home to Bristol Rovers with ten men on 8 May 2010 to win 2–1 and secure promotion. In the Championship, United were expected to struggle without the goals of Jermaine Beckford, but proved to be one of the most free-scoring sides in the division with 81 goals. However, deficiencies in defence cost them dear and they finished one place out of the Play-offs. Leaking goals continued to be a problem Grayson could not solve the following season and after a 4–1 home defeat to Birmingham City he was sacked on 1 February 2012 along with coaches Glyn Snodin and Ian Miller. Leeds were just outside the Play-off zone at the time. Three weeks later Grayson replaced Lee Clark at League One club Huddersfield.

Grayson was born at Ripon on 16 December 1969 and his brother, Paul, a former England one-day international, manages Essex County Cricket Club.

Neil Warnock 2012–

After youth coach Neil Redfearn held the reins for four games, the vastly experienced Neil Warnock was appointed by chairman Ken Bates on 18 February 2012.

Bates described it as the most important managerial appointment he had made since arriving at Leeds in 2005.

Promotion specialist Warnock said: 'I feel I have one big challenge left in me and believe Leeds is a club that should be in the Premier League. I want to be the man who is able to deliver this for a set of fans who never cease to amaze me with their numbers and their loyalty.'

The previous season the 63-year-old had led QPR to the Championship crown – his seventh promotion as a manager – but was sacked a month before joining Leeds by the London side as they struggled to adapt in the Premiership.

Born in Sheffield on 1 December 1948, he was a journeyman lower division winger with Chesterfield, Hartlepool, Rotherham, Scunthorpe, Aldershot, Barnsley, York and Crewe, making 327 career appearances.

In 1981 he was appointed manager of Gainsborough Trinity and after a spell at Burton Albion became boss at Scarborough in May 1986. In his first season, he guided the Seasiders to the Football Conference title, making them the first team to win automatic promotion to the Football League following the abolition of the re-election system.

He further enhanced his reputation at Notts County as successive promotions lifted the Magpies to Division One for the 1991–92 season. Warnock turned down a lucrative offer from Bates to manage Chelsea, but lost his job at Notts after relegation saw them miss out on the start of the Premier League.

In March 1993, he worked as a consultant at Torquay United, helping them stave off relegation from the Football League before being appointed manager at Huddersfield Town. He soon made his mark with the Terriers, as they won the Division Two Play-off Final in 1995 by beating Bristol Rovers 2–1.

A few days after that Wembley triumph he surprisingly quit to become manager of Plymouth, who had just been relegated to Division Three. Once more he made an instant impact, as Argyle clinched promotion via the Play-offs.

In February 1997, he was axed by Plymouth and had spells with Oldham (February 1997 – May 1998) and Bury (June 1998 – December 1999).

His dream move came in December 1999 when he was made boss of Sheffield United, the club he had supported as a boy. Warnock's assistant at Bramall Lane was future Leeds boss Kevin Blackwell, who also worked with Warnock at Huddersfield and Plymouth.

In 2003 the Blades reached the semi-finals of both the FA Cup and League Cup and made the Final of the First Division Play-off where they lost to Wolves – Warnock's first setback in a Play-off Final after four successes.

Three years later he guided the Blades to the Premiership as Championship runners-up but could not keep them in the top flight and Warnock, who has never been afraid to speak his mind or make tough decisions, resigned after relegation to take time out of football.

He re-emerged at Crystal Palace on October 2007 and turned round an ailing club against all the odds as the London side claimed a Play-off slot, losing to Bristol City in the semi-final. Palace had big financial troubles and after being placed into administration in January 2010 received a ten-point deduction which led to Warnock's departure.

He remained in London though, taking over at Queen's Park Rangers on 2 March 2010. His first brief was to avoid relegation, which he did, and the following season took Rangers to the Championship title and a return to the Premiership after a 15-year absence.

Leeds United Chairmen

Joe Henry junior

1919

UNITED'S first chairman, Joe Henry junior also the one who had the shortest reign in the club's history.

His father Joe Henry, of the well known Holbeck engineering firm, had fought hard to save the old Leeds City club in his capacity as Lord Mayor of Leeds (see The Leeds City Scandal). Joe Henry junior was equally anxious to keep League football alive and kicking in Leeds and was a key figure at the public meeting on Friday, 17 October 1919, which agreed to form Leeds United out of the remnants of the disgraced Leeds City club.

The following day, Joe Henry junior, a keen sponsor of Leeds City, was appointed United's chairman. His aim was to resurrect the club and that done, he stood down within a few weeks to stand aside for men of wealth to invest in the club. He later served as a member of the Holbeck ward on the City Council and was chairman of the property committee.

John Hilton Crowther

1919–24

WEST Yorkshire industrialist Hilton Crowther switched his interests from neighbouring Huddersfield Town to the new club at Elland Road and in December 1919 was installed as United's new chairman.

Crowther was a director of Crowther's, a Milnsbridge woollen manufacturer and first became involved in football when he was asked by Huddersfield Town representatives in 1909 to provide financial support in Town's bid for promotion to the Football League.

Crowther and his brothers, Leonard, Stoner and Edgar, the latter a county

golfer, all joined the Huddersfield board and made generous loans and donations to the Terriers.

But Hilton Crowther, dissatisfied with lack of public support for Huddersfield football, switched his allegiance to Leeds United, who were glad to accept promise of financial security.

Crowther was genuinely interested in expanding soccer in the region and in 1923 founded the Yorkshire Midweek League, being its president until it was disbanded in 1949.

The colourful Crowther, who was married to a much younger woman, Mona Vivian, a popular revue artiste of the 1920s, was the financial platform on which Leeds United were built. One examination of the club's accounts showed that Crowther had invested £54,000 in United – a huge sum in those days. In 1924 Crowther indicted that he wanted to be bought out by the club and stepped down as chairman. He remained on the Leeds board until his death in Blackpool on 23 March 1957. His 49 years as a director at both Leeds and Huddersfield, was only surpassed by Dick Parker, who, ironically, had joined the Huddersfield Town board during the turmoils of 1919 and remained on it until his death in 1974.

Major Albert Newby Braithwaite

1924–31

CROWTHER'S replacement was 31-year-old Major Albert Braithwaite, who went on to make a name for himself in politics.

A former pupil of Woodhouse Grove School, Bradford, and a graduate of Leeds University, he enjoyed a distinguished Army career, enlisting as a private soldier in the Leeds 'Pals' 15th Battalion West Yorkshire Regiment at the outbreak of World War One and was commissioned in the Yorkshire Hussars in 1915, becoming a specialist in trench mortar warfare. He reached the rank of major and was mentioned in dispatches, receiving the Distinguished Service Order (DSO) and the Military Cross.

He was a member of the Old Boys (Harrogate) football team and helped United launch a 'Lend Us A Fiver' campaign immediately after a 1–1 draw with Sunderland – their first-ever point in Division One – on the opening day of the 1924–25 season. He knew United needed cash as Crowther wanted £35,000 of the money he had put into the club back. The young, charismatic and articulate Braithwaite, the son of Albert Braithwaite, a former Lord Mayor of Leeds, seemed the ideal candidate to replace Crowther.

He took over just before United started their maiden season in Division One when interest in the club within the city was at its highest. However, with Crowther no longer there to bankroll the club he recognised the need to raise funds.

Major Albert Braithwaite (left) with Leeds South East MP James O'Grady and fellow United director Mark Barker before the club's first game in Division One against Sunderland in 1924.

He announced that each person attending the Sunderland game would receive a programme with an application for debentures enclosed. The day after the match, which attracted a record crowd of 33,722, he took centre stage at a packed meeting in Leeds Town Hall.

Braithwaite, a natural orator, urged supporters to chip in and support the club financially. He estimated that the previous day's game, which furnished £2,192 in gate receipts, had brought business worth £15,000 to the city that afternoon.

'It would pay Leeds people to own their own democratic club,' said the dashing major, whose other bright ideas during his chairmanship included asking a London composer to write a song for the club.

An engineer, Braithwaite was director of Sir Lindsay Parkinson and Co. Ltd and entered politics midway through his tenure as United chairman. He was elected MP for the Buckrose Division of the East Riding of Yorkshire in 1926, but remained chairman of United until 1931. He served his constituents until 1945 – the same year in which he was knighted – and was elected MP for West Harrow in April 1951. He was a political high flier but Westminster was stunned in October 1959 when the pain of a serious illness proved too much to bear and he committed suicide by an overdose in his London home, aged 66.

Eric Clarke

1931–33

TOWARDS the end of Major Braithwaite's chairmanship, he found less and less time to devote to United's affairs. He often had to miss meetings and in his absence Eric Clarke took the chair.

It was fitting that Clarke, a Leeds City Alderman and noted solicitor, should be appointed United's new chairman in August 1931 as his family had connections with the club stretching back to its Leeds City days.

Clarke's father, Sir William Henry Clarke, the city's coroner, had been the Leeds City club's solicitor and had represented it at the hearing into the illegal payments affair in 1919. The following year, Eric Clarke qualified as a solicitor after heroic service in World War One with the Yorkshire Regiment. He was mentioned in dispatches for gallantry twice and was awarded both the French Croix de Guerre and silver star and the Belgian Croix de Guerre.

He shared his father's love of football and joined the United board in 1925 at the age of 32. He spent three years as chairman of the finance committee and was regarded as the most experienced man for the job of leading United in the boardroom.

Under Clarke's stewardship, United regained their place in Division One, but after only two years he stepped down in July 1933. He devoted more time to his work on Leeds City Council on which he served for 25 years and was noted for his work on water conservation in his capacity of chairman of the Leeds Waterworks Committee. Clarke died, aged 64, on 28 January 1956.

Alfred E. Masser

1933–37

THE mantle of chairman was taken on by another Leeds City Alderman and solicitor, the flamboyant Alf Masser.

He was an original shareholder of the Leeds City club and had a spell as its vice-chairman. He left City during World War

One, but after its demise returned to help get Leeds United off the ground, chairing the public meeting in Salem Hall the day after Leeds City's players were auctioned off.

Masser, a skilful advocate whose practice was based in Park Square East in the city centre, successfully put the case for United's admission to the League to the Football League administrators in May 1920, but later stood down from the board, chiefly to concentrate on his legal business and his work for Leeds City Council.

A chairman of the Council's Parks Committee, Masser was instrumental in establishing municipal golf courses in the city and the introduction of Sunday games on the city's parks. He gave the City Council 40 years unbroken service.

The son of commercial traveller, he was educated at Churwell College, Yorkshire College and Leeds University. A keen sportsman, he was a founder of Headingley Rugby Club, serving as both captain and secretary, and was secretary of Leeds Springfield Cricket Club. Masser's sphere of influence went beyond Elland Road. He was a key figure in the Football League negotiations which obtained money for the game from the Football Pools companies in the 1930s. He also narrowly missed becoming the first United chairman to serve on the Football League Management Committee, just failing in League elections in 1937 and 1939.

Masser made an enormous contribution to United's history and when he died, on 6 October 1950, aged 73, he was still serving on the United board.

Ernest Pullan

1937–48

FORMER Football League referee Ernest Pullan was elected chairman in succession to Masser on 29 July 1937. He had been

one of United's most active directors on the playing front and had actually acted as team manager for some weeks when Dick Ray quit in March 1935.

Pullan had been chairman of United's finance committee, but as chairman during World War Two and the 1946–47 relegation season, he was in charge during difficult times for the club.

Regarded as a safe pair of hands, Pullan, who had been a Football League referee in 1919 and 1920, had a deep knowledge of the game and it was largely through his efforts that the club managed to function during wartime.

He first became involved with the club when he returned from active service in World War One. His brother, Alf, was running the family building firm of J. Pullan and Sons Ltd, which was established by their father, Joseph, in 1885 and at that time there was no work for Ernest to do, so he immersed himself in his love of football.

The business was based on the top of Beeston Hill overlooking Elland Road and

Ernest and the family maintained close links with the club. The firm even stored some of its materials under the stands at the Elland Road ground.

The building of the old Lowfields Road Stand was carried out by the Pullan firm, who also built a stand at Barnsley's ground, Oakwell, and constructed Barnsley Alhambra. Many of the houses close to the business were built by Pullans and many of them were homes for United's players.

Sam Bolton

1948–61

WHEN Pullan resigned in 1948 he was succeeded by Sam Bolton, a motor haulage contractor who had gone a long way on the road to success.

Born and bred in Leeds, he was educated at Hunslet and joined Thomas Spence Ltd, a haulage company, and went on to become its managing director. During World War One he served with the Coldstream Guards before joining the Royal Flying Corps.

A football fanatic, he played for Rothwell White Rose in the Leeds League and watched Leeds City play as a 'bob-side' youngster and went on to have trials with them.

Bolton rose from United fan to United director in 1945, becoming chairman three years later. He remained as chairman for 14 years until December 1961, although he remained on the board until his death, at the age of 82 on 18 December 1976 when he was the club's vice-chairman.

Under his chairmanship he experienced the joys of promotion, the disappointment of relegation, the despairs of the 1957 West Stand fire and the sale of John Charles to Juventus for the then British record of £65,000. Bolton was acknowledged as one of the hardest working men in the game.

An FA Council life member, he was a member of the Football League Management Committee (1964–75) and England Under-23 selector and chairman of the FA Cup Committee, best known by the public as the man who pulled out the numbered balls of the famous velvet bag to make the FA Cup draw. His devotion to football did not prevent him from serving the people of Leeds in his capacity as a City councillor. He was appointed the deputy Lord Mayor of Leeds in 1965–66 and in 1970 was appointed an Honorary Alderman. He also found time for a regular round of golf and was a member of the South Leeds and Moortown Golf Clubs.

Harry Reynolds

1961–67

ONE of the men whom Bolton invited to join the board, in 1955, Harry Reynolds, took over the helm on 11 December 1961.

A typical Tyke, he was a self-made millionaire, who was managing director of H.L. Reynolds Engineers and Steel Erectors. He did much to help United build into a soccer superpower by persuading the board

to appoint Don Revie as manager.

Revie had asked Reynolds to support his application for the vacant managerial job at Bournemouth. As Reynolds wrote down Revie's managerial virtues, he suddenly realised that Revie could do the job for Leeds, tore up his letter of support and got the rest of the United's directors to agree to Revie's appointment.

Later that year Reynolds became the new United chairman and soon pulled United's finances round from debts of £150,000 to a profit of £138,000 by the time he resigned in August 1967 because of ill health.

It was that sort of business acumen which marked Reynolds as a highly successful industrialist. His rise to the top of the financial ladder was rapid.

The son of Holbeck working-class parents, he worked as a flour boy with Leeds Co-op, a railway cleaner and a fireman before founding a steel stock holding company in Leeds and turning to metal dealing.

Rumoured to be a millionaire in the late 1950s, he lived at Hough Top, Bramley, went hunting with the Bramham Moor Hunt, played polo and became a familiar face at the captain's table on the liners *Queen Mary* and *Queen Elizabeth.*

His work for United took him to less glamorous places and would regularly visit tenement flats in Glasgow with Revie to recruit up-and-coming stars for Leeds.

The work he did for United saw him appointed as a life vice-president after his resignation. Suffering from arthritis, he travelled to London to see United win their first major trophy, the Football League Cup, in March 1968, but was unable to take his seat despite travelling by rail in a wheelchair and carrying crutches. Reynolds died in September 1974.

Albert Morris

1967–68

REYNOLDS' successor, Albert Morris, had been a director since November 1961. Prior to becoming chairman in 1967 he had been the club's finance director for three years where his experience in business proved vital.

A director of Morris Wallpapers Ltd, he was the son of Alderman Hyman Morris, Lord Mayor of Leeds in 1941–42. The family were one of the most well-known Jewish families in Leeds and Albert Morris was president of the Leeds Jewish Board of Guardians and a founder member and former treasurer of the Leeds Jewish Housing Association.

Apart from his involvement with United he was a member of Yorkshire Amateurs FC and a former captain of Moor Allerton Golf Club, close to his home in Harrogate Road.

He died on 7 April 1968 in Leeds General Infirmary, only four weeks after United beat Arsenal 1–0 at Wembley to lift the Football League Cup.

Percy Arthur Woodward

1968–72

AFTER Albert Morris' death, the club's vice-chairman Percy Woodward stepped up to become the new chairman and it was during his reign at the top that United landed their first Division One Championship.

Woodward, who was born in Leeds on 21 April 1903, had supported United as a youngster from the terraces, and was vice-president of Leeds Wanderers before joining the United board in 1946 with Harold Marjason. Within a year Woodward, who ran P.A. Woodward & Son Ltd, Packing Case Merchants & Manufacturers in Hillidge Road, Leeds, was appointed vice-chairman – a position he held for 20 years until his elevation to chairman.

Woodward's daughter, Jacqueline, married United reserve player Terry Duffy and his son, Brian, was also a part-time professional on United's books after the war. Brian Woodward later played first-team football at Hereford United and York City and from 1976 was also a United director until he resigned in protest over the sacking of manager Eddie Gray in October 1985.

Woodward senior was a well-known Leeds City councillor, serving the Beeston Ward for 15 years and was Lord Mayor of Leeds in 1961. He was chairman of South Leeds Conservative Association and president of West Hunslet Conservative Club for many years.

He remained as United's chairman until 1972 when he was succeeded by Manny Cussins, but continued as vice-chairman until his death in 1976.

Manny Cussins

1972–83

MANNY Cussins was named as chairman on 17 May 1972 and was in the boardroom hot-seat during a period of immense change at the club.

When he was appointed, he announced £500,000 improvements to the ground and in his first full season Leeds won the Division One Championship. But after the departure of Revie to take up the England job, Cussins was a central figure in the 44-day appointment and sacking of Brian Clough when he sided with the disgruntled players.

Jimmy Armfield, Jock Stein, Jimmy Adamson and Allan Clarke all came and went, but they could not add to United's collection of silverware and the club dropped back into Division Two and much of Cussins' time was spent trying to combat United's growing hooliganism problem. Cussins, a millionaire, found that

restoring United to former glories was no easy task, but it was not for the want of trying, something which was apparent throughout his life.

A native of Hull, where he was born on 26 October 1905, his appetite for work and financial success began when he was 13, pushing a handcart around to collect furniture to launch a new business. It certainly paid off. In 1954 he sold the Cussins Group for £1 million and began the John Peters chain of furniture shops which had expanded to over 100 retail outlets, a dozen clothing factories and a building business by 1975.

The John Peters Group changed its name to Waring and Gillow with Cussins remaining at the helm. He also was the head of Arncliffe Holdings, a residential property group he set up in 1971.

Cussins himself never admitted to being a rich man. 'Rich men do not work', he said, adding that retirement only turned men into cabbages.

He was co-opted on to the board at Elland Road in November 1961 at the same time as Albert Morris. He was among United's most long-serving directors when he became chairman, holding the post until December 1983 when he stepped down in favour of relative newcomer Leslie Silver. Cussins remained vice-chairman until his death in London on 5 October 1987, three weeks short of his 82nd birthday.

Leslie Silver

1983–96

LONDON-BORN Leslie Silver was originally an Arsenal fan after being mesmerised by Alex James when watching his first Highbury match in 1934 at the age of nine.

Silver, like his predecessor Cussins, was a highly successful businessman after moving to Leeds in 1940. He came out of the RAF as a warrant officer in 1947 and launched a paint firm called Kalon Paints with other members of his family, with £1,000 from his wartime gratuity and other loans and developed it into a thriving business.

Silver became chairman of Silver Paint and Lacquer (Holdings) Ltd and his firm's Home Charm Paint became one of Britain's best-known names. A former president of the Oil and Colour Chemists' Association, he was awarded the OBE in June 1982 for services to export.

His company was highly regarded on the stockmarket and in 1991 when he wanted to sell 18.5 per cent of the shares he had no difficulty finding buyers. The sale brought him nearly £12 million, leaving his family interests with another £27 million worth of shares.

Six months after being honoured, Silver was elevated from vice-chairman to chairman of Leeds United. He had been on the board at Elland Road for a relatively short time, but was quick to tackle two of the club's major problems – hooliganism and finance.

The club introduced an identity card scheme to help root out troublemakers who were dragging the club's name down and introduced a system of all-ticket away games to curb the yob element and appointed a representative of the Supporters' Club, Eric Carlisle, to the board. Major steps were taken to reshape the image of Leeds United as a family club, while, at the same time, United were able to tap into the commercial potential of the broad base of fans. The sale of Elland Road to Leeds City Council for £2.5 million, generated much-needed cash and gradually the club's shaky finances got back on an even keel.

Silver was instrumental in appointing Howard Wilkinson as manager and the winning of the Second Division Championship triggered a boom within the club. Season ticket sales rocketed as Leeds returned to the big time after Silver and Wilkinson gambled on the direct route back to the top – forking out big fees for quality players.

Although it plunged the club into the red, the gamble paid off, promotion was achieved, and the First Division Championship triumph in 1991–92 saw more cash roll into the Elland Road coffers, enabling the old Lowfields Road stand to be demolished and replaced by the imposing East Stand, while the conversion of the old Kop to the Don Revie Stand made Elland Road into an all-seater stadium that was deemed fit to stage a full England international and host three games in the 1996 European Championships.

However, the need to spend big sums of money on players and ground improvements to keep Leeds near the top of the Premiership tree ate away at the club's finances and in March 1996 Silver told shareholders that the club expected to lose between £3.5 million and £4.5 million in the forthcoming year so the board were prepared to listen to offers for the club. The 71-year-old Leslie Silver announced on 9 April 1996 that he was to resign as chairman.

Silver had suffered from heart problems and weeks before his resignation he and his wife Sheila were tied up during a robbery at their Leeds home, an incident which undoubtedly played a part in his decision to stand down. He was chancellor of Leeds Metropolitan University from 1999 to 2005.

Bill Fotherby

1996–97

LESLIE SILVER was replaced by the charismatic Bill Fotherby, who had been the club's managing director since 1988, in an acting capacity.

Fotherby, Silver and vice-chairman Peter Gilman were members of United's three-man directorate with a 33 per cent holding in the club and it was Fotherby who spearheaded the commercial drive for the new Premier League in October 1991.

Hunslet-born Fotherby had been instrumental in clinching the transfer of big-money players like Tomas Brolin and Tony Yeboah and became the first-ever salaried director of the club. He received a salary of £244,098 in 1995.

There was much speculation about the future of the club throughout the summer of 1996, with London-based media group Caspian being installed as favourites, particularly as executive director Richard Thompson resigned his chairmanship at QPR.

United's financial advisors, Rothchilds, studied takeover bids for the club, which were also believed to include one from the Yorkshire-based Conrad Leisure Group, former United player Trevor Cherry being among Conrad's backers.

But in July, Caspian were named as United's new owners, the asking price variously reported as being between £16 million and £35 million. Chris Akers, chairman of Caspian said: 'We intend to maintain Leeds' position as one of the top Premier League teams. Leeds should be well placed to strengthen the first-team squad so that the club can continue to compete at the highest level, both domestically and in Europe, for the foreseeable future.'

With Fotherby, now chairman, new directors from Caspian were welcomed on board with Robin Launders named as the club's chief executive.

Caspian Group became a PLC and changed its name to Leeds Sporting PLC in August 1996. At this time, the club had two boards of directors – one for the football club and one for the parent company.

In 1999 Fotherby became chairman of Harrogate Town, stepping down in November 2011 at the age of 80.

Peter Ridsdale

1997–2003

PETER RIDSDALE, who had been a United director since 1987 took over the chairmanship from Bill Fotherby shortly after the Caspian takeover.

Born in the Harrogate area on 11 March 1952, he had forged a business career with the Appleyard Group, Baker Perkins plc, ICL plc, Schering-Plough inc and the Del Monte Corporation. He subsequently enjoyed success with the Burton Group plc, being managing director of Top Man Ltd among other roles.

He was only 35 when he became a United director and found himself in the hot-seat ten years later.

Ridsdale enjoyed a good rapport with supporters, who were particularly impressed with the dignified way in which he handled the Galatasaray tragedy. Leeds fans Kevin Speight and Christopher Loftus were both stabbed to death in Istanbul on the eve of the 2000 UEFA Cup semi-final and the chairman visited other supporters who had been injured in attacks in the Turkish capital.

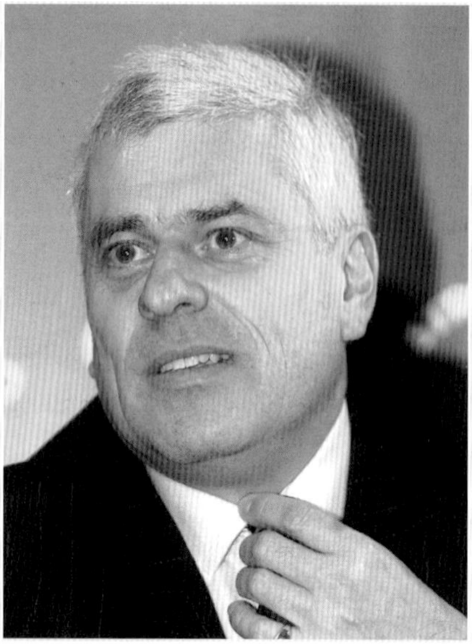

Although Caspian chairman Chris Akers had moved on, Leeds looked in secure hands with Ridsdale as chairman and two other well-respected businessmen – finance director Jeremy Fenn and commercial director Adam Pearson in place. Turnover was increasing and profits were up – United looked as though they could become a force in the Premiership for many years to come.

Caspian felt the Elland Road site could be redeveloped to create new income streams and its vision included a hotel, indoor hockey arena, exhibition centre and leisure facilities.

However, Fenn left to join Akers on his Sports Internet Group, leaving Ridsdale to become more involved with signing players. Pearson left Elland Road 18 months later and went on to become chairman at Hull City, then, later, chairman of Derby County.

The Caspian duo's policy had been to build the club up slowly, but Ridsdale, who had become both chairman of the club and the PLC in summer 1999, wanted to quicken the pace. He and O'Leary reckoned Champions League qualification would deliver their aim of turning United into a football superpower and embarked on a spending spree that took the club to the brink of disaster.

There was a plan to sell the Elland Road ground and build a bigger stadium on the outskirts of Leeds. It was a big vision and the ambition was reinforced by the arrival of some huge money signings like Rio Ferdinand, the world's most expensive defender at £18 million.

Securing a Champions League place in 2000 helped attracted more stars to Elland Road, but everything began to unravel by the failure to qualify for Europe's top club competition the following season. Some of the players were on vast wages and had been bought on a hire-purchase agreement and with no Champions League cash coming in, Ridsdale told O'Leary that some players would have to go.

All this was played out against the background of the infamous Lee Bowyer and Jonathan Woodgate assault court case and O'Leary's book – *Leeds United on Trial* – published after the 2000–01 season.

Ridsdale sacked O'Leary in June 2002 and brought in Terry Venables, but the club was now £80 million in debt. Ridsdale, had gambled and lost.

Venables was helpless as players were sold, the final straw coming when Woodgate was shipped out to Newcastle United for £9 million in order to ease the club's debts.

The former England boss Venables left soon afterwards and was quickly followed by Ridsdale.

At their Champions League peak, in Ridsdale's words United were 'living the dream' now they faced a financial nightmare. The club's debts had climbed to £103 million and the team struggling on the field.

Although it had happened on his watch, Ridsdale, the fan in the boardroom, claimed it was not all his fault and others should share responsibility. When United were relegated 15 months after his departure, Ridsdale, after a brief spell as chairman at Barnsley, was chairman at debt-ridden Cardiff City, having taken over from Sam Hamman in October 2006. The following year his book *United We Fall* gave his version of events in the Elland Road boardroom with O'Leary coming in for criticism.

Ridsdale, dubbed Publicity Pete by the media, was installed as a football consultant by crisis-hit Plymouth Argyle in October 2009 and steered the club though a High Court winding-up petition and led the hunt for new buyers. He was named acting chairman after the Pilgrims entered administration in March 2010 and he left seven months later when new buyers were found for the Devon club. On 6 December 2011 Ridsdale became chairman of Preston North End.

Professor John McKenzie

2003

DURING all the financial chaos, Professor John McKenzie, a non-executive director with responsibility for pushing the Leeds brand into the Far East, emerged as the new chairman at the end of March 2003.

The 65-year-old Ilford-born academic was seen as a safe pair of hands. His father, D.W. McKenzie had been a member of the FA international committee and president of the Isthmian League.

Professor McKenzie was a United season ticket holder who gradually built up his shareholding until he became the second largest individual shareholder with four million shares. He was invited to join the board in October 2002, and joined the plc board as a non-executive director.

A graduate of the London School of Economics, he gained a BSc from the University College of London, Bedford. In 1986 he was made rector of the London Institute and became director of international development. He was also head of Liverpool Polytechnic and held senior positions with a number of blue chip companies including Cadbury Schweppes, Unilever and SmithKline Beechams. He was also a special advisor to the Shanghai Municipal Government, the Tokyo Cultural Institute, Sarawak University in Malaysia and has a long-standing interest in the Far East.

One of his first major moves was to reveal publicly the outrageous spending which had led to United's increasing losses. The interim finance figures for the second half of 2002 showed the club lost £17.2 million before tax, while the total net debt to the end of the year was £78.9 million.

McKenzie said: 'It's like an oil tanker heading straight for the rocks and now the shareholders have put someone else on board to turn it around'.

To help cut costs, McKenzie made a mass of redundancies. He also made two key appointments – chief executive Trevor Birch, an insolvency specialist, and chief financial officer, Neil Robson, who worked for accountancy firm Ernst & Young. The

mission was to keep the Leeds United oil tanker afloat.

Professor McKenzie used his links with the Far East to drum up investors and opted to stand down as chairman of the plc at the annual meeting in December 2003 to ensure there would be no conflict of interest should he represent potential investors in talks with the club's creditors and advisors.

His nine-month reign, although short, was significant with £20 million cuts from United's costs. He remained on the football club board as a director.

Trevor Birch

2003–04

CHIEF executive Trevor Birch was appointed as United's acting-chairman on 23 December 2003 – a move welcomed by shareholders.

Birch, a former Liverpool reserve player, was Bill Shankly's last signing but didn't break into the Reds' first team and after short stints with Shrewsbury and Chester quit the professional game aged 23 to combine playing part-time football with Marine, Runcorn, Northwich and Skelmersdale with his work as a chartered accountant after qualifying at Liverpool Polytechnic.

Insolvency was his specialist area and he became chief executive of Chelsea in February 2002 when the London club was up to its neck in debt. He helped restructure its finances and helped put together the £140 million takeover by Roman Abramovich in summer 2003. The deal saw the Stamford Bridge outfit's debt virtually eradicated, so with Birch's job done, he left.

He stepped into Leeds' financial maelstrom in October 2003 as chief executive and did much to negotiate with creditors and help the club avoid administration.

His work as acting-chairman was always going to be temporary and hit a snag when a cash injection of £4.4 million from United's deputy chairman Allan Leighton failed to materialise, thus putting a subscription for shares on hold.

It was through his hard work and patient negotiation that Birch finally concluded the sale of Leeds United on 19 March 2004 to a Yorkshire-based consortium Adulant Force, fronted by accountant and insolvency expert, Gerald Krasner. The threat of administration – and possible liquidation – appeared to be over.

Birch had massively slashed the club's debts from £100 million to a more manageable £20 million and left shortly after the bargain with Adulant Force was concluded.

He is one of the few men able to come out of the whole financial meltdown saga with his reputation intact.

Shortly after leaving Leeds he was appointed chief executive at Everton, but resigned after six weeks. Since then he's been chief executive of both Derby County and Sheffield United. In February 2012, Birch was appointed administrator at cash-strapped Portsmouth.

Gerald Krasner

2004–05

DESPITE the relief of avoiding administration, United fans were still nervous about the financial future.

Adulant Force consisted of five businessmen, known as the Yorkshire Consortium, who became the new board, along with former United striker Peter Lorimer, who was an advisor on football matters.

The new club chairman was Gerald Krasner, 54, who was the consortium spokesman. He had been a United fan for 30 years and was an insolvency practitioner at accountants Bartfields in the city. Melvyn Helme, a former senior manager at NatWest Bank and property developer, was named corporate finance director.

The other directors were 26-year-old property developer Simon Morris, Leeds-born entrepreneur Melvyn Levi, the son of the late Jack Levi, a well-known Leeds solicitor, and businessman David Richmond, son of former Bradford City chairman Geoffrey, who had been a member of the Valley Parade board.

Relegation from the Premiership signalled more financial trouble and Krasner and co were still saddled with paying off former players and managers as well as agents' fees.

Championship football meant star players like Alan Smith, Mark Viduka, James Milner and Paul Robinson were sold off as the board desperately sought to reduce the club's £40 million wage bill.

Krasner organised the sale and 25-year lease-back of the Thorp Arch training ground to Manchester businessman Jacob Adler, who a few weeks later took up a similar arrangement with the Elland Road ground.

But the Yorkshire Consortium didn't have sufficient financial muscle and when the club defaulted on £2 million tax payments in January 2005 it was close to administration.

Then, out of the blue, a deal saw Ken Bates, the former Chelsea chairman, take over the club. In 2008 Krasner was appointed administrator at cash-strapped Bournemouth and fulfilled a similar role at Port Vale in 2012.

Kenneth William Bates

2005–

KEN BATES' surprise deal for Leeds United was completed in the early hours of 21 January 2005.

The often-outspoken Bates fronted the Geneva-based Sports Forward Fund (SFF) and invested about £10 million, securing a 50 per cent controlling stake in the club.

The 74-year-old's money cleared the decks with the tax man, an annual payment to bondholders of £1.4 million and other liabilities, bringing the total debt down to around £17 million.

A repayment scheme was agreed with the Inland Revenue and Customs and Excise for

other outstanding monies as the club was hauled from the brink of financial oblivion.

Despite all this, it has to be said that Bates' takeover was greeted with suspicion by some United followers.

Bates, the son of a lorry driver, was a successful businessman with interests in ready-mixed cement, sugar cane and land development. He had been chairman at Oldham and Wigan before buying a cash-crippled Chelsea in 1982 for £1.

Bates served on the Football League management committee in the mid-1980s and was an active member of the FA Executive involved in the early stages of the Wembley Stadium rebuilding project and was appointed chairman of Wembley National Stadium Ltd in 1997 but resigned four years later, citing a lack of support from the board.

On the club front, he formed Chelsea Village Limited as he went about transforming the Stamford Bridge ground with top class facilities, including a hotel. He delivered in style before selling his controlling interest in the club to Russian oil billionaire Roman Abramovich in 2003 and retired to the tax haven of Monaco.

But Bates was lured back to football the following year, showing interest in Sheffield Wednesday before pulling off his Leeds coup.

Blunt and straight to the point, Bates arrived with his long-term aides – Yvonne Todd, who became finance director, a role she had filled at Chelsea; Jayne McGuinness, who became deputy chairman; and Mark Taylor, his lawyer. The only director who remained from the old guard was former player Peter Lorimer.

The new board were quick to evaluate the club's finances. Savings were made in staff numbers and costs, like champagne in the boardroom, were reduced. Ticket prices were increased, a Members' Club formed, Yorkshire Radio launched, a subscription club TV service developed, relations with Leeds City Council and the local business community – vital for sponsorships – improved.

But failure to regain their place in the Premiership, followed by relegation to League One still left a millstone of debt around the club's neck and it went into administration, thus incurring a 10-point penalty which confirmed United's inevitable relegation.

Eventually, the club was bought by a new company formed by Bates, Taylor and chief executive Shaun Harvey only for the Football League to impose a further 15-point deduction from the start of the new campaign in League One. United appealed against the decision but lost. But for the points deduction United would have gained promotion at the first attempt but endured two more seasons in League One before finally getting back in to the Championship in 2010.

Bates regularly used his column in the matchday programme to express his views but comments about Melvyn Levi, the former United director, landed him in hot water. Levi began libel proceedings against Bates in London's High Court in June 2009.

The judge, Sir Charles Gray, ruled in favour of Levi, awarding him libel damages of £50,000 and ordered the United chairman to pay legal costs, estimated at £1.5 million.

The question of who actually owned Leeds United had repeatedly been aired by

The Guardian newspaper and the complex issue was looked into by the Football League, who in February 2010 confirmed that the club's owners passed its fit and proper persons test.

Although the actual ownership of the club had been shrouded in mystery for several years, United confirmed chairman Bates as the new owner of the club in May 2011. He bought out the previous owners FSF Limited through his company Outro Limited for an undisclosed sum.

Bates had announced further ground improvements to add to the investment in better catering facilities provided by the Billy's Bar pub and Howard's Way restaurant, plus a large conference and exhibition centre. That included 24 executive boxes and the creation of a club museum and hotel – all designed to create more income for the club – in the East Stand.

But having narrowly missed the Play-offs on their return to the Championship, Bates came in to conflict with some fans at the start of the 2011–12 season. They were unhappy at seeing several players depart and believed the club should spend more on team strengthening in an effort to reach the Premiership rather than ground developments.

Anti-Bates demonstrators at Elland Road were branded as 'morons' by the chairman, who reiterated that he was not going anywhere.

In May 2012 the club confirmed that talks were taking place regarding investment for the long-term future. The identity of the potential investor was kept under wraps.

LEEDS UNITED PRESIDENT

Earl of Harewood

1961–2011

THE Earl of Harewood became Leeds United's first president in December 1961, an honour he held until his death on 11 July 2011.

The Earl of Harewood, in his capacity as president of the FA, presents the 1969 Charity Shield to skipper Billy Bremner.

Stanley Blenkinsop, who set up the Leeds Hospitals radio service, addresses the 1947 annual meeting of the Football League.

George Henry Hubert Lascelles, seventh Earl of Harewood, elder son of the sixth Earl and Princess Mary, daughter of King George V, was born in 1923 and first became a United follower in the 1930s.

First cousin to the queen, he was an Old Etonian, who was president of the Football Association from 1963 to 1972.

After leaving Kings College, Cambridge, he became a captain in the Grenadier Guards and was wounded and captured in France. Following imprisonment at Spangenberg and Moosberg, he was sent to Colditz on the direct orders of Adolf Hitler.

A noted patron of the arts, he has been, at various times, director of the Royal Opera House, Covent Garden; artistic director of both the Edinburgh and Leeds Arts Festivals, managing director of the English National Opera, an Arts Council member, artistic advisor to the New Philharmonic Orchestra, governor of the BBC, president of the British Board of Film Censors and a former Chancellor of York University.

But his other main passion was football. If Leeds United were at home, he was at Elland Road.

Plans were in hand to name a new suite within the revamped East Stand after Lord Harewood, whose widow, Patricia, accepted an offer to become the club's patron shortly after her husband's death.

Leeds United Life Vice-Presidents

WHEN Lord Harewood was named president in 1961, two long-standing directors, **Stanley Lynam Blenkinsop** and **John Bromley**, were made vice-presidents.

Blenkinsop had served on the board for 27 years and was instrumental in establishing Leeds Hospitals radio commentaries. He set up the Leeds Cricket and Football Hospital Relays Association in 1951 after being ill in hospital and realised there was no way of following his teams fortunes from his ward bed.

Former chairman **Harry Reynolds** became a life vice-president in 1968.

Backroom Staff

AN ESSENTIAL part of the smooth running of any football club is the backroom staff and both City and United have had more than their fair share of well known, and not so well known, names working behind the scenes.

One man was around before Leeds City even moved into Elland Road – **Albert Stead.** He was trainer and groundsman when the change from rugby to soccer was made in 1905 and worked at the ground until his retirement in 1945.

However, the most famous trainer in Leeds City's days was former Loughborough left-back **George Swift,** who worked under Gilbert Gillies when the club was first formed. He represented the Football League in his days with Loughborough and was later to have a spell in charge with Southampton.

It was not until the arrival of Herbert Chapman that the club got on a proper organised footing with **Jack Chaplin**, appointed trainer in November 1913. A full-back, he had played with Chapman at Tottenham and also played for his hometown of Dundee and Manchester City.

Jack Chaplin

After a stint as Chapman's assistant, he moved on to train Bristol Rovers in March 1920, returned north to help Sheffield Wednesday in the same capacity before linking up with Chapman again at Huddersfield, where he became manager in August 1929, reverting back to trainer three years later.

Also on the staff was **Dick Murrell,** who served both City and United as trainer. He was a hard task master who would send players on endless laps around Elland Road and make them sweat off extra weight in Turkish Baths when they reported back for pre-season training.

Murrell, christened Aubrey John, but always called Dick, was a key part of the backroom staff assembled by United's first manager, Arthur Fairclough. Born in Grimsby, he played for Grimsby Town (1892–95), Grimsby All Stars, Newark, Wellingborough and Grimsby Town (1900–01) again, breaking a leg in a practice game in August 1901. He died in Leeds, aged 80, in 1951.

Bill Norman was Fairclough's assistant manager and arrived at Elland Road in June 1923 from Blackpool with his son-in-law, **Allan Ure,** who became Murrell's assistant. Norman was dubbed 'The Sergeant Major' when he had whipped the Barnsley team which won the 1912 FA Cup into shape. He spent nine years with Barnsley before becoming Huddersfield's trainer just before World War One broke out. At the end of the hostilities he became

Dick Murrell

Blackpool's first full-time manager and together with Ure moulded them into one of the fittest sides around. Despite a promising start to his managerial career, including winning the Central League Championship, Norman jumped at the chance to work under his old Barnsley mentor, Arthur Fairclough, at Leeds.

Norman helped prepare the team for promotion in 1924 but quit after relegation three years later and took charge at Hartlepool in August 1927. His toughness was legendary and according to one story he demonstrated this during a bitter Hartlepool winter when one group of timid 'Pool players were complaining about the biting cold during a training session. Norman immediately put them to shame by stripping off and rolling naked in the snow. Such bravery didn't bring Hartlepool much success on field and he left in April 1932 and resumed training at Barnsley.

Ure, born on 12 January, probably 1892, only played reserve football for Blackpool but was their trainer for years, earning a reputation as a top-class masseur and physiotherapist before joining Leeds with his father-in-law. Ure stayed at Leeds until 1928 when he returned to Blackpool and after training Barnsley was appointed Gillingham's manager in May 1937. His 12 months in charge was a disaster and the Gills voted out of the Southern Section League in preference to Ipswich.

He was trainer to Millwall in 1938 and, after the war, Bradford Park Avenue before acting as Halifax Town's physiotherapist and trainer for 10 years until his retirement in 1962.

During the reign of Dick Ray, **Arthur Campey,** the successor to Murrell became a familiar figure as he dash on to the field in his fluttering white coat to attend to injured players. In those days he was assisted by former Leeds player Harry Sherwin.

Campey made an unexpected return to United after the 1957 West Stand fire, helping fix players up with boots to replace ones which had gone up in smoke.

The colourful Campey was a hard act to follow but new trainer **Bob Roxburgh** proved more than an able replacement, giving 19 years service at Elland Road.

Born in Morpeth on 5 February 1896, Roxburgh played for Morpeth Comrades, joining Newcastle United in November 1920. A right-back, he was kept out of the team by veteran Billy Hampson, a future Leeds manager, so moved to Blackburn Rovers in May 1924 for £375. He totalled 128 appearances with Ewood Park club before taking a coaching appointment in Holland.

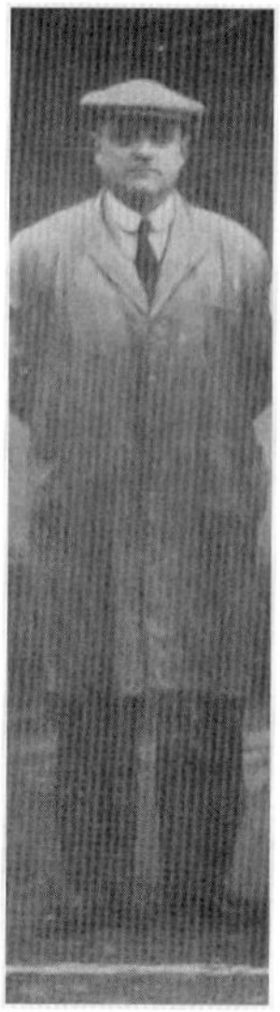

Arthur Campey

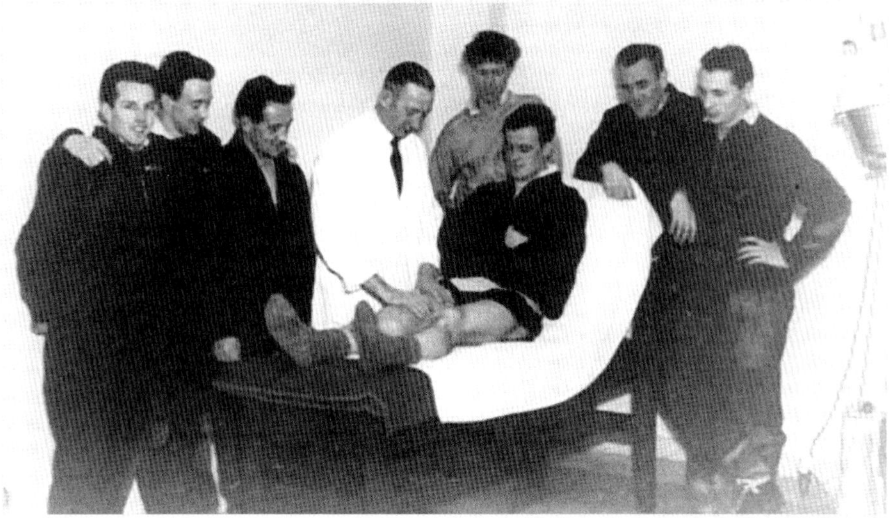

Bob Roxburgh has an audience of players as he gets to work in the treatment room.

When Hampson was appointed manager at Elland Road, he was instrumental in recruiting Roxburgh to the United staff. Roxburgh struck up a great rapport with the players and retired in November 1957 after 19 years on the training staff. He died, aged 78, in November 1974.

After World War Two, training became more technical and United were able to boast several top names on coaching staff in the late 1940s, including England internationals **Willis Edwards**, **Gordon Hodgson** and **Ken Willingham**, all former United players. Edwards was assistant trainer to Roxburgh with responsibility for looking after the reserves, Hodgson was appointed to the coaching staff during wartime before moving on to Port Vale and Willingham had a few years as a Leeds coach after retiring in 1948 as a player. He later was a coach at Halifax Town.

A fourth England international, **Sam Weaver**, also worked behind the scenes at Leeds immediately after the war. He won three England caps at wing-half and was an assistant trainer at Elland Road between summer 1947 and June 1949.

A native of Pilsley, Derbyshire, he had turned out for United in wartime games after a distinguished playing career began at Sutton Junction, Sutton Town and Hull City, who he joined in March 1928. A £2,500 move took him to Newcastle United in November 1929 and he won a Cup winners' medal with the Magpies in 1932. Another big money move saw him go to Chelsea in August 1936 for £4,000 and after guesting for Leeds, finished his playing career with Stockport County.

Weaver left Elland Road to become Millwall's trainer, a job he held until January 1954 when he had a brief spell with non-League Bromley before being appointed coach at Mansfield, where he was manager between June 1958 and January 1960, starting a seven-year stint as assistant trainer the following month. A sporting all-rounder, Weaver also played county cricket for Derbyshire and Somerset. He died, in Mansfield, on 15 April 1985, aged 74.

Fitness fanatic **Bill Lambton** was appointed United's trainer-coach by Raich Carter in November 1957 and introduced some novel training methods. He later had a three-month spell as United's manager.

Welsh international wing-half **Ivor Powell** joined the coaching staff in July 1956 and remained at Leeds until his appointment as Carlisle's manager in May 1960, a post he held for three years. He managed Bath City, coached PAOK in Greece and returned to Bath, where he coached the university's soccer team, now known as Team Bath, with great success. He was still an active coach in his 90s, was inducted into the Welsh Sports Hall of Fame in 2004 and made an MBE four years later.

Powell began his career with Bargoed in South Wales before having trials with Queen's Park Rangers but wasn't taken on. He remained in London to work and turned out for Barnet in the Isthmian League. In September 1937, QPR gave him a second chance and he made his League debut just before the war. He joined the War Reserve Police before becoming a PT instructor in Blackpool, guesting for the Seasiders. At Bloomfield Road he became big pals with Stanley Matthews, who was best man at Powell's wedding. Capped eight times by Wales, Powell also made four wartime international appearances, the last coming at Wembley in September 1943 when he was substituted and replaced by Blackpool chum Stan Mortensen.

After being posted to India, he returned to football and won a Division Three South Championship medal with QPR, then joined Aston Villa for £17,500, a record fee for a wing-half. Blighted by cartilage trouble he moved into player-management with Port Vale (August 1951) and Bradford City (May 1954), quitting as a player six months later, remaining as manager until February 1955.

He then ran a pub in the Manningham district of Bradford before United tempted him back to coaching.

The appointment of Don Revie as Leeds boss in March 1961 proved to be the turning point in the club's history and it was acknowledged that the strength of his support staff was a solid plank on which United were able to build their glory years.

Revie's able lieutenant was **Les Cocker**, a journeyman forward, who worked as a painter and decorator before becoming a professional footballer. His skills as a trainer ensured he became a Leeds legend after a modest career which began with his native Stockport where he was born on 13 March 1924. He was in the Reconnaissance Regiment in France with the 53rd Division when he played his first wartime games for County, travelling up from his Army base in Dorset to play home games.

He turned professional in August 1947, joining Accrington Stanley six years later, scoring 48 League goals in 122 games for the Peel Park club, including hat-tricks in successive games in January 1955 against Barrow and Chesterfield. He was appointed Accrington's assistant trainer in May 1957, but was re-signed four months later because of an injury crisis.

In August 1959 Cocker went to Luton as assistant trainer-coach and arrived at Elland Road with the Hatters' coach, Syd Owen, in 1960.

A fully qualified FA coach, Cocker, studied anatomy and physiology and was highly regarded, earning promotion as trainer to the England Under-23 side in November 1961. Four weeks after Revie was appointed England manager, Cocker left Leeds to become England's trainer and Revie's assistant in July 1975. He had previously assisted England during the 1970 World Cup Finals.

When Revie quit the England job for the Middle East, Cocker joined Doncaster Rovers as trainer-coach, linking up with former Leeds player Billy Bremner, who was in charge at Belle Vue. It was during one of Doncaster's training sessions that Cocker collapsed and died on 4 October 1977.

At Leeds, Cocker had whipped the Elland Road stars into shape, but it was his former Luton colleague **Syd Owen** who coached the players in the arts and skills of the game. Owen enjoyed a splendid football career culminating in three England caps, FA tours to Australia, South Africa, Rhodesia and West Indies, and an FA Cup Final appearance for Luton – his last-ever senior game.

Born in Birmingham on 29 September 1922, Owen represented Formans Road and South Birmingham Schools, worked as an engineer in his late teens and enlisted in the RAF in 1941, seeing service with his mobile radio unit in Egypt, Palestine, Sicily, Italy and Austria.

He played several representative matches for the RAF and the Central Mediterranean Forces against British Army of the Rhine before demobilisation in 1946. After a short time at Birmingham City he joined Luton in 1947. A highly mobile centre-half, he helped the Hatters to the 1959 FA Cup Final – the same year he was named Footballer of the Year. He was skipper in nine of his 12 years at Luton and had qualified as an FA coach in 1952. Soon after the Cup Final defeat against Nottingham Forest Owen was appointed Luton manager, a position he held until April 1960. Three months later he arrived at Elland Road as coach and worked daily honing the skills of the stars during Revie's glittering era.

He resigned in October 1975 because the club could not promise him a written contract, but returned, at Eddie Gray's invitation, to be chief scout in October 1982 after Ron Atkinson's arrival at Manchester United saw him lose a similar post at Old Trafford. **Maurice Lindley**, the former Everton centre-half, arrived at Leeds at the same time as Owen, as Revie's assistant manager and chief scout.

He was born in Keighley on 5 December 1915 and played for Keighley Schools, Keighley Town and Bradford City (as an amateur) before turning pro with Everton in March 1936, but actually made his name in wartime football with the RAF, regularly playing Combined Services and FA representative matches. He played one game for United as a guest in March 1944.

After the war he returned to Goodison until 1951 when he was named Swindon's coach, stepping up to manager in 1953 and staying until May 1955. Brief spells at Barry Town and Crewe (1955–58) followed before he was named Newcastle's chief scout in 1956. Two years later he joined Leeds as trainer-coach, but the following year moved to Sheffield Wednesday in a similar capacity.

Lindley rejoined Leeds in July 1960 as chief scout and proved a great ally to Revie, compiling meticulous dossiers sizing up the strengths and weaknesses of future opponents, particularly continental opposition.

Although not based at Elland Road, another vital player in Revie's supporting cast was **John Barr**, a former Third Lanark, QPR, Dunfermline and Dundee United defender. He was scouting for QPR when he was recruited by Revie in 1961 to do a similar role for Leeds – a job he did with great success, particularly in Scotland where he unearthed a roll-call of United greats – Eddie and Frank Gray, Peter Lorimer, Joe Jordan and Gordon McQueen among them.

Barr remained associated with United until his death, aged 80, in 1997.

After Revie's departure Lindley acted as caretaker manager no less than five times, but never sought the job on a full-time basis and was happy to work with a succession of managers, many of them ex-players.

When he left Elland Road in October 1981, Lindley held the title Chief Playing Staff Executive. He became chief scout, at the age of 66, at Bradford City on 5 March

Revie's dream team with the Fairs Cup, from left to right: Syd Owen, Maurice Lindley, Don Revie, Les Cocker, Bob English and Cyril Partridge.

1982, and took on the familiar mantle of caretaker manager after the dismissal of Terry Dolan and before the appointment of Terry Yorath in February 1988. He retired in 1991 and died at his home in Horsforth two years later, aged 78.

Revie's troops often embarked on long and strenuous seasons so the role of physiotherapist was crucial. Between 1959 and October 1981 it was held by ex-Army man **Bob English**.

Despite trials with Swindon in 1936 he didn't play full-time football and spent nearly 25 years with the Army Physical Training Corps, having joined up in 1933.

A preliminary FA coach, he spent a season as physiotherapist at QPR before joining Leeds, where, in the late 1970s, he became club kit convenor before becoming a victim of cost-cutting measures in October 1981.

Strength in depth was one of the features of Revie's backroom staff and York-born **Cyril Partridge** helped groom a string of youngsters into fully fledged internationals in his role as second-team trainer.

Born on 12 October 1931, he was a relatively late developer in football terms, joining QPR as a winger in August 1954. He failed to make the first team and joined Rotherham three years later, making only a handful of League games.

Future manager **Brian Doyle** also helped Leeds out briefly as a coach in the 1960s. The Mancunian, born on 15 July 1930, began as a full-back with non-League Lostock Green before joining Stoke City in March 1951. He then played for Exeter City (April 1954) and Bristol Rovers (August 1957) until injury forced his retirement in 1959.

He coached Carlisle United and served as Workington's manager between July 1968 and 1969, was a coach at Blackpool in 1971 and was manager at Stockport between March 1972 and May 1974. He died, aged 62, on 22 December 1992.

After Revie and Cocker left, Brian Clough swept through Elland Road like a new broom.

Although his assistant Peter Taylor remained at Brighton, trainer **Jimmy Gordon**, who had worked with Clough at Derby replaced the England-bound Les Cocker. Glaswegian Gordon had a great footballing pedigree. Born on 23 October 1915, he was schooled by Wishaw Juniors before joining Newcastle United as a polished wing-half in April 1935 for £50. Surprisingly overlooked by Scotland, he moved to Middlesbrough in November 1945 for £3,500, retiring 10 years later to become assistant trainer at Ayresome Park. A qualified FA coach, he joined Blackburn as trainer in 1961, moving to Derby in summer 1969 to link up with Clough, with whom he had played at Middlesbrough.

After Clough's dramatic departure from Elland Road, Gordon worked for Rolls-Royce in Derby until Clough appointed him as Nottingham Forest's trainer in January 1975. He shared in all of Forest's memorable triumphs under Clough, who asked Gordon to lead Forest out at Wembley for one of their League Cup Finals. He retired in summer 1980. After the Clough turbulence, Leeds opted for the calm of mild-mannered Jimmy Armfield as manager and he brought in one of the most experienced coaches of the post-war era, **Don Howe**.

Wolverhampton-born Howe was a fine full-back with West Bromwich Albion and Arsenal, winning 23 England caps, several with Armfield, and went on to manage both clubs.

Born on 12 October 1935, he was rejected by Wolves and joined Albion as an amateur, turning professional in November 1952. In April 1964 a £45,000 transfer took him to Highbury, where a

Jimmy Gordon in the dugout with Brian Clough.

broken leg ended his career in March 1966, so he moved into coaching, playing a major part in shaping their double-winning side of 1970–71. He also coached the Gunners to three Wembley Cup Finals and a European Cup-winners' Cup Final.

Stepping into management at The Hawthorns in July 1971, he suffered relegation in 1973 and left in April 1975, being appointed manager of Turkish side Galatasaray in May 1975. But when Armfield invited him to Leeds four months later, Howe jumped at the chance to re-enter the English game. In fact, Howe didn't stay long, returning to Arsenal as coach in August 1977, when he was also acting as Bobby Robson's assistant manager with England, and manager of the Gunners between December 1983 and March 1986.

After a spell in Saudi Arabia, Howe spent a few weeks on Bristol Rovers' coaching staff before joining Wimbledon in August 1987 as assistant to Bobby Gould and helped the Dons win the 1988 FA Cup.

Another move saw him in charge at QPR, after a period as assistant, returning to Wimbledon as coach in May 1991. He replaced Terry Butcher as manager at Coventry five months later and in 1992 was joined by Gould as they worked together as joint managers. However, within a couple of months Howe, then suffering from heart problems, accepted an offer to become Chelsea's assistant. Later he was part of Terry Venables' England coaching set-up. He retired from coaching in the summer of 2003.

Howe's departure from Leeds left a big hole in Armfield's plans, but plugged the gap by recruiting **Brian Green** in September 1977 to his coaching staff after Leeds old boy **Bobby Collins**, the youth coach, had temporarily helped with the seniors.

Although he only had modest success as a centre-forward in the lower divisions with Rochdale, Southport, Barrow, Exeter and Chesterfield, non-League Runcorn, New Brighton, Altrincham, Wisbech, Boston, Stalybridge, Ashton United and Glossop, Droylsden-born Green was highly rated as a coach.

After playing in New South Wales, Australia, for the Prague club, and coaching in Kuwait, Green returned to his old club, Southport, as player-coach and took a lot of credit for their 1972–73 Division Four Championship triumph.

He moved on to Chester, helping plot United's dramatic defeat in League Cup, before being appointed coach of the Australian national team. Back in England, he became Rochdale manager in June 1976 before his arrival at Leeds.

Subsequently, he has been assistant manager at Stockport and managed Norwegian club Bryne for several seasons. In the 1990s he was reported to be a hotel sales manager near Oldham.

After the brief 44-day reign of Scotland boss Jock Stein, United turned to Jimmy Adamson as their manager in 1978 and he brought in a new backroom staff. His assistant was **Dave Merrington**, his former playing colleague at Burnley. Merrington, born in Newcastle on 26 January 1945, went to Bristol City after his Burnley days, but did not play a first-team game there, Merrington then went into coaching and was Adamson's second in command at Sunderland prior to arriving at Leeds.

Supporting Merrington was coach **Syd Farrimond**, the former long-serving Bolton Wanderers player.

Two coaches who worked under Stein and Armfield – former Bradford City manager **Bryan Edwards** and **Jimmy McAnearney**, the former Sheffield Wednesday, Plymouth, and Watford wing-half moved on.

Dundee-born McAnearney had entered coaching with Rotherham under Tommy Docherty in May 1968, moving up to be manager between December 1968 and May 1973. He then spent two years on Sheffield Wednesday's coaching staff, acting as caretaker manager in 1975. McAnearney, whose brothers John and Tom also played League football, spent some time setting up a machine tools company in Sheffield before being appointed Scarborough's manager in 1981 and in the late 1980s was in charge at Hallam.

Edwards was born in Woodlesford, between Leeds and Wakefield, on 27 October 1930 and played for Oulton Youth Club before signing for Bolton in October 1947. An FA Cup winner in 1958, he played 518 games for Bolton before retiring to become Blackpool's assistant coach. After coaching and assisting at Plymouth, Edwards was in charge at Valley Parade between November 1971 and January 1975, then worked as Huddersfield's physiotherapist and coach until his arrival at Leeds where he ran the youth team. He returned to Bradford in July 1977, holding a variety of posts until November 1986.

After Adamson's dismissal, his number two Merrington was out of football for six months and then worked for the probation service for three years. He joined

Martin Wilkinson at a press conference with Allan Clarke.

Southampton in 1984, running the South East Counties League side and in 1990 was appointed youth-team manager, helping bring on the likes of Alan Shearer and Matthew Le Tissier. A lay preacher, he was appointed as manager of the Saints in succession to Alan Ball in July 1995 but was dismissed in June 1996. The following year he returned to The Dell as a coach under Dave Jones, but left three years later when Glenn Hoddle took over as Saints' manager, becoming first-team coach at Walsall for a short spell.

Merrington is now a Southampton summariser for BBC Radio Solent.

Former United star Allan Clarke brought the nucleus of his Barnsley staff with him when he was appointed in charge at Leeds in September 1980.

His assistant was **Martin Wilkinson**, who had failed to make the grade as a youngster with Rotherham and was working as a sales rep before joining the Barnsley coaching staff. The 34-year-old Wilkinson was sacked from his £12,000 a year job as Clarke's right-hand man at Leeds in June 1982 as part of the club's economy drive, but within a fortnight was appointed Peterborough's manager, a position he held until February 1983 when he was relieved of his duties.

Wilkinson's departure from Leeds, after relegation from Division Two, spelled the end for Clarke, whose other key man, coach **Barry Murphy**, did stay on a bit longer. Murphy was a Barnsley stalwart, clocking up more than 500 games as a full-back between July 1962 and April 1978 – including 177 consecutive League games – after going to Oakwell from South Shields. He was club captain and had a spell as player-coach.

Born in Consett on 10 February 1940, Murphy went straight into the Barnsley coaching staff after retiring and arrived at Leeds with Clarke on October 1980.

After Clarke's dismissal Murphy stayed at Elland Road for a while until becoming a sports development officer at Penistone Sports Centre in 1984.

Another of Clarke's men, chief scout **Tony Collins**, was a victim of United's financial pruning.

Born in Kensington, London on 19 March 1926, Collins played for Brentford as an amateur left winger before joining Sheffield Wednesday (November 1947), York City (July 1949), Watford (August 1950 and July 1957), Norwich City (July 1953), Torquay United (July 1955), Crystal Palace (November 1957) and Rochdale (June 1959).

He became Rochdale's manager in June 1960 and steered them to the first Football League Cup Final in 1962, losing to Norwich in a two-legged Final. He quit in September 1967 and for five years worked at Bristol City as chief scout, before doing a similar job for Leeds between 1972 and 1976. He returned to Bristol City as assistant manager and, for 19 days, caretaker manager, leaving in October 1980 to join Leeds again.

After losing his job at Leeds in October 1981, he stayed on the scouting circuit, unearthing future stars for Manchester United, QPR, Newcastle and Millwall.

Clarke's successor, Eddie Gray, immediately named his former Leeds teammate and lifelong friend **Jimmy Lumsden** as his assistant.

Lumsden was in the juniors with Gray but only made four senior appearances before playing for Southend, Morton, Cork Hibernians and Clydebank. He later worked with fellow Glaswegian Gray at Rochdale, managed Bristol City from 1990 to 1992, coached at Preston under David Moyes and followed Moyes to Everton in summer 2002.

The Gray-Lumsden partnership was supported by another former United player, **Peter Gunby**, who was on the coaching staff, and **Tony Fawthrop,** who spent a year as full-time chief scout for Gray.

Gunby was a Leeds loiner, born in the city on 20 November 1934 and signing for Leeds in September 1955 after completing his National Service. Gunby didn't make the first team and joined Bradford City in July 1956, where he played just three games, before going into non-League football after rejecting a move to QPR in 1958. He was player-manager at Harrogate Town for several years.

Jimmy Lumsden and Eddie Gray watch their team in action.

A qualified Army Physical Training Instructor, Gunby gained his FA coaching badge while working as an electrician. He was offered a part-time coaching post at Huddersfield in 1983 but soon moved to Leeds to work under Gray and was put in temporary command at Leeds when Gray was sacked in October 1985.

Also on the coaching staff at this time was **Keith Mincher**, a former schoolteacher who had a strong background in non-League football. He was one of several departures following the appointment of Billy Bremner and took over as Sheffield United's juniors' coach. Mincher later worked for Carlisle United, Nottingham Forest, Watford, Colchester United and assisted England's Under-21s as a sports psychologist.

Bremner brought in his own management team based around **Dave Bentley** and **Dave Blakey**.

Bentley, born in Worksop on 30 May 1950, was Bremner's assistant. A former Rotherham United junior, he made 250 League appearances for the Millers from July 1967 before joining Chesterfield in June 1974. A battling midfielder, he also had a month on loan with Mansfield before joining Doncaster in August 1977. It was at Doncaster that he first forged his partnership with Bremner but despite helping to take Leeds close to an FA Cup Final and promotion in 1987, the pair, along with chief scout Blakey, were replaced in October 1988. Bentley then worked as Mansfield's Football in the Community Officer.

Blakey, born in Newburn in the North-East on 22 August 1929, was signed by Chesterfield in May 1947 from Chevington Juniors and amassed a club record 613 appearances for the Spireites up to his retirement in 1966.

Also on the Bremner coaching staff were former defensive lynchpin **Norman Hunter**, who had only been appointed eight months before Bremner's sacking, and **Alan McIvor**, a part-time assistant to the Northern Intermediate League side, who had joined Leeds after being physiotherapist at Doncaster Rovers for 11 years.

Bremner's replacement, Howard Wilkinson, kept on physiotherapist **Alan Sutton**, who, had taken over from **Geoff Ladley**, who had two spells with the club, the first in 1976 and then between 1982 and 1986.

Ladley, born on 24 June 1932, went into private practice and became a lecturer at Pinderfields Hospital, Wakefield, but returned to Elland Road for a third spell in January 1993 as physiotherapist with former Bradford City reserve player Sutton, who had previously served with Halifax RL and Halifax Town, becoming his assistant. Sutton was physiotherapist to United's 1991–92 League Championship side. Ladley also worked with the England squad in the early 1970s.

Mick Hennigan

Wilkinson's second in command was **Mick Hennigan**, previously the youth coach at Sheffield Wednesday.

Born in Thrybergh, outside Rotherham, in December 1942, Hennigan played as an amateur with the Millers before joining Wednesday in March 1961 and it was at Hillsborough where he first met Wilkinson.

Hennigan never really made it as a player, contracts with Southampton (June 1962) and Brighton (July 1974) – where Wilkinson was also a player – furnished just seven appearances. He had stints with Sligo Rovers in Ireland and further afield with Durban City, Bloemfontein and Sydney Marconi before returning to South Yorkshire where he turned out for Silverwood Miners Welfare.

Although he had a modest playing career, he was supremely fit and coached at Gainsborough, Matlock and Sutton United prior to joining Sheffield Wednesday's staff in 1984 where he was youth coach.

Hennigan was the natural choice to accompany Wilkinson when he arrived at Elland Road in October 1988 and remained at Elland Road until Wilko's exit.

He then assisted Nigel Worthington at Blackpool, was youth coach at Bury, manager at Harrogate Town, youth coach and kit man at Rotherham before becoming caretaker coach of the Malawi national side in August 2005 at the age of 62.

Gunby, who had looked after the reserves and juniors since Allan Clarke's reign was kept on until retirement in 1995.

Wilkinson and Hennigan both believed that a productive youth policy should be at the heart of the club and appointed former

United defender **Paul Hart** as director of youth coaching in summer 1992. The move soon paid dividends as United lifted the FA Youth Cup for the first time in 1993.

In January 1990, **Dick Bate** a man whose clubs mirrored that of Howard Wilkinson, was appointed reserve-team coach/youth development officer.

He was a teammate of Wilkinson at Boston United in the 1970s and although he featured in the reserves at Sheffield Wednesday and York City, he didn't manage any Football League appearances and went to Alfreton Town in 1968, joining Boston three years later.

A physical education teacher, he played for Frickley Athletic for a couple of years, qualified as an FA staff coach and coached Sheffield United's youngsters between 1978 and 1980. FA North West Regional Coach between 1980 and 1985, he was assistant to the England youth team before spending two seasons as coach at Notts County.

He then spent just four months as Southend's manager until September 1987, was assistant manager at Lincoln and had two years as national coach in Malaysia before linking up with Wilkinson at Elland Road between January 1990 and January 1992. After another spell in Malaysia, he became chief coach at Hereford, where he was later assistant manager.

In 1998 he was appointed an England youth coach and also was in charge of the England National Women's team for one game against Italy in April 1998 before the appointment of Hope Powell. After 10 months as the Canadian Soccer Association's technical director he returned to England to take up a similar post with Watford in July 2006. Bate went on to become Elite Coaching Manager for the FA.

Into Bate's shoes stepped **Eddie Beaglehole**, who was no stranger to Elland Road. He had been youth development officer at Leeds for several years – apart from a stint at Doncaster Rovers – working with Don Revie, Allan Clarke and Eddie Gray at Leeds and spent 17 years as team manager and English Schools FA coach to the national Under-18 side. His son, Steve, managed Doncaster Rovers and his other son, Andy, helped at the Leeds School of Excellence.

With Premiership football demanding larger squads, the coaching staff was bolstered by the return of former favourite **Eddie Gray** in summer 1995 to help with the development of youngsters and when Gordon Strachan announced his retirement in January 1995 he helped out with coaching and there was much talk of him becoming Wilkinson's eventual successor.

Strachan was quickly persuaded to become assistant to his old Manchester United mentor, Ron Atkinson, at Coventry City, where he resumed his playing career. Former Welsh international **David Williams** added his considerable wealth of coaching experience to United's cause in summer 1995 when he arrived from Everton where he had been assistant manager to Mike Walker.

Born in Cardiff on 11 March 1955, midfield man Williams attended Howardian High School and was spotted by Bristol Rovers playing for local club Clifton Athletic. Rovers signed him in December 1975 and he made over 350 League appearances for the Pirates, being at one time the youngest player-manager in the League. He moved to Norwich as a player in May 1985, becoming player-coach two years later and assistant manager in August 1988.

The holder of five Welsh caps, he took charge of the Welsh team as caretaker manager for a game against Yugoslavia after the dismissal of Mike England, for whom he had worked as assistant.

He moved to Bournemouth as assistant manager in July 1992 after seven years at Norwich and leapt at the chance to work with Walker again at Everton in February 1994. But when Walker left Goodison, Williams also departed and was installed at Elland Road.

Another newcomer to Leeds was former Rotherham reserve goalkeeper **John Bilton** who took over as Youth Development Officer from Beaglehole in October 1995. A former Worksop and Frickley player, he has acted as a part-time coach for many non-League sides before managing Sutton United, where Hennigan did some coaching. Bilton was also a coach and scout at Doncaster and spent 25 years as an electrical engineer with British Coal before joining a micro-electronics company.

Geoff Sleight was recruited as chief scout in May 1994 and was instrumental in United signing South African duo Lucas Radebe and Philomen Musinga. Sleight has been associated with Howard Wilkinson for more than 30 years. He played in 1960–61 with Wilkinson for Yorkshire and England Grammar Schools. Born in Royston on 20 June 1943, Sleight played just two games for Bolton in 1961 before going to Australia where he played for the Prague club and featured in World Cup qualifying rounds for that country. A full-back, he returned to England to play for Buxton, then Mossley, before becoming an FA coach and managed Frickley.

The arrival of George Graham as manager in September 1996 also saw former player **David O'Leary** installed as assistant manager and **Eddie Gray** was promoted to reserve team coach. The youth team job went to **John Dungworth**, who notched a century of appearances for both Aldershot and his hometown team Rotherham. Dungworth retired at the age of 33 and after seven years on the coaching staff at Sheffield United arrived at Elland Road in summer 1997.

Alan Sutton was now assistant to **David Swift**, a Rotherham-based physiotherapist while the role of chief scout was taken by **Ian McNeill,** a Glaswegian who had played for Aberdeen, Leicester, Brighton and Southend between 1950 and 1964 before entering management with Wigan Athletic before being appointed Chelsea's assistant manager in 1981, returning to management with Shrewsbury in 1987.

But McNeill's best work was as a scout working for United, Bolton, Norwich and Chelsea. He built up extensive contacts abroad and was instrumental in recruiting Jimmy Floyd Hasselbaink for Leeds. After leaving Leeds he became Norwich's European scout in April 1999, a role he filled for about a year.

United began the 1998–99 season with former Barnsley, Rotherham, Nottingham Forest and England B goalkeeper **Alan Hill** as director of Leeds United's Football Academy which had been earmarked for a £3.3 million facelift over the next two years.

A broken arm forced Hill to quit playing at 27 and he worked as assistant youth coach, the start of a 27-year stay at the City Ground, much of it during the highly successful reign of Brian Clough.

Hill was then assistant manager to Frank Clark at both Forest and Manchester City before taking charge of the Leeds Academy, where **Steve Beaglehole,** whose dad Eddie had worked for Leeds, became Hill's assistant, working with the reserves.

Youth coaches Dungworth and **Gordon Staniforth** had left. The latter, a former England Schools international, had been a striker with Hull City, York City, Carlisle United, Plymouth Argyle and Newport County before spending nearly seven years as York's Football in the Community officer. A North Regional Coach for the PFA, he landed a youth coaching role at Leeds in October 1997 but left the following summer and became co-ordinator at York College's Football Development Centre.

Dungworth went on to join Huddersfield as reserve team coach before being first team coach from December 2006 to April 2009 and a short spell on Sheffield Wednesday's coaching staff.

At Huddersfield he was reunited with **Robin Wray**, who had worked with Leeds' Academy under both Wilkinson and Graham.

Wray had started at Huddersfield Town as a part-time youth coach, while he was a PE and history teacher at Huddersfield New College before becoming a full-time employee with the Terriers, steering them to the Final of the 1974 FA Youth Cup, a feat he repeated with Sheffield Wednesday in 1991, joining the Leeds Academy in 1994 for a four-year spell. Wray retired in 2002 after 35 years in youth coaching.

Changes continued when George Graham moved to become manager at Tottenham in October 1998 and his assistant, David O'Leary, opted to stay at Leeds and took charge of the Whites. The faithful Eddie Gray was promoted to become O'Leary's number two and former Scotland skipper **Roy Aitken** arrived to take charge of the reserves and help with the coaching of the first team. Former Celtic and Newcastle star Aitken had played 57 times for Scotland and entered management with Aberdeen, winning the 1995 Scottish League Cup before obtaining his UEFA coaching licence.

Like many clubs, a specialist goalkeeping coach was in vogue, and that was placed in the hands of **Steve Sutton** the former Nottingham Forest glovesman, who took over the role from the much-travelled **John Burridge** who played for 29 different clubs in a career spanning 30 years. Burridge turned out for Manchester City against QPR in May 1995 when he was 43 years, four months and 26 days old, making him the oldest Premier League player.

May 1999 saw the retirement of former coach Peter Gunby, who had acted as caretaker manager twice after the departures of Eddie Gray and Billy Bremner, and in later years looked after United's young players at the Thorp Arch living quarters with his wife, Maureen.

The Academy facilities at Thorp Arch were among the best in the country and in May 2000, former Manchester United and England star **Brian Kidd** was brought in above Academy director **John Seasman** as director of technical and youth development and former Bradford City stalwart **Greg Abbott** took charge of the development centres. Seasman, the former Millwall and Rotherham winger, later moved on to become a football agent.

Kidd, who also played for Arsenal, Manchester City, Everton and Bolton, was a coach on the rise. He cut his managerial teeth at Barrow and Preston before returning to Old Trafford to develop a conveyor belt of young talent like Ryan Giggs. He became Alex Ferguson's assistant in summer 1991 and enjoyed huge success before having a failed crack at management with Blackburn Rovers, being sacked in November 1999 after less than a year in charge.

Two other significant, although low-key, announcements was the return of **Ian Broomfield** as chief scout to replace Ian McNeill and the appointment of **Dave Hancock** as head physiotherapist.

Brian Kidd

Bristol-born Broomfield had an interesting back-story. After failing to make the grade as a player with Bristol City and Stockport, he had a spell in South Africa before joining the police force. He was detached to the Serious Crime and Murder Squad, tackling several high-profile cases, the most noted probably being the abduction and murder of Midlands estate agent Stephanie Slater.

Broomfield had kept his links with football with some scouting for Southampton before becoming a full-time scout at Leeds under George Graham and followed his mentor to White Hart Lane before returning to Elland Road at O'Leary's invitation.

Hancock held a diploma in sports physiotherapy from Crewe & Alsager, a masters degree in sports medicine from Queen's Medical Centre, Nottingham and a diploma in musculoskeletal physiotherapy from Sheffield Hallam University.

He was a man in demand having worked at St James' Hospital, Leeds, and assisted Wolverhampton Wanderers and Leeds Rhinos RL Club.

Leeds seemed to have a vast bank of football knowledge at their disposal behind the scenes at all levels.

Kidd, a former teammate of O'Leary's at Arsenal, appeared to be on the fast-track to the top and in March 2001 was promoted to head coach, although given his strong association with Manchester United it was not greeted with full approval from some Leeds fans.

When United's form dipped after their failure to re-qualify for the Champions League many pointed the finger at Kidd's influence, but by then United's finances were starting to fall apart and it was O'Leary who carried the can and was sacked by chairman Peter Ridsdale in summer 2002.

Venables retained Gray, Kidd and Aitken as the new season started but with players being sold left, right and centre the former England boss found himself embroiled in a relegation battle before he was sacked by Ridsdale, with whom relations had become strained, in March 2003.

Peter Reid came in and staved off relegation but further savings had to be made. United had a massive backroom staff with coaches at various levels, a physio team and strong scouting network, so with the club sinking deeper and deeper into debt it was not surprising many departed.

Kidd, who had been assisting England manager Sven-Göran Eriksson since January 2003, left Elland Road four months later and was replaced by the little-known **Kevin Blackwell,** who had worked extensively with the well-travelled manager Neil Warnock.

Kidd remained with the England set-up until Euro 2004 which he missed because he was receiving treatment for prostrate cancer. He recovered and worked as assistant manager to Neil Warnock and Bryan Robson at Sheffield United, had a brief spell with former Leeds man Paul Hart at Portsmouth before moving to Manchester City where he is currently assistant to Roberto Mancini.

Aitken opted to team up once more with O'Leary who was appointed Aston Villa's boss in June 2003 and acted as caretaker manager at Villa Park after O'Leary's dismissal in 2006 before the arrival of Martin O'Neill. In January 2007 Aitken was appointed one of Alex McLeish's assistants with the Scottish team and 10 months later followed McLeish to Birmingham City where he was one of the coaches along with ex-Leeds player Andy Watson. Aitken left St Andrew's in July 2010 to link up with O'Leary again in the United Arab Emirates as number two at

Al-Ahli but the pair were axed after only 10 months in the job.

Also out, were scout Ian Broomfield, who was replaced by Reid's former Everton teammate **Adrian Heath** who also played for Stoke, Manchester City and Espanyol in an 18-year career that included appearances for England Under-21s.

Heath had managed two of his other former clubs – Burnley and Sheffield United – and had previously assisted Reid at Sunderland.

The vacant reserve team role at Elland Road was filled by **Steve Agnew**, who had played under Reid at Sunderland. A tenacious midfielder, he played more than 200 times for his hometown club Barnsley before serving Blackburn, Leicester, Sunderland and York City. He then worked as assistant manager at Gateshead before coaching youngsters at Middlesbrough's Academy from where he arrived at Elland Road.

But with a tight budget, Reid struggled to get results and in November was axed with United at the bottom of the Premiership and was soon followed by Heath, leaving interim manager Gray and coach Blackwell at the helm. They were unable to stave off relegation and more staff cuts were made as Leeds prepared for life in the Championship.

There followed a period of financial instability and numerous changes to the coaching and support staff.

Gray left and Blackwell was promoted to the managerial hot-seat and brought in the experienced **Sam Ellis** as his assistant.

A former England Under-23 international, Ellis provided great service to Sheffield Wednesday and Lincoln as a centre-half, finishing his playing career at Watford where he became coach and assistant manager to Graham Taylor, a future England manager.

Ellis was Blackpool's manager for seven years from June 1982, was in charge at Bury, then became assistant to Peter Reid at Manchester City before managing Lincoln and assisting Stan Ternant at both Bury and Burnley.

Into the coaching set-up came **Aidy Boothroyd**, who had been a lower league full-back with Huddersfield, Bristol Rovers, Mansfield and Peterborough before making a name for himself as a coach.

Born in Baildon on 8 February 1971, injury forced him to quit playing in 1998 but he quickly made his mark at Peterborough, working his way up to become reserve team coach before moving to Norwich to work as their youth coach under Nigel Worthington. In October 2003 Boothroyd became youth development officer and technical director at West Brom but within a year snapped up the opportunity to work at Leeds.

There was also a new look to the Academy with former Ipswich, Scarborough, Hull and York defender **Neil Thompson** appointed its manager with Greg Abbot taking charge of the Under-18s. The previous Academy chief, **Andy Ritchie,** the former Leeds striker, had moved on to Barnsley to be assistant to another ex-United star, Paul Hart.

Thompson, who used to be a nappy salesman before turning professional with Hull, had managerial experience with former clubs York and Scarborough and Boston United whom he had left in February 2004.

Aidy Boothroyd

The club was rocked by the death of **Bruce Craven**, a popular member of the physio team, at the age of just 32. He died of skin cancer in February 2005 just two months after it was diagnosed.

Craven, a former Lancashire School cricketer, England Under-21 javelin thrower and Leeds Tykes RUFC player, had been a member of Dave Hancock's physio team at Thorp Arch since 1998. His death triggered several fund-raising events within the club to raise awareness of the danger of melanoma.

In March 2005 first team coach Boothroyd became the surprise choice as manager at Watford at the age of 34. Ironically, his Hornets side steamrollered United in the 2006 Championship Play-off Final at Cardiff – a result which contributed towards Blackwell's exit from Elland Road. Boothroyd left Watford by mutual consent in November 2008 and later managed Colchester (September 2009–May 2010) and Coventry (May 2010–March 2011) before being appointed boss at Northampton on 30 November 2011.

Boothroyd was replaced at Leeds by **John Carver**, who had been assistant manager to Bobby Robson at Newcastle. When Ellis did not have his contract renewed at the end of the 2005–06 season, Carver was promoted to be Blackwell's assistant and found himself installed as caretaker manager when Blackwell was fired after a poor start to the new campaign. He enjoyed a fine 3–2 win against Birmingham in his first game in charge, but poor results, including a humiliating 5–1 loss at Luton, cost him any chance of the job on a full-time basis.

Neil Thompson

While United continued their search for a new chief, **David Geddis** was elevated from the ranks to take charge for one game after Carver's departure.

Former Aston Villa and Ipswich striker Geddis, whom had worked alongside Carver on Newcastle's coaching staff, had not been reserve team coach that long at Elland Road, a position he took after scouting for Sven-Göran Eriksson's England set-up.

Geddis took charge of the team as they crashed 3–1 at home to Southend United on 24 October 2006 with the new

John Carver

management team in-waiting Dennis Wise and **Gus Poyet** watching from the stands.

Carver had left Elland Road the previous day and has since then worked with Blackwell and Ellis at Luton, coached Toronto FC in the American Major Soccer League and assisted ex-England striker Paul Mariner at Plymouth before becoming coach at Sheffield United where he was reunited with Sam Ellis as they worked with new manager Gary Speed, the former Leeds star. When Speed became the Welsh national team boss in December 2010 Carver left shortly afterwards and within a few weeks became assistant manager at Newcastle for the second time in his career.

Geddis followed Carver out of the Elland Road gates a couple of months later as the new men at the top made rapid changes. Among the early casualties were goalkeeping coach **Martin Hodge** and New Zealand-born fitness coach **Dean Riddle**, who later worked for Yorkshire County Cricket Club and Sheffield United.

Born in Southport on 4 February 1959, Hodge was a veteran of more than 600 games with Plymouth, Everton, Sheffield Wednesday, Leicester City, Hartlepool and Rochdale before hanging up his gloves in 1996. He became the Owls' goalkeeping coach and was in charge of the reserves at Hillsborough when he became Leeds' goalkeeping coach in July 2004, taking over from Steve Sutton.

Gus Poyet on the touchline with Dennis Wise.

The role of instructing United's goalkeepers went to 42-year-old **Andy Beasley**, who arrived with Wise and Poyet from Swindon. He had played in goal for Mansfield, Doncaster Rovers and Chesterfield before retiring in 1997.

The Wise-Poyet partnership also supported another former Stamford Bridge man, coach **Joe Allon**, who netted more than a century of goals with a variety of clubs ranging from Chelsea to Hartlepool where he enjoyed cult hero status.

Another Chelsea connection was to be a more lasting appointment – that of **Gwyn Williams** as technical director who had arrived at Leeds a month before Wise and Poyet were appointed. He had spent 27 years at Stamford Bridge, mainly as chief scout and is credited with discovering future England captain John Terry.

Formerly head of physical education at Drayton Manor High School in London, Williams was also assistant manager to Claudio Ranieri during his time with Chelsea and arrived at Leeds with a glowing reputation.

He had been brought in to replace Ian McNeill, who had been in his second spell as chief scout for the Whites.

However, it was not all one-way traffic from the West London club. Head physio Dave Hancock was head-hunted by the Blues in February 2007, his assistant **Harvey Sharman** moving up to oversee matters. Hancock was soon elevated to help with the England medical team and went with the squad to the 2010 World Cup.

A few weeks later former Reserves' boss Steve Agnew, uncle of Huddersfield Town striker Jordan Rhodes, left Elland Road for a second time. His first departure saw him take up the assistant manager's job at Hartlepool, but returned to Leeds as Under-18 coach, leaving to join

Middlesbrough as reserve team coach and was promoted to assistant manager at the Riverside the following year.

Agnew's post was filled by **Paul Beesley**, who played under Howard Wilkinson at Leeds in the 1990s and had been on the coaching staff at Nottingham Forest.

Despite the influx of new people, Leeds were sliding towards relegation to League One.

Despite the infamous deduction of 15 points from the start of the 2007–08 campaign, Wise and Poyet galvanised the club. Poyet, in particular, was popular with fans and players at Leeds and many Whites' supporters point to his departure as the main reason the club failed to build on winning their opening seven League games.

A free-scoring midfielder with Real Zaragoza, Chelsea and Tottenham, the Uruguayan international did a good job with Wise at Swindon and went about rebuilding Leeds with gusto but when the opportunity to become first team coach at Premiership side Spurs came along at the end of October it was an offer he could not refuse. United's results suffered post-Poyet, who was replaced at Elland Road, by Wise's old boss at Wimbledon, **Dave Bassett**.

Poyet remained at White Hart Lane until October 2009 but re-emerged as Brighton's manager in November 2009 and took the Seagulls back into the Championship with former Leeds goalkeeper Casper Ankergren a key member of his side.

Bassett brought a wealth of experience with him to Elland Road. A member of the Wimbledon side which ran the mighty Leeds team so close in the FA Cup fourth round in 1975. He was an amateur back then, working as an insurance broker, and it was off him that a Johnny Giles shot deflected into the net to settle the replay.

After the Dons were elected to the Football League he worked as a coach at Plough Lane before taking over from Dario Gradi as manager and guided them from Division Four up to the First Division with what some critics thought was a 'long ball game'.

After a brief spell as boss at Watford he was appointed manager at Sheffield United in January 1988, remaining at Bramall Lane until December 1995. Managerial spells at Crystal Palace, Barnsley, Nottingham Forest and Leicester followed before assisting Harry Redknapp at Southampton. When Redknapp left in December 2005, Wise, a senior player with the Saints, and Bassett shared the caretaker manager's role but the job went to George Burley on a permanent basis and Bassett left the Saints.

He arrived at Leeds with United 13 games into the League One season and unbeaten, but their form fell away and when Wise quit Elland Road to take up a job with Premiership side Newcastle in January 2008, Bassett and first-team coach **John Gannon** left the Whites. Gannon, another former Wimbledon player, had coaching experience with Mansfield, Chester and Notts County. He later scouted for Manchester City.

Technical director Gwyn Williams oversaw a 1–0 defeat at Southend with Joe Allon and Andy Beasley with him in the dugout before former United hero Gary McAllister was announced as the new manager.

McAllister, a Championship winner with Leeds, brought in **Steve Staunton** as his assistant and **Neil McDonald** as first team coach, and promised to provide fans with an entertaining brand of football.

Staunton, capped a record 102 times by the Republic of Ireland, played with McAllister at Liverpool and under him at Coventry. A veteran of the 1990, 1994 and 2002 World Cups, he also starred for Aston

Steve Staunton

Villa before winding up his career with Walsall where he became assistant coach.

In January 2006 he was named Eire's manager, holding the job for 21 months before being axed by the FAI in favour of Giovanni Trappatoni.

Two days after Staunton landed in Leeds, he was joined by McDonald, Lincoln City's assistant manager. The former England Under-21 international had managed Carlisle (June 2006–August 2007) and Swedish club Ostersunds for a brief period after coaching positions at Preston and Bolton and working as assistant manager to Iain Dowie at Crystal Palace. He had a 15-year playing career at the highest level with Newcastle, Everton, Oldham and Bolton.

The new management team got United back on track but after losing to Doncaster in the League One Play-off Final at Wembley, the Whites struggled for consistency the following season and McAllister, Staunton and McDonald departed in December 2008.

Staunton went on to do some scouting for Wolves before a disastrous tenure in charge of Darlington as they slid out of the Football League. Since then he's been a scout for Sunderland.

McDonald was reunited with his old Bolton mentor, Sam Allardyce at Blackburn as assistant manager and after they were dismissed by Rovers' new owners in December 2010 were named as the new management team at West Ham at the start of the 2011–12 season.

Simon Grayson was appointed as McAllister's successor and the first recruit to his support team, **Ian Miller**, joined United on Christmas Day 2008.

Miller, nicknamed 'Dusty' was well known to Grayson from his days at Blackburn and Leicester, where Miller had been a coach.

Born in Perth, Scotland, Miller played for Bury, Doncaster and Swindon but was best known for his service to Blackburn where he amassed more than 200 games in an eight-year stay before winding up his career at Port Vale and Scunthorpe. In May 1992 he headed Port Vale's youth development programme before stepping up to coach Wolves' reserves. Coaching posts at Blackburn, Blackpool, Bury and Leicester followed and was part of Sven-Göran Eriksson's scouting staff at Manchester City when he joined Grayson at Leeds as first team coach.

Miller was followed by the return of a former Elland Road favourite, **Glynn Snodin**, who shared coaching duties. The former Doncaster and Sheffield Wednesday man also played for Hearts and Barnsley before becoming chief scout at Carlisle and youth team coach at Scarborough.

He worked as assistant manager to his brother, Ian, another former United star, at Doncaster before joining Charlton Athletic's coaching staff in 2000 as reserve team manager, leading them to successive reserve league titles.

In March 2006 he was appointed Southampton's first-team coach, doubling

Glynn Snodin

as assistant manager to the Northern Ireland national side run by Nigel Worthington, another former Leeds man. Snodin then worked under Alan Curbishley at West Ham, leaving Upton Park when Curbishley left in September 2008.

However, Snodin, a cult figure at Leeds, returned to Elland Road 17 years after leaving as a player. Popular with fans, he is credited with devising the 'Leeds Salute' beloved by Whites followers.

Both Snodin and Miller lost their jobs when manager Grayson was sacked on 1 February 2012, but teamed up with their old boss three weeks later when he was installed as Huddersfield's manager.

There was a shake-up at Thorp Arch in October 2010, with Academy manager Neil Thompson and his assistant **Daryl Pugh** moved out. Gwyn Williams held the fort temporarily for four-and-a-half months before the appointment of **Chris Sulley** who was selected from more than 100 applicants for the post which saw two jobs merged in to one in the restructure. Williams was then able to return to concentrate on his position as technical director, former Leeds goalkeeper **Mervyn Day** having returned to Elland Road as chief scout three months earlier. Day, who had managerial experience at Carlisle, had worked at Charlton and West Ham with Snodin as assistant manager to Curbishley.

For Pugh, a former Doncaster, Huddersfield, Rotherham and Torquay player it was the end of a second spell with United, having previously worked as the old Centre of Excellence director for five years up to 2003. He rejoined the club in 2007 as coach to the Under-18s, a position now held by **Neil Redfearn**, before becoming Thompson's assistant in 2009.

Thompson, who had also been running United's reserves, became first-team coach at Sheffield Wednesday in February 2011 while Pugh went on to become head of the youth set-up at Bury.

The vastly experienced Redfearn, who amassed more than 850 games for a string of clubs, most notably Barnsley, took over the reserves from Thompson and continued to work as the Under-18s coach. His CV included two spells as caretaker manager with Halifax Town, player-manager at both Scarborough and Northwich Victoria before becoming youth coach, then assistant manager at York City before his switch to Leeds at the end of 2008.

After Simon Grayson and his coaching staff were dismissed, Redfearn was in temporary charge of the first team for four games until the appointment of Neil Warnock.

The vastly experienced Warnock was joined at Elland Road by 64-year-old assistant manager **Mick Jones**, a long-time partner who worked at QPR, Plymouth Argyle, Crystal Palace and Huddersfield Town. Sunderland-born Jones was a central-defender with Notts County and Peterborough United before becoming player coach with Ottawa Tigers in Canada, returning to England to become player-manager of Kettering Town.

In August 1979 he was appointed Mansfield Town's manager, then assisted Roy McFarland at Bradford City and, briefly, Derby County, before taking charge of Halifax Town for a couple of years in November 1984. Jones then assisted Noel Cantwell at Peterborough United, taking over as manager in summer 1988 until August the following year. It was at London Road that he met Warnock and, after Jones briefly scouted for Blackpool, the pair worked in tandem at Notts County (1989–93), Huddersfield Town (1993–95) and Plymouth where Jones took the manager's post after Warnock left Home Park.

Jones was dismissed by the Devon club in 1998 and he then had four successful years as Brunei's national team coach, winning the province's first Malaysia Cup the following year. In 2002 he returned to England as assistant manager of Nuneaton Borough and manager of Telford United before linking up with Warnock again in 2005 at Sheffield United, a partnership which continued at Crystal Palace, QPR and Leeds.

Warnock also brought in former Huddersfield, Port Vale, Exeter, Bury, Oldham, Burnley and Peterborough striker **Ronnie Jepson** as a coach at Elland Road.

In an 11-year professional playing career, Jepson played for Warnock at Huddersfield and first moved into coaching in 2002 with Burnley. He then assisted former Burnley boss Stan Ternant at Gillingham, where Jepson was appointed manager in November 2005. He had been consistently linked with a return to Huddersfield and that became a reality in April 2008 when he was appointed number two to his former boss Ternant but both men left Leeds Road after only six months.

After a year out of the game, Jepson was offered the position of reserve team coach at Crystal Palace by Warnock in July 2009 and the following year followed Warnock to QPR and then on to Elland Road.

The new man at the top of United's youth pyramid, Sulley, 51, had spent eight years in charge of Bolton Wanderers' Academy. As a player, he turned out for Bournemouth, Dundee United, Blackburn, Port Vale and Preston before establishing himself as a coach at Preston's Centre of Excellence prior to his switch to Bolton. Sulley left the club in April 2012.

GROUNDSMEN

ELLAND Road's turf has been tended by four long-serving groundsmen.

Albert Stead was already working at the ground when rugby league was played there before the formation of Leeds City in 1904.

He doubled as trainer and groundsman in City's early days, continuing as the latter until his retirement in 1945.

Cecil Burrows first started working for the club in the war years, taking on more of the groundsman's role after Stead's retirement and remained at Elland Road until the 1970s. He died in March 1983, aged 81.

John Reynolds held the position of head groundsman between 1972 and 1998 but did work at the Thorp Arch training centre until 2002.

A native of South Wales, he was signed up as a junior in Major Frank Buckley's reign in the early 1950s. Originally a full-back, he was switched to centre-forward and in one season netted 32 goals for United's juniors. But a serious ligament injury in a Youth Cup tie against West Brom put paid to his career and manager Raich Carter offered him the job as assistant to Burrows. Shortly before his death on 5 April 2012, aged 75, Reynolds received a Lifetime Acheivement Award at the Leeds Sports Awards.

The post of head groundsman has been occupied since 1998 by **Norman Southernwood**, the former groundsman at Halifax Town.

Leeds Administrators

WHEN the club was formed in 1904 as Leeds City, the post of secretary was part of the manager's job.

But as football expanded it became necessary for clubs to appoint a secretary to keep the club organised on a day-to-day footing and let the manager concentrate on matters on the field.

United's first full-time secretary was the bespectacled **C. Arthur Crowther**, who was appointed in 1935 and held the position until he retired in 1958 shortly after the opening of the rebuilt West Stand.

C. Arthur Crowther

Crowther's assistant was **Harry Lunn**. Ironically, most of the club records and ledgers in Crowther's care had been destroyed in the fire that had burnt down the old stand. Unfortunately, he did not enjoy a long retirement, dying in St James' Hospital, Leeds, on 10 July 1958, aged 63, two months after ending his 23-year service with the club. Beeston-born Crowther had been wing-half and secretary of Beeston Parish Church FC and was assistant secretary of the Leeds Alliance League. He served with the Army in World War One and was wounded in Italy.

He joined United as a part-time assistant in the office in 1924, becoming secretary in 1928. He received the Football League's long service medal in 1949.

Succeeding Crowther was **Cyril Williamson**, who worked under the title of general manager-secretary soon after arriving at Elland Road.

Williamson turned to professional football quite late in life, joining Leeds from the Midland Electricity Board where he was an administrative official. A Leicester man, he had a good background in football, having spent 17 years as secretary of the Leicester and Rutland County FA.

A fine amateur centre-half in the Birmingham and District League, he was a qualified referee, an FA councillor and chairman of selectors for the FA Youth International Committee, travelling to 20 countries with the Under-18 national side.

After working as secretary, he was appointed organisation and development manager by United in 1962.

Cyril Williamson

Ill health forced Williamson into early retirement in 1969 and he died, aged 76, in 1981. His role as secretary was briefly taken on by **P.L. Crowther** before the promotion of **Keith Archer** as general manager in February 1967.

In Archer's first full season United won the 1968–69 Championship and he was in office throughout the rest of the Don Revie glory days.

Keith Archer

He used to travel with the Intermediates on away trips and joined United's staff in May 1966 as assistant secretary, becoming secretary in 1972.

He gave up the secretary's job in 1982 but continued as general manager for a few more months before the impact of relegation, coupled with the recession, saw him lose his job at the age of 44 after 18 years at Elland Road. Another departure was promotions manager **Bob Baldwin**, who had done much to raise the profile of the club, particularly improving its matchday programme, and raising vital income during his six-year tenure.

Mike Dooley had worked as assistant secretary between August 1974 and July 1982, having previously been with Sheffield Wednesday. After a spell with Hull RL club, he returned to football administration with Scarborough.

Mike Lockwood, who had taken over as general manager from Archer in 1977, survived the staff cuts of 1982, but departed the following year. Lockwood had been on the Elland Road payroll for 14 years after joining from Wolves, having previously worked for Jimmy Hill's Coventry City.

Much of his work was on the commercial side, developing the club's lottery and expanding its shops and stock.

The position of secretary was now in the hands of **David Dowse**, who had held a similar position with Grimsby Town for eight years up to his appointment at Elland Road on 1 October 1982.

With United struggling financially, the post of chief executive was created in September 1983 and was filled by former RAF pilot **Terry Nash**, an assistant director with the Ministry of Defence. One of his most important jobs was to help strike a deal with Leeds City Council which saw the Elland Road ground become a community property – a move which was concluded on 1 November 1985. Nash left United four months later. His other jobs included working for the Bristol Chamber of Commerce, the Chartered Institute of Marketing and the Mansfield Area Development Association before becoming a managing director of a group of companies.

Dowse stayed at Elland Road until August 1990 and he later worked at neighbours Bradford City. His place as company secretary at Elland Road was taken by Cambridge United secretary **Nigel Pleasants**, the son of a former Ipswich Town reserve player.

Pleasants joined his hometown club Norwich City as assistant secretary in 1973 and two years later was on the shortlist for the job as deputy secretary to the Football League. He became secretary at Carrow Road in 1979 but left after 15 years service and ran a pub in the suburbs of Norwich before his appointment at Cambridge United in November 1989.

Nigel Pleasants

A member of the management committee of the Football Administratiors Association, he was involved in the discussions which set up the Premier League.

It was Pleasants who was instrumental in getting United reinstated in the European Champions Cup after he followed up rumours about Stuttgart playing an ineligible player. He checked out the nationalities of the German squad, thus starting a successful battle to get United back in the competition.

He was also heavily involved with Euro '96 which saw several games staged at Elland Road. Pleasants left Leeds in 1998 and later worked for Harrogate Town and York City, also having a spell as general manager of the Theatre Royal, Windsor, working for top theatre proprietor and Everton chairman Bill Kenwright.

Pleasants died, aged 58, after a heart attack at his home in Cromer, Norfolk, in August 2008.

Another key man involved in the European Championships at Elland Road was **Alan Roberts**, the club's general manager between 1983 and 1997.

He was a goalkeeper on United's staff as a 17-year-old and started work in the club office on a part-time basis is 1964 when he was 20. He earned promotion to administration manager in 1986 and general manager five years later.

In September 1991 he was elected chairman of the Junior and Family Supporters Association and named North East Regional Director for Euro 96.

After an absence of ten years the position of chief executive was revived after the takeover by the Caspian Group which had purchased the club from shareholders for £16 million in 1996.

Top accountant **Robin Launders** was lured by Caspian from his position as finance director at Manchester United to the chief executive's role. He arrived with an outstanding reputation, having done much to help with the redevelopment of Old Trafford and the commercialisation of Manchester United into a global brand.

But he left in April 1997 less than a year after his appointment and the chief executive's position was left dormant.

Another Caspian man, **Jeremy Fenn** was managing director of Leeds, a position he held for about three years. Previously he had qualified as a chartered accountant in 1988 and held finance director positions at several media companies.

He quit Elland Road to join the Sports Internet Group in July 1999, that company being sold to BskyB for £301 million 12 months later.

How United could have done with a slice of that sort of money, instead they were cutting costs left, right and centre, with board member and a friend of Peter Ridsdale, **Stephen Harrison** grappling with the chief executive's position a role he filled until **Trevor Birch's** arrival at the club. Birch, whose tenure is covered in the Chairmen's section of the book, left in 2004 and **Chris Middleton**, appointed by the Yorkshire Consortium, briefly held the position.

The club secretary at this time, who had replaced Pleasants, was **Ian Silvester**, who battled on through the Whites' crushing financial difficulties until 2005. He had arrived after a long association with Leicester City where he became assistant secretary in July 1986, moving up to secretary in 1994 before switching to Leeds in December 1998.

After his stint at Elland Road he worked as Liverpool's assistant secretary, then secretary before leaving Anfield in May 2011.

Since Silvester's departure from Leeds, the post of head of football administration was created and was filled by **Alison Royston**, who still holds the position today, while **Shaun Harvey** is the chief executive.

Harvey entered sports administration with Farsley Celtic before working under Geoffrey Richmond as secretary at Scarborough, then Bradford City where he became managing director. He joined Leeds in June 2004 after ten years at Valley Parade.

In May 2007, Leeds went into administration but chairman Ken Bates, his solicitor and United director Mark Taylor and Harvey formed a new company called Leeds United Football Club Limited and bought the club back. Harvey is now a United club director and company secretary and in June 2011 he was added to the Football League board of directors.

League Seasons

1904-05

West Yorkshire League

Did you know that?

15 October 1904: City did not fulfil their home game with Dewsbury & Saville because of a smallpox outbreak in Dewsbury and refused to play them at Holbeck

26 December 1904: A Boxing Day friendly home game against Huddersfield was abandoned after 72 minutes because of fog with the scores at 1-1

FA Cup

Match No.	Date	Venue	Opponents	Result	FT	HT	Scorers	Attendance
Q	Sep 17	A	Rockingham Coll.	L	1-3	0-2	Musgrave	1,000
								Appearances
								Goals

West Yorkshire League

Match No.	Date	Venue	Opponents	Result	FT	Scorers
1	Sep 1	A	Morley	D	2-2	Not Traced (1 pen)
2	3	H	Altofts	L	1-2*	Durant
3	10	A	Elland Ramdonians	L	1-2	Simpson
4	24	A	Huddersfield	W	3-1	Hefferon, Soar, Holmes
5	Oct 8	A	Mirfield	W	2-1	Morris, Other scorer not traced
6	22	A	Starbeck	D	1-1	Simpson
7	Nov 5	A	Rothwell Whi. Rose	L	1-4	Musgrave
8	19	H	Heckmondwike	L	0-3	
9	26	A	Beeston Hill P. Chur.	L	0-3	
10	Dec 3	H	Oulton	D	2-2	Simpson, G. Howard
11	10	H	Bradford City Res.	L	1-5	Sawyer
12	17	H	Rothwell Whi. Rose	W	1-0	Dixon
13	24	A	Morley	L	0-4	
14	31	A	Altofts	L	2-4	Not Traced (1 pen)
	Jan 14	H	Starbeck	D	1-1†	F. Howard
15	28	A	Dewsbury & Savile	D	0-0	
16	Mar 11	A	Elland Ramdonians	L	0-4	
17	18	A	Beeston Hill P. Chur.	W	5-1	G. Howard, Hunt, F. Howard, Spiksley 2 (1 pen)
18	18	H	Heckmondwike	L	1-3	Humberstone
19	Apr 12	H	U. Armley Chr. Chu.	D	2-2	Spiksley, Austin
20	22	A	Bradford City Res.	D	1-1	F. Howard
21	24	H	Mirfield	W	1-0	Austin
22	25	H	Huddersfield	W	1-0	Simpson
23	25	A	U. Armley Chr. Chu.	W	4-1	Dixon, Mackay, F. Howard, Clay (pen)

*At Wellington Ground, Low Road, Hunslet

† Score at 90 minutes in Hospital Cup tie - result counted in League

Scorers: Not Traced 5, F Howard 4, Simpson 4, Spiksley 3, Austin 2, Dixon 2, G Howard 2, Clay 1, Durant 1, Hefferon 1, Holmes 1, Humberston 1, Hunt 1, Mackay 1, Morris 1, Musgrave 1, Sawyer 1, Soar 1, Total 33

Leeds Hospital Cup

R1	Nov 12	H	Altofts	W	3-1	G. Howard 3 (1 pen)
R2	Jan 14	H	Starbeck	W	2-1*	F. Howard, Hunt
R3	Feb 11	A	U.Armley Chr.Chu.	L	1-2	Austin

* After extra-time

West Yorkshire Cup

R1	Jan 7	A	Bradford City Res.	L	2-3	G. Howard 2

Friendlies

Sep 5	H	Bradford City	L	0-3*	
Oct 1	A	Morley	D	1-1	Not Traced
15	H	Hull City	L	0-2	
29	H	Harrogate Cor	W	5-1	McKiernan, Eggington, Rodgers, Soar, Simpson
Nov 26	H	Burton United	W	7-2	G. Howard 4, Simpson, Lewis, F. Howard
Dec 10	A	Grimsby Town	L	0-8	
24	A	Hull City	L	2-3	G. Howard, Howe
Jan 21	H	Darlington	W	3-1	G. Howard 2, Nelson
Feb 4	H	West Brom Alb	L	0-5	
18	H	Sheffield Utd	D	2-2	Not Traced
25	H	Leicester Fosse	L	1-5	Not Traced
Mar 4	H	Hull City	L	2-5	G. Howard, Dixon
11	H	Lincoln City	L	1-3	Austin
25	H	Derby Co	L	0-2	
Apr 1	H	Preston NE	L	1-4	Austin
29	H	Barnsley	W	4-3	Verrinder 2, Austin, F. Howard

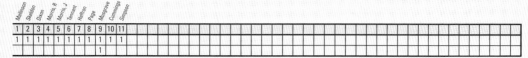

Mallinson	Skeldon	Dixon	Morris, R	Morris, J	Tennant	Heffron	Page	Musgrave	Cummings	Simpson
1	2	3	4	5	6	7	8	9	10	11
1	1	1	1	1	1	1	1	1	1	1
								1		

LEEDS' FA CUP DEBUT

JUST over a fortnight after kicking off their West Yorkshire League campaign, City contested their first FA Cup tie.

As a new club they started at rock-bottom with a preliminary round tie at Rockingham Colliery, who had finished runners-up in the Barnsley Minor Cup the previous season.

Although it was a relatively short journey to South Yorkshire, City arrived late and the match kicked off 30 minutes after schedule.

The village team, roared on by an attendance or around 1,000 attacked up their ground's slope in the first half with Meir and former Doncaster Rovers player Frank Hulley getting the final touches to goalmouth scrambles to give the home side a 2-0 half-time lead.

Leeds, whose players were drawn from a variety of the city's local clubs, were being overrun and it was no surprise when Meir added another goal with a low shot into the bottom corner.

The Colliery boys continued to attack the City goal where W.H. Mallinson, a former Sheffield Wednesday and New Brighton Tower goalkeeper kept the score down with a series of superb saves.

The reporter who covered the game for the *Hoyland Gazette* was certainly impressed by Mallinson.

"He had plenty of opportunity of showing his Leeds friends what he is capable of going. These opportunities were not wasted on him and he did show them in that they have a custodian of no mean ability.

"How on earth he saved three lightning shots in rapid succession and at different angles was simply marvellous," enthused the correspondent.

Musgrave pulled a goal back for City, but it was too little, too late, and Rockingham progressed to the next round where they lost to Sheffield side Thorpe Hesley.

Apart from Mallinson, two other players had been on the books of League clubs – Page with Liverpool and Cummings with Nottingham Forest, although neither played in the first team. Cummings stayed a few months with Leeds before joining Starbeck.

By and large, though, the Leeds boys like 'Tipper' Heffron and Tom Tennant were local amateurs thrown together to make a team who were no match for a side who played together regularly.

Rockingham Colliery: Vaines, A. Foster, Dransfield, T. Robinson, Hulley, Mann, Whitney, L. Foster, Meir, Todd, Robinson
Leeds City: W.H. Mallinson, Skeldon, H. Dixon, R. Morris, T. Morris, T. Tennant, P. Heffron, Page, Musgrave, Cummings, E. Simpson
Referee: J.H. Parkin (Sheffield) Attendance: 1,000

LEEDS' FIRST INTERNATIONALS

DESPITE their lowly status as a West Yorkshire League club, Leeds City were able to attract top quality players to the cause.

Former England internationals Fred Spiksley and Tom Morren both played in a handful of high-profile friendly games for the newly-formed club.

In effect, they became the first internationals to pull on a Leeds shirt although their stay was only brief.

Although the 34-year-old Spiksley was well past his best he was a class act and his appearances helped generate more interest in City's development.

Capped seven times by England, the left-winger shone with his home town club Gainsborough Trinity, before moving to Sheffield Wednesday where he scored a century of goals. But none of them were as the precious as the two which saw the Owls beat Wolves 2–1 in the 1896 FA Cup Final.

He arrived at Leeds after a few outings with Glossop, and after leaving City turned out for Watford before embarking on a successful coaching career, winning national championships in Sweden, Mexico and Germany, where he was interned on the outbreak of World War One. He also had a spell in Switzerland and was assistant coach at Fulham.

He died on Ladies Day at Goodwood Racecourse on 28 July 1948.

Centre-half Morren played once, and scored, for England in a 3–2 win against Ireland in Belfast on 5 March 1898. Together with Ernest 'Nudger' Needham and Rab Howell, he was a member of Sheffield United's diminutive half-back line who all played for England.

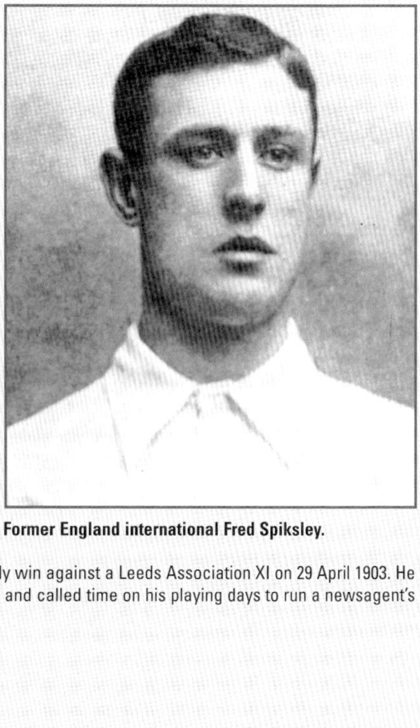

Former England international Fred Spiksley.

Sunderland-born Morren, who stood a shade over 5ft 5in, played his early football in the Middlesbrough area before joining the Blades with whom he won the Championship in 1898 and the FA Cup the following year.

Morren spent eight years at Sheffield United, his final game being a 7–3 friendly win against a Leeds Association XI on 29 April 1903. He came out of semi-retirement to have a go with Leeds City but opted not to carry on and called time on his playing days to run a newsagent's and general store in Sharrow Vale, Sheffield.

1905-06

Division Two

Manager: Gilbert Gillies

Final Position: 6th

Did you know that?

11 September 1905: Former Bradford City centre-forward Tom Drain scored City's first League goals, netting both in the 2–2 home draw with Lincoln.

3 March 1906: Dickie Morris became City's first international when he played for Wales against Scotland. City won 6–1 at home to Clapton Orient the same day, David Wilson scoring four.

31 March 1906: Because of an injury crisis, 34-year-old trainer George Swift, a former Notts County and Leicester Fosse full-back, had to turn out on the left wing at Chelsea, who won 4–0.

21 April 1906: Referee T.P. Campbell (Blackburn) was booed by City fans during the 3–1 home defeat against Manchester United after he made several controversial decisions. As the official walked off at the end of the game he was hit on the nose by a lump of concrete and a sod of earth.

Trainer George Swift was pressed into action at Chelsea on 31 March.

Match No.	Date	Venue	Opponents	Result	FT	HT	Scorers	Attendance
1	Sep 2	A	Bradford City	L	0-1	0-0		15,000
2	9	H	West Bromwich Alb	L	0-2	0-0		6,802
3	11	H	Lincoln City	D	2-2	1-1	Drain 2	3,000
4	16	A	Leicester Fosse	W	1-0	1-0	Singleton	5,000
5	23	H	Hull City	W	3-1	1-1	R. Morris 2, Hargraves	13,654
6	30	A	Lincoln City	W	2-1	1-1	Parnell (pen), Hargraves	3,000
7	Oct 14	A	Port Vale	L	0-2	0-0		1,500
8	21	H	Barnsley	W	3-2	1-2	R. Morris, Hargraves, Stacey (og)	12,000
9	Nov 11	H	Grimsby Town	W	3-0	2-0	Hargraves 2, Stringfellow	7,000
10	13	A	Burton United	D	1-1	0-0	Parnell	1,500
11	25	H	Chelsea	D	0-0	0-0		20,000
12	Dec 2	A	Gainsborough Trinity	L	1-4	1-1	Watson	2,000
13	9	H	Bristol City	D	1-1	0-1	Morgan	15,000
14	23	H	Glossop	W	1-0	1-0	Hargraves	9,000
15	26	A	Stockport County	L	1-2	1-1	Singleton	5,000
16	30	H	Bradford City	L	0-2	0-0		22,000
17	Jan 1	A	Blackpool	W	3-0	2-0	R. Morris, Wilson, Singleton	3,000
18	6	A	West Bromwich Alb	L	1-2	1-1	Wilson	2,553
19	15	A	Manchester United	W	3-0	1-0	Watson, Wilson, Singleton	6,000
20	20	H	Leicester Fosse	W	4-1	1-0	Murray (pen), Drain, Watson, Hargraves	8,000
21	27	A	Hull City	D	0-0	0-0		10,000
22	Feb 3	H	Burnley	D	1-1	0-1	Watson	7,129
23	10	A	Chesterfield	W	2-0	0-0	R. Morris, Singleton	4,000
24	17	H	Port Vale	W	3-1	1-0	Wilson, Hargraves, Parnell	9,000
25	24	A	Barnsley	L	0-3	0-1		5,000
26	27	H	Chesterfield	W	3-0	3-0	Wilson 2, Murray (pen)	2,000
27	Mar 3	H	Clapton Orient	W	6-1	3-0	Wilson 4, Hargraves, Parnell	8,000
28	10	A	Burnley	L	3-4	1-3	Wilson 2, Singleton	5,000
29	17	A	Grimsby Town	D	1-1	0-1	Murray	3,000
30	24	H	Burton United	W	2-1	1-1	Watson, Singleton	5,000
31	29	A	Clapton Orient	D	0-0	0-0		1,000
32	31	A	Chelsea	L	0-4	0-2		15,000
33	Apr 7	H	Gainsborough Trinity	W	1-0	0-0	Hargraves	12,000
34	13	H	Stockport County	D	1-1	1-0	Lavery	10,000
35	14	A	Bristol City	L	0-2	0-0		12,000
36	16	H	Blackpool	W	3-0	1-0	Hargraves 2, Watson	10,000
37	21	H	Manchester United	L	1-3	1-1	Lavery	10,000
38	28	A	Glossop	W	2-1	2-0	Parnell, Wilson	1,500
								Appearances
							One own-goal	Goals

FA Cup

Match No.	Date	Venue	Opponents	Result	FT	HT	Scorers	Attendance
P1	Oct 7	H	Morley	W	11-0	6-0	Hargraves 4, Watson 2, R. Morris 4, Parnell	3,000
P2	28	H	Mexborough	D	1-1	0-0	Hargraves	4,000
R	Nov 2	A	Mexborough	D	1-1*	1-1	Parnell	3,000
2R	6	H	Mexborough	W	3-1	2-1	Watson, R. Morris, Hargraves	5,000
P3	22	A	Hull City	D	1-1	1-1	Hargraves	3,000
R	29	H	Hull City	L	1-2	0-0	Parnell	7,186
								Appearances
								Goals

* After extra-time

League match abandoned after 53 minutes due to fog

Date	Venue	Opponents	Result	FT	HT	Scorers	Attendance
Nov 4	H	Burnley	D	1-1	1-1	R. Morris	6,000

FA Cup match abandoned after 50 minutes due to fog

Date	Venue	Opponents	Result	FT	HT	Scorers	Attendance
Nov 18	A	Hull City	D	0-0	0-0		3,000

League match abandoned after 73 minutes due to fog

Date	Venue	Opponents	Result	FT	HT	Scorers	Attendance
Dec 16	A	Manchester United	L	0-1	0-1		16,000

City prepare to embark on their first season in the Football League. Back row, left to right: Ralph Younger (director), R.S. Kirk (director), Charles Morgan, D. Whittaker (director), Dooley, John McDonald, Austin, Fred Walker, Harry Singleton, R.M. Dow (director), George Swift (trainer). Middle row: Gilbert Gillies (secretary-manager), Fred Parnell, Bob Watson, Fred Hargraves, Dick Ray, Dickie Morris, William Clay, Oliver Tordoff (director). Front row: Roy 'the City dog', Harry Stringfellow, Tom Drain, James Henderson.

Bromage, Harry	McDonald, Willie	Ray, Dick	Morgan, Charlie	Stringfellow, Harry	Henderson, James	Parnell, Fred	Watson, Bob	Hargraves, Fred	Morris, Dickie	Singleton, Harry	Drain, Tommy	Walker, Fred	Murray, David	Howard, Gordon	Wilson, David	Morris, John	Lavery, John	Swift, George	George, John	Whitley, Jack	Freeborough, Jimmy	Clay, William
1	2	3	4	5	6	7	8	9	10	11												
1	2	3	4	5	6	7	8		10	11	9											
1	2	3	4	5	6	7	8		10	11	9											
1	2	3	4	5	6	7	8	9	10	11												
1	2	3	4	5	6	7	8	9	10	11												
1	2	3	4		6	7	8	9	10	11		5										
1	2	3	4		6	7	8	9	10	11		5										
1	2	3	4	6		7	8	9	10	11		5										
1	2	3	4	5	6	7	8	9	10	11												
1	2	3	4	5	6	7	8	9	10	11												
1	2	3	4	5	6	7	8	9	10	11												
1	2	3	4	5	6	7	8	9	10	11												
1		3	4	5	6	7	8	9	10	11			2									
1		3	4		6		7	9		11		5	2	8	10							
1	2		5		6	7	4	9	10	11			3		8							
1		2	4	5	6	7	8	9	10	11			3									
1	2		4		6	7			10	11	8		3		9	5						
1		2	4		6	7	8		10	11			3		9	5						
1		3	4		6	7	8		10	11			2		9	5						
1		2	4		6	7	8	9		11	10		3			5						
1		2	4		6	7	8	10		11			3		9	5						
1		2	4		6	7	8		10	11			3		9	5						
1	3	2	4		6	7	8		10	11					9	5						
1	3	2	4		6	7		8	10	11					9	5						
1	3	2	4		6	7	8	10		11					9	5						
1	2		4		6	7	8	10		11		5	3		9							
1	2		4		6	7	8	10		11		5	3		9							
1	2		4		6	7	8	10		11		5	3		9							
1		3	4		6	7		8	10	11		5	2		9							
1		2	4		6	7	8	10		11	9	5	3									
1		2	4		6	7		8		11	9	5	3				10					
1		2		4	6	7				9	8	5	3				10	11				
1	2				6	7		9	8	11		4	3				10		5			
	2		4		6	7		9	8	11			3				10		5	1		
1	2				6	7		9	8	11		5	3				10		4			
	3		4		6	7	8	9			11		2				10		5	1		
			4			7	8			11	9	2	3				10		5	1	6	
1	2		4			7	8			11		6	3		9		10				5	
35	25	27	35	13	35	37	30	28	25	37	9	15	23	1	15	9	8	1	5	3	2	0
			1	1		5	6	12	5	7	3		3		13		2					
1	2	3	4		6	7	8	9	10	11		5										
1	2	3	4			7	6	9	10	11	8	5										
1	2	3	4		6	7	8	9	10	11		5										
1	2		4	5	6	7	8	9	10	11												3
1	2	3	4	5	6	7	8	9	10	11												
1	2	3	4	5	6	7	8	9	10	11												
6	6	5	6	3	5	6	6	6	6	6	1	3	0	0	0	0	0	0	0	0	0	1
						3	3	7	5													
1	2	3	4	5	6	7	8	9	10	11												
1	2	3	4	5	6	7	8	9	10	11												
1		3	4		6		8	9	10	11		5	2	7								

League Table

	P	W	D	L	F	A	Pts
Bristol City	38	30	6	2	83	28	66
Manchester United	38	28	6	4	90	28	62
Chelsea	38	22	9	7	90	37	53
West Bromwich Albion	38	22	8	8	79	36	52
Hull City	38	19	6	13	67	54	44
Leeds City	38	17	9	12	59	47	43
Leicester Fosse	38	15	12	11	53	48	42
Grimsby Town	38	15	10	13	46	46	40
Burnley	38	15	8	15	42	53	38
Stockport County	38	13	9	16	44	56	35
Bradford City	38	13	8	17	46	60	34
Barnsley	38	12	9	17	60	62	33
Lincoln City	38	12	6	20	69	72	30
Blackpool	38	10	9	19	37	62	29
Gainsborough Trinity	38	12	4	22	44	57	28
Glossop	38	10	8	20	49	71	28
Burslem Port Vale	38	12	4	22	49	82	28
Chesterfield	38	10	8	20	40	72	28
Burton United	38	10	6	22	34	67	26
Clapton Orient	38	7	7	24	35	78	21

1906-07

Division Two

Manager: Gilbert Gillies

Final Position: 10th

Did you know that?

City won their first piece of silverware as the Reserves lifted the West Riding Challenge Cup by beating Kippax Parish Church 2–0 with both goals coming from Alf Harwood, an amateur international who won an Amateur Cup medal in 1901 with Crook Town.

10 September 1906: John George, the city captain, only played one more game after a 5–0 defeat at the Hawthorns and was replaced by David Murray.

John Lavery scored City's opening goal of the season.

Match No.	Date	Venue	Opponents	Result	FT	HT	Scorers	Attendance
1	Sep 1	H	Bradford City	D	1-1	0-1	Lavery	20,000
2	8	A	West Bromwich Alb	L	0-5	0-2		15,504
3	10	H	Lincoln City	D	1-1	0-1	Cubberley	5,000
4	15	H	Leicester Fosse	D	1-1	1-1	Jefferson	11,000
5	22	A	Nottingham Forest	L	0-3	0-1		5,000
6	29	A	Lincoln City	D	1-1	0-0	Jefferson	4,000
7	Oct 6	A	Burton United	W	2-0	1-0	Lavery, Watson	3,000
8	13	H	Grimsby Town	W	4-3	2-2	Watson 2, D. Murray (pen), Lavery	10,000
9	20	A	Port Vale	W	2-1	0-0	Lavery, Parnell	4,000
10	27	H	Burnley	L	0-1	0-0		14,000
11	Nov 3	A	Chesterfield	L	0-1	0-0		3,000
12	10	A	Barnsley	L	0-3	0-0		4,000
13	17	H	Chelsea	L	0-1	0-1		8,000
14	24	A	Wolverhampton W	L	2-3	2-1	Lavery, D. Murray (pen)	4,500
15	Dec 1	H	Clapton Orient	W	3-2	3-1	Watson, Parnell, Mcleod	10,000
16	5	A	Blackpool	L	0-1	0-0		2,000
17	8	A	Gainsborough Trinity	L	0-1	0-1		3,000
18	15	H	Stockport County	W	6-1	3-1	McLeod, Lavery 3, Watson 2	8,000
19	22	A	Hull City	L	1-2	0-1	Lavery	10,000
20	29	A	Bradford City	D	2-2	1-1	McLeod, T. Wilson	17,000
21	Jan 1	A	Glossop	L	0-2	0-0		1,000
22	5	H	West Bromwich Alb	W	3-2	0-2	McLeod 2, Jefferson	14,000
23	19	A	Leicester Fosse	D	2-2	0-1	McLeod, Kirk	8,000
24	26	H	Nottingham Forest	L	1-4	0-3	McLeod	14,000
25	Feb 2	H	Blackpool	D	1-1	1-1	Jefferson	7,000
26	9	H	Burton United	W	3-1	1-1	McLeod 2, Parnell	7,000
27	16	A	Grimsby Town	L	0-4	0-2		4,000
28	23	H	Port Vale	W	2-0	1-0	Parnell, Watson	7,000
29	Mar 2	A	Burnley	W	2-1	0-0	Harwood, T. Wilson	5,000
30	9	H	Chesterfield	W	1-0	0-0	McLeod	10,500
31	16	H	Barnsley	W	2-1	0-1	McLeod, Watson	14,000
32	23	A	Chelsea	L	0-2	0-1		25,000
33	30	H	Wolverhampton W	W	2-0	0-0	Watson, Cubberley	15,000
34	Apr 1	H	Glossop	L	1-4	0-0	McEwan (og)	8,000
35	6	A	Clapton Orient	D	1-1	1-0	Lavery	6,000
36	13	H	Gainsborough Trinity	W	4-0	3-0	Cubberley, Lavery 2, McLeod	3,000
37	20	A	Stockport County	D	2-2	1-1	Kennedy, McLeod	3,000
38	27	H	Hull City	D	2-2	2-2	McLeod 2	7,000
								Appearances
							One own-goal	Goals

FA Cup

R1	Jan 12	A	Bristol C	L	1-4	0-3	McLeod	14,000
								Appearances
								Goals

Back row, left to right: Gilbert Gillies (secretary-manager), Charles Morgan, Fred Hargraves, Andy Clark, Fred Walker, Harry Bromage, Jimmy Freeborough, Dick Ray, Jimmy Kennedy, George Swift (trainer). Middle row: Jack Whitley, Bob Jefferson, Stan Cubberley, John Morris, David Murray, Alf Harwood, John Lavery, Harry Singleton, Willie Murray. Front row: Fred Parnell, John George, James Henderson.

Bromage, Harry	Murray, David	Clark, Andy	Morris, John	George, John	Kennedy, Jimmy	Parnell, Fred	Watson, Bob	Wilson, David	Lavery, John	Singleton, Harry	Walker, Fred	Cubberley, Stan	Murray, Willie	Whitley, Jack	Hargraves, Fred	Freeborough, Jimmy	Jefferson, Bob	Morgan, Charlie	Ray, Dick	Henderson, James	Page, George	Johnson, Garnet	McLeod, Billy	Wilson, Tommy	Pickard, Bert	Kirk, Gerald	Harwood, Alf
1	2	3	4	5	6	7	8	9	10	11																	
1	2	3		4	6	7	8	9			5	10	11														
	2	3			6	7	9		10	11		8		1	4	5											
1	2	3			6	7	8		10	11					4	5	9										
	2	3			6	7	8		10				11	1	4		9	5									
1	2	3			6	7	9				5		11		10		8	4									
1	2	3			6	7	8	9	10	11	5				4												
1	2	3			6	7	8	9	10	11	5				4												
1	2				6	7	8	9	10	11	5				4				3								
1	2	3				7	8	9	10	11	5				4					6							
1	2	3			6	7	8		11		5	10			4						9						
1	2	3			6	7			10		5		11		8			4			9						
1	2	3			6	7	8		10		5				4						9	11					
1	2	3			6	7	8		10		5		11		4								9				
1	2	3		4	6	7	8		10		5		11										9				
1	3				5	7	8		10						4	2				6	11		9				
1	3				5	7	8		10				11		4	2				6			9				
1					5	7	8		10						4	2			3				9	11	6		
1					5	7	8		10							2			3				9	11	6	4	
1					6				10			8			4	2	7		3				9	11		5	
1					5				10			8			4	2	7		3	6			9	11			
1									10	11		8			6	2	7	4	3				9			5	
1	3				6				10			8			4		7		2				9	11		5	
1	2				6				10			8					7	4	3				9	11		5	
		3				7	8					10		1	6		9	4	2					11		5	
		3			6	7	8					10		1	4				2				9	11		5	
1		3			6	7	8		10						4				2				9	11		5	
1		3			5	7	8						10		4	2				6			9	11			
1		3			5	7	10					8			4	2				6				11			9
1		3			5	7	10					8			4	2				6			9	11			
1		3			5	7	10					8			4	2				6			9	11			
1		3			5	7	10					8			4	2				6			9	11			
1		3			5	7	10					8			4	2				6			9	11			
1		3			5	7	10					8			4	2				6			9	11			
1	3				5	7			10			8			4	2				6			9	11			
1	3				5	7			10			8			4	2				6			9	11			
1	3				5	7			10			8			4	2				6			9	11			
1	3				5	7			10			8			4	2				6			9	11			
34	23	24	1	3	35	33	28	6	27	8	11	20	8	4	33	20	9	6	11	15	4	1	23	20	2	8	1
	2				1	4	9		12			3					4						15	2		1	1

1	2				6		8		10						4		7		3				9	11		5	
1	1	0	0	0	1	0	1	0	1	0	0	0	0	0	1	0	1	0	1	0	0	0	1	1	0	1	0
																							1				

League Table

	P	W	D	L	F	A	Pts
Nottingham Forest	38	28	4	6	74	36	60
Chelsea	38	26	5	7	80	34	57
Leicester Fosse	38	20	8	10	62	39	48
West Bromwich Albion	38	21	5	12	83	45	47
Bradford City	38	21	5	12	70	53	47
Wolverhampton W	38	17	7	14	66	53	41
Burnley	38	17	6	15	62	47	40
Barnsley	38	15	8	15	73	55	38
Hull City	38	15	7	16	65	57	37
Leeds City	38	13	10	15	55	63	36
Grimsby Town	38	16	3	19	57	62	35
Stockport County	38	12	11	15	42	52	35
Blackpool	38	11	11	16	33	51	33
Gainsborough Trinity	38	14	5	19	45	72	33
Glossop	38	13	6	19	53	79	32
Burslem Port Vale	38	12	7	19	60	83	31
Clapton Orient	38	11	8	19	45	67	30
Chesterfield	38	11	7	20	50	66	29
Lincoln City	38	12	4	22	46	73	28
Burton United	38	8	7	23	34	68	23

1907-08

Division Two

Manager: Gilbert Gillies

Final Position: 12th

Did you know that?

22 February 1908: Leeds were literally blown away at Lincoln as gales ripped off the roof of a stand at the Sincil Bank ground during City's 5–0 hammering.

18 April 1907: Sporting all-rounder Billy Bates made his City debut at right-back in the 3–1 win against Wolves. Son of the Yorkshire and England cricketer Willie Bates, Billy was a hard-hitting batsman with Yorkshire and Glamorgan. His son, Ted, played for and managed Southampton.

James Henderson, a noted sprinter with Morpeth Harriers, joined Preston at the end of the season.

Match No.	Date	Venue	Opponents	Result	FT	HT	Scorers	Attendance
1	Sep 2	H	Glossop	W	2-1	0-1	Lavery, Tustin (og)	4,000
2	7	A	Leicester Fosse	D	2-2	0-0	Watson, McLeod	10,000
3	9	H	Clapton Orient	W	5-2	4-0	Watson 2, Croot, Lavery 2	6,000
4	14	A	Blackpool	W	3-2	2-1	Watson, Lavery, Parnell	6,000
5	21	A	Stoke City	L	1-2	1-1	Parnell	10,000
6	28	H	West Bromwich Alb	W	1-0	1-0	McLeod	24,000
7	Oct 5	A	Bradford City	L	0-5	0-2		27,000
8	12	H	Hull City	W	3-2	1-1	McLeod 2, Watson	15,000
9	19	A	Derby County	L	1-6	1-3	Atkin (og)	10,000
10	26	H	Lincoln City	W	2-1	2-1	Parnell, McLeod	10,000
11	Nov 2	A	Fulham	L	0-2	0-1		20,000
12	9	H	Barnsley	D	1-1	1-1	McLeod	11,000
13	16	A	Chesterfield	L	3-4	2-0	Thomas 2, Parnell	4,000
14	23	H	Burnley	D	2-2	1-0	Croot, McLeod	7,000
15	30	A	Oldham Athletic	L	2-4	1-1	McLeod, Gemmell	8,000
16	Dec 14	H	Grimsby Town	W	4-1	1-0	McLeod, Croot 2, Murray (pen)	5,000
17	21	A	Wolverhampton W	L	0-2	0-1		5,000
18	25	A	Stockport County	L	1-2	1-1	McLeod	8,000
19	28	H	Gainsborough Trinity	D	0-0	0-0		8,000
20	Jan 1	A	Glossop	W	2-0	1-0	Croot, McLeod	2,000
21	4	H	Leicester Fosse	D	0-0	0-0		10,000
22	18	H	Stoke City	L	0-1	0-1		10,000
23	25	A	West Bromwich Alb	L	0-1	0-0		8,000
24	Feb 1	H	Bradford City	L	0-1	0-1		35,000
25	8	A	Hull City	L	1-4	0-3	McLeod	9,000
26	15	H	Derby County	W	5-1	2-1	Murray (pen), Croot, Lavery, McLeod 2	8,000
27	22	A	Lincoln City	L	0-5	0-3		1,000
28	29	H	Fulham	L	0-1	0-0		10,000
29	Mar 7	A	Barnsley	W	3-1	2-1	Jefferson, McLeod, Croot	5,000
30	14	H	Chesterfield	D	0-0	0-0		6,000
31	21	A	Burnley	L	0-1	0-1		7,000
32	28	H	Oldham Athletic	L	1-2	1-1	Parnell	15,000
33	Apr 4	A	Clapton Orient	D	0-0	0-0		8,000
34	11	A	Grimsby Town	L	0-2	0-0		6,000
35	17	H	Stockport County	W	3-0	1-0	Gemmell, McLeod (pen), Croot	12,000
36	18	H	Wolverhampton W	W	3-1	0-1	Parnell, Gemmell, Watson	10,000
37	20	H	Blackpool	D	1-1	1-1	Lavery	7,000
38	22	A	Gainsborough Trinity	L	1-2	1-0	McLeod	3,500
								Appearances
							Two own-goals	Goals

FA Cup

R1	Jan 11	A	Oldham Athletic	L	1-2	0-2	Parnell	14,000
								Appearances
								Goals

Back row, left to right: Bob Jefferson, Stan Cubberley, Fred Hargraves, John Lavery, Fred Croot, James Henderson. Middle row: Broad (trainer), J. Aldred, Jimmy Freeborough, Harry Bromage, Billy McLeod, Harry Kay. Front row: Jack Whitley, Tom Hynds, Fred Parnell, David Murray, Tommy Tompkins, Billy Thomas, Jimmy Thorpe, Jimmy Kennedy.

Bromage, Harry	Kay, Harry	Murray, David	Tompkins, Tom	Hynds, Tom	Henderson, James	Parnell, Fred	Watson, Bob	McLeod, Billy	Lavery, John	Croot, Fred	Thorpe, Jimmy	Cubberley, Stan	Naisby, Tom	Kennedy, Jimmy	Pickard, Bert	Jefferson, Bob	Thomas, Billy	Hargraves, Fred	Gemmell, Jimmy	Freeborough, Jimmy	Bates, Billy
1	2	3	4	5	6	7	8	9	10	11											
1	2	3	4	5	6	7	8	9	10	11											
1	2	3	4	5	6	7	8	9	10	11											
1	2	3	4	5	6	7	8	9	10	11											
1	2	3		5	6	7	8	9	10	11	4										
1	2	3	4	5		7	8	9	10	11	6										
1	2	3	4	5		7	8	9	10	11	6										
1	2	3	4	5		7	8	9		11	6	10									
1	2	3	4	5		7	8	9		11	6	10									
	2	3	4	5	6	7	8	9		11		10	1								
	2	3	4	5	6	7	8	9		11		10	1								
		2		5		7	8	9	10	11	3		1	4	6						
		2	4	5		8		9		11	3	6	1			7	10				
		3		5		8		9		11	2	6	1			7	10	4			
		3		5		7		9		11	2	6	1				10	4	8		
	2	3		5		7		9		11		6	1		4		10		8		
	2	3		5		7	4	9		11		6	1				10		8		
	2			5	4	7		9	10	11		6	1						8	3	
	2	3		5		7		9		11		6	1	4			10		8		
	2	3		5		7		9		11		6	1	4			10		8		
	2	3		5		7		9		11		6	1	4			10		8		
	2	3			4	7		9		11		6	1	5			10		8		
	2	3		5	4	7	8	9		11		6	1						10		
	2	3		5	4		8	9		11		6	1			7			10		
	2	3		5	4	7	8	9	10	11		6	1								
	2	3		5	4	7	8	9	10	11		6	1								
	2	3		5	4	7	8	9	10	11		6	1								
	2	3		5	4	7	8	9	10	11		6	1								
	2	3		5	4		8	9	10	11		6	1			7					
	2	3		5	4		8	9	10	11		6	1			7					
	2	3		5	4	8		9	10	11		6	1			7					
	2	3		5	6	7	8	9	10	11		4	1								
	2	3		5	4	7		9		11		6	1			8			10		
	2	3		5	4	7		9	10	11		6	1						8		
		3		5	4	7		9	10	11		6	1						8		2
				3	4	7	8		10	11		6	1	5					9		2
1	3			5	4		8		10	11				6		7			9		2
				3	4	7	8	9		11		6	1	5					10	2	
10	31	34	11	37	25	34	25	36	21	38	9	29	28	8	2	8	9	2	16	2	3
		2				6	6	17	6	8						1	2		3		

	2	3		5		7		9		11		6	1	4			10		8		
0	1	1	0	1	0	1	0	1	0	1	0	1	1	1	0	0	1	0	1	0	0
						1															

League Table

	P	W	D	L	F	A	Pts
Bradford City	38	24	6	8	90	42	54
Leicester Fosse	38	21	10	7	72	47	52
Oldham Athletic	38	22	6	10	76	42	50
Fulham	38	22	5	11	82	49	49
West Bromwich Albion	38	19	9	10	61	39	47
Derby County	38	21	4	13	77	45	46
Burnley	38	20	6	12	67	50	46
Hull City	38	21	4	13	73	62	46
Wolverhampton W	38	15	7	16	50	45	37
Stoke	38	16	5	17	57	52	37
Gainsborough Trinity	38	14	7	17	47	71	35
Leeds City	38	12	8	18	53	65	32
Stockport County	38	12	8	18	48	67	32
Clapton Orient	38	11	10	17	40	65	32
Blackpool	38	11	9	18	51	58	31
Barnsley	38	12	6	20	54	68	30
Glossop	38	11	8	19	54	74	30
Grimsby Town	38	11	8	19	43	71	30
Chesterfield	38	6	11	21	46	92	23
Lincoln City	38	9	3	26	46	83	21

1908-09

Division Two

Manager: Frank Scott-Walford

Final Position: 12th

Did you know that?

12 December 1908: Jimmy Gemmell scored his only hat-trick for City as they beat Wolves 5–2. But that proved to be the prelude to City's worst-ever sequence – seven successive League defeats.

Jimmy Gemmell netted a hat-trick against Wolves on 12 December.

Match No.	Date		Venue	Opponents	Result	FT	HT	Scorers	Attendance
1	Sep	5	H	Tottenham Hotspur	W	1-0	0-0	Rodger	20,000
2		7	H	Clapton Orient	D	0-0	0-0		8,000
3		12	H	Hull City	W	2-0	1-0	Rodger, Bowman	12,000
4		14	H	Barnsley	W	2-0	1-0	McLeod 2	8,000
5		19	H	Derby County	L	2-5	2-2	McLeod 2 (1 pen)	20,000
6		26	A	Blackpool	L	0-1	0-1		5,000
7	Oct	3	A	Chesterfield	L	0-2	0-0		7,000
8		10	A	Glossop	D	0-0	0-0		4,000
9		17	H	Stockport County	W	2-1	2-1	McLeod, Molyneux (og)	8,500
10		24	A	West Bromwich Alb	L	1-2	1-2	McLeod	13,554
11		31	H	Birmingham City	W	2-0	1-0	McLeod, Rodger	15,000
12	Nov	7	A	Gainsborough Trinity	D	1-1	1-1	McLeod	4,000
13		14	H	Grimsby Town	W	4-1	2-1	Gemmell 2, McLeod 2	8,000
14		21	A	Fulham	W	1-0	0-0	McLeod	18,000
15		28	H	Burnley	D	1-1	1-0	Bowman	14,000
16	Dec	12	H	Wolverhampton W	W	5-2	3-0	McLeod, Gemmell 3, Guy	14,000
17		19	A	Oldham Athletic	L	0-6	0-4		8,000
18		25	A	Bolton Wanderers	L	0-2	0-1		19,400
19		26	H	Bolton Wanderers	L	1-2	1-1	Joynes	15,000
20	Jan	1	A	Barnsley	L	1-2	1-2	Guy	6,500
21		2	A	Tottenham Hotspur	L	0-3	0-2		16,000
22		9	A	Hull City	L	1-4	0-3	McLeod	7,000
23		23	A	Derby County	L	1-5	0-3	Bowman	7,000
24		30	H	Blackpool	W	1-0	1-0	Bowman	8,000
25	Feb	13	H	Glossop	W	3-1	1-1	Croot, Burnett, Gemmell	10,000
26		20	A	Stockport County	L	0-1	0-0		6,000
27		27	H	West Bromwich Alb	D	1-1	1-1	McLeod	12,000
28	Mar	13	H	Gainsborough Trinity	L	0-2	0-1		7,000
29		20	A	Grimsby Town	W	1-0	0-0	Gemmell	5,500
30		27	H	Fulham	W	2-0	1-0	Bowman, Guy	10,000
31	Apr	3	A	Burnley	D	0-0	0-0		5,000
32		9	H	Chesterfield	W	3-0	2-0	Rodger, Gemmell, Bowman	10,000
33		10	H	Bradford PA	L	0-3	0-2		11,000
34		12	A	Birmingham City	L	0-1	0-1		3,000
35		13	A	Clapton Orient	D	0-0	0-0		3,000
36		17	A	Wolverhampton W	L	1-2	0-1	McLeod	7,000
37		24	H	Oldham Athletic	W	3-0	2-0	Burnett, Croot, Dougal	4,500
38		27	A	Bradford PA	L	0-2	0-2		6,000
									Appearances
								One own-goal	Goals

FA Cup

R1	Jan	16	A	Oldham Athletic	D	1-1	1-1	McLeod	7,000
rep		20	H	Oldham Athletic	W	2-0	1-0	McLeod (pen), Guy	19,047
R2	Feb	6	H	West Ham United	D	1-1	0-1	Burnett	31,471
Rep		11	A	West Ham United	L	1-2*	1-0	Bowman	13,000
									Appearances
									Goals

* After extra-time

Back row, left to right: John Chapman (trainer), John Watson, Harry Bromage, Tom Naisby, Stan Cubberley, Frank Scott-Walford (secretary-manager), Jabez White, David Murray, P. McKeown, Thomas Thrupp (assistant trainer). Middle row: Willie McDonald, Tom McAllister, Jimmy Gemmell, Adam Bowman, Jock Hamilton, Tom Rodger, James Kennedy. Front row: Richard Guy, James Burnett, David Dougall, Billy McLeod, Fred Croot.

Naisby, Tom	Watson, Jock	White, Jabez	McAllister, Tom	Hamilton, Jock	Cubberley, Stan	Joynes, Dickie	Gemmell, Jimmy	Bowman, Adam	Rodger, Tom	Croot, Fred	Dougal, Davie	Guy, Dickie	Kennedy, Jimmy	Burnett, Jimmy	McLeod, Billy	McDonald, Willie	Bates, Billy	Cunningham, Tom	Murray, David	Morris, Tom	Bromage, Harry
1	2	3	4	5	6	7	8	9	10	11											
1	2	3	4	5	6		8	9	10	11	7										
1	2	3	4	5	6		8	9	10	11		7									
1	2	3	4		6				10	11		7	5	8	9						
1	2	3	4	5	6				10	11		7		8	9						
1	2	3	4		6	7		9	10	11					8	5					
1	2	3		4	6	7	8		10	11			5		9						
1	2			4	6	7	8	10		11			5		9		3				
1	2	3		4	6		8	10	7	11			5		9						
1	2	3		4	6		8	10	7	11			5		9						
1	2	3	4		6	7	10		8	11			5		9						
1	2	3	4		6	7	10		8	11			5		9						
1	2	3	4		6	7	10		8	11			5		9						
1	2	3	4		6	7	10		8	11			5		9						
1	2	3	4		6	8	10	9		11		7	5								
1	2	3	4			8	10			11		7	5		9	6					
1	2	3	4				10		8	11		7	5		9	6					
1		3	4	5			10	9	8	11		7				6	2				
1	2	6	4			8	10			11		7	5		9		3				
1		3	4			8			10	11		7	5		9	6	2				
1		3	4	5					10	11		7		8	9	6	2				
1		3	4	5			10		8	11		7			9	6	2				
		2	4	5			8	9			11	7		10		6		1	3		
1	2	3	4	5			8	9		11	7			10		6					
1	2	3	4		6		8	9		11	7			10		5					
1	2	3	4		6		8	9		11	7			10		5					
1	2	3	4	5	6		8			11	7			10	9						
1	2	3	4		6		8			11		7		10	9					5	
1	2	3	4		6	10	8			11		7		9						5	
1	2	3	4		6		8	9		11		7		10						5	
1			4	3	6		8		10	11		7		9			2			5	
1			4	2			8	9	10	11		7	5			6	3				
1			4	2	6		8			11		7		10	9		3			5	
				4	6	8			10	11	7			9			3		2	5	1
				4		8			10	11	7			9		6	2		3	5	1
1	3		4	2	6				8	11				10	9		7			5	
	2	3	4		6				8	11	7			10	9					5	1
	2	3	8	5	6				10	11	7			9		4					1
33	28	31	32	21	27	15	28	15	25	37	10	18	15	18	22	14	12	1	3	9	4
						1	8	6	4	2	1	3		2	15						

1	2	3	4	5	6		8			11		7		10	9						
1	2	3	4	5	6		8			11		7		10	9						
1	2	3	4	5	6	9	8			11		7		10							
1	2	3	4	5	6		8	9		11		7		10							
4	4	4	4	4	4	1	4	1	0	4	0	4	0	4	2	0	0	0	0	0	0
								1				1		1	2						

League Table

	P	W	D	L	F	A	Pts
Bolton Wanderers	38	24	4	10	59	28	52
Tottenham Hotspur	38	20	11	7	67	32	51
West Bromwich Albion	38	19	13	6	56	27	51
Hull City	38	19	6	13	63	39	44
Derby County	38	16	11	11	55	41	43
Oldham Athletic	38	17	6	15	55	43	40
Wolverhampton W	38	14	11	13	56	48	39
Glossop	38	15	8	15	57	53	38
Gainsborough Trinity	38	15	8	15	49	70	38
Fulham	38	13	11	14	58	48	37
Birmingham	38	14	9	15	58	61	37
Leeds City	38	14	7	17	43	53	35
Grimsby Town	38	14	7	17	41	54	35
Burnley	38	13	7	18	51	58	33
Clapton Orient	38	12	9	17	37	49	33
Bradford Park Avenue	38	13	6	19	51	59	32
Barnsley	38	11	10	17	48	57	32
Stockport County	38	14	3	21	39	71	31
Chesterfield	38	11	8	19	37	67	30
Blackpool	38	9	11	18	46	68	29

1909-10

Division Two

Manager: Frank Scott-Walford

Final Position: 17th

Did you know that?

23 October 1909: Barnsley inflicted City's heaviest-ever home defeat when they triumphed 7–0 at Elland Road with goals by Ernie Gadsby (2), Harry Tufnell (2), George Lillycrop (2) and Tom Foreman. Gadsby's son, Ken, played for United after World War Two.

26 March 1910: Elland Road hosted its first FA Cup semi-final as Barnsley and Everton slogged out a 0–0 draw in front of 33,000 fans.

Cigarette card of James Tildesley, whose only City appearances were made in 1909–10.

Match No.	Date	Venue	Opponents	Result	FT	HT	Scorers	Attendance
1	Sep 1	H	Lincoln City	W	5-0	2-0	Gemmell 2, Halligan 2, Morris	6,000
2	4	A	Hull City	L	1-3	0-2	Halligan	10,000
3	11	H	Derby County	W	2-1	1-1	Croot, Halligan	12,000
4	18	A	Stockport County	D	0-0	0-0		7,000
5	25	H	Glossop	L	1-2	0-2	McLeod	12,000
6	Oct 2	A	Birmingham	W	2-1	2-0	Halligan 2	14,000
7	9	H	West Bromwich Alb	L	0-1	0-0		7,500
8	16	A	Oldham Athletic	L	1-2	0-1	Halligan	10,000
9	23	H	Barnsley	L	0-7	0-3		8,000
10	30	A	Fulham	L	1-5	0-3	Halligan	14,000
11	Nov 6	H	Burnley	W	1-0	0-0	Halligan	7,000
12	13	H	Bradford PA	L	2-3	1-3	McLeod 2	10,000
13	20	A	Wolverhampton W	L	0-5	0-2		5,500
14	27	H	Gainsborough Trinity	D	0-0	0-0		3,000
15	Dec 4	A	Grimsby Town	L	1-3	0-1	Halligan	3,000
16	11	H	Manchester City	L	1-3	1-3	McLeod	5,000
17	18	A	Leicester Fosse	L	2-6	1-2	McLeod, Halligan	12,000
18	25	H	Clapton Orient	W	2-1	1-1	Roberts, McLeod	6,000
19	27	H	Blackpool	W	3-2	2-1	McLeod, Roberts 2	10,000
20	28	A	Lincoln City	D	0-0	0-0		8,000
21	Jan 1	A	Blackpool	L	1-3	0-1	Halligan	4,000
22	8	H	Hull City	D	1-1	0-1	Gemmell	10,000
23	22	A	Derby County	L	0-1	0-1		7,000
24	Feb 5	A	Glossop	L	1-2	1-1	Roberts	1,000
25	12	H	Birmingham	W	2-1	1-0	Roberts, Croot	10,000
26	26	H	Oldham Athletic	L	3-5	1-2	McLeod, Mulholland, Croot (pen)	6,000
27	Mar 5	H	Stockport County	L	0-2	0-1		5,000
28	7	A	West Bromwich Alb	L	1-3	0-1	McLeod	6,800
29	12	H	Fulham	D	2-2	1-1	Croot 2 (1 pen)	4,000
30	17	A	Barnsley	D	1-1	1-1	McLeod	2,000
31	19	A	Burnley	L	0-3	0-0		4,000
32	26	A	Bradford PA	L	2-4	0-3	Croot (pen), McLeod	12,000
33	28	A	Clapton Orient	W	2-0	1-0	McLeod 2	7,000
34	Apr 2	H	Wolverhampton W	W	1-0	1-0	McLeod	5,000
35	9	A	Gainsborough Trinity	L	0-2	0-1		3,000
36	16	H	Grimsby Town	W	3-1	2-0	Croot 2 (1 pen), McLeod	5,000
37	23	A	Manchester City	L	0-3	0-3		15,000
38	30	H	Leicester Fosse	D	1-1	0-0	Dougal	2,000
								Appearances
							One own-goal	Goals

FA Cup

R1	Jan 15	A	Sunderland	L	0-1	0-0		18,000
								Appearances
								Goals

Back row, left to right: John Chapman (trainer), George Affleck, Tony Hogg, Harry Bromage, Tom Naisby, Morris, David Dougal, McGowan, Thomas Thrupp (assistant trainer). Middle row: Hugh Beren, Tom McAllister, Jabez White, Frank Scott-Walford (manager), John Watson, Jimmy Gemmell, Fred Croot. Front row: Ted Hamilton, James Burnett, Billy Halligan, Hugh Roberts, Tom Mulholland, Harold Bridgett.

Bromage, Harry	Watson, Jock	White, Jabez	McAllister, Tom	Morris, Tom	Cubberley, Stan	Stockton, Colin	Mulholland, Tom	Halligan, Billy	Gemmell, Jimmy	Croot, Fred	Price, Haydn	McLeod, Billy	Dougal, Davie	Joynes, Dickie	Burnett, Jimmy	Roberts, Hugh	Hamilton, Ted	Beren, Hugh	Affleck, George	Horsley, James	Naisby, Tom	Pickard, Bert	Tildesley, Jim	Bridgett, Harold	Ackerley, George	Hogg, Tony	Astill, Tommy
1	2	3	4	5	6	7	8	9	10	11																	
1	2	3	4	5	6	7	8	9	10	11																	
1	2	3	4	5		7		8	10	11	6	9															
1	2	3		5	6			9	10	11	4		7	8													
1	2	3		5	6			8	10	11	4	9	7														
1	2	3	4		5			9		11	6		7	8	10												
1	2	3	4	5	6			9	10	11				8		7											
1	2	3	4	5			8	9		11	6				10		7										
1	2	3		5	6		8	9	10	11	4						7										
1	2	3		5	6		8	9			11		7	10				4									
1		2	4		6			10	8	11		9	7						3	5							
1		2	4		6			10	8	11		9	7						3	5							
1		2		5	4			10			6	9	11	8			7		3								
	2	3		5	6			10	8	11		9	7								1	4					
	2	3	4	5	6		8	9	10	11				7							1						
1		2		5	6		8	10		11		9				7			3			4					
1	2			5	6		8	10		11		9				7		4	3								
1	2		4		6			10	8	11		9				7				5			3				
1	2		4				8		10	11		9				7			3	5		6					
1				5	6		8	9	10							7			3	4			2	11			
1	2		4	5	6			10	8	11		9				7			3								
1			4		6			10	8	11		9				7			3	5			2				
1	2		4		6			10	8			9	11			7			3	5							
1			4		6			10	8	11		9				7			3	5			2				
1			4		6			10	8	11		9				7			3	5			2				
1		2	4		6		8		10	11		9				7			3	5							
1			4		6				10	11		9		8		7			3	5			2				
1		2	4	5	6		8			11		9	10			7			3								
1		2	4		6		8		10	11		9				7			3	5							
1		2	4	5	6		8			11		9				7			3						10		
1		2			6		8		10	11		9				7		4	3	5							
		2			6		8			11		9				7			3	5		4				1	10
1		2		5	6		8			11		9	10			7			3	4							
1		2		5	6		8			11		9	10			7			3	4							
1		2		5	6		8			11		9	10			7			3	4							
1		2		5	6		8			11		9	10			7			3	4							
1		2		5	6		8			11		9				7			3	4					10		
1		2		5	6		8			11		9	10			7			3	4							
35	17	28	21	24	35	3	22	24	23	34	8	28	15	7	2	24	3	3	25	20	2	4	6	1	2	1	1
				1			1	12	3	7		15	1			6											

1			4		6			10	8	11		9				7			3	5			2				
1	0	0	1	0	1	0	0	1	1	1	0	1	0	0	0	1	0	0	1	1	0	0	1	0	0	0	0

League Table

	P	W	D	L	F	A	Pts
Manchester City	38	23	8	7	81	40	54
Oldham Athletic	38	23	7	8	79	39	53
Hull City	38	23	7	8	80	46	53
Derby County	38	22	9	7	72	47	53
Leicester Fosse	38	20	4	14	79	58	44
Glossop	38	18	7	13	64	57	43
Fulham	38	14	13	11	51	43	41
Wolverhampton W	38	17	6	15	64	63	40
Barnsley	38	16	7	15	62	59	39
Bradford Park Avenue	38	17	4	17	64	59	38
West Bromwich Albion	38	16	5	17	58	56	37
Blackpool	38	14	8	16	50	52	36
Stockport County	38	13	8	17	50	47	34
Burnley	38	14	6	18	62	61	34
Lincoln City	38	10	11	17	42	69	31
Clapton Orient	38	12	6	20	37	60	30
Leeds City	38	10	7	21	46	80	27
Gainsborough Trinity	38	10	6	22	33	75	26
Grimsby Town	38	9	6	23	50	77	24
Birmingham	38	8	7	23	42	78	23

1910-11

Division Two

Manager: Frank Scott-Walford

Final Position: 11th

Did you know that?

5 September 1910: City played their opening home game in green shirts after signing five young Irish players in the summer. Secretary-manager Frank Scott-Walford also supplied green flags to mark the centre line – the idea being to make the new boys feel at home. The kit was retained for the season. Fans got into the spirit of the gesture by shouting 'Play Up, Ireland!' during the game.

Billy Gillespie made his debut on the opening day of the season against Blackpool and went on to become a major star with Sheffield United and Ireland.

Match No.	Date	Venue	Opponents	Result	FT	HT	Scorers	Attendance
1	Sep 3	H	Blackpool	L	1-2	0-0	Enright	12,000
2	10	A	Glossop	L	1-2	0-0	Enright	8,000
3	17	H	Lincoln City	L	0-1	0-0		8,000
4	24	A	Huddersfield Town	L	2-3	1-2	Croot (pen), McLeod	7,500
5	Oct 1	H	Birmingham	D	1-1	1-0	Gillespie	8,000
6	8	A	West Bromwich Alb	L	0-2	0-2		10,000
7	15	H	Hull City	W	1-0	0-0	Gillespie	8,000
8	22	A	Fulham	L	1-2	1-1	Gillespie	11,000
9	29	H	Bradford PA	W	2-0	1-0	McLeod, Gillespie	13,000
10	Nov 5	A	Burnley	L	1-4	1-2	McLeod	8,000
11	12	H	Gainsborough Trinity	W	4-0	2-0	Enright, Gillespie 2, McLeod	5,000
12	19	A	Bolton Wanderers	L	0-3	0-0		10,000
13	26	A	Stockport County	W	4-0	2-0	Gillespie 2, McLeod, Bridgett	4,000
14	Dec 3	H	Derby County	W	3-2	1-1	Morris, Roberts 2	10,000
15	10	A	Barnsley	L	0-4	0-1		4,000
16	17	H	Leicester Fosse	L	2-3	0-1	Enright, Morris	5,000
17	24	A	Wolverhampton W	L	1-3	1-3	Gillespie	6,000
18	26	H	Chelsea	D	3-3	1-2	Roberts, Croot, McLeod	18,000
19	27	H	Clapton Orient	W	1-0	1-0	Mulholland	10,000
20	31	A	Blackpool	W	2-1	2-1	McLeod, Bridgett	1,000
21	Jan 7	H	Glossop	L	0-2	0-1		10,000
22	21	A	Lincoln City	D	1-1	0-1	Enright	5,000
23	28	H	Huddersfield Town	W	5-2	2-1	Croot 2 (1 pen), McLeod 2, Mulholland	10,000
24	Feb 4	A	Birmingham	L	1-2	1-0	McLeod	15,000
25	11	H	West Bromwich Alb	W	3-1	2-0	McLeod, Mulholland, Enright	10,700
26	18	A	Hull City	D	1-1	1-0	Enright	6,000
27	25	H	Fulham	W	3-1	1-1	Croot (pen), Enright, Mulholland	6,000
28	Mar 4	A	Bradford PA	W	2-0	1-0	Croot (pen), Mulholland	12,000
29	18	A	Gainsborough Trinity	W	2-1	0-1	Enright, Roberts	4,000
30	25	H	Bolton Wanderers	W	1-0	1-0	Mulholland	15,000
31	27	H	Burnley	D	0-0	0-0		5,500
32	Apr 1	H	Stockport County	W	4-0	2-0	McLeod 2, Mulholland 2	9,000
33	8	A	Derby County	D	2-2	2-0	Croot (pen), Mulholland	5,000
34	14	A	Chelsea	L	1-4	0-1	McLeod	50,000
35	15	H	Barnsley	D	0-0	0-0		10,000
36	17	A	Clapton Orient	L	0-1	0-0		6,000
37	22	A	Leicester Fosse	L	1-2	0-0	Croot	5,000
38	29	H	Wolverhampton W	W	1-0	0-0	Enright	6,000
								Appearances
								Goals

FA Cup

R1	Jan 14	H	Brighton & HA	L	1-3	1-1	Roberts	18,270
								Appearances
								Goals

A suited Frank Scott-Walford, sat in the middle row, with his players and staff for the 1910–11 season.

Hogg, Tony	Affleck, George	Creighton, Alec	Harkins, Jack	Morris, Tom	Cubberley, Stan	Cunningham, George	Foley, Mick	Gillespie, Billy	Enright, Joe	Croot, Fred	Horsley, James	McLeod, Billy	Roberts, Hugh	Mulholland, Tom	Bromage, Harry	White, Jabez	Kelly, Chris	Bridgett, Harold
1	2	3	4	5	6	7	8	9	10	11								
1	2	3	4	5		7	8		10	11	6	9						
1	2	3	4	5	6				10	11		9	7	8				
		3	4					9	10	11	6	8	7		1	2	5	
	2	3		5	6			9	10	11		8	7		1		4	
	2	3		5	6			9	10	11		8	7		1		4	
	2	3	4	5	6			9	10	11		8	7		1			
	2	3	4	5	6			9	10	11		8	7		1			
	2	3	4	5	6			9	10	11		8	7		1			
	2	3	4	5	6			9	10	11		8	7		1			
	2	3	4	5	6			9	10	11		8	7		1			
	2	3	4	5	6			9	10	11		8	7		1			
	2	3	4	5	6			9	10			8	7		1			11
	2	3	4	5	6			9	10			8	7		1			11
	2	3	4	5	6			9	10			8	7		1			11
	2	3		5	6			9	10		4	8	7		1			11
	2	3		5	6			9	10		4		7	8	1			11
	2	3		5	6			9	10	11	4	8	7		1			
1	3	2		5	6				10	11	4	9	7	8				
1	2	3	6	5	10						4	9	7	8				11
	2	3		5	6	7		9	10		4	8			1			11
1	2	3	4	5					10		6	9	7	8				11
1	2	3	4	5	6				10	11		9	7	8				
1	2	3	4	5	6				10	11		9	7	8				
1	2	3	4	5	6				10	11		9	7	8				
	2	3	4	5	6				10	11		9	7	8	1			
	2	3	4	5	6				10	11		9	7	8	1			
	2	3	4	5	6				10	11		9	7	8	1			
	2	3	4	5	6				10	11		9	7	8	1			
	2	3	4	5	6				10	11		9	7	8	1			
	2	3	4	5	6				10	11		9	7	8	1			
	2	3	4	5	6				10	11		9	7	8	1			
	2	3	4	5	6				10	11		9	7	8	1			
	2	3	4	5	6				10	11		9	7	8	1			
1	2	3	4	5	6				10	11		9	7	8				
1	2	3	4	5			6	9	10	11			7	8				
1	2	3	4	5	6				10	11		9	7	8				
1	2	3	4		6		5		10	11		9	7	8				
13	37	38	31	36	34	3	4	18	37	30	9	35	35	21	25	1	3	8
				2				9	10	8		14	4	9				2

	2	3	4	5	6				10			9	7	8	1			11
0	1	1	1	1	1	0	0	0	1	0	0	1	1	1	1	0	0	1
													1					

League Table

	P	W	D	L	F	A	Pts
West Bromwich Albion	38	22	9	7	67	41	53
Bolton Wanderers	38	21	9	8	69	40	51
Chelsea	38	20	9	9	71	35	49
Clapton Orient	38	19	7	12	44	35	45
Hull City	38	14	16	8	55	39	44
Derby County	38	17	8	13	73	52	42
Blackpool	38	16	10	12	49	38	42
Burnley	38	13	15	10	45	45	41
Wolverhampton W	38	15	8	15	51	52	38
Fulham	38	15	7	16	52	48	37
Leeds City	38	15	7	16	58	56	37
Bradford Park Avenue	38	14	9	15	53	55	37
Huddersfield Town	38	13	8	17	57	58	34
Glossop	38	13	8	17	48	62	34
Leicester Fosse	38	14	5	19	52	62	33
Birmingham	38	12	8	18	42	64	32
Stockport County	38	11	8	19	47	79	30
Gainsborough Trinity	38	9	11	18	37	55	29
Barnsley	38	7	14	17	52	62	28
Lincoln City	38	7	10	21	28	72	24

1911-12

Division Two

Manager: Frank Scott-Walford

Final Position: 19th

Did you know that?

30 December 1911: Former Middlesbrough full-back Alex Campbell broke his leg on his City debut – a 3–1 win against Nottingham Forest – and didn't play professional football again.

23 March 1912: The 7–2 defeat at Fulham was the heaviest City suffered on their travels. The Cottagers goals were scored by Herbert Pearce (3), Tim Coleman (2) and Fred Mavin (2).

Alex Campbell broke his leg on his City debut at Nottingham Forest.

Match No.	Date	Venue	Opponents	Result	FT	HT	Scorers	Attendance
1	Sep 2	A	Nottingham Forest	L	1-2	1-2	McLeod	10,000
2	4	A	Burnley	L	2-4	1-2	McLeod, Enright	15,000
3	9	H	Chelsea	D	0-0	0-0		15,000
4	16	A	Clapton Orient	L	1-2	0-1	McLeod	13,000
5	23	H	Bristol City	W	3-1	1-1	Croot, Enright, McLeod	10,000
6	30	A	Birmingham	L	3-4	2-2	Enright, Roberts, Croot	10,000
7	Oct 7	H	Huddersfield Town	W	2-0	1-0	McLeod, Enright	12,000
8	14	A	Blackpool	L	0-3	0-2		4,000
9	21	H	Glossop	W	2-1	1-1	Mulholland, Croot	6,000
10	28	A	Hull City	L	0-1	0-0		10,000
11	Nov 4	H	Barnsley	W	3-2	2-0	McLeod, Mulholland 2	12,000
12	11	A	Bradford PA	D	1-1	1-1	Croot (pen)	13,000
13	18	H	Fulham	L	0-2	0-1		8,000
14	25	A	Derby County	L	2-5	2-2	McLeod, Roberts	12,000
15	Dec 4	H	Grimsby Town	L	1-2	1-1	McLeod	3,000
16	9	H	Burnley	L	1-5	0-2	Gillespie pen	10,000
17	16	A	Wolverhampton W	L	0-5	0-2		8,000
18	23	H	Leicester Fosse	W	2-1	1-1	Enright 2	6,000
19	25	H	Gainsborough Trinity	D	0-0	0-0		9,000
20	26	A	Gainsborough Trinity	L	1-2	1-0	Mulholland	6,000
21	30	H	Nottingham Forest	W	3-1	2-0	Mulholland 2, Enright	8,000
22	Jan 6	A	Chelsea	L	2-4	0-0	McLeod, Foley	10,000
23	20	H	Clapton Orient	L	0-2	0-2		5,000
24	23	A	Grimsby Town	W	2-1	1-1	Johnson, Enright	3,000
25	27	A	Bristol City	L	1-4	1-3	Croot (pen)	7,000
26	Feb 10	A	Huddersfield Town	W	2-1	1-1	Mulholland 2	8,000
27	17	H	Blackpool	W	1-0	1-0	Enright	6,000
28	24	A	Glossop	L	1-2	0-1	Mulholland	3,000
29	Mar 2	H	Hull City	D	0-0	0-0		8,000
30	16	H	Bradford PA	L	1-2	1-2	Foley	10,000
31	23	A	Fulham	L	2-7	2-2	Enright, Mulholland	3,000
32	30	H	Derby County	L	0-1	0-0		4,500
33	Apr 5	H	Birmingham	D	0-0	0-0		5,000
34	6	H	Stockport County	D	1-1	0-1	Enright	4,000
35	11	A	Barnsley	W	4-3	4-1	McLeod 2, Croot 2 (2 pens)	3,000
36	15	A	Stockport County	D	3-3	2-2	McLeod 2, Mulholland	3,000
37	20	H	Wolverhampton W	D	1-1	1-1	McLeod	5,000
38	27	A	Leicester Fosse	L	1-2	0-1	Enright	10,000
								Appearances
								Goals

FA Cup

R1	Jan 13	H	Glossop	W	1-0	1-0	Roberts	21,000
R2	Feb 3	H	West Bromwich Alb	L	0-1	0-0		21,320
								Appearances
								Goals

Back row, left to right: S. Collins (trainer), John Clarkin, Albert Stead (groundsman), Sam Johnson, George Cunningham, Frank Heaney, Tony Hogg, Ted McDaniel, Les Murphy, Joe Moran, A. Roberts, Dick Roberts, William Briggs, Mick Foley, Jimmy Fortune. Middle row: Hugh Roberts, Tom Mulholland, John Harkins, Stan Cubberley, Frank Scott-Walford (manager), Tom Morris, Chris Kelly, Joe Enright, Fred Croot. Front row, on ground: Alec Creighton, George Affleck, Billy Gillespie, Harold Bridgett.

Murphy, Leslie	Affleck, George	Creighton, Alec	Harkins, Jack	Morris, Tom	Cubberley, Stan	Roberts, Hugh	Mulholland, Tom	McLeod, Billy	Gillespie, Billy	Croot, Fred	Johnson, Sam	Moran, Joe	Enright, Joe	Fortune, Jimmy	Hogg, Tony	Reinhardt, Cecil	Heaney, Frank	Bridgett, Harold	Foley, Mick	Kelly, Chris	Clarkin, John	Campbell, Alex	McDaniel, Edward
1	2	3	4	5	6	7	8	9	10	11													
1	2	3		5		7		8	9	11	4	6	10										
1	2	3	4	5	6	7		8	9				10	11									
1	2	3	4	5	6	7	8	9	10				11										
1	2	3	4	5	6	7	8	9		11			10										
1	2	3	4	5	6	7	8	9		11			10										
	2	3	4	5	6	7	8	9		11			10		1								
	2	3	4	5	6	7	8	9		11			10		1								
1	2	3	4	5	6	7	8	9		11			10										
1	2	3		5	6	7	8	9		11	4		10										
1	2	3	4	5	6	7	8	9		11			10										
1	2	3		5	6	7	8	9		11	4		10										
1	2	3		5	6	7	8	9		11		4	10										
1	2	3	4	5	6	7	8	9		11			10										
1	2	3	4	5		7	8	9		11		6	10										
1	2	3	4	5		7	8	9	10			6	11										
	3		4	5		7	8		9			6	10			1	2	11					
	2	3		5		7		9		11	4	6	10			1			8				
	2	3				7	8	9		11	4	6	10			1				5			
	2	3	4	5		7	8	9		11		6				1					10		
1	2		4	5		7	8	9		11		6	10									3	
1	2	3	4	5		7	8	9		11		6							10				
1	2	3	4	5		7	8	9		11		6	10										
1	3		4	5		7	8			11	6		10						9				2
	2		4	5		7	8	9		11	6	3	10			1							
	2	3	4	5		7	8			11		6	10			1			9				
	2	3	4	5		7	8			11		6	10			1			9				
	2	3	4	5		7	8			11		6	10			1			9				
	2	3	4	5		7	8			11		6	10			1			9				
	2	3	4	5	6	7	8	9		11						1			10				
	2	3	4	5		7	8	9		11		6	10			1							
		3	4	5		7	8			11		6	10			1	2		9				
	2		4	5	6	7	8	9				3	10		1			11					
	2		4	5	6	7	8	9				3	10		1			11					
	2		4	5	6	7	8	9		11		3	10		1								
	2		4	5	6	7	8	9		11		3	10		1								
	2		4	5	6	7	8	9		11		3	10		1								
	2		4	5	6	7	8	9		11		3	10		1								
18	37	28	32	37	20	38	35	31	6	32	7	24	34	1	8	12	2	3	9	1	1	1	1
						2	11	14	1	7	1		12						2				
1	2	3	4	5		7	8	9		11		6	10										
	2	3	4	5		7	8			11		6	10			1			9				
1	2	2	2	2	0	2	2	1	0	2	0	2	2	0	0	1	0	0	1	0	0	0	0
						1																	

League Table

	P	W	D	L	F	A	Pts
Derby County	38	23	8	7	74	28	54
Chelsea	38	24	6	8	64	34	54
Burnley	38	22	8	8	77	41	52
Clapton Orient	38	21	3	14	61	44	45
Wolverhampton W	38	16	10	12	57	33	42
Barnsley	38	15	12	11	45	42	42
Hull City	38	17	8	13	54	51	42
Fulham	38	16	7	15	66	58	39
Grimsby Town	38	15	9	14	48	55	39
Leicester Fosse	38	15	7	16	49	66	37
Bradford Park Avenue	38	13	9	16	44	45	35
Birmingham	38	14	6	18	55	59	34
Bristol City	38	14	6	18	41	60	34
Blackpool	38	13	8	17	32	52	34
Nottingham Forest	38	13	7	18	46	48	33
Stockport County	38	11	11	16	47	54	33
Huddersfield Town	38	13	6	19	50	64	32
Glossop	38	8	12	18	42	56	28
Leeds City	38	10	8	20	50	78	28
Gainsborough Trinity	38	5	13	20	30	64	23

1912-13

Division Two

Manager: Herbert Chapman

Final Position: 6th

Did you know that?

5 April 1913: Billy McLeod scored for the ninth successive League game with the only goal of the game against Nottingham Forest. He netted a record 27 League goals in the season, including hat-tricks against Lincoln and Glossop.

Evelyn Lintott was an ever-present in his City debut season.

Match No.	Date	Venue	Opponents	Result	FT	HT	Scorers	Attendance
1	Sep 7	A	Fulham	L	0-4	0-4		20,000
2	14	H	Barnsley	W	2-0	1-0	Robertson, Croot (pen)	15,000
3	21	A	Bradford PA	W	1-0	1-0	Cubberley	18,000
4	28	H	Wolverhampton W	D	2-2	0-1	McLeod, Croot (pen)	20,000
5	Oct 5	A	Leicester Fosse	D	1-1	0-0	Robertson	10,000
6	12	H	Stockport County	W	2-1	1-1	McLeod 2	15,000
7	19	A	Preston North End	L	2-3	1-2	McLeod, Enright	9,000
8	26	H	Burnley	W	4-1	1-0	Robertson 2, McLeod, Cubberley	10,000
9	Nov 2	A	Hull City	L	2-6	1-3	McLeod, Croot (pen)	10,000
10	9	H	Glossop	W	4-0	1-0	McLeod 3, Foley	12,000
11	16	A	Clapton Orient	L	0-2	0-1		10,000
12	23	H	Lincoln City	D	2-2	1-1	Robertson, Lintott	15,000
13	30	A	Nottingham Forest	W	2-1	1-1	Robertson, Roberts	8,000
14	Dec 7	H	Bristol City	D	1-1	1-1	Robertson	10,000
15	14	A	Birmingham	D	2-2	1-0	McLeod 2	20,000
16	21	H	Huddersfield Town	L	0-3	0-1		15,000
17	25	H	Grimsby Town	L	1-2	1-1	Cubberley	15,000
18	26	H	Blackpool	L	0-2	0-1		8,000
19	28	H	Fulham	L	2-3	1-1	Bainbridge, Price	10,000
20	Jan 1	A	Blackpool	W	3-0	1-0	Croot, Bainbridge, McLeod	5,000
21	4	A	Barnsley	L	0-2	0-1		5,000
22	18	H	Bradford PA	W	2-0	0-0	Foley, Speirs	10,000
23	25	A	Wolverhampton W	D	2-2	1-0	Bainbridge, McLeod	8,000
24	Feb 8	H	Leicester Fosse	W	5-1	2-0	Price 2, Speirs, Fenwick, McLeod	10,000
25	15	A	Stockport County	L	0-6	0-1		7,000
26	22	H	Preston North End	W	5-1	3-1	Affleck (pen), Fenwick 2, Bainbridge, Foley	18,000
27	Mar 1	A	Burnley	D	2-2	0-1	McLeod, Speirs	12,000
28	8	H	Hull City	W	1-0	1-0	McLeod	20,000
29	15	A	Glossop	L	1-2	1-0	McLeod	2,000
30	21	A	Grimsby Town	L	2-3	1-2	McLeod 2	8,000
31	22	H	Clapton Orient	W	3-1	2-0	Speis 2, McLeod	6,000
32	24	A	Bury	D	1-1	1-0	McLeod	10,000
33	25	H	Bury	W	4-2	1-2	McLeod 3, Speirs	17,000
34	29	A	Lincoln City	D	3-3	1-2	Speirs, McLeod, Croot	9,000
35	Apr 5	H	Nottingham Forest	W	1-0	1-0	McLeod	20,000
36	12	A	Bristol City	D	1-1	1-0	Speirs	15,000
37	19	H	Birmingham	W	4-0	1-0	Speirs 2, McLeod, Foley	8,000
38	26	A	Huddersfield Town	L	0-1	0-1		8,000
								Appearances
								Goals

FA Cup

R1	Jan 15	H	Burnley	L	2-3	1-1	McLeod, Foley	13,109
								Appearances
								Goals

FA Cup match abandoned after 50 minutes due to snow

R1	Jan 11	H	Burnley	L	2-4	2-4	McLeod, Foley	12,600

Dapper manager Herbert Chapman, back row, far right, complete with straw boater, with his Leeds City squad and support staff.

Scott, Billy	Law, George,	Ferguson, Jock	Allan, Jack	Lintott, Evelyn	Cubberley, Stan	Roberts, Hugh	Robertson, Jimmy	McLeod, Billy	Gibson, Andy	Croot, Fred	Foley, Mick	Enright, Joe	Copeland, Charlie	Affleck, George	Bainbridge, Simpson	Moran, Joe	Price, Arthur	Speirs, Jimmy	Broughton, Tom	Hogg, Tony	Bridgett, Harold	Fenwick, George
1	2	3	4	5	6	7	8	9	10	11												
1	2	3	4	5	10	7	8	9		11	6											
1	2	3	4	5	10	7	8	9		11	6											
1	2	3	4	5	10	7	8	9		11	6											
1	2	3	4	5	10	7	8	9		11	6											
1	2	3		5	4	7	8	9	10	11	6											
1	2	3		5	4		8	9	10	11	6	7										
1	2	3	4	5	10		8	9		11	6	7										
1	2	3	4	5	10	7	8	9		11	6											
1	3			5	4	7	8	9		11	6	10	2									
1	3			5	4	7	8	9		11	6	10	2									
1			4	5	10	7	8	9		11	6		2	3								
1	2	3	4	5		7	8	9	10	11	6											
1	2	3	4	5			8	9	10	11	6				7							
1	2	3	4	5	10		8	9		11	6				7							
1	2	3	4	5	10		8	9		11	6				7							
1	2	3	4	5	10		8	9		11					7	6						
1	2	3	4	5			8	9		11	6	10			7							
1	4	3		5				9		11	6		2		7		8	10				
1	2			5			8	9		11	6			3	7			10	4			
1	2			5				9		11	6			3	7		8	10	4			
				5	4			9		11	6		2	3	7		8	10		1		
	4			5			8	9			6		2	3	7			10		1	11	
	4			5				9			6		2	3	7		8	10		1		11
	4			5				9			6		2	3	7		8	10		1		11
1	4			5			8	9			6		2	3	7			10				11
1	4			5			8	9			6		2	3	7			10				11
1	4			5			8	9			6		2	3	7			10				11
	4	3		5			8	9		11	6			2	7			10		1		
	4			5				9		11	6		2	3	7		8	10		1		
	4			5			8	9		11	6		2	3	7			10		1		
	4			5			8	9		11	6		2	3	7			10		1		
	4			5				9		11	6		2	3	7		8	10		1		
	4			5				9		11	6		2	3	7		8	10		1		
	4			5			10	9		11	6		2	3	7		8			1		
	4			5				9		11	6	7	2	3			8	10		1		
				5				9		11	6		2	3	7		8	10	4	1		
	3			5				9		11	6		2		7		8	10	4	1		
24	35	17	14	38	16	11	27	38	5	32	36	6	20	19	24	1	12	19	4	14	1	5
				1	3	1	7	27		5	4	1		1	4		3	10				3

	2		4	5			8	9		11	6			3	7			10		1		
0	1	0	1	1	0	0	1	1	0	1	1	0	0	1	1	0	0	1	0	1	0	0
								1			1											

1	2		4	5			8	9		11	6			3	7			10				

League Table

	P	W	D	L	F	A	Pts
Preston North End	38	19	15	4	56	33	53
Burnley	38	21	8	9	88	53	50
Birmingham	38	18	10	10	59	44	46
Barnsley	38	19	7	12	57	47	45
Huddersfield Town	38	17	9	12	66	40	43
Leeds City	38	15	10	13	70	64	40
Grimsby Town	38	15	10	13	51	50	40
Lincoln City	38	15	10	13	50	52	40
Fulham	38	17	5	16	65	55	39
Wolverhampton W	38	14	10	14	56	54	38
Bury	38	15	8	15	53	57	38
Hull City	38	15	6	17	60	55	36
Bradford Park Avenue	38	14	8	16	60	60	36
Clapton Orient	38	10	14	14	34	47	34
Leicester Fosse	38	13	7	18	49	65	33
Bristol City	38	9	15	14	46	72	33
Nottingham Forest	38	12	8	18	58	59	32
Glossop	38	12	8	18	49	68	32
Stockport County	38	8	10	20	56	78	26
Blackpool	38	9	8	21	39	69	26

1913-14

Division Two

Manager: Herbert Chapman

Final Position: 4th

Did you know that?

29 November 1913: City enjoyed their biggest victory when they thumped bottom-of-the table Nottingham Forest 8–0 at Elland Road – ace marksman Billy McLeod scoring four of the goals. The emphatic result pushed United up into third place in the table.

7 February 1914: Ivan Sharpe played in the England amateur team's 9–1 win against Wales at Plymouth. A journalist and member of the Great Britain team which won gold at the 1912 Stockholm Olympics, he also played against Belgium, Denmark and Sweden in 1913–14.

2 March 1914: Clapton Orient fixed the kick-off of their home game against City so late, at 4.30pm, that the closing stages of the game were played in near darkness. Orient won 3–1, but City goalkeeper Billy Scott complained that he literally could not see the ball when two late goals were scored against him. The result stood but the London side were fined £25.

Match No.	Date		Venue	Opponents	Result	FT	HT	Scorers	Attendance
1	Sep	6	H	Glossop	W	3-0	1-0	Spiers, McLeod 2	8,000
2		13	A	Stockport County	L	1-2	1-0	McLeod	10,000
3		20	H	Bradford PA	W	5-1	2-0	Speirs, Price, Bainbridge 2, McLeod	23,000
4		27	A	Notts County	L	0-4	0-2		12,000
5	Oct	4	H	Leicester Fosse	W	2-1	1-1	Bainbridge, Price	18,000
6		11	A	Wolverhampton W	W	3-1	0-1	Speirs 2, Sharpe (pen)	10,000
7		18	H	Hull City	L	1-2	0-1	Speirs	20,000
8		25	A	Barnsley	W	4-1	1-0	Speirs 2, Price, McLeod	12,000
9	Nov	1	H	Bury	W	2-1	2-0	Price, Speirs	20,000
10		8	A	Huddersfield Town	D	1-1	1-1	Turner	9,000
11		15	H	Lincoln City	W	1-0	0-0	McLeod	12,000
12		22	A	Blackpool	D	2-2	1-2	Hampson, Croot	5,000
13		29	H	Nottingham Forest	W	8-0	3-0	McLeod 4, Price 2, Hampson, Speirs	14,000
14	Dec	6	A	Woolwich Arsenal	L	0-1	0-0		18,000
15		13	H	Grimsby Town	W	4-1	0-1	McLeod 2, Hampson, Price	10,000
16		20	A	Birmingham	W	2-0	1-0	McLeod, Sharpe	15,000
17		25	H	Fulham	W	2-1	2-0	McLeod, Hampson	30,000
18		26	A	Fulham	W	1-0	0-0	McLeod	25,000
19		27	A	Glossop	D	1-1	0-1	Bainbridge	2,000
20	Jan	3	H	Stockport County	W	5-1	5-0	Speirs, Jackson 2, McLeod, Sharpe	10,000
21		17	A	Bradford PA	L	1-3	1-2	McLeod	32,184
22		24	H	Notts County	L	2-4	1-4	Sharpe, Hampson	25,000
23	Feb	7	A	Leicester Fosse	L	1-5	0-3	Speirs	4,000
24		14	H	Wolverhampton W	W	5-0	1-0	McLeod 3, Speirs, Sharpe	10,000
25		21	A	Hull City	L	0-1	0-1		18,000
26		28	H	Barnsley	W	3-0	1-0	McLeod, Sharpe 2 (1 pen)	20,000
27	Mar	2	A	Clapton Orient	L	1-3	1-0	Hampson	7,000
28		7	A	Bury	D	1-1	1-1	Jackson	12,000
29		14	H	Huddersfield Town	W	5-1	2-1	Hampson, McLeod 3, Price	14,000
30		21	A	Lincoln City	L	0-1	0-1		8,000
31		28	H	Blackpool	W	2-1	2-0	McLeod, Hampson	12,000
32	Apr	4	A	Nottingham Forest	L	1-2	0-1	Law	6,000
33		10	A	Bristol City	D	1-1	1-1	McLeod	20,000
34		11	H	Woolwich Arsenal	D	0-0	0-0		25,000
35		13	H	Bristol City	W	1-0	1-0	Turner	12,000
36		14	H	Clapton Orient	D	0-0	0-0		12,000
37		18	A	Grimsby Town	W	1-0	0-0	Price	9,000
38		25	H	Birmingham	W	3-2	2-2	Price, Stuart (og), McLeod	10,000
									Appearances
								One own-goal	Goals

FA Cup

R1	Jan	10	A	Gainsborough Trinity	W	4-2	3-1	Jackson 2, Law, McLeod	14,000
R2		31	H	West Bromwich Alb	L	0-2	0-0		29,733
									Appearances
									Goals

Billy McLeod scored a club record 27 League goals for the second successive season.

Manager Herbert Chapman, still in his boater hat, with the squad which took Leeds City close to promotion to the First Division.

Hogg, Tony	Copeland, Charlie	Affleck, George	Linton, Evelyn	Hampson, John	Foley, Mick	Bainbridge, Simpson	Price, Arthur	McLeod, Billy	Speirs, Jimmy	Sharpe, Ivan	Law, George	Turner, Neil	Croot, Fred	Johnson, James	Jackson, John	Blackman, Fred	Scott, Billy	Peart, Harry	Dougherty, Joe	Lamph, Tom
1	2	3	4	5	6	7	8	9	10	11										
1	2	3	4	5	6	7	8	9	10	11										
1	2	3		5	6	7	8	9	10	11	4									
1	2	3		5	6	7	8	9	10	11	4									
1	2	3		5	6	7	8	9	10	11	4									
1	2	3		5	6	7	8	9	10	11	4									
1	2	3		5	6	7	8	9	10	11	4									
1	2	3		5	6	7	8	9	10	11	4									
1	2	3		5	6	7	8	9	10	11	4									
1		3	4	5	6		8	9	10		2	7	11							
1	2	3		5	6		8	9	10	11	4	7								
1	2	3		5	6		8	9	10	7	4		11							
1	2	3		5	6	7	10	9	8	11	4									
1	2	3		5	6	7	8	9	10	11	4									
1	2	3		5	6		8	9	10	11	4			7						
1	2	3	5		6		7	9	10	11	4				8					
1	2	3		5	6		7	9	10	11	4				8					
1	2	3		5	6	7	8	9	10	11	4									
1	2	3		5	6	7		9	10		4		11		8					
1	2	3	4	5	6	7		9	10	11					8					
1	2	3		5	6		7	9	10	11	4				8					
1	2	3		5	6	7		9	10	11	4				8					
1	2	3		5	6		8	9	10		4		11		7					
1	2	3		5	6		7	9	10	11	4				8					
1		3		5	6		7	9	10	11	4				8	2				
		3		5	6		7	9	10	11	4				8	2	1			
		3		5	6		7	9	10	11	4				8	2	1			
1		3		5	6		10	9		7	4		11		8	2				
1		3		5	6		10	9		7	4		11		8	2				
1		3		5	6		10	9		7	4		11		8	2				
1		3		5	6		10	9		7	4		11		8	2				
1		3		5	6		10	9		7	4		11		8	2				
1		3		5	6		7	9	10	11	4				8	2				
1		3		5	6		10	9		7	4		11		8	2				
1		3			6		10	9		11	4	7			8	2		5		
1		3		5	6		10			11	4	7			8	2			9	
1		3		5	10		7	9		11	4				8	2				6
1		3		5	6		7	9	10	11	4				8	2				
36	23	38	5	36	38	15	35	37	29	35	35	4	10	1	22	14	2	1	1	1
				8		4	10	27	12	7	1	2	1		3					

Hogg, Tony	Copeland, Charlie	Affleck, George	Linton, Evelyn	Hampson, John	Foley, Mick	Bainbridge, Simpson	Price, Arthur	McLeod, Billy	Speirs, Jimmy	Sharpe, Ivan	Law, George	Turner, Neil	Croot, Fred	Johnson, James	Jackson, John	Blackman, Fred	Scott, Billy	Peart, Harry	Dougherty, Joe	Lamph, Tom
1	2	3		5	6	7		9	10	11	4				8					
1		3	4	5	6	7		9	10	11	2				8					
2	1	2	1	2	2	2	0	2	2	2	2	0	0	0	2	0	0	0	0	0
								1			1				2					

League Table

	P	W	D	L	F	A	Pts
Notts County	38	23	7	8	77	36	53
Bradford Park Avenue	38	23	3	12	71	47	49
Woolwich Arsenal	38	20	9	9	54	38	49
Leeds City	38	20	7	11	76	46	47
Barnsley	38	19	7	12	51	45	45
Clapton Orient	38	16	11	11	47	35	43
Hull City	38	16	9	13	53	37	41
Bristol City	38	16	9	13	52	50	41
Wolverhampton W	38	18	5	15	51	52	41
Bury	38	15	10	13	39	40	40
Fulham	38	16	6	16	46	43	38
Stockport County	38	13	10	15	55	57	36
Huddersfield Town	38	13	8	17	47	53	34
Birmingham	38	12	10	16	48	60	34
Grimsby Town	38	13	8	17	42	58	34
Blackpool	38	9	14	15	33	44	32
Glossop	38	11	6	21	51	67	28
Leicester Fosse	38	11	4	23	45	61	26
Lincoln City	38	10	6	22	36	66	26
Nottingham Forest	38	7	9	22	37	76	23

1914-15

Division Two

Manager: Herbert Chapman

Final Position: 15th

Did you know that?

16 January 1915: Another scoring milestone for Billy McLeod. He scored five times in the 6–2 victory at Hull City.

Match No.	Date	Venue	Opponents	Result	FT	HT	Scorers	Attendance
1	Sep 2	H	Fulham	L	0-1	0-1		8,000
2	5	A	Stockport County	L	1-3	1-3	Sharpe	5,000
3	9	A	Fulham	L	0-1	0-1		5,000
4	12	H	Hull City	L	2-3	0-0	Speirs, Jackson	8,000
5	19	H	Blackpool	W	2-0	1-0	McLeod, Goodwin (pen)	8,000
6	26	A	Clapton Orient	L	0-2	0-0		9,000
7	Oct 3	H	Arsenal	D	2-2	0-0	Goodwin (pen), Speirs	10,000
8	10	A	Derby County	W	2-1	1-1	Speirs, McLeod	5,000
9	17	H	Lincoln City	W	3-1	3-0	McLeod, Speirs 2	10,000
10	24	A	Birmingham City	L	3-6	1-3	Sharpe 2, Speirs	8,000
11	31	H	Grimsby Town	W	5-0	2-0	McLeod 2, Speirs, Bainbridge, Jackson	5,000
12	Nov 7	A	Huddersfield Town	L	0-1	0-0		14,000
13	14	H	Bristol City	D	1-1	1-1	McLeod	8,000
14	21	A	Bury	D	0-0	0-0		6,000
15	28	H	Preston North End	D	0-0	0-0		7,000
16	Dec 5	A	Nottingham Forest	L	1-3	0-1	Speirs	3,000
17	12	H	Leicester Fosse	W	7-2	3-1	Bainbridge 2, McLeod 2, Price 3	5,000
18	19	A	Barnsley	L	1-2	1-1	Sharpe	3,000
19	25	A	Glossop	W	3-0	1-0	Jackson 2, McLeod	1,000
20	26	H	Glossop	W	3-0	3-0	Bainbridge, Price, McLeod	6,000
21	Jan 2	H	Stockport County	L	1-3	0-1	Speirs	7,000
22	16	A	Hull City	W	6-2	2-1	McLeod 5, Sharpe	5,000
23	23	A	Blackpool	L	0-1	0-1		6,000
24	Feb 3	H	Clapton Orient	L	0-1	0-1		4,000
25	6	A	Arsenal	L	0-2	0-2		10,000
26	13	H	Derby County	L	3-5	2-3	Edmondson, Speirs, Sharpe	5,000
27	20	A	Lincoln City	W	1-0	1-0	Edmondson	4,000
28	27	H	Birmingham City	W	2-0	1-0	Jackson, Price	7,000
29	Mar 6	A	Grimsby Town	W	5-2	2-1	Edmondson, Jackson, Sharpe, Goodwin, Price	4,000
30	13	H	Huddersfield Town	W	1-0	1-0	Sharpe	12,000
31	20	A	Bristol City	L	0-1	0-1		5,000
32	27	H	Bury	W	2-1	1-1	McLeod, Price	6,000
33	Apr 3	A	Preston North End	L	0-2	0-1		5,000
34	5	A	Wolverhampton W	L	1-5	1-2	McLeod	15,000
35	6	H	Wolverhampton W	L	2-3	2-0	McLeod, Price	5,000
36	10	H	Nottingham Forest	W	4-0	2-0	Price 3, Sharpe	4,000
37	17	A	Leicester Fosse	L	1-5	0-4	Jackson	3,000
38	24	H	Barnsley	L	0-2	0-2		5,000
								Appearances
								Goals

FA Cup

Match No.	Date	Venue	Opponents	Result	FT	HT	Scorers	Attendance
R1	Jan 9	A	Derby County	W	2-1	1-1	McLeod, Sharpe	9,417
R2	30	A	Queen's Park R	L	0-1	0-0		10,000
								Appearances
								Goals

Leeds City in their club's last peacetime season in the Football League. Back row, left to right: George Law, J.C. Whiteman (director), Tony Hogg, Fred Blackman, John Hampson, Mick Foley, Herbert Chapman (secretary-manager), Jack McQuillan. Front row: Dick Murrell (trainer), Ivan Sharpe, John Jackson, Billy McLeod, Jimmy Speirs, Ernie Goodwin, Val Lawrence.

Hogg, Tony	Bickman, Fred	McQuillan, Jack	Law, George	Peart, Harry	Foley, Mick	Bainbridge, Simpson	Jackson, John	Speirs, Jimmy	Price, Arthur	Sharpe, Ivan	Lawrence, Val	Rothwell, Alf	Cowen, Bob	Croot, Fred	Hampson, John	McLeod, Billy	Richardson, Webb	Goodwin, Ernie	Wainwright, Wilson	Affleck, George	Copeland, Charlie	Lamph, Tom	Walker, Willis	Edmondson, John	Green, Joe
1	2	3	4	5	6	7	8	9	10	11															
1	2	3	4		6			10	9	11	5	7	8												
1	2	3	5		6	7	8	10	9		4			11											
1	2	3	4				8	10	7		6			11	5	9									
1	2	3			6		8	10			4				5	9	7	11							
1	2	3			6		8	10			4				5	9	7	11							
1	2	3					8	10		7	4				5	9		11	6						
1	2	3	4	5	6		8	10		7						9		11							
1	2	3	4	5	6		8	10		7						9		11							
1	2	3	4		6		8	10		7					5	9		11							
1	2	3	4		6	7	8	10							5	9		11							
1	2	3	4		6	7	8	10		11					5	9									
1	2	3	4		6	7	8	10		11					5	9									
1	2		4			7		10	8						5	9		11	6	3					
1			4		6	7		10	8						5	9		11		3	2				
1	2		4		6	7	8	10		11					5	9				3					
1	2		4		6	7	8		10	11					5	9				3					
1	2		4		6	7	8		10	11					5	9				3					
1	2		4		6	7	8	10						11	5	9				3					
1	2		4		6	7	8		10					11	5	9				3					
1	2		4		6	7	8	10		11					5	9				3					
1	2		4		6	7	8	10		11						9				3		5			
1	2		4		6	7	8	10		11						9				3		5			
1	2		4		6	7		8	10	11					5	9				3					
		3	4		6		7	8	10	11					5					2			1	9	
	2		4	5	6			10	7	11						8				3			1	9	
	2		4		6		8		10	11					5			7		3			1	9	
	2		4		6		8		10	11					5			7		3			1	9	
	2		4		6		8		10	11					5			7		3			1	9	
	2		4		6		8		10	11					5	9		7		3			1		
		3	4		6		8		10	11					5	9		7		2			1		
		2	4		6		8		10	11					5	9		7		3			1		
		2	4		6		8		10	11					5	9		7		3			1		
	2		4		6	7	8	11	10						5	9				3			1		
		2	4	5	6	7			10				8	11		9				3			1		
		2	4	5	6		8		10	11						9		7		3			1		
		2	4		6		8		10	11					5	9		7		3			1		
	2		4		6		8	11	10						5	9		7					1		3
24	30	20	35	6	35	18	32	25	24	26	6	1	2	5	28	31	2	19	2	24	1	2	14	5	1
						4	7	10	11	9						18		3						3	

Hogg, Tony	Bickman, Fred	McQuillan, Jack	Law, George	Peart, Harry	Foley, Mick	Bainbridge, Simpson	Jackson, John	Speirs, Jimmy	Price, Arthur	Sharpe, Ivan	Lawrence, Val	Rothwell, Alf	Cowen, Bob	Croot, Fred	Hampson, John	McLeod, Billy	Richardson, Webb	Goodwin, Ernie	Wainwright, Wilson	Affleck, George	Copeland, Charlie	Lamph, Tom	Walker, Willis	Edmondson, John	Green, Joe
1	2		4	5	6	7	8	10		11						9				3					
1	2		4		6	7	8	10		11					5	9				3					
2	2	0	2	1	2	2	2	2	0	2	0	0	0	0	1	2	0	0	0	2	0	0	0	0	0
										1						1									

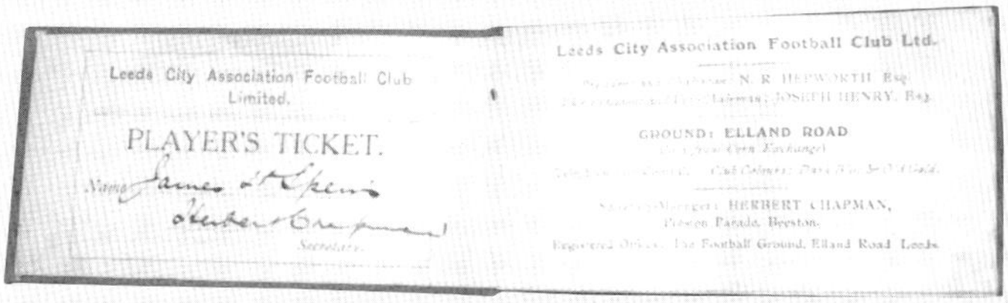

Leeds City Association Football Club Limited.
PLAYER'S TICKET.
Leeds City Association Football Club Ltd.
GROUND: ELLAND ROAD
HERBERT CHAPMAN,

Jimmy Speirs' fixture card signed by manager Herbert Chapman.

League Table

	P	W	D	L	F	A	Pts
Derby County	38	23	7	8	71	33	53
Preston North End	38	20	10	8	61	42	50
Barnsley	38	22	3	13	51	51	47
Wolverhampton W	38	19	7	12	77	52	45
Arsenal	38	19	5	14	69	41	43
Birmingham	38	17	9	12	62	39	43
Hull City	38	19	5	14	65	54	43
Huddersfield Town	38	17	8	13	61	42	42
Clapton Orient	38	16	9	13	50	48	41
Blackpool	38	17	5	16	58	57	39
Bury	38	15	8	15	61	56	38
Fulham	38	15	7	16	53	47	37
Bristol City	38	15	7	16	62	56	37
Stockport County	38	15	7	16	54	60	37
Leeds City	38	14	4	20	65	64	32
Lincoln City	38	11	9	18	46	65	31
Grimsby Town	38	11	9	18	48	76	31
Nottingham Forest	38	10	9	19	43	77	29
Leicester Fosse	38	10	4	24	47	88	24
Glossop	38	6	6	26	31	87	18

1915-16

Midland Section

Manager: Herbert Chapman

Final Positions: 10th and 1st

Did you know that?

16 October 1915: Arthur Price netted five times in a 7–1 thrashing of Barnsley but City then went the next five matches without a goal.

Arthur Price, five goals against Barnsley.

Match No.	Date		Venue	Opponents	Result	FT	HT	Scorers	Attendance
1	Sep	4	A	Derby County	W	3-1	0-1	Edmondson, Bennett, Price	3,000
2		11	H	Sheffield Wed	W	2-1	1-1	Price, Hampson	8,000
3		18	A	Bradford PA	L	3-4	1-4	Bennett, Edmondson 2	10,000
4		25	H	Lincoln City	W	2-1	2-1	Edmondson, Price	6,000
5	Oct	2	H	Hull City	W	3-1	1-1	Law, Price, Edmondson	7,000
6		9	A	Nottingham Forest	L	0-2	0-2		5,000
7		16	H	Barnsley	W	7-1	3-1	Price 5, Edmondson, Bennett	7,000
8		23	A	Leicester Fosse	L	0-4	0-3		5,000
9	Nov	6	A	Bradford City	L	0-3	0-1		5,000
10		13	H	Huddersfield Town	D	0-0	0-0		3,000
11		20	A	Grimsby Town	D	0-0	0-0		4,000
12		27	H	Notts County	L	0-4	0-2		3,000
13	Dec	4	H	Derby County	W	4-1	0-0	Edmondson 3, Walden	1,000
14		11	A	Sheffield Wed	D	0-0	0-0		3,000
15		18	H	Bradford PA	D	1-1	1-1	Price	4,000
16		25	A	Lincoln City	L	0-2	0-1		6,000
17		27	H	Sheffield United	L	2-3	1-3	Bennett, Bainbridge	6,000
18	Jan	1	A	Hull City	W	3-0	0-0	Foley, Edmondson, Price (pen)	3,000
19		8	H	Nottingham Forest	W	1-0	1-0	Bainbridge	5,000
20		15	A	Barnsley	L	1-2	1-1	Lamph	4,000
21		22	H	Leicester Fosse	W	1-0	1-0	Bainbridge	4,000
22		29	A	Sheffield United	L	1-4	1-2	Goodwin (pen)	8,000
23	Feb	5	H	Bradford City	L	0-1	0-0		10,000
24		12	A	Huddersfield Town	L	1-5	0-5	Stephenson	6,000
25		19	H	Grimsby Town	W	3-1	1-0	Peart, Sharpe, Stephenson	3,000
26	Apr	21	A	Notts County	D	1-1	1-0	Price	3,000

Midland Section Principal Tornament - Final Position: 10th

Appearances

Goals

Midland Section Subsidiary Tournament (Northern Division)

Match No.	Date		Venue	Opponents	Result	FT	HT	Scorers	Attendance
27	Mar	4	A	Rochdale	W	1-0	0-0	Wilson	4,000
28		11	H	Bradford PA	W	3-2	2-1	Stephenson 3	4,000
29		18	A	Huddersfield Town	D	1-1	1-0	Price	5,000
30		25	H	Bradford City	L	0-1	0-0		3,000
31	Apr	1	A	Barnsley	W	6-4	3-1	Peart 4, Walden, Stephenson	3,000
32		8	H	Rochdale	W	3-1	1-0	Wilson 2, Peart	3,000
33		15	A	Bradford PA	W	1-0	1-0	Price	4,000
34		22	H	Huddersfield Town	L	1-2	1-1	Stephenson	5,000
35		24	H	Barnsley	W	1-0	0-0	Stephenson	5,000
36		29	A	Bradford City	W	4-2	1-2	Price, Wilson, Sherwin, Peart (pen)	8,000

Midland Section Subsidiary Tournament (Northern Division) - Final Position: 1st

Appearances

Goals

Bradley, Bill	Law, George	Affleck, George	Lamph, Tom	Hampson, John	Foley, Mick	Walden, Fanny	Bennett Tom	Edmondson, John	Price, Arthur	Croot, Fred	Wigglesworth, A	Walker, Willis	Dowling, E	Wainwright, Arthur	Cowen, Bob	Goodwin, Ernie	Copeland, Charlie	Booth, Curtis	Bainbridge, Simpson	Dunn, John	Malcolm, Willie	Peart, Jack	Hughes, Robert	Lavery, George	Stephenson, Clem	Hewison, Bob	Sharpe, Ivan	Robinson, Stan	Jennings, William	Wilson, Willie	Williamson, John	Davison, J	Sherwin, Harry
1	2	3	4	5	6	7	8	9	10	11																							
1	2	3	4	5	6	7	8	9	10	11																							
1	2	3	4	5	6	7	8	9	10	11																							
1	4	3		5	6	7	8	9	10	11	2																						
	4	3			6	7	8	9	10	11		1	2	5																			
1	2	3		5	6	7	8	9	10	11				4																			
1	2	3	4	5	6	7	8	9	10	11																							
1	2	3	4	5	6	7	8	9	10	11																							
1	2	3	4	5	6	7		9	10						8	11																	
1	4	3	5		6	7	8	9	10							11	2																
1	4	3	5		6	7	9		10	11							2	8															
1	4	3	5		6	7			10	11						9	2	8															
	4	3		5	6	7		9	10	11		1					2	8															
	4	3	8	5	6	7		9	10	11		1					2																
	4	3		5	6	7	8	9	10	11		1					2																
	4	3		5	6	7	8	9				1					2	10	11														
	5	3			6	7	8	9	4			1						10	11	2													
		3	4	5	6	7	8	9	10			1					2		11														
	4	3		5	6	7	8	9	10			1					2		11														
	5	3	4		6	7	8	9	10			1					2		11														
	4	3	5	8	6	7		9	10			1					2		11														
	4	3	5		6	7	9		10			1				11	2				8												
	8	3	4	5	6	7	10					1					2					9	11										
		3	4	5	6	7						1						8				9	11	2	10								
		3		5	6	7						1					2	8				9			10	4	11						
		3		5	6	7			9			1					2								10	4		8	11				
11	22	26	16	19	26	26	18	19	22	13	1	15	1	2	1	4	15	7	6	1	1	3	2	1	3	2	1	1	1	0	0	0	0
	1		1	1	1	1	4	10	12							1			3			1			2		1						

Bradley, Bill	Law, George	Affleck, George	Lamph, Tom	Hampson, John	Foley, Mick	Walden, Fanny	Bennett Tom	Edmondson, John	Price, Arthur	Croot, Fred	Wigglesworth, A	Walker, Willis	Dowling, E	Wainwright, Arthur	Cowen, Bob	Goodwin, Ernie	Copeland, Charlie	Booth, Curtis	Bainbridge, Simpson	Dunn, John	Malcolm, Willie	Peart, Jack	Hughes, Robert	Lavery, George	Stephenson, Clem	Hewison, Bob	Sharpe, Ivan	Robinson, Stan	Jennings, William	Wilson, Willie	Williamson, John	Davison, J	Sherwin, Harry
		3		5	6	7			4			1					2	8					11					10		9			
		3		5	6	7			8			1					2					9			10	4				11			
		3		5	6	7			8			1					2					9			10	4				11			
		3		5	6	7			8			1					2					9			10	4				11			
		3		5	6	7			8			1					2					9			10	4				11			
		3		5	6	7			8			1					2					9			10	4				11			
		3		5	6	7			8			1					2					9			10	4				11			
		3			6	7			10			1					2								8	4	11				5	9	
		3			6	7			5			1					2						11		8	4		10		9			
		3			6	7			10			1					2					9			8	4				11			5
0	0	10	0	7	10	10	0	0	10	0	0	10	0	0	0	0	10	1	0	0	0	7	2	0	9	9	1	2	0	9	1	1	1
						1			3													6			6					4			1

1916-17

Midland Section

Manager: Herbert Chapman

Final Positions: 1st and 7th

Did you know that?

14 October 1916: Fanny Walden, an ever-present guest outside-right in 1915–16 made his final appearance v Sheffield Wednesday. The little Spurs winger at 5ft 2½in is the smallest player to play for either City or United's first team.

Pocket dynamo Fanny Walden.

Match No.	Date	Venue	Opponents	Result	FT	HT	Scorers	Attendance
1	Sep 2	H	Leicester Fosse	D	2-2	1-2	Price 2	3,000
2	9	A	Grimsby Town	W	6-1	2-1	Peart 2, C. Stephenson, Thorpe, Mayson, Price	4,000
3	16	H	Notts County	W	5-0	2-0	C. Stephenson 3, Mayson, Peart	3,000
4	23	A	Rotherham County	W	5-0	1-0	Price 4, Peart	5,000
5	30	H	Huddersfield Town	W	1-0	0-0	Peart	8,000
6	Oct 7	A	Lincoln City	W	5-2	1-2	Peart 3, Pattison, C. Stephenson	4,000
7	14	H	Sheffield Wed	W	1-0	1-0	C. Stephenson	5,000
8	21	A	Bradford PA	W	3-1	2-0	Price 2, Peart	8,000
9	28	H	Birmingham	D	1-1	0-0	Peart	6,000
10	Nov 4	A	Hull City	D	1-1	0-1	C. Stephenson	4,000
11	11	H	Nottingham Forest	W	3-1	1-1	Peart, Sherwin, C. Stephenson	5,000
12	18	A	Barnsley	L	1-4	0-3	Peart	2,000
13	25	A	Chesterfield	W	4-3	2-1	Peart 2, C. Stephenson 2	4,000
14	Dec 2	H	Sheffield United	W	2-0	2-0	Price, C. Stephenson	5,000
15	9	A	Leicester Fosse	W	4-1	0-1	Price 3, Thorpe	3,000
16	16	H	Grimsby Town	W	1-0	1-0	Price	3,000
17	23	A	Notts County	L	0-1	0-1		500
18	25	H	Bradford City	W	1-0	0-0	Mayson (pen)	10,000
19	26	A	Bradford City	W	3-0	2-0	J. Stephenson, Peart, Price	11,000
20	30	H	Rotherham County	W	2-0	2-0	Mayson, Hewison	4,000
21	Jan 6	A	Huddersfield Town	D	1-1	0-0	Trotter	7,000
22	13	H	Lincoln City	W	3-1	2-0	Peart, Price, Moore	2,000
23	20	A	Sheffield Wed	D	2-2	1-1	J. Stephenson, Peart	5,000
24	27	H	Bradford PA	D	0-0	0-0		6,000
25	Feb 3	A	Birmingham	D	1-1	0-1	Peart	15,000
26	10	H	Hull City	D	1-1	0-1	Peart	2,000
27	17	A	Nottingham Forest	D	3-3	2-2	Moore, Peart 2	3,000
28	24	H	Barnsley	W	3-0	1-0	Peart 2, C. Stephenson	6,000
29	Mar 3	H	Chesterfield	W	1-0	1-0	Peart	4,000
30	10	A	Sheffield United	D	2-2	0-0	Price, Peart	6,000

Midland Section Principal Tournament - Position: 1st

Appearances

Goals

Midland Section Subsidiary Tournament

31	Mar 17	A	Bradford PA	D	1-1	0-0	Peart	6,000
32	24	H	Huddersfield Town	L	0-2	0-1		4,000
33	31	H	Bradford City	D	1-1	1-0	Price (pen)	4,000
34	Apr 7	H	Bradford PA	L	0-2	0-0		3,000
35	9	A	Huddersfield Town	W	1-0	0-0	C. Stephenson	3,000
36	21	A	Bradford City	W	5-1	2-1	Moore 3, Peart, C. Stephenson	3,000

Midland Section Subsidiary Tournament - Position: 7th

Appearances

Goals

The Leeds City team which won the wartime Midlands Section Principal Tournament included many guest players. Back row, left to right: Harry Sherwin (Sunderland), Charlie Copeland, Bob Hewison (Sunderland), Arthur Robinson (Blackburn Rovers), Billy Hampson (Newcastle United), Levi Thorpe (Burnley). Front row: George Cripps (secretary), Clem Stephenson (Aston Villa), Billy Moore, Jack Peart (Notts County), Arthur Price, Tommy Mayson (Grimsby Town), Dick Murrell (trainer).

Walker, Willis	Copeland, Charlie	Hudson, Edward	Hewison, Bob	Hampson, John	Thorpe, Levi	McCreadie, Willie	Stephenson, Clem	Peart, Jack	Price, Arthur	Stephenson, Jimmy	Sherwin, Harry	Mayson, Tommy	Walden, Fanny	Pattison, John	Toms, Bill	James, N	Clipstone, Fred	Kaye, A	Feathers, W	Hampson, Billy	Barnshaw, Richard	Trotter, Ally	Dawson, G	Moore, Billy	Robinson, Arthur	Robinson, Stan	Hampson, Tommy	Rose, Percy	Cawley, Tom	Hudspeth, Frank
1	2	3	4	5	6	7	8	9	10	11																				
1		3	2	5	6		7	9	10	8	4	11																		
1		3	2	5	4		8	9	10	7	6	11																		
1	2	3	6	5			8	9	10	7	4	11																		
1	2	3	6	5			8	9	10		4	11	7																	
1	2		3	5			8	9	6	7	4	10		11																
1		3	2	5	6		8	9		11	4	10	7																	
1		3	2	5	6		8	9	10	7	4	11																		
1		3	2	5	6		8	9	10	7	4	11																		
1	2	3	11	5	6		8		10	7	4				9															
1	2	3	6	5			8	9	10	7	4					11														
1	2		4		6			9	8		5	11			10		3	7												
1	2	3	4		6		8	9	10	7	5	11																		
1	2		3	5	6		8	9	10	7		11							4											
1	2		4		6		8	9	10	7	5	11								3										
1	2		4		6		8	9	10	7	5	11								3										
1	2		4		6		8	9	10	7	5	11								3										
1	2		4				8	9		7	5	10								3	6	11								
1	2		4		6		8	9	10	7	5	11								3										
1	2		6	5			8	9	10	7	4	11								3										
1	2				4			9		7	5	11								3		10	6	8						
1	2				4			9	10	7	5	11								3			6	8						
	2				4		8	9		7	5	11								3			6	10	1					
	2		4		6		8	9			5	11								3				10	1	7				
	2		4		6			9	10	7	5	11								3				8	1					
	2				6			9	10	7	5	11								3		8	4		1					
	2		4		6			9	10	7	5									3				8	1	11				
	2				6		8	9	4	7	5	11								3				10	1					
	2		4		6		8	9	10	7	5	11								3							1			
			4	2	6		8	9	10	7	5	11								3							1			
22	24	11	25	14	24	1	24	29	25	27	28	26	2	1	2	1	1	1	1	16	1	3	4	7	6	2	2	0	0	0
			1		2		12	25	17	2	1	4		1								1		2						

Walker, Willis	Copeland, Charlie	Hudson, Edward	Hewison, Bob	Hampson, John	Thorpe, Levi	McCreadie, Willie	Stephenson, Clem	Peart, Jack	Price, Arthur	Stephenson, Jimmy	Sherwin, Harry	Mayson, Tommy	Walden, Fanny	Pattison, John	Toms, Bill	James, N	Clipstone, Fred	Kaye, A	Feathers, W	Hampson, Billy	Barnshaw, Richard	Trotter, Ally	Dawson, G	Moore, Billy	Robinson, Arthur	Robinson, Stan	Hampson, Tommy	Rose, Percy	Cawley, Tom	Hudspeth, Frank
			4		6		8	9		7	5						2			3				10		11	1			
			4		6		8	9	10	7	5	11					2			3							1			
			4		6		8	9	10	7	5						2			3				11			1			
			4				8		10	7	5	11								3				9			1	2	6	
			4				8		9	7	5	10								3				11			1		6	2
			2		6		8	9	4	7	5	11								3				10			1			
0	0	0	6	0	4	0	6	4	5	6	6	4	0	0	0	0	3	0	0	6	0	0	0	5	0	1	6	1	2	1
							2	2	1															3						

1917-18

Midland Section

Manager: Herbert Chapman

Final Position: 1st

Did you know that?

9 February 1918: Nottingham Forest had only 10 men for the game so Leeds loaned them Ernie Hampson who became the only Leeds player to have ever played against his own team.

9 March 1918: City concluded their League campaign in front of a large crowd paying £513, beating the highest receipts previously of £261. The 2–0 win was achieved despite Harold Millership being sent off for punching Joe Kitchen in the eye.

6 April 1918: The appearance of Walker Hampson at full-back at Bradford saw the fifth player named Hampson to appear for City in the season. Tommy was in goal with brothers Billy and Walker at full-back. The other two, John and Ernie, were also brothers.

11 May 1918: As Leeds City were crowned unofficial League champions, the combined gate proceeds of £913 of their two-leg Final with Stoke was given to the National Footballers' War Fund.

Billy Hampson, ever-present in 1917–18.

Match No.	Date		Venue	Opponents	Result	FT	HT	Scorers	Attendance
1	Sep	1	A	Sheffield Wed	W	1-0	0-0	Peart	8,000
2		8	H	Sheffield Wed	W	5-0	3-0	Price 2, C. Stephenson, Peart, Barrett	6,000
3		15	A	Bradford City	L	2-3	2-1	Wm. Hampson, C. Stephenson	4,000
4		22	H	Bradford City	W	4-0	1-0	Peart, Price 3	4,000
5		29	A	Rotherham County	W	3-0	1-0	Peart, C. Stephenson, Sherwin	5,000
6	Oct	6	H	Rotherham County	W	6-0	3-0	Price 2, Peart 2, Goodwin, Hewison	5,000
7		13	H	Lincoln City	W	3-0	0-0	Peart, C. Stephenson, S. Robinson	4,000
8		20	A	Lincoln City	W	4-0	1-0	Peart, Hewison, J. Stephenson, Moore	3,000
9		27	H	Grimsby Town	D	2-2	1-2	Peart 2	3,000
10	Nov	3	A	Grimsby Town	W	4-0	0-0	S. Robinson, Price 2, Sherwin	1,500
11		10	H	Birmingham	W	1-0	1-0	Peart	5,000
12		17	A	Birmingham	L	1-3	1-2	Cawley	20,000
13		24	H	Notts County	W	2-0	2-0	Grant, C. Stephenson	2,000
14	Dec	1	A	Notts County	W	4-2	0-0	Peart 2, Price, Sherwin	3,000
15		8	A	Barnsley	W	4-3	2-2	Peart 2, J. Hampson, Cawley	1,400
16		15	H	Barnsley	W	2-1	2-1	Peart, Hewison	3,500
17		25	H	Huddersfield Town	W	3-0	2-0	Price, Sherwin (pen), Hewison	5,000
18		26	A	Huddersfield Town	W	3-1	0-1	C. Stephenson, Peart, Price	4,000
19	Jan	5	A	Hull City	W	2-0	1-0	Price, C. Stephenson	3,000
20		12	H	Hull City	L	1-3	0-1	Price	2,000
21		19	A	Leicester Fosse	W	4-2	0-0	Sherwin, C. Stephenson, Cawley 2	3,000
22		26	H	Leicester Fosse	W	4-0	2-0	Price, Peart, Goodwin, C. Stephenson	5,000
23	Feb	2	H	Nottingham Forest	W	2-0	0-0	Wightman (og), Buchan	3,000
24		9	A	Nottingham Forest	W	1-0	1-0	Peart	3,000
25		16	H	Bradford PA	W	2-1	1-0	Cawley, C. Stephenson	7,500
26		23	A	Bradford PA	W	2-0	1-0	Sherwin (pen), Peart	7,500
27	Mar	1	A	Sheffield United	L	1-2	1-0	Hewison	18,000
28		9	H	Sheffield United	W	2-0	2-0	Cawley, C.Stephenson	15,000

Principal Tournament - Position: 1st — Appearances

One own-goal — Goals

Midland Section Subsidiary Tournament

Match No.	Date		Venue	Opponents	Result	FT	HT	Scorers	Attendance
29	Mar	16	A	Huddersfield Town	L	2-4	1-3	Price, C. Stephenson	6,500
30		23	H	Huddersfield Town	W	1-0	0-0	Cawley	6,000
31		30	H	Bradford PA	W	3-1	2-0	Price 2, C.Stephenson	1,000
32	Apr	6	A	Bradford PA	W	2-1	0-0	Wilson 2	7,000
33		13	H	Bradford City	D	0-0	0-0		3,000
34		20	A	Bradford City	D	0-0	0-0		3,000

Midland Section Subsidiary Tournament - Position: 5th — Appearances

Goals

League Championship Play-Off

Match No.	Date		Venue	Opponents	Result	FT	HT	Scorers	Attendance
35	May	4	H	Stoke	W	2-0	2-0	Hibbert, Peart	15,000
36		11	A	Stoke	L	0-1	0-0		15,000

League Championship Play-Off: Leeds City won 2-1 on aggregate — Appearances

Goals

Walker, Willis	Hewison, Bob	Hampson, Billy	Sherwin, Harry	Hampson, John	Lamph, Tommy	Barrett, PJ	Stephenson, Clem	Peart, Jack	Cawley, Tom	Robinson, Stan	Price, Arthur	Robinson, Arthur	Baines, Fred	Hampson, Tommy	Arkle, Norman	Goodwin, Ernie	Stephenson, Jimmy	Moore, Billy	Grant, W	Kirton, Billy	Hampson, Ernie	Chard (Cpl)	Millership, Harold	Buchan, Charlie	Spratt, Bert	Croot, Fred	Rutherford W	Hampson Walker	Wilson, Andy	Kettle, Billy	Hibbert, Billy
1	2	3	4	5	6	7	8	9	10	11																					
1	2	3	4	5	6	7	8	9		11	10																				
	2	3	4	5	6	7	8	9		11	10	1																			
	4	3	5		6	7	8	9		11	10	1	2																		
	4	2	5		6	7	8	9		11	10		3	1																	
	4	2	5		6		8	9			10		3	1	7	11															
	4	2	5		6		8	9		7	10		3	1		11															
	6	3	5		4		8	9			10		2	1			7	11													
1	4	2	5		6			9		11	10		3						7	8											
	4	2	5		6			9	8	11	10		3	1							7										
	4	2	5	7	6		8	9			10		3	1		11															
	4	2	5		6		8	9	7		10		3	1		11															
	4	2	5		6		8	9	7		10		3	1					11												
	4	2	5	8	6			9	7		10		3	1								11									
	4	2	5	8	6			9	7		10		3	1							11										
	4	2	5		6		8	9	7		10		3	1					11												
	4	2	5	11	6		8	9	7		10			1									3								
	4	2	5	3	6		8	9	7		10			1		11															
	4	2	5		6		8	9	7		10			1					11				3								
	4	3	5	11	6		8	9	7		10			1									2								
	4	3	5	11	6		8	9	7		10			1									2								
	4	3	5	6			8	9	7		10			1		11							2								
	4	3	5	6			8	9			10			1		11							2	7							
	4	3	5	11	6		8	9	7		10			1									2								
	4	3	5	11	6		8	9	7		10			1									2								
	4	3	5	11	6		8	9	7		10			1									2								
	4	3	5		6		8	9	7		10			1									2		11						
	4	3	5	11	6		8	9	7		10			1									2								
3	28	28	28	16	26	5	24	28	18	8	27	2	13	23	1	7	1	1	4	1	2	1	11	1	1	0	0	0	0	0	0
	5	1	6	1		1	11	20	6	2	15					2	1	1	1					1							

Walker, Willis	Hewison, Bob	Hampson, Billy	Sherwin, Harry	Hampson, John	Lamph, Tommy	Barrett, PJ	Stephenson, Clem	Peart, Jack	Cawley, Tom	Robinson, Stan	Price, Arthur	Robinson, Arthur	Baines, Fred	Hampson, Tommy	Arkle, Norman	Goodwin, Ernie	Stephenson, Jimmy	Moore, Billy	Grant, W	Kirton, Billy	Hampson, Ernie	Chard (Cpl)	Millership, Harold	Buchan, Charlie	Spratt, Bert	Croot, Fred	Rutherford W	Hampson Walker	Wilson, Andy	Kettle, Billy	Hibbert, Billy
	4	3	5	9	6		8		7		10			1									2			11					
	4	3	5	11	6		8		7		10			1									2				9				
	4	3	5	9	6		8		7		10			1							11		2								
	4	3	5		6		8		7		10			1														2	9	11	
	4	2	5		6	11	8		7		10			1														3	9		
	4	2	5		6	11	8	9	7		10			1														3			
0	6	6	6	3	6	2	6	1	6	0	6	0	0	6	0	0	0	0	0	0	1	0	3	0	0	1	1	3	2	1	0
							2		1		3																		2		

Walker, Willis	Hewison, Bob	Hampson, Billy	Sherwin, Harry	Hampson, John	Lamph, Tommy	Barrett, PJ	Stephenson, Clem	Peart, Jack	Cawley, Tom	Robinson, Stan	Price, Arthur	Robinson, Arthur	Baines, Fred	Hampson, Tommy	Arkle, Norman	Goodwin, Ernie	Stephenson, Jimmy	Moore, Billy	Grant, W	Kirton, Billy	Hampson, Ernie	Chard (Cpl)	Millership, Harold	Buchan, Charlie	Spratt, Bert	Croot, Fred	Rutherford W	Hampson Walker	Wilson, Andy	Kettle, Billy	Hibbert, Billy
	4	3	5		6			9	8		10			1		7							2								11
	4	3	5		6			9	8		10			1		7							2								11
0	2	2	2	0	2	0	0	2	2	0	2	0	0	2	0	2	0	0	0	0	0	0	2	0	0	0	0	0	0	0	2
								1																							1

1918-19

Midland Section

Manager: Herbert Chapman

Final Positions: 4th & 3rd

Did you know that?

12 October 1918: City borrowed John Smelt from Rotherham in a game where Arthur Price was one of three players sent off. The game was described as being 20 minutes of football and 70 of boxing.

25 January 1919: Only 3,000 were at Elland Road for the visit by Leicester Fosse. Due to the Spanish flu pandemic that swept the world between June 1918 and December 1920 gate takings at football matches were well down despite service personnel having returned home after the Armistice.

22 April 1919: Dick Roberts played at long last for City. A brother of Hugh Roberts, he signed for City in 1911 but never played for the first team. After war service he made his solitary appearance in Leeds colours. He played 18 times for Coventry's League team thereafter.

Aston Villa's Clem Stephenson was a star guest performer in 1918–19.

Match No.	Date		Venue	Opponents	Result	FT	HT	Scorers	Attendance
1	Sep	7	H	Notts County	W	4-1	2-0	Peart, Cawley 2, Hibbert	5,000
2		14	A	Notts County	L	2-5	0-4	Price, Peart	7,000
3		21	H	Birmingham	W	3-1	1-0	Hibbert, Cawley, E. Hampson	3,000
4		28	A	Birmingham	L	2-4	2-2	Hibbert, Peart	14,000
5	Oct	5	H	Rotherham County	W	2-1	2-0	Price, Hibbert (pen)	2,000
6		12	A	Rotherham County	W	3-0	2-0	Sherwin, McLeod, Peart	7,000
7		19	A	Lincoln City	L	0-1	0-0		4,000
8		26	H	Lincoln City	W	2-0	0-0	C. Stephenson 2	6,000
9	Nov	2	A	Grimsby Town	W	2-0	0-0	C. Stephenson, Peart	2,000
10		9	H	Grimsby Town	W	3-1	2-0	Hibbert (pen), Price, Peart	4,000
11		16	A	Bradford City	L	1-3	1-1	Peart	8,000
12		23	H	Bradford City	W	2-1	0-0	J. Hampson 2	7,500
13		30	A	Sheffield Wed	W	2-0	0-0	Hall, Peart	10,000
14	Dec	7	H	Sheffield Wed	D	1-1	0-0	Hall	9,000
15		14	H	Hull City	D	0-0	0-0		5,000
16		21	A	Hull City	L	1-2	0-1	Peart	4,500
17		25	H	Huddersfield Town	D	1-1	1-0	Price (pen)	5,000
18		26	A	Huddersfield Town	W	1-0	0-0	Price (pen)	10,000
19		28	H	Coventry City	L	0-1	0-0		6,000
20	Jan	11	H	Barnsley	W	4-0	3-0	Hall, Price, C. Stephenson 2	6,000
21		18	A	Barnsley	W	1-0	0-0	Hall	7,000
22		25	H	Leicester Fosse	W	4-2	1-0	C. Stephenson, Price 2, Peart	3,000
23	Feb	1	A	Leicester Fosse	D	0-0	0-0		4,000
24		8	A	Nottingham Forest	W	2-0	2-0	C. Stephenson, Peart	10,000
25		15	H	Nottingham Forest	L	0-4	0-2		11,000
26		22	A	Bradford PA	W	3-1	2-0	Peart, C. Stephenson, Hall	5,000
27	Mar	1	H	Bradford PA	L	2-5	1-3	Hall, C. Stephenson	10,000
28		8	H	Sheffield United	W	2-1	2-0	Peart, Hall	8,000
29		15	A	Sheffield United	L	0-1	0-1		22,000
30	Apr	22	A	Coventry City	W	3-1	0-1	Peart, McLeod, Hall (pen)	9,000

Principal Tournament - Position: 4th

Appearances

Goals

Midland Section Subsidiary Tournament

Match No.	Date		Venue	Opponents	Result	FT	HT	Scorers	Attendance
31	Mar	22	H	Huddersfield Town	W	3-0	0-1	Peart 2, McLeod	9,000
32		29	A	Huddersfield Town	L	0-1	0-0		8,000
33	Apr	5	A	Bradford PA	L	0-5	0-3		12,000
34		12	H	Bradford PA	W	3-1	1-1	McLeod, J. Stephenson, Hall	6,000
35		19	A	Bradford City	L	1-2	0-1	Bainbridge	16,000
36		26	H	Bradford City	W	3-0	1-0	McLeod 2, Bainbridge	7,000

Midland Section Subsidiary Tournament - Position: 3rd

Appearances

Goals

Walker, Willis	Millership, Harold	Hampson, Billy	McLachlan, Albert	Sherwin, Harry	Lamph, Tommy	Hampson, Ernie	Hibbert, Billy	Peart, Jack	Hampson, John	Cawley, Tom	Cook, Walter	Price, Arthur	Robinson, Stan	Hewison, Bob	Copeland, Charlie	Smelt, John	McLeod, Billy	Bavin, Arthur	Stephenson, Clem	Hugall, Jimmy	Hall, Tom	Moore, Billy	Linfoot, Fred	Gough, Harold	Scott, E	Lounds, Herbert	Cartwright, James	Rutherford, A	Voysey, Clem	Curry, Tom	Bainbridge, Simpson	Roberts, Dick	Sutcliffe, Charles	Stephenson Jimmy	Edmondson, John
1	2	3	4	5	6	7	8	9	10	11																									
	2	3		5	4	11	8	9	6	7	1	10																							
	2	3		5	6	11	9		4	7	1	10	8																						
	2	3		5	6	11	8	9	4	7	1	10																							
	2	3		5	6		8	9	11	7	1	10		4																					
		3		5				9	4	7	1	10	11		2	6	8																		
		3		5	6		8	8	2	7	1	10	11					4																	
1		3		5	6		11	9	4	7		10			2				8																
1	2	3	6	5			11	9	4	7		10							8																
1	2	3		5	6		11	9	4	7		10							8																
	2	3	4	5	6		10	9	11	7	1						8																		
	2	3	4	5	6			9	11	7										1	8	10													
1	2	3	6	5	4		10	9	11								7				8														
	2	3	4	5	6		10	9	11	7	1										8														
	3		6	5			11	9	4		1	10			2						8		7												
	2	3	6	5	4		11	9			1	10									8		7												
	3	2	6	5	4			9	11			10					7				8			1											
	3	2	6	5	4			9	11			10					7				8			1											
	2	3		5	4			9	6		1	10					7				8				11										
1	2	3	6	5	4			9	11			10							8		7														
1	2	3	6		4			9	5	11		10							8		7														
1	2	3	6		4			9	5			10							8		7					11									
1	2	3			4			9	5	10		6							8		7					11									
1	2	3	6		4			9	5			10							8		7						11								
1	2	3	4		6			9				10			5				8		7						11								
1	2	3	6		4			9				10							8		7						11	5							
1	2	3			4			9	5			10							8		7						11		6						
1	2	3			4			9	11			10							8		7							5		6					
1	2	3	6		4			9	11								10		8		7							5							
1	2		6		4			9	5								10				8					7					11	3			
16	27	28	18	20	27	4	14	29	27	15	11	23	3	1	4	1	8	1	13	1	19	1	2	2	1	3	4	3	1	1	1	1	0	0	0
				1		1	4	14	2	2		8					2		9		7														

1	2	3	6		4			9	11								10		8				5			7									
1	2	3	6		4			9	11								10		8		7		5												
	2	3	6		4			9	5										8		10										11		1	7	
1	2	3	6						5								9		8		10		4								11			7	
1	2		6		4			9	3								10		8				5			7					11				
	2	3	6		4				5								10		8							7					11		1		9
4	6	5	6	0	5	0	0	4	6	0	0	0	0	0	0	0	5	0	6	0	3	0	4	0	0	3	0	0	0	0	4	0	2	2	1
								2									4				1										2			1	

1919-20

Division Two

Manager: Herbert Chapman

Final Position: Expelled

Match No.	Date	Venue	Opponents	Result	FT	HT	Scorers	Attendance
1	Aug 30	A	Blackpool	L	2-4	2-4	Macleod 2	10,000
2	Sep 3	H	Coventry City	W	3-0	2-0	McLeod 2, Bainbridge	8,000
3	6	H	Blackpool	W	1-0	1-0	Edmondson	10,000
4	11	A	Coventry City	W	4-0	1-0	McLeod 2, Edmondson, Bainbridge	12,000
5	13	H	Hull City	L	1-2	1-0	Bainbridge	10,000
6	20	A	Hull City	D	1-1	0-1	Edmondson	8,000
7	27	H	Wolverhampton W	D	1-1	1-1	Price (pen)	12,000
8	Oct 4	A	Wolverhampton W	W	4-2	0-2	Lamph, McLeod 3	15,000

Port Vale took over remaining fixtures

Appearances

Goals

Midland League

Manager: Dick Ray

Final Position: 12th

No.	Date	Venue	Opponents	Result	FT	HT	Scorers Match	Attendance
1	Nov 22	H	Barnsley Res	D	0-0			3,000
2	29	H	Rotherham Town	D	2-2		Ellson, Smith	
3	Dec 6	H	Worksop Town	L	3-4		Ellson 2 (1 pen), Riddick	
4	13	A	Sheffield Utd Res	L	0-4			
5	20	H	Lincoln City Res	W	2-0		Birtles, Bedford	4,000
6	25	H	Halifax Town	D	3-3		Buckley, Parsons, Mason	
7	Jan 1	A	Barnsley Res	L	1-2		Birtles	1,000
8	3	A	Lincoln City Res	L	0-4			1,000
9	10	A	Chesterfield Mun	L	3-4		White 2, Birtles	
10	17	H	Sheffield Wed Res	W	1-0		Mason	4,000
11	24	A	Castleford Town	D	0-0			
12	31	H	Hull City Res	W	1-0		Birtles	
13	Feb 5	A	Hull City Res	L	1-2		White	2,000
14	7	A	Mexborough Town	L	0-2			3,000
15	14	A	Halifax Town	D	0-0			
16	21	H	Castleford Town	W	6-0		Mason 2, Fawcett, Ellson, Birtles, Rodgers	5,000
17	23	A	Sheffield Wed Res	L	2-5		Birtles, Anstead	1,500
18	28	A	Notts County Res	D	1-1		Bedford	
19	Mar 1	A	Rotherham Town	L	1-3		Not Traced	4,000
20	6	H	Notts County Res	W	2-0		Plows, Fawcett	4,000
21	13	H	Rotherham Co Res	D	3-3		Bedford, Rodgers 2 (1 pen)	3,000
22	20	A	Rotherham Co Res	W	1-0		Ellson	3,000
23	24	H	Grimsby Town Res	D	1-1		Ellson	
24	27	A	Worksop Town	L	0-2			
25	Apr 3	A	Silverwood Colliery	W	4-1*		Bedford 3, Fawcett	2,000
26	5	A	Gainsborough Trin	L	1-2		Butler	3,000
27	6	A	Grimsby Town Res	W	2-0		Butler, Bedford	
28	8	A	Scunthorpe United	L	2-3		Mason, Butler	3,000
29	14	H	Silverwood Colliery	W	3-1		Mason, Butler 2	
30	17	H	Sheffield Utd Res	L	1 2		Butler	8,000
31	21	H	Mexborough Town	W	4-2		Rodgers (pen), Ellson, Butler, Fawcett	
32	24	H	Chesterfield Mun	L	0-2			5,000
33	28	H	Scunthorpe United	D	0-0			
34	May 1	H	Gainsborough Trin	W	6-0		White, Rodgers, Ellson, Makes, Foster 2	3,000

* at Millmoor, Rotherham

Scorers: Ellson 8, Bedford 7, Butler 7, Birtles 6, Mason 6, Rodgers 5, Fawcett 4, White 4, Foster 2, Anstead 1, Buckley 1, Makes 1, Parsons 1, Plows 1, Riddick 1, Smith 1, Not Traced 1, Total 57

Friendlies

Date	Venue	Opponents	Result	FT	Scorers	Attendance
Nov 15	H	Yorkshire Amateurs	W	5-2	Hunt, Moiser, Heslop, Birds, Rodgers	
Dec 26	A	Scarborough	D	1-1	Not Traced	
27	H	Bradford Park Av	W	3-2	Birtles 2, Rodgers	2,000
Feb 9	H	Crewe Alexandra	H	0-5		
Mar 27	H	Yorkshire Amateurs	W	3-1	White, Jones, Buckley	
Apr 2	H	Bradford City	W	1-0	Butler	7,000
3	H	Newcastle City	W	5-0	Jones 2, Barnsby 2, Watson (og)	2,000
5	H	Bradford Park Av	L	1-2	McGee (pen)	4,000
6	H	Rotherham Am	W	3-0	Booth 2, McGee	
10	H	Halifax Town	D	1-1	Butler	

Did you know that?

4 October 1919: Due to a rail strike City travelled to their last ever fixture by charabanc.

Harold Millership, a full-back signed from Blackpool, played in all eight City fixtures before the club was expelled from the Football League. He went on to play six times for Wales as a Rotherham County player.

Welsh international Harold Millership.

Did you know that?

24 April 1920: Chesterfield Municipal, previously known as Chesterfield Town, effectively clinched the Midland League title at Elland Road with a 2–0 win with both goals coming from Haydn Kemp.

Walker, Willis	Millership, Harold	Hampson, John	Lamph, Tommy	Hopkins, William	Foley, Mick	Lounds, Herbert	Price, Arthur	Short, Billy	McLeod, Billy	Bainbridge, Simpson	Edmondson, John	Affleck, George	Kirton, Billy	Goodwin, Ernie
1	2	3	4	5	6	7	8	9	10	11				
1	2	3	4	5	6	7	8	9	10	11				
1	2	3	4	5	6	7		8	10	11	9			
1	2	3	4	5		7	6	8	10	11	9			
1	2	3	4	5		7	6	8	10	11	9			
1	2	3	4	5	6	7	8		10	11	9			
1	2		4	5	6	7	8		10	11	9	3		
1	2	5	4			7	6		10		9	3	8	11
8	8	7	8	7	5	8	7	5	8	7	6	2	1	1
			1				1		9	3	3			

THE MIDLAND LEAGUE

THE honour of scoring Leeds United's first competitive goal fell to schoolmaster Merton Ellson.

After Leeds City's ignominious exit from the Football League, the hastily assembled Leeds United were welcomed into the Midland League two months after the start of the 1919–20 season.

United were playing catch-up from the start and after just one friendly match, a 5–2 victory against Yorkshire Amateurs, they kicked off their Midland League campaign with a goalless draw against Barnsley at Elland Road in front of 3,000 supporters.

The following week they drew 2–2 at home with Rotherham Town, the experienced Ellson getting the opener. The inside-right, who served with the Middlesex Regiment in the Great War, probably played as an amateur because of his teaching duties.

Ellson, known as Matt to his teammates, had previously played for Frickley Athletic, as had another of Leeds United's new recruits, right-winger George Mason. Both men were to remain with United for their maiden season in the Football League, along with Hull-born forward Walter Butler, who had been among the goals with the Leeds Steelworks side.

Ellson finished the campaign as United's top scorer in the Midland League with a modest eight goals and performed well in United's first season back in Division Two before rejoining Frickley then moving to Halifax Town. Mason remained at Elland Road until 1923 when he joined Swindon Town.

The Midland League provided a good grounding for many players, including a youthful Ernie Hart, a stylish teenager, who went on to captain United and England. Dozens of trialists – Barnsley forward Tommy Birtles and Tom Heslop (Bolton Wanderers) among them – were put to the test by the Leeds management.

The Midland League was a well-established League founded at the Maypole Hotel, Nottingham on 17 April 1889. Leeds City first joined it in 1905–06 when the reserves finished 12th and they remained members until the club were booted out of the Football League on 13 October 1919.

The new Leeds United were invited to join the Midland League 18 days later as Leeds City reserves' replacement and fulfilled their entire 34-game programme to finish in a creditable 12th place. United also played 10 friendly games so squeezed in 44 games in just over six months before their election to the Football League.

United fielded a reserve side in the Midland League in 1920–21 before being elected to the Central League the following season.

Former Frickley Athletic men Merton Ellson (below), and George Mason (left), played for United in both the Midland League and the Football League.

League Table

	P	W	D	L	F	A	Pts
Chesterfield Municipal	34	24	5	5	78	35	53
Sheffield United Res	34	20	11	3	73	28	51
Scunthorpe United	34	18	7	9	71	39	43
Worksop Town	34	20	3	11	71	52	43
Mexborough Town	34	18	6	10	60	45	42
Sheffield Wed. Res	34	16	6	12	50	44	38
Rotherham Town	34	14	8	12	83	71	36
Castleford Town	34	14	8	12	53	46	36
Hull City Res	34	16	2	16	74	59	34
Grimsby Town Res	34	14	5	15	66	64	33
Rotherham County Res	34	13	5	16	60	57	31
Leeds United	34	11	9	14	57	55	31
Notts County Res	34	10	11	13	50	56	31
Halifax Town	34	13	4	17	52	70	30
Lincoln City Res	34	8	7	19	43	83	23
Barnsley Res	34	6	9	19	46	72	21
Silverwood Colliery	34	6	7	21	38	89	19
Gainsborough Trinity	34	7	3	24	37	95	17

1920-21

Division Two

Manager: Arthur Fairclough

Final Position: 14th

Did you know that?

1 September 1920: Len Armitage, who scored United's first-ever League goal, was the grandson of Yorkshire and England cricketer Tom Armitage. Len's brother, Tom, a Sheffield Wednesday reserve, died in hospital five days after being injured in a match at Hillsborough.

1 December 1920: Amateur star Ivan Sharpe became the first man to play for both Leeds City and Leeds United when he turned out against Coventry. A sports journalist and author, he wrote a column in the United programme in the 1950s. The only other man to play for both Leeds clubs was Tommy Lamph, who got into the United side a couple of months after Sharpe.

11 December 1920: Bob Thompson, a winner of Edinburgh's famous Powderhall Sprint, netted United's first hat-trick as Notts County are beaten 3–0 at Elland Road.

Len Armitage, scorer of United's first League goal.

Match No.	Date	Venue	Opponents	Result	FT	HT	Scorers	Attendance
1	Aug 28	A	Port Vale	L	0-2	0-1		15,000
2	Sep 1	H	South Shields	L	1-2	1-2	Armitage	16,958
3	4	H	Port Vale	W	3-1	1-1	Best, Ellson 2	15,000
4	8	A	South Shields	L	0-3	0-1		15,000
5	11	A	Leicester City	D	1-1	1-0	Ellson	16,000
6	18	H	Leicester City	W	3-1	2-1	Ellson, Goldthorpe 2 (1 pen)	11,000
7	25	A	Blackpool	L	0-1	0-0		8,000
8	Oct 2	H	Blackpool	W	2-0	1-0	Walton, Mason	10,000
9	9	A	Sheffield Wed	L	0-2	0-1		20,000
10	16	H	Sheffield Wed	W	2-0	1-0	Thompson, Ellson	15,000
11	23	A	Hull City	W	1-0	0-0	Thompson	10,000
12	30	H	Hull City	D	1-1	1-1	Ellson	20,000
13	Nov 6	A	Stoke	L	0-4	0-3		10,000
14	13	H	Stoke	D	0-0	0-0		15,000
15	27	A	Coventry City	D	1-1	1-1	Lyon	18,000
16	Dec 1	H	Coventry City	W	4-0	0-0	Thompson 2, Ellson, Mason	10,000
17	4	A	Notts County	W	2-1	0-1	Lyon, Mason	14,000
18	11	H	Notts County	W	3-0	1-0	Thompson 3	12,000
19	18	A	Birmingham	L	0-1	0-0		20,000
20	25	H	Fulham	D	0-0	0-0		25,000
21	27	A	Fulham	L	0-1	0-1		30,000
22	Jan 1	H	Birmingham	W	1-0	0-0	Baker (pen)	24,000
23	8	H	Rotherham County	W	1-0	1-0	Ellson	18,000
24	15	A	Wolverhampton W	L	0-3	0-1		20,000
25	22	H	Wolverhampton W	W	3-0	1-0	Thompson 2, Lyon	14,000
26	29	H	West Ham United	L	1-2	1-2	Thompson	15,000
27	Feb 5	A	West Ham United	L	0-3	0-1		23,000
28	12	A	Stockport County	L	1-3	1-1	Thompson	9,000
29	19	H	Stockport County	L	0-2	0-1		20,000
30	26	A	Clapton Orient	L	0-1	0-0		17,000
31	Mar 5	H	Clapton Orient	W	2-1	0-0	Musgrove, Baker (pen)	18,000
32	12	A	Bury	D	1-1	0-0	Howarth	10,000
33	19	H	Bury	W	1-0	1-0	Musgrove	16,000
34	26	H	Bristol City	L	0-1	0-1		20,000
35	28	A	Cardiff City	L	0-1	0-0		30,000
36	29	H	Cardiff City	L	1-2	1-1	Howarth	20,000
37	Apr 2	A	Bristol City	D	0-0	0-0		24,000
38	9	H	Barnsley	D	0-0	0-0		13,000
39	16	A	Barnsley	D	1-1	1-1	Howarth	12,000
40	23	H	Nottingham Forest	D	1-1	0-1	Howarth	12,000
41	30	A	Nottingham Forest	L	0-1	0-1		8,000
42	May 7	A	Rotherham County	W	2-0	1-0	Howarth 2 (1 pen)	10,000
								Appearances
								Goals

FA Cup

Q1	Sep 11	H	Boothtown	W	5-2	2-1	Armitage 2, O'Doherty 3	1,500
Q2	25	H*	Leeds Steelworks	W	7-0	3-0	Butler 3, Thompson, Hart, O'Doherty, Waterhouse	3,000
								Appearances
								Goals

*Steelworks ceded ground advantage

Leeds then withdrew from the competition

Leeds United in their maiden Football League season. Back row, left to right: Mark Barker (director), J. Hilton Crowther (chairman), Bert Duffield, George Cooper, Ernie Hart, Brown, Harold Jacklin, Billy Down, Dick Coope, Jimmy Walton, H. Jeffery, Albert Stead (assistant trainer), Dick Murrell (trainer), Arthur Fairclough (secretary-manager). Middle row: Jimmy Frew, Spencer, John Lyon, Merton Ellson, Bob Thompson, George Stuart, Ernie Goldthorpe, P. Reynolds. Front row: Len Armitage, George Mason, Jim Baker, Arthur Tillotson, Bob Musgrove, Jock McGee, Jerry Best.

Down, Billy	Duffield, Bert	Tillotson, Arthur	Musgrove, Robert	Baker, Jim	Walton, Jimmy	Mason, George	Goldthorpe, Ernie	Thompson, Robert	Lyon, Jack	Best, Jerry	Ellson, Merton	Armitage, Len	Frew, Jimmy	Hill, George	Brock, John	Boardman, Billy	Sharpe, Ivan	Wood, Basil	Smelt, Alf	Hart, Ernie	Stuart, George	Butler, Walter	Lamph, Tommy	Howarth, Tommy	Powell, Sam	Rodgerson, Ralph	Jacklin, Harold	Coope, Dick	McGee, Jock	Cooper, George	Waterhouse, Fred	O'Doherty, Eugene
1	2	3	4	5	6	7	8	9	10	11																						
1	2	3	4	5	6	7			10	11	8	9																				
1	2		4	5	6	7			10	11	8	9	3																			
1	2		4	5	6		9		10	11	8		3	7																		
1	2		4	5	6		9		10	11	8		3	7																		
1	2		4	5	6	7	9		10	11	8		3																			
1	2		4	5	6	7	9		10	11	8		3																			
1	2		4	5	6	7	9		10	11	8		3																			
1	2		4	5	6	7			10	11	8	9	3																			
1	2		4	5	6	7		9	10		8		3		11																	
1	2		4	5	6	7		9	10	11	8		3																			
1	2		4	5	6	7			10	11	8	9	3																			
1	2		4	5	6	7			10		8	9	3			11																
1	2		4	5	6	7		9	10		8		3			11																
1	2		4	5	6	7		9	10		8		3	11																		
1	2		4	5	6	7		9	10		8		3				11															
1	2		4	5	6	7		9	10		8		3	11																		
1	2		4	5	6	7		9	10		8		3	11																		
1	2		4	5	6	7		9	10		8		3	11																		
1	2		4	5	6	7		9	10		8		3					11														
1	2		4	5	6	7		9	10		8		3	11																		
1	2		4	5	6	7		9	10		8		3					11														
1	2		4	5	6	7		9	10		8		3					11														
1	2		4	5	6	7		9	10		8		3					11														
1	2		4	5	6	7		9	10		8		3					11														
1	2		4	5	6			9	10		8		3		7			11														
1	2		4	5	6			9	10				3		7	8		11														
1	2		4	5	6			9	10						7	8		11	3													
1	2			4		7		9			8		3					11		5	6	10										
1	2		8	5	6	7		9			10		3					11					4									
1	2		8	5	6	7		9			10		3					11					4									
1	2		8	5	6			7			10		3					11					4	9								
1	2		8	5	6			7			10		3					11					4	9								
1	2			5	6	7					10		3		8			11					4	9								
1	2			5	6	7					10		3		8			11					4	9								
1	2		4	5	6	7			10				3					11						9	8							
1	2		4	3	6	7			10									11		5				9	8							
1	2		4	5	6	7			10		8		3					11						9								
1	2		4	5	6	7			10		8		3					11						9								
1	2			5	6	7			10		8							11		4				9		3						
1	8			4	6	7					10		2					11		5				9		3						
1	2			4	6	7						8						11		5				9	10	3						
42	42	2	36	42	41	35	6	23	33	11	36	6	36	7	6	4	1	22	1	5	1	1	6	11	3	3	0	0	0	0	0	0
			2	2	1	4	2	11	2	1	8	1												6								

Down, Billy	Duffield, Bert	Tillotson, Arthur	Musgrove, Robert	Baker, Jim	Walton, Jimmy	Mason, George	Goldthorpe, Ernie	Thompson, Robert	Lyon, Jack	Best, Jerry	Ellson, Merton	Armitage, Len	Frew, Jimmy	Hill, George	Brock, John	Boardman, Billy	Sharpe, Ivan	Wood, Basil	Smelt, Alf	Hart, Ernie	Stuart, George	Butler, Walter	Lamph, Tommy	Howarth, Tommy	Powell, Sam	Rodgerson, Ralph	Jacklin, Harold	Coope, Dick	McGee, Jock	Cooper, George	Waterhouse, Fred	O'Doherty, Eugene
								11				9								5	4	10					1	2	3	6	7	8
								9						11					3	5	4	10					1	2		6	7	8
0	0	0	0	0	0	0	0	2	0	0	0	1	0	1	0	0	0	0	1	2	2	2	0	0	0	0	2	2	1	2	2	2
								1				2								1		3								1	4

League Table

	P	W	D	L	F	A	Pts
Birmingham	42	24	10	8	79	38	58
Cardiff City	42	24	10	8	59	32	58
Bristol City	42	19	13	10	49	29	51
Blackpool	42	20	10	12	54	42	50
West Ham United	42	19	10	13	51	30	48
Notts County	42	18	11	13	55	40	47
Clapton Orient	42	16	13	13	43	42	45
South Shields	42	17	10	15	61	46	44
Fulham	42	16	10	16	43	47	42
Sheffield Wednesday	42	15	11	16	48	48	41
Bury	42	15	10	17	45	49	40
Leicester City	42	12	16	14	39	46	40
Hull City	42	10	20	12	43	53	40
Leeds United	42	14	10	18	40	45	38
Wolverhampton W	42	16	6	20	49	66	38
Barnsley	42	10	16	16	48	50	36
Port Vale	42	11	14	17	43	49	36
Nottingham Forest	42	12	12	18	48	55	36
Rotherham County	42	12	12	18	37	53	36
Stoke	42	12	11	19	46	56	35
Coventry City	42	12	11	19	39	70	35
Stockport County	42	9	12	21	42	75	30

1921-22

Division Two

Manager: Arthur Fairclough

Final Position: 8th

Did you know that?

11 February 1922: Billy Poyntz, a close season signing from Llanelli, becomes the first United player to be sent off – in the 2–1 loss at Bury. The following Saturday he scored a hat-trick in a 3–0 win against Leicester, just hours after getting married.

Jimmy Walton's only goal of the season came in the opening day win against Port Vale.

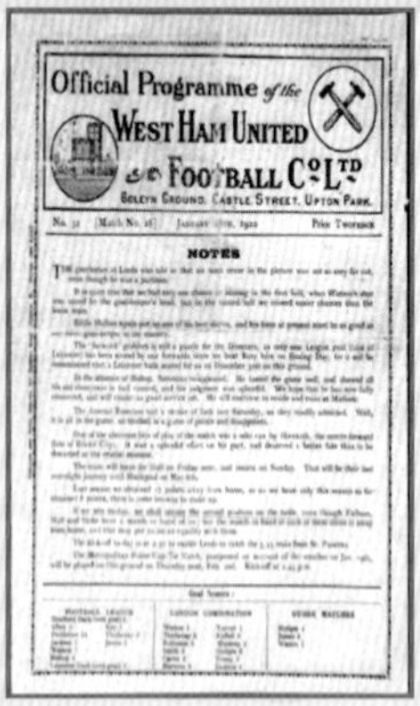

A programme from United's visit to West Ham on 28 January 1921.

Match No.	Date	Venue	Opponents	Result	FT	HT	Scorers	Attendance
1	Aug 27	H	Port Vale	W	2-1	2-1	Howarth, Walton	18,000
2	29	A	Bristol City	D	0-0	0-0		16,000
3	Sep 3	A	Port Vale	W	1-0	1-0	Howarth	18,000
4	5	H	Bristol City	W	3-0	2-0	Howarth 2, Moore	18,000
5	10	H	Blackpool	D	0-0	0-0		18,000
6	17	A	Blackpool	W	3-1	0-1	Howarth, Wood, Mason	15,000
7	24	H	Clapton Orient	W	2-0	1-0	Wood, Howarth	20,000
8	Oct 1	A	Clapton Orient	L	2-4	1-0	Howarth (pen), Moore	20,000
9	8	H	South Shields	D	0-0	0-0		20,000
10	15	A	South Shields	W	1-0	0-0	Howarth	15,000
11	22	H	Stoke	L	1-2	0-2	Howarth	10,000
12	29	A	Stoke	L	0-3	0-0		15,000
13	Nov 5	H	Bradford PA	W	3-0	2-0	Howarth (pen), Armitage, Mason	18,000
14	12	A	Bradford PA	W	1-0	0-0	Howarth	20,000
15	19	A	Hull City	L	0-1	0-1		12,800
16	26	H	Hull City	L	0-2	0-2		20,000
17	Dec 3	A	Notts County	L	1-4	0-2	Howarth	12,000
18	10	H	Notts County	D	1-1	1-0	Moore	16,000
19	17	H	Crystal Palace	D	0-0	0-0		10,000
20	24	A	Crystal Palace	W	2-1	2-0	Swan, Moore	10,000
21	26	H	Sheffield Wed	D	1-1	0-1	Swan	20,540
22	27	A	Sheffield Wed	L	1-2	1-1	Howarth	25,000
23	31	H	Rotherham County	L	0-2	0-2		12,000
24	Jan 14	A	Rotherham County	L	0-1	0-0		6,000
25	21	H	West Ham United	D	0-0	0-0		7,000
26	28	A	West Ham United	D	1-1	0-1	Armitage	20,000
27	Feb 4	H	Bury	W	2-0	0-0	Armitage, Poyntz	5,000
28	11	A	Bury	L	1-2	0-0	Armitage	10,000
29	20	H	Leicester City	W	3-0	2-0	Poyntz 3	5,000
30	25	A	Leicester City	D	0-0	0-0		14,000
31	Mar 4	H	Derby County	W	2-1	1-0	Swan 2	12,000
32	11	A	Derby County	L	0-2	0-2		9,000
33	18	A	Coventry City	L	0-1	0-1		15,000
34	25	H	Coventry City	W	5-2	1-0	Armitage 2, Swan 3	10,000
35	Apr 1	A	Barnsley	D	2-2	0-2	Swan, Armitage	12,660
36	8	H	Barnsley	W	4-0	2-0	Swan 2, Gittins (og), Poyntz	10,000
37	14	H	Fulham	W	2-0	1-0	Poyntz, Coates	20,000
38	15	A	Wolverhampton W	D	0-0	0-0		10,000
39	17	A	Fulham	W	1-0	1-0	Armitage	20,000
40	22	H	Wolverhampton W	D	0-0	0-0		7,000
41	29	A	Nottingham Forest	L	0-1	0-1		16,000
42	May 6	H	Nottingham Forest	D	0-0	0-0		10,000
								Appearances
							One own-goal	Goals

FA Cup

Match No.	Date	Venue	Opponents	Result	FT	HT	Scorers	Attendance
R1	Jan 7	A	Swindon Town	L	1-2	1-1	Swan	16,000
								Appearances
								Goals

Back row, left to right: Jim Baker, Dick Murrell (trainer), Ernie Hart, Billy Down, Mark Barker (director), Ralph Rodgerson, J. Hilton Crowther (chairman), Jimmy Walton. Front row: George Mason, Bert Duffield, Tommy Howarth, Merton Ellson, Basil Wood, Jimmy Frew.

Whalley, Fred	Duffield, Bert	Rodgerson, Ralph	Baker, Jim	Sherwin, Harry	Walton, Jimmy	Clark, Wallace	Armitage, Len	Howarth, Tommy	Moore, Jim	Wood, Basil	Hart, Ernie	Mason, George	Coates, Walter	Frew, Jimmy	Poyntz, Billy	Swan, Jack	Down, Billy	Jacklin, Harold	Gascoigne, Tom	Ellson, Merton	Potts, Joe	Powell, Sam	Robson, Bill
1	2	3	4	5	6	7	8	9	10	11													
1	2	3	4	5	6	7	8	9	10	11													
1	2	3	4	5	6	7	8	9	10	11													
1	2	3	4		6		8	9	10	11	5	7											
1	2	3	4		6		8	9	10	11	5	7											
1	2	3	4		6		8	9	10	11	5	7											
1	2	3	4		6		8	9	10	11	5		7										
1		3	4		6		8	9	10	11	5		7	2									
1	2	3	4		6		8	9	10	11	5		7										
1	2	3	4		6		8	9	10	11	5		7										
1	2	3	4		6		8	9	10	11	5		7										
1	2	3	6	4			8		10	11	5	7			9								
1	2		6	4			8	9	10	11	5	7		3									
1	2		6	4			8	9	10	11	5	7		3									
1	2		6	4				9	8	11	5	7		3		10							
1		3	6	4			8	9	10	11	5	7		2									
	2		6	4			8	9	10	11	5	7		3			1						
	2		6	5				9	8	11		7		3				1	4	10			
	2		5		6	11			8			7			9			1	4		3	10	
	2	3	5		6			9	8	11		7				10		1	4				
1	2	3	5		6			9	8	11		7				10			4				
1		3	6				8	9		11	5	7		2		10			4				
1	2	3	5					9	8	11		7		6		10			4				
1	2	3	5	4	6		8	9		11		7				10							
1	2	3	5	4	6			9		11			7		8	10							
1	2	3	6	4			9			11	5		7		8	10							
1	2	3	6	4			9			11	5		7		8	10							
1	2	3	6	4			9			11	5		7		8	10							
1		3	6	4			9		11		5		7	2	8	10							
1	2		6	4			9		10	11	5		7	3	8								
1	2		6	4			9	8	11		5		7	3		10							
1	2		6	4				9	8	11	5		7	3		10							
1	2		6		4			9		11	5		7	3		10							8
1	2		6	4			9			11	5		7	3		10							8
1	2		6	4		11	9				5		7	3	8	10							
1	2		6	4		11	9				5		7	3	8	10							
1	2		6	4		11	9				5		7	3	8	10							
1	2		6	4		11	9				5		7	3	8	10							
1	2		6	4		11	9				5		7	3	8	10							
1	2		6	4		11	9			7	5			3	8	10							
1		2	6	4				9	8	11	5	7		3		10							
1	2		6	4				9		11	5			3	8							10	7
38	37	24	42	28	17	10	31	28	27	34	32	17	20	23	15	22	1	3	6	1	1	2	3
					1		8	13	4	2		2	1		6	10							

1	2	3	5	4	6		8	9	11			7				10							
1	1	1	1	1	1	0	1	1	1	0	0	1	0	0	0	1	0	0	0	0	0	0	0
																1							

League Table

	P	W	D	L	F	A	Pts
Nottingham Forest	42	22	12	8	51	30	56
Stoke	42	18	16	8	60	44	52
Barnsley	42	22	8	12	67	52	52
West Ham United	42	20	8	14	52	39	48
Hull City	42	19	10	13	51	41	48
South Shields	42	17	12	13	43	38	46
Fulham	42	18	9	15	57	38	45
Leeds United	42	16	13	13	48	38	45
Leicester City	42	14	17	11	39	34	45
Sheffield Wednesday	42	15	14	13	47	50	44
Bury	42	15	10	17	54	55	40
Derby County	42	15	9	18	60	64	39
Notts County	42	12	15	15	47	51	39
Crystal Palace	42	13	13	16	45	51	39
Clapton Orient	42	15	9	18	43	50	39
Rotherham County	42	14	11	17	32	43	39
Wolverhampton W	42	13	11	18	44	49	37
Port Vale	42	14	8	20	43	57	36
Blackpool	42	15	5	22	44	57	35
Coventry City	42	12	10	20	51	60	34
Bradford Park Avenue	42	12	9	21	46	62	33
Bristol City	42	12	9	21	37	58	33

1922-23

Division Two

Manager: Arthur Fairclough

Final Position: 7th

Did you know that?

4 November 1922: Percy Whipp scored a hat-trick on his debut in a 3–0 win against West Ham. A £750 signing from Sunderland, he finished the season as top scorer with 16 League and Cup goals.

19 February 1923: An England trial game at Elland Road was called off because the pitch was covered in a blanket of snow.

Future England international Ernie Hart only missed one game.

Match No.	Date	Venue	Opponents	Result	FT	HT	Scorers	Attendance
1	Aug 26	H	Blackpool	D	1-1	0-1	Swan	18,000
2	28	A	Southampton	W	1-0	0-0	Swan	16,000
3	Sep 2	A	Blackpool	L	0-1	0-1		15,000
4	4	H	Southampton	W	1-0	0-0	Harris	6,000
5	9	H	Stockport County	W	2-0	0-0	Walton, Armitage	12,000
6	16	A	Stockport County	L	1-2	0-2	Armitage	14,000
7	23	H	Bradford City	W	1-0	0-0	Harris	20,000
8	30	A	Bradford City	W	2-0	0-0	Swan, Harris	22,000
9	Oct 7	A	Clapton Orient	L	0-3	0-2		14,000
10	14	H	Clapton Orient	D	0-0	0-0		15,000
11	21	H	Leicester City	D	0-0	0-0		12,000
12	28	A	Leicester City	L	1-2	0-2	Harris	20,000
13	Nov 4	H	West Ham United	W	3-1	1-1	Whipp 3 (1 pen)	12,000
14	11	A	West Ham United	D	0-0	0-0		14,000
15	18	H	South Shields	L	0-1	0-1		12,000
16	25	A	South Shields	W	2-0	2-0	Whipp, Poyntz	18,000
17	Dec 2	H	Wolverhampton W	W	1-0	1-0	Walton	14,000
18	9	A	Wolverhampton W	W	1-0	1-0	Hart	16,000
19	16	A	Coventry City	W	2-1	0-0	Richmond 2	12,000
20	23	H	Coventry City	W	1-0	1-0	Whipp	10,000
21	25	A	Bury	D	1-1	1-1	Whipp	20,000
22	26	H	Bury	D	0-0	0-0		27,000
23	30	A	Port Vale	W	2-1	1-0	Whipp 2	8,000
24	Jan 6	H	Port Vale	W	2-1	2-1	Whipp 2	15,000
25	20	A	Manchester United	D	0-0	0-0		25,000
26	27	H	Manchester United	L	0-1	0-0		25,000
27	Feb 10	A	Barnsley	L	0-1	0-0		11,000
28	17	H	Sheffield Wed	D	0-0	1-2		14,000
29	24	H	Barnsley	D	1-1	0-0	Swan	8,000
30	Mar 3	H	Hull City	D	2-2	1-2	Swan 2	12,000
31	10	A	Hull City	L	1-3	0-0	Swan	14,000
32	17	A	Crystal Palace	L	0-1	0-0		15,000
33	19	A	Sheffield Wed	L	1-3	1-2	Powell	11,000
34	24	H	Crystal Palace	W	4-1	1-1	Whipp, Swan, Powell, Sherwin	8,000
35	30	H	Rotherham County	W	2-0	1-0	Powell, Whipp	12,000
36	31	A	Fulham	L	0-3	0-2		16,000
37	Apr 2	A	Rotherham County	L	1-3	1-1	Harris (pen)	10,000
38	7	H	Fulham	D	1-1	0-0	Whipp	10,000
39	14	A	Notts County	L	0-1	0-1		10,000
40	21	H	Notts County	W	3-0	2-0	Whipp 2, Powell	8,000
41	28	A	Derby County	W	1-0	1-0	Noble	5,000
42	May 5	H	Derby County	W	1-0	1-0	Powell (pen)	4,000
								Appearances
								Goals

FA Cup

Round	Date	Venue	Opponents	Result	FT	HT	Scorers	Attendance
R1	Jan 13	A	Portsmouth	D	0-0	0-0		26,046
Rep	17	H	Portsmouth	W	3-1	1-1	Whipp, Armitage, Swan	21,240
R2	Feb 3	A	Bolton Wanderers	L	1-3	1-0	Swan	43,389
								Appearances
								Goals

Back row, left to right: Bert Duffield, Ernie Hart, Jimmy Frew, Fred Whalley, Tom Gascoigne, Joe Harris. Front row: Bobby Mason, Jimmy Walton, Jim Baker, Sam Powell, Len Armitage.

Whalley, Fred	Duffield, Bert	Frew, Jimmy	Sherwin, Harry	Hart, Ernie	Baker, Jim	Mason, George	Poyntz, Billy	Howarth, Tommy	Swan, Jack	Harris, Joe	Robson, Bill	Armitage, Len	Walton, Jimmy	Powell, Sam	Gascoigne, Tom	Clark, Wallace	Potts, Joe	Dark, Alf	Noble, Alan	Whipp, Percy	Richmond, Joe	Bell, Tom	Armand, Jack	Coates, Walter	Smith, Len
1	2	3	4	5	6	7	8	9	10	11															
1	2	3	4	5	6	7	8	9	10	11															
1	2	3	4	5	6	7	8	9	10	11															
1	2	3	4	5	6	7		9		11	8	10													
1	2	3	4	5	6	7				11		9	8	10											
1	2	3		5	6	7				11		9	8	10	4										
1	2	3	4	5	6	7	8		10	11		9													
1	2	3	4	5	6	7	8		10	11		9													
1	2	3	4	5	6	7	8		10			9				11									
1	2			5	6	7	8	9	10	11					4		3								
1	2		4	5	6	7	8	9	10	11							3								
1	2		4	5	6	7	9		10	11							3	8							
1	2		4	5	6		9		10	11							3		7	8					
1	2		4	5	6		9		10	11							3		7	8					
1	2		4	5	6		9		10	11							3		7	8					
1	2		4	5	6		9			11			10				3		7	8					
1	2		4	5	6		9			11			10				3		7	8					
1	2	3	4	5	6					11			10						7	8	9				
1	2	3	4	5	6								10			11			7	8	9				
1	2	3	4	5	6								10			11			7	8	9				
1	2		4	5	6					11		9	10						7	8		3			
1	2	3	4	5	6	7				11			10							8	9				
1	2	3	4	5	6					11		9	10						7	8					
1	2	3	4	5	6					11		9	10						7	8					
1	2	3		5	6				10	11		9			4				7	8					
1	2	3	4	5	6				10	11									7	8			9		
1	2	3		5	6				10	11		9			4				7	8					
1	2	3		5	6					11					4				7	8	9		10		
1	2	3		5	6				10	11					4				7	8			9		
1	2	3	4		5				10	11					6				7	8			9		
1	2	3		5	6				9	11					4				7	8			10		
1	2	3		5	6				10	11					4				7	8			9		
1	2	3		5	6					11	8			9	4				7				10		
1	2	3	4	5	6				10	11				9					7	8					
1	2	3	4	5	6				10	11				9					7	8					
1	2	3		5	6				10	11				9	4					8				7	
1		3		5	6				10	11				9			2	4	7	8					
1	2	3		5	6					11	8			9				4	7	10					
1	2	3	4	5	6					11	8			9					7	10					
1	2	3	4	5	6					11	8			9					7	10					
1	2	3		5	6					11	8			9					7	10					4
1	2	3		5	6					11	8			9					7	10					4
42	41	33	28	41	42	13	14	6	23	39	7	11	11	12	11	3	9	3	28	29	5	1	7	1	2
			1	1			1		8	5		2	2	5					1	15	2				

1	2	3	4	5	6					11		9	10						7	8					
1	2	3	4	5	6				10	11		9							7	8					
1	2	3	4	5	6				10	11		9							7	8					
3	3	3	3	3	3	0	0	0	2	3	0	3	1	0	0	0	0	0	3	3	0	0	0	0	0
									2			1								1					

League Table

	P	W	D	L	F	A	Pts
Notts County	42	23	7	12	46	34	53
West Ham United	42	20	11	11	63	38	51
Leicester City	42	21	9	12	65	44	51
Manchester United	42	17	14	11	51	36	48
Blackpool	42	18	11	13	60	43	47
Bury	42	18	11	13	55	46	47
Leeds United	42	18	11	13	43	36	47
Sheffield Wednesday	42	17	12	13	54	47	46
Barnsley	42	17	11	14	62	51	45
Fulham	42	16	12	14	43	32	44
Southampton	42	14	14	14	40	40	42
Hull City	42	14	14	14	43	45	42
South Shields	42	15	10	17	35	44	40
Derby County	42	14	11	17	46	50	39
Bradford City	42	12	13	17	41	45	37
Crystal Palace	42	13	11	18	54	62	37
Port Vale	42	14	9	19	39	51	37
Coventry City	42	15	7	20	46	63	37
Clapton Orient	42	12	12	18	40	50	36
Stockport County	42	14	8	20	43	58	36
Rotherham County	42	13	9	20	44	63	35
Wolverhampton W	42	9	9	24	42	77	27

1923-24

Division Two

Manager: Arthur Fairclough

Final Position: 1st

Did you know that?

3 November 1923: United made it a club record seven wins on the bounce by beating Bradford City. The following week goalkeeper Billy Down kept a sixth successive clean sheet in a 0–0 draw at Bradford City. At the turn of the year United were top of Division Two.

22 December 1923: United's 3–0 defeat at Bury on 22 December was the first game missed by skipper Jim Baker since they were elected to the Football League – a run of 167 League and Cup games.

Bill Menzies made his first appearance in a 10-year career with Leeds at Oldham on Christmas Day.

Match No.	Date	Venue	Opponents	Result	FT	HT	Scorers	Attendance
1	Aug 25	A	Stoke	D	1-1	1-0	Noble	12,000
2	27	H	Crystal Palace	W	3-0	3-0	Fullam, Noble, Whipp	10,000
3	Sep 1	H	Stoke	D	0-0	0-0		12,900
4	5	A	Crystal Palace	D	1-1	0-1	Whipp	8,000
5	8	A	Leicester City	L	0-2	0-1		18,000
6	15	H	Leicester City	L	1-2	0-1	Swan	15,000
7	22	A	Hull City	W	2-1	1-1	Swan 2	11,500
8	29	H	Hull City	W	5-2	5-1	Richmond 3, Swan, Harris	12,000
9	Oct 6	A	Clapton Orient	W	1-0	1-0	Richmond	25,000
10	13	H	Clapton Orient	W	1-0	0-0	Harris	15,000
11	20	A	Port Vale	W	1-0	0-0	Richmond	10,000
12	27	H	Port Vale	W	3-0	1-0	Swan 2, Richmond	12,000
13	Nov 3	H	Bradford City	W	1-0	0-0	Whipp	17,000
14	10	A	Bradford City	D	0-0	0-0		25,000
15	17	H	Barnsley	W	3-1	2-1	Swan 2, Whipp	12,000
16	24	A	Barnsley	W	3-1	1-0	Harris, Richmond 2	12,000
17	Dec 1	H	Manchester United	D	0-0	0-0		20,000
18	8	A	Manchester United	L	1-3	0-2	Whipp	30,000
19	15	H	Bury	L	1-2	0-0	Whipp (pen)	17,000
20	22	A	Bury	L	0-3	0-1		10,000
21	25	A	Oldham Athletic	D	2-2	2-1	Richmond 2	17,000
22	26	H	Oldham Athletic	W	5-0	3-0	Swan 2, Richmond, Whipp 2	12,000
23	Jan 5	A	South Shields	L	0-2	0-1		10,000
24	19	A	Sheffield Wed	D	0-0	0-0		18,000
25	26	H	Sheffield Wed	W	1-0	1-0	Swan	15,000
26	Feb 9	H	Coventry City	W	3-1	2-1	Armand, Richmond, Harris	11,239
27	16	A	Bristol City	W	1-0	1-0	Swan	14,000
28	27	H	South Shields	W	2-1	1-0	Whipp, Armand	8,000
29	Mar 1	A	Southampton	W	1-0	0-0	Hart	8,000
30	8	H	Southampton	W	3-0	0-0	Shelley (og), Swan, Harris	15,000
31	10	A	Coventry City	L	1-2	1-1	Sherwin	6,000
32	15	H	Fulham	W	3-0	1-0	Swan 2, Coates	18,000
33	19	H	Bristol City	D	0-0	0-0		8,000
34	22	A	Fulham	W	2-0	2-0	Fullam, Whipp	17,000
35	29	H	Blackpool	D	0-0	0-0		25,000
36	Apr 5	A	Blackpool	D	1-1	1-0	Richmond	14,000
37	12	H	Derby County	D	1-1	0-0	Whipp	20,000
38	18	A	Stockport County	D	1-1	1-0	Richmond	15,000
39	19	A	Derby County	L	0-2	0-1		21,622
40	21	H	Stockport County	W	4-0	1-0	Swan 2, Richmond, Harris	22,500
41	26	H	Nelson	W	1-0	0-0	Coates	20,000
42	May 3	A	Nelson	L	1-3	0-3	Swan	10,000
								Appearances
							One own-goal	Goals

FA Cup

Match No.	Date	Venue	Opponents	Result	FT	HT	Scorers	Attendance
R1	Jan 12	H	Stoke	W	1-0	0-0	Whipp	26,574
R2	Feb 2	A	West Ham United	D	1-1	0-1	Coates	30,123
Rep	6	H	West Ham United	W	1-0	0-0	Whipp	31,071
R3	23	A	Aston Villa	L	0-3	0-2		51,238
								Appearances
								Goals

Second Division champions. Back row, left to right: Harry Sherwin, Arthur Fairclough (manager), Bert Duffield, Dick Murrell (trainer), Billy Down, John Armand, Bill Menzies, Bill Norman (assistant manager). Front row: Walter Coates, Percy Whipp, Joe Richmond, Jim Baker, Jack Swan, Joe Harris, Ernie Hart.

Whalley, Fred	Duffield, Bert	Speak, George	Sherwin, Harry	Mason, Bobby	Baker, Jim	Noble, Alan	Whipp, Percy	Richmond, Joe	Fullam, Bob	Harris, Joe	Powell, Sam	Frew, Jimmy	Lambert, Jack	Swan, Jack	Down, Billy	Baker, Len	Gascoigne, Tom	Coates, Walter	Hart, Ernie	Armand, Jack	Menzies, Bill	Johnson, Bill	Bell, Albert	Smith, Len	Allen, Jack
1	2	3	4	5	6	7	8	9	10	11															
1	2	3	4	5	6	7	8	9	10	11															
1	2	3	4	5	6	7	8		10	11	9														
1	2	3	4	5	6	7	8	9	10	11															
1	2		4	5	6	7	10			11	9	3	8												
1	2	3	4	5	6	7	8	9		11				10											
	2	3	4		6	7	8	9		11				10	1	5									
	2	3	4		6	7	8	9		11				10	1	5									
	2	3			6	7	8	9		11				10	1	5	4								
	2	3			6		8	9		11				10	1	5	4	7							
	2	3	4		6		8	9		11				10	1			7	5						
	2		4		6		8	9		11		3		10	1			7	5						
	2		4		6		8	9		11		3		10	1			7	5						
	2	3	4		6		8	9		11				10	1			7	5						
	2	3	4		6		8	9		11				10	1			7	5						
	2	3	4		6		8	9		11				10	1			7	5						
	2	3	4		6		8	9		11				10	1			7	5						
	2	3	4		6		8	9		11				10	1			7	5						
	2	3	4		6		8	9		11				10	1			7	5						
	2	3		4		7				11	9			10	1	6			5	8					
	2		4			7		9		11				10	1	6			5	8	3				
	2	3			4	7	8	9						10	1	6			5	11					
	2	3			4	7	8	9		11				10	1	6			5						
	2		4	5	6		8	9		11				10	1					7	3				
	2		4	5	6	7	8			11	9			10	1						3				
	2			5	6			9		11		3		10	1		4	7		8					
	2		4		6		8	9		11				10	1			7	5		3				
1	2		4		6	7	8			11				10					5	9	3				
			4		6	7	8			11				10					5	9	3	1	2		
	2	3	4		6	7	8	9		11				10	1				5						
	2		4		6	7	8	9		11				10	1				5		3				
	2		4		6		8	9		11				10				7	5		3	1			
	2		4		6		8	9		11				10	1			7	5		3				
	2	3		5			8		10	7				9	1	4								6	11
	2				4		8		10	7				9	1				5		3			6	11
	2				4	7	8	9		11				10	1				5		3			6	
			4		2	7	8	9		11				10	1				5		3			6	
		3			4	7	8	9		11				10	1				5		2			6	
		3	4				8	9	10	11								7	5		2	1		6	
	2				4		8	9		11				10	1			7	5		3			6	
	2				4		8	9		11				10	1			7	5		3			6	
	2		4				8	9		11				10	1			7	5		3			6	
7	38	23	30	11	37	21	39	34	7	41	4	4	1	36	32	9	3	18	28	7	17	3	1	9	2
			1			2	11	15	2	6				18				2	1	2					

Whalley, Fred	Duffield, Bert	Speak, George	Sherwin, Harry	Mason, Bobby	Baker, Jim	Noble, Alan	Whipp, Percy	Richmond, Joe	Fullam, Bob	Harris, Joe	Powell, Sam	Frew, Jimmy	Lambert, Jack	Swan, Jack	Down, Billy	Baker, Len	Gascoigne, Tom	Coates, Walter	Hart, Ernie	Armand, Jack	Menzies, Bill	Johnson, Bill	Bell, Albert	Smith, Len	Allen, Jack
	2	3	4		6		8	9		11				10	1				5	7					
	2	3	4		6		8	9		11				10	1			7	5						
	2	3	4		6		8	9		11				10	1			7	5						
	2		4		6		8	9		11				10	1			7	5		3				
0	4	3	4	0	4	0	4	4	0	4	0	0	0	4	4	0	0	3	4	1	1	0	0	0	0
							2											1							

League Table

	P	W	D	L	F	A	Pts
Leeds United	42	21	12	9	61	35	54
Bury	42	21	9	12	63	35	51
Derby County	42	21	9	12	75	42	51
Blackpool	42	18	13	11	72	47	49
Southampton	42	17	14	11	52	31	48
Stoke	42	14	18	10	44	42	46
Oldham Athletic	42	14	17	11	45	52	45
Sheffield Wednesday	42	16	12	14	54	51	44
South Shields	42	17	10	15	49	50	44
Clapton Orient	42	14	15	13	40	36	43
Barnsley	42	16	11	15	57	61	43
Leicester City	42	17	8	17	64	54	42
Stockport County	42	13	16	13	44	52	42
Manchester United	42	13	14	15	52	44	40
Crystal Palace	42	13	13	16	53	65	39
Port Vale	42	13	12	17	50	66	38
Hull City	42	10	17	15	46	51	37
Bradford City	42	11	15	16	35	48	37
Coventry City	42	11	13	18	52	68	35
Fulham	42	10	14	18	45	56	34
Nelson	42	10	13	19	40	74	33
Bristol City	42	7	15	20	32	65	29

1924-25

Division One

Manager: Arthur Fairclough

Final Position: 18th

Did you know that?

27 September 1924: The 41,800 which witnessed a 1–1 draw with neighbours Huddersfield Town was a ground record for Elland Road.

25 December 1924: When United beat Aston Villa 6–0 on Christmas Day 1924 all the goals came in the second half. On Boxing Day United lost 2–1 at Villa Park.

Jim Baker shakes hands with his brother Alf, the Arsenal skipper, at Highbury where Leeds crashed 6–1 on 20 December.

Match No.	Date	Venue	Opponents	Result	FT	HT	Scorers	Attendance
1	Aug 30	H	Sunderland	D	1-1	1-1	Swan	33,722
2	Sep 1	A	Notts County	L	0-1	0-1		16,000
3	6	A	Cardiff City	L	0-3	0-0		30,000
4	10	H	Notts County	D	1-1	0-0	Swan	18,000
5	13	H	Preston North End	W	4-0	3-0	Swan 2, Thom, Harris	20,000
6	17	H	Everton	W	1-0	1-0	Thom	22,000
7	20	A	Burnley	D	1-1	1-1	Thom	23,000
8	27	H	Huddersfield Town	D	1-1	1-0	Swan	41,800
9	Oct 4	H	Birmingham	L	0-1	0-1		24,000
10	11	A	West Bromwich Alb	L	1-3	1-0	Robson	21,332
11	18	H	Tottenham H	W	1-0	1-0	Whipp	23,000
12	25	A	Blackburn Rovers	W	3-2	2-0	Robson 2, Swan	20,000
13	Nov 1	H	West Ham United	W	2-1	1-0	Richmond (pen), Swan	17,000
14	8	A	Sheffield United	D	1-1	0-1	Swan	30,000
15	15	H	Newcastle United	D	1-1	1-0	Whipp	30,000
16	22	A	Liverpool	L	0-1	0-0		20,000
17	29	H	Nottingham Forest	D	1-1	0-0	Robson	20,000
18	Dec 6	A	Bury	L	0-1	0-0		15,000
19	13	H	Manchester City	L	0-3	0-2		15,000
20	20	A	Arsenal	L	1-6	0-4	Whipp	30,000
21	25	H	Aston Villa	W	6-0	0-0	Whipp 3, Swan 2, Hart	24,000
22	26	A	Aston Villa	L	1-2	0-1	Swan	50,000
23	27	A	Sunderland	L	1-2	1-2	Richmond	18,000
24	Jan 3	H	Cardiff City	D	0-0	0-0		19,000
25	17	A	Preston North End	W	4-1	0-1	Whipp 2, Powell 2	15,000
26	24	H	Burnley	L	0-2	0-1		15,000
27	31	A	Huddersfield Town	L	0-2	0-1		12,000
28	Feb 7	A	Birmingham	D	0-0	0-0		20,000
29	14	H	West Bromwich Alb	L	0-1	0-1		18,500
30	28	H	Blackburn Rovers	D	1-1	1-1	Noble	17,000
31	Mar 7	A	West Ham United	D	0-0	0-0		15,000
32	9	A	Tottenham H	L	1-2	1-0	Armand	12,000
33	14	H	Sheffield United	D	1-1	1-1	Harris	25,000
34	21	A	Newcastle United	L	1-4	1-2	Wainscoat	15,000
35	28	H	Liverpool	W	4-1	2-1	Wainscoat, Armand, Harris, Jennings	25,000
36	Apr 4	A	Nottingham Forest	L	0-4	0-3		5,000
37	10	A	Bolton Wanderers	L	0-1	0-1		25,000
38	11	H	Bury	W	1-0	0-0	Jennings	25,000
39	14	H	Bolton Wanderers	W	2-1	1-1	Wainscoat, Jennings	30,000
40	18	A	Manchester City	L	2-4	1-1	Wainscoat, Whipp	14,000
41	25	H	Arsenal	W	1-0	1-0	Whipp	20,000
42	May 2	A	Everton	L	0-1	0-1		10,000
								Appearances
								Goals

FA Cup

R3	Jan 10	A	Liverpool	L	0-3	0-1		39,000
								Appearances
								Goals

Back row, from left to right: Josh Atkinson, Dick Murrell (trainer), George Speak, Dave Russell, Bill Menzies, Val Riley, Ernie Hart. Front row: Joe Harris, Sam Powell, Jim Baker, Fred Graver, Percy Whipp, Alan Noble.

Down, Billy	Duffield, Bert	Menzies, Bill	Sherwin, Harry	Hart, Ernie	Baker, Jim	Noble, Alan	Whipp, Percy	Richmond, Joe	Swan, Jack	Harris, Joe	Duxbury, Tom	Thom, Jock	Graver, Fred	Clark, Jimmy	Coates, Walter	Johnson, Bill	Speak, George	Robson, Cud	Smith, Len	Moore, Bill	Armand, Jack	Mason, Bobby	Baker, Len	Powell, Sam	Russell, David	Atkinson, Josh	Martin, Jack	Jennings, Tom	Edwards, Willis	Wainscoat, Russell
1	2	3	4	5	6	7	8	9	10	11																				
1	2	3		5					10	7	4	8	9	11					6											
1	2	3	4	5	6		8	9	10	11					7															
1	2	3	4	5	6		8	9	10	11					7															
1	2	3	4	5	6		8		10	11		9			7															
1	2	3	4	5	6		8		10	11		9			7															
1	2	3	4	5	6		8		10	11		9			7															
1	2	3	4	5	6		8		10	11		9			7															
	2	3	4	5	6		8		10	11		9			7	1														
	2			5	6		8	9	10	11	4					1	3	7												
	2	3	4	5	6		8		10	11		9				1		7												
	2	3		5	4		8	9	10	11						1		7	6											
	2	3		5	4		8	9	10	11						1		7	6											
	2	3		5	4		8	9	10	11						1		7	6											
	2	3		5	4		8	9	10	11								7	6	1										
	2	3		5	4		8	9	10	11								7	6	1										
1	2	3	4	5			8	9	10	11								7	6											
1	2	3		5	4	7	8	9	10	11									6											
1	2	3		5	4		8		10	11								7	6		9									
1	2	3		5	6		9		10	11								7			8	4								
	2	3	4	5			9		10	11								7	6	1	8									
		2			4				10	11							3	7	6	1	8		5	9						
	2		4	5				9	10	11			8				3	7	6	1										
	2	3	4	5			8	9	10	11								7	6	1										
1	2	3		5	4		8	9		11								7	6					10						
1	2	3			4		8	9		11								7	6			5		10						
	2	3		5	4		8		10	11					7									9	1	6				
		2		5	4	7	8			11			9				3							10	1	6				
1		2		5	4	7	8		9	11							3							10		6				
1	2	3		5	4	7	9		10	11											8					6				
1	2	3			6	4		9		7				10							8	5					11			
1	2	3			6	4		9		7				10							8	5					11			
1	2	3			4	7				11									6		8	5		10				9		
1	2	3		5						11								7			8					6		9	4	10
	2	3		5			7			11											8				1	6		9	4	10
	2	3		5			7			11											8				1	6		9	4	10
	2	3		5			7			11											8				1	6		9	4	10
	2	3		5		7	8			11															1	6		9	4	10
	2	3		5		7	8			11															1	6		9	4	10
	2	3		5		7	8			11															1	6		9	4	10
	2	3		5			8			11											7				1	6		9	4	10
1	2	3		5			8			11											7					6		9	4	10
21	39	40	13	37	28	11	35	17	27	42	2	7	3	3	8	6	5	17	16	6	14	5	1	7	9	13	2	10	9	9
				1		1	10	2	11	3		3						4			2			2				3		4

Down, Billy	Duffield, Bert	Menzies, Bill	Sherwin, Harry	Hart, Ernie	Baker, Jim	Noble, Alan	Whipp, Percy	Richmond, Joe	Swan, Jack	Harris, Joe	Duxbury, Tom	Thom, Jock	Graver, Fred	Clark, Jimmy	Coates, Walter	Johnson, Bill	Speak, George	Robson, Cud	Smith, Len	Moore, Bill	Armand, Jack	Mason, Bobby	Baker, Len	Powell, Sam	Russell, David	Atkinson, Josh	Martin, Jack	Jennings, Tom	Edwards, Willis	Wainscoat, Russell
1		2	4	5			9		10	11							3	7	6		8									
1	0	1	1	1	0	0	1	0	1	1	0	0	0	0	0	0	1	1	1	0	1	0	0	0	0	0	0	0	0	0

League Table

	P	W	D	L	F	A	Pts
Huddersfield Town	42	21	16	5	69	28	58
West Bromwich Albion	42	23	10	9	58	34	56
Bolton Wanderers	42	22	11	9	76	34	55
Liverpool	42	20	10	12	63	55	50
Bury	42	17	15	10	54	51	49
Newcastle United	42	16	16	10	61	42	48
Sunderland	42	19	10	13	64	51	48
Birmingham	42	17	12	13	49	53	46
Notts County	42	16	13	13	42	31	45
Manchester City	42	17	9	16	76	68	43
Cardiff City	42	16	11	15	56	51	43
Tottenham Hotspur	42	15	12	15	52	43	42
West Ham United	42	15	12	15	62	60	42
Sheffield United	42	13	13	16	55	63	39
Aston Villa	42	13	13	16	58	71	39
Blackburn Rovers	42	11	13	18	53	66	35
Everton	42	12	11	19	40	60	35
Leeds United	42	11	12	19	46	59	34
Burnley	42	11	12	19	46	75	34
Arsenal	42	14	5	23	46	58	33
Preston North End	42	10	6	26	37	74	26
Nottingham Forest	42	6	12	24	29	65	24

1925-26

Division One

Manager: Arthur Fairclough

Final Position: 19th

Did you know that?

26 December 1925: Goalkeeper Richard Thornton was left punch-drunk on Boxing Day in his only United appearance. Leeds lost 6–3 at Burnley, whose goals all came in the first half.

13 February 1926: Tom Jennings became the first United player to net 20 League goals in a season, reaching the milestone in a 2–1 defeat at Manchester United. He finished the League campaign with 26.

1 March 1926: Willis Edwards became United's first England player as he featured in the 3–1 loss against Wales. He was the 500th player to be capped by England.

6 March 1926: The long-serving Jim Baker played his final game, a 1–1 draw against Everton at Elland Road, before joining Nelson.

1 May 1926: United's 4–1 home win against Tottenham kept them up at the expense of Manchester City who lost 3–2 at Newcastle and went down with Notts County.

Wilf Chadwick hit the winner against Leicester at Elland Road.

Match No.	Date	Venue	Opponents	Result	FT	HT	Scorers	Attendance
1	Aug 29	A	Notts County	L	0-1	0-1		18,155
2	31	H	Bolton Wanderers	W	2-1	1-0	Jennings, Harris	24,188
3	Sep 5	H	Aston Villa	D	2-2	1-1	Jennings 2	29,501
4	7	A	Bolton Wanderers	L	0-1	0-1		23,343
5	12	A	Leicester City	W	3-1	0-1	Jennings, Turnbull 2	23,592
6	16	H	Newcastle United	W	2-0	1-0	Jennings, Jackson	21,291
7	19	H	West Ham United	W	5-2	1-1	Whipp, Jennings 2, Wainscoat 2	16,433
8	26	A	Arsenal	L	1-4	0-2	Wainscoat	32,531
9	Oct 3	H	Manchester United	W	2-0	1-0	Jennings, Wainscoat	26,265
10	10	A	Liverpool	D	1-1	1-0	Wainscoat	30,088
11	17	H	Huddersfield Town	L	0-4	0-3		33,008
12	24	A	Everton	L	2-4	0-3	Jennings, Wainscoat	28,660
13	31	H	Bury	L	2-3	1-0	Hart, Jackson	15,008
14	Nov 7	A	Blackburn Rovers	D	2-2	2-0	Hart, Jennings	9,190
15	14	H	Cardiff City	W	1-0	0-0	Turnbull	19,360
16	21	A	Sheffield United	L	0-2	0-0		22,327
17	28	H	West Bromwich Alb	L	0-1	0-1		14,774
18	Dec 5	A	Birmingham	L	1-2	1-2	Jennings	13,435
19	12	H	Manchester City	L	3-4	1-1	Armand 2 (1 pen), Chadwick	18,762
20	19	A	Tottenham Hotspur	L	2-3	0-1	Armand 2 (1 pen)	19,200
21	25	H	Burnley	D	2-2	1-2	Turnbull, Whipp	23,325
22	26	A	Burnley	L	3-6	1-6	Whipp, Armand, Jennings	22,207
23	Jan 1	A	Sunderland	W	3-1	0-0	Armand (pen), Townsley, Jennings	29,527
24	2	H	Notts County	W	2-1	0-1	Armand (pen), Whipp	14,615
25	23	H	Leicester City	W	1-0	1-0	Chadwick	19,569
26	30	A	West Ham United	L	2-4	2-4	Jennings 2	17,246
27	Feb 3	A	Aston Villa	L	1-3	1-3	Jennings	11,573
28	6	H	Arsenal	W	4-2	4-0	Jennings 3, Chadwick	26,239
29	13	A	Manchester United	L	1-2	1-1	Jennings	29,584
30	20	H	Liverpool	D	1-1	1-0	Jennings	24,158
31	27	A	Huddersfield Town	L	1-3	0-1	Wainscoat	26,248
32	Mar 6	H	Everton	D	1-1	1-1	Wainscoat	18,163
33	13	A	Bury	W	2-0	1-0	Armand, Jennings	15,226
34	20	H	Blackburn Rovers	W	2-1	0-1	Fell, Armand	22,419
35	27	A	Cardiff City	D	0-0	0-0		18,300
36	Apr 3	H	Sheffield United	W	2-0	2-0	Jennings, Turnbull	26,262
37	5	A	Newcastle United	L	0-3	0-1		16,666
38	6	H	Sunderland	L	0-2	0-2		27,345
39	10	A	West Bromwich Alb	L	0-3	0-3		11,358
40	17	H	Birmingham	D	0-0	0-0		12,186
41	27	A	Manchester City	L	1-2	0-2	Jennings	43,475
42	May 1	H	Tottenham Hotspur	W	4-1	1-1	Turnbull, Jennings 2, Whipp	16,158
								Appearances
								Goals

FA Cup

Match No.	Date	Venue	Opponents	Result	FT	HT	Scorers	Attendance
R3	Jan 9	A	Middlesbrough	L	1-5	0-2	Armand (pen)	29,000
								Appearances
								Goals

League match abandoned after 82 minutes due to fog

Match No.	Date	Venue	Opponents	Result	FT	HT	Scorers	Attendance
	Jan 16	A	Aston Villa	L	0-1	0-0		12,930

Johnson, Bill	Duffield, Bert	Menzies, Bill	Edwards, Willis	Hart, Ernie	Atkinson, Josh	Turnbull, Bobby	Whipp, Percy	Jennings, Tom	Wainscoat, Russell	Harris, Joe	Allan, Jimmy	Baker, Jim	Jackson, Billy	Smith, Len	Armand, Jack	Sissons, Albert	Mears, Frank	Kirkpatrick, Jim	Chadwick, Wilf	Townsley, Tom	Thornton, Dick	Fell, Jackie	Potts, Jimmy	Roberts, Harry	Reed, George
1	2	3	4	5	6	7	8	9	10	11															
1	2	3	4	5	6	7	8	9	10	11															
1	2	3	4	5	6	7	8	9	10	11															
1		3	4	5			8	9	10	7	2	6	11												
1	2	3	4	5		7	8	9	10			6	11												
1	2	3	4	5		7	8	9	10			6	11												
1		3	4	5		7	8	9	10		2		11	6											
1		3	4	5		7	8	9	10		2		11	6											
1		3	4	5		7	8	9	10		2	6	11												
1		3	4	5		7	8	9	10		2	6	11												
1	2	3	4	5			8	9	10			6	11		7										
1		3	4	5		7		9	10		2	6	11		8										
1		3	4	5	6			9			2		11		8	7	10								
1		3	4	5	6	10	8	9			2		11			7									
1			4	5	6	10	8	9			2		11			7		3							
1			4	5	6	11	8	9			2					7		3	10						
1			4	5	6	7	8	9			2		11					3	10						
1			4	5	6	7	8	9			2		11					3	10						
1		3	4	5	6	7		9			2		11		8				10						
1			4		5	7	8	9			2		11	6	10			3							
1			4		6	7	8	9			2		11		10			3		5					
			4		2	7	8	9					11	6	10			3		5	1				
1		3	4		6	7	8	9			2		11		10					5					
1		3	4		6	7	8	9			2		11		10					5					
1		3	4	5	6	7		9			2		11		8				10						
1		3	4		6	7		9	10		2		11						8	5					
1		3	4		6	7		9	10		2		11						8	5					
1		3	4		6	7		9	10		2		11						8	5					
1		3	4		6	7		9	10		2								8	5		11			
1		3	4			7		9	10		2		11	6	8					5					
		3	4				8	9	10		2	6	11			7				5			1		
		3	4				8	9	10		2	6	11			7				5			1		
		6		5		7		9	10		3				8					4		11	1	2	
		3	4	5		7		9	10		2				8					6		11	1		
		3	4	5		7		9	10		2				8					6		11	1		
		3	4	5		7		9	10		2				8					6		11	1		
		3	4	5		7		9	10		2				8					6		11	1		
		3	4			7		9	10		2				11				8	5			1		6
		3	4	5		7	8	9			2								10	6		11	1		
		3			4	7	8	9			2		11	6					10	5			1		
		3	4		6	7	8	9			2		11						10	5			1		
		3	4		6	7	8	9			2		11						10	5			1		
29	6	35	40	26	23	37	27	42	25	4	35	9	30	6	17	6	1	7	14	21	1	7	12	1	1
				2		6	5	26	8	1			2		9				3	1		1			

1		3	4		6	7	8	9			2		11		10					5					
1	0	1	1	0	1	1	1	1	0	0	1	0	1	0	1	0	0	0	0	1	0	0	0	0	0
															1										

1		3	4		6	7		9			2		11		8				10	5					

League Table

	P	W	D	L	F	A	Pts
Huddersfield Town	42	23	11	8	92	60	57
Arsenal	42	22	8	12	87	63	52
Sunderland	42	21	6	15	96	80	48
Bury	42	20	7	15	85	77	47
Sheffield United	42	19	8	15	102	82	46
Aston Villa	42	16	12	14	86	76	44
Liverpool	42	14	16	12	70	63	44
Bolton Wanderers	42	17	10	15	75	76	44
Manchester United	42	19	6	17	66	73	44
Newcastle United	42	16	10	16	84	75	42
Everton	42	12	18	12	72	70	42
Blackburn Rovers	42	15	11	16	91	80	41
West Bromwich Albion	42	16	8	18	79	78	40
Birmingham	42	16	8	18	66	81	40
Tottenham Hotspur	42	15	9	18	66	79	39
Cardiff City	42	16	7	19	61	76	39
Leicester City	42	14	10	18	70	80	38
West Ham United	42	15	7	20	63	76	37
Leeds United	42	14	8	20	64	76	36
Burnley	42	13	10	19	85	108	36
Manchester City	42	12	11	19	89	100	35
Notts County	42	13	7	22	54	74	33

1926-27

Division One

Manager: Arthur Fairclough

Final Position: 21st

Did you know that?

2 April 1927: The prolific Tom Jennings made the most of changes to the offside law by becoming the first Leeds player to reach 30 goals in a season with the first of his brace against West Brom. He went on to smash his own scoring record, set the previous season, by ramming home 35 League goals, but could not prevent United from relegation to Division Two.

Leading marksman Tom Jennings.

Match No.	Date	Venue	Opponents	Result	FT	HT	Scorers	Attendance
1	Aug 28	H	Bolton Wanderers	L	2-5	0-2	Wainscoat, Turnbull	23,699
2	30	H	Cardiff City	D	0-0	0-0		14,242
3	Sep 4	A	Manchester United	D	2-2	2-1	Jennings, Wainscoat (pen)	26,338
4	6	A	Cardiff City	L	1-3	1-2	Whipp	13,653
5	11	H	Derby County	W	1-0	0-0	Jennings	17,411
6	15	H	Aston Villa	W	3-1	2-1	Armand, Jennings, Sissons	13,792
7	18	A	Sheffield United	L	0-1	0-1		19,940
8	25	H	Arsenal	W	4-1	2-1	Jennings 3, Wainscoat	20,544
9	Oct 2	A	Liverpool	W	4-2	2-1	Jennings 4	30,942
10	9	H	Blackburn Rovers	W	4-1	2-0	Jennings 4	16,304
11	16	A	Leicester City	L	2-3	2-2	Jennings 2 (1 pen)	27,753
12	23	H	Everton	L	1-3	1-1	Jennings	24,867
13	30	A	Huddersfield Town	L	1-4	1-0	Jennings	29,679
14	Nov 6	H	Sunderland	D	2-2	1-1	Jennings, Duggan	15,667
15	13	A	West Bromwich Alb	W	4-2	2-2	Mitchell 2, Whipp, Armand	10,269
16	20	H	Bury	W	4-1	2-0	Jennings 3, Mitchell	18,332
17	27	A	Birmingham	L	0-2	0-1		19,707
18	Dec 4	H	Tottenham Hotspur	D	1-1	0-0	Armand	24,470
19	11	A	West Ham United	L	2-3	1-0	Armand, Menzies	20,924
20	18	H	Sheffield Wed	W	4-1	3-0	Edwards, Jennings, Mitchell, Whipp	20,722
21	27	H	Newcastle United	L	1-2	1-1	Jennings	48,590
22	28	A	Aston Villa	L	1-5	1-3	Armand	43,963
23	Jan 1	A	Newcastle United	L	0-1	0-0		51,343
24	15	A	Bolton Wanderers	L	0-3	0-3		19,149
25	22	H	Manchester United	L	2-3	1-1	Jennings 2 (1 pen)	16,816
26	Feb 5	H	Sheffield United	D	1-1	0-0	Jennings	18,348
27	12	A	Arsenal	L	0-1	0-1		25,961
28	19	A	Derby County	L	0-1	0-1		14,597
29	23	H	Liverpool	D	0-0	0-0		13,776
30	26	A	Blackburn Rovers	L	1-4	0-2	White	16,149
31	Mar 5	H	Leicester City	D	1-1	1-1	Jennings	21,420
32	12	A	Everton	L	1-2	1-0	Jennings	57,440
33	19	H	Huddersfield Town	D	1-1	1-0	Turnbull	36,364
34	26	A	Sunderland	L	2-6	0-2	Wainscoat 2	12,288
35	apr 2	H	West Bromwich Alb	W	3-1	1-0	Jennings 2, Wainscoat	20,176
36	9	A	Bury	L	2-4	0-3	Wainscoat, Jennings	12,489
37	15	A	Burnley	L	2-3	0-1	Turnbull, Jennings	21,099
38	16	H	Birmingham	W	2-1	0-0	Turnbull, Jennings	18,703
39	19	H	Burnley	L	0-2	0-1		18,740
40	23	A	Tottenham Hotspur	L	1-4	1-2	Jennings	17,745
41	30	H	West Ham United	W	6-3	3-1	Turnbull, White, Wainscoat 4	10,997
42	May 7	A	Sheffield Wed	L	0-1	0-0		12,027

Appearances
Goals

FA Cup

R3	Jan 8	H	Sunderland	W	3-2	2-2	Jennings 2 (1 pen), Duggan	31,000
R4	29	H	Bolton Wanderers	D	0-0	0-0		42,694
Rep	Feb 2	A	Bolton Wanderers	l	0-3	0-3		46,686

Appearances
Goals

Potts, Jimmy	Allan, Jimmy	Menzies, Bill	Edwards, Willis	Townsley, Tom	Atkinson, Josh	Turnbull, Bobby	Chadwick, Wilf	Jennings, Tom	Wainscoat, Russell	Jackson, Billy	Hart, Ernie	Sissons, Albert	Whipp, Percy	Fell, Jackie	Armand, Jack	Kirkpatrick, Jim	Roberts, Harry	Duggan, Harry	Robinson, David	Mitchell, Tom	Reed, George	White, Jock	Mears, Frank
1	2	3	4	5	6	7	8	9	10	11													
1	2	3	4	5	6	7	8	9	10	11													
1	2	3	4	6				9	10	11	5	7	8										
1	2	3	4	6				9	10		5	7	8	11									
1	2	3	4	6				9			5	7	8	11	10								
1	2	6	4	5				9				7	8	11	10	3							
1	2	6	4	5		11		9				7	8		10	3							
1	2	6	4	5		11		9	10			7			8	3							
1	3	6	4	5				9				7	8	11			2	10					
1		6		5	4	11		9	10			7					2	8	3				
1	3	6	4	5		11		9	10			7					2	8					
1	3	6	4	5		11		9	10			7					2	8					
1	3	6	4	5		7		9	10					11			2	8					
1	3	6	4	5		7		9	10								2	8		11			
1		3	4	5	6			9				7	8		10		2			11			
1		3	4	5	6			9				7	8		10		2			11			
1		3		5	6			9			4	7	8		10		2			11			
1		3	4	5	6			9				7	8		10		2			11			
1		3	4	5	6			9				7	8		10		2			11			
1		3	4	5		7		9					8		10		2			11	6		
1		3	4	5		7		9					8		10		2			11	6		
1	3		4	5		7		9					8		10		2			11	6		
1	3		4	5		7		9					8		10		2			11	6		
1	3		4	5		7		9							10		2	8		11	6		
1		3	4	5				9				7			10		2	8		11	6		
1		3	4	5		7		9	10						8		2			11	6		
1		3		4		7		9	10		5						2			11	6	8	
1		3	4	5		7		9	10								2			11	6	8	
1			4	5	6	7		9						11	10		2		3			8	
1			4	5		7									10		2		3	11	6	8	9
1			4	5		7		9	10								2		3	11	6	8	
1		3	4	5		7		9	10								2			11	6	8	
1		3		5	4	7		9	10								2			11	6	8	
1		3	4	5		7		9	10								2			11	6	8	
1	3			5	4	7		9	10	11							2				6	8	
1	3		4	5		7		9	10	11							2				6	8	
1	3		4	5		7		9	10	11							2				6	8	
1	3		4	5		7		9	10	11							2				6	8	
1		3	4	5		7		9	10	11							2				6	8	
1		3	4	5		7		9	10								2			11	6	8	
1	3		4	5		7		9	10								2			11	6	8	
1	3		4	5		7		9	10								2			11	6	8	
42	22	30	37	42	11	31	2	41	25	8	5	16	15	6	18	3	34	8	4	23	22	16	1
		1	1			5		35	11			1	3		5			1		4		2	

1		3	4	5		7		9							10		2	8		11	6		
1		3	4	5				9	8			7			10		2			11	6		
1	2		4	5				9	10								3			11	6	8	7
3	1	2	3	3	0	1	0	3	2	0	0	1	0	0	2	0	3	1	0	3	3	1	1
								2										1					

League Table

	P	W	D	L	F	A	Pts
Newcastle United	42	25	6	11	96	58	56
Huddersfield Town	42	17	17	8	76	60	51
Sunderland	42	21	7	14	98	70	49
Bolton Wanderers	42	19	10	13	84	62	48
Burnley	42	19	9	14	91	80	47
West Ham United	42	19	8	15	86	70	46
Leicester City	42	17	12	13	85	70	46
Sheffield United	42	17	10	15	74	86	44
Liverpool	42	18	7	17	69	61	43
Aston Villa	42	18	7	17	81	83	43
Arsenal	42	17	9	16	77	86	43
Derby County	42	17	7	18	86	73	41
Tottenham Hotspur	42	16	9	17	76	78	41
Cardiff City	42	16	9	17	55	65	41
Manchester United	42	13	14	15	52	64	40
Sheffield Wednesday	42	15	9	18	75	92	39
Birmingham	42	17	4	21	64	73	38
Blackburn Rovers	42	15	8	19	77	96	38
Bury	42	12	12	18	68	77	36
Everton	42	12	10	20	64	90	34
Leeds United	42	11	8	23	69	88	30
West Bromwich Albion	42	11	8	23	65	86	30

1927-28

Division Two

Manager: Dick Ray

Final Position: 2nd

Did you know that?

19 November 1927: In a Central League match against Bolton Wanderers at Elland Road, Charlie Keetley scored seven times in a 10–1 win.

25 April 1928: A new attendance record crowd of 48,470 saw the title decider against Manchester City. Both sides were already promoted but City won, Tommy Tait scoring the only goal. United, who counted record receipts of £3,083 from that game, finished the campaign with a club record 98 goals from their 42 Second Division games.

It proved a breakthrough season for young forward Charlie Keetley.

Match No.	Date	Venue	Opponents	Result	FT	HT	Scorers	Attendance
1	Aug 27	A	South Shields	W	5-1	0-0	Wainscoat, Mitchell, White 2, Jennings	9,826
2	29	H	Barnsley	D	2-2	0-1	White, Jennings	21,219
3	Sep 3	H	Southampton	W	2-0	1-0	Wainscoat 2	19,479
4	10	H	Nottingham Forest	W	4-0	3-0	Turnbull, Jennings, Wainscoat, Mitchell	19,478
5	17	A	Manchester City	L	1-2	1-0	Jennings	40,931
6	24	H	Hull City	W	2-0	0-0	Jennings, Wainscoat	21,943
7	26	A	Barnsley	L	1-2	0-1	Mitchell	13,038
8	Oct 1	A	Preston North End	L	1-5	1-1	White	16,966
9	8	H	Swansea Town	W	5-0	3-0	Jennings 2 (1 pen), Turnbull, White 2	18,697
10	15	A	Fulham	D	1-1	0-1	White	16,704
11	22	A	Grimsby Town	L	2-3	2-3	Jennings, Wainscoat	11,909
12	29	H	Oldham Athletic	W	1-0	1-0	Mitchell	17,615
13	Nov 5	A	Notts County	D	2-2	2-1	Jennings 2	9,866
14	12	H	Reading	W	6-2	2-0	Wainscoat, Turnbull 2, White 2, Jennings	17,257
15	19	A	Blackpool	W	2-0	1-0	Mitchell 2	9,008
16	26	H	West Bromwich Alb	L	1-2	1-1	Townsley	23,690
17	Dec 3	A	Clapton Orient	L	1-2	1-1	Mitchell	12,838
18	10	H	Chelsea	W	5-0	1-0	Jennings 4, White	22,059
19	17	A	Bristol City	W	2-1	0-1	Wainscoat, White	18,236
20	24	H	Stoke City	W	5-1	2-1	Jennings 2, White, Turnbull, Hart	12,889
21	26	A	Port Vale	W	2-1	1-1	Wainscoat, White	18,869
22	27	H	Port Vale	W	3-0	1-0	Wainscoat, Jennings 2	32,275
23	31	H	South Shields	W	3-0	2-0	Turnbull, Wainscoat, Keetley	12,752
24	Jan 7	A	Southampton	W	4-1	0-0	White 2, Wainscoat, Keetley	13,966
25	21	A	Nottingham Forest	D	2-2	0-1	White, Keetley	13,133
26	28	H	Bristol City	W	3-2	2-0	Keetley 3	15,534
27	Feb 4	A	Hull City	L	1-3	0-0	Jennings	12,502
28	11	H	Preston North End	L	2-4	0-3	Wainscoat 2	24,276
29	18	A	Swansea Town	D	1-1	0-1	Jennings	13,444
30	25	H	Fulham	W	2-1	0-0	White, Wainscoat	17,358
31	Mar 3	H	Grimsby Town	D	0-0	0-0		23,567
32	10	A	Oldham Athletic	W	1-0	0-0	Keetley	22,029
33	17	H	Notts County	W	6-0	5-0	Keetley 3, Turnbull, Armand, White	17,643
34	24	A	Reading	W	1-0	0-0	Keetley	13,098
35	31	H	Blackpool	W	4-0	2-0	Wainscoat 2, Mitchell, Armand	19,630
36	Apr 7	A	West Bromwich Alb	W	1-0	0-0	Turnbull	23,644
37	9	A	Wolverhampton W	D	0-0	0-0		25,251
38	10	H	Wolverhampton W	W	3-0	2-0	Keetley 2, White	29,821
39	14	H	Clapton Orient	W	4-0	1-0	Keetley 3, White	22,884
40	21	A	Chelsea	W	3-2	2-0	Keetley 2, White	47,562
41	25	H	Manchester City	L	0-1	0-1		48,470
42	May 5	A	Stoke City	L	1-5	0-3	Wainscoat	12,401
								Appearances
								Goals

FA Cup

R3	Jan 14	A	Manchester City	L	0-1	0-0		50,473
								Appearances
								Goals

Potts, Jimmy	Roberts, Harry	Menzies, Bill	Edwards, Willis	Townsley, Tom	Reed, George	Turnbull, Bobby	White, Jock	Jennings, Tom	Wainscoat, Russell	Mitchell, Tom	Hart, Ernie	Sissons, Albert	Allan, Jimmy	Baker, Aaron	Coutts, Tom	Atkinson, Josh	Keetley, Charlie	Robinson, David	Johnson, Bill	Stacey, Alex	Armand, Jack
1	2	3	4	5	6	7	8	9	10	11											
1	2	3	4	5	6	7	8	9	10	11											
1		3	4	2	6	7	8	9	10	11	5										
1		3	4	2	6	7	8	9	10	11	5										
1		3	4	2	6	7	8	9	10	11	5										
1		3	4	2	6		8	9	10	11	5	7									
1	2	3	4	5	6	7	8	9	10	11											
1	2		4	5	6	7	8	9	10	11			3								
1	2			5	6	7	8	9	10	11			3	4							
1	2			5	6	7	8	9	10	11			3	4							
1	2			5	6	7	8	9	10	11			3		4						
1		3		5	6	7	8	9	10	11			2			4					
1		3		5	6	7	8	9	10	11			2			4					
1		3		5	6	7	8	9	10	11			2			4					
1		3		5	6	7	8	9	10	11			2			4					
1		3		5	6	7	8	9	10	11			2			4					
1			4	2	6	7	8	9	10	11	5		3								
1			4	2	6	7	8	9	10	11	5		3								
1			4	2	6	7	8	9	10	11	5		3								
1		3	4	2	6	7	8	9	10	11	5										
1		3	4	2	6	7	8	9	10	11	5										
1		3	4	2	6	7	8	9	10	11	5										
1		3	4	2	6	7	8		10	11	5						9				
1		3	4	2	6		8		10	11	5	7					9				
1		3	4	2	6		8		10	11	5	7					9				
1			4	2	6	7	8		10	11	5						9	3			
1			4	2	6		8	9	10	11	5	7	3								
		3	4	2	6		8		10	11	5	7					9		1		
		3	4	2	6		8	9	10	11	5	7							1		
		3	4	2	6		8	9	10	11	5	7							1		
		3	4	2	6		8	9	10	11	5	7							1		
1		3		2	6	7	8		10	11	5						9			4	
1		3	4	2	6	7	8			11	5						9				10
1		3	4	2	6	7	8		10	11	5						9				
1		3		2	6	7			10	11	5						9			4	8
1		3	4	2	6	7	8		10	11	5						9				
1		3	4	2	6	7	8		10	11	5						9				
1		3	4	2	6	7	8		10	11	5						9				
1		3	4	2	6	7	8		10	11	5						9				
1		3	4	2	6	7	8		10	11	5						9				
1		3	4	2	6	7	8		10	11	5						9				
1		3	4	2	6	7	8		10	11	5						9				
38	7	33	32	42	42	34	41	26	41	42	30	8	13	2	1	5	16	1	4	2	2
				1		8	21	21	18	8	1						18				2

1		3	4	2	6	7	8	9	10	11	5										
1	0	1	1	1	1	1	1	1	1	1	1	0	0	0	0	0	0	0	0	0	0

League Table

	P	W	D	L	F	A	Pts
Manchester City	42	25	9	8	100	59	59
Leeds United	42	25	7	10	98	49	57
Chelsea	42	23	8	11	75	45	54
Preston North End	42	22	9	11	100	66	53
Stoke City	42	22	8	12	78	59	52
Swansea Town	42	18	12	12	75	63	48
Oldham Athletic	42	19	8	15	75	51	46
West Bromwich Albion	42	17	12	13	90	70	46
Port Vale	42	18	8	16	68	57	44
Nottingham Forest	42	15	10	17	83	84	40
Grimsby Town	42	14	12	16	69	83	40
Bristol City	42	15	9	18	76	79	39
Barnsley	42	14	11	17	65	85	39
Hull City	42	12	15	15	41	54	39
Notts County	42	13	12	17	68	74	38
Wolverhampton W	42	13	10	19	63	91	36
Southampton	42	14	7	21	68	77	35
Reading	42	11	13	18	53	75	35
Blackpool	42	13	8	21	83	101	34
Clapton Orient	42	11	12	19	55	85	34
Fulham	42	13	7	22	68	89	33
South Shields	42	7	9	26	56	111	23

1928-29

Division One

Manager: Dick Ray

Final Position: 13th

Did you know that?

17 November 1928: United lost 2–0 at Sheffield Wednesday without defensive stars Willis Edwards and Ernie Hart who were in the England side which won 3–2 against Wales in Swansea – the first time two United players were in the same England team.

9 February 1929: West Ham forward Vic Watson was the scourge of the United defence, scoring six times – the best individual tally against Leeds – as the Peacocks crashed 8–2 at Upton Park. Three months earlier he scored a hat-trick at Elland Road – and more followed the next season.

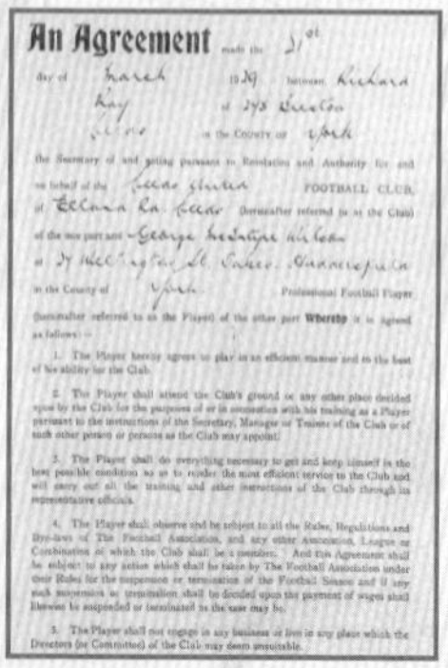

Sign please....The contract of George Wilson, who joined United from neighbours Huddersfield.

Match No.	Date	Venue	Opponents	Result	FT	HT	Scorers	Attendance
1	Aug 25	H	Aston Villa	W	4-1	2-0	Keetley 3, Wainscoat	26,588
2	27	H	Bury	W	3-1	0-0	Armand, Wainscoat 2	18,354
3	Sep 1	A	Leicester City	D	4-4	3-2	Keetley 2, Turnbull, Armand	27,507
4	8	H	Manchester United	W	3-2	1-2	Wainscoat, Keetley, Armand	28,723
5	15	A	Huddersfield Town	L	1-6	0-2	Wainscoat pen	39,869
6	22	A	Liverpool	D	1-1	1-1	Wainscoat	37,417
7	29	H	West Ham United	W	4-1	3-0	Jennings 2, Wainscoat, White	29,423
8	Oct 6	A	Newcastle United	L	2-3	2-1	Wainscoat, Jennings	39,166
9	13	H	Burnley	W	2-1	0-1	White, Jennings	29,565
10	20	H	Manchester City	W	4-1	2-1	White 3, Wainscoat	32,866
11	27	A	Everton	W	1-0	0-0	Wainscoat	41,504
12	Nov 3	H	Portsmouth	W	3-2	1-2	Wainscoat, Jennings, White	29,022
13	10	A	Bolton Wanderers	L	1-4	0-2	Turnbull	16,308
14	17	H	Sheffield Wed	L	0-2	0-1		25,519
15	24	A	Derby County	W	4-3	4-1	White, Keetley, Mitchell, Wainscoat	16,601
16	Dec 1	H	Sunderland	L	0-3	0-0		30,082
17	8	A	Blackburn Rovers	W	1-0	0-0	Keetley	17,333
18	15	H	Arsenal	D	1-1	1-1	Keetley	20,293
19	22	A	Birmingham	L	1-5	1-2	Turnbull	16,057
20	25	H	Cardiff City	W	3-0	0-0	Keetley, White, Hart	28,188
21	26	A	Cardiff City	L	1-2	1-2	Turnbull	20,409
22	29	A	Aston Villa	L	0-1	0-1		31,565
23	Jan 1	A	Bury	D	2-2	0-0	Turnbull, Wainscoat	21,696
24	5	H	Leicester City	W	4-3	2-1	Keetley 3, Turnbull	18,870
25	19	A	Manchester United	W	2-1	0-1	Keetley, Hart	21,995
26	Feb 2	H	Liverpool	D	2-2	1-1	Done (og), Jennings	18,780
27	9	A	West Ham United	L	2-8	2-2	Wainscoat, Jennings	18,055
28	16	H	Newcastle United	D	0-0	0-0		16,036
29	23	A	Burnley	L	0-5	0-3		13,506
30	Mar 2	A	Manchester City	L	0-3	0-1		33,921
31	9	H	Everton	W	3-1	1-1	Keetley 3	22,459
32	16	A	Portsmouth	W	2-0	1-0	Mitchell, Wainscoat	17,700
33	30	A	Sheffield Wed	L	2-4	0-2	Wainscoat, Keetley	30,655
34	Apr 1	A	Sheffield United	D	1-1	0-0	Keetley	20,400
35	2	H	Sheffield United	W	2-0	2-0	Jennings, White	20,119
36	6	H	Derby County	D	1-1	1-1	Mitchell	19,985
37	13	A	Sunderland	L	1-2	1-1	Keetley	12,208
38	20	H	Blackburn Rovers	L	0-1	0-1		17,201
39	27	A	Arsenal	L	0-1	0-1		21,465
40	29	H	Bolton Wanderers	D	2-2	1-2	Wainscoat 2	12,877
41	May 1	H	Huddersfield Town	L	1-2	0-2	Jennings	17,291
42	4	H	Birmingham	L	0-1	0-1		8,151
								Appearances
							One own-goal	Goals

FA Cup

Round	Date	Venue	Opponents	Result	FT	HT	Scorers	Attendance
R3	Jan 12	A	Exeter City	D	2-2	1-1	Keetley, Menzies	13,500
Rep	16	H	Exeter City	W	5-1	2-1	Lowton (og), Wainscoat, Reed, Cochrane, Keetley	23,000
R4	26	A	Huddersfield Town	L	0-3	0-3		53,700
								Appearances
							One own-goal	Goals

Back row, left to right: Willis Edwards, John White, Tom Townsley, Jimmy Potts, George Reed, Bill Menzies, Ernie Hart. Front row: Bobby Turnbull, Tom Jennings, Charlie Keetley, Russell Wainscoat, Tom Mitchell.

Potts, Jimmy	Townsley, Tom	Menzies, Bill	Edwards, Willis	Hart, Ernie	Reed, George	Turnbull, Bobby	Armand, Jack	Keetley, Charlie	Wainscoat, Russell	Mitchell, Tom	Roberts, Harry	Jennings, Tom	Buck, Teddy	White, Jock	Cochrane, Tom	Milburn, George	Stacey, Alex	Gribben, Bill	McNestry, George	Wilson, James	Longden, Eric	Wilson, George	Underwood, Ben	Firth, Joe
1	2	3	4	5	6	7	8	9	10	11														
1	2	3	4	5	6	7	8	9	10	11														
1	2	3	4	5	6	7	8	9	10	11														
1	2	3	4	5	6	7	8	9	10	11														
1	4	3		5	6	7	8		10	11	2	9												
1	2	3		5	6	7			10	11		9	4	8										
1	2	3	4	5	6	7			10	11		9		8										
1	2	3	4	5	6	7			10	11		9		8										
1	2	3	4	5	6	7			10	11		9		8										
1	2	3	4	5		7			10			9	6	8	11									
1	2	3	4	5	6	7			10			9		8	11									
1	2	3	4	5	6	7			10			9		8	11									
1	2	3	4	5	6	7	10					9		8	11									
1	5	3			6	7	10					9	4	8	11	2								
1	2	3	4	5	6	7		9	10	11				8										
1	2	3	4	5	6	7		9	10	11				8										
1	2	3			6			9	10	11				8			4	5	7					
1	2	3			6	7		9	10	11				8			4	5						
1	2	3		5	6	7		9	10	11				8			4							
1	2	3		5	6	7		9	10	11				8			4							
1	2	3		5	6	7		9	10	11			4	8										
1	2	3		5	6	7		9	10				4	8	11									
	2	3		5	6	7		9	10				4	8	11					1				
1	2	3		5	6	7		9	10	11			4	8										
1	2	3	4	5	6	7		9	10					8	11									
	2	3	4	5	6	7		8	10			9			11					1				
	2		4	5	6	7		8	10	11	3	9								1				
1	2		4	5	6	7	11	8	10			9				3								
1	5	3	4		6	7		8	10	11		9				2								
1	2	3	4		6	7	8	9	10	11								5						
1	2	3	4	5	6	7		9	10	11				8										
1	2	3	4	5	6	7		9	10	11				8										
1	2	3	4	5	6	7		9	10	11				8										
1			4					9	10		2		6	8	11	3			7		5			
1		3	4	5	6	7			10	11	2	9		8										
1		3	4	5	6	7		9	10	11	2			8										
1	2	3		5	6	7		9		11				8			4				10			
1	2	3	4	5	6	7		9	10	11				8										
1	2	3	4	5	6	7		9	10	11												8		
1	2	3	4	5	6	7			10	11		9										8		
1	2	3	4	5	6	7			10	11		9										8		
1								9	10		2				11	3	4		7		5		6	8
39	38	38	29	35	39	39	9	29	39	30	6	17	8	28	11	5	6	3	3	3	3	3	1	1
				2		6	3	20	18	3		9		9										

Potts, Jimmy	Townsley, Tom	Menzies, Bill	Edwards, Willis	Hart, Ernie	Reed, George	Turnbull, Bobby	Armand, Jack	Keetley, Charlie	Wainscoat, Russell	Mitchell, Tom	Roberts, Harry	Jennings, Tom	Buck, Teddy	White, Jock	Cochrane, Tom	Milburn, George	Stacey, Alex	Gribben, Bill	McNestry, George	Wilson, James	Longden, Eric	Wilson, George	Underwood, Ben	Firth, Joe
1	2	3	4	5	6	7		9	10	11				8										
1	2	3	4	5	6	7		9	10					8	11									
	2	3	4	5	6	7		9	10					8	11					1				
2	3	3	3	3	3	3	0	3	3	1	0	0	0	3	2	0	0	0	0	1	0	0	0	0
		1			1			2	1						1									

League Table

	P	W	D	L	F	A	Pts
Sheffield Wednesday	42	21	10	11	86	62	52
Leicester City	42	21	9	12	96	67	51
Aston Villa	42	23	4	15	98	81	50
Sunderland	42	20	7	15	93	75	47
Liverpool	42	17	12	13	90	64	46
Derby County	42	18	10	14	86	71	46
Blackburn Rovers	42	17	11	14	72	63	45
Manchester City	42	18	9	15	95	86	45
Arsenal	42	16	13	13	77	72	45
Newcastle United	42	19	6	17	70	72	44
Sheffield United	42	15	11	16	86	85	41
Manchester United	42	14	13	15	66	76	41
Leeds United	42	16	9	17	71	84	41
Bolton Wanderers	42	14	12	16	73	80	40
Birmingham	42	15	10	17	68	77	40
Huddersfield Town	42	14	11	17	70	61	39
West Ham United	42	15	9	18	86	96	39
Everton	42	17	4	21	63	75	38
Burnley	42	15	8	19	81	103	38
Portsmouth	42	15	6	21	56	80	36
Bury	42	12	7	23	62	99	31
Cardiff City	42	8	13	21	43	59	29

1929-30

Division One

Manager: Dick Ray

Final Position: 5th

Did you know that?

25 September 1929: David Mangnall netted 10 goals in United's 13–0 thrashing of Stockport County in a Northern Midweek League game at Elland Road.

11 January 1930: United notched a club record 8–1 win by thrashing Crystal Palace in the FA Cup, Russell Wainscoat scoring a hat-trick.

25 January 1930: That man Vic Watson scored all West Ham's goals as Leeds were beaten 4–1 in the FA Cup and netted a hat-trick as United lost at Upton Park two months later to take his tally against United to 16 goals in four games.

9 April 1930: The 3,950 attendance to see a Charlie Keetley hat-trick beat Sheffield Wednesday was the lowest to witness a League game at Elland Road.

Dave Mangnall.

Match No.	Date	Venue	Opponents	Result	FT	HT	Scorers	Attendance
1	Aug 31	A	Arsenal	L	0-4	0-0		41,855
2	Sep 7	H	Aston Villa	W	4-1	3-1	Roberts 2 (2 pens), Longden, Jennings	23,649
3	11	A	Everton	D	1-1	0-1	Turnbull	24,098
4	14	A	Huddersfield Town	L	0-1	0-1		28,287
5	16	H	Everton	W	2-1	0-1	Wainscoat, Jennings	16,667
6	21	A	Sheffield Wed	W	2-1	2-0	Wainscoat, Jennings	21,353
7	23	H	Portsmouth	W	1-0	1-0	White	14,027
8	28	H	Burnley	W	3-0	1-0	Wainscoat, Hart, White	26,676
9	Oct 5	A	Sunderland	W	4-1	1-1	Mangnall 2, Wainscoat, Turnbull	23,503
10	12	H	Bolton Wanderers	W	2-1	2-0	Turnbull, Mangnall	29,749
11	19	H	Birmingham	W	1-0	0-0	Turnbull	20,067
12	26	A	Leicester City	D	2-2	2-2	Mitchell, Mangnall	27,242
13	Nov 2	H	Grimsby Town	W	6-0	4-0	White, Wainscoat 2, Turnbull, Mangnall, Reed	24,013
14	9	A	Sheffield United	L	2-3	2-2	Turnbull, Mangnall	25,359
15	16	H	West Ham United	L	1-3	0-1	Wainscoat	18,582
16	23	A	Liverpool	L	0-1	0-1		30,643
17	30	H	Middlesbrough	L	1-2	0-2	Reed	19,508
18	Dec 7	A	Blackburn Rovers	L	1-2	0-1	Mitchell	13,504
19	14	H	Newcastle United	W	5-2	3-1	Wainscoat, Longden 2, Jennings 2	21,097
20	21	A	Manchester United	L	1-3	1-3	Longden	15,054
21	25	H	Derby County	W	2-1	1-0	Longden, Wainscoat	25,360
22	26	A	Derby County	L	0-3	0-1		30,307
23	28	H	Arsenal	W	2-0	2-0	Jennings 2	29,167
24	Jan 4	A	Aston Villa	W	4-3	4-1	Jennings 2, White, Wainscoat	32,476
25	18	H	Huddersfield Town	L	0-1	0-1		40,789
26	Feb 1	A	Burnley	W	3-0	0-0	Duggan, Jennings 2	12,505
27	8	H	Sunderland	W	5-0	3-0	Cochrane, Wainscoat 2, Jennings, Longden	22,377
28	15	A	Bolton Wanderers	L	2-4	1-2	Jennings, Duggan	18,104
29	22	A	Birmingham	L	0-1	0-0		17,703
30	Mar 1	H	Leicester City	L	1-2	0-2	Jennings	18,486
31	8	A	Grimsby Town	W	2-1	0-0	Firth, Jennings	16,591
32	15	H	Sheffield United	D	2-2	0-2	Turnbull, Wainscoat	7,569
33	22	A	West Ham United	L	0-3	0-1		18,351
34	29	H	Liverpool	D	1-1	1-0	Wainscoat	14,178
35	Apr 5	A	Middlesbrough	D	1-1	0-0	Keetley	14,136
36	9	H	Sheffield Wed	W	3-0	2-0	Keetley 3	3,950
37	12	H	Blackburn Rovers	W	4-2	3-0	Longden, Keetley, Hart, Mitchell	15,451
38	19	A	Newcastle United	L	1-2	0-1	Keetley	23,066
39	21	A	Manchester City	L	1-4	0-1	Keetley	23,578
40	22	H	Manchester City	W	3-2	2-2	Turnbull, Keetley, Wainscoat	16,636
41	26	H	Manchester United	W	3-1	3-1	Keetley 2, Firth	10,596
42	May 3	A	Portsmouth	D	0-0	0-0		13,925
								Appearances
								Goals

FA Cup

R3	Jan 11	H	Crystal Palace	W	8-1	3-0	Wainscoat 3, White 2, Jennings 2, Turnbull	31,418
R4	25	A	West Ham United	L	1-4	1-3	Jennings	31,000
								Appearances
								Goals

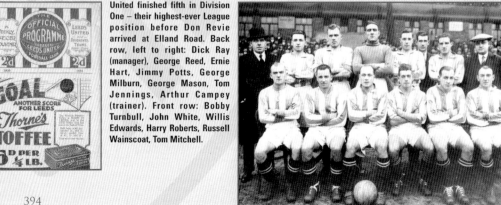

United finished fifth in Division One – their highest-ever League position before Don Revie arrived at Elland Road. Back row, left to right: Dick Ray (manager), George Reed, Ernie Hart, Jimmy Potts, George Milburn, George Mason, Tom Jennings, Arthur Campey (trainer). Front row: Bobby Turnbull, John White, Willis Edwards, Harry Roberts, Russell Wainscoat, Tom Mitchell.

Potts, Jimmy	Roberts, Harry	Menzies, Bill	Edwards, Willis	Hart, Ernie	Underwood, Ben	Turnbull, Bobby	Longden, Eric	Jennings, Tom	Wainscoat, Russell	Mitchell, Tom	Johnson, Bill	Reed, George	White, Jock	Milburn, Jack	Mangnall, Dave	Stacey, Alex	Townsley, Tom	Furness, Billy	Keetley, Charlie	Duggan, Harry	Cochrane, Tom	Firth, Joe	Milburn, George
1	2	3	4	5	6	7	8	9	10	11													
	2	3	4	5	6	7	8	9	10	11	1												
	2	3	4	5	6	7	8	9	10	11	1												
	2	3	4	5		7	8		10	11	1	6	9										
	2		4	5		7		9	10	11	1	6	8	3									
	2		4	5		7		9	10	11	1	6	8	3									
	2		4	5		7		9	10	11	1	6	8	3									
	2		4	5		7			10	11	1	6	8	3	9								
	2		4	5		7			10	11	1	6	8	3	9								
	2		4	5		7			10	11	1	6	8	3	9								
	2					7			10	11	1	6	8	3	9	4	5						
	2		4	5		7			10	11	1	6	8	3	9								
	2					7			10	11	1	6	8	3	9	4	5						
	2		4	5		7			10	11	1	6	8	3	9								
	2		4	5		7			10	11	1	6	8	3	9								
	2		4	5		7			10	11	1	6	8	3	9								
1	2		4	5		7		9		11		6	8	3				10					
1	2		4	5		7	8	9	10	11		6		3									
1	2		4	5		7	8	9	10	11		6		3									
1	2		4	5		7	8	9	10	11		6		3									
1	2		4	5		7	8		10	11		6		3					9				
1	2				6	7	8	9	10	11				3		4	5						
1	2		4			7		9	10	11		6	8	3			5						
1	2		4	5		7		9	10	11		6	8	3									
1	2		4	5		7		9	10	11		6	8	3									
1		3	4				8	9	10			6		2			5			7	11		
1		3	4				8	9	10			6		2			5			7	11		
1		3	4				8	9	10			6		2			5			7	11		
		3	4	5		7	8	9	10	11	1	6		2									
	2		4			7		9		11	1	6		3			5	10				8	
	2		4			7	5	9	10	11	1	6		3								8	
	2		4			7	5	9	10		1	6		3							11	8	
	2		4			7	8	9	10		1	6		3			5				11		
		3	4			7	5	9	10		1	6		2				8			11		
		3	4	5			8		10	7	1	6		2					9		11		
		3	4	5			8		10	11	1	6		2					9	7			
		3	4	5			8		10	11	1	6		2					9	7			
		3	4	5			8		10	11	1	6		2					9	7			
		3	4	5		7	8		10	11	1	6		2					9				
1	2		4	5		7			10			6		3					9		11	8	
1	2		4	5		7			10			6		3					9		11	8	
1			4	5		7	6		10					3					9		11	8	2
16	31	14	39	30	4	35	23	23	40	33	26	37	17	38	9	3	9	3	9	6	10	6	1
	2			2		9	7	14	15	3		2	4		6				10	2	1	2	

Potts, Jimmy	Roberts, Harry	Menzies, Bill	Edwards, Willis	Hart, Ernie	Underwood, Ben	Turnbull, Bobby	Longden, Eric	Jennings, Tom	Wainscoat, Russell	Mitchell, Tom	Johnson, Bill	Reed, George	White, Jock	Milburn, Jack	Mangnall, Dave	Stacey, Alex	Townsley, Tom	Furness, Billy	Keetley, Charlie	Duggan, Harry	Cochrane, Tom	Firth, Joe	Milburn, George
1	2		4	5		7		9	10	11		6	8	3									
1	2		4	5		7		9	10	11		6	8	3									
2	2	0	2	2	0	2	0	2	2	2	0	2	2	2	0	0	0	0	0	0	0	0	0
						1		2	3				2										

League Table

	P	W	D	L	F	A	Pts
Sheffield Wednesday	42	26	8	8	105	57	60
Derby County	42	21	8	13	90	82	50
Manchester City	42	19	9	14	91	81	47
Aston Villa	42	21	5	16	92	83	47
Leeds United	42	20	6	16	79	63	46
Blackburn Rovers	42	19	7	16	99	93	45
West Ham United	42	19	5	18	86	79	43
Leicester City	42	17	9	16	86	90	43
Sunderland	42	18	7	17	76	80	43
Huddersfield Town	42	17	9	16	63	69	43
Birmingham	42	16	9	17	67	62	41
Liverpool	42	16	9	17	63	79	41
Portsmouth	42	15	10	17	66	62	40
Arsenal	42	14	11	17	78	66	39
Bolton Wanderers	42	15	9	18	74	74	39
Middlesbrough	42	16	6	20	82	84	38
Manchester United	42	15	8	19	67	88	38
Grimsby Town	42	15	7	20	73	89	37
Newcastle United	42	15	7	20	71	92	37
Sheffield United	42	15	6	21	91	96	36
Burnley	42	14	8	20	79	97	36
Everton	42	12	11	19	80	92	35

1930-31

Division One

Manager: Dick Ray

Final Position: 21st

Did you know that?

20 September 1930: The 7–3 win at Blackpool is the only time United have scored seven times in a League away match. On the mark were Billy Furness 2, Charlie Keetley 2, (1 pen), Tom Cochrane 2 and Bobby Turnbull.

2 May 1931: Despite beating Derby 3–1, United were relegated along with Manchester United as their big rivals for the drop, Blackpool, drew 2–2 with Manchester City.

England international Bobby Turnbull.

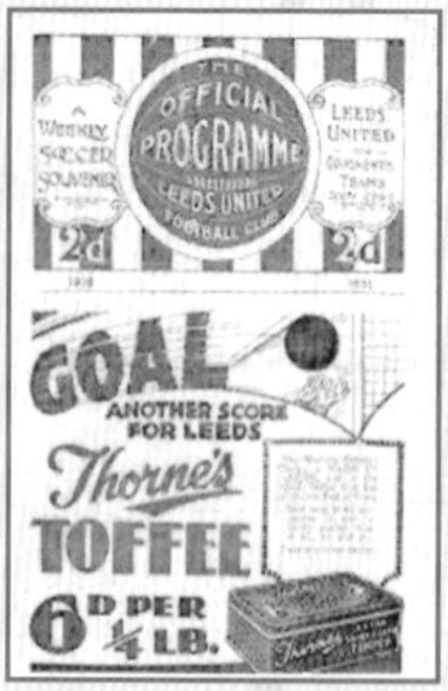

Match No.	Date	Venue	Opponents	Result	FT	HT	Scorers	Attendance
1	Aug 30	H	Portsmouth	D	2-2	2-1	Turnbull, Keetley	15,900
2	Sep 3	A	Derby County	L	1-4	1-3	Wainscoat	13,924
3	6	A	Arsenal	L	1-3	0-1	Furness	40,828
4	8	H	Manchester City	W	4-2	3-1	Cochrane, Keetley 3 (1 pen)	12,295
5	13	H	Blackburn Rovers	W	4-2	3-2	Keetley, Duggan, Furness, Wainscoat	11,837
6	17	A	Manchester City	L	0-1	0-1		17,051
7	20	A	Blackpool	W	7-3	5-0	Furness 2, Keetley 2 (1 pen), Cochrane 2, Turnbull	25,473
8	27	H	Huddersfield Town	L	1-2	1-1	Wainscoat	30,625
9	Oct 4	H	Sunderland	L	0-3	0-1		16,378
10	11	A	Leicester City	L	0-4	0-1		19,405
11	18	A	Liverpool	L	0-2	0-2		25,637
12	25	H	Middlesbrough	W	7-0	3-0	Mitchell, Duggan 2, Wainscoat 2, Jennings 2	18,116
13	Nov 1	A	Newcastle United	L	1-4	1-2	Jennings	13,534
14	8	H	Sheffield Wed	L	2-3	1-2	Jennings, Hart	22,040
15	15	A	West Ham United	D	1-1	0-1	Wainscoat	16,612
16	22	H	Chelsea	L	2-3	1-1	Wainscoat, Duggan	13,602
17	29	A	Grimsby Town	L	0-2	0-1		6,783
18	Dec 6	H	Bolton Wanderers	W	3-1	2-0	Turnbull, Wainscoat, Keetley	7,595
19	13	A	Aston Villa	L	3-4	1-3	Turnbull, Keetley 2	26,272
20	20	H	Manchester United	W	5-0	2-0	Waiscoat, Turnbull 3, Furness	11,282
21	25	A	Birmingham	W	1-0	0-0	Furness	24,991
22	26	H	Birmingham	W	3-1	2-1	Keetley, Furness 2	12,381
23	27	A	Portsmouth	D	1-1	1-1	Keetley	18,530
24	jan 1	A	Manchester United	D	0-0	0-0		9,875
25	17	A	Blackburn Rovers	L	1-3	1-1	Hydes	11,975
26	28	H	Blackpool	D	2-2	2-1	Hart, Turnbull	7,750
27	31	A	Huddersfield Town	L	0-3	0-1		13,044
28	Feb 7	A	Sunderland	L	0-4	0-2		25,765
29	18	H	Leicester City	L	1-3	1-3	Duggan	5,572
30	21	H	Liverpool	L	1-2	0-1	Wainscoat	15,570
31	28	A	Middlesbrough	L	0-5	0-3		15,707
32	Mar 7	H	Newcastle United	W	1-0	1-0	Turnbull (pen)	6,845
33	11	H	Arsenal	L	1-2	0-2	Turnbull (pen)	12,212
34	14	A	Sheffield Wed	L	1-2	0-1	Wainscoat	14,562
35	21	H	West Ham United	W	3-0	1-0	Turnbull (pen), Alderson 2	11,611
36	28	A	Chelsea	L	0-1	0-0		25,446
37	Apr 4	H	Grimsby Town	D	0-0	0-0		14,951
38	6	A	Sheffield United	D	1-1	1-1	Copping	12,948
39	7	H	Sheffield United	W	4-0	2-0	Keetley 2, Thorpe (og), Wainscoat	13,315
40	11	A	Bolton Wanderers	L	0-2	0-1		15,438
41	18	H	Aston Villa	L	0-2	0-1		10,388
42	May 2	H	Derby County	W	3-1	2-0	Keetley 2, Green	11,190
								Appearances
							One own-goal	Goals

FA Cup

Round	Date	Venue	Opponents	Result	FT	HT	Scorers	Attendance
R3	Jan 10	H	Huddersfield Town	W	2-0	0-0	Hydes, Furness	41,103
R4	24	H	Newcastle United	W	4-1	2-0	Furness, Wainscoat 2, Mitchell	40,261
R5	Feb 14	A	Exeter City	L	1-3	0-2	Mitchell	19,130
								Appearances
								Goals

This was the season United reached the fifth round of the FA Cup for the first time, only to lose at Third Division South club Exeter City. Ten weeks later United were relegated from Division One. Back row, left to right: Wilf Copping, George Milburn, Jimmy Potts, Ernie Hart, Jack Milburn, Willis Edwards. Front row: Bobby Turnbull, Billy Furness, Charlie Keetley, Russell Wainscoat, Tom Mitchell.

Johnson, Bill	Roberts, Harry	Milburn, Jack	Edwards, Willis	Hart, Ernie	Copping, Wilf	Turnbull, Bobby	Longden, Eric	Keetley, Charlie	Wainscoat, Russell	Cochrane, Tom	Mitchell, Tom	Potts, Jimmy	Milburn, George	Duggan, Harry	Firth, Joe	Jennings, Tom	Furness, Billy	Townsley, Tom	Hornby, Cyril	Underwood, Ben	Hydes, Arthur	Green, Harry	Brown, Vic	Menzies, Bill	Alderson, Tom	Danskin, Bob
1	2	3	4	5	6	7	8	9	10	11																
1	2	3	4	5	6	7	8	9	10		11															
		3	4	5	6					11		1	2	7	8	9	10									
		3	4		6			9		11		1	2	7	8		10	5								
		3	4		6			9	10	11		1	2	7			8	5								
		3	4		6			9	10	11		1	2	7			8	5								
		3	4	5	6	7		9	10	11		1	2				8									
		3	4	5	6	7		9	10	11		1	2				8									
		3	4	5	6	7		9	10	11		1					8	2								
		3	4	5	6			9			11	1	2	7			10		8							
		3	4	5	6			9			11	1		7			10	2	8							
	2	3	4	5	6				10		11	1		7		9	8									
	2	3	4	5	6				10		11	1		7		9	8									
	2	3	4	5	6				10	11		1		7		9	8									
1		3	4	5	6				10	11			2	7		9	8									
1		3	4	5	6				10	11			2	7		9	8									
		3	4	5	6	7		9	10	11		1	2				8									
		3	4	5	6	7		9	10		11	1	2				8									
		3	4	5	6	7		9	10		11	1	2				8									
		3	4	5	6	7		9	10		11	1	2				8									
		3	4	5	6	7		9	10		11	1	2				8									
		3	4	5	6	7		9	10		11	1	2				8									
		3			6	7		9		11		1	2				8	5	10	4						
		3	4	5	6	7			10		11	1	2			9	8									
		3	4	5	6	7			10		11	1	2				8				9					
		3	4	5	6	7		9	10		11	1	2				8									
		3		5	6	7		9	10		11	1	2				8		4							
		3	4	5	6			9		11		1	2				8		10			7				
		3	4		6				10	11		1		7				5	8		9		2			
		2	4	5	6	7			10	11		1				9	8							3		
		2	4	5	6			9		11		1					10		8			7		3		
		2	4	5	6	7		9		11		1					10		8					3		
		2	4	5	6	7		9	10	11		1							8					3		
		2	4	5	6	7		9	10	11		1					8							3		
		2	4	5	6	7			10	11		1					8							3	9	
		2	4	5	6	7			10	11		1					8							3	9	
		2	4	5	6	7			10	11		1					8							3	9	
		2	4	5	6	7		9	10	11		1					8							3		
		2	4	5	6	7		9	10	11		1												3	8	
		2	4	5	6	7		9	10	11		1					8							3		
		2	4	5	6	7		9	10	11		1					8							3		
			4		6			9		11		1	2				10		8			7		3		5
4	5	41	40	36	42	27	2	29	33	28	14	38	22	12	2	8	37	7	10	1	2	3	1	13	4	1
				2	1	11		16	12	3	1			5		4	8				1	1			2	

Johnson, Bill	Roberts, Harry	Milburn, Jack	Edwards, Willis	Hart, Ernie	Copping, Wilf	Turnbull, Bobby	Longden, Eric	Keetley, Charlie	Wainscoat, Russell	Cochrane, Tom	Mitchell, Tom	Potts, Jimmy	Milburn, George	Duggan, Harry	Firth, Joe	Jennings, Tom	Furness, Billy	Townsley, Tom	Hornby, Cyril	Underwood, Ben	Hydes, Arthur	Green, Harry	Brown, Vic	Menzies, Bill	Alderson, Tom	Danskin, Bob
		3	4	5	6	7			10	11		1	2				8								9	
		3	4	5	6	7		9	10	11		1	2				8									
		3	4	5	6	7			10	11		1	2				8								9	
0	0	3	3	3	3	3	0	1	3	3	0	3	3	0	0	0	3	0	0	0	0	0	0	0	2	0
									2	2							2								1	

League Table

	P	W	D	L	F	A	Pts
Arsenal	42	28	10	4	127	59	66
Aston Villa	42	25	9	8	128	78	59
Sheffield Wednesday	42	22	8	12	102	75	52
Portsmouth	42	18	13	11	84	67	49
Huddersfield Town	42	18	12	12	81	65	48
Derby County	42	18	10	14	94	79	46
Middlesbrough	42	19	8	15	98	90	46
Manchester City	42	18	10	14	75	70	46
Liverpool	42	15	12	15	86	85	42
Blackburn Rovers	42	17	8	17	83	84	42
Sunderland	42	16	9	17	89	85	41
Chelsea	42	15	10	17	64	67	40
Grimsby Town	42	17	5	20	82	87	39
Bolton Wanderers	42	15	9	18	68	81	39
Sheffield United	42	14	10	18	78	84	38
Leicester City	42	16	6	20	80	95	38
Newcastle United	42	15	6	21	78	87	36
West Ham United	42	14	8	20	79	94	36
Birmingham	42	13	10	19	55	70	36
Blackpool	42	11	10	21	71	125	32
Leeds United	42	12	7	23	68	81	31
Manchester United	42	7	8	27	53	115	22

1931-32

Division Two

Manager: Dick Ray

Final Position: 2nd

Did you know that?

21 November 1931: A crushing 5–0 win at Burnley set a club record nine successive wins as United moved into top spot. They eventually finished runners-up to Wolves.

9 January 1932: United lost 3–1 against QPR in the FA Cup in front of 41,097 at the White City, the biggest attendance ever to see a Rangers home game.

Great servants Russell Wainscoat and Tom Townsley left United at the end of the season.

Match No.	Date		Venue	Opponents	Result	FT	HT	Scorers	Attendance
1	Aug	29	A	Swansea Town	W	2-0	2-0	Firth, Green	16,175
2		31	A	Port Vale	W	2-1	1-0	Wainscoat, Green	16,874
3	Sep	5	H	Barnsley	L	0-1	0-1		13,078
4		7	H	Millwall	L	0-1	0-1		8,388
5		12	A	Notts County	D	1-1	1-1	Cochrane	12,630
6		14	A	Millwall	W	3-2	1-1	Keetley, Furness, Cochrane	11,844
7		19	H	Plymouth Argyle	D	0-0	0-0		10,782
8		26	A	Bristol City	W	2-0	1-0	Furness, Keetley	9,157
9	Oct	3	H	Oldham Athletic	W	5-0	3-0	Keetley 3, Cochrane 2	12,336
10		10	A	Bury	W	4-1	1-0	Firth, Duggan, Hart, Keetley	16,353
11		17	H	Wolverhampton W	W	2-1	0-1	Furness, Keetley	13,825
12		24	A	Charlton Athletic	W	1-0	0-0	Furness	11,303
13		31	H	Stoke City	W	2-0	1-0	Cochrane, Furness	15,524
14	Nov	7	A	Manchester United	W	5-2	1-0	Duggan, Firth 2, Keetley, Furness	9,512
15		14	H	Preston North End	W	4-1	2-1	Firth 2, Furness, Keetley	15,439
16		21	A	Burnley	W	5-0	3-0	Cochrane 2, Furness, Firth 2	12,767
17		28	H	Chesterfield	D	3-3	3-1	Keetley 2, Furness	13,483
18	Dec	5	A	Nottingham Forest	D	3-3	3-2	Keetley 2, Furness	12,214
19		12	H	Tottenham Hotspur	W	1-0	1-0	Green	15,689
20		19	A	Southampton	L	1-2	0-1	Duggan	11,736
21		25	A	Bradford PA	L	0-3	0-1		32,421
22		26	H	Bradford PA	W	3-2	2-1	Duggan, Keetley 2	34,005
23	Jan	2	H	Swansea Town	W	3-2	2-1	Keetley, Firth, Danskin	12,885
24		16	A	Barnsley	W	2-0	1-0	Keetley, Firth	9,136
25		23	H	Notts County	D	2-2	2-1	Keetley 2	14,562
26		30	A	Plymouth Argyle	L	2-3	1-1	Firth, Hydes	28,426
27	Feb	6	H	Bristol City	W	1-0	0-0	Firth	10,677
28		13	A	Oldham Athletic	L	1-2	1-0	Keetley	6,496
29		20	H	Bury	W	1-0	1-0	Firth	13,748
30		27	A	Wolverhampton W	D	1-1	1-1	Cochrane	34,520
31	Mar	5	H	Charlton Athletic	W	2-0	1-0	Firth, Keetley	11,092
32		12	A	Stoke City	W	4-3	1-1	Bennett 2, Keetley, Hornby	17,981
33		19	H	Manchester United	L	1-4	1-2	Bennett	13,644
34		26	A	Preston North End	D	0-0	0-0		12,151
35		28	A	Bradford City	L	1-4	0-1	Bennett	22,354
36		29	H	Bradford City	D	1-1	0-0	Hydes	18,277
37	Apr	2	H	Burnley	W	3-1	1-1	Cochrane, Furness, Hydes	13,037
38		9	A	Chesterfield	D	1-1	1-0	Duggan	11,992
39		16	H	Nottingham Forest	D	1-1	1-1	J. Milburn (pen)	12,195
40		23	A	Tottenham Hotspur	L	1-3	1-1	Furness	17,285
41		30	H	Southampton	W	1-0	1-0	Keetley	13,401
42	May	7	H	Port Vale	L	0-2	0-1		9,588
									Appearances
									Goals

FA Cup

R3	Jan	9	A	Queen's Park R	L	1-3	0-2	J. Milburn (pen)	41,097
									Appearances
									Goals

Potts, Jimmy	Milburn, Jack	Menzies, Bill	Edwards, Willis	Hart, Ernie	Copping, Wilf	Green, Harry	Firth, Joe	Keetley, Charlie	Wainscoat, Russell	Cochrane, Tom	Stacey, Alex	Danskin, Bob	Milburn, George	Hydes, Arthur	Furness, Billy	Duggan, Harry	Turnbull, Bobby	Hornby, Cyril	Bennett, Bill	Moore, Stan	Mahon, Jack	Wilkinson, Charlie	Neal, Tom
1	2	3	4	5	6	7	8	9	10	11													
1	2	3			6	7	8	9	10	11	4	5											
1	2	3	4	5	6	7	8	9	10	11													
1	3		4		6	7	8			11		5	2	9	10								
1	3		4	5	6		8	9		11			2		10	7							
1	3		4	5	6		8	9		11			2		10	7							
1	2	3	4	5	6		8	9		11					10	7							
1	2	3	4	5	6		8	9		11					10	7							
1	2	3	4	5	6		8	9		11					10	7							
1	2	3	4	5	6		8	9		11					10	7							
1	2	3		5	6		8	9		11	4				10	7							
1	2	3	4	5	6		8	9		11					10	7							
1	2	3	4	5	6		8	9		11					10	7							
1	2	3		5	6		8	9		11	4				10	7							
1	2	3	4	5	6		8	9		11					10	7							
1	2	3	4	5	6		8	9		11					10	7							
1	2	3	4	5	6		8	9		11					10		7						
1	2	3	4	5	6		8	9		11					10	7							
1	2	3	4	5	6	7	8	9		11					10								
1	2	3	4	5	6		8	9		11					10	7							
1	3			5	6		8			11	4		2	9	10	7							
1		3		5	6		8	9		11			2			7		4	10				
1	3		4		6		8	9		11		5	2			7			10				
	3		4	5	6		8	9		11			2			7			10	1			
	3		4	5	6		8	9		11			2	10		7				1			
	3			5	6	7	8	9					2	10				4		1	11		
	2	3		5	6		8	9		11				10		7		4		1			
	2	3		5	6		8	9		11						7		4	10	1			
	2	3		5	6		8	9		11						7		4	10	1			
	3			5	6			9		11	4		2			7		8	10	1			
	3			5	6		8	9		11	4		2			7			10	1			
	3		4	5	6			9		11			2			7		8	10	1			
	3			5	6			9		11	4		2			7		8	10	1			
1	2		4	5	6			9		11					10	7		8				3	
1	2			5	6			9		11	4					7		8	10			3	
1	2	3	4	5	6					10				9		7		8			11		
1	2	3	4	5		7				11				9	10	8							6
1	2	3		5		7		9		11	4				10	8							6
1	2	3	4	5	6	7		9		11					10	8							
1	2	3	4	5	6		8			11				9	10	7							
1	2	3	4	5	6		8	9		11					10	7							
1	2	3	4		6		8	9		11		5			10	7							
32	41	28	28	38	40	9	33	37	3	41	9	4	13	8	25	35	1	11	10	10	2	2	2
	1			1		3	14	23	1	9		1		3	12	5		1	4				

	2	3	4		6		8	9		11		5				7			10	1			
0	1	1	1	0	1	0	1	1	0	1	0	1	0	0	0	1	0	0	1	1	0	0	0
	1																						

League Table

	P	W	D	L	F	A	Pts
Wolverhampton W	42	24	8	10	115	49	56
Leeds United	42	22	10	10	78	54	54
Stoke City	42	19	14	9	69	48	52
Plymouth Argyle	42	20	9	13	100	66	49
Bury	42	21	7	14	70	58	49
Bradford Park Avenue	42	21	7	14	72	63	49
Bradford City	42	16	13	13	80	61	45
Tottenham Hotspur	42	16	11	15	87	78	43
Millwall	42	17	9	16	61	61	43
Charlton Athletic	42	17	9	16	61	66	43
Nottingham Forest	42	16	10	16	77	72	42
Manchester United	42	17	8	17	71	72	42
Preston North End	42	16	10	16	75	77	42
Southampton	42	17	7	18	66	77	41
Swansea Town	42	16	7	19	73	75	39
Notts County	42	13	12	17	75	75	38
Chesterfield	42	13	11	18	64	86	37
Oldham Athletic	42	13	10	19	62	84	36
Burnley	42	13	9	20	59	87	35
Port Vale	42	13	7	22	58	89	33
Barnsley	42	12	9	21	55	91	33
Bristol City	42	6	11	25	39	78	23

1932-33

Division One

Manager: Dick Ray

Final Position: 8th

Did you know that?

27 December 1932: The 56,796 crowd which saw United and Arsenal battle out a 0–0 draw over the festive period smashed the Elland Road attendance record which was set in 1927–28. The new mark was to stand for 35 years. The Leeds board were delighted to bank record receipts of £3,508.

6 May 1933: Brothers George and Jack Milburn completed all 42 League games as full-back partners.

Jack Milburn.

George Milburn.

Match No.	Date	Venue	Opponents	Result	FT	HT	Scorers	Attendance
1	Aug 27	H	Derby County	L	0-2	0-1		16,344
2	29	A	Blackpool	L	1-2	1-1	Roper	20,313
3	Sep 3	A	Blackburn Rovers	D	1-1	0-0	Cochrane	13,010
4	5	H	Blackpool	W	3-1	2-1	Keetley, Copping, Furness	9,171
5	10	H	Huddersfield Town	H	1-1	1-0	Keetley	23,882
6	17	H	Sheffield Wed	W	3-2	2-1	Keetley 2, Duggan	17,977
7	24	A	West Bromwich Alb	W	1-0	1-0	Keetley	26,497
8	Oct 1	H	Birmingham	D	1-1	1-0	Duggan	14,193
9	8	A	Sunderland	D	0-0	0-0		9,651
10	15	H	Manchester City	W	2-1	2-1	Hydes, J. Milburn (pen)	16,898
11	22	A	Sheffield United	D	0-0	0-0		13,842
12	29	H	Wolverhampton W	W	2-0	2-0	O'Grady, Hydes	11,486
13	Nov 5	A	Liverpool	W	1-0	1-0	Duggan	25,464
14	12	H	Leicester City	D	1-1	0-1	Hydes	12,426
15	19	A	Portsmouth	D	3-3	0-2	J. Milburn (pen), Furness, Cochrane	17,579
16	26	H	Chelsea	W	2-0	1-0	Hydes 2	19,709
17	Dec 3	A	Newcastle United	L	1-3	0-0	Hydes	20,965
18	10	H	Aston Villa	D	1-1	1-0	Hydes	23,794
19	17	A	Middlesbrough	W	1-0	0-0	Keetley	9,341
20	24	H	Bolton Wanderers	W	4-3	3-0	Hydes 2, Keetley, Furness	15,804
21	26	A	Arsenal	W	2-1	1-1	Keetley 2	55,876
22	27	H	Arsenal	D	0-0	0-0		56,796
23	31	A	Derby County	L	1-5	1-1	Keetley	13,375
24	Jan 7	H	Blackburn Rovers	W	3-1	1-1	Furness, Keetley, Mahon	14,043
25	21	A	Huddersfield Town	D	2-2	2-1	O'Grady, Furness	18,619
26	Feb 4	H	West Bromwich Alb	D	1-1	0-0	Hydes	19,696
27	8	A	Sheffield Wed	L	0-2	0-2		9,585
28	11	A	Birmingham	L	1-2	0-2	Hydes	22,157
29	22	H	Sunderland	L	2-3	2-1	Hydes, Duggan	7,971
30	Mar 4	H	Sheffield United	L	1-3	0-0	Hydes	13,448
31	11	A	Wolverhampton W	D	3-3	0-2	Keetley 3	24,901
32	18	H	Liverpool	W	5-0	1-0	Bradshaw (og), Mahon 2, Hydes, Duggan	12,268
33	25	A	Leicester City	L	1-3	0-2	Furness	13,669
34	Apr 1	H	Portsmouth	L	0-1	0-0		9,839
35	5	A	Manchester City	D	0-0	0-0		16,789
36	8	A	Chelsea	L	0-6	0-1		31,095
37	15	H	Newcastle United	W	6-1	3-1	Fowler 2, Mahon 2, Copping, Hydes	14,967
38	17	A	Everton	W	1-0	1-0	Hydes	21,265
39	18	H	Everton	W	1-0	1-0	Duggan	19,663
40	22	A	Aston Villa	D	0-0	0-0		21,238
41	29	H	Middlesbrough	L	0-1	0-1		9,006
42	May 6	A	Bolton Wanderers	L	0-5	0-3		10,048
								Appearances
							One own-goal	Goals

FA Cup

R3	Jan 14	A	Newcastle United	W	3-0	2-0	Hydes 3	47,554
R4	28	A	Tranmere Rovers	D	0-0	0-0		20,000
Rep	Feb 1	H	Tranmere Rovers	W	4-0	1-0	J. Milburn (pen), Mahon, Cochrane, Hydes	25,000
R5	18	A	Everton	L	0-2	0-1		58,073
								Appearances
								Goals

Potts, Jimmy	Milburn, George	Milburn, Jack	Edwards, Willis	Hart, Ernie	Copping, Wilf	Green, Harry	Firth, Joe	Hydes, Arthur	Furness, Billy	Mahon, Jack	Stacey, Alex	Roper, Harry	Cochrane, Tom	Keetley, Charlie	Duggan, Harry	O'Grady, Harry	Neal, Tom	Hornby, Cyril	Fowler, Alan	Moore, Stan
1	2	3	4	5	6	7	8	9	10	11										
1	2	3		5	6	7		9	10		4	8	11							
1	2	3		5	6	7	8		10		4		11	9						
1	2	3		5	6			8	10		4		11	9	7					
1	2	3		5	6			8	10		4		11	9	7					
1	2	3		5	6			8	10		4		11	9	7					
1	2	3		5	6			8	10		4		11	9	7					
1	2	3		5	6	7		8	10		4		11		9					
1	2	3		5	6			8	10		4		11	9	7					
1	2	3		5	6			8	10		4		11	9	7					
1	2	3		5	6			8	10		4		11	9	7					
1	2	3		5	6			9	10		4		11		7	8				
1	2	3		5	6			9	10		4		11		7	8				
1	2	3		5	6			9	10		4		11		7	8				
1	2	3		5	6			9	10		4		11		7	8				
1	2	3		5	6			9	10		4		11		7	8				
1	2	3		5	6	7		8	10		4		11	9						
1	2	3	4	5	6			8	10	7			11	9						
1	2	3		5	6			8	10	7	4		11	9						
1	2	3		5	6			8	10	7	4		11	9						
1	2	3		5	6			8	10	7	4		11	9						
1	2	3	4	5	6			8	10				11	9	7					
1	2	3	4	5	6			8	10	7			11	9						
1	2	3	4	5	6			8	10	7			11	9						
1	2	3	4	5	6				10	7			11	9		8				
1	2	3	4	5				9	10	7			11			8	6			
1	2	3	4					9	10	7			11			8	6	5		
1	2	3	4	5				8	10	7			11				6		9	
1	2	3	4	5	6		8	9	10				11		7					
1	2	3	4	5	6		8	9	10				11		7					
	2	3	4	5	6			8	10				11	9	7					1
	2	3	4	5	6			8	10	11				9	7					1
	2	3	4	5	6			8	10	11				9	7					1
	2	3	4		6		8		10	11				9	7			5		1
	2	3	4	5	6			8	10	11				9	7					1
	2	3	4	5	6			8	10	11				9	7					1
	2	3	4	5	6			8	10	11					7				9	1
	2	3	4	5	6			8	10	11					7				9	1
	2	3	4	5	6			8	10	11					7				9	1
	2	3	4	5	6			8	10	11					7				9	1
	2	3	4	5	6			8	10	11					7				9	1
	2	3	4		6			8	10	11				9	7			5		1
30	42	42	23	39	39	5	5	39	42	22	19	1	30	24	28	8	3	3	6	12
		2			2			16	6	5		1	2	14	6	2			2	

1	2	3	4	5	6			8	10	7			11	9						
1	2	3	4	5	6			8	10	7			11	9						
1	2	3	4	5	6			9	10	7			11			8				
1	2	3	4	5	6			8	10				11	9	7					
4	4	4	4	4	4	0	0	4	4	3	0	0	4	3	1	1	0	0	0	0
		1						4		1			1							

League Table

	P	W	D	L	F	A	Pts
Arsenal	42	25	8	9	118	61	58
Aston Villa	42	23	8	11	92	67	54
Sheffield Wednesday	42	21	9	12	80	68	51
West Bromwich Albion	42	20	9	13	83	70	49
Newcastle United	42	22	5	15	71	63	49
Huddersfield Town	42	18	11	13	66	53	47
Derby County	42	15	14	13	76	69	44
Leeds United	42	15	14	13	59	62	44
Portsmouth	42	18	7	17	74	76	43
Sheffield United	42	17	9	16	74	80	43
Everton	42	16	9	17	81	74	41
Sunderland	42	15	10	17	63	80	40
Birmingham	42	14	11	17	57	57	39
Liverpool	42	14	11	17	79	84	39
Blackburn Rovers	42	14	10	18	76	102	38
Manchester City	42	16	5	21	68	71	37
Middlesbrough	42	14	9	19	63	73	37
Chelsea	42	14	7	21	63	73	35
Leicester City	42	11	13	18	75	89	35
Wolverhampton W	42	13	9	20	80	96	35
Bolton Wanderers	42	12	9	21	78	92	33
Blackpool	42	14	5	23	69	85	33

1933-34

Division One

Manager: Dick Ray

Final Position: 9th

Did you know that?

7 April 1934: The 8–0 win against Leicester City at Elland Road was a club record beating the previous best – a 7–0 thumping of Middlesbrough on 25 October 1930. Ironically, Arthur Hydes, United's top scorer, did not play and missed out on the goal feast.

Arthur Hydes.

Match No.	Date		Venue	Opponents	Result	FT	HT	Scorers	Attendance
1	Aug	26	A	Blackburn Rovers	L	2-4	1-2	Hydes, Cochrane	10,130
2		28	H	Middlesbrough	W	5-2	2-2	Hydes 4, Roper	10,896
3	Sep	2	H	Newcastle United	W	3-0	1-0	J. Milburn (pen), Cochrane, Hydes	17,721
4		9	A	Huddersfield Town	D	0-0	0-0		18,976
5		16	A	Derby County	L	1-3	1-2	Hydes	16,584
6		23	H	West Bromwich Alb	W	3-0	1-0	Hydes 2, G. Shaw (og)	17,364
7		30	A	Birmingham	L	0-4	0-3		21,566
8	Oct	7	H	Sheffield Wed	W	2-1	2-1	Fowler 2	16,165
9		14	A	Manchester City	W	1-0	0-0	Fowler	22,413
10		21	H	Portsmouth	W	1-0	0-0	Fowler	18,255
11		28	A	Sunderland	L	2-4	2-3	Fowler, Keetley	14,578
12	Nov	4	H	Aston Villa	L	2-4	0-1	Hornby, Furness (pen)	20,148
13		11	A	Liverpool	L	3-4	2-1	Hydes, Fowler, Duggan	26,181
14		18	H	Tottenham Hotspur	D	0-0	0-0		19,681
15		25	A	Leicester City	D	2-2	2-1	Duggan, Hydes	14,022
16	Dec	2	H	Stoke City	W	2-0	2-0	Keetley, Hydes	12,601
17		9	A	Sheffield United	L	1-2	0-0	Furness	11,113
18		16	H	Wolverhampton W	D	3-3	2-1	Keetley 2, Duggan	11,013
19		23	A	Chelsea	D	1-1	0-1	Keetley	18,157
20		25	H	Arsenal	L	0-1	0-1		33,192
21		26	A	Arsenal	L	0-2	0-1		22,817
22		30	H	Blackburn Rovers	W	4-0	3-0	Hydes 3, Furness	10,722
23	Jan	1	A	Middlesbrough	L	1-2	0-1	Hydes	16,071
24		6	A	Newcastle United	L	0-2	0-0		21,587
25		20	H	Huddersfield Town	D	1-1	0-1	J. Milburn (pen)	24,957
26		31	H	Derby County	L	0-2	0-1		11,790
27	Feb	3	A	West Bromwich Alb	W	3-0	2-0	Roper, Mahon 2	13,343
28		10	H	Birmingham	W	1-0	1-0	Furness	14,753
29		24	H	Manchester City	W	3-1	2-0	Firth, Mahon, Furness	15,761
30		26	A	Sheffield Wed	W	2-0	1-0	Firth, Keetley	6,546
31	Mar	7	A	Portsmouth	L	1-2	1-1	Copping	10,568
32		10	H	Sunderland	W	3-1	2-0	Cochrane, Duggan, Furness	7,333
33		24	H	Liverpool	W	5-1	3-1	Mahon, Firth 2, Duggan 2	12,907
34		30	H	Everton	D	2-2	1-1	Duggan 2	19,951
35		31	A	Tottenham Hotspur	L	1-5	1-2	Keetley	29,574
36	Apr	2	A	Everton	L	0-2	0-2		25,624
37		7	H	Leicester City	W	8-0	4-0	Duggan 2, Mahon 2, Furness 2, Firth 2	11,871
38		14	A	Stoke City	W	2-1	1-1	Duggan, Firth	16,262
39		21	H	Sheffield United	D	1-1	0-0	Holmes (og)	10,815
40		28	A	Wolverhampton W	L	0-2	0-1		5,571
41		30	A	Aston Villa	L	0-3	0-1		9,849
42	May	5	H	Chelsea	W	3-1	2-0	Mahon, Firth, Cochrane	6,092
									Appearances
								Two own-goals	Goals

FA Cup

R3	Jan	13	H	Preston North End	L	0-1	0-1		29,158
									Appearances
									Goals

Back row, left to right: Cyril Hornby, George Milburn, Stan Moore, Fred Jones, Jack Milburn, Wilf Copping. Front row: Johnny Mahon, Harry Roper, Ernie Hart, Charlie Keetley, Billy Furness, Tom Cochrane.

Moore, Stan	Milburn, George	Milburn, Jack	Stacey, Alex	Edwards, Willis	Copping, Wilf	Duggan, Harry	Roper, Harry	Hydes, Arthur	Furness, Billy	Cochrane, Tom	Wilkinson, Charlie	Turner, Charlie	Hart, Ernie	Fowler, Alan	Neal, Tom	Green, Harry	Keetley, Charlie	Hornby, Cyril	Sproston, Bert	Firth, Joe	Mahon, Jack
1	2	3	4	5	6	7	8	9	10	11											
1	2		4		6	7	8	9	10	11	3	5									
1	2	3	4		6	7	8	9	10	11		5									
1	2	3	4		6	7	8	9	10	11		5									
1	2	3	4		6	7	8	9	10	11		5									
1	2	3	4		6	7	8	9	10	11			5								
1	2	3	4		6	7	8	9	10	11			5								
1	2	3	4		6	7	8		10	11			5	9							
1	2	3	4				8		10	11			5	9	6	7					
1	2	3	4		6	7	8		10	11			5	9							
1	2	3	4		6	7			10	11			5	9			8				
1	2	3	4		6	7			10	11			5	9				8			
1	2	3		4	6	7	8		10	11			5	9							
1	2	3		4	6	7	8		10	11			5	9							
1	2	3		4	6	7		9	10	11			5				8				
1	2	3		4	6	7		9	10	11			5				8				
1	2	3		4	6	7		9	10	11			5				8				
1	2	3		4	6	7		9	10	11			5				8				
1		3		4	6	7		9	10	11			5				8		2		
1		3		4	6	7		9	10	11			5				8		2		
1		3			6	7		9	10	11		5						4	2	8	
1		3			6	7		9	10	11			5					4	2	8	
1		3			6	7		9	10	11			5					4	2	8	
1	2	3			6	7		9	10	11			5					4		8	
1	2	3			6		8		10			5		9		7		4			11
1	2	3			6		8		10	11		5		9				4			7
1	2	3			6		8		10	11			5				9	4			7
1	2	3					8		10	11			5				9	4		6	7
1	2	3			6				10	11			5				9	4		8	7
1	2	3			6				10	11			5				9	4		8	7
1	2	3			6				10	11			5				9	4		8	7
1	2	3			6	9			10	11			5					4		8	7
1	2	3			6	9			10	11			5					4		8	7
1	2	3			6	9			10	11			5					4		8	7
1	2	3			6	9				11			5				10	4		8	7
1	2	3			6	9			10	11			5				8	4			7
1	2	3		4	6	9			10	11			5							8	7
1	2	3		4		9			10	11		5						6		8	7
1	2	3		4	6	9			10	11			5							8	7
1	2	3		4	6	9			10	11			5							8	7
1	2	3		4	6				10	11			5				9			8	7
1	2	3		4		9			10	11			5					6		8	7
42	37	41	12	15	38	33	14	19	41	41	1	8	33	9	1	2	15	19	5	18	18
		2			1	11	2	16	8	4				6			7	1		8	7

1	2	3			6	7			10	11			5				9	4		8	
1	1	1	0	0	1	1	0	0	1	1	0	0	1	0	0	0	1	1	0	1	0

League Table

	P	W	D	L	F	A	Pts
Arsenal	42	25	9	8	75	47	59
Huddersfield Town	42	23	10	9	90	61	56
Tottenham Hotspur	42	21	7	14	79	56	49
Derby County	42	17	11	14	68	54	45
Manchester City	42	17	11	14	65	72	45
Sunderland	42	16	12	14	81	56	44
West Bromwich Albion	42	17	10	15	78	70	44
Blackburn Rovers	42	18	7	17	74	81	43
Leeds United	42	17	8	17	75	66	42
Portsmouth	42	15	12	15	52	55	42
Sheffield Wednesday	42	16	9	17	62	67	41
Stoke City	42	15	11	16	58	71	41
Aston Villa	42	14	12	16	78	75	40
Everton	42	12	16	14	62	63	40
Wolverhampton W	42	14	12	16	74	86	40
Middlesbrough	42	16	7	19	68	80	39
Leicester City	42	14	11	17	59	74	39
Liverpool	42	14	10	18	79	87	38
Chelsea	42	14	8	20	67	69	36
Birmingham	42	12	12	18	54	56	36
Newcastle United	42	10	14	18	68	77	34
Sheffield United	42	12	7	23	58	101	31

1934-35

Division One

Manager: Dick Ray then Billy Hampson

Final Position: 18th

Did you know that?

27 August 1934: The season could hardly have got off to a worse start. After losing their opening game 4–2 at home to Middlesbrough, United crashed 8–1 at Stoke two days later with Stanley Matthews scoring four times. It was United's heaviest defeat in the club's history and came just seven games after recording their best-ever win.

22 September 1934: United ditched their blue and white stripes and appeared in blue and gold halved shirts for the first time in the 3–0 home defeat against Liverpool.

29 September 1934: United's 2–0 victory against West Riding rivals Huddersfield Town was their first against the Terriers in 17 attempts.

Willis Edwards passed through the 300 League games barrier.

Match No.	Date	Venue	Opponents	Result	FT	HT	Scorers	Attendance
1	Aug 25	H	Middlesbrough	L	2-4	1-1	Mills 2	15,949
2	27	A	Stoke City	L	1-8	1-4	Hornby	24,568
3	Sep 1	A	Blackburn Rovers	D	1-1	0-1	J. Milburn (pen)	12,316
4	3	H	Stoke City	W	4-2	3-1	Cochrane, Mahon, Furness, Duggan	8,932
5	8	H	Arsenal	D	1-1	0-1	Furness	29,447
6	15	A	Portsmouth	D	0-0	0-0		17,470
7	22	H	Liverpool	L	0-3	0-2		10,877
8	29	H	Huddersfield Town	W	2-0	1-0	Duggan 2	12,298
9	Oct 6	A	West Bromwich Alb	L	3-6	1-3	J. Milburn (pen), Duggan, Mahon	15,843
10	13	H	Sheffield Wed	D	0-0	0-0		16,860
11	20	H	Everton	W	2-0	1-0	Hydes, Furness	16,731
12	27	A	Grimsby Town	L	2-3	1-1	Hydes 2	10,940
13	Nov 3	H	Chelsea	W	5-2	3-2	McAulay (og), Furness, Hydes 2, Mahon	13,295
14	10	A	Wolverhampton W	W	2-1	1-1	J. Milburn (pen), Mahon	13,602
15	17	H	Sunderland	L	2-4	0-1	Duggan, Furness	24,141
16	24	A	Leicester City	L	0-1	0-1		12,785
17	Dec 1	H	Derby County	W	4-2	1-2	Furness 2, Hydes 2	16,565
18	8	A	Aston Villa	D	1-1	0-1	Hydes	31,682
19	15	H	Preston North End	D	3-3	3-2	Hornby, Duggan 2	13,342
20	22	A	Tottenham Hotspur	D	1-1	1-0	Furness	23,662
21	25	H	Manchester City	L	1-2	0-0	J. Milburn (pen)	24,810
22	26	A	Manchester City	L	0-3	0-1		51,387
23	29	A	Middlesbrough	D	3-3	2-2	Hydes 2, Mahon	15,615
24	Jan 5	H	Blackburn Rovers	W	5-1	1-0	Hydes 3, Firth, Furness	13,832
25	19	A	Arsenal	L	0-3	0-2		37,026
26	Feb 2	A	Liverpool	L	2-4	2-1	Hydes 2	21,201
27	9	A	Huddersfield Town	L	1-3	0-1	Mahon	18,413
28	20	H	West Bromwich Alb	W	4-1	4-1	J. Milburn (pen), Mahon 2, Duggan	7,408
29	23	A	Sheffield Wed	L	0-1	0-0		19,591
30	Mar 2	H	Portsmouth	W	3-1	1-0	Hydes 2, G. Milburn	13,450
31	6	A	Everton	D	4-4	2-2	Hydes 2, Stephenson 2	10,441
32	9	H	Grimsby Town	W	3-1	1-0	Hodgson (og), Hydes, J. Milburn (pen)	15,458
33	16	A	Chelsea	L	1-7	1-5	J. Kelly	35,698
34	23	H	Wolverhampton W	D	1-1	0-1	Hornby	9,001
35	30	A	Sunderland	L	0-3	0-1		19,118
36	Apr 6	H	Leicester City	L	0-2	0-1		12,086
37	13	A	Derby County	W	2-1	1-1	Furness 2	11,041
38	19	H	Birmingham	D	1-1	0-1	Furness	14,786
39	20	H	Aston Villa	D	1-1	0-1	Furness	16,234
40	22	A	Birmingham	L	1-3	0-2	Furness	18,008
41	27	A	Preston North End	W	2-0	2-0	Duggan, Hydes	11,758
42	May 4	H	Tottenham Hotspur	W	4-3	3-1	Furness 2, Hydes, Hart	7,668
								Appearances
							Two own-goals	Goals

FA Cup

R3	Jan 12	H	Bradford PA	W	4-1	2-0	Hydes 2, Furness, Mahon	35,444
Rep	26	A	Norwich City	D	3-3	2-0	Mahon, Duggan, Cochrane	13,710
R4	30	H	Norwich City	L	1-2	1-1	Hydes	27,269
								Appearances
								Goals

League match abandoned after 53 minutes due to waterlogged pitch

	Feb 16	H	Portsmouth	W	1-0	1-0	J. Kelly	6,635

Back row, left to right: Willis Edwards, Fred Mills, George Milburn, Stan Moore, Jack Milburn, Cyril Hornby. Front row: Harry Duggan, Joe Firth, Ernie Hart, Billy Furness, Tom Cochrane. Insets: Bert Sproston (left) and Reg Savage.

Moore, Stan	Milburn, George	Milburn, Jack	Edwards, Willis	Hart, Ernie	Hornby, Cyril	Duggan, Harry	Firth, Joe	Mills, Fred	Furness, Billy	Cochrane, Tom	Worsley, Bert	Savage, Reg	Keetley, Charlie	Neal, Tom	Mahon, Jack	Kelly, Mick	Sproston, Bert	Wilcockson, Stan	Roper, Harry	Hydes, Arthur	Turner, Charlie	McDougall, Jock	Kelly, Jack	Stephenson, Eric	Daniels, John	Abel, Bobby
1	2	3	4	5	6	7	8	9	10	11																
1	2	3	4	5	6		8	9	10	11	7															
	2	3		5	6		8	4	10	11	7	1	9													
	2	3		5		9		4	10	11		1		6	7	8										
		3		5		9		4	10	11		1		6	7		2	8								
		3		5		9		4	10	11		1		6	7		2	8								
		3		5	6	9		4	10	11		1			7		2	8								
		3		5	8	9		4	10	11		1		6	7		2									
		3		5	8	9		4	10	11		1		6	7		2									
		3		5		9		4	10	11		1		6	7		2		8							
		3		5	6			4	10	11		1			7		2		8	9						
		3		5	6	8		4	10	11		1			7		2			9						
		3		5	6	8		4	10	11		1			7		2			9						
		3			6	8		4	10	11		1			7		2			9	5					
		3			6	8		4	10	11		1			7		2			9	5					
1		3				8		4	10	11					7		2	6		9		5				
1		3	4		6	8			10	11					7		2			9		5				
1		3	4		6	8			10	11					7		2			9	5					
1		3	4		6	8			10	11					7		2			9	5					
1		3	4		6	8			10	11					7		2			9	5					
1		3	4		6	8			10	11					7		2			9		5				
1		3	4		6	8			10	11					7	9	2					5				
1		3	4			8			10	11				6	7		2			9		5				
1		3	4				8		10	11				6	7		2			9		5				
1		3	4	5			8		10	11				6	7		2			9						
1	2	3	4	5	6		8			11					7				10	9						
1	2	3	4	5	6	8	10			11					7								9			
	2	3	4	5	6	7				10		1			11					9			8			
	2	3	4	5	6	7				10		1			11					9			8			
	2	3	4	5	6	7						1			11					9			8	10		
		3	4	5	6					11	7	1					2			9			8	10		
	2	3	4		6	7				11		1								9		5	8	10		
	2	3	4	5	6	7			10	11										9			8		1	
	2	3	4	5	6	7				11		1								9			8	10		
		3	4		6	7			10	11		1					2			9		5	8			
		3	4		6	7			10	11		1					2			9		5	8			
	2	3	4	5	6	8			10	11		1			7					9						
	2	3	4	5	6	8			10	11		1			7					9						
			4		6	8			10	11		1			7		2			9		5				3
	2	3	4	9	6	7			10	11		1								8		5				
	2	3	4	5	6	8			10	11		1			7					9						
	2	3	4	5	6	8			10	11		1			7					9						
14	17	41	28	27	34	35	7	16	34	41	3	27	1	9	32	2	25	4	3	30	5	11	10	4	1	1
	1	6		1	3	9	1	2	16	1					8					22			1	2		

Moore, Stan	Milburn, George	Milburn, Jack	Edwards, Willis	Hart, Ernie	Hornby, Cyril	Duggan, Harry	Firth, Joe	Mills, Fred	Furness, Billy	Cochrane, Tom	Worsley, Bert	Savage, Reg	Keetley, Charlie	Neal, Tom	Mahon, Jack	Kelly, Mick	Sproston, Bert	Wilcockson, Stan	Roper, Harry	Hydes, Arthur	Turner, Charlie	McDougall, Jock	Kelly, Jack	Stephenson, Eric	Daniels, John	Abel, Bobby
1		3	4			8			10	11				6	7		2			9		5				
1		3		4		8			10	11				6	7		2			9		5				
1		3	4				8			11				6	7		2			9		5	10			
3	0	3	2	1	0	2	1	0	2	3	0	0	0	3	3	0	3	0	0	3	0	3	1	0	0	0
						1			1	1					2					3						

Moore, Stan	Milburn, George	Milburn, Jack	Edwards, Willis	Hart, Ernie	Hornby, Cyril	Duggan, Harry	Firth, Joe	Mills, Fred	Furness, Billy	Cochrane, Tom	Worsley, Bert	Savage, Reg	Keetley, Charlie	Neal, Tom	Mahon, Jack	Kelly, Mick	Sproston, Bert	Wilcockson, Stan	Roper, Harry	Hydes, Arthur	Turner, Charlie	McDougall, Jock	Kelly, Jack	Stephenson, Eric	Daniels, John	Abel, Bobby
1	2	3	4	5	6	7				10					11					9			8			

League Table

	P	W	D	L	F	A	Pts
Arsenal	42	23	12	7	115	46	58
Sunderland	42	19	16	7	90	51	54
Sheffield Wednesday	42	18	13	11	70	64	49
Manchester City	42	20	8	14	82	67	48
Grimsby Town	42	17	11	14	78	60	45
Derby County	42	18	9	15	81	66	45
Liverpool	42	19	7	16	85	88	45
Everton	42	16	12	14	89	88	44
West Bromwich Albion	42	17	10	15	83	83	44
Stoke City	42	18	6	18	71	70	42
Preston North End	42	15	12	15	62	67	42
Chelsea	42	16	9	17	73	82	41
Aston Villa	42	14	13	15	74	88	41
Portsmouth	42	15	10	17	71	72	40
Blackburn Rovers	42	14	11	17	66	78	39
Huddersfield Town	42	14	10	18	76	71	38
Wolverhampton W	42	15	8	19	88	94	38
Leeds United	42	13	12	17	75	92	38
Birmingham	42	13	10	19	63	81	36
Middlesbrough	42	10	14	18	70	90	34
Leicester City	42	12	9	21	61	86	33
Tottenham Hotspur	42	10	10	22	54	93	30

1935-36

Division One

Manager: Billy Hampson

Final Position: 11th

Did you know that?

9 November 1935: United produced possibly their best 45 minutes ever when they led Sheffield Wednesday 6–1 at Elland Road, Harry Duggan scoring a hat-trick. The game finished 7–2 after an even second half.

15 February 1936: The biggest crowd ever to witness a game at Bramall Lane, 68,287, saw the Blades defeat Leeds 3–1 in the fog.

Bert Sproston established himself as one of the country's best right-backs.

Bramall Lane's biggest attendance of 68,287 saw Leeds take on Sheffield United in the FA Cup.

Match No.	Date	Venue	Opponents	Result	FT	HT	Scorers	Attendance
1	Aug 31	A	Stoke City	L	1-3	0-1	J. Milburn	22,552
2	Sep 4	H	Birmingham	D	0-0	0-0		13,271
3	7	H	Blackburn Rovers	L	1-4	0-1	Hydes	14,514
4	11	A	Birmingham	L	0-2	0-1		14,298
5	14	A	Chelsea	L	0-1	0-1		35,720
6	18	H	Arsenal	D	1-1	0-0	J. Kelly	24,283
7	21	H	Liverpool	W	1-0	0-0	J. Milburn (pen)	17,931
8	28	A	Grimsby Town	W	1-0	1-0	J. Kelly	11,236
9	Oct 5	H	Huddersfield Town	D	2-2	1-2	J. Milburn (pen), Brown	33,224
10	12	H	West Bromwich Alb	D	1-1	1-0	J. Milburn (pen)	21,657
11	19	A	Middlesbrough	D	1-1	0-1	J. Milburn (pen)	12,256
12	26	H	Aston Villa	W	4-2	1-2	Brown 2, J. Kelly 2	19,358
13	Nov 2	A	Wolverhampton W	L	0-3	0-1		22,243
14	9	H	Sheffield Wed	W	7-2	6-1	J. Kelly, Cochrane, Duggan 3, Edwards, J. Milburn (pen)	19,897
15	16	A	Portsmouth	D	2-2	1-2	Duggan, Furness	15,120
16	23	H	Bolton Wanderers	W	5-2	2-0	Duggan, Brown 2, J. Kelly, Furness	22,973
17	30	A	Brentford	D	2-2	2-2	Cochrane, Brown	23,914
18	Dec 7	H	Derby County	W	1-0	1-0	Brown	21,331
19	14	A	Everton	D	0-0	0-0		28,901
20	21	H	Preston North End	L	0-1	0-1		17,749
21	26	A	Sunderland	L	1-2	1-0	J. Milburn (pen)	25,296
22	28	H	Stoke City	W	4-1	3-1	Brown 2, J. Kelly, J. Milburn (pen)	18,621
23	Jan 4	A	Blackburn Rovers	W	3-0	2-0	Duggan, Brown, J. Kelly	13,110
24	18	H	Chelsea	W	2-0	1-0	Brown, Furness	18,999
25	Feb 1	H	Grimsby Town	L	1-2	0-2	Hodgson (og)	24,212
26	8	A	Huddersfield Town	W	2-1	1-0	J. Kelly, Brown	20,862
27	19	A	West Bromwich Alb	L	2-3	0-2	Furness, Stephenson	7,939
28	22	H	Middlesbrough	L	0-1	0-1		21,055
29	29	A	Sheffield Wed	L	0-3	0-0		6,316
30	Mar 7	H	Brentford	L	1-2	1-1	Brown	10,509
31	14	A	Aston Villa	D	3-3	2-2	Furness, Brown, J. Kelly	37,382
32	18	A	Liverpool	L	1-2	0-1	Brown	16,210
33	21	H	Portsmouth	W	1-0	1-0	J. Milburn (pen)	13,031
34	28	A	Bolton Wanderers	L	0-3	0-1		21,289
35	Apr 4	H	Wolverhampton W	W	2-0	1-0	Hydes, J. Kelly	10,754
36	10	A	Manchester City	W	3-1	0-1	Hydes 2, J. Kelly	17,175
37	11	A	Derby County	L	1-2	1-1	J. Kelly	15,585
38	13	H	Manchester City	D	1-1	0-0	Furness	38,733
39	18	H	Everton	W	3-1	2-1	J. Kelly, Brown 2	13,738
40	22	H	Sunderland	W	3-0	0-0	Brown (pen), J. Kelly, Cochrane	16,682
41	25	A	Preston North End	L	0-5	0-2		10,927
42	May 2	A	Arsenal	D	2-2	2-2	Furness (pen), Hydes	25,920
								Appearances
							One own-goal	Goals

FA Cup

R3	Jan 11	A	Wolverhampton W	D	1-1	0-1	McDougall	39,176
Rep	15	H	Wolverhampton W	W	3-1	0-0	J. Kelly, Cochrane, Duggan	35,637
R4	28	H	Bury	W	3-2	0-2	Brown 2, Duggan	19,633
R5	Feb 15	A	Sheffield United	L	1-3	1-1	Furness	68,287
								Appearances
								Goals

FA Cup match abandoned after 76 minutes due to fog

	Jan 25	H	Bury	W	2-1	1-1	Furness, J. Kelly	30,000

Back row, left to right: Bert Sproston, Bob Kane, Albert McInroy, Mick Kelly, Tom Cochrane. Front row: Jim Makinson, Sammy Armes, Jack Milburn, Billy Furness, Bobby Browne, Eric Stephenson.

McInroy, Albert	Milburn, George	Milburn, Jack	Edwards, Willis	Hart, Ernie	Hornby, Cyril	Duggan, Harry	Kelly, Jack	Hydes, Arthur	Furness, Billy	Cochrane, Tom	Sproston, Bert	McDougall, Jock	Stephenson, Eric	Savage, Reg	Neal, Tom	Mahon, Jack	Kelly, Mick	Brown, George	Browne, Bobby	Armes, Sammy	Kane, Bob	Makinson, Jim	Hargreaves, Jack	Turner,Jack	Carr, Jimmy
1	2	3	4	5	6	7	8	9	10	11															
1		3	4		6	7		9	10	11	2	5	8												
1		3	4	5	6	7		9	10	11	2		8												
		3	4			8				11	2	5	10	1	6	7	9								
1		3	4		6					11	2	5	10			7	9	8							
1		3	4		6		9			11	2	5	10			7		8							
1		3	4		6		9			11	2	5	10			7		8							
1		3	4		6	7	9			11	2	5	10					8							
1		3	4		6	7	9			11	2	5	10					8							
1		3	4		6	7	9		10	11	2	5						8							
1		3	4		6	7	9		10	11	2	5						8							
1		3	4			7	9		10	11	2	5						8	6						
1		3	4			7	9		10	11	2	5						8	6						
1		3	4			7	9		10	11	2	5						8	6						
1		3	4			7	9		10	11	2	5						8	6						
1		3	4			7	9		10	11	2	5						8	6						
1		3	4			7	9		10	11	2	5						8	6						
1		3	4			7	9		10	11	2	5						8	6						
1		3	4			7		9	10	11	2	5						8	6						
1		3	4			7	9		10	11	2	5						8	6						
1		3	4			7	9		10	11	2	5						8	6						
1		3	4			7	9		10	11	2	5						8	6						
1		3	4			7	9		10	11	2	5						8	6						
1		3	4			7	9		10	11	2	5						8	6						
1		3	4	5	6		9		10	11	2							8		7					
1		3	4				9		10	11	2							8	6	7	5				
1		3					9		8	11	2		10						6	7	5	4			
1		3					9		10	11	2				6			8		7	5	4			
1		3	4				9		10		2	5						8	6	7			11		
1		3	4				9				2	5	10		6			8		7			11		
1	2	3	4				9		10	11		5						8	6					7	
1		3	4				9		10	11	2	5			6			8						7	
1		3	4			7			10	11	2							8	6		5				9
1		3	4			7			10	11	2							8	6		5				9
1		3	4			7	9	8	10	11	2								6		5				
1		3	4			7	9	8	10	11	2				6						5				
1		3		6			9	8		11	2	5						10				4		7	
1		3	4			7	9	8	10	11	2								6		5				
1		3	4			7	9		10	11	2							8	6		5				
1	3		4			7	9		10	11	2	5						8	6						
1	3		4			7		9	10	11	2							8	6		5				
1	3		4				9	8	10	11	2	5							6	7					
41	5	39	39	4	11	29	34	10	34	40	40	29	10	1	5	4	2	33	25	7	10	3	2	3	2
		9	1			6	15	5	7	3			1					18							

1		3	4			7	9		10	11	2	5						8	6						
1		3	4			7	9		10	11	2	5						8	6						
1		3	4			7	9		10	11	2	5						8	6						
1		3	4				9		10	11	2	5						8	6	7					
4	0	4	4	0	0	3	4	0	4	4	4	4	0	0	0	0	0	4	4	1	0	0	0	0	0
						2	1		1	1		1						2							

1		3	4			7	9		10	11	2	5						8	6						

League Table

	P	W	D	L	F	A	Pts
Sunderland	42	25	6	11	109	74	56
Derby County	42	18	12	12	61	52	48
Huddersfield Town	42	18	12	12	59	56	48
Stoke City	42	20	7	15	57	57	47
Brentford	42	17	12	13	81	60	46
Arsenal	42	15	15	12	78	48	45
Preston North End	42	18	8	16	67	64	44
Chelsea	42	15	13	14	65	72	43
Manchester City	42	17	8	17	68	60	42
Portsmouth	42	17	8	17	54	67	42
Leeds United	42	15	11	16	66	64	41
Birmingham	42	15	11	16	61	63	41
Bolton Wanderers	42	14	13	15	67	76	41
Middlesbrough	42	15	10	17	84	70	40
Wolverhampton W	42	15	10	17	77	76	40
Everton	42	13	13	16	89	89	39
Grimsby Town	42	17	5	20	65	73	39
West Bromwich Albion	42	16	6	20	89	88	38
Liverpool	42	13	12	17	60	64	38
Sheffield Wednesday	42	13	12	17	63	77	38
Aston Villa	42	13	9	20	81	110	35
Blackburn Rovers	42	12	9	21	55	96	33

1936-37

Division One

Manager: Billy Hampson

Final Position: 19th

Did you know that?

3 March 1936: Former Liverpool and England forward Gordon Hodgson, newly signed from Aston Villa for £1,500, made his debut in a 7–1 defeat at Everton. He scored the only Leeds goal.

20 March 1937: Young Welsh winger Aubrey Powell broke his leg at Deepdale. The sound of the fracture was said to be like a gunshot round the ground. It was to be another 18 months before he played in the first team.

Winger Sammy Armes' only goal came in the victory against Brentford at the end of October.

Match No.	Date	Venue	Opponents	Result	FT	HT	Scorers	Attendance
1	Aug 29	H	Chelsea	L	2-3	0-2	J. Milburn 2 (1 pen)	19,379
2	Sep 2	A	Manchester City	L	0-4	0-1		24,726
3	5	A	Stoke City	L	1-2	0-1	Stephenson	19,193
4	9	H	Manchester City	D	1-1	0-0	Hargreaves	13,933
5	12	H	Charlton Athletic	W	2-0	0-0	Edwards, Brown	13,789
6	16	A	Portsmouth	L	0-3	0-2		12,222
7	19	A	Grimsby Town	L	1-4	0-1	Betmead (og)	11,217
8	26	H	Liverpool	W	2-0	0-0	Furness, Hargreaves	16,861
9	Oct 3	A	Huddersfield Town	L	0-3	0-1		18,654
10	10	A	Birmingham	L	1-2	1-0	Hydes	23,833
11	17	H	Everton	W	3-0	2-0	Thomson, Stephenson, Hydes	16,861
12	24	A	Bolton Wanderers	L	1-2	0-1	Thomson	20,411
13	31	H	Brentford	W	3-1	3-1	Armes, Stephenson, Hydes	21,498
14	Nov 7	A	Arsenal	L	1-4	0-2	Thomson	32,535
15	14	H	Preston North End	W	1-0	1-0	Hydes	15,651
16	21	A	Sheffield Wed	W	2-1	1-1	Hydes 2	18,411
17	28	H	Manchester United	W	2-1	1-0	Stephenson, Thomson	17,610
18	Dec 5	A	Derby County	L	3-5	2-4	Buckley 2, Hydes	15,557
19	19	A	Sunderland	L	1-2	1-1	Ainsley	23,633
20	25	H	Middlesbrough	W	5-0	2-0	Hydes, Ross (og), Ainsley 2, Buckley	30,647
21	26	A	Chelsea	L	1-2	1-0	Hydes	27,761
22	28	A	Middlesbrough	L	2-4	1-2	Hydes, Powell	14,191
23	Jan 2	H	Stoke City	W	2-1	1-1	Buckley, Ainsley	13,506
24	9	A	Charlton Athletic	L	0-1	0-0		26,760
25	23	H	Grimsby Town	W	2-0	1-0	Hydes, Furness	11,752
26	30	A	Liverpool	L	0-3	0-0		11,252
27	Feb 6	H	Huddersfield Town	W	2-1	1-0	Edwards, Mountford (og)	28,930
28	13	H	Birmingham	L	0-2	0-2		13,674
29	27	H	Bolton Wanderers	D	2-2	1-2	Edwards, Furness	15,090
30	Mar 3	A	Everton	L	1-7	0-2	Hodgson	17,064
31	6	A	Brentford	L	1-4	0-3	Powell	16,588
32	13	H	Arsenal	L	3-4	1-2	Thomson, Hodgson, Buckley	25,148
33	20	A	Preston North End	L	0-1	0-1		18,050
34	27	H	Sheffield Wed	D	1-1	0-1	Ainsley	20,776
35	29	A	West Bromwich Alb	L	0-3	0-2		31,247
36	30	H	West Bromwich Alb	W	3-1	3-1	Hodgson 2, Stephenson	16,016
37	Apr 3	A	Manchester United	D	0-0	0-0		34,429
38	10	H	Derby County	W	2-0	2-0	Stephenson, Hodgson	20,228
39	17	A	Wolverhampton W	L	0-3	0-1		13,688
40	21	H	Wolverhampton W	L	0-1	0-0		14,220
41	24	H	Sunderland	W	3-0	2-0	Furness, Hodgson, J. Milburn (pen)	22,234
42	May 1	H	Portsmouth	W	3-1	2-0	Furness, Kelly, J. Milburn (pen)	15,034
								Appearances
							Three own-goals	Goals

FA Cup

R3	Jan 16	A	Chelsea	L	0-4	0-2		34,589
								Appearances
								Goals

League match abandoned after 83 minutes due to fog

	Dec 12	H	Wolverhampton W	L	0-1	0-1		11,987

Back row, left to right: Willis Edwards, Bert Sproston, Albert McInroy, George Milburn, Jack Milburn, Bobby Browne. Front row: Sammy Armes, Eric Stephenson, Jock McDougall, Arthur Hydes, Billy Furness, Arthur Buckley.

McIlroy, Albert	Sproston, Bert	Milburn, Jack	Edwards, Willis	McDougall, Jock	Browne, Bobby	Duggan, Harry	Brown, George	Kelly, Jack	Furness, Billy	Cochrane, Tom	Milburn, George	Armes, Sammy	Stephenson, Eric	Hargreaves, Jack	Kane, Bob	Holley, Tom	Hydes, Arthur	Buckley, Arthur	Mills, Fred	Turner, Jack	Thomson, John	Ainsley, George	Powell, Aubrey	Savage, Reg	Makinson, Jim	Trainor, Jack	Gadsby, Ken	Hodgson, Gordon
1	2	3	4	5	6	7	8	9	10	11																		
1		3	4	5	6			9	8		2	7	10	11														
1		3	4					9	8		2	7	10	11	5	6												
1		3			6			9	8		2	7	10	11	5	4												
1		3	4		6		9		8		2	7	10	11	5													
1		3	4		6		9		8		2	7	10	11	5													
1		3	4				9		8		2	7	10	11	5	6												
1		3	4		6			9	8		2	7	10	11	5													
1	2	3	4		6			9	8	11		7	10		5													
1	2	3	4	5	6				10			7	8				9	11										
1		3	4	5							2		10				9	11	6	7	8							
1	2	3	4	5									10				9	11	6	7	8							
1	2	3	4	5								7	10				9	11	6		8							
1	2	3	4	5								7	10				9	11	6		8							
1	2	3	4	5								7	10				9	11	6		8							
1	2	3	4	5								7	10				9	11	6		8							
1	2	3	4	5								7	10				9	11	6		8							
1	2	3	4	5								7	10				9	11	6		8							
1	2	3	4	5					10								9	11	6	7		8						
	2	3							10						5		9	11	6			8	7	1	4			
	2	3							10						5		9	11	6			8	7	1	4			
	2		4						10		3				5		9	11	6			8	7	1				
	2		4						10		3				5			11	6			8	7	1		9		
	2										3				5		10	11	6			8	7	1	4	9		
1	2	3	4						10			7			5		9	11	6			8						
1	2	3	4		6				10			7			5		9	11				8						
1	2	3	4						10						5		9	11	6			8	7					
1	2	3	4						10					11	5		9		6			8	7					
1	2	3	4					9	10			7			5			11	6			8						
1	2		4						10							5		11	6			8	7				3	9
1		3	4					8	10		2					5		11	6				7					9
		3	4						10		2				5			11	6		8		7	1				9
		3	4						10		2				5			11	6		8		7	1				9
		3	4		6				10		2				5			11	7			8		1				9
		3			6						2		10		5			11	4	7	8			1				9
		3	4		6								10		5			11	2	7	8			1				9
		3	4		6								10		5			11	2	7	8			1				9
		3	4		6								10		5			11	2	7	8			1				9
		3	4										10		5	6		11	2	7	8			1				9
	2	3	4												5		8	11	6	7	10			1				9
		3			6			8	10			7		11	5				2					1	4			9
		3			6			8	10			7		11		5			2					1	4			9
26	23	38	35	12	16	1	4	10	27	2	16	20	22	10	27	7	19	30	31	9	16	13	11	16	5	2	1	13
		4	3				1	1	5			1	6	2			11	5			5	5	2					6
	2		4								3				5		10	11	6			8	7	1		9		
0	1	0	1	0	0	0	0	0	0	0	1	0	0	0	1	0	1	1	1	0	0	1	1	1	0	1	0	0
1	2	3	4	5				8				7	10				9	11	6									

League Table

	P	W	D	L	F	A	Pts
Manchester City	42	22	13	7	107	61	57
Charlton Athletic	42	21	12	9	58	49	54
Arsenal	42	18	16	8	80	49	52
Derby County	42	21	7	14	96	90	49
Wolverhampton W	42	21	5	16	84	67	47
Brentford	42	18	10	14	82	78	46
Middlesbrough	42	19	8	15	74	71	46
Sunderland	42	19	6	17	89	87	44
Portsmouth	42	17	10	15	62	66	44
Stoke City	42	15	12	15	72	57	42
Birmingham	42	13	15	14	64	60	41
Grimsby Town	42	17	7	18	86	81	41
Chelsea	42	14	13	15	52	55	41
Preston North End	42	14	13	15	56	67	41
Huddersfield Town	42	12	15	15	62	64	39
West Bromwich Albion	42	16	6	20	77	98	38
Everton	42	14	9	19	81	78	37
Liverpool	42	12	11	19	62	84	35
Leeds United	42	15	4	23	60	80	34
Bolton Wanderers	42	10	14	18	43	66	34
Manchester United	42	10	12	20	55	78	32
Sheffield Wednesday	42	9	12	21	53	69	30

1937-38

Division One

Manager: Billy Hampson

Final Position: 9th

Did you know that?

23 February 1938: Numbers were worn by players for the first time at Elland Road. The Football League introduced numbering at the start of the 1939–40 season which was interrupted by the outbreak of World War Two. The FA had experimented with numbers several times before that, the FA Amateur XI game against the Combined Universities game at Leeds being one of them.

19 March 1938: Goalkeeper Jim Twomey made his United debut against Blackpool three days after making his bow for Ireland against Wales.

30 April 1938: Rugby returned to Elland Road when Hunslet beat Leeds 8–2 in the Rugby League Championship in front of a massive 54,112 crowd.

Match No.	Date		Venue	Opponents	Result	FT	HT	Scorers	Attendance
1	Aug	28	A	Charlton Athletic	D	1-1	1-0	Hodgson	30,979
2	Sep	1	H	Chelsea	W	2-0	1-0	Armes, Barber (og)	18,858
3		4	H	Preston North End	D	0-0	0-0		22,513
4		8	A	Chelsea	L	1-4	0-2	Hodgson	17,300
5		11	A	Grimsby Town	D	1-1	0-0	Hodgson	9,328
6		15	H	Portsmouth	W	3-1	1-1	Hodgson 2, Ainsley	12,579
7		18	H	Huddersfield Town	W	2-1	1-0	Milburn (pen), Armes	33,200
8		25	H	Liverpool	W	2-0	1-0	Armes, Ainsley	21,477
9	Oct	2	A	West Bromwich Alb	L	1-2	0-1	Milburn (pen)	25,609
10		9	H	Birmingham	W	1-0	1-0	Ainsley	20,698
11		16	A	Everton	D	1-1	0-1	Armes	26,035
12		23	H	Wolverhampton W	L	1-2	0-2	Buckley	13,304
13		30	A	Leicester City	W	4-2	2-1	Hodgson 2, Milburn (pen), Buckley	18,833
14	Nov	6	H	Blackpool	D	1-1	0-0	Buckley	18,438
15		13	A	Derby County	D	2-2	0-1	Thomson, Hodgson	15,966
16		20	H	Bolton Wanderers	D	1-1	0-1	Hodgson	23,687
17		27	A	Arsenal	L	1-4	1-2	Stephenson	34,350
18	Dec	4	H	Sunderland	W	4-3	1-3	Stephenson 3, Hodgson	15,340
19		11	A	Brentford	D	1-1	1-0	Hodgson	18,184
20		18	H	Manchester City	W	2-1	1-0	Stephenson, Buckley	22,144
21		25	H	Middlesbrough	W	5-3	4-2	Hodgson 2, Buckley, Stephenson, Thomson	37,020
22		27	A	Middlesbrough	L	0-2	0-1		34,640
23	Jan	1	H	Charlton Athletic	D	2-2	1-2	Stephenson, Buckley	26,433
24		15	A	Preston North End	L	1-3	1-2	Thomson	14,032
25		26	H	Grimsby Town	D	1-1	1-0	Buckley	10,512
26		29	A	Huddersfield Town	W	3-0	3-0	Armes, Buckley, Thomson	16,677
27	Feb	5	A	Liverpool	D	1-1	1-1	Hodgson	34,468
28		12	H	West Bromwich Alb	W	1-0	0-0	Hodgson	21,819
29		19	A	Birmingham	L	2-3	2-2	Hodgson, Thomson	20,403
30		26	H	Everton	D	4-4	3-2	Hodgson 4	23,497
31	Mar	5	A	Wolverhampton W	D	1-1	0-0	Sproston	38,849
32		12	H	Leicester City	L	0-2	0-2		19,839
33		19	A	Blackpool	L	2-5	1-1	Ainsley, Hodgson	18,029
34		26	H	Derby County	L	0-2	0-1		19,911
35	Apr	2	A	Bolton Wanderers	D	0-0	0-0		18,492
36		9	H	Arsenal	L	0-1	0-0		29,365
37		16	A	Sunderland	D	0-0	0-0		21,450
38		18	A	Stoke City	W	1-0	0-0	Mould (og)	25,114
39		19	H	Stoke City	W	2-1	0-0	Ainsley, Stephenson	17,896
40		23	H	Brentford	W	4-0	2-0	Hodgson 3, Ainsley	17,840
41		30	A	Manchester City	L	2-6	1-3	Hodgson, Buckley	26,732
42	May	7	A	Portsmouth	L	0-4	0-3		29,571
									Appearances
								Two own-goals	Goals

FA Cup

R3	Jan	8	H	Chester	W	3-1	2-1	Armes, Buckley, Ainsley	37,155
R4		22	A	Charlton Athletic	L	1-2	0-2	Hodgson	50,516
									Appearances
									Goals

Les Goldberg, who later changed his surname to Gaunt, made his debut in a thrilling win against Sunderland in December.

Back row, left to right: Billy Hampson (manager), Bert Sproston, Jim Makinson, Reg Savage, Jack Milburn, Bobby Browne, Tom Holley. Front row: Sammy Armes, George Ainsley, Gordon Hodgson, Eric Stephenson, Arthur Buckley.

Savage, Reg	Sproston, Bert	Milburn, Jack	Makinson, Jim	Holley, Tom	Browne, Bobby	Armes, Sammy	Ainsley, George	Hodgson, Gordon	Stephenson, Eric	Buckley, Arthur	Kelly, Jack	Mills, Fred	Thonson, John	Edwards, Willis	Turner, Jack	Kane, Bob	Goldberg, Les	Trainor, Jack	Hargreaves, Jack	Twomey, Bill	Cochrane, Dave	Kelly, Dominic	Francis, Cliff
1	2	3	4	5	6	7	8	9	10	11													
1	2	3	4	5	6	7	8	9	10	11													
1	2	3	4	5	6	7	8	9	10	11													
1	2	3	4	5	6	7	8	9	10	11													
1	2	3	4	5	6	7	8	9	10	11													
1	2	3	4	5	6	7	8	9	10	11													
1	2	3	4	5	6	7	8	9	10	11													
1	2	3	4	5	6	7	8	9	10	11													
1	2	3	4	5	6	7	8		10	11	9												
1	2	3	4	5	6	7	8		10	11	9												
1	2	3	4	5		7	8			11	9	6	10										
1		3	6	5		7	8			11	9	2	10	4									
1	2	3	4	5	6		8	9	10	11					7								
1	2	3	4	5	6			9	10	11	8				7								
1	2	3	4	5	6	7		9	10	11			8										
1		3	4		6	7		9	10	11		2	8			5							
1	2	3	4	5		7		9	10	11		6	8										
1		3	4			7		9	10	11		6	8			5	2						
1		3	4			7		9	10	11		6	8			5	2						
1	2	3	4			7		9	10	11		6	8			5							
1	2	3	4			7		9	10	11		6	8			5							
1	2	3	4			7			10			6	8			5		9	11				
1	2	3	4			7		9	10	11		6	8			5							
1	2	3	4		6	7	8	9		11			10			5							
1	2	3	4			7	8	9	10	11		6				5							
1	2	3	4	5	6	7		9	10	11			8										
1	2	3	4	5	6	7		9	10				8						11				
1	2	3	4	5	6	7		9	10	11			8										
1	2	3	4	5	6	7		9	10				8						11				
1	2	3	4	5	6	7		9	10				8						11				
1	2	3	4	5	6	7		9	10				8						11				
1	2	3	4		6	7	9		10				8			5			11				
	2	3	4	5	6	7	8	9	10										11	1			
	2	3	4	5			8	9	10	11		6								1	7		
	2	3			6	7	8	9	10	11				4						1		5	
		3			6	7	8	9		11				4			2			1		5	10
	2	3	4		6	7	8	9	10	11						5				1			
	2	3	4		6	7	8	9	10	11						5				1			
	2	3	4		6	7	8	9	10	11						5				1			
	2	3	4		6	7	8	9	10	11						5				1			
	2	3	4		6	7	8	9	10	11										1		5	
	2	3	4		6	7	8	9	10	11										1		5	
32	37	42	40	24	31	39	26	36	38	35	5	12	19	3	2	14	3	1	7	10	1	4	1
	1	3				5	6	25	8	9			5										

Savage, Reg	Sproston, Bert	Milburn, Jack	Makinson, Jim	Holley, Tom	Browne, Bobby	Armes, Sammy	Ainsley, George	Hodgson, Gordon	Stephenson, Eric	Buckley, Arthur	Kelly, Jack	Mills, Fred	Thonson, John	Edwards, Willis	Turner, Jack	Kane, Bob	Goldberg, Les	Trainor, Jack	Hargreaves, Jack	Twomey, Bill	Cochrane, Dave	Kelly, Dominic	Francis, Cliff
1	2	3	4			7	8	9	10	11		6				5							
1	2	3	4			7	8	9	10	11		6				5							
2	2	2	2	0	0	2	2	2	2	2	0	2	0	0	0	2	0	0	0	0	0	0	0
						1		1		2													

League Table

	P	W	D	L	F	A	Pts
Arsenal	42	21	10	11	77	44	52
Wolverhampton W	42	20	11	11	72	49	51
Preston North End	42	16	17	9	64	44	49
Charlton Athletic	42	16	14	12	65	51	46
Middlesbrough	42	19	8	15	72	65	46
Brentford	42	18	9	15	69	59	45
Bolton Wanderers	42	15	15	12	64	60	45
Sunderland	42	14	16	12	55	57	44
Leeds United	42	14	15	13	64	69	43
Chelsea	42	14	13	15	65	65	41
Liverpool	42	15	11	16	65	71	41
Blackpool	42	16	8	18	61	66	40
Derby County	42	15	10	17	66	87	40
Everton	42	16	7	19	79	75	39
Huddersfield Town	42	17	5	20	55	68	39
Leicester City	42	14	11	17	54	75	39
Stoke City	42	13	12	17	58	59	38
Birmingham	42	10	18	14	58	62	38
Portsmouth	42	13	12	17	62	68	38
Grimsby Town	42	13	12	17	51	68	38
Manchester City	42	14	8	20	80	77	36
West Bromwich Albion	42	14	8	20	74	91	36

1938-39

Division One

Manager: Billy Hampson

Final Position: 13th

Did you know that?

1 October 1938: Gordon Hodgson, 34, set a United record by netting five times in United's 8–2 thrashing of Leicester City.

Five-goal Gordon Hodgson.

Match No.	Date	Venue	Opponents	Result	FT	HT	Scorers	Attendance
1	Aug 27	H	Preston North End	W	2-1	0-0	Hodgson, Buckley	19,255
2	31	H	Birmingham	W	2-0	0-0	Ainsley, Buckley	13,578
3	Sep 3	A	Charlton Athletic	L	0-2	0-0		30,383
4	5	A	Stoke City	D	1-1	0-1	Hodgson	16,052
5	10	H	Bolton Wanderers	L	1-2	1-0	Hodgson	20,381
6	17	A	Huddersfield Town	W	1-0	1-0	Hodgson	19,793
7	24	A	Liverpool	L	0-3	0-0		32,197
8	Oct 1	H	Leicester City	W	8-2	3-0	Hodgson 5, Cochrane, Milburn (pen), Hargreaves	15,001
9	8	A	Middlesbrough	W	2-1	0-1	Armes, Hodgson	23,009
10	15	H	Wolverhampton W	W	1-0	0-0	Thomson	25,860
11	22	A	Everton	L	0-4	0-3		30,747
12	29	H	Portsmouth	D	2-2	1-0	Ainsley, Rowe (og)	18,055
13	Nov 5	A	Arsenal	W	3-2	1-2	Stephenson 2, Buckley	39,092
14	12	H	Brentford	W	3-2	2-0	Hodgson 2, Buckley	22,555
15	19	A	Blackpool	W	2-1	0-1	Hodgson, Hargreaves	16,612
16	26	H	Derby County	L	1-4	1-2	Buckley	34,158
17	Dec 3	A	Grimsby Town	L	2-3	0-3	Armes, Powell	11,202
18	10	H	Sunderland	D	3-3	2-2	Ainsley, Hargreaves, Powell	20,853
19	17	A	Aston Villa	L	1-2	0-1	Hargreaves	28,990
20	24	A	Preston North End	L	0-2	0-2		18,424
21	26	H	Chelsea	D	1-1	1-1	Edwards	27,586
22	27	A	Chelsea	D	2-2	1-1	Hodgson, Stephenson	32,692
23	31	H	Charlton Athletic	W	2-1	1-0	Hodgson, Cochrane	18,774
24	Jan 14	A	Bolton Wanderers	D	2-2	1-2	Hodgson, Goslin (og)	14,893
25	28	H	Liverpool	D	1-1	0-0	Hodgson	13,679
26	Feb 4	A	Leicester City	L	0-2	0-0		12,618
27	11	H	Middlesbrough	L	0-1	0-0		18,273
28	18	A	Wolverhampton W	L	1-4	0-1	Sutherland	31,977
29	25	H	Everton	L	1-2	1-0	Ainsley	21,728
30	Mar 8	A	Portsmouth	L	0-2	0-2		14,469
31	11	H	Arsenal	W	4-2	1-1	Stephenson (pen), Powell, Hodgson, Hargreaves	22,160
32	18	A	Brentford	W	1-0	0-0	Hargreaves	21,480
33	25	H	Blackpool	W	1-0	0-0	Cochrane	21,818
34	Apr 1	A	Derby County	L	0-1	0-0		11,278
35	7	A	Manchester United	D	0-0	0-0		35,564
36	8	H	Grimsby Town	L	0-1	0-0		19,700
37	10	H	Manchester United	W	3-1	2-0	Ainsley, Hodgson, Buckley	13,771
38	15	A	Sunderland	L	1-2	0-0	Ainsley	10,913
39	19	H	Huddersfield Town	W	2-1	0-0	Hodgson, Powell	12,006
40	22	H	Aston Villa	W	2-0	0-0	Hargreaves 2	14,241
41	29	A	Birmingham	L	0-4	0-2		12,522
42	May 6	H	Stoke City	D	0-0	0-0		12,048
								Appearances
							Two own-goals	Goals

FA Cup

R3	Jan 17	H	Bournemouth	W	3-1	2-1	Stephenson, Hargreaves, Cochrane	10,114
Rep	21	H	Huddersfield Town	L	2-4	2-0	Hodgson, Cochrane	43,702
								Appearances
								Goals

League Jubilee Fund

	Aug 20	H	Huddersfield Town	D	1-1	0-1	Milburn (pen)	7,352

League match abandoned after 63 minutes due to snow

	Jan 25	H	Huddersfield Town	L	0-1	0-1		3,896

A United line-up from the last full season before World War Two. Players in kit only, back row, left to right: George Ainsley, Jim Makinson, Reg Savage, Jack Milburn, Tom Holley. Front row: Sammy Armes, Bill Parry, Gordon Hodgson, Eric Stephenson. Arthur Buckley, Bobby Browne.

Twomey, Jim	Milburn, Jack	Gadsby, Ken	Makinson, Jim	Holley, Tom	Browne, Bobby	Armes, Sammy	Ainsley, George	Hodgson, Gordon	Stephenson, Eric	Buckley, Arthur	Goldberg, Les	Edwards, Willis	Kane, Bob	Cochrane, Dave	Thomson, John	Powell, Aubrey	Hargreaves, Jack	Mills, Fred	Parry, Bill	Hampson, Tom	Savage, Reg	Sutherland, Harry	Copping, Wilf	Scaife, George	Dunderdale, Len	Henry, Gerry
1	2	3	4	5	6	7	8	9	10	11																
1	2	3	4	5	6	7	8	9	10	11																
1	2	3	4	5	6	7	8	9	10	11																
1	3		6				8	9	10	11	2	4	5	7												
1	3		4		6	7	8	9	10	11	2		5													
1	2	3	4	5	6	7		9	10	11					8											
1	2	3	4	5	6	7		9		11					8	10										
1	2	3	4	5	6			9						7	8	10	11									
1	2	3		5		7		9				4			8	10	11	6								
1	2	3		5				9				4		7	8	10	11	6								
1	2	3		5				9				4		7	8	10	11	6								
1	2	3		5	6	7	9		10	11		4				8										
1	2	3		5	6		9		10	11		4		7		8										
1	2	3		5	6		8	9	10	11		4		7												
1	2	3		5	6			9	10			4		7		8	11									
1	2	3		5	6			9	10	11		4		7		8										
1	2	3		5	6	7		9	10	11		4				8										
1	2	3		5			9		10			4		7		8	11	6								
1	2	3		5	6		8	9	10			4		7			11									
1	2	3		5	6		8	9	10			4		7			11									
1		3		5			9		10		2	4		7		8	11		6							
1		3		5		7		9	10		2					8	11		6	4						
1		3		5				9	10		2	4		7		8	11		6							
	2	3	4	5		7	8	9	10								11		6		1					
1		3		5		7		9	10		2	4				8	11	6								
1		3		5			8	9	10		2	4		7			11		6							
1	2	3						9	10				5	7		8	11	4	6							
1		3							10		2		5	7		8	11	4		6		9				
		3	4				8		10		2		5	7			11	6			1	9				
1		3	4	5			8		10		2			7			11					9	6			
1		3	4	5				9	10					7		8	11						6	2		
1			4	5				9	10		2			7		8	11						6	3		
1			4	5					10		2			7		8	11						6	3	9	
1				5					10		2	4		7		8	11						6	3	9	
1		3	4	5			8		10								11						6	2	9	7
		3		5			8	9				4		7		10	11				1		6	2		
1		3	4	5			10	9		11				7		8							6	2		
1		3	4	5	6		10	9		11	2			7		8										
1		3	4	5				9	10	11	2			7		8							6			
1		3	4	5				9	10					7		8	11						6	2		
1		3	4	5				9	10					7		8	11						6	2		
1		3		5				9	10	11	2	4				8							6			7
39	22	37	20	37	16	12	20	32	34	16	16	20	5	28	6	28	26	8	6	2	3	3	12	9	3	2
	1					2	6	20	4	6		1		3	1	4	8					1				

	2	3		5				9	10			4		7		8	11		6		1					
	2	3		5				9	10			4		7		8	11		6		1					
0	2	2	0	2	0	0	0	2	2	0	0	2	0	2	0	2	2	0	2	0	2	0	0	0	0	0
								1	1					2			1									

1	2	3	6	5		7	8	9	10	11		4							

1		3		5		7		9	10		2	4				8	11	6	

League Table

	P	W	D	L	F	A	Pts
Everton	42	27	5	10	88	52	59
Wolverhampton W	42	22	11	9	88	39	55
Charlton Athletic	42	22	6	14	75	59	50
Middlesbrough	42	20	9	13	93	74	49
Arsenal	42	19	9	14	55	41	47
Derby County	42	19	8	15	66	55	46
Stoke City	42	17	12	13	71	68	46
Bolton Wanderers	42	15	15	12	67	58	45
Preston North End	42	16	12	14	63	59	44
Grimsby Town	42	16	11	15	61	69	43
Liverpool	42	14	14	14	62	63	42
Aston Villa	42	16	9	17	71	60	41
Leeds United	42	16	9	17	59	67	41
Manchester United	42	11	16	15	57	65	38
Blackpool	42	12	14	16	56	68	38
Sunderland	42	13	12	17	54	67	38
Portsmouth	42	12	13	17	47	70	37
Brentford	42	14	8	20	53	74	36
Huddersfield Town	42	12	11	19	58	64	35
Chelsea	42	12	9	21	64	80	33
Birmingham	42	12	8	22	62	84	32
Leicester City	42	9	11	22	48	82	29

1939-40

Regional League North-East Division

Manager: Billy Hampson

Final Position: 5th

Did you know that?

2 September 1939: United's 1–0 home defeat to Sheffield United in front of only 9,779 fans left Leeds at the bottom of the table without a goal to their name after three games. War was declared the following day and League football suspended.

6 April 1940: Alf Stephens took over brother Bill's number-nine shirt for the game v Bradford and scored. The brothers both ended up as prisoners-of-war and were the first twins at Elland Road until Rod and Ray Wallace surpassed them by being the first pair to appear in the League for the club.

8 June 1940: Just days after the BEF evacuation from Dunkirk, only 200 turned out to see the last game v Newcastle United.

Norman Wharton, who kept goal in the final two games of the abandoned Football League season.

Match No.	Date	Venue	Opponents	Result	FT	HT	Scorers	Attendance
1	Oct 28	H	Bradford City	W	3-0	2-0	Hodgson 2, Brown	3,000
2	Nov 4	A	Hull City	W	3-0	0-0	Powell, Hodgson, McGraw	3,000
3	11	A	Darlington	W	3-1	1-1	McGraw, Hodgson, Brown	5,727
4	18	H	Hartlepools United	W	2-1	0-1	Holley, Hodgson	4,000
5	25	A	York City	D	1-1	1-1	Henry	4,000
6	Dec 2	H	Huddersfield Town	D	0-0	0-0		4,000
7	9	A	Bradford PA	L	1-3	0-1	Hodgson (pen)	4,000
8	23	H	Middlesbrough	W	3-1	2-0	Cochrane, Powell, Henry	5,000
9	Jan 6	A	Newcastle United	L	0-3	0-1		6,000
10	Mar 9	H	Darlington	W	3-2	1-1	Cochrane, Stephenson (pen), Henry	4,000
11	16	A	Hartlepools United	L	1-2	0-1	J.W. Stephens	1,500
12	23	H	York City	W	3-1	1-1	Short 2, Powell	3,000
13	30	A	Huddersfield Town	L	1-2	1-2	Short	5,833
14	Apr 6	H	Bradford PA	W	5-2	1-1	Powell, McGraw, A. Stephens, Cochrane 2	3,000
15	13	A	Middlesbrough	D	1-1	1-1	A. Stephens	1,000
16	May 25	A	Halifax Town	L	2-3	2-0	Henry 2	600
17	June 1	H	Hull City	W	3-1	0-1	Henry, Cochrane 2	500
18	8	H	Newcastle United	L	1-3	1-2	Cochrane	200
								Appearances
								Goals

League War Cup

R3	Apr 20	H	Sheffield Wed	W	6-3	3-1	Thompson, A. Stephens 3, Hargreaves 2	8,065
rep	27	A	Sheffield Wed	L	2-3	0-2	Powell, Hodgson	9,506
R4	May 4	A	Sunderland	D	0-0	0-0		11,226
R5	11	H	Sunderland	L	0-1	0-1		9,000
								Appearances
								Goals

Football League (Season abandoned due to Second World War)

1	Aug 26	A	Preston North End	D	0-0	0-0		20,491
2	30	H	Charlton Athletic	L	0-1	0-0		12,049
3	Sep 2	H	Sheffield United	L	0-1	0-0		9,779
								Appearances
								Goals

League Jubilee Fund

	Aug 19	A	Huddersfield Town	L	0-5	0-2		4,630

Swindin, George	Goldberg, Les	Gadsby, Ken	Makinson, Jim	Holley, Tom	Thompson, Les	Henry, Gerry	Powell, Aubrey	Hodgson, Gordon	McGraw, Jim	Brown, John	Browne, Bobby	Hargreaves, Jack	Milburn, Jim	Stephenson, Eric	Copping, Wilf	Cochrane, Dave	Edwards, Willis	Lee, Alex	Stephens, Bill	Milburn, Jack	Short, John	Stephens, Alf	Buckley, Arthur	Murgatroyd, Arthur	Saxon, A	Ainsley, George	Twomey, Jim	Dunderdale, Len	Wharton, Norman	Kane, Bob
1	2	3	4	5	6	7	8	9	10	11																				
1	2	3	4	5	6	7	8	9	10	11																				
1	2	3	4	5	6	7	8	9	10	11																				
1	2	3	4	5		7		9	8	11	6	10																		
1	2	3	4	5	6	7	8	9	10	11																				
1	2		4		5	7	8	9		11	6		3	10																
1	2	3	4		5	7	8	9	10		6	11																		
1	2	3	4	5		9	8			11				10	6	7														
1	2	3		5	9		8		10	11					6	7	4													
	2	3	4	5	6	11	8							10		7		1	9											
		3	4	5	6	11								10		7		1	9	2	8									
	2	3	4	5			7					11		10	6			1	9		8									
		3	4	5	6		8					11				7		1	9	2	10									
	2	3	4	5	6		8		10							7		1				9	11							
		3		5	6	11			10							7	4	1		2	8	9								
			4		6	9		5	10			11				7		1		3	8			2						
			4		6	9		5	10			11				7		1		2	8			3						
			4		6	9		5	10							7		1		2	8			3	11					
9	12	14	16	13	15	14	12	10	12	8	3	6	1	5	3	10	2	9	4	6	7	2	1	3	1	0	0	0	0	0
				1		6	4	6	3	2				1		7			1		3	2								

	2	3	4	5	6		8					11		10		7		1				9								
	2	3	4	5	6		7	9				11		10				1				8								
	2	3		5	6							11		10		7	4	1				9				8				
		3	6		5	8		9	10			11				7	4	1		2										
0	3	4	3	3	4	1	2	2	1	0	0	4	0	3	0	3	2	4	0	1	0	3	0	0	0	1	0	0	0	0
					1		1	1				2										2								

	2	3		5							4	11		10	6	7										8	1	9		
	2	3		5			8				4			10	6	7							11			9			1	
		3					8	9			4		2	10	6	7							11						1	5
0	2	3	0	2	0	0	2	1	0	0	3	1	1	3	3	3	0	0	0	0	0	0	2	0	0	2	1	1	2	1

	2	3		5										10	6	7	4						11			8	1	9		

1940-41

North Regional League

Manager: Billy Hampson

Final Position: 15th

Did you know that?

25 December 1940: United beat Bradford Park Avenue 2–1 in a game played on Christmas morning. Len Shackleton appeared for both Bradford teams in the same day when he turned out for City against Huddersfield in the afternoon.

11 January 1941: Goalkeeper Alex Lee was injured and, in those days before substitutes, played out on the wing. The young airman found the net twice but his replacement in goals was not so successful and conceded three times as Leeds lost 3–2 to Chesterfield.

17 May 1941: Jim Makinson completed a wartime rarity for any club by being an ever-present in the season 1940–41.

Len Shackleton, two games in one day.

Match No.	Date	Venue	Opponents	Result	FT	HT	Scorers	Attendance
1	Aug 31	H	Bradford City	D	2-2	1-0	Stephenson, Sutherland	3,000
2	Sep 7	A	Newcastle United	L	0-1	0-1		4,000
3	14	H	Huddersfield Town	W	5-2	4-2	Short 2, Hodgson, Young (og), Powell	3,000
4	21	H	Manchester City	D	0-0	0-0		5,000
5	28	A	Everton	L	1-5	1-1	Baird	3,000
6	Oct 5	A	Huddersfield Town	D	1-1	0-0	Jack Milburn (pen)	3,368
7	12	A	Rotherham United	D	0-0	0-0		4,208
8	19	A	Bradford City	W	6-3	3-2	Hodgson 3, Powell 2, Short	3,000
9	Nov 2	A	Barnsley	L	0-3	0-1		1,244
10	9	H	Middlesbrough	W	2-1	2-1	Townsend, Stephenson	2,000
11	16	H	Bradford City	W	6-0	3-0	Jack Milburn (pen), Mahon, Stephenson, Townsend 2, Hodgson	2,500
12	23	H	Hull City	W	3-2	1-1	Townsend 2, Mahon	3,000
13	30	H	Newcastle United	W	3-2	2-1	Townsend 2, Stephenson	3,000
14	Dec 7	H	Burnley	D	1-1	1-1	Hargreaves	3,000
15	14	A	Chesterfield	L	0-3	0-1		1,000
16	21	A	Halifax Town	D	2-2	2-2	McGraw, Townsend	3,000
17	25	H	Bradford PA	W	2-1	1-0	Hodgson, Townsend	4,500
18	28	H	Chesterfield	L	1-2	1-0	Short	4,000
19	Jan 4	A	Chesterfield*	W	4-2	2-1	Townsend 2, Henry, Stephenson	2,000
20	11	H	Chesterfield*	L	2-3	0-0	Lee 2	5,000
21	18	A	Hull City	L	1-4	1-0	McGraw	1,500
22	Mar 22	H	Sheffield Wed	W	3-2	1-2	Hargreaves, Makinson, Burditt	1,500
23	29	A	Rochdale	W	3-2	1-1	Burditt, Ainsley, Makinson	800
24	Apr 5	A	Doncaster Rovers	W	4-1	2-0	Henry, Edwards, Hargreaves 2	4,000
25	12	A	Manchester City	D	1-1	0-1	Hargreaves	3,000
26	14	H	Bury	D	2-2	1-1	Henry, Hargreaves	2,400
27	26	H	Sheffield United	W	2-0	1-0	Hargreaves, Burditt	2,000
28	May 3	A	Newcastle United	L	2-3	1-2	Short 2	2,000
29	10	H	Huddersfield Town*	W	1-0	1-0	Powell	4,000
30	17	A	Middlesbrough*	L	2-3	1-3	Jim Milburn (pen), Short	3,000

* Games also in the West Riding Cup.

Appearances

One own-goal — Goals

League War Cup

Match No.	Date	Venue	Opponents	Result	FT	HT	Scorers	Attendance
31	Feb 15	A	Halifax Town	W	3-2	1-0	Townsend 3	4,000
32	Mar 1	H	Halifax Town	D	2-2	1-0	Hodgson, Edwards	5,000
33	8	A	Middlesbrough	L	0-2	0-0		9,000
34	15	H	Middlesbrough	D	2-2	0-2	Henry, Jack Milburn	5,000

Appearances

Goals

Lee, Alex	Milburn, Jim	Gadsby, Ken	Makinson, Jim	Holley, Tom	Thompson, Les	Henry, Gerry	Powell, Aubrey	Sutherland, Harry	Stephenson, Eric	Houldershaw, Rex	Milburn, Jack	Short, John	Hodgson, Gordon	Hargreaves, Jack	Stacey, Alex	Edwards, Willis	Baird, Horace	McTavish, Hugh	Goslin, Harry	Howitt, Harry	McGraw, Jim	Heaton, Billy	Townsend, Len	Mahon, Jack	Ainsley, George	Hodgson, John	Dempsey, Alan	Farrage, Tom	Copping, Wilf	Daniels, John	Baker, Harold	Brown, John	Burditt, George	Goldberg, Les	Jackett, Stan	Spike, Septimus	Meens, Harold
1	2	3	4	5	6	7	8	9	10	11																											
1		3	4	5	6	7		9	10	11	2	8																									
1		3	6		5		7		10		2	8	9	11	4																						
1		3	6		5		7		10		2	9				4	8	11																			
1		3	4	5	6	7			10		2		9	11			8																				
1		3	6	5					10		2	8	9	11					4	7																	
1		3	6	5					10	11	2		9			4				7	8																
1			6	2	5		7		10	11	3	8	9			4																					
1		3	6	5					10		2	8				4				7	9	11															
1		3	6	5			7		10		2	8				4						11	9														
1		3	6	5					10		2		8			4				7			9	11													
1		3	6	5	4				10		2		8			7							9	11													
1		3	6	5					10		2	7	8	11		4							9														
1		3	6	5	4				10		2		9	11		7					8																
		3	6	5	4						2	8		11		7							9		10	1											
1		3	6	5	4						2		8			7					10		9				11										
1		3	6	5			7				2		8								10		9				4	11									
1		3	6	5							2	10	8										9	7			4	11									
1		3	6	5		7	8		10		2								4				9	11													
1		3	6			7			10		2		8						4				9	11					5								
		3	4			9	8				2										10			11					6	1	5	7					
1			5			7			10		2			11		4					3		8						6				9				
	2		6			7			10				5	11		4									8				3	1			9				
	2	3	4			8			10				5	11		7													6	1			9				
	2	3	4				8		10				5	11											7				6	1			9				
	3		4	5		8	10							11		7													6	1			9	2			
	2		6	5		7	8		10					11															3	1			9		4		
	2		6	5		9			10			8	7	11							4									1						3	
	2		6	5		7	8		10					11		4													3	1			9				
	2	3	4			7	8					11									10								6	1			9				5
20	9	23	30	21	10	14	13	2	23	4	21	12	17	14	1	16	2	1	3	4	9	2	11	6	3	1	3	2	10	9	1	1	8	1	1	1	1
2	1		2			3	4	1	5		2	7	6	7		1	1				2		11	2	1								3				
1		3	4	5		7			10		2		8										9					11	6								
1		3	4	5					10		2		9	11		7					8								6								
1			6	5		7			10		2		8	11		4													3				9				
1			6	5		7	8		10		2		9	11		4													3								
4	0	2	4	4	0	3	1	0	4	0	4	0	4	3	0	3	0	0	0	0	1	0	1	0	0	0	0	1	4	0	0	0	1	0	0	0	0
						1					1		1			1							3														

1941-42

Football League Northern Section

Manager: Billy Hampson

Final Position: 26th

Did you know that?

14 March 1942: Gerry Henry scored his second haul of four goals in a game for the season against Doncaster and ended the season with an impressive 28 goals in 33 appearances.

Gerry Henry.

Match No.	Date	Venue	Opponents	Result	FT	HT	Scorers	Attendance
1	Aug 30	H	York City	W	2-0	1-0	Henry 2	3,000
2	Sep 6	A	York City	L	0-1	0-0		4,000
3	13	A	Gateshead	L	2-3	1-3	Henry, Short	4,000
4	20	H	Gateshead	W	5-1	4-1	Henry 2, Short 2, Hargreaves	2,500
5	27	H	Sunderland	L	1-2	0-0	Short	3,000
6	Oct 4	A	Sunderland	L	1-6	1-2	Stephenson	10,000
7	11	A	Bradford PA	L	0-6	0-2		3,000
8	18	H	Bradford PA	W	4-0	2-0	Hargreaves, Henry, Adam, Powell	2,000
9	25	A	Chesterfield	L	0-3	0-0		1,500
10	Nov 1	H	Chesterfield	D	2-2	1-1	Henry, Hargreaves	3,000
11	8	H	Middlesbrough	L	2-3	2-0	Hargreaves 2	2,000
12	15	A	Middlesbrough	W	2-1	1-1	Powell, Hargreaves	4,000
13	22	A	Newcastle United	L	2-4	2-2	Hargreaves, Shanks (pen)	4,500
14	29	H	Newcastle United	W	5-2	1-1	Hargreaves, Henry 4	3,000
15	Dec 6	H	Bradford City	W	4-2	3-1	Gregory (og), Henry, Powell, Lichfield	1,500
16	13	A	Bradford City	L	0-5	0-4		2,000
17	20	A	Huddersfield Town	L	2-4	1-1	Henry 2	2,063
18	25	H	Huddersfield Town	W	2-1	1-0	Henry, McGraw	6,000

First Championship 38 teams.

Appearances

One own-goal — Goals

Football League Northern Section (Second Championship)

Match No.	Date	Venue	Opponents	Result	FT	HT	Scorers	Attendance
19	Dec 27	A	Rotherham United†	L	1-3	1-1	Powell	3,606
20	Jan 3	H	Lincoln City†	W	5-1	0-1	Henry 3, Turner, Jack Milburn (pen)	3,000
21	10	A	Rochdale†	L	0-2	0-0		2,000
22	17	H	Rochdale†	W	5-0	2-0	Knight 2, Adam, Henry 2	3,000
23	Feb 14	H	Barnsley†	W	3-2	2-0	Adam 2, Henry	2,500
24	21	A	Blackburn Rovers†	L	0-1	0-1		1,000
25	28	H	Blackburn Rovers†	L	0-1	0-0		5,200
26	Mar 14	H	Doncaster Rovers†	W	6-1	4-0	Knight, Ainsley, Henry 4	3,000
27	21	A	Barnsley†	L	2-3	1-3	Powell, Harper (og)	4,500
28	28	A	Doncaster Rovers†	L	0-1	0-0		1,225
29	Apr 4	H	Sheffield Wed	L	1-2	1-1	McGraw	3,000
30	6	A	Halifax Town*	L	1-6	1-3	Asquith	2,000
31	11	H	Halifax Town*	W	3-1	0-0	Henry, Holley, Ainsley	2,000
32	18	A	Huddersfield Town*	L	1-5	1-1	Henry	1,636
33	25	A	Middlesbrough*	W	3-2	1-2	Adam, Hepplewhite (og), Jim Milburn (pen)	2,500
34	May 2	H	Chesterfield*	W	1-0	1-0	Henry	2,000
35	9	H	Middlesbrough*	L	1-2	1-0	Adam	2,000

Second Championship 22 teams (+29 teams including Leeds United failed to qualify by playing fewer than 18 games).

† League War Cup Qualifing Competition.

* Combined Counties Cup.

All counted in the League.

Appearances

Two own-goals — Goals

Lee, Alex	Goldberg, Les	Murgatroyd, Arthur	Stanton, Reg	Holley, Tom	Makinson, Jim	Livingstone, Archie	Powell, Aubrey	Henry, Gerry	Lichfield, Eric	Hargreaves, Jack	Fowler, Norman	Bratley, George	Short, John	Brown, John	Copping, Wilf	Stephenson, Eric	McGraw, Jim	Maddison, Ralph	Ramsey, J	Adam, Colin	Daniels, John	Keeping, Alex	Haddow, John	Milburn, Jim	Knight, Arnold	Heaton, Billy	Spike, Sepimus	Shanks, Robert	Harvey, Peter	Gadsby, Ken	Spink, Ken	Watson, George	Milburn, Jack	Williams, Billy	Turner, Jack	Sellar, Ray	Taylor, Walter	Ramsden, Bernard	Bush, Tom	Ainsley, George	McClure, William	Attwell, Reg	Vickers, Harry	Eastham, Harry	Warburton, George	Asquith, Beaumont	Scaife, George	Wesley, John	Shaftoe, John	Kidd, William	Clarke, Reg	Burton, Stan
1	2	3	4	5	6	7	8	9	10	11																																										
1		3	4	5	6	7	8	9	10	11	2																																									
1		3	4		6		8	9	10	11	2	5	7																																							
1				5	4		8	9	10	11	2		7	3	6																																					
1				5	4		8	9		11	2		7	3	6	10																																				
1				5	4		8	9		11	2		7			10	3	6																																		
1	2			5	4		8	9	10		3				6				7	11																																
				5	6		8	9		10	2								7	11	1	3	4																													
				5	6		8	9		7					3	10				11	1		4	2																												
				5	4		8	9		7					3	10				11	1			2	6																											
				5	4		8	9	7	10					2						1	3			6	11																										
					4		8	9	7	10	2									11	1						3	5	6																							
					6		7	9		10			8							11	1		4				2	5		3																						
					4		8	9	7	10	3				6					11	1						2	5																								
11					6		8	9	7		3									10	1		4				2	5																								
					6		8	9	7		3									11	1		4		10		2	5																								
					4		8	9	2		3									10	1		6			11		5			7																					
				5	4		8	9	7								10			11	1			2	6							3																				
8	2	3	3	11	18	2	18	18	12	13	12	1	5	2	7	4	2	1	2	11	11	2	6	3	4	2	5	6	1	1	1	1	0	0	0	0	0	0	0	0	0	0	0	0	0	0	0	0	0	0	0	0
							3	15	1	8			4			1	1			1								1																								

Lee, Alex	Goldberg, Les	Murgatroyd, Arthur	Stanton, Reg	Holley, Tom	Makinson, Jim	Livingstone, Archie	Powell, Aubrey	Henry, Gerry	Lichfield, Eric	Hargreaves, Jack	Fowler, Norman	Bratley, George	Short, John	Brown, John	Copping, Wilf	Stephenson, Eric	McGraw, Jim	Maddison, Ralph	Ramsey, J	Adam, Colin	Daniels, John	Keeping, Alex	Haddow, John	Milburn, Jim	Knight, Arnold	Heaton, Billy	Spike, Sepimus	Shanks, Robert	Harvey, Peter	Gadsby, Ken	Spink, Ken	Watson, George	Milburn, Jack	Williams, Billy	Turner, Jack	Sellar, Ray	Taylor, Walter	Ramsden, Bernard	Bush, Tom	Ainsley, George	McClure, William	Attwell, Reg	Vickers, Harry	Eastham, Harry	Warburton, George	Asquith, Beaumont	Scaife, George	Wesley, John	Shaftoe, John	Kidd, William	Clarke, Reg	Burton, Stan
				5	4		8	9	7		2				3		10			11	1				6																											
				5	4		7	9		11					6						1									3			2	8	10																	
				5	4		8	9	10						6					11	1			2											3	7																
				5	6		8	9			3									11	1			4	10								2				7															
				5	4		8	9							6					11	1			2	10					3							7															
					6			9												11	1			4	10					3							7	2	5	8												
					5		8	9		7							3			11	1				10															4	2	6										
							7	9									11				1				6					2								3	5	8			4	10								
				3	4		7	9		11											1				6													2	5	8				10								
					5		8	9		7							2			11	1																	3		4			6	10								
					4		8			11							10				1			5									2					3					6		7	9						
				5	4		8			11							10				1			2																			6			9	3	7				
				5	4			9												11	1			2	10													3		8			6		7							
				5	6		8	9	10			4								11	1			3									2					7														
				5				7									10			11	1			6														3	4	8	2								9			
				5	6		7	9									3			11	1			4																8										2	10	
	2				4			9					10							11	1			3	6															8	5											7
0	1	0	0	11	15	0	13	15	3	6	2	1	1	0	4	0	8	0	0	12	17	0	0	11	9	0	0	0	0	4	0	0	4	1	2	1	3	8	4	9	3	1	5	3	2	2	1	1	1	1	1	1
				1			2	13									1			5				1	3								1		1					2						1						

1942-43

Football League Northern Section

Manager: Billy Hampson

Final Position: 43rd

Did you know that?

21 November 1942: The rumour that Bolton's Stan Hanson had been posted with the Army to the Leeds area led to the bizarre guest appearance of another soldier, Sid Anson, at outside-right against York City. Despite the shortcomings of the amateur player, Leeds won 2–1.

30 January 1943: Leeds beat Newcastle 7–2 at Elland Road a week after losing 9–0 at St James' Park for the first team's heaviest ever defeat at any level. Incredibly, earlier in the season, Leeds had lost at home to Newcastle 7–1 with a much changed team a week after winning 5–3 away.

Match No.	Date	Venue	Opponents	Result	FT	HT	Scorers	Attendance
1	Aug 29	H	Middlesbrough	L	0-1	0-1		3,000
2	Sep 5	A	Middlesbrough	L	0-2	0-0		3,500
3	12	A	Gateshead	L	1-3	0-3	Short	3,000
4	19	H	Gateshead	L	1-2	0-0	Powell	3,000
5	26	A	Newcastle United	W	5-3	3-2	Wakefield, Short 2, Rutherford, Brown	6,000
6	Oct 3	H	Newcastle United	L	1-7	0-3	Powell	3,000
7	10	H	Doncaster Rovers	W	6-0	3-0	Powell 2, Short 2, Rutherford, Wakefield	3,000
8	17	A	Doncaster Rovers	D	2-2	1-2	Hargreaves, Henry (pen)	2,000
9	24	H	Sunderland	L	1-2	1-0	Wakefield	4,000
10	31	A	Sunderland	L	1-4	1-1	Powell	3,000
11	Nov 7	H	Bradford PA	D	1-1	0-0	Powell	3,000
12	14	A	Bradford PA	L	0-1	0-0		4,465
13	21	H	York City	W	2-1	1-1	Henry, R. Houldershaw	4,000
14	28	A	York City	L	1-3	0-2	Wakefield	5,000
15	Dec 5	H	Halifax Town	D	1-1	0-0	Wakefield	1,000
16	12	A	Halifax Town	L	1-5	1-1	Fallaize	4,000
17	19	A	Huddersfield Town	L	1-4	0-1	Henry	2,286
18	25	H	Huddersfield Town	D	3-3	1-1	Wakefield 2, Henry	4,000

First Championship 48 teams.

Appearances

Goals

Football League Northern Section (Second Championship)

Manager: Billy Hampson

Final Position: 47th

Match No.	Date	Venue	Opponents	Result	FT	HT	Scorers	Attendance
19	Dec 26	A	Barnsley†	L	1-2	0-1	Rutherford	6,000
20	Jan 2	H	Barnsley†	L	1-3	1-2	Powell	2,000
21	9	H	Huddersfield Town†	L	2-4	1-1	Powell, R. Houldershaw	1,000
22	16	A	Huddersfield Town†	L	1-4	1-2	Powell	1,179
23	23	A	Newcastle United†	L	0-9	0-3		7,000
24	30	H	Newcastle United†	W	7-2	2-2	Powell 4, Henry, Ainsley 2	2,000
25	Feb 6	A	Bradford PA†	L	1-2	0-0	Henry	4,500
26	13	H	Bradford PA†	D	2-2	1-1	Rutherford, Henry	3,000
27	20	A	Bradford City†	L	0-1	0-1		4,287
28	27	H	Bradford City†	L	1-5	1-1	Rutherford	3,000
29	Mar 6	H	Middlesbrough*	W	3-2	1-1	Wakefield 2, R. Houldershaw	2,000
30	13	A	Middlesbrough*	W	3-2	1-0	Lawn, Henry 2	2,500
31	20	H	Newcastle United	L	1-3	0-1	Short	2,500
32	27	A	Newcastle United	W	5-4	0-2	Short, Powell 2, Rutherford, Williams	8,000
33	Apr 3	H	Bradford PA*	W	2-0	1-0	Smith, Jim Milburn	3,000
34	10	A	Bradford PA*	L	2-5	1-1	Argue, Powell	3,908

Second Championship 54 teams.

† League War Cup Qualifing Competition.

* Combined Counties Cup.

All counted in the League.

Appearances

Goals

Liverpool and England defender Bill Jones guested for Leeds in 1942–43.

Daniels, John	Fowler, Norman	Gadsby, Ken	Vickers, Harry	Bush, Tom	McInnes, John	Powell, Aubrey	Taylor, Phil	Henry, Gerry	Eastham, Harry	Patterson, George	Holley, Tom	Knight, Arnold	Jones, Bill	Butterworth, Frank	Short, John	Kinghorn, William	Goldberg, Les	Rutherford, Eddie	Milburn, Jack	McGraw, Jim	Wakefield, Albert	Brown, John	Scaife, George	Kirby, Dennis	Clutterbuck, Jack	O'Farrell, John	Tindall, John	Milburn, Jim	Poxon, John	Moss, Amos	Hargreaves, Jack	Robbins, Horace	Lambert, Ray	Houldershaw, Rex	Simpson, John	Marshall, Dennis	Warren, Ray	Anson, Sid	Ainsley, George	Campbell, Robson	Harston, John	Sturrock, William	Fallaize, Reg	Houldershaw, Harry	D'Arcy, Lawrence	Woffinden, Richard	Harper, Bernard
1	2	3	4	5	6	7	8	9	10	11																																					
1	3			2	4	7	8	9	10	11	5	6																																			
1	3				4	8		9	7			6	2	5	10	11																															
1						8		9		10	5	6	3	4		11	2	7																													
1						8					5	6		4	10			7	2	3	9	11																									
1						8		7			5									3	9		2	4	6	10	11																				
1						8					5	6		4	10			7	2		9	11						3																			
1						8		10						5				7		3	9							2	4	6	11																
1		3				8		10			5			4				7			9	11						2				6															
1		3				8		7			5			4	10				2		9												6	11													
1						8		10			5										9							2	4	6				11	3	7											
1						8		7			5			4						3	9								10	6				11	2												
1						8		10				6							2									3		4				11			5	7	9								
1						8		7				6								3	9							2						11			5		10	4							
1						8						6		4				7		3	9													11					10		2	5					
1						8						6		4				7		3																			10		2	5	9	11			
1						8		9				6		4				7		2																			10					11	3	5	
1		3				8		9				6								2	10								5					11					4								7
18	3	4	1	2	3	18	2	14	3	3	9	11	2	11	4	2	1	8	4	9	11	3	1	1	1	1	1	6	4	4	1	1	1	7	2	1	2	1	6	1	2	2	1	2	1	1	1
						6		4							5			2			7	1									1			1													

Daniels, John	Gadsby, Ken	McGraw, Jim	Lambert, Ray	Milburn, Jim	Knight, Arnold	Rutherford, Eddie	Powell, Aubrey	Henry, Gerry	Wakefield, Albert	Houldershaw, Rex	Bedford, Harold	Moss, Amos	Butterworth, Frank	Ainsley, George	Milburn, Jack	Warren, Ray	Whittle, Roger	Short, John	Wilcox, George	Dunn, William	Wheeler, Stan	Jones Bill (WH)	Wilkinson, Ken	Edwards, Willis	Fallaize, Reg	Holley, Tom	Rhodes, Arthur	Argue, James	Hick, Jack	Lawn, Maurice	Harris, William	Dainty, Albert	Wildon, Norman	Taylor, Walter	Williams, Tom	Pyke, R	Binns, Cliff	Harper, Bernard	Smith, Gavin	Boyes, Walter	Bokas, Frank
1	2	3	4	5	6	7	8	9	10	11																															
1		3			6		8	7	9	11	2	4	5	10																											
1		3			6	7	8		9	11		4	5	10	2																										
1		3			6	7	8	10	9	11			2	4		5																									
1		3			6	11	7	9					5	10		4	2	8																							
1		10			6	11	8	7					5	9					2	3	4																				
1		3			6	11	8	7	9			4	5	10					2																						
1					6	11	8	7	10				5									2	3	4	9																
1		3			6	11	8	7	10				4			2									9	5															
1		3			6	11	8	7	10				5		2												4	9													
1	3			2	6	7		9	10	11																	4	8	5												
1	3			2	6		8	7	10	11		5															4			9											
1		3	6			11		7					5					8												9	2	4	10								
1					6	7	10						5			4		8													3			2	9	11					
				3	6		8	9																			4	10						2			1	5	7	11	
					6		8									2		10				3						9									1	5	7	11	4
14	3	10	2	4	15	12	14	13	10	6	1	4	11	6	2	5	1	4	2	1	1	2	1	1	2	1	4	4	1	2	2	1	1	2	1	1	2	2	2	2	1
				1		4	10	5	2	2				2				2										1		1					1				1		

1943-44

Football League Northern Section

Manager: Billy Hampson

Final Position: 27th

Did you know that?

11 September 1943: After three games Leeds had leaked 17 goals and scored only three for the worst start to any season ever.

11 March 1944: In the home win against Sheffield United, the Leeds guest centre-half was Maurice Lindley of Everton who was to return to Elland Road two decades later as one of Don Revie's closest assistants.

Everton winger Walter Boyes was one of the star guest performers of the season.

Match No.	Date	Venue	Opponents	Result	FT	HT	Scorers	Attendance
1	Aug 28	A	Sunderland	L	1-7	1-3	Wakefield	4,000
2	Sep 4	H	Sunderland	L	1-5	0-2	Tremelling	4,000
3	11	H	Bradford City	L	1-5	0-4	Boyes (pen)	2,000
4	18	A	Bradford City	D	3-3	2-2	Henry 2, Boyes (pen)	6,000
5	25	H	Middlesbrough	W	3-0	1-0	Stevens, Jameson, Henry	3,000
6	Oct 2	A	Middlesbrough	D	3-3	0-1	Powell, Henry, Short	3,000
7	9	H	Gateshead	W	5-2	3-0	Henry, Tremelling 3, Boyes	3,000
8	16	A	Gateshead	W	4-3	1-2	Short, Henry, Powell 2	3,000
9	23	A	Doncaster Rovers	D	3-3	2-2	Knight 2, Henry	8,264
10	30	H	Doncaster Rovers	D	2-2	2-2	Henry (pen), Fallaize	5,000
11	Nov 6	A	Bradford PA	L	1-6	0-3	Henry	5,301
12	13	H	Bradford PA	D	2-2	0-0	Henry, Hindle	6,000
13	20	A	York City	W	3-1	0-1	Henry 2, Knight	4,708
14	27	H	York City	W	1-0	1-0	Knight	4,000
15	Dec 4	A	Halifax Town	L	1-2	0-1	Brown	3,000
16	11	H	Halifax Town	W	4-0	3-0	Knight, Boyes, Dorling, Hindle (pen)	4,000
17	18	H	Huddersfield Town	L	0-3	0-1		5,000
18	25	A	Huddersfield Town	L	0-3	0-1		7,792

First Championship 50 teams.

Appearances

Goals

Football League Northern Section (Second Championship)

Manager: Billy Hampson

Final Position: 35th

Match No.	Date	Venue	Opponents	Result	FT	HT	Scorers	Attendance
19	Dec 26	A	Bradford PA†	L	1-2	1-1	Powell	13,186
20	Jan 1	H	Bradford PA†	W	3-1	1-1	Hindle, Powell, Antonio	7,200
21	8	H	Barnsley†	W	2-0	1-0	Antonio, Henry	7,000
22	15	A	Barnsley†	L	2-3	1-1	Henry 2	4,347
23	22	A	Huddersfield Town†	L	1-4	1-2	Hindle	1,810
24	29	H	Huddersfield Town†	W	2-0	2-0	Boyes, Antonio	8,000
25	Feb 5	A	Bradford City†	D	3-3	0-2	Antonio 2, Boyes	4,800
26	12	H	Bradford City†	W	2-0	1-0	Hindle, Boyes	8,000
27	19	H	York City†	W	2-1	1-1	Mahon, Henry	7,000
28	26	A	York City†	L	1-8	1-4	Knight	5,176
29	Mar 4	A	Sheffield United‡	L	1-3	0-1	Boyes	12,000
30	11	H	Sheffield United‡	W	1-0	0-0	Davies	15,000
31	18	A	Derby County	D	2-2	0-1	Curry 2	6,000
32	Apr 1	A	Chesterfield*	W	3-1	1-1	Davie 2, Gadsby	1,000
33	8	H	Chesterfield*	W	1-0	1-0	Steele	4,500
34	10	A	Rotherham United	L	3-5	1-1	Tatton, Powell, Short	8,000
35	15	H	Halifax Town*	D	2-2	1-2	Tatton, Davie	6,000
36	22	A	Halifax Town*	L	2-5	2-3	Steele, Davie	4,000

Second Championship 50 teams.

† League War Cup Qualifying Competition.

‡ League War Cup Knockout (2 legs).

* Combined Counties Cup.

All counted in the League.

Appearances

Goals

Daniels, John	Gadsby, Ken	Stokes, Ernie	Butterworth, Frank	Glover, Arthur	Knight, Arnold	Henry, Gerry	Powell, Aubrey	Rodgers, William	Ainsley, George	Wakefield, Albert	Poland, George	Wilcox, George	Makinson, Jim	Paton, Tom	Tremelling, Jack	Wright, Horace	Boyes, Walter	Hirst, Hubert	McGraw, Jim	Padgett, Herbert	Lawn, Maurice	Jones, Syd	Fallaize, Reg	Attwell, Reg	Stevens, Tom	Jameson, Percy	Hindle, Tom	Milburn, Jim	Short, John	Rhodes, Arthur	O'Neill, Tom	Challinor, Jack	Kirton, John	Ward, Tim	Holley, Tom	Thompson, Les	Houldershaw, Harry	Bowen, James	Sharp, Norman	Kirby, Dennis	Mahon, Jack	Jordan, Clarrie	Galley, Tom	Goldberg, Les	Walker, Jack	Brown, John	McKellar, Walter	Tatton, Billy	Dorling, George	Moule, Jack	Dewis, George
1	2	3	4	5	6	7	8	9	10	11																																									
	3				6		8	7			1	2	4	5	9	10	11																																		
1			5		6	7							4			10	11	2	3	8	9																														
	3		5			9	8				1		4			10	11		6			2	7																												
1	3		5			7						2					11		4					6	8	9	10																								
1		3	5		6	9	7						4				11										10	2	8																						
1		3	5			7							6		9		11		2								10		8	4																					
			5			9	7				1		6				11		2								10		8	4	3																				
			5		9	7					1						11		8			2					10					3	4	6																	
1		3	4			9							6									2	8				10								5	7	11														
		3	5			9	7				1		6				11										10									4		2	8												
			5			8					1						11										10	2				3	6							4	7	9									
			5		9	7	8				1						11		3								10	2												6			4								
1			5		9	7	8										11										10					3								6				2	4						
1			5			7							6						2								10					3													4	8	9	11			
	2		5		9	7	8				1						11		3								10																4						6		
	2		5		9	7	8				1						11										10					3	6										4								
1	3				6		8						5				11										10	2					4																	7	9
9	7	5	16	1	10	16	11	2	1	1	9	2	10	1	2	3	15	1	9	1	1	3	2	1	1	1	14	4	3	2	1	5	4	1	1	2	1	1	1	3	1	1	3	1	2	1	1	1	1	1	1
					5	12	3			1					4		4						1		1	1	2		2																	1		1			

Daniels, John	Milburn, Jim	Gadsby, Ken	Kirton, John	Butterworth, Frank	Knight, Arnold	Henry, Gerry	Powell, Aubrey	Dewis, George	Hindle, Tom	Boyes, Walter	Challinor, Jack	Dorling, George	Antonio, George	Milburn, Jack	Makinson, Jim	McGraw, Jim	Poland, George	Thompson, Les	Davies, Cecil	Goldberg, Les	Holley, Tom	Moule, Jack	Ward, Tim	Mahon, Jack	Rosier, Alf	Hodgson, John	Corbett, Norman	Milburn, George	Galley, Tom	Lindley, Maurice	Goodburn, Harold	Dutchman, John	Curry, Robert	Yeomanson, Jack	Davie, John	Short, John	Steele, Fred	Tatton, Billy	Farrell, Arthur	Williams, Cyril
1	2	3	4	5	6	7	8	9	10	11																														
1		2		5	6	9	7		10	11	3	4	8																											
1	2			5	6	9	7		10	11	3	4	8																											
1					6	9	7			11	3	4	8	2	5	10																								
				5	6	9	7		10	11			8			3	1	2	4																					
1				4		9	7		10	11	3		8		6					2	5																			
1				6		9			10	11			8	2	4	3					5	7																		
1				5		8			10	11	3			2	4								6	7	9															
1				5		7			10		3		8			2			6				4	11	9															
				5	9				10	11	3		8			2			4					7		1	6													
1				5		9	7		10	11			8	3					6									2	4											
1				4		9	7		10	11			8			3			6									2		5										
1	5					7									4	3								11	9			2			6	8	10							
1		3		5	10	7	8			11				2					6															4	9					
1				5		7					3									2			6											4	9	8	10	11		
1				5		7	10									3				2														4	9	8		11	6	
1				5	10	7	8								6	3																		4	9			11		2
1			6	5		7				11	3				4																			2	8		9	10		
16	3	3	2	16	8	17	11	1	11	13	9	3	10	5	7	9	1	1	6	3	2	1	3	4	3	1	1	3	1	1	1	1	1	5	5	2	2	4	1	1
		1			1	4	3		3	4			5						1					1									2		4	1	2	2		

1944-45

Football League Northern Section

Manager: Billy Hampson

Final Position: 22nd

Did you know that?

25 November 1944: As the Leeds bus drove down a dark deserted rural road after a trip to play Hartlepools, a projectile shot through the bus leaving bullet-like holes on either side. No shot had been heard and the incident remained a mystery.

21 May 1945: Despite losing 6–1, United scored a record 106 goals for the season, a higher total than the League football best of 98 in 1927–28.

Match No.	Date	Venue	Opponents	Result	FT	HT	Scorers	Attendance
1	Aug 26	A	Bradford PA	L	3-4	1-2	Jack Milburn (pen), Henry, Sutherland	8,416
2	Sep 2	H	Bradford PA	D	3-3	1-1	Jack Milburn (pen), Yeomanson, Sutherland	6,000
3	9	H	Sunderland	L	0-1	0-1		8,000
4	16	A	Sunderland	L	1-5	1-0	Mahon	8,000
5	23	A	Middlesbrough	L	2-3	1-1	Ainsley 2	4,500
6	30	H	Middlesbrough	W	4-2	3-0	Mahon 2, Hindle, Coyne	8,000
7	Oct 7	H	Hull City	W	5-2	4-1	Coyne 2, Mahon, Hindle, Henry	8,000
8	14	A	Hull City	D	0-0	0-0		5,000
9	21	H	Newcastle United	W	2-1	2-1	Coyne 2	8,000
10	28	A	Newcastle United	W	4-2	2-0	Hindle, Morton, Short, Ainsley	25,000
11	Nov 4	A	Bradford City	W	6-2	2-1	Hindle 2, Ainsley 3, Coyne	6,657
12	11	H	Bradford City	W	4-1	2-0	Ainsley 3, Hindle	8,760
13	18	H	Hartlepools United	W	6-2	4-0	Short 3, Hindle 2, Ainsley	9,000
14	25	A	Hartlepools United	L	0-3	0-1		4,940
15	Dec 2	A	Huddersfield Town	L	2-4	1-3	Henry, Moule	7,880
16	9	H	Huddersfield Town	L	2-3	2-2	Henry, Moule	14,000
17	16	H	York City	W	3-1	1-0	Henry 3	5,000
18	23	A	York City	W	6-3	2-0	Hindle 3, Short 2, Moule	4,871

First Championship 54 teams.

Appearances
Goals

Sunderland's Eddie Burbanks was a popular guest and was later to join United.

Football League Northern Section (Second Championship)

Manager: Billy Hampson

Final Position: 32nd

Match No.	Date	Venue	Opponents	Result	FT	HT	Scorers	Attendance
19	Dec 26	H	Bradford City†	W	9-1	5-0	Hindle 3, Short 2, Henry, Mahon, Burbanks, Weaver (pen)	3,500
20	30	A	Bradford City†	L	2-6	2-0	Mahon, Henry	7,672
21	Jan 6	H	Barnsley†	L	0-1	0-1		12,000
22	13	A	Barnsley†	L	0-5	0-2		6,989
23	20	A	York City†	W	5-0	1-0	Moule, Dunderdale 2, Hindle 2	1,000
24	27	H	York City†	W	4-3	1-2	Moule, Henry, Hindle, Bubanks	6,000
25	Feb 3	H	Hull City†	W	6-1	2-0	Coyne, Hindle 2, Henry 2, Weaver (pen)	8,000
26	10	A	Hull City†	D	1-1	0-0	Campbell	4,000
27	17	A	Bradford PA†	L	2-5	2-2	Hindle, Henry	10,198
28	24	H	Bradford PA†	L	0-2	0-1		15,000
29	Mar 3	H	Sheffield Wed	W	4-3	3-1	Henry 3, Hindle	7,000
30	10	H	Preston North End	W	3-1	1-1	Hindle 2, Coyne	8,500
31	17	A	Sheffield Wed	D	1-1	1-1	Henry	7,000
32	24	H	Grimsby Town	D	1-1	0-0	Knight	7,000
33	Apr 2	H	Chesterfield	L	0-2	0-1		6,500
34	9	A	Grimsby Town	L	0-3	0-0		6,000
35	14	H	Hull City	W	6-2	3-1	Henry 2, Hindle 2, Coyne, Moule	2,000
36	21	A	Barnsley	W	3-1	1-0	Knight 2, Hartson (og)	3,380
37	28	H	Barnsley	L	1-3	0-2	Moule	4,000
38	May 5	A	Sheffield United	L	0-6	0-3		4,000
39	12	H	Sheffield United	W	4-1	4-0	Jim Milburn, Hindle, Ward, Henry	4,000
40	21	A	Chesterfield	L	1-6	1-3	Morton	4,000

Second Championship 60 teams.
† League War Cup Qualifying Competition (games also counted in the League).

One own-goal

Appearances
Goals

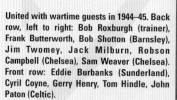

United with wartime guests in 1944–45. Back row, left to right: Bob Roxburgh (trainer), Frank Butterworth, Bob Shotton (Barnsley), Jim Twomey, Jack Milburn, Robson Campbell (Chelsea), Sam Weaver (Chelsea). Front row: Eddie Burbanks (Sunderland), Cyril Coyne, Gerry Henry, Tom Hindle, John Paton (Celtic).

Daniels, John	Milburn, Jack	Gadsby, Ken	Yeomanson, Jack	Butterworth, Frank	Knight, Arnold	Mahon, Jack	Henry, Gerry	Sutherland, Harry	Hindle, Tom	Calverley, Alf	Sharples, Ken	Pickering, Bill	Weaver, Sam	Dutchman, John	Hodgson, John	Kirby, Dennis	Howe, Arthur	Short, John	Ainsley, George	Burbanks, Eddie	Hardaker, Neville	Coyne, Cyril	McGraw, Jim	James, John	Byrom, Tom	Booth, Sammy	Campbell, Robson	Birch, Walter	Moule, Jack
1	2	3	4	5	6	7	8	9	10	11																			
1	2	3	4	5	6		8	9	10	11	7																		
1			2	5	4	11	7	9	10			3	6	8															
		2		5		11	7		10			3			1	4	6	8	9										
		3	2	5	4	7			10				6		1			8	9	11									
1			2	5	4	7			10				6						9	11	3	8							
1			2	5		11	7		10				6			4			9			8	3						
1		3	2	5		7			10				6			4			9	11		8							
1				5			7		10							4	6		9	11	3	8	2						
1				5		11	7		10				6			4			9			8	2	3					
1				5		11	7		10				6						9			8	3		2	4			
1				5	6	11	7		10										9			8			2	4	3		
1	2			5		11	7		10									8	9				3		4		6		
1	3		2	5		11	7		10				6					9				8			4				
1				5		11	9		10				6									8	3				4	2	7
1				5	4	10	9						6							11		8	3				2		7
1	2			5	4		9		10											11		8	3				6		7
1		3	2		4				10				6					9		11		8					5		7
16	5	6	9	17	9	14	14	3	17	2	1	2	11	1	2	5	2	5	10	7	2	12	8	1	4	2	6	1	4
	2		1			5	7	2	11									6	10			6							3

Daniels, John	Yeomanson, Jack	Gadsby, Ken	Knight, Arnold	Butterworth, Frank	Weaver, Sam	Mahon, Jack	Short, John	Henry, Gerry	Hindle, Tom	Burbanks, Eddie	Moule, Jack	Coyne, Cyril	McGraw, Jim	Gleave, Colin	Paton, John	Goldberg, Les	Dunderdale, Len	Bokas, Frank	Milburn, Jack	Campbell, Robson	Houldershaw, Rex	Shotton, Bob	Twomey, Jim	Glover, Arthur	Harper, Ken	Hargreaves, Jack	Forde, Steve	Normanton, Sid	Fearnley, Harry	Duthoit, Jack	Crookes, Geoff	Benn, Alf	Powell, Aubrey	Cherry, D	Milburn, Jim	Ruecroft, Jacob	Ward, Tom	Hulbert, J	Downing, H	Morton, Norman	Stephens, Bill
1	2	3	4	5	6	7	8	9	10	11																															
1	2	3	4	5	6	11		9	10		7	8																													
1	2			5	6	7		9	10			8	3	4	11																										
1	3			5	6	7		8	10					4	11	2	9																								
1	3			5	6		8		10		7				11	2	9	4																							
1	3			5				8	10	11	7						9	4	2	6																					
1				5	6	7		9	10			8	3						2	4	11																				
1				5		7		9	10			8	3					4	2	6	11																				
1				5		7		9	10			8	4						3	6	11	2																			
1				5		7		9	10			8						4	3	6	11	2																			
		3		5				9	10		7	8							2	6	11		1	4																	
				5	6			9	10	11		8			7				2	4		3	1																		
				5	6			9	10		7	8								4		3	1		2	11															
	2		11	5	6			9	10		7	8								4		3	1																		
1			4	5	6		8		10	11	7									2							3	9													
			4	5				8	10	11	7	6					9		2				1				3														
		3	4	5	6			9	10		7	8																	1	2	11										
			9	5	6				10		11	7								3									1	2		4	8								
				5	4			9	10		7	8								3									1	2	11			6							
			4		6				10		7	8	3						5									9	1	2	11										
		3	11		6			7	10			8								4									1						2	5	9				
		3	4		6		10					8																	1							5		2	7	9	11
11	7	6	10	19	16	8	4	17	21	5	12	17	5	2	4	2	4	4	9	13	5	5	5	1	1	1	2	2	6	4	3	1	1	1	1	2	1	1	1	1	1
			3		2	2	2	13	15	2	4	3					2			1															1		1			1	

1945-46

Football League Northern Section

Manager: Billy Hampson

Final Position: 22nd

Did you know that?

4 February 1946: An FA Cup fourth round replay between Middlesbrough and Blackpool attracted a 30,000 crowd to Elland Road – up to nearly half of whom did not pay to get in. Even though all but four of the 36 turnstiles were open, spectators sneaked in though big gaps in hoardings near the main stand. The roof of the Supporters' Club, on which fans had been standing, also partially collapsed, but no one was hurt. The club later appealed to the gatecrashers to send a minimum charge of 1s 6d to United so it could be passed on to charity.

1 May 1946: The season ended with a win over Bradford but United had conceded a massive 119 goals over the 42 games.

Burnley's Jackie Chew was among the season's guest players.

Match No.	Date		Venue	Opponents	Result	FT	HT	Scorers	Attendance
1	Aug	25	A	Chesterfield	L	1-3	1-0	Hindle	7,229
2	Sep	1	H	Chesterfield	L	1-3	0-3	Short	7,339
3		8	H	Barnsley	L	1-2	0-1	Powell	8,561
4		13	A	Stoke City	L	1-2	0-2	Hindle	6,882
5		15	A	Barnsley	L	2-3	1-1	Henry, Hindle	10,055
6		22	A	Everton	W	2-0	1-0	Grainger, Henry	19,711
7		29	H	Everton	L	2-3	0-1	Short, Hindle	13,541
8	Oct	6	H	Bolton Wanderers	W	2-1	0-1	Grainger, Hindle	11,836
9		13	A	Bolton Wanderers	L	0-6	0-3		17,770
10		20	H	Preston North End	W	2-1	0-1	Dutchman, Henry	11,782
11		27	A	Preston North End	L	2-8	0-3	Chew, Henry	12,344
12	Nov	3	H	Burnley	L	1-2	1-0	Ainsley	11,387
13		10	A	Burnley	W	3-2	2-0	Ainsley, Henry, Short	6,925
14		17	H	Manchester United	D	3-3	2-1	Ainsley, Short, Henry	12,013
15		24	A	Manchester United	L	1-6	1-2	Whalley (og)	21,312
16	Dec	1	H	Sunderland	W	4-2	2-2	Ainsley, Grainger, Stelling (og), Dutchman	9,509
17		8	A	Sunderland	L	1-5	1-3	Grainger	10,106
18		15	H	Sheffield United	L	2-4	1-3	J.W. Stephens, Henry	10,401
19		22	A	Sheffield United	L	2-6	1-1	Ainsley, Grainger	14,926
20		25	H	Middlesbrough	W	1-0	0-0	Grainger	12,217
21		26	A	Middlesbrough	L	1-4	1-2	Ainsley	23,019
22		29	H	Stoke City	D	0-0	0-0		22,219
23	Jan	12	H	Blackpool	L	1-2	1-0	Ainsley	14,372
24		19	A	Blackpool	L	2-4	2-1	Ainsley 2	8,734
25		26	A	Grimsby Town	L	2-3	1-2	Ainsley, Henry	10,105
26	Feb	2	H	Liverpool	W	3-0	1-0	Henry 2 (1 pen), Ainsley	11,881
27		9	H	Bury	D	3-3	1-0	Hindle 2, Ainsley (pen)	13,474
28		16	A	Bury	L	1-3	1-0	Grainger	8,623
29		23	A	Blackburn Rovers	D	0-0	0-0		6,048
30	Mar	2	H	Blackburn Rovers	L	1-4	0-3	Ainsley (pen)	10,752
31		9	H	Grimsby Town	D	2-2	2-1	Henry, Heaton	8,000
32		16	A	Bradford PA	L	4-9	1-5	Ainsley 2, McGraw, Grainger	11,302
33		23	A	Manchester City	L	1-5	1-3	Heaton	20,000
34		30	H	Manchester City	L	1-3	1-1	Price	10,000
35	Apr	6	H	Newcastle United	L	0-3	0-1		14,000
36		10	A	Liverpool	D	1-1	0-1	Grainger	10,620
37		13	A	Newcastle United	D	1-1	1-0	Ainsley	25,000
38		20	H	Huddersfield Town	W	3-2	3-1	Briggs (og), Powell, Heaton	15,000
39		22	H	Sheffield Wed	L	0-1	0-0		14,000
40		23	A	Sheffield Wed	L	0-2	0-1		14,000
41		27	A	Huddersfield Town	L	2-3	1-1	Ainsley 2	4,622
42	May	1	H	Bradford PA	W	3-2	2-0	Hindle, Ainsley 2	10,000
									Appearances
								Three own-goals	Goals

FA Cup

R3	Jan	5	D	Middlesbrough	D	4-4	1-2	Henry, Ainsley, Hardwick (og), Short	18,000
		9	L	Middlesbrough	L	2-7	1-7	Grainger, Ainsley	23,878

Leeds lost 11-6 on aggregate

	Appearances
One own-goal	Goals

Parker, William	Milburn, Jack	Oliver, Harry	Duffy, Robert	Butterworth, Frank	Coyne, Cyril	Henry, Gerry	Blair, Doug	Stephens, Bill	Hindle, Tom	Glackin, Tom	Duthoit, Jack	Jones, Syd	Moule, Jack	Short, John	Crookes, Geoff	Hodgson, John	Powell Aubrey	Grainger, Dennis	Hudson, George	Iceton, Lloyd	Jones, Eric	Laidman, Fred	Chew, Jackie	Stephens, Alf	Burbanks, Eddie	Gadsby, Ken	Buckley, Arthur	Alberry, Bill	Dutchman, John	Walker, Jack	Westlake, Frank	Price, Arthur	Ainsley, George	Skidmore, William	McGraw, Jim	Holley, Tom	Barton, Teddy	Laking, George	Heaton, Billy	Pope, Alf	Browne, Bobby	Smith, Jack	Collier, Austin	Fearnley, Harry	Milburn, Jim	Knight, Arnold	Goldberg, Les	Batey, Dick	Pogson, Donald			
1	2	3	4	5	6	7	8	9	10	11																																									
1			4	5	6			9	10		2	3	7	8	11																																						
	2		4	5	6			9	10			3		8		1	7	11																																			
			4	5	6			8	10			3				1		7	2	9	11																															
	2		4	5	6	7			10			3		8		1		11		9																																	
			4	5	6	9			10			3				1		7	2			8	11																														
			4	5	6	9			10			3		7		1			2			8	11																														
			4	5	6				10			3				1		7	2				8	9	11																													
			4	5	6	9		8				2				1		7									3	11																									
			4		6	9					2	7			1		11					10			3		5	8																						
			4	5	6	9					3				1		7	2			8	10								11																					
			4	5	6				10		2		8		1									11							3	7	9																		
			4	5	6	7			10					8		1		11	2																9	3																	
			4	5	6	7			10					8		1		11	2																9	3																	
			4			7			10		2			8		1		11																	9		3	5	6																
				4		7			10		2					1		11												8				9		3	5	6																
				4		7		10			2					1		11												8				9		3	5	6																
				4	6	7		10			2			8		1		11								3								9			5																	
				4	6	7			10		2					1	8	11								3								9			5																	
					6	7			10		2					1	8	11								3							4	9			5																	
									10		2			8		1	7	11								3							4	9			5	6																
				4	6				10		2			8		1	7																			9			5		3	11													
						8			10		2					1		7																	4	9			5			11	3	6											
						7		8	10		2					1																			4	9			5			11		6	3										
					6	8			10		2					1		7																	4	9			5			11			3										
					6	8			10		2					1		7																	4	9			5			11			3										
					6			8	10		2					1		7																	4	9			5			11			3										
					6	8			10		2					1		7																	4	9			5			11			3										
						8		9	10		2		7			1																			4				5			11		6	3										
						7		8	10		2					1		11																	4	9			5				6	3										
					6	8			10							1		7																	4	9		3	5			11			2										
					6	8			10							1		7																		9		3	5			11			2	4									
						8			10									7																	4	9			5			11			2		1	3	6							
						8			10							1		7																	4	9			5			11			2			3	6							
						7			10							1	8	11																		9			5								4		3		2	6					
																1	8	7																	4	9			5			11						3	10	2	6					
																1	8	7																	4	9			5			11						3	10	2	6					
																1	8	7																	4	9			5			11						3	10	2	6					
						9												8	7																	4				5			11					1	3	10	2	6					
						9			10								8	7																	4				5			11					1	3		2	6					
									10							1	8	7																	4	9			5			11						2			6	3			
						8			10									7																	4	9			5			11					1	3		2	6					
2	3	1	15	18	24	30	1	11	33	1	17	11	3	11	1	36	12	35	7	2	1	3	6	1	2	6	1	1	3	1	1	21	28	2	5	28	4	1	19	1	4	11	2	4	10	6	7	8	1			
						11		1	8					4			2	9					1						2			1	20		1				3													
				4	6	7			10		2			8		1		11								3								9			5																	
				5	4	7			10		2			8		1		11								3							6	9																			
0	0	0	0	2	2	2	0	0	2	0	2	0	0	2	0	2	0	2	0	0	0	0	0	0	0	2	0	0	0	0	0	1	2	0	0	1	0	0	0	0	0	0	0	0	0	0	0	0	0			
						1								1				1																2																			

1946-47

Division One

Manager: Billy Hampson

Final Position: 22nd

Did you know that?

31 August 1946: The legendary Tom Finney made his debut in Preston North End's 3–2 win against United.

18 January 1947: United beat Chelsea 2–1 with goals from Gerry Henry (penalty) and Dave Cochrane, but United only picked up two draws in their remaining 17 League games to finish bottom of Division One.

20 January 20 1947: Three new directors were elected to the United board – Harold Marjason, Percy Woodward and Robert Wilkinson.

10 March 1947: It was not only the first team who were having a bad season. United's reserves lost 11–0 at Blackpool in the Central League.

26 May 1947: A 4–1 defeat at Everton in the final game of the season saw United finish with 30 defeats and only 18 points – both unwanted records.

Relegation was not much to write home about but the players' autographs were legible.

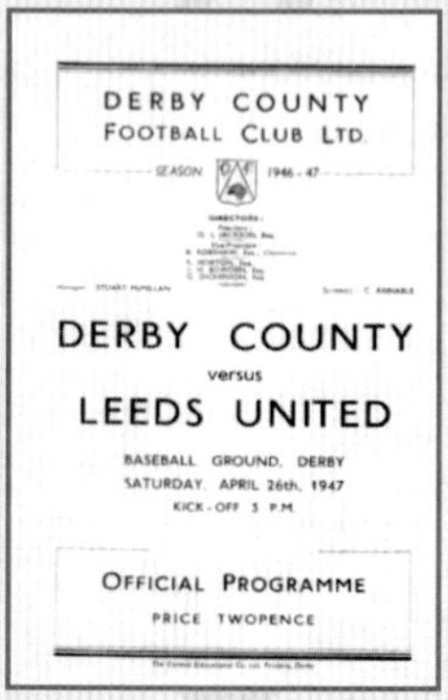

Match No.	Date	Venue	Opponents	Result	FT	HT	Scorers	Attendance
1	Aug 31	A	Preston North End	L	2-3	1-2	Grainger 2	25,311
2	Sep 4	H	Charlton Athletic	L	0-2	0-2		22,857
3	7	H	Sheffield United	D	2-2	1-1	Powell, Henry	28,543
4	14	A	Chelsea	L	0-3	0-1		57,184
5	16	A	Stoke City	L	2-5	1-2	Ainsley 2	21,141
6	21	H	Bolton Wanderers	W	4-0	3-0	Cochrane, Ainsley, Short 2	25,739
7	25	A	Charlton Athletic	L	0-5	0-4		16,488
8	28	A	Liverpool	L	0-2	0-1		51,042
9	Oct 5	H	Huddersfield Town	W	5-0	3-0	Ainsley 3, Powell, Short	30,622
10	12	H	Grimsby Town	W	1-0	0-0	Powell	28,877
11	19	A	Wolverhampton W	L	0-1	0-1		40,113
12	26	H	Blackburn Rovers	L	0-1	0-0		28,683
13	Nov 2	A	Portsmouth	L	1-4	1-1	Ainsley	25,984
14	9	H	Everton	W	2-1	0-1	Powell, Short	22,992
15	16	A	Arsenal	L	2-4	1-1	Ainsley 2	36,377
16	23	H	Blackpool	W	4-2	1-0	Powell 2, Ainsley, Grainger	25,829
17	30	A	Brentford	D	1-1	1-1	Cochrane	20,352
18	Dec 7	H	Sunderland	D	1-1	0-1	Cochrane	25,784
19	14	A	Aston Villa	L	1-2	0-2	Powell	29,410
20	21	H	Derby County	L	1-2	0-1	Henry (pen)	21,320
21	25	H	Middlesbrough	D	3-3	0-1	Milburn, Short, Cochrane	28,742
22	26	A	Middlesbrough	L	0-3	0-1		45,336
23	28	H	Preston North End	L	0-3	0-2		33,433
24	Jan 4	A	Sheffield United	L	2-6	0-3	Cochrane, Ainsley	31,947
25	18	H	Chelsea	W	2-1	1-0	Henry (pen), Cochrane	37,884
26	Feb 1	H	Liverpool	L	1-2	0-1	Grainger	25,430
27	3	A	Bolton Wanderers	L	0-2	0-1		6,278
28	22	H	Wolverhampton W	L	0-1	0-0		30,313
29	Mar 1	A	Blackburn Rovers	L	0-1	0-0		28,371
30	22	H	Arsenal	D	1-1	0-0	Grainger	32,190
31	29	A	Blackpool	L	0-3	0-2		14,501
32	Apr 5	H	Brentford	L	1-2	1-1	Henry (pen)	23,962
33	7	A	Manchester United	L	1-3	1-1	Cochrane	41,912
34	8	H	Manchester United	L	0-2	0-1		15,528
35	12	A	Sunderland	L	0-1	0-1		30,429
36	19	H	Aston Villa	D	1-1	0-1	Clarke	22,291
37	26	A	Derby County	L	1-2	1-1	Powell	10,994
38	May 3	H	Stoke City	L	1-2	0-0	Short	21,714
39	10	A	Huddersfield Town	L	0-1	0-1		20,596
40	17	A	Grimsby Town	L	1-4	0-2	Short	10,795
41	24	H	Portsmouth	L	0-1	0-1		14,097
42	26	A	Everton	L	1-4	1-2	Powell	21,001
								Appearances
								Goals

FA Cup

R3	Jan 11	A	West Bromwich Alb	L	1-2	1-2	Ainsley	31,007
								Appearances
								Goals

Hodgson, John	Goldberg, Les	Milburn, Jim	Price, Arthur	Holley, Tom	Batey, Bob	Cochrane, Dave	Powell, Aubrey	Henry, Gerry	Short, John	Grainger, Dennis	Ainsley, George	Bannister, Eddie	Hindle, Tom	Kane, Bob	Browne, Bobby	Browning, Len	Heaton, Billy	Fearnley, Harry	Twomey, Jim	Gadsby, Ken	Martin, Con	Clarke, Harry	Willingham, Ken	Hodgkinson, Eddie
1	2	3	4	5	6	7	8	9	10	11														
1	2	3	4	5	6	7	8	9	10	11														
1	2	3	4	5	6	7	8	9	10	11														
1	2	3	4	5	6	7	8		10	11	9													
1		3	4		6	7	8			11	9	2	10	5										
1		3			5	7	8	4	10	11	9	2			6									
1		3			5	7	8	4	10	11		2			6	9								
1		3	6	5			8	4	9	7		2	10				11							
		3		5		7	8	4	10	11	9	2			6			1						
		3		5		7	8	4	10	11	9	2			6			1						
		3		5		7		4	8	11	9	2	10		6			1						
		3		5	6	7	8	4	10	11	9	2						1						
		3		5		7	8	4	10	11	9	2			6			1						
		3		5		7	8	4	10	11	9	2			6			1						
		3		5		7	8	4	10	11	9	2			6			1						
	2			5		7	8	4	10	11	9				6				1	3				
	2			5		7	8	4	10	11	9						6		1	3				
	2			5		7	8	4	10	11	9				6				1	3				
	2			5		7	8	4	10	11	9				6				1	3				
	2			5		7		4	8		9		10		6		11		1	3				
	2	4		5		7	8		10	11	9				6				1	3				
	2	4		5		7			8	11	9		10		6			1		3				
		2		5		7	8		9	11		4	10		6			1		3				
	2	4		5		7	8		10	11	9				6				1		3			
1		2		5		7	8	4	10	11	9	3									6			
1		2		5		7	8	4	10	11	9	3									6			
1		2		5		7	8	4	10	11	9	3			6									
1		2		5		7	8	4	10	11		3									6	9		
1		2		5		7		4		11	8	3	10								6	9		
1		2		5		7	8	10		11		3									6	9	4	
1		2		5		7		4		11	8	3	10								6	9		
1		2		5		7		10			8	3					11				6	9	4	
1		2		5		7		6			8	3	10				11					9	4	
		2		5		7		6			8	3	10				11		1			9		4
1		2		5		7	8	6					10				11			3		9	4	
		2		5		7	8	10							6		11		1	3		9	4	
		2		5		7	8	10							6		11		1	3		9	4	
		2		5			8	6	10	7							11		1	3		9	4	
		2		5		7	8	6	10								11		1	3		9	4	
		2		5		7	8	6	10								11		1	3		9	4	
		2		5			8	6	10	7	9						11		1	3			4	
				5			7	6	10		9	2					11		1	3		8		4
18	12	36	6	39	8	38	34	36	32	32	28	23	11	1	19	1	14	9	15	16	8	14	10	2
		1				7	9	4	7	5	11											1		

		2		5		7	8	4	10	11	9								1	3	6			
0	0	1	0	1	0	1	1	1	1	1	1	0	0	0	0	0	0	0	1	1	1	0	0	0
											1													

League Table

	P	W	D	L	F	A	Pts
Liverpool	42	25	7	10	84	52	57
Manchester United	42	22	12	8	95	54	56
Wolverhampton W	42	25	6	11	98	56	56
Stoke City	42	24	7	11	90	53	55
Blackpool	42	22	6	14	71	70	50
Sheffield United	42	21	7	14	89	75	49
Preston North End	42	18	11	13	76	74	47
Aston Villa	42	18	9	15	67	53	45
Sunderland	42	18	8	16	65	66	44
Everton	42	17	9	16	62	67	43
Middlesbrough	42	17	8	17	73	68	42
Portsmouth	42	16	9	17	66	60	41
Arsenal	42	16	9	17	72	70	41
Derby County	42	18	5	19	73	79	41
Chelsea	42	16	7	19	69	84	39
Grimsby Town	42	13	12	17	61	82	38
Blackburn Rovers	42	14	8	20	45	53	36
Bolton Wanderers	42	13	8	21	57	69	34
Charlton Athletic	42	11	12	19	57	71	34
Huddersfield Town	42	13	7	22	53	79	33
Brentford	42	9	7	26	45	88	25
Leeds United	42	6	6	30	45	90	18

1947-48

Division Two

Manager: Willis Edwards

Final Position: 18th

Did you know that?

30 August 1947: Albert Wakefield scored on his debut as United won 2–1 at Southampton – their first League win on opposition soil since 18 March 1939 when they beat Brentford.

1 May 1947: Although Bury were demolished 5–1 by an Albert Wakefield hat-trick and a double from Dave Cochrane, United finished in 18th place in Division Two, their lowest placing since joining the League.

Former England star Ken Willingham retired at the end of the season.

Match No.	Date	Venue	Opponents	Result	FT	HT	Scorers	Attendance
1	Aug 23	H	Leicester City	W	3-1	1-0	Short, Ainsley 2	26,519
2	27	A	Barnsley	L	0-3	0-0		23,440
3	30	A	Southampton	W	2-1	2-0	Smith (og), Wakefield	21,023
4	Sep 3	H	Barnsley	W	4-1	1-0	Wakefield 2, Short, Cochrane	36,501
5	6	A	Fulham	L	2-3	0-3	Short, Wakefield	26,247
6	10	H	Plymouth Argyle	W	5-0	1-0	Short, Powell 3, Heaton (pen)	29,396
7	13	H	Coventry City	W	2-1	1-1	Powell 2	30,462
8	17	A	Plymouth Argyle	L	0-1	0-1		21,126
9	20	A	Newcastle United	L	2-4	1-1	Wakefield, Cochrane	57,275
10	27	H	Birmingham City	L	0-1	0-0		37,135
11	Oct 4	A	West Bromwich Alb	L	2-3	0-3	Heaton, Wakefield	30,479
12	11	H	Doncaster Rovers	D	0-0	0-0		34,775
13	18	A	Nottingham Forest	L	0-1	0-1		22,380
14	25	H	Bradford PA	W	2-0	2-0	Wakefield 2	31,532
15	Nov 1	A	Cardiff City	D	0-0	0-0		36,851
16	8	H	Sheffield Wed	D	2-2	2-1	Wakefield 2	32,547
17	15	A	Tottenham Hotspur	L	1-3	0-2	Cochrane (pen)	41,563
18	22	H	Millwall	W	2-1	0-0	Powell 2	24,160
19	29	A	Chesterfield	L	0-3	0-1		15,501
20	Dec 6	H	West Ham United	W	2-1	1-0	Short, Martin	21,866
21	13	A	Bury	D	1-1	0-1	Wakefield	13,104
22	20	A	Leicester City	L	0-2	0-0		22,252
23	26	H	Luton Town	L	0-2	0-1		28,597
24	27	A	Luton Town	L	1-6	0-2	Cochrane	16,964
25	Jan 3	H	Southampton	D	0-0	0-0		23,794
26	17	H	Fulham	L	0-1	0-1		29,640
27	24	H	Newcastle United	W	3-1	2-1	Cochrane, Wakefield 2	30,367
28	31	A	Coventry City	W	2-1	2-0	Wakefield 2	22,269
29	Feb 14	A	Birmingham City	L	1-5	0-2	Chisholm	39,955
30	21	H	West Bromwich Alb	W	3-1	1-0	Hindle, Pemberton (og), Chisholm	22,333
31	28	A	Doncaster Rovers	L	0-3	0-2		26,569
32	Mar 6	H	Nottingham Forest	D	2-2	2-1	Powell, Wakefield	27,018
33	13	A	Bradford PA	L	1-3	1-2	Powell	21,060
34	20	H	Cardiff City	W	4-0	2-0	Chisholm 2, Powell, Short	34,276
35	26	A	Brentford	L	0-3	0-1		30,538
36	27	A	Sheffield Wed	L	1-3	1-1	Short	38,736
37	29	H	Brentford	D	1-1	1-1	Bannister (pen)	26,775
38	Apr 3	H	Tottenham Hotspur	L	1-3	1-1	Wakefield	24,891
39	10	A	Millwall	D	1-1	0-1	Chisholm	21,426
40	17	H	Chesterfield	W	3-0	1-0	Hindle, Chisholm, Wakefield	28,794
41	24	A	West Ham United	L	1-2	1-1	Chisholm	13,594
42	May 1	H	Bury	W	5-1	1-0	Wakefield 3, Cochrane 2	17,573
								Appearances
							Two own-goals	Goals

FA Cup

R3	Jan 10	A	Blackpool	L	0-4	0-2		28,500
								Appearances
								Goals

United looked to rebuild in Division Two in 1947–48.

Twomey, Jim	Milburn, Jim	Gadsby, Ken	Henry, Gerry	Holley, Tom	Martin, Con	Cochrane, Dave	Powell, Aubrey	Ainsley, George	Short, John	Heaton, Billy	Wakefield, Albert	Hindle, Tom	Willingham, Ken	Ingham, Tony	Kirby, Dennis	Grainger, Dennis	Dunn, Jimmy	Hodgkinson, Eddie	Windle, Billy	Bullions, Jim	Morton, Norman	Bannister, Eddie	Chisholm, Ken	Hodgson, John	McCabe, Jim	Fearnley, Harry
1	2	3	4	5	6	7	8	9	10	11																
1	2	3	4	5	6	7	8	9	10	11																
1	2	3	4	5	6	7			8	11	9	10														
1	2	3	4	5	6	7	8		10	11	9															
1	2	3	4	5	6	7	8		10	11	9															
1	2	3		5	6	7	8		10	11	9		4													
1	2	3		5	6	7	8		10	11	9		4													
1	2	3		5	6	7	8		10	11	9		4													
1	2	3		5	6	7	8		10	11	9		4													
1	2	3		5	6	7			8	11	9	10	4													
1	2	3					8		10	11	9		4	5	6	7										
1	2	3		5	6	7	8		10	11	9		4													
1	2	3		5	10	7			8	11	9		4		6											
1	2	3			5	7	8			10	9		4		6	11										
1		3			5	7	8			10	9		4		6	11	2									
1		3			5	7	8			10	9		4		6	11	2									
1		3	4		5	7	8			10	9				6	11	2									
1	3			5	6	7	8			10	9						2	4	11							
1	3			5	6	7	8		10	11	9						2			4						
1		3		5	6	7	8		10	11	9						2			4						
1		3		5	10		7		8	11	9				6		2			4						
1		3		5	6	7	8		10	11	9						2			4						
1	3			5	6	7	8				9	10					2		11	4						
1	2	3		5	10	7	8					11			6					4	9					
1	2	3			5	7	8			10	9	11	6							4						
1	2				5	7	8				9	11	6							4		3	10			
1	2				5	7	8				9	11	6							4		3	10			
1	2				5	7	8				9	11	6							4		3	10			
1	2				5	7	8				9	11	6							4		3	10			
	2				5	7	8				9	11	6							4		3	10	1		
1	2				5	7	8				9	11	6							4		3	10			
1	2				5	7	8				9	11	6							4		3	10			
1	2	3			5	7	8				9	11								4			10		6	
1	2				3	7	8		9			11	6							4			10		5	
1	2				3		8		9		7	11	6							4			10		5	
1					3		8		9		7	11	6				2			4			10		5	
						7	8		9			11	6				2			4		3	10		5	1
	2	3				7	8				9	11	6							4			10		5	1
	3			5		7	8				9	11					2			4			10		6	1
	3			5		7	8				9	11					2			4			10		6	1
	3			5		7	8				9	11					2			4			10		6	1
	3			5		7	8			11	9						2			4			10		6	1
35	34	24	6	23	35	38	39	2	21	24	37	21	24	1	8	5	15	1	2	24	1	8	17	1	10	6
					1	7	10	2	7	2	21	2										1	1			

1	2	3		9	5	7	8				10	11	6							4						
1	1	1	0	1	1	1	1	0	0	0	1	1	1	0	0	0	0	0	0	1	0	0	0	0	0	0

League Table

	P	W	D	L	F	A	Pts
Birmingham City	42	22	15	5	55	24	59
Newcastle United	42	24	8	10	72	41	56
Southampton	42	21	10	11	71	53	52
Sheffield Wednesday	42	20	11	11	66	53	51
Cardiff City	42	18	11	13	61	58	47
West Ham United	42	16	14	12	55	53	46
West Bromwich Albion	42	18	9	15	63	58	45
Tottenham Hotspur	42	15	14	13	56	43	44
Leicester City	42	16	11	15	60	57	43
Coventry City	42	14	13	15	59	52	41
Fulham	42	15	10	17	47	46	40
Barnsley	42	15	10	17	62	64	40
Luton Town	42	14	12	16	56	59	40
Bradford Park Avenue	42	16	8	18	68	72	40
Brentford	42	13	14	15	44	61	40
Chesterfield	42	16	7	19	54	55	39
Plymouth Argyle	42	9	20	13	40	58	38
Leeds United	42	14	8	20	62	72	36
Nottingham Forest	42	12	11	19	54	60	35
Bury	42	9	16	17	58	68	34
Doncaster Rovers	42	9	11	22	40	66	29
Millwall	42	9	11	22	44	74	29

1948-49

Division One

Manager: Frank Buckley

Final Position: 15th

Did you know that?

4 September 1948: Coventry's 'new look' with smart red shirts and white trim left them with red faces and feeling blue after a 4–1 defeat at Elland Road.

30 October 1948: United's amateur inside forward Brian Close played in the England Youth team's 3–1 defeat by Scotland in Aberdeen. He made his debut for Yorkshire County Cricket Club against Cambridge University at the end of the season and later opted to play the summer game on a full-time basis, going on to captain England.

19 April 1949: The legendary John Charles first came to the public's attention as the 17-year-old Welshman made his senior debut in a friendly on Easter Tuesday in a 0–0 draw against Queen of the South.

Len Browning was top scorer.

Match No.	Date	Venue	Opponents	Result	FT	HT	Scorers	Attendance
1	Aug 21	A	Leicester City	L	2-6	2-2	Chisholm, Short	34,937
2	25	H	Brentford	D	0-0	0-0		26,625
3	28	H	Luton Town	W	2-0	0-0	Chisholm 2	25,463
4	Sep 1	A	Brentford	W	3-1	2-0	Milburn (pen), Short, Chisholm	19,212
5	4	H	Coventry City	W	4-1	2-0	Chisholm 2, Short 2	29,557
6	8	H	Tottenham H	D	0-0	0-0		37,640
7	11	A	Sheffield Wed	L	1-3	1-1	Cochrane	31,735
8	13	A	Tottenham H	D	2-2	1-2	Milburn, Cochrane	33,793
9	18	H	Lincoln City	W	3-1	2-0	Wakefield, Milburn (pen), Cochrane	33,963
10	25	A	Chesterfield	L	1-3	1-2	Wakefield	15,150
11	Oct 2	H	West Bromwich Alb	L	1-3	0-2	Marsh	33,706
12	9	A	Bradford PA	D	1-1	1-1	Chisholm	25,587
13	16	H	Southampton	D	1-1	0-0	Cochrane	34,959
14	23	A	Barnsley	D	1-1	1-1	Browning	26,240
15	30	H	Grimsby Town	W	6-3	3-1	Burden 2, Milburn (pen), Heaton, Chisholm, Browning	33,581
16	Nov 6	A	Nottingham Forest	D	0-0	0-0		24,237
17	13	H	Fulham	D	1-1	0-0	Browning	26,240
18	20	A	Plymouth Argyle	L	1-2	1-0	Heaton	24,752
19	Dec 4	A	Cardiff City	L	1-2	1-1	Browning	31,973
20	11	H	Queen's Park R	L	1-2	0-1	Burden	26,420
21	18	H	Leicester City	W	3-1	1-0	Heaton 2, Chisholm	22,600
22	25	A	West Ham United	L	2-3	0-2	Holley, Browning	20,660
23	26	H	West Ham United	L	1-3	1-2	Chisholm	32,577
24	Jan 1	A	Luton Town	D	0-0	0-0		15,310
25	15	A	Coventry City	L	1-4	0-4	Browning	23,670
26	22	H	Sheffield Wed	D	1-1	1-0	Cochrane	42,053
27	29	H	Blackburn Rovers	W	1-0	0-0	McMorran	32,963
28	Feb 5	A	Lincoln City	D	0-0	0-0		18,060
29	12	H	Bury	L	0-1	0-0		27,063
30	19	H	Chesterfield	W	1-0	0-0	Browning	29,362
31	Mar 5	H	Bradford PA	W	4-2	3-1	Browning 2, Iggleden, Cochrane	22,477
32	12	A	Southampton	L	1-2	0-1	Webber (og)	25,736
33	19	H	Barnsley	W	4-1	3-1	Moss, McMorran, Browning 2	29,701
34	26	A	Grimsby Town	L	1-5	0-3	Browning	15,848
35	Apr 2	H	Nottingham Forest	W	1-0	0-0	Iggleden	23,932
36	6	A	West Bromwich Alb	L	0-1	0-0		28,662
37	9	A	Fulham	L	0-1	0-0		23,961
38	16	H	Plymouth Argyle	W	1-0	1-0	Browning	24,326
39	18	A	Bury	L	1-3	0-1	McMorran	15,305
40	23	A	Blackburn Rovers	D	0-0	0-0		18,873
41	30	H	Cardiff City	D	0-0	0-0		19,945
42	May 7	A	Queen's Park R	L	0-2	0-0		16,730
								Appearances
							One own-goal	Goals

FA Cup

Match No.	Date	Venue	Opponents	Result	FT	HT	Scorers	Attendance
R3	Jan 8	H	Newport County	L	1-3	1-2	Browning	31,500
								Appearances
								Goals

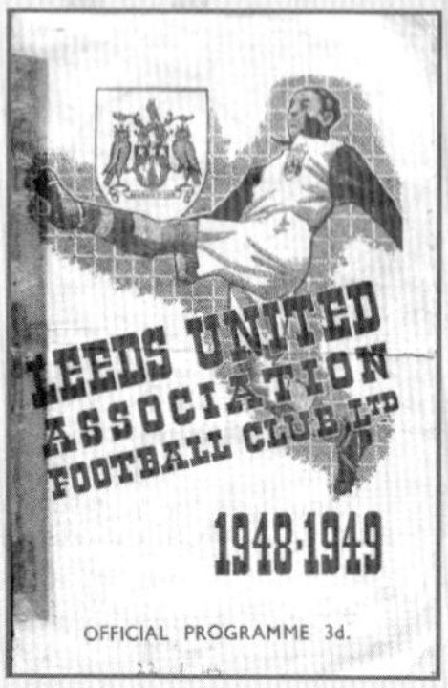

Major Frank Buckley, fourth from left on seated row, with his first Leeds United squad.

Twomey, Jim	Dunn, Jimmy	Milburn, Jim	Bullions, Jim	Holley, Tom	McCabe, Jim	Hindle, Tom	Short, John	Wakefield, Albert	Chisholm, Ken	Heaton, Billy	Martin, Con	Cochrane, Dave	Burden, Tommy	McAdam, David	Lomas, Albert	Marsh, Cliff	Fearnley, Harry	Browning, Len	Depear, Roly	Williams, John	Iggleden, Ray	Searson, Harry	McMorran, Eddie	Moss, Jack	Rudd, Jimmy	Edwards, Walter	Bannister, Eddie	Ingham, Tony	Charles, John
1	2	3	4	5	6	7	8	9	10	11																			
1	2	3	4	5	6	7	8	9	10	11																			
1	2	3	4	5	6	7	8	9	10	11																			
1	2	3		5	4	11	8	9	10		6	7																	
1	2	3		5	4	11	8	9	10		6	7																	
1	2	3		5	4	11	8	9	10		6	7																	
1	2	3		5	4	11	9		10		6	7	8																
1	2	3		5	4	11		9	10			7	8	6															
1	2	3		5	4	11		9	10			7	8	6															
1	2	3		5	4	11		9	10			7	8	6															
	2	3		5	4				10	11		7	9	6	1	8													
	2	3		5	4	7		9	10	11			8	6			1												
	2	3		5	4			9	10	11		7	8	6			1												
	2	3		5	4				10	11		7	8	6			1	9											
	2	3		5	4				10	11		7	8	6			1	9											
	2	3		5	4				10	11		7	8	6			1	9											
	2	3		5	4				10	11		7	8	6			1	9											
	2	3		5	4				10	11		7	8	6			1	9											
	2	3		5	4				10	11		7	8	6			1	9											
	2	3		5	4			9	10	11		7	8	6			1												
	2	3			6				10	11		7	8	4			1	9	5										
	2	3		5	6				10	11		7	8	4			1	9											
	6	3							10	11		7	8	4			1	9	5	2									
	2	3	4							11		7		6		10	1	9	5		8								
	2	3			4					11		7	10	6				9	5		8	1							
	2	3		5	4					11		7	8	6							10	1	9						
	2	3		5	4					11		7	8	6							10	1	9						
	2	3		5	4					11		7	6								10	1	9	8					
	2	3		5	4							7	6								9	1	11	8	10				
	2	3		5	4							7	6					8			10	1	9		11				
	2	3		5	4							7	6					9			10	1	8		11				
	2	3	4	5								7	6			8		9			10	1			11				
	2	3	4	5								7	6					9				1	8	10	11				
	2	3	6	5									4					9			8	1		10	11	7			
	2	3	4	5	8							7	6					9			10	1			11				
		3		5	4							7	6					9			8	1		10		11	2		
		3			5							7	6					9			11	1	8	10			2	4	
	2	3	4		5							7	6					9			10	1	8		11				
	2	3	4		5							7	6					9			10	1	8		11				
		3			4							7	6					9			10	1	8		11		2		5
		3			4							7	6					9				1	8	10	11		2		5
		3			4							7	6			8		9				1		10	11		2		5
10	37	42	10	32	37	11	7	12	23	21	4	37	35	20	1	4	13	24	4	1	16	18	12	8	12	2	5	1	3
		3		1			4	2	10	4		6	3			1		13			2		3	1					

	2	3	4		6					11		7	8			10	1	9	5										
0	1	1	1	0	1	0	0	0	0	1	0	1	1	0	0	1	1	1	1	0	0	0	0	0	0	0	0	0	0
																		1											

League Table

	P	W	D	L	F	A	Pts
Fulham	42	24	9	9	77	37	57
West Bromwich Albion	42	24	8	10	69	39	56
Southampton	42	23	9	10	69	36	55
Cardiff City	42	19	13	10	62	47	51
Tottenham Hotspur	42	17	16	9	72	44	50
Chesterfield	42	15	17	10	51	45	47
West Ham United	42	18	10	14	56	58	46
Sheffield Wednesday	42	15	13	14	63	56	43
Barnsley	42	14	12	16	62	61	40
Luton Town	42	14	12	16	55	57	40
Grimsby Town	42	15	10	17	72	76	40
Bury	42	17	6	19	67	76	40
Queen's Park Rangers	42	14	11	17	44	62	39
Blackburn Rovers	42	15	8	19	53	63	38
Leeds United	42	12	13	17	55	63	37
Coventry City	42	15	7	20	55	64	37
Bradford Park Avenue	42	13	11	18	65	78	37
Brentford	42	11	14	17	42	53	36
Leicester City	42	10	16	16	62	79	36
Plymouth Argyle	42	12	12	18	49	64	36
Nottingham Forest	42	14	7	21	50	54	35
Lincoln City	42	8	12	22	53	91	28

1949-50

Division Two

Manager: Frank Buckley

Final Position: 5th

Did you know that?

14 January 1950: Highlight of the season was a thumping 3–0 win over runaway champions Tottenham as goals by Dave Cochrane (2) and Ray Iggleden ended Spurs' 22-match unbeaten run.

4 March 1950: A fleet of 150 coaches and thousands more fans made their way to Highbury as United played in the FA Cup sixth round for the first time. London Underground had to call out more ticket collectors to cope with the huge crowd. United lost 1–0 to Arsenal.

Dave Cochrane, who netted twice against Spurs at Elland Road.

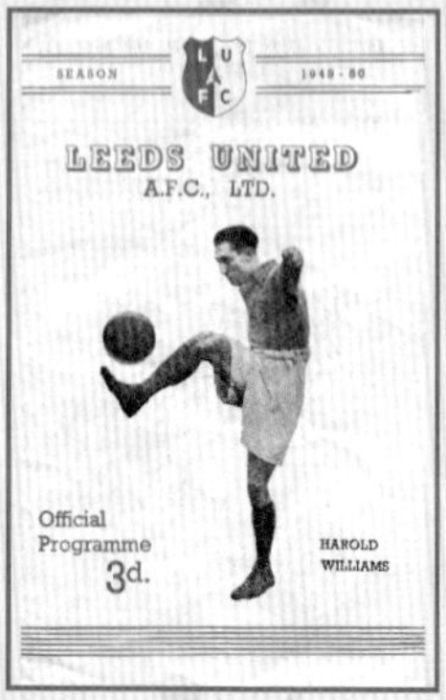

Match No.	Date		Venue	Opponents	Result	FT	HT	Scorers	Attendance
1	Aug	20	H	Queen's Park R	D	1-1	0-1	Milburn (pen)	31,589
2		22	A	West Ham United	L	1-3	0-2	Rudd	24,728
3		27	A	Preston North End	D	1-1	1-0	Burden	31,378
4		31	H	West Ham United	D	2-2	0-1	Cochrane, Dudley	29,732
5	Sep	3	H	Swansea Town	L	1-2	1-2	Dudley	29,767
6		5	A	Sheffield United	W	1-0	1-0	Browning	22,126
7		10	A	Tottenham Hotspur	L	0-2	0-0		48,274
8		14	H	Sheffield United	L	0-1	0-1		23,199
9		17	A	Southampton	L	1-2	0-2	P. Harrison	23,214
10		24	H	Coventry City	D	3-3	2-1	McMorran, Dudley, Cochrane	22,590
11	Oct	1	A	Luton Town	L	0-1	0-0		15,291
12		8	H	Cardiff City	W	2-0	1-0	Dudley, Browning	25,523
13		15	A	Blackburn Rovers	W	1-0	1-0	Dudley	22,038
14		22	H	Brentford	W	1-0	1-0	Dudley	27,342
15		29	A	Hull City	L	0-1	0-0		47,638
16	Nov	5	H	Sheffield Wed	D	1-1	1-1	Williams	33,733
17		12	A	Plymouth Argyle	W	2-1	1-1	Frost, Charles (pen)	21,923
18		19	H	Chesterfield	D	0-0	0-0		24,409
19		26	A	Bradford PA	W	2-1	2-0	Dudley, Frost	18,401
20	Dec	3	H	Leicester City	D	1-1	0-1	P. Harrison	26,768
21		10	A	Bury	L	0-2	0-1		13,381
22		17	A	Queen's Park R	D	1-1	1-1	Dudley	13,256
23		24	H	Preston North End	W	3-1	1-0	Browning, Dudley, Quigley (og)	41,303
24		26	A	Barnsley	D	1-1	0-0	Milburn	27,017
25		27	H	Barnsley	W	1-0	0-0	Williams	47,817
26		31	A	Swansea Town	W	2-1	1-1	Williams, Browning	23,192
27	Jan	14	H	Tottenham Hotspur	W	3-0	1-0	Cochrane 2, Iggleden	50,476
28		21	H	Southampton	W	1-0	0-0	Williams	38,646
29	Feb	4	A	Coventry City	W	4-0	3-0	Williams 2, Iggleden, Browning	22,990
30		18	H	Luton Town	W	2-1	1-0	Browning, Iggleden	37,263
31		25	A	Cardiff City	L	0-1	0-0		28,423
32	Mar	11	A	Brentford	D	0-0	0-0		22,231
33		18	H	Hull City	W	3-0	1-0	Williams, McMorran, Milburn (pen)	49,465
34		25	A	Sheffield Wed	L	2-5	2-2	Browning, Williams	50,485
35	Apr	1	H	Bradford PA	D	0-0	0-0		31,062
36		7	A	Grimsby Town	L	0-2	0-0		22,511
37		8	A	Leicester City	D	1-1	0-0	McMorran	33,881
38		10	H	Grimsby Town	W	1-0	1-0	Milburn (pen)	17,991
39		15	H	Plymouth Argyle	D	1-1	1-0	Williams	24,132
40		22	A	Chesterfield	L	1-3	0-3	Dudley	11,346
41		26	H	Blackburn Rovers	W	2-1	1-1	Dunn, Williams	12,538
42		29	H	Bury	W	4-1	1-1	Dudley 2, Moss, Cochrane	8,913
									Appearances
								One own-goal	Goals

FA Cup

R3	Jan	7	A	Carlisle United	W	5-2	5-1	Browning, Dudley 2, Williams, Cochrane	22,832
R4		28	H	Bolton Wanderers	D	1-1	1-0	Williams	51,488
Rep	Feb	1	A	Bolton Wanderers	W	3-2*	1-0	Dudley 2, Browning	29,440
R5		11	H	Cardiff City	W	3-1	2-1	Williams, Cochrane, Iggleden	53,099
R6	Mar	4	A	Arsenal	L	0-1	0-0		62,273
									Appearances
									Goals

* After extra-time (score at 90 minutes 2-2)

Back row, left to right: Jimmy Dunn, Jim McCabe, John Charles, Harold Searson, Tommy Burden, Jim Milburn. Front row: Harold Williams, Eddie McMorran, Len Browning, Frank Dudley, Jimmy Rudd.

Season, Harry	Dunn, Jimmy	Milburn, Jim	McCabe, Jim	Charles, John	Burden, Tommy	Williams, Harold	McMorran, Eddie	Browning, Len	Moss, Jack	Rudd, Jimmy	Dudley, Frank	Casey, Tom	Cochrane, Dave	Hilton, Joe	McAdam, David	Harrison, Ralph	Ingham, Tony	Iggleden, Ray	Frost, Des	Wilkins, George	Harrison, Peter	Bannister, Eddie	Bullions, Jim	Kerfoot, Eric	Taylor, Frank
1	2	3	4	5	6	7	8	9	10	11															
1	2	3	4	5	6	7	8	9		11	10														
1	2	3	4	5	8	11			10		9	6	7												
1	2	3	4	5	8				10	11	9	6	7												
1	2	3	4	5	8					11	9	6	7	10											
1	2	3		5	4			8	10	11	9		7		6										
1	2	3		5	4			9	10		8		7		6	11									
1	2	3		5	4			9			8		7			11	6	10							
1	2	3		5	4						9		7		6				8	10	11				
1	2	3		5	6		8				9		7		4					10	11				
1	2	3	4	5	6	7	8			11	9									10					
1	2		4	5	6	11	8	9			10		7									3			
1	2		4	5	6	11	8	9			10		7									3			
1	2		4	5	6	11	8	9			10		7									3			
1	2		4	5	6	11	8	9			10		7									3			
1	2		4	5	6	11	8	9			10		7									3			
1	2		4	5	6		8	9			11		7						10			3			
1	2	3	4	5	6		8	9			11		7						10						
1	2	3	4	5	6	11	8				10		7						9						
1	2	3	4	5	6	11	8				10								9		7				
1	2	3		5	6	7	8	9			11								10				4		
1	2	3		5	6	11	8	9			10										7			4	
1	2	3		5	6	7	8	9			10													4	11
1	2	3		5	6	7		9			10							8						4	11
1	2	3		5	6	11	8	9			10		7											4	
1	2	3		5	6	11	8	9			10		7											4	
1	2	3		5	6	11		9			10		7					8						4	
1	2	3		5	6	11		9			10		7					8						4	
1	2	3	4	5	6	11		9			10		7					8							
1	2	3	4	5	6	11		9			10		7					8							
1	2	3	4	5	6	11		9			10		7					8							
1	2	3	4	5	6	11	8	9			7							10							
1	2	3	4	5	6	11	8	9			7							10							
1	2	3	4	5	6	11	8	9					7					10							
1	2	3	4	5	6	11		9			10		7					8							
1	2	3	4	5	6	7		9				11						8	10						
1		3	4	5	6		10	9										8	7			2			11
1		3	4	5	6	7	9				11							8	10			2			
1	2	3	4	5	6	11	9				10		7					8							
1	2	3	4	5	6	11			10		9		7					8							
1	2	3		5	6	11	8		10		9		7											4	
1	2	3		5	6	11	8		10		9		7											4	
42	40	36	27	42	42	32	26	29	8	6	38	4	29	1	4	2	1	16	9	3	4	8	1	9	3
	1	4		1	1	10	3	7	1	1	12		5					3	2		2				

Season, Harry	Dunn, Jimmy	Milburn, Jim	McCabe, Jim	Charles, John	Burden, Tommy	Williams, Harold	McMorran, Eddie	Browning, Len	Moss, Jack	Rudd, Jimmy	Dudley, Frank	Casey, Tom	Cochrane, Dave	Hilton, Joe	McAdam, David	Harrison, Ralph	Ingham, Tony	Iggleden, Ray	Frost, Des	Wilkins, George	Harrison, Peter	Bannister, Eddie	Bullions, Jim	Kerfoot, Eric	Taylor, Frank
1	2	3	4	5	6	11	8	9			10		7												
1	2	3	4	5	6	11	8	9			10		7												
1	2	3	4	5	6	11		9			10		7					8							
1	2	3	4	5	6	11		9			10		7					8							
1	2	3	4	5	6	11		9			10		7					8							
5	5	5	5	5	5	5	2	5	0	0	5	0	5	0	0	0	0	3	0	0	0	0	0	0	0
						3		2			4		2					1							

League Table

	P	W	D	L	F	A	Pts
Tottenham Hotspur	42	27	7	8	81	35	61
Sheffield Wednesday	42	18	16	8	67	48	52
Sheffield United	42	19	14	9	68	49	52
Southampton	42	19	14	9	64	48	52
Leeds United	42	17	13	12	54	45	47
Preston North End	42	18	9	15	60	49	45
Hull City	42	17	11	14	64	72	45
Swansea Town	42	17	9	16	53	49	43
Brentford	42	15	13	14	44	49	43
Cardiff City	42	16	10	16	41	44	42
Grimsby Town	42	16	8	18	74	73	40
Coventry City	42	13	13	16	55	55	39
Barnsley	42	13	13	16	64	67	39
Chesterfield	42	15	9	18	43	47	39
Leicester City	42	12	15	15	55	65	39
Blackburn Rovers	42	14	10	18	55	60	38
Luton Town	42	10	18	14	41	51	38
Bury	42	14	9	19	60	65	37
West Ham United	42	12	12	18	53	61	36
Queen's Park Rangers	42	11	12	19	40	57	34
Plymouth Argyle	42	8	16	18	44	65	32
Bradford Park Avenue	42	10	11	21	51	77	31

1950-51

Division Two

Manager: Frank Buckley

Final Position: 5th

Did you know that?

31 March 1951: Grenville Hair made his debut in a 2–1 win against Leicester City – the start of a 14-year career with United.

Frank Dudley netted a hat-trick at Leicester in November.

Match No.	Date	Venue	Opponents	Result	FT	HT	Scorers	Attendance
1	Aug 19	H	Doncaster Rovers	W	3-1	3-0	Dudley 2, Browning	40,208
2	21	A	Coventry City	L	0-1	0-0		30,213
3	26	A	Brentford	W	2-1	2-1	Williams, Burden	20,381
4	30	H	Coventry City	W	1-0	0-0	Browning	28,938
5	Sep 2	H	Blackburn Rovers	L	0-1	0-1		32,799
6	7	A	Swansea Town	L	2-4	0-2	Dudley, Browning	19,501
7	9	A	Southampton	L	0-2	0-2		25,806
8	16	H	Barnsley	D	2-2	0-1	Browning, Williams	37,633
9	23	A	Sheffield United	D	2-2	1-0	Dudley, Hughes	28,872
10	30	H	Luton Town	W	2-1	0-1	Dudley, Browning	21,209
11	Oct 7	H	Bury	D	1-1	0-1	Williams	28,859
12	14	A	Preston North End	L	0-2	0-1		35,578
13	21	H	Chesterfield	W	2-0	2-0	Browning, Iggleden	23,032
14	28	A	Queen's Park R	L	0-3	0-2		15,935
15	Nov 4	H	Manchester City	D	1-1	0-1	Dudley	30,764
16	11	A	Leicester City	W	5-1	1-1	Burden, Dudley 3, Williams	26,573
17	18	H	Notts County	L	0-1	0-1		29,728
18	25	A	Grimsby Town	D	2-2	1-0	Browning 2	15,561
19	Dec 2	H	Birmingham City	W	3-0	2-0	Milburn, Browning, Burden	23,355
20	9	A	Cardiff City	L	0-1	0-1		23,716
21	16	A	Doncaster Rovers	D	4-4	1-2	Harrison 2, Dudley, Browning	16,745
22	23	H	Brentford	W	1-0	0-0	Dudley	19,839
23	25	A	West Ham United	L	1-3	0-2	Harrison	19,519
24	26	H	West Ham United	W	2-0	0-0	Browning 2	33,162
25	Jan 13	H	Southampton	W	5-3	2-0	Williams, Browning 3, Burden	29,253
26	20	A	Barnsley	W	2-1	0-0	Milburn (pen), Glover (og)	21,967
27	Feb 3	H	Sheffield United	W	1-0	1-0	Browning	28,438
28	10	A	Blackburn Rovers	L	1-2	1-1	Harrison	25,496
29	17	A	Luton Town	W	3-2	1-1	Iggleden, Stevenson, Browning	13,323
30	24	A	Bury	W	1-0	0-0	Stevenson	13,517
31	Mar 3	H	Preston North End	L	0-3	0-1		42,114
32	10	A	Chesterfield	L	0-1	0-1		9,856
33	17	H	Queen's Park R	D	2-2	1-0	Milburn, Browning	18,094
34	23	A	Hull City	L	0-2	0-1		46,701
35	24	A	Manchester City	L	1-4	0-2	Harrison	35,149
36	26	H	Hull City	W	3-0	1-0	Charles 2, Stevenson	27,887
37	31	H	Leicester City	W	2-1	2-1	Burden 2	14,397
38	Apr 7	A	Notts County	D	0-0	0-0		23,466
39	14	H	Grimsby Town	W	1-0	1-0	Charles	15,524
40	21	A	Birmingham City	W	1-0	1-0	Stevenson	23,809
41	28	H	Cardiff City	W	2-0	0-0	Iggleden, Hollyman (og)	14,765
42	May 5	H	Swansea Town	W	2-0	1-0	Iggleden, Browning	11,213
								Appearances
							Two own-goals	Goals

FA Cup

Match No.	Date	Venue	Opponents	Result	FT	HT	Scorers	Attendance
R3	Jan 6	H	Middlesbrough	W	1-0	1-0	Browning	45,583
R4	27	A	Manchester United	L	0-4	0-4		55,434
								Appearances
								Goals

Festival of Britain

Match No.	Date	Venue	Opponents	Result	FT	HT	Scorers	Attendance
	May 9	H	Rapid Vienna	D	2-2	1-1	Iggleden, Hughes	18,000
	14	H	FC Haarlem	W	2-0	1-0	Miller, Harrison	9,362
								Appearances
								Goals

Back row, left to right: John Charles, Eric Kerfoot, Jimmy Dunn, Frank Dudley, Harold Searson, Jim Milburn. Front row: Dave Cochrane, Ray Iggleden, Tommy Burden, Len Browning, Harold Williams.

Searson, Harry	Dunn, Jimmy	Milburn, Jim	Kerfoot, Eric	Charles, John	Burden, Tommy	Cochrane, Dave	Iggleden, Ray	Browning, Len	Dudley, Frank	Williams, Harold	Moss, Jack	McCabe, Jim	Harrison, Peter	Frost, Des	Hughes, Charlie	Scott, John	Miller, George	Stevenson, Ernie	Kirk, Roy	Vickers, Peter	McNeish, Sam	Hair, Grenville	Ross, Bobby
1	2	3	4	5	6	7	8	9	10	11													
1	2	3	4	5	6	7		9	10	11	8												
1	2	3	4		6			9	10	11	8	5	7										
1	2	3	4		6			9	10	11		5	7	8									
1	2	3	4	5	8			9	10	11		6	7										
1	2	3	4	5	6			9	10	11	8		7										
1	2	3	4	5	6			9	10	11	8		7										
1	2	3	4	5	6		8	9	10	7					11								
1	2	3	4	5	6		8	9	10	7					11								
1	2	3	4	5	6		8	9	10				7		11								
1	2	3	4	5	6		8	9	10	7					11								
1	2	3	4	5	6		8		9	7	10				11								
1	2	3	4	5	6		8	9	11		10		7										
1	2	3	4	5	6		8	9	11	7	10												
	2	3	6	5	8			9	10			4	7		11	1							
	2	3	6	5	8			9	10	11		4	7			1							
	2	3	6	5	8			9	10	11		4	7			1							
	2	3	6	5	10		8	9	7	11		4				1							
	2	3	6	5	8		10	9	11	7		4				1							
	2	3	6	5	8		10	9	11	7		4				1							
1	2	3		5	6			9	10	11		4	7				8						
	2	3		5	6			9	10	11		4	7			1	8						
	2	3		5	6			9	10	11		4	7			1	8						
1	2	3		5	6			9	10	11		4	7				8						
1	2	3		5	6			9	10	11		4	7				8						
1	2	3		5	6			9	10	11		4	7				8						
	2	3	6	5			8	9		11		4	7			1		10					
	2	3			6		8	9		11		4	7			1		10	5				
	2	3			6		8	9				4	7		11	1		10	5				
	2	3	6	5			8	9				4	7		11	1		10					
	2	3		5	6		8	9		7		4			11	1		10					
	2	3		5	6			9		11		4	7			1	8	10					
	2	3	4	5	6			9		7					11	1	8			10			
	2	3	4	5	6			9					7		11	1	8			10			
	2	3	6	9	8					11		4	7			1			5		10		
1	2	3	4	9	6		8			11			7					10	5				
1		2	6		9		8			11		4	7					10	5			3	
1		2	6	5	9		8			11		4	7					10				3	
1	2	3	6	9			8			11		4	7					10	5				
1	2	3	6		9		8			11		4	7					10	5				
1	2	3	6		9		8			11		4	7					10	5				
1	2	3			6		8	9		11		4	7					10	5				
25	40	42	31	34	39	2	23	34	26	36	7	28	30	1	11	17	9	13	9	2	1	2	0
		3		3	6		4	19	11	5			5		1			4					

1	2	3		5	6			9	10	11		4	7				8						
1	2	3		5	6		8	9	10	11		4	7										
2	2	2	0	2	2	0	1	2	2	2	0	2	2	0	0	0	1	0	0	0	0	0	0
								1															

1	2	3		9	6		8			11		4	7		10				5				
			4	5	6			9		11			7		10	1	8					3	2
1	1	1	1	2	2	0	1	1	0	2	0	1	2	0	2	1	1	0	1	0	0	1	1
							1						1		1		1						

League Table

	P	W	D	L	F	A	Pts
Preston North End	42	26	5	11	91	49	57
Manchester City	42	19	14	9	89	61	52
Cardiff City	42	17	16	9	53	45	50
Birmingham City	42	20	9	13	64	53	49
Leeds United	42	20	8	14	63	55	48
Blackburn Rovers	42	19	8	15	65	66	46
Coventry City	42	19	7	16	75	59	45
Sheffield United	42	16	12	14	72	62	44
Brentford	42	18	8	16	75	74	44
Hull City	42	16	11	15	74	70	43
Doncaster Rovers	42	15	13	14	64	68	43
Southampton	42	15	13	14	66	73	43
West Ham United	42	16	10	16	68	69	42
Leicester City	42	15	11	16	68	58	41
Barnsley	42	15	10	17	74	68	40
Queen's Park Rangers	42	15	10	17	71	82	40
Notts County	42	13	13	16	61	60	39
Swansea Town	42	16	4	22	54	77	36
Luton Town	42	9	14	19	57	70	32
Bury	42	12	8	22	60	86	32
Chesterfield	42	9	12	21	44	69	30
Grimsby Town	42	8	12	22	61	95	28

1951-52

Division Two

Manager: Frank Buckley

Final Position: 6th

Did you know that?

9 February 1952: Before the home game against Rotherham, respects were paid to King George VI, who died three days earlier. After the hymn *Abide With Me* there was a minute's silence followed by the National Anthem.

Left-half and skipper Tommy Burden only missed a couple of games.

Match No.	Date	Venue	Opponents	Result	FT	HT	Scorers	Attendance
1	Aug 18	H	Brentford	D	1-1	1-0	Browning	20,268
2	22	A	Birmingham City	D	1-1	0-1	Stevenson	17,081
3	25	A	Doncaster Rovers	L	0-2	0-1		22,222
4	29	H	Birmingham City	D	1-1	1-1	Iggleden	15,098
5	Sep 1	H	Everton	L	1-2	1-0	Miller	16,873
6	8	A	Southampton	D	0-0	0-0		19,682
7	12	H	Cardiff City	W	2-1	1-0	Hughes, Milburn	12,860
8	15	H	Sheffield Wed	W	3-2	1-1	Browning 2, Tyrer	20,016
9	22	A	West Ham United	L	0-2	0-1		19,464
10	29	A	Rotherham United	L	2-4	0-1	Iggleden 2	21,352
11	Oct 6	H	Sheffield United	W	3-1	1-1	Iggleden 2, Mills	26,915
12	13	A	Barnsley	L	1-3	1-1	Iggleden	15,565
13	20	H	Hull City	W	2-0	1-0	Iggleden, Harrison	24,656
14	27	A	Blackburn Rovers	W	3-2	1-1	Harrison, Fidler, Iggleden	20,631
15	Nov 3	H	Queen's Park R	W	3-0	2-0	Iggleden, Fidler, Williams	22,875
16	10	A	Notts County	W	2-1	1-0	Fidler, Kerfoot	25,307
17	17	H	Luton Town	D	1-1	1-1	Iggleden	27,405
18	24	A	Bury	W	2-1	2-0	Fidler, Iggleden	11,836
19	Dec 1	H	Swansea Town	D	1-1	0-1	Mills	17,957
20	8	A	Coventry City	L	2-4	0-1	Williams, Kerfoot	14,621
21	15	A	Brentford	L	1-2	0-0	Mills	17,957
22	22	H	Doncaster Rovers	D	0-0	0-0		21,793
23	25	A	Leicester City	W	2-1	0-0	Iggleden, Mills	24,498
24	26	H	Leicester City	W	2-1	1-1	Fidler 2	29,422
25	29	A	Everton	L	0-2	0-1		37,616
26	Jan 5	H	Southampton	D	1-1	1-0	Fidler	25,319
27	19	A	Sheffield Wed	W	2-1	0-0	Iggleden 2	42,354
28	26	H	West Ham United	W	3-1	2-0	Milburn, Kirk, Iggleden	32,297
29	Feb 9	H	Rotherham United	W	3-0	0-0	Stewart, Milburn, Iggleden	47,985
30	16	A	Sheffield United	L	0-3	0-1		36,265
31	Mar 1	H	Barnsley	W	1-0	0-0	Mills	32,221
32	8	A	Hull City	L	2-3	1-2	Stewart, Williams	28,767
33	15	H	Blackburn Rovers	W	1-0	1-0	Iggleden	29,226
34	22	A	Queen's Park R	D	0-0	0-0		15,195
35	29	H	Notts County	W	1-0	0-0	Barritt	12,867
36	Apr 5	A	Luton Town	L	1-2	0-2	Iggleden	11,460
37	11	A	Nottingham Forest	D	1-1	1-1	Williams	28,808
38	12	H	Bury	W	2-1	0-0	Mills 2	23,004
39	14	H	Nottingham Forest	D	0-0	0-0		26,511
40	19	A	Swansea Town	L	1-4	1-4	Williams	18,206
41	26	H	Coventry City	W	3-1	2-0	Dorman (og), Kerfoot, Fidler	16,322
42	May 3	A	Cardiff City	L	1-3	0-2	Iggleden	45,925
								Appearances
							One own-goal	Goals

FA Cup

R3	Jan 12	A	Rochdale	W	2-0	1-0	Kirk 2	21,475
R4	Feb 2	H	Bradford	W	2-0	1-0	Milburn, Iggleden	50,645
R5	23	H	Chelsea	D	1-1	1-1	Milburn, Iggleden	52,328
Rep	27	A	Chelsea	D	1-1*	0-0	Kirk	60,851
2R	Mar 3	N	Chelsea	L	1-5†	1-2	Mills	30,504
								Appearances
								Goals

* After extra-time (score at 90 minutes 1-1)
† At Villa Park, Birmingham

Back row, left to right: Jim McCabe, Jimmy Dunn, Brian Taylor, Roy Kirk, Jim Milburn. Front row: Peter Harrison, Ray Iggleden, Len Browning, Tommy Burden, Ernie Stevenson, Harold Williams.

Scott, John	Dunn, Jimmy	Milburn, Jim	McCabe, Jim	Kirk, Roy	Burden, Tommy	Williams, Harold	Iggleden, Ray	Browning, Len	Stevenson, Ernie	Hughes, Charlie	Taylor, Brian	Harrison, Peter	Finlay, Jock	Barritt, Ron	Miller, George	Kerfoot, Eric	Mollatt, Ron	Tyrer, Arthur	Hudson, Billy	Mills, Don	Ross, Bobby	Searson, Harry	Hair, Grenville	Fidler, Frank	Charles, John	Stewart, Gordon
1	2	3	4	5	6	7	8	9	10	11																
	2	3	4	5	6	11	8	9	10		1	7														
	2	3	4	5	6		8		10		1	11	7	9												
	2	3	4	5	6	11	8				1	7		9	10											
	2	3	5	9	6	11	8				1	7			10	4										
	2	3		5	6	7	8	9		10	1						4	11								
	2	3		5	6		8	9		10	1						4	11	7							
	2	3		5	6		8	9		10	1						4	11	7							
	2	3		5	6		8	9		10	1						4	11	7							
	2	3		5	6	7	8	9			1					4		11		10						
	2			5	6	11	10	9			1	7				4				8	3					
	2			5	6	11	10	9			1	7				4				8	3					
				5	6	11	10					7		9		4				8	2	1	3			
				5	6	11	10					7				4				8	2	1	3	9		
				5	6	11	10					7				4				8	2	1	3	9		
	2			5	6	11	10					7				4				8		1	3	9		
	2			5	6	11	10					7				4				8		1	3	9		
	2			5	6	11	10					7				4				8		1	3	9		
	2				6	11	10					7				4				8		1	3	9	5	
	2			4		11	10					7				6				8		1	3	9	5	
	2		4			11	10					7				6				8		1	3	9	5	
	2				6	11	10					7				4				8		1	3	9	5	
	2				6	11	10					7				4				8		1	3	9	5	
	2				6	11						7			10	4				8		1	3	9	5	
	2				6	11	10					7				4				8		1	3	9	5	
	2				6	11	10					7				4				8		1	3	9	5	
	2			7	6	11	10							9	8	4						1	3		5	
	2	9		7	6	11	10									4						1	3		5	8
	2	9		7	6	11	10									4						1	3		5	8
	2	9		7	6	11	10									4						1	3		5	8
	2			9	6	7	10			11						4				8		1	3		5	
1	2	9		5	6	11	10					7				4							3			8
1	2		5		6	11	10			3		7				4								9		8
1	2				6		10			3		7				4			11					9	5	8
1	2		5		6	11	10			3		7		9		4				8						
1	2				6	11	10					7		9		4				8			3		5	
1	2		5		6	11	10					7				4				8			3		9	
1	2		5		6	11	10					7				4				8			3		9	
1	2		5		6	11	10					7				4							3		9	8
1		9	5		6	11	10			3		7				4				8			2			
1		2	5		6	11	10					7				4				8			3	9		
1		2	5		6	11	10					7				4				8			3	9		
12	36	17	14	25	40	37	41	9	3	10	11	31	1	6	4	34	4	5	4	25	5	19	27	17	18	7
		3		1		5	19	3	1	1		2		1	1	3		1		7				8		2

Scott, John	Dunn, Jimmy	Milburn, Jim	McCabe, Jim	Kirk, Roy	Burden, Tommy	Williams, Harold	Iggleden, Ray	Browning, Len	Stevenson, Ernie	Hughes, Charlie	Taylor, Brian	Harrison, Peter	Finlay, Jock	Barritt, Ron	Miller, George	Kerfoot, Eric	Mollatt, Ron	Tyrer, Arthur	Hudson, Billy	Mills, Don	Ross, Bobby	Searson, Harry	Hair, Grenville	Fidler, Frank	Charles, John	Stewart, Gordon
	2			7	6	11	10									4				8		1	3	9	5	
	2	9		7	6	11	10									4						1	3		5	8
	2	9		7	6	11	10									4				8		1	3		5	
	2			9	6	7	10			11						4						1	3		5	8
	2			9	6	7	10			11						4				8		1	3		5	
0	5	2	0	5	5	5	5	0	0	2	0	0	0	0	0	5	0	0	0	3	0	5	5	1	5	2
		2		3			1													1						

League Table

	P	W	D	L	F	A	Pts
Sheffield Wednesday	42	21	11	10	100	66	53
Cardiff City	42	20	11	11	72	54	51
Birmingham City	42	21	9	12	67	56	51
Nottingham Forest	42	18	13	11	77	62	49
Leicester City	42	19	9	14	78	64	47
Leeds United	42	18	11	13	59	57	47
Everton	42	17	10	15	64	58	44
Luton Town	42	16	12	14	77	78	44
Rotherham United	42	17	8	17	73	71	42
Brentford	42	15	12	15	54	55	42
Sheffield United	42	18	5	19	90	76	41
West Ham United	42	15	11	16	67	77	41
Southampton	42	15	11	16	61	73	41
Blackburn Rovers	42	17	6	19	54	63	40
Notts County	42	16	7	19	71	68	39
Doncaster Rovers	42	13	12	17	55	60	38
Bury	42	15	7	20	67	69	37
Hull City	42	13	11	18	60	70	37
Swansea Town	42	12	12	18	72	76	36
Barnsley	42	11	14	17	59	72	36
Coventry City	42	14	6	22	59	82	34
Queen's Park Rangers	42	11	12	19	52	81	34

1952-53

Division Two

Manager: Frank Buckley

Final Position: 10th

Did you know that?

15 November 1952: United's home game against Nottingham Forest was called off after 10 minutes at 0–0 because of fog. No other Leeds game at Elland Road has been abandoned since.

25 April 1953: Jack Charlton made his League debut in a 1–1 draw at Doncaster – the first of his record 629 League appearances.

Local lad Jack Marsden made his debut in the win against Lincoln in March.

Match No.	Date	Venue	Opponents	Result	FT	HT	Scorers	Attendance
1	Aug 23	A	Huddersfield Town	L	0-1	0-0		35,230
2	28	A	Bury	D	2-2	0-1	Iggleden, Langley	12,274
3	30	H	Plymouth Argyle	D	1-1	1-1	Rundle (og)	25,067
4	Sep 3	H	Bury	W	2-0	1-0	Iggleden, Langley	14,623
5	6	A	Rotherham United	L	1-3	1-1	Iggleden	14,900
6	10	H	Birmingham City	L	0-1	0-0		14,133
7	13	H	Fulham	W	2-0	2-0	Smith, Mills	18,371
8	17	A	Birmingham City	D	2-2	1-1	Hastie 2	18,371
9	20	A	West Ham United	D	2-2	0-1	Iggleden, Tyrer	22,437
10	24	H	Southampton	D	1-1	0-0	Iggleden	13,299
11	27	H	Leicester City	L	0-1	0-1		19,724
12	Oct 4	A	Notts County	L	2-3	1-3	Iggleden, Southwell (og)	22,836
13	11	A	Sheffield United	L	1-2	1-2	Nightingale	33,683
14	18	H	Barnsley	W	4-1	2-0	Nightingale 2, Charles, Mills	22,155
15	25	A	Lincoln City	D	1-1	1-1	Charles	15,491
16	Nov 1	H	Hull City	W	3-1	1-1	Charles 3	25,538
17	8	A	Blackburn Rovers	D	1-1	1-0	Charles	22,510
18	22	A	Everton	D	2-2	2-2	Charles 2	28,664
19	29	H	Brentford	W	3-2	1-1	Charles 3	16,077
20	Dec 6	A	Doncaster Rovers	D	0-0	0-0		15,744
21	13	H	Swansea Town	W	5-1	4-0	Charles 2 (1 pen), Nightingale, Iggleden 2	21,065
22	20	H	Huddersfield Town	W	2-1	1-0	Iggleden, Charles	34,365
23	26	A	Luton Town	L	0-2	0-1		19,480
24	27	H	Luton Town	D	2-2	1-2	Charles, Langley	31,634
25	Jan 3	A	Plymouth Argyle	W	1-0	0-0	Iggleden	27,149
26	17	H	Rotherham United	W	4-0	2-0	Charles 3, Nightingale	24,048
27	24	A	Fulham	L	1-2	0-1	Tyrer	21,210
28	Feb 7	H	West Ham United	W	3-2	1-1	Iggleden, Charles 2	17,680
29	14	A	Leicester City	D	3-3	3-1	Meek, Charles 2	21,754
30	21	H	Notts County	W	3-1	1-0	Burden, Iggleden, McCall	22,922
31	28	H	Sheffield United	L	0-3	0-2		39,858
32	Mar 7	A	Barnsley	D	2-2	0-0	Charles, McCall	11,536
33	14	H	Lincoln City	W	2-1	1-0	Meek 2	18,293
34	21	A	Hull City	L	0-1	0-1		25,387
35	28	H	Blackburn Rovers	L	0-3	0-2		10,644
36	Apr 4	A	Nottingham Forest	L	1-2	0-1	Nightingale	18,734
37	6	A	Southampton	D	2-2	1-1	Nightingale 2	17,704
38	11	H	Everton	W	2-0	1-0	Forrest, Meek	15,363
39	16	A	Swansea Town	L	2-3	2-1	Meek, Charles	21,262
40	18	A	Brentford	D	3-3	2-2	Charles 2, Forrest	12,783
41	22	H	Nottingham Forest	W	2-1	0-1	Burden, Kerfoot	11,497
42	25	H	Doncaster Rovers	D	1-1	0-1	Kerfoot	12,715
								Appearances
							Two own-goals	Goals

FA Cup

R3	Jan 10	A	Brentford	L	1-2	1-2	Charles	22,650
								Appearances
								Goals

League match abandoned after 10 minutes due to fog

	Nov 15	H	Nottingham Forest	D	0-0	N/A		15,729

Back row, left to right: Jim McCabe, Eric Kerfoot, Jimmy Dunn, Jack Scott, Grenville Hair, Tommy Burden. Front row: George Meek, Albert Nightingale, John Charles, Ray Iggleden, Harold Williams.

Scott, John	Dunn, Jimmy	Hair, Grenville	Kerfoot, Eric	Charles, John	Burden, Tommy	Williams, Harold	Iggleden, Ray	Mills, Don	McCall, Andy	Tyrer, Arthur	Fidler, Frank	Langley, Jim	Smith, Barry	Hastie, Ken	Stewart, Gordon	McCabe, Jim	Meek, George	Nightingale, Albert	Mollatt, Ron	Marsden, Jack	Forrest, Bobby	Charlton, Jack
1	2	3	4	5	6	7	8	9	10	11												
1	2	3	4	5	6	7	10		8		9	11										
1	2	3	4	5	6	7	10		8		9	11										
1	2	3	4	5	6	7	10		8		9	11										
1	2	3	4	5	6	7	10		8		9	11										
1	2	3	4	5	6	7	10	8			9	11										
1	2	3	4	5	6	7	10	8		11			9									
1	2	3	4	5	6	7	10	8		11				9								
1	2	3	4	5	6	7	10	8		11				9								
1	2	3	4	5	6	7	10	8		11				9								
1	2	3	4	5	6	7	10	8		11			9									
1	2	3	4	5	6	7	10			11				9	8							
1	2	3	4	9	6	11	10									5	7	8				
1	2	3	4	9	6	7		8		11						5		10				
1	2	3	4	9	6	7		8		11						5		10				
1	2	3	4	9	6	11	10									5	7	8				
1	2	3	4	9	6	11	8									5	7	10				
1	2	3	4	9	6	11	10									5	7	8				
1	2	3	4	9	6		10			11						5	7	8				
1	2	3	4	9	6		10			11						5	7	8				
1	2	3	4	9	6		10			11						5	7	8				
1	2	3	4	9	6		10			11						5	7	8				
1	2	3	4	9	6		10			11						5	7	8				
1	2	3	4	9	6		10					11				5	7	8				
1	2	3	4	9	6		10			11						5	7	8				
1	2	3	4	9	6		10			11						5	7	8				
1	2	3	4	9	6		10			11						5	7	8				
1	2	3	4	9	6		10			11						5	7	8				
1	2	3	4	9	6		10		8	11						5	7					
1	2		4	9	6		10		8	11		3				5	7					
1	2		4	9	6		10		8	11		3				5	7					
1	2	3		9	4		10		8			11				5	7		6			
1	2	3		9	6		10		7								11	8	4	5		
1	2	3		9	6		10		7								11	8	4	5		
1	2	3	4	9	6		7								10		11	8		5		
1	2	3	4		6		10		7								11	8		5	9	
1	2	3	4		6		10		7								11	8		5	9	
1	2	3	4	8	6				7								11	10		5	9	
1	2	3	4	9	6				7								11	8		5	10	
1	2	3	4	8	6		7									5	11	10			9	
1	2	3	4	8	6		7									5	11	10			9	
1	2	3	4	9	6		10		7								11	8				5
42	42	40	39	40	42	18	38	9	16	21	5	9	2	4	2	22	28	26	3	7	6	1
			2	26	2		12	2	2	2		3	1	2			5	8			2	

1	2	3	4	9	6		10			11						5	7	8				
1	1	1	1	1	1	0	1	0	0	1	0	0	0	0	0	1	1	1	0	0	0	0
				1																		

1	2	3	4	9	6	11	10									5	7	8				

League Table

	P	W	D	L	F	A	Pts
Sheffield United	42	25	10	7	97	55	60
Huddersfield Town	42	24	10	8	84	33	58
Luton Town	42	22	8	12	84	49	52
Plymouth Argyle	42	20	9	13	65	60	49
Leicester City	42	18	12	12	89	74	48
Birmingham City	42	19	10	13	71	66	48
Nottingham Forest	42	18	8	16	77	67	44
Fulham	42	17	10	15	81	71	44
Blackburn Rovers	42	18	8	16	68	65	44
Leeds United	42	14	15	13	71	63	43
Swansea Town	42	15	12	15	78	81	42
Rotherham United	42	16	9	17	75	74	41
Doncaster Rovers	42	12	16	14	58	64	40
West Ham United	42	13	13	16	58	60	39
Lincoln City	42	11	17	14	64	71	39
Everton	42	12	14	16	71	75	38
Brentford	42	13	11	18	59	76	37
Hull City	42	14	8	20	57	69	36
Notts County	42	14	8	20	60	88	36
Bury	42	13	9	20	53	81	35
Southampton	42	10	13	19	68	85	33
Barnsley	42	5	8	29	47	108	18

1953-54

Division Two

Manager: Raich Carter

Final Position: 10th

Did you know that?

9 November 1953: The first floodlit game was played at Elland Road when Scottish side Hibernian were beaten 4–1 in a friendly in front of a 31,500 crowd. The lights cost £7,000.

24 April 1954: Eddie Burbanks became the oldest player in United's history when he skippered the side against one of his former clubs, Hull City, three weeks after his 41st birthday. It finished 1–1, John Charles netting for Leeds to finish the season with a club record 42 League goals.

John Charles in the thick of the action against Everton at Goodison Park.

Match No.	Date	Venue	Opponents	Result	FT	HT	Scorers	Attendance
1	Aug 19	H	Notts County	W	6-0	3-0	Charles 4, Williams, Nightingale	18,432
2	22	H	Rotherham United	W	4-2	2-2	Charles 3, Nightingale	24,309
3	27	A	Swansea Town	L	3-4	0-2	Charles, Nightingale, Burbanks	26,408
4	29	A	Leicester City	L	0-5	0-2		21,984
5	Sep 2	H	Swansea Town	W	3-2	2-1	Nightingale, Charles 2	20,949
6	5	H	Stoke City	D	1-1	0-1	Charles	27,571
7	7	A	Plymouth Argyle	D	1-1	0-1	Charles	20,356
8	12	A	Fulham	W	3-1	1-1	Charles 2, Williams	26,044
9	16	H	Plymouth Argyle	D	1-1	0-1	Williams	20,621
10	19	H	West Ham United	L	1-2	0-1	Charles	28,635
11	26	A	Lincoln City	L	0-2	0-1		17,979
12	Oct 3	A	Birmingham City	D	3-3	3-1	Charles, Iggleden, Kerfoot	26,434
13	10	H	Bristol Rovers	D	3-3	1-3	Forrest 3	19,386
14	17	A	Brentford	L	1-2	0-2	Charles	18,329
15	24	H	Derby County	W	3-1	2-0	Charles 2, Nightingale	26,430
16	31	A	Blackburn Rovers	D	2-2	0-1	Williams, Nightingale	25,272
17	Nov 7	H	Doncaster Rovers	W	3-1	0-1	Nightingale 3	26,830
18	14	A	Bury	D	4-4	3-3	Charles 3, Nightingale	11,915
19	21	H	Oldham Athletic	W	2-1	2-0	Forrest, Nightingale	26,747
20	28	A	Everton	L	1-2	1-1	Charles	55,970
21	Dec 5	H	Hull City	D	0-0	0-0		21,070
22	12	A	Notts County	L	0-2	0-0		17,552
23	19	A	Rotherham United	W	4-2	1-1	Charles 3 (1 pen), Iggleden	13,145
24	25	A	Nottingham Forest	L	2-5	2-3	Nightingale, Charles	19,725
25	26	H	Nottingham Forest	L	0-2	0-0		22,135
26	Jan 2	H	Leicester City	W	7-1	5-0	Iggleden 3, Williams, Charles, Nightingale, Tyrer	21,532
27	16	A	Stoke City	L	0-4	0-2		26,794
28	23	H	Fulham	L	1-2	1-0	Charles	20,170
29	Feb 6	A	West Ham United	L	2-5	1-1	Iggleden, McCall	15,585
30	13	H	Lincoln City	W	5-2	3-0	Charles 3, Iggleden, Nightingale	15,325
31	20	H	Birmingham City	D	1-1	0-1	Burden	22,803
32	27	A	Bristol Rovers	D	1-1	1-0	Nightingale	26,846
33	Mar 6	H	Brentford	W	4-0	0-0	Charles 2, Nightingale, Williams	16,501
34	13	A	Derby County	W	2-0	2-0	Forrest 2	12,773
35	20	H	Blackburn Rovers	W	3-2	1-1	McCall, Nightingale, Charles (pen)	24,915
36	27	A	Oldham Athletic	L	2-4	2-1	Williams, Charles	18,067
37	Apr 3	H	Everton	W	3-1	1-1	Williams, Forrest, Kerfoot	22,581
38	10	A	Doncaster Rovers	D	0-0	0-0		12,472
39	16	A	Luton Town	D	1-1	1-1	Charles	16,129
40	17	H	Bury	L	3-4	3-3	Charles 2 (1 pen), Forrest	17,156
41	19	H	Luton Town	W	2-1	0-0	Charles 2 (1 pen)	13,930
42	24	A	Hull City	D	1-1	1-1	Charles	18,619
								Appearances
								Goals

FA Cup

Match No.	Date	Venue	Opponents	Result	FT	HT	Scorers	Attendance
R3	Jan 9	H	Tottenham Hotspur	D	3-3	3-2	Iggleden, Charles, Ramsey (og)	41,465
Rep	13	A	Tottenham Hotspur	L	0-1	0-1		35,023
								Appearances
							One own-goal	Goals

Back row, left to right: Eric Kerfoot, Jimmy Dunn, Roy Wood, Grenville Hair, Jack Marsden. Front row: Harold Williams, Albert Nightingale, John Charles, Tommy Burden, Ray Iggleden, Arthur Tyrer.

Scott, John	Dunn, Jimmy	Hair, Grenville	Kerfoot, Eric	McCabe, Jim	Burden, Tommy	Williams, Harold	Nightingale, Albert	Charles, John	Iggleden, Ray	Burbanks, Eddie	Wheatley, Tom	McCall, Andy	Mollatt, Ron	Marsden, Jack	Willis, George	Forrest, Bobby	Wood, Roy	Tyrer, Arthur	Flynn, Peter	Webb, Bobby	Davies, Byron	Dawson, Bobby
1	2	3	4	5	6	7	8	9	10	11												
1	2	3	4	5	6	7	8	9	10	11												
1	2	3	4	11	6	7	8	5	10	9												
1	2	3	4	5	6	7	8	9	10	11												
	2	3	4	5	6	11	8	9	10	7	1											
	2	3	4	5	6	7	8	9	10	11	1											
	2	3	4	5	6	7	8	9		11	1	10										
	2	3	4	5	6	7	8	9		11	1	10										
	2	3	4	5	6	7	8	9		11	1	10										
	2	3	4	5	6	7	8	9		11	1	10										
1	2	3	4	5		7	8	9		11		10	6									
1	2	3	4		8		7	9	10				6	5	11							
1	2	3	4	5	8		7		10				6		11	9						
1	2	3	4	5	10		7	9					6		11	8						
	2	3	4		6	7	8	9	10					5			1	11				
	2	3	4		6	7	8	9	10					5			1	11				
	2	3	4		6	7	8	9	10					5			1	11				
	2	3	4		6	7	8	9	10					5			1	11				
	2	3	4		6	7	8		10					5		9	1	11				
	2	3	4		6	7	8	9	10					5			1	11				
	2	3	4		6	7	8	9	10					5			1	11				
	2	3	4		6	7	8	9	10					5			1	11				
	2	3	4		6	7	8	9	10					5			1	11				
	2	3	4		6	7	8	9	10					5			1	11				
	2	3	4		6	7	8	9	10	11				5			1					
1	2	3	4		6	7	8	9	10					5				11				
1	2	3	4		6	7		9	10			8		5				11				
1	2	3	4		6	7		9	10					5				11	8			
1	2	3	8	4	6	11		9	10			7		5								
1	2	3	4		6	11	8	9	10			7		5								
1	2	3	4		6	11	8	9	10			7		5								
1	2	3	4		6	11	8	9	10			7		5								
1	2	3	4		6	11	8	9				7		5						10		
1	2	3	4		6	11	8					7		5		9				10		
1	2	3	4		6	11	8	9				7		5		10						
1	2	3	4		6	11	8	9				7		5		10						
1	2	3	4		6	11	8	9	7					5		10						
1	2	3	4		6	11	8	9	7					5		10						
1	2	3	4		6	11	8	9				7		5		10						
1	2	3	4		6		8	9	11			7		5		10						
1	2	3	4		6	11	8	9	10			7									5	
1		3	4				8	9	10	11		7	6	5								2
25	41	42	42	14	40	37	39	39	31	13	6	18	5	28	3	10	11	13	1	2	1	1
			2		1	8	17	42	7	1		2				8		1				

1	2	3	4		6	7	8	9	10					5				11				
1	2	3	4		6	7	8	9	10					5				11				
2	2	2	2	0	2	2	2	2	2	0	0	0	0	2	0	0	0	2	0	0	0	0
								1	1													

League Table

	P	W	D	L	F	A	Pts
Leicester City	42	23	10	9	97	60	56
Everton	42	20	16	6	92	58	56
Blackburn Rovers	42	23	9	10	86	50	55
Nottingham Forest	42	20	12	10	86	59	52
Rotherham United	42	21	7	14	80	67	49
Luton Town	42	18	12	12	64	59	48
Birmingham City	42	18	11	13	78	58	47
Fulham	42	17	10	15	98	85	44
Bristol Rovers	42	14	16	12	64	58	44
Leeds United	42	15	13	14	89	81	43
Stoke City	42	12	17	13	71	60	41
Doncaster Rovers	42	16	9	17	59	63	41
West Ham United	42	15	9	18	67	69	39
Notts County	42	13	13	16	54	74	39
Hull City	42	16	6	20	64	66	38
Lincoln City	42	14	9	19	65	83	37
Bury	42	11	14	17	54	72	36
Derby County	42	12	11	19	64	82	35
Plymouth Argyle	42	9	16	17	65	82	34
Swansea Town	42	13	8	21	58	82	34
Brentford	42	10	11	21	40	78	31
Oldham Athletic	42	8	9	25	40	89	25

1954-55

Division Two

Manager: Raich Carter

Final Position: 4th

Did you know that?

11 September 1954: Albert Nightingale scored a hat-trick as United beat Swansea 5–2 – the start of a 34-match unbeaten League run at Elland Road.

Roy Wood established himself as United's number one and went on to make 139 successive League appearances.

Albert Nightingale struck twice as United won 2–1 at Blackburn in December.

Match No.	Date	Venue	Opponents	Result	FT	HT	Scorers	Attendance
1	Aug 21	A	Hull City	W	2-0	1-0	Brook, Charles	32,071
2	25	H	Rotherham United	L	2-4	1-2	Charles 2	25,021
3	28	H	Lincoln City	L	2-3	0-2	Toner, Vickers	22,326
4	30	A	Rotherham United	L	0-3	0-1		17,799
5	Sep 4	A	Bury	L	3-5	1-1	McCall, Charles, May (og)	15,357
6	8	H	Stoke City	L	0-1	0-1		20,295
7	11	H	Swansea Town	W	5-2	3-1	Nightingale 3, Kerfoot, Brook	20,040
8	13	A	Stoke City	W	1-0	1-0	Forrest	19,311
9	18	H	Nottingham Forest	D	1-1	1-0	Forrest	22,402
10	25	A	Ipswich Town	W	2-1	1-1	Williams, Nightingale	16,716
11	Oct 2	H	Birmingham City	W	1-0	0-0	Forrest	21,200
12	9	A	Derby County	W	4-2	3-1	Brook 2, McCall 2	20,214
13	16	H	West Ham United	W	2-1	0-0	Ripley, Forrest	21,074
14	23	A	Bristol Rovers	L	1-5	1-2	Brook	24,568
15	30	H	Plymouth Argyle	W	3-2	2-2	Williams, Nightingale, McCall	20,613
16	Nov 6	A	Port Vale	W	1-0	1-0	Nightingale	16,062
17	13	H	Doncaster Rovers	W	1-0	1-0	Ripley	15,757
18	20	A	Notts County	W	2-1	1-0	Nightingale 2	14,519
19	27	H	Liverpool	D	2-2	0-1	Forrest, Charles (pen)	22,263
20	Dec 4	A	Blackburn Rovers	W	2-1	0-0	Nightingale 2	26,187
21	11	H	Fulham	D	1-1	0-0	Charles	30,714
22	18	H	Hull City	W	3-0	1-0	Brook, Nightingale, Forrest	23,991
23	25	H	Middlesbrough	D	1-1	0-0	Forrest	26,344
24	27	A	Middlesbrough	L	0-1	0-1		45,271
25	Jan 1	A	Lincoln City	L	0-2	0-1		12,231
26	15	H	Bury	W	1-0	1-0	Lydon	8,954
27	22	A	Swansea Town	L	0-2	0-0		19,637
28	Feb 5	A	Nottingham Forest	D	1-1	0-1	Charles	14,074
29	12	H	Ipswich Town	W	4-1	1-0	Brook 2, Vickers 2	12,038
30	26	H	Derby County	W	1-0	0-0	Charles (pen)	16,994
31	Mar 2	A	Birmingham City	L	0-2	0-0		10,774
32	5	A	West Ham United	L	1-2	0-1	Forrest	19,664
33	12	H	Bristol Rovers	W	2-0	2-0	Brook, Forrest	16,922
34	19	A	Plymouth Argyle	L	1-3	1-1	Brook	19,968
35	26	H	Port Vale	W	3-0	0-0	Henderson, Ripley, Charles (pen)	8,831
36	Apr 2	A	Doncaster Rovers	W	1-0	0-0	Brook	12,740
37	8	A	Luton Town	D	0-0	0-0		25,775
38	9	H	Notts County	W	2-0	0-1	Brook, Nightingale	24,564
39	11	H	Luton Town	W	4-0	2-0	Brook, Charles 2 (2 pens), Henderson	29,583
40	16	A	Liverpool	D	2-2	0-0	Meek, Brook	34,950
41	23	H	Blackburn Rovers	W	2-0	1-0	Brook 2	39,208
42	30	A	Fulham	W	3-1	0-1	Smith (og), Henderson, Nightingale	21,400
								Appearances
							Two own-goals	Goals

FA Cup

R3	Jan 8	H	Torquay United	D	2-2	0-2	Kerfoot, Charles	28,150
Rep	12	A	Torquay United	L	0-4	0-1		12,000
								Appearances
								Goals

Back row, left to right: Bob Roxburgh (trainer), Harold Brook, Archie Gibson, Jimmy Dunn, Roy Wood, Eric Kerfoot, Grenville Hair. Front row: Andy McCall, Albert Nightingale, John Charles, Bobby Forrest, George Meek.

Scott, John	Dunn, Jimmy	Hair, Grenville	Kerfoot, Eric	Marsden, Jack	Burden, Tommy	Toner, Jim	Nightingale, Albert	Charles, John	Brook, Harold	McCall, Andy	Williams, Harold	Charlton, Jack	Vickers, Peter	Forrest, Bobby	Ripley, Keith	Wood, Roy	Mollatt, Ron	Iggleden, Ray	Lydon, Micky	Gibson, Archie	Webb, Bobby	Meek, George	Henderson, Jock
1	2	3	4	5	6	7	8	9	10	11													
1	2	3	4	5	6	10	8	9		11	7												
1	2	3	4		6	7	8	9			11	5	10										
1	2	3	4	5	6		8	9		11	7		10										
1	2	3	4	5	6	7		9		11			10	8									
1	2	3	6				7	5	8	11			10	9	4								
1	2	3	6				8	5	10	11	7			9	4								
1	2	3	6				8	5	10	11	7			9	4								
1	2	3	6				8	5	10	11	7			9	4								
1	2	3	6	5			8		10	11	7			9	4								
1	2	3	6				8	5	10	11	7			9	4								
1	2	3	6				8	5	10	11	7			9	4								
1	2	3	6	5			8		10	11	7			9	4								
1	2	3	6	5			8	9	10	11	7				4								
	2	3	6				8	5	10	11	7			9	4	1							
	2	3	6				8	5	10	11	7			9	4	1							
	2	3	4				8	5	10	11	7			9	6	1							
	2	3	6				8	5	10	11	7			9	4	1							
	2	3	6				8	5	10	11	7			9	4	1							
	2	3	6				8	5	10	11	7			9	4	1							
	2	3	6			7	8	5		11			10	9	4	1							
	2	3	6				8	5	10	11	7			9	4	1							
	2	3					8	5	10	11	7			9	4	1	6						
	2	3					8	5	10	11	7			9	4	1	6						
	2	3					8	5	10	11	7			9	4	1	6						
	2	3	6			7		5	10					9		1	4	8	11				
	2	3	6			7		5	10					9		1	4	8	11				
	2	3	6					5	10	11	7		8	9	4	1							
	2	3	6				8	5	9	11	7		10		4	1							
	2	3	6				8	5	9		7				4	1		10	11				
	2	3	6				8	5	9		7					1		10	11	4			
	2	3	6				8	5	9	11				10		1				4	7		
	2	3	6				8	5	9	7				10		1				4		11	
	2	3	6				8	5	9		7					1				4		11	10
	2	3	6				7	5	9						8	1				4		11	10
	2	3	6				7	5	9						8	1				4		11	10
	2	3	6				8	5	9						7	1				4		11	10
	2	3	6				8	5	9		7					1				4		11	10
	2	3	6				8	5	9		7					1				4		11	10
	2	3	6				8	5	9		7					1				4		11	10
	2	3	6				8	5	9		7					1				4		11	10
	2	3	6				8	5	9		7					1				4		11	10
14	42	42	39	7	5	7	38	40	37	28	31	1	7	25	26	28	5	4	4	12	1	10	9
			1			1	13	11	16	4	2		3	9	3				1			1	3

	2	3	6	5			8	9	10	11	7				4	1							
	2	3	6	5			8	9	10	11	7				4	1							
0	2	2	2	2	0	0	2	2	2	2	2	0	0	0	2	2	0	0	0	0	0	0	0
			1					1															

League Table

	P	W	D	L	F	A	Pts
Birmingham City	42	22	10	10	92	47	54
Luton Town	42	23	8	11	88	53	54
Rotherham United	42	25	4	13	94	64	54
Leeds United	42	23	7	12	70	53	53
Stoke City	42	21	10	11	69	46	52
Blackburn Rovers	42	22	6	14	114	79	50
Notts County	42	21	6	15	74	71	48
West Ham United	42	18	10	14	74	70	46
Bristol Rovers	42	19	7	16	75	70	45
Swansea Town	42	17	9	16	86	83	43
Liverpool	42	16	10	16	92	96	42
Middlesbrough	42	18	6	18	73	82	42
Bury	42	15	11	16	77	72	41
Fulham	42	14	11	17	76	79	39
Nottingham Forest	42	16	7	19	58	62	39
Lincoln City	42	13	10	19	68	79	36
Port Vale	42	12	11	19	48	71	35
Doncaster Rovers	42	14	7	21	58	95	35
Hull City	42	12	10	20	44	69	34
Plymouth Argyle	42	12	7	23	57	82	31
Ipswich Town	42	11	6	25	57	92	28
Derby County	42	7	9	26	53	82	23

1955-56

Division Two

Manager: Raich Carter

Final Position: 2nd

Did you know that?

25 February 1956: United make it a club record 34 League games without defeat at Elland Road by seeing off Sheffield Wednesday, 2–1. The run was ended by Blackburn a fortnight later.

21 April 1956: The biggest home crowd of the season, 49,274, saw United come from behind to beat promotion rivals Bristol Rovers and move above the Pirates into second place on goal average. United won their last two games at Rotherham and Hull to seal promotion for the fourth time – each occasion being a leap year.

Eric Kerfoot was ever-present.

Match No.	Date		Venue	Opponents	Result	FT	HT	Scorers	Attendance
1	Aug	20	A	Barnsley	L	1-2	1-1	Brook	19,341
2		22	H	Bury	W	1-0	0-0	Henderson	19,722
3		27	H	Middlesbrough	W	2-0	1-0	Nightingale, Brook	22,535
4		30	A	Bury	L	0-1	0-1		11,674
5	Sep	3	A	Bristol City	W	1-0	0-0	Forrest	31,060
6		5	H	Hull City	W	1-0	1-0	Ripley	17,524
7		10	H	West Ham United	D	3-3	2-2	Ripley, Nightingale, Meek	21,855
8		17	A	Port Vale	L	0-2	0-1		21,348
9		24	H	Rotherham United	W	4-1	3-1	Nightingale, Ripley 3	23,763
10	Oct	1	A	Swansea Town	D	1-1	0-1	Brook	29,477
11		8	H	Nottingham Forest	W	3-0	2-0	Ripley, Brook, Charles	21,272
12		15	A	Sheffield Wed	L	0-4	0-2		27,640
13		22	H	Lincoln City	W	1-0	1-0	Overfield	17,378
14		29	A	Bristol Rovers	L	1-4	0-1	Brook	24,575
15	Nov	5	H	Stoke City	W	1-0	1-0	Charles	21,261
16		12	A	Plymouth Argyle	L	3-4	1-2	Robertson (og), Williams, Charles	19,122
17		19	H	Liverpool	W	4-2	1-2	Overfield, Charles 2, Brook	22,596
18		26	A	Leicester City	L	2-5	0-3	Charles 2 (2 pens)	30,196
19	Dec	3	H	Doncaster Rovers	W	3-0	1-0	Hutchinson, Charles, Overfield	21,769
20		10	A	Blackburn Rovers	W	3-2	1-2	Overfield, Charles 2 (1 pen)	18,898
21		17	H	Barnsley	W	3-1	1-0	Hutchinson 2, Williams	23,493
22		24	A	Middlesbrough	L	3-5	2-3	Hutchinson, Charles, Vickers	19,416
23		26	H	Notts County	W	1-0	0-0	Brook	24,869
24		27	A	Notts County	L	1-2	1-0	Charles	23,910
25		31	H	Bristol City	W	2-1	2-0	Hutchinson, Brook	31,751
26	Jan	14	A	West Ham United	D	1-1	1-1	Charles	20,000
27		21	H	Port Vale	D	1-1	0-1	Brook	23,680
28	Feb	11	H	Swansea Town	D	2-2	0-2	Charles (pen), Nightingale	20,089
29		25	H	Sheffield Wed	W	2-1	1-0	Charles, Forrest	43,268
30		28	A	Liverpool	L	0-1	0-0		21,068
31	Mar	3	A	Lincoln City	D	1-1	0-0	Charles (pen)	13,713
32		10	H	Blackburn Rovers	L	1-2	1-1	Charles	28,380
33		17	A	Stoke City	L	1-2	1-1	Brook	22,784
34		24	H	Plymouth Argyle	W	4-2	2-1	Brook, Nightingale, Charles 2	12,348
35		30	A	Fulham	W	2-1	1-1	Brook, Charles	25,459
36		31	A	Nottingham Forest	L	0-2	0-1		19,448
37	Apr	2	H	Fulham	W	6-1	3-1	Charles 3, Nightingale 2, Brook	20,115
38		7	H	Leicester City	W	4-0	3-0	Overfield, Brook, Charles 2 (1 pen)	26,408
39		14	A	Doncaster Rovers	W	2-1	2-1	Charles, Nightingale	18,404
40		21	H	Bristol Rovers	W	2-1	2-1	Charles, Overfield	49,274
41		23	A	Rotherham United	W	2-0	0-0	Nightingale 2	20,013
42		28	A	Hull City	W	4-1	1-1	Charles 2 (1 pen), Brook 2	31,123
									Appearances
								One own-goal	Goals

FA Cup

R3	Jan	7	H	Cardiff City	L	1-2	0-0	Brook	40,000
									Appearances
									Goals

United signed off the 1955–56 season with promotion to Division One. This team photograph shows the side which began the season at Barnsley. Back row, left to right: Eric Kerfoot, Jimmy Dunn, Roy Wood, Archie Gibson, Grenville Hair. Front row: Harold Williams, Albert Nightingale, Harold Brook, John Charles, Jock Henderson, George Meek.

Wood, Roy	Dunn, Jimmy	Hair, Grenville	Gibson, Archie	Charles, John	Kerfoot, Eric	Williams, Harold	Nightingale, Albert	Brook, Harold	Henderson, Jock	Meek, George	Ripley, Keith	Forrest, Bobby	Charlton, Jack	Ashall, Jimmy	Marsden, Jack	Overfield, Jack	Vickers, Peter	Hutchinson, George
1	2	3	4	5	6	7	8	9	10	11								
1	2	3	4	5	6	7	8	9	10	11								
1	2	3	4	5	6	7	8	9	10	11								
1	2	3	4	5	6	7	8	9	10	11								
1	2	3	4	5	6	7		9		11	8	10						
1	2	3	4	5	6		7	9		11	8	10						
1	2	3	4	5	6	7	10	9		11	8							
1	2	3	4	5	6	7	10	9		11	8							
1	2	3		4	6	7	10	9		11	8		5					
1	2			4	6	11	7	9	10		8		5	3				
1	2			4	6		10	9		7	8		5		3	11		
1	2			4	6		10	9		7	8		5		3	11		
1	2	3			6		8	9		7	4	10	5			11		
1	2	3		9	6			10	8	7	4		5			11		
1	2	3		9	6		8			7	4	10	5			11		
1	2	3		9	6	7	8				4	10	5			11		
1	2	3		9	6	7		8			4		5			11	10	
1	2	3		9	6	7					4	8	5			11	10	
1	2	3		9	6	7	4						5			11	10	8
1	2	3	4	9	6	7							5			11	10	8
1	2	3	4	9	6	7							5			11	10	8
1	2	3	4	9	6	11							5			7	8	10
1	2	3	4	9	6			8					5			11	10	7
1	2	3	4	9	6			8					5			11	10	7
1	2	3	4	9	6			8					5			11	10	7
1	2	3	4	9	6			8					5			11	10	7
1	2		4	9	6			10					5	3		11	8	7
1	2		4	9	6		8			7	10		5	3		11		
1	2		4	8	6		10			7		9	5	3		11		
1	2		4	8	6		10			7		9	5	3		11		
1	2		4	8	6			10		11		9	5	3				7
1	2	3	4	8	6			10				9	5			11		7
1	2	3	4	8	6	7		10				9	5			11		
1	2	3	4	8	6	7	10	9		11			5					
1	2	3	4	8	6	7	10	9					5			11		
1	2	3	4	8	6			9		7		10	5			11		
1	2	3	4	8	6		10	9		7			5			11		
1	2	3	4	8	6		10	9		7			5			11		
1	2	3		8	6		10	9		7	4		5			11		
1	2	3		8	6		10	9		7	4		5			11		
1	2	3		8	6		10	9		7	4		5			11		
1	2	3		8	6		10	9		7	4		5			11		
42	42	34	27	41	42	19	26	32	6	26	19	12	34	6	2	30	11	11
				29		2	10	16	1	1	6	2				6	1	5

1	2	3	4	5	6	7		8					9			11	10	
1	1	1	1	1	1	1	0	1	0	0	0	0	1	0	0	1	1	0
								1										

League Table

	P	W	D	L	F	A	Pts
Sheffield Wednesday	42	21	13	8	101	62	55
Leeds United	42	23	6	13	80	60	52
Liverpool	42	21	6	15	85	63	48
Blackburn Rovers	42	21	6	15	84	65	48
Leicester City	42	21	6	15	94	78	48
Bristol Rovers	42	21	6	15	84	70	48
Nottingham Forest	42	19	9	14	68	63	47
Lincoln City	42	18	10	14	79	65	46
Fulham	42	20	6	16	89	79	46
Swansea Town	42	20	6	16	83	81	46
Bristol City	42	19	7	16	80	64	45
Port Vale	42	16	13	13	60	58	45
Stoke City	42	20	4	18	71	62	44
Middlesbrough	42	16	8	18	76	78	40
Bury	42	16	8	18	86	90	40
West Ham United	42	14	11	17	74	69	39
Doncaster Rovers	42	12	11	19	69	96	35
Barnsley	42	11	12	19	47	84	34
Rotherham United	42	12	9	21	56	75	33
Notts County	42	11	9	22	55	82	31
Plymouth Argyle	42	10	8	24	54	87	28
Hull City	42	10	6	26	53	97	26

1956-57

Division One

Manager: Raich Carter

Final Position: 8th

Did you know that?

18 August 1956: United made a flying start on their return to Division One by crushing Everton 5–1, Jack Overfield netting after only two minutes and Harold Brook scoring a 21-minute hat-trick. Overfield failed to score again all season despite playing every game.

18 September 1956: Fire destroyed the West Stand wiping out the club offices, dressing-rooms, boardroom, press-box, floodlighting generators, kit, physio equipment and playing records.

22 April 1957: John Charles, making his final appearance before his record-breaking £53,000 move to Juventus scored twice as Sunderland, captained by Don Revie, were beaten 3–1.

Jimmy Dunn didn't miss a League game for the third successive season.

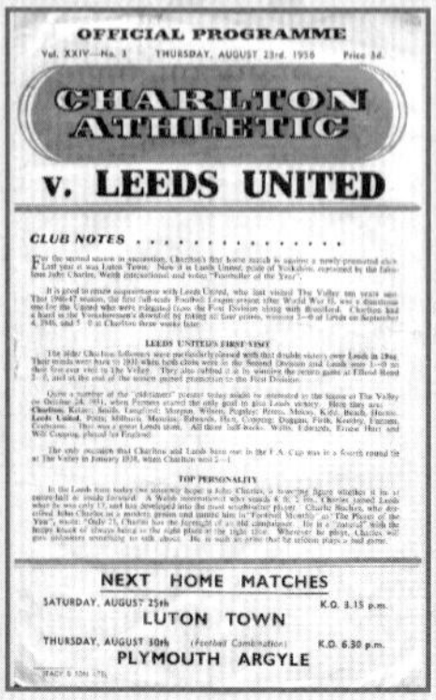
OFFICIAL PROGRAMME

CHARLTON ATHLETIC

v. LEEDS UNITED

CLUB NOTES

NEXT HOME MATCHES

LUTON TOWN

PLYMOUTH ARGYLE

Match No.	Date	Venue	Opponents	Result	FT	HT	Scorers	Attendance
1	Aug 18	H	Everton	W	5-1	5-0	Overfield, Charles, Brook 3	31,379
2	23	A	Charlton Athletic	W	2-1	1-1	Charles 2	23,299
3	25	A	Tottenham Hotspur	L	1-5	1-3	Ripley	51,212
4	29	H	Charlton Athletic	W	4-0	2-0	Forrest 2, Charles, Brook	34,444
5	Sep 1	H	Chelsea	D	0-0	0-0		38,679
6	5	A	Manchester City	L	0-1	0-1		34,185
7	8	H	Bolton Wanderers	W	3-2	1-1	Meek, Charles, Brook	40,010
8	12	H	Manchester City	W	2-0	1-0	Charles, Brook	35,068
9	15	A	Wolverhampton W	W	2-1	0-0	Charles 2	40,824
10	22	H	Aston Villa	W	1-0	1-0	Charles	35,388
11	29	A	Luton Town	D	2-2	1-1	Charles 2	20,949
12	Oct 6	A	Cardiff City	L	1-4	2-1	Forrest	38,333
13	13	H	Birmingham City	D	1-1	0-0	Ripley	34,460
14	20	A	Burnley	D	0-0	0-0		26,440
15	27	H	Preston North End	L	1-2	0-0	Wilson (og)	36,571
16	Nov 3	A	Newcastle United	W	3-2	1-1	McKenna 2, Charles	49,034
17	10	H	Sheffield Wed	W	3-1	1-1	Charles 3	31,857
18	17	A	Manchester United	L	2-3	1-1	McKenna, Charles (pen)	52,401
19	24	H	Arsenal	D	3-3	0-3	Charles 2, Forrest	39,113
20	Dec 1	A	West Bromwich Alb	D	0-0	0-0		29,000
21	8	H	Portsmouth	W	4-1	1-1	Charles 2, Ripley 2	29,866
22	15	A	Everton	L	1-2	1-1	Ripley	33,765
23	25	A	Blackpool	D	1-1	0-1	Brook	20,517
24	26	H	Blackpool	W	5-0	3-0	Brook 3, Charles 2	22,689
25	29	A	Chelsea	D	1-1	0-1	Armstrong (og)	43,860
26	Jan 12	A	Bolton Wanderers	L	3-5	2-4	Charles 2, Meek	25,705
27	19	H	Wolverhampton W	D	0-0	0-0		32,910
28	Feb 2	A	Aston Villa	D	1-1	1-0	Forrest	39,432
29	9	H	Luton Town	L	1-2	0-2	Charles	25,646
30	16	H	Cardiff City	W	3-0	0-0	McKenna, Charles, Forrest	21,695
31	23	A	Preston North End	L	0-3	0-2		14,036
32	Mar 2	H	Tottenham Hotspur	D	1-1	0-0	Charles	33,895
33	9	A	Portsmouth	W	5-2	3-2	Charles 2, Crowe 2, Meek	23,596
34	11	H	Burnley	D	1-1	1-0	Charles	31,956
35	16	H	Newcastle United	D	0-0	0-0		32,541
36	26	A	Sheffield Wed	W	3-2	1-2	Charles 3	33,205
37	30	H	Manchester United	L	1-2	1-1	Charles	47,216
38	Apr 6	A	Arsenal	L	0-1	0-1		40,388
39	13	H	West Bromwich Alb	D	0-0	0-0		20,905
40	19	A	Sunderland	L	0-2	0-1		56,551
41	20	A	Birmingham City	L	2-6	2-4	Charles 2	30,642
42	22	H	Sunderland	W	3-1	0-0	Charles 2, Brook	
								Appearances
							Two own-goals	Goals

FA Cup

Match No.	Date	Venue	Opponents	Result	FT	HT	Scorers	Attendance
R3	Jan 5	H	Cardiff City	L	1-2	0-0	Charles	34,237
								Appearances
								Goals

Back row, left to right: Eric Kerfoot, Keith Ripley, Jimmy Dunn, Roy Wood, Grenville Hair, Jack Charlton. Front row: George Meek, Albert Nightingale, John Charles, Harold Brook, Jack Overfield.

Wood, Roy	Dunn, Jimmy	Hair, Grenville	Gibson, Archie	Charlton, Jack	Kerfoot, Eric	Meek, George	Charles, John	Brook, Harold	Nightingale, Albert	Overfield, Jack	Ripley, Keith	Forrest, Bobby	Marsden, Jack	Crowe, Chris	McKenna, Frank	O'Brien, George
1	2	3	4	5	6	7	8	9	10	11						
1	2	3	4	5	6	7	8	9		11	10					
1	2	3	4	5	6	7	8	9		11	10					
1	2	3		5	6	7	8	9		11	4	10				
1	2	3		5	6	7	8	9		11	4	10				
1	2	3	4	5	6	7	8	9		11		10				
1	2	3	4		6	7	8	9		11		10	5			
1	2	3	4		6	7	8	9		11		10	5			
1	2	3	4		6	7	8	9		11		10	5			
1	2	3	4		6	7	8	9		11		10	5			
1	2	3	4		6	7	8	9		11		10	5			
1	2	3	4		6	7	8			11	9	10	5			
1	2	3	4		6	7	8			11	10	9	5			
1	2	3	4	5	6	7				11	10	9		8		
1	2	3	4	5	6	7				11	10	9		8		
1	2	3	4	5	6	7	8			11		10			9	
1	2	3	4	5	6	7	8			11		10			9	
1	2	3	4	5	6	7	8			11		10			9	
1	2	3	4	5	6	7	8			11		10			9	
1	2	3	4	5	6	7	8	9		11		10				
1	2	3	4	5	6	7	8			11	9	10				
1	2	3	4	5	6	7	8			11	9	10				
1	2	3	4	5	6	7	8	9		11		10				
1	2	3	4	5	6	7	8	9		11		10				
1	2	3	4	5	6	7	8	9		11		10				
1	2	3	4		6	7	8	9		11			5	10		
1	2	3	4		6	7	8	9		11	10		5			
1	2	3	4		6	7	8	9		11			5	10		
1	2	3	4		6	7	8			11		9	5	10		
1	2	3	4		6		8	9		11		10	5		7	
1	2	3	4		6		8	9		11			5	10	7	
1	2	3	4		6	7	8	9		11		10	5			
1	2	3	4		6	7	9	10		11			5	8		
1	2	3	4		6	7	9			11		10	5	8		
1	2	3	4		6	7	9	10		11			5			8
1	2	3	4	5	6	7	9			11				8		10
1	2	3	4	5	6	7	9			11				8		10
1	2	3	4	5	6	7	9			11				8		10
1	2	3	4		6	7	9			11			5	8		10
1	2	3	4		6	7	9	8		11			5			10
1	2	3	4		6	7	9			11			5	8		10
1	2	3	4		6	7	9	8		11			5			10
42	42	42	40	21	42	40	40	25	1	42	11	26	21	13	6	8
						3	38	11		1	5	6		2	4	

1	2	3	4	5	6	7	8	9		11		10				
1	1	1	1	1	1	1	1	1	0	1	0	1	0	0	0	0
							1									

League Table

	P	W	D	L	F	A	Pts
Manchester United	42	28	8	6	103	54	64
Tottenham Hotspur	42	22	12	8	104	56	56
Preston North End	42	23	10	9	84	56	56
Blackpool	42	22	9	11	93	65	53
Arsenal	42	21	8	13	85	69	50
Wolverhampton W	42	20	8	14	94	70	48
Burnley	42	18	10	14	56	50	46
Leeds United	42	15	14	13	72	63	44
Bolton Wanderers	42	16	12	14	65	65	44
Aston Villa	42	14	15	13	65	55	43
West Bromwich Albion	42	14	14	14	59	61	42
Chelsea	42	13	13	16	73	73	39
Birmingham City	42	15	9	18	69	69	39
Sheffield Wednesday	42	16	6	20	82	88	38
Everton	42	14	10	18	61	79	38
Luton Town	42	14	9	19	58	76	37
Newcastle United	42	14	8	20	67	87	36
Manchester City	42	13	9	20	78	88	35
Portsmouth	42	10	13	19	62	92	33
Sunderland	42	12	8	22	67	88	32
Cardiff City	42	10	9	23	53	88	29
Charlton Athletic	42	9	4	29	62	120	22

1957-58

Division One

Manager: Raich Carter

Final Position: 17th

Did you know that?

23 August 1957: The rebuilt West Stand was used for the first time as United reserves drew 2–2 with Blackpool reserves.

3 January 1958: United were knocked out of the FA Cup by Cardiff City at Elland Road for the third year running – each of those games being won by the Welsh side, 2–1.

Hugh Baird was top scorer with 20 goals.

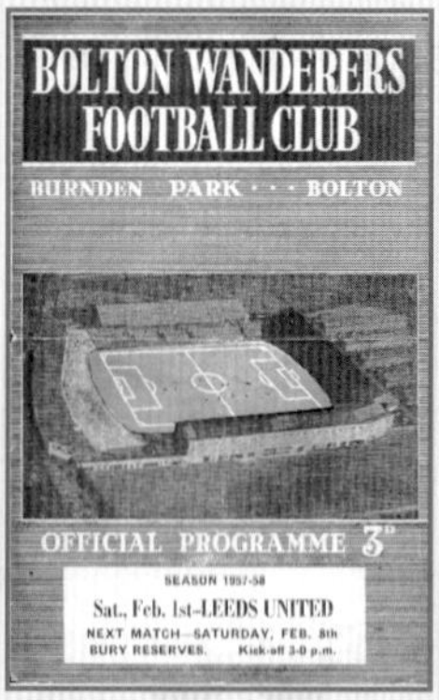

Match No.	Date	Venue	Opponents	Result	FT	HT	Scorers	Attendance
1	Aug 24	A	Blackpool	L	0-3	0-0		26,700
2	26	A	Aston Villa	L	0-2	0-0		25,693
3	31	H	Leicester City	W	2-1	0-0	Baird (pen), Overfield	26,660
4	Sep 4	H	Aston Villa	W	4-0	1-0	Baird 2, O'Brien, Brook	22,685
5	7	A	Manchester United	L	0-5	0-1		50,842
6	11	H	Luton Town	L	0-2	0-0		21,972
7	14	H	Nottingham Forest	L	1-2	1-1	Overfield	25,556
8	18	A	Luton Town	D	1-1	1-1	Overfield	16,887
9	21	H	Bolton Wanderers	W	2-1	1-0	Meek, Baird	18,379
10	25	H	Sunderland	W	2-1	1-1	Baird, Gibson	17,600
11	28	A	Arsenal	L	1-2	1-2	Brook	39,538
12	Oct 5	H	Wolverhampton W	D	1-1	1-1	Baird	28,635
13	12	A	Portsmouth	W	2-1	1-1	Baird, Brook	23,534
14	19	H	West Bromwich Alb	D	1-1	1-0	Forrest	24,614
15	26	A	Tottenham Hotspur	L	0-2	0-1		33,860
16	Nov 2	H	Preston North End	L	2-3	2-3	Baird 2 (2 pens)	23,832
17	9	A	Sheffield Wed	L	2-3	1-3	Ripley, Forrest	21,469
18	16	H	Manchester City	L	2-4	1-3	Kerfoot, Baird	23,855
19	23	A	Burnley	L	1-3	1-2	Baird (pen)	24,144
20	30	H	Birmingham City	D	1-1	1-0	Cush	21,358
21	Dec 7	A	Chelsea	L	1-2	0-0	Baird	17,038
22	14	H	Newcastle United	W	3-0	2-0	Forrest, Crowe, Overfield	23,363
23	21	H	Blackpool	W	2-1	1-0	Cush, Forrest	32,411
24	26	A	Sunderland	L	1-2	1-1	Crowe	34,875
25	28	A	Leicester City	L	0-3	0-1		31,747
26	Jan 11	H	Manchester United	D	1-1	1-0	Baird	39,401
27	18	A	Nottingham Forest	D	1-1	1-1	Baird	23,368
28	Feb 1	A	Bolton Wanderers	W	2-0	2-0	Forrest, Cush	18,558
29	19	A	Wolverhampton W	L	2-3	1-2	Peyton, Forrest	35,527
30	22	H	Portsmouth	W	2-0	1-0	Baird 2	26,713
31	Mar 8	H	Tottenham Hotspur	L	1-2	0-1	Baird	23,429
32	12	A	West Bromwich Alb	L	0-1	0-1		16,412
33	15	A	Preston North End	L	0-3	0-2		21,353
34	19	H	Arsenal	W	2-0	1-0	Meek, Peyton	25,948
35	22	H	Burnley	W	1-0	0-0	Meek	24,994
36	29	A	Manchester City	L	0-1	0-1		21,962
37	Apr 4	A	Everton	W	1-0	1-0	Baird	32,679
38	5	H	Sheffield Wed	D	2-2	1-1	Meek, Baird	26,212
39	7	H	Everton	W	1-0	0-0	Forrest	25,188
40	12	A	Birmingham City	D	1-1	0-0	O'Brien	23,112
41	19	H	Chelsea	D	0-0	0-0		20,515
42	26	A	Newcastle United	W	2-1	1-0	Baird, O'Brien	32,594
								Appearances
								Goals

FA Cup

R3	Jan 4	H	Cardiff City	L	1-2	1-2	Forrest	30,374
								Appearances
								Goals

Back row, left to right: Jack Charlton, Jimmy Dunn, Roy Wood, Grenville Hair, Archie Gibson, Hugh Baird. Front row: Chris Crowe, George O'Brien, Eric Kerfoot, George Meek, Jack Overfield.

Wood, Roy	Dunn, Jimmy	Hair, Grenville	Gibson, Archie	Charlton, Jack	Kerfoot, Eric	Crowe, Chris	O'Brien, George	Baird, Hugh	Meek, George	Overfield, Jack	Forrest, Bobby	Ripley, Keith	Brook, Harold	Marden, Jack	Ashall, Jimmy	Cush, Wilbur	Francis, Gerry	Nimmo, Billy	Peyton, Noel
1	2	3	4	5	6	7	8	9	10	11									
1	2	3	4	5	6		8	9	7	11	10								
1	2	3	4	5	6		8	9	7	11	10								
1	2	3		5	6		8	9	7	11		4	10						
1	2	3			6		8	9	7	11		4	10	5					
1	2			3	6		8	9	7	11		4	10	5					
1	2		4	5	6			9	7	11	8		10		3				
1	2		4	5	6			9	7	11	8		10		3				
1			4	5	2	8		9	7	11	10	6			3				
1			4	5	6	8		9	7	11	10			2	3				
1			4	5	2			9	7	11	10	6	8		3				
1			4	5	2	8		9	7	11	10	6			3				
1			4	5	2		8	9	7	11		6	10		3				
1		2		5	4			9	7	11	8	6	10		3				
1		2		5	4		8	9	7	11		6	10		3				
1	2	3	4	5	6		10	9	7	11		8							
1	2	3	4	5	6	7		8	11		10	9							
1	2	3		5	4	7		9	11		10	8				6			
1	2	3	8	5	4	10		9	7	11						6			
1	2	3	4	5	6	10		9	11							8	7		
1	2	3	4	5	6	10		9	7	11						8			
1	2	3	4	5	6	10			7	11	9					8			
1	2	3	4	5	6	10			7	11	9					8			
1	2	3	4	5	6	10			7	11	9					8			
1	2	3	4	5	6	7		9		11	10					8			
1	2	3	4	5	6			9	7	11	10					8			
1	2	3	4	5	6			9	7	11	10					8			
	2	3		5	6			9	7	11	10					4		1	8
1	2	3		5	6			9	7	11	10					4			8
1	2	3		5	6			9	7	11	10					4			8
1	2	3		5	6			9	7	11	10					4			8
1	2	3		5	6		10	9	7	11						4			8
1	2	3		5	6			9	7	11	10					4			8
1	2	3		5	6	7	10	9	11							4			8
1	2	3		5	6	7	10	9	11							4			8
1	2	3	4	5	6	7	10	9	11										8
1	2	3	4	5	6	7	8	9		11	10								
1	2	3	4		6		10	9	7	11				5					8
1	2	3		5	6		10	9	7	11	8					4			
1	2	3		5	6	8	10	9	7	11						4			
1	2	3		5	6	8	10	9	7	11						4			
1	2	3	4	5	6		10	9	7	11									8
41	35	34	25	40	42	19	19	39	40	36	24	12	9	4	9	21	1	1	11
			1		1	2	3	20	4	4	7	1	3			3			2

1	2	3	4	5	6	10			7	11	9					8			
1	1	1	1	1	1	1	0	0	1	1	1	0	0	0	0	1	0	0	0
											1								

League Table

	P	W	D	L	F	A	Pts
Wolverhampton W	42	28	8	6	103	47	64
Preston North End	42	26	7	9	100	51	59
Tottenham Hotspur	42	21	9	12	93	77	51
West Bromwich Albion	42	18	14	10	92	70	50
Manchester City	42	22	5	15	104	100	49
Burnley	42	21	5	16	80	74	47
Blackpool	42	19	6	17	80	67	44
Luton Town	42	19	6	17	69	63	44
Manchester United	42	16	11	15	85	75	43
Nottingham Forest	42	16	10	16	69	63	42
Chelsea	42	15	12	15	83	79	42
Arsenal	42	16	7	19	73	85	39
Birmingham City	42	14	11	17	76	89	39
Aston Villa	42	16	7	19	73	86	39
Bolton Wanderers	42	14	10	18	65	87	38
Everton	42	13	11	18	65	75	37
Leeds United	42	14	9	19	51	63	37
Leicester City	42	14	5	23	91	112	33
Newcastle United	42	12	8	22	73	81	32
Portsmouth	42	12	8	22	73	88	32
Sunderland	42	10	12	20	54	97	32
Sheffield Wednesday	42	12	7	23	69	92	31

1958-59

Division One

Manager: Bill Lambton

Final Position: 15th

Did you know that?

29 November 1958: Future boss Don Revie made his debut in a 3–2 home win against Newcastle.

27 December 1958: When Archie Gibson was sent off v West Bromwich Albion he was the first Leeds player to be dismissed in a League match since Billy Poyntz on 11 February 1922. A total of 1,259 League games had been played between the dismissals.

28 February 1959: Full-back John Kilford made his debut in a 1–1 draw with Portsmouth. After giving up football he was ordained into the church.

11 April 1959: United dropped a clanger in the programme against Blackburn introducing Headington United boss Arthur Turner as 'Our New Manager'. He opted to stay with the Oxford club rather than take over from Bill Lambton at Elland Road.

Match No.	Date	Venue	Opponents	Result	FT	HT	Scorers	Attendance
1	Aug 23	A	Bolton Wanderers	L	0-4	0-1		25,922
2	26	H	Luton Town	D	1-1	0-1	Crowe (pen)	25,498
3	30	H	Burnley	D	1-1	0-0	Forrest	22,739
4	Sep 3	A	Luton Town	D	1-1	0-1	Baird	13,497
5	6	A	Preston North End	W	2-1	1-1	Baird (pen), Overfield	22,765
6	10	H	Birmingham City	D	0-0	0-0		25,228
7	13	H	Leicester City	D	1-1	1-0	Meek	23,847
8	17	A	Birmingham City	L	1-4	1-2	Forrest	24,068
9	20	A	Everton	L	2-3	0-2	Cush, Crowe	31,105
10	27	H	Arsenal	W	2-1	0-1	Crowe (pen), Overfield	33,961
11	Oct 4	A	Manchester City	L	1-2	0-2	Leivers (og)	31,989
12	11	A	Portsmouth	L	0-2	0-0		22,570
13	18	H	Aston Villa	D	0-0	0-0		21,088
14	25	A	Tottenham Hotspur	W	3-2	1-2	Cush, O'Brien, Overfield	38,691
15	Nov 1	H	Manchester United	L	1-2	1-0	Shackleton	48,574
16	8	A	Chelsea	L	0-2	0-1		33,357
17	15	H	Blackpool	D	1-1	0-1	Crowe	29,252
18	22	A	Blackburn Rovers	W	4-2	1-1	Shackleton 3, Humphries	28,727
19	29	H	Newcastle United	W	3-2	0-1	Overfield, Crowe, Scott (og)	23,732
20	Dec 6	A	West Ham United	W	3-2	2-0	Crowe (pen), Overfield, Bond (og)	22,022
21	13	H	Nottingham Forest	W	1-0	0-0	Crowe	26,341
22	20	H	Bolton Wanderers	L	3-4	1-3	Crowe (pen), Gibson, Shackleton	28,534
23	26	A	West Bromwich Alb	W	2-1	0-1	Humphries, Crowe (pen)	34,878
24	27	H	West Bromwich Alb	L	0-1	0-0		44,929
25	Jan 3	A	Burnley	L	1-3	1-1	Shackleton	26,013
26	17	H	Preston North End	L	1-3	0-1	Revie	22,043
27	31	A	Leicester City	W	1-0	0-0	Shackleton	23,376
28	Feb 7	H	Everton	W	1-0	1-0	Shackleton	18,200
29	14	A	Wolverhampton W	L	2-6	2-4	Shackleton, Overfield	26,790
30	21	H	Manchester City	L	0-4	0-1		18,515
31	24	A	Arsenal	L	0-1	0-1		30,034
32	28	H	Portsmouth	D	1-1	1-0	Cush	14,900
33	Mar 7	A	Aston Villa	L	1-2	0-0	Overfield	27,631
34	14	H	Tottenham Hotspur	W	3-1	3-0	Crowe, Shackleton, Overfield	17,010
35	21	A	Manchester United	L	0-4	0-1		45,473
36	28	H	Chelsea	W	4-0	2-0	O'Brien 2, Shackleton, Crowe	16,676
37	31	H	Wolverhampton W	L	1-3	1-2	Crowe	35,819
38	Apr 4	A	Blackpool	L	0-3	0-1		14,089
39	11	H	Blackburn Rovers	W	2-1	1-1	Shackleton, Charlton	15,232
40	18	A	Newcastle United	D	2-2	1-0	Revie, Peyton	19,321
41	22	A	Nottingham Forest	W	3-0	3-0	Shackleton 3	18,650
42	25	H	West Ham United	W	1-0	0-0	Shackleton	11,257
								Appearances
							Three own-goals	Goals

FA Cup

Match No.	Date	Venue	Opponents	Result	FT	HT	Scorers	Attendance
R3	Jan 10	A	Luton Town	L	1-5	0-1	Shackleton	18,354
								Appearances
								Goals

Irish international Wilbur Cush was the star of the season.

Back row, left to right: Jim Ashall, Archie Gibson, Roy Wood, Jack Charlton, Grenville Hair. Front row: Billy Humphries, Chris Crowe, Don Revie, Wilbur Cush, Alan Shackleton, Jack Overfield.

Wood, Roy	Dunn, Jimmy	Hair, Grenville	Gibson, Archie	Charlton, Jack	Cush, Wilbur	Crowe, Chris	Peyton, Noel	Forrest, Bobby	O'Brien, George	Overfield, Jack	Ashall, Jimmy	Baird, Hugh	Kerfoot, Eric	Meek, George	Marsden, Jack	Humphries, Billy	Shackleton, Alan	Revie, Don	McConnell, Peter	Mitchell, Ron	Burgin, Ted	Kemp, John	Kilford, John
1	2	3	4	5	6	7	8	9	10	11													
1	2	3	4	5	6	7	8	9	10	11													
1		3	4	5	6	7	8	10		11	2	9											
1		3	4	5	10			8		11	2	9	6	7									
1		3	4	5	10			8		11	2	9	6	7									
1		3	4	5	10			8		11	2	9	6	7									
1		3	4	5	10			8		11	2	9	6	7									
1		3	4		6	8		9	10	11	2			7	5								
1		3	4		6	8		9	10	11	2			7	5								
1		3	6	5	4	8	10	9		11	2					7							
1		3	4	5		8	10		6	11	2	9				7							
1		3	4	5	8	10		9	6	11	2					7							
1		3	6	5	4	8		9	10	11	2					7							
1		3	6	5	4	8		9	10	11	2					7							
1		3	6	5	4	8			10	11	2					7	9						
1		3	6	5	4	8			10	11	2			7			9						
1		3	6	5	4	8		10		11	2					7	9						
1		3	6	5	4	8		10		11	2					7	9						
1		3	6	5	4	8				11	2					7	9	10					
1		3	6	5	4	8				11	2					7	9	10					
1		3	6	5	4	8				11	2					7	9	10					
1	3		6	5		8				11	2					7	9	10	4				
1		3	6	5	4	8				11	2					7	9	10					
1		3	6	5	4	8				11	2					7	9	10					
1		3	6	5	4	8				11	2					7	9	10					
1		3	6	5	4				10					11		7	9	8		2			
		3		5	4	8				11			6			7	9	10		2	1		
		3		5	4	8				11			6			7	9	10		2	1		
		3		5	6				10	11			4			7	9	8		2	1		
		3	6	5	4	8					2					7	9	10			1	11	
		3	6	5	4	8				11	2					7	9	10			1		
			6	5	8				10		2			11		7	9	4			1		3
	2			5	10	8			6	11	3		4	7			9				1		
	2			5	10	8				11	3		6	7			9	4			1		
	2			5	10	8				11	3		6	7			9	4			1		
		3	4	5		8			10	11	2		6	7			9				1		
		3	4	5		8			10	11	2		6	7			9				1		
		3		5		8			10	11	2		6			7	9		4		1		
	2	3		5	8	7							6	11			9	10	4		1		
	2	3			5	7	10						6	11			9	8	4		1		
	2	3		5		7	10						6	11			9	8	4		1		
	2	3		5	6	7	10							11			9	8	4		1		
26	10	37	31	39	36	35	8	15	17	35	32	6	16	18	2	23	28	20	6	4	16	1	1
			1	1	3	12	1	2	3	8		2		1		2	16	2					

1		3	6	5	4	8				11	2					7	9	10					
1	0	1	1	1	1	1	0	0	0	1	1	0	0	0	0	1	1	1	0	0	0	0	0
																	1						

League Table

	P	W	D	L	F	A	Pts
Wolverhampton W	42	28	5	9	110	49	61
Manchester United	42	24	7	11	103	66	55
Arsenal	42	21	8	13	88	68	50
Bolton Wanderers	42	20	10	12	79	66	50
West Bromwich Albion	42	18	13	11	88	68	49
West Ham United	42	21	6	15	85	70	48
Burnley	42	19	10	13	81	70	48
Blackpool	42	18	11	13	66	49	47
Birmingham City	42	20	6	16	84	68	46
Blackburn Rovers	42	17	10	15	76	70	44
Newcastle United	42	17	7	18	80	80	41
Preston North End	42	17	7	18	70	77	41
Nottingham Forest	42	17	6	19	71	74	40
Chelsea	42	18	4	20	77	98	40
Leeds United	42	15	9	18	57	74	39
Everton	42	17	4	21	71	87	38
Luton Town	42	12	13	17	68	71	37
Tottenham Hotspur	42	13	10	19	85	95	36
Leicester City	42	11	10	21	67	98	32
Manchester City	42	11	9	22	64	95	31
Aston Villa	42	11	8	23	58	87	30
Portsmouth	42	6	9	27	64	112	21

1959-60

Division One

Manager: Jack Taylor

Final Position: 21st

Did you know that?

19 March 1960: New signing from Manchester United Freddie Goodwin found himself marking Denis Law who was making his Manchester City debut after signing from Huddersfield. Law netted but United won 4–3.

30 April 1960: Relegated United beat Nottingham Forest 1–0 on the final day of the campaign – the clean sheet ensuring they avoided the ignomy of conceding the most goals in a season. They let in 92, 46 of them at home, an unwanted record shared by the class of 1934–35.

Match No.	Date		Venue	Opponents	Result	FT	HT	Scorers	Attendance
1	Aug	22	H	Burnley	L	2-3	2-1	Charlton, Cush (pen)	20,233
2		26	A	Leicester City	L	2-3	1-3	Crowe, Cush	24,790
3		29	A	Luton Town	W	1-0	1-0	Revie	15,822
4	Sep	2	H	Leicester City	D	1-1	0-1	Crowe	18,384
5		5	A	West Ham United	W	2-1	1-1	Crowe 2 (1 pen)	27,777
6		9	A	Manchester United	L	0-6	0-3		48,619
7		12	H	Chelsea	W	2-1	0-1	Crowe 2	17,011
8		16	H	Manchester United	D	2-2	1-2	Cush, Crowe	34,048
9		19	A	West Bromwich Alb	L	0-3	0-0		26,364
10		26	H	Newcastle United	L	2-3	2-1	McCole, Revie	28,306
11	Oct	3	A	Birmingham City	L	0-2	0-1		25,301
12		10	H	Everton	D	3-3	2-1	Crowe (pen), Francis, McCole	19,122
13		17	A	Blackpool	D	3-3	1-2	McCole 2, Francis	22,301
14		24	H	Blackburn Rovers	L	0-1	0-1		17,159
15		31	A	Bolton Wanderers	D	1-1	1-0	McCole	20,183
16	Nov	7	H	Arsenal	W	3-2	1-1	Peyton 2, McCole	21,617
17		14	A	Wolverhampton W	L	2-4	1-3	Crowe, Peyton	21,546
18		21	H	Sheffield Wed	L	1-3	0-2	McCole	21,260
19		28	A	Nottingham Forest	L	1-4	1-1	Revie	21,366
20	Dec	5	H	Fulham	L	1-4	1-1	McCole	18,846
21		12	A	Manchester City	D	3-3	2-1	Revie, Crowe, Gibson	19,715
22		19	A	Burnley	W	1-0	1-0	Overfield	17,398
23		26	H	Tottenham Hotspur	L	2-4	1-1	McCole 2	36,037
24		28	A	Tottenham Hotspur	W	4-1	1-1	McCole 2, Cameron, Meek	54,170
25	Jan	2	H	Luton Town	D	1-1	1-1	McCole	19,921
26		16	H	West Ham United	W	3-0	1-0	Crowe, McCole, Meek	15,284
27		23	A	Chelsea	W	3-1	1-1	McCole 2, Peyton	18,963
28	Feb	6	H	West Bromwich Alb	L	1-4	0-2	McCole (pen)	23,729
29		13	A	Newcastle United	L	1-2	1-1	Revie	16,148
30		27	A	Fulham	L	0-5	0-0		23,355
31	Mar	5	H	Blackpool	L	2-4	2-1	McCole, Meek	23,127
32		9	H	Birmingham City	D	3-3	2-1	Revie 2, Bremner	8,557
33		19	H	Manchester City	W	4-3	2-2	McCole 2 (2 pens), Bremner, Peyton	32,545
34		26	A	Arsenal	D	1-1	0-0	Gibson	19,597
35	Apr	2	H	Wolverhampton W	L	0-3	0-1		29,492
36		9	A	Sheffield Wed	L	0-1	0-1		27,073
37		16	H	Bolton Wanderers	W	1-0	0-0	Charlton	19,272
38		18	A	Preston North End	D	1-1	0-0	Gibson	15,879
39		19	H	Preston North End	W	2-1	0-1	Charlton, Francis	23,764
40		23	A	Everton	L	0-1	0-1		37,885
41		27	A	Blackburn Rovers	L	2-3	1-2	Meek, McCole	18,295
42		30	H	Nottingham Forest	W	1-0	1-0	McCole (pen)	11,699
									Appearances
									Goals

FA Cup

R3	Jan	9	A	Aston Villa	L	1-2	1-1	McCole	43,421
									Appearances
									Goals

Despite relegation, Jack Charlton was a rock in

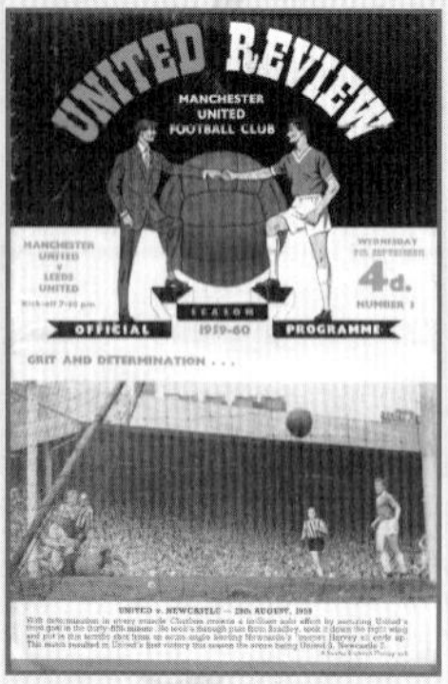

Leeds crshed 6–0 at Old Trafford.

Back row, left to right: Jim Ashall, Jack Overfield, Ted Burgin, Jack Charlton, Grenville Hair. Front row: George Meek, John McCole, Wilbur Cush, Bobby Cameron, Chris Crowe, Archie Gibson.

Burgin, Ted	Ashall, Jimmy	Hair, Grenville	McConnell, Peter	Charlton, Jack	Cush, Wilbur	Humphries, Billy	Revie, Don	Shackleton, Alan	Crowe, Chris	Meek, George	Overfield, Jack	Cameron, Bobby	Francis, Gerry	Peyton, Noel	Kilford, John	Gibson, Archie	McCole, John	Wood, Roy	Caldwell, Terry	Bremner, Billy	Humphreys, Alan	Goodwin, Freddie
1	2	3	4	5	6	7	8	9	10	11												
1	2	3	4	5	6		8	9	10	7	11											
1	2	3	4	5	6		9		10	7	11	8										
1	2	3	4	5	6		9		10	7	11	8										
1	2	3	4	5	6		9		10	7	11	8										
1	2	3		5	6		4			8	11	9	7	10								
1	2			5	6		9		10	7	11	8			3	4						
1	2			5	6		9		10	7	11			8	3	4						
1	2	3		5	6				10	7	11	8				4	9					
	2	3		5	6	7	8		10		11					4	9	1				
	2	3		5			8		7		11	6		10		4	9	1				
	2	3		5	6				10		11	8	7			4	9	1				
1	2	3		5	6		8		10		11		7			4	9					
1	2	3		5	6		8		10		11		7			4	9					
1	2	3		5			8		11			4	7	10		6	9					
1	2	3		5			8		11			4	7	10		6	9					
1	2	3	6	5			8		7	11		4		10			9					
1	2	3		5	6		8		7			4	11	10			9					
1	2	3	4	5			8		7	11		10				6	9					
1		3		5	4		8		10	7	11					6	9		2			
1		3		5	4		8		10	7	11					6	9		2			
1		3		5	4				10	7	11	8				6	9		2			
1		3		5	4				10	7		8	11			6	9		2			
1	2	3		5	4				7	11		8		10		6	9					
1	2	3		5	4				7	11		8		10		6	9					
	2	3		5	4		8		7	11				10		6	9	1				
	2	3		5	4		8			11				10		6	9	1		7		
	2	3		5	4		8			11				10		6	9	1		7		
	2	3		5	4		8		7	11				10		6	9	1				
	2	3		5	4		8		7	11				10		6	9				1	
	2			5	4		8		10	11					3	6	9			7	1	
	2		4		5		8			11				10	3	6	9			7	1	
1	2	3		5			8			11				10		4	9			7		6
1	2	3		5			8			11				10		4	9			7		6
1	2	3		5	9		8			11				10		4				7		6
1	2	3		5			8			11		10				4	9			7		6
1	2			5			8			11		10				4	9		3	7		6
1	2			5	10		8			11			7			4	9		3			6
1	2			5	10		8			11			7			4	9		3			6
1	2			5			8			11		10				4	9		3	7		6
1	2			5			8			11			7	10		4	9		3			6
1	2			5								8	11	10		4	9		3	7		6
32	38	32	8	41	30	2	35	2	28	33	16	21	12	20	4	34	33	7	10	11	3	10
				3	3		7		11	4	1	1	3	5		3	22			2		

Burgin, Ted	Ashall, Jimmy	Hair, Grenville	McConnell, Peter	Charlton, Jack	Cush, Wilbur	Humphries, Billy	Revie, Don	Shackleton, Alan	Crowe, Chris	Meek, George	Overfield, Jack	Cameron, Bobby	Francis, Gerry	Peyton, Noel	Kilford, John	Gibson, Archie	McCole, John	Wood, Roy	Caldwell, Terry	Bremner, Billy	Humphreys, Alan	Goodwin, Freddie
	2	3		5	4				7	11		8		10		6	9	1				
0	1	1	0	1	1	0	0	0	1	1	0	1	0	1	0	1	1	1	0	0	0	0
																	1					

League Table

	P	W	D	L	F	A	Pts
Burnley	42	24	7	11	85	61	55
Wolverhampton W	42	24	6	12	106	67	54
Tottenham Hotspur	42	21	11	10	86	50	53
West Bromwich Albion	42	19	11	12	83	57	49
Sheffield Wednesday	42	19	11	12	80	59	49
Bolton Wanderers	42	20	8	14	59	51	48
Manchester United	42	19	7	16	102	80	45
Newcastle United	42	18	8	16	82	78	44
Preston North End	42	16	12	14	79	76	44
Fulham	42	17	10	15	73	80	44
Blackpool	42	15	10	17	59	71	40
Leicester City	42	13	13	16	66	75	39
Arsenal	42	15	9	18	68	80	39
West Ham United	42	16	6	20	75	91	38
Everton	42	13	11	18	73	78	37
Manchester City	42	17	3	22	78	84	37
Blackburn Rovers	42	16	5	21	60	70	37
Chelsea	42	14	9	19	76	91	37
Birmingham City	42	13	10	19	63	80	36
Nottingham Forest	42	13	9	20	50	74	35
Leeds United	42	12	10	20	65	92	34
Luton Town	42	9	12	21	50	73	30

1960-61

Division Two

Manager: Jack Taylor to March 1961 then Don Revie OBE

Final Position: 14th

Did you know that?

17 September 1960: United, managed by Jack Taylor, played in all-white with a blue and gold trim for the first time in the 4–4 draw with Middlesbrough. This was before Don Revie made the change permanent the following season.

5 December 1960: United's fourth round Football League Cup tie at Southampton didn't finish until 10.10pm after two floodlight failures. The Saints led 4–0, but Leeds fought back to level, only to be beaten by a last-minute goal by Derek Reeves – his fifth of the match.

Don Revie took over as player-manager.

Match No.	Date		Venue	Opponents	Result	FT	HT	Scorers	Attendance
1	Aug	20	A	Liverpool	L	0-2	0-2		43,041
2		24	H	Bristol Rovers	D	1-1	0-1	McCole	11,330
3		27	H	Rotherham United	W	2-0	0-0	Hawksby, McCole	16,480
4		29	A	Bristol Rovers	D	4-4	4-0	Hawksby, Grainger, Peyton, McCole	18,864
5	Sep	3	A	Southampton	W	4-2	1-1	Grainger, Cameron, Francis, McCole	21,862
6		7	H	Leyton Orient	L	1-3	0-2	Cameron	17,363
7		10	H	Huddersfield Town	L	1-4	1-0	Cameron (pen)	22,146
8		14	A	Leyton Orient	W	1-0	0-0	Revie	8,505
9		17	H	Middlesbrough	D	4-4	3-2	Stonehouse (og), Goodwin, Cameron (pen), McCole	17,799
10		24	A	Brighton & HA	L	1-2	0-1	McCole	16,276
11	Oct	1	H	Ipswich Town	L	2-5	2-1	McCole 2	13,502
12		8	A	Sunderland	W	3-2	2-0	Peyton, Francis, McCole	22,296
13		15	H	Plymouth Argyle	W	2-1	2-0	Grainger, Francis	12,229
14		22	A	Norwich City	L	2-3	1-2	Bremner 2	18,970
15		29	H	Charlton Athletic	W	1-0	1-0	Grainger	14,014
16	Nov	5	A	Sheffield United	L	2-3	0-1	Cameron (pen), Francis	17,565
17		12	H	Stoke City	L	0-1	0-0		13,486
18		19	A	Swansea Town	L	2-3	1-1	McCole, Cameron	11,140
19	Dec	3	A	Lincoln City	W	3-2	1-1	McCole, Bremner, Peyton	5,678
20		10	H	Portsmouth	D	0-0	0-0		9,421
21		17	H	Liverpool	D	2-2	1-0	Murray, Bremner	11,929
22		24	A	Derby County	W	3-2	1-0	McCole, Bremner 2	15,185
23		27	H	Derby County	D	3-3	1-0	McCole, Murray, Charlton	18,517
24		31	A	Rotherham United	W	3-1	1-0	McCole, Lambert (og), Waterhouse (og)	12,557
25	Jan	14	H	Southampton	W	3-0	0-0	Cameron, Francis 2	14,039
26		21	A	Huddersfield Town	W	1-0	1-0	McCole	18,938
27	Feb	4	A	Middlesbrough	L	0-3	0-2		16,593
28		10	H	Brighton & HA	W	3-2	1-1	McCole, Charlton, Goodwin	12,598
29		18	A	Ipswich Town	L	0-4	0-3		13,125
30		25	H	Sunderland	L	2-4	1-4	Smith, Bremner	15,136
31	Mar	4	A	Plymouth Argyle	L	1-3	0-0	Grainger	14,878
32		8	H	Luton Town	L	1-2	0-1	Cameron (pen)	9,995
33		11	H	Norwich City	W	1-0	0-0	Smith	11,294
34		18	A	Portsmouth	L	1-3	1-1	Charlton	16,230
35		25	H	Sheffield United	L	1-2	1-1	Shaw (og)	13,688
36	Apr	1	A	Luton Town	D	1-1	1-0	Bremner	11,137
37		3	A	Scunthorpe United	L	2-3	1-2	Charlton 2 (1 pen)	8,725
38		8	H	Swansea Town	D	2-2	1-0	Charlton 2	11,862
39		15	A	Stoke City	D	0-0	0-0		7,130
40		22	H	Lincoln City	W	7-0	3-0	McCole 2 (1 p), Bell, Peyton, McConnell, Bremner, Drysdale (og)	8,432
41		25	H	Scunthorpe United	D	2-2	2-0	McCole 2	6,975
42		29	A	Charlton Athletic	L	0-2	0-0		9,081
									Appearances
								Five own-goals	Goals

FL Cup

R2	Sep	28	H	Blackpool	D	0-0	0-0		13,064
Rep	Oct	5	A	Blackpool	W	3-1*	1-1	Revie, Grainger, McCole	9,614
R3	Nov	23	A	Chesterfield	W	4-0	1-0	McCole, Cameron (pen), Bremner, Peyton	2,021
R4	Dec	5	A	Southampton	L	4-5	0-3	Peyton, McCole, Charlton, Cameron (pen)	13,448
									Appearances
									Goals

* After extra-time (score at 90 minutes 1-1)

FA Cup

R3	Jan	7	A	Sheffield Wed	L	0-2	0-1		34,821
									Appearances
									Goals

This United side crashed 4–1 at home to neighbours Huddersfield Town on 10 September 1960. Back row, left to right: Jim Ashall, Bobby Cameron, Alan Humphreys, Jack Charlton, Grenville Hair, Freddie Goodwin. Front row: Tommy Murray, Noel Peyton, Don Revie, John McCole, Colin Grainger.

Burgin, Ted	Ashall, Jimmy	Jones, Alf	Smith, Eric	Charlton, Jack	Goodwin, Freddie	Bremner, Billy	Revie, Don	McCole, John	Fitzgerland, Peter	Grainger, Colin	Hair, Grenville	Francis, Gerry	Peyton, Noel	Cameron, Bobby	Hawksby, John	Murray, Tommy	Bell, Willie	Humphreys, Alan	Caldwell, Terry	McGugan, Jackie	Wright, Ronnie	McConnell, Peter	Kilford, John	Carling, Terry	Johanneson, Albert	Martin, Geoff
1	2	3	4	5	6	7	8	9	10	11																
1		2	4	5	6		8	9		11	3	7	10													
1		2		5	6			9		11	3	7	10	4	8											
1		2		5	6			9		11	3	7	10	4	8											
1	2			5	6			9		11	3	7	10	4		8										
1	2			5		8	7	9		11	3		10	4			6									
	2			5	6		8	9		11	3		10	4		7		1								
1				5	6		8	9		11	3		10	4		7			2							
1				5	6			9		11	3	7	10	4	8				2							
1				5	6		8	9		11	3	7	10	4					2							
1				5	6		8	9		11	3	7		4						2	10					
				5	6		8	9		11	3	7	10	4				1	2							
				5	6		8	9		11	3	7	10	4				1	2							
				5		8			9	11	3	7	10	4			6	1	2							
				5	6	8			9	11	3	7	10	4				1	2							
				5	6	8		9		11	3	7	10	4				1	2							
				5	6	8	10		9	11	3	7		4				1	2							
				5	6	8		9		11	3	7		4	10			1	2							
		2		5	6	8		9		11	3	7	10	4				1								
		2		5	6	8		9		11	3		10	4		7		1								
		2		5	6	10	4	9		11	3			8		7		1								
		2		5	6	10	4	9		11	3	8				7		1								
		2		5	6	10	4	9		11	3	8				7		1								
		2	4	5	6	10		9		11	3	7		8				1								
		2		5	6	10	8	9		11	3	7		4				1								
		2	8	5	6	10		9		11	3	7		4				1								
		2	8	5	6	10		9		11	3	7		4				1								
		2	8	5	6	10		9		11	3	7		4				1								
		2	8	5	6	10		9			3	7		4	11			1								
		2	8	5	6	10		9		11	3	7		4				1								
		2	8	5	6	10		9		11	3	7		4				1								
		2			5	8		9		11	3	7	10	4				1				6				
		2	8	5		10		9	7			11		4				1				6	3			
		2		9	5	10			8	11		7		4				1				6	3			
			4	9	5	8		10		11	2	7						1				6	3			
			4	9	5	8		10			2	7			11							6	3	1		
			4	9	5	8			7		2		10		11							6	3	1		
			4	9	5	8			7		2		10					1				6	3		11	
			4	5		7		9			2	8	10					1				6	3		11	
			4	5		7		9			2		10				6	1				8	3		11	
			4	5		7		9			2		10				6					8	3	1	11	
			4	9	5	7					2		10				6					8	3	1	11	
10	4	20	18	41	36	31	14	35	8	33	39	31	23	30	7	7	5	28	10	1	1	11	10	4	5	0
			2	7	2	9	1	20		5		6	4	8	2	2	1					1				

Burgin, Ted	Ashall, Jimmy	Jones, Alf	Smith, Eric	Charlton, Jack	Goodwin, Freddie	Bremner, Billy	Revie, Don	McCole, John	Fitzgerland, Peter	Grainger, Colin	Hair, Grenville	Francis, Gerry	Peyton, Noel	Cameron, Bobby	Hawksby, John	Murray, Tommy	Bell, Willie	Humphreys, Alan	Caldwell, Terry	McGugan, Jackie	Wright, Ronnie	McConnell, Peter	Kilford, John	Carling, Terry	Johanneson, Albert	Martin, Geoff
1				5	6		8	9		11	3	7		4					2		10					
				5	6		8	9		11	3	7	10	4				1	2							
		2		5	6	7	8	9			3		10	4										1		11
		2		5	6	8		9		11	3	7	10	4				1								
1	0	2	0	4	4	2	3	4	0	3	4	3	3	4	0	0	0	2	2	0	1	0	0	1	0	1
				1		1	1	3		1			2	2												

Burgin, Ted	Ashall, Jimmy	Jones, Alf	Smith, Eric	Charlton, Jack	Goodwin, Freddie	Bremner, Billy	Revie, Don	McCole, John	Fitzgerland, Peter	Grainger, Colin	Hair, Grenville	Francis, Gerry	Peyton, Noel	Cameron, Bobby	Hawksby, John	Murray, Tommy	Bell, Willie	Humphreys, Alan	Caldwell, Terry	McGugan, Jackie	Wright, Ronnie	McConnell, Peter	Kilford, John	Carling, Terry	Johanneson, Albert	Martin, Geoff
		2	4	5	6	10		9		11	3	7		8				1								
0	0	1	1	1	1	1	0	1	0	1	1	1	0	1	0	0	0	1	0	0	0	0	0	0	0	0

League Table

	P	W	D	L	F	A	Pts
Ipswich Town	42	26	7	9	100	55	59
Sheffield United	42	26	6	10	81	51	58
Liverpool	42	21	10	11	87	58	52
Norwich City	42	20	9	13	70	53	49
Middlesbrough	42	18	12	12	83	74	48
Sunderland	42	17	13	12	75	60	47
Swansea Town	42	18	11	13	77	73	47
Southampton	42	18	8	16	84	81	44
Scunthorpe United	42	14	15	13	69	64	43
Charlton Athletic	42	16	11	15	97	91	43
Plymouth Argyle	42	17	8	17	81	82	42
Derby County	42	15	10	17	80	80	40
Luton Town	42	15	9	18	71	79	39
Leeds United	42	14	10	18	75	83	38
Rotherham United	42	12	13	17	65	64	37
Brighton & Hove Albion	42	14	9	19	61	75	37
Bristol Rovers	42	15	7	20	73	92	37
Stoke City	42	12	12	18	51	59	36
Leyton Orient	42	14	8	20	55	78	36
Huddersfield Town	42	13	9	20	62	71	35
Portsmouth	42	11	11	20	64	91	33
Lincoln City	42	8	8	26	48	95	24

1961-62

Division Two

Manager: Don Revie OBE

Final Position: 19th

Did you know that?

25 November 1961: Billy Bremner put Leeds 2–1 up in 64 minutes with a penalty retaken as 'keeper Alan Boswell had moved. It was reordered by Mr F.W. Cooper, the substitute referee, after Mr R.H. Windle had to go on the line after being hit by a clearance by Jimmy Dudley of Walsall.

7 April 1962: Grenville Hair ended his long wait for his first United goal, scoring against Middlesbrough in his 411th League appearance – the equivalent of three weeks and 16 hours non-stop football.

Grenville Hair finally got on the scoresheet – against Middlesbrough in April.

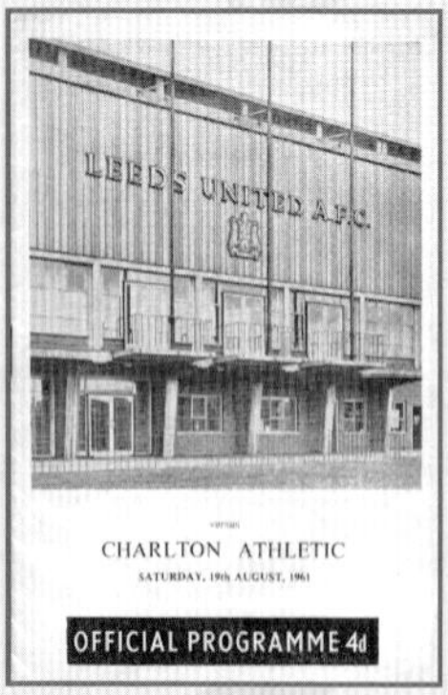

Match No.	Date	Venue	Opponents	Result	FT	HT	Scorers	Attendance
1	Aug 19	H	Charlton Athletic	W	1-0	0-0	Bremner	12,916
2	22	A	Brighton & HA	W	3-1	1-1	Peyton, Bremner, Mayers	22,744
3	26	A	Liverpool	L	0-5	0-1		42,450
4	30	H	Brighton & HA	D	1-1	1-0	Bremner	12,642
5	Sep 2	H	Rotherham United	L	1-3	0-1	McCole	12,610
6	6	A	Norwich City	L	0-2	0-0		26,860
7	9	A	Sunderland	L	1-2	0-2	McCole	30,737
8	16	H	Stoke City	W	3-1	2-1	McCole, Peyton, Bremner	9,578
9	20	H	Norwich City	L	0-1	0-1		10,948
10	23	A	Bristol Rovers	L	0-4	0-2		13,676
11	30	H	Preston North End	L	1-2	0-1	Charlton	9,360
12	Oct 7	A	Plymouth Argyle	D	1-1	1-1	McConnell	10,144
13	14	H	Huddersfield Town	W	1-0	1-0	Charlton	19,162
14	21	A	Swansea Town	L	1-2	1-0	McConnell	11,091
15	28	H	Southampton	D	1-1	1-0	McConnell	10,145
16	Nov 4	A	Luton Town	L	2-3	1-1	Revie, Bremner (pen)	10,341
17	11	H	Leyton Orient	D	0-0	0-0		7,967
18	18	A	Middlesbrough	W	3-1	1-0	Mayers, Bremner, Charlton	10,758
19	25	H	Walsall	W	4-1	1-1	Charlton 2, Bremner (pen), Peyton	10,999
20	Dec 2	A	Derby County	D	3-3	2-1	Peyton, Mayers, Bell	16,408
21	16	A	Charlton Athletic	L	1-3	1-2	Bremner (pen)	9,459
22	23	H	Liverpool	W	1-0	0-0	Bremner	17,214
23	26	H	Scunthorpe United	L	1-4	1-2	Charlton	19,481
24	Jan 12	A	Rotherham United	L	1-2	1-0	McAdams	6,207
25	20	H	Sunderland	W	1-0	1-0	Smith	17,763
26	27	H	Newcastle United	L	0-1	0-1		17,120
27	feb 3	A	Stoke City	L	1-2	0-0	Peyton	21,935
28	10	H	Bristol Rovers	D	0-0	0-0		9,108
29	20	A	Scunthorpe United	L	1-2	0-2	Mayers (pen)	9,186
30	24	H	Plymouth Argyle	L	2-3	1-1	Charlton, Mayers	8,554
31	Mar 3	A	Huddersfield Town	L	1-2	1-1	Charlton	16,799
32	10	H	Swansea Town	W	2-0	1-0	Collins, McAdams	17,314
33	17	A	Southampton	L	1-4	1-2	Lawson	11,924
34	24	H	Luton Town	W	2-1	0-1	Bremner 2	13,078
35	31	A	Leyton Orient	D	0-0	0-0		13,290
36	Apr 7	H	Middlesbrough	W	2-0	1-0	Hair, Gates (og)	16,116
37	9	A	Preston North End	D	1-1	1-0	Cunningham (og)	10,492
38	14	A	Walsall	D	1-1	0-1	Johanneson	9,005
39	20	A	Bury	D	1-1	0-1	Charlton	11,313
40	21	H	Derby County	D	0-0	0-0		11,922
41	24	H	Bury	D	0-0	0-0		21,482
42	28	A	Newcastle United	W	3-0	1-0	Johanneson, McAdams, Keith (og)	21,708
								Appearances
							Three own-goals	Goals

FL Cup

R2	Sep 13	H	Brentford	W	4-1	2-0	McCole 4	4,517
R3	Oct 4	H	Huddersfield Town	W	3-2	1-0	Bremner (pen), Charlton, McConnell	10,023
R4	Dec 12	A	Rotherham United	D	1-1	0-1	Charlton	10,899
rep	Jan 15	H	Rotherham United	L	1-2	0-1	Johanneson (pen)	6,385
								Appearances
								Goals

FA Cup

R3	Jan 6	H	Derby County	D	2-2	1-1	Charlton, Peyton	27,089
Rep	10	A	Derby County	L	1-3	1-1	McAdams	28,168
								Appearances
								Goals

Don Revie embarked on his first full season in management in 1961–62. Here his United squad are assembled in front of the open Spion Kop at Elland Road. Back row, left to right: Syd Owen (coach), Les Cocker (trainer), John Hawksby, Alan Humphreys, John Kilford, Jack Charlton, Eric Thompson, Mike Addy, Gary Sprake, Peter Metcalfe, Paul Reaney, Rod Johnson, Bob English (physiotherapist), Don Revie (manager). Middle row: Billy Bremner, Francis, Derek Mayers, Eric Smith, Tom Hallett, Terry Carling, Albert Johanneson, Willie Bell. Front row: Norman Hunter, Terry Casey, Grenville Hair, Alf Jones, Hugh Ryden, John McCole, Bobby Cameron, Colin Grainger, Noel Peyton, Peter McConnell, Terry Cooper.

Humphreys, Alan	Smith, Eric	Hair, Grenville	Cameron, Bobby	Charlton, Jack	Goodwin, Freddie	Mayers, Derek	Bremner, Billy	McCole, John	Peyton, Noel	Johanneson, Albert	McConnell, Peter	Carling, Terry	Francis, Gerry	Revie, Don	Bell, Willie	Hawksby, John	Younger, Tommy	Jones, Alf	Kilford, John	McAdams, Billy	Casey, Terry	Lawson, Ian	Mason, Cliff	Collins, Bobby	Sprake, Gary	Addy, Mike
1	2	3	4	5	6	7	8	9	10	11																
1	2	3		5	6	7	8	9	10	11	4															
1	2	3		5	6	7	8	9	10	11	4															
	2	3	4	5	6		9		10	11	8	1	7													
1	2	3	4	5	6		8	9	10	11			7													
1	2	3		5	6	7	8	9	10	11				4												
1	2	3			5	7	8	9	10	11				4	6											
1	4	2		5	6	7	8	9	10						3	11										
1	4	2		5	6	7	8	9	10						3	11										
1	4	2		5	6	7		9	10				8		3	11										
	4			5	6	7		9	10				8		3	11	1	2								
	4	3		9	5		8		7		10				6	11	1	2								
	4	2		9	5		8		7		10				6	11	1		3							
	4	2		9	5				7		10			8	6	11	1		3							
	4	2		9	5		7		11		10			8	6		1		3							
	4	2		9	5		7		11		10			8	6		1		3							
	4	2			5	7	8		10		6			9	3	11	1									
	4	2		9	5	7	8		10		6				3	11	1									
	4	2		9	5	7	8		10		6				3	11	1									
		2		9	5	7	8		10		4				6	11	1		3							
	4	2			5	7	8		10		6				3	11	1			9						
	4	2		9	5	11	7		10		6				3		1			8						
	4	2		9	5	11	7		10		6				3		1			8						
	2				5	7	8		10		6					11	1		3	9	4					
	8				5		7		10		6				3	11	1	2		9	4					
	8				5		7		10	11	6				3		1	2		9	4					
	4	2		9	5		7		10		6				3	11	1			8						
	4	2		9	5	7	8		10		6				3	11	1									
	4	2		9	5	7	8		10		6				3	11	1									
	6	2	4	9	5	7	8				10				3	11	1									
	6	3	4	9	5		7		11					8			1	2				10				
	6	2	4		5		7									11	1			9		10	3	8		
	6	2	4		5		7									11				9		10	3	8	1	
	6	2		5	4		7		10							11	1					9	3	8		
	6	2		5	4		7		10							11	1					9	3	8		
	6	2		5	4		7		10							11	1					9	3	8		
	6	2		5			7		10		4					11	1					9	3	8		
	6	2		5	4		7		10	11							1					9	3	8		
	6	2		5	4		7		10	11							1					9	3	8		
	6	2		5	4		7		10	11							1					9	3	8		
	6	2		5	4		7			11							1			9		10	3	8		
	6	2		5	4		7			11					10		1			9			3	8		
9	41	38	7	34	41	20	39	10	37	13	23	1	4	7	24	24	31	5	6	11	3	11	11	11	1	0
	1	1		9		5	11	3	5	2	3			1	1					3		1		1		

1	4	2		5	6	7	8	9	10						3	11										
	4	2		9	5		8		7		10				6	11	1		3							
		2		9	5	7	8		10		6				3	11	1				4					
	4				5		7		8	11	6					10	1	2	3							9
1	3	3	0	3	4	2	4	1	4	1	3	0	0	0	3	4	3	1	2	0	1	0	0	0	0	1
				2			1	4		1	1															

	4	2		9	5	11	7		10		6				3		1			8						
	4	2		9	5	11	7		10		6				3		1			8						
0	2	2	0	2	2	2	2	0	2	0	2	0	0	0	2	0	2	0	0	2	0	0	0	0	0	0
				1					1											1						

League Table

	P	W	D	L	F	A	Pts
Liverpool	42	27	8	7	99	43	62
Leyton Orient	42	22	10	10	69	40	54
Sunderland	42	22	9	11	85	50	53
Scunthorpe United	42	21	7	14	86	71	49
Plymouth Argyle	42	19	8	15	75	75	46
Southampton	42	18	9	15	77	62	45
Huddersfield Town	42	16	12	14	67	59	44
Stoke City	42	17	8	17	55	57	42
Rotherham United	42	16	9	17	70	76	41
Preston North End	42	15	10	17	55	57	40
Newcastle United	42	15	9	18	64	58	39
Middlesbrough	42	16	7	19	76	72	39
Luton Town	42	17	5	20	69	71	39
Walsall	42	14	11	17	70	75	39
Charlton Athletic	42	15	9	18	69	75	39
Derby County	42	14	11	17	68	75	39
Norwich City	42	14	11	17	61	70	39
Bury	42	17	5	20	52	76	39
Leeds United	42	12	12	18	50	61	36
Swansea Town	42	12	12	18	61	83	36
Bristol Rovers	42	13	7	22	53	81	33
Brighton & Hove Albion	42	10	11	21	42	86	31

1962-63

Division Two

Manager: Don Revie OBE

Final Position: 5th

Did you know that?

8 September 1962: Seventeen-year-old Rod Johnson made a scoring debut and was carried off as a youthful United won 2–0 at Swansea. The match also saw debuts for Norman Hunter and Paul Reaney.

29 September 1962: Revie's policy of giving youth a chance reached new heights as Peter Lorimer becomes United's youngest player at 15 years 289 days in the 1–1 home draw with Southampton.

15 December 1962: Christmas came early for Don Weston who scored a debut hat-trick in the 3–1 win against Stoke after his move from Rotherham. It was the Potters first defeat in 18 League games.

2 March 1963: United beat Derby 3–1 in their first game in 41 days as Britain emerged from the grip of the big freeze.

6 March 1963: The FA Cup victory over Stoke ended a run of 16 consecutive FA Cup ties without a win.

Don Weston scored a debut hat-trick.

Match No.	Date		Venue	Opponents	Result	FT	HT	Scorers	Attendance
1	Aug	18	A	Stoke City	W	1-0	1-0	Storrie	27,188
2		22	H	Rotherham United	L	3-4	0-2	Storrie, Charles, Johanneson	14,199
3		25	H	Sunderland	W	1-0	0-0	Bremner	17,753
4		28	A	Rotherham United	L	1-2	0-1	Charles	19,508
5	Sep	1	A	Huddersfield Town	D	1-1	1-1	Charles	34,946
6		5	H	Bury	L	1-2	1-0	Bremner	28,313
7		8	A	Swansea Town	W	2-0	1-0	Johnson, Bremner	17,696
8		15	H	Chelsea	W	2-0	1-0	Johanneson 2	27,520
9		18	A	Bury	L	1-3	0-2	Storrie	18,876
10		22	A	Luton Town	D	2-2	2-1	Storrie, Collins	8,958
11		29	H	Southampton	D	1-1	0-1	Storrie	25,408
12	Oct	6	H	Middlesbrough	L	2-3	1-1	Hunter, Bremner	28,222
13		13	A	Derby County	D	0-0	0-0		14,246
14		20	H	Newcastle United	W	1-0	1-0	Johanneson	23,386
15		27	A	Walsall	D	1-1	1-0	Johanneson	7,353
16	Nov	3	H	Norwich City	W	3-0	2-0	Storrie, Bell, Johanneson	15,919
17		10	A	Grimsby Town	D	1-1	1-0	Storrie	9,183
18		17	H	Plymouth Argyle	W	6-1	3-0	Johanneson, Storrie 3, Collins, Bremner	15,301
19		24	A	Preston North End	L	1-4	1-3	Bell	13,145
20	Dec	1	H	Portsmouth	D	3-3	2-2	Storrie, Collins, Johanneson	15,519
21		8	A	Cardiff City	D	0-0	0-0		11,334
22		15	H	Stoke City	W	3-1	2-1	Weston 3	19,331
23		22	A	Sunderland	L	1-2	0-1	Bremner	40,252
24	Mar	2	H	Derby County	W	3-1	1-1	Weston, Storrie, Charlton (pen)	22,912
25		9	A	Newcastle United	D	1-1	1-0	Storrie	29,570
26		13	H	Walsall	W	3-0	2-0	Johanneson, Storrie 2	17,077
27		23	A	Norwich City	L	2-3	0-3	Collins, Johanneson	26,154
28		30	H	Grimsby Town	W	3-0	1-0	Bremner, Collins 2	13,938
29	Apr	3	H	Scunthorpe United	W	1-0	0-0	Bremner	15,783
30		6	A	Plymouth Argyle	L	1-3	1-2	Storrie	8,992
31		13	H	Preston North End	W	4-1	1-0	Bremner 2, Storrie, Collins	16,016
32		15	A	Charlton Athletic	W	2-1	2-0	Charlton, Hunter	13,538
33		16	H	Charlton Athletic	W	4-1	3-0	Weston, Henderson, Johanneson, Storrie	24,646
34		20	A	Portsmouth	L	0-3	0-2		7,773
35		23	A	Scunthorpe United	W	2-0	1-0	Lawson 2	7,794
36		27	H	Cardiff City	W	3-0	1-0	Storrie 3	19,752
37		30	A	Chelsea	D	2-2	2-2	Lawson 2	24,387
38	May	4	H	Luton Town	W	3-0	1-0	Storrie 2, Weston	23,781
39		6	A	Middlesbrough	L	1-2	0-2	Johanneson	17,365
40		11	H	Huddersfield Town	L	0-1	0-1		28,501
41		15	A	Southampton	L	1-3	0-2	Weston	11,619
42		18	H	Swansea Town	W	5-0	3-0	Storrie 2, Lawson, Collins, Johanneson	11,314
									Appearances
									Goals

FL Cup

R2	Sep	26	H	Crystal Palace	W	2-1	0-0	Charlton, Storrie	7,274
R3	Oct	17	A	Blackburn Rovers	L	0-4	0-2		7,680
									Appearances
									Goals

FA Cup

R3	Mar	6	H	Stoke City	W	3-1	2-0	Collins, Reaney, Hair	36,873
R4		16	A	Middlesbrough	W	2-0	0-0	Storrie, Johanneson	39,672
R5		19	A	Nottingham Forest	L	0-3	0-1		36,392
									Appearances
									Goals

Back row, left to right: Jack Charlton, Peter McConnell, Ian Lawson, Tommy Younger, Cliff Mason, Grenville Hair, Freddie Goodwin. Front row: Eric Smith, Billy Bremner, Jim Storrie, John Charles, Bobby Collins, Albert Johanneson. Inset: Gary Sprake, Norman Hunter, Willie Bell, Don Weston.

Younger, Tommy	Hair, Grenville	Mason, Cliff	Goodwin, Freddie	Charlton, Jack	Smith, Eric	Bremner, Billy	Storrie, Jim	Charles, John	Collins, Bobby	Johanneson, Albert	Bell, Willie	Lawson, Ian	Hawksby, John	Sprake, Gary	Reaney, Paul	Hunter, Norman	Peyton, Noel	Johnson, Rod	Addy, Mike	Lorimer, Peter	Henderson, Tommy	Weston, Don	Williamson, Brian	Wright, Barrie	Greenhoff, Jimmy	Hallett, Tom
1	2	3	4	5	6	7	8	9	10	11																
1	2	3	4	5	6	7	8	9	10	11																
1	2	3	4	5		7	8	9	10	11	6															
1	2	3		5		4	8	9	10		6	7	11													
1	2	3		5	4	7	8	9	10	11	6															
1	2	3		5	4	7	8	9	10	11	6															
		3		5	4	8			10	11				1	2	6	7	9								
		3		5	4	8		9	10	11				1	2	6	7									
		3		5		4	8	9	10	11				1	2	6	7									
		3		5		8	9		10	11				1	2	6		7	4							
		3		5			8	9	10	11				1	2	6			4	7						
	3	7		5		8	9	4	10	11				1	2	6										
		3		5			8	9	10	11	4		7	1	2	6										
		3		5					10	11	4		7	1	2	6	8	9								
		3		5			8		10	11	4		7	1	2	6		9								
		3	5			8	9		10	11	4		7	1	2	6										
		3	5			8	9		10	11	4			1	2	6					7					
	2	3		5		8	9		10	11	4			1		6					7					
		3		5		8	9		10	11	4			1	2	6					7					
		3		5		8	9		10	11	4			1	2	6					7					
	3			5			9		10	11	4			1	2	6	8				7					
	3			5			9		10	11	4			1	2	6					7	8				
	3			5		10	9			11	4			1	2	6					7	8				
	3			5			9		10	11	4			1	2	6					7	8				
	3			5			9		10	11	4			1	2	6					7	8				
	3			5			9		10	11	4			1	2	6					7	8				
	3			5		8	9		10	11	4			1	2	6						7				
	3			5		8	9		10	11	4				2	6						7	1			
	3			5		8	9		10	11	4				2	6						7	1			
	3			5		8	9		10	11	4				2	6						7	1			
				5		8	9		10	11	4			1	2	6					7			3		
				5		8	9		10	11	4			1	2	6					7			3		
				5			9		10	11	4			1	2	6					7	8		3		
	3			5			9		10	11	4			1	2	6	8				7					
	3		5				9		10	11	4	8		1	2	6					7					
	3		5				9		10	11	4	8		1	2	6					7					
	3			5			9		10	11	4	8		1	2	6					7					
	3			5			9		10	11	4			1	2	6					7	8				
			4	5			9		10	11	3			1	2	6					7	8				
	3			5					10	11	4	9		1	2	6					7	8				
	3			5		8	9		10	11				1	2	6						7			4	
	3			5			9		10	11		8		1	2	6						7			4	
6	26	20	8	38	6	24	38	11	41	41	32	6	5	33	35	36	6	4	2	1	20	15	3	3	2	0
				2		10	25	3	8	13	2	5				2		1			1	7				

	2	3		5			8					9	11	1		6	10	7	4							
		3					8				4	9	11	1	2	6	10	7								5
0	1	2	0	1	0	0	2	0	0	0	1	2	2	2	1	2	2	2	1	0	0	0	0	0	0	1
				1			1																			

	3			5			9		10	11	4			1	2	6					7	8				
	3			5			9		10	11	4			1	2	6					7	8				
	3			5			9		10	11	4			1	2	6					7	8				
0	3	0	0	3	0	0	3	0	3	3	3	0	0	3	3	3	0	0	0	0	3	3	0	0	0	0
	1						1		1	1					1											

League Table

	P	W	D	L	F	A	Pts
Stoke City	42	20	13	9	73	50	53
Chelsea	42	24	4	14	81	42	52
Sunderland	42	20	12	10	84	55	52
Middlesbrough	42	20	9	13	86	85	49
Leeds United	42	19	10	13	79	53	48
Huddersfield Town	42	17	14	11	63	50	48
Newcastle United	42	18	11	13	79	59	47
Bury	42	18	11	13	51	47	47
Scunthorpe United	42	16	12	14	57	59	44
Cardiff City	42	18	7	17	83	73	43
Southampton	42	17	8	17	72	67	42
Plymouth Argyle	42	15	12	15	76	73	42
Norwich City	42	17	8	17	80	79	42
Rotherham United	42	17	6	19	67	74	40
Swansea Town	42	15	9	18	51	72	39
Portsmouth	42	13	11	18	63	79	37
Preston North End	42	13	11	18	59	74	37
Derby County	42	12	12	18	61	72	36
Grimsby Town	42	11	13	18	55	66	35
Charlton Athletic	42	13	5	24	62	94	31
Walsall	42	11	9	22	53	89	31
Luton Town	42	11	7	24	61	84	29

1963-64

Division Two

Manager: Don Revie OBE

Final Position: 1st

Did you know that?

4 January 1964: United's FA Cup victory at Cardiff was marred by a triple leg break for defender Freddie Goodwin which put an end to his career. Goodwin also played cricket for Lancashire.

18 April 1964: Promoted United's draw with Plymouth ensured they completed a season undefeated at Elland Road for the first time in the club's history.

25 April 1964: United put on a champion display with a 2–0 win at Charlton to finish the season with 63 points, the best tally by any Second Division side since Tottenham in 1920.

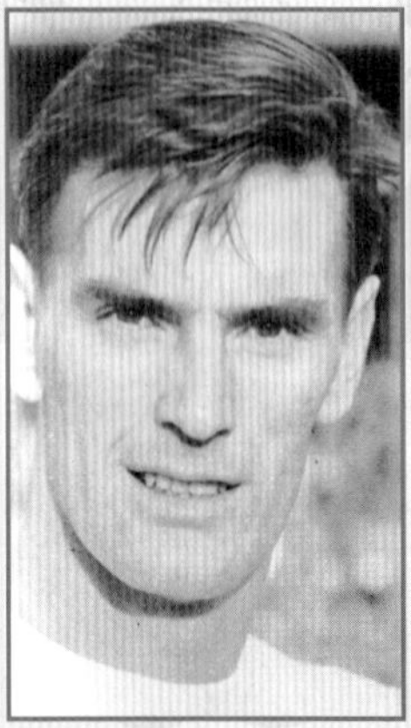

Alan Peacock rounded off the season in champion style with both goals at Charlton.

Match No.	Date		Venue	Opponents	Result	FT	HT	Scorers	Attendance
1	Aug	28	H	Rotherham United	W	1-0	0-0	Weston	22,517
2		31	H	Bury	W	3-0	1-0	Collins, Storrie, Johanneson	26,041
3	Sep	3	A	Rotherham United	D	2-2	0-0	Charlton, Johanneson	14,178
4		7	A	Manchester City	L	2-3	1-1	Johanneson, Lawson	29,186
5		11	H	Portsmouth	W	3-1	1-0	Storrie, Weston, Bremner	24,926
6		14	H	Swindon Town	D	0-0	0-0		33,301
7		18	A	Portsmouth	D	1-1	0-0	Henderson	12,569
8		21	A	Cardiff City	D	0-0	0-0		16,117
9		28	H	Norwich City	W	4-2	2-0	Weston 2, Johanneson, Collins (pen)	22,804
10	Oct	1	A	Northampton Town	W	3-0	2-0	Lawson, Weston, Collins	15,079
11		5	A	Scunthorpe United	W	1-0	0-0	Lawson	10,793
12		9	H	Middlesbrough	W	2-0	1-0	Hunter, Collins	36,919
13		12	A	Huddersfield Town	W	2-0	0-0	Giles, Weston	31,220
14		19	H	Derby County	D	2-2	0-2	Charlton, Weston	29,864
15		26	A	Southampton	W	4-1	4-0	Lawson 2, Giles, Johanneson	18,036
16	Nov	2	H	Charlton Athletic	D	1-1	1-0	Charlton	32,344
17		9	A	Grimsby Town	W	2-0	1-0	Lawson, Weston	12,194
18		16	H	Preston North End	D	1-1	0-0	Johanneson	33,841
19		23	A	Leyton Orient	W	2-0	0-0	Collins, Johanneson	12,072
20		30	H	Swansea Town	W	2-1	1-1	Johanneson, Bell	21,870
21	Dec	7	A	Plymouth Argyle	W	1-0	1-0	Johanneson	9,918
22		14	H	Northampton Town	D	0-0	0-0		21,108
23		21	A	Bury	W	2-1	1-0	Lawson, Weston	7,453
24		26	H	Sunderland	D	1-1	0-0	Lawson	41,167
25		28	A	Sunderland	L	0-2	0-2		55,046
26	Jan	11	H	Manchester City	W	1-0	0-0	Weston	33,737
27		18	A	Swindon Town	D	2-2	1-2	Giles, Hunter	19,015
28	Feb	1	H	Cardiff City	D	1-1	1-1	Johanneson	28,039
29		8	A	Norwich City	D	2-2	0-0	Weston, Peacock	20,843
30		15	H	Scunthorpe United	W	1-0	1-0	Johanneson	28,868
31		22	H	Huddersfield Town	D	1-1	1-0	Storrie	36,439
32	Mar	3	A	Preston North End	L	0-2	0-1		35,612
33		7	H	Southampton	W	3-1	1-1	Lawson, Collins, Johanneson	24,077
34		14	A	Middlesbrough	W	3-1	1-1	Lawson, Peacock, Giles	15,986
35		21	H	Grimsby Town	W	3-1	1-1	Lawson, Bremner, Peacock	25,351
36		27	A	Newcastle United	W	1-0	1-0	Giles	55,038
37		28	A	Derby County	D	1-1	0-0	Peacock	16,757
38		30	H	Newcastle United	W	2-1	1-1	Weston, Johanneson	40,105
39	Apr	4	H	Leyton Orient	W	2-1	1-0	Giles, Weston	30,920
40		11	A	Swansea Town	W	3-0	3-0	Peacock 2, Giles	14,321
41		18	H	Plymouth Argyle	D	1-1	1-0	Bell	34,725
42		25	A	Charlton Athletic	W	2-0	1-0	Peacock 2	21,323
									Appearances
									Goals

FL Cup

R2	Sep	25	H	Mansfield Town	W	5-1	2-0	Lawson 2, Johanneson 2, Bell	9,843
R3	Oct	22	H	Swansea Town	W	2-0	1-0	Lawson, Storrie	10,748
R4	Nov	27	A	Manchester City	L	1-3	1-1	Weston	10,769
									Appearances
									Goals

FA Cup

R3	Jan	4	A	Cardiff City	W	1-0	0-0	Bremner	13,932
R4		25	H	Everton	D	1-1	1-0	Lawson	48,826
Rep		28	A	Everton	L	0-2	0-1		66,167
									Appearances
									Goals

Second Division champions. Back row, left to right: Billy Bremner, Paul Reaney, Gary Sprake, Jack Charlton, Norman Hunter, Willie Bell. Front row: Johnny Giles, Don Weston, Bobby Collins, Alan Peacock, Albert Johanneson.

Sprake, Gary	Reaney, Paul	Bell, Willie	Bremner, Billy	Charlton, Jack	Hunter, Norman	Weston, Don	Lawson, Ian	Storrie, Jim	Collins, Bobby	Johanneson, Albert	Giles, Johnny	Hair, Grenville	Henderson, Tommy	Goodwin, Freddie	Wright, Barrie	Madeley, Paul	Williamson, Brian	Peacock, Alan	Greenhoff, Jimmy	Cooper, Terry	Hawksby, John	Lorimer, Peter	Smith, Eric
1	2	3	4	5	6	7	8	9	10	11													
1	2	3	4	5	6	8		9	10	11	7												
1	2	3	4	5	6	8		9	10	11	7												
1	2	3	4	5	6	8	10	9		11	7												
1	2		4	5	6	8		9	10	11	7	3											
1	2		4	5	6	8		9	10	11	7	3											
1	2		4	5	6	8		9	10		7	3	11										
1	2		4	5	6	8		9	10		7	3	11										
1	2		4		6	8		9	10	11	7	3		5									
1	2	3	4		6	9	8		10	11	7			5									
1	2	3	4		6	9	8		10	11	7			5									
1	2	3	4	5	6	9	8		10	11	7												
1	2	3	4	5	6	9	8		10	11	7												
1	2	3	4	5	6	9	8		10	11	7												
1	2	3	4	5	6	9	8		10	11	7												
1	2	3	4	5	6	9	8		10	11	7												
1	2	3	4		6	9	8		10	11	7			5									
1	2	3	4		6		8	9	10	11	7			5									
1		3	4		6	9	8		10	11	7			5	2								
1	2	3	4		6	9	8		10	11	7			5									
1	2	3	4		6	8		9	10	11	7			5									
1	2	3	4		6	8		9	10	11	7			5									
1	2	3	4		6	8	9		10	11	7			5									
1	2	3	4		6	8	9		10	11	7			5									
1	2	3	4		6	7	9	8	10		11			5									
1	2	3	4		6	8	9		10	11	7					5							
	2	3	4		6	8	9		10	11	7					5	1						
1	2	5	4		6	8	9		10	11	7				3								
1	2	3	4		6	8			10	11	7					5		9					
1	2		4		6	8			10	11	7	3				5		9					
1	2		4	5	6			8	10	11	7	3						9					
1	2	4		5	6			8	10	11	7	3						9					
1	2	3		5	6	7	8		10	11								9	4				
1	2	3		5	6		8		10	11	7							9	4				
1	2	3	4	5	6		8		10	11	7							9					
1	2	3	4	5	6		8		10	11	7							9					
1	2	3	4	5	6		8		10	11	7							9					
1	2	3	4	5	6	8			10	11	7							9					
1	2	3	4	5	6	8			10	11	7							9					
1	2	3	4	5	6	8			10		7							9		11			
1	2	3	4	5	6	8			10	11	7							9					
1	2	3	4	5	6	8			10		7							9		11			
41	41	35	39	25	42	35	24	15	41	37	40	8	2	12	2	4	1	14	2	2	0	0	0
		2	3	3	2	13	11	3	6	13	7		1					8					

1	2	4		5	6	9	8		10	11		3	7										
1	2	3	6	5			10	9		11	7								4			8	
1		3			6	8		9			10	2	7	5							11		4
3	2	3	1	2	2	2	2	2	1	2	2	2	2	1	0	0	0	0	1	0	1	1	1
		1				1	3	1		2													

1	2	3	4		6	8	9			11	10		7	5									
1	2	3	4		6		9		10	11	8		7			5							
1	2	3	4		6		9		10		8		7			5					11		
3	3	3	3	0	3	1	3	0	2	2	3	0	3	1	0	2	0	0	0	0	1	0	0
			1				1																

League Table

	P	W	D	L	F	A	Pts
Leeds United	42	24	15	3	71	34	63
Sunderland	42	25	11	6	81	37	61
Preston North End	42	23	10	9	79	54	56
Charlton Athletic	42	19	10	13	76	70	48
Southampton	42	19	9	14	100	73	47
Manchester City	42	18	10	14	84	66	46
Rotherham United	42	19	7	16	90	78	45
Newcastle United	42	20	5	17	74	69	45
Portsmouth	42	16	11	15	79	70	43
Middlesbrough	42	15	11	16	67	52	41
Northampton Town	42	16	9	17	58	60	41
Huddersfield Town	42	15	10	17	57	64	40
Derby County	42	14	11	17	56	67	39
Swindon Town	42	14	10	18	57	69	38
Cardiff City	42	14	10	18	56	81	38
Leyton Orient	42	13	10	19	54	72	36
Norwich City	42	11	13	18	64	80	35
Bury	42	13	9	20	57	73	35
Swansea Town	42	12	9	21	63	74	33
Plymouth Argyle	42	8	16	18	45	67	32
Grimsby Town	42	9	14	19	47	75	32
Scunthorpe United	42	10	10	22	52	82	30

1964-65

Division One

Manager: Don Revie OBE

Final Position: 2nd

Did you know that?

7 November 1964: United's tough reputation was enhanced at Goodison Park where referee Ken Stokes took both teams off for 10 minutes during the first half to allow tempers to cool after a series of flare-ups. Revie's men won 1–0 and Everton were later fined £250 after their furious fans hurled missiles on to the pitch.

2 January 1965: Victory over Sunderland took United to the top of the First Division for the first time in the club's history.

8 May 1965: Billy Bremner became the first Leeds player to represent Scotland when he played in a 0–0 draw with Spain at Hampden Park.

Billy Bremner, the first Leeds player to be capped by Scotland.

Match No.	Date	Venue	Opponents	Result	FT	HT	Scorers	Attendance
1	Aug 22	A	Aston Villa	W	2-1	1-1	Johanneson, Charlton	28,000
2	26	H	Liverpool	W	4-2	2-1	Yeats (og), Weston, Bremner, Giles	36,005
3	29	H	Wolverhampton W	W	3-2	1-2	Storrie 2, Charlton	34,538
4	Sep 2	A	Liverpool	L	1-2	1-0	Collins	52,548
5	5	A	Sunderland	D	3-3	2-0	Storrie, Bell, Johanneson	48,858
6	7	A	Blackpool	L	0-4	0-2		26,310
7	12	H	Leicester City	W	3-2	0-2	Bremner 2 (1 pen), Johanneson	32,300
8	16	H	Blackpool	W	3-0	2-0	Collins 2, Hunter	35,973
9	19	A	Chelsea	L	0-2	0-1		38,006
10	26	H	Nottingham Forest	L	1-2	1-0	Storrie	32,776
11	30	H	Fulham	D	2-2	1-1	Storrie 2	31,260
12	Oct 10	A	Stoke City	W	3-2	1-2	Storrie 2, Greenhoff	27,561
13	17	H	Tottenham Hotspur	W	3-1	2-1	Belfitt, Giles, Bell (pen)	41,464
14	24	A	Burnley	W	1-0	1-0	Bell	24,329
15	31	H	Sheffield United	W	4-1	0-1	Collins, Storrie, Johanneson, Belfitt	33,357
16	Nov 7	A	Everton	W	1-0	1-0	Bell	43,605
17	11	H	Arsenal	W	3-1	1-1	Charlton, Belfitt, Storrie	38,620
18	14	H	Birmingham City	W	4-1	2-1	Storrie, Charlton, Collins, Giles (pen)	32,030
19	21	A	West Ham United	L	1-3	0-3	Belfitt	28,150
20	28	H	West Bromwich Alb	W	1-0	1-0	Johnson	29,553
21	Dec 5	A	Manchester United	W	1-0	0-0	Collins	53,374
22	12	H	Aston Villa	W	1-0	1-0	Johanneson	27,339
23	19	A	Wolverhampton W	W	1-0	0-0	Johnson	17,126
24	26	H	Blackburn Rovers	D	1-1	1-1	Storrie	45,341
25	28	A	Blackburn Rovers	W	2-0	2-0	Storrie, Johanneson	24,511
26	Jan 2	H	Sunderland	W	2-1	0-0	Charlton, Hunter	43,808
27	16	A	Leicester City	D	2-2	1-2	Charlton, Johnson	23,230
28	23	H	Chelsea	D	2-2	1-1	Storrie, Giles	47,109
29	Feb 6	A	Nottingham Forest	D	0-0	0-0		36,596
30	13	A	Arsenal	W	2-1	1-1	Giles, Weston	32,132
31	27	A	Tottenham Hotspur	D	0-0	0-0		42,202
32	Mar 13	A	Fulham	D	2-2	1-1	Peacock, Collins	24,704
33	15	H	Burnley	W	5-1	1-1	Collins 2, Charlton 2, Johanneson	38,506
34	20	H	Everton	W	4-1	2-1	Johanneson 2, Bremner, Peacock	29,701
35	Apr 3	H	West Ham United	W	2-1	0-0	Peacock, Bremner	41,918
36	5	H	Stoke City	W	3-1	3-0	Weston 2, Greenhoff	38,133
37	12	A	West Bromwich Alb	W	2-1	0-1	Peacock 2	20,007
38	17	H	Manchester United	L	0-1	0-1		52,368
39	19	A	Sheffield Wed	L	0-3	0-2		39,054
40	20	H	Sheffield Wed	W	2-0	2-0	Storrie, Giles (pen)	45,065
41	24	A	Sheffield United	W	3-0	1-0	Storrie, Bremner, Peacock	32,928
42	26	A	Birmingham City	D	3-3	0-1	Giles (pen), Reaney, Charlton	16,644
								Appearances
							One own-goal	Goals

FL Cup

R2	Sep 23	H	Huddersfield Town	W	3-2	2-1	Hunter, Storrie, Belfitt	9,837
R3	Oct 14	H	Aston Villa	L	2-3	1-1	Johanneson, Collins	10,656
								Appearances
								Goals

FA Cup

R3	Jan 9	H	Southport	W	3-0	1-0	Greenhoff, Johanneson, Johnson	31,297
R4	30	H	Everton	D	1-1	0-0	Storrie	50,051
Rep	Feb 2	A	Everton	W	2-1	0-0	Charlton, Weston	65,940
R5	20	H	Shrewsbury Town	W	2-0	1-0	Giles (pen), Johanneson	47,740
R6	Mar 10	A	Crystal Palace	W	3-0	0-0	Peacock 2, Storrie	45,384
SF	27	N	Manchester United	D	0-0*	0-0		65,000
Rep	31	N	Manchester United	W	1-0#	0-0	Bremner	46,300
R5	May 10	N	Liverpool	L	1-2†	0-0	Bremner	100,000
								Appearances
								Goals

*At Hillsborough, Sheffield

At the City Ground, Nottingham

† At Wembley, London, after extra-time (score at 90 minutes 0-0)

This squad took United within a hairsbreadth of a famous League and FA Cup double. Back row, left to right: Billy Bremner, Paul Madeley, Willie Bell, Gary Sprake, Paul Reaney, Norman Hunter, Jimmy Greenhoff, Don Weston. Front row: Jim Storrie, Johnny Giles, Terry Cooper, Bobby Collins, Alan Peacock, Jack Charlton, Albert Johanneson, Rod Johnson.

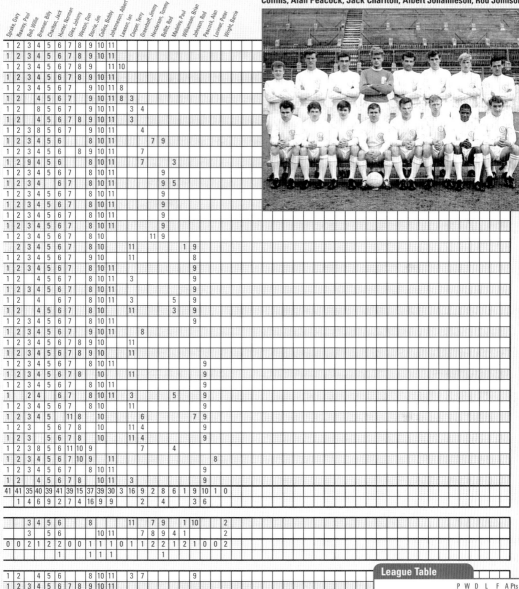

Sprake, Gary	Reaney, Paul	Bell, Willie	Bremner, Billy	Charlton, Jack	Hunter, Norman	Giles, Johnny	Weston, Don	Storrie, Jim	Collins, Bobby	Johanneson, Albert	Lawson, Ian	Cooper, Terry	Greenhoff, Jimmy	Henderson, Tommy	Belfitt, Rod	Madeley, Paul	Williamson, Brian	Johnson, Rod	Peacock, Alan	Lorimer, Peter	Wright, Barrie
1	2	3	4	5	6	7	8	9	10	11											
1	2	3	4	5	6	7	8	9	10	11											
1	2	3	4	5	6	7	8	9		11	10										
1	2	3	4	5	6	7	8	9	10	11											
1	2	3	4	5	6	7		9	10	11	8										
1	2		4	5	6	7		9	10	11	8	3									
1	2		8	5	6	7		9	10	11		3	4								
1	2		4	5	6	7	8	9	10	11		3									
1	2	3	8	5	6	7		9	10	11			4								
1	2	3	4	5	6			8	10	11				7	9						
1	2	3	4	5	6		8	9	10	11			7								
1	2	9	4	5	6			8	10	11			7			3					
1	2	3	4	5	6	7		8	10	11					9						
1	2	3	4		6	7		8	10	11					9	5					
1	2	3	4	5	6	7		8	10	11					9						
1	2	3	4	5	6	7		8	10	11					9						
1	2	3	4	5	6	7		8	10	11					9						
1	2	3	4	5	6	7		8	10	11					9						
1	2	3	4	5	6	7		8	10					11	9						
	2	3	4	5	6	7		8	10			11					1	9			
1	2	3	4	5	6	7		9	10			11						8			
1	2	3	4	5	6	7		8	10	11								9			
1	2		4	5	6	7		8	10	11		3						9			
1	2	3	4	5	6	7		8	10	11								9			
1	2		4		6	7		8	10	11		3				5		9			
1	2		4	5	6	7		8	10			11				3		9			
1	2	3	4	5	6	7		8	10	11								9			
1	2	3	4	5	6	7		9	10	11			8								
1	2	3	4	5	6	7	8	9	10			11									
1	2	3	4	5	6	7	8	9	10			11									
1	2	3	4	5	6	7		8	10	11									9		
1	2	3	4	5	6	7	8		10			11							9		
1	2	3	4	5	6	7		8	10	11									9		
1		2	4		6	7		8	10	11		3				5			9		
1	2	3	4	5	6	7		8	10			11							9		
1	2	3	4	5		11	8		10				6					7	9		
1	2	3		5	6	7	8		10			11	4						9		
1	2	3		5	6	7	8		10			11	4						9		
1	2	3	8	5	6	11	10	9					7			4					
1	2	3	4	5	6	7	10	9		11										8	
1	2	3	4	5	6	7		8	10	11									9		
1	2		4	5	6	7	8		10	11		3							9		
41	41	35	40	39	41	39	15	37	39	30	3	16	9	2	8	6	1	9	10	1	0
	1	4	6	9	2	7	4	16	9	9			2		4			3	6		

Sprake, Gary	Reaney, Paul	Bell, Willie	Bremner, Billy	Charlton, Jack	Hunter, Norman	Giles, Johnny	Weston, Don	Storrie, Jim	Collins, Bobby	Johanneson, Albert	Lawson, Ian	Cooper, Terry	Greenhoff, Jimmy	Henderson, Tommy	Belfitt, Rod	Madeley, Paul	Williamson, Brian	Johnson, Rod	Peacock, Alan	Lorimer, Peter	Wright, Barrie
		3	4	5	6			8				11		7	9		1	10			2
		3		5	6				10	11			7	8	9	4	1				2
0	0	2	1	2	2	0	0	1	1	1	0	1	1	2	2	1	2	1	0	0	2
					1			1	1	1					1						

Sprake, Gary	Reaney, Paul	Bell, Willie	Bremner, Billy	Charlton, Jack	Hunter, Norman	Giles, Johnny	Weston, Don	Storrie, Jim	Collins, Bobby	Johanneson, Albert	Lawson, Ian	Cooper, Terry	Greenhoff, Jimmy	Henderson, Tommy	Belfitt, Rod	Madeley, Paul	Williamson, Brian	Johnson, Rod	Peacock, Alan	Lorimer, Peter	Wright, Barrie
1	2		4	5	6			8	10	11		3	7					9			
1	2	3	4	5	6	7	8	9	10	11											
1	2	3	4	5	6	7	8	9	10			11									
1	2	3	4	5	6	7	8	9	10	11											
1	2	3	4	5	6	7		8	10			11							9		
1	2	3	4	5	6	7		8	10	11									9		
1	2	3	4	5	6	7		8	10			11							9		
1	2	3	4	5	6	7		8	10	11									9		
8	8	7	8	8	8	7	3	8	8	5	0	4	1	0	0	0	0	1	4	0	0
			2	1		1	1	2		2			1					1	2		

League Table

	P	W	D	L	F	A	Pts
Manchester United	42	26	9	7	89	39	61
Leeds United	42	26	9	7	83	52	61
Chelsea	42	24	8	10	89	54	56
Everton	42	17	15	10	69	60	49
Nottingham Forest	42	17	13	12	71	67	47
Tottenham Hotspur	42	19	7	16	87	71	45
Liverpool	42	17	10	15	67	73	44
Sheffield Wednesday	42	16	11	15	57	55	43
West Ham United	42	19	4	19	82	71	42
Blackburn Rovers	42	16	10	16	83	79	42
Stoke City	42	16	10	16	67	66	42
Burnley	42	16	10	16	70	70	42
Arsenal	42	17	7	18	69	75	41
West Bromwich Albion	42	13	13	16	70	65	39
Sunderland	42	14	9	19	64	74	37
Aston Villa	42	16	5	21	57	82	37
Blackpool	42	12	11	19	67	78	35
Leicester City	42	11	13	18	69	85	35
Sheffield United	42	12	11	19	50	64	35
Fulham	42	11	12	19	60	78	34
Wolverhampton W	42	13	4	25	59	89	30
Birmingham City	42	8	11	23	64	96	27

1965-66

Division One

Manager: Don Revie OBE

Final Position: 2nd

Did you know that?

1 September 1965: Substitutes for injured players were introduced by the Football League and Rod Johnson became the first United number-12 when he replaced Jack Charlton in the 2–0 win against Aston Villa.

19 February 1966: Substitute Terry Hibbitt came on for his debut and scored with his first touch in the 4–0 romp at Nottingham Forest.

5 May 1966: The 4,554 attendance at Highbury which witnessed United's 3–0 win is Arsenal's lowest gate in the top flight. The poor turn out was put down to torrential rain in London, coupled with live TV screening of the Liverpool v Borussia Dortmund European Cup-Winners' Cup Final at Hampden Park.

Terry Hibbitt scored for Leeds with his first touch at Nottingham Forest.

Match No.	Date	Venue	Opponents	Result	FT	HT	Scorers	Attendance
1	Aug 21	H	Sunderland	W	1-0	0-0	Hunter	36,348
2	23	A	Aston Villa	W	2-0	1-0	Peacock, Cooper	33,836
3	28	A	West Ham United	L	1-2	1-1	Peacock	27,995
4	Sep 1	H	Aston Villa	W	2-0	2-0	Peacock 2	33,575
5	4	H	Nottingham Forest	W	2-1	2-0	Bell, Lorimer	35,427
6	8	A	Tottenham Hotspur	L	2-3	2-2	Lorimer, Clayton (og)	48,114
7	11	H	Sheffield United	D	2-2	0-2	Bremner, Hunter	33,249
8	15	H	Tottenham Hotspur	W	2-0	1-0	Bremner, Charlton	41,920
9	18	A	Leicester City	D	3-3	1-1	Peacock 2, Madeley	23,276
10	25	H	Blackburn Rovers	W	3-0	3-0	Lorimer 2, Cooper	31,098
11	Oct 9	A	Sheffield Wed	D	0-0	0-0		35,105
12	16	H	Northampton Town	W	6-1	3-1	Lorimer 2, Bremner, Charlton, Peacock, Storrie	33,748
13	23	A	Stoke City	W	2-1	2-0	Peacock, O'Grady	30,093
14	30	H	Burnley	D	1-1	0-0	Storrie	41,628
15	Nov 6	A	Chelsea	L	0-1	0-1		39,373
16	13	H	Arsenal	W	2-0	1-0	Bremner, Giles	36,383
17	20	A	Everton	D	0-0	0-0		36,291
18	Dec 11	H	West Bromwich Alb	W	4-0	2-0	Giles 2, Storrie, O'Grady	33,140
19	27	A	Liverpool	W	1-0	1-0	Lorimer	53,430
20	28	H	Liverpool	L	0-1	0-1		49,192
21	Jan 1	H	Sheffield Wed	W	3-0	1-0	Storrie, Peacock, Gray	34,841
22	8	A	West Bromwich Alb	W	2-1	1-0	Peacock, Giles (pen)	24,900
23	12	H	Manchester United	D	1-1	1-0	Storrie	49,762
24	15	H	Stoke City	D	2-2	2-0	O'Grady, Storrie	34,802
25	29	A	Sunderland	L	0-2	0-1		35,942
26	Feb 5	H	West Ham United	W	5-0	2-0	Hunter 2, Lorimer, Bremner, Storrie	33,312
27	19	A	Nottingham Forest	W	4-0	3-0	Lorimer 2, Hibbitt, Giles (pen)	26,283
28	26	A	Sheffield United	D	1-1	1-1	Bell	35,682
29	Mar 5	A	Northampton Town	L	1-2	1-2	O'Grady	21,548
30	12	H	Leicester City	W	3-2	0-0	Charlton 2, Hunter	35,957
31	19	A	Blackburn Rovers	W	3-2	0-0	Bremner, Lorimer, Storrie	25,398
32	26	H	Blackpool	L	1-2	0-0	Charlton	30,727
33	28	A	Blackpool	L	0-1	0-0		19,017
34	Apr 4	H	Chelsea	W	2-0	1-0	Bremner, Hinton (og)	37,784
35	8	A	Fulham	W	3-1	1-0	Bremner, Johanneson, Storrie	38,960
36	12	H	Fulham	L	0-1	0-0		33,968
37	16	H	Everton	W	4-1	1-0	Charlton, Lorimer, Storrie, Johanneson	25,200
38	30	H	Newcastle United	W	3-0	1-0	Lorimer, Storrie, McGrath (og)	29,531
39	May 5	A	Arsenal	W	3-0	2-0	Storrie 2, Greenhoff	4,554
40	7	A	Burnley	W	1-0	0-0	Elder (og)	32,238
41	16	A	Newcastle United	L	0-2	0-1		21,660
42	19	A	Manchester United	D	1-1	0-0	Reaney	35,008
								Appearances
								Sub appearances
							Four own-goals	Goals

FL Cup

	Date	Venue	Opponents	Result	FT	HT	Scorers	Attendance
R2	Sep 22	H	Hartlepools United	W	4-2	1-0	Cooper, Johnson, Belfitt, Storrie	11,081
R3	Oct 13	H	West Bromwich Alb	L	2-4	1-4	Madeley, Belfitt	13,455
								Appearances
								Goals

FA Cup

	Date	Venue	Opponents	Result	FT	HT	Scorers	Attendance
R3	Jan 22	H	Bury	W	6-0	4-0	Lorimer 3 (1 pen), Reaney, Greenhoff, Giles	30,386
R4	Feb 12	A	Chelsea	L	0-1	0-1		57,947
								Appearances
								Goals

Inter-Cities Fairs Cup

	Date	Venue	Opponents	Result	FT	HT	Scorers	Attendance
R1	Sep 29	H	Torino	W	2-1	1-0	Bremner, Peacock	33,852
	Oct 6	A	Torino	D	0-0	0-0		26,000
R2	Nov 24	A	SC Leipzig	W	2-1	0-0	Lorimer, Bremner	8,000
	Dec 1	H	SC Leipzig	D	0-0	0-0		32,111
R3	Feb 2	H	Valencia	D	1-1	0-1	Lorimer	34,414
	16	A	Valencia	W	1-0	0-0	O'Grady	45,000
R4	Mar 2	H	Ujpesti Dósza	W	4-1	4-0	Cooper, Bell, Storrie, Bremner	40,462
	9	A	Ujpesti Dósza	D	1-1	0-1	Lorimer	30,000
SF	Apr 20	A	Real Zaragoza	L	0-1	0-0		35,000
	27	H	Real Zaragoza	W	2-1	1-0	Johanneson, Charlton	24,008
Rep	May 11	H	Real Zaragoza	L	1-3	0-3	Charlton	43,046
								Appearances
								Goals

Back row, left to right: Billy Bremner, Willie Bell, Paul Madeley, Gary Sprake, Paul Reaney, Norman Hunter, Jimmy Greenhoff. Front row: Don Weston, Terry Cooper, Johnny Giles, Jim Storrie, Alan Peacock, Bobby Collins, Jack Charlton, Alber Johanneson.

Sprake, Gary	Reaney, Paul	Bell, Willie	Bremner, Billy	Charlton, Jack	Hunter, Norman	Giles, Johnny	Weston, Don	Peacock, Alan	Collins, Bobby	Cooper, Terry	Lorimer, Peter	Johanneson, Albert	Johnson, Rod	Madeley, Paul	Storrie, Jim	O'Grady, Mike	Greenhoff, Jimmy	Gray, Eddie	Belfitt, Rod	Hibbitt, Terry	Harvey, David	Bates, Mick	Davey, Nigel	Wright, Barrie	Hawkins, Dennis	Williamson, Brian
1	2	3	4	5	6	7	8	9	10	11																
1	2	3	4	5	6	7	8	9	10	11																
1	2	3	4	5	6	10	7	9		11	8															
1	2	3	4	**5**	6	7		9	10		8	11	S*													
1	2	**3**	4	5	6	7		9	10	S*	8	11														
1	2		4	5	6	7		9	10	3	8	11														
1	2		4	5	6	7		9	10	3	8	**11**	S*													
1	2		4	5	6	7		9	10	3	8	**11**		S*												
1	2		4	5	6	7		9	10	11	8			3												
1	2		4	5	6	7		9	10	11	8			3												
1	2		4	5	6	7		9			8		10	3	11											
1	2	3	4	5	6	10		9			8				7	11										
1	2	3	4	5	6	10		9			8				7	11										
1	2	3	4	5	**6**	10		9			8			S*	7	11										
1	2	3	4	5	6	10		9			8		11		7											
1	2		4	5	6	10		**9**		S*	8			3	7	11										
1	2	9	4	5	6	10					8			3	7	11										
1	2	3	4	5	6	10		9			8				7	11										
1	2	3	4	5	6	**10**		9			8			S*	7	11										
1	2	3	10	5	6			9			8			4	7	11										
1	2	3	4	5	6			9							8	11	7	10								
1	2	3	4	5	6	10		9							8	11	7									
1	2	3	4	5	6	10		9							8	11	7									
1	2	3	4	5	6	10		9				11			8	7										
1	2	3	4		6	10		**9**			8	11	S*	5		7										
1	**2**	3	4	5	6	10					8			S*	7	11			9							
1	2	3	4	5	6	10					8			**9**	7	11				S*						
1	2	3	4	5	6	10				11	9				7	8										
1	2	3	4	5	6	10				11	8				9	7										
1	2		4	5	6	10				3	8				9	11	7									
1	2		4	5	6	10				3	8				9	11	7									
1	2	3		5	6	10				11	8				9	7		4								
1	2	3	4	5	6	10									8	11		7	9							
1	2	3	4	5	6	10					8	11		**9**		7	S*									
1	2	3	4	5	6	10					8	11			9	7										
	2	3	4	5	6	10					8	11			9	**7**	S*				1					
		2	8	5	6	**10**				3	8	11			9		4	S*			1					
1	2	3	4	5	6	10					8				9	11	7									
1	2	3	4	5	6	10					8				9	11	7									
1	2	3	4	5	6	10				S*	8				9	11	**7**									
1	2	3	4	5	6	10				11	8				9	7										
1	2	5	4			8			10			11			7	6	3		9							
40	41	33	41	40	41	40	3	24	10	15	34	12	2	9	30	29	10	3	3	0	2	0	0	0	0	0
										3			3	4			2	1		1						
	1	2	8	6	5	6		10		2	13	1		1	13	4	1	1		1						

Sprake, Gary	Reaney, Paul	Bell, Willie	Bremner, Billy	Charlton, Jack	Hunter, Norman	Giles, Johnny	Weston, Don	Peacock, Alan	Collins, Bobby	Cooper, Terry	Lorimer, Peter	Johanneson, Albert	Johnson, Rod	Madeley, Paul	Storrie, Jim	O'Grady, Mike	Greenhoff, Jimmy	Gray, Eddie	Belfitt, Rod	Hibbitt, Terry	Harvey, David	Bates, Mick	Davey, Nigel	Wright, Barrie	Hawkins, Dennis	Williamson, Brian
1	2			5	6	7				11			4	3	8				9			10				
		3					7			11			10	5	4				8		1		2	6	9	
1	1	1	0	1	1	1	1	0	0	2	0	0	2	2	2	0	0	0	2	0	1	1	1	1	1	0
										1			1	1	1				2							

Sprake, Gary	Reaney, Paul	Bell, Willie	Bremner, Billy	Charlton, Jack	Hunter, Norman	Giles, Johnny	Weston, Don	Peacock, Alan	Collins, Bobby	Cooper, Terry	Lorimer, Peter	Johanneson, Albert	Johnson, Rod	Madeley, Paul	Storrie, Jim	O'Grady, Mike	Greenhoff, Jimmy	Gray, Eddie	Belfitt, Rod	Hibbitt, Terry	Harvey, David	Bates, Mick	Davey, Nigel	Wright, Barrie	Hawkins, Dennis	Williamson, Brian
	2	3	4	5	6	10		9			8	11					7									1
1	2	3	4	5	6	10					8			9	7	11										
1	2	2	2	2	2	2	0	1	0	0	2	1	0	1	1	1	1	0	0	0	0	0	0	0	0	1
	1					1					3						1									

Sprake, Gary	Reaney, Paul	Bell, Willie	Bremner, Billy	Charlton, Jack	Hunter, Norman	Giles, Johnny	Weston, Don	Peacock, Alan	Collins, Bobby	Cooper, Terry	Lorimer, Peter	Johanneson, Albert	Johnson, Rod	Madeley, Paul	Storrie, Jim	O'Grady, Mike	Greenhoff, Jimmy	Gray, Eddie	Belfitt, Rod	Hibbitt, Terry	Harvey, David	Bates, Mick	Davey, Nigel	Wright, Barrie	Hawkins, Dennis	Williamson, Brian
1	2		4	5	6	11		7	8	9	10			3												
1	2		4	5	6	11		7	8	9	10			3												
1	2	3	4	5	6	10					9			8	7	11										
1	2	3	4	5	6	10		9			8				7	11										
1	2	3	4	5	6	10					8				7	11			9							
1	2	3	4	5	6	10					8			9	7	11										
1	2	3	4	5	6	10				11	8				9	7										
1	2	3	4	5	6	10				11	8				9	7										
1	2	3	4	5	6	10						11			9		7	8								
1	2	3	4	5	6	10						11			9		7	8								
1	2	3	4	5	6	10					8				9	11	7									
11	11	9	11	11	11	11	0	3	2	4	9	2	0	4	9	7	3	2	1	0	0	0	0	0	0	0
		1	3	2				1		1	3	1			1	1										

League Table

	P	W	D	L	F	A	Pts
Liverpool	42	26	9	7	79	34	61
Leeds United	42	23	9	10	79	38	55
Burnley	42	24	7	11	79	47	55
Manchester United	42	18	15	9	84	59	51
Chelsea	42	22	7	13	65	53	51
West Bromwich Albion	42	19	12	11	91	69	50
Leicester City	42	21	7	14	80	65	49
Tottenham Hotspur	42	16	12	14	75	66	44
Sheffield United	42	16	11	15	56	59	43
Stoke City	42	15	12	15	65	64	42
Everton	42	15	11	16	56	62	41
West Ham United	42	15	9	18	70	83	39
Blackpool	42	14	9	19	55	65	37
Arsenal	42	12	13	17	62	75	37
Newcastle United	42	14	9	19	50	63	37
Aston Villa	42	15	6	21	69	80	36
Sheffield Wednesday	42	14	8	20	56	66	36
Nottingham Forest	42	14	8	20	56	72	36
Sunderland	42	14	8	20	51	72	36
Fulham	42	14	7	21	67	85	35
Northampton Town	42	10	13	19	55	92	33
Blackburn Rovers	42	8	4	30	57	88	20

1966-67

Division One

Manager: Don Revie OBE

Final Position: 4th

Did you know that?

7 November 1966: United crashed to their worst-ever League Cup defeat, 7–0 at West Ham.

22 February 1967: Bury signed Bobby Collins, a key factor in United's revival, on a free transfer.

15 March 1967: The Elland Road attendance record was set in the fifth round FA Cup replay with Sunderland.

20 March 1967: Two Sunderland players, David Herd and George Mulhall, were sent off as United beat the Rokerites 2–1 in a stormy FA Cup fourth round second replay at Hull.

Bobby Collins left Elland Road on a free transfer to Bury.

Match No.	Date		Venue	Opponents	Result	FT	HT	Scorers	Attendance
1	Aug	20	A	Tottenham Hotspur	L	1-3	1-1	Giles	43,844
2		24	H	West Bromwich Alb	W	2-1	2-1	Bell, Giles	35,102
3		27	H	Manchester United	W	3-1	2-0	Reaney, Lorimer, Madeley	45,092
4		31	A	West Bromwich Alb	L	0-2	0-1		22,303
5	Sep	3	A	Burnley	D	1-1	1-0	Gray	30,757
6		7	H	Sunderland	W	2-1	2-1	Giles (pen), Johanneson	37,646
7		10	H	Nottingham Forest	D	1-1	1-0	Gray	35,634
8		17	A	Fulham	D	2-2	1-1	Lorimer, Johanneson	19,985
9		24	H	Everton	D	1-1	1-0	Giles (pen)	38,486
10	Oct	1	A	Stoke City	D	0-0	0-0		28,987
11		8	A	Aston Villa	L	0-3	0-2		19,188
12		15	H	Arsenal	W	3-1	2-0	Bell, Madeley, Giles	31,481
13		29	H	Southampton	L	0-1	0-0		32,232
14	Nov	5	A	Arsenal	W	1-0	1-0	Charlton	24,227
15		12	H	Leicester City	W	3-1	0-0	Giles 2, Greenhoff	33,803
16		19	A	Liverpool	L	0-5	0-1		50,764
17		26	H	West Ham United	W	2-1	1-1	Giles, Johanneson	37,382
18	Dec	3	A	Sheffield Wed	D	0-0	0-0		35,264
19		10	H	Blackpool	D	1-1	0-0	Greenhoff	28,466
20		17	H	Tottenham Hotspur	W	3-2	3-0	Greenhoff 2, Gray	29,853
21		24	A	Newcastle United	W	2-1	1-1	O'Grady, Johanneson	29,160
22		26	H	Newcastle United	W	5-0	2-0	Lorimer 2, Charlton, Storrie, Cooper	40,680
23		31	A	Manchester United	D	0-0	0-0		53,486
24	Jan	7	H	Burnley	W	3-1	0-0	Greenhoff, Johanneson 2	37,465
25		14	A	Nottingham Forest	L	0-1	0-1		43,899
26		21	H	Fulham	W	3-1	1-0	Giles, Greenhoff, Johanneson	32,015
27	Feb	4	A	Everton	L	0-2	0-0		48,738
28		11	H	Stoke City	W	3-0	2-0	Bell, Lorimer, Belfitt	37,370
29		25	H	Aston Villa	L	0-2	0-1		34,398
30	Mar	4	A	Southampton	W	2-0	2-0	Charlton, Giles	26,150
31		18	H	Manchester City	D	0-0	0-0		34,366
32		25	A	Blackpool	W	2-0	0-0	Bremner, Charlton	22,548
33		27	A	Sheffield United	W	4-1	1-0	Giles (pen), Peacock, Bremner, Matthewson (og)	25,701
34		28	H	Sheffield United	W	2-0	0-0	Charlton, Peacock	38,755
35	Apr	1	H	Chelsea	W	1-0	0-0	Lorimer	39,728
36		10	A	Leicester City	D	0-0	0-0		15,437
37		22	A	West Ham United	W	1-0	1-0	Lorimer	25,500
38	May	3	H	Liverpool	W	2-1	0-1	Giles (pen), Greenhoff	36,547
39		6	A	Chelsea	D	2-2	2-1	Lorimer, Belfitt	35,882
40		8	A	Manchester City	L	1-2	0-1	Belfitt	24,924
41		13	A	Sunderland	W	2-0	0-0	Gray, Lorimer	23,686
42		15	H	Sheffield Wed	W	1-0	1-0	Hibbitt	23,052
									Appearances
									Sub appearances
								One own-goal	Goals

FL Cup

R2	Sep	13	H	Newcastle United	W	1-0	1-0	Peacock	18,131
R3	Oct	4	A	Preston North End	D	1-1	0-0	Storrie	15,049
Rep		12	H	Preston North End	W	3-0	1-0	Lorimer 2 (1 pen), Greenhoff	17,221
R4	Nov	7	A	West Ham United	L	0-7	0-4		27,474
									Appearances
									Sub appearances
									Goals

FA Cup

R3	Jan	28	H	Crystal Palace	W	3-0	2-0	O'Grady, Bell, Johanneson	37,768
R4	Feb	18	H	West Bromwich Alb	W	5-0	4-0	Lorimer 2, Madeley, Belfitt 2	41,329
R5	Mar	11	A	Sunderland	D	1-1	1-1	Charlton	55,763
Rep		15	H	Sunderland	D	1-1*	1-1	Giles	57,892
2n Rep		20	N	Sunderland	W	2-1#	1-0	Belfitt, Giles (pen)	40,546
R6	Apr	8	H	Manchester City	W	1-0	0-0	Charlton	48,877
SF		29	N	Chelsea	L	0-1†	0-1		62,378

* After extra-time (score at 90 minutes 1-1) # At Boothferry Park, Hull
† At Villa Park, Birmingham

Appearances
Sub appearances
Goals

Inter-Cities Fairs Cup

R2	Oct	18	A	DWS Amsterdam	W	3-1	2-0	Bremner, Johanneson, Greenhoff	7,000
		26	H	DWS Amsterdam	W	5-1	3-0	Johanneson 3, Giles (pen), Madeley	27,096
R3	Jan	18	H	Valencia	D	1-1	1-1	Greenhoff	40,644
	Feb	8	A	Valencia	W	2-0	1-0	Giles, Lorimer	45,000
QF	Mar	22	A	Bologna	L	0-1	0-0		18,000
	Apr	19	H	Bologna	W	1-0*	1-0	Giles (pen)	42,126
SF	May	19	H	Kilmarnock	W	4-2	4-2	Belfitt 3, Giles (pen)	43,189
		24	A	Kilmarnock	D	0-0	0-0		28,000
F	Aug	30	A	Dynamo Zagreb	L	0-2	0-1		40,000
	Sep	6	H	Dynamo Zagreb	D	0-0	0-0		35,604

* After extra-time (score at 90 minutes 1-1 on aggregate - Leeds won toss of a disc)

Appearances
Goals

Glasgow Charity Cup

	Aug	10	N	Glasgow Select XI	D	1-1*	0-0	Giles	18,000

* At Hampden Park, Glasgow (Trophy was shared)

Back row, left to right: Norman Hunter, Alan Peacock, Jack Charlton, Paul Madeley, Eddie Gray, Rod Belfitt. Middle row: Don Revie (manager), Willie Bell, Mike O'Grady, David Harvey, Gary Sprake, Albert Johanneson, Rod Johnson, Jimmy Greenhoff. Front row: Paul Reaney, Bobby Collins, Johnny Giles, Billy Bremner, Jim Storrie, Peter Lorimer, Terry Cooper.

Sprake, Gary	Reaney, Paul	Bell, Willie	Bremner, Billy	Madeley, Paul	Hunter, Norman	Lorimer, Peter	Collins, Bobby	Belfitt, Rod	Giles, Johnny	Greenhoff, Jimmy	Cooper, Terry	Johanneson, Albert	Gray, Eddie	Charlton, Jack	Bates, Mick	Storrie, Jim	Peacock, Alan	O'Grady, Mike	Harvey, David	Sibbald, Bobby	Hibbitt, Terry	Johnson, Rod	Lumsden, Jimmy	Hawkins, Dennis
1	2	3	4	5	6	7	8	9	**10**	11	S*													
1	2	3	4	5	6	9	**8**		10	7	S	11												
1	2	5	4	9	6	7			10		3	11	8											
1	2	3	4	9	6	7			10	11			8	5										
1	2	5	4	9	6	7					3	11	10		8									
1	2	5	4	9	6	7			10	S*	3	**11**	8											
1	2		4	9	5	7			10		3	11	**6**		8	S*								
1	2	3	4	8	6	7		9	10			11		5										
1	2	3	4	S*	6	7			10			**11**	8	5			9							
1	2	3	4	6					10			11	8	5		7	9							
1	2	3	4	8	**6**	S*			10			11	9	5		7								
1	2	3	4	9	6				10	8		11		5				7						
	2	3	4	9	6	S*			7	8		**11**	10	5					1					
	2	3	4	7	6			8	10	9				5				11	1					
1	2	3	4		6				10	9	11		8	5				7						
1	2	3	4	8	6				10	9	11			5				7						
1	2	3	4		6	8			**10**	9		11		5		S*		7						
1	2	3	4		**6**	8	10			9		11		5		S*		7						
1	2	3	4		6	7	10			9		11	8	5										
1	2	3	4		6		10			9		11	8	5				7						
1	2	3	4		6		10			9		11	8	5				7						
1	2	3	4		6	8					11		10	5		9		7						
1	2	3	4		6	8				**9**	S*	11	10	5				7						
1	2	3	4		6	8				9		11	10	5				7						
1	2	3	4		6	8				9	S*	**11**	10	5				7						
1	2		4	5	6				8	9	3	11	10					7						
1	2	3	4	7	6	9			8		**11**		10	5						S*				
1		3	4	2	6	8	7	9				**11**	10	5							S*			
1	2	3		4	6	8		9	7	S*			10	5							**11**			
1	2	3	4	8	6	7		S*	10	9			**11**	5										
1	2	3		4	6	8				9				5	10						11	7		
1	2	3	4	8	6				10		11			5	7		9							
1	2	3	4	8	6				10		11			5	7		9							
1	2	3	4	8	6				10	7	11			5			9							
1	2	3	4	8	6	7			10	9	11			5										
1	2	5	4	3	6			8	7	9	11		10											
1	2		4	5	6	7		8		9	3	**11**	10		S*									
1	2	3	4		5	7			6	8	9		10		11									
1	2	3			5	8		9	10	4	11		6		7									
1	2	5			6	11		8	10	9	3		4									7		
1	2	3		5	6	8		S*	10	**9**	11		4					7						
	2		S*					10			3		**6**		7		5		1		11	9	4	8
39	41	38	36	27	40	27	7	10	29	27	20	22	29	28	8	3	6	14	3	0	3	3	1	1
			1	1		2		2		2	4				1	3				1	1			
	1	3	2	2		9		3	12	7	1	7	4	5		1	2	1			1			

	2	3	4	8	6	7			10			11		5			9							
1	2	3	4	6					10	11			8	5		7	9		1					
1	2	3	4	10	6	8				9		11		5				7	1					
	2	3	4	7	6			8	10	**9**				5	S*			11						
2	4	4	4	4	3	2	0	1	3	3	0	2	1	4	0	1	2	2	2	0	0	0	0	0
															1									
						2				1						1	1							

1	2	3	4	S*	6				8	**9**		11	10	5				7						
1	2	3		4	6	8		9	7				10	5	S*			**11**						
1	2	3	4	7	6	11		8	10	9				5										
1	2	3	4		6	7		8	10	9	S*	**11**		5										
1	2	3	4		6	7		8	10	9	11			5										
1	2	3	4	8	6	7			10	S*			11	5			**9**							
1	2	3	4	5	6	S*		**8**	7	9	11		10											
7	7	7	6	4	7	5	0	5	7	5	2	2	4	6	0	0	1	2	0	0	0	0	0	0
				1		1				1	1				1									
		1		1		2		3	2			1		2				1						

1	2	3	4	9	6				10	8		11		5				7						
1	2	3	4	8	6				10	9		11		5		7								
1	2		4	3	6		10		7	9	11		8	5										
1		3	4	2	6			9	7	8			10	5							11			
1	2	3	4	9	6			8	10	7	11			5										
1	2		4	3	6			8	7	9	11		10	5										
1	2	3	4	5	6	8		9	10				11					7						
1	2	3	4	5	6	7		9	10		11		8											
1	2		4		6	8		9			3		10	5	7			11						
1	7	2	4		6			8	10	9	3			5				11						
10	9	7	10	8	10	3	1	7	9	7	6	2	6	8	1	1	0	4	0	0	1	0	0	0
			1	1		1		3	4	2		4												

1	2	3	4	S*	6	9	8		10				11	**5**		7								

League Table

	P	W	D	L	F	A	Pts
Manchester United	42	24	12	6	84	45	60
Nottingham Forest	42	23	10	9	64	41	56
Tottenham Hotspur	42	24	8	10	71	48	56
Leeds United	42	22	11	9	62	42	55
Liverpool	42	19	13	10	64	47	51
Everton	42	19	10	13	65	46	48
Arsenal	42	16	14	12	58	47	46
Leicester City	42	18	8	16	78	71	44
Chelsea	42	15	14	13	67	62	44
Sheffield United	42	16	10	16	52	59	42
Sheffield Wednesday	42	14	13	15	56	47	41
Stoke City	42	17	7	18	63	58	41
West Bromwich Albion	42	16	7	19	77	73	39
Burnley	42	15	9	18	66	76	39
Manchester City	42	12	15	15	43	52	39
West Ham United	42	14	8	20	80	84	36
Sunderland	42	14	8	20	58	72	36
Fulham	42	11	12	19	71	83	34
Southampton	42	14	6	22	74	92	34
Newcastle United	42	12	9	21	39	81	33
Aston Villa	42	11	7	24	54	85	29
Blackpool	42	6	9	27	41	76	21

1967-68

Division One

Manager: Don Revie OBE

Final Position: 4th

Did you know that?

22 September 1967: Mick Jones became Leeds' first £100,000 player after signing from Sheffield United.

3 October 1967: United set a new club record by beating Spora Luxembourg 9–0 in the Fairs Cup.

7 October 1967: The day after Tommy Docherty was sacked as Chelsea manager, Leeds thrashed his old side at Elland Road with all seven goals scored by different players, setting a League record.

2 March 1968: Brian Greenhoff was a ballboy at Wembley when United, including his older brother Jimmy, won the Football League Cup by beating Arsenal.

4 May 1968: Although they lost 2–1 at home to Liverpool, Mick Jones' goal meant that United had scored at Elland Road in every League game – a feat only achieved once before in 1955–56.

Mick Jones became Leeds' first £100,000 signing.

Match No.	Date	Venue	Opponents	Result	FT	HT	Scorers	Attendance
1	Aug 19	H	Sunderland	D	1-1	1-1	Greenhoff	36,252
2	23	A	Manchester United	L	0-1	0-0		53,016
3	26	A	Wolverhampton W	L	0-2	0-0		35,368
4	Sep 2	H	Fulham	W	2-0	2-0	Belfitt 2	25,760
5	9	A	Southampton	D	1-1	0-0	Lorimer	25,522
6	16	A	Everton	W	1-0	1-0	Gray	53,159
7	20	H	Burnley	W	2-1	1-1	Lorimer 2	32,944
8	23	H	Leicester City	W	3-2	2-2	Lorimer 2 (1 pen), Greenhoff	37,084
9	30	A	West Ham United	D	0-0	0-0		28,940
10	Oct 7	H	Chelsea	W	7-0	4-0	Johanneson, Greenhoff, Charlton, Lorimer, Gray, Hinton (og), Bremner	40,460
11	14	A	West Bromwich Alb	L	0-2	0-0		21,300
12	25	H	Newcastle United	W	2-0	1-0	Lorimer, Johanneson	30,347
13	28	A	Manchester City	L	0-1	0-0		39,713
14	Nov 4	H	Arsenal	W	3-1	1-0	Lorimer (pen), Jones, Gray	31,632
15	8	H	Manchester United	W	1-0	1-0	Greenhoff	43,999
16	11	A	Sheffield United	L	0-1	0-0		24,715
17	18	H	Coventry City	D	1-1	1-0	Lorimer	32,469
18	25	A	Nottingham Forest	W	2-0	0-0	Greenhoff, Lorimer	29,750
19	Dec 2	H	Stoke City	W	2-0	1-0	Lorimer, Madeley	29,988
20	9	A	Liverpool	L	0-2	0-2		39,675
21	16	A	Sunderland	D	2-2	1-1	Greenhoff, Gray	21,189
22	23	H	Wolverhampton W	W	2-1	0-1	Jones, Charlton	28,376
23	26	A	Sheffield Wed	W	1-0	1-0	Giles (pen)	51,055
24	30	H	Sheffield Wed	W	3-2	2-0	Greenhoff, Gray, Hunter	36,409
25	Jan 6	A	Fulham	W	5-0	3-0	Greenhoff 3, Jones 2	24,419
26	13	H	Southampton	W	5-0	2-0	Madeley 2, Lorimer, Jones, Hibbitt	31,474
27	20	H	Everton	W	2-0	0-0	Jones, Giles (pen)	44,119
28	Feb 3	A	Leicester City	D	2-2	0-1	Madeley, Giles	30,081
29	10	H	West Ham United	W	2-1	1-1	Lorimer 2	41,814
30	Mar 13	H	Nottingham Forest	D	1-1	0-1	Bremner	32,508
31	16	A	Newcastle United	D	1-1	0-0	Hunter	45,190
32	20	A	Chelsea	D	0-0	0-0		47,470
33	23	H	Manchester City	W	2-0	0-0	Charlton, Giles	51,818
34	Apr 6	H	Sheffield United	W	3-0	0-0	Madeley, Giles 2 (2 pens)	31,039
35	12	A	Tottenham Hotspur	L	1-2	1-1	Madeley	56,597
36	13	A	Coventry City	W	1-0	0-0	Hibbitt	38,778
37	17	H	Tottenham Hotspur	W	1-0	0-0	Lorimer (pen)	50,000
38	20	H	West Bromwich Alb	W	3-1	1-0	Gray (pen), Madeley, Charlton	38,334
39	23	A	Stoke City	L	2-3	0-2	Charlton, Greenhoff	23,999
40	May 4	H	Liverpool	L	1-2	1-0	Jones	44,553
41	7	A	Arsenal	L	3-4	2-2	Lorimer, Jones, Giles	25,043
42	11	A	Burnley	L	0-3	0-1		13,247
								Appearances
								Sub appearances
							One own-goal	Goals

FL Cup

Round	Date	Venue	Opponents	Result	FT	HT	Scorers	Attendance
R2	Sep 13	H	Luton Town	W	3-1	0-0	Lorimer 3 (1 pen)	11,473
R3	Oct 11	H	Bury	W	3-0	2-0	Charlton, Johanneson, Greenhoff	20,927
R4	Nov 15	A	Sunderland	W	2-0	1-0	Greenhoff 2	29,536
R5	Dec 13	H	Stoke City	W	2-0	2-0	Bremner, Lorimer	31,904
SF	Jan 17	A	Derby County	W	1-0	0-0	Giles (pen)	31,904
	Feb 7	H	Derby County	W	3-2	2-1	Belfitt 2, Gray	29,367
F	Mar 2	N	Arsenal	W	1-0*	1-0	Cooper	97,887

*At Wembley, London

Appearances
Sub appearances
Goals

FA Cup

Round	Date	Venue	Opponents	Result	FT	HT	Scorers	Attendance
R3	Jan 27	A	Derby County	W	2-0	0-0	Charlton, Lorimer	39,753
R4	Feb 17	H	Nottingham Forest	W	2-1	2-1	Jones, Giles	51,739
R5	Mar 9	H	Bristol City	W	2-0	2-0	Jones, Lorimer	45,227
R6	30	H	Sheffield United	W	1-0	1-0	Madeley	48,322
SF	Apr 27	N	Everton	L	0-1*	0-1		63,000

* At Old Trafford, Manchester

Appearances
Sub appearances
Goals

Inter-Cities Fairs Cup

Round	Date	Venue	Opponents	Result	FT	HT	Scorers	Attendance
R1	Oct 3	A	Spora Luxembourg	W	9-0	4-0	Lorimer 4 (1 pen), Bremner, Greenhoff 2, Madeley, Jones	2,500
	17	H	Spora Luxembourg	W	7-0	2-0	Johanneson 3, Greenhoff 2, Cooper, Lorimer	15,196
R2	Nov 29	A	Partizan Belgrade	W	2-1	1-0	Lorimer, Belfitt	8,000
	Dec 6	H	Partizan Belgrade	D	1-1	1-0	Lorimer	34,258
R3	20	H	Hibernian	W	1-0	1-0	Gray	31,522
	Jan 10	A	Hibernian	D	1-1	0-1	Charlton	40,503
QF	Mar 26	A	Rangers	D	0-0	0-0		60,000
	Apr 9	H	Rangers	W	2-0	2-0	Giles (pen), Lorimer	50,498
SF	May 1	A	Dundee	D	1-1	1-1	Madeley	30,000
	15	H	Dundee	W	1-0	0-0	Gray	23,830
F	Aug 7	H	Ferencvaros	W	1-0	1-0	Jones	25,268
	Sep 11	A	Ferencvaros	D	0-0	0-0		75,000

Appearances
Sub appearances
Goals

Back row, left to right: Don Revie (manager), Alan Peacock, Willie Bell, Jack Charlton, Gary Sprake, Paul Madeley, Norman Hunter, Rod Belfitt, Les Cocker (trainer). Front row: Terry Cooper, Paul Reaney, Albert Johanneson, Billy Bremner, Jimmy Greenhoff, Johnny Giles, Peter Lorimer, Eddie Gray.

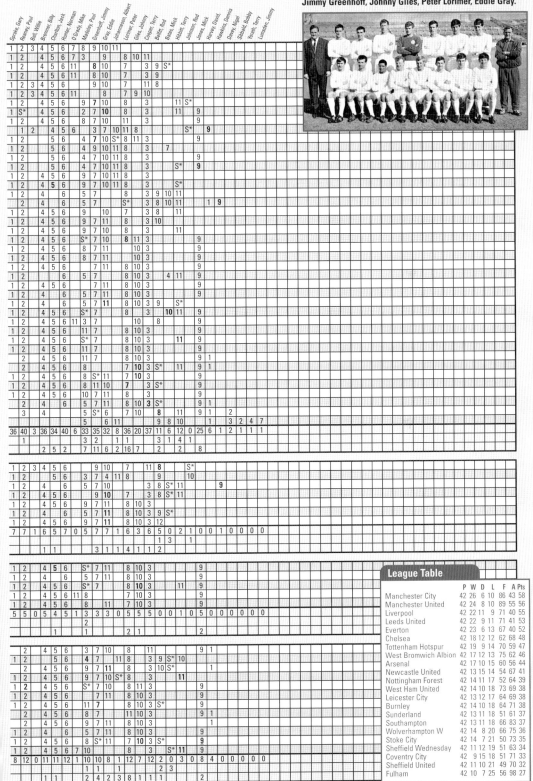

Sprake, Gary	Reaney, Paul	Bell, Willie	Bremner, Billy	Charlton, Jack	Hunter, Norman	O'Grady, Mike	Madeley, Paul	Greenhoff, Jimmy	Gray, Eddie	Johanneson, Albert	Lorimer, Peter	Giles, Johnny	Cooper, Terry	Belfitt, Rod	Bates, Mick	Hibbitt, Terry	Johnson, Rod	Jones, Mick	Harvey, David,	Hawkins, Dennis	Davey, Nigel	Sibbald, Bobby	Yorath, Terry	Lumsden, Jimmy
1	2	3	4	5	6	7	8	9	10	11														
1	2		4	5	6	7	3		9		8	10	11											
1	2		4	5	6	11		**8**	10		7		3	9	S*									
1	2		4	5	6	11		8	10		7		3	9										
1	2	3	4	5	6			9	10		7		11	8										
1	2	3	4	5	6	11			8		7	9	10											
1	2		4	5	6		9	**7**	10		8		3			11	S*							
1	S*		4	5	6		2	7	**10**		8		3			11		9						
1	2		4	5	6		8	7	10		11		3					9						
	1	2		4	5	6		3	7	10	11	8					S*		**9**					
1	2			5	6		4	**7**	10	S*	8	11	3					9						
1	2			5	6		4	9	10	11	8		3		7									
1	2			5	6		4	7	10	11	8		3					9						
1	2			5	6		4	7	10	11	8		3			S*		**9**						
1	2		4	5	6		9	7	10	11	8		3											
1	2		4	**5**	6		9	7	10	11	8		3			S*								
1	2		4		6		5	7			8		3	9	10	11								
	2		4		6		5	7			S*		3	8	10	11			1	**9**				
1	2		4	5	6		9		10		7		3	8		11								
1	2		4	5	6		9	7	11		8		3	10										
1	2		4	5	6		9	7	10		8		3			11								
1	2		4	5	6		S*	7	10		**8**	11	3					9						
1	2		4	5	6		8	7	11			10	3					9						
1	2		4	5	6		8	7	11			10	3					9						
1	2		4	5	6			7	11		8	10	3					9						
1	2				6		5	7			8	10	3		4	11		9						
1	2		4	5	6			7	11		8	10	3					9						
1	2		4		6		5	7	11		8	10	3					9						
1	2		4		6		5	7	**11**		8	10	3	9		S*								
1	2		4	5	6		S*	7			8		3		**10**	11		9						
1	2		4	5	6	11	3	7				10		8				9						
1	2		4	5	6		11	7			8	10	3					9						
1	2		4	5	6		S*	7			8	10	3			**11**		9						
1	2		4	5	6		11	7			8	10	3					9						
	2		4	5	6		11	7			8	10	3					9	1					
	2		4	5	6		8				7	**10**	3	S*		11		9	1					
1	2		4	5	6		8	S*	11		7	**10**	3					9						
1	2		4	5	6		8	11	10		**7**		3	S*				9						
1	2		4	5	6		10	7	11		8		3					9						
	2		4		6		5	7	11		8	10	**3**	S*				9	1					
	3		4				5	S*	6		7	10		**8**		11		9	1		2			
							5		6	11				9	8	10			1		3	2	4	7
36	40	3	36	34	40	6	33	35	32	8	36	20	37	11	6	12	0	25	6	1	2	1	1	1
	1						3	2		1	1			3	1	4	1							
			2	5	2		7	11	6	2	16	7		2		2		8						

1	2	3	4	5	6			9	10		7		11	**8**			S*							
1	2			5	6		3	7	4	11	8			9			10							
1	2		4		6		5	7	10				3	8	S*	11				**9**				
1	2		4	5	6			9	**10**		7		3	8	S*	11								
1	2		4	5	6		9	7	11		8	10	3											
1	2		4		6		5	7	**11**		8	10	3	9	S*									
1	2		4	5	6		9	7	**11**		8	10	3	12										
7	7	1	6	5	7	0	5	7	7	1	6	3	6	5	0	2	1	0	0	1	0	0	0	0
														1	3		1							
			1	1				3	1	1	4	1	1	2										

1	2		4	**5**	6		S*	7	11		8	10	3					9						
1	2		4		6		5	7	11		8	10	3					9						
1	2		4	5	6		S*	7			8	**10**	3			11		9						
1	2		4	5	6	11	8				7	10	3					9						
1	2		4	5	6		8		11		7	10	3					9						
5	5	0	5	4	5	1	3	3	3	0	5	5	5	0	0	1	0	5	0	0	0	0	0	0
							2																	
				1			1				2	1						2						

	2		4	5	6		3	7	10		8		11					9	1					
1	2			5	6		**4**	7		11	8		3	9	S*	10								
	2		4	5	6		9	7	**11**		8		3	10	S*				1					
1	2		4	5	6		9	7	10	S*	8		3			**11**								
1	**2**		4	5	6		S*	7	10		8	11	3					9						
1	2		4	5	6			7	11		8	10	3					9						
1	2		4	5	6		11	**7**			8	10	3	S*				9						
	2		4	5	6		8	7			11	10	3					9	1					
	2		4	5	6		9	7	11		8	10	3						1					
1	2		4		6		5	7	11		8	10	3					9						
1	2		4	5	6		8	S*	11		7	**10**	3	S*				**9**						
1	2		4	5	6	7	10				8		3		S*	**11**		9						
8	12	0	11	11	12	1	10	10	8	1	12	7	12	2	0	3	0	8	4	0	0	0	0	0
							1	1		1				2	3									
			1	1			2	4	2	3	8	1	1	1				2						

League Table

	P	W	D	L	F	A	Pts
Manchester City	42	26	6	10	86	43	58
Manchester United	42	24	8	10	89	55	56
Liverpool	42	22	11	9	71	40	55
Leeds United	42	22	9	11	71	41	53
Everton	42	23	6	13	67	40	52
Chelsea	42	18	12	12	62	68	48
Tottenham Hotspur	42	19	9	14	70	59	47
West Bromwich Albion	42	17	12	13	75	62	46
Arsenal	42	17	10	15	60	56	44
Newcastle United	42	13	15	14	54	67	41
Nottingham Forest	42	14	11	17	52	64	39
West Ham United	42	14	10	18	73	69	38
Leicester City	42	13	12	17	64	69	38
Burnley	42	14	10	18	64	71	38
Sunderland	42	13	11	18	51	61	37
Southampton	42	13	11	18	66	83	37
Wolverhampton W	42	14	8	20	66	75	36
Stoke City	42	14	7	21	50	73	35
Sheffield Wednesday	42	11	12	19	51	63	34
Coventry City	42	9	15	18	51	71	33
Sheffield United	42	11	10	21	49	70	32
Fulham	42	10	7	25	56	98	27

1968-69

Division One

Manager: Don Revie OBE

Final Position: 1st

Did you know that?

24 August 1968: Fire at the City Ground forced the abandonment of United's game with Nottingham Forest at half-time with the score at 1–1.

11 September 1968: United became the first British winners of the Inter-Cities Fairs Cup with a 0–0 draw in Hungary after beating Ferencvaros 1–0 in the first leg.

23 October 1968: Both United and Fairs Cup opponents Standard Liege took to the Elland Road pitch in all white strips. The colour clash meant the game started 18 minutes late and United, clad in all blue, came from 2–0 down to win 3–2 thanks to a late Billy Bremner goal.

1 May 1969: Johnny Giles' winner against Nottingham Forest ensured United finished with 67 points – a League record under the old two points for a win system.

Johnny Giles' record-breaking goal against Nottingham Forest.

Match No.	Date		Venue	Opponents	Result	FT	HT	Scorers	Attendance
1	Aug	10	A	Southampton	W	3-1	2-1	Lorimer, Jones, Hibbitt	25,479
2		14	H	Queen's Park R	W	4-1	1-1	Jones, Giles, Reaney, Hibbitt	31,612
3		17	H	Stoke City	W	2-0	1-0	Jones, Johanneson	30,383
4		20	A	Ipswich Town	W	3-2	2-1	O'Grady, Belfitt, Hibbitt	30,382
5		28	H	Sunderland	D	1-1	1-1	Belfitt	37,797
6		31	H	Liverpool	W	1-0	1-0	Jones	38,929
7	Sep	7	H	Wolverhampton W	W	2-1	0-1	Cooper, Charlton	31,227
8		14	A	Leicester City	D	1-1	0-1	Madeley	28,564
9		21	H	Arsenal	W	2-0	2-0	Charlton, O'Grady	39,946
10		28	A	Manchester City	L	1-3	0-2	O'Grady	45,006
11	Oct	5	A	Newcastle United	W	1-0	1-0	Charlton	41,915
12		9	A	Sunderland	W	1-0	1-0	Jones	33,853
13		12	H	West Ham United	W	2-0	1-0	Giles (pen), Lorimer	40,786
14		19	A	Burnley	L	1-5	1-2	Bremner	26,423
15		26	H	West Bromwich Alb	D	0-0	0-0		33,926
16	Nov	2	A	Manchester United	D	0-0	0-0		53,839
17		9	H	Tottenham Hotspur	D	0-0	0-0		38,995
18		16	A	Coventry City	W	1-0	1-0	Madeley	33,224
19		23	H	Everton	W	2-1	1-1	Giles (pen), Gray	41,716
20		30	A	Chelsea	D	1-1	0-0	O'Grady	43,286
21	Dec	7	H	Sheffield Wed	W	2-0	1-0	Lorimer 2	32,718
22		14	A	West Ham United	D	1-1	1-0	Gray	27,418
23		21	H	Burnley	W	6-1	4-0	Lorimer 2, Bremner, Jones, Giles, Gray	31,409
24		26	H	Newcastle United	W	2-1	2-0	Lorimer (pen), Madeley	42,000
25	Jan	11	H	Manchester United	W	2-1	1-0	Jones, O'Grady	48,145
26		18	A	Tottenham Hotspur	D	0-0	0-0		42,396
27		24	A	Queen's Park R	W	1-0	1-0	Jones	26,163
28	Feb	1	H	Coventry City	W	3-0	1-0	O'Grady, Bremner 2	32,314
29		12	H	Ipswich Town	W	2-0	1-0	Belfitt, Jones	24,229
30		15	H	Chelsea	W	1-0	0-0	Lorimer	35,789
31		25	A	Nottingham Forest	W	2-0	1-0	Lorimer, Jones	36,249
32	Mar	1	H	Southampton	W	3-2	1-2	Giles (pen), Jones, Kirkup (og)	33,205
33		8	A	Stoke City	W	5-1	3-0	Jones, Bremner 2, O'Grady 2	24,327
34		29	A	Wolverhampton W	D	0-0	0-0		27,986
35	Apr	1	A	Sheffield Wed	D	0-0	0-0		34,278
36		5	H	Manchester City	W	1-0	0-0	Giles	43,176
37		9	A	West Bromwich Alb	D	1-1	0-1	Gray	28,959
38		12	A	Arsenal	W	2-1	2-1	Jones, Giles	43,715
39		19	H	Leicester City	W	2-0	1-0	Jones, Gray	38,391
40		22	A	Everton	D	0-0	0-0		59,000
41		28	A	Liverpool	D	0-0	0-0		53,750
42		30	H	Nottingham Forest	W	1-0	0-0	Giles	46,508

Appearances
Sub appearances
One own-goal — Goals

FL Cup

R2	Sep	4	H	Charlton Athletic	W	1-0	0-0	Jones	18,860
R3		25	H	Bristol City	W	2-1	1-0	Johanneson, Jones	16,359
R4	Oct	16	A	Crystal Palace	L	1-2	0-1	Madeley	26,217

Appearances
Sub appearances
Goals

FA Cup

R3	Jan	4	A	Sheffield Wed	D	1-1	1-1	Lorimer (pen)	52,111
Rep		8	H	Sheffield Wed	L	1-3	1-1	Johanneson	48,234

Appearances
Sub appearances
Goals

Inter-Cities Fairs Cup

R1	Sep	18	A	Standard Liege	D	0-0	0-0		35,000
	Oct	23	H	Standard Liege	W	3-2	0-1	Charlton, Lorimer, Bremner	24,178
R2	Nov	13	H	Napoli	W	2-0	2-0	Charlton 2	26,967
		27	A	Napoli	D	0-0	0-0		15,000
R3	Dec	13	H	Hannover 96	W	5-1	2-0	O'Grady, Hunter, Lorimer 2, Charlton	25,162
	Feb	4	A	Hannover 96	W	2-1	2-0	Belfitt, Jones	15,000
QF	Mar	5	H	Ulpest Dósza	L	0-1	0-0		30,906
		19	A	Ujpest Dósza	L	0-2	0-0		40,000

Appearances
Sub appearances
Goals

League match abandoned after 45 minutes due to stand fire

	Aug	24	A	Nottingham Forest	D	1-1	1-1	Belfitt	31,126

Back row, left to right: Paul Madeley, Mike O'Grady, David Harvey, Gary Sprake, Jack Charlton, Norman Hunter. Middle row: Albert Johanneson, Rod Belfitt, Mick Jones, Terry Hibbitt, Eddie Gray, Peter Lorimer, Don Revie (manager). Front row: Paul Reaney, Terry Cooper, Johnny Giles, Billy Bremner, Jimmy Greenhoff, Mick Bates, Les Cocker (trainer).

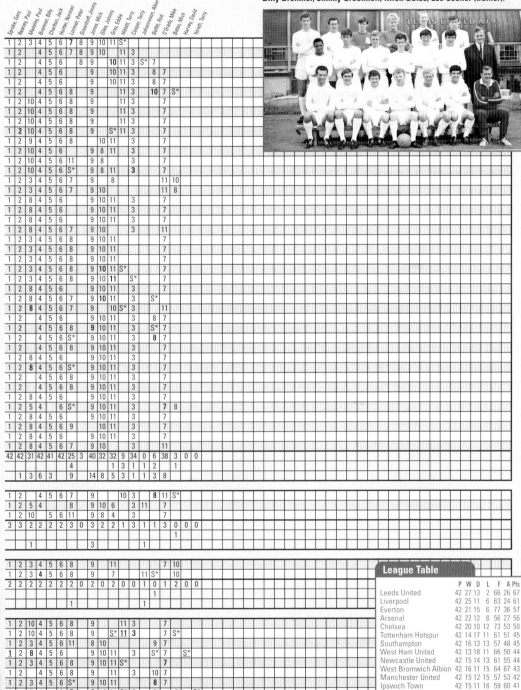

Sprake, Gary	Reaney, Paul	Madeley, Paul	Bremner, Billy	Charlton, Jack	Hunter, Norman	Lorimer, Peter	Greenhoff, Jimmy	Jones, Mick	Giles, Johnny	Gray, Eddie	Hibbitt, Terry	Cooper, Terry	Johanneson, Albert	Belfitt, Rod	O'Grady, Mike	Bates, Mick	Harvey, David	Yorath, Terry
1	2	3	4	5	6	**7**	8	9	10	11	S*							
1	2		4	5	6	7	8	9	10		11	3						
1	2		4	5	6		8	9		**10**	11	3	S*	7				
1	2		4	5	6			9		10	11	3		8	7			
1	2		4	5	6			9		10	11	3		8	7			
1	2		4	5	6	8		9			11	3		**10**	7	S*		
1	2	10	4	5	6	8		9			11	3			7			
1	2	10	4	5	6	8		9			11	3			7			
1	2	10	4	5	6	8		9			11	3			7			
1	**2**	10	4	5	6	8		9		S*	11	3			7			
1	2	9	4	5	6	8			10	11		3			7			
1	2	10	4	5	6			9	8	11		3			7			
1	2	10	4	5	6	11		9	8			3			7			
1	2	10	4	5	6	S*		9	8	11		**3**			7			
1	2	3	4	5	6	7		9		8					11	10		
1	2	3	4	5	6	7		9	10						11	8		
1	2	8	4	5	6			9	10	11		3			7			
1	2	8	4	5	6			9	10	11		3			7			
1	2	8	4	5	6			9	10	11		3			7			
1	2	8	4	5	6	7		9	10			3			11			
1	2	3	4	5	6	8		9	10	11					7			
1	2	3	4	5	6	8		9	10	11					7			
1	2	3	4	5	6	8		9	10	11					7			
1	2	3	4	5	6	8		9	**10**	11	S*				7			
1	2	3	4	5	6	8		9	10	**11**		S*			7			
1	2	8	4	5	6			9	10	11		3			7			
1	2	8	4	5	6	7		9	**10**	11		3		S*				
1	2	**8**	4	5	6	7		9		10	S*	3			11			
1	2		4	5	6			9	10	11		3		8	7			
1	2		4	5	6	8		**9**	10	11		3		S*	7			
1	2		4	5	6	S*		9	10	11		3		**8**	7			
1	2		4	5	6	8		9	10	11		3			7			
1	2	8	4	5	6			9	10	11		3			7			
1	2	**8**	4	5	6	S*		9	10	11		3			7			
1	2		4	5	6	8		9	10	11		3			7			
1	2		4	5	6	8		9	10	11		3			7			
1	2	8	4	5	6			9	10	11		3			7			
1	2	5	4		6	S*		9	10	11		3			**7**	8		
1	2	8	4	5	6			9	10	11		3			7			
1	2	8	4	5	6	9			10	11		3			7			
1	2	8	4	5	6			9	10	11		3			7			
1	2	8	4	5	6	7		9	10			3			11			
42	42	31	42	41	42	25	3	40	32	32	9	34	0	6	38	3	0	0
						4				1	3	1	1	2		1		
	1	3	6	3		9		14	8	5	3	1	1	3	8			

Sprake, Gary	Reaney, Paul	Madeley, Paul	Bremner, Billy	Charlton, Jack	Hunter, Norman	Lorimer, Peter	Greenhoff, Jimmy	Jones, Mick	Giles, Johnny	Gray, Eddie	Hibbitt, Terry	Cooper, Terry	Johanneson, Albert	Belfitt, Rod	O'Grady, Mike	Bates, Mick	Harvey, David	Yorath, Terry
1	2		4	5	6	7		9			10	3		**8**	11	S*		
1	2	5	4			8		9	10	6		3	11		7			
1	2	10		5	6	11		9	8	4		3			7			
3	3	2	2	2	2	3	0	3	2	2	1	3	1	1	3	0	0	0
																1		
		1						3					1					

Sprake, Gary	Reaney, Paul	Madeley, Paul	Bremner, Billy	Charlton, Jack	Hunter, Norman	Lorimer, Peter	Greenhoff, Jimmy	Jones, Mick	Giles, Johnny	Gray, Eddie	Hibbitt, Terry	Cooper, Terry	Johanneson, Albert	Belfitt, Rod	O'Grady, Mike	Bates, Mick	Harvey, David	Yorath, Terry
1	2	3	4	5	6	8		9		11					7	10		
1	2	3	**4**	5	6	8		9		7			11	S*		10		
2	2	2	2	2	2	2	0	2	0	2	0	0	1	0	1	2	0	0
														1				
						1							1					

Sprake, Gary	Reaney, Paul	Madeley, Paul	Bremner, Billy	Charlton, Jack	Hunter, Norman	Lorimer, Peter	Greenhoff, Jimmy	Jones, Mick	Giles, Johnny	Gray, Eddie	Hibbitt, Terry	Cooper, Terry	Johanneson, Albert	Belfitt, Rod	O'Grady, Mike	Bates, Mick	Harvey, David	Yorath, Terry
1	2	10	4	5	6	8		9			11	3			7			
1	2	10	4	5	6	8		9		S*	**11**	**3**			7	S*		
1	2	3	4	5	6	11		8	10					9	7			
1	2	**8**	4	5	6			9	10	11		3		S*	7		S*	
1	2	3	4	5	6	8		9	10	11	S*				**7**			
1	2		4	5	6	8		9		11		3		10	7			
1	2	3	4	5	6	S*		9	10	11				**8**	7			
1		5	4		6	**7**		**9**	10	11	S*	3		8		2		S*
8	7	7	8	7	8	6	0	8	5	5	2	5	0	4	7	1	0	0
						1				1	2			1		1	1	1
			1	4	1	3		1						1	1			

Sprake, Gary	Reaney, Paul	Madeley, Paul	Bremner, Billy	Charlton, Jack	Hunter, Norman	Lorimer, Peter	Greenhoff, Jimmy	Jones, Mick	Giles, Johnny	Gray, Eddie	Hibbitt, Terry	Cooper, Terry	Johanneson, Albert	Belfitt, Rod	O'Grady, Mike	Bates, Mick	Harvey, David	Yorath, Terry
1	2		4	5	6			9		10	11	3		8	7			

League Table

	P	W	D	L	F	A	Pts
Leeds United	42	27	13	2	66	26	67
Liverpool	42	25	11	6	63	24	61
Everton	42	21	15	6	77	36	57
Arsenal	42	22	12	8	56	27	56
Chelsea	42	20	10	12	73	53	50
Tottenham Hotspur	42	14	17	11	61	51	45
Southampton	42	16	13	13	57	48	45
West Ham United	42	13	18	11	66	50	44
Newcastle United	42	15	14	13	61	55	44
West Bromwich Albion	42	16	11	15	64	67	43
Manchester United	42	15	12	15	57	53	42
Ipswich Town	42	15	11	16	59	60	41
Manchester City	42	15	10	17	64	55	40
Burnley	42	15	9	18	55	82	39
Sheffield Wednesday	42	10	16	16	41	54	36
Wolverhampton W	42	10	15	17	41	58	35
Sunderland	42	11	12	19	43	67	34
Nottingham Forest	42	10	13	19	45	57	33
Stoke City	42	9	15	18	40	63	33
Coventry City	42	10	11	21	46	64	31
Leicester City	42	9	12	21	39	68	30
Queen's Park Rangers	42	4	10	28	39	95	18

1969-70

Division One

Manager: Don Revie OBE

Final Position: 2nd

Did you know that?

9 August 1969: Allan Clarke, United's £165,000 record signing from Leicester, netted on his League debut, a 3–1 victory against Tottenham.

26 August 1969: The 1–1 draw with Burnley stretched United's unbeaten League run to a record 34 games. It was also Jack Charlton's 500th League appearance.

28 February 1970: The 2–0 win against Crystal Palace took United to a record-breaking 39 home League games without defeat – a sequence ended four weeks later by Southampton.

30 March 1970: United's scorer in the infamous Easter Monday defeat at Derby when Don Revie fielded a reserve side was centre-half David Kennedy. He played twice more – once in Europe – before ending his career with Lincoln. United were fined £5,000 for not fielding their strongest side at the Baseball Ground.

4 April 1970: Centre-half John Faulkner, signed from non-League Sutton United after Leeds knocked them out of the FA Cup, scored an own-goal on his debut against Burnley. The game, a week before the FA Cup final, is best remembered for two outstanding Eddie Gray goals.

New record signing Allan Clarke.

Match No.	Date	Venue	Opponents	Result	FT	HT	Scorers	Attendance
1	Aug 9	H	Tottenham Hotspur	W	3-1	1-0	Bremner, Clarke, Giles (pen)	35,804
2	13	H	Arsenal	D	0-0	0-0		37,164
3	16	A	Nottingham Forest	W	4-1	0-0	Clarke, Giles (pen), Gray, Lorimer	34,290
4	19	A	Arsenal	D	1-1	0-1	Lorimer	45,160
5	23	H	Newcastle United	D	1-1	1-0	Jones	40,403
6	26	A	Burnley	D	1-1	1-1	Jones	28,000
7	30	A	Everton	L	2-3	0-2	Bremner, Clarke	51,797
8	Sep 6	H	Manchester United	D	2-2	1-0	Sadler (og), Bremner	44,271
9	13	A	Sheffield Wed	W	2-1	2-1	Clarke, Gray	31,998
10	20	H	Chelsea	W	2-0	1-0	Giles (pen), Lorimer	33,130
11	27	A	Coventry City	W	2-1	2-1	Clarke, Gray	36,091
12	Oct 4	H	Stoke City	W	2-1	1-0	Giles 2 (2 pens)	35,860
13	11	A	West Bromwich Alb	D	1-1	0-1	Jones	33,688
14	18	A	Crystal Palace	D	1-1	1-1	Lorimer	31,910
15	25	H	Derby County	W	2-0	2-0	Clarke 2	44,183
16	29	H	Nottingham Forest	W	6-1	2-1	Lorimer 3, Charlton, Bates, Hibbitt	29,636
17	Nov 1	A	Sunderland	D	0-0	0-0		31,842
18	8	H	Ipswich Town	W	4-0	2-0	Giles, Jones, Hunter, Gray	26,497
19	15	A	Southampton	D	1-1	1-0	Jones	23,963
20	19	H	Sunderland	W	2-0	1-0	Jones, Lorimer	25,890
21	22	H	Liverpool	D	1-1	1-1	Giles (pen)	43,293
22	29	A	Manchester City	W	2-1	1-0	Gray, Jones	44,590
23	Dec 6	H	Wolverhampton W	W	3-1	2-0	Holsgrove (og), Charlton, Clarke	33,090
24	13	H	Sheffield Wed	W	2-0	0-0	Clarke 2	31,114
25	17	H	West Ham United	W	4-1	2-0	Lorimer 2, Clarke, Giles	30,699
26	26	A	Newcastle United	L	1-2	0-2	Giles	54,527
27	27	H	Everton	W	2-1	2-0	Jones 2	46,770
28	Jan 10	A	Chelsea	W	5-2	1-2	Clarke, Cooper, Giles (pen), Lorimer, Jones	57,221
29	17	H	Coventry City	W	3-1	2-0	Clarke 2, Charlton	34,295
30	26	A	Manchester United	D	2-2	0-0	Jones, Bremner	60,514
31	31	A	Stoke City	D	1-1	1-1	Giles	35,908
32	Feb 10	H	West Bromwich Alb	W	5-1	3-1	Gray, Jones, Giles 2, Lorimer	31,515
33	14	A	Tottenham Hotspur	D	1-1	0-1	Lorimer	41,713
34	28	H	Crystal Palace	W	2-0	1-0	Jones 2	37,138
35	Mar 7	A	Liverpool	D	0-0	0-0		51,435
36	21	A	Wolverhampton W	W	2-1	1-0	Jones, Clarke	35,057
37	28	H	Southampton	L	1-3	0-0	Lorimer	38,370
38	30	A	Derby County	L	1-4	0-2	Kennedy	41,011
39	Apr 2	A	West Ham United	D	2-2	1-2	Clarke 2	26,140
40	4	H	Burnley	W	2-1	1-1	Gray 2	24,691
41	18	H	Manchester City	L	1-3	0-1	Belfitt	22,932
42	21	A	Ipswich Town	L	2-3	1-3	Hibbitt, Gray	16,875
								Appearances
								Sub appearances
							Two own-goals	Goals

FL Cup

R2	Sep 2	A	Fulham	W	1-0	1-0	Charlton	20,446
R3	24	H	Chelsea	D	1-1	0-0	Madeley	21,933
Rep	Oct 6	A	Chelsea	L	0-2	0-0		38,485
								Appearances
								Sub appearances
								Goals

FA Cup

R3	Jan 3	H	Swansea Town	W	2-1	0-1	Giles (pen), Jones	30,246
R4	24	A	Sutton United	W	6-0	3-0	Clarke 4, Lorimer 2	14,000
R5	Feb 7	H	Mansfield Town	W	2-0	2-0	Giles, Clarke	48,093
R6	21	A	Swindon Town	W	2 0	2 0	Clarke 2	27,500
SF	Mar 14	N	Manchester United	D	0-0*	0-0		55,000
Rep	23	N	Manchester United	D	0-0#	0-0		62,500
2Rep	26	N	Manchester United	W	1-0†	1-0	Bremner	56,000
F	Apr 11	N	Chelsea	D	2-2‡	1-1	Charlton, Jones	100,000
F Rep	29	N	Chelsea	L	1-2√	1-0	Jones	62,078
								Appearances
								Sub appearances
								Goals

* At Hillsborough, Sheffield # At Villa Park, Birmingham a.e.t.
† At Burnden Park, Bolton ‡ At Wembley, London a.e.t.
√ At Old Trafford, Manchester a.e.t
(Score at 90 minutes at Wembley 2-2 and at Old Trafford 1-1)

European Cup

R1	Sep 17	H	Lyn Oslo	W	10-0	5-0	O'Grady, Jones 3, Clarke 2, Giles 2, Bremner 2	25,979
	Oct 1	A	Lyn Oslo	W	6-0	3-0	Belfitt 2, Hibbitt 2, Jones, Lorimer	7,595
R2	Nov 12	H	Ferencvaros	W	3-0	3-0	Giles, Jones 2	37,291
	26	A	Ferencvaros	W	3-0	1-0	Jones 2, Lorimer	5,400
QF	Mar 4	A	Standard Liege	W	1-0	0-0	Lorimer	38,000
	18	H	Standard Liege	W	1-0	0-0	Giles (pen)	48,775
SF	Apr 1	H	Celtic	L	0-1	0-1		45,505
	15	A	Celtic	L	1-2*	1-0	Bremner	136,505
								Appearances
								Sub appearances
								Goals

* At Hampden Park, Glasgow

FA Charity Shield

	Aug 2	H	Manchester City	W	2-1	0-0	Charlton, Gray	39,835

Treble chasing United relied on this powerful squad in a gruelling 1969–70 season. Back row, left to right: Norman Hunter, Peter Lorimer, Mike O'Grady, Eddie Gray, Allan Clarke, David Harvey, Gary Sprake, Mick Jones, Paul Madeley, Rod Belfitt. Front row: Terry Hibbitt, Mick Bates, Paul Reaney, Johnny Giles, Billy Bremner, Albert Johanneson.

Sprake, Gary	Reaney, Paul	Madeley, Paul	Bremner, Billy	Charlton, Jack	Hunter, Norman	O'Grady, Mike	Lorimer, Peter	Clarke, Allan	Giles, Johnny	Gray, Eddie	Cooper, Terry	Jones, Mick	Yorath, Terry	Bates, Mick	Hibbitt, Terry	Belfitt, Rod	Harvey, David	Davey, Nigel	Lumsden, Jimmy	Peterson, Paul	Kennedy, David	Galvin, Chris	Johanneson, Albert	Faulkner, John
1	2	3	4	5	6	7	8	9	10	11														
1	2	5	4		6	7	8	9	10	11	3													
1	2	5	4		6		7	8	10	11	3	9												
1	2	5	4		6		7	8	10	11	3	9												
1	2	5	4		6		7	8	10	11	3	9												
1	2	7	4	5	6			8	10	11	3	9												
1	2	7	4	5	6		S*	10	8	**11**	3	9												
1	2	7	4	5	6	S*	8		10	**11**	3	9												
1	2	7	4	5	6			8	10	11	3	9												
1	2	7	4	**5**	6	11	S*	8	10		3	9												
1	2	5	4		6		7	8	10	11	3	9												
1	2	7	4	5	6		S*	8	**10**	11	3	9												
1	2	8	4	5	6		7		10	11	**3**	9	S*											
1	2	3	4	5	6		7		10	11		9	**8**	S*										
1	2	3	4	5	6		7	8		**11**		9		10	S*									
1	2	3	4	5	6		7	**8**		11		9		10	S*									
1	2	3	4	5	6		7			11		9		10		8								
1	2	3		5	6		7		10	4		9	S*	8	**11**									
1	2	3	4	5	6		7		10			9	S*	8	**11**									
1	2	8	4	5	6		7			11	3	9	S*	**10**										
1	2	8	4	5	6		7		10	11	3	9												
1	2	8	4	5	6		7		10	11	3	9												
1	2	11	4	5	6		7	8	10		3	9												
1	2	9	4	5	6		7	8	10		3				11									
1	2	11	4	5	6		7	8	10		3	9												
1	2	11	4	5	6		7	10	8		3	9												
1	2	11	4	5	6		7	8	10		3	9												
1	2	11	4	5	6		7	**8**	10		3	9		S*										
1	2	11	4	**5**	6		7	8	10		3	9		S*										
	2	11	4	5	6		7	8	10		3	9					1							
1	2	11	4	5	6		7	8	10		3	9												
1	2	8	4	5	6		7		10	11	3	9												
1	2	8	4	5	6		7		10	11	3	9												
1	2	3	4	5	6		7	**8**	10	11	S*	9												
1	2	9	4	5	6		7	8	10	11	3													
1	2	4		**5**			7	8		11	3	9	6	10		S*								
1		3		5			7	8		6			4	10	11	9		**2**	S*					
													6	8	10	9	1	2	4	3	5	7	11	
1	2	5					7	8	11	6			4	10	S*	**9**		3						
		4					7			6			2	8	11		1			3		10	9	5
			4				7	8		6	3			10	11	9	1	2		S*				**5**
							8			6			4	10	11	9	1	2		3	5	7		
37	37	39	35	32	35	3	36	28	32	30	29	32	7	13	8	6	5	5	1	3	2	3	2	2
						1	3				1		4	3	3	1			1	1				
			4	3	1		14	17	13	9	1	15		1	2	1					1			
	2	4		5			7			6	3	9		8	11	10	1							
1	2	5	4		6		7		10		3	9		S*	**11**	8								
	2	10	4	5	6		7			11	3	9				8	1							
1	3	3	2	2	2	0	3	0	1	2	3	3	0	1	2	3	2	0	0	0	0	0	0	0
														1										
		1		1																				
1	2	11	4	5	6		7	8	10		3	9												
	2	11	4	5	6		7	8	10		3	9					1							
1	2		4	5	6		7	8	10	11	3	9												
1	2	7	4	5	6			8	10	11	3	9												
1	2	11	4	5	6		**7**	8	10	S*	3	9												
1	2	6	4	5			7	8	10	11	**3**	9		S*										
1	2	6	4	5			7	8	10	11	3	9												
1	2	4	5	6	7	8	10	11	3	9														
	2	4	5	6	7	8	10	11	3	9							1							
7	9	8	9	9	7	2	8	9	9	6	7	7					2							
										1				1										
			1	1			2	7	2			3												
1	2	7	4	5	6	11		8	**10**		3	9		S*										
1	2	5	4				7			6	3	9		10	11	8								
1	2	3	4	5	6		7		10	11		9		8										
1	2	8	4	5	6		7		10	**11**	3	9										S*		
1	2	11	4	5	6		7	8	10		3	9												
1	2	11	4	5	6		7	8	10		3	9												
1	2	6	**4**	5			7	8	10	11	3	9		S*										
1		2	4	5	6		**7**	8	10	11	3	9		S*			S*							
8	7	8	8	7	6	1	7	5	7	5	7	8	0	2	1	1	0	0	0	0	0	0	0	0
														3			1					1		
			3			1	3	2	4			8			2	2								
1	2	7	4	5	6		S*	8	10	11	3	**9**												

League Table

	P	W	D	L	F	A	Pts
Everton	42	29	8	5	72	34	66
Leeds United	42	21	15	6	84	49	57
Chelsea	42	21	13	8	70	50	55
Derby County	42	22	9	11	64	37	53
Liverpool	42	20	11	11	65	42	51
Coventry City	42	19	11	12	58	48	49
Newcastle United	42	17	13	12	57	35	47
Manchester United	42	14	17	11	66	61	45
Stoke City	42	15	15	12	56	52	45
Manchester City	42	16	11	15	55	48	43
Tottenham Hotspur	42	17	9	16	54	55	43
Arsenal	42	12	18	12	51	49	42
Wolverhampton W	42	12	16	14	55	57	40
Burnley	42	12	15	15	56	61	39
Nottingham Forest	42	10	18	14	50	71	38
West Bromwich Albion	42	14	9	19	58	66	37
West Ham United	42	12	12	18	51	60	36
Ipswich Town	42	10	11	21	40	63	31
Southampton	42	6	17	19	46	67	29
Crystal Palace	42	6	15	21	34	68	27
Sunderland	42	6	14	22	30	68	26
Sheffield Wednesday	42	8	9	25	40	71	25

1970-71

Division One

Manager: Don Revie OBE

Final Position: 2nd

Did you know that?

15 August 1970: Mick Jones' stunning header – his 100th League goal – earned a 1–0 win at Manchester United.

29 August 1970: United made it their best start to a season with a fifth straight victory, easing to a 3–0 win at Burnley where Allan Clarke opened the scoring after just 21 seconds.

17 April 1971: United's title hopes suffered a huge blow as West Brom, without an away win for 16 months, claim a controversial 2–1 win at Elland Road. The second Albion goal was offside, prompting some fans to go on to the pitch and manhandle referee Ray Tinkler. Their actions saw United hit with a four-game home ban from the start of 1971–72.

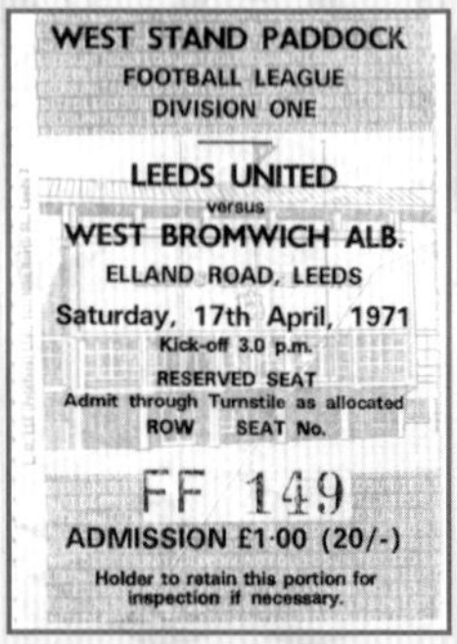

This match had severe repercussions for United.

Match No.	Date	Venue	Opponents	Result	FT	HT	Scorers	Attendance
1	Aug 15	A	Manchester United	W	1-0	1-0	Jones	59,365
2	19	A	Tottenham Hotspur	W	2-0	0-0	Giles, Gray	39,927
3	22	H	Everton	W	3-2	1-2	Bremner 2, Giles	46,718
4	26	H	West Ham United	W	3-0	1-0	Jones, Giles (pen), Belfitt	42,677
5	29	A	Burnley	W	3-0	3-0	Clarke 2, Jones	26,006
6	Sep 1	A	Arsenal	D	0-0	0-0		47,749
7	5	H	Chelsea	W	1-0	0-0	Clarke	47,662
8	12	A	Stoke City	L	0-3	0-1		22,592
9	19	H	Southampton	W	1-0	1-0	Giles (pen)	32,713
10	26	A	Nottingham Forest	D	0-0	0-0		31,537
11	Oct 3	H	Huddersfield Town	W	2-0	1-0	Lorimer 2 (1 pen)	36,498
12	10	A	West Bromwich Alb	D	2-2	1-1	Clarke, Jones	37,255
13	17	H	Manchester United	D	2-2	1-0	Belfitt, Charlton	50,190
14	24	A	Derby County	W	2-0	0-0	Lorimer, Clarke	32,797
15	31	H	Coventry City	W	2-0	1-0	Charlton, Giles	31,670
16	Nov 7	A	Crystal Palace	D	1-1	1-0	Lorimer	37,963
17	14	H	Blackpool	W	3-1	1-0	Madeley, Charlton, Giles	32,921
18	18	H	Stoke City	W	4-1	2-1	Madeley, Clarke, Lorimer, Giles (pen)	30,549
19	21	A	Wolverhampton W	W	3-2	3-1	Madeley, Clarke, Holsgrove (og)	41,048
20	28	H	Manchester City	W	1-0	0-0	Clarke	43,511
21	Dec 5	A	Liverpool	D	1-1	0-0	Madeley	51,357
22	12	H	Ipswich Town	D	0-0	0-0		29,675
23	19	A	Everton	W	1-0	1-0	Charlton	47,393
24	26	H	Newcastle United	W	3-0	1-0	Clarke, Giles 2 (2 pens)	46,758
25	Jan 9	H	Tottenham Hotspur	L	1-2	1-1	Clarke	43,907
26	16	A	West Ham United	W	3-2	1-0	Hunter, Giles, Belfitt	34,396
27	30	A	Manchester City	W	2-0	2-0	Clarke, Charlton	43,517
28	Feb 6	H	Liverpool	L	0-1	0-1		48,425
29	20	H	Wolverhampton W	W	3-0	1-0	Madeley, Clarke, Giles (pen)	37,273
30	23	A	Ipswich Town	W	4-2	1-2	Lorimer, Clarke 2, Giles (pen)	27,264
31	26	A	Coventry City	W	1-0	0-0	Lorimer	40,012
32	Mar 6	H	Derby County	W	1-0	0-0	Lorimer	36,467
33	13	A	Blackpool	D	1-1	0-1	Lorimer	27,401
34	20	H	Crystal Palace	W	2-1	1-1	Giles, Lorimer	31,876
35	27	A	Chelsea	L	1-3	0-2	Cooper	58,462
36	Apr 3	H	Burnley	W	4-0	2-0	Clarke 4	31,192
37	10	A	Newcastle United	D	1-1	0-0	Lorimer	49,640
38	12	A	Huddersfield Town	D	0-0	0-0		43,011
39	17	H	West Bromwich Alb	L	1-2	0-1	Clarke	36,812
40	24	A	Southampton	W	3-0	2-0	Hollywood (og), Jones 2	30,001
41	26	H	Arsenal	W	1-0	0-0	Charlton	48,350
42	May 1	H	Nottingham Forest	W	2-0	2-0	Bremner, Lorimer	43,083
								Appearances
								Sub appearances
							Two own-goals	Goals

FL Cup

Round	Date	Venue	Opponents	Result	FT	HT	Scorers	Attendance
R2	Sep 8	A	Sheffield United	L	0-1	0-0		29,573
								Appearances
								Sub appearances
								Goals

FA Cup

Round	Date	Venue	Opponents	Result	FT	HT	Scorers	Attendance
R3	Jan 11	A	Rotherham United	D	0-0	0-0		24,000
Rep	18	H	Rotherham United	W	3-2	1-2	Lorimer 2, Giles	36,890
R4	23	H	Swindon Town	W	4-0	2-0	Jones 3, Clarke	36,895
R5	Feb 13	A	Colchester United	L	2-3	0-2	Hunter, Giles	16,000
								Appearances
								Sub appearances
								Goals

Inter-Cities Fairs Cup

Round	Date	Venue	Opponents	Result	FT	HT	Scorers	Attendance
R1	Sep 15	A	Sarpsborg	W	1-0	0-0	Lorimer	8,769
	29	H	Sarpsborg	W	5-0	1-0	Charlton 2, Bremner 2, Lorimer	19,283
R2	Oct 21	H	Dynamo Dresden	W	1-0	0-0	Lorimer (pen)	21,292
	Nov 4	A	Dynamo Dresden	L	1-2	1-1	Jones	35,000
R3	Dec 2	H	Sparta Prague	W	6-0	5-0	Clarke, Chovanec (og), Bremner, Gray 2, Charlton	25,843
	9	A	Sparta Prague	W	3-2	3-0	Gray, Clarke, Belfitt	30,000
QF	Mar 10	H	Vitoria Setubal	W	2-1	1-1	Lorimer, Giles (pen)	27,143
	24	A	Vitoria Setubal	D	1-1	1-0	Lorimer	30,000
SF	Apr 14	A	Liverpool	W	1-0	0-0	Bremner	52,877
	28	H	Liverpool	D	0-0	0-0		40,462
F	May 28	A	Juventus	D	2-2	1-0	Madeley, Bates	45,000
	Jun 3	H	Juventus	D	1-1	1-1	Clarke	42,483
								Appearances
								Sub appearances
							One own-goal	Goals

Inter-Cities Fairs Cup - Match abandoned after 51 minutes due to waterlogged pitch

Round	Date	Venue	Opponents	Result	FT	HT	Scorers	Attendance
F	May 26	A	Juventus	D	0-0	0-0		46,501

Back row, left to right: Chris Galvin, Terry Yorath, David Harvey, Mick Jones, Gary Sprake, Jack Charlton, Allan Clarke, Norman Hunter, Eddie Gray, Paul Madeley. Front row: Rod Belfitt, Paul Reaney, Peter Lorimer, Johnny Giles, Billy Bremner, Terry Cooper, Mick Bates, Terry Hibbitt.

Sprake, Gary	Madeley, Paul	Cooper, Terry	Bremner, Billy	Charlton, Jack	Hunter, Norman	Lorimer, Peter	Clarke, Allan	Jones, Mick	Giles, Johnny	Gray, Eddie	Bates, Mick	Belfitt, Rod	Yorath, Terry	Hibbitt, Terry	Reaney, Paul	Harvey, David	Davey, Nigel	Galvin, Chris	Kennedy, David	Jordan, Joe
1	2	3	4	5	6	7	8	9	10	11										
1	2	3	4	5	6	7	8	9	10	11										
1	2	3	4	5	6	7	8	9	10	11										
1	2	3		5	6	7	8	9	**10**	11	4	S*								
1	2	3	4	5	6	7	8	9		11	10									
1	2	3	4	5	6	7	8	9		11	10									
1	2	3	4	5	6	7	8	9		11	10									
1	2	3	4		6	7	8	9		11	10		5							
1	2	3	4	5	6	7	8	9	10	11										
1	2	3	4	5	6	7	8	9	10	11										
1	2	3	4	5	6	7	8	9		**11**	10			S*						
1	11	3	4	5	6	7	8	9			10				2					
1	11	3	4	5	6	7	8				**10**	9		S*	2					
1	11	3	4	5	6	7	8	9				10					2			
1	11	3	4	5	6	7	8	9	10								2			
1	11	3		5	6	7	8	9	10		4						2			
1	2	3		5	6	7	8	9	10	11	4									
1	11	3		5	6	7	8	**9**	10		4	S*					2			
1	4	3		5	6	7	8	**9**	10		11	S*					2			
1	2	3	4	5	6	7	8		10	11	9									
1	2	3	4	5	6	7	8	9	10	**11**					S*					
1	11	3	4	5	6	7	8	9	10						2					
	11	3	4	5	6	7	**8**	9	10		S*				2	1				
1	11	3	4	5	6	7	8	9	10						2					
1	11	3	4	5	6	7	8	9	10						2					
1	7	3		5	6		8	**9**	10		4	S*	11		2					
1	7	3		**5**	6		8	9	10		4	S*	11		2					
	11	3		5	6	7	8	9	10		4				2	1				
	2	3	4	5	6	7	8	9	10		11					1				
	2	3	**4**	5	6	7	8	9	10		11	S*				1				
	11	3		5	6	7	8	9	10		4			S*	**2**	1				
	11			5	6	7		9	10		4	8			3	1	2			
	11	3		5	6	7	8	9	10		4				2	1				
	11	3		5	6	**7**	8	9	10		4	S*			2	1				
1	11	3		5	6	7	8	9	10		4				2					
1	11	3		5	6	7	8	**9**	10		4	S*			2					
1	11	3		5	6	7	8	9	10		**4**	S*			2					
1	11	3		5	6	**7**	8	9	10		4	S*			2					
1		3	7	5	6		8	9	10	11	**4**				2		S*			
1	2	3	4	5	6		8	9	10	11	7									
1	2	3	4	5	6		8	9	10	11	7									
1	2	3	4	5	6	7	8	9	10	11										
34	41	41	26	41	42	37	41	40	34	18	29	3	3	0	18	8	6	0	0	0
											1	10		3	1		1			
	5	1	3	6	1	12	19	6	13	1		3								

Sprake, Gary	Madeley, Paul	Cooper, Terry	Bremner, Billy	Charlton, Jack	Hunter, Norman	Lorimer, Peter	Clarke, Allan	Jones, Mick	Giles, Johnny	Gray, Eddie	Bates, Mick	Belfitt, Rod	Yorath, Terry	Hibbitt, Terry	Reaney, Paul	Harvey, David	Davey, Nigel	Galvin, Chris	Kennedy, David	Jordan, Joe
1	2	3	4	**5**	6	7	8	9		11	10	S*								
1	1	1	1	1	1	1	1	1	0	1	1	0	0	0	0	0	0	0	0	0
												1								

Sprake, Gary	Madeley, Paul	Cooper, Terry	Bremner, Billy	Charlton, Jack	Hunter, Norman	Lorimer, Peter	Clarke, Allan	Jones, Mick	Giles, Johnny	Gray, Eddie	Bates, Mick	Belfitt, Rod	Yorath, Terry	Hibbitt, Terry	Reaney, Paul	Harvey, David	Davey, Nigel	Galvin, Chris	Kennedy, David	Jordan, Joe
1	11	3	4	5	6	7	8	9	10						2					
1	11	**3**	4	5	6	7	8		10		S*	9			2					
1	11			5	6	**7**	8	9	10		4				2		3	S*		
1	11	3		5	6	7	8	9	10		4				2					
4	4	3	2	4	4	4	4	3	4	0	2	1	0	0	4	0	1	0	0	0
											1							1		
					1	2	1	3	2											

Sprake, Gary	Madeley, Paul	Cooper, Terry	Bremner, Billy	Charlton, Jack	Hunter, Norman	Lorimer, Peter	Clarke, Allan	Jones, Mick	Giles, Johnny	Gray, Eddie	Bates, Mick	Belfitt, Rod	Yorath, Terry	Hibbitt, Terry	Reaney, Paul	Harvey, David	Davey, Nigel	Galvin, Chris	Kennedy, David	Jordan, Joe
1	2	3	4			7		9		6	10	8		11					5	
1	2	**3**	4	5	6	7	8			11	10	9			S*					
	11	3	4	5	6	7	8	9				10				1	2			
1	3		4	5	6	7	8	9	10		11						2			
1	2	3	4	5	6	7	8		10	11		**9**			S*					
1	5	3	4		**6**	7	8			11	10	9	S*		2	S*				
	11			5	6	7		**9**	10		4	8	S*		3	1	**2**			S*
S*	11	3		5	6	7	8	9	10		4				2	**1**				
1	11	3	4	5	6		8	9	10		7				**2**		S*			
1	2	3	4	5	6		**8**	**9**	10	11	7				S*					S*
1	11	3	4	5	6	7	8	**9**	10		S*				2					
1	**11**	3	4	5	6	7	8	9	10		S*				2					
9	12	10	10	10	11	10	10	9	8	5	8	6	0	1	6	3	3	0	1	0
1											2		2		3	1	1			2
	1		4	3		5	3	1	1	3	1	1								

Sprake, Gary	Madeley, Paul	Cooper, Terry	Bremner, Billy	Charlton, Jack	Hunter, Norman	Lorimer, Peter	Clarke, Allan	Jones, Mick	Giles, Johnny	Gray, Eddie	Bates, Mick	Belfitt, Rod	Yorath, Terry	Hibbitt, Terry	Reaney, Paul	Harvey, David	Davey, Nigel	Galvin, Chris	Kennedy, David	Jordan, Joe
1	2	3	4	5	6	7	8	9	10	**11**			S*							

League Table

	P	W	D	L	F	A	Pts
Arsenal	42	29	7	6	71	29	65
Leeds United	42	27	10	5	72	30	64
Tottenham Hotspur	42	19	14	9	54	33	52
Wolverhampton W	42	22	8	12	64	54	52
Liverpool	42	17	17	8	42	24	51
Chelsea	42	18	15	9	52	42	51
Southampton	42	17	12	13	56	44	46
Manchester United	42	16	11	15	65	66	43
Derby County	42	16	10	16	56	54	42
Coventry City	42	16	10	16	37	38	42
Manchester City	42	12	17	13	47	42	41
Newcastle United	42	14	13	15	44	46	41
Stoke City	42	12	13	17	44	48	37
Everton	42	12	13	17	54	60	37
Huddersfield Town	42	11	14	17	40	49	36
Nottingham Forest	42	14	8	20	42	61	36
West Bromwich Albion	42	10	15	17	58	75	35
Crystal Palace	42	12	11	19	39	57	35
Ipswich Town	42	12	10	20	42	48	34
West Ham United	42	10	14	18	47	60	34
Burnley	42	7	13	22	29	63	27
Blackpool	42	4	15	23	34	66	23

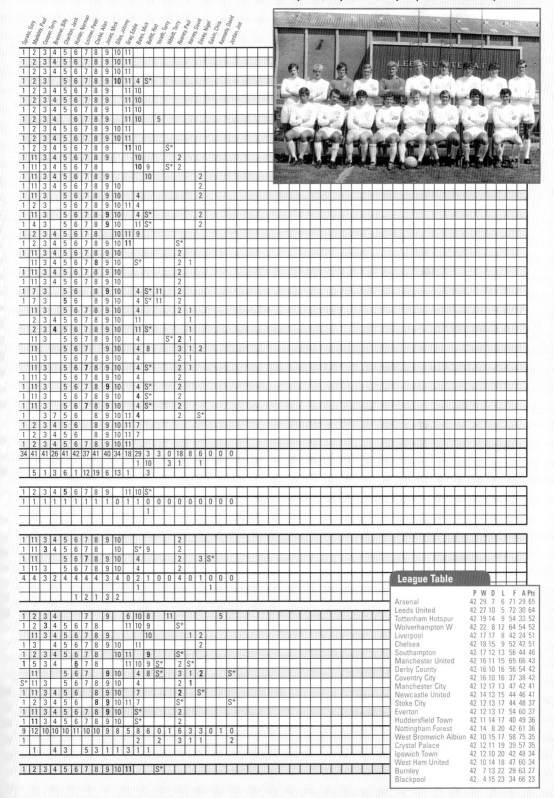

1971-72

Division One

Manager: Don Revie OBE

Final Position: 2nd

Did you know that?

25 August 1971: United's second game in exile saw them draw 1–1 with Tottenham at Hull, the first Division One game ever played at Boothferry Park.

3 November 1971: West Brom's Asa Hartford joined Leeds for a record £177,000 and trained with his new teammates. Three hours before his debut against Leicester the following Saturday the move was called off owning to Hartford's undiscovered medical condition – a tiny hole in his heart had been found in his medical check-up. Hartford returned to West Brom and went on to have a long career, including 50 appearances for Scotland.

8 April 1972: Terry Cooper broke a leg in the 3–0 win at Stoke and missed out on United's FA Cup Final triumph against Arsenal the following month. Reserve left-back Nigel Davey fractured a leg on the same day against West Brom in the Central League.

29 April 1972: The single *Leeds United*, recorded by the squad to mark reaching the FA Cup Final, entered the singles charts at No. 31, rising to 10 during its 10 week stay. The B side, *Leeds! Leeds! Leeds!* is better known as *Marching On Together*.

Big hit...United's single.

Match No.	Date	Venue	Opponents	Result	FT	HT	Scorers	Attendance
1	Aug 14	A	Manchester City	W	1-0	0-0	Lorimer	38,566
2	17	A	Sheffield United	L	0-3	0-0		40,725
3	21	H	Wolverhampton W	D	0-0	0-0		20,686
4	25	H	Tottenham Hotspur	D	1-1	0-1	Bremner	25,099
5	28	A	Ipswich Town	W	2-0	2-0	Lorimer, Belfitt	26,689
6	Sep 1	H	Newcastle United	W	5-1	2-0	Charlton, Lorimer, Giles (pen), Yorath, Madeley	18,623
7	4	H	Crystal Palace	W	2-0	2-0	Madeley, Giles (pen)	18,715
8	11	A	Arsenal	L	0-2	0-1		51,196
9	18	H	Liverpool	W	1-0	0-0	Lorimer	41,381
10	25	A	Huddersfield Town	L	1-2	1-1	Charlton	26,340
11	Oct 2	H	West Ham United	D	0-0	0-0		30,942
12	9	A	Coventry City	L	1-3	0-2	Parker (og)	32,183
13	16	H	Manchester City	W	3-0	1-0	Clarke, Jones, Lorimer	36,004
14	23	H	Everton	W	3-2	1-1	Cooper, Charlton, Lorimer	34,208
15	30	A	Manchester United	W	1-0	1-0	Lorimer	53,960
16	Nov 6	H	Leicester City	W	2-1	0-1	Bremner, Lorimer	39,877
17	13	A	Southampton	L	1-2	0-1	Giles	25,331
18	20	H	Stoke City	W	1-0	1-0	Lorimer	32,012
19	27	A	Nottingham Forest	W	2-0	1-0	Lorimer, Clarke	29,463
20	Dec 4	H	West Bromwich Alb	W	3-0	1-0	Giles 2, Lorimer	32,521
21	11	A	Chelsea	D	0-0	0-0		45,867
22	18	A	Crystal Palace	D	1-1	1-0	Lorimer	31,456
23	27	H	Derby County	W	3-0	2-0	Gray, Lorimer 2	44,214
24	Jan 1	A	Liverpool	W	2-0	0-0	Clarke, Jones	53,847
25	8	H	Ipswich Town	D	2-2	0-1	Bremner, Clarke	32,194
26	22	H	Sheffield United	W	1-0	1-0	Clarke	41,038
27	29	A	Tottenham Hotspur	L	0-1	0-0		46,774
28	Feb 12	A	Everton	D	0-0	0-0		45,935
29	19	H	Manchester United	W	5-1	0-0	Jones 3, Clarke, Lorimer	45,399
30	Mar 4	H	Southampton	W	7-0	2-0	Clarke 2, Lorimer 3, Charlton, Jones	34,275
31	11	H	Coventry City	W	1-0	1-0	Charlton	43,154
32	22	A	Leicester City	D	0-0	0-0		32,152
33	25	H	Arsenal	W	3-0	3-0	Clarke, Jones, Lorimer	45,055
34	27	H	Nottingham Forest	W	6-1	1-1	Lorimer 2, Gray 2, Clarke 2	40,866
35	31	A	West Ham United	D	2-2	0-2	Gray 2	41,003
36	Apr 1	A	Derby County	L	0-2	0-1		39,450
37	5	H	Huddersfield Town	W	3-1	1-0	Jones, Lorimer, Gray	46,148
38	8	A	Stoke City	W	3-0	1-0	Jones 2, Lorimer	35,123
39	19	A	Newcastle United	L	0-1	0-0		42,006
40	22	A	West Bromwich Alb	W	1-0	0-0	Giles (pen)	39,724
41	May 1	H	Chelsea	W	2-0	1-0	Bremner, Jones	46,565
42	8	A	Wolverhampton W	L	1-2	0-1	Bremner	53,379

Elland Road closed by FA Order for four games:
Matches 3 & 7 were played at Leeds Road, Huddersfield; Match 4 at Boothferry Park, Hull; Match 6 at Hillsborough, Sheffield.

Appearances
Sub appearances
Goals

FL Cup

R2	Sep 8	A	Derby County	D	0-0	0-0		34,023
Rep	27	H	Derby County	W	2-0	1-0	Lorimer 2	28,132
R3	Oct 6	A	West Ham United	D	0-0	0-0		35,890
Rep	20	H	West Ham United	L	0-1*	0-0		26,504

* After extra-time

Appearances
Sub appearances
Goals

FA Cup

R3	Jan 15	H	Bristol Rovers	W	4-1	3-0	Giles 2 (1 pen), Lorimer 2	33,565
R4	Feb 5	A	Liverpool	D	0-0	0-0		56,300
Rep	9	H	Liverpool	W	2-0	1-0	Clarke 2	45,821
R5	26	A	Cardiff City	W	2-0	1-0	Giles 2	50,000
R6	Mar 18	H	Tottenham Hotspur	W	2-1	1-1	Clarke, Charlton	43,937
SF	Apr 15	N	Birmingham City	W	3-0†	2-0	Jones 2, Lorimer	55,000
F	May 6	N	Arsenal	W	1-0‡	0-0	Clarke	100,000

† At Hillsborough, Sheffield
‡ At Wembley, London

Appearances
Sub appearances
Goals

UEFA Cup

R1	Sep 15	A	Lierse	W	2-0	1-0	Galvin, Lorimer	17,000
	29	H	Lierse	L	0-4	0-3		18,680

Appearances
Sub appearances
Goals

Inter-Cities Fair-Cities Cup Play-off

R1	Sep 22	A	Barcelona	L	1-2*	0-0	Jordan	35,000

* At Nou Camp, Barcelona for permanent possession of the old trophy

Sprake, Gary	Reaney, Paul	Cooper, Terry	Bremner, Billy	Charlton, Jack	Hunter, Norman	Lorimer, Peter	Clarke, Allan	Belfitt, Rod	Giles, Johnny	Madeley, Paul	Bates, Mick	Jones, Mick	Yorath, Terry	Harvey, David	Jordan, Joe	Galvin, Chris	Edwards, Keith	Mann, Jimmy	Gray, Eddie	Davey, Nigel	Failkner, John	Shaw, John
1	2	3	4	5	6	7	8	9	10	11												
1	2		4	5	6	7	8	9	10	3	11											
1	2	3	4	5	6	7	8		**10**	11	S*	9										
1	2	3	4	5	6	7	8			11	10	9										
1	2	3	4	5	6	7	8	**9**		11	10		S*									
1	2	3	4	5	6	7	8	**9**	10	11			S*									
1	2	3	4	5	6	7	8	9	10	11												
	2		4	5	6	7	8	**9**	10	11			3	1	S*							
1	2	3	4	5	6	7		**9**	10	11					S*	8						
1	**2**	3	4	5	6	7		9	10	11						8	S*					
1	2	3		5	6	7		9	10	11			4			S*		**8**				
1	2	3	4	5	6	7		9	10	11			**8**		S*							
	2	3	4	5	6	7	**8**		10	11		9		1	S*							
1	2	3	4	5	6	7	9		**10**	11					8				S*			
1	2	3	4	5	6	7		S*	10	11					**9**				8			
1	2	3	4	5	6	7			10	11					9				8			
1	2	3	4	5	6	7			10	11					9				8			
1		3	4	5	6	7	8		10	2		9							11			
1		3	4	5	6	7	8		10	2		9							11			
1	S*	3	4	5	6	7	8		10	2		9							**11**			
1		3	4	5	6	7	8		10	2		9							11			
1		3	4	5	6	7	8		10	2		9							11			
1		3	4	5	6	7	8		10	2		9							11			
1	2	3	4		6	7	8		10	5	S*	9							**11**			
1	S*	3	4	**5**	6	7	8		10	2		9							11			
1		3	4	5	6	7	8		10	2		9							11			
1		3	4	5	6	7	8		10	2		9							11			
1	**2**	3	4	5	6	7	8		10	9					S*				11			
1		3	4	5	6	7	8		10	2		9							11			
1	2		4	5	6	7	8		10	3		9							11			
1	2		4	5	6	7	8		10	3		9							11			
1		3	4	5	6	7	8		10	2		9							11			
1	2	3	4	5	6	7	8		10	11		9										
1	2	3	4	5	6	7	8			11		**9**	S*						10			
1	2	3	4	5	6	7	8			11	S*				**9**				10			
1	2	3	4	5	6	7	8		10	9									11			
1	S*	3	4	5	6	7	**8**		10	2		9							11			
	S*	3	4	5	6	7	**8**		10	2		9		1					11			
	2		4	5	6	7	8		10	3		9		1					11			
	2		4	5	6	7	**8**		10	3	11	9		1	S*							
	2		4	5	6	7	**8**		10	3	11	9		1	S*							
	2		4	5	6	7	**8**		10	3	9		S*	1					11			
35	29	34	41	41	42	42	35	10	38	42	6	24	3	7	5	2	0	1	25	0	0	0
	4							4			3		4		7	1	1	1	1			
		1	5	5		23	11	1	6	2		11	1						6			

	2		4	5	6	7	8	9	10	11			3	1								
1	2	3	**4**	5	6	7		9	10	11			8					S*				
1		3	4	5	6	7		9	10	11			8							2		
	2	3	4	5	6	7	8		10	11		**9**		1					S*			
2	3	3	4	4	4	4	2	3	4	4	0	1	3	2	0	0	0	0	0	1	0	0
																		1	1			
						2																

1	2	3	4		6	7			10	5	8				**9**	S*			11			
1	2	3	4		6	7	8		10	5	11	9										
1	**2**	3	4	5	6	7	8		10	9					S*				11			
1		3	4	5	6	7	8		10	2		9							11			
1	S*	**3**	4	5	6	7	8		10	2		9							11			
	2		4	5	6	7	8		10	3		9		1					11			
	2		4	5	6	7	8		10	3		9		1					11			
5	5	5	7	5	7	7	6	0	7	7	2	5	0	2	1	0	0	0	6	0	0	0
	1														1	1						
				1		3	4		4			2										

1	2		4		6	7		9	10		11		3			8					5	
S*	2	3			S*	7		9		6	10		4			11		**8**			5	**1**
1	2	1	1	0	1	2	0	2	1	1	2	0	2	0	0	2	0	1	0	0	2	1
1					1																	
						1										1						

1	2		4	5	6	7		9	10						8	11				3		

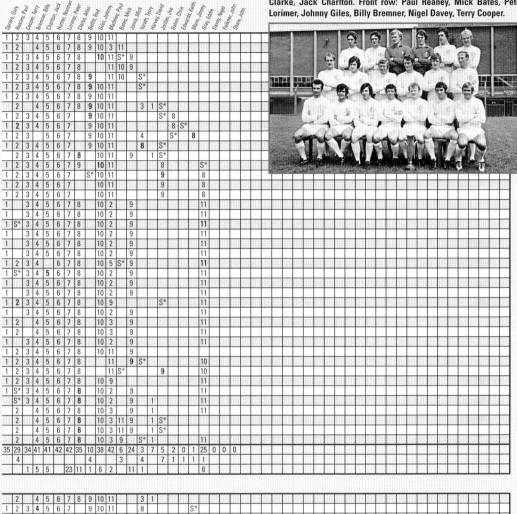

United, with the Fairs Cup at Billy Bremner's feet, face the cameras before the 1971–72 season. Back row, left to right: Rod Belfitt, Norman Hunter, Gary Sprake, David Harvey, Joe Jordan, Terry Yorath. Middle row: John Faulkner, Chris Galvin, Mick Jones, Paul Madeley, Allan Clarke, Jack Charlton. Front row: Paul Reaney, Mick Bates, Peter Lorimer, Johnny Giles, Billy Bremner, Nigel Davey, Terry Cooper.

League Table

	P	W	D	L	F	A	Pts
Derby County	42	24	10	8	69	33	58
Leeds United	42	24	9	9	73	31	57
Liverpool	42	24	9	9	64	30	57
Manchester City	42	23	11	8	77	45	57
Arsenal	42	22	8	12	58	40	52
Tottenham Hotspur	42	19	13	10	63	42	51
Chelsea	42	18	12	12	58	49	48
Manchester United	42	19	10	13	69	61	48
Wolverhampton W	42	18	11	13	65	57	47
Sheffield United	42	17	12	13	61	60	46
Newcastle United	42	15	11	16	49	52	41
Leicester City	42	13	13	16	41	46	39
Ipswich Town	42	11	16	15	39	53	38
West Ham United	42	12	12	18	47	51	36
Everton	42	9	18	15	37	48	36
West Bromwich Albion	42	12	11	19	42	54	35
Stoke City	42	10	15	17	39	56	35
Coventry City	42	9	15	18	44	67	33
Southampton	42	12	7	23	52	80	31
Crystal Palace	42	8	13	21	39	65	29
Nottingham Forest	42	8	9	25	47	81	25
Huddersfield Town	42	6	13	23	27	59	25

1972-73

Division One

Manager: Don Revie OBE

Final Position: 3rd

Did you know that?

12 August 1972: United endured a nightmare opening to the season as goalkeeper David Harvey and Mick Jones were both carried off at Stamford Bridge. Peter Lorimer went in goal and 10-man Leeds crashed 4–0 to Chelsea.

7 October 1972: One of United's best displays of the season saw them rout Brian Clough's champions, Derby County, 5–0.

28 April 1973: Jack Charlton, 37, played his 629th, and last game for United in a 3–1 defeat at Southampton.

Jack Charlton was finally able to call it a day and put his feet up.

Match No.	Date	Venue	Opponents	Result	FT	HT	Scorers	Attendance
1	Aug 12	A	Chelsea	L	0-4	0-1		51,102
2	15	A	Sheffield United	W	2-0	1-0	Colquhoun (og), Giles (pen)	40,159
3	19	H	West Bromwich Alb	W	2-0	1-0	Clarke, Giles (pen)	36,555
4	23	H	Ipswich Town	D	3-3	2-2	Jordan 2, Giles (pen)	32,461
5	26	A	Tottenham Hotspur	D	0-0	0-0		41,191
6	30	H	Southampton	W	1-0	0-0	Bremner	31,401
7	Sep 2	H	Norwich City	W	2-0	2-0	Jordan, Charlton	34,261
8	9	A	Stoke City	D	2-2	1-0	Lorimer, Clarke	26,705
9	16	H	Leicester City	W	3-1	0-1	Clarke, Jones, Bates	33,930
10	23	A	Newcastle United	L	2-3	2-2	Clarke, Jones	38,962
11	30	H	Liverpool	L	1-2	1-1	Jones	46,468
12	Oct 7	H	Derby County	W	5-0	3-0	Giles 2, Clarke, Bremner, Lorimer	36,477
13	14	A	Everton	W	2-1	1-0	Jones, Jordan	47,821
14	21	H	Coventry City	D	1-1	0-0	Charlton	36,240
15	28	A	Wolverhampton W	W	2-0	2-0	E. Gray, Lorimer	33,731
16	Nov 4	A	Ipswich Town	D	2-2	1-2	Charlton, Lorimer	27,566
17	11	H	Sheffield United	W	2-1	0-0	Clarke 2	31,600
18	18	A	Crystal Palace	D	2-2	0-2	Jones, Giles	30,107
19	25	H	Manchester City	W	3-0	0-0	Cherry, Lorimer, Clarke	39,879
20	Dec 2	A	Arsenal	L	1-2	1-0	Lorimer (pen)	39,108
21	9	H	West Ham United	W	1-0	1-0	Jones	30,270
22	16	H	Birmingham City	W	4-0	1-0	Clarke 2, Lorimer, Jones	25,285
23	23	A	Manchester United	D	1-1	0-1	Clarke	46,382
24	26	H	Newcastle United	W	1-0	0-0	Jordan	45,486
25	Jan 6	H	Tottenham Hotspur	W	2-1	2-0	Jones, Lorimer (pen)	32,404
26	20	A	Norwich City	W	2-1	2-0	Jordan, Clarke	27,447
27	27	H	Stoke City	W	1-0	0-0	Clarke	33,487
28	Feb 10	A	Leicester City	L	0-2	0-1		35,976
29	17	H	Chelsea	D	1-1	1-0	Jones	41,781
30	Mar 3	A	Derby County	W	3-2	1-1	Lorimer 2 (2 pens), Clarke	38,100
31	10	H	Everton	W	2-1	1-1	Clarke, Lorimer	39,663
32	24	H	Wolverhampton W	D	0-0	0-0		39,078
33	28	A	West Bromwich Alb	D	1-1	1-0	Clarke	33,057
34	31	A	Manchester City	L	0-1	0-0		35,772
35	Apr 2	A	Coventry City	W	1-0	1-0	Reaney	24,383
36	14	A	West Ham United	D	1-1	0-0	Clarke	38,804
37	18	H	Manchester United	L	0-1	0-0		45,450
38	21	H	Crystal Palace	W	4-0	3-0	Bremner, Lorimer, F.T. Gray, Clarke	31,173
39	23	A	Liverpool	L	0-2	0-0		55,738
40	28	A	Southampton	L	1-3	0-0	Hunter	24,108
41	30	A	Birmingham City	L	1-2	1-1	Jordan	34,449
42	May 9	H	Arsenal	W	6-1	2-0	Lorimer 3 (1 pen), Bremner, Jordan 2	25,088
								Appearances
								Sub appearances
							One own-goal	Goals
FL Cup								
R2	Sep 6	H	Burnley	W	4-0	0-0	Lorimer 2, Jones, Cherry	20,857
R3	Oct 4	A	Aston Villa	D	1-1	1-0	Charlton	46,185
Rep	11	H	Aston Villa	W	2-0	2-0	Nicholl (og), Jones	28,894
R4	31	A	Liverpool	D	2-2	1-1	Jones, Lorimer	44,609
Rep	Nov 22	H	Liverpool	L	0-1	0-0		34,856
								Appearances
								Sub appearances
							One own-goal	Goals
FA Cup								
R3	Jan 13	A	Norwich City	D	1-1	1-1	Lorimer	32,310
Rep	17	H	Norwich City	D	1-1*	0-1	Giles	36,087
2 Rep	29	N	Norwich City	W	5-0#	4-0	Clarke 3, Jones, Lorimer	33,225
R4	Feb 3	H	Plymouth Argyle	W	2-1	0-0	Clarke, Bates	38,374
R5	24	H	West Bromwich Alb	W	2-0	2-0	Clarke 2	39,229
R6	Mar 17	A	Derby County	W	1-0	1-0	Lorimer	38,350
SF	Apr 7	N	Wolverhampton W	W	1-0†	0-0	Bremner	52,505
F	May 5	N	Sunderland	L	0-1‡	0-1		100,000
* After extra-time # At Villa Park, Birmingham								Appearances
† At Maine Road, Manchester ‡ At Wembley, London								Sub appearances
								Goals
European Cup-Winners' Cup								
R1	Sep 13	A	Ankaragucu	D	1-1	1-0	Jordan	20,000
	27	H	Ankaragucu	W	1-0	0-0	Jones	22,411
R2	Oct 25	A	Carl Zeiss Jena	D	0-0	0-0		18,000
	Nov 8	H	Carl Zeiss Jena	W	2-0	0-0	Cherry, Jones	26,855
QF	Mar 7	H	Rapid Bucharest	W	5-0	3-0	Giles, Clarke, Lorimer 2, Jordan	25,702
	21	A	Rapid Bucharest	W	3-1	2-0	Bates, Jones, Jordan	25,000
SF	Apr 11	H	Hadjuk Split	W	1-0	1-0	Clarke	32,051
	25	A	Hadjuk Split	D	0-0	0-0		30,000
F	May 16	N	AC Milan	L	0-1*	0-1		40,154
* At Kaftantzoglio, Salonika								Appearances
								Sub appearances
								Goals

Back row, left to right: Trevor Cherry, Paul Madeley, Mick Jones, Roy Ellam, Joe Jordan, Jack Charlton. Middle row: Paul Reaney, Chris Galvin, David Harvey, Gary Sprake, Norman Hunter, Allan Clarke. Front row: Peter Lorimer, Johnny Giles, Billy Bremner, Mick Bates, Eddie Gray, Terry Yorath.

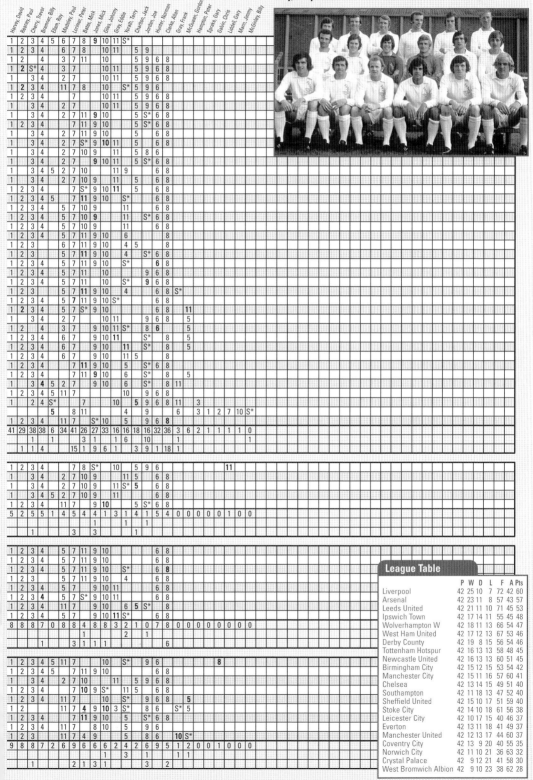

Harvey, David	Reaney, Paul	Cherry, Trevor	Bremner, Billy	Ellam, Roy	Madeley, Paul	Lorimer, Peter	Bates, Mick	Jones, Mick	Giles, Johnny	Gray, Eddie	Yorath, Terry	Charlton, Jack	Jordan, Joe	Hunter, Norman	Clarke, Allan	Gray, Frank	McQueen, Gordon	Hampton, Peter	Sprake, Gary	Galvin, Chris	Liddell, Gary	Mann, Jimmy	McGinley, Billy
1	2	3	4	5	6	7	8	**9**	10	11	S*												
1	2	3	4		6	7	8		10	11		5	9										
1	2		4		3	7	11		10			5	9	6	8								
1	**2**	S*	4		3	7			10	11		5	9	6	8								
1		3	4		2	7			10	11		5	9	6	8								
1	**2**	3	4		11	7	8		10		S*	5	9	6									
1	2	3	4			7			10	11		5	9	6	8								
1		3	4		2	7			10	11		5	9	6	8								
1		3	4		2	7	11	**9**	10			5	S*	6	8								
1	2	3	4			7	11	9	10			5	S*	6	8								
1		3	4		2	7	11	9	10			5		6	8								
1		3	4		2	7	S*	9	**10**	11		5		6	8								
1		3	4		2	7	10	9		11		5	8	6									
1		3	4		2	7		**9**	10	11		5	S*	6	8								
1		3	4	5	2	7	10			11	9			6	8								
1		3	4		2	7	10	9		11		5		6	8								
1	2	3	4			7	S*	9	10	**11**		5		6	8								
1	2	3	4	5		7	**11**	9	10		S*			6	8								
1	2	3	4		5	7	10	9			11			6	8								
1	2	3	4		5	7	10	**9**			11		S*	6	8								
1	2	3	4		5	7	10	9			11			6	8								
1	2	3	4		5	7	11	9	10		6				8								
1	2	3			6	7	11	9	10		4	5			8								
1	2	3			5	7	**11**	9	10		4		S*	6	8								
1	2	3	4		5	7	11	9	10		S*			**6**	8								
1	2	3	4		5	7	11		10				9	6	8								
1	2	3	4		5	7	11		10		S*		**9**	6	8								
1	2	3			5	7	**11**	9	10		4			6	8	S*							
1	2	3	4		5	**7**	11	9	10	S*				6	8								
1	**2**	3	4		5	7	S*	9	10						6	8		**11**						
1		3	4		2	7			10	11			9	6	8		5						
1	2		4		3	7		9	10	11	S*		8	**6**			5						
1	2	3	4		6	7		9	10	**11**			S*		8		5						
1	2	3	4		6	7		9	10		**11**		S*		8		5						
1	2	3	4		6	7		9	10		11	5			8								
1	2	3	4			7	**11**	9	10		5		S*	6	8								
1	2	3	4			7	11	**9**	10		6		S*		8		5						
1		3	**4**	5	2	7		9	10		6		S*		8	11							
1	2	3	4	5	11	7					10		9	6	8								
1		2	4	S*			7			10		**5**	9	6	8	11		3					
				5		8	11				4		9			6		3	1	2	7	10	S*
1	2	3	4		11	7		S*	10		5		9	6	**8**								
41	29	38	38	6	34	41	26	27	33	16	16	18	16	32	36	3	6	2	1	1	1	1	0
		1		1			3	1		1	6		10			1							1
	1	1	4			15	1	9	6	1		3	9	1	18	1							

Harvey, David	Reaney, Paul	Cherry, Trevor	Bremner, Billy	Ellam, Roy	Madeley, Paul	Lorimer, Peter	Bates, Mick	Jones, Mick	Giles, Johnny	Gray, Eddie	Yorath, Terry	Charlton, Jack	Jordan, Joe	Hunter, Norman	Clarke, Allan	Gray, Frank	McQueen, Gordon	Hampton, Peter	Sprake, Gary	Galvin, Chris	Liddell, Gary	Mann, Jimmy	McGinley, Billy
1	2	3	4			7	8	S*		10		5	9	6							**11**		
1		3	4		2	7	10	9			11	5		6	8								
1		3	4		2	7	10	9		11	S*	**5**		6	8								
1		3	4	5	2	7	10	9		11					6	8								
1	2	3	4		11	7		9	**10**			5	S*	6	8								
5	2	5	5	1	4	5	4	4	1	3	1	4	1	5	4	0	0	0	0	0	1	0	0
								1			1		1										
		1				3		3				1										

Harvey, David	Reaney, Paul	Cherry, Trevor	Bremner, Billy	Ellam, Roy	Madeley, Paul	Lorimer, Peter	Bates, Mick	Jones, Mick	Giles, Johnny	Gray, Eddie	Yorath, Terry	Charlton, Jack	Jordan, Joe	Hunter, Norman	Clarke, Allan	Gray, Frank	McQueen, Gordon	Hampton, Peter	Sprake, Gary	Galvin, Chris	Liddell, Gary	Mann, Jimmy	McGinley, Billy
1	2	3	4		5	7	11	9	10					6	8								
1	2	3	4		5	7	11	9	10					6	8								
1	2	3	4		5	7	11	9	10		S*			6	**8**								
1	2	3			5	7	11	9	10		4			6	8								
1	2	3	4		5	7		9	10	11				6	8								
1	2	3	**4**		5	7	S*	9	10	11				6	8								
1	2	3	4		11	7		9	10		6	**5**	S*		8								
1	2	3	4		5	7		9	10	**11**	S*			6	8								
8	8	8	7	0	8	8	4	8	8	3	2	1	0	7	8	0	0	0	0	0	0	0	0
							1				2		1										
			1			3	1	1	1						6								

Harvey, David	Reaney, Paul	Cherry, Trevor	Bremner, Billy	Ellam, Roy	Madeley, Paul	Lorimer, Peter	Bates, Mick	Jones, Mick	Giles, Johnny	Gray, Eddie	Yorath, Terry	Charlton, Jack	Jordan, Joe	Hunter, Norman	Clarke, Allan	Gray, Frank	McQueen, Gordon	Hampton, Peter	Sprake, Gary	Galvin, Chris	Liddell, Gary	Mann, Jimmy	McGinley, Billy
1	2	3	4	5	11	7			10		S*		9	6						**8**			
1	2	3	4	5		7	11	9	10					6	8								
1		3	4		2	7	10			11		5	9	6	8								
1	2	3	4			7	**10**	9	S*		11	5		6	8								
1	2	3	4		11	7			10		S*		9	6	8		**5**						
1	2				11	7	**4**	9	**10**	3	S*		8	6		S*	5						
1	2	3	4			7	**11**	9	10		5		S*	6	8								
1	2	3	4		11	7		8	10		5		9	6									
1	2	3			11	7	4	9			5		8	6		**10**	S*						
9	8	8	7	2	6	9	6	6	6	2	4	2	6	9	5	1	2	0	0	1	0	0	0
									1		3		1			1	1						
		1				2	1	3	1				3		2								

League Table

	P	W	D	L	F	A	Pts
Liverpool	42	25	10	7	72	42	60
Arsenal	42	23	11	8	57	43	57
Leeds United	42	21	11	10	71	45	53
Ipswich Town	42	17	14	11	55	45	48
Wolverhampton W	42	18	11	13	66	54	47
West Ham United	42	17	12	13	67	53	46
Derby County	42	19	8	15	56	54	46
Tottenham Hotspur	42	16	13	13	58	48	45
Newcastle United	42	16	13	13	60	51	45
Birmingham City	42	15	12	15	53	54	42
Manchester City	42	15	11	16	57	60	41
Chelsea	42	13	14	15	49	51	40
Southampton	42	11	18	13	47	52	40
Sheffield United	42	15	10	17	51	59	40
Stoke City	42	14	10	18	61	56	38
Leicester City	42	10	17	15	40	46	37
Everton	42	13	11	18	41	49	37
Manchester United	42	12	13	17	44	60	37
Coventry City	42	13	9	20	40	55	35
Norwich City	42	11	10	21	36	63	32
Crystal Palace	42	9	12	21	41	58	30
West Bromwich Albion	42	9	10	23	38	62	28

1973-74

Division One

Manager: Don Revie OBE

Final Position : 1st

Did you know that?

20 October 1973: One of the most bizarre incidents in the club's history occurred when a pantomime horse got on the Elland Road pitch during the game against Liverpool. The nag – two Sheffield University students publicising their rag week – was apprehended and escorted in front of the Kop who sang *I'll Say Goodbye To My Horse* to the tune of *Bless 'Em All*.

3 November 1973: Youth team goalkeeper Glan Letheran became an instant hero as United knocked Hibernian out of the UEFA Cup on penalties at Easter Road. With David Harvey injured and David Stewart ineligible, John Shaw started but broke two fingers and was replaced at half-time by 17-year-old Letheran, who survived the 45 minutes and extra-time without being beaten.

9 February 1974: United's 2–0 victory at Old Trafford made it a record 29 games without defeat from the start of the season beating the previous best of 28 set by Liverpool way back in 1893–94. Two weeks later the Whites' tremendous run came to an end at Stoke, who came from 2–0 down to win 3–2.

27 April 1974: Newly crowned champions United finish the season in style as Allan Clarke scored the only goal of the game at QPR in front of the biggest-ever attendance at Loftus Road, 35,353.

Penalty shoot-out hero Glan Letheran.

Match No.	Date	Venue	Opponents	Result	FT	HT	Scorers	Attendance
1	Aug 25	H	Everton	W	3-1	1-0	Bremner, Giles, Jones	39,325
2	28	A	Arsenal	W	2-1	0-1	Lorimer, Madeley	47,429
3	Sep 1	A	Tottenham Hotspur	W	3-0	3-0	Bremner 2, Clarke	42,801
4	5	H	Wolverhampton W	W	4-1	2-1	Lorimer 2 (1 pen), Jones, Bremner	39,946
5	8	H	Birmingham City	W	3-0	2-0	Lorimer 3 (1 pen)	39,736
6	11	A	Wolverhampton W	W	2-0	2-0	Jones, Clarke	36,980
7	15	A	Southampton	W	2-1	1-0	Clarke 2	27,770
8	22	H	Manchester United	D	0-0	0-0		47,058
9	29	A	Norwich City	W	1-0	1-0	Giles	31,993
10	Oct 6	H	Stoke City	D	1-1	1-0	Jones	36,562
11	13	A	Leicester City	D	2-2	2-2	Jones, Bremner	36,978
12	20	H	Liverpool	W	1-0	1-0	Jones	44,911
13	27	A	Manchester City	W	1-0	0-0	Bates	45,346
14	Nov 3	H	West Ham United	W	4-1	2-0	Bates, Jones 2, Clarke	36,869
15	10	A	Burnley	D	0-0	0-0		37,894
16	17	H	Coventry City	W	3-0	1-0	Clarke, Jordan, Bremner	35,552
17	24	A	Derby County	D	0-0	0-0		36,003
18	Dec 1	H	Queen's Park R	D	2-2	0-1	Bremner, Jones	32,194
19	8	A	Ipswich Town	W	3-0	0-0	Yorath, Jones, Clarke	27,110
20	15	A	Chelsea	W	2-1	1-0	Jordan, Jones	40,768
21	22	H	Norwich City	W	1-0	0-0	Yorath	34,747
22	26	A	Newcastle United	W	1-0	1-0	Madeley	54,474
23	29	A	Birmingham City	D	1-1	0-1	Jordan	50,451
24	Jan 1	H	Tottenham Hotspur	D	1-1	1-0	Jones	46,545
25	12	H	Southampton	W	2-1	1-0	Jones, Jordan	35,000
26	19	A	Everton	D	0-0	0-0		55,811
27	Feb 2	H	Chelsea	D	1-1	0-1	Cherry	41,510
28	5	H	Arsenal	W	3-1	0-1	Simpson (og), Jordan 2	26,778
29	9	A	Manchester United	W	2-0	0-0	Jones, Jordan	60,025
30	23	A	Stoke City	L	2-3	2-2	Bremner, Clarke	39,598
31	26	H	Leicester City	D	1-1	1-0	Lorimer (pen)	30,489
32	Mar 2	H	Newcastle United	D	1-1	0-0	Clarke	46,611
33	9	H	Manchester City	W	1-0	1-0	Lorimer (pen)	36,578
34	16	A	Liverpool	L	0-1	0-0		56,003
35	23	H	Burnley	L	1-4	1-2	Clarke	39,335
36	30	A	West Ham United	L	1-3	1-0	Clarke	37,480
37	Apr 5	H	Derby County	W	2-0	1-0	Lorimer, Bremner	37,838
38	13	A	Coventry City	D	0-0	0-0		35,182
39	15	H	Sheffield United	D	0-0	0-0		41,140
40	16	A	Sheffield United	W	2-0	0-0	Lorimer 2 (1 pen)	39,972
41	20	H	Ipswich Town	W	3-2	2-1	Lorimer, Bremner, Clarke	44,015
42	27	A	Queen's Park R	W	1-0	0-0	Clarke	35,353
								Appearances
								Sub appearances
							One own-goal	Goals

FL Cup

R2	Oct 8	A	Ipswich Town	L	0-2	0-1		26,385
								Appearances
								Sub appearances
								Goals

FA Cup

R3	Jan 5	A	Wolverhampton W	D	1-1	0-0	Lorimer (pen)	38,132
Rep	9	H	Wolverhampton W	W	1-0	0-0	Jones	42,747
R4	26	A	Peterborough U	W	4-1	4-0	Lorimer, Jordan 2, Yorath	28,000
R5	Feb 16	A	Bristol City	D	1-1	1-0	Bremner	37,000
Rep	19	H	Bristol City	L	0-1	0-0		47,128
								Appearances
								Sub appearances
								Goals

UEFA Cup

R1	Sep 19	A	Stromsgodset	D	1-1	1-0	Clarke	16,276
	Oct 3	H	Stromsgodset	W	6-1	3-1	Clarke 2, Jones 2, F.T. Gray, Bates	18,711
R2	21	H	Hibernian	D	0-0	0-0		27,145
	Nov 3	A	Hibernian	D	0-0*	0-0		36,051
R3	28	H	Vitoria Setubal	W	1-0	0-0	Cherry	14,196
	Dec 12	A	Vitoria Setubal	L	1-3	0-0	Liddell	25,000
								Appearances
								Sub appearances
								Goals

* After extra-time. Won 5-4 on penalties

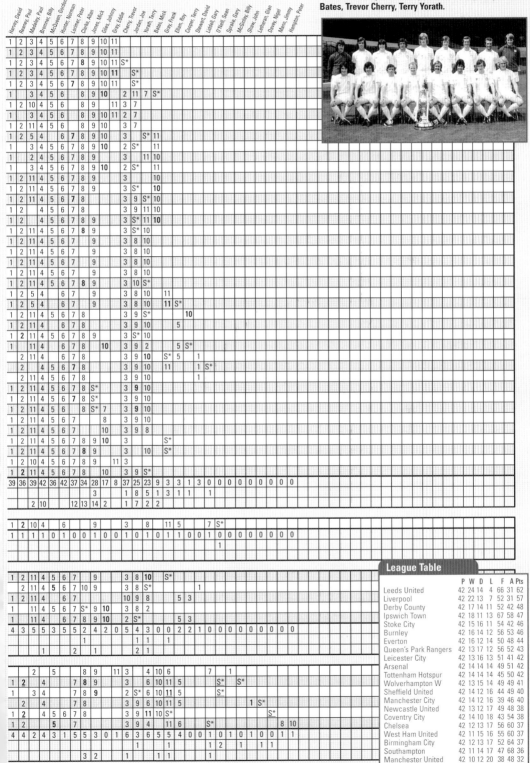

Champions for the second time, 1973–74 vintage. Back row, left to right: David Harvey, Joe Jordan, Eddie Gray, Gordon McQueen, Allan Clarke, Paul Madeley, Paul Reaney, David Stewart. Front row: Frank Gray, Peter Lorimer, Johnny Giles, Billy Bremner, Terry Cooper, Mick Bates, Trevor Cherry, Terry Yorath.

Harvey, David	Reaney, Paul	Madeley, Paul	Bremner, Billy	McQueen, Gordon	Hunter, Norman	Lorimer, Peter	Clarke, Allan	Jones, Mick	Giles, Johnny	Gray, Eddie	Cherry, Trevor	Jordan, Joe	Yorath, Terry	Bates, Mick	Gray, Frank	Ellam, Roy	Cooper, Terry	Stewart, David	Liddell, Gary	O'Neill, Sean	Sprake, Gary	McGinlay, Billy	Shaw, John	Letheran, Glan	Davey, Nigel	Mann, Jimmy	Hampton, Peter
1	2	3	4	5	6	7	8	9	10	11																	
1	2	3	4	5	6	7	8	9	10	11																	
1	2	3	4	5	6	7	**8**	9	10	11	S*																
1	2	3	4	5	6	7	8	9	10	**11**		S*															
1	2	3	4	5	6	**7**	8	9	10	11		S*															
1		3	4	5	6		8	9	**10**		2	11	7	S*													
1	2	10	4	5	6		8	9		11	3	7															
1		3	4	5	6		8	9	10	11	2	7															
1	2	11	4	5	6		8	9	10		3	7															
1	2	5	4		6	**7**	8	9	10		3		S*	11													
1		3	4	5	6	7	8	9	**10**		2	S*		11													
1		2	4	5	6	7	8	9			3		11	10													
1		3	4	5	6	7	8	9	**10**		2	S*		11													
1	2	11	4	5	6	7	8	9			3			10													
1	2	11	4	5	6	7	8	9			3	S*		**10**													
1	2	11	4	5	6	**7**	8				3	9	S*	10													
1	2		4	5	6	7	8				3	9	11	10													
1	2		4	5	6	7	8	9			3	S*	11	**10**													
1	2	11	4	5	6	7	**8**	9			3	S*	10														
1	2	11	4	5	6	7		9			3	8	10														
1	2	11	4	5	6	7		9			3	8	10														
1	2	11	4	5	6	7		9			3	8	10														
1	2	11	4	5	6	7		9			3	8	10														
1	2	11	4	5	6	7	**8**	9			3	10	S*														
1	2	5	4		6	7		9			3	8	10		11												
1	2	5	4		6	7		9			3	8	10		**11**	S*											
1	2	11	4	5	6	7	8				3	9	S*				**10**										
1	2	11	4		6	7	8				3	9	10			5											
1	**2**	11	4	5	6	7	8	9			3	S*	10														
1		11	4		6	7	8		**10**		3	9	2			5	S*										
	2	11	4		6	7	8				3	9	**10**		S*	5		1									
	2		4	5	6	**7**	8				3	9	10		11			1	S*								
	2	11	4	5	6	7	8				3	9	10					1									
1	2	11	4	5	6	7	8	S*			3	**9**	10														
1	2	11	4	5	6	**7**	8	S*			3	9	10														
1	2	11	4	5	6		8	S*	7		3	**9**	10														
1	2	11	4	5	6	7			8		3	9	10														
1	2	11	4	5	6	7			10		3	9	8														
1	2	11	4	5	6	7	8	9	**10**		3				S*												
1	2	11	4	5	6	7	**8**	9			3		10		S*												
1	2	10	4	5	6	7	8	9		11	3																
1	**2**	11	4	5	6	7	8		10		3	9	S*														
39	36	39	42	36	42	37	34	28	17	8	37	25	23	9	3	3	1	3	0	0	0	0	0	0	0	0	0
								3			1	8	5	1	3	1	1		1								
		2	10			12	13	14	2		1	7	2	2													

1	**2**	10	4		6			9			3		8		11	5			7	S*							
1	1	1	1	0	1	0	0	1	0	0	1	0	1	0	1	1	0	0	1	0	0	0	0	0	0	0	0
																				1							

1	2	11	4	5	6	7		9			3	8	**10**		S*												
	2	11	4	**5**	6	7	10	9			3	8	S*					1									
1	2	11	4		6	7					10	9	8			5	3										
1		11	4	5	6	7	S*	9	**10**		3	8	2														
1		11	4		6	7	8	9	**10**		2	S*				5	3										
4	3	5	5	3	5	5	2	4	2	0	5	4	3	0	0	2	2	1	0	0	0	0	0	0	0	0	0
							1					1	1		1												
			1			2		1				2	1														

		2		5			8	9		11	3		4	10	6				7		1						
1	**2**		4			7	**8**	9			3		6	10	11	5				S*		S*					
1		3	4			7	8	**9**			2	S*	6	10	11	5				S*							
	2		4			7	8				3	9	6	10	11	5							**1**	S*			
1	**2**		4	5	6	7	8				3	9	**11**	10	S*										S*		
1	2			**5**		7					3	9	4		11	6			S*							8	10
4	4	2	4	3	1	5	5	3	0	1	6	3	6	5	5	4	0	0	1	0	1	0	1	0	0	1	1
												1			1				1	2		1		1	1		
							3	2			1			1	1				1								

League Table

	P	W	D	L	F	A	Pts
Leeds United	42	24	14	4	66	31	62
Liverpool	42	22	13	7	52	31	57
Derby County	42	17	14	11	52	42	48
Ipswich Town	42	18	11	13	67	58	47
Stoke City	42	15	16	11	54	42	46
Burnley	42	16	14	12	56	53	46
Everton	42	16	12	14	50	48	44
Queen's Park Rangers	42	13	17	12	56	52	43
Leicester City	42	13	16	13	51	41	42
Arsenal	42	14	14	14	49	51	42
Tottenham Hotspur	42	14	14	14	45	50	42
Wolverhampton W	42	13	15	14	49	49	41
Sheffield United	42	14	12	16	44	49	40
Manchester City	42	14	12	16	39	46	40
Newcastle United	42	13	12	17	49	48	38
Coventry City	42	14	10	18	43	54	38
Chelsea	42	12	13	17	56	60	37
West Ham United	42	11	15	16	55	60	37
Birmingham City	42	12	13	17	52	64	37
Southampton	42	11	14	17	47	68	36
Manchester United	42	10	12	20	38	48	32
Norwich City	42	7	15	20	37	62	29

1974-75

Division One

Manager: Brian Clough until September then Jimmy Armfield CBE

Final Position: 9th

Did you know that?

10 August 1974: The FA Charity Shield against Liverpool at Wembley was Brian Clough's first game in charge of Leeds. Billy Bremner and Kevin Keegan were sent off for fighting, the game finished 1–1 and United lost 6–5 on penalties, goalkeeper David Harvey missing the decisive kick.

14 August 1974: United broke their transfer record with the £250,000 signing of Nottingham Forest's Duncan McKenzie

14 September 1974: Just days after Brian Clough's dismissal, Maurice Lindley takes charge of the team for the game at Burnley where United lost 2–1 and see Gordon McQueen and Clarets forward Ray Hankin, later to join Leeds, sent off.

Johnny Giles made his final Leeds appearance in the European Cup Final.

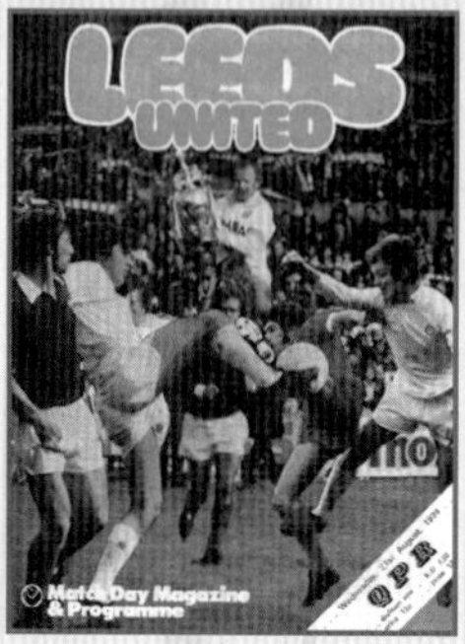

Match No.	Date		Venue	Opponents	Result	FT	HT	Scorers	Attendance
1	Aug	17	A	Stoke City	L	0-3	0-0		33,534
2		21	H	Queen's Park R	L	0-1	0-1		31,497
3		24	H	Birmingham City	W	1-0	0-0	Clarke	30,820
4		27	A	Queen's Park R	D	1-1	1-0	Yorath	24,965
5		31	A	Manchester City	L	1-2	1-1	Clarke	37,919
6	Sep	7	H	Luton Town	D	1-1	1-1	Clarke	26,450
7		14	A	Burnley	L	1-2	1-0	Lorimer	25,122
8		21	H	Sheffield United	W	5-1	2-0	Clarke 2, McQueen, Lorimer (pen), Yorath	33,382
9		28	A	Everton	L	2-3	1-2	Clarke, Yorath	41,824
10	Oct	5	H	Arsenal	W	2-0	0-0	McKenzie 2	32,784
11		12	A	Ipswich Town	D	0-0	0-0		29,815
12		15	A	Birmingham City	L	0-1	0-0		36,513
13		19	H	Wolverhampton W	W	2-0	1-0	Clarke, McKenzie	31,224
14		26	A	Liverpool	L	0-1	0-0		54,996
15	Nov	2	H	Derby County	L	0-1	0-0		33,551
16		9	A	Coventry City	W	3-1	2-0	O'Hare, Hindley (og), Bremner	25,414
17		16	H	Middlesbrough	D	2-2	2-1	McKenzie 2	45,488
18		23	A	Carlisle United	W	2-1	0-1	Jordan, McKenzie	19,975
19		30	H	Chelsea	W	2-0	1-0	Cherry, Clarke	30,441
20	Dec	4	H	Tottenham Hotspur	W	2-1	1-0	McKenzie, Lorimer (pen)	25,832
21		7	A	West Ham United	L	1-2	0-1	McKenzie	39,562
22		14	H	Stoke City	W	3-1	1-0	McQueen, Lorimer, Yorath	34,685
23		21	A	Newcastle United	L	0-3	0-0		32,535
24		26	H	Burnley	D	2-2	1-1	Jordan, Lorimer	34,724
25		28	A	Leicester City	W	2-0	2-0	F.T. Gray, McKenzie	29,699
26	Jan	11	H	West Ham United	W	2-1	1-1	Clarke, McKenzie	40,099
27		18	A	Chelsea	W	2-0	1-0	McKenzie, Yorath	34,733
28	Feb	1	H	Coventry City	D	0-0	0-0		33,901
29		8	A	Derby County	D	0-0	0-0		33,641
30		22	A	Middlesbrough	W	1-0	1-0	Clarke	39,500
31		25	H	Carlisle United	W	3-1	1-0	Lorimer, Clarke, E. Gray	32,346
32	Mar	1	H	Manchester City	D	2-2	1-1	Lorimer 2	47,489
33		15	H	Everton	D	0-0	0-0		50,084
34		22	A	Luton Town	L	1-2	0-2	Jordan	23,048
35		29	H	Newcastle United	D	1-1	0-1	Clarke	40,994
36		31	H	Leicester City	D	2-2	1-0	Clarke, Giles	29,898
37	Apr	1	A	Sheffield United	D	1-1	1-0	Madeley	38,442
38		5	H	Liverpool	L	0-2	0-1		34,971
39		12	A	Arsenal	W	2-1	1-0	Clarke, Hunter	36,619
40		19	H	Ipswich Town	W	2-1	1-1	Cherry, Harris	30,174
41		26	A	Wolverhampton W	D	1-1	0-1	F.T. Gray	34,875
42		28	A	Tottenham Hotspur	L	2-4	0-1	Jordan, Lorimer	49,886
									Appearances
									Sub appearances
								One own-goal	Goals

FL Cup

R2	Sep	10	A	Huddersfield Town	D	1-1	0-0	Lorimer	15,013
Rep		24	H	Huddersfield Town	D	1-1*	0-0	Clarke	18,496
2Rep	Oct	7	H	Huddersfield Town	W	2-1	0-0	Bates, Lorimer (pen)	14,599
R3		9	A	Bury	W	2-1	1-0	Lorimer, Cherry	16,354
R4	Nov	13	A	Chester	L	0-3	0-1		19,000
									Sub appearances
									Goals

* After extra-time (score 1-1 after 90 minutes)

FA Cup

R3	Jan	4	H	Cardiff City	W	4-1	4-0	E. Gray, Clarke 2, McKenzie	31,572
R4		25	H	Wimbledon	D	0-0	0-0		46,230
Rep	Feb	10	A	Wimbledon	W	1-0†	0-0	Bassett (og)	45,071
R5		18	A	Derby County	W	1-0	0-0	Nish (og)	35,298
R6	Mar	8	A	Ipswich Town	D	0-0	0-0		38,010
Rep		11	H	Ipswich Town	D	1-1*	0-1	McKenzie	50,074
2Rep		25	N	Ipswich Town	D	0-0*‡	0-0		35,195
3Rep		27	N	Ipswich Town	L	2-3‡	1-1	Clarke, Giles	19,510
									Sub appearances
								Two own-goals	Goals

* After extra-time (score 1-1 after 90 minutes) † At Selhurst Park, London
‡ At Filbert Street, Leicester

European Cup

R1	Sep	18	H	FC Zurich	W	4-1	3-0	Clarke 2, Lorimer (pen), Jordan	20,012
	Oct	2	A	FC Zurich	L	1-2	1-2	Clarke	16,500
R2		23	A	Ujpest Dosza	W	2-1	2-1	Lorimer, McQueen	20,000
	Nov	6	H	Ujpest Dosza	W	3-0	1-0	McQueen, Bremner, Yorath	28,091
R3	Mar	5	H	Anderlecht	W	3-0	2-0	Jordan, McQueen, Lorimer	43,195
		19	A	Anderlecht	W	1-0	0-0	Bremner	29,091
SF	Apr	9	H	Barcelona	W	2-1	1-0	Bremner, Clarke	50,393
		23	A	Barcelona	D	1-1	1-0	Lorimer	110,000
F	May	28	N	Bayern Munich	L	0-2†	0-0		48,374
									Appearances
									Sub appearances
									Goals

† At Parc des Princes, Paris

FA Charity Shield

	Aug	10	N	Liverpool	D	1-1*	0-1	Cherry	67,000

* At Wembley, London. Lost 6-5 on penalties

Challenge Match

	May	19	A	Scotland U-23	L	2-3‡	2-3	Lorimer 2	9,978

‡ At Hampden Park, Glasgow

Facing the camera at the start of 1974–75 – minus new manager Brian Clough. Back row, left to right: Paul Madeley, Norman Hunter, Trevor Cherry, Joe Jordan, Gordon McQueen, David Stewart, David Harvey, Eddie Gray, Allan Clarke, Paul Reaney. Front row: Peter Lorimer, Johnny Giles, Billy Bremner, Terry Cooper, Mick Bates, Frank Gray, Terry Yorath.

Harvey, David	Reaney, Paul	Cooper, Terry	Bremner, Billy	McQueen, Gordon	Cherry, Trevor	Lorimer, Peter	Madeley, Paul	Jordan, Joe	Giles, Johnny	McKenzie, Duncan	Bates, Mick	McGovern, John	Hunter, Norman	Clarke, Allan	O'Hare, John	Yorath, Terry	Gray, Frank	Stewart, David	Gray, Eddie	Hampton, Peter	Stevenson, Byron	Liddell, Gary	Letheran, Glan	Harris, Carl	Thomas, Gwyn
1	2	3	4	5	6	7	8	9	10	11															
1	2	3		5	6	7	8	9	10	11	4														
1	2			5	3	7	**11**	S*	10			4	6	8	9										
1	2			5	3	7			10			4	6	8	9	11									
1	2			5	3	7	S*		10			4	6	8	9	**11**									
1	2			5	3	7	11		10			4	6	8	9										
1	2			5	3	7	11	9	10				6	8		4									
1	2			5	3	7	11	9	10				6	8		4									
1	2				3	7	5	9			10		6	8		4	11								
1	2	**3**		5		7	11	9	10	8	S*		6			4									
1	2	11		5	3	7		9	10				6	8		4									
1	2	11		5	3	7		9	10				6	8		4									
1	2	3		5		7	11	9	S*	10			**6**	8		4									
1	2	3		5		7	11	9	**10**	8			6	S*		4									
1	2	3		5		**7**	11		10	S*			6	8	9	4									
1	2	11	4	5	3	7	10							8	9	6									
1	2	3	4	5			11	9	10	7				8		6									
1	2		4	5	3		6	9	10	7				8		11									
1	2		4	5	3		6	9	10	7				8		11									
	2		4	5	3	10	6	9		7				8		11		1							
1	2		4	5	3	10	6	9		7				8		11									
1	2		4	5	3	10	6	9	S*	7				8		**11**									
1	2		4	5	3	10	6	9		7				8		11									
1	2		4	5		10	6	**9**	S*	7				8		11	3								
	2		4	5		9	6		10	7				8		11	3	1							
1	2		4	5		9	6		10	7				8			3		11						
1	2		4	5		9	6		10	7				**8**		S*	3		11						
1	2		4	5		7	6			9				8		10	3		11						
1	2		4	**5**	S*	7	6			9				8		10	3		11						
	2	11	4			7	5	9	10				6	8			3	1							
	2		4			7	6	9	10				5	8			3	1	11						
	2		4			7	5	S*		9			6	8		10	3	1	11						
			4		2	7	5			9			6	8		10	3	1	11						
	2			**5**	S*		4	**9**	10	7			6			8	3	1	11						
	2		4		**3**		5	9	10	7			6	8			11	1		S*					
	2		4				5	9	10	7			6	**8**		11	3	1		S*					
			4			7	5			9			6			10	3	1	11		2	8			
			4	5	S*	7	2	9		8			6			10	**3**	1	11						
	2		4	5	3	S*	11	9	10	7			6	8				1							
	2		4	5	3	7	8		**10**				6			9			11				1	S*	
	2		4	5	3	7	6							**8**		10	11	1						9	S*
	2		4		3	7	**5**	9					6			10	8	1	11					S*	
27	39	11	27	33	24	35	38	26	26	26	2	4	25	33	6	32	18	14	12	0	1	1	1	1	0
					3	1		3	3	1	1			1		1				2				2	
			1	2	2	9	1	4	1	11			1	14	1	5	2		1					1	

1	2			5	3	7	11	9	10		4		6	8																
1	2				3	7	5	9	**10**	11	S*		6	8		4														
1	2			5	3	7	11			8	**10**		6		9	4	S*													
	2	8	**4**	5	3	7	S*	9		11			6			10		1												
1	2	3	**10**	5	6	7	11	9			S*			8		4														
Appearances					4	5	2	2	4	5	5	4	4	2	3	2	0	4	3	1	4	0	1	0	0	0	0	0	0	0
							1				2						1													
					1	3					1			1																

1	**2**		4	5	S*	7	6		10	9				8			3		11													
1	2		4	5		9	6		10	7						8	3		11													
1	2		4				6	9	10	7				8		5	3		11													
	2		4	5			6	9		7				8		10	3	1	11													
			4	5			2	9	10				6	8		7	3	1	11													
	2		4			7	5	9	10	S*			6	8		11	3	1														
	2		4			**7**	5	9	10	S*			6	8		11	3	1														
	2		4				5	9	10	S*			6	8		**11**	3	1	7													
		Appearances					3	7	0	8	4	0	4	8	6	7	4	0	0	4	7	0	7	8	5	6	0	0	0	0	0	0
					1					3																						
									1	2				3					1													

1	2	3		5		7	11	9	10				6	8		4									
1	2				3	7	5	9			10		6	8		4	**11**			S*					
1	2	3		5		7	11	9	10	8			6			4									
1	2	3	9	5	S*	**7**	11		10				**6**	8		4								S*	
			4	5		7	2	9	10				6	8		S*	3	1	11						
	2		4	5		7	11	9					6	8		10	3	1							
	2		4	5			6	9	10					8		7	3	1	11						
			4	5	2	11	7	9					6	8		10	3	1							
	2		4			7	5	9	10				6	8		**11**	3	1	S*						
4	7	3	6	7	2	8	9	8	6	1	1	0	8	8	0	8	6	5	2	0	0	0	0	0	0
					1											1			1	1				1	
			3	3			4	2						4		1									

1	2		4	5	3	7		9	10	S*			6	**8**					11						

1	**2**		4		S*	7	5	**9**		S*			6	8		10	3		11				S*		

League Table

	P	W	D	L	F	A	Pts
Derby County	42	21	11	10	67	49	53
Liverpool	42	20	11	11	60	39	51
Ipswich Town	42	23	5	14	66	44	51
Everton	42	16	18	8	56	42	50
Stoke City	42	17	15	10	64	48	49
Sheffield United	42	18	13	11	58	51	49
Middlesbrough	42	18	12	12	54	40	48
Manchester City	42	18	10	14	54	54	46
Leeds United	42	16	13	13	57	49	45
Burnley	42	17	11	14	68	67	45
Queen's Park Rangers	42	16	10	16	54	54	42
Wolverhampton W	42	14	11	17	57	54	39
West Ham United	42	13	13	16	58	59	39
Coventry City	42	12	15	15	51	62	39
Newcastle United	42	15	9	18	59	72	39
Arsenal	42	13	11	18	47	49	37
Birmingham City	42	14	9	19	53	61	37
Leicester City	42	12	12	18	46	60	36
Tottenham Hotspur	42	13	8	21	52	63	34
Luton Town	42	11	11	20	47	65	33
Chelsea	42	9	15	18	42	72	33
Carlisle United	42	12	5	25	43	59	29

1975-76

Division One

Manager: Jimmy Armfield CBE

Final Position: 5th

Did you know that?

1 November 1975: *Match of the Day* viewers see Norman Hunter and Derby's Francis Lee slug it out in a punch-up which continued in the tunnel after they were dismissed at the Baseball Ground by referee Derek Nippard.

20 December 1975: Allan Clarke's winner against Aston Villa was his 100th goal for United.

Norman Hunter, whose famous punch-up with Francis Lee was caught on camera.

Match No.	Date		Venue	Opponents	Result	FT	HT	Scorers	Attendance
1	Aug	16	A	Aston Villa	W	2-1	1-1	Lorimer 2 (1 pen)	46,026
2		20	A	Norwich City	D	1-1	0-0	Cherry	25,301
3		23	H	Ipswich Town	W	1-0	0-0	Lorimer	30,912
4		26	H	Liverpool	L	0-3	0-1		36,186
5		30	A	Sheffield United	W	2-0	1-0	McKenzie, Clarke	29,996
6	Sep	6	H	Wolverhampton W	W	3-0	2-0	McQueen, Clarke, McKenzie	24,460
7		13	A	Stoke City	L	2-3	0-2	Lorimer 2 (1 pen)	23,129
8		20	H	Tottenham Hotspur	D	1-1	1-0	Lorimer	27,372
9		27	A	Burnley	W	1-0	1-0	Cherry	23,190
10	Oct	4	H	Queen's Park R	W	2-1	0-0	Clarke, Lorimer	30,943
11		11	H	Manchester United	L	1-2	0-1	Clarke, Lorimer	40,264
12		18	A	Birmingham City	D	2-2	2-2	Cherry, Hunter	33,775
13		25	H	Coventry City	W	2-0	0-0	Yorath, Clarke	25,946
14	Nov	1	A	Derby County	L	2-3	1-2	Cherry, McKenzie	33,107
15		8	H	Newcastle United	W	3-0	2-0	McKenzie 2, Yorath	39,304
16		15	A	Middlesbrough	D	0-0	0-0		33,000
17		22	H	Birmingham City	W	3-0	1-0	Bremner, McKenzie 2	26,640
18		29	H	Everton	W	5-2	3-1	Lorimer 2 (1 pen), Clarke 2, E. Gray	30,879
19	Dec	6	A	Arsenal	W	2-1	0-0	McKenzie 2	36,003
20		13	A	Ipswich Town	L	1-2	0-0	McKenzie	26,858
21		20	H	Aston Villa	W	1-0	1-0	Clarke	29,118
22		26	A	Manchester City	W	1-0	0-0	Madeley	48,077
23		27	H	Leicester City	W	4-0	1-0	Clarke, McKenzie 2, Lorimer	45,139
24	Jan	10	H	Stoke City	W	2-0	2-0	McKenzie, Bremner	36,906
25		17	A	Wolverhampton W	D	1-1	1-0	McAlle (og)	34,925
26		31	H	Norwich City	L	0-3	0-1		27,254
27	Feb	7	A	Liverpool	L	0-2	0-1		54,525
28		21	H	Middlesbrough	L	0-2	0-1		32,994
29		23	A	West Ham United	D	1-1	0-0	McKenzie	28,025
30		28	A	Coventry City	W	1-0	0-0	F.T. Gray	25,563
31	Mar	2	H	Derby County	D	1-1	1-1	F.T. Gray (pen)	40,608
32		9	H	West Ham United	D	1-1	0-0	Jordan	28,453
33		13	A	Manchester United	L	2-3	0-2	Cherry, Bremner	59,429
34		20	A	Everton	W	3-1	0-0	Bremner, Jordan, Harris	28,566
35		27	H	Arsenal	W	3-0	2-0	Clarke 2, Bremner	26,657
36		31	A	Newcastle United	W	3-2	2-1	Oates (og), Cherry, Harris	32,685
37	Apr	3	H	Burnley	W	2-1	1-1	McKenzie, Hampton	25,384
38		10	A	Tottenham Hotspur	D	0-0	0-0		40,359
39		14	H	Sheffield United	L	0-1	0-0		22,799
40		17	H	Manchester City	W	2-1	0-1	McNiven, Harris	33,514
41		20	A	Leicester City	L	1-2	0-0	McKenzie	24,240
42		24	A	Queen's Park R	L	0-2	0-0		31,002
									Appearances
									Sub appearances
								Two own-goals	Goals

FL Cup

Round	Date		Venue	Opponents	Result	FT	HT	Scorers	Attendance
R2	Sep	9	H	Ipswich Town	W	3-2	3-1	McKenzie, Lorimer (pen), Clarke	15,318
R3	Oct	8	H	Notts County	L	0-1	0-0		19,122
									Appearances
									Sub appearances
									Goals

FA Cup

Round	Date		Venue	Opponents	Result	FT	HT	Scorers	Attendance
R3	Jan	3	A	Notts County	W	1-0	1-0	Clarke	31,129
R4		24	H	Crystal Palace	L	0-1	0-1		43,116
									Appearances
									Sub appearances
									Goals

Back row, left to right: Jimmy Armfield (manager), Duncan McKenzie, Joe Jordan, Gordon McQueen, David Harvey, David Stewart, Paul Madeley, Norman Hunter, Paul Reaney. Front row: Terry Yorath, Frank Gray, Eddie Gray, Peter Lorimer, Trevor Cherry, Billy Bremner, Allan Clarke.

Harvey, David	Reaney, Paul	Gray, Frank	Bremner, Billy	McQueen, Gordon	Cherry, Trevor	Lorimer, Peter	Clarke, Allan	McKenzie, Duncan	Yorath, Terry	Madeley, Paul	Hunter, Norman	Gray, Eddie	Harris, Carl	Stewart, David	Jordan, Joe	Stevenson, Byron	Parkinson, Keith	Bates, Mick	Hampton, Peter	McNiven, David
1	2	3	4	5	6	7	8	9	10	11										
1	2	3	4	5	6	7	8	9	10	11										
1	2	3		5	6	7	8	9	10		4	11								
1	2	3	4	5	6	7	8	9	10	11										
1		3	4	5	2	7	8	9	10	11	6									
1		3	4	5	2	7	8	9	10	11	6									
1		3	4	5	2	7	8	**9**	10	11	6		S*							
1		3	4	5	2	7	8	9	10	11	6	S*								
1	2	3	9		6	7	8		10	5	4	11								
1	S*	3	4	**5**	2	7	8	9	10	11	6									
	2	3	4		7		8	**9**	10	5	6	11	S*	1						
1	2	3	4		7		8	9	10	5	6	11								
1	2	3	4		11	7	8	9	10	5	6									
1	2	3	4		5	7	8	9	10	11	6									
1	2	3	4	**5**	8	7		9	10	6		11	S*							
1	2	3	4		6	7	8	9	10	5		11								
1	2	3	4		6	7	8	9	10	5		11								
1	2	3	4		6	7	8	9	**10**	5		11			S*					
1	2	3	4		6	7	8	9	10	5		11								
1	2	3	4		6	7	8	9	10	5		11								
1	2	3	4		6	7	8	9	10	5		11								
1	2	3	4		6	7	8	9	10	5		11								
1	**2**	3	4		10	7	8	9		5	6	11	S*							
1	2	**3**	4		11	7	8	9	10	5	6		S*							
1	2	3	4		11	7	8	9	10	5	6									
1	2	3			4	**7**	8	9	10	5	6	11			S*					
1	**2**	3				4	8	7	10	5	6	11			9	S*				
1	2	3				**4**	8	7	10	5	6	11			9		S*			
1	2	3			8			7	10	5	6	11			9			4		
1	2	3			8		S*	7	10	5	6	**11**			9			4		
1	2	3			11		8	7	10	5	6				9			4		
1	**2**	3			11		8	7	10	5	6	S*			9			4		
1		3	4		2	10	8	7	5		6	11			9					
1		3	4		2		8		10	5	6	11	7		9					
1	2	3	4		10		8	S*		5	6	11	7		**9**					
1	2	3	4		10		8			5	6	11	7		9					
	2	3	4		10			8	**11**	5	6		7	1	9				S*	
1		3	4		2		8	10			6	11	7		9		5			
1		3	4		2	S*	8	9		10	6	11	**7**				5			
1		3	4		2			10		8	6	11	7		9		**5**			S*
1		3	4		2			10	8	5	6	**11**	7		9					S*
1	2	**3**	4		8	S*		10		5	6	11	7		9					
40	31	42	34	10	40	27	35	38	35	39	31	27	9	2	15	0	3	4	0	0
	1					2	1	1				2	5		2	1			1	2
		2	5	1	6	10	11	16	2	1	1	1	3		2				1	1

1		3	4		2	7	8	9	10	5	6	11								
1	2	10	4		3	7		9		5	6	11	S*							**8**
2	1	2	2	0	2	2	1	2	1	2	2	2	0	0	0	0	0	0	0	1
													1							
						1	1	1												

1	2	3	4		6	7	8	9	11	5	10									
1	2	3	**4**		6	7	8	9	10	5	S*	11								
2	2	2	2	0	2	2	2	2	2	2	1	1	0	0	0	0	0	0	0	0
											1									
							1													

League Table

	P	W	D	L	F	A	Pts
Liverpool	42	23	14	5	66	31	60
Queen's Park Rangers	42	24	11	7	67	33	59
Manchester United	42	23	10	9	68	42	56
Derby County	42	21	11	10	75	58	53
Leeds United	42	21	9	12	65	46	51
Ipswich Town	42	16	14	12	54	48	46
Leicester City	42	13	19	10	48	51	45
Manchester City	42	16	11	15	64	46	43
Tottenham Hotspur	42	14	15	13	63	63	43
Norwich City	42	16	10	16	58	58	42
Everton	42	15	12	15	60	66	42
Stoke City	42	15	11	16	48	50	41
Middlesbrough	42	15	10	17	46	45	40
Coventry City	42	13	14	15	47	57	40
Newcastle United	42	15	9	18	71	62	39
Aston Villa	42	11	17	14	51	59	39
Arsenal	42	13	10	19	47	53	36
West Ham United	42	13	10	19	48	71	36
Birmingham City	42	13	7	22	57	75	33
Wolverhampton W	42	10	10	22	51	68	30
Burnley	42	9	10	23	43	66	28
Sheffield United	42	6	10	26	33	82	22

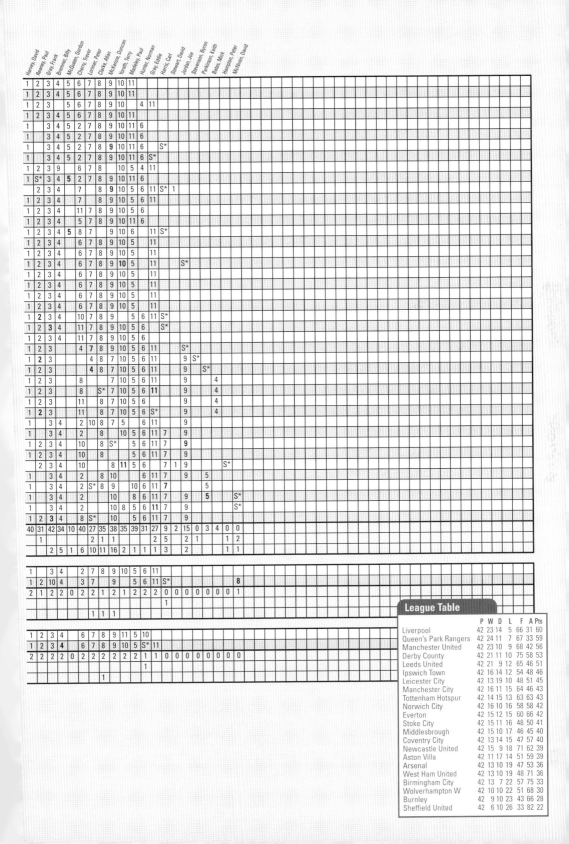

1976-77

Division One

Manager: Jimmy Armfield CBE

Final Position: 10th

Did you know that?

18 December 1976: Former Chairman Sam Bolton died at the age of 82.

5 February 1977: Peter Lorimer, usually so deadly from the spot, missed two penalties against Middlesbrough, but United still won 2–1.

23 March 1977: United's 3–2 win against Norwich saw both full-backs, Paul Reaney and Peter Hampton, get on the scoresheet – just over two months after they both scored in a 5–2 thumping of the Canaries in the FA Cup.

Paul Reaney netted Cup and League goals against Norwich.

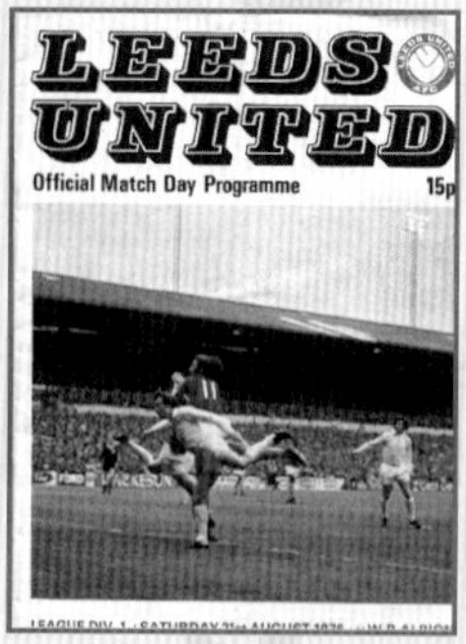

Match No.	Date	Venue	Opponents	Result	FT	HT	Scorers	Attendance
1	Aug 21	H	West Bromwich Alb	D	2-2	0-2	Harris, Clarke	40,248
2	24	A	Birmingham City	D	0-0	0-0		35,399
3	28	A	Coventry City	L	2-4	1-1	F.T. Gray, Currie	18,227
4	Sep 4	H	Derby County	W	2-0	2-0	E. Gray, Cherry	33,352
5	11	A	Tottenham Hotspur	L	0-1	0-1		35,525
6	18	H	Newcastle United	D	2-2	0-0	McNiven, Harris	35,089
7	25	A	Middlesbrough	L	0-1	0-0		25,000
8	Oct 2	H	Manchester United	L	0-2	0-2		44,512
9	6	A	West Ham United	W	3-1	1-1	E. Gray, Lorimer, Harris	21,909
10	16	A	Norwich City	W	2-1	0-0	F.T. Gray, E. Gray	25,217
11	23	H	Liverpool	D	1-1	0-0	McNiven	44,696
12	30	H	Arsenal	W	2-1	1-0	Cherry, Jordan	33,566
13	Nov 6	A	Everton	W	2-0	0-0	McQueen, Jordan	33,618
14	10	H	Stoke City	D	1-1	0-0	Lorimer	29,199
15	20	A	Ipswich Town	D	1-1	0-0	McQueen	30,096
16	27	H	Leicester City	D	2-2	1-2	Lorimer, McNiven	29,713
17	Dec 11	H	Aston Villa	L	1-3	0-1	McNiven	31,232
18	27	H	Manchester City	L	0-2	0-2		48,708
19	29	A	Sunderland	W	1-0	0-0	Jordan	26,999
20	Jan 3	A	Arsenal	D	1-1	0-0	Clarke	44,090
21	22	A	West Bromwich Alb	W	2-1	2-0	E. Gray, McQueen	25,958
22	Feb 2	H	Birmingham City	W	1-0	1-0	McQueen	22,805
23	5	H	Coventry City	L	1-2	1-1	Jordan	26,058
24	12	A	Derby County	W	1-0	0-0	Jordan	28,350
25	19	H	Tottenham Hotspur	W	2-1	2-1	Jordan, Clarke	26,858
26	Mar 2	A	Newcastle United	L	0-3	0-0		31,995
27	5	H	Middlesbrough	W	2-1	0-0	McQueen 2	32,152
28	8	A	Queen's Park R	D	0-0	0-0		20,386
29	12	A	Manchester United	L	0-1	0-1		60,612
30	23	H	Norwich City	W	3-2	1-2	Reaney, Hampton, Jordan	18,700
31	Apr 2	A	Liverpool	L	1-3	0-2	McQueen	48,791
32	8	A	Manchester City	L	1-2	1-1	Jordan	47,727
33	9	H	Sunderland	D	1-1	0-0	Cherry	32,966
34	12	A	Stoke City	L	1-2	0-0	Jordan	17,960
35	16	H	Ipswich Town	W	2-1	2-1	McGhie, Clarke (pen)	28,578
36	26	H	West Ham United	D	1-1	0-0	Jordan	16,891
37	30	H	Bristol City	W	2-0	1-0	Thomas, E. Gray	21,461
38	May 4	H	Everton	D	0-0	0-0		22,175
39	7	A	Aston Villa	L	1-2	1-0	McNiven	38,205
40	10	A	Bristol City	L	0-1	0-0		23,587
41	14	H	Queen's Park R	L	0-1	0-1		22,226
42	16	A	Leicester City	W	1-0	1-0	F.T. Gray	13,642
								Appearances
								Sub appearances
								Goals

FL Cup

R2	Sep 1	A	Stoke City	L	1-2	1-0	Currie	22,559
								Appearances
								Sub appearances
								Goals

FA Cup

R3	Jan 8	H	Norwich City	W	5-2	5-1	Clarke, Reaney, Jordan, McQueen, Hampton	28,130
R4	29	A	Birmingham City	W	2-1	0-0	Jordan, Clarke	38,000
R5	Feb 26	H	Manchester City	W	1-0	0-0	Cherry	47,731
R6	Mar 19	A	Wolverhampton W	W	1-0	1-0	E,Gray	50,000
SF	Apr 23	N	Manchester United	L	1-2†	0-2	Clarke (pen)	55,000
								Appearances
								Sub appearances
								Goals

† At Hillsborough, Sheffield

United, unusually, face the camera at the start of 1976–77 in their away strip. Several of the 15 internationals pictured here moved on during the course of the campaign, including Billy Bremner, Norman Hunter and Terry Yorath. Back row, left to right: Don Howe (coach), Paul Reaney, Tony Currie, Norman Hunter, David Harvey, Jimmy Armfield, David Stewart, Gordon McQueen, Joe Jordan, Trevor Cherry, Geoff Ladley (physiotherapist). Front row: Frank Gray, Paul Madeley, Allan Clarke, Billy Bremner, Terry Yorath, Peter Lorimer, Eddie Gray.

Harvey, David	Reaney, Paul	Gray, Frank	Cherry, Trevor	Madeley, Paul	Hunter, Norman	Lorimer, Peter	Clarke, Allan	McNiven, David	Currie, Tony	Gray, Eddie	Harris, Carl	Yorath, Terry	Bremner, Billy	Jordan, Joe	McQueen, Gordon	Hampton, Peter	Hankin, Ray	Stevenson, Byron	Stewart, David	Thomas, Gwyn	McGhie, Billy	Whyte, David
1	2	3	4	5	6	**7**	8	9	10	11	S*											
1	2	3	4	5	6		8	9	10	11		7										
1	2	3	7	5	6		8		10	11			4	9								
1	2	3	7	5	6		8	9	10	11			4									
1	2	3	7	5	6		8	9	10	11			4									
1	2	3	7	5	6		8	9	**10**	11	S*		4									
1	2	3	7	8	6	4		9		**11**	10				5	S*						
1	2	3	7	4	**6**	S*	8		10	11				9	5							
1	2	10	7	4	6	8				**11**	S*			9	5	3						
1	2	6	7	4		8			10	11				9	5	3						
1	2	**10**	4	6		7		S*	8	11				9	5	3						
1	2	6	7	4		**8**		S*	10	11				9	5	3						
1	2	6	7	**4**					10	11	S*			9	5	3	8					
1	2	6	4			7			10	11				9	5	3	8					
1	2	6	4			7			10	11				9	5	3	8					
1	2	6	4			7		S*	**10**	11				9	5	3	8					
1	2	6	4			7		8		11				9	5	3		10				
1	2	10	4	6		7	8			11				9	5	3						
1		10	6	4		7	8			11				9	5	3		2				
1	2	7	**4**	6		S*	8		10	11				9	5	3						
1	2	7	4	6			8		10	11				9	5	3						
1	2	7	4	6			8		10	11				9	5	3						
1	2	7	4	6		10	8			11	S*			9	5	**3**						
1	2	7	4	6		11	8		10					9	5	3						
1	2	7	4	6			8		10	11				9	5	3						
1	2	7	4	6			8	S*	**10**	11				9	5	3						
	2	7	**4**	6		S*	8		10	11				9	5	3			1			
	2	7	4	6		10	**8**			11				9	5			3	1	S*		
	2	7	4	6		8		S*	**10**	11				9	5	3			1			
	2	7	4	6		S*	8		10	**11**				9	5	3			1			
		7	6	4		**8**			10	11				9	5	3		2	1	S*		
	2	7	4	6		8			10	11				9	5	3			1			
	2	7	4	6		8			10	**11**	S*			9	5	3			1			
	2	7	4	6		8			10		11			9	5	3			1			
	2	3	4	6		S*	8		10		7			**9**	5				1		11	
			4	6				8	10	11	7			9	5	3		2	1			
		3	4	6					10	11	S*			**9**	5			2	1	7	8	
		3	4	6				8	10	11	9				5			2	1	7		
		8	4	6				**9**	10		11				5	3		2	1	7		S*
		9	4	6				8	10	11	S*				5	3		2	1	**7**		
		9	4	6				8	10	11	S*			**7**		3		2	1			5
	2	9	4	6		5		8	10		11					3			1	7		
26	34	41	42	38	9	21	20	13	35	37	7	1	4	32	34	30	4	10	16	5	2	1
						5		5			9					1				2		1
	1	3	3			3	4	5	1	5	3			10	7	1				1	1	
	2	3	7	5	6		8		10		11		4	9					1			
0	1	1	1	1	1	0	1	0	1	0	1	0	1	1	0	0	0	0	1	0	0	0
									1													
1	2	4		6		7	8		10	11				9	5	3						
1	2	7	4	6			8		10	11				9	5	3						
1	2	7	4	6			8		10	11				9	5	3						
	2	7	4	6			8		10	11				9	5	3			1			
	2	**7**	4	6		S*	8		10	11				9	5	3			1			
3	5	5	4	5	0	1	5	0	5	5	0	0	0	5	5	5	0	0	2	0	0	0
						1																
	1		1				3			1				2	1	1						

League Table

	P	W	D	L	F	A	Pts
Liverpool	42	23	11	8	62	33	57
Manchester City	42	21	14	7	60	34	56
Ipswich Town	42	22	8	12	66	39	52
Aston Villa	42	22	7	13	76	50	51
Newcastle United	42	18	13	11	64	49	49
Manchester United	42	18	11	13	71	62	47
West Bromwich Albion	42	16	13	13	62	56	45
Arsenal	42	16	11	15	64	59	43
Everton	42	14	14	14	62	64	42
Leeds United	42	15	12	15	48	51	42
Leicester City	42	12	18	12	47	60	42
Middlesbrough	42	14	13	15	40	45	41
Birmingham City	42	13	12	17	63	61	38
Queen's Park Rangers	42	13	12	17	47	52	38
Derby County	42	9	19	14	50	55	37
Norwich City	42	14	9	19	47	64	37
West Ham United	42	11	14	17	46	65	36
Bristol City	42	11	13	18	38	48	35
Coventry City	42	10	15	17	48	59	35
Sunderland	42	11	12	19	46	54	34
Stoke City	42	10	14	18	28	51	34
Tottenham Hotspur	42	12	9	21	48	72	33

1977-78

Division One

Manager: Jimmy Armfield CBE

Final Position: 9th

Did you know that?

7 September 1977: David Stewart saved a penalty on his one and only appearance for Scotland, who lost 1–0 in Berlin to East Germany. Arthur Graham made his international debut in the same match.

7 January 1978: Crowd trouble flared during the 2–1 FA Cup home defeat against Manchester City. Referee Colin Seel pleaded for sanity over the public address system during a 20–minute break in play as mounted police tackle troublemakers. Leeds were banned from staging home FA Cup games for three seasons.

Eddie Gray scored his only United treble as Leicester were demolished 5–1.

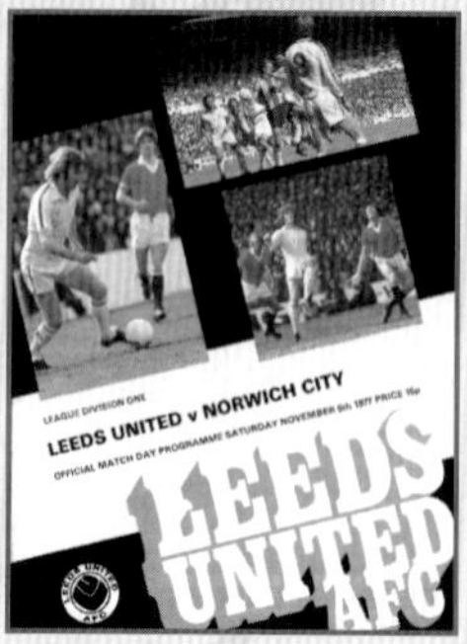

Match No.	Date		Venue	Opponents	Result	FT	HT	Scorers	Attendance
1	Aug	20	A	Newcastle United	L	2-3	1-2	Hankin, Lorimer (pen)	36,491
2		24	H	West Bromwich Alb	D	2-2	0-0	Jordan, McQueen	21,000
3		27	H	Birmingham City	W	1-0	0-0	Hankin	24,551
4	Sep	3	A	Coventry City	D	2-2	2-1	Hankin, McQueen	21,479
5		10	H	Ipswich Town	W	2-1	0-0	Hankin 2	24,280
6		17	A	Derby County	D	2-2	0-1	Lorimer, Graham	24,274
7		24	H	Manchester United	D	1-1	0-0	Hankin	33,514
8	Oct	1	A	Chelsea	W	2-1	1-0	Lorimer, Hankin	35,427
9		5	H	Aston Villa	D	1-1	0-1	McQueen	27,797
10		8	A	Bristol City	L	2-3	1-1	Hankin 2	26,215
11		15	H	Liverpool	L	1-2	1-1	Thomas	45,500
12		22	A	Middlesbrough	L	1-2	0-1	Harris	27,516
13		29	A	Leicester City	D	0-0	0-0		20,128
14	Nov	5	H	Norwich City	D	2-2	1-2	Lorimer 2	24,345
15		12	A	Manchester City	W	3-2	0-1	Jordan, Graham, Hankin	42,651
16		19	H	Nottingham Forest	W	1-0	1-0	Hankin	42,925
17		26	A	West Ham United	W	1-0	0-0	Hankin	26,883
18	Dec	3	H	Queen's Park R	W	3-0	1-0	Needham (og), Flynn, Currie	26,597
19		10	A	Arsenal	D	1-1	0-0	McQueen	40,162
20		17	H	Manchester City	W	2-0	1-0	McQueen, Cherry	37,380
21		26	A	Wolverhampton W	L	1-3	1-0	Jordan	27,704
22		27	H	Everton	W	3-1	2-0	Hankin 2, Lorimer	45,560
23		31	A	West Bromwich Alb	L	0-1	0-0		24,249
24	Jan	2	H	Newcastle United	L	0-2	0-1		36,643
25		14	A	Birmingham City	W	3-2	0-0	Graham 3	23,703
26		21	H	Coventry City	W	2-0	2-0	Hankin, Harris	27,062
27	Feb	4	A	Ipswich Town	W	1-0	0-0	E. Gray	24,023
28		25	H	Chelsea	W	2-0	0-0	F.T. Gray, Currie	25,263
29	Mar	1	A	Manchester United	W	1-0	0-0	Clarke	49,101
30		4	H	Bristol City	L	0-2	0-0		24,830
31		11	A	Liverpool	L	0-1	0-0		48,233
32		18	H	Middlesbrough	W	5-0	2-0	Hankin, Graham 2, Clarke 2	21,145
33		25	A	Everton	L	0-2	0-1		45,020
34		27	H	Wolverhampton W	W	2-1	1-1	Graham, Hankin	24,440
35		28	H	Leicester City	W	5-1	2-0	Hankin, F.T. Gray, E. Gray 3	21,145
36	Apr	1	A	Norwich City	L	0-3	0-1		19,615
37		8	H	West Ham United	L	1-2	1-1	Graham	22,953
38		12	H	Derby County	W	2-0	0-0	E. Gray, Hankin	16,531
39		15	A	Nottingham Forest	D	1-1	1-0	F.T. Gray (pen)	38,662
40		22	H	Arsenal	L	1-3	1-3	Currie	33,263
41		26	A	Aston Villa	L	1-3	0-1	Hankin	30,524
42		29	A	Queen's Park R	D	0-0	0-0		23,993
									Appearances
									Sub appearances
								One own-goal	Goals

FL Cup

R2	Aug	31	A	Rochdale	W	3-0	1-0	Jordan, Cherry, Harris	8,644
R3	Oct	26	H	Colchester United	W	4-0	2-0	Jordan, Graham, Lorimer, Hankin	17,713
R4	Nov	30	A	Bolton Wanderers	W	3-1	0-0	Graham, Jordan, F.T. Gray	33,766
R5	Jan	18	H	Everton	W	4-1	3-1	Currie, Lorimer 2 (1 pen), E. Gray	35,020
SF	Feb	8	H	Nottingham Forest	L	1-3	1-2	E. Gray	43,222
		22	A	Nottingham Forest	L	2-4	2-1	F.T. Gray, Graham	38,131
									Appearances
									Sub appearances
									Goals

FA Cup

R3	Jan	7	H	Manchester City	L	1-2	0-0	F.T. Gray (pen)	38,517
									Appearances
									Sub appearances
									Goals

Back row, left to right: Jimmy Armfield (manager), Paul Reaney, Allan Clarke, Joe Jordan, Ray Hankin, David Harvey, David Stewart, Gordon McQueen, Tony Currie, Byron Stevenson, Arthur Graham. Front row: Paul Madeley, Eddie Gray, Peter Lorimer, Frank Gray, Trevor Cherry, Peter Hampton, Carl Harris, David McNiven.

Stewart, David	Reaney, Paul	Cherry, Trevor	Lorimer, Peter	McQueen, Gordon	Madeley, Paul	Gray, Eddie	McNiven, David	Hankin, Ray	Currie, Tony	Graham, Arthur	Gray, Frank	Jordan, Joe	Harris, Carl	Stevenson, Byron	Thomas, Gwyn	Parkinson, Keith	Harvey, David	Flynn, Brian	Hampton, Peter	Clarke, Allan	Parker, Neil	Hart, Paul
1	2	3	4	5	6	7	8	**9**	10	11	S*											
1	2	3	4	5	6	7	8		10	11		9										
1	2	3	4	5	6			8	10	11	7	9										
1	**2**	3	4	5	6			8	10	11	7	9	S*									
1		2	4	5	6	7		8	10	11	3	9		S*								
1		2	4	5	6	7		8	10	11	3	9										
1		2	4	5	6	**7**		8	10	11	3	9		S*								
1		2	4	5	6	7		8	10	11	3	9										
1		2	4	5	6	7		8	10	11	3	9										
1		2	4	5	6	7		8	10	11	3	9										
1		6	4	5		7		8	10	**11**	3			2	9	S*						
		7	4		6			8	10		3	9	11	2		5	1					
		2	4	5	6	10			8	7	3	9	11				1					
		2	4	5	6	**7**		8		11	3	9	S*				1	10				
		2	4	5	6			8		11	3	9	7				1	10				
		2			5			8	10	11	3	9	7			6	1	4				
		2			6			8	4	11	3	9	7			5	1	10				
	2	8		5	6				4	11	3	9	7				1	10				
	2	**8**		5	6	9			4	11	3		7				1	10				
	2	8		5	6	S*		9	4	11	3		7				1	10				
	2	4	S*	5	6			8		11	3	9	7				1	10				
1		2	4	5	6			8		11	3	9	7					10				
1		2	4	5	6			8		11	3	9	7					10				
1		2	4	5	6	S*			8	**11**	3	9	7					10				
	2	6	4			7		9	8	11	3					5	1	10				
	2	9	4		6	11		8	10		3		**7**			5	1	S*				
		2	4		6	7		8	9	11	3					5	1	10				
1	2	5			6			8	9	11	7							4	3	10		
	2	5			6			8	9	11	7						1	4	3	10		
	2	5			6				9	11	7				8	S*	1	4	3	10		
		6						8	9	11	7			2			1	4	**3**	10	S*	5
		6	4		2			8	9	11	3		S*				1	7		10		5
		6	7		2	8			9	11	3						1	4	S*	**10**		5
		6	7		2	10		8	9	11	3						1	4				5
		6	S*		**2**	9		8		11	10		7				1	4	3			5
	2	6	9			8				11	10		7		S*		1	**4**	3			5
	2		7		6	8			9	11	3		10				1	4				5
		6			2	8		9	10	11	7						1	4	3			5
1		6			2	8		9	10	11	7							4	3			5
1		6			2	**9**		8	10	11	7							4	3	S*		5
		6			2	S*		8	10	11	7						1	4	**3**	9		5
		6			2	7		8	10	11	3						1	4		9		5
17	15	41	26	21	38	24	2	33	35	40	40	20	16	3	2	6	25	28	10	8	0	12
			2			3					1		3	2	1	2		1	1	1	1	
		1	6	5		5		20	3	9	3	3	2		1			1		3		

Stewart, David	Reaney, Paul	Cherry, Trevor	Lorimer, Peter	McQueen, Gordon	Madeley, Paul	Gray, Eddie	McNiven, David	Hankin, Ray	Currie, Tony	Graham, Arthur	Gray, Frank	Jordan, Joe	Harris, Carl	Stevenson, Byron	Thomas, Gwyn	Parkinson, Keith	Harvey, David	Flynn, Brian	Hampton, Peter	Clarke, Allan	Parker, Neil	Hart, Paul
1	2	6	7	5	4			8	10	**11**	3	9	S*									
		2	4		6	10		8		7	3	9	11			5	1					
	2	10			6			**8**	4	11	3	9	7			5	1		S*			
	2	7	4		6	10		8	9	11	3					5	1					
	2	7	**4**		6	10		8	9	11	3		S*			5	1					
1	2	4			6	7		8	9	11	5								3	10		
2	5	6	4	1	6	4	0	6	5	6	6	3	2	0	0	4	4	0	1	1	0	0
													2						1			
		1	3			2		1	1	3	2	3	1									

Stewart, David	Reaney, Paul	Cherry, Trevor	Lorimer, Peter	McQueen, Gordon	Madeley, Paul	Gray, Eddie	McNiven, David	Hankin, Ray	Currie, Tony	Graham, Arthur	Gray, Frank	Jordan, Joe	Harris, Carl	Stevenson, Byron	Thomas, Gwyn	Parkinson, Keith	Harvey, David	Flynn, Brian	Hampton, Peter	Clarke, Allan	Parker, Neil	Hart, Paul
	2	4		5	6			8	9	11	3		7				1	10		S*		
0	1	1	0	1	1	0	0	1	1	1	1	0	1	0	0	0	1	1	0	0	0	0
																				1		
											1											

League Table

	P	W	D	L	F	A	Pts
Nottingham Forest	42	25	14	3	69	24	64
Liverpool	42	24	9	9	65	34	57
Everton	42	22	11	9	76	45	55
Manchester City	42	20	12	10	74	51	52
Arsenal	42	21	10	11	60	37	52
West Bromwich Albion	42	18	14	10	62	53	50
Coventry City	42	18	12	12	75	62	48
Aston Villa	42	18	10	14	57	42	46
Leeds United	42	18	10	14	63	53	46
Manchester United	42	16	10	16	67	63	42
Birmingham City	42	16	9	17	55	60	41
Derby County	42	14	13	15	54	59	41
Norwich City	42	11	18	13	52	66	40
Middlesbrough	42	12	15	15	42	54	39
Wolverhampton W	42	12	12	18	51	64	36
Chelsea	42	11	14	17	46	69	36
Bristol City	42	11	13	18	49	53	35
Ipswich Town	42	11	13	18	47	61	35
Queen's Park Rangers	42	9	15	18	47	64	33
West Ham United	42	12	8	22	52	69	32
Newcastle United	42	6	10	26	42	78	22
Leicester City	42	5	12	25	26	70	22

1978-79

Division One

Manager: Jock Stein CBE until October then Jimmy Adamson

Final Position: 5th

Did you know that?

23 August 1978: The four new floodlight pylons stood at 260ft and were the highest in Britain. They each held 220 lamps which were used that night for the first time.

24 March 1979: Andy Ritchie scored a hat-trick for Manchester United as Leeds crashed 4–1 at Old Trafford. Ritchie joined the Whites four years later.

17 May 1979: Liverpool's 3–0 win at Elland Road saw the Reds capture their 11th title and beat United's record points tally of 67, set 10 years earlier, by a point.

Top scorer John Hawley.

Match No.	Date	Venue	Opponents	Result	FT	HT	Scorers	Attendance
1	Aug 19	A	Arsenal	D	2-2	1-1	Currie, Cherry	42,057
2	23	H	Manchester United	L	2-3	1-2	Hart, F.T. Gray (pen)	36,845
3	26	H	Wolverhampton W	W	3-0	2-0	Hankin, F.T. Gray (pen), Currie	26,267
4	Sep 2	A	Chelsea	W	3-0	1-0	Graham, Hawley 2	30,099
5	9	A	Manchester City	L	0-3	0-2		40,125
6	16	H	Tottenham Hotspur	L	1-2	0-1	Graham	36,062
7	23	A	Coventry City	D	0-0	0-0		27,365
8	30	H	Birmingham City	W	3-0	1-0	Flynn, F.T. Gray (pen), Hankin	23,331
9	Oct 7	A	Bolton Wanderers	L	1-3	1-0	Graham	27,751
10	14	H	West Bromwich Alb	L	1-3	1-1	Stevenson	25,931
11	21	A	Norwich City	D	2-2	1-0	F.T. Gray, Hawley	19,981
12	28	H	Derby County	W	4-0	3-0	Flynn, Hart, Hankin, Hawley	25,449
13	Nov 4	A	Liverpool	D	1-1	1-0	Hawley	51,857
14	11	H	Arsenal	L	0-1	0-1		33,961
15	18	A	Wolverhampton W	D	1-1	1-1	Currie	18,961
16	22	H	Chelsea	W	2-1	2-1	Graham, Hankin	24,088
17	25	H	Southampton	W	4-0	2-0	Graham, Currie, Golac (og), Madeley	23,592
18	Dec 2	A	Ipswich Town	W	3-2	2-1	Hankin, Harris, Cherry	22,526
19	9	H	Bristol City	D	1-1	1-1	Flynn	22,529
20	16	A	Everton	D	1-1	1-0	Hawley	37,997
21	23	H	Middlesbrough	W	3-1	1-1	Hawley, E. Gray, Currie	27,146
22	26	A	Aston Villa	D	2-2	0-2	E. Gray 2	40,973
23	30	A	Queen's Park R	W	4-1	1-0	Hawley 2, Harris, E. Gray	17,435
24	Jan 13	H	Manchester City	D	1-1	1-0	Hawley	36,303
25	20	A	Tottenham Hotspur	W	2-1	1-0	Hart, Hankin	36,828
26	Feb 3	H	Coventry City	W	1-0	1-0	Currie	22,928
27	10	A	Birmingham City	W	1-0	1-0	F.T. Gray (pen)	17,620
28	24	A	West Bromwich Alb	W	2-1	2-1	Graham 2	26,426
29	Mar 3	H	Norwich City	D	2-2	1-0	Hawley 2	23,038
30	10	A	Derby County	W	1-0	0-0	Hawley	22,800
31	24	A	Manchester United	L	1-4	0-3	Hankin	51,191
32	31	A	Southampton	D	2-2	1-0	Hawley 2	21,805
33	Apr 7	H	Ipswich Town	D	1-1	1-0	Cherry	24,153
34	10	A	Middlesbrough	L	0-1	0-1		23,260
35	14	H	Aston Villa	W	1-0	1-0	Hart	24,281
36	16	A	Nottingham Forest	D	0-0	0-0		37,397
37	21	H	Everton	W	1-0	0-0	Currie	29,125
38	25	H	Bolton Wanderers	W	5-1	2-0	Cherry, F.T. Gray (pen), Hart, Harris, Hawley	20,218
39	28	A	Bristol City	D	0-0	0-0		25,388
40	May 4	H	Queen's Park R	W	4-3	1-2	Graham, Hankin 2, Cherry	20,121
41	15	H	Nottingham Forest	L	1-2	0-1	Cherry	33,544
42	17	H	Liverpool	L	0-3	0-2		41,324

Appearances
Sub appearances
One own-goal — Goals

FL Cup

R2	Aug 29	A	West Bromwich Alb	D	0-0	0-0		25,064
Rep	Sep 6	H	West Bromwich Alb	D	0-0*	0-0		29,316
2Rep	Oct 2	N	West Bromwich Alb	W	1-0†	1-0	Hart	8,164
R3	10	A	Sheffield United	W	4-1	2-0	Currie, F.T. Gray, E. Gray 2	40,899
R4	Nov 7	A	Queen's Park R	W	2-0	0-0	Hawley, Hankin	22,769
R5	Dec 3	H	Luton Town	W	4-1	1-0	Cherry, Currie, E. Gray, F.T. Gray	28,177
SF	Jan 24	H	Southampton	D	2-2	1-0	Currie, Hankin	33,415
	30	A	Southampton	L	0-1	0-1		23,645

* After extra-time
† At Maine Road, Manchester

Appearances
Sub appearances
Goals

FA Cup

R3	Jan 18	A	Hartlepools United	W	6-2	3-1	Hart, Graham, E. Gray 2, Harris, F.T. Gray (pen)	16,000
R4	Feb 26	N	West Bromwich Alb	D	3-3†	0-1	F.T. Gray, Graham, Harris	34,000
Rep	Mar 1	A	West Bromwich Alb	L	0-2*	0-0		31,101

* After extra-time (score at 90 minutes 0-0)
† At The Hawthorns, West Bromwich

Appearances
Sub appearances
Goals

Harvey, David	Madeley, Paul	Gray, Frank	Flynn, Brian	Hart, Paul	Cherry, Trevor	Harris, Carl	Gray, Eddie	Hawley, John	Currie, Tony	Graham, Arthur	Stevenson, Byron	Hankin, Ray	Stewart, David	Hampton, Peter	Lorimer, Peter	Thomas, Gwyn	Parkinson, Keith	Hird, Kevin
1	2	3	4	5	6	7	8	9	10	11								
1	6	3	4	5		7	9		10	11	2	8						
	6	3	4	5		**7**	8	S*	10	11	2	9	1					
	6	3	4	5				9	10	11	2	8	1	7				
	6	**3**	4	5	7	S*		9		11	2	8	1	10				
1	6	3	4	5	10	7				11	2	8			9			
1	6	3	4	5	10	7				11	2	8			9			
1	6	10	4	5	3	7				11	2	8			**9**	S*		
1	6	10	4	5	3	7	9			11	2	8						
1	6	9	4	5	3		7		10	11	2	8						
1	6	3	4	5	2		7	9	10	11		8						
1	6	3	4	5	2		7	9	10	11		8						
1	6	3	4	5	2		7	9	10	11		8						
1	6	3	4	5	2	**7**		9	10	11		8						
1	6	3	4	5	2		7	9	10	11		8						
1	6	3	4	5	2		7	9	10	11		8						
1	6	3	4	5	2		7	9	10	11		8						
1	6	3	4	5	2	11	7	9	10			8						
1	6		4	5	2	11	7		10		3	8				9		
1	6	3	4	5	2	11	7	9	10			8						
1	6	3	4	5	2	7	8	9	10	11								
1	6	3	4	5	2	8	7	9	10	11								
1	6	**3**	4	5	2	11	7	9	10	8							S*	
1	6	3	4	5	2	11	7	9	10	8								
1		3	4	5		11		9	10	8	2	7					6	
1	6	7	4		2	9			10	11	3	8					5	
1	6	7	4	5	2	**8**	S*	9	10	11	3							
1	6	11	4	5	2	**7**		9	10	8	3						S*	
1	6	3	4		2	7		9	10	11							5	8
1	**6**	3	4	5	2	7	S*	9	10	11								8
1		**8**	4	5	3	7	6	9	10	11		S*						2
1		3	4	5	6		7	9	10	11		8						2
1	6	3	4	5	2		7	9	**10**	11		8						S*
1	10	3	4	5	6		7	9		11	S*	**8**						2
1	6	3	4	5	2	S*	**7**	9		11		8						10
1	10	3	4	5	6	7		9		**11**				8				2
1	9	3	4	5	6	7			10	11		8						2
1	6	3	4	5	8	7		S*	10	11		**9**						2
1	6	3		5	4	7	10			11		9		8				2
1	6	3	4	5	8	7		S*	10	**11**		9						2
1	6	3	4	5	8	**7**	S*	9	10	11								2
1	6	3	4	5	8	7	10	9		11								2
39	39	41	41	40	38	29	25	29	32	39	14	29	3	4	3	1	3	13
						2	3	3			1	1				1	2	1
	1	6	3	5	6	3	4	16	7	8	1	9						

Harvey, David	Madeley, Paul	Gray, Frank	Flynn, Brian	Hart, Paul	Cherry, Trevor	Harris, Carl	Gray, Eddie	Hawley, John	Currie, Tony	Graham, Arthur	Stevenson, Byron	Hankin, Ray	Stewart, David	Hampton, Peter	Lorimer, Peter	Thomas, Gwyn	Parkinson, Keith	Hird, Kevin
	2	3	4	5				9	10	11	6	8	1	7				
	6	3	4	5	7		S*	9	**10**	11	2	8	1					
1	6	10	4	5	3		9			11	2	8			S*	**7**		
1		9	4	5	3		7		10	11	2	8		6				
1	6	3	4	5	2		7	9	10	11		8						
1	6	3	4	5	2	11	7	9	10			8						
1	6	3	4	5	2	S*	7	9	10	**11**		8						
1	6	3	4	5	2	S*	7	**9**	10	11		8						
6	7	8	8	8	7	1	6	6	7	7	4	8	2	2	0	1	0	0
						2	1								1			
		2		1	1		3	1	3			2						

Harvey, David	Madeley, Paul	Gray, Frank	Flynn, Brian	Hart, Paul	Cherry, Trevor	Harris, Carl	Gray, Eddie	Hawley, John	Currie, Tony	Graham, Arthur	Stevenson, Byron	Hankin, Ray	Stewart, David	Hampton, Peter	Lorimer, Peter	Thomas, Gwyn	Parkinson, Keith	Hird, Kevin
1	6	3	4	5	2	11	7	9	10	8								
1	6	3	4	5	2	7		9	10	11	8							
1	6	3	4		2	7		9	10	11	**8**					S*	5	
3	3	3	3	2	3	3	1	3	3	3	2	0	0	0	0	0	1	0
																1		
		2		1		2	2			2								

League Table

	P	W	D	L	F	A	Pts
Liverpool	42	30	8	4	85	16	68
Nottingham Forest	42	21	18	3	61	26	60
West Bromwich Albion	42	24	11	7	72	35	59
Everton	42	17	17	8	52	40	51
Leeds United	42	18	14	10	70	52	50
Ipswich Town	42	20	9	13	63	49	49
Arsenal	42	17	14	11	61	48	48
Aston Villa	42	15	16	11	59	49	46
Manchester United	42	15	15	12	60	63	45
Coventry City	42	14	16	12	58	68	44
Tottenham Hotspur	42	13	15	14	48	61	41
Middlesbrough	42	15	10	17	57	50	40
Bristol City	42	15	10	17	47	51	40
Southampton	42	12	16	14	47	53	40
Manchester City	42	13	13	16	58	56	39
Norwich City	42	7	23	12	51	57	37
Bolton Wanderers	42	12	11	19	54	75	35
Wolverhampton W	42	13	8	21	44	68	34
Derby County	42	10	11	21	44	71	31
Queen's Park Rangers	42	6	13	23	45	73	25
Birmingham City	42	6	10	26	37	64	22
Chelsea	42	5	10	27	44	92	20

1979-80

Division One

Manager: Jimmy Adamson

Final Position: 11th

Did you know that?

18 August 1979: New £370,000 record signing Alan Curtis scored twice on his debut in a 2–2 draw with Bristol City.

4 September 1979: Arsenal dished out a 7–0 League Cup thumping to equal West Ham's feat 13 years earlier.

17 November 1979: Seventeen-year-old local lad Terry Connor came on as substitute to score the only goal against West Brom at Elland Road.

22 March 1980: There are demonstrations against manager Jimmy Adamson after the 0–0 draw against Coventry before Elland Road's lowest League crowd for 17 years.

Teenage substitute Terry Connor had a dream goalscoring debut against West Brom.

Match No.	Date	Venue	Opponents	Result	FT	HT	Scorers	Attendance
1	Aug 18	A	Bristol City	D	2-2	1-1	Curtis 2	22,845
2	22	H	Everton	W	2-0	0-0	Hird, Harris	30,000
3	25	A	Norwich City	L	1-2	1-2	Hart	18,444
4	Sep 1	H	Arsenal	D	1-1	1-0	Hart	23,245
5	8	A	Nottingham Forest	D	0-0	0-0		26,914
6	15	H	Liverpool	D	1-1	0-0	Curtis	39,779
7	22	A	Bolton Wanderers	D	1-1	0-0	Gray (pen)	21,724
8	29	H	Manchester City	L	1-2	0-0	Hankin	29,592
9	Oct 6	H	Ipswich Town	W	2-1	0-1	Cherry, Hird (pen)	19,342
10	13	A	Brighton & HA	D	0-0	0-0		27,002
11	20	H	Tottenham Hotspur	L	1-2	1-1	Hankin	25,203
12	27	A	Southampton	W	2-1	1-1	Entwistle, Curtis	23,259
13	Nov 3	H	Bristol City	L	1-3	1-1	Gray	17,376
14	10	A	Coventry City	L	0-3	0-1		19,402
15	13	A	Everton	L	1-5	0-4	Hird	23,000
16	17	H	West Bromwich Alb	W	1-0	0-0	Connor	17,481
17	24	A	Aston Villa	D	0-0	0-0		29,736
18	Dec 1	H	Crystal Palace	W	1-0	1-0	Hird	21,330
19	8	A	Manchester United	D	1-1	1-0	Connor	57,478
20	15	H	Wolverhampton W	W	3-0	2-0	Connor, Graham, Hamson	21,227
21	21	A	Stoke City	W	2-0	2-0	Connor, Harris	16,878
22	26	A	Middlesbrough	L	1-3	1-2	Entwistle	23,259
23	29	H	Norwich City	D	2-2	2-1	Hird, Hankin	23,493
24	Jan 1	H	Derby County	W	1-0	0-0	Hird	24,271
25	12	A	Arsenal	W	1-0	0-0	Connor	32,799
26	19	H	Nottingham Forest	L	1-2	1-1	Connor	29,816
27	Feb 9	H	Bolton Wanderers	D	2-2	1-1	Hird (pen), Graham	16,428
28	16	A	Manchester City	D	1-1	1-0	Graham	34,392
29	23	H	Brighton & HA	D	1-1	0-0	Flynn	17,216
30	Mar 1	A	Tottenham Hotspur	L	1-2	0-1	Chandler	35,331
31	8	H	Southampton	W	2-0	2-0	Hart, Parlane	21,169
32	14	A	Ipswich Town	L	0-1	0-0		23,140
33	19	A	Liverpool	L	0-3	0-1		37,008
34	22	H	Coventry City	D	0-0	0-0		16,967
35	29	A	West Bromwich Alb	L	1-2	1-2	Chandler	18,898
36	Apr 2	H	Middlesbrough	W	2-0	1-0	Cherry, Flynn	17,906
37	5	A	Derby County	L	0-2	0-2		22,745
38	8	H	Stoke City	W	3-0	1-0	Parlane, Harris 2	15,541
39	12	A	Crystal Palace	L	0-1	0-0		25,318
40	19	H	Aston Villa	D	0-0	0-0		15,840
41	26	A	Wolverhampton W	L	1-3	0-1	Flynn	22,746
42	May 3	H	Manchester United	W	2-0	1-0	Parlane, Hird (pen)	39,625
								Appearances
								Sub appearances
								Goals

FL Cup

R2	Aug 29	H	Arsenal	D	1-1	0-0	Stevenson (pen)	23,421
	Sep 4	A	Arsenal	L	0-7	0-3		35,129
								Appearances
								Sub appearances
								Goals

FA Cup

R3	Jan 5	H	Nottingham Forest	L	1-4	0-2	Lloyd (og)	35,945
								Appearances
								Sub appearances
							One own-goal	Goals

Names up in lights. United set for the 1979–80 season. Back row, left to right: Alan Curtis, Gary Hamson, Paul Madeley, John Hawley, Eddie Gray. Middle row: Dave Merrington (assistant manager), Keith Parkinson, David Hart, John Lukic, Ray Hankin, Byron Stevenson, Syd Farrimond (coach). Front row: Carl Harris, Kevin Hird, Peter Hampton, Jimmy Adamson (manager), Trevor Cherry, Arthur Graham, Brian Flynn.

Harvey, David	Hird, Kevin	Stevenson, Byron	Flynn, Brian	Parkinson, Keith	Hampton, Peter	Curtis, Alan	Cherry, Trevor	Hankin, Ray	Harris, Carl	Graham, Arthur	Hart, Paul	Greenhoff, Brian	Hawley, John	Madeley, Paul	Gray, Eddie	Chandler, Jeff	Hamson, Gary	Lukic, John	Entwistle, Wayne	Connor, Terry	Firm, Neil	Parlane, Derek	Dickinson, Martin	Thomas, Gwyn
1	2	3	4	5	6	7	8	9	10	11														
1	2	6	4		3	10	8	9	7	11	5													
1	2	6	4	S*	**3**	10	8	9	7	11	5													
1	2	3	4	6		10	8			11	5	7	9											
1	2		4		3	10	8	9		11	5			6	7									
1	2		4		3	10	8	9		11	5			6	7									
1	2		4		3	10	8	9		11	5	S*		6	**7**									
1	2				3	10	8	9	7	11	5	4		**6**		S*								
1	2		4	6	3	10	8	9		11		5					7							
	2	6	4	5	3	10	8	9		11							7	1						
	2		4		3	10	8	9				**5**		6	7	S*		1	11					
		2		5	3	10	8	9						6	7	4		1	11					
		3			**4**	10	2	9	S*		5			6	11	7		1	8					
	7	3	**4**			10	2	9			5	8		6	11			1	S*					
	7	3				10	2				5	4		6	11		9	1	8					
	4	3				10	2		11		5			**6**	7		8	1	9	S*				
	7	3				10	2			8	5	6			11		4	1		9				
	8	3				10	2			11	5	6			7		4	1		9				
	8	3				10	2		S*	11	5	6			7		**4**	1		9				
	8	3				10	2			11	5	6			7		4	1		9				
	8	3				10	2		**11**		5	6			7		4	1	S*	9				
	8	3				10	2		11		5	**6**			7		4	1	S*	9				
	8	3					2	10	11		5			6	7		4	1		9				
	8	3					2	10	11		5			6	7		4	1		9				
	8	3			11		2					5		6	7		4	1	10	9				
	8	3			11		2			S*		5		6	7		4	1	**10**	9				
	8		4		3		2	7		11		5		6			10	1		9				
	8		4		3		2			11		5		6	7			1		9	10			
	8	2	4		10		3			11		**6**			7		S*	1		9	5			
		3	4				**2**			11	5				7	8	10	1	S*	9	6			
	2		4	3						11	5			6	7	8		1		9		10		
	8		4	3			2			11	5			6	**7**	S*		1		9		10		
	8		4	3			2			**11**	5			6		S*	10	1		9		7		
	2			3			8			11	5			6		4	7	1		9		10		
	2		4	**3**			7			11	5	S*		6	8	9		1				10		
	2		4				8			11	5	3			7	9		1				10	6	
	2		4				3			**11**	5	6			7	9		1		S*		10	8	
	2		4				3		9		5			6	7	8		1				10	11	
	2	3							11		5			6	7	8		1		9			4	10
	2	3							11		**5**	6			7	8		1		S*		9	4	10
	2	S*	4				8					3		6		7		1		10		9	**5**	11
	2	10	4				3		7	11		5		6		8		1				9		
9	39	25	24	10	17	22	39	16	13	26	30	22	1	25	30	13	18	33	7	20	3	11	6	3
		1		1					2	1		2				4	1		4	3				
	8		3			4	2	3	4	3	3				2	2	1		2	6		3		

Harvey, David	Hird, Kevin	Stevenson, Byron	Flynn, Brian	Parkinson, Keith	Hampton, Peter	Curtis, Alan	Cherry, Trevor	Hankin, Ray	Harris, Carl	Graham, Arthur	Hart, Paul	Greenhoff, Brian	Hawley, John	Madeley, Paul	Gray, Eddie	Chandler, Jeff	Hamson, Gary	Lukic, John	Entwistle, Wayne	Connor, Terry	Firm, Neil	Parlane, Derek	Dickinson, Martin	Thomas, Gwyn
1	2	6	4		3	10	8		7	11	5	9												
1	2	6	4		3	10	8	7	S*	11	5	**9**												
2	2	2	2	0	2	2	2	1	1	2	2	2	0	0	0	0	0	0	0	0	0	0	0	0
									1															
		1																						

Harvey, David	Hird, Kevin	Stevenson, Byron	Flynn, Brian	Parkinson, Keith	Hampton, Peter	Curtis, Alan	Cherry, Trevor	Hankin, Ray	Harris, Carl	Graham, Arthur	Hart, Paul	Greenhoff, Brian	Hawley, John	Madeley, Paul	Gray, Eddie	Chandler, Jeff	Hamson, Gary	Lukic, John	Entwistle, Wayne	Connor, Terry	Firm, Neil	Parlane, Derek	Dickinson, Martin	Thomas, Gwyn
	8	3				**10**	2		11		5			6	7		4	1	S*	9				
0	1	1	0	0	0	1	1	0	1	0	1	0	0	1	1	0	1	1	0	1	0	0	0	0
																			1					

League Table

	P	W	D	L	F	A	Pts
Liverpool	42	25	10	7	81	30	60
Manchester United	42	24	10	8	65	35	58
Ipswich Town	42	22	9	11	68	39	53
Arsenal	42	18	16	8	52	36	52
Nottingham Forest	42	20	8	14	63	43	48
Wolverhampton W	42	19	9	14	58	47	47
Aston Villa	42	16	14	12	51	50	46
Southampton	42	18	9	15	65	53	45
Middlesbrough	42	16	12	14	50	44	44
West Bromwich Albion	42	11	19	12	54	50	41
Leeds United	42	13	14	15	46	50	40
Norwich City	42	13	14	15	58	66	40
Crystal Palace	42	12	16	14	41	50	40
Tottenham Hotspur	42	15	10	17	52	62	40
Coventry City	42	16	7	19	56	66	39
Brighton & Hove Albion	42	11	15	16	47	57	37
Manchester City	42	12	13	17	43	66	37
Stoke City	42	13	10	19	44	58	36
Everton	42	9	17	16	43	51	35
Bristol City	42	9	13	20	37	66	31
Derby County	42	11	8	23	47	67	30
Bolton Wanderers	42	5	15	22	38	73	25

1980-81

Division One

Manager: Jimmy Adamson until October then Allan Clarke

Final Position: 9th

Match No.	Date	Venue	Opponents	Result	FT	HT	Scorers	Attendance
1	Aug 16	H	Aston Villa	L	1-2	1-1	Stevenson (pen)	23,401
2	19	A	Middlesbrough	L	0-3	0-1		19,470
3	23	A	Norwich City	W	3-2	1-0	Hart, Graham, Connor	17,800
4	30	H	Leicester City	L	1-2	0-0	Hart	18,530
5	Sep 6	A	Stoke City	L	0-3	0-3		12,729
6	13	H	Tottenham Hotspur	D	0-0	0-0		21,947
7	20	H	Manchester United	D	0-0	0-0		32,539
8	27	A	Sunderland	L	1-4	0-2	Parlane	29,619
9	Oct 4	A	Ipswich Town	D	1-1	0-0	Sabella	24,087
10	8	H	Manchester City	W	1-0	0-0	Harris	19,134
11	11	H	Everton	W	1-0	0-0	Curtis	25,601
12	18	A	Wolverhampton W	L	1-2	1-1	Connor	20,699
13	22	A	Nottingham Forest	L	1-2	1-2	Harris	25,033
14	25	H	Crystal Palace	W	1-0	1-0	Connor	19,208
15	Nov 1	A	Coventry City	L	1-2	0-2	Connor	13,970
16	8	H	Arsenal	L	0-5	0-2		20,855
17	12	H	Middlesbrough	W	2-1	0-0	Hird 2 (1 pen)	17,382
18	15	A	Aston Villa	D	1-1	1-1	Sabella	29,106
19	22	A	Southampton	L	1-2	1-2	Graham	20,278
20	29	H	Brighton & HA	W	1-0	0-0	Harris	14,333
21	Dec 6	A	West Bromwich Alb	W	2-1	1-1	Harris, Graham	17,771
22	13	H	Nottingham Forest	W	1-0	0-0	Greenhoff	21,882
23	20	A	Manchester City	L	0-1	0-0		31,866
24	26	H	Birmingham City	D	0-0	0-0		19,214
25	27	A	Liverpool	D	0-0	0-0		44,086
26	Jan 10	H	Southampton	L	0-3	0-1		21,007
27	17	A	Leicester City	W	1-0	0-0	Hart	16,094
28	31	H	Norwich City	W	1-0	0-0	Harris	15,836
29	Feb 7	A	Tottenham Hotspur	D	1-1	0-1	Harris	32,372
30	14	H	Stoke City	L	1-3	1-1	Flynn	16,530
31	21	H	Sunderland	W	1-0	0-0	Harris	23,236
32	28	A	Manchester United	W	1-0	0-0	Flynn	45,733
33	Mar 14	A	Everton	W	2-1	0-1	Parlane, Harris	23,014
34	21	H	Wolverhampton W	L	1-3	1-1	Harris	19,252
35	28	A	Crystal Palace	W	1-0	1-0	Parlane	15,053
36	31	H	Ipswich Town	W	3-0	2-0	Hird, Harris, Hart	26,462
37	Apr 4	H	Coventry City	W	3-0	1-0	Stevenson, Parlane, Flynn	15,882
38	11	A	Arsenal	D	0-0	0-0		29,339
39	18	H	Liverpool	D	0-0	0-0		39,206
40	21	A	Birmingham City	W	2-0	1-0	Parlane, Hird (pen)	14,505
41	May 2	A	Brighton & HA	L	0-2	0-1		27,577
42	6	H	West Bromwich Alb	D	0-0	0-0		17,218
								Appearances
								Sub appearances
								Goals

FL Cup

R2	Aug 27	A	Aston Villa	L	0-1	0-1		24,238
	Sep 3	H	Aston Villa	L	1-3	1-2	Graham	12,236
								Appearances
								Sub appearances
								Goals

FA Cup

R3	Jan 3	H	Coventry City	D	1-1	0-1	Hird (pen)	24,523
Rep	6	A	Coventry City	L	0-1	0-0		22,057
								Appearances
								Sub appearances
								Goals

Did you know that?

16 August 1980: Alex Sabella became the first South American to play for United in the opening day defeat at home to Aston Villa which saw Byron Stevenson score from the spot after just 177 seconds.

8 November 1980: Arsenal condemned United to their heaviest home League defeat since World War Two with a 5–0 hammering. It also proved to be Paul Madeley's 730th and final game for the club as he went off injured.

The versatile Paul Madeley retired after an 18-year career at Elland Road.

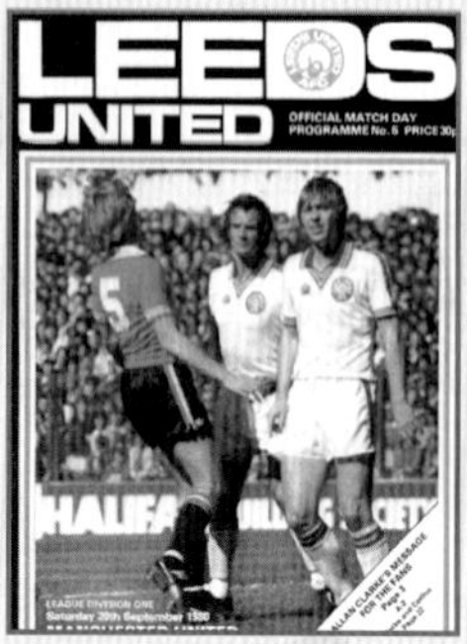

Just weeks after this team shot was taken before the 1980–81 season manager Jimmy Adamson departed. Back row, left to right: Byron Stevenson, Neil Firm, Paul Hart, John Lukic, Paul Madeley, Derek Parlane. Middle row: Dave Merrington (assistant manager), Syd Farrimond (coach), Terry Connor, Alex Sabella, Eddie Gray, Martin Dickinson, Alan Curtis, Peter Hampton, Jimmy Adamson (manager). Front row: Arthur Graham, Brian Flynn, Jeff Chandler, Trevor Cherry, Carl Harris, Kevin Hird.

Lukic, John	Cherry, Trevor	Stevenson, Byron	Flynn, Brian	Hart, Paul	Greenhoff, Brian	Gray, Eddie	Harris, Carl	Curtis, Alan	Sabella, Alex	Graham, Arthur	Parlane, Derek	Connor, Terry	Chandler, Jeff	Madeley, Paul	Hamson, Gary	Thomas, Gwyn	Hird, Kevin	Firm, Neil	Parkinson, Keith	Butterworth, Aiden	Dickinson, Martin
1	2	3	4	5	6	**7**	8	9	10	11	S*										
1	2	3	4	5	6	7		9		11	S*	**8**	10								
1	2		4	5	3				10	11		9	7	6	**8**	S*					
1	2		4	5	3				10	11		9	7	6	8						
1	2		4	5	3		S*		10	11	7	9		**6**	8						
1	4	3		5					10	11	8	**9**	7		S*		2	6			
1	7	3	4	5		10				11	9	8					2	6			
1	7	3	4	5		10	S*			11	9	8					2	**6**			
1	6		4	5	2	3	7	8	10	11	9										
1	6		4	5	2	3	7	8	10	11	**9**				S*						
1	6		4	5	2	3	7	8	10	11					9						
1	6		4	5	2	**3**	7	8	10			11			9		S*				
1	6		4	5	2	3	**7**		10			9	11			S*	8				
1	6		4	5	2	10	7			11		9		3			8				
1	6		4	5	2	10	7			11		9		3			8				
1	6		4	5	2	10	S*			11	7	9		**3**			8				
1	6		4	5	2	3	7		10	11		9					8				
1	6		4	5	2	3	7		10	11		**9**			S*		8				
1	6		4	5	2	3	7		10	11					9		8				
1	6		4	5	2	3	7		10	11		9					8				
1	6		4	5	2	3	7		10	11		9					8				
1	6		4	5	2	3	7		10	11	S*	**9**					8				
1	6		4	5	2	3	7		10	11		9					8				
1	6		4	5	2	3	7		10	**11**	S*	9					8				
1	6		4	5		3	7		10	11	8	**9**			S*		2				
1	6		4	5		3	S*		10	11	**7**		9		8		2				
1	6		4	5	2	3	7		**10**	11		9	S*				8				
1	6		4	5	2	3	7		10	11		9					8				
1	6	S*	4	5	2	3	7			11		9	**10**				8				
1	6		4	5	2	3	7		S*	11	10	**9**					8				
1	6	10	4	5	2	3	7			11	9						8				
1	6	10	4	5	2	3	7			11	9						8				
1	6	10	4		2	3	7			11	9						8		5		
1	6	10	4		2	3	7			11	9	S*	**8**						5		
1	6	10	4	5		3	8			11	9						7		2		
1	6	10	4	5	2	3	7			11	9						8				
1		10	4	5	2	3	7			11	**9**						8	6		S*	
1	6	10	4	5	2	3	7			11	9						8				
1	6	10	4	5	2	3	7			11	9						8				
1	6	10	4	**5**	2	3	7			11	9						8	S*			
1	6	10	4		2	3	**7**			11	9	S*					8	5			S*
1	6	**10**	4		2	3	7			11	9	5					8				
42	41	17	41	38	36	38	33	6	22	40	22	25	8	6	7	0	32	5	3	0	0
		1					4		1		4	2	1		4	2	1	1		1	1
		2	3	4	1		10	1	2	3	5	4					4				

1	2		4	5	3				10	11		9	8	6		7					
1	2		4	5	3		S*		10	11	7	9		6	**8**						
2	2	0	2	2	2	0	0	0	2	2	1	2	1	2	1	1	0	0	0	0	0
							1														
										1											

1	6		4	5	**2**	3			10	11	7	9			S*		8				
1	6		4	5		2			10	11	7		8		9		3				
2	2	0	2	2	1	2	0	0	2	2	2	1	1	0	1	0	2	0	0	0	0
															1						
																	1				

League Table

	P	W	D	L	F	A	Pts
Aston Villa	42	26	8	8	72	40	60
Ipswich Town	42	23	10	9	77	43	56
Arsenal	42	19	15	8	61	45	53
West Bromwich Albion	42	20	12	10	60	42	52
Liverpool	42	17	17	8	62	42	51
Southampton	42	20	10	12	76	56	50
Nottingham Forest	42	19	12	11	62	44	50
Manchester United	42	15	18	9	51	36	48
Leeds United	42	17	10	15	39	47	44
Tottenham Hotspur	42	14	15	13	70	68	43
Stoke City	42	12	18	12	51	60	42
Manchester City	42	14	11	17	56	59	39
Birmingham City	42	13	12	17	50	61	38
Middlesbrough	42	16	5	21	53	61	37
Everton	42	13	10	19	55	58	36
Coventry City	42	13	10	19	48	68	36
Sunderland	42	14	7	21	52	53	35
Wolverhampton W	42	13	9	20	43	55	35
Brighton & Hove Albion	42	14	7	21	54	67	35
Norwich City	42	13	7	22	49	73	33
Leicester City	42	13	6	23	40	67	32
Crystal Palace	42	6	7	29	47	83	19

1981-82

Division One

Manager: Allan Clarke

Final Position: 20th

Did you know that?

29 August 1981: United played in sponsored shirts for the first time as RFW was emblazoned across the players' chests in the 5–1 opening day hammering at Swansea. RFW were RF Winder, a Pudsey electrical firm.

3 October 1981: Steve Balcombe scored a superb solo goal on his only League appearance to earn a 1–1 draw with Aston Villa.

5 December 1981: After eight successive away defeats Leeds called in a hypnotist during the week and won 2–1 at Stoke. Sadly the effect soon wore off.

15 May 1982: Late goals by Gary Hamson and Kevin Hird earned a dramatic 2–1 victory against Brighton and ended an unwanted record 10-game run without a League win at Elland Road. Three days later United were relegated.

Gary Hamson was on target in United's dramatic final home game of the season.

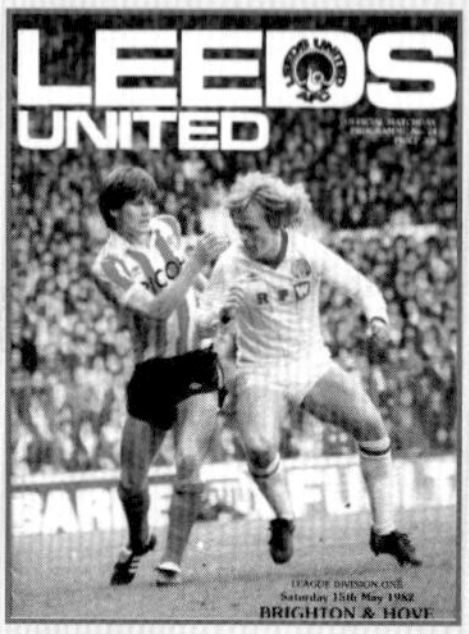

Match No.	Date		Venue	Opponents	Result	FT	HT	Scorers	Attendance
1	Aug	29	A	Swansea City	L	1-5	1-1	Parlane	23,489
2	Sep	2	H	Everton	D	1-1	1-1	Graham	26,502
3		5	H	Wolverhampton W	W	3-0	1-0	Graham 3	20,216
4		12	A	Coventry City	L	0-4	0-2		13,065
5		19	H	Arsenal	D	0-0	0-0		21,410
6		23	A	Manchester City	L	0-4	0-2		35,077
7		26	A	Ipswich Town	L	1-2	1-0	Barnes	22,319
8		30	A	Manchester United	L	0-1	0-0		47,019
9	Oct	3	H	Aston Villa	D	1-1	0-1	Balcombe	21,065
10		10	A	Liverpool	L	0-3	0-2		35,840
11		17	H	West Bromwich Alb	W	3-1	0-0	Graham, Cherry, Connor	19,164
12		24	H	Sunderland	W	1-0	0-0	E. Gray	25,220
13		31	A	Nottingham Forest	L	1-2	1-1	Butterworth	25,272
14	Nov	7	H	Notts County	W	1-0	1-0	Butterworth	19,552
15		21	A	Southampton	L	0-4	0-3		21,127
16		28	H	West Ham United	D	3-3	1-0	Graham, Hird (pen), Cherry	25,637
17	Dec	5	A	Stoke City	W	2-1	2-0	Graham, Hamson	13,901
18		12	H	Tottenham Hotspur	D	0-0	0-0		28,780
19	Jan	16	H	Swansea City	W	2-0	1-0	Stevenson, Butterworth	18,700
20		30	A	Arsenal	L	0-1	0-1		22,408
21	Feb	6	H	Coventry City	D	0-0	0-0		16,385
22		20	H	Ipswich Town	L	0-2	0-0		20,287
23		27	H	Liverpool	L	0-2	0-1		33,689
24	Mar	2	A	Brighton & HA	L	0-1	0-1		12,857
25		10	H	Manchester City	L	0-1	0-0		20,797
26		13	A	Sunderland	W	1-0	0-0	Worthington	20,285
27		16	A	Wolverhampton W	L	0-1	0-1		11,729
28		20	H	Nottingham Forest	D	1-1	1-1	Worthington (pen)	18,036
29		27	A	Notts County	L	1-2	1-0	Worthington	13,316
30	Apr	3	H	Manchester United	D	0-0	0-0		31,118
31		6	A	Middlesbrough	D	0-0	0-0		15,494
32		10	A	Birmingham City	W	1-0	0-0	Hart	14,497
33		13	H	Middlesbrough	D	1-1	0-1	Parlane	20,458
34		17	H	Southampton	L	1-3	1-3	Worthington	21,353
35		24	A	West Ham United	L	3-4	1-0	Connor, Graham, Flynn	24,748
36		28	A	Aston Villa	W	4-1	1-1	Graham, Worthington 2, Connor	20,566
37	May	1	H	Stoke City	D	0-0	0-0		17,775
38		4	A	Everton	L	0-1	0-0		17,137
39		8	A	Tottenham Hotspur	L	1-2	0-1	Worthington	35,020
40		12	H	Birmingham City	D	3-3	2-2	Worthington 2 (1 pen), Connor	18,583
41		15	H	Brighton & HA	W	2-1	0-1	Hamson, Hird	19,831
42		18	A	West Bromwich Alb	L	0-2	0-0		23,118
									Appearances
									Sub appearances
									Goals

FL Cup

R2	Oct	7	H	Ipswich Town	L	0-1	0-0		16,994
		27	A	Ipswich Town	L	0-3	0-3		16,494
									Appearances
									Sub appearances
									Goals

FA Cup

R3	Jan	2	A	Wolverhampton W	W	3-1	1-1	Hamson, Hird, E. Gray	20,923
R4		28	A	Tottenham Hotspur	L	0-1	0-0		46,126
									Appearances
									Sub appearances
									Goals

Back row, left to right: Derek Parlane, Brian Greenhoff, John Lukic, David Seaman, Paul Hart, Neil Firm. Middle row: Geoff Ladley (physiotherapist), Carl Harris, Kevin Hird, Arthur Graham, Terry Connor, Alex Sabella, Eddie Gray, Bob English (kit manager), Peter Gunby (coach). Front row: Martin Wilkinson (assistant manager), Peter Barnes, Byron Stevenson, Allan Clarke (manager), Trevor Cherry, Brian Flynn, Barry Murphy (coach).

Lukic, John	Hird, Kevin	Gray, Frank	Flynn, Brian	Hart, Paul	Cherry, Trevor	Harris, Carl	Graham, Arthur	Parlane, Derek	Gray, Eddie	Barnes, Peter	Greenhoff, Brian	Stevenson, Byron	Firm, Neil	Connor, Terry	Hamson, Gary	Thomas, Gwyn	Arins, Tony	Balcombe, Steve	Burns, Kenny	Butterworth, Aiden	Aspin, Neil	Worthington, Frank
1	2	3	4	5	6	7	8	9	10	11												
1			4	5	6	7	8	9	3	11	2	10										
1	S*		4		6	7	8	9	3	11	**2**	10	5									
1	S*		4		6	**7**	8		3	11	2	10	5	9								
1		5	4		6	7	8		3	11	2	10		9								
1	8	5	4		6	7			**3**	11	2	10		9	S*							
1	10	3	4		6	7	8			11	**2**	5				9	S*					
1	2	3	**4**		6	7	8			11		5		S*	10	9						
1	4	3		5	6	7	8			11		2			10			9				
1	2	3		5	6	7	8		10	11		S*			**4**	9						
1	4	3		5	2	**7**	8			11	S*			9	10				6			
1	4	3		5	2		8		7	11				9	10				6			
1	4	3		5	2		8		7			11			10				6	9		
1	2	3		5	6		8		7	11		4			10					9		
1		3	4	5	2		8			11		7			10				6	9		
1	11	3		5	2	7	8					4			10				6	9		
1	11	3		5	2	7	8					4			10				6	9		
1	11	3		5	2	7	8					4		S*	10				6	**9**		
1	11	3		5	2		**8**		7		S*	4			10				6	9		
1	**11**	3		5	2	S*	8		7			4			10				6	9		
1	11	3	4	5	2		8	9	7				6		10							
1	2	3		5			8	9	10	11		4								7	6	
1	7	3		5	2		8		**10**	11		4		S*					6	9		
1	11	3	S*	**5**	2	7	8				4			10					6	9		
1	4				6	11			3		2			10		8			5	7		9
1	4	11			5			7	3		2			10		8			6			9
1	4	11			5	S*		7	3		**2**			10		8			6			9
1	2	4			5		8	**7**	3	11				10		S*			6			9
1	2	10		5	6		4		3	11				7		8						9
1	2	4		5	6		8		3	11				10		7						9
1	4	3		5	2		8	11						10		7			6			9
1	2			5			8	7	3	11				10		4			6			9
1	**2**	**3**		5			8	7		11				10		4			6	S*		9
1	2	**3**		5		S*	8	7		11				10	4				6			9
1	2	3	4	5	6		8		7	11				S*						**10**		9
1	2	3	4	5	6		8		7	11				10								9
1	**2**	3	4	5	6		8		7	11				10					S*			9
1		3	4	5	2		8		7	11				10					6			9
1	S*	3	4	5	2		8		7	11				10					**6**			9
1	2	3	**4**	5	6		8		7	11				10		S*						9
1	2			5	6		8		7	11				10	3	4						9
1	2	S*		5	6		8		7	11				**10**	9	4			3			
42	35	35	16	32	38	16	38	12	30	30	10	18	3	23	17	13	0	1	22	13	1	17
	3	1	1			3					2	1		4	1	2	1		1	1		
	2		1	1	2		9	2	1	1		1		4	2			1		3		9

1	4	3		5	6	7	8		10	11		2						9				
1	**4**	3		5		7	8		6	11	2	S*		9	10							
2	2	2	0	2	1	2	2	0	2	2	1	1	0	1	1	0	0	1	0	0	0	0
												1										

1	11	3		5	2		8		7			4			10				6	9		
1	11	3	S*	5	2		8		7			**4**			10				6	9		
2	2	2	0	2	2	0	2	0	2	0	0	2	0	0	2	0	0	0	2	2	0	0
			1																			
	1								1						1							

League Table

	P	W	D	L	F	A	Pts
Liverpool	42	26	9	7	80	32	87
Ipswich Town	42	26	5	11	75	53	83
Manchester United	42	22	12	8	59	29	78
Tottenham Hotspur	42	20	11	11	67	48	71
Arsenal	42	20	11	11	48	37	71
Swansea City	42	21	6	15	58	51	69
Southampton	42	19	9	14	72	67	66
Everton	42	17	13	12	56	50	64
West Ham United	42	14	16	12	66	57	58
Manchester City	42	15	13	14	49	50	58
Aston Villa	42	15	12	15	55	53	57
Nottingham Forest	42	15	12	15	42	48	57
Brighton & Hove Albion	42	13	13	16	43	52	52
Coventry City	42	13	11	18	56	62	50
Notts County	42	13	8	21	61	69	47
Birmingham City	42	10	14	18	53	61	44
West Bromwich Albion	42	11	11	20	46	57	44
Stoke City	42	12	8	22	44	63	44
Sunderland	42	11	11	20	38	58	44
Leeds United	42	10	12	20	39	61	42
Wolverhampton W	42	10	10	22	32	63	40
Middlesbrough	42	8	15	19	34	52	39

1982-83

Division Two

Manager: Eddie Gray MBE

Final Position: 8th

Match No.	Date	Venue	Opponents	Result	FT	HT	Scorers	Attendance
1	Aug 28	A	Grimsby Town	D	1-1	0-0	Connor	16,137
2	Sep 4	H	Wolverhampton W	D	0-0	0-0		16,462
3	8	A	Leicester City	W	1-0	0-0	Butterworth	12,963
4	11	A	Sheffield Wed	W	3-2	2-0	Worthington 2, Butterworth	29,050
5	18	H	Derby County	W	2-1	1-1	F.T. Gray, Worthington	16,889
6	25	A	Fulham	L	2-3	1-1	Thomas, Graham	12,798
7	Oct 2	H	Cambridge United	W	2-1	1-1	Butterworth, Hird	14,910
8	9	A	Chelsea	D	0-0	0-0		25,358
9	16	H	Carlisle United	D	1-1	1-1	Hart	14,141
10	20	H	Burnley	W	3-1	2-1	Worthington, Butterworth, Hird	13,827
11	23	A	Blackburn Rovers	D	0-0	0-0		12,040
12	30	H	Newcastle United	W	3-1	1-0	Worthington, Burns, Butterworth	26,570
13	Nov 6	H	Charlton Athletic	L	1-2	0-1	Connor	15,148
14	13	A	Crystal Palace	D	1-1	1-1	Connor	11,673
15	20	H	Middlesbrough	D	0-0	0-0		18,482
16	27	A	Barnsley	L	1-2	1-1	Butterworth	21,530
17	Dec 4	H	Queen's Park R	L	0-1	0-0		11,528
18	11	A	Rotherham United	W	1-0	0-0	Gavin	13,034
19	18	H	Shrewsbury Town	D	1-1	1-0	Hird	8,741
20	26	A	Oldam Athletic	D	2-2	1-1	Burns, Sheridan	15,658
21	28	H	Bolton Wanderers	D	1-1	0-0	Graham	16,180
22	Jan 1	A	Middlesbrough	D	0-0	0-0		17,000
23	3	A	Wolverhampton W	L	0-3	0-1		22,567
24	15	H	Grimsby Town	W	1-0	0-0	Butterworth	13,583
25	22	A	Derby County	D	3-3	1-0	Graham 2, Hart	17,005
26	Feb 12	A	Cambridge United	D	0-0	0-0		6,909
27	19	H	Chelsea	D	3-3	1-1	Butterworth, F.T. Gray (pen), Graham	19,365
28	26	A	Carlisle United	D	2-2	2-0	Connor, Butterworth	6,419
29	Mar 5	H	Blackburn Rovers	W	2-1	1-1	F.T. Gray (pen), Hird	12,280
30	12	A	Newcastle United	L	1-2	0-1	Connor	24,580
31	19	A	Charlton Athletic	W	1-0	0-0	Sheridan	8,229
32	26	H	Crystal Palace	W	2-1	0-1	Ritchie, F.T. Gray (pen)	13,973
33	Apr 2	A	Bolton Wanderers	W	2-1	1-0	Butterworth, Hart	10,784
34	5	H	Oldham Athletic	D	0-0	0-0		18,442
35	9	A	Burnley	W	2-1	1-1	Ritchie, Scott (og)	12,149
36	16	H	Fulham	D	1-1	1-0	Wright	24,328
37	23	A	Queen's Park R	L	0-1	0-1		19,573
38	27	H	Sheffield Wed	L	1-2	1-1	Ritchie	16,591
39	30	H	Barnsley	D	0-0	0-0		15,344
40	May 2	H	Leicester City	D	2-2	1-0	O'Neill (og), F.T. Gray (pen)	14,442
41	7	A	Shrewsbury Town	D	0-0	0-0		6,052
42	14	H	Rotherham United	D	2-2	0-1	Butterworth, Donnelly	14,958
								Appearances
								Sub appearances
							Two own-goals	Goals

FL Cup

Round	Date	Venue	Opponents	Result	FT	HT	Scorers	Attendance
R2	Oct 6	H	Newcastle United	L	0-1	0-1		24,012
	27	A	Newcastle United	W	4-1*	1-1	Saunders (og), Worthington, Butterworth, Connor	24,173
R3	Nov 10	H	Huddersfield Town	L	0-1	0-0		24,215
								Appearances
								Sub appearances
							One own-goal	Goals

* After extra-time (score 2-1, agg 2-2 after 90 minutes)

FA Cup

Round	Date	Venue	Opponents	Result	FT	HT	Scorers	Attendance
R3	Jan 8	H	Preston North End	W	3-0	1-0	Sheridan, Connor, Graham	16,816
R4	29	A	Arsenal	D	1-1	0-0	Nicholas (og)	33,930
Rep	Feb 2	H	Arsenal	D	1-1*	0-0	Butterworth	24,410
2Rep	9	A	Arsenal	L	1-2	0-0	Connor	26,802
								Appearances
								Sub appearances
							One own-goal	Goals

* After extra-time (score 0-0 after 90 minutes)

Did you know that?

18 December 1982: A meagre 8,741 fans at a ghostly Elland Road witnessed a 1–1 draw with Shrewsbury as the terraces were closed – as they had been for the previous game against QPR – by order of the FA as punishment for serious crowd trouble against Newcastle in October.

1 February 1983: Gales blew off part of the Lowfields Road Stand roof and a section had to be closed for the following night's FA Cup replay against Arsenal to go ahead.

5 March 1983: John Lukic made his 146th successive League appearance in a 2–1 win against Blackburn, but was dropped after putting in a transfer request and joined Arsenal in the summer.

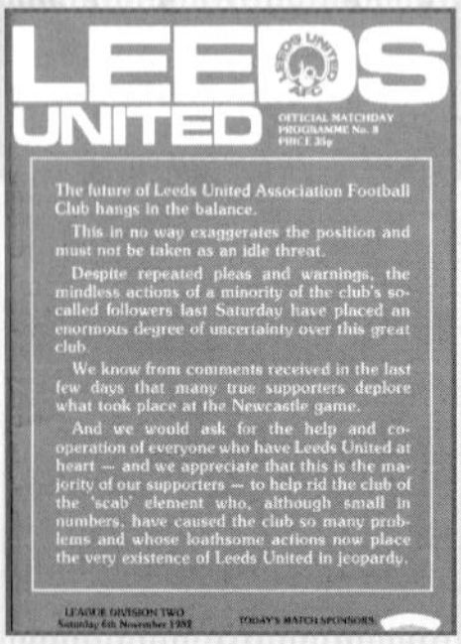

LEEDS UNITED

OFFICIAL MATCHDAY PROGRAMME No. 8
PRICE 35p

The future of Leeds United Association Football Club hangs in the balance.

This in no way exaggerates the position and must not be taken as an idle threat.

Despite repeated pleas and warnings, the mindless actions of a minority of the club's so-called followers last Saturday have placed an enormous degree of uncertainty over this great club.

We know from comments received in the last few days that many true supporters deplore what took place at the Newcastle game.

And we would ask for the help and co-operation of everyone who have Leeds United at heart — and we appreciate that this is the majority of our supporters — to help rid the club of the 'scab' element who, although small in numbers, have caused the club so many problems and whose loathsome actions now place the very existence of Leeds United in jeopardy.

LEAGUE DIVISION TWO
Saturday 6th November 1982

TODAY'S MATCH SPONSORS

United had to read the riot act to their own fans after several incidents of terrace trouble.

Youngster Aidan Butterworth topped the scoring charts.

Back row, left to right: Gary Hamson, Derek Parlane, Martin Dickinson, Frank Gray, Gwyn Thomas, Peter Barnes. Middle row: Peter Gunby (reserve team coach), Keith Mincher (youth coach), Aidan Butterworth, Kevin Hird, Paul Hart, John Lukic, David Seaman, Frank Worthington, Kenny Burns, Barry Murphy (first team coach), Geoff Ladley (physiotherapist). Front row: Brian Flynn, Trevor Cherry, Eddie Gray (player-manager), Jimmy Lumsden (assistant manager), Terry Connor, Arthur Graham.

Lukic, John	Hird, Kevin	Gray, Eddie	Dickinson, Martin	Hart, Paul	Thomas, Gwyn	Connor, Terry	Butterworth, Aiden	Worthington, Frank	Gray, Frank	Graham, Arthur	Cherry, Trevor	Parlane, Derek	Burns, Kenny	Gavin, Mark	Flynn, Brian	Sheridan, John	Aspin, Neil	McNab, Neil	Donnelly, John	Harvey, David	Ritchie, Andy	Wright, Tommy	Brown, Tony	Sellars, Scott	Hamson, Gary
1	2	3	4	5	6	7	8	9	10	11															
1	2	3	4	5	6	**7**	8	9	10	11	S*														
1	7	3	4	5	6		8	9	10	11	2														
1	7	**3**	4	5	6	S*	8	9	10	11	2														
1	**7**	3	4	5	6		8	9	10	11	2	S*													
1	7	**3**	4	5	6		8	9	10	11	2		S*												
1	7		**2**	5	6		8	9	10	11	3		4	S*											
1	7	3		5	6		8	9	10	11	2		4												
1	7	3		5	6	S*	8	9	**10**	11	2				4										
1	7	3		5	6		8	9	10	11	2		4												
1	7	3		5	6		8	9	10	11	2		4												
1	**7**	3	5		6	S*	8	9	10	11	2		4												
1	7	3	5		6	S*	8	9	10	11	**2**		4												
1	7			5	10	8		9	3	11	2		6		4										
1	7			5	10	8	S*	**9**	3	11	2		6			4									
1	7			5	10	8	9		3	11	2		6			4									
1	S*		2	5			9		3	11	10		6	**8**		4	7								
1	7		2	5	10		9		3	11			6	8		4									
1	7		4	5	2		9		3				6	11		8		10							
1	7		2	5	10		9		3	11			6			4		8							
1	7		**2**	5	10		8		3	11			6	S*		4	9								
1				5	10	8	9		3	11			6			4	2	7							
1	S*			5	10	8	9		**3**	11			6			4	2	7							
1	S*	**3**		5		8	9		10	11			6			4	2	7							
1	S*	3		5	**7**	8	9		10	11			6			4	2								
1	S*	3	**6**	5	7	8	9		10	11						4	2								
1	S*	3	6	5	**7**	8	9		10	11						4	2								
1	S*	3	6	5	7	9	8		10	11						**4**	2								
1	S*		6	5	**7**	9	8		3	11						4	2		10						
	7		6	5		9	8		3	11			10			4	**2**		S*	1					
	7		6	5	2	8	9		3	11						4			10	1					
	7		6	5	2		8		3	11						4			10	1	9				
	7		6	5	2		9		3	11						4			10	1	8				
	7	S*	6	5	2		**8**		3	11						4			10	1	9				
	7	8	6	5	2				3	11						4			10	1	9				
	7	8	6	5	2				3	11						4	S*		10	1		**9**			
	7	8	6	5	2				3	11				S*		4			**10**	1	9				
	7		6	5	**2**		8		3	11				S*		4			10	1	9				
	7		6	5	2		8		3	11						4			10	1	9				
			6		7		8		3							4	2		10	1	9	11	5		
			6	5	7		**8**		3							4	2		10	1	9	S*		11	
	S*		6	5	7		8		3	**11**							2		10	1	9	4			
29	30	20	31	39	39	15	37	15	42	39	15	0	19	3	2	27	14	5	13	13	10	3	1	1	0
	9	1			2	4	1				1	1	1	4			1		1			1			
	4			3	1	5	11	5	5	5			2	1					1		3	1			

1	7	3		5	6	S*	8	9	10	11	**2**		4												
1	7	**3**		5	6	S*	8	9	10	11	2		4												
1	S*	**3**		5	6	7	8	9	10	11	2		4												
3	2	3	0	3	3	1	3	3	3	3	3	0	3	0	0	0	0	0	0	0	0	0	0	0	0
	1					2																			
						1	1	1																	

1	S*	3		5	10	8	9			11			6			**4**	2	7							
1	S*	3	6	5	4	8	9		10	11							2								**7**
1	7	3	6	5	4	9	8		10	11							2								
1		3	6	5	7	9	8		10	11						4	2								
4	1	4	3	4	4	4	4	0	3	4	0	0	1	0	0	2	4	1	0	0	0	0	0	0	1
	2																								
						2	1			1						1									

League Table

	P	W	D	L	F	A	Pts
Queen's Park Rangers	42	26	7	9	77	36	85
Wolverhampton W	42	20	15	7	68	44	75
Leicester City	42	20	10	12	72	44	70
Fulham	42	20	9	13	64	47	69
Newcastle United	42	18	13	11	75	53	67
Sheffield Wednesday	42	16	15	11	60	47	63
Oldham Athletic	42	14	19	9	64	47	61
Leeds United	42	13	21	8	51	46	60
Shrewsbury Town	42	15	14	13	48	48	59
Barnsley	42	14	15	13	57	55	57
Blackburn Rovers	42	15	12	15	58	58	57
Cambridge United	42	13	12	17	42	60	51
Derby County	42	10	19	13	49	58	49
Carlisle United	42	12	12	18	68	70	48
Crystal Palace	42	12	12	18	43	52	48
Middlesbrough	42	11	15	16	46	67	48
Charlton Athletic	42	13	9	20	63	86	48
Chelsea	42	11	14	17	51	61	47
Grimsby Town	42	12	11	19	45	70	47
Rotherham United	42	10	15	17	45	68	45
Burnley	42	12	8	22	56	66	44
Bolton Wanderers	42	11	11	20	42	61	44

1983-84

Division Two

Manager: Eddie Gray MBE

Final Position: 10th

Did you know that?

29 August 1983: Andy Watson marked his second Leeds appearance with a goal after 20 seconds as Brighton were beaten 3–2.

5 October 1983: Chester, 92nd in the League, embarrassed United with a 1–0 League Cup win at Elland Road in front of just 8,176 fans. Leeds won the return leg 4–1.

9 November 1983: To mark his first call-up to the Welsh squad for a European Championship game against Bulgaria, Gwyn Thomas received a carriage clock from vice-chairman Leslie Silver before the Milk Cup tie against Oxford. Injury later forced Thomas to pull out of the squad and he never played for his country.

24 April 1984: Peter Lorimer became United's goalscoring record holder when his penalty hit the back of the Oldham net, moving him past John Charles with 155 goals.

Record goalscorer Peter Lorimer.

Match No.	Date		Venue	Opponents	Result	FT	HT	Scorers	Attendance
1	Aug	27	H	Newcastle United	L	0-1	0-1		30,806
2		29	H	Brighton & HA	W	3-2	2-1	Watson, F.T. Gray, Sheridan	13,303
3	Sep	3	A	Middlesbrough	D	2-2	1-0	F.T. Gray (pen), McCluskey	12,793
4		6	A	Grimsby Town	L	0-2	0-1		8,000
5		10	H	Cardiff City	W	1-0	0-0	McCluskey	12,336
6		17	A	Fulham	L	1-2	0-0	Ritchie	10,055
7		24	H	Manchester City	L	1-2	0-0	Ritchie	21,918
8	Oct	1	A	Shrewsbury Town	L	1-5	1-0	Ritchie	6,289
9		8	A	Sheffield Wed	L	1-3	0-1	F.T. Gray (pen)	26,814
10		14	H	Cambridge United	W	3-1	1-0	Hird, Watson, Donnelly	9,923
11		22	A	Barnsley	W	2-0	0-0	Donnelly, Barnes	18,236
12		29	H	Portsmouth	W	2-1	1-0	Watson, Barnes	16,254
13	Nov	5	H	Crystal Palace	D	1-1	0-1	McCluskey	14,847
14		12	A	Blackburn Rovers	D	1-1	1-0	Donnelly	9,556
15		19	A	Derby County	D	1-1	0-0	Ritchie	16,726
16		26	H	Chelsea	D	1-1	0-0	McCluskey	20,680
17	Dec	3	A	Carlisle United	L	0-1	0-0		6,845
18		15	A	Charlton Athletic	L	0-2	0-1		6,285
19		26	H	Huddersfield Town	L	1-2	0-2	Wright	23,791
20		27	A	Oldham Athletic	L	2-3	1-0	Wright, F.T. Gray	8,393
21		31	H	Middlesbrough	W	4-1	1-0	Sellars, McCluskey 2, Wright	14,215
22	Jan	2	A	Manchester City	D	1-1	1-0	Bond (og)	34,441
23		21	H	Fulham	W	1-0	1-0	Watson	11,421
24	Feb	4	H	Shrewsbury Town	W	3-0	2-0	Watson 2, Brown	10,628
25		11	A	Cardiff City	W	1-0	0-0	McCluskey	9,407
26		15	H	Swansea City	W	1-0	0-0	Lorimer	10,031
27		18	A	Portsmouth	W	3-2	1-2	Wright, Watson, Lorimer (pen)	13,911
28		25	H	Barnsley	L	1-2	1-0	Wright	19,138
29	Mar	3	A	Crystal Palace	D	0-0	0-0		8,077
30		10	H	Blackburn Rovers	W	1-0	0-0	Butterworth	12,857
31		17	H	Grimsby Town	W	2-1	1-1	Aspin, Sellars	14,412
32		24	A	Brighton & HA	L	0-3	0-2		12,605
33		28	A	Newcastle United	L	0-1	0-1		30,877
34		31	H	Sheffield Wed	D	1-1	0-0	Ritchie	25,343
35	Apr	7	A	Cambridge United	D	2-2	0-0	Barnes, Sellars	4,700
36		14	H	Derby County	D	0-0	0-0		12,549
37		21	A	Huddersfield Town	D	2-2	1-0	Wright, Barnes	16,270
38		24	H	Oldham Athletic	W	2-0	0-0	Ritchie, Lorimer (pen)	9,576
39		28	A	Chelsea	L	0-5	0-3		33,447
40	May	5	H	Carlisle United	W	3-0	0-0	Gavin, Ritchie, McCluskey	8,278
41		7	A	Swansea City	D	2-2	1-0	Wright, Lorimer	5,498
42		12	H	Charlton Athletic	W	1-0	0-0	Wright	13,254
									Appearances
									Sub appearances
								One own-goal	Goals

FL Cup

R2	Oct	5	H	Chester City	L	0-1	0-1		8,176
		26	A	Chester City	W	4-1	1-0	Ritchie 2, Burns, Barnes	8,044
R3	Nov	9	H	Oxford United	D	1-1	0-1	McCluskey	13,349
Rep		23	A	Oxford United	L	1-4	0-3	Burns	13,389
									Appearances
									Sub appearances
									Goals

FA Cup

R3	Jan	7	H	Scunthorpe United	D	1-1	1-0	Wright	17,130
Rep		10	A	Scunthorpe United	D	1-1*	0-0	Wright	13,129
2 Rep		16	A	Scunthorpe United	L	2-4	1-2	Wright, Ritchie	13,312
									Appearances
									Sub appearances
									Goals

* After extra-time (score 0-0 after 90 minutes)

Back row, left to right: Keith Mincher (youth coach), Andy Watson, John Donnelly, Tony Brown, Neil Aspin, George McCluskey, Peter Gunby (reserve team coach). Middle row: Geoff Ladley (physiotherapist), Scott Sellars, Mark Gavin, Tommy Wright, John Sheridan, David Harvey, Gary Hamson, Kevin Hird, Andy Ritchie, Gwyn Thomas, Barry Murphy (first team coach). Front row: Peter Barnes, Aidan Butteworth, Jimmy Lumsden (assistant manager), Eddie Gray (player-manager), Martin Dickinson, Frank Gray.

Harvey, David	Thomas, Gwyn	Gray, Frank	Sheridan, John	Brown, Tony	Dickinson, Martin	Watson, Andy	McCluskey, George	Ritchie, Andy	Donnelly, John	Barnes, Peter	Butterworth, Aiden	Hamson, Gary	Aspin, Neil	Gavin, Mark	Hughes, Phil	Gray, Eddie	Burns, Kenny	Wright, Tommy	Hird, Kevin	McGoldrick, John	Sellars, Scott	Lormer, Peter	Irwin, Denis	Thompson, Nigel
1	2	3	4	5	6	**7**	8	9	10	11	S*													
1	2	3	7	5	6	4	8	9		11	S*	**10**												
1	10	3	7	5	6	4	8	9	S*	**11**			2											
1	10	3	7	5	6	4	8		S*		9		**2**	11										
	2	3	10	5	6	4	8	**9**			S*			11	1	7								
	2	3	10	5	6	4	8	9			S*			11	1	**7**								
1	2	3	7	5	6		**8**	9	10					11			4	S*						
1	2	3	7	**5**	6	S*	8	9	10					11			4							
1	11	3	7		6	**4**	8	9	10	S*							5		2					
1	11	3	7		6	4	8	9	10								5		2					
1	11	3	**7**		6	4	8	9	10	S*							5		2					
1	7	3		6		4	8	9	10	11			2				5							
1	7	3			6	**4**	8	9	10	11	S*		2				5							
1		3			6	4	8	9	10	11			2				5	7						
1	7	3			6	4	8	9	10	11							5			2				
1	7	3			6	4	8	9	10	11							5			2				
1	**7**	3		6	2	4	8	9	10	11		S*					5							
1		3			6	**4**	8	9	10	11		S*					5	7		2				
1		3			6		8	9	**10**			4					5	7	S*	2	11			
1		3			6		**8**	9	10			4	5					7	S*	2	11			
1		3			6		**8**	9	10			4	5					7		2	11	S*		
1		3			6		**8**	9	10			4	5					7		2	11	S*		
1						4		9		11		3	5					7	2		8	10	6	
1				5	6	4	S*	9		11		3						7	2		**8**	10		
1				5	6	4	S*	9		**11**		3						7	2		8	10		
1				5	6	4	S*	9		**11**		3						7	2		8	10		
1				5	6	4	S*	**9**		11		3						7	2		8	10		
1		6		5		4	**9**			11		3		S*				7	2		8	10		
1	S*			5		4				11				9		**3**		7	2		8	10	6	
1					6	**4**		9		11	S*	3	5					7	2		8	10		
1				5	6			9		11		3	4					7	2		8	10		
1		**3**		5	6			9		11	S*		4					7	2		8	10		
1					6			9		11	7	3	5						2		8	10	4	
1					6			9		11	7	3	5						2		8	10	4	
1				6				9		11	7	3	5					S*	**2**		8	10	4	
1					6			9	**4**	11		3	5	S*				7			8	10	2	
1					6	4	S*	9	**10**	11		3	5					7				8	2	
1					6	4		9	8			3	5	11				7				10	2	
1					6	4	S*	9				3	5	11				7			**8**	10	2	
1				6		4	S*	9	8			3	5	**11**				7				10	2	
1				6		4	S*	**9**	8			3		11				7				10	2	5
1				6		4	9		8			3	5			11		7				10	2	
40	16	24	11	22	34	30	24	38	23	25	4	23	21	10	2	4	13	23	16	7	19	20	12	1
	1					1	8		2	2	7	2		2				2	2			2		
		4	1	1		7	8	7	3	4	1		1	1				8	1		3	4		

1	10	3			6	4	S*	9			8			**11**			5		7	2				
1	7	3			6	4	8	9	10	11			2				5							
1	7	3			6	4	8	**9**	10	11			2	S*			5							
1	7	3			6	4	8	9	10	11							5	S*		**2**				
4	4	4	0	0	4	4	3	4	3	3	1	0	2	1	0	0	4	0	1	2	0	0	0	0
							1							1				1						
							1	2		1							2							

1		**3**			6		8	9	10			4	5					7		2	11	S*		
1					6	4	8	9				3	5					7		2	11	10		
1		4					8	9		11		3	5					7		2		10	6	
3	0	2	0	0	2	1	3	3	1	1	0	3	3	0	0	0	0	3	0	3	2	2	1	0
																						1		
								1										3						

League Table

	P	W	D	L	F	A	Pts
Chelsea	42	25	13	4	90	40	88
Sheffield Wednesday	42	26	10	6	72	34	88
Newcastle United	42	24	8	10	85	53	80
Manchester City	42	20	10	12	66	48	70
Grimsby Town	42	19	13	10	60	47	70
Blackburn Rovers	42	17	16	9	57	46	67
Carlisle United	42	16	16	10	48	41	64
Shrewsbury Town	42	17	10	15	49	53	61
Brighton & Hove Albion	42	17	9	16	69	60	60
Leeds United	42	16	12	14	55	56	60
Fulham	42	15	12	15	60	53	57
Huddersfield Town	42	14	15	13	56	49	57
Charlton Athletic	42	16	9	17	53	64	57
Barnsley	42	15	7	20	57	53	52
Cardiff City	42	15	6	21	53	66	51
Portsmouth	42	14	7	21	73	64	49
Middlesbrough	42	12	13	17	41	47	49
Crystal Palace	42	12	11	19	42	52	47
Oldham Athletic	42	13	8	21	47	73	47
Derby County	42	11	9	22	36	72	42
Swansea City	42	7	8	27	36	85	29
Cambridge United	42	4	12	26	28	77	24

1984-85

Division Two

Manager: Eddie Gray MBE

Final position: 7th

Did you know that?

19 January 1985: Teenager Tommy Wright scored his first senior hat-trick as Notts County were beaten 5–2. His father, Thomas Wright, and cousin, Jackie Sinclair, both played for Scotland. Tommy's brother, Barry, was a National Hunt jockey.

2 March 1985: John Stiles, son of World Cup winner Nobby and nephew of Leeds legend Johnny Giles, made his League debut in a goalless draw at Middlesbrough.

John Stiles made his League debut against Middlesbrough.

Match No.	Date	Venue	Opponents	Result	FT	HT	Scorers	Attendance
1	Aug 25	A	Notts County	W	2-1	1-1	Wright 2	12,196
2	27	H	Fulham	W	2-0	0-0	McCluskey, Wright	14,207
3	Sep 1	H	Wolverhampton W	W	3-2	1-1	Wright 2, Lorimer	17,843
4	8	A	Grimsby Town	W	2-0	0-0	McCluskey, Lorimer	13,290
5	12	A	Cardiff City	L	1-2	0-1	Sellars	6,893
6	15	H	Portsmouth	L	0-1	0-0		19,438
7	22	A	Crystal Palace	L	1-3	0-2	Sellars	19,460
8	29	H	Oldham Athletic	W	6-0	1-0	Wright, Ritchie 3 (1 pen), Sheridan, Linighan	14,290
9	Oct 6	H	Sheffield United	D	1-1	0-0	Lorimer (pen)	25,547
10	13	A	Barnsley	L	0-1	0-1		16,199
11	20	A	Huddersfield Town	L	0-1	0-0		15,257
12	27	H	Middlesbrough	W	2-0	1-0	Lorimer (pen), Ritchie	14,838
13	Nov 3	A	Charlton Athletic	W	3-2	1-1	Sheridan, McCluskey, Gavin	6,950
14	10	H	Carlisle United	D	1-1	1-1	Dickinson	13,327
15	17	H	Brighton & HA	W	1-0	1-0	Ritchie	13,127
16	24	A	Oxford United	L	2-5	2-1	Wright, Lorimer	12,192
17	Dec 1	H	Wimbledon	W	5-2	2-1	Wright, Ritchie 3, Sellars	10,899
18	8	A	Shrewsbury Town	W	3-2	2-2	Ritchie 2, Linighan	6,358
19	15	H	Birmingham City	L	0-1	0-0		15,854
20	22	A	Wolverhampton W	W	2-0	1-0	Gray, McCluskey	9,259
21	26	A	Blackburn Rovers	L	1-2	0-1	McCluskey	20,149
22	29	H	Cardiff City	D	1-1	1-0	Lorimer (pen)	11,798
23	Jan 1	H	Manchester City	D	1-1	1-1	Ritchie	22,626
24	19	H	Notts County	W	5-0	1-0	Sheridan, Wright 3, Irwin	11,369
25	Feb 2	A	Oldham Athletic	D	1-1	0-1	Lorimer (pen)	8,824
26	9	H	Grimsby Town	D	0-0	0-0		12,517
27	23	H	Charlton Athletic	W	1-0	0-0	Lorimer	10,644
28	26	A	Carlisle United	D	2-2	0-1	Wright, Aspin	5,484
29	Mar 2	A	Middlesbrough	D	0-0	0-0		8,781
30	9	H	Huddersfield Town	D	0-0	0-0		18,607
31	12	A	Portsmouth	L	1-3	1-2	Sheridan	16,208
32	16	H	Barnsley	W	2-0	0-0	Lorimer, Sellars	13,091
33	23	A	Sheffield United	L	1-2	0-1	Ritchie	21,468
34	30	A	Fulham	W	2-0	0-0	Wright 2	7,901
35	Apr 6	H	Blackburn Rovers	D	0-0	0-0		15,829
36	8	A	Manchester City	W	2-1	0-0	Baird, Sellars	33,553
37	13	H	Crystal Palace	W	4-1	1-0	Baird, Sellars, Sheridan 2	12,286
38	20	A	Brighton & HA	D	1-1	1-1	Sellars	17,279
39	27	H	Oxford United	W	1-0	0-0	Baird	17,992
40	May 4	A	Wimbledon	D	2-2	1-0	Baird 2	6,638
41	6	H	Shrewsbury Town	W	1-0	0-0	Baird	12,423
42	11	A	Birmingham City	L	0-1	0-1		24,847
								Appearances
								Sub appearances
								Goals
FL Cup								
R2	Sep 25	A	Gillingham	W	2-1	1-1	Wright, Ritchie	8,881
	Oct 10	H	Gillingham	W	3-2	1-1	Gavin, Sellars, Lorimer	11,109
R3	31	H	Watford	L	0-4	0-1		21,221
								Appearances
								Sub appearances
								Goals
FA Cup								
R3	Jan 4	H	Everton	L	0-2	0-1		21,211
								Appearances
								Sub appearances
								Goals

Back row, left to right: Martin Dickinson, Neil Aspin, Andy Linighan, Tony Brown, George McCluskey, John Donnelly. Middle row: Geoff Ladley (physiotherapist), Keith Mincher (youth coach), John Stiles, John Sheridan, David Harvey, Phil Hughes, Denis Irwin, Peter Lorimer, Mark Gavin, Peter Gunby (reserve team coach). Front row: Andy Ritchie, Frank Gray, Scott Sellars, Eddie Gray (manager), Jimmy Lumsden (assistant manager), Tommy Wright, Gary Hamson, Andy Watson.

Harvey, David	Irwin, Denis	Hamson, Gary	Watson, Andy	Linighan, Andy	Aspin, Neil	Wright, Tommy	Sheridan, John	McCluskey, George	Lorimer, Peter	Gray, Frank	Gavin, Mark	Sellars, Scott	Ritchie, Andy	Dickinson, Martin	Donnelly, John	Ell, Roger	Hughes, Phil	Day, Mervyn	Stiles, John	Brown, Tony	Baird, Ian	Simmonds, Lyndon
1	2	**3**	4	5	6	7	8	9	10	11	S*											
1	2		4	5	6	7	8	9	10	3		11										
1	2		4	5	6	7	8	9	10	3		11										
1	2		4	5	6	7	8	9	10	3		11										
1	2		**4**	5	6	7	8	9	10	3	S*	11										
1	2		4	5	6	7	8	**9**	10	3		11	S*									
1	2		4	5	6	7	**8**		10	3	S*	11	9									
1	2			5		7	8		10	3	11	4	9	6								
1	2			5		7	8		10	3	11	4	9	6								
1	2			5		7	8	S*	10	3	**11**	4	9	6								
1	2			5		7	**8**		10	3	11	4	9	6	S*							
1	2			5		7	8		10	3	11	4	9	6								
1		3		5	2	7	8	9	10		11	4		6								
1	2	3		5		7	8	**9**	10		11	4	S*	6								
1	2	3		5		7	8		10	11		4	9	6								
1	2	3		5		7	8		10	11	S*	**4**	9	6								
1	2	3		5	6	7	8		**10**	11		4	9			S*						
1	2	3		5	6	7	8			11		4	9	10								
1	2	3		5	6	7	8			11		4	9	10								
	2	3		5	6	7	8	9	10	11		4					1					
	2	3		5	6	7	8	9	10	11		4					1					
1	2	3		5	6	7	8	9	10	11		4										
	2	3		5	6	7	8	S*	10	11		4	**9**				1					
	2	3		5	6	7	8	S*	10	**11**		4	9				1					
	2	3		5	6	7	8		10	11		4	9					1				
	2	3		5	6	7	8	S*	10	11		**4**	9					1				
	2	3		5	6	7	8	S*	10	11		**4**	9					1				
	2	3		5	6	7	8	4	10	11			9					1				
	2	3		5	6	7	8		10	11			9					1	4			
	2	3		5	6	7	8		10	11		4	9					1				
	2	**3**		5		S*	8		10	11		4	9					1		6	7	
	2	3		5		7	8		10	11		4		6				1			9	
	2	3		5	6	7	8		10	11		4	S*					1			9	
	2	3		5	6	7	8	S*	10	**11**		4	9					1				
	2	3		5	6	7	8	**11**	10			4	9					1				S*
	2	3		5	6	7	8		10	11		4						1			9	
	2	3		5	6	7	8		10	11		4						1			9	
	2	3		5	6	7	8		10	11		4						1			9	
	2	3		5	6	7	8		10	11		4						1			9	
	2	3		5	6	7	8		**10**	11		4	S*					1			9	
	2	3		5	6	**7**	8		10	11		4	S*					1			9	
	2	3		5	**6**	7	8		10	11		4	S*					1			9	
20	41	31	7	42	32	41	42	13	40	39	7	39	22	12	0	0	4	18	1	1	10	0
						1		6			4		6		1	1						1
	1			2	1	14	6	5	9	1	7	7	12	1							6	

1	2			5		7	8		10	3	11	4	9	6								
1	2			5		7	8		10	3	11	4	9	6								
1	2			5		7	8	S*	10	3	11	**4**	9	6								
3	3	0	0	3	0	3	3	0	3	3	3	3	3	3	0	0	0	0	0	0	0	0
								1														
						1			1		1	1	1									

	2	3		5	6	7	8	**9**	10	11	S*	4					1					
0	1	1	0	1	1	1	1	1	1	1	0	1	0	0	0	0	1	0	0	0	0	0
											1											

League Table

	P	W	D	L	F	A	Pts
Oxford United	42	25	9	8	84	36	84
Birmingham City	42	25	7	10	59	33	82
Manchester City	42	21	11	10	66	40	74
Portsmouth	42	20	14	8	69	50	74
Blackburn Rovers	42	21	10	11	66	41	73
Brighton & Hove Albion	42	20	12	10	54	34	72
Leeds United	42	19	12	11	66	43	69
Shrewsbury Town	42	18	11	13	66	53	65
Fulham	42	19	8	15	68	64	65
Grimsby Town	42	18	8	16	72	64	62
Barnsley	42	14	16	12	42	42	58
Wimbledon	42	16	10	16	71	75	58
Huddersfield Town	42	15	10	17	52	64	55
Oldham Athletic	42	15	8	19	49	67	53
Crystal Palace	42	12	12	18	46	65	48
Carlisle United	42	13	8	21	50	67	47
Charlton Athletic	42	11	12	19	51	63	45
Sheffield United	42	10	14	18	54	66	44
Middlesbrough	42	10	10	22	41	57	40
Notts County	42	10	7	25	45	73	37
Cardiff City	42	9	8	25	47	79	35
Wolverhampton W	42	8	9	25	37	79	33

1985-86

Division Two

Manager: Eddie Gray MBE until October then Billy Bremner

Final Position: 14th

Did you know that?

13 September 1985: An extraordinary general meeting of the club's shareholders agreed to set in motion plans to sell the freehold of the Elland Road stadium to Leeds City Council to ease the club's £1.5 million overdraft.

23 November 1985: United supporters turned out in force for the 2–1 win at Carlisle despite an FA ban on Leeds fans attending away games after trouble at a recent match at Millwall. Hundreds were at Brunton Park and Wimbledon a fortnight later, so the FA lifted the ban, although an all-ticket ruling remained.

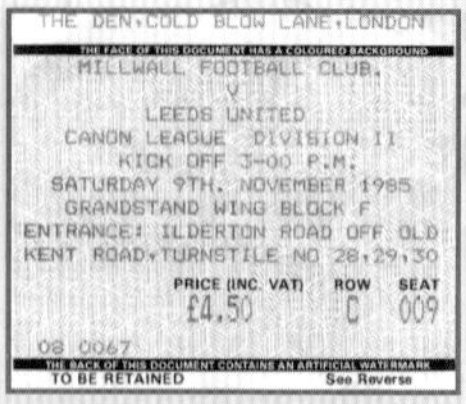
THE DEN, COLD BLOW LANE, LONDON

THE FACE OF THIS DOCUMENT HAS A COLOURED BACKGROUND

MILLWALL FOOTBALL CLUB.

V

LEEDS UNITED

CANON LEAGUE DIVISION II

KICK OFF 3-00 P.M.

SATURDAY 9TH. NOVEMBER 1985

GRANDSTAND WING BLOCK F

ENTRANCE: ILDERTON ROAD OFF OLD KENT ROAD, TURNSTILE NO 28,29,30

PRICE (INC. VAT)	ROW	SEAT
£4.50	C	009

08 0067

THE BACK OF THIS DOCUMENT CONTAINS AN ARTIFICIAL WATERMARK

TO BE RETAINED See Reverse

Four policemen were injured in clashes between Leeds and Millwall fans at The Den, prompting a ban on United's away support which had to be lifted because it was unenforceable.

Match No.	Date		Venue	Opponents	Result	FT	HT	Scorers	Attendance
1	Aug	17	A	Fulham	L	1-3	1-0	Lorimer	5,772
2		21	H	Wimbledon	D	0-0	0-0		12,426
3		24	H	Hull City	D	1-1	0-0	Baird	16,689
4		26	A	Stoke City	L	2-6	0-1	Aspin, Snodin	7,047
5		31	H	Charlton Athletic	L	1-2	1-1	Lorimer (pen)	10,860
6	Sep	4	A	Brighton & HA	W	1-0	0-0	McCluskey	9,798
7		7	A	Shrewsbury Town	W	3-1	1-0	Wright, McCluskey, Baird	4,168
8		14	H	Sunderland	D	1-1	0-1	Sheridan	19,693
9		21	H	Bradford City	W	2-1	0-0	Lorimer, Sellars	21,104
10		28	H	Sheffield United	D	1-1	0-1	Baird	15,622
11	Oct	5	A	Huddersfield Town	L	1-3	1-2	Baird	9,983
12		12	H	Middlesbrough	W	1-0	1-0	Lorimer (pen)	14,117
13		19	H	Grimsby Town	D	1-1	0-1	Baird	11,244
14		27	A	Barnsley	L	0-3	0-1		8,302
15	Nov	2	H	Portsmouth	W	2-1	0-1	Simmonds 2 (1 pen)	15,672
16		9	A	Millwall	L	1-3	0-1	Ritchie	9,158
17		16	H	Crystal Palace	L	1-3	0-2	McCluskey	10,378
18		23	A	Carlisle United	W	2-1	0-0	Linighan, Ritchie	3,504
19		30	H	Norwich City	L	0-2	0-1		11,480
20	Dec	7	A	Wimbledon	W	3-0	2-0	Snodin, Baird, Dickinson	3,492
21		14	H	Fulham	W	1-0	0-0	Sheridan	9,998
22		22	A	Hull City	L	1-2	1-2	Sheridan	11,852
23		26	A	Blackburn Rovers	L	0-2	0-2		8,666
24		28	H	Brighton & HA	L	2-3	0-1	Baird, Snodin	13,110
25	Jan	1	H	Oldham Athletic	W	3-1	1-1	Baird 2, Ritchie	10,830
26		11	A	Sunderland	L	2-4	0-1	Baird, Sheridan	15,139
27		16	A	Charlton Athletic	L	0-4	0-3		4,333
28	Feb	1	H	Stoke City	W	4-0	1-0	Stiles, Baird, Swan 2	10,425
29		8	A	Grimsby Town	L	0-1	0-0		6,382
30		15	H	Barnsley	L	0-2	0-0		11,765
31	Mar	8	H	Huddersfield Town	W	2-0	1-0	Ormsby, Snodin	14,667
32		15	A	Middlesbrough	D	2-2	1-1	Simmonds, Rennie	6,889
33		22	H	Shrewsbury Town	D	1-1	0-0	Rennie	9,641
34		28	A	Oldham Athletic	L	1-3	0-1	Ritchie	4,937
35		31	H	Blackburn Rovers	D	1-1	0-0	Ritchie	9,919
36	Apr	5	A	Portsmouth	W	3-2	0-1	Ritchie 2, Baird	14,430
37		9	A	Bradford City	W	1-0	1-0	Aspin	10,751
38		12	H	Millwall	W	3-1	2-1	Sellars, Swan, Ritchie	15,067
39		19	A	Crystal Palace	L	0-3	0-1		6,285
40		22	A	Sheffield United	L	2-3	1-1	Ritchie, Snodin	9,158
41		26	H	Carlisle United	W	2-0	1-0	Ritchie 2	13,868
42	May	3	A	Norwich City	L	0-4	0-1		17,942
									Appearances
									Sub appearances
								One own-goal	Goals

FM Cup

Round	Date		Venue	Opponents	Result	FT	HT	Scorers	Attendance
Grp	Oct	14	A	Manchester City	L	1-6	0-3	Lorimer (pen)	4,029
Grp		16	H	Sheffield United	D	1-1	0-0	Sellars	2,274
									Appearances
									Sub appearances
									Goals

FL Cup

Round	Date		Venue	Opponents	Result	FT	HT	Scorers	Attendance
R2	Sep	25	H	Walsall	D	0-0	0-0		8,869
	Oct	8	A	Walsall	W	3-0	2-0	Linighan, Snodin 2	7,085
R3		30	H	Aston Villa	L	0-3	0-1		15,444
									Appearances
									Sub appearances
									Goals

FA Cup

Round	Date		Venue	Opponents	Result	FT	HT	Scorers	Attendance
R3	Jan	4	A	Peterborough U	L	0-1	0-0		10,137
									Appearances
									Sub appearances
									Goals

Back row, left to right: Martin Dickinson, Andy Ritchie, George McCluskey, Andy Linighan, Neil Aspin, Ian Baird. Middle row: Keith Mincher (youth coach), Gary Hamson, Peter Lorimer, Mervyn Day, Trevor Swinburne, Ian Snodin, John Stiles, Geoff Ladley (physiotherapist). Front row: John Sheridan, Tommy Wright, Jimmy Lumsden (assistant manager), Eddie Gray (manager), Peter Gunby (reserve team coach), Scott Sellars, Denis Irwin.

Day, Mervyn	Irwin, Denis	Hamson, Gary	Snodin, Ian	Linighan, Andy	Aspin, Neil	McCluskey, George	Sheridan, John	Baird, Ian	Lorimer, Peter	Sellars, Scott	Wright, Tommy	Dickinson, Martin	Phelan, Terry	Ritchie, Andy	Swinburne, Trevor	McGregor, John	Simmonds, Lyndon	Caswell, Brian	Robinson, Ronnie	Stiles, John	Thompson, Nigel	Eli, Roger	Swan, Peter	Harle, David	Rennie, David	Ormsby, Brendan	Taylor, Bob
1	2	3	4	5	6	7	8	9	10	11																	
1	2	3	4	5	6	7	8	9	10	11																	
1	2	3	4	5	6	7	8	9	**10**	11	S*																
1	2	3	4	5	6	**7**	8	9	10	11	S*																
1	2	3	4	5	6	S*	8	**9**	10	11	7																
1	2	3	4	5	6	9	8		10		7	11															
1	2		4	5	6	9	8	S*	10		7	**11**	3														
1	2		4	5	6	11	8	9	10	S*	**7**		3														
1	2		4	**5**	6	7	8	9	10	11	S*		3														
1	2		4	5			8	9	10	11	7	6	3														
1	2		4	5		S*	8	9	10	11	7	**6**	3														
1	2	4		5	6	7	8	9	10		S*		3	**11**													
	2	4		5	6	7		9	10			8	3	11	1												
1		8	4	5	6	7		9	10			2	3	11													
1	2	10		5	6		8	9					3	7		4	11										
1		11		5	6	10	8	9				2	3	7		4											
1		10	4	5	6	9	8					S*	3	7		2	11										
1		10	4	5		9	8					11		7		6		2	3								
		10	4	6		9	8					11		7	1	5	S*	2	**3**								
1		10	4	6	5			9				11		7				2	3	8							
1	2	10	4	6	5		8	9				11		7					3								
1		10	4	5	6	**9**	8					11	S*	7				2	3								
1		10	4	**6**	5	9	8			S*		11	3	7				2									
1	2	10	4		5		8	9		S*		11		7							3	**6**					
1	2	10	4		5			**9**		3		11		7									6	8			
1	2	3	4	5	6		10	9				11		7										8			
1	2	11	4		6		10	9				5		7				3							8		
1		10	4		5			9						7				2	3	11			8		6		
1		10	4		5			9				S*		7				**2**	3	11			8		6		
1		10	4		5			9					S*	7					3	2			8	**11**	6		
1			4		2		8	9									7		3	11			10		6	5	
1			4		2		8	9						S*			7		**3**	11			10		6	5	
1		3	4		2		8	9									7			11			10		6	5	
1		3	4		2		8	9						11			7						10		6	5	
1		3	4		2	7	8	9						11									10		6	5	
1			4		2	7	8	9						11					3				10		6	5	
1			4		2	**7**	8	9						11					3	S*			10		6	5	
1			4		2					**7**				9			S*		3	8			10		6	5	11
1			4		2		8	9		S*				11					3				10		6	5	**7**
1			4		2			9		8				11					3	7			10		6	5	
1		3	**4**		2		S*	9		8				7						11			10		6	5	
1		3			2			9		8				7					4	11			10		6	5	
40	19	30	37	24	38	20	31	34	14	13	6	17	12	28	2	5	6	8	16	11	1	1	16	3	16	12	2
						2	1	1		4	4	2	2	1			2			1							
			5	1	2	3	4	12	4	2	1	1		11			3			1			3		2	1	

Day, Mervyn	Irwin, Denis	Hamson, Gary	Snodin, Ian	Linighan, Andy	Aspin, Neil	McCluskey, George	Sheridan, John	Baird, Ian	Lorimer, Peter	Sellars, Scott	Wright, Tommy	Dickinson, Martin	Phelan, Terry	Ritchie, Andy	Swinburne, Trevor	McGregor, John	Simmonds, Lyndon	Caswell, Brian	Robinson, Ronnie	Stiles, John	Thompson, Nigel	Eli, Roger	Swan, Peter	Harle, David	Rennie, David	Ormsby, Brendan	Taylor, Bob
1	2	4		**5**	6	**7**	8	9	10	11			3				S*						S*				
1	**2**			5	**6**		8	9	10	4			3				7			S*	11		S*				
2	2	1	0	2	2	1	2	2	2	2	0	0	2	0	0	0	1	0	0	0	1	0	0	0	0	0	0
																	1			1			2				
									1	1																	

Day, Mervyn	Irwin, Denis	Hamson, Gary	Snodin, Ian	Linighan, Andy	Aspin, Neil	McCluskey, George	Sheridan, John	Baird, Ian	Lorimer, Peter	Sellars, Scott	Wright, Tommy	Dickinson, Martin	Phelan, Terry	Ritchie, Andy	Swinburne, Trevor	McGregor, John	Simmonds, Lyndon	Caswell, Brian	Robinson, Ronnie	Stiles, John	Thompson, Nigel	Eli, Roger	Swan, Peter	Harle, David	Rennie, David	Ormsby, Brendan	Taylor, Bob
1	2		4	5		**7**	8	9	10	11	S*	6	3														
1	2	11	4	5		S*	8	9	10			**6**	3	7													
1	2	11	4	5	6	10	8	9				3		7													
3	3	2	3	3	1	2	3	3	2	1	0	3	2	2	0	0	0	0	0	0	0	0	0	0	0	0	0
						1					1																
			2	1																							

Day, Mervyn	Irwin, Denis	Hamson, Gary	Snodin, Ian	Linighan, Andy	Aspin, Neil	McCluskey, George	Sheridan, John	Baird, Ian	Lorimer, Peter	Sellars, Scott	Wright, Tommy	Dickinson, Martin	Phelan, Terry	Ritchie, Andy	Swinburne, Trevor	McGregor, John	Simmonds, Lyndon	Caswell, Brian	Robinson, Ronnie	Stiles, John	Thompson, Nigel	Eli, Roger	Swan, Peter	Harle, David	Rennie, David	Ormsby, Brendan	Taylor, Bob
1	2	10	4	6	5		S*	9		3		11		7									**8**				
1	1	1	1	1	1	0	0	1	0	1	0	1	0	1	0	0	0	0	0	0	0	0	1	0	0	0	0
							1																				

League Table

	P	W	D	L	F	A	Pts
Norwich City	42	25	9	8	84	37	84
Charlton Athletic	42	22	11	9	78	45	77
Wimbledon	42	21	13	8	58	37	76
Portsmouth	42	22	7	13	69	41	73
Crystal Palace	42	19	9	14	57	52	66
Hull City	42	17	13	12	65	55	64
Sheffield United	42	17	11	14	64	63	62
Oldham Athletic	42	17	9	16	62	61	60
Millwall	42	17	8	17	64	65	59
Stoke City	42	14	15	13	48	50	57
Brighton & Hove Albion	42	16	8	18	64	64	56
Barnsley	42	14	14	14	47	50	56
Bradford City	42	16	6	20	51	63	54
Leeds United	42	15	8	19	56	72	53
Grimsby Town	42	14	10	18	58	62	52
Huddersfield Town	42	14	10	18	51	67	52
Shrewsbury Town	42	14	9	19	52	64	51
Sunderland	42	13	11	18	47	61	50
Blackburn Rovers	42	12	13	17	53	62	49
Carlisle United	42	13	7	22	47	71	46
Middlesbrough	42	12	9	21	44	53	45
Fulham	42	10	6	26	45	69	36

1986-87

Division Two

Manager: Billy Bremner

Final Position: 4th

Did you know that?

7 September 1986: United's hooligan problem reared its ugly head again as fighting broke out at Odsal Stadium where a fish and chip van was overturned and caught fire. The game was held up for 20 minutes and the stadium cleared before the teams completed the final few minutes with no fans in the ground. Bradford won 2–0.

5 January 1987: Skipper Ian Snodin was sold for a United record of £840,000 to Everton.

Ian Snodin was sold to Everton.

Back row, left to right: Andy Ritchie, Neil Aspin, Mervyn Day, Ronnie Sinclair, Bob Taylor, Peter Swan, Peter Haddock. Middle row: Peter Gunby (coach), Barry Murphy, Dave Bentley (assistant manager), Jack Ashurst, Ian Baird, Nigel Thompson, David Rennie, Brendan Ormsby, Ronnie Robinson, Billy Bremner (manager). Front row: John Stiles, Lyndon Simmonds, Russell Doig, Ian Snodin, Tommy Wright, John Buckley, Keith Edwards.

Match No.	Date	Venue	Opponents	Result	FT	HT	Scorers	Attendance
1	Aug 23	A	Blackburn Rovers	L	1-2	1-0	Ritchie	8,346
2	25	H	Stoke City	W	2-1	1-1	Sheridan, Baird	13,334
3	30	H	Sheffield United	L	0-1	0-1		18,294
4	Sep 2	A	Barnsley	W	1-0	1-0	Baird	6,839
5	6	A	Huddersfield Town	D	1-1	1-0	Sheridan	9,306
6	13	H	Reading	W	3-2	0-2	Edwards, Ritchie, Buckley	12,248
7	20	A	Bradford City	L	0-2	0-1		13,525
8	27	H	Hull City	W	3-0	1-0	Ritchie (pen), Baird, Ormsby	13,551
9	Oct 4	A	Plymouth Argyle	D	1-1	0-0	Baird	11,923
10	11	H	Crystal Palace	W	3-0	0-0	Sheridan (pen), Ormsby, Edwards	14,316
11	18	H	Portsmouth	W	3-1	0-0	Sheridan (pen), Ritchie, Baird	21,361
12	25	A	Grimsby Town	D	0-0	0-0		7,223
13	Nov 1	H	Shrewsbury Town	W	1-0	0-0	Aspin	14,966
14	8	A	Millwall	L	0-1	0-1		6,869
15	15	H	Oldham Athletic	L	0-2	0-0		21,052
16	21	A	Birmingham City	L	1-2	0-0	Sheridan	7,836
17	29	H	Derby County	W	2-0	1-0	Sheridan, Edwards	19,129
18	Dec 6	A	West Bromwich Alb	L	0-3	0-1		19,853
19	13	H	Brighton & HA	W	3-1	1-0	Sheridan, Snodin, Baird	12,014
20	21	A	Stoke City	L	2-7	0-5	Baird, Sheridan (pen)	12,358
21	26	H	Sunderland	D	1-1	0-1	Bennett (og)	21,286
22	27	A	Oldham Athletic	W	1-0	1-0	Ritchie	8,477
23	Jan 1	A	Ipswich Town	L	0-2	0-1		14,125
24	3	H	Huddersfield Town	D	1-1	0-1	Baird	17,983
25	24	H	Blackburn Rovers	D	0-0	0-0		14,452
26	Feb 7	A	Sheffield United	D	0-0	0-0		12,494
27	14	H	Barnsley	D	2-2	1-0	Baird, Sheridan	14,216
28	28	H	Bradford City	W	1-0	0-0	Edwards	21,802
29	Mar 7	H	Grimsby Town	W	2-0	1-0	Ritchie, Sheridan (pen)	14,270
30	10	A	Portsmouth	D	1-1	0-1	Adams	13,745
31	21	A	Crystal Palace	L	0-1	0-0		8,781
32	28	H	Plymouth Argyle	W	4-0	2-0	Sheridan (pen), Baird 3	18,618
33	Apr 4	H	Millwall	W	2-0	1-0	Baird, Ritchie	18,304
34	8	A	Hull City	D	0-0	0-0		9,531
35	14	A	Shrewsbury Town	W	2-0	1-0	Sheridan, Pearson	4,186
36	18	H	Ipswich Town	W	3-2	2-1	McDonald, Sheridan, Ormsby	24,839
37	20	A	Sunderland	D	1-1	0-1	Pearson	14,725
38	22	A	Reading	L	1-2	0-2	Pearson	7,415
39	25	H	Birmingham City	W	4-0	0-0	Sheridan, Baird 2, Edwards	19,100
40	May 2	A	Derby County	L	1-2	0-2	Ashurst	20,087
41	4	H	West Bromwich Alb	W	3-2	2-0	Sheridan (pen), Pearson, Ormsby	24,688
42	9	A	Brighton & HA	W	1-0	0-0	Edwards	8,139
								Appearances
								Sub appearances
							One own-goal	Goals

FM Cup

R1	Oct 1	H	Bradford City	L	0-1*	0-0		3,960

* after extra-time

Appearances
Sub appearances
Goals

FL Cup

R2	Sep 23	A	Oldham Athletic	L	2-3	2-0	Aspin, Taylor	5,569
	Oct 8	H	Oldham Athletic	L	0-1	0-0		11,449

Appearances
Sub appearances
Goals

FA Cup

R3	Jan 11	N	Telford United	W	2-1†	1-0	Baird 2	6,460
rR4	Feb 3	A	Swindon Town	W	2-1	1-1	Quinn (og), Baird	14,031
R5	21	H	Queen's Park R	W	2-1	1-0	Baird, Ormsby	31,324
R6	Mar 15	A	Wigan Athletic	W	2-0	0-0	Stiles, Adams	12,479
SF	Apr 12	N	Coventry City	L	2-3‡	1-0		51,372

† At the Hawthorns, West Bromwich
‡ At Hillsborough, Sheffield, after extra-time (score at 90 minutes 2-2)

Appearances
Sub appearances
One own-goal — Goals

League Play-offs

SF	May 14	H	Oldham Athletic	W	1-0	0-0	Edwards	29,472
	17	A	Oldham Athletic	L	1-2†	0-1	Edwards	19,216
F	23	A	Charlton Athletic	L	0-1	0-0		16,680
	25	H	Charlton Athletic	W	1-0	0-0	Ormsby	31,395
Rep	29	N	Charlton Athletic	L	1-2‡	0-0	Sheridan	18,000

† Won on away goals rule after extra-time (score 1-2 after 90 minutes)
‡ Played at St Andrew's, Birmingham, after extra-time (score 0-0 after 90 minutes)

Appearances
Sub appearances
Goals

Sinclair, Ronnie	Haddock, Peter	Caswell, Brian	Snodin, Ian	Ormsby, Brendan	Rennie, David	Ritchie, Andy	Stiles, John	Baird, Ian	Edwards, Keith	Ashurst, Jack	Swan, Peter	Aspin, Neil	Thompson, Nigel	Sheridan, John	Buckley, John	Day, Mervyn	Robinson, Ronnie	Taylor, Bob	Doig, Russell	Adams, Micky	Pearson, John	McDonald, Bobby	Aizlewood, Mark	Wright, Tommy
1	2	3	4	**5**	6	7	8	9	10	11	S*													
1			4		6	11	7	9	10	5		2	3	8										
1	3		4		6	11	7	9	10	5		2		8										
1	3		4		6	11	7	9	10	5		2		8										
1	3				6	11	**7**	9	10	5	4	2		8	S*									
1	3				6	11	7	9	10	5	**4**	2		8	S*									
1	3		**4**		6	11	7		10	5	S*	2		8	9									
	3			4	6	11	7	9	10	5		2		8		1								
	3			4	6	11	7	9	10	5		2		8		1								
				4	6	11	7	9	10	5		2		8		1	3							
				4	6	11	7	9	10	5		2		8		1	3							
				4	6	11	**7**	9	10	5		2	S*	8		1	3							
1	**7**			4	6	11		9	10	5		2		8	S*		3							
	S*		4	6	**7**	11		9	10	5		2		8		1	3							
			4	6		11		9		5		2		8	7	1	3	10						
			4	6				9	10	5		2	7	8		1	3	11						
			4	6		11	7	9	10	5		2		**8**		1	3		S*					
			4	6	**11**	S*	7	9	10	5		2		8		1	3							
			4	6	11		S*	9	10	5		2		8		1	3		**7**					
					11	S*		9	10	5	6	2	4	8		1	**3**		7					
					3	11		9	10	5	6	2	4	8	7	1								
			4	6	11	10	3	9			5	2		8	7	1								
			4	6	11	10	3	9	S*	5		2		8	**7**	1								
			4	6	11	7	3	9	10	5		2		8		1								
				6	8	7	4	10		5		2			**11**	1			S*	3	9			
				6			7	10		5		2		8		1				11	9	3	4	
				6			**7**	10	S*	5		2		8		1				11	9	3	4	
				6		7	**11**	10	S*	5		2		8		1					9	3	4	
					6	7			10	5		2		8		1				11	9	3	4	
				6			7	10		5		2		8		1				11	9	3	4	
				6			7	10		5		2		8		1				11	9	3	4	
				6		7		10	S*	5		2		**8**		1				11	9	3	4	
				6		7		10		5		2		8		1				11	9	3	4	
				6		7	S*	10		5		2		8		1				11	9	3	**4**	
				6		7		10		5		2		8		1				11	9	3	4	
				6		7		10		5		2		8		1				11	9	3	4	
				6		**7**	S*	10		5		2		8		1				11	9	3	4	
				6				10	7	5		2		8		1				11	9	3	4	
				6				10	7	5		2		8		1				11	9	3	4	
				6	**4**		7	10	S*	5		2		8		1				11	9	3		
				6			7	10		5		2		8		1				11	9	3	4	
	4			6			7	10	S*	5		2		8		1				11	**9**	3		
8	10	1	14	33	24	29	26	40	24	41	5	41	4	40	6	34	11	2	2	17	18	17	15	0
	1					2	3		6		2		1		3				2					
			1	4		7		15	6	1		1		15	1					1	4	1		

	3			**4**	6		7		10	5		2	S*	8	11	1		9						
0	1	0	0	1	1	0	1	0	1	1	0	1	0	1	1	1	0	1	0	0	0	0	0	0
													1											

1					6	11	4		9	5	10	2	3	8				**7**						S*
				4	6	11	**7**	9	10	5		2	3	8		1		S*						
1	0	0	0	1	2	2	2	1	2	2	1	2	2	2	0	1	0	1	0	0	0	0	0	0
																		1						1
												1						1						

				6	4	7	3	9	10	5		2		8		1			11					
				6	11	7	**4**	10	S*	5		2		8		1				3	9			
				6	**4**	11	7	10	S*	5		2		8	S*	1				3	9			
					6	7	4		10	5	11	2		8		1				3	9			
	S*			6	11	7	**4**	10	S*	5		2		8		1				3	**9**			
0	0	0	0	4	5	5	5	4	2	5	1	5	0	5	0	5	0	0	1	4	4	0	0	0
	1								3							1								
				1	1		1	4	1											1				

				6		**7**		10	S*	5		2		8		1				11	9	3	4	
				6			**7**	10	S*	5		2		8		1				11	9	3	4	
				6		S*		10	7	5		2		8		1				11	**9**	3	4	
				6		**7**		10	S*	5		2		8		1		9		11		3	4	
				6			7	10	S*	5		2		8		1				11	9	3	4	
0	0	0	0	5	0	2	2	5	1	5	0	5	0	5	0	5	0	1	0	5	4	5	5	0
						1			4															
				1					2					1										

League Table

	P	W	D	L	F	A	Pts
Derby County	42	25	9	8	64	38	84
Portsmouth	42	23	9	10	53	28	78
Oldham Athletic	42	22	9	11	65	44	75
Leeds United	42	19	11	12	58	44	68
Ipswich Town	42	17	13	12	59	43	64
Crystal Palace	42	19	5	18	51	53	62
Plymouth Argyle	42	16	13	13	62	57	61
Stoke City	42	16	10	16	63	53	58
Sheffield United	42	15	13	14	50	49	58
Bradford City	42	15	10	17	62	62	55
Barnsley	42	14	13	15	49	52	55
Blackburn Rovers	42	15	10	17	45	55	55
Reading	42	14	11	17	52	59	53
Hull City	42	13	14	15	41	55	53
West Bromwich Albion	42	13	12	17	51	49	51
Millwall	42	14	9	19	39	45	51
Huddersfield Town	42	13	12	17	54	61	51
Shrewsbury Town	42	15	6	21	41	53	51
Birmingham City	42	11	17	14	47	59	50
Sunderland	42	12	12	18	49	59	48
Grimsby Town	42	10	14	18	39	59	44
Brighton & Hove Albion	42	9	12	21	37	54	39

1987-88

Division Two

Manager: Billy Bremner

Final Position: 7th

Did you know that?

15 September 1987: Peter Mumby, brother of Bradford Northern and Great Britain Rugby League star Keith Mumby, made his League debut in a 0–0 draw at Huddersfield.

1 January 1988: Gary Williams finally scored his first career goal. After 240 League games for Aston Villa and 19 for Leeds he netted in the New Year's Day victory against Bradford City.

Gary Williams notched his first career goal.

Match No.	Date		Venue	Opponents	Result	FT	HT	Scorers	Attendance
1	Aug	16	A	Barnsley	D	1-1	0-0	Taylor	9,778
2		19	H	Leicester City	W	1-0	0-0	Sheridan (pen)	21,034
3		22	H	Reading	D	0-0	0-0		19,286
4		29	A	Bradford City	D	0-0	0-0		11,428
5		31	H	West Bromwich Alb	W	1-0	0-0	Sheridan	19,847
6	Sep	5	A	Ipswich Town	L	0-1	0-0		11,163
7		12	H	Hull City	L	0-2	0-0		18,205
8		15	A	Huddersfield Town	D	0-0	0-0		9,085
9		19	A	Middlesbrough	L	0-2	0-1		12,051
10		26	H	Manchester City	W	2-0	1-0	De Mange, Snodin	25,358
11		30	H	Stoke City	D	0-0	0-0		17,208
12	Oct	3	A	Blackburn Rovers	D	1-1	0-0	Taylor	7,675
13		10	H	Aston Villa	L	1-3	1-1	Taylor	20,741
14		17	A	Plymouth Argyle	L	3-6	2-2	Taylor, Snodin 2	9,358
15		20	A	Oldham Athletic	D	1-1	0-1	Swan	6,312
16		24	H	Bournemouth	W	3-2	3-0	Taylor, Swan, Rennie	15,253
17		31	A	Sheffield United	D	2-2	0-1	Snodin, Swan	12,095
18	Nov	7	H	Shrewsbury Town	W	2-1	1-0	Stiles, Taylor	13,760
19		14	A	Millwall	L	1-3	0-0	McLeary (og)	8,014
20		21	H	Swindon Town	W	4-2	3-1	Rennie, Davison, Taylor, Haddock	15,457
21		28	A	Crystal Palace	L	0-3	0-1		8,749
22	Dec	5	H	Birmingham City	W	4-1	2-0	Sheridan (pen), Davison, Swan, Taylor	15,977
23		12	A	Reading	W	1-0	0-0	Sheridan (pen)	6,505
24		19	H	Huddersfield Town	W	3-0	1-0	Sheridan 2, Davison	20,111
25		26	A	Manchester City	W	2-1	1-1	Redmond (og), Batty	30,153
26		28	H	Middlesbrough	W	2-0	1-0	Davison, Swan	34,186
27	Jan	1	H	Bradford City	W	2-0	1-0	Williams, Snodin	36,004
28		3	A	Hull City	L	1-3	1-3	Swan	14,694
29		16	H	Barnsley	L	0-2	0-1		19,028
30		30	A	West Bromwich Alb	W	4-1	2-0	Sheridan, Williams, Pearson, Davison	9,008
31	Feb	6	H	Ipswich Town	W	1-0	1-0	Pearson	19,564
32		13	A	Leicester City	L	2-3	1-1	Williams, Sheridan (pen)	11,937
33		23	A	Stoke City	L	1-2	0-1	Pearson	10,129
34		27	H	Blackburn Rovers	D	2-2	2-0	Sheridan (pen), Snodin	23,843
35	Mar	5	H	Plymouth Argyle	W	1-0	0-0	Baird	18,115
36		12	A	Aston Villa	W	2-1	2-0	Swan, Taylor	19,677
37		19	H	Sheffield United	W	5-0	1-0	Swan, Pearson 3, Sheridan	22,376
38		26	A	Bournemouth	D	0-0	0-0		9,147
39	Apr	2	A	Shrewsbury Town	L	0-1	0-0		7,369
40		6	H	Millwall	L	1-2	0-1	Sheridan (pen)	24,241
41		23	H	Oldham Athletic	D	1-1	0-0	Snodin	13,442
42		30	A	Swindon Town	W	2-1	2-1	Baird 2	8,299
43	May	2	H	Crystal Palace	W	1-0	1-0	Sheridan (pen)	13,217
44		6	A	Birmingham City	D	0-0	0-0		6,024
									Appearances
									Sub appearances
								Two own-goals	Goals

FM Cup

R1	Nov	25	H	Sheffield United	W	3-0	0-0	Rennie, Taylor, Noteman	4,425
R2	Dec	8	A	Millwall	L	0-2	0-1		5,034
									Appearances
									Sub appearances
									Goals

FL Cup

R2	Sep	23	H	York City	D	1-1	0-0	Snodin	11,527
	Oct	6	A	York City	W	4-0	1-0	Sheridan 2, Taylor, Mumby	5,996
R3		28	H	Oldham Athletic	D	2-2	1-0	Swan 2	15,600
Rep	Nov	4	A	Oldham Athletic	A	2-4*	0-0	Snodin, Taylor	7,058

* After extra-time (score at 90 minutes 2-2)

Appearances
Sub appearances
Goals

FA Cup

R3	Jan	9	H	Aston Villa	L	1-2	0-1	Davison	29,002
									Appearances
									Sub appearances
									Goals

Back row, left to right: Jack Ashurst, David Rennie, John Pearson, Mervyn Day, Neil Aspin, Peter Swan, Peter Haddock, Middle row: David Bentley (assistant manager), Nigel Thompson, Bobby McDonald, John Buckley, John Sheridan, Ronnie Sinclair, Brendan Ormsby, Bob Taylor, Gary Williams, Dave Blakey (chief scout), Billy Bremner (manager). Front row: Alun Sutton (physiotherapist), John Stiles, Glynn Snodin, Micky Adams, Mark Aizlewood, David Batty, Russell Doig, Keith Edwards, Peter Gunby (coach).

Day, Mervyn	Aspin, Neil	Adams, Micky	Aizlewood, Mark	Ashurst, Jack	Rennie, David	Williams, Gary	Sheridan, John	Pearson, John	Taylor, Bob	Snodin, Glynn	Edwards, Keith	Haddock, Peter	Buckley, John	Doig, Russell	Stiles, John	Grayson, Simon	Mumby, Peter	De Mange, Ken	Melrose, Jim	Swan, Peter	McDonald, Bobby	Batty, David	Davison, Bobby	Baird, Ian	Brockie, Vince	Maguire, Peter	Noteman, Kevin
1	2	3	4	5	6	7	8	9	**10**	11	S*																
1	2	3	4	5	6	7	8	9	**10**	**11**	S*	S*															
1	2	3	4	5	6	7	8	**9**			10	11	S*														
1	2	3	4	5	6	7	8	9	10			11															
1	2	3	4	5	6	**7**	8	S*	10		**9**	11		S*													
1	2	3	4	5	6	7	8	S*	**10**		9	11															
1	2	3	**4**	5	6		8	9		11	10	S*			7												
1	2	3		5	6		8	9		**7**	S*	11			S*	**4**	10										
1	2	3		5	6		8	9	**10**	11	S*	**4**			S*		7										
1	2	3		5	**6**		8	S*	10	11		4					S*	7	**9**								
1	2	3		5	6		8	S*	**10**	11		4						7	**9**								
1	2	3		5	6		8	10	S*	11		4						7	**9**								
1	S*	3		5	6		8		**9**	11		2			**4**		10	7	S*								
1	2	**3**		5		**6**	8	**10**	9	11		4			S*			7		S*							
1	2	3		5		8		**10**	9	11		6			4			7		S*							
1		3		5	6	4	8		9	11		2						7		10							
1		3		5		2	8		9	11		6		7				4		10							
1				5	7	2			9	11		6			8			4		10	3						
1				5	3	2		7	9	11		6			8			4		10							
1		3		5	8	**2**			9	11		6			S*			4				7	10				
1		3		5	**8**	2			9	11		6						4		S*		7	10				
1	2	3		5		4	8		9	11		6								S*		7	**10**				
1	2	3		5			8		9			6						4		11		7	10				
1	2	3		5		4	8		9			6								11		7	10				
1	2	3		5		4	8			**11**		6			S*					9		7	10				
1	2	3		5		4	8			11		6								9		7	10				
1	2	3		5		4	8			11		6								9		7	10				
1	2	3		5		4	**8**		S*	**11**		6			S*					9		7	10				
1	2	3		5		4	8		**9**			6					S*	S*		11		**7**	10				
1	2	3		5	**11**	4	8	9	S*			6						7					10				
1	2	3		5	7	4	8	9		11		6											10				
1	2	3		5	7	4	8	9	S*			**6**										11	10				
1		3	4	5		2	8	9		11		6										7	10				
1		3	4	5	S*	2	8	9	10	11		**6**										7					
1		3	4	5	S*	**2**	8	10		11										6		7		9			
1			**4**	5	S*	2		10	8	11		3								6		7		9			
1			**4**	5		2	S*	10	8	11		3								6		7		9			
1		3	4	5		2	S*	10		**11**		**8**								6		7	S*	9			
1		3	4	5		**2**	8	**10**	11	S*		7								6		S*		9			
1		3	4	5			8	S*	**11**	S*		2								6		7	**10**	9			
1		3	4	5	10		8		S*	11		2								**6**		7		9			
1		3			6		8	S*	**10**	11		2			4					5		7		9			
1		3	S*		6		8	S*		11					**4**					5		7		9	2	**10**	
1		**3**			6		8			11						4				5		7		9	2	10	S*
44	25	40	16	41	25	31	36	21	27	33	4	38	0	1	7	2	3	14	3	21	1	22	15	10	2	2	0
	1		1		3		2	7	5	2	4	2	1	1	6		2	1	1	4		1	1				1
					2	3	12	6	9	7		1			1			1		8		1	5	3			

1		3		5	8				9			6				2		4				7	10				11
1	2			5			8	S*	9	11		**6**			**S***			4		3		7	10				
2	1	1	0	2	1	0	1	0	2	1	0	2	0	0	0	1	0	2	0	1	0	2	2	0	0	0	1
								1							1												
					1				1																		1

1	2	3		5	6	**7**	8	**9**	10	11				S*	4		S*										
1		3		5	6		8	**9**	10	**11**		4		S*	2		S*	7									
1	**2**	3		5		4	8		9	11		6			S*			7		10							
1				5		2	8		9	11		6		**7**	S*			4	S*	**10**	3						
4	2	3	0	4	2	3	4	2	4	4	0	3	0	1	2	0	0	3	0	2	1	0	0	0	0	0	0
														2	2		2		1								
							2		2	2							1			2							

1	2	3		5		4	8		9	**11**		6							S*			7	10				
1	1	1	0	1	0	1	1	0	1	1	0	1	0	0	0	0	0	0	0	0	0	1	1	0	0	0	0
																			1								
																							1				

League Table

	P	W	D	L	F	A	Pts
Millwall	44	25	7	12	72	52	82
Aston Villa	44	22	12	10	68	41	78
Middlesbrough	44	22	12	10	63	36	78
Bradford City	44	22	11	11	74	54	77
Blackburn Rovers	44	21	14	9	68	52	77
Crystal Palace	44	22	9	13	86	59	75
Leeds United	44	19	12	13	61	51	69
Ipswich Town	44	19	9	16	61	52	66
Manchester City	44	19	8	17	80	60	65
Oldham Athletic	44	18	11	15	72	64	65
Stoke City	44	17	11	16	50	57	62
Swindon Town	44	16	11	17	73	60	59
Leicester City	44	16	11	17	62	61	59
Barnsley	44	15	12	17	61	62	57
Hull City	44	14	15	15	54	60	57
Plymouth Argyle	44	16	8	20	65	67	56
Bournemouth	44	13	10	21	56	68	49
Shrewsbury Town	44	11	16	17	42	54	49
Birmingham City	44	11	15	18	41	66	48
West Bromwich Albion	44	12	11	21	50	69	47
Sheffield United	44	13	7	24	45	74	46
Reading	44	10	12	22	44	70	42
Huddersfield Town	44	6	10	28	41	100	28

1988-89

Division Two

Manager: Billy Bremner until September then Howard Wilkinson

Final Position: 10th

Did you know that?

8 October 1988: Cars in the club car park were damaged during a 2,000-strong demonstration by fans after managerless United lost 1–0 at home to Watford. Within 48 hours Howard Wilkinson was installed as Billy Bremner's successor.

1 April 1989: Carl Shutt showed he was no April fool by scoring a debut hat-trick against Bournemouth after his £50,000 move from Sheffield Wednesday.

1 May 1989: After scoring the winner against Walsall, Mark Aizlewood stuck two fingers up to his barrackers on the Kop. He was immediately stripped of the captaincy by Howard Wilkinson and never played for Leeds again.

Carl Shutt netted a hat-trick on his debut.

Match No.	Date	Venue	Opponents	Result	FT	HT	Scorers	Attendance
1	Aug 27	H	Oxford United	D	1-1	1-1	Snodin	22,038
2	Sep 3	A	Portsmouth	L	0-4	0-2		15,263
3	10	H	Manchester City	D	1-1	0-0	Blake	23,677
4	17	A	Bournemouth	D	0-0	0-0		7,922
5	21	H	Barnsley	W	2-0	0-0	Davison, Hilaire	17,370
6	24	H	Chelsea	L	0-2	0-2		26,080
7	Oct 1	A	Brighton & HA	L	1-2	1-0	Baird	7,109
8	4	A	Sunderland	L	1-2	0-1	Davison	12,671
9	8	H	Watford	L	0-1	0-0		15,657
10	16	A	Swindon Town	D	0-0	0-0		9,234
11	22	H	Leicester City	D	1-1	1-0	Hilaire	17,263
12	26	A	Bradford City	D	1-1	1-0	Davison	13,048
13	29	H	Hull City	W	2-1	1-0	Sheridan, Baird	17,536
14	Nov 5	A	Ipswich Town	W	1-0	1-0	Sheridan (pen)	11,750
15	12	H	West Bromwich Alb	W	2-1	2-1	Aizlewood, Baird	20,442
16	19	A	Oldham Athletic	D	2-2	1-1	Davison 2	8,824
17	22	A	Birmingham City	D	0-0	0-0		6,168
18	26	H	Stoke City	W	4-0	2-0	Baird 2, Davison, Sheridan (pen)	19,933
19	Dec 3	A	Walsall	W	3-0	1-0	Davison 2, Whitlow	6,885
20	10	H	Shrewsbury Town	L	2-3	0-2	Sheridan (pen), Davison	19,967
21	17	A	Crystal Palace	D	0-0	0-0		9,847
22	26	H	Blackburn Rovers	W	2-0	2-0	Baird, Davison	31,622
23	31	H	Plymouth Argyle	W	2-0	0-0	Baird, Snodin	24,043
24	Jan 2	A	Manchester City	D	0-0	0-0		33,034
25	14	H	Birmingham City	W	1-0	0-0	Hilaire	21,937
26	21	A	Oxford United	L	2-3	2-2	Blake, Hilaire	7,928
27	Feb 4	H	Sunderland	W	2-0	1-0	Davison, Sheridan (pen)	31,985
28	11	A	Watford	D	1-1	0-1	Pearson	13,439
29	18	A	Leicester City	W	2-1	2-1	Davison, Snodin	14,151
30	25	H	Swindon Town	D	0-0	0-0		22,651
31	Mar 1	H	Bradford City	D	3-3	2-2	Blake, Hilaire, Baird	33,325
32	5	A	West Bromwich Alb	L	1-2	1-2	Adams	15,914
33	11	H	Ipswich Town	L	2-4	0-1	Hiaire, Blake	19,639
34	14	A	Hull City	W	2-1	1-1	Baird, Davison	8,887
35	19	A	Barnsley	D	2-2	1-1	Aizlewood, Sheridan (pen)	11,578
36	25	H	Portsmouth	W	1-0	0-0	Baird	27,049
37	27	A	Blackburn Rovers	L	0-2	0-0		11,533
38	Apr 1	H	Bournemouth	W	3-0	1-0	Shutt 3	21,095
39	5	H	Crystal Palace	L	1-2	1-2	Shutt	25,604
40	9	A	Plymouth Argyle	L	0-1	0-0		9,365
41	15	H	Brighton & HA	W	1-0	1-0	A. Williams	14,915
42	22	A	Chelsea	L	0-1	0-0		30,337
43	29	A	Stoke City	W	3-2	1-2	Sheridan (pen), Davison, Strachan	9,051
44	May 1	H	Walsall	W	1-0	0-0	Aizlewood	13,280
45	6	H	Oldham Athletic	D	0-0	0-0		14,459
46	13	A	Shrewsbury Town	D	3-3	2-2	Strachan 2 (1 pen), Rennie	4,693

Appearances
Sub appearances
Goals

FM Cup

R1	Nov 9	H	Shrewsbury Town	W	3-1	1-1	Davison 2, Aizlewood	3,220
R2	29	A	Millwall	L	0-2	0-1		4,242

Appearances
Sub appearances
Goals

FL Cup

R2	Sep 27	A	Peterborough U	W	2-1	2-1	Snodin, Baird	4,979
	Oct 12	H	Peterborough U	W	3-1	1-0	Davison, Hilaire, Sheridan (pen)	8,894
R3	Nov 2	H	Luton Town	L	0-2	0-1		19,447

Appearances
Sub appearances
Goals

FA Cup

R3	Jan 7	A	Brighton & HA	W	2-1	0-0	Baird 2	10,900
R4	28	A	Nottingham Forest	L	0-2	0-1		28,107

Appearances
Sub appearances
Goals

Day, Mervyn	Haddock, Peter	Adams, Mickey	Aizlewood, Mark	Blake, Noel	Ashurst, Jack	Stiles, John	Hilaire, Vince	Baird, Ian	Pearson, John	Snodin, Glynn	Davison, Bobby	Rennie, David	Taylor, Bob	Williams, Gary	Batty, David	Sheridan, John	Aspin, Neil	Williams, Andy	Whitlow, Mike	Andrews, Ian	Swan, Peter	Fairclough, Chris	Strachan, Gordon	Shutt, Carl	Kerr, Dylan	Speed, Gary	Mumby, Peter	Ormsby, Brendan
1	2	3	4	5	6	7	8	9	10	11	S*	S*																
1	2	3	4	5	6	8	11	9	10		S*		7															
1		3	4	5	6		11	9	S*		10			2	7	8	S*											
1	S*	3	4	5	6		11		S*		10		9	2	7	8												
1	S*	3	4	5	6		11	9			10			2	7	8												
1	4	3		5	6		11	9	S*	S*	10			2	7	8												
1		3	4	5			11	9	10	8		6		2	7	S*												
1	2	3		5		4	11	9	S*		10	6			7	8	S*											
1		3		5		4	11	9	S*	S*	10	6			7	8	2											
1			4	5	S*		11	9	S*	3	10	6			7	8	2											
1			4	5		S*	11	9	S*	3	10	6			7	8	2											
1			4	5		S*	11	9	S*	3	10	6			7	8	2											
1			4	5		S*	11	9	S*	3	10	6			7	8	2											
1			4	5		S*	11	9	S*	3	10	6			7	8	2											
1			4	5			11	9	S*	3	10	6			7	8	2	S*										
1			4	5			11	9	S*	3	10	6			7	8	2	S*										
1		S*	4	5			11	9		3	10	6	S*			8	2	7										
1			4	5			11	9		3	10	6			S*	8	2		7									
1			4	5			11	9		3	10	6				8	2	S*	7									
1			4	5			11	9		3	10	6	S*			8	2		7									
			4	5			11	9		3	10	6	S*			8	2	S*	7	1								
1			4	5			11	9	S*	3	10	6				8	2	S*	7									
1			4	5			11	9	S*	3	10	6				8	2		7									
1			4	5			11	9	S*	3	10	6			S*	8	2		7									
1			4	5			11	9	S*	3	10	6					2	8	7									
1			4	5			11	9	S*	3	10	6				8	2	S*	7									
1		4		5			11	9		3	10	6			7	8	2											
1		4		5			11	9	S*	3	10	6			7	8	2	S*										
1		4	S*	5			11	9	S*	3	10	6			7	8	2											
1		4	S*	5			11	9	S*	3	10	6			7	8	2											
1		4	S*	5			11	9		3	10	6			7	8	2											
1		4	S*	5			11	9	S*	3	10	6		2	7	8												
1			4	5			11	9	S*	3	10	6		2	7	8			S*									
1			4				11	9	S*	3	10			2	7	8	6		S*		5							
1	2		4	5			11		9	3	10		S*			8	6	S*	7									
1			4	5			11	9	S*	3	10					8	2	S*				6	7					
1			4	5			11	9	10	3					S*	8	2	S*				6	7					
1			4	5				9		3						8	2	S*	11			6	7	10				
1			4				11	9	S*	3		5				8	2					6	7	10				
1				5				9	S*	3		S*			8		2	4	11			6	7	10				
1	2		3	5					9		10	S*				8		4	11			6	7		S*			
1			4	5				9	S*		10					S*	2	8	11			6	7		3			
1	S*		4	5			11	9			10				S*	8		2	3			6	7					
1	S*		4	5			11	9			10				S*	8		2	3			6	7					
1	2			5		S*	11	9				4			8				3			6	7			10	S*	
1	2			5		S*	11	9				10			8				3			6	7		S*			4
45	8	15	34	44	6	4	42	43	6	33	37	30	2	8	25	38	31	7	18	1	1	11	11	3	1	1	0	1
	4	1	4		1	6			27	2	2	3	4		5	2	2	11	2						2		1	
		1	3	4			6	10	1	3	14	1				7		1	1				3	4				

1			4	5			11	9			10	6	S*		7	8	2		3									
1	S*		4	5			11	9	S*	3	10	6				8	2		7									
2	0	0	2	2	0	0	2	2	0	1	2	2	0	0	1	2	2	0	2	0	0	0	0	0	0	0	0	0
	1								1				1															
			1								2																	

1	S*	3	4	5			11	9	10	8		6		2	7													
1			4	5			11	9	S*	3	10	6			7	8	2											
1			4	5			11	9		3	10	6			7	8	2											
3	0	1	3	3	0	0	3	3	1	3	2	3	0	1	3	2	2	0	0	0	0	0	0	0	0	0	0	0
	1								1																			
							1	1		1	1					1												

1	S*		4	5			11	9	S*	3	10	6				8	2	7										
1		10		5			11	9		3	S*	6		S*	7	8	2				4							
2	0	1	1	2	0	0	2	2	0	2	1	2	0	0	1	2	2	1	0	0	1	0	0	0	0	0	0	0
	1								1		1			1														
								2																				

League Table

	P	W	D	L	F	A	Pts
Chelsea	46	29	12	5	96	50	99
Manchester City	46	23	13	10	77	53	82
Crystal Palace	46	23	12	11	71	49	81
Watford	46	22	12	12	74	48	78
Blackburn Rovers	46	22	11	13	74	59	77
Swindon Town	46	20	16	10	68	53	76
Barnsley	46	20	14	12	66	58	74
Ipswich Town	46	22	7	17	71	61	73
West Bromwich Albion	46	18	18	10	65	41	72
Leeds United	46	17	16	13	59	50	67
Sunderland	46	16	15	15	60	60	63
Bournemouth	46	18	8	20	53	62	62
Stoke City	46	15	14	17	57	72	59
Bradford City	46	13	17	16	52	59	56
Leicester City	46	13	16	17	56	63	55
Oldham Athletic	46	11	21	14	75	72	54
Oxford United	46	14	12	20	62	70	54
Plymouth Argyle	46	14	12	20	55	66	54
Brighton & Hove Albion	46	14	9	23	57	66	51
Portsmouth	46	13	12	21	53	62	51
Hull City	46	11	14	21	52	68	47
Shrewsbury Town	46	8	18	20	40	67	42
Birmingham City	46	8	11	27	31	76	35
Walsall	46	5	16	25	41	80	31

1989-90

Division Two

Manager: Howard Wilkinson

Final Position: 1st

Did you know that?

21 October 1989: In one of the light-hearted moments of a tense promotion season, hard man Vinnie Jones brings down five-year-old mascot Robert Kelly in the area during the warm-up against Wolves much to the hilarity of the Kop.

1 November 1989: Bobby Davison scored in his fifth successive League game to give United a 2–1 win against Plymouth, equalling a feat achieved by Peter Lorimer 19 years earlier.

20 January 1990: Mervyn Day celebrated his 600th League appearance by saving a Wayne Biggins penalty as United defeated Stoke City 2–0.

Six hundred up for Mervyn Day.

Second Division champions.

Match No.	Date	Venue	Opponents	Result	FT	HT	Scorers	Attendance
1	Aug 19	A	Newcastle United	L	2-5	2-1	Davison, Baird	24,482
2	23	H	Middlesbrough	W	2-1	1-0	Davison, Parkinson (og)	25,004
3	26	H	Blackburn Rovers	D	1-1	0-1	Fairclough	25,045
4	Sep 2	A	Stoke City	D	1-1	0-1	Strachan	10,915
5	9	H	Ipswich Town	D	1-1	1-0	Jones	22,972
6	16	A	Hull City	W	1-0	1-0	Baird	11,620
7	23	H	Swindon Town	W	4-0	2-0	Strachan 3 (1 pen), Davison	21,694
8	27	H	Oxford United	W	2-1	2-0	Davison, Sterland	24,097
9	30	A	Port Vale	D	0-0	0-0		11,156
10	Oct 7	A	West Ham United	W	1-0	1-0	Jones	23,539
11	14	H	Sunderland	W	2-0	2-0	Davison, Fairclough	27,815
12	17	A	Portsmouth	D	3-3	0-0	Davison, Whitlow, Sterland	10,260
13	21	H	Wolverhampton W	W	1-0	1-0	Davison	28,204
14	28	A	Bradford City	W	1-0	0-0	Davison	12,527
15	Nov 1	H	Plymouth Argyle	W	2-1	1-1	Strachan (pen), Davison	26,791
16	4	H	Bournemouth	W	3-0	2-0	Baird, Strachan (pen), Fairclough	26,484
17	11	A	Leicester City	L	3-4	2-0	Baird, Williams, Strachan (pen)	18,032
18	18	H	Watford	W	2-1	0-1	Fairclough, Williams	26,921
19	25	A	West Bromwich Alb	L	1-2	0-2	Fairclough	15,116
20	Dec 2	H	Newcastle United	W	1-0	0-0	Baird	31,715
21	9	A	Middlesbrough	W	2-0	2-0	Shutt, Fairclough	19,686
22	16	H	Brighton & HA	W	3-0	3-0	Strachan, Hendrie, Jones	24,070
23	26	A	Sheffield United	D	2-2	1-2	Sterland, Shutt	31,254
24	30	A	Barnsley	L	0-1	0-1		14,485
25	Jan 1	H	Oldham Athletic	D	1-1	0-1	Hendrie	30,217
26	13	A	Blackburn Rovers	W	2-1	0-1	Chapman, Strachan	14,485
27	20	H	Stoke City	W	2-0	0-0	Strachan (pen), Hendrie	29,318
28	Feb 4	A	Swindon Town	L	2-3	1-1	Strachan (pen), Hendrie	16,208
29	10	H	Hull City	W	4-3	2-1	Hendrie, Jones, Varadi, Strachan	29,977
30	17	A	Ipswich Town	D	2-2	2-1	Chapman 2	17,102
31	24	H	West Bromwich Alb	D	2-2	1-0	Kamara, Chapman	30,004
32	Mar 3	A	Watford	L	0-1	0-1		13,468
33	7	H	Port Vale	D	0-0	0-0		28,756
34	10	A	Oxford United	W	4-2	0-2	Chapman 2, Varadi, Fairclough	8,397
35	17	H	West Ham United	W	3-2	2-0	Chapman 2, Strachan	32,356
36	20	A	Sunderland	W	1-0	1-0	Sterland	17,851
37	24	H	Portsmouth	W	2-0	1-0	Jones, Chapman	27,600
38	31	A	Wolverhampton W	L	0-1	0-1		22,419
39	Apr 7	H	Bradford City	D	1-1	0-0	Speed	32,316
40	10	A	Plymouth Argyle	D	1-1	1-1	Chapman	11,382
41	13	A	Oldham Athletic	L	1-3	0-1	Davison	16,292
42	16	H	Sheffield United	W	4-0	1-0	Strachan 2 (1 pen), Chapman, Speed	32,727
43	21	A	Brighton & HA	D	2-2	1-0	Speed, I. Chapman (og)	11,359
44	25	H	Barnsley	L	1-2	1-0	Fairclough	31,700
45	28	H	Leicester City	W	2-1	1-0	Sterland, Strachan	32,597
46	May 5	A	Bournemouth	W	1-0	0-0	Chapman	9,918
								Appearances
								Sub appearances
							Two own-goals	Goals

FM Cup

R1	Nov 8	H	Blackburn Rovers	W	1-0	1-0	Davison	5,070
R2	28	A	Barnsley	W	2-1	2-1	Strachan (pen), Williams	6,136
R3	Dec 19	A	Stoke City	D	2-2*	0-1	Shutt 2	5,792
R4	Jan 17	A	Aston Villa	L	0-2	0-0		17,543

* After extra-time (score at 90 minutes 1-1), Leeds won 5-4 on penalties

Appearances
Sub appearances
Goals

FL Cup

R2	Sep 19	A	Oldham Athletic	L	1-2	1-2	Strachan	8,415
	Oct 3	H	Oldham Athletic	L	1-2	0-2	Fairclough	18,092

Appearances
Sub appearances
Goals

FA Cup

R3	Jan 6	H	Ipswich Town	L	0-1	0-0		26,766

Appearances
Sub appearances
Goals

Day, Mervyn	Sterland, Mel	Beglin, Jim	Thomas, Mickey	McClelland, John	Haddock, Peter	Strachan, Gordon	Batty, David	Baird, Ian	Davison, Bobby	Hendrie, John	Whitlow, Mike	Shutt, Carl	Fairclough, Chris	Jones, Vinnie	Speed, Gary	Blake, Noel	Williams, Andy	Turner, Chris	Pearson, John	Kerr, Dylan	Snodin, Glynn	Chapman, Lee	Kamara, Chris	Varadi, Imre	O'Donnell, Chris	Hilaire, Vince	Edwards, Neil
1	2	3	**4**	5	6	7	8	9	**10**	11	S*	S*															
1	2		**4**		6	7	8	9	10	11	3	S*	5	S*													
1	2		**4**		6	7	8	9	**10**	11	3	S*	5	S*													
1	2				6	7	8	9	**10**	11	3		5	4	S*												
1	2				6	7	8	9	10	**11**	3		5	4	S*												
1	2					7	8	9	10	11	**3**		6	4		5	S*										
1	2				6	7	8	9	10	**11**	3			4		5	S*										
1	2				6	7	8	9	10	11	3			**4**		5	S*										
1	2				6	7	8	9	**10**		3	S*		**4**	S*	5	11										
1	2				6	7	8	9	**10**		3	S*	5	4			11										
1	2				6	7	8	9	10		3		5	4			11										
1	2				6	7	8	9	10		3		5	4			11										
1	2				6	**7**	8	9	10		3	S*	5	4	S*		11										
1	2				6	7	8	9	10		3		5	4	S*		**11**										
1	2				6	7	8	9	10		3		5	**4**	S*		11										
1	2				6	7	8	9	10		3		5	4	S*		**11**										
1	2				6	7	8	9	10		3	S*	5	4			11										
	2				6	7	8	9	**10**		3	S*	5	4			11	1									
	2				6	7	8	9	10		3	S*	5	**4**	S*		**11**	1									
1	2					7	8	9	10		3	S*	5	4		6	**11**										
1	2					7	8				3	10	6	4		5	11		9								
1	2				6	7	8	S*		**11**	3	**10**	5	4	S*				9								
1	2					7	8	9		11	3	10	6	4		5											
1	2				6	7	8	9		**11**	**3**	10	5	4					S*	S*							
1	2				6	7	8	**9**		11		**10**	5	4					S*	3	S*						
1	**2**	S*			6	7	8		10	11	3		5	4								9					
1		2			6	7	8		**10**	11	3		5	4					S*			9					
1		2			6	7	8			11	**3**		5	4	S*				S*	**10**		9					
1		**3**			6	7	8			11			5	4								**9**	2	10	S*	S*	
1		3			6	7	8			**11**			5	4								9	2	10		S*	
1		3			6	7	8			**11**			5	4								9	2	10		S*	
1	2	3			6	7	8			S*			5	4	S*							9	**11**	**10**			
1	2	3			6	7	8			**11**			5	4	S*							9		10			
1	2	**3**			6	7				S*			5	4	**8**					S*	11	9		10			
1	2				6	7				**11**		S*	5	4	8					S*	3	9		**10**			
1	2				6	7	8		S*	S*			5	4	11						**3**	9		**10**			
1	2	3			6	**7**	8			S*	S*		5	4	11							9		**10**			
1	2				6	7	8			S*	3		5	4	**11**							9	S*	**10**			
1	2	3			6	7	8		S*	**10**			5	4	11							9					
1	2	3			6	7	8		S*	**10**			5	4	11							9					
1	2	3			**6**	7	8		S*				5	4	S*							9	11	**10**			
1	2	3		6		7			**10**			S*	5	4	11							9	8				
1	2	3		6		7	S*					S*	5	4	11							9	**8**	**10**			
1	2	3			6	7						**10**	5	4	11				S*			9	8				
1	2	3			6	7	S*		**10**				5	**4**	11							9	8	S*			
1	2	3			6	7	S*		**10**			**S***	5	4	11							9	8				
44	41	18	3	3	40	46	39	23	25	22	27	6	42	43	12	7	13	2	2	2	3	21	10	12	0	0	0
		1					3	1	4	5	2	14		2	13		3		5	3	1		1	1	1	3	
	5					16		5	10	5	1	2	8	5	3		2					12	1	2			

Day, Mervyn	Sterland, Mel	Beglin, Jim	Thomas, Mickey	McClelland, John	Haddock, Peter	Strachan, Gordon	Batty, David	Baird, Ian	Davison, Bobby	Hendrie, John	Whitlow, Mike	Shutt, Carl	Fairclough, Chris	Jones, Vinnie	Speed, Gary	Blake, Noel	Williams, Andy	Turner, Chris	Pearson, John	Kerr, Dylan	Snodin, Glynn	Chapman, Lee	Kamara, Chris	Varadi, Imre	O'Donnell, Chris	Hilaire, Vince	Edwards, Neil
1	**2**				6	7	8	9	10		3		5	4	S*		11										
	2				**6**	7	8	9	**10**		3	S*	5	4			11			S*							1
1	2				6	7	8	10		11	**3**	S*		4		5			**9**	S*							
1		**10**			6	7	8	9		**11**	3		5	4		2			S*	S*							
3	3	1	0	0	4	4	4	4	2	2	4	0	3	4	0	2	2	0	1	0	0	0	0	0	0	0	1
												2			1				1	3							
						1			1			2					1										

Day, Mervyn	Sterland, Mel	Beglin, Jim	Thomas, Mickey	McClelland, John	Haddock, Peter	Strachan, Gordon	Batty, David	Baird, Ian	Davison, Bobby	Hendrie, John	Whitlow, Mike	Shutt, Carl	Fairclough, Chris	Jones, Vinnie	Speed, Gary	Blake, Noel	Williams, Andy	Turner, Chris	Pearson, John	Kerr, Dylan	Snodin, Glynn	Chapman, Lee	Kamara, Chris	Varadi, Imre	O'Donnell, Chris	Hilaire, Vince	Edwards, Neil
1	2				6	7	8	9	**10**	11	3		**5**	4		S*	S*										
1	2				6	7	8	9	10		3		S*	**4**	S*	**5**	11										
2	2	0	0	0	2	2	2	2	2	1	2	0	1	2	0	1	1	0	0	0	0	0	0	0	0	0	0
													1		1	1	1										
						1							1														

Day, Mervyn	Sterland, Mel	Beglin, Jim	Thomas, Mickey	McClelland, John	Haddock, Peter	Strachan, Gordon	Batty, David	Baird, Ian	Davison, Bobby	Hendrie, John	Whitlow, Mike	Shutt, Carl	Fairclough, Chris	Jones, Vinnie	Speed, Gary	Blake, Noel	Williams, Andy	Turner, Chris	Pearson, John	Kerr, Dylan	Snodin, Glynn	Chapman, Lee	Kamara, Chris	Varadi, Imre	O'Donnell, Chris	Hilaire, Vince	Edwards, Neil
1	2				6	7	8	**9**		11		**10**	5	4					S*	3	S*						
1	1	0	0	0	1	1	1	1	0	1	0	1	1	1	0	0	0	0	0	1	0	0	0	0	0	0	0
																			1		1						

League Table

	P	W	D	L	F	A	Pts
Leeds United	46	24	13	9	79	52	85
Sheffield United	46	24	13	9	78	58	85
Newcastle United	46	22	14	10	80	55	80
Swindon Town	46	20	14	12	79	59	74
Blackburn Rovers	46	19	17	10	74	59	74
Sunderland	46	20	14	12	70	64	74
West Ham United	46	20	12	14	80	57	72
Oldham Athletic	46	19	14	13	70	57	71
Ipswich Town	46	19	12	15	67	66	69
Wolverhampton W	46	18	13	15	67	60	67
Port Vale	46	15	16	15	62	57	61
Portsmouth	46	15	16	15	62	65	61
Leicester City	46	15	14	17	67	79	59
Hull City	46	14	16	16	58	65	58
Watford	46	14	15	17	58	60	57
Plymouth Argyle	46	14	13	19	58	63	55
Oxford United	46	15	9	22	57	66	54
Brighton & Hove Albion	46	15	9	22	56	72	54
Barnsley	46	13	15	18	49	71	54
West Bromwich Albion	46	12	15	19	67	71	51
Middlesbrough	46	13	11	22	52	63	50
Bournemouth	46	12	12	22	57	76	48
Bradford City	46	9	14	23	44	68	41
Stoke City	46	6	19	21	35	63	37

1990-91

Division One

Manager: Howard Wilkinson

Final Position: 4th

Did you know that?

11 November 1990: United are on ITV's live programme *The Match* for the first time and win many Sunday afternoon armchair admirers in a 3–2 win at Manchester City.

11 May 1991: Lee Chapman's double in the 4–3 defeat at Nottingham Forest took his total to 31, the best haul by a First Division player that season and reached a career tally of 200 goals in League and Cup matches.

Lee Chapman piled in 21 League goals.

Back in the big time. United look forward to their first season since 1982.

Match No.	Date	Venue	Opponents	Result	FT	HT	Scorers	Attendance
1	Aug 25	A	Everton	W	3-2	2-0	Fairclough, Speed, Varadi	34,412
2	28	H	Manchester United	D	0-0	0-0		29,172
3	Sep 1	H	Norwich City	W	3-0	2-0	Chapman 2, Varadi	25,684
4	8	A	Luton Town	L	0-1	0-1		10,185
5	15	H	Tottenham Hotspur	L	0-2	0-0		31,342
6	23	A	Sheffield United	W	2-0	0-0	Pearson, Strachan	26,078
7	29	H	Arsenal	D	2-2	1-1	Chapman, Strachan (pen)	30,085
8	Oct 6	A	Crystal Palace	D	1-1	0-0	Speed	21,676
9	20	H	Queen's Park R	L	2-3	2-2	Whtye, Chapman	27,443
10	27	A	Aston Villa	D	0-0	0-0		24,219
11	Nov 3	H	Nottingham Forest	W	3-1	2-0	Chapman, Strachan (pen), McAllister	30,409
12	11	A	Manchester City	W	3-2	2-0	Chapman, Shutt, Strachan	27,782
13	17	H	Derby County	W	3-0	2-0	Chapman, Strachan, Speed	27,868
14	24	A	Coventry City	D	1-1	1-0	Chapman	16,183
15	Dec 1	H	Southampton	W	2-1	2-0	Fairclough, Shutt	29,341
16	8	A	Manchester United	D	1-1	0-0	Sterland	40,927
17	16	H	Everton	W	2-0	2-0	Strachan (pen), Shutt	27,775
18	23	A	Sunderland	W	1-0	0-0	Sterland	23,773
19	26	H	Chelsea	W	4-1	1-0	Sterland, Chapman 2, Whitlow	30,893
20	29	H	Wimbledon	W	3-0	3-0	Chapman, Speed, Sterland	29,292
21	Jan 1	A	Liverpool	L	0-3	0-2		36,975
22	12	A	Norwich City	L	0-2	0-1		17,786
23	19	H	Luton Town	W	2-1	1-0	Strachan (pen), Fairclough	27,010
24	Feb 2	A	Tottenham Hotspur	D	0-0	0-0		32,253
25	Mar 2	A	Southampton	L	0-2	0-1		16,858
26	9	H	Coventry City	W	2-0	1-0	Davison, Whyte	28,880
27	17	A	Arsenal	L	0-2	0-0		26,218
28	23	H	Crystal Palace	L	1-2	1-1	Speed	28,556
29	30	A	Chelsea	W	2-1	2-0	Shutt, Fairclough	17,585
30	Apr 2	H	Sunderland	W	5-0	3-0	Chapman 2, Shutt, Speed 2	28,132
31	6	A	Wimbledon	W	1-0	1-0	Chapman	6,800
32	10	H	Manchester City	L	1-2	1-1	McAllister	28,757
33	13	H	Liverpool	L	4-5	0-4	Chapman 3, Shutt	31,460
34	17	A	Queen's Park R	L	0-2	0-0		10,998
35	23	A	Derby County	W	1-0	1-0	Shutt	12,666
36	May 4	H	Aston Villa	W	5-2	2-1	Price (og), Chapman 2, Whyte, Shutt	29,188
37	8	H	Sheffield United	W	2-1	1-0	Sterland, Shutt	28,978
38	11	A	Nottingham Forest	L	3-4	1-2	Chapman 2, Shutt	25,067
								Appearances
								Sub appearances
							One own-goal	Goals

FM Cup

Round	Date	Venue	Opponents	Result	FT	HT	Scorers	Attendance
R2	Dec 19	A	Wolverhampton W	W	2-1	1-0	Varadi, McAllister	11,080
R3	Jan 22	H	Derby County	W	2-1	2-0	Shutt, Chapman	6,334
SF(N)	Feb 20	H	Manchester City	W	2-0*	0-0	Williams, Strachan	11,898
F(N)	Mar 19	H	Everton	D	3-3	2-3	Sterland, Chapman 2	13,387
	21	A	Everton	L	1-3*	1-0	Sterland	12,603
								Appearances
								Sub appearances
								Goals

* After extra-time (Northern Area Final 2nd Leg score 1-1 after 90 minutes)

FL Cup

Round	Date	Venue	Opponents	Result	FT	HT	Scorers	Attendance
R2	Sep 26	A	Leicester City	L	0-1	0-1		13,744
	Oct 10	H	Leicester City	W	3-0	0-0	Walsh (og), Speed, Strachan	19,090
R3	31	H	Oldham Athletic	W	2-0	2-0	Chapman, Speed	26,327
R4	Nov 27	A	Queen's Park R	W	3-0	3-0	McAllister, Fairclough, Chapman	15,832
R5	Jan 16	H	Aston Villa	W	4-1	1-0	Chapman 2, Mcallister, Speed	28,176
SF	Feb 10	A	Manchester United	L	1-2	0-0	Whyte	34,050
	24	H	Manchester United	L	0-1	0-0		32,014
								Appearances
								Sub appearances
							One own-goal	Goals

FA Cup

Round	Date	Venue	Opponents	Result	FT	HT	Scorers	Attendance
R3	Jan 6	A	Barnsley	D	1-1	0-0	Sterland	22,424
Rep	9	H	Barnsley	W	4-0	2-0	Smith (og), Chapman, McAllister, Strachan (pen)	19,773
R4	27	A	Arsenal	D	0-0	0-0		30,905
Rep	30	H	Arsenal	D	1-1*	0-0	Chapman	27,753
2R	Feb 13	A	Arsenal	D	0-0*	0-0		30,433
3R	16	H	Arsenal	L	1-2	0-2	Chapman	27,190
								Appearances
								Sub appearances
							One own-goal	Goals

* After extra-time (score at 90 minutes in first replay 1-1)

Lukic, John	Sterland, Mel	Snodin, Glynn	Batty, David	Fairclough, Chris	Whyte, Chris	Strachan, Gordon	Varadi, Imre	Chapman, Lee	McAllister, Gary	Speed, Gary	Kamara, Chris	Haddock, Peter	Whitlow, Mike	Jones, Vinnie	Pearson, John	Shutt, Carl	Williams, Andy	Davison, Bobby	McClelland, John	Day, Mervyn	Beglin, Jim	Kerr, Dylan
1	2	3	4	5	6	7	8	9	10	11	S*	S*										
1	2	S*	4	5	6	7	8	9	10	11		3										
1	2	3	4	5	6	7	8	9	10	11		S*	S*									
1	2	3	4		6	7	S*	9	10	S*		5	11	8								
1	2	S*	4	5	6	7	8	9	10	11		S*	3									
1	2		4	5	6	7	8	9	10	11		3			S*							
1	2	11	4	5	6	7		9	10	S*		3			8							
1	2		4	5	6	7		9	10	11		3			8							
1	2	3	4	5	6	7		9	10	11	S*				8	S*						
1	2		4	5	6	7		9	10	11	3				8							
1	2	S*	4	5	6	7		9	10	11	3					8						
1	2		4	5	6	7		9	10	11	3				S*	8						
1	2		4	5	6	7		9	10	11	3					8						
1	2		4	6	5	7		9	10	11	3	S*			S*	8						
1	2		4	5	6	7		9	10	11		3			S*	8	S*					
1	2		4	5	6	7		9	10	11		3				8						
1	2	S*	4	5	6	7		9	10	11		3				8						
1	2	S*	4	5	6	7		9	10	11		3				8						
1	2	3	4	5	6	7		9	10	11			S*			8						
1	2	3	4	5	6	7		9	10	11			S*		S*	8						
1	2	3	4	5	6	7		9	10	11			S*		S*	8						
1	2	3	4	5	6	7		9	10	S*			11		S*	8						
1	2	3	4	5	6	7		9	10	11		S*				8						
1	2	S*		5	6	7		9	10	11		3	4		S*		8					
1	2		4	5	6			9	10	11			3			8	7	S*				
1	2		4	5	6	7		9	10	11			3			S*		8				
1	2		4	5	6	7		9	10	11			3			S*		8				
1	2		4	5	6	7		9	10	11			3		S*	8	S*					
1	2		4	5	6	7		9	10	11			3			8	S*					
1	2		4		6	7		9	10	11			3			8			5			
1	2		4		6	7		9	10	11			3			8	S*		5			
1	2		4		6			9	10	11			3			8	7	S*	5			
1	2		4	5	6	7		9	10	11			3			8						
1	2		4	5	6	7		9	10	11			3			8	S*					
1	2	3	4	5	6	7		9	10	11						8	S*					
1	2	3	4	5	6			9	10	11						8	7	S*				
1	2	3	4	5	6			9	10	11						8	7					
1	2	3	4	5	6	7		9	10	11						8	S*					
38	38	14	37	34	38	34	5	38	38	35	5	10	14	1	4	25	5	2	3	0	0	0
		6					1			3	2	5	4		9	3	7	3				
	5			4	3	7	2	21	2	7			1		1	10		1				

Lukic, John	Sterland, Mel	Snodin, Glynn	Batty, David	Fairclough, Chris	Whyte, Chris	Strachan, Gordon	Varadi, Imre	Chapman, Lee	McAllister, Gary	Speed, Gary	Kamara, Chris	Haddock, Peter	Whitlow, Mike	Jones, Vinnie	Pearson, John	Shutt, Carl	Williams, Andy	Davison, Bobby	McClelland, John	Day, Mervyn	Beglin, Jim	Kerr, Dylan
	2	3		5		7	8		10	11		6			9		S*			1	4	S*
1	2	3	4		6	7	S*	9		11		5				8	10					
1	2		4	5	6	7		9	10	11			3			8	S*	S*				
1	2		4	5	6	7		9	10	S*			3			S*	11	8				
1	2		4	5	6	7		9	10	S*			3			8	11	S*				
4	5	2	4	4	4	5	1	4	4	3	0	2	3	0	1	3	3	1	0	1	1	0
							1			2						1	2	2				1
	2					1	1	3	1							1	1					

Lukic, John	Sterland, Mel	Snodin, Glynn	Batty, David	Fairclough, Chris	Whyte, Chris	Strachan, Gordon	Varadi, Imre	Chapman, Lee	McAllister, Gary	Speed, Gary	Kamara, Chris	Haddock, Peter	Whitlow, Mike	Jones, Vinnie	Pearson, John	Shutt, Carl	Williams, Andy	Davison, Bobby	McClelland, John	Day, Mervyn	Beglin, Jim	Kerr, Dylan
1	2		4	5	6	7	8	9	10	11			3		S*		S*					
	2		4	5	6	7		9	10	11	S*	3			8	S*				1		
1		3	4	5	6	7		9	10	11	2				8							
1	2	S*	4	5	6	7		9	10	11		3				8						
1	2	3	4	5	6	7		9	10	11		S*			S*	8						
1	2			5	6	7		9	10	11		3	4				8					
1	2		4	5	6	7		9	10	11		3	S*		S*	8						
6	6	2	6	7	7	7	1	7	7	7	1	4	2	0	2	3	1	0	0	1	0	0
		1									1	1	1		3	1	1					
				1	1	1		4	2	3												

Lukic, John	Sterland, Mel	Snodin, Glynn	Batty, David	Fairclough, Chris	Whyte, Chris	Strachan, Gordon	Varadi, Imre	Chapman, Lee	McAllister, Gary	Speed, Gary	Kamara, Chris	Haddock, Peter	Whitlow, Mike	Jones, Vinnie	Pearson, John	Shutt, Carl	Williams, Andy	Davison, Bobby	McClelland, John	Day, Mervyn	Beglin, Jim	Kerr, Dylan
1	2	3	4	5		7		9	10	11			S*		S*	8			6			
1	2	3	4	5		7		9	10	11			S*		S*	8			6			
1	2		4	5	6	7		9	10	11		3			S*	8						
1	2	S*	4	5	6	7		9	10	11		3			8							
1	2		4	5	6	7		9	10	11		3	S*			8		S*				
1	2		4	5	6	7		9	10	11		3				8		S*				
6	6	2	6	6	4	6	0	6	6	6	0	4	0	0	1	5	0	0	2	0	0	0
		1											3		3			2				
	1					1		3	1													

League Table

	P	W	D	L	F	A	Pts
Arsenal	38	24	13	1	74	18	83
Liverpool	38	23	7	8	77	40	76
Crystal Palace	38	20	9	9	50	41	69
Leeds United	38	19	7	12	65	47	64
Manchester City	38	17	11	10	64	53	62
Manchester United	38	16	12	10	58	45	59
Wimbledon	38	14	14	10	53	46	56
Nottingham Forest	38	14	12	12	65	50	54
Everton	38	13	12	13	50	46	51
Tottenham Hotspur	38	11	16	11	51	50	49
Chelsea	38	13	10	15	58	69	49
Queen's Park Rangers	38	12	10	16	44	53	46
Sheffield United	38	13	7	18	36	55	46
Southampton	38	12	9	17	58	69	45
Norwich City	38	13	6	19	41	64	45
Coventry City	38	11	11	16	42	49	44
Aston Villa	38	9	14	15	46	58	41
Luton Town	38	10	7	21	42	61	37
Sunderland	38	8	10	20	38	60	34
Derby County	38	5	9	24	37	75	24

1991-92

Division One

Manager: Howard Wilkinson

Final Position: 1st

Did you know that?

17 August 1991: United's opening game of the season at Crystal Palace was called off because ground works at Selhurst Park had not been completed.

7 September 1991: Midfielder David Batty scored his first goal in three years nine months as United thumped Manchester City 3–0.

26 October 1991: An own-goal by Oldham's Brian Kilcline sent United to the top of Division One for the first time since winning the title in 1974.

Inspirational skipper Gordon Strachan led United to their third title.

Howard Wilkinson, the last English man to manage a League champion squad with his heroes of 1991–92.

Match No.	Date	Venue	Opponents	Result	FT	HT	Scorers	Attendance
1	Aug 20	H	Nottingham Forest	W	1-0	1-0	McAllister	29,457
2	24	H	Sheffield Wed	D	1-1	0-0	Hodge	30,260
3	28	A	Southampton	W	4-0	1-0	Speed 2, Strachan 2 (2 pens)	15,847
4	31	A	Manchester United	D	1-1	1-0	Chapman	43,778
5	Sep 3	H	Arsenal	D	2-2	0-1	Strachan (pen), Chapman	29,396
6	7	H	Manchester City	W	3-0	2-0	Dorigo, Batty, Strachan (pen)	29,986
7	14	A	Chelsea	W	1-0	0-0	Shutt	23,439
8	18	A	Coventry City	D	0-0	0-0		15,488
9	21	H	Liverpool	W	1-0	1-0	Hodge	32,917
10	28	A	Norwich City	D	2-2	0-0	Dorigo, Speed	15,828
11	Oct 1	A	Crystal Palace	L	0-1	0-0		18,298
12	5	H	Sheffield United	W	4-3	3-0	Hodge 2, Sterland 2 (1 pen)	28,362
13	19	A	Notts County	W	4-2	2-1	Chapman, Hodge, Whyte, McAllister	12,964
14	26	H	Oldham Athletic	W	1-0	0-0	Kilcline (og)	28,199
15	Nov 2	A	Wimbledon	D	0-0	0-0		7,025
16	16	H	Queen's Park R	W	2-0	0-0	Sterland, Wallace	27,087
17	24	A	Aston Villa	W	4-1	1-0	Wallace, Sterland, Chapman 2	23,666
18	30	H	Everton	W	1-0	0-0	Wallace	30,043
19	Dec 7	A	Luton Town	W	2-0	0-0	Wallace, Speed	11,550
20	14	H	Tottenham Hotspur	D	1-1	1-1	Speed	31,404
21	22	A	Nottingham Forest	D	0-0	0-0		27,170
22	26	H	Southampton	D	3-3	2-0	Hodge 2, Speed	29,053
23	29	H	Manchester United	D	1-1	0-0	Sterland (pen)	32,638
24	Jan 1	A	West Ham United	W	3-1	2-1	Chapman 2, McAllister	21,766
25	12	A	Sheffield Wed	W	6-1	3-1	Chapman 3, Dorigo, Whitlow, Wallace	32,228
26	18	H	Crystal Palace	D	1-1	1-1	Fairclough	27,717
27	Feb 1	H	Notts County	W	3-0	1-0	Sterland, Batty, Wallace	27,224
28	8	A	Oldham Athletic	L	0-2	0-1		18,409
29	23	A	Everton	D	1-1	0-0	Keown (og)	19,248
30	29	H	Luton Town	W	2-0	0-0	Cantona, Chapman	28,231
31	Mar 3	H	Aston Villa	D	0-0	0-0		28,896
32	7	A	Tottenham Hotspur	W	3-1	1-0	Wallace, Newsome, McAllister	27,622
33	11	A	Queen's Park R	L	1-4	1-1	Speed	14,641
34	14	H	Wimbledon	W	5-1	3-0	Chapman 3, Wallace, Cantona	26,760
35	22	A	Arsenal	D	1-1	0-0	Chapman	27,844
36	28	H	West Ham United	D	0-0	0-0		31,101
37	Apr 4	A	Manchester City	L	0-4	0-2		30,239
38	11	H	Chelsea	W	3-0	0-0	Wallace, Chapman, Cantona	31,363
39	18	A	Liverpool	D	0-0	0-0		37,186
40	20	H	Coventry City	W	2-0	0-0	Fairclough, McAllister (pen)	26,582
41	26	A	Sheffield United	W	3-2	1-1	Wallace, Newsome, Gayle (og)	32,000
42	May 2	H	Norwich City	W	1-0	1-0	Wallace	32,673
								Appearances
								Sub appearances
							Three own-goals	Goals

FM Cup

R2	Oct 22	H	Nottingham Forest	L	1-3	0-2	Wallace	6,145
								Appearances
								Sub appearances
								Goals

FL Cup

R2	Sep 24	A	Scunthorpe United	D	0-0	0-0		8,392
	Oct 8	H	Scunthorpe United	W	3-0	0-0	Sterland (pen), Chapman, Speed	14,558
R3	29	H	Tranmere Rovers	W	3-1	0-0	Chapman 2, Shutt	18,266
R4	Dec 4	A	Everton	W	4-1	2-1	Speed, Chapman, Wallace 2	25,467
R5	Jan 8	H	Manchester United	L	1-3	1-1	Speed	28,886
								Appearances
								Sub appearances
								Goals

FA Cup

R3	Jan 15	H	Manchester United	L	0-1	0-1		31,819
								Appearances
								Sub appearances
								Goals

Lukic John	McClelland, John	Dorigo, Tony	Batty, David	Fairclough, Chris	Whyte, Chris	Strachan, Gordon	Wallace, Rod	Chapman, Lee	McAllister, Gary	Speed, Gary	Hodge, Steve	Sterland, Mel	Wetherall, David	Shutt, Carl	Varadi, Imre	Whitlow, Mike	Kamara, Chris	Newsome, Jon	Kelly, Gary	Davison, Bobby	Cantona, Eric	Agana, Tony	Snodin, Glynn	Grayson, Simon	Williams, Andy
1	2	3	4	5	6	7	8	9	10	11															
1	**2**	3	4	5	6	7	8	9	10	**11**	S*	S*													
1	2	3	4	**5**	6	7	8	9	**10**	11	S*	S*													
1	5	3	4		6	7	8	9	**10**	11	S*	2													
1	5	**3**	4		6	7	8	9	10	11	S*	**2**	S*												
1	5	3	4		6	7	**8**	9	10	11	S*	2													
1	5	3	4		6	**7**		9	10	11	S*	2		8											
1	5	3	4		6	7		9	10	11	S*	2		**8**											
1	5	3	4		6	7		9	10	**11**	8	2		S*											
1	5	3	4		6			9	10	11	**8**	2		S*	**7**	S*									
1	5	3	4		6			9	**10**	11	8	2		S*	**7**	S*									
1	5	3	4	S*	6			9	**10**	11	7	**2**		8		S*									
1		3	4	5	6	7		**9**	**S***	11	10	2		8			S*								
1		3	4	5	6	**7**	8	9	10	**11**		2		S*			S*								
1		3		5	6	7	**8**	9	10	11		2		4				S*							
1		3	4	5	6	7	8	9	10	**11**		2			S*										
1	11	3	4	5	6	7	8	9	10			2													
1	S*	3	4	5	6	7	8	9	10	**11**	**S***	2													
1		3	4	5	6	7	8	9	10	11		2													
1	5	3	4		6	7	8	9	10	11		2													
1	5	3	4		6	**7**	8	9	10	11		2							S*						
1	5	3	4		6		8	9	10	11	7	2													
1		3	**4**	5	6	7	8	9	10	11	S*	2													
1		3	4	5	6	7	8	9	10	11		2													
1		3		5	6		8	9	10	11	**4**	2		**7**		S*				S*					
1		3	4	5	6	7	8		**10**	11	**9**	2				S*				S*					
1		3	4	5	6	**7**	8		10	11	9	**2**				S*			S*						
1		3	4	5	6	7	8		10	11	**9**	**2**				S*					S*				
1		3	4	5	6	7	**8**		10	11		2		S*							9				
1		**3**	4	5	6	7	**8**	9	10	11		2									S*	S*			
1	S*		4	**5**	6	7		9	10	11		2				3					S*	**8**			
1			4	5	6	7	8	9	10	11		**2**				**3**		S*			S*				
1			4	5	6	7	8	9	**10**	11						3		2			S*				
1			4	5	6	**7**	8	9	10	11				S*				2			3				
1		3	4	5	6	7	8	9	10	11											2				
1		3	4	5		7	**8**	9	10	11	S*							6			2				
1		3	4	5	6	7	8	9	10	11											2				
1		3	4	5	6	7	**8**	9	10	11	**2**							S*			S*				
1		3	4	5	6		8	9	10	11	**7**							2			S*				
1		3	4	5	6	**7**	**8**	9	10	11				S*				2			S*				
1		3	4	5	6	**7**	8	9	**10**	11				S*				2			S*				
1		3	4	5	6	S*	8	**9**	10	11	S*							2			**7**				
42	16	38	40	30	41	35	34	38	41	41	12	29	0	6	2	3	0	7	0	0	6	1	0	0	0
	2			1		1			1		11	2	1	8	1	7	2	3	2	2	9	1			
		3	2	2	1	4	11	16	5	7	7	6		1		1		2			3				

1		3	4	5	6		S*			11		**2**		8			**10**	**7**					9	S*	
1	0	1	1	1	1	0	0	0	0	1	0	1	0	1	0	0	1	1	0	0	0	0	1	0	0
							1																	1	
							1																		

1	5	3	4		6	**7**		9	10	11	8	2		S*											
1	5	3	4	S*	6			9		11	7	2		**8**					S*						**10**
1		3		5	6	7	**11**	9	10		**4**	2		8			S*								S*
1		3	4	5	6	**7**	8	9	10	11	S*	2													
1	S*	**3**	4	5	6	7	8	**9**	10	11	S*	2													
5	2	5	4	3	5	4	3	5	4	4	3	5	0	2	0	0	0	0	0	0	0	0	0	0	1
	1			1							2			1			1		1						1
							2	4		3		1		1											

1		3		5	6		8	9	10	11	**4**	2				S*				S*					**7**
1	0	1	0	1	1	0	1	1	1	1	1	1	0	0	0	0	0	0	0	0	0	0	0	0	1
																1				1					

League Table

	P	W	D	L	F	A	Pts
Leeds United	42	22	16	4	74	37	82
Manchester United	42	21	15	6	63	33	78
Sheffield Wednesday	42	21	12	9	62	49	75
Arsenal	42	19	15	8	81	46	72
Manchester City	42	20	10	12	61	48	70
Liverpool	42	16	16	10	47	40	64
Aston Villa	42	17	9	16	48	44	60
Nottingham Forest	42	16	11	15	60	58	59
Sheffield United	42	16	9	17	65	63	57
Crystal Palace	42	14	15	13	53	61	57
Queen's Park Rangers	42	12	18	12	48	47	54
Everton	42	13	14	15	52	51	53
Wimbledon	42	13	14	15	53	53	53
Chelsea	42	13	14	15	50	60	53
Tottenham Hotspur	42	15	7	20	58	63	52
Southampton	42	14	10	18	39	55	52
Oldham Athletic	42	14	9	19	63	67	51
Norwich City	42	11	12	19	47	63	45
Coventry City	42	11	11	20	35	44	44
Luton Town	42	10	12	20	38	71	42
Notts County	42	10	10	22	40	62	40
West Ham United	42	9	11	22	37	59	38

1992-93

Premiership

Manager: Howard Wilkinson

Final Position: 17th

Did you know that?

21 November 1992: David Rocastle made his long-awaited first League start since his record £2 million move from Arsenal against his old employers who sunk 3–0 at Elland Road.

8 May 1993: Rod Wallace scored a hat-trick in the 3–3 draw at Coventry, but failure to record a victory meant the defending champions had gone the entire League season without winning on their travels.

Record £2 million signing David Rocastle.

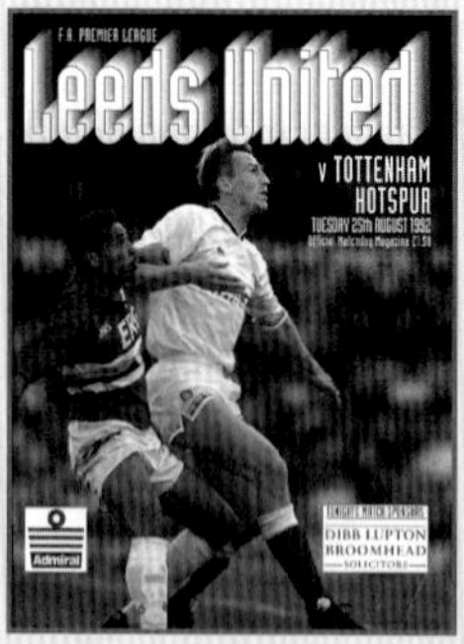

Match No.	Date	Venue	Opponents	Result	FT	HT	Scorers	Attendance
1	Aug 15	H	Wimbledon	W	2-1	1-0	Chapman 2	25,795
2	19	A	Aston Villa	D	1-1	0-0	Speed	29,151
3	22	A	Middlesbrough	L	1-4	0-2	Cantona	18,649
4	25	H	Tottenham Hotspur	W	5-0	3-0	Wallace, Cantona 3, Chapman	28,218
5	29	H	Liverpool	D	2-2	1-1	McAllister, Chapman	29,597
6	Sep 1	A	Oldham Athletic	D	2-2	0-0	Cantona 2	13,848
7	6	A	Manchester United	L	0-2	0-2		31,296
8	13	H	Aston Villa	D	1-1	0-1	Hodge	27,817
9	19	A	Southampton	D	1-1	0-1	Speed	16,229
10	26	H	Everton	W	2-0	0-0	McAllister (pen), Chapman	27,915
11	Oct 3	A	Ipswich Town	L	2-4	0-3	Stockwell (og), Speed	21,200
12	17	H	Sheffield United	W	3-1	1-0	Chapman, Speed, Whyte	29,706
13	24	A	Queen's Park R	L	1-2	0-0	Strachan	19,326
14	31	H	Coventry City	D	2-2	0-1	Chapman, Fairclough	28,018
15	Nov 7	A	Manchester City	L	0-4	0-2		27,255
16	21	H	Arsenal	W	3-0	0-0	Fairclough, Chapman, McAllister	30,516
17	29	A	Chelsea	L	0-1	0-0		24,345
18	Dec 5	H	Nottingham Forest	L	1-4	0-1	Speed	29,364
19	12	H	Sheffield Wed	W	3-1	1-1	Speed, Chapman, Varadi	29,770
20	20	A	Crystal Palace	L	0-1	0-1		14,462
21	26	A	Blackburn Rovers	L	1-3	1-2	McAllister	19,910
22	28	H	Norwich City	D	0-0	0-0		30,282
23	Jan 9	H	Southampton	W	2-1	0-1	Chapman, Speed	26,071
24	16	A	Everton	L	0-2	0-1		21,031
25	30	H	Middlesbrough	W	3-0	0-0	Strandli, Batty, Fairclough	30,344
26	Feb 6	A	Wimbledon	L	0-1	0-0		6,704
27	8	H	Manchester United	D	0-0	0-0		34,166
28	13	H	Oldham Athletic	W	2-0	1-0	McAllister (pen), Chapman	27,654
29	20	A	Tottenham Hotspur	L	0-4	0-2		32,040
30	24	A	Arsenal	D	0-0	0-0		21,061
31	27	H	Ipswich Town	W	1-0	0-0	Dorigo (pen)	28,848
32	Mar 13	H	Manchester City	W	1-0	1-0	Rocastle	30,840
33	21	A	Nottingham Forest	D	1-1	1-1	Wallace	25,148
34	24	H	Chelsea	D	1-1	1-0	Wetherall	28,135
35	Apr 6	A	Sheffield United	L	1-2	1-1	Strandli	20,562
36	10	H	Blackburn Rovers	W	5-2	2-0	Strachan 3 (2 pens), Wallace, Chapman	31,791
37	14	A	Norwich City	L	2-4	1-3	Chapman, Wallace	18,613
38	17	H	Crystal Palace	D	0-0	0-0		27,545
39	21	A	Liverpool	L	0-2	0-0		34,992
40	May 1	H	Queen's Park R	D	1-1	0-1	Hodge	31,408
41	4	A	Sheffield Wed	D	1-1	1-0	King (og)	26,855
42	8	A	Coventry City	D	3-3	1-2	Wallace 3	19,591

Appearances
Sub appearances
Two own-goals — Goals

FL Cup

R2	Sep 22	H	Scunthorpe United	W	4-1	2-0	Strachan, Chapman, Speed, Shutt	10,113
	Oct 27	A	Scunthorpe United	D	2-2	1-2	Wallace, Chapman	7,419
R3	Nov 10	A	Watford	L	1-2	0-0	McAllister	18,035

Appearances
Sub appearances
Goals

FA Cup

R3	Jan 2	H	Charlton Athletic	D	1-1	0-0	Speed	21,287
Rep	13	A	Charlton Athletic	W	3-1	1-0	Speed, Garland (og), McAllister	8,337
R4	25	A	Arsenal	D	2-2	2-0	Speed, Chapman	26,516
Rep	Feb 3	H	Arsenal	L	2-3*	0-0	Shutt, McAllister	26,449

* After extra-time (score at 90 minutes 2-2)

Appearances
Sub appearances
One own-goal — Goals

European Cup

R1	Sep 16	A	VfB Stuttgart	L	0-3	0-0		38,000
	30	H	VfB Stuttgart	W	4-1*	2-1	Speed, McAllister (pen), Cantona, Chapman	20,457
PO	Oct 9	N	VfB Stuttgart	W	2-1†	1-1	Strachan, Shutt	7,400
R2	21	A	Rangers	L	1-2	1-2	McAllister	43,251
	Nov 4	H	Rangers	L	1-2	0-1	Cantona	25,118

* Tie awarded 3-0 to Leeds as Stuttgart played a fourth foreign player
† At Nou Camp, Barcelona

Appearances
Sub appearances
Goals

Charity Shield

	Aug 8	N	Liverpool	W	4-3	2-1	Cantona 3, Dorigo	61,291

At Wembley, London

Appearances
Sub appearances
Goals

Lukic, John	Newsome, Jon	Dorigo, Tony	Batty, David	Fairclough, Chris	Whyte, Chris	Cantona, Eric	Wallace, Rod	Chapman, Lee	McAllister, Gary	Speed, Gary	Strachan, Gordon	Hodge, Steve	Sellars, Scott	Wetherall, David	Shutt, Carl	Rocastle, David	Day, Mervyn	Wallace, Ray	Varadi, Imre	Sterland, Mel	Strandli, Frank	Bowman, Rob	Kerslake, David	Forrester, Jamie	Kerr, Dylan	Tinkler, Mark	Sharp, Kevin	Whelan, Noel	Beeney, Mark
1	2	3	4	5	6	7	8	9	10	11	S*	S*																	
1	2	3	4	5	6	7	8	9	10	11	S*	S*																	
1	2	3	4	5	6	7	8	9	10	11	S*	S*																	
1	2	3	4	5	6	7	8	9	10	11																			
1	2	3	4	5	6	7	8	9	10	11	S*	S*																	
1	2	3	4	5	6	7	8	9	10	11		S*																	
1	2	3	4	5	6	7	8	9	10	11	S*	S*																	
1	2		4	5	6	7		9	10	11	8	S*	3																
1		3	4	5	6			9	10	11	7	8	S*	2	S*														
1		3	4	5	6	8		9	10	11	7		2		S*														
1		3	4	5	6	8		9	10	11	7		2			S*													
1	2	3	4	5	6	8		9	10	11	7				S*														
1	2	3	4	5	6		8	9	10	11	7				S*	S*													
1	2	3	4	5	6	S*	8	9	10	11	7					S*													
	2			5	6	8	9	S*	10	11	7	4		3			1												
1	2	3		5	6		8	9	10	11	7				S*	4													
1	2	3		5	6		8	9	10	11	7					4													
1	2	3		5			8	9	10	11	7	S*			S*	4		6											
1	2	3		5	6		8	9	10	11	7	S*				4			S*										
1	2	3		5	6		8	9	10	11	7	S*				4			S*										
1	S*	3	4	5	6			9	10	11	7								8	2									
1	S*	3	4	5				9	10	11	7			6					8	2									
1	S*	3		5			4	9	10	11	7			6	8	S*				2									
	2	3	4	S*	6		S*	9	10	11	7			5	8		1												
1		3	4	5	6		9		10	11	7			2	8	S*					S*								
1	5	3	4		6			9	10	11			2		S*	7					8	S*							
1	5	3	4		6			9	10	11		S*	2		8						S*	7							
1	5	3	4		6		8	9	10	11		S*	2		S*							7							
1	5	3	4		6		8	9	10	11		7				S*					S*	2							
1	S*	3	4	2	6		8	S*	10	11	7			5							9								
1	2	3	4	5			8	S*		11	7			6				10			9								
1	S*	3	4	5			8	S*		11		10		6		7					9		2						
1	6	3	4				8	9		11		10		5		7							2	S*					
1	6	3	4				8	9		11	S*	10		5		7					S*		2						
1					6				10	11	7	S*		5							9		2	8	3	4			
1	S*			5	6		8	9		11	7												2	10	3	4			
1	S*			5	6		8	9		11	7	S*											2	10	3	4			
1	6						8	9	10	11	7			5									2	4		S*	3		
1	5				6		8	9		11	7				10	4		S*					2				3		
1	5		4		6		8	9				10				7		2			S*			11		S*	3		
1	5		4		6		8	9				10						2							S*	11	3	7	
	5	3	4		6		8	9				10			7	S*		2							S*	11			1
39	30	33	30	29	34	12	31	36	32	39	25	9	6	13	6	11	2	5	2	3	5	3	8	5	3	5	4	1	1
	7			1		1	1	4			6	14	1		8	7		1	2		5	1		1	2	2			

1		3	4		6			9	10	11	7	S*	5	2	8	S*													
1	2		4	5	S*		8	9	10	11	7		S*	6											3				
1	2			5	6	8	4	9	10	11	7					S*									3				
3	2	1	2	2	2	1	2	3	3	3	3	0	1	2	1	0	0	0	0	0	0	0	0	0	2	0	0	0	0
					1							1	1			2													
							1	2	1	1	1				1														

1	S*	3	4	5			S*	9	10	11	7			6	8					2									
		3		S*	6		4	9	10	11	7			5	8	S*	1			2									
1		3	4	5	6		S*	9	10	11	7			2	8	S*													
1		3	4	2	6		S*	9	10	11	7			5	8	S*													
3	0	4	3	3	3	0	1	4	4	4	4	0	0	4	4	0	1	0	0	2	0	0	0	0	0	0	0	0	0
	1			1			3									3													
								1	2	3					1														

1		3	4	5	6	7		9	10	11	8	S*			S*	2													
1		3	4	5	6	8		9	10	11	7		2																
1	2	3	4	5	6	8		9	10	11	7				S*														
1	2	3	4	5	6	8	S*	9	10	11	7					S*													
1	2	3		5	6	8	S*	9	10	11	7	S*				4													
5	3	5	4	5	5	5	0	5	5	5	5	0	1	0	0	2	0	0	0	0	0	0	0	0	0	0	0	0	0
							2					2			2	1													
						2		1	2	1	1				1														

1	2	3	4	5	6	7	8	9	10	11	S*	S*																	
1	1	1	1	1	1	1	1	1	1	1	0	0	0	0	0	0	0	0	0	0	0	0	0	0	0	0	0	0	0
											1	1																	
		1				3																							

League Table

	P	W	D	L	F	A	Pts
Manchester United	42	24	12	6	67	31	84
Aston Villa	42	21	11	10	57	40	74
Norwich City	42	21	9	12	61	65	72
Blackburn Rovers	42	20	11	11	68	46	71
Queen's Park Rangers	42	17	12	13	63	55	63
Liverpool	42	16	11	15	62	55	59
Sheffield Wednesday	42	15	14	13	55	51	59
Tottenham Hotspur	42	16	11	15	60	66	59
Manchester City	42	15	12	15	56	51	57
Arsenal	42	15	11	16	40	38	56
Chelsea	42	14	14	14	51	54	56
Wimbledon	42	14	12	16	56	55	54
Everton	42	15	8	19	53	55	53
Sheffield United	42	14	10	18	54	53	52
Coventry City	42	13	13	16	52	57	52
Ipswich Town	42	12	16	14	50	55	52
Leeds United	42	12	15	15	57	62	51
Southampton	42	13	11	18	54	61	50
Oldham Athletic	42	13	10	19	63	74	49
Crystal Palace	42	11	16	15	48	61	49
Middlesbrough	42	11	11	20	54	75	44
Nottingham Forest	42	10	10	22	41	62	40

1993-94

Premiership

Manager: Howard Wilkinson

Final Position: 5th

Did you know that?

14 August 1993: United players had their names on the back of their shirts for the first time as Brian Deane's last-gasp goal earned a point at Manchester City.

11 September 1993: The 2–0 win at Southampton was United's first League away victory since the title-clinching Sunday at Bramall Lane 25 games ago.

28 January 1994: The new East Stand was officially opened by the Lord Chief Justice, Lord Taylor.

4 April 1994: United's second goal, scored by Rod Wallace, in the 4–0 romp at QPR was the 1,000th Premier League goal.

17 April 1994: A brace by Rod Wallace gave United a 2–0 win over Spurs with Rod winning the BBC *Match of the Day* Goal of the Season award for his breathtaking run down the left before curling the ball home in style.

3 May 1994: The 2–2 draw with Sheffield Wednesday was the last time fans were able to stand on the Kop. Seats were installed during the summer.

Rod Wallace scored *Match of the Day*'s Goal of the Season.

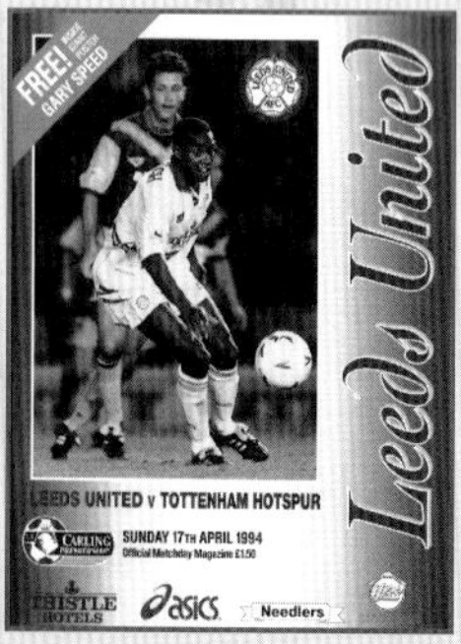

Match No.	Date	Venue	Opponents	Result	FT	HT	Scorers	Attendance
1	Aug 14	A	Manchester City	D	1-1	0-0	Deane	32,366
2	17	H	West Ham United	W	1-0	0-0	Speed	34,588
3	21	H	Norwich City	L	0-4	0-2		32,008
4	24	A	Arsenal	L	1-2	0-1	Strachan	29,042
5	28	A	Liverpool	L	0-2	0-2		44,068
6	30	H	Oldham Athletic	W	1-0	1-0	Strachan	28,717
7	Sep 11	A	Southampton	W	2-0	0-0	Deane, Speed	13,511
8	18	H	Sheffield United	W	2-1	2-1	McAllister, Strachan	33,879
9	25	A	Coventry City	W	2-0	1-0	Wallace 2	13,933
10	Oct 2	H	Wimbledon	W	4-0	2-0	Speed 2, McAllister 2	30,255
11	17	A	Ipswich Town	D	0-0	0-0		17,532
12	23	H	Blackburn Rovers	D	3-3	0-1	McAllister (pen), Newsome, Sherwood (og)	37,827
13	30	A	Sheffield Wed	D	3-3	1-2	Fairclough, Wallace, Speed	31,892
14	Nov 6	H	Chelsea	W	4-1	0-0	Deane, Wallace 2, Rocastle	35,050
15	20	A	Tottenham Hotspur	D	1-1	0-0	Deane	31,275
16	23	A	Everton	D	1-1	0-0	Wallace	17,102
17	27	H	Swindon Town	W	3-0	0-0	Deane, Wallace, Speed	32,630
18	Dec 4	H	Manchester City	W	3-2	2-0	Wallace, Speed, Deane	33,820
19	8	A	West Ham United	W	1-0	0-0	Wallace	20,468
20	13	A	Norwich City	L	1-2	0-1	Wallace	16,586
21	18	H	Arsenal	W	2-1	1-1	McAllister, Adams (og)	37,289
22	22	A	Newcastle United	D	1-1	0-0	Fairclough	36,388
23	29	H	Queen's Park R	D	1-1	0-0	Hodge	39,124
24	Jan 1	A	Manchester United	D	0-0	0-0		44,724
25	15	H	Ipswich Town	D	0-0	0-0		31,317
26	23	A	Blackburn Rovers	L	1-2	0-1	Speed	17,475
27	Feb 6	A	Aston Villa	L	0-1	0-0		26,919
28	19	H	Liverpool	W	2-0	1-0	Wetherall, McAllister	40,029
29	28	A	Oldham Athletic	D	1-1	1-0	McAllister	11,136
30	Mar 5	H	Southampton	D	0-0	0-0		30,829
31	13	A	Sheffield United	D	2-2	1-0	Speed, Deane	19,425
32	16	H	Aston Villa	W	2-0	1-0	Wallace, Deane	33,126
33	19	H	Coventry City	W	1-0	0-0	Wallace	30,023
34	26	A	Wimbledon	L	0-1	0-1		9,035
35	Apr 1	H	Newcastle United	D	1-1	0-1	Fairclough	40,005
36	4	A	Queen's Park R	W	4-0	2-0	Deane, Wallace, White 2	15,365
37	17	H	Tottenham Hotspur	W	2-0	0-0	Wallace 2	33,658
38	23	A	Chelsea	D	1-1	1-0	Speed	18,544
39	27	H	Manchester United	L	0-2	0-0		41,127
40	30	H	Everton	W	3-0	0-0	McAllister, Watson (og), White	35,487
41	May 3	H	Sheffield Wed	D	2-2	0-1	White, Wallace	33,575
42	7	A	Swindon Town	W	5-0	2-0	Deane 2, Wallace, White, Fairclough	17,228
								Appearances
								Sub appearances
							Three own-goals	Goals

FL Cup

R2	Sep 21	A	Sunderland	L	1-2	1-1	Speed	17,101
	Oct 6	H	Sunderland	L	1-2	0-2	Whelan	22,165
								Appearances
								Sub appearances
								Goals

FA Cup

R3	Jan 8	H	Crewe Alexandra	W	3-1	1-1	Deane, Forrester 2	23,475
R4	29	A	Oxford United	D	2-2	1-2	Speed, Wetherall	11,029
Rep	Feb 9	H	Oxford United	L	2-3*	0-0	Strachan, White	22,167
								Appearances
								Sub appearances
								Goals

* After extra-time (score at 90 minutes 2-2)

Challenge Match

	July 23	A	League of Ireland	D	2-2†	0-0	Shutt, Speed	7,000

† At Tolka Park, Dublin

Lukic, John	Kelly, Gary	Dorigo, Tony	Batty, David	Fairclough, Chris	O'Leary, David	Strachan, Gordon	Whelan, Noel	Deane, Brian	McAllister, Gary	Speed, Gary	Wallace, Rod	Newsome, Jon	Beeney, Mark	Wetherall, David	Strandli, Frank	Rocastle, David	Hodge, Steve	Pemberton, John	Forrester, Jamie	Sharp, Kevin	Wallace, Ray	White, David	Tinkler, Mark	Ford, Mark	Tobin, Steve	Shutt, Carl
1	2	3	4	5	6	**7**	8	9	10	11	S*															
1	2	3	4	5	6	**7**	**8**	9	10	11	S*	S*														
1	2	3	4	5	**6**	7	8	9	10	11		S*														
1	2	3	4	5		7	**8**	9	10	11	S*	6														
1	2	3	4	5		7	S*	9	10	11	**8**	6														
	2	3	4			7		9	10	11	8	6	1	5												
	2	3	4			7		9	10	11	**8**	6	1	5	S*											
	2	3	4	5		7		9	10	11	**8**		1	6	S*											
	2	3		5		7		9	10	11	8	4	1	6												
	2	3		5		7		9	10	11	**8**	4	1	6	S*											
	2	3		5				9	10	11	8	4	1	6	S*	**7**										
	2	3	S*	5			S*	9	10	11	8	4	1	**6**		**7**										
	2	3		5				9	10	11	8	4	1	6		**7**	S*									
	2	3		5				9	10	11	8	4	1	6		7										
	2	3		5			S*	9	10	11	8		1	6		**7**		4								
	2	3		5			S*	9	10	11	8		1	6		**7**		4								
	2	3		5		7		9	10	11	8		1	6				**4**	S*							
	2	3		5		7	S*	9	10	11	**8**		1	6						**4**	S*					
	2	3		5		7		9	10	**11**	8		1	6				S*		4						
	2	3		5		7	S*	9	10		8		1	6			11			**4**						
	2	3		5		**7**		9	10		8	4	1	6		S*	11									
	2	3		5			**7**	9	10		8	4	1				11	6		S*						
	2	3		5		7		9	10		**8**	4	1				11			S*		6				
	2	3		5		7		9	10			4	1				**11**	6		S*		8				
	2	3		5		7		9	10	S*		4	1	S*			11		**8**			**6**				
	2	3		5		7	S*	9	10	11		4	1					S*	**8**			**6**				
	2	3		5		7	S*	9	10	11		4	1				8					**6**				
1	2	3		5	**6**	7		9	10	11	**8**	S*		4								S*				
1	2	3		5		7		9	10	11	8	6		4												
1	2	3		5	6	7		**9**	10	11	8			4								S*				
1	2	3		5	6	7		9	10	11	8			4												
1	2	3		5	**6**	7		9	10	11	8	S*		4												
1	2	3		5		7		9	10	11	8	6		4												
1	2	3		5		7		9	10	11	8	**6**		4								S*				
1	2	3		5		7		9	10	11	8	6		**4**								S*				
1	2	**3**		5				9	10	11	8	6		4								7	S*			
1	2			5				9	10	11	8	6		4						3		7				
1	2			5		S*		9	10	11	8	6		4						3		**7**				
1	2	**3**		5		7	S*	9	10	11	8	6		**4**				S*								
1	2			5	6	7	**9**		10	11	**8**			4						3		S*	S*			
1	2			5	6	7		9	10	**11**	8			4						**3**		S*	S*			
1	2			5	6	**7**	S*	9	10		8			4				3				**11**		S*		
20	42	37	8	40	10	32	6	41	42	35	34	25	22	31	0	6	7	6	2	7	0	9	0	0	0	0
			1			1	10			1	3	4		1	4	1	1	3	1	3	1	6	3	1		
				4		3		11	8	10	17	1		1		1	1					5				

	2	3		5		7		9	10	11	8		1	6			4									
	2	3		5		**7**	8	9	10	11		4	1	**6**	S*	S*										
0	2	2	0	2	0	2	1	2	2	2	1	1	2	2	0	0	1	0	0	0	0	0	0	0	0	0
															1	1										
							1			1																

	2	3		5		7		9	10			4	1				11		8			6				
	2	3		5		7		9	10	11	**8**	**4**	1	S*			S*					6				
	2	3		5		7		**9**	10	11		4	1	S*	**8**				S*			6				
0	3	3	0	3	0	3	0	3	3	2	1	3	3	0	1	0	1	0	1	0	0	3	0	0	0	0
														2			1		1							
						1		1		1				1					2			1				

	2	3	4			7			10	11	8	6	1	5											**9**	S*

League Table

	P	W	D	L	F	A	Pts
Manchester United	42	27	11	4	80	38	92
Blackburn Rovers	42	25	9	8	63	36	84
Newcastle United	42	23	8	11	82	41	77
Arsenal	42	18	17	7	53	28	71
Leeds United	42	18	16	8	65	39	70
Wimbledon	42	18	11	13	56	53	65
Sheffield Wednesday	42	16	16	10	76	54	64
Liverpool	42	17	9	16	59	55	60
Queen's Park Rangers	42	16	12	14	62	61	60
Aston Villa	42	15	12	15	46	50	57
Coventry City	42	14	14	14	43	45	56
Norwich City	42	12	17	13	65	61	53
West Ham United	42	13	13	16	47	58	52
Chelsea	42	13	12	17	49	53	51
Tottenham Hotspur	42	11	12	19	54	59	45
Manchester City	42	9	18	15	38	49	45
Everton	42	12	8	22	42	63	44
Southampton	42	12	7	23	49	66	43
Ipswich Town	42	9	16	17	35	58	43
Sheffield United	42	8	18	16	42	60	42
Oldham Athletic	42	9	13	20	42	68	40
Swindon Town	42	5	15	22	47	100	30

1994-95

Premiership

Manager: Howard Wilkinson

Final Position: 5th

Did you know that?

16 October 1994: The old Kop was officially renamed the Don Revie Stand in a ceremony featuring Don's widow, Elsie, club president Lord Harwood and members of Revie's great squad.

17 January 1995: Substitute Phil Masinga scored a nine-minute hat-trick in extra-time to see off brave Walsall in an FA Cup third round replay.

1 February 1995: Blackburn goalkeeper Tim Flowers was sensationally sent off after two minutes at Ewood Park but United fell behind moments later to an Alan Shearer penalty. Leeds salvaged a point with a Gary McAllister spot-kick.

9 April 1995: United won at Anfield for the first time in 23 years with a Brian Deane goal.

Howard Wilkinson and his new signings, from left to right, Nigel Worthington, Lucas Radebe, Phil Masinga and Carlton Palmer.

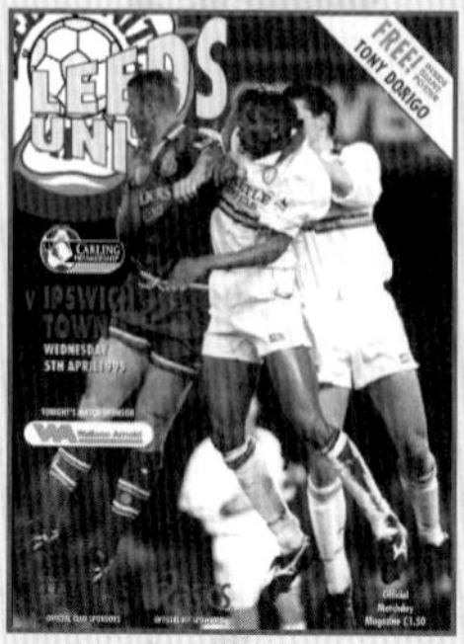

Match No.	Date	Venue	Opponents	Result	FT	HT	Scorers	Attendance
1	Aug 20	A	West Ham United	D	0-0	0-0		18,610
2	23	H	Arsenal	W	1-0	0-0	Whelan	34,318
3	27	H	Chelsea	L	2-3	2-1	Masinga, Whelan	32,212
4	30	A	Crystal Palace	W	2-1	1-0	White, Whelan	14,453
5	Sep 11	H	Manchester United	W	2-1	1-0	Wetherall, Deane	39,120
6	17	A	Coventry City	L	1-2	0-0	Speed	15,383
7	26	A	Sheffield Wed	D	1-1	1-1	McAllister	23,227
8	Oct 1	H	Manchester City	W	2-0	1-0	Whelan 2	30,938
9	8	A	Norwich City	L	1-2	0-0	Wallace	17,390
10	15	H	Tottenham Hotspur	D	1-1	0-1	Deane	39,362
11	24	H	Leicester City	W	2-1	1-0	McAllister, Whelan	28,479
12	29	A	Southampton	W	3-1	0-1	Wallace 2, Maddison (og)	15,202
13	Nov 1	A	Ipswich Town	L	0-2	0-1		15,534
14	5	H	Wimbledon	W	3-1	3-1	Wetherall, White, Speed	27,246
15	19	A	Queen's Park R	L	2-3	0-2	McDonald (og), Deane	17,416
16	26	H	Nottingham Forest	W	1-0	0-0	Whelan	37,709
17	Dec 5	A	Everton	L	0-3	0-1		25,906
18	10	H	West Ham United	D	2-2	2-1	Worthington, Deane	28,987
19	17	A	Arsenal	W	3-1	1-0	Masinga 2, Deane	38,100
20	26	H	Newcastle United	D	0-0	0-0		39,337
21	31	H	Liverpool	L	0-2	0-1		38,468
22	Jan 2	A	Aston Villa	D	0-0	0-0		35,038
23	14	H	Southampton	D	0-0	0-0		28,969
24	24	H	Queen's Park R	W	4-0	2-0	Masinga 2, White, Deane	28,750
25	Feb 1	A	Blackburn Rovers	D	1-1	0-1	McAllister (pen)	28,561
26	4	A	Wimbledon	D	0-0	0-0		10,211
27	22	H	Everton	W	1-0	0-0	Yeboah	30,793
28	25	A	Manchester City	D	0-0	0-0		22,892
29	Mar 4	H	Sheffield Wed	L	0-1	0-1		33,774
30	11	A	Chelsea	W	3-0	2-0	Yeboah 2, McAllister	20,174
31	15	A	Leicester City	W	3-1	1-1	Yeboah 2, Palmer	20,068
32	18	H	Coventry City	W	3-0	1-0	Wallace, Yeboah, Gould (og)	29,231
33	22	A	Nottingham Forest	L	0-3	0-3		26,299
34	Apr 2	A	Manchester United	D	0-0	0-0		43,712
35	5	H	Ipswich Town	W	4-0	4-0	Speed, Yeboah 3	28,565
36	9	A	Liverpool	W	1-0	1-0	Deane	37,454
37	15	H	Blackburn Rovers	D	1-1	0-1	Deane	39,426
38	17	A	Newcastle United	W	2-1	2-1	Yeboah, McAllister (pen)	35,626
39	29	H	Aston Villa	W	1-0	0-0	Palmer	32,973
40	May 6	H	Norwich City	W	2-1	0-1	McAllister (pen), Palmer	31,981
41	9	H	Crystal Palace	W	3-1	2-0	Yeboah 2, Wetherall	30,963
42	14	A	Tottenham Hotspur	D	1-1	0-1	Deane	33,040
								Appearances
								Sub appearances
							Three own-goals	Goals

FL Cup

R2	Sep 21	H	Mansfield Town	L	0-1	0-1		7,844
	Oct 4	A	Mansfield Town	D	0-0	0-0		7,227
								Appearances
								Sub appearances
								Goals

FA Cup

R3	Jan 7	A	Walsall	D	1-1	0-1	Wetherall	8,691
Rep	17	H	Walsall	W	5-2*	2-1	Deane, Wetherall, Masinga 3	17,881
R4	28	H	Oldham Athletic	W	3-2	2-0	White, Palmer, Masinga	25,010
R5	Feb 19	A	Manchester United	L	1-3	0-2	Yeboah	42,744

* After extra-time (score at 90 minutes 2-2)

Appearances
Sub appearances
Goals

Lukic, John	Kelly, Gary	Worthington, Nigel	Palmer, Carlton	Wetherall, David	White, David	Strachan, Gordon	Wallace, Rod	Deane, Brian	McAllister, Gary	Speed, Gary	Masinga, Phil	Whelan, Noel	Fairclough, Chris	Pemberton, John	Tinkler, Mark	Radebe, Lucas	Dorigo, Tony	Yeboah, Tony	Couzens, Andy	Sharp, Kevin
1	2	3	4	5	6	7	**8**	9	10	11	S*									
1	2	3	4	5	6	**7**	8		10	11	9	S*								
1	2	3	4	5	6		8		10	11	9	7								
1	2	3	4	5	6		8		10	11	**9**	7	S*							
1	2	3	4	5	**6**		8	S*	10	11	**9**	7	S*							
1	2	3	4	**5**		7	8		10	11	**9**	6	S*	S*						
1	2	3	4	5			8	9	10	11	**7**	S*			**6**	S*				
1	2	3	4	6			8	**9**	10	11		7	5	S*						
1	2	**6**	4	5			8	9	10	11		**7**	S*	S*			3			
1	**2**	6	4	5			8	9	10	11		7		S*			3			
1	2	6	4	5			8	9	10	11		7					3			
1	2	6	4	5			8	9	10	11		7				S*	**3**			
1	2	3	4	5	**6**		8	9	10	11	S*	7								
1	2	3	4	5	**6**		8	**9**	10	11	S*	7				S*				
1	2	3	4	5	S*		8	9	10	11		7				**6**				
1	2		4	5	6		**8**	9	10	11	S*	**7**		S*			3			
1	2		4	5	6		8	9	10	11		7					3			
1	2	**11**	4	5	S*	7		9	10			8			6		3			
1	2		4	5	S*			9		11	10	**8**		7		6	3			
1	2	S*	4	5	7	S*			10	11	**9**	8		**6**			3			
1	2	S*		5	S*	**7**			10	11	9	8		6		4	**3**			
1	2	3		5	7		S*	9	10	11	**8**			6		4				
1	2	3	4	5	**7**		S*	9	10	11	S*			6		**8**				
1	2	3	4	5	7			9	10	11	**8**			6				S*		
1	2	S*	4		7			9	10	11	**8**			6		**5**	3	S*		
1	2	11	4		7			9	10		8			6		5	3			
1	2	S*		5	7				10	11	8			6		**4**	3	9		
1	2	6	4	5	7			S*	10	11	8						3	**9**		
1	2		4	5			**7**	9	10	11	S*			6			3	8		
1	2		4	5			7	9	10	11				6			3	8		
1	2		4	5			7	9	10	11				6			3	8		
1	2		4				7	9	10	11					6	**5**	3	8	S*	
1	**2**		4		S*		7	9	10	11				6			3	8	5	
1	2	S*	4	5			**7**	**9**	10			S*		6			3	8	11	
1	**2**		4	5			7	9	10	11				6			3	8	S*	
1	2		4	5			7	9	10	11				6			3	8		
1	2		4	5			**7**	9	10	11		S*		6			3	8		
1	2	S*	4	5	**7**			9	10	11	S*			6			3	**8**		
1	2		4	5			7	9	10	11				6			3	8		
1	2		4	5			**7**	9	10	11		S*		6			3	**8**		S*
1	2		4	5			7	9	10	11				6			3	8		
1	2		4	5			**7**	9	10	11				6			3	8		S*
42	42	21	39	38	18	5	30	33	41	39	15	18	1	22	3	9	28	16	2	0
		6			5	1	2	2			7	5	4	5		3		2	2	2
		1	3	3	3		4	9	6	3	5	7						12		

1	2	3	4		**7**		8	S*	10	11	**9**	6	5			S*				
1	2	3	**4**	6			**7**	9	10	11		8	**5**	S*			S*			
2	2	2	2	1	1	0	2	1	2	2	1	2	2	0	0	0	0	0	0	0
								1						1		1	1			

1	2	3	4	5	**7**		S*	9	10	11	S*			6		**8**				
1	2	3	**4**	5			**7**	9	10	11	S*	8		6		S*				
1	2	3	4	5	7			9	10	11	**8**			6				S*		
1	2	S*		5	7		**8**		10	11	**9**	4		6			3	S*		
4	4	3	3	4	3	0	2	3	4	4	2	2	0	4	0	1	1	0	0	0
		1					1				2					1		2		
			1	2	1			1			4							1		

League Table

	P	W	D	L	F	A	Pts
Blackburn Rovers	42	27	8	7	80	39	89
Manchester United	42	26	10	6	77	28	88
Nottingham Forest	42	22	11	9	72	43	77
Liverpool	42	21	11	10	65	37	74
Leeds United	42	20	13	9	59	38	73
Newcastle United	42	20	12	10	67	47	72
Tottenham Hotspur	42	16	14	12	66	58	62
Queen's Park Rangers	42	17	9	16	61	59	60
Wimbledon	42	15	11	16	48	65	56
Southampton	42	12	18	12	61	63	54
Chelsea	42	13	15	14	50	55	54
Arsenal	42	13	12	17	52	49	51
Sheffield Wednesday	42	13	12	17	49	57	51
West Ham United	42	13	11	18	44	48	50
Everton	42	11	17	14	44	51	50
Coventry City	42	12	14	16	44	62	50
Manchester City	42	12	13	17	53	64	49
Aston Villa	42	11	15	16	51	56	48
Crystal Palace	42	11	12	19	34	49	45
Norwich City	42	10	13	19	37	54	43
Leicester City	42	6	11	25	45	80	29
Ipswich Town	42	7	6	29	36	93	27

1995-96

Premiership

Manager: Howard Wilkinson

Final Position: 13th

Did you know that?

21 August 1995: Tony Yeboah's thunderbolt beat Liverpool 1–0 and became *Match of the Day's* Goal of the Season.

14 October 1995: John Lukic's 400th game for United saw him on the end of a 3–0 drubbing against his former club Arsenal.

13 January 1996: On-loan Lee Chapman, 36, was sent off against West Ham on his second United debut, but two Tomas Brolin goals, his first at Elland Road, sealed a 2–0 win.

29 March 1996: Defender Lucas Radebe played in goal for the second half of the 1–0 home defeat against Middlesbrough because of a head injury to John Lukic.

2 May 1996: A 3–1 loss at Tottenham equalled United's worst ever run of seven League defeats set in 1946–47.

Goalkeeper John Lukic completed 400 games for Leeds.

Match No.	Date	Venue	Opponents	Result	FT	HT	Scorers	Attendance
1	Aug 19	A	West Ham United	W	2-1	0-1	Yeboah 2	22,901
2	21	H	Liverpool	W	1-0	0-0	Yeboah	36,007
3	26	H	Aston Villa	W	2-0	1-0	Speed, White	35,086
4	30	A	Southampton	D	1-1	0-0	Dorigo	15,212
5	Sep 9	A	Tottenham Hotspur	L	1-2	0-1	Yeboah	30,034
6	16	H	Queen's Park R	L	1-3	0-2	Wetherall	31,505
7	23	A	Wimbledon	W	4-2	3-1	Palmer, Yeboah 3	13,307
8	30	H	Sheffield Wed	W	2-0	1-0	Yeboah, Speed	33,899
9	Oct 14	H	Arsenal	L	0-3	0-1		38,332
10	21	A	Manchester City	D	0-0	0-0		26,390
11	28	H	Coventry City	W	3-1	2-1	McAllister 3 (1 pen)	30,025
12	Nov 4	A	Middlesbrough	D	1-1	1-1	Deane	29,467
13	18	H	Chelsea	W	1-0	0-0	Yeboah	36,209
14	25	A	Newcastle United	L	1-2	1-0	Deane	36,572
15	Dec 2	H	Manchester City	L	0-1	0-0		33,249
16	9	H	Wimbledon	D	1-1	0-1	Jobson	27,994
17	16	A	Sheffield Wed	L	2-6	1-3	Brolin, Wallace	24,573
18	24	H	Manchester United	W	3-1	2-1	McAllister (pen), Yeboah, Deane	39,801
19	27	A	Bolton Wanderers	W	2-0	1-0	Brolin, Wetherall	18,414
20	30	A	Everton	L	0-2	0-1		40,009
21	Jan 1	H	Blackburn Rovers	D	0-0	0-0		31,285
22	13	H	West Ham United	W	2-0	1-0	Brolin 2	30,472
23	20	A	Liverpool	L	0-5	0-1		40,254
24	31	A	Nottingham Forest	L	1-2	0-1	Palmer	24,465
25	Feb 3	A	Aston Villa	L	0-3	0-2		35,982
26	Mar 2	H	Bolton Wanderers	L	0-1	0-1		30,106
27	6	A	Queen's Park R	W	2-1	2-1	Yeboah 2	13,991
28	13	A	Blackburn Rovers	L	0-1	0-0		23,358
29	17	H	Everton	D	2-2	2-1	Deane 2	29,422
30	30	H	Middlesbrough	L	0-1	0-1		31,788
31	Apr 3	H	Southampton	W	1-0	0-0	Deane	26,077
32	6	A	Arsenal	L	1-2	0-1	Deane	37,619
33	8	H	Nottingham Forest	L	1-3	1-2	Wetherall	29,220
34	13	A	Chelsea	L	1-4	0-3	McAllister	22,131
35	17	A	Manchester United	L	0-1	0-0		48,382
36	29	H	Newcastle United	L	0-1	0-1		38,562
37	May 2	H	Tottenham Hotspur	L	1-3	1-2	Wetherall	30,024
38	5	A	Coventry City	D	0-0	0-0		22,767

Appearances
Sub appearances
Goals

FL Cup

R2	Sep 19	H	Notts County	D	0-0	0-0		12,384
	Oct 3	A	Notts County	W	3-2	1-1	McAllister, Couzens, Speed	12,477
R3	25	A	Derby County	W	1-0	0-0	Speed	16,030
R4	Nov 29	H	Blackburn Rovers	W	2-1	2-0	Deane, Yeboah	26,006
R5	Jan 10	H	Reading	W	2-1	2-1	Masinga, Speed	21,023
SF	Feb 11	A	Birmingham City	W	2-1	0-1	Yeboah, Whyte (og)	24,781
	25	H	Birmingham City	W	3-0	0-0	Masinga, Yeboah, Deane	35,435
F	Mar 24	N	Aston Villa	L	0-3†	0-1		77,056

† Played at Wembley, London

Appearances
Sub appearances
One own-goal — Goals

FA Cup

R3	Jan 7	A	Derby County	W	4-2	0-0	Speed, Deane, McAllister, Yeboah	16,155
R4	Feb 14	A	Bolton Wanderers	W	1-0	1-0	Wallace	16,694
R5	21	H	Port Vale	D	0-0	0-0		18,607
Rep	27	A	Port Vale	W	2-1	0-1	McAllister 2	14,023
R6	Mar 10	H	Liverpool	D	0-0	0-0		24,632
Rep	20	A	Liverpool	L	0-3	0-0		30,812

Appearances
Sub appearances
Goals

UEFA Cup

R1	Sep 12	A	AS Monaco	W	3-0	1-0	Yeboah 3	14,000
	26	H	AS Monaco	L	0-1	0-1		24,501
R2	Oct 17	H	PSV Eindhoven	L	3-5	1-3	Speed, Palmer, McAllister	24,846
	31	A	PSV Eindhoven	L	0-3	0-2		25,750

Appearances
Sub appearances
Goals

Lukic, John	Kelly, Gary	Dorigo, Tony	Palmer, Carlton	Pemberton, John	Wetherall, David	Deane, Brian	Wallace, Rod	Yeboah, Tony	McAllister, Gary	Speed, Gary	Whelan, Noel	Worthington, Nigel	Beesley, Paul	White, David	Masinga, Phil	Tinkler, Mark	Couzens, Andy	Jobson, Richard	Sharp, Kevin	Ford, Mark	Brolin, Tomas	Bowman, Rob	Beeney, Mark	Radebe, Lucas	Chapman, Lee	Gray, Andy	Harte, Ian	Maybury, Alan	Kewell, Harry	Blunt, Jason	Jackson, Mark
1	2	3	4	5	6	7	8	9	10	11	S*	S*	S*																		
1	2	3	4	5	6	7	8	9	10	11	S*																				
1	2	3	4	5	6	7	8	9	10	11				S*																	
1	2	3	4	5	6	7	8	9	10	11		S*		S*																	
1	2	3	4	5	6	7		9	10	11	S*			8																	
1	2		4	5	6	7		9	10	11	8	3	S*	S*																	
1	2		4	5	6	8		9	10	11			3		7	S*															
1	2		4		5	S*		9	10	11			3		7	8	6														
1	2	3	4	5	6	8	S*	9		11						7	10														
1	2		4	5	6	7	8	9	10		S*	3					11														
1	3		4	2	6	7		9	10	11	8						S*	5	S*												
1	2		4	5	6	8		9	10		7	3						11													
1	2	3	4		6	8	S*	9	10	11							7	5													
1	2	3	4		6	8		9	10	11								5		7	S*	S*									
1	2	3	4	S*	6	8		9	10		S*							5		7	11										
1		3	4	2	6	8	S*	9	10	11								5			7										
1	2	3	4		6	S*	S*	9	10	11							8	5			7										
	2	3	4		6	8	S*	9	10	11								5			7		1								
	2	3			6	8		9	10	11								5		4	7		1	S*							
	2	3			6	8	S*		10	11		S*			9			5		4	7		1								
	2		4			8	S*	9	10	11		3						5		6	7		1								
	2	3	4		5		8		10	11							S*			6	7		1		9	S*	S*				
	2		4		5	S*	8		10	11		3					S*			6	7		1		9						
	2	3	4			9	8		10	11						S*	6	5			7	S*	1			S*					
		3	4	5		9	8		10	11		S*				S*	7					6	1					2			
1			4		6	11	8	9	10			3	5				S*				7			2		S*					
1			4		6			9	10			2	5		S*					8	7			3		11					
1	2		4		6	9	8		10			3	5								S*			7		11					
1	3		4	2		9	S*								S*	6	8			10	7			5		11					
1	3		4	2	6	9	S*		10	11														5		7			8	S*	S*
1	2		4		6	S*	S*		10	11											9			5		7			3	8	
1	2		4		6	9			10	11											8			5		7	3				
1	3		4		5	9	S*		10	11											8			2		7	S*			6	
1	2		4	6	5	9			10	11											8			S*		7	3				
	2		4		6	9			10	11		3	5		S*	S*				8			1	S*		7					
	2				6	9	S*		10	11		3	4		S*					8			1	5		7					
1	2		4		6				10			3	5		9	7	S*			8						11					
1	2		4		6		8		10			3			9	7	S*							5		11					
28	34	17	35	16	34	30	12	22	36	29	3	12	8	1	5	5	8	12	0	12	17	1	10	10	2	12	2	1	2	2	0
				1		4	12				5	4	2	3	4	4	6		1		2	2		3		3	2			1	1
		1	2		4	7	1	12	5	2				1				1			4										

Lukic, John	Kelly, Gary	Dorigo, Tony	Palmer, Carlton	Pemberton, John	Wetherall, David	Deane, Brian	Wallace, Rod	Yeboah, Tony	McAllister, Gary	Speed, Gary	Whelan, Noel	Worthington, Nigel	Beesley, Paul	White, David	Masinga, Phil	Tinkler, Mark	Couzens, Andy	Jobson, Richard	Sharp, Kevin	Ford, Mark	Brolin, Tomas	Bowman, Rob	Beeney, Mark	Radebe, Lucas	Chapman, Lee	Gray, Andy	Harte, Ian	Maybury, Alan	Kewell, Harry	Blunt, Jason	Jackson, Mark
1	2		4	5	6	8		9	10	11		3	S*	7												S*					
1	2		4		5	8	S*	9	10	11		S*	3			7	6														
1	2		4	5	6	8		9	10	11	S*	3	7																		
1	2	3	4		5	8		9	10	11	S*									6	7	S*									
	2	3	4		5		8		10	11					9		S*			6	7		1				S*				
1	2	3	4		6	S*	8	9	10	11			5							7				S*							
1	2	3	4		6		8	9	10	11			5		7						S*			S*							
1	2		4	5	6	S*		9	10	11										8	S*			3		7					
7	8	4	8	3	8	4	3	7	8	8	0	2	4	1	2	1	1	0	0	4	2	0	1	1	0	1	0	0	0	0	0
						2	1				2	1	1				1				2	1		2		1	1				
						2		3	1	3					2		1														

Lukic, John	Kelly, Gary	Dorigo, Tony	Palmer, Carlton	Pemberton, John	Wetherall, David	Deane, Brian	Wallace, Rod	Yeboah, Tony	McAllister, Gary	Speed, Gary	Whelan, Noel	Worthington, Nigel	Beesley, Paul	White, David	Masinga, Phil	Tinkler, Mark	Couzens, Andy	Jobson, Richard	Sharp, Kevin	Ford, Mark	Brolin, Tomas	Bowman, Rob	Beeney, Mark	Radebe, Lucas	Chapman, Lee	Gray, Andy	Harte, Ian	Maybury, Alan	Kewell, Harry	Blunt, Jason	Jackson, Mark
	2	3	4		6	9	S*	8	10	11								5		7			1								
1	2	3	4		6	S*	8	9	10	11			5							7				S*							
1	2	3	4		6	S*	8	9	10	11			5							7											
1	2	3	4		6	11	8	9	10				5		7						S*					S*					
1	2		4	S*	6	S*		9	10			3	5							11	8			7							
1	2		4	6		9		8	10	11		3								7				5		S*					
5	6	4	6	1	5	3	3	6	6	4	0	2	4	0	1	0	0	1	0	5	1	0	1	2	0	0	0	0	0	0	0
					1	3	1														1			1		2					
						1	1	1	3	1																					

Lukic, John	Kelly, Gary	Dorigo, Tony	Palmer, Carlton	Pemberton, John	Wetherall, David	Deane, Brian	Wallace, Rod	Yeboah, Tony	McAllister, Gary	Speed, Gary	Whelan, Noel	Worthington, Nigel	Beesley, Paul	White, David	Masinga, Phil	Tinkler, Mark	Couzens, Andy	Jobson, Richard	Sharp, Kevin	Ford, Mark	Brolin, Tomas	Bowman, Rob	Beeney, Mark	Radebe, Lucas	Chapman, Lee	Gray, Andy	Harte, Ian	Maybury, Alan	Kewell, Harry	Blunt, Jason	Jackson, Mark
1	2	3	4	5	6	8		9	10	11	7	S*																			
1	2		4	5	6	8		9	10	11		3		7		S*	S*														
1	2	3	4	5	6	8	S*	9	10	11	7	S*					S*														
1	2		4	5	6			9	10	11	8	3		S*					S*	S*		7									
4	4	2	4	4	4	3	0	4	4	4	3	2	0	1	0	0	0	0	0	0	0	1	0	0	0	0	0	0	0	0	0
							1					2		1		1	2		1	1											
			1					3	1	1																					

League Table

	P	W	D	L	F	A	Pts
Manchester United	38	25	7	6	73	35	82
Newcastle United	38	24	6	8	66	37	78
Liverpool	38	20	11	7	70	34	71
Aston Villa	38	18	9	11	52	35	63
Arsenal	38	17	12	9	49	32	63
Everton	38	17	10	11	64	44	61
Blackburn Rovers	38	18	7	13	61	47	61
Tottenham Hotspur	38	16	13	9	50	38	61
Nottingham Forest	38	15	13	10	50	54	58
West Ham United	38	14	9	15	43	52	51
Chelsea	38	12	14	12	46	44	50
Middlesbrough	38	11	10	17	35	50	43
Leeds United	38	12	7	19	40	57	43
Wimbledon	38	10	11	17	55	70	41
Sheffield Wednesday	38	10	10	18	48	61	40
Coventry City	38	8	14	16	42	60	38
Southampton	38	9	11	18	34	52	38
Manchester City	38	9	11	18	33	58	38
Queen's Park Rangers	38	9	6	23	38	57	33
Bolton Wanderers	38	8	5	25	39	71	29

1996-97

Premiership

Manager: Howard Wilkinson until September then George Graham

Final Position: 11th

Did you know that?

7 September 1996: The returning Eric Cantona scored and missed a penalty as Manchester United won 4–0 at Elland Road. Howard Wilkinson, who had bought and sold the French star, was sacked two days later.

14 September 1996: Andy Couzens scored just 51 seconds into George Graham's reign but United lost 2–1 at Coventry.

23 November 1996: Gary Kelly scored his first Leeds goal in the 2–0 win at Southampton in his 165th United appearance.

11 May 1997: Brian Deane's goal earned United a 1–1 draw which condemned opponents Middlesbrough to relegation. United only scored 28 Premiership goals, the lowest by any club avoiding relegation from the top tier.

Gary Kelly finally broke his United scoring duck.

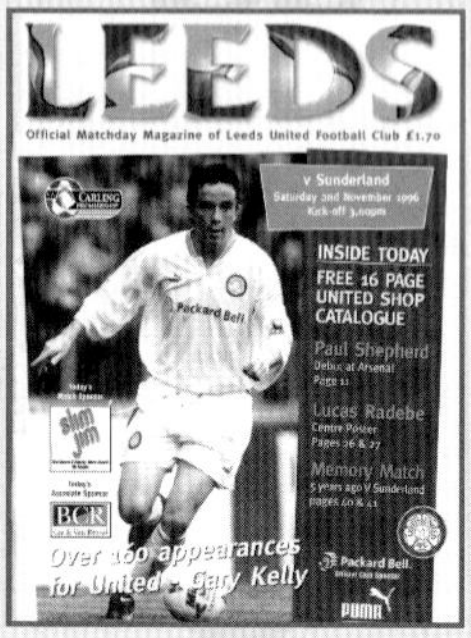

Match No.	Date	Venue	Opponents	Result	FT	HT	Scorers	Attendance
1	Aug 17	A	Derby County	D	3-3	1-0	Laursen (og), Harte, Bowyer	17,925
2	20	H	Sheffield Wed	L	0-2	0-1		31,008
3	26	H	Wimbledon	W	1-0	0-0	Sharpe	25,860
4	Sep 4	A	Blackburn Rovers	W	1-0	1-0	Harte	23,226
5	7	H	Manchester United	L	0-4	0-1		39,694
6	14	A	Coventry City	L	1-2	1-0	Couzens	17,298
7	21	H	Newcastle United	L	0-1	0-0		36,070
8	28	A	Leicester City	L	0-1	0-0		20,359
9	Oct 12	H	Nottingham Forest	W	2-0	0-0	Wallace 2	29,255
10	19	A	Aston Villa	L	0-2	0-0		39,051
11	26	A	Arsenal	L	0-3	0-2		38,076
12	Nov 2	H	Sunderland	W	3-0	1-0	Ford, Sharpe, Deane	31,450
13	16	H	Liverpool	L	0-2	0-1		39,981
14	23	A	Southampton	W	2-0	0-0	Kelly, Sharpe	15,241
15	Dec 1	H	Chelsea	W	2-0	2-0	Deane, Rush	32,596
16	7	A	Middlesbrough	D	0-0	0-0		30,018
17	14	H	Tottenham Hotspur	D	0-0	0-0		33,783
18	21	A	Everton	D	0-0	0-0		36,954
19	26	H	Coventry City	L	1-3	1-3	Deane	36,465
20	28	A	Manchester United	L	0-1	0-1		55,256
21	Jan 1	A	Newcastle United	L	0-3	0-1		36,489
22	11	H	Leicester City	W	3-0	2-0	Bowyer, Rush 2	29,480
23	20	A	West Ham United	W	2-0	0-0	Kelly, Bowyer	19,441
24	29	H	Derby County	D	0-0	0-0		27,523
25	Feb 1	H	Arsenal	D	0-0	0-0		35,596
26	19	A	Liverpool	L	0-4	0-3		38,957
27	22	A	Sunderland	W	1-0	0-0	Bowyer	21,846
28	Mar 1	H	West Ham United	W	1-0	0-0	Sharpe	30,575
29	8	H	Everton	W	1-0	1-0	Molenaar	32,055
30	12	H	Southampton	D	0-0	0-0		25,913
31	15	A	Tottenham Hotspur	L	0-1	0-1		33,040
32	22	A	Sheffield Wed	D	2-2	2-1	Sharpe, Wallace	30,373
33	Apr 7	H	Blackburn Rovers	D	0-0	0-0		27,322
34	16	A	Wimbledon	L	0-2	0-1		7,979
35	19	A	Nottingham Forest	D	1-1	0-1	Deane	25,565
36	22	H	Aston Villa	D	0-0	0-0		26,884
37	May 3	A	Chelsea	D	0-0	0-0		27,135
38	11	H	Middlesbrough	D	1-1	0-0	Deane	38,569
								Appearances
								Sub appearances
							One own-goal	Goals

FL Cup

Round	Date	Venue	Opponents	Result	FT	HT	Scorers	Attendance
R2	Sep 18	H	Darlington	D	2-2	1-1	Wallace 2	15,711
Rep	24	A	Darlington	W	2-0	2-0	Wallace, Harte	6,298
R3	Oct 23	H	Aston Villa	L	1-2	0-0	Sharpe	15,803
								Appearances
								Sub appearances
								Goals

FA Cup

Round	Date	Venue	Opponents	Result	FT	HT	Scorers	Attendance
R3	Jan 14	A	Crystal Palace	D	2-2	2-1	Deane, Andersen (og)	21,052
Rep	25	H	Crystal Palace	W	1-0	1-0	Wallace	21,903
R4	Feb 4	A	Arsenal	W	1-0	1-0	Wallace	38,115
R5	15	H	Portsmouth	L	2-3	0-1	Bowyer 2	35,604
								Appearances
								Sub appearances
							One own-goal	Goals

Martyn, Nigel	Kelly, Gary	Sharpe, Lee	Palmer, Carlton	Radebe Lucas	Jobson, Richard	Ford, Mark	Couzens, Andy	Rush, Ian	Deane, Brian	Bowyer, Lee	Wetherall, David	Tinkler, Mark	Harte, Ian	Hateley, Mark	Gray, Andy	Wallace, Rod	Blunt, Jason	Jackson, Mark	Boyle, Wes	Dorigo, Tony	Beesley, Paul	Shepherd, Paul	Halle, Gunnar	Kewell, Harry	Yeboah, Tony	Molenaar, Robert	Beeney, Mark	Lilley, Derek	Laurent, Pierre
1	2	3	4	5	6	7	8	9	10	11	S*	S*	S*																
1	2	3	4	5	6	7		9		11	S*	S*	8	10	S*														
1	S*	3	4	S*	5		2	9		11	6	7	8	10															
1	2	10	4	S*	5	7	S*	9		11	6		3		S*	8													
1	2	10	4	S*	5	7		9		11	6		3	S*	S*	8													
1	2		4		5	S*	7	9			6		3	10	11	8	S*												
1	2	10	4		5	7	11	9			6		3			8		S*	S*										
1	2	10	4	S*	5	7	11				6		3			9		8											
1	2	3		4	5	7	11	9			6			10		8		S*		S*									
1	2	11	4	3	5	7	S*	9			6			10		8					S*								
1	2	11	4	5		7	8	9	S*				3								6	10							
1	2	3		4		7	S*	9	10	11	5					8					6								
1	2	3	4	5		7		9	10	11						8		S*			6								
1	2	3	4	5		7		9	10	11	S*							8			6								
1	2	3	4	8		7		9	10	11	5										6								
1	2	3	4	8		7		9	10	11	5							S*			6								
1	2		4	5		7		9	10	11						8		S*			6		3	S*					
1	2	11	4	8				9	10	7	5							S*			6		3						
1	2		4	8				9	10	11	5							7		S*	6		3		S*				
1	2		4	5				9	10	11					S*			8		3			6		7				
1	2		4	8				9	10	11	5				S*	S*		7		3	6								
1	2							9	10	11	5					8		7		3	6					4			
1	2		4	8				9	10	11	6							7					3			5			
	2		4	8				S*	10	11						9		7		3			6			5	1		
1	2			4				9	10	11					S*	8		7		3			6			5			
1	2		4	10				S*	9	11			S*			8		7		3			6			5			
1	2	11		4				9	10	7			S*			S*				3			6		8	5			
1		3	S*	8				9	10	11	6		4										2		7	5			
1		3	4					9	10	11	6		8										2		7	5			
1	2	3	4					9	10	11	6									S*			8		7	5			
1	2	11		4				9	10	7										3			6		8	5			
1	2	11		4				9	10	7	S*		S*			8				3			6			5			
1	2	11						9	10	7	5					8		4		3			6					S*	S*
1	S*	11		4				9	10	7	5					8				3			6			2		S*	S*
1	2	11	S*	4					10	8	5					S*				3			6					9	7
1	2		4	8				9		10	5					S*				3			6					7	11
1	2		4	8				9	10	11	5									3			6					7	
1	2	11		4				9	10	7	5					S*				3			6					8	
37	34	26	26	28	10	15	7	34	27	32	25	1	10	5	1	17	0	11	0	15	11	1	20	0	6	12	1	4	2
	2		2	4		1	3	2	1		4	2	4	1	6	5	1	6	1	3	1			1	1			2	2
	2	5				1	1	3	5	4			2			3										1			

1	2	11			5	4	10	9			6		3		7	8	S*												
1	2	9	4		5	7	10				6		3		11	8													
1	2	11	4	3	5	7	10	9			S*		S*			8					6								
3	3	3	2	1	3	3	3	2	0	0	2	0	2	0	2	3	0	0	0	0	1	0	0	0	0	0	0	0	0
											1		1				1												
		1											1			3													

1	2	S*		4				9	10	11	5					8		7		3	6								
1	2		4	5				9	10	11						8		7		3			6						
1	2		4					S*	9	11	S*		10			8		7		3			6			5			
1	2		4	10				S*	9	11						8		7		3			6			5			
4	4	0	3	3	0	0	0	2	4	4	1	0	1	0	0	4	0	4	0	4	1	0	3	0	0	2	0	0	0
		1						2			1																		
									1	2						2													

League Table

	P	W	D	L	F	A	Pts
Manchester United	38	21	12	5	76	44	75
Newcastle United	38	19	11	8	73	40	68
Arsenal	38	19	11	8	62	32	68
Liverpool	38	19	11	8	62	37	68
Aston Villa	38	17	10	11	47	34	61
Chelsea	38	16	11	11	58	55	59
Sheffield Wednesday	38	14	15	9	50	51	57
Wimbledon	38	15	11	12	49	46	56
Leicester City	38	12	11	15	46	54	47
Tottenham Hotspur	38	13	7	18	44	51	46
Leeds United	38	11	13	14	28	38	46
Derby County	38	11	13	14	45	58	46
Blackburn Rovers	38	9	15	14	42	43	42
West Ham United	38	10	12	16	39	48	42
Everton	38	10	12	16	44	57	42
Southampton	38	10	11	17	50	56	41
Coventry City	38	9	14	15	38	54	41
Sunderland	38	10	10	18	35	53	40
Middlesbrough	38	10	12	16	51	60	39
Nottingham Forest	38	6	16	16	31	59	34

1997-98

Premiership

Manager: George Graham

Final Position: 5th

Did you know that?

7 December 1997: Billy Bremner, captain in the great Revie era died in hospital, aged 54.

13 December 1997: Despite having Gary Kelly and Alf Inge Haaland sent off in the first half, United forced a 0–0 draw in a match of eight bookings at third-placed Chelsea.

United were stunned by the death of legendary skipper Billy Bremner.

Match No.	Date		Venue	Opponents	Result	FT	HT	Scorers	Attendance
1	Aug	9	H	Arsenal	D	1-1	1-1	Hasselbaink	37,993
2		13	A	Sheffield Wed	W	3-1	2-0	Wallace 2, Ribeiro	31,520
3		23	H	Crystal Palace	L	0-2	0-1		29,108
4		26	H	Liverpool	L	0-2	0-1		39,878
5		30	A	Aston Villa	L	0-1	0-0		39,027
6	Sep	14	A	Blackburn Rovers	W	4-3	4-3	Wallace 2, Molenaar, Hopkin	21,956
7		20	H	Leicester City	L	0-1	0-1		29,442
8		24	A	Southampton	W	2-0	1-0	Molenaar, Wallace	15,102
9		27	H	Manchester United	W	1-0	1-0	Wetherall	39,943
10	Oct	4	A	Coventry City	D	0-0	0-0		17,771
11		18	H	Newcastle United	W	4-1	3-0	Ribeiro, Kewell, Beresford (og), Wetherall	39,865
12		25	A	Wimbledon	L	0-1	0-1		15,718
13	Nov	1	A	Tottenham Hotspur	W	1-0	1-0	Wallace	26,441
14		8	H	Derby County	W	4-3	2-3	Wallace, Kewell, Hasselbaink (pen), Bowyer	33,572
15		23	H	West Ham United	W	3-1	0-0	Hasselbaink 2, Haaland	29,447
16		29	A	Barnsley	W	3-2	1-2	Haaland, Wallace, Lilley	18,690
17	Dec	6	H	Everton	D	0-0	0-0		34,872
18		13	A	Chelsea	D	0-0	0-0		34,779
19		20	H	Bolton Wanderers	W	2-0	0-0	Ribeiro, Hasselbaink	31,184
20		26	A	Liverpool	L	1-3	0-0	Haaland	43,854
21		28	H	Aston Villa	D	1-1	0-0	Hasselbaink	36,909
22	Jan	10	A	Arsenal	L	1-2	0-0	Hasselbaink	38,018
23		17	H	Sheffield Wed	L	1-2	0-0	Pembridge (og)	33,596
24		31	A	Crystal Palace	W	2-0	2-0	Wallace, Hasselbaink	25,248
25	Feb	7	A	Leicester City	L	0-1	0-1		21,344
26		22	A	Newcastle United	D	1-1	0-0	Wallace	36,511
27		28	H	Southampton	L	0-1	0-0		28,926
28	Mar	4	H	Tottenham Hotspur	W	1-0	1-0	Kewell	31,802
29		11	H	Blackburn Rovers	W	4-0	0-0	Bowyer, Hasselbaink, Haaland 2	32,935
30		15	A	Derby County	W	5-0	3-0	Laursen (og), Halle, Bowyer, Kewell, Hasselbaink	30,217
31		30	A	West Ham United	L	0-3	0-2		24,107
32	Apr	4	H	Barnsley	W	2-1	1-1	Hasselbaink, Moses (og)	37,749
33		8	H	Chelsea	W	3-1	2-1	Haselbaink 2, Wetherall	37,246
34		11	A	Everton	L	0-2	0-2		37,099
35		18	A	Bolton Wanderers	W	3-2	2-0	Haaland, Halle, Haselbaink	25,000
36		25	H	Coventry City	D	3-3	2-2	Hasselbaink 2, Kewell	36,868
37	May	3	A	Manchester United	L	0-3	0-2		55,167
38		10	H	Wimbledon	D	1-1	0-0	Haaland	38,445
									Appearances
									Sub appearances
								Four own-goals	Goals

FL Cup

R2	Sep	17	H	Bristol City	W	3-1	1-0	Wetherall, Hasselbaink (pen), Ribeiro	8,806
		30	A	Bristol City	L	1-2	1-1	Hasselbaink	10,857
R3	Oct	15	A	Stoke City	W	3-1*	0-0	Kewell, Wallace 2	16,203
R4	Nov	18	H	Reading	L	2-3	1-1	Wetherall, Bowyer	15,069

* After extra-time (score after 90 minutes 1-1)

Appearances
Sub appearances
Goals

FA Cup

R3	Jan	3	H	Oxford United	W	4-0	2-0	Radebe, Hasselbaink (pen), Kewell 2	20,568
R4		24	H	Grimsby Town	W	2-0	1-0	Molenaar, Hasselbaink	29,598
R5	Feb	14	H	Birmingham City	W	3-2	2-0	Wallace, Hasselbaink 2	35,463
R6	Mar	7	H	Wolverhampton W	L	0-1	0-0		39,902

Appearances
Sub appearances
Goals

Martyn, Nigel	Kelly, Gary	Robertson, David	Halle, Gunnar	Radebe, Lucas	Wetherall, David	Hopkin, David	Wallace, Rod	Hasselbaink, Jimmy F	Ribeiro, Bruno	Bowyer, Lee	Haaland, Alf Inge	Kewell, Harry	Molenaar, Robert	Lilley, Derek	Maybury, Alan	Beeney, Mark	Matthews, Lee	McPhail, Stephen	Harte, Ian	Hiden, Martin	Jackson, Mark
1	2	3	4	5	6	7	8	9	10	11	S*	S*									
1	2	3	4		6	7	8	9	10	11	S*		5	S*							
1	2	3	4	S*	6	7	8	9	10	11	S*	S*	5								
1	2	3	4	5		7	8	9	10		11		6								
1	2	3	S*	5	6	7	8	9	10		4	11		S*							
1	2	3	4	5	6	7	8	9	S*			10	11	S*							
1	2	3	4	5	6		8	9	10	11	7	S*	S*	S*							
1	2	3	4		6	7	8		10	S*	11	9	5								
1	2	3	4	5	6	7	8		10		11	9	S*								
1	2	3	4	5	6	7	8	9	10		11			S*							
1	2	3	4	5	6	7	8		10	S*	11	9									
1		3	2	5	6	7	8		10	11	4	9		S*	S*						
1	4	3		5	6	7	8		10		11	9			2						
1	4	3		5	6	7	8	S*	10	S*	11	9			2						
1	2	3	4	5	6		8	9	10	11	7										
1	2	3	4	5	6		8	9	10	11	7		S*	S*	S*						
1	2	3	4	5	6		8	S*	10	11	7	9									
1	2	3	4	5	6	7	8	9	10		11			S*							
1	2	3	4		6	7	8	9	10	S*	11		5								
1	2	3	4		6	7	8	9	10		11		5								
1		3		5	6		8	9	10	11		7	4	S*	2						
1	4		3	5	6		8	S*	10	11	7	9	S*	S*	2						
	4	3	S*	8	6	7	S*	9	10			11	5	S*	2	1					
1	2	3		5	6	7	8	9	10		S*	11	4				S*				
1	2	3	6		5	7	8	9	10		4	11			S*			S*			
1	4		3		6		8	9	10		7	11	5		2						
1			4			7	8	9	10			11	5		2		S*		3	6	
1			4			7	8	9		11		10	5		2		S*	S*	3	6	
1	2			5	6	7		9		11	8	10							3	4	
1	2		4	8				9		11	7	10	5					S*	3	6	
1	4		8		S*		S*	9	10	11	7		5		2				3	6	
1	2		7		6			9	10	11		8	5					S*	3	4	
1	2		7	8	6			9		11	S*	10	5						3	4	
1	2		7	8	6			9		11	S*	10	5	S*					3	4	
1	2		7	5	6			9		11	8	10							3	4	
1	2		7		5	S*	8	9		11	4	10							3	6	
1	2		7	5	6	S*		9		11	8	10							3	4	
1	2		4	5	6	S*	8	9		11	7	10		S*					3		S*
37	34	24	31	26	33	22	29	30	28	21	26	26	18	0	9	1	0	0	12	11	0
			2	1	1	3	2	3	1	4	6	3	4	13	3		3	4			1
			2		3	1	10	16	3	3	7	5	2	1							

1	2	3	4	5	6	7	8	9	S*			10	11								
1	2	3		4	6	7	8	9		11	10		5	S*							
1	2	3	4	5	6	7	8		10	S*	11	9		S*							
1		3		5	6	7	8	9	10	11	4		S*	S*	2						
4	3	4	2	4	4	4	4	3	2	2	3	2	2	0	1	0	0	0	0	0	0
									1	1			1	3							
					2		2	2	1	1		1									

1	4		3	11	6		8	9		7		10	5	S*	2	S*			S*		
1	2	3			6	4	8	9	10	7		11	5								
1	4		3		5		8	9	10	7	6	11			2				S*		
1	S*		4	5			8	9	10		7	11	6						3	2	
4	3	1	3	2	3	1	4	4	3	3	2	4	3	0	2	0	0	0	1	1	0
	1													1		1			2		
				1			1	4				2	1								

League Table

	P	W	D	L	F	A	Pts
Arsenal	38	23	9	6	68	33	78
Manchester United	38	23	8	7	73	26	77
Liverpool	38	18	11	9	68	42	65
Chelsea	38	20	3	15	71	43	63
Leeds United	38	17	8	13	57	46	59
Blackburn Rovers	38	16	10	12	57	52	58
Aston Villa	38	17	6	15	49	48	57
West Ham United	38	16	8	14	56	57	56
Derby County	38	16	7	15	52	49	55
Leicester City	38	13	14	11	51	41	53
Coventry City	38	12	16	10	46	44	52
Southampton	38	14	6	18	50	55	48
Newcastle United	38	11	11	16	35	44	44
Tottenham Hotspur	38	11	11	16	44	56	44
Wimbledon	38	10	14	14	34	46	44
Sheffield Wednesday	38	12	8	18	52	67	44
Everton	38	9	13	16	41	56	40
Bolton Wanderers	38	9	13	16	41	61	40
Barnsley	38	10	5	23	37	82	35
Crystal Palace	38	8	9	21	37	71	33

1998-99

Premiership

Manager: George Graham to October 1998 then David O'Leary

Final Position: 4th

Did you know that?

29 September 1998: United managed to stay awake to beat Maritimo on penalties to progress in the UEFA Cup. The game kicked off late to accommodate Portuguese television and Lee Sharpe's winning kick went in at 11.45pm – the latest finish ever to a Leeds game.

14 December 1998: David Batty's second debut for United in the 2–0 win against Coventry ended in disappointment as he went off with a rib injury which kept him out for three months.

Jimmy Floyd Hasselbaink topped the scoring charts for successive seasons.

Match No.	Date		Venue	Opponents	Result	FT	HT	Scorers	Attendance
1	Aug	15	A	Middlesbrough	D	0-0	0-0		34,160
2		24	H	Blackburn Rovers	W	1-0	1-0	Hasselbaink	30,541
3		29	A	Wimbledon	D	1-1	0-0	Bowyer	16,473
4	Sep	8	H	Southampton	W	3-0	1-0	Marshall (og), Harte, Wijnhard	30,637
5		12	A	Everton	D	0-0	0-0		36,687
6		19	H	Aston Villa	D	0-0	0-0		33,162
7		26	A	Tottenham Hotspur	D	3-3	2-1	Halle, Hasselbaink, Wijnhard	35,535
8	Oct	3	H	Leicester City	L	0-1	0-0		32,120
9		17	A	Nottingham Forest	D	1-1	0-0	Halle	23,911
10		25	H	Chelsea	D	0-0	0-0		35,833
11		31	A	Derby County	D	2-2	2-1	Molenaar, Kewell	27,034
12	Nov	8	H	Sheffield Wed	W	2-1	1-1	Hasselbaink, Woodgate	30,012
13		14	A	Liverpool	W	3-1	0-0	Smith, Hasselbaink 2	44,305
14		21	H	Charlton Athletic	W	4-1	1-0	Hasselbaink, Bowyer, Smith, Kewell	32,487
15		29	A	Manchester United	L	2-3	1-1	Hasselbaink, Kewell	55,172
16	Dec	5	H	West Ham United	W	4-0	1-0	Bowyer 2, Molenaar, Hasselbaink	36,315
17		14	H	Coventry City	W	2-0	1-0	Hopkin, Bowyer	31,799
18		20	A	Arsenal	L	1-3	0-1	Hasselbaink	38,025
19		26	A	Newcastle United	W	3-0	1-0	Kewell, Bowyer, Hasselbaink	36,759
20		29	H	Wimbledon	D	2-2	1-1	Ribeiro, Hopkin	39,901
21	Jan	9	A	Blackburn Rovers	L	0-1	0-1		27,620
22		16	H	Middlesbrough	W	2-0	2-0	Smith, Bowyer	37,394
23		30	A	Southampton	L	0-3	0-1		15,236
24	Feb	6	H	Newcastle United	L	0-1	0-0		40,202
25		17	A	Aston Villa	W	2-1	2-0	Hasselbaink 2	37,510
26		20	H	Everton	W	1-0	0-0	Korsten	36,344
27	Mar	1	A	Leicester City	W	2-1	1-0	Kewell, Smith	18,101
28		10	H	Tottenham Hotspur	W	2-0	1-0	Smith, Kewell	34,561
29		13	A	Sheffield Wed	W	2-0	1-0	Hasselbaink, Hopkin	28,142
30		20	H	Derby County	W	4-1	3-1	Bowyer, Hasselbaink, Korsten, Harte	38,992
31	Apr	3	H	Nottingham Forest	W	3-1	1-0	Hasselbaink, Harte, Smith	39,645
32		12	H	Liverpool	D	0-0	0-0		39,372
33		17	A	Charlton Athletic	D	1-1	1-1	Woodgate	20,043
34		25	H	Manchester United	D	1-1	1-0	Hasselbaink	40,255
35	May	1	A	West Ham United	W	5-1	2-0	Hasselbaink, Smith, Harte (pen), Bowyer, Haaland	25,997
36		5	A	Chelsea	L	0-1	0-0		34,762
37		11	H	Arsenal	W	1-0	0-0	Hasselbaink	40,124
38		16	A	Coventry City	D	2-2	1-0	Wijnhard, Hopkin	23,049
									Appearances
									Sub appearances
								One own-goal	Goals

FL Cup

R3	Oct	28	H	Bradford City	W	1-0	1-0	Kewell	27,561
R4	Nov	11	A	Leicester City	L	1-2	1-0	Kewell	20,161
									Appearances
									Sub appearances
									Goals

FA Cup

R3	Jan	2	A	Rushden & Diamonds	D	0-0	0-0		6,431
Rep		13	H	Rushden & Diamonds	W	3-1	1-1	Smith 2, Hasselbaink	39,159
R4		23	A	Portsmouth	W	5-1	2-1	Wetherall, Harte, Kewell, Ribeiro, Wijnhard	18,864
R5	Feb	13	H	Tottenham Hotspur	D	1-1	0-0	Harte	39,696
Rep		24	A	Tottenham Hotspur	L	0-2	0-0		32,307
									Appearances
									Sub appearances
									Goals

Martyn, Nigel	Hiden, Martin	Harte, Ian	Haaland, Alf-Inge	Radebe, Lucas	Molenaar, Robert	Hopkin, David	Wijnhard, Clyde	Sharpe, Lee	Kewell, Harry	Bowyer, Lee	Lilley, Derek	Hasselbaink, Jimmy F	Wetherall, David	Ribeiro, Bruno	Halle, Gunnar	McPhail, Stephen	Granville, Danny	Woodgate, Jonathan	Robinson, Paul	Smith, Alan	Batty, David	Korsten, Wim	Jones, Matt	Knarvik, Tommy
1	2	3	4	5	6	7	8	9	10	11	S*													
1	2	3	4	5	6	7	8	S*	10	11		9												
1	2	3	4	5	6	7	8		10	11		9												
1	2	3	4	5	6	7	8		10	11		9	S*	S*										
1	2	3	4	5	6	7	8		10	11	S*	9		S*										
1	2	3	S*	5	6	7		S*	10	11		9		8	4									
1	2	3		5	6	7	8		10	11		9	S*		4									
1	2	3	10		6		8	7	S*	11		9	5		4	S*	S*							
1	2			5	6	7	S*		10	11		9		S*	S*	8	3	4						
	2		S*	5	6	7	S*		10	11		9				8	3	4	1					
		3		5	6	7	S*		10	11		9	S*		2	8		4	1					
1	2	3	S*		6	7	S*		10	11		9	5			8		4						
1	5	3			6	7	8		10	11		9			2			4		S*				
1	5	3			6	7	8		10	11		9			2			4		S*				
1	5	3	6			7			10			9	S*	11	2	8		4	S*	S*				
		3	2	5	6	7	S*		10	11		9				S*		4	1	8				
1		3		5	6	7			10	11		9			S*	S*		2		8	4			
1		3	6		5	7			10	11		9	S*		2		8	4		S*				
1		3	6			7			10	11		9	5	8	2	S*		4		S*				
1		3	6			7			10	11		9	5	8	2	S*		4						
1			6			7			10	11		9	5	8	2	S*	3	4		S*				
1		2	S*	5		7			10	11		9	6			4	3			8		S*		
1		3	2	5		7			10	11		9	6					4		8				
1		2	6	5		7	8		10	11					S*		3	4		9		S*		
1		3	4	5		7			10			9	6		2		S*					8	11	
1		3	4	5		7			10	11		9	6		2					S*		8	S*	
1		3	2	5		7			10	11		9	6	S*						8		4		
1		3	2	5					10	11		9	6					4		7	8			
1		3	2	5		7			10	11		9	S*					6		8	4	S*		
1		3	2	5		7			10	11		9				6		4				8	S*	
1		3		5		7			10	11		9	6	4				2		8			S*	
1		3		5		7			10	11		9		S*	2			6		8	4		S*	
1		3	S*	5		7			10	11		9	6					2		8	4		S*	
1		3		5			S*		10	11		9	S*			7		6		8	4		2	
1		3	2	5			S*		10	11		9		S*		7		6		8	4			
1		3	2	5		S*			10	11		9				7		6		8	4			
1		3	2	5		7			10	11		9						6		8	4			
		S*	2	5		S*	8		S*			9	6	10		7	3		1		4		11	
34	14	34	24	29	17	32	11	2	36	35	0	36	14	7	14	11	7	25	4	15	10	4	3	0
		1	5			2	7	2	2		2		7	6	3	6	2		1	7		3	5	
		4	1		2	4	3		6	9		18		1	2			2		7		2		

Martyn, Nigel	Hiden, Martin	Harte, Ian	Haaland, Alf-Inge	Radebe, Lucas	Molenaar, Robert	Hopkin, David	Wijnhard, Clyde	Sharpe, Lee	Kewell, Harry	Bowyer, Lee	Lilley, Derek	Hasselbaink, Jimmy F	Wetherall, David	Ribeiro, Bruno	Halle, Gunnar	McPhail, Stephen	Granville, Danny	Woodgate, Jonathan	Robinson, Paul	Smith, Alan	Batty, David	Korsten, Wim	Jones, Matt	Knarvik, Tommy
				5	6	7			10	11		9			2	8	3	4	1					
1	2	3			5	7	8		10	11		9		4				6						
1	1	1	0	1	2	2	1	0	2	2	0	2	0	1	1	1	1	2	1	0	0	0	0	0
										2														

Martyn, Nigel	Hiden, Martin	Harte, Ian	Haaland, Alf-Inge	Radebe, Lucas	Molenaar, Robert	Hopkin, David	Wijnhard, Clyde	Sharpe, Lee	Kewell, Harry	Bowyer, Lee	Lilley, Derek	Hasselbaink, Jimmy F	Wetherall, David	Ribeiro, Bruno	Halle, Gunnar	McPhail, Stephen	Granville, Danny	Woodgate, Jonathan	Robinson, Paul	Smith, Alan	Batty, David	Korsten, Wim	Jones, Matt	Knarvik, Tommy
1		6	4			7	8		10	11		9			2		3	5		S*				
1		2	S*	5		7			10	11		9	6				3	4		8				
1		4				7	S*		10			9	6	8	2		3	5				11	S*	S*
1		3	2	5		7			10	11		9	6					4		8		S*		
1		3	2	5		7			10	11		9	6		S*			4		S*		8		
5	0	5	3	3	0	5	1	0	5	4	0	5	4	1	2	0	3	5	0	2	0	2	0	0
			1				1								1					2		1	1	1
		2					1		1			1	1	1						2				

League Table

	P	W	D	L	F	A	Pts
Manchester United	38	22	13	3	80	37	79
Arsenal	38	22	12	4	59	17	78
Chelsea	38	20	15	3	57	30	75
Leeds United	38	18	13	7	62	34	67
West Ham United	38	16	9	13	46	53	57
Aston Villa	38	15	10	13	51	46	55
Liverpool	38	15	9	14	68	49	54
Derby County	38	13	13	12	40	45	52
Middlesbrough	38	12	15	11	48	54	51
Leicester City	38	12	13	13	40	46	49
Tottenham Hotspur	38	11	14	13	47	50	47
Sheffield Wednesday	38	13	7	18	41	42	46
Newcastle United	38	11	13	14	48	54	46
Everton	38	11	10	17	42	47	43
Coventry City	38	11	9	18	39	51	42
Wimbledon	38	10	12	16	40	63	42
Southampton	38	11	8	19	37	64	41
Charlton Athletic	38	8	12	18	41	56	36
Blackburn Rovers	38	7	14	17	38	52	35
Nottingham Forest	38	7	9	22	35	69	30

1999-2000

Premiership

Manager: David O'Leary

Final Position: 3rd

Did you know that?

7 August 1999: The Billy Bremner statue was unveiled outside Elland Road.

21 October 1999: A club record 10 successive wins was set by the 4–1 UEFA Cup victory against Lokomotiv Moscow.

25 November 1999: United's 3,000-mile round trip to Moscow was in vain as temperatures plunged to -27 in the Russian capital leaving the Spartak pitch unplayable.

16 April 2000: In the wake of the Galatasaray murders, Arsenal's players presented their Leeds counterparts with bouquets before the kick-off, but the sympathy ended there as the Gunners handed Leeds a 4–0 thumping.

14 May 2000: A 0–0 draw at West Ham was enough to secure a Champions League place as former player David Wetherall's goal for Bradford City beat Euro rivals Liverpool.

Goals flowed in the O'Leary era. Here Alan Smith, centre, celebrates with Ian Harte and Michael Bridges.

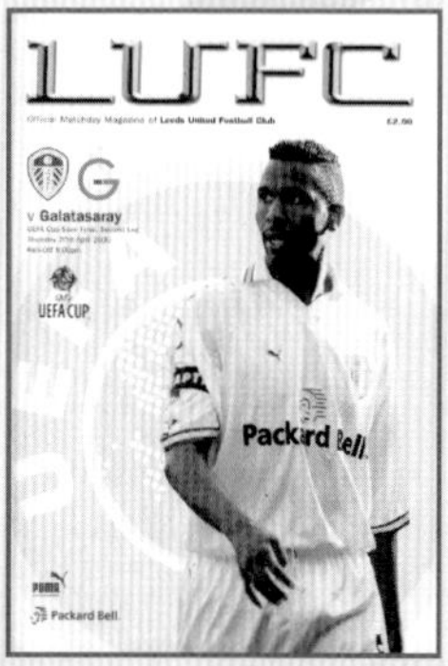

Match No.	Date	Venue	Opponents	Result	FT	HT	Scorers	Attendance
1	Aug 7	H	Derby County	D	0-0	0-0		40,118
2	11	A	Southampton	W	3-0	1-0	Bridges 3	15,206
3	14	A	Manchester United	L	0-2	0-0		55,187
4	21	H	Sunderland	W	2-1	0-1	Bowyer, Mills	39,064
5	23	H	Liverpool	L	1-2	1-1	Song (og)	39,703
6	28	A	Tottenham Hotspur	W	2-1	0-1	Smith, Harte	36,012
7	Sep 11	A	Coventry City	W	4-3	3-2	Bowyer, Huckerby, Harte (pen), Bridges	21,528
8	19	H	Middlesbrough	W	2-0	1-0	Bridges, Kewell	34,122
9	25	H	Newcastle United	W	3-2	2-1	Bowyer, Kewell, Bridges	40,192
10	Oct 3	A	Watford	W	2-1	1-1	Bridges, Kewell	19,677
11	16	H	Sheffield Wed	W	2-0	0-0	Smith 2	39,437
12	24	A	Everton	D	4-4	2-3	Bridges 2, Kewell, Woodgate	37,355
13	30	H	West Ham United	W	1-0	0-0	Harte	40,190
14	Nov 7	A	Wimbledon	L	0-2	0-1		18,747
15	20	H	Bradford City	W	2-1	0-0	Smith, Harte (pen)	39,937
16	28	H	Southampton	W	1-0	0-0	Bridges	39,288
17	Dec 5	A	Derby County	W	1-0	0-0	Harte (pen)	29,455
18	19	A	Chelsea	W	2-0	0-0	McPhail 2	35,106
19	26	H	Leicester City	W	2-1	2-1	Bridges, Bowyer	40,105
20	28	A	Arsenal	L	0-2	0-1		38,096
21	Jan 3	H	Aston Villa	L	1-2	0-1	Kewell	40,027
22	23	A	Sunderland	W	2-1	1-0	Wilcox, Bridges	41,633
23	Feb 5	A	Liverpool	L	1-3	0-1	Bowyer	44,793
24	12	H	Tottenham Hotspur	W	1-0	1-0	Kewell	40,127
25	20	H	Manchester United	L	0-1	0-0		40,160
26	26	A	Middlesbrough	D	0-0	0-0		34,800
27	Mar 5	H	Coventry City	W	3-0	2-0	Kewell, Bridges, Wilcox	38,710
28	12	A	Bradford City	W	2-1	1-0	Bridges 2	18,276
29	19	H	Wimbledon	W	4-1	3-1	Bakke 2, Harte (pen), Kewell	39,256
30	26	A	Leicester City	L	1-2	1-1	Kewell	21,059
31	Apr 1	H	Chelsea	L	0-1	0-0		40,162
32	9	A	Aston Villa	L	0-1	0-1		33,889
33	16	H	Arsenal	L	0-4	0-1		39,307
34	23	A	Newcastle United	D	2-2	2-1	Bridges, Wilcox	36,448
35	30	A	Sheffield Wed	W	3-0	1-0	Hopkin, Briges, Kewell	23,416
36	May 3	H	Watford	W	3-1	2-1	Bridges, Duberry, Huckerby	36,324
37	8	H	Everton	D	1-1	1-0	Bridges	37,713
38	14	A	West Ham United	D	0-0	0-0		26,044
								Appearances
								Sub appearances
							One own-goal	Goals

FL Cup

R3	Oct 13	H	Blackburn Rovers	W	1-0	0-0	Mills	24,353
R4	Dec 15	A	Leicester City	D	0-0*	0-0		16,125
								Appearances
								Sub appearances
								Goals

* After extra-time. Lost 4-2 on penalties

FA Cup

R3	Dec 12	H	Port Vale	W	2-0	0-0	Bakke 2	11,912
R4	Jan 9	A	Manchester City	W	5-2	3-2	Bakke, Smith, Kewell 2, Bowyer	29,240
R5	30	A	Aston Villa	L	2-3	2-1	Harte, Bakke	30,026
								Appearances
								Sub appearances
								Goals

UEFA Cup

R1	Sep 14	A	Partizan Belgrade	W	3-1†	2-1	Bowyer 2, Radebe	4,950
	30	H	Partizan Belgrade	W	1-0	0-0	Huckerby	39,806
R2	Oct 21	H	Lokomotiv Moscow	W	4-1	2-0	Bowyer 2, Smith, Kewell	37,814
	Nov 4	A	Lokomotiv Moscow	W	3-0	3-0	Harte (pen), Bridges 2	8,000
R3	Dec 2	A	Spartak Moscow	L	1-2‡	1-1	Kewell	5,485
	9	H	Spartak Moscow	W	1-0*	0-0	Radebe	39,732
R4	Mar 2	A	Roma	D	0-0	0-0		37,726
	9	H	Roma	W	1-0	0-0	Kewell	39,149
QF	16	H	Slavia Parague	W	3-0	1-0	Wilcox, Kewell, Bowyer	39,519
	23	A	Slavia Parague	L	1-2	0-0	Kewell	13,460
SF	Apr 6	A	Galatasaray	L	0-2	0-2		18,000
	20	H	Galatasaray	D	2-2	1-2	Bakke 2	38,406
								Appearances
								Sub appearances
								Goals

† At Abe Lenstra, Heerenveen, Holland

‡ At Georgi Asparhukov Stadium, Sofia, Bulgaria

* Won on away goals rule

Martyn, Nigel	Mills, Danny	Harte, Ian	Batty, David	Radebe, Lucas	Woodgate, Jonathan	Hopkin, David	Smith, Alan	Bridges, Michael	Kewell, Harry	Bowyer, Lee	McPhail, Stephen	Duberry, Michael	Jones, Matt	Bakke, Eirik	Huckerby, Darren	Hiden, Martin	Kelly, Gary	Haaland, Alf Inge	Wilcox, Jason
1	2	3	4	5	6	7	8	9	10	11	S*								
1	2	3	8	5	6	7		9	10	11		4	S*	S*					
1	2	3	8	5	6	S*		9	10	11		4		S*	7	S*			
1	2	3	4	5	6	7	S*	9	10	11					8				
1	2	3	4	5	6	7	S*	9	10	11				S*	8				
1	2	3	8	5	6	S*	7	9	10	11		4			S*		S*		
1	2	3	4	5	S*	7		9	10	11		6			8		S*		
1	2	3	4	5	6	7	8	9	10	11					S*		S*		
1		3	4	5	6		8	9	10	11				7	S*		2	S*	
1	S*	3	4	5	6	7	8	9	10					11	S*		2	S*	
1	2		4	5	6		8	9	10	11	7				S*		3		
1		3	4	5	6		8	9	10	11	7				S*		2		
1		3	4	5	6		8	9	10	11	7				S*		2		
1		3	4	5	6	S*	9		10	11	7	S*		S*	8		2		
1		3	4	5	6		8	9		11	7			10	S*		2		
1	6	3	4		5		8	9	10	11	7			S*	S*		2		
1		3		5	6		S*	9	10	11	7		S*	4	8		2		
1		3		5	6			9	10	11	7		S*	4	8		2		S*
1		3		5	6			9	10	11	7			4	8		2		S*
1		3		5	6		8	9	10	11	7		S*	4			2		S*
1		3			6		8	9	10			5	11	4	S*		2	7	S*
1		3			6			9	10	8	7	5		4	S*		2		11
1		3			6		9	S*	10	8	7	5		4	S*		2		11
1		3			6		9		10	7		5	8	4	S*		2	S*	11
1		3		5	6		9		10	7			8	4			2		11
1	2	3		5	6	7	9	S*	10	8					S*			4	11
1		3		5	6			9	10	8	7		S*	4	S*		2	S*	11
1		3		5		S*	10	9		8	7			4	S*		2	6	11
1		3		5		7	S*	9	10		8		S*	4	S*		2	6	11
1		3		5	6			9	10		7			4	S*		2	8	11
1		3		5	6		9		10	8	7			4	S*		2		11
1		3		5	6			9	10	8	7			4	S*		2		11
1		3			6		8	9	10	11	7			4			2	5	S*
1	2	3		5				9	10	S*	7	6		4	S*			8	11
1	3			5		7		9	10			6	8	4	S*		2	S*	11
1	3			5	S*		S*	9	10	11	7	6		4	8		2		
1	3				5			9	10	8	7	6		4	S*		2	S*	11
1	3			5	6		S*	9	10	S*	7		8	4	S*		2		11
38	16	33	16	31	32	10	20	32	36	31	23	12	5	24	9	0	28	7	15
	1				2	4	6	2		2	1	1	6	5	24	1	3	6	5
	1	6			1	1	4	19	10	5	2	1		2	2				3

1	2		4	5	6	7	8	9	10		S*			11	S*		3		
1		3	4	5	6			9	10	11	7	S*	S*	8			2		
2	1	1	2	2	2	1	1	2	2	1	1	0	0	2	0	0	2	0	0
											1	1	1		1				
	1																		

1		3		5	6		9	S*	10	11	7		S*	4	8		2		
1		3		5	6		9		10	8	7			4	S*		2		11
1	S*	3			6		S*	9	10	8	7	5		4	S*		2		11
3	0	3	0	2	3	0	2	1	3	3	3	1	0	3	1	0	3	0	2
	1						1	1					1		2				
		1					1		2	1				4					

1	2	3	4	5	6	7	S*	9	10	11							8		
1		3	4	5	6	7	S*	9	10	11			S*	S*	8		2		
1		3	4	5	6		8	9	10	11	7				S*		2		
1		3	4	5	6	S*		9	10	11	7			8	S*		2	S*	
1		3			6			9	10	11	7	5		8	S*		2	4	
1		3		5	6		8	9	10	11	7			4	S*		2		
1		3		5	6		S*	9	10	11			8	7			2	4	
1		3		5			S*	9	10	8	7		S*	6	S*		2	4	11
1		3		5			S*	9	10	8	7			6	S*		2	4	11
1		3		5	6		S*	9	10		7		11	8			2	4	
1		3		5	6			9	10	11	7		8	4	S*		2		S*
1	2	3		5	6			9	10	8	7			4	S*				11
12	2	12	4	11	10	2	2	12	12	11	9	1	3	9	1	0	11	5	3
						1	6						2	1	8			1	1
		1		2			1	2	5	5				2	1				1

League Table

	P	W	D	L	F	A	Pts
Manchester United	38	28	7	3	97	45	91
Arsenal	38	22	7	9	73	43	73
Leeds United	38	21	6	11	58	43	69
Liverpool	38	19	10	9	51	30	67
Chelsea	38	18	11	9	53	34	65
Aston Villa	38	15	13	10	46	35	58
Sunderland	38	16	10	12	57	56	58
Leicester City	38	16	7	15	55	55	55
West Ham United	38	15	10	13	52	53	55
Tottenham Hotspur	38	15	8	15	57	49	53
Newcastle United	38	14	10	14	63	54	52
Middlesbrough	38	14	10	14	46	52	52
Everton	38	12	14	12	59	49	50
Coventry City	38	12	8	18	47	54	44
Southampton	38	12	8	18	45	62	44
Derby County	38	9	11	18	44	57	38
Bradford City	38	9	9	20	38	68	36
Wimbledon	38	7	12	19	46	74	33
Sheffield Wednesday	38	8	7	23	38	70	31
Watford	38	6	6	26	35	77	24

2000-01

Premiership

Manager: David O'Leary

Final Position: 4th

Did you know that?

8 November 2000: Gary Kelly led United's 6,000-strong army of fans on a post-match karaoke of Leeds songs in the San Siro after the 1–1 draw earned qualification for the second phase of the Champions League.

21 November 2000: United agreed an £18 million world record fee for a defender with West Ham for Rio Ferdinand.

17 March 2001: Mark Viduka scored United's fastest ever goal in the Premiership in 11.1 seconds against Charlton. Only Ledley King (10.0) and Alan Shearer (10.4) have scored quicker goals in the Premiership.

7 May 2001: United were stunned to hear that Lee Bowyer would miss the following day's Champions League semi-final second leg in Valencia for allegedly stamping on a Spanish player in the goalless first leg. It had not been seen by the match referee but had been imposed by UEFA after reviewing video evidence.

Mark Viduka was quick off the mark at Charlton. Here he hammers in a shot against Anderlecht.

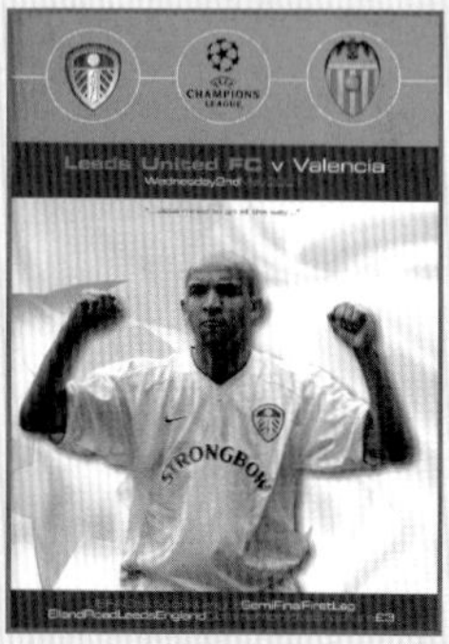

Match No.	Date	Venue	Opponents	Result	FT	HT	Scorers	Attendance
1	Aug 19	H	Everton	W	2-0	2-0	Smith 2	40,010
2	26	A	Middlesbrough	W	2-1	2-0	Bowyer, Smith	31,626
3	Sep 5	H	Manchester City	L	1-2	0-2	Bowyer	40,055
4	9	A	Coventry City	D	0-0	0-0		20,363
5	16	H	Ipswich Town	L	1-2	1-1	Bowyer	35,552
6	23	A	Derby County	D	1-1	1-0	Harte	26,248
7	30	H	Tottenham Hotspur	W	4-3	0-1	Viduka 2, Smith 2	37,562
8	Oct 14	H	Charlton Athletic	W	3-1	1-0	Smith, Viduka 2	38,837
9	21	A	Manchester United	L	0-3	0-1		67,523
10	29	A	Bradford City	D	1-1	0-1	Viduka	17,364
11	Nov 4	H	Liverpool	W	4-3	1-2	Viduka 4	40,055
12	12	A	Chelsea	D	1-1	0-0	Viduka	35,121
13	18	H	West Ham United	L	0-1	0-1		40,005
14	26	H	Arsenal	W	1-0	0-0	Dacourt	38,084
15	Dec 2	A	Leicester City	L	1-3	0-3	Viduka	21,489
16	9	A	Southampton	L	0-1	0-1		15,225
17	16	H	Sunderland	W	2-0	1-0	Bowyer, Viduka	40,053
18	23	H	Aston Villa	L	1-2	0-1	Woodgate	39,714
19	26	A	Newcastle United	L	1-2	1-2	Dacourt	52,118
20	Jan 1	H	Middlesbrough	D	1-1	0-1	Keane (pen)	39,251
21	13	A	Manchester City	W	4-0	1-0	Bakke, Bowyer, Keane 2	34,288
22	20	H	Newcastle United	L	1-3	1-2	Keane	40,005
23	24	A	Aston Villa	W	2-1	1-1	Bowyer, Harte (pen)	29,355
24	31	H	Coventry City	W	1-0	0-0	Keane	36,555
25	Feb 3	A	Ipswich Town	W	2-1	2-0	Venus (og), Keane	22,016
26	7	A	Everton	D	2-2	0-1	Harte, Dacourt	34,224
27	10	H	Derby County	D	0-0	0-0		38,789
28	24	A	Tottenham Hotspur	W	2-1	1-1	Harte (pen), Bowyer	36,070
29	Mar 3	H	Manchester United	D	1-1	0-0	Viduka	40,055
30	17	A	Charlton Athletic	W	2-1	1-1	Viduka, Smith	20,043
31	31	A	Sunderland	W	2-0	1-0	Smith, Viduka	46,833
32	Apr 7	H	Southampton	W	2-0	1-0	Kewell, Keane	39,267
33	13	A	Liverpool	W	2-1	2-0	Ferdinand, Bowyer	44,116
34	21	A	West Ham United	W	2-0	1-0	Keane, Ferdinand	26,041
35	28	H	Chelsea	W	2-0	0-0	Keane, Viduka	39,253
36	May 5	A	Arsenal	L	1-2	0-1	Harte	38,142
37	13	H	Bradford City	W	6-1	5-1	Viduka, Harte, Bakke, Smith, Kewell, Bowyer	38,300
38	19	H	Leicester City	W	3-1	1-1	Smith 2, Harte	39,905
								Appearances
								Sub appearances
							One own-goal	Goals

FL Cup

R3	Oct 31	A	Tramere Rovers	L	2-3*	2-0	Huckerby 2	11,681
								Appearances
								Sub appearances
								Goals

* After extra-time (score at 90 minutes 2-2)

FA Cup

R3	Jan 6	H	Barnsley	W	1-0	1-0	Viduka	32,386
R4	27	H	Liverpool	L	0-2	0-0		37,108
								Appearances
								Sub appearances
								Goals

European Cup

3Q	Aug 9	H	1860 Munich	W	2-1	1-0	Smith, Harte (pen)	33,769
	23	A	1860 Munich	W	1-0	0-0	Smith	45,000
St1H	Sep 13	A	Barcelona	L	0-4	0-2		85,000
	19	H	AC Milan	W	1-0	0-0	Bowyer	35,398
	26	H	Besiktas	W	6-0	3-0	Bowyer 2, Viduka, Matteo, Bakke, Huckerby	34,485
	Oct 18	A	Besiktas	D	0-0	0-0		20,000
	24	H	Barcelona	D	1-1	1-0	Bowyer	36,721
	Nov 8	A	AC Milan	D	1-1	1-0	Matteo	52,289
St2D	22	H	Real Madrid	L	0-2	0-0		36,794
	Dec 5	A	Lazio	W	1-0	0-0	Smith	42,450
	Feb 13	H	Anderlecht	W	2-1	0-0	Harte, Bowyer	36,064
	21	A	Anderlecht	W	4-1	3-0	Smith 2, Viduka, Harte	28,000
	Mar 6	A	Real Madrid	L	2-3	1-2	Smith, Viduka	40,000
	14	H	Lazio	D	3-3	2-2	Bowyer, Wilcox, Viduka	36,741
QF	Apr 3	H	Deportivo La Coruna	W	3-0	1-0	Harte, Smith, Ferdinand	35,508
	17	A	Deportivo La Coruna	L	0-2	0-1		35,600
SF	May 2	H	Valencia	D	0-0	0-0		36,437
	8	A	Valencia	L	0-3	0-1		53,000
								Appearances
								Sub appearances
								Goals

Martyn, Nigel	Kelly, Gary	Harte, Ian	Bakke, Eirik	Radebe, Lucas	Woodgate, Jonathan	Dacourt, Olivier	Smith, Alan	Bridges, Michael	Viduka, Mark	Bowyer, Lee	Mills, Danny	Huckerby, Darren	Duberry, Michael	Jones, Matt	Evans, Gareth	McPhail, Stephen	Wilcox, Jason	Matteo, Dominic	Hay, Danny	Robinson, Paul	Burns, Jacob	Ferdinand, Rio	Kewell, Harry	Batty, David	Keane, Robbie	Hackworth, Tony	Maybury, Alan
1	2	3	4	5	6	7	8	9	10	11	S*	S*															
1	2	3	4	S*	6	7	8	9	10	11	S*		5	S*													
1	2	3		5		7	8	9	10	11			6	4	S*												
1	2	3		5		7	8	9		11		10	6			4	S*										
1	2	3				7	8	9		11	6	10	5			4											
1	2	3	4	5		7	8	9		10	S*		6			S*		11									
1	2	3	4	5		7	8	S*	9	10	6					S*		11	S*								
1	2	3	4		5		8		9	10	6							11		S*	7						
	2				6		8		9	11		S*		10		4		3	5	1	7						
	2	3	4		6	7	8		9	10								11	5	1	S*						
	2	3	4		6	7	8		9	11								5	S*	1	10						
	2	3	4	5		7	8		9	10	6	S*						11		1							
	2	3	4	5		7	8		9	10	6	S*						11		1							
	2	3	4	5	6	7	8		9	10							11			1							
	2			4	6	7	8		9	11				10			S*	3		1		5	S*				
	2		4		6	7	8		9	10							11	3		1		5	S*				
	2		4		6	7	8		9	11		S*						3		1		5	10	S*			
	2		7	4	6		8		9	11								3		1		5	10		S*		
	2		4		6	7	8		9	11								3		1		5	10	S*	S*		
	2			6		7	S*		9	10							11	3		1		5		4	8		
			4	6		7	8		9	10	2						11	3		1		5			S*		
			4	5	6	7	S*		9	10	2						11	3		1					8		
	2	3	4		6	7	S*		9	10							S*	11		1		5		S*	8		
1		3	4	6					9	10	2						11					5		7	8		
1		3	S*	6		7	S*		9	10	2							11				5		4	8		
1		3	S*	6		7	S*		9	10	2						S*	11				5		4	8		
1		2	S*	6		7	S*		9	10							11	3				5	S*	4	8		
1		3	11			7			9	10	2							6				5	S*	4	8		
1		3		6		7	S*		9	10	2							11				5	S*	4	8		
1		3				7	8		9	10	2						S*	6				5	11	4			
1	S*	3	S*	6		7	8		9	10	2											5	11	4	S*		
1		3	7						9	10	2						S*	6				5	11	4	8		
1		3				7	8		9	10	2						S*	6				5	11	4	S*		
1	S*	3	8			7				10	2						S*	6				5	11	4	9		
1		3	S*			7	8		9	10	2							6				5	11	4	S*		
1	2	3	4			7			9	10						S*	S*	6				5	11		8		
1		3	4			7	8		9	10	2					S*		6				5	11				
1		3	4			7	8		9	10	2						S*	6				5	11				
23	22	29	24	19	14	33	26	6	34	38	20	2	5	3	0	3	7	30	2	15	3	23	12	13	12	0	0
	2		5	1			7	1			3	5		1	1	4	10		2	1	1		5	3	6		
		7	2		1	3	11		17	9												2	2		9		

Martyn, Nigel	Kelly, Gary	Harte, Ian	Bakke, Eirik	Radebe, Lucas	Woodgate, Jonathan	Dacourt, Olivier	Smith, Alan	Bridges, Michael	Viduka, Mark	Bowyer, Lee	Mills, Danny	Huckerby, Darren	Duberry, Michael	Jones, Matt	Evans, Gareth	McPhail, Stephen	Wilcox, Jason	Matteo, Dominic	Hay, Danny	Robinson, Paul	Burns, Jacob	Ferdinand, Rio	Kewell, Harry	Batty, David	Keane, Robbie	Hackworth, Tony	Maybury, Alan
	2	3	4	S*	6		S*		9			8		10				11	5	1	7					S*	
0	1	1	1	0	1	0	0	0	1	0	0	1	0	1	0	0	0	1	1	1	1	0	0	0	0	0	0
				1			1																			1	
												2															

Martyn, Nigel	Kelly, Gary	Harte, Ian	Bakke, Eirik	Radebe, Lucas	Woodgate, Jonathan	Dacourt, Olivier	Smith, Alan	Bridges, Michael	Viduka, Mark	Bowyer, Lee	Mills, Danny	Huckerby, Darren	Duberry, Michael	Jones, Matt	Evans, Gareth	McPhail, Stephen	Wilcox, Jason	Matteo, Dominic	Hay, Danny	Robinson, Paul	Burns, Jacob	Ferdinand, Rio	Kewell, Harry	Batty, David	Keane, Robbie	Hackworth, Tony	Maybury, Alan
			11	6		7	8		9		2							3		1		5	S*	4	10		
1	2	3	7		6		S*		9	10								11				5		4	8		
1	1	1	2	1	1	1	1	0	2	1	1	0	0	0	0	0	0	2	0	1	0	2	0	2	2	0	0
							1																1				
									1																		

Martyn, Nigel	Kelly, Gary	Harte, Ian	Bakke, Eirik	Radebe, Lucas	Woodgate, Jonathan	Dacourt, Olivier	Smith, Alan	Bridges, Michael	Viduka, Mark	Bowyer, Lee	Mills, Danny	Huckerby, Darren	Duberry, Michael	Jones, Matt	Evans, Gareth	McPhail, Stephen	Wilcox, Jason	Matteo, Dominic	Hay, Danny	Robinson, Paul	Burns, Jacob	Ferdinand, Rio	Kewell, Harry	Batty, David	Keane, Robbie	Hackworth, Tony	Maybury, Alan
1	2	3	4	5		7	8	9	10	11	S*		6														
1	2	3		10	5		8		9	11	6	S*	4	7	S*												
1	2	3		5		7	8	9			6		4			10		11	S*							S*	
1	2	3	4			7	8	9		10	6		5					11									
1	2	3	4	5		7	8		9	10	6	S*				S*		11									
	2	3	4		5			8	9	10	6	S*				S*		11		1	7						
	2	3	4		5	7	8		9	10	6							11		1	S*						
	2	3	4	5		7	8		9	10	6							11		1							
	7	3		5	6		8		9	10	2						S*	11		1	4						
	2		4	5	6	7	8		9	10							11	3		1			S*				
1		3	S*	6		7	8		9	10	2							11				5	S*	4			
1		3	10	6		7	8		9		2							11				5	S*	4			
1	S*	2	11	6		7	8		9								S*	3				5	10	4			
	2	3							9	8	5						11	6		1	4		10	S*		S*	7
1		3				7	8		9	10	2						S*	6				5	11	4			
1		3	S*			7	8		9	10	2							6				5	11	4			
1		3				7	8		9	10	2							6				5	11	4			
1		3	10			7	8		9		2							6				5	11	4			
12	11	17	10	10	5	14	16	4	16	14	15	0	4	1	0	1	2	16	0	6	3	7	6	7	0	0	1
	1		2								1	3			1	2	3		1		1		3	1		2	
		4	1				7		4	6	1						1	2				1					

League Table

	P	W	D	L	F	A	Pts
Manchester United	38	24	8	6	79	31	80
Arsenal	38	20	10	8	63	38	70
Liverpool	38	20	9	9	71	39	69
Leeds United	38	20	8	10	64	43	68
Ipswich Town	38	20	6	12	57	42	66
Chelsea	38	17	10	11	68	45	61
Sunderland	38	15	12	11	46	41	57
Aston Villa	38	13	15	10	46	43	54
Charlton Athletic	38	14	10	14	50	57	52
Southampton	38	14	10	14	40	48	52
Newcastle United	38	14	9	15	44	50	51
Tottenham Hotspur	38	13	10	15	47	54	49
Leicester City	38	14	6	18	39	51	48
Middlesbrough	38	9	15	14	44	44	42
West Ham United	38	10	12	16	45	50	42
Everton	38	11	9	18	45	59	42
Derby County	38	10	12	16	37	59	42
Manchester City	38	8	10	20	41	65	34
Coventry City	38	8	10	20	36	63	34
Bradford City	38	5	11	22	30	70	26

2001-02

Premiership

Manager: David O'Leary

Final Position: 5th

Did you know that?

4 November 2002: United made it 11 games unbeaten since the start of the Premiership season as Harry Kewell netted a late winner against Tottenham.

12 January 2002: Despite an Alan Smith goal after 29 seconds at Newcastle, Leeds lost 3–1 and were knocked off the top of the Premiership.

8 March 2002: United announced a pre-tax loss of £13.8 million for the six months up to 31 December.

9 April 2002: Jonathan Woodgate suffered a broken jaw in his hometown of Middlesbrough and was ruled out for the rest of the season.

Eirik Bakke played in the World Cup with Norway at the end of the season.

Match No.	Date	Venue	Opponents	Result	FT	HT	Scorers	Attendance
1	Aug 18	H	Southampton	W	2-0	0-0	Bowyer, Smith	39,715
2	21	A	Arsenal	W	2-1	1-1	Harte, Viduka	38,062
3	25	A	West Ham United	D	0-0	0-0		24,517
4	Sep 8	H	Bolton Wanderers	D	0-0	0-0		40,153
5	16	A	Charlton Athletic	W	2-0	1-0	Keane, Mills	20,451
6	23	H	Derby County	W	3-0	1-0	Bakke, Kewell 2	39,155
7	30	A	Ipswich Town	W	2-1	0-1	Keane, Venus (og)	22,628
8	Oct 12	A	Liverpool	D	1-1	1-0	Kewell	44,352
9	21	H	Chelsea	D	0-0	0-0		40,171
10	27	A	Manchester United	D	1-1	0-0	Viduka	67,555
11	Nov 4	H	Tottenham Hotspur	W	2-1	0-0	Harte, Kewell	40,203
12	18	A	Sunderland	L	0-2	0-0		46,017
13	25	H	Aston Villa	D	1-1	1-1	Smith	40,159
14	Dec 2	A	Fulham	D	0-0	0-0		20,918
15	9	A	Blackburn Rovers	W	2-1	0-0	Kewell 2	28,309
16	16	H	Leicester City	D	2-2	1-0	Kewell, Viduka	38,337
17	19	H	Everton	W	3-2	2-0	Viduka, Fowler 2	40,201
18	22	H	Newcastle United	L	3-4	1-1	Bowyer, Viduka, Harte	40,287
19	26	A	Bolton Wanderers	W	3-0	2-0	Fowler 3	27,060
20	29	A	Southampton	W	1-0	0-0	Bowyer	31,622
21	Jan 1	H	West Ham United	W	3-0	2-0	Viduka 2, Fowler	39,322
22	12	A	Newcastle United	L	1-3	1-1	Smith	52,130
23	20	H	Arsenal	D	1-1	1-1	Fowler	40,143
24	30	A	Chelsea	L	0-2	0-2		40,615
25	Feb 3	H	Liverpool	L	0-4	0-1		40,216
26	9	A	Middlesbrough	D	2-2	1-0	Bakke, Fowler	30,221
27	24	H	Charlton Athletic	D	0-0	0-0		39,374
28	Mar 3	A	Everton	D	0-0	0-0		33,226
29	6	H	Ipswich Town	W	2-0	0-0	Fowler, Harte (pen)	39,414
30	17	H	Blackburn Rovers	W	3-1	2-0	Fowler 2, Kewell	39,857
31	23	A	Leicester City	W	2-0	2-0	Viduka, Fowler	18,976
32	30	H	Manchester United	L	3-4	1-3	Viduka, Harte, Bowyer	40,058
33	Apr 1	A	Tottenham Hotspur	L	1-2	0-2	Viduka	35,167
34	7	H	Sunderland	W	2-0	1-0	Craddock (og), Keane	39,195
35	13	A	Aston Villa	W	1-0	1-0	Viduka	40,039
36	20	H	Fulham	L	0-1	0-0		39,811
37	27	A	Derby County	W	1-0	1-0	Bowyer	30,735
38	May 11	H	Middlesbrough	W	1-0	0-0	Smith	40,218
								Appearances
								Sub appearances
							Two own-goals	Goals

FL Cup

R3	Oct 9	A	Leicester City	W	6-0	3-0	Keane 3, Bakke, Viduka, Kewell	16,316
R4	Nov 28	H	Chelsea	L	0-2	0-0		33,841
								Appearances
								Sub appearances
								Goals

FA Cup

R3	Jan 6	A	Cardiff City	L	1-2	1-1	Viduka	22,009
								Appearances
								Sub appearances
								Goals

UEFA Cup

R1	Sep 20	A	Maritimo	L	0-1	0-1		10,500
	27	H	Maritimo	W	3-0	2-0	Keane, Kewell, Bakke	38,125
R2	Oct 18	H	Troyes	W	4-2	3-1	Viduka 2, Bowyer 2	40,015
	Nov 1	A	Troyes	L	2-3	1-2	Viduka, Keane	15,000
R3	22	A	Grasshoppers	W	2-1	0-1	Harte, Smith	15,000
	Dec 6	H	Grasshoppers	D	2-2	2-1	Kewell, Keane	40,014
R4	Feb 21	A	PSV Eindhoven	D	0-0	0-0		32,000
	28	H	PSV Eindhoven	L	0-1	0-0		39,755
								Appearances
								Sub appearances
								Goals

Martyn, Nigel	Mills, Danny	Harte, Ian	Batty, David	Ferdinand, Rio	Matteo, Dominic	Dacourt, Olivier	Keane, Robbie	Viduka, Mark	Kewell, Harry	Bowyer, Lee	Bakke, Eirik	Smith, Alan	Kelly, Gary	Woodgate, Jonathan	Maybury, Alan	Wilcox, Jason	McPhail, Stephen	Johnson, Seth	Fowler, Robbie	Dubberry, Michael
1	2	3	4	5	6	7	8	9	10	11	S*	S*								
1	2	3	S*	5	6	7		9	10	11	4	8	S*	S*						
1	2	3	4	5	6	7	8	9	10	11				S*	S*					
1		3	4	5	6	7	8	9	10		S*		2			11				
1	2	3	4	5	6	7	8	9	10	11							S*			
1	2	3	4	5	6		8	9	10	11	7									
1	2	3	4	5	6		8	9	10	11	7									
1	2	3	S*	5	6	7	8	9	10	11	4									
1	2	3		5	6	7	8	9	10	11	4	S*								
1	2	3	S*	5	6	7	8	9	10	11	4	S*								
1	2	3	S*	5	6	7	8	9	10	11	4	S*						S*		
1	2	3	4	5	6	7	8				11	9						10		
1	2	3	4	5	6		8				7	9				11		10		
1	6	3	4	5		S*		9	7			8	2					11	10	
1	2	3	4	5		11		9	10				7			S*			8	6
1	2	3	4	5	6			9	10		S*		7					11	8	
1	2	3	4	5	6		S*	9	10		S*		7					11	8	
1	6	3	4	5				9	10	7	S*		2					11	8	
1		S*	4	5	3			9		11	7	8	2	6		S*			10	
1	2	3	4	5				9		11		8	7	6		S*			10	
1	2	3	4	5				9		11		8	7	6		S*			10	
1	2		4		3			9		11		8	7	6		S*		10		5
1	2		4	5	3			9		7				6		11		10	8	
1		S*	4	5	3		S*	9	S*	7			2	6		11		10	8	
1		3	4	5	6	7	S*	9	10	11			2			S*			8	
1		3	4	5	6	7		9	10		11		2			S*			8	
1		3	S*	5	6	7	8	9	11		4		2						10	
1		3	4		6			9	11		7	8	2						10	5
1		3	4	5	6		S*	9	11		7	8	2						10	
1	2	3	4	5		7	S*	9	11		S*	8		6		S*			10	
1	2	3	4		6	7		9	11			8		5				S*	10	
1	2	3	4		6		S*	9	11	S*	S*	8		5				7	10	
1	2	3	4		6		S*	9		11	7	8		5					10	
1	2	3	4		6		S*	9		11	7	8		5					10	
1	5	3	4		6		10	9		11	7	8	2							
1	2	3	4	5	6		9			11	7	8							10	
1		3	S*	5	6		S*		11	7	4	8	2					10	9	
1		3		5	6		9		11	7	4	8	2			S*		10		
38	28	34	30	31	32	16	16	33	26	24	20	19	19	11	0	4	0	12	22	3
		2	6			1	9		1	1	7	4	1	2	1	9	1	2		
	1	5					3	11	8	5	2	4							12	

Martyn, Nigel	Mills, Danny	Harte, Ian	Batty, David	Ferdinand, Rio	Matteo, Dominic	Dacourt, Olivier	Keane, Robbie	Viduka, Mark	Kewell, Harry	Bowyer, Lee	Bakke, Eirik	Smith, Alan	Kelly, Gary	Woodgate, Jonathan	Maybury, Alan	Wilcox, Jason	McPhail, Stephen	Johnson, Seth	Fowler, Robbie	Dubberry, Michael
1	2	3		5		7	8	9	10	11	4	S*		6			S*			S*
1	2	3	4	5	6	7	8				10	9	S*			11	S*			S*
2	2	2	1	2	1	2	2	1	1	1	2	1	0	1	0	1	0	0	0	0
												1	1				2			2
							3	1	1		1									

Martyn, Nigel	Mills, Danny	Harte, Ian	Batty, David	Ferdinand, Rio	Matteo, Dominic	Dacourt, Olivier	Keane, Robbie	Viduka, Mark	Kewell, Harry	Bowyer, Lee	Bakke, Eirik	Smith, Alan	Kelly, Gary	Woodgate, Jonathan	Maybury, Alan	Wilcox, Jason	McPhail, Stephen	Johnson, Seth	Fowler, Robbie	Dubberry, Michael
1	2	3	4	5				9		11		8	7	6					10	S*
1	1	1	1	1	0	0	0	1	0	1	0	1	1	1	0	0	0	0	1	0
																				1
								1												

Martyn, Nigel	Mills, Danny	Harte, Ian	Batty, David	Ferdinand, Rio	Matteo, Dominic	Dacourt, Olivier	Keane, Robbie	Viduka, Mark	Kewell, Harry	Bowyer, Lee	Bakke, Eirik	Smith, Alan	Kelly, Gary	Woodgate, Jonathan	Maybury, Alan	Wilcox, Jason	McPhail, Stephen	Johnson, Seth	Fowler, Robbie	Dubberry, Michael
1		3	4	5	6	7	8	9	10				2			S*	11			
1	2	3	4	5	6	7	8	9	10		11									
1	2	3	S*	5	6	7	8	9	10	11	4	S*								
1	2	3	4	5	6	7	8	9	10		11					S*				
1	2	3	4	5	6	7	9				10	8				11				
1	6	3	4	5		7	10	9	11			8	2							
1	2	3		5	6	7		9	10	11	4	8								
1	2	3		5	6			9	10	11	4	8	7							
8	7	8	5	8	7	7	6	7	7	3	6	4	3	0	0	1	1	0	0	0
			1									1				2				
		1					3	3	2	2	1	1								

League Table

	P	W	D	L	F	A	Pts
Arsenal	38	26	9	3	79	36	87
Liverpool	38	24	8	6	67	30	80
Manchester United	38	24	5	9	87	45	77
Newcastle United	38	21	8	9	74	52	71
Leeds United	38	18	12	8	53	37	66
Chelsea	38	17	13	8	66	38	64
West Ham United	38	15	8	15	48	57	53
Aston Villa	38	12	14	12	46	47	50
Tottenham Hotspur	38	14	8	16	49	53	50
Blackburn Rovers	38	12	10	16	55	51	46
Southampton	38	12	9	17	46	54	45
Middlesbrough	38	12	9	17	35	47	45
Fulham	38	10	14	14	36	44	44
Charlton Athletic	38	10	14	14	38	49	44
Everton	38	11	10	17	45	57	43
Bolton Wanderers	38	9	13	16	44	62	40
Sunderland	38	10	10	18	29	51	40
Ipswich Town	38	9	9	20	41	64	36
Derby County	38	8	6	24	33	63	30
Leicester City	38	5	13	20	30	64	28

2002-03

Premiership

Manager: Terry Venables until March then Peter Reid

Final Position: 15th

Did you know that?

28 September 2002: Arsenal's 4–1 win at Elland Road created an all-time record of scoring in 47 consecutive games, remaining unbeaten in 23 away matches and 29 Premiership matches.

26 December 2002: James Milner became the Premiership's youngest scorer at 16 years 356 days when he netted the winner at Sunderland – a mark since passed by Everton's James Vaughan.

31 January 2003: Cash-strapped Leeds sold Jonathan Woodgate to Newcastle for £9 million on transfer deadline day.

4 May 2003: In-form Mark Viduka's unexpected late winner in the penultimate game of the season at Arsenal guaranteed United's Premiership survival.

Jonathan Woodgate was sold to Newcastle for £9 million.

Match No.	Date	Venue	Opponents	Result	FT	HT	Scorers	Attendance
1	Aug 17	H	Manchester City	W	3-0	2-0	Barmby, Viduka, Keane	40,195
2	24	A	West Bromwich Alb	W	3-1	1-0	Kewell, Bowyer, Viduka	26,598
3	28	H	Sunderland	L	0-1	0-0		39,929
4	31	A	Birmingham City	L	1-2	0-1	Bowyer	27,364
5	Sep 11	A	Newcastle United	W	2-0	1-0	Viduka, Smith	51,730
6	14	H	Manchester United	W	1-0	0-0	Kewell	39,622
7	22	A	Blackburn Rovers	L	0-1	0-1		25,415
8	28	H	Arsenal	L	1-4	0-2	Kewell	40,199
9	Oct 6	A	Aston Villa	D	0-0	0-0		33,505
10	19	H	Liverpool	L	0-1	0-0		40,197
11	26	A	Middlesbrough	D	2-2	1-1	Viduka (pen), Bowyer	34,723
12	Nov 3	H	Everton	L	0-1	0-0		40,168
13	10	A	West Ham United	W	4-3	4-1	Barmby, Kewell 2, Viduka	33,297
14	17	H	Bolton Wanderers	L	2-4	1-1	Smith, Kewell	36,627
15	24	A	Tottenham Hotspur	L	0-2	0-2		35,720
16	Dec 1	H	Charlton Athletic	L	1-2	1-0	Kewell	35,547
17	7	A	Fulham	L	0-1	0-1		17,499
18	16	A	Bolton Wanderers	W	3-0	2-0	Mills, Fowler, Wilcox	23,201
19	21	H	Southampton	D	1-1	0-0	Kewell	36,687
20	26	A	Sunderland	W	2-1	0-1	Milner, Fowler (pen)	44,029
21	29	H	Chelsea	W	2-0	2-0	Gallas (og), Milner	40,143
22	Jan 1	H	Birmingham City	W	2-0	1-0	Bakke, Viduka	40,044
23	11	A	Manchester City	L	1-2	0-1	Kewell	34,884
24	18	H	West Bromwich Alb	D	0-0	0-0		39,708
25	28	A	Chelsea	L	2-3	1-0	Kewell, Lucic	39,741
26	Feb 1	A	Everton	L	0-2	0-0		40,153
27	8	H	West Ham United	W	1-0	1-0	Seth Johnson	40,126
28	22	H	Newcastle United	L	0-3	0-1		40,025
29	Mar 5	A	Manchester United	L	1-2	0-1	Viduka	67,626
30	15	H	Middlesbrough	L	2-3	1-2	Viduka 2	39,073
31	23	A	Liverpool	L	1-3	1-2	Viduka	43,021
32	Apr 5	A	Charlton Athletic	W	6-1	3-1	Kewell 2, Harte (pen), Viduka 3 (1 pen)	26,317
33	12	H	Tottenham Hotspur	D	2-2	1-2	Viduka 2 (1 pen)	39,580
34	19	A	Southampton	L	2-3	0-2	Kewell, Barmby	32,032
35	22	H	Fulham	W	2-0	1-0	Viduka 2	37,220
36	26	H	Blackburn Rovers	L	2-3	1-1	Viduka, Smith	38,122
37	May 4	A	Arsenal	W	3-2	1-1	Kewell, Harte, Viduka	38,127
38	11	H	Aston Villa	W	3-1	1-1	Harte, Barmby, Viduka	40,205
								Appearances
								Sub appearances
							One own-goal	Goals

FL Cup

R3	Nov 5	A	Sheffield United	L	1-2	1-0	Yates (og)	26,663
								Appearances
								Sub appearances
							One own-goal	Goals

FA Cup

R3	Jan 4	A	Scunthorpe United	W	2-0	1-0	Viduka (pen), Bakke	8,329
R4	25	A	Gillingham	D	1-1	0-0	Smith	11,093
Rep	Feb 4	H	Gillingham	W	2-1	1-0	Viduka, Bakke	29,359
R5	16	A	Crystal Palace	W	2-1	1-1	Kelly, Kewell	24,512
R6	Mar 9	A	Sheffield United	L	0-1	0-0		24,633
								Appearances
								Sub appearances
								Goals

UEFA Cup

R1	Sep 19	H	Metalurg Zapor	W	1-0	0-0	Smith	30,000
	Oct 3	A	Metalurg Zapor	D	1-1	0-1	Barmby	7,000
R2	31	H	Hapoel Tel Aviv	W	1-0	0-0	Kewell	31,867
	Nov 14	A	Hapoel Tel Aviv	W	4-1*	1-1	Smith 4	3,000
R3	26	A	Malaga	D	0-0	0-0		35,000
	Dec 12	H	Malaga	L	1-2	1-1	Bakke	34,123
								Appearances
								Sub appearances
								Goals

* At Artemio Franchi Stadium, Florence

Robinson, Paul	Mills, Danny	Harte, Ian	Bakke, Eirik	Radebe, Lucas	Matteo, Dominic	Barmby, Nick	Smith, Alan	Viduka, Mark	Kewell, Harry	Bowyer, Lee	Keane, Robbie	Johnson, Seth	Woodgate, Jonathan	Dacourt, Olivier	McPhail, Stephen	Kelly, Gary	McMaster, Jamie	Duberry, Michael	Lucic, Teddy	Bridges, Michael	Wilcox, Jason	Milner, James	Burns, Jacob	Fowler, Robbie	Okon, Paul	Bravo, Raul	Kilgannon, Matt	Johnson, Simon	Richardson, Frazer
1	2	3	4	5	6	7	8	9	10	11	S*	S*																	
1	2	3	4	S*	6	7	8	9	10	11	S*		5																
1	2	3	4	5	6	7	8	9	10	11	S*			S*															
1	2	3	4		6	7	8	9	10	11			5	S*															
1	2	3	S*		6	7	8	9	10	11			5	4															
1	2	3	S*	S*	6	7	8	9	10	11			5	4	S*														
1	2	3	4	5		7	8	9		10			6	11	S*	S*	S*												
1	3		4	5	6		8	9	10	11				7	S*	2		S*											
1	2	3	4		6	7	9	S*	10	11			5		8														
1	2	3	4			7	9	S*	10	11			5	S*	8				6										
1	2		S*	5		7	8	9	10	11			6		4				3	S*									
1	2	S*	4	5		7	8	9	10	11			6				S*		3	S*									
1		3	4	5		7		9	10	8					S*	2			6	S*	11	S*							
1						7	8	9	10				5		4	2		S*	3		11	S*	6						
1			4				9	S*	10	7			5		8	2			3		11	S*	6						
1		3	4				9		10	7			5		8	2		6		S*	11			S*					
1	S*	3	4				9						5		8	2		6		10	11	S*		S*	7				
1	2	3	4						10			S*	5			7			6		11			9	8				
1	2	3					8	S*	10				5			7			6		11			9	4				
1	5	3	4				8	9	10							2		S*	6		11	S*		S*	7				
1	6		4				8	9	10			S*	5			2			3		11	S*		S*	7				
1	6	3	4				8	9	10				5			2					11	S*			7				
1	6		4		3		8	9	10			S*	5			2					11	S*		S*	7				
1			4	5	6		8	9	10			S*				2			3		11	S*		S*	7				
1	5		4		6		8	9	10			S*				2			3		11	S*			7				
1	5	S*	4	S*	6		8	9	10							2			3		11	S*			7				
1	2		10		6							4				7	S*	5			11	9			8	3	S*		
1	2			5		S*	9		10			4				7		6	S*		11	S*			8	3			
1	2	3		5		10	8	9				7			S*				6			S*			4	11			
1	2		4	5		10	8	9											6		11	S*			7	3			
1	2	S*	4	5		7	10	9									S*		6		11	S*			8	3			
1	2	3	4	5	11		8	9	10							7		6			S*	S*						S*	
1	2	3	4	5	11		8	9	10							7		6			S*	S*							
1	5	3	4		7	S*	8	9	10							2		6			11								
1	2	3	4		6		8	9	10							7		5			11								
1	2	3	4		6		8	9	10							7		5			11							S*	
1	2	3	8	5	6			9	10							7		4			11							S*	
1	2	3	8	5	6	S*		9							S*	7		4			11						S*	10	
38	32	24	31	16	20	16	33	29	31	15	0	3	18	4	7	24	0	11	16	1	23	1	2	2	15	5	0	1	0
	1	3	3	3		3		4			3	6		3	6	1	4	3	1	4	2	17		6			2	3	
	1	3	1			4	3	20	14	3	1	1							1		1	2		2					

1	2	3	4			7		9	10	8			5		S*			S*	6	S*	11								
1	1	1	1	0	0	1	0	1	1	1	0	0	1	0	0	0	0	0	1	0	1	0	0	0	0	0	0	0	0
															1			1		1									

1	6		4		3		8	9	10			S*	5			2					11	S*		S*	7				
1			4	5	6		8	9	10							2			3		11				7				
1	2	3	4	5	6			9				10				7		S*			11	S*			8				
1	2	3		5		S*	9		10			4				7		6	S*		11	S*			8				
1	2	3	S*	5		S*	8	9	10			7							6			S*			4	11			
5	4	3	3	4	3	0	4	4	4	0	0	3	1	0	0	4	0	1	2	0	4	0	0	0	5	1	0	0	0
			1			2						1						1	1			4		1					
			2				1	2	1							1													

1		3	4	6			8	9	10	11			5	7	S*	2				S*									
1	5	3	4		6	7	9		10	11					8	2		S*											
1	S*	3	4	6		11	8	9	10				5	7	S*	2				S*									
1		3	4	5		7	9		10	8					S*	2		6			11						S*		S*
1		3	4				9		10	7			5		8	2		6			11								
1	2		4				8			10			5			3		6		9	11			S*	7				
6	2	5	6	3	1	3	6	2	5	5	0	0	4	2	2	6	0	3	0	1	3	0	0	0	1	0	0	0	0
	1														3			1		2				1			1		1
			1			1	5		1																				

League Table

	P	W	D	L	F	A	Pts
Manchester United	38	25	8	5	74	34	83
Arsenal	38	23	9	6	85	42	78
Newcastle United	38	21	6	11	63	48	69
Chelsea	38	19	10	9	68	38	67
Liverpool	38	18	10	10	61	41	64
Blackburn Rovers	38	16	12	10	52	43	60
Everton	38	17	8	13	48	49	59
Southampton	38	13	13	12	43	46	52
Manchester City	38	15	6	17	47	54	51
Tottenham Hotspur	38	14	8	16	51	62	50
Middlesbrough	38	13	10	15	48	44	49
Charlton Athletic	38	14	7	17	45	56	49
Birmingham City	38	13	9	16	41	49	48
Fulham	38	13	9	16	41	50	48
Leeds United	38	14	5	19	58	57	47
Aston Villa	38	12	9	17	42	47	45
Bolton Wanderers	38	10	14	14	41	51	44
West Ham United	38	10	12	16	42	59	42
West Bromwich Albion	38	6	8	24	29	65	26
Sunderland	38	4	7	27	21	65	19

2003-04

Premiership

Manager: Peter Reid until January then Eddie Gray MBE

Final Position: 19th

Did you know that?

23 August 2003: At 16 years 129 days Aaron Lennon became the Premiership's youngest player when he came on as a substitute in the 2–1 defeat at Tottenham. Fulham's Matthew Briggs is the current holder of that record.

15 September 2003: Brazilian World Cup winner Roque Junior made his debut in a 4–0 hammering at Leicester. In his five League starts for Leeds, United let in 20 goals.

24 September 2003: Paul Robinson became the first goalkeeper to score for Leeds when his last-gasp header against Swindon took the Coca-Cola Cup tie into extra-time, United winning 4–3 on penalties.

2 May 2004: Mark Viduka scored and was sent off as a 4–1 defeat at Bolton confirms United's relegation.

Goalscoring goalkeeper Paul Robinson.

Match No.	Date	Venue	Opponents	Result	FT	HT	Scorers	Attendance
1	Aug 17	H	Newcastle United	D	2-2	1-1	Viduka, Smith	36,766
2	23	A	Tottenham Hotspur	L	1-2	1-1	Smith	34,350
3	26	H	Southampton	D	0-0	0-0		34,721
4	30	A	Middlesbrough	W	3-2	1-0	Sakho, Camara, Viduka	30,414
5	Sep 15	A	Leicester City	L	0-4	0-2		30,460
6	20	H	Birmingham City	L	0-2	0-0		34,305
7	28	A	Everton	L	0-4	0-3		39,151
8	Oct 4	H	Blackburn Rovers	W	2-1	2-0	Seth Johnson 2	35,039
9	18	H	Manchester United	L	0-1	0-0		40,153
10	25	A	Liverpool	L	1-3	1-1	Smith	43,599
11	Nov 1	H	Arsenal	L	1-4	0-3	Smith	36,491
12	8	A	Portsmouth	L	1-6	1-2	Smith	20,122
13	22	H	Bolton Wanderers	L	0-2	0-2		36,558
14	29	A	Charlton Athletic	W	1-0	1-0	Milner	26,425
15	Dec 6	H	Chelsea	D	1-1	1-0	Pennant	36,305
16	14	H	Fulham	W	3-2	1-0	Duberry, Viduka, Matteo	30,544
17	22	A	Manchester City	D	1-1	1-0	Viduka	47,126
18	26	H	Aston Villa	D	0-0	0-0		38,513
19	28	A	Wolverhampton W	L	1-3	1-1	Duberry	29,139
20	Jan 7	A	Newcastle United	L	0-1	0-1		52,130
21	10	H	Tottenham Hotspur	L	0-1	0-0		35,365
22	17	A	Southampton	L	1-2	0-2	Kilgallon	31,976
23	31	H	Middlesbrough	L	0-3	0-0		35,970
24	Feb 7	A	Aston Villa	L	0-2	0-1		39,171
25	10	H	Wolverhampton W	W	4-1	2-1	Smith, Matteo, Milner, Viduka	36,867
26	21	A	Manchester United	D	1-1	0-0	Smith	67,744
27	29	H	Liverpool	D	2-2	2-2	Bakke, Viduka	39,932
28	Mar 13	A	Fulham	L	0-2	0-0		17,104
29	22	H	Manchester City	W	2-1	1-1	McPhail, Viduka (pen)	36,998
30	27	A	Birmingham City	L	1-4	1-1	Viduka	29,069
31	Apr 5	H	Leicester City	W	3-2	2-0	Duberry, Viduka, Smith	34,036
32	10	A	Blackburn Rovers	W	2-1	1-0	Caldwell, Viduka	26,611
33	13	H	Everton	D	1-1	0-1	Milner	39,835
34	16	A	Arsenal	L	0-5	0-3		38,094
35	25	H	Portsmouth	L	1-2	0-1	Harte (pen)	39,273
36	May 2	A	Bolton Wanderers	L	1-4	1-0	Viduka (pen)	27,420
37	8	H	Charlton Athletic	D	3-3	2-1	Kilgallon, Pennant, Smith (pen)	38,986
38	15	A	Chelsea	L	0-1	0-1		41,281
								Appearances
								Sub appearances
								Goals

FL Cup

R2	Sep 24	H	Swindon Town	D	2-2*	0-1	Harte, Robinson	29,211
R3	Oct 28	H	Manchester United	L	2-3†	0-0	Roque Junior 2	37,546
								Appearances
								Sub appearances
								Goals

* After extra-time. Won 4-3 on penalties
† After extra-time (score at 90 minutes 1-1)

FA Cup

R3	Jan 4	H	Arsenal	L	1-4	1-1	Viduka	31,207
								Appearances
								Sub appearances
								Goals

Robinson, Paul	Kelly, Garry	Matteo, Dominic	Morris, Jody	Radebe, Lucas	Camara, Zoumana	Sakho, Lamine	Smith, Alan	Viduka, Mark	Johnson, Seth	Wilcox, Jason	Domi, Didier	Batty, David	Lennon, Aaron	Pennant, Jermaine	Harte, Ian	Richardson, Frazer	Roque Junior	Olembe, Salomon	Bridges, Michael	Milner, James	Barmby, Nick	Duberry, Michael	Chapuis, Cyril	McPhail, Stephen	Kilgallon, Matt	Bakke, Eirik	Carson, Scott	Caldwell, Stephen	Johnson, Simon
1	2	3	4	5	6	7	8	9	10	11	S*	S*																	
1	2	3	4	5	6	7	8	9	10	11	S*		S*	S*															
1	2	5	4		6	11	8	9	10	S*		S*		7	3	S*													
1	2	6	4	S*	5	11	8	9	10				S*	7	3														
1	2		4	S*	6	11	8	9	10		5		S*	7			3	S*											
1	2		4		6	11	8	9					S*	7	3		5	10											
1	2	3	4		6	11	8	9	10				S*	7			5	S*	S*										
1	2	5	4		6	S*	8	9	11			10		7				3	S*										
1	2	5			6	S*	8	9	10			4	S*	7				3	S*	11									
1	2	5			6	S*	8	9	10			4	S*	7				3		11	S*								
1	2				6	11	8		10			4	S*	7			5	3	9	S*									
1	2	5	8			S*	9		10					7			6	3	S*	11		4							
1			8	5	2	11		9	10			4			3			S*		7	S*	6	S*						
1	2	4		5			8	9				10		7	3					11		6							
1	2	4		5			8	9	S*		S*			7	3					11		6		10					
1	2	4		5			8	9				10		7	3					11		6							
1	2	4		5			8	9				10		7	3				S*	11		6		S*	S*				
1	2	4					8	9				10	S*	7	3					11		6			5	S*			
1	2	4				S*	8	9						7	3					S*		6		11	5	10			
1	2	4				S*		9	10			8		7	3			S*	S*	11		6			5				
1	2	4				S*		9						7	3			8	S*	S*	10	6			5	11			
1	2		8		6		9		10					7	3				S*	11					5	4			
1	2	4	S*				9		10					7	3				S*	8		6			5	11	S*		
1	2	4					8	9	10		3		S*	7		S*				11						6		5	
1	2	4					8	9	10		3			7	S*					11						6		5	
	2	4				S*	9		10		3			7						11				8		6	1	5	
1	2	4					8	9	10		3			7						11				S*		6		5	S*
1	2	4					8	9	10		3			7						11				6				5	S*
1	2	4					8	9	10		3			7						11				6				5	
1	2	4					8	9	10		3			7						11				6				5	S*
1	2	4					8	9	10		3			7	S*					11		6						5	
1	2	4					8	9	10					7	3					11		6		S*		S*		5	
1	2	4		10			8	9						7	3					11		6						5	
1	2	4		10			8	9						7	3					11	S*	6						5	S*
1	2	4		10			9						S*	7	3					11	S*	6		S*				5	8
1	2	4					8	9		S*				7	3					11		6		10				5	
1	2	4		S*			9			S*				7	3	11				10		6		8	5				
	2	4		5			9			11				S*	3	7		8		10	S*	6					1		
36	37	33	11	11	13	9	35	30	24	3	9	10	0	34	21	2	5	8	1	27	1	19	0	8	7	8	2	13	1
			1	3		8			1	3	3	2	11	2	2	2		4	9	3	5		1	4	1	2	1		4
		2			1	1	9	11	2					2	1					3		3		1	2	1		1	

1	2			S*	5		8			11	S*	4	7		3		6	10	S*				9							
1	2				5	7	8		10		S*		S*		3		6	4	9	11			S*							
2	2	0	0	0	2	1	2	0	1	1	0	1	1	0	2	0	2	2	1	1	0	0	1	0	0	0	0	0	0	
				1							2		1						1				1							s
1															1		2													

1		4				S*	8	9				10	S*		3	2				11		6			5	7			
1	0	1	0	0	0	0	1	1	0	0	0	1	0	0	1	1	0	0	0	1	0	1	0	0	1	1	0	0	0
						1							1																
								1																					

League Table

	P	W	D	L	F	A	Pts
Arsenal	38	26	12	0	73	26	90
Chelsea	38	24	7	7	67	30	79
Manchester United	38	23	6	9	64	35	75
Liverpool	38	16	12	10	55	37	60
Newcastle United	38	13	17	8	52	40	56
Aston Villa	38	15	11	12	48	44	56
Charlton Athletic	38	14	11	13	51	51	53
Bolton Wanderers	38	14	11	13	48	56	53
Fulham	38	14	10	14	52	46	52
Birmingham City	38	12	14	12	43	48	50
Middlesbrough	38	13	9	16	44	52	48
Southampton	38	12	11	15	44	45	47
Portsmouth	38	12	9	17	47	54	45
Tottenham Hotspur	38	13	6	19	47	57	45
Blackburn Rovers	38	12	8	18	51	59	44
Manchester City	38	9	14	15	55	54	41
Everton	38	9	12	17	45	57	39
Leicester City	38	6	15	17	48	65	33
Leeds United	38	8	9	21	40	79	33
Wolverhampton W	38	7	12	19	38	77	33

2004-05

Championship

Manager: Kevin Blackwell

Final Position: 14th

Did you know that?

25 July 2004: Sixteen-year-old Simon Walton had a debut to remember – scoring a penalty in a high-profile pre-season game against Valencia and minutes later was sent off for two bookable offences.

3 November 2004: Jermaine Wright scored what is thought to be the quickest goal at Elland Road, hitting the back of the Burnley net after 12 seconds.

20 November 2004: Brian Deane joined a select band of United goal heroes as he scored four in the 6–1 demolition of QPR.

5 April 2005: Swift action by physio Dave Hancock helped save Paul Butler's life after the United skipper was knocked unconscious and swallowed his tongue in the home game against Sheffield United.

Paul Butler's season came to a premature end when he was knocked unconscious against Sheffield United.

Match No.	Date	Venue	Opponents	Result	FT	HT	Scorers	Attendance
1	Aug 7	H	Derby County	W	1-0	0-0	Richardson	30,459
2	10	A	Gillingham	L	1-2	0-2	Pugh	10,739
3	14	A	Wolverhampton, W	D	0-0	0-0		28,397
4	21	H	Nottingham Forest	D	1-1	1-0	Guppy	31,808
5	29	A	Sheffield United	L	0-2	0-0		22,959
6	Sep 11	H	Coventry City	W	3-0	1-0	Carlisle, Joachim, Pugh	26,725
7	14	A	Plymouth Argyle	W	1-0	1-0	Keith (og)	20,555
8	18	A	Crewe Alexandra	D	2-2	0-0	Pugh 2	9,095
9	24	H	Sunderland	L	0-1	0-0		28,926
10	28	H	Stoke City	D	0-0	0-0		25,759
11	Oct 2	A	Cardiff City	D	0-0	0-0		17,006
12	16	H	Preston North End	W	1-0	0-0	Pugh	30,458
13	19	A	Reading	D	1-1	1-1	Walton	22,230
14	23	A	Brighton & HA	L	0-1	0-0		6,716
15	31	H	Wigan Athletic	L	0-2	0-0		27,432
16	Nov 3	H	Burnley	L	1-2	1-2	Wright	27,490
17	6	A	Preston North End	W	4-2	3-0	Deane, Healy 2, Walton	18,531
18	13	A	Ipswich Town	L	0-1	0-0		29,955
19	20	H	Queen's Park R	W	6-1	5-1	Healy, Deane 4, Wright	29,739
20	24	H	Watford	D	2-2	1-1	Wright, Carlisle	24,585
21	29	A	Rotherham United	L	0-1	0-0		8,860
22	Dec 4	H	Leicester City	L	0-2	0-0		27,384
23	10	A	West Ham United	D	1-1	0-0	Healy (pen)	30,684
24	19	H	Millwall	D	1-1	1-0	Oster	26,265
25	26	A	Sunderland	W	3-2	1-1	Lennon, Deane, Joachim	43,253
26	28	H	Plymouth Argyle	W	2-1	0-0	Gilbert (og), Healy	34,496
27	Jan 1	H	Crewe Alexandra	L	0-2	0-1		32,302
28	3	A	Coventry City	W	2-1	1-0	Blake, Healy	19,084
29	15	H	Cardiff City	D	1-1	1-0	Walton	29,548
30	22	A	Stoke City	W	1-0	0-0	Thomas (og)	18,372
31	26	A	Derby County	L	0-2	0-0		25,648
32	29	H	Brighton & HA	D	1-1	1-0	Carlisle	27,033
33	Feb 5	A	Burnley	W	1-0	0-0	Einarsson	17,789
34	12	H	Reading	W	3-1	1-0	Healy, Hulse 2	30,034
35	19	A	Wigan Athletic	L	0-3	0-1		17,177
36	26	H	West Ham United	W	2-1	0-0	Hulse, Derry	34,115
37	Mar 6	A	Millwall	D	1-1	0-1	Hulse	12,510
38	12	H	Gillingham	D	1-1	0-1	Hulse	27,995
39	16	A	Nottingham Forest	D	0-0	0-0		25,101
40	Apr 2	H	Wolverhampton, W	D	1-1	0-1	Derry	29,773
41	5	H	Sheffield United	L	0-4	0-2		28,936
42	9	A	Watford	W	2-1	1-1	Hulse, Carlisle	16,306
43	16	A	Queen's Park R	D	1-1	1-0	Seth Johnson	18,182
44	23	H	Ipswich Town	D	1-1	1-1	Spring	29,607
45	May 1	A	Leicester City	L	0-2	0-2		26,593
46	8	H	Rotherham United	D	0-0	0-0		30,900
								Appearances
								Sub appearances
							Three own-goals	Goals

FL Cup

R1	Aug 24	H	Huddersfield Town	W	1-0	1-0	Pugh	30,115
R2	Sep 21	H	Swindon Town	W	1-0	1-0	Ricketts	18,476
R3	Oct 26	A	Portsmouth	L	1-2	1-2	Deane	15,215
								Appearances
								Sub appearances
								Goals

FA Cup

R3	Jan 8	A	Birmingham City	L	0-3	0-2		25,159
								Appearances
								Sub appearances
								Goals

Sullivan, Neil	Kelly, Gary	Kilgallon, Matt	Walton, Simon	Butler, Paul	Duberry, Michael	Richardson, Frazer	Pugh, Danny	Ricketts, Michael	Joachim, Julian	Wright, Jermaine	Radebe, Lucas	Deane, Brian	Guppy, Steve	Crainey, Stephen	Carlisle, Clark	McMaster, Jamie	Lennon, Aaron	Spring, Matthew	Gregan, Sean	Ormerod, Brett	Healy, David	Johnson, Simon	Oster, John	Woods, Martin	Einarsson, Gylfi	Blake, Nathan	Griffit, Leandre	Bakke, Eirik	Gray, Michael	Hulse, Rob	Derry, Shaun	King, Marlon	Johnson, Seth	Moore, Ian	Cadamarteri, Danny	Keogh, Andy
1	2	3	4	5	6	7	8	9	10	11	S*	S*																								
1	2	3	4	5	6	7	8	9	10	11		S*	S*																							
1	2		S*	5	6	7	8	9	S*	11	4	10	S*	3																						
1	2		S*	5		7	4	S*	10	8		9	11	3	6	S*																				
1	2			5	6	7	4	9	10	11		8		3		S*	S*																			
1	2		4	5		7	8	S*	10	11		9		3	6	S*																				
1	2		4	5		7	8	S*	10	11		9		3	6	S*		S*																		
1	2			5		7	8	S*	10	11		9		3	6	S*			4																	
1	2			5		7	8	S*	S*	11		9		3	6				4	10																
1	2			5		7	8		S*	11		9		3	6				4	10																
1	2			5		7	8	S*	S*	11		9		3	6				4	10																
1	2	3	11	5		7	8	9				S*			6		S*	S*	4	10																
1	2	3	11	5		7	8	9	S*			S*			6			S*	4	10																
1	2	3	11	5		7	8	9				S*			6		S*	S*	4	10																
1	2	3	5			7	8		S*	S*		9			6		S*		4		10	11														
1	2	3		5			8	S*	11	7		9			6		S*		4		10	S*														
1	2		3	5		S*	8			7		9			6				4		10		11													
1	2		3	5			8		S*	7		9			6				4		10		11													
1	2		3	5		S*	8		S*	7		9			6		S*		4		10		11													
1	2		3	5			8		S*	7		9			6				4		10		11													
1	2	3	8	5		S*		9	S*	7					6		S*		4		10		11													
1	2	3	8	5		S*			S*	7		9			6	S*			4		10		11													
1	2	3	S*	5		7	8		S*	6		9				S*			4		10		11													
1	2	6	S*	5		7	3		S*	8		9							4		10		11													
1	2	6		5		7	3	S*	S*	11		9					8	4			10			S*												
1	2	6		5		7	3		S*	11		9			S*		8		4		10															
1	2	6	S*	5		7	3	S*		11							8		4		10				S*	9										
1		6	7			2	3		S*	11					5		8	S*	4		10					9										
1	2	6	4	5		7	3		9	11					S*		8	S*			10															
1	2			5		7	3	S*	S*	11		9			6		8		4		10															
1	2		S*	5		3	8	9	11	7		S*			6				4		10						S*									
1	2		8	5		3						9			6		7	S*	4		10				11			S*								
1	2			5			S*	S*		11		9			6		7		4		10				8				3							
1	2			5		S*	S*	S*		11					6		7		4		10				8				3	9						
1	2			5		S*				11					6		7		4		10								3	9	8					
1	2	6	11	5			S*								S*		7		4		10								3	9	8					
1	2	6	11	5											S*		7		4		10								3	9	8	S*	S*			
1	2	6	11	5		S*				8		S*					7		4		10								3	9		S*				
1	2	6	11	5		4	3			8		S*			S*		7				10									9			S*			
1		6	2	5			3										7	S*			S*				S*					9	4	8	11	10		
1		6	2	5			3								S*		7		S*		10									9	4	8	11	S*		
1	2	6				S*									5		7		4		10								3	9	8	S*	11	S*		
1	2					S*	S*								5		7	S*	4						8				3	9	6	10	11			
1	2	6	S*			11				S*					5			7	4						8				3	9		S*		10		
1	2	6				11	S*								5		S*	7	4						8				3	9		S*		10		
1	2	5				S*	3			8	S*						7	6	4											9		11		10		
46	43	26	23	39	4	28	33	9	10	33	1	23	1	9	29	0	19	4	34	6	27	1	8	0	6	2	0	0	10	13	7	4	4	4	0	0
			7			10	5	12	17	2	2	8	2		6	7	8	9	1		1	1		1	2		1	1				5	2	2		
			3			1	5		2	3		6	1		4		1	1			7		1		1	1				6	2		1			

1	2			5		7	8	9	10	4			11	3	6	S*																				
1	2	3	S*	5			8	9	10			S*			6	11		4	7																S*	
1	2		3			7	8	S*	10			9			5		S*	6	4			11														S*
3	3	1	1	2	0	2	3	2	3	1	0	1	1	1	3	1	0	2	2	0	0	1	0	0	0	0	0	0	0	0	0	0	0	0	0	0
			1					1				1				1	1																		1	1
							1	1				1																								

1	2	6	7		5	3	S*		S*	11							8	4			10					9										
1	1	1	1	0	1	1	0	0	0	1	0	0	0	0	0	0	1	1	0	0	1	0	0	0	0	1	0	0	0	0	0	0	0	0	0	0
							1		1																											

League Table

	P	W	D	L	F	A	Pts
Sunderland	46	29	7	10	76	41	94
Wigan Athletic	46	25	12	9	79	35	87
Ipswich Town	46	24	13	9	85	56	85
Derby County	46	22	10	14	71	60	76
Preston North End	46	21	12	13	67	58	75
West Ham United	46	21	10	15	66	56	73
Reading	46	19	13	14	51	44	70
Sheffield United	46	18	13	15	57	56	67
Wolverhampton W	46	15	21	10	72	59	66
Millwall	46	18	12	16	51	45	66
Queen's Park Rangers	46	17	11	18	54	58	62
Stoke City	46	17	10	19	36	38	61
Burnley	46	15	15	16	38	39	60
Leeds United	46	14	18	14	49	52	60
Leicester City	46	12	21	13	49	46	57
Cardiff City	46	13	15	18	48	51	54
Plymouth Argyle	46	14	11	21	52	64	53
Watford	46	12	16	18	52	59	52
Coventry City	46	13	13	20	61	73	52
Brighton & Hove Albion	46	13	12	21	40	65	51
Crewe Alexandra	46	12	14	20	66	86	50
Gillingham	46	12	14	20	45	66	50
Nottingham Forest	46	9	17	20	42	66	44
Rotherham United	46	5	14	27	35	69	29

2005-06

Championship

Manager: Kevin Blackwell

Final Position: 5th

Did you know that?

7 August 2005: David Healy scored twice to give United a flying start to the new season in a Sunday home fixture against Millwall, who had no fans at the game as they rejected travelling on organised coaches.

10 December 2005: Peter Ridsdale returned to Elland Road for the first time since resigning as United chairman to see his new club, Cardiff, gain their first League win at Leeds since 1921.

25 February 2006: Gary Kelly celebrated his 500th game as United beat Luton 2–1.

Opening day scorer David Healey.

Match No.	Date	Venue	Opponents	Result	FT	HT	Scorers	Attendance
1	Aug 7	H	Millwall	W	2-1	1-0	Healy 2 (1 pen)	20,440
2	9	A	Cardiff City	L	1-2	1-0	Blake	15,231
3	13	A	Luton Town	D	0-0	0-0		10,102
4	20	H	Wolverhampton W	W	2-0	1-0	Lewis, Hulse	21,229
5	27	A	Norwich City	W	1-0	0-0	Hulse	25,015
6	Sep 10	H	Brighton & HA	D	3-3	0-1	Healy 2, Douglas	21,212
7	13	A	Sheffield Wed	L	0-1	0-1		29,986
8	17	A	Queen's Park R	W	1-0	1-0	Hulse	15,523
9	24	H	Ipswich Town	L	0-2	0-1		21,676
10	28	H	Derby County	W	3-1	3-0	Hulse 3	18,353
11	Oct 1	A	Watford	D	0-0	0-0		16,050
12	15	A	Burnley	W	2-1	0-0	Lewis, Hulse	16,174
13	18	H	Southampton	W	2-1	2-1	Hulse, Blake	18,881
14	21	H	Sheffield United	D	1-1	0-0	Richardson	23,600
15	29	A	Reading	D	1-1	0-0	Healy	22,012
16	Nov 1	A	Crewe Alexandra	L	0-1	0-1		7,220
17	5	H	Preston North End	D	0-0	0-0		22,289
18	19	A	Southampton	W	4-3	0-3	Butler, Blake, Healy (pen), Miller	30,173
19	22	H	Burnley	W	2-0	0-0	Healy (pen), Blake	21,318
20	26	A	Millwall	W	1-0	0-0	May (og)	8,134
21	Dec 3	H	Leicester City	W	2-1	1-0	Healy, Kilgallon	21,402
22	10	H	Cardiff City	L	0-1	0-1		20,597
23	17	A	Wolverhampton W	L	0-1	0-1		26,821
24	26	H	Coventry City	W	3-1	1-0	Douglas, Blake, Cresswell	24,291
25	28	A	Stoke City	W	1-0	0-0	Lewis	20,408
26	31	H	Hull City	W	2-0	1-0	Douglas 2	26,387
27	Jan 2	A	Plymouth Argyle	W	3-0	0-0	Cresswell, Blake, Hulse (pen)	17,726
28	14	A	Brighton & HA	L	1-2	1-1	Blake (pen)	7,415
29	21	H	Sheffield Wed	W	3-0	0-0	Butler, Cresswell 2	27,843
30	31	A	Ipswich Town	D	1-1	0-0	Healy (pen)	25,845
31	Feb 4	H	Queen's Park R	W	2-0	1-0	Cresswell, Butler	21,807
32	11	A	Derby County	D	0-0	0-0		27,000
33	14	H	Watford	W	2-1	0-1	Blake 2 (1 pen)	22,007
34	18	A	Leicester City	D	1-1	1-1	Blake (pen)	25,497
35	25	H	Luton Town	W	2-1	0-0	Douglas, Lewis	23,644
36	Mar 4	A	Crystal Palace	W	2-1	1-0	Blake, Hulse	23,843
37	11	H	Norwich City	D	2-2	1-0	Hulse, Lewis	24,993
38	18	A	Coventry City	D	1-1	0-1	Healy (pen)	26,643
39	21	H	Crystal Palace	L	0-1	0-1		24,507
40	25	H	Stoke City	D	0-0	0-0		21,452
41	Apr 1	A	Hull City	L	0-1	0-0		23,486
42	8	H	Plymouth Argyle	D	0-0	0-0		20,650
43	15	H	Reading	D	1-1	0-0	Hulse	24,535
44	18	A	Sheffield United	D	1-1	1-1	Healy	29,329
45	22	H	Crewe Alexandra	W	1-0	0-0	Healy	21,046
46	30	A	Preston North End	L	0-2	0-1		19,350
								Appearances
								Sub appearances
							One own-goal	Goals

FL Cup

R1	Aug 23	H	Oldham Athletic	W	2-0	2-0	Ricketts, Richardson	14,970
R2	Sep 20	A	Rotherham United	W	2-0	2-0	Cresswell 2	5,445
R3	Oct 25	A	Blackburn Rovers	L	0-3	0-0		15,631
								Appearances
								Sub appearances
								Goals

FA Cup

R3	Jan 7	A	Wigan Athletic	D	1-1	0-0	Hulse	10,980
Rep	17	H	Wigan Athletic	D	3-3*	1-1	Healy 2 (1 pen), Kelly	15,243
								Appearances
								Sub appearances
								Goals

* After extra-time (score at 90 minutes 2-2). Lost 4-2 on penalties

FL Play-offs

SF	May 5	H	Preston North End	D	1-1	0-0	Lewis	35,239
	8	A	Preston North End	W	2-0	0-0	Hulse, Richardson	20,383
F	21	N	Watford	L	0-3†	0-1		64,736
								Appearances
								Sub appearances
								Goals

† At the Millenium Stadium, Cardiff

Sullivan, Neil	Kelly, Gary	Harding, Dan	Bakke, Eirik	Butler, Paul	Derry, Shaun	Wright, Jermaine	Gregan, Sean	Healey, David	Blake, Robbie	Lewis, Eddie	Richardson, Frazer	Ricketts, Michael	Kilgallon, Matt	Bennett, Ian	Einarsson, Gylfi	Hulse, Rob	Douglas, Jonathan	Cresswell, Richard	Crainey, Stephen	Moore, Ian	Pugh, Danny	Miller, Liam	Walton, Simon	Beckford, Jermaine	Griffiths, Joel	Graham, Danny	Stone, Steve	Rui Marques, Manuel
1	2	3	4	5	6	7	8	9	10	11	S*	S*																
1	2	3	4	5	6	7	8	9	10	11	S*	S*	S*															
	2	3	4	5	6	7	8	S*	9	11	S*	10		1	S*													
	2	3		5	6		8	S*	9	11	7	S*		1	4	10	S*											
	2	3		5	6		8	9		11	7			1	4	10	S*	S*										
	2	3		5	6		8	9	S*	11	7			1	4	10	S*	S*										
1	2			5	6		8	9	S*	11	S*				7	S*	4	10	3									
1	2			5	6		8	9		11					7	10	4	S*	3									
1	2			5	6		8		S*	11	S*				7	9	4	10	3	S*								
1	2			5	6		8		S*	11	7		S*			9	4	10	3	S*								
1	2			5	6		8	S*	9	11	7		3			10	4			S*	S*							
1	2	3		5	6		8	S*	9	11	7				S*	10	4			S*								
1	2	3		5	6		8	S*	9	11	7		S*		S*	10	4											
1	2	3		5	6			S*	9	11	7		8		S*	10	4			S*								
1	2	3		5	6			S*	9	11	7		8			10	4			S*	S*							
1	2	3		5	6			9	S*	11	S*		8			10	4			7	S*							
1	2	3		5	6			9	S*	11	7		8			10	S*			S*		4						
1	2	3		5	6			S*	9	11	7		8			10						4						
1	2	3		5	6			9	7	11	S*		8			10	S*				S*	4						
1	2	3			6		8	9	7	11			5			10	S*			S*		4						
1	2	3		5				9	7	11	S*		6			10				S*	S*	4	8					
1	2	3		5			8	9	7	11			6			10	S*			S*	S*	4						
1		3		5	6			9	7	11			8				S*	10		S*		4	2					
1	2	3		5	6			9	7	11	S*		8			S*	4	10										
1	2	3		5	6			9	7	11			8			S*	4	10				S*						
1	2			5	6			S*	9	11			8			S*	4	10	3		S*	7						
1	2			5	6				9	11			8			S*	4	10	3			7						
1	2			5	6			S*	9	11			8			S*	4	10	3		S*	7						
1	2			5	6		8	S*	9	11							4	10	3			7	S*					
1	2			5	6		8	S*		11						10	4	9	3			7						
1	2			5	6		8	9	S*	11						S*	4	10	3			7						
1	2			5	6		8		9	11						10	4		3	S*	S*	7						
1	2			5	6		8	S*	9	11						10	4	S*	3			7						
1	2		6	5			8	S*	9	11						10	4		3	S*		7						
1	2		S*	5			6	9	8	11						10	4		3	S*		7						
1	2			5	6		8	S*	9	11						10	4		3		S*	7						
1	2		S*	5	6		8	S*	9	11						10	4		3			7						
1	2			5	6			S*	9	11			8			10	4		3	S*		7						
1	2		S*	5	6			9	S*	11			8			10	4		3			7		S*				
1	2			5	6		8	9	S*	11						10	4		3			7		S*	S*			
1	2			5	6		8	S*	9	11	S*					10	4		3			7				S*		
1	2			5	6		8	9	7	S*	11					10	4		3			S*		S*				
1	2		11	5	6			9					8			10	4		3	S*		7		S*		S*		
1	2		11	5	6			9					8			10	4		3	S*	S*	7						
1	2		4	5	6			9	S*	11			8						3	S*		7				10	S*	
1							6	9	8		2		5				4			7	3		10	S*	S*		11	
42	44	20	7	44	41	3	28	24	31	42	13	1	22	4	6	32	32	12	24	2	1	26	3	0	0	1	1	0
			3					18	10	1	10	3	3		4	7	8	4		18	11	2	1	5	2	2	1	
				3				12	11	5	1		1			12	5	5				1						

Sullivan, Neil	Kelly, Gary	Harding, Dan	Bakke, Eirik	Butler, Paul	Derry, Shaun	Wright, Jermaine	Gregan, Sean	Healey, David	Blake, Robbie	Lewis, Eddie	Richardson, Frazer	Ricketts, Michael	Kilgallon, Matt	Bennett, Ian	Einarsson, Gylfi	Hulse, Rob	Douglas, Jonathan	Cresswell, Richard	Crainey, Stephen	Moore, Ian	Pugh, Danny	Miller, Liam	Walton, Simon	Beckford, Jermaine	Griffiths, Joel	Graham, Danny	Stone, Steve	Rui Marques, Manuel
1							5	9	S*		7	10	6		8		4		3		11							2
1					S*		5				2		6		8	10	4	9	3	7	11							
1		3		5			4	9	10	S*	2		6		8	S*	S*			7	11							
3	0	1	0	1	0	0	3	2	1	0	3	1	3	0	3	1	2	1	2	2	3	0	0	0	0	0	0	1
					1				1	1						1	1											
											1	1						2										

Sullivan, Neil	Kelly, Gary	Harding, Dan	Bakke, Eirik	Butler, Paul	Derry, Shaun	Wright, Jermaine	Gregan, Sean	Healey, David	Blake, Robbie	Lewis, Eddie	Richardson, Frazer	Ricketts, Michael	Kilgallon, Matt	Bennett, Ian	Einarsson, Gylfi	Hulse, Rob	Douglas, Jonathan	Cresswell, Richard	Crainey, Stephen	Moore, Ian	Pugh, Danny	Miller, Liam	Walton, Simon	Beckford, Jermaine	Griffiths, Joel	Graham, Danny	Stone, Steve	Rui Marques, Manuel
1	2			5	6			S*	9	11			8			10	4	S*	3			7						
1	2			5				9	S*	11			8		S*	10	4	S*	3			7	6					
2	2	0	0	2	1	0	0	1	1	2	0	0	2	0	0	2	2	0	2	0	0	2	1	0	0	0	0	0
								1	1						1			2										
	1							2								1												

Sullivan, Neil	Kelly, Gary	Harding, Dan	Bakke, Eirik	Butler, Paul	Derry, Shaun	Wright, Jermaine	Gregan, Sean	Healey, David	Blake, Robbie	Lewis, Eddie	Richardson, Frazer	Ricketts, Michael	Kilgallon, Matt	Bennett, Ian	Einarsson, Gylfi	Hulse, Rob	Douglas, Jonathan	Cresswell, Richard	Crainey, Stephen	Moore, Ian	Pugh, Danny	Miller, Liam	Walton, Simon	Beckford, Jermaine	Griffiths, Joel	Graham, Danny	Stone, Steve	Rui Marques, Manuel
1	2		8		6		4	9	S*	11			5			10		S*	3			7					S*	
1	2				6		8			11	7		5			9	4	S*	3			10					S*	
1	2		S*	5	6		8	S*	S*	11	7		3			9	4					10						
3	3	0	1	1	3	0	3	1	0	3	2	0	3	0	0	3	2	0	2	0	0	3	0	0	0	0	0	0
			1					1	2									2									2	
										1	1					1												

League Table

	P	W	D	L	F	A	Pts
Reading	46	31	13	2	99	32	106
Sheffield United	46	26	12	8	76	46	90
Watford	46	22	15	9	77	53	81
Preston North End	46	20	20	6	59	30	80
Leeds United	46	21	15	10	57	38	78
Crystal Palace	46	21	12	13	67	48	75
Wolverhampton W	46	16	19	11	50	42	67
Coventry City	46	16	15	15	62	65	63
Norwich City	46	18	8	20	56	65	62
Luton Town	46	17	10	19	66	67	61
Cardiff City	46	16	12	18	58	59	60
Southampton	46	13	19	14	49	50	58
Stoke City	46	17	7	22	54	63	58
Plymouth Argyle	46	13	17	16	39	46	56
Ipswich Town	46	14	14	18	53	66	56
Leicester City	46	13	15	18	51	59	54
Burnley	46	14	12	20	46	54	54
Hull City	46	12	16	18	49	55	52
Sheffield Wednesday	46	13	13	20	39	52	52
Derby County	46	10	20	16	53	67	50
Queen's Park Rangers	46	12	14	20	50	65	50
Crewe Alexandra	46	9	15	22	57	86	42
Millwall	46	8	16	22	35	62	40
Brighton & Hove Albion	46	7	17	22	39	71	38

2006-07

Championship

Manager: Kevin Blackwell unitil November then Dennis Wise

Final Position: 24th

Did you know that?

3 February 2007: Tom Elliott became the first schoolboy to play for Leeds when he came on as a substitute in the 2–1 loss at Norwich, a game which saw Jonny Howson score his first Leeds goal.

6 May 2007: Rob Bayly was sent off on his full debut in the 2–0 defeat at Derby which confirmed United's relegation to the third tier of English football for the first time. When Fabian Delph came on for his debut as a substitute he became the 44th player used that season, equalling the record highest number set in 2004–05 by Kidderminster Harriers.

England Under-21 international defender Matthew Kilgallon joined Sheffield United for £1.75 million in January.

Match No.	Date	Venue	Opponents	Result	FT	HT	Scorers	Attendance
1	Aug 5	H	Norwich City	W	1-0	1-0	Healy (pen)	22,417
2	8	A	Queen's Park R	D	2-2	0-0	Lewis, Horsfield	13,996
3	13	A	Crystal Palace	L	0-1	0-0		17,218
4	19	H	Cardiff City	L	0-1	0-0		18,246
5	27	A	Sheffield Wed	W	1-0	0-0	Healy (pen)	23,792
6	Sep 10	H	Wolverhampton W	L	0-1	0-0		16,268
7	13	H	Sunderland	L	0-3	0-2		23,037
8	16	A	Coventry City	L	0-1	0-1		22,146
9	23	H	Birmingham City	W	3-2	2-1	Healy 2 (1 pen), Tebily (og)	18,898
10	30	A	West Bromwich Alb	L	2-4	0-1	Hosfield, Stone	21,435
11	Oct 14	H	Stoke City	L	0-4	0-1		18,173
12	17	H	Leicester City	L	1-2	0-1	Butler	16,477
13	21	A	Luton Town	L	1-5	1-1	Foxe	10,260
14	28	H	Southend United	W	2-0	1-0	Moore, Blake	19,528
15	31	A	Preston North End	L	1-4	0-2	Healy	16,168
16	Nov 4	A	Barnsley	L	2-3	2-1	Derry, Blake	16,943
17	11	H	Colchester United	W	3-0	1-0	Blake 2 (1 pen), Cresswell	17,628
18	18	H	Southampton	L	0-3	0-1		19,647
19	25	A	Plymouth Argyle	W	2-1	1-1	Blake, Lewis	17,088
20	28	A	Burnley	L	1-2	0-0	Healy	15,061
21	Dec 2	H	Barnsley	D	2-2	2-2	Kandol, Ehiogu	21,378
22	9	H	Derby County	L	0-1	0-1		20,087
23	16	A	Ipswich Town	L	0-1	0-1		23,661
24	23	H	Hull City	D	0-0	0-0		22,578
25	26	A	Sunderland	L	0-2	0-0		40,116
26	30	A	Stoke City	L	1-3	1-1	Moore	18,128
27	Jan 1	H	Coventry City	W	2-1	1-1	Healy, Douglas	18,158
28	20	H	West Bromwich Alb	L	2-3	1-3	Flo, Thompson	20,019
29	30	A	Hull City	W	2-1	1-1	Heath, Thompson	24,311
30	Feb 3	A	Norwich City	L	1-2	1-0	Howson	25,018
31	10	H	Crystal Palace	W	2-1	1-0	Heath, Blake	19,228
32	17	A	Cardiff City	L	0-1	0-1		16,544
33	20	H	Queen's Park R	D	0-0	0-0		29,593
34	24	A	Wolverhampton W	L	0-1	0-0		24,314
35	27	A	Birmingham City	L	0-1	0-1		18,363
36	Mar 3	H	Sheffield Wed	L	2-3	0-2	Bullen (og), Cresswell	25,297
37	10	H	Luton Town	W	1-0	0-0	Cresswell	27,138
38	13	A	Leicester City	D	1-1	1-1	Blake	25,165
39	17	A	Southend United	D	1-1	0-1	Healy	11,274
40	30	H	Preston North End	W	2-1	0-1	Blake, Healy	18,433
41	Apt 7	H	Plymouth Argyle	W	2-1	1-1	Healy, Michalik	30,034
42	9	A	Colchester United	L	1-2	0-0	Lewis	5,916
43	14	H	Burnley	W	1-0	1-0	Heath	23,528
44	21	A	Southampton	L	0-1	0-0		29,012
45	28	H	Ipswich Town	D	1-1	1-0	Cresswell	31,269
46	May 6	A	Derby County	L	0-2	0-1		31,183

* Deducted 10 points by Football League

Appearances
Sub appearances
Two own-goals — Goals

FL Cup

R1	Aug 22	H	Chester City	W	1-0	0-0	Bakke	10,013
R2	Sep 19	H	Barnet	W	3-1	1-0	Blake, Moore 2	7,220
R3	Oct 24	H	Southend United	L	1-3	1-2	Moore	10,449

Appearances
Sub appearances
Goals

FA Cup

R3	Jan 6	A	West Bromwich Alb	L	1-3	0-2	Robinson (og)	16,957

Appearances
Sub appearances
One own-goal — Goals

Warner, Tony	Kelly, Gary	Crainey, Stephen	Derry, Shaun	Butler, Paul	Kilgallon, Matt	Stone, Steve	Bakke, Erik	Healy, David	Horsfield, Geoff	Lewis, Eddie	Moore, Ian	Westlake, Ian	Carole, Seb	Richardson, Frazer	Blake, Robbie	Beckford, Jermaine	Foxe, Hayden	Douglas, Jonathan	Nicholls, Kevin	Gregan, Sean	Sullivan Neil	Wright, Alan	Cresswell, Richard	Johnson, Adam	Stack, Graham	Einarsson, Gylfi	Heath, Matt	Kandol, Tresor	Ehiogu, Ugo	Howson, Jonathan	Elliott, Robbie	Rui Marques, Manuel	Sá, Armando	Thompson, Alan	Flo, Tore Andre	Elliott, Tom	Ankergren, Casper	Johnson, Jemal	Kishishev, Radostin	Michalik, Lubomir	Gray, Michael	Bayly, Robert	Delph, Fabian
1	2	3	4	5	6	7	8	9	10	11	S*	S*	S*																														
1	2	3	4	5	6	7	8	9	10	11	S*	S*	S*																														
1	2	3	4	5	6	7		9	10	11	S*	8	S*	S*																													
1	2	3	4	5	6	7	S*	9		11		8	S*		10	S*																											
1	2	3	4	5	6			9		11	10	8	7				S*																										
1	2	3		5	6	S*		9		11	10	8	7			S*		4																									
1	2	3		5	6	7		9	10	11		8	S*		S*			4	S*																								
1	2	3		5	6	S*		9	10			8	7		S*			S*	11	4																							
1	2	3	4	5	6	S*		9	10	11	S*	S*						7	8																								
1	2	3	4	5	6	S*		9	10	11	S*	S*						7	8																								
	2		4	5	6	S*		9	10	11		8			S*			7			1	3	S*																				
	2	3	4	5	6			9			11	S*			S*		S*	7			1		10	8																			
	2	3	4	5				S*		S*	S*	8			9		6	7			1		10	11																			
	2		4	5	6			9		3	11	S*		S*	S*			7					10	8	1																		
	2		4	5	6			9	S*	3	7	8			S*								10	11	1																		
	2		4	5	6			9	10	3		8			11			7					S*	S*	1	S*																	
		2	8		6				9	3	S*	S*			11	S*	4	7					10		1		5																
		3	4		6			9	10	11	S*				8	S*	2	7							1		5																
		3	4		6					11	9	8	S*		10		2	7							1		5	S*															
		3	4					S*	S*	11	9	8			10		2	7							1		5	S*	6														
		3	4					S*		11	9	8	S*	S*	10			2							1		5	7	6														
		3	4					9		11	S*		S*		8		2	7							1		5	10	6														
			4					S*	S*	11	9	3	S*	2			6	7	8						1		5	10															
1			4					S*		11	_	3		2	9			7									5	10	6	8													
1			8		S*			S*		11	S*	3		2		9	4	7									5	10	6														
1			4					9		11	10	3		2				7									5	S*	6	8													
								9		11	10	S*		2	8		5	7	4		1							S*		S*	3	6											
								9		11	S*				7		5		4		1					S*		S*			3	6	2	8	10								
		S*						9		11				3	S*			7			1					S*	5	10		4		6	2	8									
											S*			2	9			7	4		1						5	10		8		6	3	11		S*							
										3	9	8		2	11		S*	7	4				S*				5	10				6	S*				1						
								S*		3	9	8			11		S*	7	4				S*				5	10				6	2				1						
								9		3					8		S*	7	4				10				5			S*		6	2	11			1	S*					
								9		3	S*		11	2	8			7	4				10				5					6				S*	1						
								9		3	S*			2	11			7	4				10		1		5			8		6	S*					S*					
								9		3	8		S*	2	S*			7					10		1		5			4		6							11				
								S*		3	S*		4	2	9			7					10				5						S*				1	8	11	6			
								S*			S*		4	2	9			7					10				5						3	S*			1	8	11	6			
								S*		11	S*			2	8			7					10				5	9			3						1		4	6			
								9		11	_			2	8			7					10				5				S*	S*					1		4	6	3		
								9		11	S*			2	8			7					10				5					S*		S*			1		4	6	3		
								9		11					S*			7									5	10				2		8			1		4	6	3		
								9		11				2	7								10				5					S*	S*	8			1		4	6	3		
								9		11				2	7		S*						10				5	S*			3	6	S*	8			1		4				
								9		11	S*			2	7		5						10					S*			S*	6	_	8			1		4		3		
													7		9		5						10							S*	6	2		8		S*	1	11			3	4	S*
13	16	18	23	16	18	5	2	31	11	40	14	19	7	19	27	1	12	34	12	1	7	1	18	4	12	0	26	11	6	6	5	14	6	9	1	0	14	3	10	7	6	1	0
		1			1	5	1	10	3	1	19	8	10	3	9	4	6	1	1				4	1		3		7		3	2	3	5	2		3		2					1
			1	1		1		10	2	3	2				8		1	1					4				3	1	1	1				2	1					1			

		3			S*		4	S*		11	S*	8	7	2	10	9	5			6	1																						
	2	3	S*		6	7			9	11	S*				10		5	4	8		1									S*													
1	2	3		5	6			9		11	10	4		8	S*			7					S*																			S*	
1	2	3	0	1	2	1	1	1	1	3	1	2	1	2	2	1	2	2	1	1	2	0	0	0	0	0	0	0	0	0	0	0	0	0	0	0	0	0	0	0	0	0	0
			1		1			1			2				1								1							1												1	
							1				3				1																												

			S*					9		11	10				7		5		4		1						6			8	3	2	S*		S*								
0	0	0	0	0	0	0	0	1	0	1	1	0	0	0	1	0	1	0	1	0	1	0	0	0	0	0	1	0	0	1	1	1	0	0	0	0	0	0	0	0	0	0	0
			1																														1		1								

League Table

	P	W	D	L	F	A	Pts
Sunderland	46	27	7	12	76	47	88
Birmingham City	46	26	8	12	67	42	86
Derby County	46	25	9	12	62	46	84
West Bromwich Albion	46	22	10	14	81	55	76
Wolverhampton	46	22	10	14	59	56	76
Southampton	46	21	12	13	77	53	75
Preston North End	46	22	8	16	64	53	74
Stoke City	46	19	16	11	62	41	73
Sheffield Wednesday	46	20	11	15	70	66	71
Colchester United	46	20	9	17	70	56	69
Plymouth Argyle	46	17	16	13	63	62	67
Crystal Palace	46	18	11	17	59	51	65
Cardiff City	46	17	13	16	57	53	64
Ipswich Town	46	18	8	20	64	59	62
Burnley	46	15	12	19	52	49	57
Norwich City	46	16	9	21	56	71	57
Coventry City	46	16	8	22	47	62	56
Queen's Park Rangers	46	14	11	21	54	68	53
Leicester City	46	13	14	19	49	64	53
Barnsley	46	15	5	26	53	85	50
Hull City	46	13	10	23	51	67	49
Southend United	46	10	12	24	47	80	42
Luton Town	46	10	10	26	53	81	40
Leeds United*	46	13	7	26	46	72	36

*Leeds United deducted 10 points

2007-08

League One

Manager: Dennis Wise to January then Gary McAllister MBE

Final Position: 5th

Did you know that?

29 September 2007: Hopes of a club record-breaking eight successive victories from the start of the season ended at Gillingham where referee Danny McDermid sent off strikers Tresor Kandol and Jermaine Beckford. Nine-man United held on to their 1–0 lead until Ian Cox's last-minute equaliser.

3 May 2008: The final day Elland Road attendance of 38,256 against Gillingham was the highest in the Football League that season by a wide margin.

The free-scoring Jermaine Beckford helped steer United to the Play-off Final at Wembley.

Match No.	Date		Venue	Opponents	Result	FT	HT	Scorers	Attendance
1	Aug	11	A	Tranmere Rovers	W	2-1	0-1	Heath, Kandol	11,008
2		18	H	Southend United	W	4-1	1-0	Thompson, Flo, Rui Marques, Beckford	24,036
3		25	A	Nottingham Forest	W	2-1	1-0	Kandol, Beckford	25,237
4	Sep	1	H	Luton Town	W	1-0	1-0	Kandol	26,856
5		8	H	Hartlepool United	W	2-0	1-0	Kandol, Beckford	26,877
6		14	A	Bristol Rovers	W	3-0	1-0	Beckford 2, Kandol	11,833
7		22	H	Swansea City	W	2-0	0-0	Beckford, Prutton	29,467
8		29	A	Gillingham	D	1-1	1-0	Carole	8,719
9	Oct	2	A	Oldham Athletic	W	1-0	0-0	Westlake	10,054
10		6	H	Yeovil Town	W	1-0	0-0	De Vries	27,808
11		13	H	Leyton Orient	D	1-1	0-1	Carole	29,177
12		20	A	Brighton & HA	W	1-0	0-0	Kandol	8,691
13		27	H	Millwall	W	4-2	1-0	Prutton, Beckford, Douglas 2	30,319
14	Nov	3	A	Carlisle United	L	1-3	1-0	Beckford	16,668
15		6	A	Bournemouth	W	3-1	1-1	Kandol 2, Carole	9,632
16		17	H	Swindon Town	W	2-1	1-0	Beckford 2 (1 pen)	27,900
17		25	A	Cheltenham Town	L	0-1	0-0		7,043
18	Dec	4	H	Port Vale	W	3-0	1-0	Prutton, Beckford, Flo	20,301
19		8	H	Huddersfield Town	W	4-0	1-0	Douglas, Beckford 2, Flo	32,501
20		15	A	Walsall	D	1-1	0-0	Thompson	10,102
21		22	H	Bristol Rovers	W	1-0	0-0	Howson	27,863
22		26	A	Hartlepool United	D	1-1	0-1	Beckford	7,784
23		29	A	Swansea City	L	2-3	1-3	Beckford, Thompson	19,010
24	Jan	1	H	Oldham Athletic	L	1-3	0-3	Constantine	25,906
25		5	H	Northampton Town	W	3-0	1-0	Richardson, Rui Marques, Weston	24,472
26		14	A	Crewe Alexandra	W	1-0	1-0	Beckford	6,771
27		19	H	Doncaster Rovers	L	0-1	0-1		31,402
28		26	A	Luton Town	D	1-1	1-0	Huntington	9,297
29		29	A	Southend United	L	0-1	0-1		9,819
30	Feb	2	H	Tranmere Rovers	L	0-2	0-0		24,907
31		9	A	Northampton Town	D	1-1	1-0	Howson	7,260
32		12	H	Nottingham Forest	D	1-1	0-0	Beckford (pen)	29,552
33		23	H	Crewe Alexandra	D	1-1	0-0	Kandol	21,223
34	Mar	1	A	Swindon Town	W	1-0	1-0	Kandol	13,270
35		8	H	Bournemouth	W	2-0	1-0	Johnson, Kilkenny	21,199
36		11	H	Cheltenham Town	L	1-2	0-1	Elding	20,257
37		15	A	Port Vale	D	3-3	2-0	Rio Marques, Freedman 2	7,908
38		22	H	Walsall	W	2-0	1-0	Beckford 2	19,095
39		29	H	Brighton & HA	D	0-0	0-0		22,575
40	Apr	1	A	Doncaster Rovers	W	1-0	1-0	Sheehan	15,001
41		5	A	Leyton Orient	W	2-0	1-0	Johnson, Beckford	7,602
42		12	H	Carlisle United	W	3-2	0-1	Freedman 2, Howson	28,530
43		15	A	Huddersfield Town	L	0-1	0-0		16,413
44		19	A	Millwall	W	2-0	0-0	Prutton, Hughes	13,895
45		25	A	Yeovil Town	W	1-0	1-0	Freedman	9,527
46	May	3	H	Gillingham	W	2-1	0-1	Johnson, Kandol	38,256

* Deducted 15 points by Football League

Appearances
Sub appearances
Goals

FL Cup

R1	Aug	14	A	Macclesfield Town	W	1-0	0-0	Westlake	3,422
R2		28	A	Portsmouth	L	0-3	0-1		8,502

Appearances
Sub appearances
Goals

FA Cup

R1	Nov	9	A	Hereford United	D	0-0	0-0		5,924
Rep		20	H	Hereford United	L	0-1	0-1		11,315

Appearances
Sub appearances
Goals

FL Trophy

R2	Oct	9	A	Darlington	W	1-0	0-0	Huntington	7,891
QF			H	Bury	L	1-2	1-2	Constantine	18,809

Appearances
Sub appearances
Goals

Play-offs

	May	12	H	Carlisle United	L	1-2	0-1	Freedman	36,297
		15	A	Carlisle United	W	2-0	1-0	Howson 2	12,873
F		25	N	Doncaster Rovers	L	0-1†	0-0		75,132

† At Wembley, London

Appearances
Sub appearances
Goals

Ankergren, Casper	Richardson, Frazer	Lewis, Eddie	Westlake, Ian	Heath, Matt	Rui Marques, Manuel	Weston, Curtis	Thompson, Alan	Beckford, Jermaine	Kandol, Tresor	Hughes, Andy	Flo, Tore Andre	Howson, Jonathan	Douglas, Jonathan	Prutton, David	Parker, Ben	Carole, Seb	Clapham, Jamie	Huntington, Paul	De Vries, Mark	Andrews, Wayne	Da Costa, Filipe	Constantine, Leon	Kishishev, Radostin	Lucas, David	Kilkenny, Neil	Kenton, Darren	Sweeney, Peter	Johnson, Bradley	Sheehan, Alan	Michalik, Lubomir	Elding, Anthony	Freedman, Dougie	Gardner, Scott	Delph, Fabian	Elliott, Tom	Ameobi, Tomi	Bayly, Robert	Madden, Simon
1	2	3	4	5	6	7	8	9	10	11	S*	S*																										
1	2		11	5	6		8	9	10	3	S*		4	7	S*	S*																						
1	2			5	6		8	9	10		S*	S*	4	7	S*	11	3																					
1	2			5	6		8	9	10	3			4	7		11	S*																					
1	2		S*	5	6			9	10	8		4		7		11	3	S*																				
1	2		S*	5	6			9	10	8			4	7		11	3	S*																				
1	2		S*	5	6			9	10	8	S*		4	7		11	3																					
1	2		S*	5	6	S*		9	10	8			4	7		11	3	S*																				
1	2		S*	5	6		8			3			4	7		11			9	10																		
1	2		S*	5	6			9	10	8	S*		4	7		11	3		S*																			
1	2		S*	5	6		8	9	10	4				7		11	3		S*		S*																	
1	2		S*	5	6			9	10	8			4	7		11	3		S*																			
1	2		8	5	6	S*		9	10				4	7		11	3				S*																	
1	2			5	6			9	10	8			4	7		11	3	S*			S*	S*																
1	2			5	6	S*		9	10	8			4	7		11	3				S*																	
1	2			5	6			9	10	8		4		7		11	3		S*			S*	S*															
	2		S*	5	6			9	10	8	S*		4	7	3	11			S*					1														
1	2		11	5	6		S*	9	10	3	S*	S*	4	7									8															
1	2		11	5	6			9	10	3	S*	S*	4	7		S*							8															
1	2		11	5	6		S*	9		3	S*	S*	4	7								10	8															
1	2		11	5	6		8	9	10	3	S*	4		7		S*							S*															
1	2		11	5	6		S*	9	10	3	S*	4		7		S*							8															
1	2		11	5	6	S*	3	9	10	8	S*	4		S*		7																						
1	2			5	6		8	9	10	3	S*			7	S*	11						S*	4															
1	2		11		6	S*		9	S*	8	10			7	3	S*		5							4													
1	2							9	S*	8	10			7	3			5							4	6	11	S*										
1	2			S*		S*		9	S*	8	10				3			5							4	6	11	7										
1	2		S*					9	10	8	S*			7	3			5								6	11	4										
	2							9	10	11	S*			7	3	S*		5						1	4	6	8	S*										
				5				9		8	S*	4		7		S*		S*						1		3		11	2	6	10							
1					6			9	10	8	S*	4		7												3	S*	11	2	5								
1					6			9	10	8	S*	4		7												3	S*	11	2	5	S*							
1	2				6				10		9	4		7		S*										3	8	S*	11	5	S*							
1	2				6		S*	9	10			8		7											4	3		11		5								
1	3				6			9	10	S*		8		7											4	2		11		5	S*	S*						
1	3				6			9	10	S*		8		7											4	2		11		5	S*	S*						
1					6			9	S*	3		8		7		S*									4	2		11		5		10						
1					6			9	S*			8	S*	7											4	2		11	3	5		10						
1					6			9	S*			8	S*	7											4	2		11	3	5	S*	10						
1	2							9		S*		8	7					6							4			11	3	5		10						
1	2							9	S*	S*		8	7	S*				6							4			11	3	5		10						
1	2							9	S*	S*		8	7	S*				6							4	3		11		5		10						
1	2								9	S*		8	7	S*		S*		6							4	3		11		5		10						
1	2								S*	S*		8		7				6							4		S*	11	3	5	9	10						
1	2				S*					S*		8	7	S*				6							4			11	3	5	9	10						
1					S*				10	8			4	7		S*		6									3	11		5	9		2	S*				
43	39	1	10	25	34	1	9	40	32	32	4	21	22	38	6	17	12	12	1	1	0	1	5	3	16	16	6	18	10	17	4	9	1	0	0	0	0	0
			10	1	2	6	4		9	8	18	5	2	5	3	11	1	5	5		4	3	2				3	3			5	2		1				
	1		1	1	3	1	3	20	11	1	3	3	3	4		3		1	1			1			1			3	1		1	5						

Ankergren, Casper	Richardson, Frazer	Lewis, Eddie	Westlake, Ian	Heath, Matt	Rui Marques, Manuel	Weston, Curtis	Thompson, Alan	Beckford, Jermaine	Kandol, Tresor	Hughes, Andy	Flo, Tore Andre	Howson, Jonathan	Douglas, Jonathan	Prutton, David	Parker, Ben	Carole, Seb	Clapham, Jamie	Huntington, Paul	De Vries, Mark	Andrews, Wayne	Da Costa, Filipe	Constantine, Leon	Kishishev, Radostin	Lucas, David	Kilkenny, Neil	Kenton, Darren	Sweeney, Peter	Johnson, Bradley	Sheehan, Alan	Michalik, Lubomir	Elding, Anthony	Freedman, Dougie	Gardner, Scott	Delph, Fabian	Elliott, Tom	Ameobi, Tomi	Bayly, Robert	Madden, Simon
1		3	S*	5		S*		S*	10			8	7	4	6	11																	2		9			
1	2			5	6			S*	10			8	7	4	3	11																		S*		9	S*	
2	1	1	0	2	1	0	0	0	2	0	0	2	2	2	2	2	0	0	0	0	0	0	0	0	0	0	0	0	0	0	0	0	1	0	1	1	0	0
			1			1		2																										1			1	
			1																																			

Ankergren, Casper	Richardson, Frazer	Lewis, Eddie	Westlake, Ian	Heath, Matt	Rui Marques, Manuel	Weston, Curtis	Thompson, Alan	Beckford, Jermaine	Kandol, Tresor	Hughes, Andy	Flo, Tore Andre	Howson, Jonathan	Douglas, Jonathan	Prutton, David	Parker, Ben	Carole, Seb	Clapham, Jamie	Huntington, Paul	De Vries, Mark	Andrews, Wayne	Da Costa, Filipe	Constantine, Leon	Kishishev, Radostin	Lucas, David	Kilkenny, Neil	Kenton, Darren	Sweeney, Peter	Johnson, Bradley	Sheehan, Alan	Michalik, Lubomir	Elding, Anthony	Freedman, Dougie	Gardner, Scott	Delph, Fabian	Elliott, Tom	Ameobi, Tomi	Bayly, Robert	Madden, Simon
1				5	6	7		9	10			8		4	3	11	S*	2			S*	S*																
1	2		4	5		S*		9	10	11		8			3	7		6				S*		S*														
2	1	0	1	2	1	1	0	2	2	1	0	2	0	1	2	2	0	2	0	0	0	0	0	0	0	0	0	0	0	0	0	0	0	0	0	0	0	0
						1											1				1	2		1														

Ankergren, Casper	Richardson, Frazer	Lewis, Eddie	Westlake, Ian	Heath, Matt	Rui Marques, Manuel	Weston, Curtis	Thompson, Alan	Beckford, Jermaine	Kandol, Tresor	Hughes, Andy	Flo, Tore Andre	Howson, Jonathan	Douglas, Jonathan	Prutton, David	Parker, Ben	Carole, Seb	Clapham, Jamie	Huntington, Paul	De Vries, Mark	Andrews, Wayne	Da Costa, Filipe	Constantine, Leon	Kishishev, Radostin	Lucas, David	Kilkenny, Neil	Kenton, Darren	Sweeney, Peter	Johnson, Bradley	Sheehan, Alan	Michalik, Lubomir	Elding, Anthony	Freedman, Dougie	Gardner, Scott	Delph, Fabian	Elliott, Tom	Ameobi, Tomi	Bayly, Robert	Madden, Simon
	2		11	6		7	8					4			3		S*	5	9	10	S*			1												S*		
				S*	6				S*			4	7	S*	3	11		5	9		8	10		1														2
0	1	0	1	1	1	1	1	0	0	0	0	2	1	0	2	1	0	2	2	1	1	1	0	2	0	0	0	0	0	0	0	0	0	0	0	0	0	1
				1					1					1			1				1															1		
																		1				1																

Ankergren, Casper	Richardson, Frazer	Lewis, Eddie	Westlake, Ian	Heath, Matt	Rui Marques, Manuel	Weston, Curtis	Thompson, Alan	Beckford, Jermaine	Kandol, Tresor	Hughes, Andy	Flo, Tore Andre	Howson, Jonathan	Douglas, Jonathan	Prutton, David	Parker, Ben	Carole, Seb	Clapham, Jamie	Huntington, Paul	De Vries, Mark	Andrews, Wayne	Da Costa, Filipe	Constantine, Leon	Kishishev, Radostin	Lucas, David	Kilkenny, Neil	Kenton, Darren	Sweeney, Peter	Johnson, Bradley	Sheehan, Alan	Michalik, Lubomir	Elding, Anthony	Freedman, Dougie	Gardner, Scott	Delph, Fabian	Elliott, Tom	Ameobi, Tomi	Bayly, Robert	Madden, Simon
1	2							9	S*	S*		8	7	11		S*		6							4			3		5		10						
1	2							9				8	7	11				6							4			3		5		10						
1	2							9	S*	S*		8	7	11				6							4			3		5		10						
3	3	0	0	0	0	0	0	3	0	0	0	3	3	3	0	0	0	3	0	0	0	0	0	0	3	0	0	3	0	3	0	3	0	0	0	0	0	0
									2	2						1																						
												2																				1						

League Table

	P	W	D	L	F	A	Pts
Swansea	46	27	11	8	82	42	92
Nottingham Forest	46	22	16	8	64	32	82
Doncaster Rovers	46	23	11	12	68	41	80
Carlisle United	46	23	11	12	64	46	80
Leeds United*	46	27	10	9	72	38	76
Southend United	46	22	10	14	70	55	76
Brighton & Hove Albion	46	19	12	15	57	49	69
Oldham Athletic	46	18	13	15	58	46	67
Northampton Town	46	17	15	14	60	55	66
Huddersfield Town	46	20	6	20	50	62	66
Tranmere Rovers	46	18	11	17	52	47	65
Walsall	46	16	16	14	51	45	64
Swindon Town	46	16	13	17	62	56	61
Leyton Orient	46	16	12	18	49	62	60
Hartlepool United	46	15	9	22	63	66	54
Bristol Rovers	46	12	17	17	45	56	53
Millwall	46	14	10	22	45	60	52
Yeovil Town	46	14	10	22	38	59	52
Cheltenham Town	46	13	12	21	42	64	51
Crewe Alexandra	46	12	14	20	47	65	50
Bournemouth**	46	17	7	22	62	72	48
Gillingham	46	11	13	22	44	73	46
Port Vale	46	9	11	26	47	81	38
Luton Town***	46	11	10	25	43	63	33

*Leeds United deducted 15 points
**Bournemouth deducted 10 points
***Luton Town deducted 10 points

2008-09

League One

Manager: Gary McAllister MBE until December then Simon Grayson

Final Position: 4th

Did you know that?

30 November 2008: United lost to non-League opposition in the FA Cup for the first time when they were beaten 1–0 at Histon.

2 May 2009: Robert Snodgrass netted United's 100th goal of the season with a spectacular scissor kick in the 3–0 triumph against Northampton. It was the 11th successive League win at Elland Road, the club's best run for 40 years.

United came unstuck at muddy non-League Histon in the FA Cup. Here Robert Snodgrass is tackled by a home defender.

Match No.	Date		Venue	Opponents	Result	FT	HT	Scorers	Attendance
1	Aug	9	A	Scunthorpe United	W	2-1	0-0	Showunmi, Beckford	8,315
2		16	H	Oldham Athletic	L	0-2	0-0		24,631
3		23	A	Yeovil Town	D	1-1	1-0	Becchio	6,580
4		30	H	Bristol Rovers	D	2-2	1-2	Elliott (og), Beckford	21,024
5	Sep	6	H	Crewe Alexandra	W	5-2	2-0	Delph, Sheehan, Douglas, Beckford, Robinson	20,075
6		13	A	Swindon Town	W	3-1	1-1	Beckford 2, Kilkenny	13,001
7		20	A	Carlisle United	W	2-0	1-0	Becchio, Beckford	12,148
8		27	H	Hereford United	W	1-0	0-0	Robinson	25,676
9	Oct	4	A	Peterborough U	L	0-2	0-0		13,191
10		11	H	Brighton & HA	W	3-1	2-0	Becchio, Beckford 2	22,726
11		18	A	Millwall	L	1-3	1-1	Becchio	13,041
12		21	H	Leyton Orient	W	2-1	2-1	Purches (og), Becchio	18,990
13		25	H	Walsall	W	3-0	0-0	Becchio, Delph 2	22,422
14		28	A	Southend United	L	0-1	0-1		10,132
15	Nov	1	A	Cheltenham United	W	1-0	1-0	Becchio	5,726
16		15	H	Huddersfield Town	L	1-2	1-0	Snodgrass	32,028
17		22	H	Hartlepool United	W	4-1	1-1	Beckford 2, Delph, Becchio	21,182
18		26	A	Northampton Town	L	1-2	0-1	Beckford	6,008
19	Dec	6	A	Tranmere Rovers	L	1-2	1-1	Showunmi	8,700
20		13	H	Colchester United	L	1-2	1-1	Snodgrass	19,625
21		20	A	Milton Keynes Dons	L	1-3	0-2	Snodgrass	17,073
22		26	H	Leicester City	D	1-1	0-1	Snodgrass	33,580
23		28	A	Stockport County	W	3-1	1-1	Becchio, Delph, Christie	10,723
24	Jan	10	H	Carlisle United	L	0-2	0-2		22,411
25		17	A	Brighton & HA	W	2-0	0-0	Trundle, Delph	7,096
26		24	H	Peterborough U	W	3-1	0-0	Beckford 2, Howson	22,766
27		27	H	Southend United	W	2-0	2-0	Rui Marques, Naylor	20,392
28		31	A	Walsall	L	0-1	0-1		8,920
29	Feb	9	H	Millwall	W	2-0	1-0	Beckford 2	19,314
30		14	A	Huddersfield Town	L	0-1	0-1		20,928
31		17	A	Hereford United	L	0-2	0-1		6,120
32		21	H	Cheltenham United	W	2-0	0-0	Howson 2	20,131
33		28	H	Scunthorpe United	W	3-2	2-1	Beckford 2, Johnson	24,921
34	Mar	2	A	Oldham Athletic	D	1-1	0-0	Becchio	7,835
35		7	A	Bristol Rovers	D	2-2	1-1	Becchio, Snodgrass	10,293
36		10	H	Yeovil Town	W	4-0	2-0	Beckford 3, Kilkenny	18,847
37		14	H	Swindon Town	W	1-0	0-0	Beckford	21,765
38		21	A	Crewe Alexandra	W	3-2	3-0	Kilkenny, Becchio, Snodgrass	7,138
39		28	H	Milton Keynes Dons	W	2-0	1-0	Beckford 2	27,649
40	Apr	4	A	Colchester United	W	1-0	1-0	Becchio	9,559
41		7	A	Leyton Orient	D	2-2	1-0	Snodgrass 2 (1 pen)	6,943
42		11	H	Stockport County	W	1-0	1-0	Howson	24,967
43		13	A	Leicester City	L	0-1	0-0		25,507
44		18	H	Tranmere Rovers	W	3-1	2-1	Beckford, Kilkenny, Becchio	24,360
45		25	A	Hartlepool United	W	1-0	0-0	Beckford	6,402
46	May	2	H	Northampton Town	W	3-0	1-0	Becchio, Beckford, Snodgrass	34,214

Appearances
Sub appearances
Two own-goals — Goals

FL Cup

R1	Aug	12	A	Chester City	W	5-2	5-1	Beckford 3, Snodgrass, Robinson	3,644
R2		26	H	Crystal Palace	W	4-0	2-0	Douglas, Beckford, Becchio, Showunmi	10,765
R3	Sep	23	H	Hartlepool United	W	3-2	1-2	Snodgrass, Showunmi, Robinson	14,599
R4	Nov	11	A	Derby County	L	1-2	1-2	Becchio	18,540

Appearances
Sub appearances
Goals

FA Cup

R1	Nov	7	H	Northampton Town	D	1-1	1-1	Robinson (pen)	9,531
Rep		17	A	Northampton Town	W	5-2	4-1	Beckford 3, Hughes (og), Parker	3,960
R2		30	A	Histon	L	0-1	0-1		4,500

Appearances
Sub appearances
One own-goal — Goals

FL Trophy

R1	Sep	2	H	Bradford City	W	2-1	2-0	Robinson (pen), Becchio	20,128
R2	Oct	8	A	Rotherham United	L	2-4	1-2	Howson, Showunmi	4,658

Appearances
Sub appearances
Goals

Play-offs

	May	9	A	Millwall	L	0-1	0-0		13,228
		14	H	Millwall	D	1-1	0-0	Becchio	37,036

Appearances
Sub appearances
Goals

Ankergren, Casper	Richardson, Frazer	Sheehan, Alan	Howson, Jonathan	Huntington, Paul	Rui Marques, Manuel	Prutton, David	Snodgrass, Robert	Beckford, Jermaine	Showunmi, Enoch	Robinson, Andy	Becchio, Luciano	Hughes, Andy	Delph, Fabian	Douglas, Jonathan	Lucas, David	Johnson, Bradley	Kilkenny, Neil	Michalik, Lubomir	Telfer, Paul	White, Aidan	Parker, Ben	Christie, Malcolm	Assoumani, Mansoor	Trundle, Lee	Dickinson, Carl	Naylor, Richard	Grella, Mike	Dickinson, Liam	Sodje, Sam	Webb, Jonathan
1	2	3	4	5	6	7	8	9	10	11	S*	S*																		
1	2	3	4	5	6	7	8	9	10	11	S*		S*																	
1	2	3	4	5	6	7	8	9	S*	11	10		S*	S*																
	2		S*	5			S*	9	S*		10	8	11	7	1	3	4	6												
	2	3	S*				S*	9		S*	10	7	11	8	1		4	6	5											
	2	3	S*		6	S*	S*	9			10	11	8	7	1		4		5											
	2		S*		6		S*	9		S*	10	11	8	7	1		4		5	3										
	2		4		6		S*	9		11	10	S*	8	7	1				5	3										
1	2		4		6		S*	9		11	10		8	7			S*		5	3	S*									
	2				6			9			10	8	11	7	1		4	5		3										
	2				6		S*	9	S*		10	11	8	7	1		4	5		3										
	2		8			S*		9		S*	10		11	7	1		4	6	5		3									
1	2		8			S*	S*	9		S*	10		11	7			4	6	5		3									
1	2		8				S*	9		S*	10		11	7			4	6	5		3									
1	2		8			S*	S*	9		S*	10		11	7			4	6	5		3									
1	2		S*			S*	9	S*		8	10		11	7			4	6	5		3									
						7	S*	9		8	10	2	11	4	1			6	5		3									
			S*			7	S*	9		11	10	2	4	8	1			6	5		3									
	2	3	4		6	7	8		9		10			11	1		S*		5											
		3	_		6	7	9		S*		10	2	11	8	1		4		5			S*								
	S*	3	8		6		9		S*		10		11	7	1		4	5					2							
1	2	3	S*		6	7	S*	9		11	10	S*	4	8				5												
1	2	3	S*		6	S*	8	9			10	11	4	7				5				S*								
1	2	3			6		8			S*	10	11	4	7		S*		5				9		S*						
1	2		S*		6					S*	10	8	4	7		11						S*		9	3	5				
1			S*		6		S*	S*		8	10	2	4	7		11								9	3	5				
1			S*		6		S*	9		8	S*	2	4	7		11								10	3	5				
1			S*		6		S*	9		8	S*	2	4	7		11								10	3	5				
1			S*		6		8	9		11	S*	2	4	7		S*								10	3	5				
1			S*		6		8			11	9	2	4	7				S*						10	3	5	S*			
1			8		6	S*	7			11	9		4			S*					3			10	2	5	S*			
1			8		6		10			11	9	2	4	7			S*				3			S*		5	S*			
1			8		6		10	9		11			4	2		S*	7	S*			3			S*		5				
1					6		7	9			10		4	2		11	8				3					5				
1			4		6	S*	7	9			10		11	2			8				3					5				
1			8		6		7	9			10		11	2		S*	4				3					5	S*			
1			8		6		7	9			10		11	2		S*	4				3					5	S*	S*		
1			8		6		7				10		11	2		S*	4	S*			3					5	S*	9		
1			8				7	9			10	S*	11	2			4	S*			3					5		S*	6	
1			8				7	9		S*	10	S*	11	2			4				3					5		S*	6	
1			8		6		7			S*	10	S*	11	2			4				3					5		9		
1			8		6		7			S*	10		11	2			4				3					5	S*	9		
1			8				7			S*	10	S*	11	2			4				3					5	S*	9	6	
1			8				7	9		11	10	S*		2		S*	4				3					5	S*		6	
1			8					9		7	10	S*		2		11	4				3					5	S*	S*	6	
1	S*		8		6		S*	9		7	10		11	2			4				3					5	S*			
33	21	11	26	4	32	8	25	32	3	20	40	18	40	42	13	7	27	15	14	5	23	1	1	7	7	22	0	4	5	0
	2		14			8	17	2	5	12	5	9	2	1		8	3	4			1	3		3			11	4		
		1	4		1		9	26	2	2	15		6	1		1	4					1		1		1				

1	2	3	4	5	6		8	9	S*	11	10		7	S*		S*														
	2		S*					9	S*		10	8	11	7	1	S*	4	6	5	3										
1			8	5		7	9	S*	10	11	S*	2	S*				4	6			3									
1	2		S*				9	S*		8	10		11	7			4	6	5	S*	3									
3	3	1	2	2	1	1	3	2	1	3	3	2	3	2	1	0	3	3	2	1	2	0	0	0	0	0	0	0	0	0
			2					2	2		1		1	1		2				1										
							2	4	2	2	2			1																

1	2		4				9		S*	8	10		11	7				6	5	S*	3									
			8			7		9	S*		S*	2		11	1		4	6	5		3	10								S*
	2	3	S*		5		8		S*	11	10	9	4	7	1			6												
1	2	1	2	0	1	1	2	1	0	2	2	2	2	3	2	0	1	3	2	0	2	1	0	0	0	0	0	0	0	0
			1						3		1									1										1
								3		1											1									

	2		8	5	6	7	9		10	11	S*		S*		1	S*	4			3										
		S*	8		6	7	9	S*	10	11	S*	2			1		4	5			3									
0	1	0	2	1	2	2	2	0	2	2	0	1	0	0	2	0	2	1	0	1	1	0	0	0	0	0	0	0	0	0
		1						1			2		1			1														
			1						1	1	1																			

1			8				7	9		S*	10		11	2		S*	4				3					5			6	
1			8				7	9		S*	10		11	2		S*	4				3					5	S*		6	
2	0	0	2	0	0	0	2	2	0	0	2	0	2	2	0	0	2	0	0	0	2	0	0	0	0	2	0	0	2	0
										2						2											1			
											1																			

League Table

	P	W	D	L	F	A	Pts
Leicester City	46	27	15	4	84	39	96
Peterborough United	46	26	11	9	78	54	89
Milton Keynes Dons	46	26	9	11	83	47	87
Leeds United	46	26	6	14	77	49	84
Millwall	46	25	7	14	63	53	82
Scunthorpe United	46	22	10	14	82	63	76
Tranmere Rovers	46	21	11	14	62	49	74
Southend United	46	21	8	17	58	61	71
Huddersfield Town	46	18	14	14	62	65	68
Oldham Athletic	46	16	17	13	66	65	65
Bristol Rovers	46	17	12	17	79	61	63
Colchester United	46	18	9	19	58	58	63
Walsall	46	17	10	19	61	66	61
Leyton Orient	46	15	11	20	45	57	56
Swindon Town	46	12	17	17	68	71	53
Brighton & Hove Albion	46	13	13	20	54	69	52
Yeovil Town	46	12	15	19	41	66	51
Stockport County*	46	16	12	18	59	57	50
Hartlepool United	46	13	11	22	66	79	50
Carlisle United	46	12	14	20	56	69	50
Northampton Town	46	12	13	21	60	64	49
Crewe Alexandra	46	12	10	24	59	82	46
Cheltenham Town	46	9	12	25	51	91	39
Hereford United	46	9	7	30	42	79	34

*Stockport County deducted 10 points

2009-10

League One

Manager: Simon Grayson

Final Position: 2nd

Did you know that?

5 September 2009: Goals by Mike Grella and Lubomir Michalik beat Stockport 2–0 as United made it the best-ever start to a season with eight victories on the bounce, bettering Don Revie's 1973–74 title winners.

19 September 2009: United made it a club record 15 successive League home wins by beating Gillingham 4–1.

24 April 2010: MK Dons had three players sent off – Matthias Doumbe, David McCracken and Peter Leven – as they crashed 4–1 at Elland Road.

Fans mob Andy Hughes after the promotion-clinching win against Bristol Rovers.

Match No.	Date	Venue	Opponents	Result	FT	HT	Scorers	Attendance
1	Aug 6	H	Exeter City	W	2-1	1-0	Beckford 2	27,681
2	15	A	Wycombe W	W	1-0	0-0	Becchio	8,400
3	18	A	Walsall	W	2-1	0-0	Johnson, Beckford	8,483
4	22	H	Tranmere Rovers	W	3-0	2-0	Johnson, Beckford, Becchio	21,692
5	29	A	Colchester United	W	2-1	0-0	Johnson, Beckford	8,810
6	Sep 5	H	Stockport County	W	2-0	2-0	Grella, Michalik	22,870
7	11	A	Southend United	D	0-0	0-0		10,123
8	19	H	Gillingham	W	4-1	2-0	Johnson 2, Howson, Beckford	21,026
9	26	A	Milton Keynes Dons	W	1-0	0-0	Snodgrass	16,713
10	29	H	Carlisle United	D	1-1	1-0	Beckford	19,673
11	Oct 3	H	Charlton Athletic	D	0-0	0-0		31,838
12	19	H	Norwich City	W	2-1	1-1	Johnson, Beckford	19,912
13	24	A	Millwall	L	1-2	1-1	Kisnorbo	14,165
14	27	A	Bristol Rovers	W	4-0	1-0	Beckford 2, Vokes, Kandol	11,448
15	31	H	Yeovil Town	W	4-0	1-0	Johnson, Gradel, Beckford, Kandol	24,482
16	Nov 21	A	Brighton & HA	W	3-0	2-0	Snodgrass, Beckford, Kilkenny	7,615
17	24	H	Leyton Orient	W	1-0	0-0	Gradel	19,744
18	Dec 1	A	Oldham Athletic	W	2-0	1-0	Kilkenny, Becchio	7,793
19	5	H	Huddersfield Town	D	2-2	1-0	Snodgrass, Gradel	36,723
20	12	A	Brentford	D	0-0	0-0		9,031
21	19	H	Southampton	W	1-0	0-0	Snodgrass	25,948
22	26	H	Hartlepool United	W	3-1	2-1	Beckford 2, Becchio	30,191
23	28	A	Stockport County	W	4-2	1-1	Snodgrass, Beckford, Bromby	7,768
24	Jan 9	H	Wycombe W	D	1-1	1-0	Howson	24,383
25	16	A	Exeter City	L	0-2	0-1		8,549
26	26	A	Swindon Town	L	0-3	0-1		14,508
27	30	H	Colchester United	W	2-0	1-0	Beckford 2 (1 pen)	23,425
28	Feb 6	A	Hartlepool United	D	2-2	1-0	Becchio 2	5,115
29	13	A	Leyton Orient	D	1-1	0-0	Daniels (og)	8,013
30	16	H	Walsall	L	1-2	0-0	McSheffrey	18,941
31	20	H	Brighton & HA	D	1-1	0-0	Snodgrass	24,120
32	23	H	Oldham Athletic	W	2-0	0-0	Becchio 2	17,635
33	27	A	Huddersfield Town	D	2-2	0-1	Howson, Becchio	21,764
34	Mar 6	H	Brentford	D	1-1	0-0	Beckford	25,445
35	9	A	Tranmere Rovers	W	4-1	3-1	Snodgrass, Beckford 2 (1 pen), Becchio	8,346
36	13	A	Southampton	L	0-1	0-1		30,794
37	22	H	Millwall	L	0-2	0-1		21,348
38	27	A	Norwich City	L	0-1	0-0		25,445
39	Apr 3	H	Swindon Town	L	0-3	0-1		27,881
40	5	A	Yeovil Town	W	2-1	2-0	Naylor 2	6,308
41	10	H	Southend United	W	2-0	0-0	Gradel, Becchio	21,650
42	13	A	Carlisle United	W	3-1	1-1	Becchio 2, Gradel	8,728
43	17	A	Gillingham	L	2-3	1-3	Becchio, Beckford (pen)	9,649
44	24	H	Milton Keynes Dons	W	4-1	2-1	Becchio, Gradel, Beckford 2 (1 pen)	25,964
45	May 1	A	Charlton Athletic	L	0-1	0-0		23,198
46	8	H	Bristol Rovers	W	2-1	0-0	Howson, Beckford	38,234
								Appearances
								Sub appearances
							One own-goal	Goals

FL Cup

R1	Aug 10	A	Darlington	W	1-0	0-0	Showunmi	4,487
R2	24	H	Watford	W	2-1*	1-0	Snodgrass 2	14,681
R3	Sep 22	H	Liverpool	L	0-1	0-0		38,168
								Appearances
								Sub appearances
								Goals

* After extra-time

FA Cup

R1	Nov 7	A	Oldham Athletic	W	2-0	1-0	Howson, Grella	5,552
R2	29	A	Kettering Town	D	1-1	0-0	Beckford	4,837
Rep	Dec 8	H	Kettering Town	W	5-1*	1-0	Becchio, Grella 2, Kandol, Beckford	10,670
R3	Jan 3	A	Manchester United	W	1-0	1-0	Beckford	74,526
R4	23	A	Tottenham Hotspur	D	2-2	0-1	Beckford 2 (1 pen)	35,750
Rep	Feb 3	H	Tottenham Hotspur	L	1-3	1-1	Becchio	37,704
								Appearances
								Sub appearances
								Goals

* After extra-time

FL Trophy

R2	Oct 6	H	Darlington	W	2-1	2-1	Robinson, Kandol	8,429
QF	Nov 10	H	Grimsby Town	W	3-1	2-0	Lancashire (og), Kilkenny, Beckford	10,430
SF	Dec 15	H	Accrington Stanley	W	2-0	1-0	Ephraim, Kilkenny	12,696
NF	Jan 19	H	Carlisle United	L	1-2	0-1	Crowe	13,011
	Feb 9	A	Carlisle United	W	3-2*	0-1	Snodgrass, Crowe, Grella	9,430
								Appearances
								Sub appearances
							One own-goal	Goals

* Lost 6-5 on penalties

Higgs, Shane	Crowe, Jason	Parker, Ben	Doyle, Micky	Rui Marques, Manuel	Kisnorbo, Patrick	Johnson, Bradley	Howson, Jonathan	Beckford, Jermaine	Becchio, Luciano	Snodgrass, Robert	Hughes, Andy	Robinson, Andy	Showunmi, Enoch	Prutton, David	Kilkenny, Neil	Grella, Mike	Michalik, Lubomir	Bromby, Leigh	Ankergren, Casper	Naylor, Richard	Vokes, Sam	Kandol, Tresor	Gradel, Max	White, Aidan	Capaldi, Tony	Ephraim, Hogan	Lowry, Shane	McSheffrey, Gary	Dickov, Paul	Collins, Neill	Watt, Sanchez	Huntington, Paul	Somma, Davide	Martin, David
1	2	3	4	5	6	7	8	9	10	11	S*	S*	S*																					
1	2		4	5	6	7	8	9	10	11	3		S*	S*																				
1	2		4	5	6	7	8	9	10	11	3	S*		S*	S*																			
1	2		4	5	6	7	8	9	10	11	3	S*			S*	S*																		
1	2		4	5	6	7	8	9	10	11	3		S*	S*			S*																	
1	2		4			7	8		10	11	3	S*	S*		S*	9	6	5																
1	2		4		6	7	8	9	10	11	3				S*	S*	S*	5																
1	2		4		6	7	8	9	10	11	3				S*	S*	S*	5																
1	2		4		6	7	8	9		11	3	S*				10	S*	5	S*															
			4		6	7	8	9	10	11	3		S*	S*	S*			2	1	5														
			4		6	7	8	9	10		3	S*	S*		11	S*		2	1	5														
1	2		4			7	8	9		11	3							6	S*	5	10	S*	S*											
			4		6	7	8	9		11	3				S*			2	1	5	10	S*	S*											
			4		6	7	8	9		11	3				S*			2	1	5	10	S*	S*											
			4		6	7	8	9		11	3				S*			2	1	5	10	S*	S*											
			4		3		11	9		7	2		S*	S*	8		6	5	1		10		S*											
			2		6		8	9		11	3				7	S*	4	5	1		10		S*	S*										
	2						8		S*	S*				7	4	S*	6	5	1		10		9		3	11								
	2		7				8	9	S*	11					4		6	5	1		10		S*		3	S*								
	S*		2		6		8	9	10		11				4			5	1			S*	7		3	S*								
			4		6	S*	8	9	10	11	3				7			2	1	5			S*											
			3		6	S*	8	9	10	11	7				4			2	1	5		S*	S*											
			3		6	7	S*	9	10	11	8				4			2	1	5		S*	S*											
	2		3		6	7	8	9	10	11					4	S*			1	5			S*	S*										
			3		6	7	S*	9	10	11	8				4	S*		2	1	5			S*											
	2		4		6	11	8	9	S*	10	3				7		S*	5	1				S*											
			3			S*	8	9	10	11							6	4	1	5			S*				2	7						
			4			S*	8	9	10	S*							6	2	1	5			7				3	11						
	2					11	S*		10	9					4	S*		3	1	5			7	S*			6	8						
	2					7	S*	9	10	8					4	S*		3	1	5			S*				6	11						
			3		5	7	8	9	S*	S*	11				4				1	2			S*				6	10						
			4		5	S*	8	9	10	11	7					S*			1	2			S*	3			6							
			3		5	S*	4	9	10	11	7								1	2		S*					6	8						
			3		6	S*	4	9	10	11	7						S*	5	1					2				8	S*					
			3		6		4	9	10	11	7								1	5		S*	S*	2				8	S*					
			3		6		4	9	10	11	7				S*			S*	1	5			S*	2				8						
			3		6	7	4		10	11	8				S*			2	1	5			S*	S*					9					
1			3			S*	4	9	10	11	7				8	S*				2		S*					6			5				
1		S*	3				4	9		11	7				8	10				2			S*				6		S*	5				
1			3			S*	4	9		10	11				8			2		5			7							6	S*			
1			3			S*	4	9	S*	10	11				8			2		5			7							6	S*			
1			3				4	S*	10	9	11				8	S*		2		5			7							6				
1		S*	3				4	S*	10	9	11				8			2		5			7							6	S*			
1		3				7	S*	S*	10	11	6				4					2			9					S*		5	8			
1			3			7		S*	10	11	8				4	S*				2			9				6			5	S*			
1			3			11	S*	9	10	S*	8				4			2					7				6			5	S*			
19	16	2	42	5	29	26	39	38	32	40	38	0	0	1	24	3	7	31	27	29	8	0	11	4	3	1	11	9	1	9	1	0	0	0
	1	2				10	6	4	5	4	1	6	7	5	11	14	6	1	2			10	21	4		2		1	3		5			
					1	7	4	25	15	7					2	1	1	1		2	1	2	6					1						

1	2		4			11	8		S*	7	3	S*	10		S*	9	6															5		
1	2		4	5	6	7	8	9	S*	11	3		S*		S*	10																		
1	2		4		6	7	8	9	10	11	3		S*		S*	S*	5																	
3	3	0	3	1	2	3	3	2	1	3	3	0	1	0	0	2	2	0	0	0	0	0	0	0	0	0	0	0	0	0	0	1	0	0
									2			1	2		3	1																		
										2			1																					

			7		6	11	8	9		10	3				4	S*		5	1	2				S*										
	2		4				8	9	S*	11					7	10	6	5	1						3									
			4				8	9	10	11	3				7	S*	6	5	1			S*		2	S*									
	2		4		6	11	8	9	10	S*	3				7		S*	5	1					S*										
	2		4		6	11	8	9	S*	10	3				7			5	1					S*										
	S*		4			7	8	9	10	11	3					S*	6	2	1	5				S*										
0	3	0	6	0	3	4	6	6	3	5	5	0	0	0	5	1	3	6	6	2	0	0	0	1	1	0	0	0	0	0	0	0	0	0
	1								2	1						3	1					1		4	1									
							1	5	2							3						1												

						S*					3	11	S*	7	4	8	6	5	1	2		9		10									S*	
						11		9		8	3	S*	S*	S*	4		5		1	6	10		7	2										
	2				S*					11	3			7	4	10	6			5	S*	9	S*			8								1
	2					7	8	9	S*	11	3				4	10		6	1	5														
	2		4			S*	8		10	7					S*	S*	6		1	5			9				3	11						
0	3	0	1	0	0	2	2	2	1	4	4	1	0	2	4	3	4	2	4	5	1	2	2	2	0	1	1	1	0	0	0	0	0	1
					1	2			1			1	2	1	1	1					1		1										1	
	2							1		1		1			2	1						1				1								

League Table

	P	W	D	L	F	A	Pts
Norwich City	46	29	8	9	89	47	95
Leeds United	46	25	11	10	77	44	86
Millwall	46	24	13	9	76	44	85
Charlton Athletic	46	23	15	8	71	48	84
Swindon Town	46	22	16	8	73	57	82
Huddersfield Town	46	23	11	12	82	56	80
Southampton*	46	23	14	9	85	47	73
Colchester United	46	20	12	14	64	52	72
Brentford	46	14	20	12	55	52	62
Walsall	46	16	14	16	60	63	62
Bristol Rovers	46	19	5	22	59	70	62
Milton Keynes Dons	46	17	9	20	60	68	60
Brighton & Hove Albion	46	15	14	17	56	60	59
Carlisle United	46	15	13	18	63	66	58
Yeovil Town	46	13	14	19	55	59	53
Oldham Athletic	46	13	13	20	39	57	52
Leyton Orient	46	13	12	21	53	63	51
Exeter City	46	11	18	17	48	60	51
Tranmere Rovers	46	14	9	23	45	72	51
Hartlepool United**	46	14	11	21	59	67	50
Gillingham	46	12	14	20	48	64	50
Wycombe	46	10	15	21	56	76	45
Southend United	46	10	13	23	51	72	43
Stockport County	46	5	10	31	35	95	25

*Southampton deducted 10 points
**Hartlepool United deducted 3 points

2010-11

Championship

Manager: Simon Grayson

Final Position: 7th

Did you know that?

28 September 2010: United, 4–1 up just before half-time, lost 4–6 to Preston, who became the first visiting team to hit six goals at Elland Road. It was United's highest scoring defeat and equalled the record of aggregate record of 10 goals in a game.

28 February 2011: *The King's Speech* won the Oscar for best film. The opening sequences of the movie were shot at Elland Road.

Jonny Howson opens the scoring in the 4–1 win against Nottingham Forest.

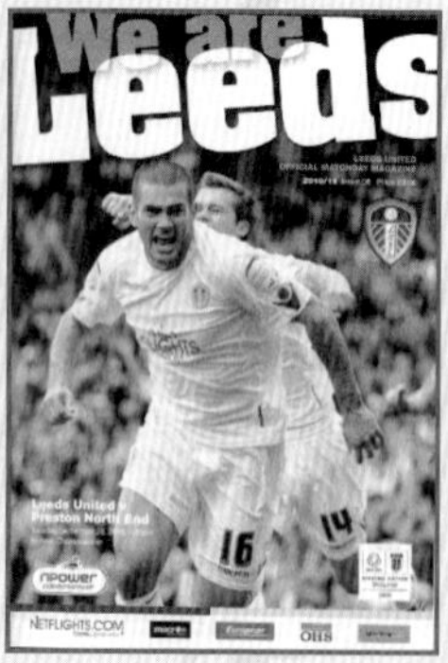

Match No.	Date	Venue	Opponents	Result	FT	HT	Scorers	Attendance
1	Aug 7	H	Derby County	L	1-2	1-2	Becchio	26,761
2	15	A	Nottingham Forest	D	1-1	1-1	Sam	24,986
3	21	H	Millwall	W	3-1	1-1	Sam, Somma 2	25,067
4	28	A	Watford	W	1-0	1-0	Naylor	14,039
5	Sep 11	H	Swansea City	W	2-1	0-1	Johnson, Becchio	26,453
6	14	A	Barnsley	L	2-5	1-1	Howson, Somma	20,309
7	17	A	Doncaster Rovers	D	0-0	0-0		13,293
8	25	H	Sheffield United	W	1-0	0-0	Johnson	33,622
9	28	H	Preston North End	L	4-6	4-2	Becchio, Bruce, Somma 2	22,727
10	Oct 2	A	Ipswich Town	L	1-2	0-1	Snodgrass	23,105
11	16	A	Middlesbrough	W	2-1	1-0	Somma, Becchio	23,550
12	19	H	Leicester City	L	1-2	0-0	Becchio	22,775
13	25	H	Cardiff City	L	0-4	0-1		20,747
14	30	A	Scunthorpe United	W	4-1	1-1	Gradel, Howson 3	8,122
15	Nov 6	A	Coventry City	W	3-2	2-0	Howson, Snodgrass, Gradel (pen)	28,184
16	9	H	Hull City	D	2-2	1-1	Johnson, O'Brien	24,906
17	13	H	Bristol City	W	3-1	0-0	Becchio 3	27,567
18	20	A	Norwich City	D	1-1	1-0	Gradel	26,315
19	27	A	Reading	D	0-0	0-0		23,677
20	Dec 4	H	Crystal Palace	W	2-1	0-1	Becchio 2	25,476
21	11	A	Burnley	W	3-2	0-2	Gradel, Becchio, Howson	20,453
22	18	H	Queen's Park R	W	2-0	1-0	Gradel 2	29,426
23	26	A	Leicester City	D	2-2	1-0	Gradel, Snodgrass	30,919
24	28	H	Portsmouth	D	3-3	2-1	Gradel, Howson, Johnson	31,556
25	Jan 1	H	Middlesbrough	D	1-1	0-1	Becchio	30,452
26	4	A	Cardiff City	L	1-2	0-1	Snodgrass	25,010
27	15	H	Scunthorpe United	W	4-0	3-0	Watt, Gradel, Johnson, Somma	25,446
28	22	A	Portsmouth	D	2-2	0-1	Becchio, Somma	20,040
29	Feb 1	A	Hull City	D	2-2	1-2	Snodgrass, Somma	24,110
30	5	H	Coventry City	W	1-0	0-0	Somma	27,033
31	12	A	Bristol City	W	2-0	1-0	Snodgrass, Gradel	18,000
32	19	H	Norwich City	D	2-2	1-1	Becchio, Somma	31,601
33	22	H	Barnsley	D	3-3	2-1	Becchio, Gradel 2 (1 pen)	26,289
34	26	A	Swansea City	L	0-3	0-1		19,309
35	Mar 5	H	Doncaster Rovers	W	5-2	1-1	Gradel 2, Howson 2, Becchio	27,027
36	8	A	Preston North End	W	2-1	1-0	Kilkenny, Paynter	15,269
37	12	H	Ipswich Town	D	0-0	0-0		27,432
38	19	A	Sheffield United	L	0-2	0-0		23,728
39	Apr 2	H	Nottingham Forest	W	4-1	0-0	Howson, Becchio, Gradel 2	29,524
40	9	A	Millwall	L	2-3	0-2	Becchio, O'Brien	16,724
41	12	A	Derby County	L	1-2	0-0	Gradel	27,252
42	16	H	Watford	D	2-2	0-0	Becchio, Deeney (og)	30,240
43	22	H	Reading	D	0-0	0-0		24,564
44	25	A	Crystal Palace	L	0-1	0-1		20,142
45	30	H	Burnley	W	1-0	1-0	McCormack	31,186
46	May 7	A	Queen's Park R	W	2-1	1-1	Gradel, McCormack	18,234
								Appearances
								Sub appearances
							One own-goal	Goals

FL Cup

R1	Aug 10	H	Lincoln City	W	4-0	3-0	Howson, Becchio, Sam, Kilkenny (pen)	12,602
R2	24	H	Leicester City	L	1-2	1-0	Somma	16,509
								Appearances
								Sub appearances
								Goals

FA Cup

R3	Jan 8	A	Arsenal	D	1-1	0-0	Snodgrass (pen)	59,520
Rep	19	H	Arsenal	L	1-3	1-2	Johnson	38,232
								Appearances
								Sub appearances
								Goals

Schmeichel, Kasper	Connolly, Paul	Bessone, Fede	Howson, Jonathan	Collins, Neill	Naylor, Richard	Johnson, Bradley	Kilkenny, Neil	Watt, Sanchez	Becchio, Luciano	Sam, Lloyd	White, Aidan	Clayton, Adam	Grella, Mike	Somma, Davide	Hughes, Andy	Gradel, Max	McCormack, Ross	Higgs, Shane	Bruce, Alex	Snodgrass, Robert	McCartney, George	Faye, Amdi	Brown, Jason	Bromby, Leigh	Nunez, Ramon	O'Brien, Andy	Paynter, Billy	Parker, Ben	Lichaj, Eric	Bannan, Barry	Livermore, Jake	Kisnorbo, Patrick
1	2	3	4	5	6	7	8	9	10	11	S*	S*	S*																			
1	2	3	4	5	6	7	8	9	10	11		S*																				
1	2	3	4	5	6	7	8	9	10	11				S*	S*																	
1	2	3	4	5	6	7	8	9	10	11					S*	S*	S*															
	2	3	4	5	6	7	8	9	10	S*				S*		11	S*	1														
	2	3	4	5	6	7	8		10	11				S*	S*	9	S*	1														
			4	5		7	8	S*			3			10	2	11	9	1	6	S*												
			4	5		7	S*		10	11				9	2	8	S*	1	6	S*	3											
			4	5		7	S*	S*	10	11		S*		9	2	8		1	6		3											
			4	5	6	7	8	S*	S*					9				1	2	11	3	10	S*									
	2		4	5	6	S*		7	10					9	S*					11	3	8	1	S*								
	2		4	5	6	S*	S*	7	10					9		S*				11	3	8	1									
1	2		4	5		7			10			S*		9		S*			6	11	3	8			S*							
1	2		4			S*	8		10							9			6	11	3	7			S*	5	S*					
	2		4	5		S*	8		10					S*	S*	9				11	3	7	1			6						
1	2		4			7	8		10	S*				S*		9			5	11	3					6	S*					
1	2		4			7	8		S*	S*				10		9			5	11	3					6	S*					
1	2		4	S*		7	8		10	S*						9	S*		5	11	3					6						
1	2		4			7	8		10	S*						9	S*		5	11	3					6	S*					
1			4			7	8		10	S*					2	9	S*		5	11	3					6	S*					
1	2		4	5		7	8		10							9	S*		6	11	3	S*										
1	2		4	5		7	8		10	S*						9			6	11	3			S*			S*					
1	2		4	5		7	8		10							9	S*			11	3	S*				6	S*					
1	2		4	5		7			S*	S*						8	9			11	3					6	10					
1	2		4	5		7	S*	S*	10	S*					3	8	9			11						6						
1	2		4	5		7		S*	S*	S*						8	9			11						6	10	3				
1	2		4			7		8	10					S*		9	S*		5	11	3					6	S*					
1	2		4			7		8	10					S*		9			5	11	3			6								
1	2		4			7			10	S*				9		8	S*		5	11	3					6	S*					
1	2		4			7	S*		10					9		8			5	11	3			S*		6	S*					
1			4			7	8		10					S*		9	S*		5	11	3					6			2			
1			4			7	8		10					S*		9			5	11	3					6	S*		2			
1			4			7	8	S*	10					S*		9			5	11	3					6			2			
1			4				8	S*	10					9		7			5	11	3					6	S*	S*	2			
1			4		S*	7	8	S*	10							9				11	3			5		6	S*		2			
1			4		S*	7	8		S*							9				11	3			5		6	10		2	S*		
1			4			7	8		S*							9				11	3			5		6	10		2	S*		
1			4			7		S*	10					S*		9				11	3			5		6	S*		2	8		
1			4			7	S*		10					S*		9				11	3			5		6			2	8	S*	
1	2		4			7			10					S*		9	S*			11				5		6			3	S*	8	
1	2		4			S*	8		10					S*		9	S*							5		6			3	11	7	
1			4			7	8		S*					10		9	S*			11	3			5		6			2	S*		
1	2		4		5	7	S*	S*						S*		9				11						6	10		3		8	
1	2		4		5	7	S*	S*						S*		9				11						6	10		3		8	
1			4		5	7	8	S*								11	9			S*	3			S*		6	10		2			
1	2		4		5	7	8	S*						S*		11	9									6	10		3			S*
37	30	6	46	20	13	40	29	9	34	7	1	0	0	12	5	38	6	6	21	34	32	6	3	9	0	30	8	1	16	3	4	0
				1	2	5	8	13	7	11	1	4	1	17	5	3	15			3		2	1	4	2		14	1		4	1	1
			10		1	5	1	1	19	2				11		18	2		1	6						2	1					

1	2	3	4	5		7	8	9	10	11	S*		S*		S*				6													
	2	3	4	5		11	8	S*	10					9	S*	7		1	6													
1	2	2	2	2	0	2	2	1	2	1	0	0	0	1	0	1	0	1	2	0	0	0	0	0	0	0	0	0	0	0	0	0
								1			1		1		2																	
			1				1		1	1				1																		

1	2		4			7		8	10					S*	S*	9			5	11				S*		6		3				
1	2		4			7		8		S*				S*		9			5	11				S*		6	10	3				
2	2	0	2	0	0	2	0	2	1	0	0	0	0	0	0	2	0	0	2	2	0	0	0	0	0	2	1	2	0	0	0	0
										1				2	1									2								
						1														1												

League Table

	P	W	D	L	F	A	Pts
Queen's Park Rangers	46	24	16	6	71	32	88
Norwich City	46	23	15	8	83	58	84
Swansea	46	24	8	14	69	42	80
Cardiff City	46	23	11	12	76	54	80
Reading	46	20	17	9	77	51	77
Nottingham Forest	46	20	15	11	69	50	75
Leeds United	46	19	15	12	81	70	72
Burnley	46	18	14	14	65	61	68
Millwall	46	18	13	15	62	48	67
Leicester City	46	19	10	17	76	71	67
Hull City	46	16	17	13	52	51	65
Middlesbrough	46	17	11	18	68	68	62
Ipswich Town	46	18	8	20	62	68	62
Watford	46	16	13	17	77	71	61
Bristol City	46	17	9	20	62	65	60
Portsmouth	46	15	13	18	53	60	58
Barnsley	46	14	14	18	55	66	56
Coventry City	46	14	13	19	54	58	55
Derby County	46	13	10	23	58	71	49
Crystal Palace	46	12	12	22	44	69	48
Doncaster Rovers	46	11	15	20	55	81	48
Preston North End	46	10	12	24	54	79	42
Sheffield United	46	11	9	26	44	79	42
Scunthorpe United	46	12	6	28	43	87	42

2011-12

Championship

Manager: Simon Grayson until February then Neil Warnock

Final Position: 14th

Did you know that?

2 November 2011: The 5–0 home defeat to Blackpool equalled the highest losing margin set on 8 November 1980 when Arsenal won by the same score.

The 11 home League defeats is the worst in the club's history and included a 7–3 loss to Nottingham Forest who became the first side to score seven times at Elland Road.

A record nine different players received red cards during the campaign – Max Gradel, Jonny Howson, Aidan White, Patrick Kisnorbo, Tom Lees, Paul Connolly, Zac Thompson, Michael Brown and Darren O'Dea.

Ross McCormack.

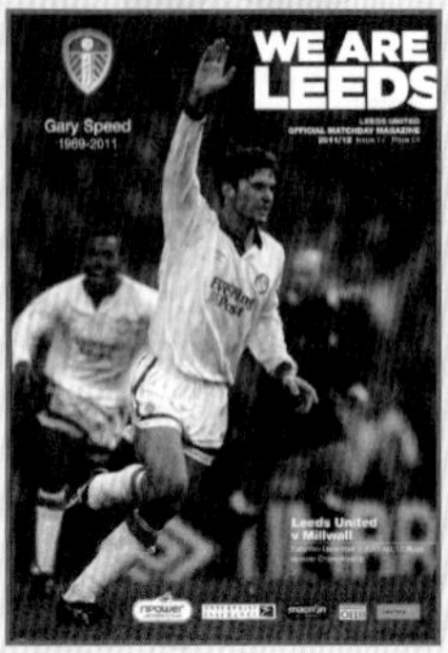

Match No.	Date	Venue	Opponents	Result	FT	HT	Scorers	Attendance
1	Aug 6	A	Southampton	L	1-3	0-2	Gradel (pen)	25,860
2	13	H	Middlesborough	L	0-1	0-1		25,650
3	16	H	Hull City	W	4-1	2-1	McCormack, Lees, Snodgrass, Nunez	22,363
4	21	A	West Ham United	D	2-2	0-1	McCormack, Clayton	28,252
5	27	A	Ipswich Town	L	1-2	1-0	McCormack	19,758
6	Sep 10	H	Crystal Palace	W	3-2	1-2	McCormack 2, Becchio	23,916
7	17	H	Bristol City	W	2-1	1-1	Clayton, McCormack	22,655
8	23	A	Brighton & HA	D	3-3	2-0	Keogh, McCormack 2	20,646
9	Oct 1	H	Portsmouth	W	1-0	1-0	Pugh	22,476
10	14	A	Doncaster Rovers	W	3-0	1-0	Pugh, McCormack, Lees	12,962
11	18	H	Coventry City	D	1-1	1-0	O'Dea	21,528
12	22	A	Peterborough U	W	3-2	1-1	Keogh, Clayton, O'Dea	12,880
13	26	A	Birmingham City	L	0-1	0-1		21,426
14	30	H	Cardiff City	D	1-1	0-1	Snodgrass	20,270
15	Nov 2	H	Blackpool	L	0-5	0-3		22,423
16	6	A	Leicester City	W	1-0	0-0	Clayton	27,720
17	19	A	Burnley	W	2-1	0-1	Snodgrass 2	17,226
18	26	H	Barnsley	L	1-2	0-2	McCormack	25,900
19	29	A	Nottingham Forest	W	4-0	2-0	Snodgrass, Howson, Becchio, Clayton	23,577
20	Dec 3	H	Millwall	W	2-0	0-0	Snodgrass 2	27,161
21	10	A	Watford	D	1-1	0-1	Snodgrass pen	13,573
22	17	H	Reading	L	0-1	0-1		23,162
23	26	A	Derby County	L	0-1	0-0		33,010
24	31	A	Barnsley	L	1-4	0-1	Becchio	17,499
25	Jan 2	H	Burnley	W	2-1	0-0	Easton (og), McCormack	27,295
26	14	A	Crystal Palace	D	1-1	0-1	Snodgrass	17,796
27	21	H	Ipswich Town	W	3-1	0-1	Snodgrass, McCormack, Becchio	22,844
28	31	H	Birmingham City	L	1-4	1-1	McCormack	19,628
29	Feb 4	A	Bristol City	W	3-0	1-0	Snodgrass, McCormack, Becchio	15,257
30	11	H	Brighton & HA	L	1-2	0-0	Becchio	23,171
31	14	A	Coventry City	L	1-2	1-1	McCormack	15,704
32	18	H	Doncaster Rovers	W	3-2	0-1	Townsend, Clayton, Becchio	21,131
33	25	A	Portsmouth	D	0-0	0-0		17,571
34	Mar 3	H	Southamton	L	0-1	0-1		20,901
35	6	A	Hull City	D	0-0	0-0		22,676
36	10	A	Middlesborough	W	2-0	2-0	Snodgrass, Becchio	21,301
37	17	H	West Ham United	D	1-1	0-0	Becchio	33,366
38	20	H	Nottingham Forest	L	3-7	1-2	Snodgrass (pen), Becchio, Brown	21,367
39	24	A	Millwall	W	1-0	0-0	McCormack	14,309
40	31	H	Watford	L	0-2	0-1		21,766
41	Apr 6	A	Reading	L	0-2	0-0		22,775
42	9	H	Derby County	L	0-2	0-1		21,363
43	14	H	Peterborough U	W	4-1	1-1	Paynter 2, McCormack 2	19,469
44	17	A	Blackpool	L	0-1	0-0		14,134
45	21	A	Cardiff City	D	1-1	0-1	Becchio	25,109
46	28	H	Leicester City	L	1-2	0-1	Webber	25,664
								Appearances
								Sub appearances
							One own goal	Goals

FL Cup

R2	Aug 9	H	Bradford City	W	3-2	0-1	Nunez 2, McCormack	17,667
R3	23	A	Doncaster Rovers	W	2-1	1-1	Nunez 2	8,505
R4	Sep 20	H	Manchester United	L	0-3	0-3		31,031
								Appearances
								Sub appearances
								Goals

FA Cup

R3	Jan 9	A	Arsenal	L	0-1	0-0		59,615
								Appearances
								Sub appearances
								Goals

Lonergan, Andy	Connolly, Paul	Kisnorbo, Patrick	Howson, Jonathan	O'Brien, Andy	O'Dea, Darren	Gradel, Max	Brown, Michael	McCormack, Ross	Clayton, Adam	Snodgrass, Robert	Paynter, Billy	Nunez, Ramon	Sam, Lloyd	Lees, Tom	Bromby, Leigh	Thompson, Zac	White, Aidan	Keogh, Andy	Taylor, Charlie	Becchio, Luciano	Forssell, Mikail	Pugh, Danny	Varynen, Mika	Rachubka, Paul	Cairns, Alex	McCarthy, Alex	Bruce, Alex	Townsend, Andros	Delph, Fabian	Smith, Adam	Rogers, Robbie	Webber Danny	Robinson.Paul	Parker, Ben
1	2	3	4	5	6	7	8	9	10	11	S*	S*	S*																					
1		3	4		6	7	8	9	10	11		S*	S*	2	5	S*																	
1		5			6		8	9	10	11		10	S*	2		S*	3	7															
1		5	4		6	7		9	10	11		S*	S*	2			3	8															
1		5	4	S*	6	7		9	10	11		S*	S*	2			3	8															
1		5	4		6		8	9		11		6	S*	2				7	3	S*	S*												
1		5	4		6			9	10	11		8		2	S*		3	7		S*	S*												
1			4		6			9	10	11				2	5		3	7		S*	S*	8	S*										
1	2		4		6			9	10	11				5			3	7		S*	S*	8	S*										
1	2		4		6			9	10	11				5			3	7		S*		8	S*	S*									
	2		4		6			9	10	11				5			3	7		S*	S*	8	S*	1									
	2		4		6			9	10			S*	S*	5			3	11		S*		8	7	1									
	2		4		6			9	10	11			S*	5			3	7		S*		8	S*	1									
	2	S*	4		6			9	10	11			S*	5			3	7		S*		8		1									
	2	5	4					9	10	11				6			3	7		S*		8	S*	1	S*								
	2	6	4	5			S*	9	10	11					S*		3	7		S*		8				1							
	2	5	4		6			9	10	7		S*	11	S*			3	8		S*						1							
	2	5	4					9	8	7		S*	11	6			3	S*		10		S*				1							
	2	5	4				8	S*	7	11		S*		6			3	S*		9		10				1							
	2	5	4				8		7	11			S^	6			3	S*		9		10				1							
	2	5						S*	10	7			11	6			3	8		9		4	S*			1							
1	2	5					8	9	7	11			S*	6			3	S*		10		4	S*										
1	S*	5			6		8	9	7	11		S*		2			3	S*		10		4											
1	2	5			6		8	9	S*			10					3	7		S*		11	4										
1		5			6			S*	8			9	S*			2	3			10	S*	11				4	7						
1					6		8	9	4	S*				5		2	3			10	S*	11					7						
1					6			9	4	11				5		2	S*			S*	10	3						7	8					
1					6			9	4	11				5		2	3			10								7	8					
1					6			9	4	11				5			3			10		7							8	2				
1					6			9	4	11		S*		5			3			10		7						S*	8	2				
1				S*	6		S*	9	4	11		S*		5			3			10		7							8	2				
1					6		S*	9	4	11				5			7			10	S*	3					2	8			S*			
1					6		8	9	4	11				5	S*		7			10		3					2							
1	S*				6		8	9	4	11			S*	5	2		7			10		3										S*		
1	2				6		8	9	4	11			S*	5						10		3										7		
1	2				6		8	9	4	11				5			7			10	S*	S*										S*	3	
1	2				6		8	9	4	11				5			7			10	S*											S*	3	
1	2				6		8	9	4	11	S*			5			7			10		S*										S*	3	
1	S*				6		8	9	4	11				5			7			10							2					S*	3	
1	2						8	9	4	11		S*		5			7			10	S*						6					S*	3	
1							8	9		11				5	2	6				10	S*	7					4				S*	S*	3	
1	2				6		8	9		11	S*	7		5						10		4									S*	S*	3	
1	2				6			9	4	11	10			5					3	S*		8									7	S*	S*	
1	S*				6			9	4	11	10			5	2					S*	S*	8										7	3	
1	S*							9	7	11		S*		5	2	6				10		8					4					S*	3	
1	2						8	9	7	11				5		6				10	S*	3					4					S*		
35	24	18	19	2	35	4	21	42	42	42	2	6	3	41	6	7	35	17	2	25	1	31	2	5	0	6	8	5	5	3	1	2	9	0
	4			2			1	3	1	1	3	10	14	1	3	2	1	5		16	14	3	8	1	1			1			3	11	1	
			1		2	1	1	18	6	13	2	1		2				2		11		2						1				1		

1	2	5	4		6		8	9	10			11	7	S*	S*				S*															3
	2	S*	4	5		S*		9	10			11	7			6	3	8	S*					1										
1				5	6			9	10	11		S*		4	2		3	7		8	S*		S*											
2	2	1	2	2	2	0	1	3	3	1	0	2	2	1	1	1	2	2	0	1	0	0	0	1	0	0	0	0	0	0	0	0	0	1
		1				1						1		1	1				2		1		1											
								1				4																							

1					6		S*	S*	10			8		5		2	3			9	S*	11	4					7						
1	0	0	0	0	1	0	0	0	1	0	0	1	0	1	0	1	1	0	0	1	0	1	1	0	0	0	0	1	0	0	0	0	0	0
							1	1													1													

League Table

	P	W	D	L	F	A	Pts
Reading	46	27	8	11	69	41	89
Southampton	46	26	10	10	85	46	88
West Ham Utd	46	24	14	8	81	48	86
Birmingham	46	20	16	10	78	51	76
Blackpool	46	20	15	11	79	59	75
Cardiff City	46	19	18	9	66	53	75
Middlesbrough	46	18	16	12	52	51	70
Hull City	46	19	11	16	47	44	68
Leicester City	46	18	12	16	66	55	66
Brighton	46	17	15	14	52	52	66
Watford	46	16	16	14	56	64	64
Derby County	46	18	10	18	50	58	64
Burnley	46	17	11	18	61	58	62
Leeds United	46	17	10	19	65	68	61
Ipswich Town	46	17	10	19	69	77	61
Millwall	46	15	12	19	55	57	57
Crystal Palace	46	13	17	16	46	51	56
Peterborough	46	13	11	22	67	77	50
Nottm Forest	46	14	8	24	48	63	50
Bristol City	46	12	13	21	44	68	49
Barnsley	46	13	9	24	49	74	48
Portsmouth	46	13	11	22	50	59	40
Coventry City	46	9	13	24	41	65	40
Doncaster	46	8	12	26	43	80	36

Leeds City's League Record Against Other Clubs 1905–20

Leeds City have played 36 clubs in the Football League in their short history. Below is a record against each club. Clubs are listed by name as they were called when Leeds City last played them. Some clubs are known differently now (eg Clapton Orient is now Leyton Orient) and some clubs have later modified their titles (eg Birmingham and Stoke later added City). In addition some clubs have left the Football League over the years. The 1919–20 season is included as the games were not expunged with the playing record taken over by Port Vale.

		HOME					AWAY				
	P	W	D	L	F	A	W	D	L	F	A
ARSENAL	4	0	2	0	2	2	0	0	2	0	3
BARNSLEY	20	6	2	2	16	15	3	1	6	14	22
BIRMINGHAM	14	5	2	0	14	4	2	1	4	13	16
BLACKPOOL	22	7	2	2	16	9	4	1	6	16	18
BOLTON WANDERERS	4	1	0	1	2	2	0	0	2	0	5
BRADFORD CITY	6	0	1	2	1	4	0	1	2	2	8
BRADFORD PA	12	3	0	3	12	9	2	1	3	7	10
BRISTOL CITY	10	2	3	0	7	4	0	2	3	3	9
BURNLEY	16	2	4	2	10	11	1	2	5	10	19
BURTON UNITED	4	2	0	0	5	2	1	1	0	3	1
BURY	6	3	0	0	8	4	0	3	0	2	2
CHELSEA	8	0	3	1	3	4	0	0	4	3	14
CHESTERFIELD	8	3	1	0	7	0	1	0	3	5	7
CLAPTON ORIENT	20	6	2	2	20	10	1	4	5	5	11
COVENTRY CITY	2	1	0	0	3	0	1	0	0	4	0
DERBY COUNTY	12	3	0	3	15	15	1	1	4	8	20
FULHAM	16	3	1	4	11	11	2	0	6	6	21
GAINSBOROUGH TRINITY	14	3	3	1	9	2	1	1	5	6	13
GLOSSOP	20	7	0	3	20	11	3	2	5	12	12
GRIMSBY TOWN	18	7	0	2	29	11	4	1	4	13	16
HUDDERSFIELD TOWN	10	4	0	1	13	6	1	1	3	5	7
HULL CITY	22	5	3	3	17	13	1	3	7	14	25
LEICESTER FOSSE	18	5	3	1	24	11	1	3	5	12	25

		HOME					AWAY				
	P	**W**	**D**	**L**	**F**	**A**	**W**	**D**	**L**	**F**	**A**
LINCOLN CITY	16	4	3	1	16	8	2	4	2	8	12
MANCHESTER CITY	2	0	0	1	1	3	0	0	1	0	3
MANCHESTER UNITED	2	0	0	1	1	3	1	0	0	3	0
NOTTINGHAM FOREST	10	4	0	1	17	5	1	0	4	5	11
NOTTS COUNTY	2	0	0	1	2	4	0	0	1	0	4
OLDHAM ATHLETIC	6	1	0	2	7	7	0	0	3	3	12
PORT VALE	4	2	0	0	5	1	1	0	1	2	3
PRESTON NORTH END	4	1	1	0	5	1	0	0	2	2	5
STOCKPORT COUNTY	20	6	2	2	25	11	1	3	6	13	21
STOKE	2	0	0	1	0	1	0	0	1	1	2
TOTTENHAM HOTSPUR	2	1	0	0	1	0	0	0	1	0	3
WEST BROMWICH ALBION	12	3	1	2	8	7	0	0	6	3	15
WOLVERHAMPTON W	20	6	3	1	23	10	2	1	7	14	30
TOTALS	**388**	**106**	**42**	**46**	**375**	**221**	**38**	**37**	**119**	**217**	**405**

City Career Records 1905–19

Below are the career records (League, FA Cup, and League Cup) of every City first-team player since the club's first League match in 1905. The years given are the first years of seasons. Thus, 1906 means 1906–07. The 1904–05 FA Cup first preliminary round tie versus Rockingham Colliery (lost 3–1) is not included below. The team on 17 September 1904 was W.H. Mallinson, Skeldon, H. Dixon, R. Morris, J. Morris, T. Tennant, P. Heffron, Page, Musgrave (scorer), Cummings, Simpson. Both R. Morris and J. Morris played for City in the following season but their totals below are not credited with this game.

		LEAGUE		FA CUP		TOTAL	
Player	**Played**	**App**	**Gls**	**App**	**Gls**	**App**	**Gls**
ACKERLEY, G.	1909	2	0	0	0	2	0
AFFLECK, G.	1909–19	182	1	9	0	191	1
ALLAN, J.	1912–14	14	0	1	0	15	0
ASTILL, T.	1908–11	1	0	0	0	1	0
BAINBRIDGE, S.	1912–19	64	15	5	0	69	15
BATES, W.E.	1907–09	15	0	0	0	15	0
BEREN, H.G.	1909–10	3	0	0	0	3	0
BLACKMAN, F.E.	1914–19	44	0	2	0	46	0
BOWMAN, A.	1908–09	15	6	1	1	16	7
BRIDGETT, H.	1909–13	13	2	1	0	14	2
BROMAGE, H.	1905–11	143	0	9	0	152	0
BROUGHTON, T.W.	1912–13	4	0	0	0	4	0
BURNETT, J.J.	1908–10	20	2	4	1	24	3
CAMPBELL, A.	1911	1	0	0	0	1	0
CLARK, A.	1906	24	0	0	0	24	0
CLARKIN, J.	1911	1	0	0	0	1	0
CLAY, W.E.	1905	0	0	1	0	1	0
COPELAND, C.W.	1912–14	44	0	1	0	45	0
COWEN, R.W.	1914	2	0	0	0	2	0
CREIGHTON, A.	1910–11	66	0	3	0	69	0
CROOT, F.R.	1907–14	218	38	9	0	227	38
CUBBERLEY, S.M.	1906–12	181	6	7	0	188	6
CUNNINGHAM, G.P.	1910	3	0	0	0	3	0
CUNNINGHAM, T.	1908	1	0	0	0	1	0
DOUGAL, D.W.	1908–09	25	2	0	0	25	2
DOUGHERTY, J.	1913	1	0	0	0	1	0

Player	Played	LEAGUE App	LEAGUE Gls	FA CUP App	FA CUP Gls	TOTAL App	TOTAL Gls
DRAIN, T.	1905	9	3	1	0	10	3
EDMONDSON, J.	1914–19	11	6	0	0	11	6
ENRIGHT, J.	1910–12	77	23	3	0	80	23
FENWICK, G.	1912	5	3	0	0	5	3
FERGUSON, J.	1912	17	0	0	0	17	0
FOLEY, M.	1910–19	127	6	6	1	133	7
FORTUNE, J.J.	1911	1	0	0	0	1	0
FREEBOROUGH, J.	1905–07	24	0	0	0	24	0
GEMMELL, J.	1907–09	67	14	6	0	73	14
GEORGE, J.S.	1905–06	8	0	0	0	8	0
GIBSON, A.	1912	5	0	0	0	5	0
GILLESPIE, W.B.	1910–11	24	10	0	0	24	10
GOODWIN, E.W.	1914–19	20	3	0	0	20	3
GREEN, J.	1914	1	0	0	0	1	0
GUY, R.W.	1908	18	3	4	1	22	4
HALLIGAN, W.	1909	24	12	1	0	25	12
HAMILTON, E.M.	1909	3	0	0	0	3	0
HAMILTON, J.	1908	21	0	4	0	25	0
HAMPSON, J.	1913–19	71	8	3	0	74	8
HARGRAVES, J.F.	1905–07	63	12	7	7	70	19
HARKINS, J.A.	1910–11	63	0	3	0	66	0
HARWOOD, A.	1906	1	1	0	0	1	1
HEANEY, F.	1911	2	0	0	0	2	0
HENDERSON, J.T.	1905–07	75	0	5	0	80	0
HOGG, A.	1909	96	0	5	0	101	0
HOPKINS, W.	1919	7	0	0	0	7	0
HORSLEY, J.T.	1909–10	29	0	1	0	30	0
HOWARD, G.	1905	1	0	0	0	1	0
HYNDS, T.	1907	37	0	1	0	38	0
JACKSON, J.B.	1913–14	54	10	4	2	58	12
JEFFERSON, R.W.	1906–07	17	5	1	0	18	5
JOHNSON, G.J.W.	1906	1	0	0	0	1	0
JOHNSON, J.T.	1913	1	0	0	0	1	0
JOHNSON, S.	1911	7	1	0	0	7	1
JOYNES, R.A.	1908–09	22	1	1	0	23	1
KAY, H.	1907	31	0	1	0	32	0
KELLY, C.	1910–11	4	0	0	0	4	0
KENNEDY, J.J.	1906–08	58	1	2	0	60	1
KIRK, G.	1906	8	1	1	0	9	1
KIRTON, W.J.	1919	1	0	0	0	1	0
LAMPH, T.	1913–19	11	1	0	0	11	1

Player	Played	LEAGUE App	LEAGUE Gls	FA CUP App	FA CUP Gls	TOTAL App	TOTAL Gls
LAVERY, J.	1905–07	56	20	1	0	57	20
LAW, G.	1912–14	105	1	5	1	110	2
LAWRENCE, V.	1914	6	0	0	0	6	0
LINTOTT, E.H.	1912–13	43	1	2	0	45	1
LOUNDS, H.E.	1919	8	0	0	0	8	0
McALLISTER, T.	1908–09	53	0	5	0	58	0
McDANIEL, E.	1911	1	0	0	0	1	0
McDONALD, J.	1905	25	0	6	0	31	0
McDONALD, W.	1908	14	0	0	0	14	0
McLEOD, W.	1906–19	289	171	12	6	301	177
McQUILLAN, J.	1914	20	0	0	0	20	0
MILLERSHIP, H.	1919	8	0	0	0	8	0
MORAN, J.	1911–12	25	0	2	0	27	0
MORGAN, C.	1905	41	1	6	0	47	1
MORRIS, J.	1905	10	0	0	0	10	0
MORRIS, R.	1905	25	5	6	5	33	10
MORRIS, T.H.	1908–11	106	3	3	0	109	3
MULHOLLAND, T.S.	1909–11	78	21	3	0	81	21
MURPHY, L.A.	1911	18	0	1	0	19	0
MURRAY, D.B.	1905–08	83	7	2	0	85	7
MURRAY, W.B.	1906	8	0	0	0	8	0
NAISBY, T.H.	1907–09	63	0	5	0	68	0
PAGE, G.	1906	4	0	0	0	4	0
PARNELL, G.F.	1905	104	15	7	4	111	19
PEART, H.	1913–14	7	0	1	0	8	0
PICKARD, H.	1906–09	8	0	0	0	8	0
PRICE, A.	1912–19	78	25	0	0	78	25
PRICE, I.H.	1909	8	0	0	0	8	0
RAY, R.	1905–06	38	0	6	0	44	0
REINHARDT, C.G.	1911	12	0	1	0	13	0
RICHARDSON, W.F.	1914	2	0	0	0	2	0
ROBERTS, H.P.	1909–12	108	13	4	2	112	15
ROBERTSON, J.	1912	27	7	1	0	28	7
RODGER, T.	1908	25	4	0	0	25	4
ROTHWELL, A.	1914	1	0	0	0	1	0
SCOTT, W.	1912–13	26	0	0	0	26	0
SHARPE, I.G.	1913–14	61	16	4	1	65	17
SHORT, W.	1919	5	0	0	0	5	0
SINGLETON, H.B.	1905–06	45	7	6	0	51	7
SPEIRS, J.H.	1912–14	73	32	5	0	78	32
STOCKTON, C.M.	1909	3	0	0	0	3	0

Player	Played	LEAGUE App	LEAGUE Gls	FA CUP App	FA CUP Gls	TOTAL App	TOTAL Gls
STRINGFELLOW, H.	1905	13	1	3	0	16	1
SWIFT, G.H.	1905	1	0	0	0	1	0
THOMAS, W.	1907	9	2	1	0	10	2
THORPE, J.	1907	9	0	0	0	9	0
TILDESLEY, J.	1909	6	0	1	0	7	0
TOMPKINS, T.	1907	11	0	0	0	11	0
TURNER, N.M.	1913	4	2	0	0	4	2
WAINWRIGHT, W.	1914	2	0	0	0	2	0
WALKER, F.	1905	26	0	3	0	29	0
WALKER, W.	1914–19	22	0	0	0	22	0
WATSON, J.	1908	45	0	4	0	49	0
WATSON, R.	1905–07	83	21	7	3	90	24
WHITE, J.W.	1908–10	60	0	4	0	64	0
WHITLEY, J.	1905–06	7	0	0	0	7	0
WILSON, D.	1905–06	21	13	0	0	21	13
WILSON, T.C.	1906	20	2	1	0	21	2
Own-goals			6		0		6
TOTALS		**4,268**	**592**	**231**	**35**	**4,499**	**627**

Wartime Appearances

Leeds City World War One Appearances and Goalscorers

Player	Team	App	Goals
Affleck, George	Leeds City	36	
Arkle, Norman	Juniors	1	
Bainbridge, Simpson	Leeds City	11	5
Baines, Fred	Leeds City	13	
Barnshaw, Richard	Aberdare	1	
Barrett, P.J. (Pte)	Army	7	1
Bavin, Arthur	Lincoln City	1	
Bennett, Tom	Newcastle United	18	4
Booth, Curtis	Newcastle United	8	
Bradley, Bill	Newcastle United	11	
Buchan, Charlie M.	Arsenal	1	1
Cartwright, James E.	Manchester City	4	
Cawley, Tom E.	Rotherham	43	9
Chard, (Cpl)	Army	1	
Clipstone, Fred	Northampton Town	4	
Cook, Walter	Leeds City	11	
Copeland, Charlie W.	Leeds City	53	
Cowen, Bob W.	Leeds City	1	
Croot Fred R.	Leeds City	14	
Curry, Tom	Newcastle United	1	
Davison, J.	Newcastle United	1	
Dawson, G.	Preston North End	4	
Dowling, E.		1	
Dunn, John	Leeds City	1	
Edmondson, John	Leeds City	20	10
Feathers, W.		1	
Foley, Mick	Leeds City	36	1
Goodwin, Ernie	Leeds City	13	3
Gough, Harold	Sheffield United	2	
Grant, W. (Cpl)	Army	4	1
Hall, Tom	Newcastle United	22	8
Hampson, Ernie	Northampton Town	7	1
Hampson, John	Leeds City	92	4
Hampson, Tommy	Accrington Stanley	39	
Hampson, Walker	Burnley	3	

Player	Team	App	Goals
Hampson, Wm 'Billy'	Newcastle United	91	1
Hewison, Bob	Sunderland	79	6
Hibbert, Billy	Newcastle United	16	5
Hudson, Edward K.	Manchester United	11	
Hudspeth, Fred C.	Newcastle United	1	
Hugall, Jim C.	Clapton Orient	1	
Hughes, Robert	Northampton Town	4	
James, N.	Portsmouth	1	
Jennings, William	Notts County	1	
Kaye, A.	Barnsley	1	
Kettle, Billy	Juniors	1	
Kirton, Billy J.	Leeds City	1	
Lamph, Tommy	Leeds City	82	1
Lavery, George D.		1	
Law, George	Leeds City	22	1
Linfoot, Fred	Leeds City	6	
Lounds, Herbert	Leeds City	6	
McCreadie, Willie	Leeds City	1	
McLachlan, Albert	Aberdeen	24	
McLeod, Billy	Leeds City	13	6
Malcolm, Willie	Dunipace	1	
Mayson, Tommy	Grimsby Town	30	4
Millership, Harry	Leeds City	49	
Moore, Billy G.B.	Sunderland	14	6
Pattison, John M.	Hull City	1	1
Peart, Jack G.	Notts County	107	71
Price, Arthur	Leeds City	120	59
Roberts, Dick	Leeds City	1	
Robinson, Arthur	Blackburn Rovers	8	
Robinson, Stan	Bradford PA	17	2
Rose, Percy		1	
Rutherford, A.		3	
Rutherford, W.		1	
Scott, E.		1	
Sharpe, Ivan G.	Glossop	2	1
Sherwin, Harry	Sunderland	91	9
Smelt, John	Rotherham	1	
Spratt, A.	Sheffield United	1	
Stephenson, Clem	Aston Villa	91	44
Stephenson, Jimmy	Aston Villa	36	4
Sutcliffe, Charlie S.	Leeds City	2	
Toms, Bill	Eccles Borough	2	

Player	Team	App	Goals
Thorpe, Levi	Burnley	28	2
Trotter, Ally	Jarrow	3	1
Voysey, Clem R.	Arsenal	1	
Wainwright, Arthur H.	Leeds City	2	
Walden, Fred I. 'Fanny'	Tottenham	38	2
Walker, Willis	Leeds City	70	
Williamson, John R.	Newcastle United	1	
Wilson, Andy, W.	Middlesbrough	2	2
Wilson, Willie	Hearts	9	4
Wrigglesworth, A.		1	
Own-goal*			1
Totals		**1,584**	**281**

* Wightman, *Nottingham Forest*

Leeds United World War Two Appearances and Goalscorers

Player	Team	App	Goals
Adam, Colin	Leicester City	23	6
Ainsley, George E.	Leeds United	64	35
Alberry, Bill E.	Leeds United	1	
Anson, Sidney	Army	1	
Antonio, George R.	Stoke City	10	5
Argue, Jimmy	Chelsea	4	1
Asquith, Beaumont	Barnsley	2	1
Attwell, Reg	West Ham United	2	
Baird, Henry	Huddersfield Town	2	1
Baker, Harold	Bradford PA	1	
Barton, Edward V. 'Teddy'	ex-Tranmere Rovers	4	
Batey, N. Bob	Preston North End	8	
Bedford, Harold	Amateur	1	
Bean, Alf	Lincoln City	1	
Binns, Cliff H.	Barnsley	2	
Birch, Walter	Rochdale	1	
Blair, Doug	Blackpool	1	
Bokas, Frank	Barnsley	5	
Booth, W. Sammy	Cardiff City	2	
Boyes, Walter E.	Everton	30	8
Bratley, George	Hull City	2	
Brown, John M.	Leeds United	15	4
Browne, Bobby, J.	Leeds United	7	
Buckley, Arthur	Leeds United	2	

Player	Team	App	Goals
Burbanks, W. Eddie	Sunderland	14	2
Burditt, George L.	Doncaster Rovers	9	3
Burton, Stanley	Wolverhampton W	1	
Bush, Tom W.	Liverpool	6	
Butterworth, Frank	Leeds United	108	
Byrom, Tom	Tranmere Rovers	4	
Calverley, Alf	Huddersfield Town	2	
Campbell, Robson	Charlton Athletic	20	1
Challinor, Jack	Stoke City	14	
Cherry, D.	Leeds United	1	
Chew, Jackie	Burnley	6	1
Clarke, Reg L.	Aldershot	1	
Clutterback, Jack	Wolverhampton W	1	
Cochrane, David	Leeds United	13	7
Collier, Austin	York City	2	
Copping, Wilf	Leeds United	28	
Corbett, Norman G.	West Ham United	1	
Coyne, Cyril	Leeds United	53	9
Crookes, Geoffrey	Leeds United	4	
Curry, Robert	Sheffield United	1	2
Dainty, Albert	Preston North End	1	
Daniels, John F.	Tranmere Rovers	121	
D'arcy, Lawrence	Folkestone	1	
Davie, John	Brighton & HA	5	4
Davies, Cecil J.	Barrow	6	1
Dempsey, Alan	Amateur	3	
Dewis, George	Leicester City	2	
Dorling, George	Tottenham Hotspur	4	1
Dowen, John S.	Hull City	1	
Downing, H.		1	
Duffy, Robert	Blackpool	15	
Dunderdale, W. Len	Leeds United	4	2
Dunn, William M.	Southampton	1	
Dutchman, John A.	Leeds United	5	2
Duthoit, Jack	Leeds United	21	
Eastham, Harry	Liverpool	6	
Edwards, Willis	Leeds United	24	2
Fallaize, Reg	Halifax Town	5	2
Farrage, Tom O.	Birmingham City	3	
Farrell, Arthur	Bradford PA	1	
Fearnley, Harrison L.	Leeds United	10	
Forde, Steve	West Ham United	2	

Player	Team	App	Goals
Fowler, H. Norman	Middlesbrough	17	
Gadsby, Ken J.	Leeds United	84	1
Galley, Tom	Wolverhampton W	4	
Glackin, Tom	Amateur	1	
Gleave, Colin	Stockport County	2	
Glover, Arthur	Barnsley	2	
Goldberg, Les	Leeds United	33	
Goodburn, H.		1	
Goslin, Harry A.	Bolton Wanderers	3	
Grainger, Dennis	Leeds United	35	9
Haddow, Johnny B.	Rangers	6	
Hardaker, Neville G.	Leeds United	2	
Hargreaves, Jack	Leeds United	48	18
Harper, Bernard	Barnsley	3	
Harper, Ken	Walsall	1	
Harris, William	Watford	2	
Harston, John	Wolverhampton W	2	
Harvey, Peter	West Ham United	1	
Heaton, Billy H.	Leeds United	23	3
Henry, Gerry R.	Leeds United	186	94
Hick, Jack B.	Bristol City	1	
Hindle, Tom	Leeds United	96	39
Hirst, Hubert	Bradford PA	1	
Hodgson, Gordon	Leeds United	33	14
Hodgson, John	Leeds United	40	
Holley, Tom	Leeds United	104	2
Houldershaw, Harry	Leeds United	3	
Houldershaw, Rex	Leeds United	22	3
Howitt, Harry	Armley Christ Church	4	
Howe, Arthur K.B.	Leeds United	2	
Hudson, George	Portsmouth	7	
Hulbert, J.		1	
Iceton, O. Lloyd	Preston North End	2	
Jackett, Stan		1	
James, John	Bradford PA	1	
Jameson, Percy	Darlington	1	1
Jones, Bill	Barnsley	2	
Jones, Bill 'W.H.'	Liverpool	2	
Jones, Eric N.	Brentford	1	
Jones, Syd	Arsenal	14	
Jordan, Clarrie	Doncaster Rovers	1	
Keeping, Alex E.M.	Fulham	2	

Player	Team	App	Goals
Kidd, William E.	Chesterfield	1	
Kinghorn, William J.D.	Liverpool	2	
Kirby, Dennis	Leeds United	9	
Kirton, John	Stoke City	6	
Knight, Arnold W.	Leeds United	82	12
Laidman, Fred	Sunderland	3	
Laking, George	Middlesbrough	1	
Lambert, Ray	Liverpool	3	
Lawn, Maurice	Leeds United	3	1
Lee, Alec	Leeds United	45	2
Lichfield, Eric	Newcastle United	15	1
Lindley, W. Maurice	Everton	1	
Livingstone, R. Archie	Weymouth	2	
McClure, Duncan	Kilmarnock	3	
McGraw, James	Leeds United	88	8
McInnes, John S.	Liverpool	3	
McKellor, Walter	Huddersfield Town	1	
McTavish, Hugh	Watford	1	
Maddison, Ralph	Bishop Auckland	1	
Mahon, Jack	Huddersfield Town	33	10
Makinson, Jim	Leeds United	103	2
Marshall, Dennis	Leeds United	1	
Meens, Harold	Hull City	1	
Milburn, George W.	Chesterfield	3	
Milburn, Jack	Norwich City	64	6
Milburn, Jim	Leeds United	52	4
Morton, Norman	Sunderland	1	1
Moss, Amos	Aston Villa	8	
Moule, Jack	Leeds United	21	7
Murgatroyd, Arthur	Whitkirk	8	
Normanton, Sidney	Barnsley	2	
O'Farrell, John	Hamilton Accies	1	
O'Neill, Tom H.	Newcastle United	1	
Oliver, Harry S.	Hartlepools United	1	
Padgett, Herbert	Sheffield Wednesday	1	
Parker, William	Wolverhampton W	2	
Paton, John	Celtic	4	
Patterson, George L.	Liverpool	3	
Pickering, Bill	Sheffield Wednesday	2	
Pogson, Donald	Leeds United	1	
Poland, George	Liverpool	10	
Pope, Alf	Halifax Town	1	

Player	Team	App	Goals
Powell, Aubrey	Leeds United	126	38
Poxon, John	Dulwich Hamlet	4	
Price, Arthur	Leeds United	21	1
Pike, R.D.	Wrexham	1	
Ramsden, Bernard	Liverpool	8	
Ramsey, J.	Hearts	2	
Rhodes, Arthur	Cardiff City	6	
Robbins, Horace S.	Dulwich Hamlet	1	
Rodgers, William	Blackburn Rovers	2	
Rozier, Alf	Fulham	3	
Ruecroft, Jacob	Halifax Town	2	
Rutherford, Eddie	Rangers	20	6
Saxon, Albert	Yorkshire Amateurs	1	
Scaife, George	Leeds United	2	
Sellar, Raymond	Welsh Guards	1	
Shafto, Johnny	Liverpool	1	
Shanks, Robert	Crystal Palace	6	1
Sharp, Norman	Everton	1	
Sharples, Kenneth	Amateur	1	
Short, John D.	Leeds United	58	36
Shotton, Bob	Barnsley	5	
Simpson, John	Huddersfield Town	2	
Skidmore, William	Wolverhampton W	2	
Smith, Gavin	Barnsley	2	1
Smith, Jack	Chelsea	11	
Spike, Septimus	Newcastle United	6	
Spink, Ken	Yorkshire Stormcocks	1	
Stacey, Alec	ex-Leeds United	1	
Stanton, Reg	West Ham United	3	
Steel, Fred C.	Stoke City	2	2
Stephens, Alf	Leeds United	6	5
Stephens, J. Bill	Leeds United	16	2
Stephenson, J. Eric	Leeds United	39	7
Stevens, Tom	Northampton Town	1	1
Stokes, Ernie	Southend United	5	
Sturrock, William	Forfar Athletic	2	
Sutherland Harry	Leeds United	5	3
Swindin, George	Arsenal	9	
Tatton, Billy	Leeds United	5	2
Taylor, Leslie T.	Isthmian League	3	
Taylor, Phil H.	Liverpool	2	
Taylor, Walter	Grimsby Town	2	

Player	Team	App	Goals
Thompson, Leslie	Leeds United	32	1
Tindall, John E.	Amateur	1	
Townsend, Len	Brentford	12	14
Tremelling, Jack	Wolverhampton W	2	4
Turner, John	Bristol City	2	1
Twomey, Jim F.	Leeds United	5	
Vickers, Harry	Leeds United	6	
Wakefield, Albert	Leeds United	22	10
Walker, Jack	St Mirren	3	
Warburton, George	Chester	2	
Ward, Tim V.	Derby County	4	
Ward, Tom A.	Sheffield Wednesday	1	1
Warren, Ray	Bristol Rovers	7	
Watson, George		1	
Weaver, Sam	Chelsea	27	2
Wesley, John C.	Bradford PA	1	
Westlake, Frank	Sheffield Wednesday	1	
Wheeler, S.		1	
Whittle, J. Roger	Port Vale	1	
Wilcocks, George E.	Derby County	4	
Wildon, Norman	Middlesbrough	1	
Wilkinson, Ken	Huddersfield Town	1	
Williams, Billy	West Bromwich A	1	
Williams, Cyril E.	Bristol City	1	
Williams, Tom	Cardiff City	1	1
Woffinden, Richard	Wolverhampton W	3	
Yeomanson, Jack	Leeds United	20	1
Own-goals*			8
Totals		**2,673**	**486**

* Briggs, *Huddersfield Town*; Gregory, *Bradford City*; Harper, *Barnsley*; Harston, *Barnsley*; Heppelwhite, *Middlesbrough*; Stelling, *Sunderland*; Whalley, *Manchester United*; Young, *Huddersfield Town*

Fallen Heroes

World War One

Although war was declared a month before the 1914–15 season got underway, the Football League pottered on as normal. Fixtures and dates were arranged, transfer fees fixed and the go-ahead given to player benefit matches at its management committee meeting on 6 August.

However, as the British Expeditionary Force landed in France two weeks later, the League gave permission for clubs to play games in aid of war relief funds. But football's authorities drew the line at calling off the season, claiming it should carry on as normal as possible to help the nation bear its sorrow.

Rugby union had already ceased and as the weeks wore on more pressure came to bear on the League to call a halt to the season. Gradually, fans began to vote with their feet and attendances started to decline. At Elland Road only three games topped 10,000 or more, far lower than 1913–14.

With gate receipts falling against the backdrop of wholesale slaughter on the continent, players' wages were cut but clubs – and the League – were running out of money. Many players had also signed up with the Footballers' Battalion, which was formed in December 1914, others were involved with munitions work and away trips to matches by train were becoming increasingly difficult because of travel restrictions.

The season was completed, but the League bowed to the inevitable and on 3 July 1915 the official suspension of League football was announced at a conference in Blackpool. However, football was played in an ad-hoc fashion throughout hostilities, Leeds City being one of the most successful clubs.

Among those who had joined the Footballers' Battalion was former England centre-half and future Leeds United manager Major Frank Buckley who was seriously injured when metal shrapnel hit him in the chest and punctured his lungs. Buckley was sent to a military hospital in Kent and after operating on him, surgeons were able to remove the shrapnel, but his lungs were so badly damaged that he was never able to play football again.

By January 1917 Buckley was back at the Front and was mentioned in dispatches for the bravery he showed during the hand-to-hand fighting that took place during the offensive at Argentvillers. The Germans used poison gas during the battle and the Major's lungs were unable to cope and he was sent back home to recuperate.

The brave Buckley survived World War One but the players in this chapter who had played for Leeds City did not return home.

Several City, and soon to be United players, served in the war on land and sea and made valuable contributions to the war effort. In factories geared for war, men like Herbert Chapman ensured those at the front line were supplied while full-back Jack McQuillan had his playing career ended when a grinding machine exploded at the factory in Hull where he was working.

John Anderson Harkins

(10 April 1881–22 April 1916)

Glasgow-born Jack was a member of the famous Black Watch Regiment (Royal Highlanders) before he became a professional footballer. Middlesbrough bought him out of the Army in September 1906 after seeing him shine against Celtic in a Scottish Cup tie and gave him his First Division debut the following month against Newcastle.

After falling out of favour, he had spells with Broxburn Athletic and Bathgate, where he had previously lived and worked in the steel industry, before joining Leeds City in August 1910. A solid right-half, he notched up 63 League games for City in two seasons.

Shortly before joining Darlington in 1912, Jack lodged with winger Jimmy Thackeray, with whom he played at Middlesbrough, at Great Horton when Thackeray was playing for Bradford City.

He then linked up with his former Leeds manager Frank Scott-Walford at Coventry, who were then in the Southern League, for the 1914–5 season.

Jack rejoined his old Scottish regiment, the Black Watch and was a corporal with F Company 2nd Battalion who landed at the port of Basra in Persia, what is today Iraq, shortly after Christmas 1915. Basra, the key to the Persian oilfields, had just fallen to British troops after a 10-day battle with Ottoman forces.

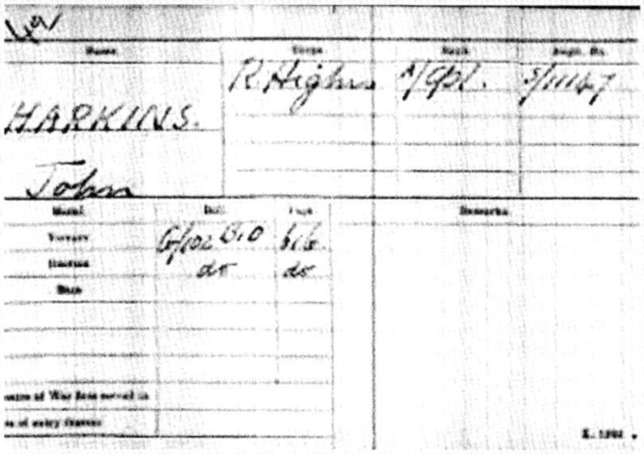

HARKINS.
John

Jack Harkins' medal card.

The Black Watch pushed about 100 miles further north to Amara where Corporal Jack Harkins was killed in action on 22 April 1916, aged 34. The son of James and Jane Harkins, he left a widow, Lily, at their home in Cranston Street, Edinburgh.

He was buried in Amara War Cemetery, alongside 4,620 other men.

Gerald Kirk

(14 July 1883–24 April 1915)

Sporting all-rounder Gerald played football for fun but seriously enough to turn out for Leeds City and neighbours Bradford City in League football. His father, Alfred, was a successful engineer, and Gerald was born into a relatively wealthy family in Bramley, just outside Leeds, on 14 July 1883.

His early education was in Ilkley, but from the age of 12 he boarded at Pocklington School, near York, before leaving in his late teens to return to the family home in Ingleton in the Yorkshire Dales.

He captained Ingleton FC, leading them to the Lancaster and District League title in 1903. His performances at centre-half attracted the interest of Bradford City and he signed for them in April 1905 on amateur terms. He played 40 Division Two games for the Bantams in just over a year, scoring a couple of goals, before transferring to Leeds City, still retaining his amateur status.

Gerald made his debut in a 2–1 defeat at Hull on 22 December but could not secure a regular place in the first team and returned to Valley Parade in September 1907.

He played just three more games for Bradford before going back to play for Ingleton where he was a pillar of the community.

Apart from being an excellent firearms shot, keen cricketer and tennis player, Gerald was a sidesman at St Mary's Church, was secretary of the local Conservative Club and Ingleton Farmers' Association and an ardent follower of the Vale of Lune Hounds.

He and his wife, Sarah Jane, were living in Carnforth on the Lancashire coast when war was declared and he enlisted in the Kings Own Royal Lancaster Regiment on 2 September 1914 and became a Second Lieutenant on 3 January 1915, entering a training camp at Didcot in Oxfordshire.

2nd lieutenant Gerald Kirk with members of the Pals Company of the 5th Battalion at Didcot in September 1914. He is second from left, middle row.

Picture: King's Own Royal Regiment Museum, Lancaster.

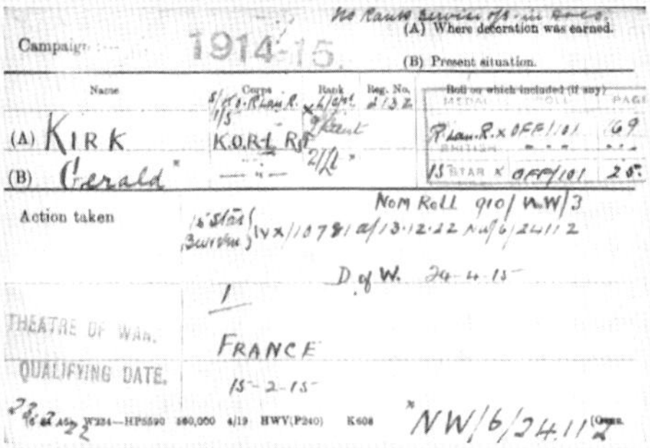
Campaign 1914-15
(A) Where decoration was earned.
(B) Present situation.
Name | Corps | Rank | Reg. No. | Roll on which included (if any)
(A) KIRK | K.O.R.L. R. | 2/Lt
(B) Gerald
Action taken
Nom Roll 910/N.W/3
D of W. 24-4-15
THEATRE OF WAR. FRANCE
QUALIFYING DATE. 15-2-15
NW/6/24112

Gerald Kirk's medal card.

The following month Gerald landed at Le Havre with the 5th Battalion who took part in a great charge with Canadian forces at Ypres in Belgium on 23 April. Lt Kirk was severely wounded at Wieltje and died the following day in a military hospital at Poperinghe.

His commanding officer, Capt Gerald W. Sharpe, said: 'He died a noble and gallant death, leading his platoon across an absolute inferno of shot and shell. He was wounded through the chest by a bullet. Four of his men carried him back to the dressing station where he was made as comfortable as possible and he was the first to be sent off in the motor ambulance.'

Another glowing tribute was made by Col Lord Richard Cavendish, who wrote: 'He was mortally wounded when bravely leading his men against a very strong position of the enemy. Although he had only been in the battalion a comparatively short time, he had endeared himself to us all, and he will be deeply mourned and long remembered. He had proved himself an extremely efficient officer.'

Gerald was buried, aged 32, in Poperinghe Old Military Cemetery and on 9 March 1916 a memorial tablet was unveiled to his memory at St Mary's Church in Ingleton.

Evelyn Henry Lintott

(2 November 1883–1 July 1916)

Evelyn, like Gerald Kirk, was also a gentleman footballer, but one who reached the height of his sport. A schoolteacher by profession, he was an England international and the first head of what is now the Professional Footballers' Association.

A centre-half with Herbert Chapman's City team in 1912–13, he was one of the first, and most high profile, footballers to join up after the outbreak of the war.

The son of a cattle salesman, Evelyn was born in Godalming, Surrey, on 2 November 1883. He attended King Edward VI Grammar School in Guildford and St Luke's Training College in Exeter. After qualifying as a teacher,

Amateur star Evelyn Lintott in his playing days wearing his England strip.

he played as an amateur, captaining Woking in 1905–06, representing Surrey and playing briefly for Plymouth Argyle.

His football life took off when he joined QPR in the Southern League after taking a teaching post in Willesden in north London. He won five amateur caps and made three full appearances for England's senior side in 1908 before joining Bradford City in November of that year; the £1,000-plus helping the Hoops out of serious financial difficulties.

While at Valley Parade he made four more England appearances and worked for a sports kit manufacturer before returning to teaching in the Dudley Hill area of Bradford. He was also involved with the Association Football Players' Union, later to become the PFA, and was elected the organisation's chairman. His brother, Frederick, a sports journalist with the *Bradford Daily Telegraph*, edited the union's magazine.

It was quite a coup for Leeds when Evelyn joined the Elland Road roster on 7 June 1912 and was ever-present in his first season when City finished sixth in Division Two.

A few weeks after war broke out, Evelyn enlisted at Leeds on 14 September 1914, even though he lived close to Valley Parade in neighbouring Bradford. He joined up with the 15th Battalion West Yorkshire Regiment (Prince of Wales Own), known as the Leeds Pals, whose ranks also included Yorkshire County cricketers Roy Kilner and Major William Booth.

After training in the Yorkshire Dales around Masham, Evelyn was promoted to sergeant and by the end of the year had risen to the rank of lieutenant, the first professional footballer to gain a commission.

Evelyn's regiment sailed on the liner *Empress of Britain* – which two weeks after the sinking of the *Titanic* also struck an iceberg but escaped with minor damage – from Liverpool to Egypt to guard the Suez Canal, arriving at Port Said just before Christmas 1915.

After three months in Egypt, his regiment boarded the troopship *Asconia* for France, landing at Marseilles and was transported to the front for the assault on the Somme where Evelyn was cut down, aged 33, struck in the chest by machine gun fire at 3pm on the first day of the battle on 1 July 1916.

The *Yorkshire Post* reported: 'Lt Lintott's end was particularly gallant. Tragically, he was killed leading his platoon of the 15th West Yorkshire Regiment, The Leeds Pals, over the top. He led his men with great dash and when hit the first time declined to take the count. Instead, he drew his revolver and called for further effort. Again he was hit but struggled on but a third shot finally bowled him over.'

Evelyn achieved the rank of lieutenant.

His body was never found, but is commemorated on the Thiepval Memorial to the Missing which has 72,000 names of British and Commonwealth soldiers killed during the Battle of the Somme who have no known grave.

THOMAS HENRY MORRIS

(14 September 1884–24 March 1916)

Centre-half Tom was the longest-serving Leeds City player to die in World War One, clocking up more than a century of appearances for the Peacocks. He came to Elland Road from Brighton with manager Frank Scott-Walford for whom he later played at Coventry.

The son of a Grimsby fish dock foreman, Tom signed for his hometown team in February 1906 from local side Haycroft Rovers but moved to Brighton the following May and arrived at Leeds in March 1909 to link up with his old boss.

He spent more than four seasons at Elland Road and a football annual of 1913, the year he left to become player-coach at Scunthorpe and Lindsay United, described him as 'a fearless, tireless hard-working centre-half. Tackles well and passes to advantage. Served his clubs with credit and distinction'.

After a season in the Midland League with Scunthorpe he hooked up with his old mentor Scott-Walford, who was helping keep Coventry afloat in the Southern League out of his own pocket. Tom had been ever-present at Highfield Road until he enlisted in March 1915.

He served with the 2nd Battalion of the Lincolnshire Regiment, known as The Poachers, and met his fate during the German spring offensive of 1918.

Rising to the rank of sergeant, he was among the men who were in the muddy waterlogged trenches near Passchendaele before they marched overnight on 18/19 January to Wieltje then on by motor bus to Waton where the Lincolnshires were transferred to the 62nd Brigade as part of the 5th Allied Army.

The Allies knew through information from prisoners that a German attack, centring on the strategic village of Pozieres, was imminent, and when it arrived its scale stunned British forces. On 21 March gas and explosive shells from guns of every calibre rained down on the Lincolnshires in a four-hour bombardment as the Germans advanced in thick fog.

Through the gloom, the enemy could be seen moving towards the Allied lines with stretchers packed with ammunition – a ploy which helped extend the fighting for three days.

Tom Morris, the Lincolnshire-born centre-half.

The British were driven back across the former Somme battlefields by overwhelming numbers and it was on the final day of the fighting near Bapaume, Palm Sunday, 24 March, that Tom was killed in action. His name in inscribed on the Pozieres Memorial which encloses the British cemetery.

DAVID BRUCE MURRAY

(4 December 1882–10 December 1915)

David was one of the few players for whom Leeds City paid a transfer fee during their first season of League football. A former Rangers reserve, he is also one of the rare number to play for both Liverpool and Everton.

He was born in Cathcart, Glasgow, on 4 December 1882 and was a good enough junior to be signed by the Ibrox club but after making little impact made his breakthrough in 1903–04 after joining Everton. He played twice at left-back in Division One that season, moving in the summer to Liverpool where he won a Division Two Championship medal.

Leeds signed him for £150 in December 1905 and he put in four years solid defensive service at Elland Road, making 83 League appearances and scoring seven goals – six of them from the penalty spot.

A cigarette card of David Murray, along with his service record.

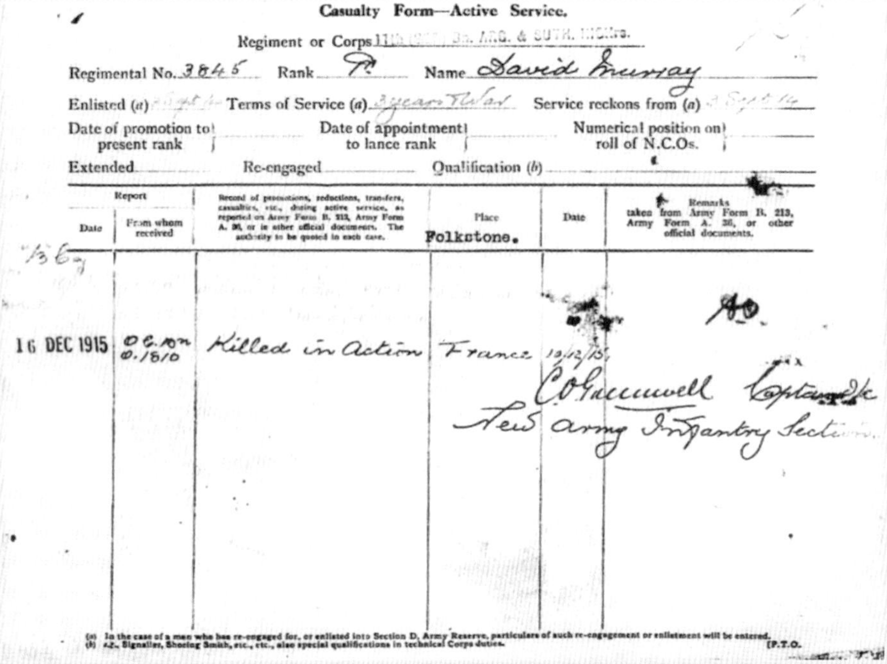

Casualty Form—Active Service.

Regiment or Corps 11th (S.) Bn. ARG. & SUTH. HIGHrs.

Regimental No. 3845 Rank Pte Name David Murray

Enlisted (a) 3 Sept 14 Terms of Service (a) 3 years the War Service reckons from (a) 3 Sept 14

Date of promotion to present rank Date of appointment to lance rank Numerical position on roll of N.C.Os.

Extended Re-engaged Qualification (b)

Report Date	From whom received	Record of promotions, reductions, transfers, casualties, etc., during active service, as reported on Army Form B. 213, Army Form A. 36, or in other official documents. The authority to be quoted in each case.	Place Folkstone.	Date	Remarks taken from Army Form B. 213, Army Form A. 36, or other official documents.
16 DEC 1915	O.C. 10th O.1810	Killed in Action	France	10/12/15	A.O.

C.O. Greenwell Captain
New Army Infantry Section.

(a) In the case of a man who has re-engaged for, or enlisted into Section D, Army Reserve, particulars of such re-engagement or enlistment will be entered.
(b) e.g., Signaller, Shoeing Smith, etc., etc., also special qualifications in technical Corps duties. [P.T.O.

David moved on to Mexborough Town in 1909 and also had a brief spell at Burslem Port Vale before working as a miner in Mexborough where he boarded with William Sleight and his wife, Elizabeth, at 13 Garden Street. He enlisted for Kitchener's Army in Mexborough on 3 September 1914 and served as a private with Argyll and Sutherland Highlanders (Princess Louise's).

He fought with The Thin Red Line, as they were known, after they landed at Boulogne on 9 July 1915. David's Battalion was dispatched to the front and he was killed in action near Loos on 10 December 1915, six days after his 33rd birthday.

His landlady, Mrs Sleight, successfully applied for his British War and Victory medals to be sent to her at Mexborough, describing David as an 'adopted son' in the Army paperwork. It is not known if this adoption was official.

JAMES HAMILTON SPEIRS

(22 March 1886–30 August 1917)

Scottish international Jimmy Speirs won the Military Medal for the bravery he displayed in battle. Along with Evelyn Lintott he was the most well-known of the Leeds City men to lay down their life for king and country in World War One.

Like Lintott, Jimmy was signed by Herbert Chapman from Bradford City where he enjoyed legendary status by scoring the goal that beat Newcastle United in the 1911 FA Cup Final replay at Old Trafford.

A native of the Govanhill district of Glasgow, he came from a mining family and began his career with Annandale and Maryhill while working as a clerk. He stepped up in class to join Glasgow giants Rangers in August 1905. He made his sole appearance for Scotland three years later in a 2–1 win against Wales at Dens Park, Dundee. After a year with Clyde he moved south in September 1909 to Bradford City where he was made captain.

His arrival at Elland Road from neighbouring Bradford in summer 1913 for £1,400, a huge fee for the era, caught the Leeds public's imagination and he didn't disappoint.

Jimmy Speirs, the Scottish international, feted on a cigarette card.

Jimmy kitted out in the uniform of the Queen's Own 7th Battalion Cameron Highlanders.

Leading the team by example, he scored 32 League goals and creating countless others for Billy McLeod, in two seasons.

His final game for City was a 2–0 home defeat at the hands of Barnsley on 24 April 1915 by which time the war was well underway.

Just over three weeks after the season had finished, 29-year-old Jimmy volunteered in Glasgow to enlist in the Queen's Own 7th Battalion Cameron Highlanders. He was older than most recruits and had he not volunteered may never have fought as conscription was only a year away and he would have been exempt because he was married with two small children.

Instead, Jimmy chose to serve his country and was immediately posted to a reserve battalion in Inverness before heading to France in March 1916, moving up the ranks to corporal before being wounded in his left elbow by either a bullet or shrapnel in heavy fighting in autumn 1916. He was not sent home and after convalescing in France was awarded the Military Medal for bravery in the field at Grand Rullecourt – an act that also saw him promoted to sergeant – although there is no detail about what deed Jimmy did to earn the honour.

The Cameron Highlanders were in the thick of the action at Passchendaele in summer 1917 and Speirs was declared wounded and missing in action on 20 August and a few days later presumed dead.

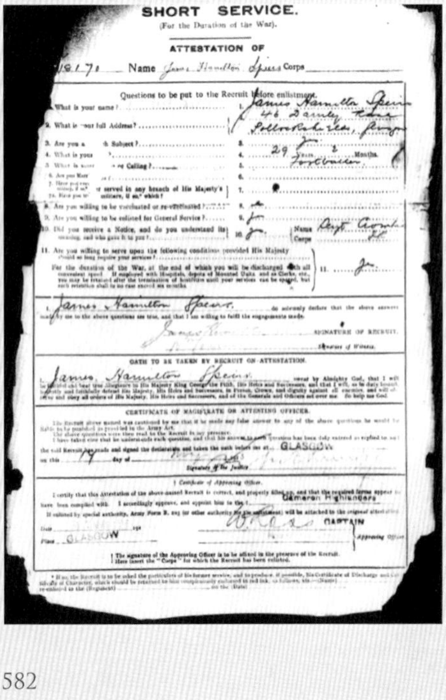

SHORT SERVICE.

(For the Duration of the War).

ATTESTATION OF

Name James Hamilton Speirs Corps

Questions to be put to the Recruit before enlistment.

1. What is your name? — 1. James Hamilton Speirs
2. What is your full Address? — 2. 46 Darnley Place, Pollokshields, Glasgow
3. Are you a British Subject? — 3. Yes
4. What is your Age? — 4. 29 Years 2 Months
5. What is your Trade or Calling? — 5. Footballer
6. Are you Married? — 6.
7. Have you ever served in any branch of His Majesty's Forces, naval or military, if so, which? — 7.
8. Are you willing to be vaccinated or re-vaccinated? — 8.
9. Are you willing to be enlisted for General Service? — 9. Yes
10. Did you receive a Notice, and do you understand its meaning, and who gave it to you? — 10. Yes. Name: Sergt. Cameron
11. Are you willing to serve upon the following conditions provided His Majesty should so long require your services? For the duration of the War, at the end of which you will be discharged with all convenient speed. — 11. Yes.

I, James Hamilton Speirs, do solemnly declare that the above answers made by me to the above questions are true, and that I am willing to fulfil the engagements made.

SIGNATURE OF RECRUIT.

Signature of Witness.

OATH TO BE TAKEN BY RECRUIT ON ATTESTATION.

I, James Hamilton Speirs, swear by Almighty God, that I will be faithful and bear true Allegiance to His Majesty King George the Fifth, His Heirs and Successors, and that I will, as in duty bound, honestly and faithfully defend His Majesty, His Heirs and Successors, in Person, Crown, and dignity against all enemies, and will observe and obey all orders of His Majesty, His Heirs and Successors, and of the Generals and Officers set over me. So help me God.

CERTIFICATE OF MAGISTRATE OR ATTESTING OFFICER.

The Recruit above named was cautioned by me that if he made any false answer to any of the above questions he would be liable to be punished as provided in the Army Act.

The above questions were then read to the Recruit in my presence.

I have taken care that he understands each question, and that his answer to each question has been duly entered as replied to, and the said Recruit has made and signed the declaration and taken the oath before me at GLASGOW on this 14 day of May 1915

Signature of the Justice

Certificate of Approving Officer.

I certify that this Attestation of the above-named Recruit is correct, and properly filled up, and that the required forms appear to have been complied with. I accordingly approve, and appoint him to the Cameron Highlanders

If enlisted by special authority, Army Form B. 203 (or other authority for the enlistment) will be attached to the original attestation.

Date 191

Place GLASGOW

W. Ross CAPTAIN Approving Officer

The signature of the Approving Officer is to be affixed in the presence of the Recruit.

Here insert the "Corps" for which the Recruit has been enlisted.

Jimmy's call-up papers.

The *Bradford Weekly Telegraph* reported he had been hit in the thigh during an advance, and managed to crawl into a shell-hole. 'There he was attended to for a short time, but the Cameron Highlanders did not return from their raid that way, so he was not seen again.'

His body was later found and identified and is buried about four miles north east of Ypres in Dochy Farm New British Cemetery where about 1,500 men were interred. His medals were sent to his widow, Bessie, who received a war pension of 25 shillings and 5d a week for her and Jimmy's children, nine-year-old James and Elizabeth, five.

WORLD WAR TWO

War was declared on Sunday 3 September 1939, a day after clubs had completed their third game of the season. It was no great surprise to anyone as several players had already been called up for military training and, unlike in World War One, the League acted decisively. Telegrams were sent to clubs stating that the competition had been suspended.

Regional competitions were held and Leeds United were among the clubs to soldier on. In fact, only six clubs – Aston Villa, Derby County, Exeter City, Gateshead, Ipswich Town and Sunderland opted to close down.

However, many of United's players and former players saw active service and those below are known to have paid the ultimate price.

ALAN FOWLER

(20 November 1911–10 July 1944)

Local boy star Alan was a forward who was tipped for the top. The Rothwell-born youngster was an England Schools international who was playing for Whitehall Printeries when he signed for Leeds on his 16th birthday.

But in the late 1930s competition was hot at Elland Road with Tom Jennings, Charlie Keetley and Arthur Hydes banging in the goals. Young Fowler had to bide his time and was loaned back to the Printeries and had a spell with Brodsworth Main to gain experience. In 15 senior games for United he scored eight goals but it was only when he joined Swindon Town in May 1934 that he reached his full potential.

Leeds-born forward Alan Fowler from a team line-up at Swindon where his name is on a plaque at the County Ground.

Standing at just 5ft 6in and weighing less than 10 stone, he had great dribbling skills and scored 102 goals – including a hat-trick against Luton in the first six minutes – in 224 appearances in six years with the Robins.

Alan briefly returned to Leeds to play wartime football, but his wife Emily and parents, Joseph and Phyllis, remained in the West Country so he returned to Swindon to enlist and found himself in the Dorsetshire Regiment.

Because of his natural fitness, Alan became a sergeant PT instructor with the Dorsets who were part of the 43rd (Wessex) Division, which also included two battalions from the Wiltshire Regiment, and others from the south-west.

Long before embarking for France, he distinguished himself in 1941, reported the local Swindon paper, by saving three men's lives, as well as his own, while priming grenades.

The Wessex Division had arrived in France on 24 June, and a little over two weeks later were earmarked to take part in Operation Jupiter, which was the breakout after the British liberated the Normandy city of Caen.

Alan's battalion had orders to liberate the towns of Eterville and Martot, south-west of the city, as part of an operation to capture Hill 112 – a position of great strategic importance. Fighting for the hill was intense and Fowler died of wounds on the first day of engagement, 10 July 1944.

How he received those wounds is controversial with one published writer, using an eye-witness account, suggesting Alan was the victim of 'friendly fire' after the British assault began with a massive bombardment of enemy positions when air-support Typhoon fighters, inadvertently dropped two bombs in the middle of the 4 Dorset's B Company.

Alan is buried at Baneville-la-Campagne war cemetery about five miles east of Caen. His father was assistant groundsman at the County Ground where there is a plaque on the North Stand dedicated to Fowler and other Swindon players who died serving their country.

MAURICE HUBERT LAWN

(22 October 1923–7 August 1944)

Centre-forward Maurice Lawn was the youngest of the United players to lose their lives fighting for their country. Maurice died in what was one of the conflict's most horrific incidents which was not widely reported at the time.

He was the 20-year-old son of mill worker Herbert Lawn, who lived in Rothesay Terrace, one of the Holbeck back-to-back houses close to Elland Road, before the family moved to nearby 12 Euston Grove. A former pupil of Ingram Road School, he played for Leeds City Schools and Whitehall Printeries and worked at Dunn's Hatters in Boar Lane in the city centre.

Maurice made the first of his appearances for United, scoring in a 3–2 win at Middlesbrough on 13 March 1943, and retained his place for the following week's game against Newcastle at Elland Road, Leeds losing 3–1. His final game came in the following season – a 5–1 defeat at Bradford City on 11 September – and less than a year later died off the coast of Normandy.

Maurice was a trooper with 15th Scottish Regiment whose units started to land in France about a week after D-Day, 6 June. His regiment were attached to the Royal Armoured Corps and played a key role in the overland push to force the Germans back in the thick of combat at Odon River and Mont Picon.

Trooper Lawn was part of a reconnaissance party clearing an area near Galet and La Mancelliere on 2 August 1944 when they came under heavy machine gun fire. Several men were hit and Maurice provided cover as the group withdrew, but was shot in the stomach.

He made it back to safety and was taken to a field hospital from where he was moved aboard the hospital ship SS *Amsterdam*, a former London and North East Railways ship which was anchored off Caen.

The vessel had been commissioned and fully kitted out with medical wards and operating theatres. *Amsterdam* had made several successful Channel crossings between Normandy and Southampton and saved many lives but on the foggy morning of 7 August – five days after he had been wounded – stricken Trooper Lawn was helpless as the ship struck a mine off Juno Beach and rapidly sank.

He was one of 55 wounded men who drowned, along with 30 medical staff and 11 German prisoners of war.

The 15th Scottish Regiment had the honour of leading the final river crossing into Germany over the Rhine, Maurice Lawn, whose name is inscribed on the Bayeux Memorial, was, sadly, not among them.

ROBERT MONTGOMERY

(18 April 1922–30 January 1944)

Promising United centre-forward Robert Montgomery was killed when leading a bombing raid on a German ball bearing factory at Schweinfurt. He had earlier made his mark in the Elland Road junior ranks after signing from Irish side Portadown, the club which supplied winger Davy Cochrane, in September 1938.

Although a North Irishman, born at Enniskillen, County Fermanagh, Bob gained a scholarship to attend Sligo Grammar School where he shone at rugby winning a Connaught province cap. But he also excelled at football and was spotted by Portadown playing for Armagh Whites, an Armagh Summer League side, against Eden Villa. He had trials with the Ports in 1937 before returning to school and the following year scored a hat-trick for the Portadown club in a trial game after scoring 16 goals for Killyrea in the Summer League.

He looked a star in the making and marked his senior Portadown debut with a goal in a 4–0 win against Larne. That match was watched by United manager Billy Hampson who was running the rule over another Portadown player, George Black. Hampson switched his attention to the 5ft 10in, 12st, 16-year-old amateur forward and the deal was sealed a few days later on 7 September 1938 when Hampson met Portadown manager Tom Sloan and two of his directors at Ibrox Park when the Scottish League beat the Irish League 6–1.

Although he didn't make the first team, Bob was a regular in the Leeds side which were runners-up in the Yorkshire League in 1938–39 and had played for the reserves four times before volunteering.

Rising Irish star Robert Montgomery died after a raid on German territory.

'Monty' enlisted on 23 July 1941 with the Birmingham Reserve with the RAF with the hope of becoming a pilot. He did much of his pilot training in Canada before returning to England for further training at Whitley Bay in Northumberland. After a posting to RAF Scampston, Robert was discharged to a commission as a Pilot Officer on 14 January 1944.

He joined 49 Squadron and on 27 April 1944 flew his Lancaster crew on their 19th mission. The target were the ball bearing factories of Schweinfurt in Bavaria. The industrial units were a key part of the German war machine, helping to build engines and generators for tanks.

The raid was dangerous as it took place by moonlight and PO Montgomery's Lancaster JB679 was shot down on their return by a German fighter over France. Five of the seven-man crew, including Robert, were killed. All are buried beside each other in Bure Churchyard, Meuse, west of Nancy. They were one of 21 Lancasters who failed to return from the operation.

Of Robert's other crew, Sgt Richard Mitchell and Flight-Sergeant John Baker were able to parachute to safety. Baker was captured and became a prisoner of war while Mitchell managed to evade the Germans and with help from French civilians made his way to Switzerland and eventually back to England where he re-enlisted.

Robert was aged 22 when he was killed and on 25 February 2009, Bonhams of Chester auctioned his 1937 Connaught rugby cap and the Yorkshire League runners'-up medal he won with United.

Joseph Eric Stephenson

(4 September 1914–8 September 1944)

England international inside-forward Eric Stephenson was the highest-ranked of any Leeds player to be killed in combat. A major in the 3rd Gurkha Rifles, he was the only England international of his day to die while serving in World War Two.

The son of a Kent engineer, Eric's family moved from East London to Leeds when he was young, and he played for Oakwood Stormcocks and Leeds Schools before joining Harrogate, then a Northern League club, in 1931. Although most of his games were in the reserves the 17-year-old showed sufficient promise to be signed by Leeds on amateur terms, turning pro in September 1934.

A small, neat, probing inside-forward, he was capped twice by England in 1938 – a 1–0 defeat at the hands of Scotland at Wembley and a 7–0 thumping of Ireland at Maine Road. He also went on England's 1939 continental tour of Italy, Yugoslavia and Romania but didn't play.

Eric, who played 155 games for Leeds scoring 22 goals, joined up as a physical training instructor with the Army at Aldershot but was able to turn out for Leeds while he was based

LEEDS UNITED A.F.C. · LTD.

"At the going down of the sun and in the morning, we will remember them."

THE LATE

Major JOSEPH ERIC STEPHENSON

2nd K.E.O. GURKHA RIFLES

Killed in Action, 8th September, 1944

England international Eric Stephenson, one of the most high-profile players to die on active service in World War Two.

Michael
He endured hardness as a good soldier of Jesus Christ.
Major Joseph Eric Stephenson. I.A. Killed in action. Burma. 1944.
This window is a tribute to his memory from his wife and children.

Eric's name is honoured in stained glass at Lidgett Park Methodist Church, Leeds, where he was a worshipper.

with the Manchester Regiment in Malton, North Yorkshire. He played in representative games for the Army, FA and Football League and was named as a reserve for the England v Scotland game at Newcastle in February 1941.

But Eric was soon to leave football way behind him. After taking an Officer Cadet Training Unit course he gained his commission and went to India in 1942. He joined the 2nd King Edward VII Own Gurkha Rifles, known as the Sirmoor Rifles. They were part of a group known as the Chindits who were formed and trained by Major General Orde Wingate, specifically to operate behind enemy lines.

Eric, who had risen to the rank of major, was a part of this guerrilla force and was among those who made a famous 350-mile incursion into Japanese-held Burma territory. It was extremely dangerous jungle warfare in which disease, as well as enemy fire, claimed thousands of lives, Eric among them. He was killed in action four days after his 30th birthday and is buried in Taukhyan War Cemetary. His memory is permanently remembered, though, near his Leeds home in Chelwood Drive.

Eric was a member of Lidgett Park Methodist Church and was a lieutenant in the 30th Leeds Company Boys' Brigade. His church commissioned a Belfast company to make a stained-glass window of seven lights commemorating Eric and three other servicemen who lost their lives in World War Two, and three women. The Gurkha Rifles' regimental badge is depicted with the inscription below an image of St Michael: 'He endured hardness as a good soldier of Jesus Christ. Major Joseph Eric Stephenson. Killed in action Burma 1944. This window is a tribute to his memory from his wife and children.'

Leeds United did not forget their man either. On 27 May 1947 a benefit match against Glasgow Celtic was held at Elland Road, attracting 19,000 spectators. The Scottish side won 3–1 and the proceeds from the game went to Stephenson's widow, Olive, and their children, Janet and Rosalind.

Eric's brother, Ernest Frank Stephenson, was also killed on active service in August 1943.

LESLIE THOMPSON

(14 February 1922–29 August 1944)

Schoolboy star Leslie Thompson was born in Little Houghton, near Barnsley, to coal hewer Albert and Gladys Thompson and was killed in action before his unquestioned football talent could bear its full fruit.

The Thompsons lived in Little Houghton and Leslie went to school at neighbouring Great Houghton. A wing-half, he played for Dearne Valley and Yorkshire Schools, scoring for the county in a 5–3 win against Lancashire in 1936. That earned him a trial for The Rest against England Schools at Kettering and he did so well that he was elevated to the national schoolboy side to face Wales, the first of three caps that year.

Leslie joined Leeds in 1937 from Middlecliffe Rovers, the club which had produced Wilf Copping and Ken Gadsby. Although he had not made a senior appearance for United by the start of World War Two, he was on the groundstaff and made his debut on 28 October 1939 in a 3–0 win over Bradford City at Elland Road at left-half.

He joined the RAF Volunteer Reserve and after training was based at East Kirkby, Lincolnshire, from where he flew on several missions, often with Canadian airmen.

Former England Schools international Leslie Thompson, back row, far right, and his fellow crew members who were shot down over Denmark.

Leslie was a wireless operator and gunner, and on the night of 26 August 1944 took off in Lancaster ME650 of 630 squadron. The raid was at the extreme range for the planes, involving a round trip of 1,900 miles but Wireless Officer Air Gunner Thompson and his five crew members did not make it home along with three other Allied planes.

Leslie is buried in Skarrild Churchyard where there is a memorial to the fallen airmen.

It was the crew's 12th operation and they were on their way back from a bombing raid on Konigsberg in what was then East Prussia in the early hours when they were attacked by a night fighter. The Lancaster was shot down over Skarrild, Denmark, which was occupied by the Germans, and crashed in a farmer's field with the loss of all on board. Locals reported that the Lancaster's final act was to shoot down their attacker.

A German working party were digging a grave for the crew in the field when Constable Egon Christensen persuaded the military to allow the bodies to be buried in the local churchyard rather than the field. Christensen borrowed a horse-drawn carriage, put the bodies on board and covered them with the Danish flag.

A grave at the churchyard had been prepared and two large coffins had been placed in it. The carriage was parked next to it and Constable Christensen climbed down in the grave and one, by one, the seven bodies were handed down to him and placed in the coffins.

When this grim task was done, Vicar Henrik Ingerslev officiated at the grave side ceremony. The Germans allowed about 50 attending Danes to sing one hymn and before the end of the day the grave was covered with flowers.

Each year on the evening of 5 May – on the day of the liberation of Denmark – a ceremony is held at Skarrild Cemetery in honour of the fliers.

At least two players who guested for United in the war, **Harry Goslin** and **Tom Farrage** were also killed in action. Both men played three times in United colours during the war.

Goslin played for Bolton Wanderers and in early 1939 joined the Territorial Army, and inspired 14 other Bolton players to do the same. When war was declared, out of 35 Bolton players, 32 went into uniform, and the others worked in coal mines or munitions factories.

Lieutenant Goslin transferred to the 53 Field Regiment Royal Artillery and was wounded in action in Italy and died on 18 December 1943 and is buried in the Sangro River War Cemetery.

Birmingham left-winger Farrage was a member of the 10th Battalion Parachute Regiment and was involved in the Battle of Arnhem. He was killed on 23 September 1944 and is honoured on the Groesbeek Memorial in Holland.

Several United players were involved in the Services, some seeing action abroad and others being restricted to British camps.

Tom Holley and **Billy Heaton** were on active service in India and **Jim Milburn** was wounded in Belgium where Welsh international Aubrey Powell was also stationed.

Goalkeeper **Alex Lee**, who left Leeds for Northampton Town during the war, was awarded the Air Force Medal.

Bob Kane was with the Royal Artillery in Gibraltar and **Albert Wakefield** was in Italy where his displays in services' football prompted several Italian clubs to try to sign him. **Wilf Copping** was involved in the North African campaign while the **Stephens** twins, **Alf** and **Bill**, who turned out in wartime games, were both Royal Engineers and were taken prisoner, ending up in the same PoW camp.

Another captive was the **Earl of Harewood**, the future United president, who was a captain in the Grenadier Guards. He was wounded and captured shortly after D Day and from November 1944 was held in Colditz after direct orders from Adolf Hitler.

Anyone who knows of any Leeds players who were killed in action, but are not recorded in this book, can contact the authors via the publishers, DB Books, so they can be included in any future *Complete Record* of the club.

Leeds United's League Record Against Other Clubs 1920–2012

Leeds United have played 88 clubs in the Football League since 1920–21. Below is their record against each club. Some clubs changed their names (eg Small Heath became Birmingham then Birmingham City) and some clubs modified their titles (eg Leicester Fosse became Leicester City). In all cases except Wimbledon (now non-League AFC Wimbledon), the current name used by each club covers all games played under previous names. The totals do not include the abandoned season of 1939–40 or any League Play-off games since 1986–87.

		HOME					AWAY				
	P	W	D	L	F	A	W	D	L	F	A
AFC BOURNEMOUTH	8	4	0	0	11	2	2	2	0	4	1
ARSENAL	100	25	14	11	84	61	13	10	27	54	93
ASTON VILLA	80	17	15	8	63	38	10	11	19	45	63
BARNSLEY	50	11	8	6	45	29	6	7	12	32	44
BIRMINGHAM CITY	84	22	12	8	62	31	6	11	25	37	79
BLACKBURN ROVERS	82	22	11	8	74	43	15	10	16	58	62
BLACKPOOL	38	9	7	3	36	22	5	4	10	25	35
BOLTON WANDERERS	48	12	6	6	51	39	6	4	14	28	50
BRADFORD CITY	20	7	3	0	20	8	4	4	2	9	9
BRADFORD PA	10	4	1	0	12	4	2	1	2	5	8
BRENTFORD	26	7	4	2	24	12	3	6	4	16	20
BRIGHTON & HA	34	9	6	2	30	19	6	4	7	20	20
BRISTOL CITY	24	7	2	3	18	12	6	4	2	15	7
BRISTOL ROVERS	16	4	4	0	13	8	2	3	3	16	20
BURNLEY	52	16	5	5	53	30	12	5	9	38	40
BURY	42	13	3	5	38	18	5	7	9	31	39
CAMBRIDGE UNITED	4	2	0	0	5	2	0	2	0	2	2
CARDIFF CITY	40	9	7	4	26	13	1	6	13	10	28
CARLISLE UNITED	16	4	3	1	14	8	4	2	2	14	11
CHARLTON ATHLETIC	40	11	5	4	34	18	10	2	8	25	28
CHELSEA	90	28	12	5	89	32	11	13	21	47	75
CHELTENHAM TOWN	4	1	0	1	3	2	1	0	1	1	1
CHESTERFIELD	10	3	2	0	9	3	0	1	4	3	11

		HOME					AWAY				
	P	W	D	L	F	A	W	D	L	F	A
COLCHESTER UNITED	6	2	0	1	6	2	2	0	1	4	3
COVENTRY CITY	80	29	9	2	82	27	14	12	14	50	55
CREWE ALEXANDRA	8	2	1	1	7	5	2	1	1	6	5
CRYSTAL PALACE	50	16	4	5	44	21	5	10	10	19	28
DERBY COUNTY	94	28	10	9	78	39	14	13	20	62	78
DONCASTER ROVERS	20	6	3	1	19	8	4	4	2	11	10
EVERTON	104	36	12	4	101	45	11	17	24	49	87
EXETER CITY	2	1	0	0	2	1	0	0	1	0	2
FULHAM	46	12	6	5	37	20	8	4	11	33	35
GILLINGHAM	6	2	1	0	7	3	0	1	2	4	6
GRIMSBY TOWN	38	12	5	2	34	11	4	5	10	21	35
HARTLEPOOL UNITED	6	3	0	0	9	2	1	2	0	4	3
HEREFORD UNITED	2	1	0	0	1	0	0	0	1	0	2
HUDDERSFIELD TOWN	58	12	9	8	45	33	5	8	16	24	46
HULL CITY	42	13	6	2	43	18	7	4	10	23	27
IPSWICH TOWN	60	16	9	5	53	34	10	7	13	38	43
LEICESTER CITY	112	30	13	13	119	69	14	18	24	75	101
LEYTON ORIENT	22	7	3	1	16	7	4	3	4	12	13
LINCOLN CITY	12	5	0	1	20	7	1	3	2	5	8
LIVERPOOL	100	17	14	19	67	69	7	11	32	34	95
LUTON TOWN	42	12	5	4	33	20	3	10	8	21	33
MANCHESTER CITY	94	25	8	14	76	56	12	9	26	48	84
MANCHESTER UNITED	92	15	15	16	61	57	8	17	21	37	70
MIDDLESBROUGH	82	21	9	11	82	46	10	15	16	45	64
MILLWALL	24	8	1	3	22	12	4	2	6	15	19
MILTON KEYNES DONS	4	2	0	0	6	1	1	0	1	2	3
NELSON	2	1	0	0	1	0	0	0	1	1	3
NEWCASTLE UNITED	86	22	10	11	80	44	11	7	25	52	80
NORTHAMPTON TOWN	8	3	1	0	12	1	1	1	2	6	5
NORWICH CITY	44	12	6	4	34	26	5	5	12	27	42
NOTTINGHAM FOREST	78	19	12	8	65	42	8	17	14	46	49
NOTTS COUNTY	32	12	3	1	40	7	5	3	8	20	25
OLDHAM ATHLETIC	36	11	4	3	33	11	4	8	6	24	29
OXFORD UNITED	6	2	1	0	4	2	1	0	2	8	10
PETERBOROUGH UNITED	4	2	0	0	7	2	1	0	1	3	4
PLYMOUTH ARGYLE	38	12	6	1	40	16	6	4	9	26	32
PORTSMOUTH	52	16	6	4	47	26	5	10	11	33	56
PORT VALE	20	7	2	1	20	6	6	2	2	12	10
PRESTON NORTH END	44	9	4	9	38	37	5	4	13	23	47
QUEEN'S PARK RANGERS	44	10	6	6	43	24	7	7	8	24	27
READING	14	3	3	1	13	7	2	3	2	5	6

			HOME						AWAY		
	P	**W**	**D**	**L**	**F**	**A**	**W**	**D**	**L**	**F**	**A**
ROTHERHAM UNITED	28	8	2	4	29	18	5	1	8	20	24
SCUNTHORPE UNITED	12	4	1	1	12	8	4	0	2	12	7
SHEFFIELD UNITED	70	18	10	7	64	37	8	12	15	45	54
SHEFFIELD WEDNESDAY	80	21	11	8	74	44	13	8	19	53	69
SHREWSBURY TOWN14	4	2	1	11	6	3	2	2	12	12	
SOUTHAMPTON	88	25	12	7	71	34	19	7	18	69	62
SOUTH SHIELDS	10	2	1	2	6	4	3	0	2	8	6
SOUTHEND UNITED	8	4	0	0	10	1	0	2	2	1	3
STOCKPORT COUNTY	10	4	0	1	9	2	2	1	2	10	9
STOKE CITY	84	25	11	6	74	31	14	7	21	57	93
SUNDERLAND	82	22	10	9	71	46	14	6	21	49	68
SWANSEA CITY	34	13	3	1	45	16	4	3	10	27	38
SWINDON TOWN	16	5	2	1	14	6	4	2	2	15	10
TOTTENHAM HOTSPUR	88	21	14	9	68	46	9	12	23	51	77
TRANMERE ROVERS	6	2	0	1	6	3	2	0	1	7	4
WALSALL	12	5	0	1	14	3	2	3	1	8	5
WATFORD	14	3	2	2	11	10	3	3	1	7	5
WEST BROMWICH ALBION	74	18	10	9	63	40	13	5	19	48	63
WEST HAM UNITED	98	33	10	6	105	49	14	17	18	69	85
WIGAN ATHLETIC	2	0	0	1	0	2	0	0	1	0	3
WIMBLEDON	24	8	4	0	31	10	3	4	5	11	12
WOLVERHAMPTON W	78	23	9	7	66	31	9	10	20	37	64
WYCOMBE WANDERERS	2	0	1	0	1	1	1	0	0	1	0
YEOVIL TOWN	6	3	0	0	9	0	2	1	0	4	2
TOTALS	**3,572**	**992**	**452**	**342**	**3,225**	**1,766**	**499**	**472**	**815**	**2,108**	**2,901**

Leeds in Other Leagues

West Yorkshire League

See page 344

Season	P	W	D	L	F	A	Pts	Pos
1904–05	24	7	7	10	34	49	21	11th

North Eastern League

Leeds City became the founder members of the North Eastern League at a meeting in Newcastle United's boardroom on 5 May 1906. Together with major clubs from the North-East, City fielded an A team or third XI, but stayed only two seasons because of the high travelling costs.

Season	P	W	D	L	F	A	Pts	Pos
1906–07	18	9	4	5	33	20	22	4th
1907–08	24	13	3	8	64	46	29	4th

Midland League

Leeds City entered a reserve side in the Midland League for the first time in 1905–06 and finished in a respectable mid-table position. In 1913–14, City Reserves finished bottom, but were re-elected and the following season were runners-up, one point behind champions Rotherham County. After City were disbanded by FA order in 1919, newly formed Leeds United were invited to take over from City Reserves and were elected to the Midland League on 31 October. In 1920–21, United were elected to the Football League and their Reserves played in the Midland League for one more season before joining to the Central League.

Season	*P*	*W*	*D*	*L*	*F*	*A*	*Pts*	*Pos*
1905–06	34	10	8	16	60	81	28	12th
1906–07	38	16	10	12	67	64	42	8th
1907–08	38	14	9	15	61	72	37	11th
1908–09	38	12	4	22	56	90	28	18th
1909–10	42	18	6	18	60	75	42	10th
1910–11	38	13	9	16	66	68	35	12th
1911–12	36	18	6	12	57	49	42	5th
1912–13	38	18	7	13	68	52	43	5th
1913–14	34	8	4	22	45	75	20	18th
1914–15	38	24	5	9	99	42	53	2nd
1919–20	34	11	9	14	57	55	31	12th
1920–21	38	15	8	15	49	51	38	12th

Central League

United entered the Central League for the first time in 1921–22 and put in some respectable performances throughout the 1920s, but had to wait until 1936–37 for their first Championship. The Reserves, led by George Milburn, went into their last game of the season against bottom-of-the-table Oldham at Elland Road on 28 April, needing one point to pip Preston for the title. They did it in style, goals from George Ainsley, Jack Hargreaves and John Thomson clinching an easy 3–0 win. The United A team won the Yorkshire League Cup on the same night. As a tribute to the Reserves' achievement, they represented United in the West Riding Cup Final the following week against Bradford City.

After the war, United Reserves had a dismal Central League record, finishing bottom five times in 13 years. Even during Revie's days, when United's second-teamers were reckoned to be the strongest in the land, they struggled to make an impact in the Central League. When it was split into two divisions in 1982–83, United were in the top flight but were relegated the following season before regaining their place 12 months later when three points for a win was introduced for the first time.

Season	P	W	D	L	F	A	Pts	Pos
1921–22	42	14	15	13	61	60	43	10th
1922–23	42	23	7	12	74	45	53	5th
1923–24	42	17	7	18	64	58	41	11th
1924–25	42	20	7	15	64	55	47	8th
1925–26	42	20	4	18	103	71	44	7th
1926–27	42	23	7	12	89	70	53	4th
1927–28	42	21	8	13	112	60	50	3rd
1928–29	42	14	14	14	89	77	42	9th
1929–30	42	23	7	12	108	60	53	5th
1930–31	42	23	5	14	118	78	51	5th
1931–32	42	20	8	14	92	69	48	8th
1932–33	42	19	9	14	77	63	47	8th
1933–34	42	20	6	16	72	63	46	10th
1934–35	42	19	12	11	77	71	50	4th
1935–36	42	18	7	17	91	82	43	12th
1936–37	42	29	4	9	95	52	62	1st
1937–38	42	15	12	15	58	59	42	9th
1938–39	42	13	10	19	71	84	36	16th
1945–46	40	12	11	17	59	80	35	15th
1946–47	42	12	8	22	71	118	32	19th
1947–48	42	12	6	22	48	86	32	22nd
1948–49	42	8	5	29	40	89	21	22nd
1949–50	42	11	7	24	43	84	29	20th
1950–51	42	12	13	17	43	56	37	17th
1951–52	42	16	12	14	65	58	44	6th
1952–53	42	12	15	15	55	59	39	15th
1953–54	42	10	3	29	48	106	23	22nd
1954–55	42	10	9	23	58	100	29	20th
1955–56	42	12	6	24	71	92	30	20th
1956–57	42	8	10	24	42	85	26	22nd
1957–58	42	14	4	24	70	95	32	21st

1958–59	42	12	10	20	64	82	34	17th
1959–60	42	6	9	27	49	113	21	22nd
1960–61	42	10	10	22	58	109	30	19th
1961–62	42	14	8	20	57	93	36	17th
1962–63	42	13	11	18	54	76	37	16th
1963–64	42	12	12	18	47	54	36	16th
1964–65	42	12	13	17	56	71	37	15th
1965–66	42	9	11	22	52	61	29	19th
1966–67	42	16	8	18	65	63	40	12th
1967–68	42	10	11	21	48	69	31	18th
1968–69	42	12	12	18	42	57	36	15th
1969–70	42	9	16	17	40	74	34	16th
1970–71	42	11	17	14	52	56	39	15th
1971–72	42	12	15	15	47	43	39	13th
1972–73	42	15	7	20	50	55	37	18th
1973–74	42	11	13	18	43	63	35	17th
1974–75	42	14	14	14	56	60	42	11th
1975–76	42	21	9	12	76	52	51	5th
1976–77	42	19	10	13	84	54	48	7th
1977–78	42	16	12	14	69	60	44	8th
1978–79	42	14	16	12	50	49	44	9th
1979–80	42	9	9	24	47	75	27	20th
1980–81	42	10	20	12	42	56	40	12th
1981–82	42	18	5	19	60	53	41	11th
Division One								
1982–83	30	6	11	13	30	49	23	11th
1983–84	30	7	7	16	37	51	28	14th
Division Two								
1984–85	34	21	3	10	85	37	66	3rd
Division One								
1985–86	34	16	3	15	63	70	51	7th
1986–87	34	17	3	14	64	61	54	8th
1987–88	34	15	5	14	58	56	50	6th
1988–89	34	13	7	14	59	59	46	9th
1989–90	34	14	8	12	62	49	50	9th

Pontins League

In 1990–91 the Central League was sponsored by Pontins and renamed. United ended a 61-year wait for the reserve title when they clinched the premier division title in 1997–98. They went into the final week of the season needing to win the last two games to prevent Manchester United retaining the title. A Jonathan Woodgate goal saw them beat Everton at Halifax and then stormed to a 5–0 win over Blackburn Rovers at Elland Road with goals by David Hopkin (2), Derek Lilley (2) and an Andy Gray penalty.

Season	P	W	D	L	F	A	Pts	Pos
1990–91	34	11	12	11	44	47	45	9th
1991–92	34	14	11	9	47	41	53	5th
1992–93	34	15	8	11	59	44	53	4th
1993–94	34	13	8	13	42	48	47	9th
1994–95	34	19	4	11	53	37	61	3rd
1995–96	34	17	8	9	40	32	59	4th
1996–97	24	10	4	10	29	34	34	5th
Premier Division								
1997–98	24	15	3	6	50	27	48	1st
1998–99	24	9	3	12	40	43	30	7th

FA Premier Reserve League

There was a shake-up in the reserve team structure in 1999–2000 with the advent of the FA Premier Reserve League with United in the Northern Section.

North Section

Season	P	W	D	L	F	A	Pts	Pos
1999–2000	24	10	6	8	48	38	36	7th
2000–01	22	11	4	7	40	24	37	3rd
2001–02	24	10	4	10	25	33	34	8th
2002–03	28	10	11	7	45	37	41	7th
2003–04	26	10	7	9	40	40	37	8th
2004–05	28	7	7	14	31	52	28	13th
2005–06	28	9	11	8	27	31	38	9th

Pontins Holiday League

After the senior side's relegation from the Premiership the reserves went back into the Pontins League, then rebranded the Pontins Holiday League.

Division One Central

Season	P	W	D	L	F	A	Pts	Pos
2006–07	22	7	7	8	33	35	28	6th
Division One East								
2007–08	22	8	6	8	33	29	30	6th

Totesport.com Reserve League

The league acquired a new sponsor Totesport.com ahead of the 2008–09 season. United's second string won their last 11 fixtures that season to overhaul Huddersfield Town and lift the title. They retained their crown the following season by taking a maximum 15 points from their last five matches to overtake Hartlepool and Middlesbrough on the final day of the campaign.

Unhappy with the lack of testing fixtures, United pulled out of the league after the 2010–11 season and opted to play 'friendly' games, sometimes behind closed doors for the 2011–12 season.

East Division

Season	P	W	D	L	F	A	Pts	Pos
2008–09	16	13	0	3	27	8	39	1st
2009–10	18	11	3	4	46	22	36	1st
2010–11	14	7	2	5	36	23	23	3rd

Yorkshire League

United entered an A team in the Yorkshire League for the first time in 1929–30 and won the title the following year, although they lost the traditional Championship match against York City Reserves 5–1.

United gained revenge over City on 2 May 1931 by winning the Play-off in a subsidiary competition between the winners of Groups A and B, 5–4. For the next two seasons the League was divided into two competitions but no more honours came United's way until they beat Selby Town 2–1 in the Yorkshire League Cup Final at Goole on 28 April 1937, with goals from Jimmy Carr and Sammy Armes. Two seasons later, United were in the Final again at Goole, but this time went down 2–1 to Barnsley A, John Short scoring United's goal. There was consolation the following week when, as runners-up, United beat Sheffield Wednesday A 1–0 in the Championship match.

United reached the Final in 1947 but were thrashed 4–0 by York and also had left-winger Arnold Knight sent-off. In 1949–50, the Yorkshire League was split into divisions with United going into Division One – a status they lost in 1953.

After a few more 'yo–yo' seasons, United pulled out of the Yorkshire League until returning in 1961 for one last season in Division Three when the League season was followed by a supplementary Cup competition run on a League basis.

Season	*P*	*W*	*D*	*L*	*F*	*A*	*Pts*	*Pos*
1929–30	26	17	6	3	86	29	40	2nd
1930–31	22	19	1	2	103	29	39	1st
First Competition								
1931–32	12	6	2	4	28	18	14	3rd
Second Competition								
1931–32	12	4	4	4	33	20	12	4th
First Competition								
1932–33	18	12	3	3	45	25	27	2nd
Second Competition								
1932–33	12	6	2	4	32	25	14	3rd
Back to one League								
1933–34	24	12	3	9	57	45	27	5th
1934–35	34	19	8	7	90	59	46	4th
1935–36	38	20	6	12	112	70	46	6th
1936–37	36	17	7	14	114	75	39	8th
1937–38	38	18	6	14	83	54	42	7th
1938–39	38	30	1	7	125	47	61	2nd
1946–47	38	15	4	19	83	99	34	15th

1947–48	38	12	8	18	78	93	32	16th
1948–49	38	17	5	16	85	93	39	9th
Division One								
1949–50	34	11	7	16	62	67	29	14th
1950–51	34	12	2	20	68	104	26	14th
1951–52	34	14	6	14	77	77	34	8th
1952–53	34	12	5	17	65	80	29	15th
Division Two								
1953–54	30	19	3	8	97	40	41	5th
1954–55	30	20	3	7	86	38	43	4th
Division One								
1955–56	34	9	6	19	52	77	24	17th
Division Two								
1956–57	32	16	5	11	86	49	37	7th
1957–58	26	8	5	13	42	60	21	10th
Division Three								
1961–62	16	8	0	8	39	35	16	3rd
1961–62 Cup	16	9	2	5	51	36	20	3rd

Yorkshire League Cup Finals

28 April 1937 v Selby Town at Goole, 2–1, *Carr, Armes, Howieson*
27 April 1939 v Barnsley A at Goole, 1–2, *Short*
6 June 1947 v York City Res at York, 0–4

Northern Intermediate League

United were founder members of the Northern Intermediate League in 1949–50 when the juniors achieved the 'double'. For first few years League games occupied the first part of the season with a Challenge Cup, also run on a League basis, operating in the latter part. The top four clubs in the Challenge Cup table qualified for the semi-finals with the winners meeting in the Final. As the League expanded in the mid-1950s, the Cup was run on a straight-forward knockout basis.

Season	P	W	D	L	F	A	Pts	Pos
1949–50								
1950–51								
The Northern Intermediate League had no record of the above seasons								
Cup	10	2	1	7	16	24	5	10th
1951–52	20	10	6	4	60	35	26	3rd
Cup	10	5	1	4	26	18	11	4th
1952–53	20	9	3	8	43	41	21	4th
Cup	10	5	3	2	20	12	13	3rd
1953–54	20	11	5	4	44	30	27	1st
Cup	10	6	2	2	27	14	14	2nd
1954–55	24	18	3	3	66	25	39	1st

Cup	12	5	3	4	29	25	13	6th
1955–56	26	10	4	12	47	58	24	7th
Cup	13	4	4	5	24	19	12	9th
1956–57	28	14	6	8	59	51	34	5th
1957–58	28	7	4	17	48	61	18	12th
1958–59	28	12	5	11	53	46	29	8th
1959–60	30	12	6	12	56	49	30	9th
1960–61	30	12	2	16	54	67	26	10th
1961–62	32	18	5	9	66	31	41	5th
1962–63	24	12	3	9	44	38	27	6th
1963–64	32	16	4	12	68	47	36	7th
1964–65	32	21	2	9	68	45	44	4th
1965–66	32	25	3	4	92	25	53	1st
1966–67	28	10	9	9	52	41	29	7th
1967–68	32	5	10	17	28	51	20	13th
1968–69	34	14	11	9	70	48	39	7th
1969–70	34	26	4	4	89	19	56	2nd
1970–71	28	16	7	5	61	27	39	3rd
1971–72	30	11	8	11	44	41	30	9th
1972–73	30	19	3	8	65	25	41	4th
1973–74	32	15	7	10	54	39	37	6th
1974–75	32	19	8	5	69	30	46	3rd
1975–76	30	13	12	5	51	49	31	7th
1976–77	28	13	7	8	36	34	33	7th
1977–78	30	13	8	9	38	24	34	6th
1978–79	30	8	7	15	54	52	23	11th
1979–80	30	15	5	10	59	38	35	4th
1980–81	34	17	5	12	67	41	39	7th
1981–82	30	14	9	7	60	40	37	5th
1982–83	30	14	4	12	56	44	32	8th
1983–84	28	16	5	7	46	24	37	5th
1984–85	28	18	1	9	79	53	37	3rd
1985–86	34	12	8	14	77	56	32	10th
1986–87	34	21	5	8	68	38	68	3rd
1987–88	34	20	4	10	82	52	64	3rd
1988–89	34	20	7	7	85	40	67	3rd
1989–90	34	13	10	11	68	64	49	8th
1990–91	34	21	6	7	63	25	69	2nd
1991–92	34	19	8	7	75	39	65	2nd
1992–93	32	18	7	7	85	41	61	3rd
1993–94	30	16	4	10	50	43	52	3rd
1994–95	32	19	8	5	84	47	65	3rd
1995–96	30	21	4	5	100	34	62	2nd

1996–97	34	28	3	3	112	23	87	1st
1997–98	34	14	4	16	60	57	46	9th

United's Successes in the Northern Intermediate League Cup

Some fairly well-known names have played their part in bringing the Northern Intermediate Cup to Elland Road. Many went on to break into United's first team like the inspirational Billy Bremner but one player who slipped through the net was John Scales, a scorer in the 1984 triumph against Newcastle. He was a forward at Leeds, but later played for Wimbledon, Liverpool, Tottenham and England as a defender.

United's successes in the Final have been:

6 May 1950 v Rotherham United (h) 2–1 *Webb 2 (1 pen)*
3 May 1952 v Rotherham United (h) 4–1 *Webb 2, Smith, Vickers*
13 April 1959 v Newcastle United 1st leg (h) 4–1 *Harvey 2, Hawksby, Howieson*
20 April 1959 v Newcastle United 2nd leg (a) 3–3 *Bremner, McCall* – Leeds won 7–4 on aggregate
27 April 1965 v Sheffield Wednesday 1st leg (a) 2–2 *Hawkins 2*
29 April 1965 v Sheffield Wednesday 2nd leg (h) 1–0 *Hibbitt* – Leeds won 3–0 on aggregate
2 May 1966 v Sheffield United 1st leg (a) 1–0 *Bates*
12 May 1966 v Sheffield United 2nd leg (h) 3–1 *Hawkins 2, Sibbald (pen)* – Leeds won 4–1 on aggregate
24 April 1975 v Sunderland 1st leg (a) 0–0
6 May 1975 v Sunderland 2nd leg (h) 3–0 *McNiven 3* – Leeds won 3–0 on aggregate
15 May 1984 v Newcastle United 1st leg (h) 4–0 *Sellars, Opp own-goal, Wright 2*
18 May 1984 v Newcastle United 2nd leg (a) 2–1 *Scales, Simmonds* – Leeds won 6–1 on aggregate
10 May 1996 v Newcastle United (n*) 2–0 *Elliott (og), Matthews*

* The 1996 Final was played at Bootham Crescent, York, as a one game Final because work was being done at Elland Road and St James' Park to prepare for the European Championships.

FA Premier Youth League

This League only operated for one season before the FA Premier Academy League was set up. The new Academy Leagues had two age groups, Under-19 and Under-17.

Northern Conference

Season	P	W	D	L	F	A	Pts	Pos
1997–98	22	5	11	6	44	44	26	5th

FA Academy Under-19 League

Group C

Season	P	W	D	L	F	A	Pts	Pos
1998–99	22	10	3	9	34	37	33	4th

Qualified for Play-offs, losing 3–0 at home to Wimbledon in the first round.

Group A

1999–2000	22	7	4	11	32	48	25	5th
2000–01	28	11	5	12	39	47	38	7th

Group D

2001–02	28	13	6	9	52	45	45	5th

Group B

2002–03	28	11	5	12	32	38	38	6th
2003–04	26	12	5	9	36	27	41	3rd

FA Academy Under-17 League

Group C

Season	P	W	D	L	F	A	Pts	Pos
1998–99	22	11	4	7	55	33	37	2nd

Qualified for Play-off beating Charlton Athletic 4–1 at home in the first round, and losing at home to Liverpool 5–4 on penalties after their second round game. Finished 1–1 after extra-time.

Group A

1999–2000	22	9	0	13	46	52	27	5th
2000–01	24	8	7	9	36	44	31	5th

Group D

2001–02	24	11	7	6	39	24	40	3rd

Group 9 Play-offs

	3	2	1	0	8	1	7	1st

Qualified for Play-off quarter-finals winning 2–1 at Aston Villa. Lost 2–0 at home to Manchester United in the semi-finals.

Group B

2002–03	22	16	2	4	54	24	50	1st

Group 8 Play-offs

2002–03	4	4	0	0	8	1	12	1st

Qualified for Play-off quarter-finals, winning 2–1 at Sheffield United. Beat Arsenal 1–0 at home in the semi-finals and won the Final at Manchester City 1–0 after extra-time.

2003–04	26	12	7	7	45	30	42	1st

Qualified for Play-off quarter-finals, losing 3–1 at home to Tottenham Hotspur.

FA Academy Under-18 League

Group D

Season	P	W	D	L	F	A	Pts	Pos
2004–05	28	12	4	12	50	43	40	4th
2005–06	28	16	5	7	51	26	53	2nd
2006–07	28	16	4	8	50	37	52	3rd
2007–08	28	13	6	9	53	38	45	3rd
2008–09	28	9	5	14	41	43	32	6th
2009–10	28	10	5	13	38	53	35	5th
2010–11	28	10	4	14	30	51	34	7th
2011–12	28	16	5	7	60	31	53	7th

Leeds United Ladies

Leeds United Ladies were formed in 1989 and spent seven years in the Yorkshire and Humberside League before joining the Northern Division of the National League.

After winning the title in 2001, when Stacey Daniel was named Northern Division Player of the Year, they were promoted to the National Division and did well in their first season under Manager of the Year Mark Hodgson.

His work was built upon by Julie Chipchase as the Ladies developed into one of the best teams outside London, supplying England with several international players, including Sue Smith and Sophie Walton, sister of United player Simon.

The girls reached the finals of the Women's FA Cup and the Premier League Cup twice, losing on each occasion to Arsenal.

The youth teams amalgamated with the Leeds United Girls Centre of Excellence in summer 2007 to form one organisation feeding into the open age team.

When Leeds United ran into its well-publicised financial difficulties, funding to the Ladies team, which played at Thorp Arch, was cut. The Ladies, managed by Rick Passmoor, went into partnership with Leeds Metropolitan University and became Leeds Carnegie in 2008 and won the Premier League Cup in 2010, beating Everton 3–1 at Rochdale.

The link with the university ended after two years and the Ladies club had its funding and Super League application withdrawn in January 2010. Its future looked in doubt but in stepped Leeds United in July and the club adopted the Leeds United name once more.

It is now independently funded by local businesses and supporters.

Leeds United Ladies League record since 1998

Season	P	W	D	L	F	A	Pts	Pos
Northern Division								
1998–99	18	9	5	4	67	29	32	3rd
1999–2000	22	12	3	7	48	30	39	3rd
2000–01	22	18	2	2	75	18	56	1st
National Division								
2001–02	18	7	5	6	36	37	26	4th
2002–03	18	5	4	9	33	42	19	7th
2003–04	18	8	4	6	32	28	28	4th
2004–05	18	8	2	8	31	34	26	6th
2005–06	18	4	6	8	27	36	18	7th
2006–07	22	12	1	9	50	44	40	5th
2007–08	22	12	4	6	45	33	40	3rd
2010–11	14	5	3	6	17	17	18	4th
2011–12	18	13	2	3	36	10	41	2nd

Leeds United Ladies Women's FA Cup record

Leeds United Ladies have twice reached the Final, losing on both occasions to Arsenal.

1 May 2006 (at Upton Park, West Ham)
Arsenal Ladies 5 *(Lucy Ward og 3, Julie Fleeting 34, Rachael Yankey 35, Kelly Smith pen 73, Lianne Sanderson 77)*
Leeds United Ladies 0
Leeds United Ladies: Fay, Cook (Walton 52), Culvin, Emmanuel, Haigh, Ward, Clarke, Burke, Walker (Panesar 85), Preston (Owen 85), Smith.
Ref: Phil Crossley (Kent) *Att:* 13,452

5 May 2008 (at City Ground, Nottingham)
Arsenal Ladies 4 *(Kelly Smith 53, 83, Jayne Ludlow 59, Lianne Sanderson 60)*
Leeds United Ladies 1 *(Jess Clarke 69)*
Leeds United Ladies: Telford, Bradley, Wright (Bonner 86), Holtham, S. Smith, Houghton, Clarke, Moore (Sutcliffe 60), Barr, Culvin (Thackray 86), Walton
Att: 24,582 (record for Women's FA Cup Final)

The full record of Leeds United Ladies – not including Leeds Carnegie – in the competition is:
1995–96
Round 1 v Sunderland (a) 1–2
1996–97
Round 1 v Kirklees (a) 3–1
Round 2 v Rochdale (a) 7–0
Round 3 v Aston Villa (h) 2–5
1997–98
Round 1 v Chester-le-Street (a) 8–3
Round 2 v Blyth Spartans (a) 3–6
1998–99
Round 2 v Sheffield Wednesday 2–3
1999–2000
Round 3 v Stockport County (h) 9–0
Round 4 v Wimbledon (h) 2–1
Round 5 v Southampton Saints (h) 3–2
Round 6 v Wolverhampton Wanderers (a) 1–0
Semi-final v Croydon (h) 1–2
2000–01
Round 3 v Huddersfield Town (h) 8–0
Round 4 v Arsenal (a) 3–5
2001–02
Round 4 v Newcastle United (a) 4–2
Round 5 v Arsenal (a) 0–3
2002–03
Round 4 v Merthyr Tydfil (h) 4–0
Round 5 v Aston Villa (h) 0–3

2003–04
Round 4 v Doncaster Rovers Belles (a) 1–2
2004–05
Round 4 v Blackburn Rovers (a) 4–1
Round 5 v Arsenal (h) 1–3
2005–06
Round 4 v Doncaster Rovers Belles (h) 2–1
Round 5 v Everton (h) 3–1
Round 6 v Birmingham City (a) 3–1
Semi-final v Liverpool (h) 2–0
Final v Arsenal (at Upton Park) 0–5
2006–07
Round 4 v Sunderland (a) 3–1
Round 5 v Cardiff City (a) 2–1
Round 6 v Blackburn Rovers (a) 1–2
2007–08
Round 4 v Bristol Academy (a) 1–1* – Leeds won 4–3 on penalties
Round 5 v Chelsea (a) 1–1* – Leeds won 6–5 on penalties
Round 6 v Cardiff City (a) 5–1
Semi-final v Everton (a) 0–0* – Leeds won 5–4 on penalties
Final v Arsenal (at City Ground, Nottingham) 1–4
2010–11
Round 3 v Blackburn Rovers (h) 0–0* – Blackburn won 5–4 on penalties
2011–12
Round 3 v Watford (a) 6–1
Round 4 v Coventry City (a) 2–1
Round 5 v Bristol Academy (a) 0–3

Leeds United Ladies Premier League Cup record

Leeds United Ladies have got through to the Final twice in 2007 and 2012 but the trophy eluded them on both occasions.

They went down to a last-minute goal to Arsenal Ladies in 2007 and five years later were defeated 2–1 by Sunderland.

4 March 2007
(at Glanford Park, Scunthorpe)
Arsenal Ladies 1 *(Jayne Ludlow 90)*
Leeds United Ladies 0
Leeds United: Fay, Bradley, Culvin, McArthur, Wright, Preston, Emmanuel, Smith, Walton, Ward (Clarke 63), Burke (Sutcliffe 73).
Ref: D. Roberts, *Att:* 3,688.

5 May 2012
(at Sixfields Stadium, Northampton)
Leeds United Ladies 1 *(Carey Huegett pen 90)*
Sunderland Ladies 2 *(Natalie Gutteridge 9, 66)*
Leeds United: Draycott, Emmonds (Johnson 51), Sharp, Birkby (Lipman 51), Sykes, Huegett, Rich (Danby 68), Galton, Holmes, Turner, Holbrook.
Ref: Paul Forrester, *Att:* 641.

Leeds United Ladies full record – not including Leeds Carnegie – in the competition is:
1998–99
Round 1 v Ilkeston Town (h) 3–0
Round 2 v Garswood Saints (a) 2–3
1999–2000
Prelim Round v Birmingham City (h) 2–0
Round 1 v Coventry City (a) 5–0
Round 2 v Bangor City (a) 3–4
2000–01
Round 1 v Ilkeston Town (h) 6–0
Round 2 v Wimbledon (a) 1–0
Round 3 v Millwall Lionesses (a) 1–2
2001–02
Round 1 v Fulham (a) 0–8
2002–03
Round 1 v Lincoln City (a) 4–2
Round 2 v Arsenal (a) 0–3
2003–04
Round 1 v Bristol City (h) 3–1
Round 2 v Everton (h) 7–0
Round 3 v Fulham (h) 2–3
2004–05
Round 1 v Blackburn Rovers (a) 3–0
Round 2 v Fulham (h) 2–3
2005–06
Round 1 v Bristol Academy (h) 1–2
2006–07
Round 1 v Cardiff City (h) 4–0
Round 2 v Barnet (h) 2–0
Round 3 v Millwall Lionesses (h) 2–1
Semi-final v Charlton Athletic (a) 2–2*
Leeds won on penalties
Final v Arsenal (at Scunthorpe) 0–1
2007–08
Round 1 v Liverpool (a) 0–2
2010–11
Group stage v Sunderland (a) 1–1
Group stage v Newcastle United (h) 4–1
Group stage v Leeds City Vixens (h) 3–1
Round 1 v Sunderland (a) 1–3 (aet)
2011–12
Group stage v Sheffield FA (a) 1–0
Group stage v Sunderland (a) 1–1
Group stage v Leeds City Vixens (h) walkover
Round 1 v Derby County (h) 4–1
Round 2 v Charlton Athletic (a) 5–2
Semi-final v Coventry City (a) 2–0
Final v Sunderland (at Northampton) 1–2

Leeds United In Other Competitions

WEST RIDING SENIOR CUP

The first trophy ever to be taken back to Elland Road was the West Riding Challenge Cup, won by Leeds City Reserves in 1907 when two goals by Alf Harwood gave them victory over Kippax Parish Church, a team from the West Yorkshire League.

City also figured in the first West Riding Senior Cup Final in 1910, but were well beaten by Bradford. The Senior Cup competition had replaced the Challenge Cup and both United and City have been regular finalists.

LEEDS CITY IN THE FINAL

1910–11

1 November v Bradford (Valley Parade) 1–5 (0–3)

McLeod

Bromage, Affleck, Creighton, Harkins, T. Morris, Cubberley, Roberts, McLeod, Gillespie, Enright, Croot.

Att: 3,000

1914–15

11 November v Hull City (Elland Road) 1–0 (0–0)

Speirs

Hogg, Blackman, McQuillan, Law, J. Hampson, Foley, Bainbridge, Jackson, McLeod, Speirs, Sharpe.

Att: 1,000 (Hampson was sent off)

1918–19

17 May v Huddersfield Town (Valley Parade) 0–0 (0–0)

Sutcliffe, Millership, W. Hampson, Lamph, J. Hampson, McLachlan, Hall, C. Stephenson, Peart, McLeod, Bainbridge.

Att: 10,000

Replay

24 May v Huddersfield Town (Valley Parade) 2–0 (2–0)

C. Stephenson 2

Sutcliffe, Millership, W. Hampson, Lamph, J. Hampson, Hall, Stephenson, Peart, McLeod, Bainbridge.

Att: 10,000

The Leeds teams included guest players Clem Stephenson (Huddersfield Town), Jack Peart (Notts County) and Tom Hall (Newcastle). Goalkeeper Charlie Sutcliffe didn't play a first-team game for Leeds.

LEEDS UNITED IN THE FINAL

1921–22

13 May v Huddersfield Town (Valley Parade) 0–1 (0–0)

Whalley, J.W. Baker, Frew, Sherwin, Hart, Walton, Coates, Poyntz, Armitage, Swan, Clark.

Att: 8,500

1922–23

25 October v Halifax Town (Elland Road) 1–0 (0–0)

Poyntz

Whalley, Duffield, J. Potts, Sherwin, Hart, L.H. Baker, Mason, Dark, Poyntz, Swan, Harris.

Att: 6,000

1923–24

10 May v Bradford (Elland Road) 1–2 (0–0)

Richmond

Down, Duffield, Menzies, L.H. Baker, Hart, J.W. Baker, Coates, Whipp, Richmond, Swan, Harris.

Att: 12,000

1925–26

8 May v Huddersfield Town (Park Avenue) 4–1 (0–1)

Jennings 3, Jackson

Att: 10,700

Local FA has no record of teams and because of the 1926 General Strike there were no newspapers.

1926–27

14 May v Bradford (Park Avenue) 2–3 (2–1)

Jennings, Wainscoat

J.F. Potts, Roberts, Allan, Edwards, Townsley, Reed, Tumbull, White, Jennings, Wainscoat, Mitchell.

Att: 11,082

1927–28

12 May v Bradford (Elland Road) 4–2 (3–2)

Mitchell, Hart, Turnbull, Keetley

J.F. Potts, Roberts, Menzies, Edwards, Hart, Reed, Turnbull, White, Keetley, Wainscoat, Mitchell.

Att: 10,000

1928–29

11 May v Halifax Town (Valley Parade) 4–0 (2–0)

Duggan 2, Keetley 2

J.F. Potts, Roberts, Menzies, Underwood, Townsley, Reed, Duggan, Keetley, Jennings, Wainscoat, Mitchell.

Att: 3,500

1929–30

10 May v Huddersfield Town (Elland Road) 0–1 (0–0)

J.F. Potts, Roberts, J.Milburn, Edwards, Hart, Stacey, Tumbull, Longden, Keetley, Wainscoat, Cochrane.

Att: 10,000

1930–31

9 May v Huddersfield Town (Valley Parade) 0–1 (0–1)

J.F. Potts, G.W. Milburn, Menzies, Edwards, Danskin, Copping, Green, Homby, Keetley, Furness, Cochrane.

Att: 5,900

1932–33

26 April v Huddersfield Town (Valley Parade) 0–1 (0–1)

Moore, G.W. Milburn, J. Milburn, Edwards, Hart, Copping, Duggan, Firth, Fowler, Hydes, Mahon.

Att: 2,700 (Hart was sent off)

1936–37

3 May v Bradford City (Elland Road) 4–2 aet (2–1; 90 min 2–2)

Kelly, Hargreaves 2, Trainor

United fielded a reserve team to mark winning the Central League. Among those who played were G.W. Milburn, Thomson, Furness, Kelly, Trainor, Turner, Hargreaves.

Att: 1,500

1949–50
6 May v Bradford City (Valley Parade) 2–3 (1–3)
Dudley, Kerfoot
Searson, Dunn, J. Milburn, McCabe, Charles, Kerfoot, Cochrane, Iggleden, McMorran, Dudley, Williams.
Att: 14,372

1950–51
12 May v Bradford (Elland Road) 0–4 (0–3)
Searson, Dunn, J. Milburn, McCabe, Kirk, Burden, P. Harrison, Iggleden, Charles, Stevenson, Williams.
Att: 15,000

1951–52
8 October v Halifax Town (Elland Road) 2–1 (1–0)
Charles 2
Scott, Dunn, Hair, Kerfoot, McCabe, Burden, Meek, Tyrer, Charles, Iggleden, Williams.
Att: 3,500
Final held over until following season.

1953–54
15 March v Huddersfeld Town (Elland Road) 2–1 (1–1)
Nightingale, Charles
Scott, Dunn, Hair, Kerfoot, Marsden, Burden, McCall, Nightingale, Charles, Forrest, Williams.
Att: 23,000

1954–55
8 May v Bradford (Elland Road) 2–1 (0–0)
Smith, Nightingale
Wood, Dawson, Dunn, Gibson, Charles, Kerfoot, Williams, Nightingale, Smith, Henderson, Meek.
Att: 4,000

1955–56
28 November v Huddersfield Town (Elland Road) 5–2 (3–1)
Charles 4, Vickers
Wood, Dunn, Hair, Nightingale, Charlton, Kerfoot, Williams, Hutchinson, Charles, Vickers, Overfield.
Att: 12,500

1956–57
26 November v Halifax Town (Elland Road) 3–1 (2–1)
Ripley 3
Wood, Dunn, Hair, Rich, Charlton, Gibson, Meek, Charles, Ripley, Crowe, Overfield.
Att: 3,500

1957–58
25 November v Bradford City (Valley Parade) 2–2 (2–0)
Crowe, Baird
Wood, Stanley, Hair, Ripley, Charlton, Cush, Francis, Gibson, Baird, Crowe, Overfield.
Att: 8,858

Replay
1 May v Bradford City (Elland Road) 4–0 (0–0)
Baird (pen), Overfield, Charlton, Crowe
Wood, Dunn, Hair, Gibson, Charlton, Cush, Meek, Crowe, Baird, Forrest, Overfield.
Att: 6,037

1959–60
9 May v Bradford (Elland Road) 1–1 (0–0)
McCole
Humphreys, Ashall, Caldwell, Gibson, Charlton, Goodwin, Bremner, Francis, McCole, Hawksby, Meek.
Att: 5,500

Replay
12 May v Bradford (Park Avenue) 3–1 (1–1)
McCole 2, Goodwin
Humphreys, Ashall, Caldwell, McConnell, Charlton, Goodwin, Brernner, Francis, McCole, Hawksby, Meek.
Att: 5,766

1960–61
9 May v Bradford (Park Avenue) 4–2 (2–1)
Bremner 2, Peyton, Hawksby
Carling, Jones, Kilford, Smith, Charlton, Bell, Johanneson, McConnell, Bremner, Peyton, Hawksby.
Att: 10,023

1963–64
7 May v Bradford City (Elland Road) 4–1 (3–1)
Collins 2, Cooper, Storrie
Sprake, Reaney, Bell, Bremner, Charlton, Hunter, Giles, Storrie, Peacock, Collins, Cooper.
Att: 11,084

1965–66
20 May v Bradford (Park Avenue) 4–0 (4–0)
O'Grady 2, Johanneson, Thomas (og)
Sprake, Reaney, Cooper, Bremner, Bell, Greenhoff, O'Grady, Lorimer, Storrie, Collins, Johanneson.
Att: 9,013

1968–69
16 May v Huddersfield Town (Park Avenue) 2–1(1–0)
Lorimer, Hunter
Sprake, Reaney, Cooper, Giles, Yorath, Hunter, Bates, Lorimer, Jones, Belfitt, Hibbitt.
Att: 10,794

1971–72
12 May v Halifax Town (Elland Road) 4–3 (2–2)
Lorimer 3, Jordan
Sprake, Reaney, O'Neill, Bremner, Saunders, Yorath, Lorimer, Mann, Jordan, Bates (Hampton), Galvin.
Att: 6,256

1972–73
21 August v Halifax Town (Elland Road) 2–1 (1–1)
Lorimer (pen), Jones
Harvey, Reaney, Cherry, Bremner, McQueen, Hunter, Lorimer, Clarke, Jones, Giles, Bates.
Att: 4,650
Final held over until following season.

1975–76
15 November v Huddersfield Town (Elland Road) 2–0 (1–0)
Hankin 2
Harvey, Reaney, F.T. Gray, McGhie, Parkinson, Stevenson, Lorimer (Thomas), McNiven, Hankin, Currie, Liddell.
Att: 2,971
Final held over until following season.

1976–77
10 October v Bradford City (Valley Parade) 5–2 (3–0)
McNiven, Lorimer 2 (1 pen), Thomas 2
Harvey, Stevenson, F.T. Gray, Lorimer (Felix), Parkinson, Firm, Harris, Whyte, Thomas, Currie (Parker), McNiven.
Att: 4,695

Final held over until following season. Gary Felix didn't play a first-team game for Leeds.

1977–78

On 4 May 1978, United were due to play Huddersfield Town in the Final but refused to alter a tour programme to Switzerland. Leeds were fined £2,000 and Huddersfield awarded the game.

1979–80

6 May v Bradford City (Valley Parade) 4–1 (0–0)
Harris, Graham 3
Smith, Hird, Stevenson, Flynn, Firm, Madeley, Harris, Chandler, Parlane (Connor), E. Gray, Graham.
Att: 3,255

1981–82

23 August v Halifax Town (Elland Road) 3–2 aet (0–1; 90 mins 2–2)
Worthington (pen), Butterworth, F.T. Gray
Lukic, Hird, Cherry, Flynn, Hart, Burns (Aspin), Sheridan, Parlane (Butterworth), Worthington, F.T. Gray, Graham.
Att: 1,228

Final held over from previous season.

No competition was held in 1982–83. In 1983 the competition was played as a pre-season mini-league with a revolutionary points scoring system. Two points were awarded for the team who won the first half, two points to the team winning the second half and a further two points for winning the match. United won the competition in the first season of the new format, Bradford City winning it for the next four years.

1983

13 August v Huddersfield Town (h) 2–1 (1–0)
Ritchie, Sheridan
Harvey, Hird, F.T. Gray, Watson (Sellars), Brown, Dickinson, Thomas (Donnelly), McCluskey, Ritchie, Sheridan, Barnes.
Att: 3,761

16 August v Halifax Town (a) 0–2 (0–1)
Harvey, Hird, F.T. Gray, Sheridan (Aspin), Brown, Dickinson, Sellars (Gavin), McCluskey, Ritchie, Donnelly, Barnes.
Att: 1,402

20 August v Bradford City (h) 2–0 (1–0)
Donnelly Ritchie
Harvey, Hird, Hamson, Watson, Brown, F.T. Gray, Thomas, McCluskey (Butterworth), Ritchie, Donnelly, Barnes.
Att: 3,108

1984

11 August v Bradford City (a) 0–2 (0–0)
Harvey, Irwin, F.T. Gray, Watson, Linighan, Aspin, Wright, Sheridan, Ritchie, Lorimer, Sellars.
Att: 3,079

13 August v Huddersfield Town (a) 1–0 (1–0)
McCluskey
Harvey, Irwin, Hamson, Watson, Linighan, Aspin, Wright, Sheridan, McCluskey, Lorimer, Sellars.
Att: 1,726

15 August v Halifax Town (h) 3–1 (2–0)
Lorimer 3
Hughes, Irwin, Hamson, Watson, Linighan, Aspin, Wright, Sheridan, McCluskey, Lorimer, Sellars.
Att: 1,469

1985

5 August v Huddersfield Town (h) 2–1 (0–0)
Baird, Lorimer (pen)
Swinburne; Irwin, Hamson, Snodin, Bentley, Aspin, McCluskey, Sheridan, Baird, Lorimer, Sellars.
Att: 2,134

David Bentley didn't play a first-team game for Leeds.

7 August v Halifax Town (a) 6–0 (2–0)
McCluskey 2, Baird 2, Sellars 2
Day, Irwin, Hamson, I. Snodin, Linighan, Aspin, McCluskey, Sheridan, Baird, Lorimer, Sellars.
Att: 1,473

10 August v Bradford City (h) 2–4 (1–2)
McCluskey Sheridan
Day, Irwin, Hamson, I. Snodin, Linighan, Aspin, McCluskey, Sheridan, Baird, Lorimer, Sellars.
Att: 4,692

1986

6 August v Bradford City (at Odsal) 0–3 (0–1)
Day, Haddock (Stiles), Caswell (Robinson), I. Snodin, Aspin, Rennie, Doig, Sheridan, Ritchie, Ashurst, Swan.
Att: 2,276

9 August v Halifax Town (a) 3–0 (2–0)
Edwards 2, Ritchie
Day (Sinclair), Aspin (Stiles), Caswell, I. Snodin, Hazell, Rennie, Buckley (Doig), Sheridan, Edwards, Ashurst, Ritchie.
Att: 2,308

12 August v Huddersfield Town (a) 2–2 (1–1)
Buckley Ormsby
Sinclair, Aspin, Caswell, Snodin, Hazell (Ormsby), Rennie, Buckley (Doig), Sheridan, Edwards, Ashurst, Ritchie.
Att: 1,365

Bob Hazell (former Wolves, QPR and Leicester) was on trial, but didn't sign and went on to play for Reading and Port Vale.

1987

1 August v Halifax Town (h) 1–0 (1–0)
G. Willlams
Day, Aspin, Haddock, Aizlewood, Ashurst (Rennie), G. Williams(Grayson), Batty, Sheridan, Pearson (Edwards), Taylor (Ritchie), G. Snodin.
Att: 2,606

3 August v Huddersfield Town (h) 3–2 (2–0)
G. Snodin 2, Sheridan
Day, Aspin, Haddock (Rennie), Aizlewood, Ashurst, Ritchie (Doig), Batty, Sheridan, Pearson, Edwards, G. Snodin (Speed).
Att: 3,101

7 August v Bradford City (h) 2–2 (1–2)
Doig, G. Snodin (pen)
Day, Aspin, Adams, Rennie, Ashurst, Williams, Batty, Doig, Pearson, Edwards, G. Snodin.
Att: 4,566

There was a break from the West Riding Senior Cup for three seasons as clubs in the County FA joined the pre-season Yorkshire and Humberside Cup. The West Riding Senior Cup competition was restored in 1991.

1991

31 July v Bradford City (a) 1–0 (1–0)
Fairclough
Day, McClelland, G. Snodin, Wetherall, Fairclough, Speed, Strachan (Dorigo), Davison (Varadi), Chapman, McAllister, Rod Wallace.
Att: 3,630

This game doubled as Maurice Lindley's Testimonial game.

7 August v Halifax Town (h) 0–2 (0–2)
O'Dowd, Ray Wallace, Whitlow, Kerr, Wetherall, Curtis, Grayson (Sterland), Williams, Davison (Nicholson), Varadi, G. Snodin.
Att: 2,174

Tony O'Dowd, Len Curtis and Steve Nicholson didn't play a first-team game for Leeds.

10 August v Huddersfield Town (h) 0–1 (0–1)
Day; Sterland, Whitlow, Kerr, Wetherall, Curtis, Ray Wallace (A. Williams) Grayson, Davison, Varadi, G. Snodin.
Att: 1,678

The competition was won by Bradford City. This was the last time United entered the West Riding Senior Cup which was retained in 1992 by Bradford City, who beat Huddersfield Town 1–0 in the Final at Leeds Road, the goal being scored by former United player Peter Mumby, who was on loan from Huddersfield.

YORKSHIRE AND HUMBERSIDE CUP

The Yorkshire and Humberside Cup was first played for as a pre-season tournament in 1988. The competition was formed as a result of a partnership between the Sports Council and 12 of the region's top professional clubs, the relevant County Football Associations and the Sports Aid Foundation (Yorkshire and Humberside). In effect, the new competition replaced the West Riding Senior Cup, North Riding Senior Cup and Hallamshire Cup competitions. The 12 clubs in the Yorkshire and Humberside Cup were split into two groups of six. Each club played three matches with the winners of each group going through to the Final. United were in Group A in the competition's first season, along with Huddersfield Town, Scarborough, Barnsley, Scunthorpe United and York City. United were one of the favourites to win the competition, but did badly and failed to reach the Final. Scarborough won Group A but lost in the Final to Sheffield United, the Group B winners, 2–1 after extra-time at the McCain Stadium, Scarborough, on 13 September. The 64lb trophy was presented at the Final by Leeds director Maxwell Holmes, the chairman of the Yorkshire and Humberside Cup competition.

1988

13 August v York City (h) 0–0 (0–0)
Day, Aspin (G. Williams), Adams, Aizlewood, Blake, Ormsby, Batty, Hilaire, Baird, Swan (Davison), G. Snodin.
Att: 2,908

16 August v Huddersfield Town (a) 0–1 (0–1)
Day, G. Williams, Adams, Aizlewood, Blake, Ormsby, Stiles, Hilaire, Baird (Pearson), Davison, G. Snodin.
Att: 2,407

20 August v Barnsley (h) 1–1 (0–0)
Rennie
Day; Aspin, Adams, Aizlewood, Blake, Ormsby (Ashurst), G. Williams, Rennie (Batty), Baird, Pearson, Hilaire.
Att: 2,657

1989

5 August v Rotherham United (h) 1–1 (0–1)
Whitlow
Day, Sterland, Whitlow, Jones, McClelland, Fairclough, Strachan, Batty, Baird, G. Snodin (Speed), Hendrie.
Att: 4,735

8 August v Doncaster Rovers (h) 2–0 (0–0)
Hendrie, Speed
Day; Sterland (G. Williams), Whitlow, Grayson, McClelland, Haddock, Strachan (Parsley), Batty, Speed, Davison, Hendrie.
Att: 3,562
Neil Parsley didn't play a first-team game for Leeds.

11 August v Halifax Town (a) 1–2 (1–1)
Hendrie
Edwards, Sterland, Whitlow (G. Williams), Speed, McClelland, Haddock, Strachan, Batty, Baird (Grayson), Davison, Hendrie.
Att: The match was played behind closed doors at The Shay because improvements were being done to the ground.

The competition was won by Hull City, who beat Bradford City in the Final.

1990
11 August v Hull City (a) 1–2 (1–2)
McAllister
Lukic, Sterland, G. Snodin, Haddock (Varadi), Fairclough, Whyte, Strachan, Batty (A. Williams), Chapman, McAllister, Speed.
Att: 3,111

13 August v Scarborough (a) 2–0 (0–0)
Chapman, Whyte
Day, Sterland, G. Snodin, Jones, Fairclough (Haddock), Whyte, Strachan, Varadi, Chapman (Pearson), McAllister, Speed.
Att: 3,608

18 August v Lincoln City (a) 4–1 (0–0)
Williams, Sterland, Snodin, Varadi
Lukic, Sterland, G. Snodin, Kamara, Whyte, Haddock, Strachan, Batty (Jones), Pearson, Varadi, Speed (A. Williams).
Att: 4,661

The competition was won by Halifax Town, who won 3–2 at Rotherham in the Final.

TRANSPENNINE EXPRESS TROPHY

United fielded a mixture of reserves and juniors in this pre-season invitation tournament in 1993 which also involved Liverpool, Tottenham Hotspur and Sheffield Wednesday. Tottenham, who beat Sheffield Wednesday 2–1 in their semi-final, won the competition. Liverpool took third place with a 4–3 win over Wednesday. Both United matches were played at Queensgate, Bridlington.

1993
27 July v Liverpool (at Bridlington) 4–0 (3–0)
Shutt, Chapman 2, Ford
Beeney, Couzens, Oliver, Hodge, Wetherall,Whyte, Shutt, Ray Wallace, Chapman, Tobin, Ford.

29 July v Tottenham Hotspur (at Bridlington) 0–2 (0–1)
Beeney, Couzens, Sharp, Hodge, Wetherall, Whyte, Shutt, Tinkler, Chapman, Forrester, Ford.
Simon Oliver and Steve Tobin didn't play a first-team game for Leeds.

RYEDALE TROPHY

This competition effectively succeeded the Transpennine Trophy with all the games being played at Ryedale Stadium, the home of York Rugby League Club. The format was unchanged and Tottenham retained the trophy. The following year, the tournament was won by Nottingham Forest, who beat Tottenham 2–0.

1994

30 July v Sheffield Wednesday 2–2 (1–1)
Hodge 2, Forrester (pen)
Pettinger, Couzens, Sharp, Ford, Ray Wallace, Jackson, Wharton, Hodge, A. Brown (Gray), Forrester, Smithard.

31 July v Tottenham Hotspur 0–2 aet (0–0; 90 mins 0–0)
Pettinger, Couzens, Sharp, Ford, Ray Wallace, Jackson (O'Shea), Wharton, Blunt, A. Brown (Shepherd), Forrester, Smithard.

1995

5 August v Tottenham Hotspur 1–4 (0–1)
Ford
Pettinger; Marks, Fidler, Bowman, O'Shea, Smithard, Wharton, A Brown (Masinga), Forrester, Sharp (Blunt).

6 August v Sheffield Wednesday 0–0 (0–0)
Pettinger, Smithard, Fidler (Shepherd), Blunt, O'Shea, Jackson (Maybury), Wharton, Ford, Grant, Lowndes (A. Brown), Gray.
Paul Pettinger, Jamie Marks, Paul Wharton, Andrew Brown, Matthew Smithard, Alan O'Shea, Richard Fidler, Tony Grant and Nathan Lowndes didn't play a first-team game for Leeds.

PRE-SEASON TOURNAMENTS

United have figured in many tournaments, often used for pre-season fine tuning, which have taken them to many parts of Europe and beyond.

Here are a selection of some of the more high-profile competitions in which they have figured.

The details have been drawn from a variety of sources, so not all referees, attendances and half-times have been obtained.

Amsterdam 701 Tournament

All the games for this four-team competition were played at the Olympic Stadium, Amsterdam.

United found themselves up against a familiar face in Duncan McKenzie in their opening game as he was making his first senior outing for Anderlecht since his move from Elland Road.

But it was the Whites' new signing Tony Currie who caught the eye, opening the scoring with a diving header and spraying some great passes around the field. The Belgians hit back through Rob Rensenbrink, Peter Ressel and Ludo Coeck before Carl Harris added a last-minute consolation.

Hosts Ajax beat Borussia Moenchengladbach in the other match so United faced the German champions in the third-fourth place Play-off.

Eddie Gray gave United the lead inside a minute, but as in the previous match they fell 3–1 behind. Gray grabbed his second just after an hour and a late equaliser by Allan Clarke sent the game to penalties which Leeds lost 3–1, Currie being the only successful scorer while Frank Gray, Trevor Cherry and Norman Hunter all missed.

Anderlecht won the Final by beating Ajax 3–1.

6 August 1976 v Anderlecht 2–3 (1–2)
Currie, Harris
Stewart, Reaney, F.T. Gray (Hampton), Bremner, Madeley, Hunter, Cherry, Lorimer (Harris), Clarke, Currie, Yorath
Ref: Jan Beck (Holland)
Att: 40,000

8 August 1976 v Borussia Moenchengladbach 3–3 (1–2) Leeds lost 3–1 on penalties
E. Gray 2, Clarke
Stewart, Stevenson, F.T. Gray, Bremner (Hampton), Madeley, Hunter, Cherry, Currie, Clarke, Yorath, E. Gray
Ref: Gerrie Berrevots (Holland)
Att: 35,000

Edi Naegli Tournament
This tournament, played in 1980, honoured the cigar-smoking Edi Naegli, FC Zurich's colourful department store owning president, who died the previous year. He had been president of the Swiss club since 1957.

All the games were played at the Letzigrund Stadium, one of the world's most famous athletics venues.

United went down to a Hans Pfister goal for Grasshoppers in their opening game and finished last when they were beaten on penalties by the host club after Alex Sabella had wiped out Jurica Jerkovic's opener

Eintracht Frankfurt were the tournament winners, beating FC Zurich 3–1 and Grasshoppers 2–1 in the Final.

1 August 1980 v Grasshoppers 0–1
Lukic, Hird, Stevenson (Greenhoff), Flynn (Connor), Hart, Cherry, E. Gray (Hamson), Sabella, Parlane, Curtis, Graham.
Ref: Gottlieb Barmettler (Zurich)
Att: 2,000

2 August 1980 v FC Zurich 1–1 Leeds lost 3–2 on penalties
Sabella
Lukic, Cherry (Graham), Stevenson, Greenhoff, Hart, Hird, Sabella, Hamson, Parlane, Connor, Curtis.
Ref: Rudolf Affolter (Switzerland)
Att: 3,000

Ikast SDS Cup
This week-long tournament hosted by Danish side Ikast was the beginning of one of the busiest pre-seasons ever.

The hosts were beaten by a Neil Firm header from a Brian Greenhoff cross in the opening game of the six-team competition. United were then held by the Polish champions Widzew Lodz, Brian Flynn cancelling out Miroslav Sajewicz's opener.

The draw meant they failed to reach the final and lost to FC Utrecht of Holland in the Play-off for third place, Bert Gozems netting with a twice-taken 12th minute free-kick. The other teams taking part were Start from Norway and German side Eintract Braunschweig.

After the three games in Denmark, Leeds played a one-off game in Germany, losing 3–2 to Cologne, then took part in a tournament in Gibraltar before jetting off to Canada to play in a competition in Toronto.

22 July 1981 v Ikast FS 1–0 (0–0)
Firm
Lukic, Greenhoff (Connor), E. Gray, Flynn, Firm, Cherry, Harris, Hird, Parlane, Stevenson, Graham.
Att: 6,500

24 July 1981 v Widzew Lodz 1–1 (0–1)
Flynn
Lukic, F.T. Gray, E. Gray, Flynn, Firm, Cherry, Harris (Hart), Hird, Parlane, Stevenson, Graham.

26 July 1981 v FC Utrecht 0–1 (0–1)
Lukic, Hird, F.T. Gray, Firm, Hart, Cherry, Flynn, Stevenson, Harris, Parlane, Connor.

Gibraltar Tournament

This tournament had been played each year since 1970 with all matches played in the southern Spanish city of La Línea de la Concepción, near Gibraltar.

United did well to beat Gijon in their opener but were overpowered by Real Madrid in the final by goals from San Jose Isidoro, Carlos Santillana and former West Brom favourite Laurie Cunningham.

8 August 1981 v Sporting Gijon 3–2

Parlane 2, Flynn

Lukic, Greenhoff (Connor), F.T. Gray, Flynn, Hart, Cherry, Harris, Hird, Parlane, E. Gray, Graham.

Ref: Ausocua Sanz (Spain)

9 August 1981 v Real Madrid 0–3

Lukic, Hird, F.T. Gray, Flynn, Hart, Cherry, Harris, Connor (Stevenson), Parlane, E. Gray, Graham.

Ref: Guruceta Muro (Spain)

Toronto International Tournament

The club's new record signing, Peter Barnes, joined United while they were in Gibraltar and made his debut against Ecuador's Barcelona Sporting at the Varsity Stadium, home of Toronto Blizzard, where all the games were played. It was certainly a bizarre introduction to life with Leeds who had Paul Hart sent off just before half-time. When Alcides de Oliveira put the South Americans ahead, United looked out of it, but substitute Terry Connor equalised for 10-man Leeds to take the game into extra time.

The teams were eight minutes away from a penalty shootout when Alcides dived in the box and referee Gordon Arrowsmith waved 'play on'. He was immediately jostled by Barcelona's players and manager Humberto Maschio, who stormed on to the pitch to confront the official.

In the melee, a kick was aimed at Arrowsmith, who slumped to the ground, but recovered to red card Maschio and player Carlos Torres Garces before leaving the field with his linesmen – the match had been abandoned.

Allan Clarke took his players to the dressing room where tournament organiser Frank Alvarek tried to persuade Leeds to settle the match on penalties – an offer Clarke declined as his team were already in the bath.

It was not until they got back to their hotel that United were officially informed that they would meet Portuguese champions Benfica in the final which was settled by a 75th minute penalty by Nene.

14 August 1981 v Barcelona (Ecuador) 1–1 (0–0) match abandoned after extra-time

Connor

Lukic, Greenhoff (Stevenson), F.T. Gray, Flynn (Firm), Hart, Cherry, Harris (Sabella), Graham, Parlane (Connor), E. Gray, Barnes.

Ref: Gordon Arrowsmith (Ontario)

16 August 1981 v Benfica 0–1 (0–0)

Lukic, Greenhoff, F.T. Gray, Flynn, Firm, Cherry, Sabella, Graham, Connor, E. Gray (Stevenson), Barnes (Harris).

Marbella Tournament

This well-established tournament, first played in 1962, proved one of the most popular among the pre-season travelling Leeds supporters, boosted by a large number of servicemen from nearby Gibraltar.

However, United found themselves out of their depth at the Estadio Municipal de Utrera Molina. They lost to Castilla – Real Madrid's reserves – before folding to the hosts in the third-fourth Play-off.

Belenenses of Portugal beat Castilla 4–2 in the Final.

18 August 1984 v CF Castilla 0–3 (0–1)
Harvey, Irwin, Hamson, Watson, Linighan, Aspin, Wright, Sheridan, Ritchie, F.T. Gray, Sellars (Gavin).

19 August 1984 v Malaga 2–5 (0–3)
Watson, Ritchie
Harvey, Irwin, Hamson, Watson, Linighan, Aspin, McCluskey, Sheridan, Ritchie (Wright), F.T. Gray, Gavin.

Makita Trophy Tournament

United hosted the 1992 Makita Trophy Tournament, a high profile pre-season invitation competition which had been held at Wembley in previous years.

There was an added edge to the competition as United, the English champions, had been drawn against one of the participants, VfB Stuttgart, in the European Cup and the teams were scheduled to meet in the semi-final of the Makita tournament.

United fell behind to a Fritz Walter strike, but two goals in three minutes midway through the second half by Rod Wallace and David Rocastle edged out the German side. Italian team Sampdoria beat Nottingham Forest 2–0 in their semi-final match on the same day.

Sven Göran-Eriksson's Sampdoria beat United in the final with a Vladimir Jugovic goal, although the match is probably best remembered by a David Batty challenge which saw one of the Italians splattered into an advertising hoarding.

Stuttgart beat Forest 1–0 in the third/fourth Play-off game.

1 August 1992 v VfB Stuttgart (h) 2–1 (0–1)
Wallace, Rocastle
Lukic; Newsome, Dorigo, Hodge, Sellars (Batty), Whyte, Rocastle (Cantona), Rod Wallace, Chapman, McAllister, Speed.
Ref: Gerald Ashby (Worcester)
Att: 12,500

2 August v Sampdoria (h) 0-1 (0-1)
Lukic, Newsome (Whyte), Dorigo, Batty, Fairclough, Hodge, Rocastle (Cantona), Rod Wallace, Chapman, McAllister, Speed.
Ref: Joe Worrall (Warrington)
Att: 15,000

New Year Tournament

This three-team competition, held in the Italian city of Florence, certainly broke the mould – it was held in mid-season with games of one half of 45 minutes all staged on one day.

It featured Fiorentina, Inter Milan and United, who had not won an away game all season in defence of their Division One title.

They did not improve on that record in the Tourneo Di Capadanno (New Year Tournament), losing both their games 2–0.

They kicked off at 7.30pm against Inter with Norwegian striker Frank Strandli making his debut and were sunk by goals from Nicola Berti (17) and Darko Pancev (37). An hour later United faced the hosts who won courtesy of a Francesco Baiano double (12 and 36 minutes). Gordon Strachan was sent off against Fiorentina, who went on to beat Inter 1–0 with a goal from Argentinian World Cup star Gabriel Batistuta to win the tournament.

About the only positive to come out of the competition, screened live by Eurosport, was the £200,000 United received for taking part.

6 January 1993 v Inter Milan (a) 0–2
Day, Newsome, Wetherall, Whyte, Fairclough, Sellars, Rocastle, Hodge, Varadi, Strandli, Rod Wallace.
Ref: Piero Ceccarini (Livorno)

6 January 1993 v Fiorentina (a) 0–2
Lukic, Sterland, Newsome, Whyte, Fairclough, Dorigo, Strachan, McAllister, Speed, Shutt, Chapman
Ref: Marcello Nicchi (Arezzo)
Att: 12,222 (for the three 45-minute matches)

Mitsubishi Tournament

United flew to Malaysia to take part in this tournament which marked the opening of 69,372 capacity Stadium Sah Alam where all the games were played.

Leeds played an Australian Olympic XI and Brazilian side Flamenco, the eventual winners. Other teams involved were Dundee United, Bayern Munich and a Selangor FA XI.

David White put United ahead against the Olyroos, Joe Piteri equalised and Phil Masinga came off the bench to claim an 80th minute winner.

Leeds came from behind against the Brazilians to level with a Noel Whelan goal 15 minutes from the end, but an error by goalkeeper Mark Beeney saw Flamenco into the Final where they beat Bayern Munich.

19 July 1994 v Australia Olympic XI 2–1 (1–1)
White, Masinga
Lukic, Worthington, Wetherall, Palmer, Dorigo, White (Strachan), Tinkler, McAllister, Speed, Wallace, Deane (Masinga).

21 July 1994 v Flamengo 1–2 (0–1)
Whelan
Beeney, Pemberton, O'Leary, Palmer, Worthington, Strachan, Tinkler, McAllister, Sharpe, Masinga, Whelan.

United Bank Challenge

After the signing of Lucas Radebe and Phil Masinga, United's popularity in South Africa had soared so they were obvious choices to take part in the United Bank Challenge tournament.

When the Leeds squad landed at Johannesburg they were mobbed by fans who carried striker Masinga shoulder high through the terminal.

He was made captain for the day against his old side Mamelodi Sundowns, but United lost to a late Kenneth Neimach goal in high altitude at the Loftus Versfelt Stadium in Pretoria.

It was also a struggle three days later in Johannesburg's Ellis Park with United stretched by Portuguese side Benfica, particularly after the second half dismissal of David Wetherall.

After 90 minutes the goal-less game went straight to penalties with both sides scoring five each before a break in proceedings to allow a parachute display, which was part of the build-up to the Final, to take place. After what seemed an age, Noel Whelan finally got to take what was the sixth Leeds kick which he put against the bar, leaving Nassar Hassan to hit the winning spot-kick.

Kaiser Chiefs, the former club of Radebe, who didn't feature because of injury, lost 3–0 to the Sundowns in the Final.

27 July 1995 v Mamelodi Sundowns 0–1 (0–0)
Lukic, Kelly, Dorigo (Worthington), White (Tinkler), Pemberton, Wetherall, Masinga (Whelan), Deane, Wallace, McAllister, Speed.
Att: 45,000

30 July 1995 v Benfica 0–0 (0–0) Leeds lost 5–6 on penalties

Beeney, Kelly, Worthington, Tinkler, Pemberton, Wetherall, Deane, Wallace, Yeboah, McAllister, Speed. Subs: Whelan, Lukic, Masinga, Sharpe, Couzens.

Freiburg Tournment

Nigel Martyn made his Leeds debut in the opener in Bahlingen against German fifth division side Freiburger FC and was left rooted to the spot when he was beaten by a 30-yarder after only five minutes. He also brought down a forward to enable Achim Hausen to score from the spot, but a couple of Brian Deane goals ensured it was all-square at half-time.

Ian Rush, who had scored the only goal in the pre-tournament game against Pforzheim, nabbed a couple in the second half to spare United's blushes.

SC Freiburg beat Bahlingen 4–1 in the other game and promptly won the Bente-Turnier Trophy for the ninth time in 12 seasons by defeating Leeds 2–1 in the Final.

Alain Sutter scored early on for the Bundeslegia side, Rush equalised on 36 minutes but a Stefan Muller header slipped through Mark Beeney's grasp in the final minute to hand the Germans their silverware.

2 August 1996 v Freiburger FC 4–2 (2–2)

Deane 2, Rush 2

Martyn, Couzens, Harte (Wallace), Bowman, Jackson, Beesley, Blunt (Bowyer), Tinkler (Palmer), Yeboah (Rush), Deane (Kelly), Gray.

3 August 1996 v Sporting Club Freiburg 1–2 (1–1)

Rush

The Leeds team included Beeney, Kewell, Rush, Bowyer and Yeboah, the latter going off after 70 minutes.

Carlsberg Trophy

United were invited to take part in the inaugural tournament at Lansdowne Road, Dublin, in 1998 alongside Liverpool, Italian side Lazio and Irish champions St Patrick's Athletic.

Trailing to a 78th minute goal by Rosario Aquino, United were heading to defeat against Lazio before Lee Bowyer headed a late equaliser. The game went to penalties with Ian Harte, Derek Lilley, Lee Bowyer and Lee Matthews on target to clinch victory.

The final saw defeat for United as Patrik Berger and Michael Owen struck twice in as many minutes in the second period.

31 July 1998 v Lazio 1–1 (0–0) Leeds won 4–2 on penalties

Bowyer

Martyn, Kelly, Harte, Ribeiro (McPhail), Radebe, Molenaar, Halle, Bowyer, Hasselbaink (Lilley), Hopkin (Matthews), Granville.

Ref: Dick O'Hanlon (Waterford)

August 1 1998 v Liverpool 0-2 (0-0)

Martyn, Hiden, Harte (Ribeiro), Haaland, Radebe, Molenaar, Halle (Kelly), Bowyer (Hopkin), Hasselbaink, Matthews, McPhail (Granville).

Att: 28,000

Dublin Tournament

The competition was jointly hosted by Shelbourne and St Patrick's Athletic with all the games played at Tolka Park.

The tournament was a major disappointment as United lost Michael Duberry with a fractured jaw after only ten minutes of the opening game against Villa, managed by former boss David O'Leary. The game was 30 minutes late in starting as Villa arrived late because of a delay to their flight.

Trialist striker Lamine Sakho and Didier Domi made their Leeds debuts but United fell behind to goals by Hassan Kachloul and Thomas Hitzlesperger. Nick Barmby and Ian Harte levelled to take the game to penalties but Harte and Stephen McPhail failed from the spot.

United were beaten by Irish part-timers Shelbourne the following day to finish with the wooden spoon and earned the wrath of manager Peter Reid who criticised his players' attitude.

Villa beat St Patrick's Athletic 6–0 in the Final.

9 August 2003 v Aston Villa 2–2 (0–0)
Villa won 4-2 on penalties
Barmby, Harte
Robinson, Kelly (Mills), Duberry (Radebe), Camara, Matteo (Woods), Milner (Barmby), Morris (Harte), Seth Johnson (McPhail), Wilcox (Domi), Smith (McMaster), Sakho (Lennon).
Ref: Paul McKeon (Dublin)

10 August v Shelbourne 0–2 (0–2)
Martyn, Mills, Camara, Matteo, Domi, Barmby (Milner), McPhail (Woods), Morris, Wilcox (Harte), Sakho (Lennon), McMaster.
Ref: Paul Tuite (Dublin)

MERCANTILE CREDIT FOOTBALL FESTIVAL

To celebrate the centenary of the Football League in 1988 a variety of events were staged by the Football League, the centrepiece being the Mercantile Credit Football Festival. The Final of the festival was played at Wembley on 17 April 1988 – exactly 100 years to the day that officials from 12 clubs met at the Royal Hotel, Manchester, to form the first football competition in the world.

The Football League came up with the concept that 16 clubs – eight from Division One, four from Division Two and two each from Divisions Three and Four should qualify for the finals.

Qualification was based on the number of points teams gained in their first League fixtures between the start of November and the end of February. Provision was made that in the case of clubs not fulfilling 15 League fixtures during the specified period, points were to be allocated on a pro-rata basis for any missing games, if necessary, to establish qualification.

Leeds picked up 30 points to qualify as the third team in Division Two behind Blackburn Rovers and Aston Villa.

League fixtures for 16 and 17 April were cancelled to allow the event to be staged at Wembley. Because of the number of matches to be played, games were only 40 minutes long in rounds one and two, and an hour in the semi-final and final.

Leeds were drawn against Nottingham Forest and lost 3–0. Forest went on to beat Sheffield Wednesday 3–2 on penalties in the final after neither side scored in normal time.

Many critics were quick to point out that the contrived nature of the competition had failed to grip the public's imagination. Only 40,000 entered the stadium with 20,000 being the maximum attendance at any one time.

16 April 1998 v Nottingham Forest 0–3 (0–2)
Day, G. Williams, Adams, (G. Snodin), Aizlewood, Ashurst, Rennie, Batty, Sheridan, Baird, Taylor (Pearson), Grayson. Subs (not used): Swan, Stiles, Sinclair.
Ref: Gary Aplin (Kendal)

Leeds United Players' Testimonial Matches

TESTIMONIAL matches for a top-level professional footballer are fairly scarce in the modern era.

But before the days of astronomical wages and expensive season tickets, a testimonial game was one way of saying thanks to a loyal one-club man, the sort of player who is a rare commodity these days.

The last two Leeds players to be recognised – Gary Kelly and Lucas Radebe – both made their matches into charity fund-raisers.

That had not always been the case as footballers have not always been richly rewarded. Even the men in the Don Revie era, although well paid, didn't live a millionaire lifestyle.

Before World War Two clubs, Leeds City and Leeds United included, would often earmark the gate receipts from a League game to go to a particular player. It is only since the war, particularly after the introduction of floodlights which enabled testimonial games to be played in midweek without upsetting League schedules, that they became a feature of the domestic game.

United have had their fair share of these games, some played more seriously than others, and the matches played for Leeds players past and present involving United are recorded here. Line-ups, scorers, referees, attendances and half-times are given where ever possible.

Eric Stephenson

25 May 1947 v Celtic (h) 1–3 (0–1)

Dodds

England international Eric Stephenson, who was killed in action in Burma, was the most high-profile of all the Leeds players who died in World War Two.

This match was held as a benefit game with all the proceeds going to his widow Olive and their children.

United include guest players Jimmy Baxter and Jimmy Kelly (Barnsley), Peter Doherty (Huddersfield) and Jock Dodds (Everton), who scored the Leeds goal. Jimmy Sirrell, George Hazlett and Joe Rae netted for Celtic.

Further details of Stephenson's career in the War are in the Fallen Heroes section.

Leeds United: Twomey, Milburn, Gadsby, Henry, Holley, Baxter, Powell, Short, Dodds, Doherty, Kelly.

Celtic: Ugolini, Hogg, McAra, McPhail, Corbett, McAuley, Quinn, Sirrell, Rae, Evans, Hazlett.

Ref: Arthur Luty (Leeds) *Att:* 19,000

Arthur Crowther, Willis Edwards and Bob Roxburgh

19 April 1950 v Wolverhampton Wanderers (h) 1–1 (0–0)

Dudley

FA Cup holders Wolves and their England captain Billy Wright were the star attractions for this game to honour three United stalwarts – secretary Arthur Crowther, former player, manager and coach Willis Edwards and coach Bob Roxburgh.

The game was organised by Leeds manager Major Frank Buckley, who maintained good contacts with his former employers at Molineux. Eight of the Wolves team were signed by him and after the match a dinner was held at the Queen's Hotel to honour the beneficiaries who shared the £1,493 gate receipts.

Leeds United: Searson, Dunn, Milburn, McCabe, Charles, Burden, Cochrane, Iggleden, Dudley, Frost, Williams.

Wolverhampton Wanderers: Parsons, Pritchard, Springthorpe, Russell, Chatham, Wright, Smith, Smythe, Swinbourne, Pye, Mullen.

Ref: Arthur Ellis (Halifax) *Att:* 19,000

Jack Scott and Jack Marsden

14 March 1956 v All Stars XI (h) 5–2 (2–1)

Brook, Charles 3, Forrest

As testimonials go this was a bit of a disaster for one of the beneficiaries – goalkeeper Jack Scott.

Bitter weather saw a low turn out and poor Scott dislocated a finger after only four minutes. His hand need a couple of stitches after punching the ball in an incident which led to Leeds boss Raich Carter putting the All Stars ahead.

John Charles went in goal for United for 10 minutes while Roy Wood got ready to take over between the sticks. Charles then banged in a hat-trick after Harold Brook netted United's equaliser. Carter grabbed his second before Bobby Forrest completed the scoring.

The United side included a couple of juniors who didn't make the first team – Freddie Spridgeon and Derek Powell, a youngster from Dursley, near Gloucester – while the All Stars included some of the greatest names of the post-war era including Carter, former England captain George Hardwick, Bill Shankly and Peter Doherty.

Because gate receipts were disappointing, the Leeds directors opted to top it up out of their own pockets for two players, who, despite not being first team regulars, had given the club loyal service.

Leeds United: Scott (Wood), Dunn, Spridgeon, Gibson, Charlton, Powell, Crowe, Charles, Forrest, Brook, Overfield.

All Stars: Swindin, Beattie, Barnes, Shankly, Boot, Watson, Broome, Carter, Lawton, Doherty, Mitten.

Ref: Ronnie Leigh (Leeds) *Att:* 6,000

Len Browning

1 October 1956 v Sheffield United/Wednesday XI (a) 1–7 (0–4)

Hickson

Former Leeds forward Len Browning was struck by tuberculosis which brought a premature end to his playing career in October 1953.

He left Elland Road in 1951 to join Sheffield United and this match between a Sheffield XI against a Leeds United/Huddersfield Town XI was played at Bramall Lane in driving rain and christened the Blades' new floodlights.

The steel city men hammered their West Yorkshire counterparts who included Leeds' new South African signing John Roos in their line-up. He had arrived a couple of weeks earlier from the Peninsula club in Cape Town with a big goalscoring reputation but the inside forward didn't break into the Leeds first team.

The visitors goal was scored by Huddersfield's Dave Hickson four minutes from the end by which time Hawksworth (28, 58), Watson (31, 63), Alan Finney (42, 44) and Jimmy Hagan (65) had destroyed the West Yorkshire combination.

The match generated gates receipts of £1,517 for Browning who later helped the Whites as a video analyst.

Sheffield XI: Burgin, Staniforth, Mason, McAnearney, Barras, Hoyland, Finney, Hagan, Hawksworth, Shiner, Watson.

Leeds United/Huddersfield Town: Wood, Charlton, Hair, McGarry, Marsden, Quested, McKenna, Charles, Hickson, Roos, Metcalfe.

Ref: A. Murdoch (Sheffield) *Att:* 17,337

Willis Edwards and Bob Roxburgh

17 October 1960 v All Stars (h) 4–2 (2–0)

Revie 2, Fitzgerald 2

The Italian Football League refused permission for John Charles to play for United so the Juventus star hoped to fly from Turin to kick the game off.

But his plans of honouring his former coaches were dashed by thick fog which put paid to any chance of him flying to England. The fog, followed by heavy rain, also reduced the attendance for a game in which saw United continuing to wear their newly adopted all-white kit.

Don Revie, fresh from winning the Professional Footballers' Golf Championship a second time, netted twice as did Peter Fitzgerald, who came on after 20 minutes when John McCole was injured after a collision with Joe Shaw. Ron Staniforth and Danny Clapton scored for the Stars.

Leeds United: Humphreys, Caldwell, Hair, McConnell, McGugan, Bell, Bremner, Revie, McCole (Fitzgerald), Peyton, Grainger.

All Stars: Wood (Huddersfield Town), Staniforth (Barrow), Shaw (Sheffield United – McCullough, Arsenal), Scoular (Newcastle United), Franklin (ex-Stoke City and Hull City), Adamson (Burnley), Clapton (Arsenal), Welsh (Leicester City), Liddell (Liverpool), McIlroy (Burnley), Mullen (Wolverhampton Wanderers).

Att: 8,009

Tommy Younger

21 May 1963 v Tommy Younger XI (h) 2–5 (2–2)

Johanneson, Lawson

Scottish international goalkeeper Tommy Younger finished his distinguished career at Leeds who hosted his testimonial.

The former Hibernian, Liverpool and Stoke man was kept on by United as a scout before he moved to Canada to take up a coaching role with Toronto City.

He was later chairman at Hibernian and president of the Scottish FA.

One of United's substitutes, who came on for Rod Johnson, was Glasgow Schools player Jim McAlliog, who had just signed for the club as an amateur. Four months later he joined Chelsea and went on to star for Sheffield Wednesday and Wolves, winning five Scottish caps.

Scorers for Younger's victorious team were Mike O'Grady, who later was to play for Leeds, Liverpool duo Ian St John and Roger Hunt, Alex Harley and Pat Quinn.

Leeds United: Sprake, Reaney, Hair (Wright), Greenhoff, Bell, Hunter, Henderson, Lawson, Storrie, Johnson (McAlliog), Johanneson.

Tommy Younger XI: Trautmann (ex-Manchester City), Gratrix (Blackpool), Wilson (Huddersfield Town), Yeats (Liverpool), Swan (Sheffield Wednesday), Robson (Fulham), Douglas (Blackburn Rovers), Quinn (Blackpool – Hunt Liverpool), St John (Liverpool – Harley Manchester City), Melia (Liverpool – Gray Manchester City), O'Grady (Huddersfield Town).

Ref: Arthur Luty (Leeds) *Att:* 8,969

Grenville Hair

15 November 1965 v All Stars XI (h) 4–2 (1–2) match abandoned after 75 minutes

Gray, Lorimer 2, Cooper

This game was put on at the fifth attempt and had to be abandoned after 75 minutes because of fog.

Fixture congestion meant the fixture to honour a man who had spent 17 years at Elland Road had to be postponed four times.

Full-back Hair was player-manager of Wellington Town when the game was played and the fog saw a poor turn out. The gate receipts amounted to £1,250 but United added 100 guineas to boost the total.

Billy Bremner played at centre-forward, a role he had filled against Arsenal the previous Saturday, while the outstanding performer for the All Stars was goalkeeper Gordon Banks, who played the first 45 minutes.

Leeds United: Sprake, Reaney, Bell, Cooper, Charlton, Hunter (Gray), Storrie, Lorimer, Bremner, Giles, O'Grady.

All Stars XI: Banks (Leicester City – Walters, Blackpool), Hair (Wellington Town), Shaw (Sheffield United), Allen (Stoke City), Anderson (Newcastle United), Mobley (Sheffield Wednesday), Appleton (Leicester City), Wilson (Preston North End), Lofthouse (ex-Bolton Wanderers), Milburn (ex-Newcastle United), Dougan (Leicester City), Birchenall (Sheffield United), Mudie (ex-Blackpool), Finch (Luton Town).

Ref: Arthur Holland (Barnsley) *Att:* 6,203

Peter Fitzgerald

7 August 1967 v Waterford (a) 4–2 (3–1)

Giles (2, 1 pen), Gray, O'Grady

Although only a bit-part player at Leeds, Peter Fitzgerald was granted a testimonial by Waterford six years after he left Elland Road.

Fitzgerald, who played for Eire five times, began his career with Waterford and was signed for United by Jack Taylor from Dutch club Sparta Rotterdam but only made eight appearances in his one-year stay at Leeds.

Don Revie sold the forward to Chester for £5,500 in summer 1961 and Fitzgerald rejoined his hometown club in September 1963. Revie sent a strong side to Kilcohan Park to honour a player who also went on to manage Waterford. He was one of six brothers to play for the League of Ireland club.

On their arrival, the United party were given a civic reception by the Mayor of Waterford but the goodwill didn't always extend to the pitch with Gary Sprake having a dust up with one of the home team after what he thought was a bad challenge while Billy Bremner and Jimmy McGeogh gave no quarter in their tackles.

United's class eventually told with two Johnny Giles goals – one from the spot, an Eddie Gray piledriver and a Mike O'Grady effort putting them in charge. John O'Neill and Mick Lynch, a substitute for Argentinian trialist Louis Fullone, netted for the home side.

Waterford: Thomas, Bryan, Griffin, Ferguson, Morrissey, McGeough, O'Neill, Casey, Hale, Fullone (Lynch), Matthews.

Leeds United: Sprake, Reaney, Bell, Bremner, Charlton, Hunter, O'Grady, Gray, Madeley, Giles, Cooper.

Ref: James Quinn (Ireland) *Att:* 'A near record'

Grenville Hair

30 July 1968 v Bradford City (a) 4–0 (1–0)

Charlton, Hunter, Madeley, Cooper (og)

Just two-and-a-half years after playing a testimonial for Grenville Hair, United played another one for his dependents after his untimely death.

The game was played at Valley Parade, home of Bradford City where former United stalwart Hair, was trainer. He collapsed and died supervising a Paraders training session on 7 March 1968 and the match was organised to raise funds for his wife, Jill, and two sons, Anthony and Kenneth, generating gate receipts of more than £2,000.

Leeds United: Sprake, Reaney, Cooper, Bremner, Charlton, Hunter, Lorimer, Madeley, Jones, Giles, Gray (Greenhoff).

Bradford City: Liney (Pollard), Atkins, Cooper, Stowell (Bayliss), Hallett, Swallow, Hall, Ham (Middleton), Leighton, Bayliss (Rackstraw), Walker.

Ref: Frank Cowan (Oldham) *Att:* 10,607

John Charles

8 December 1971 v John Charles All Stars XI (a) 5–8 (3–4)

Clarke, Jones, Lorimer, Sprake (pen), Jordan

Goals flowed in this feast of football at Cardiff's Ninian Park to mark the end of the great John Charles's playing career.

Even goalkeeper Gary Sprake got in on the act with a penalty in the 65th minute, sending Bournemouth's Fred Davies the wrong way. United's other marksmen were Allan Clarke (27), Mick Jones (30), Peter Lorimer (42) and Joe Jordan (70).

King Charles, who had parted company as Hereford's player-manager a few months earlier, had finally called it a day and although he could not play because of flu there was no shortage of household names in his side.

On target for the All Stars were John Toshack (9, 15), Ted Macdougall (23, 79), Gil Reece (46, 53), Jimmy Greaves (89) and Johnny Haynes, the former Fulham and England star, who crashed in a 25-yard drive on 33 minutes.

The Leeds team below was taken from the Yorkshire Post report of the game, but differs to the pre-match line-up given by local Welsh papers. Reports of the game vary widely and it is assumed Greaves, who started the match, and later substituted, returned at some stage to score the final goal.

Leeds United: Sprake, Reaney, Cooper, Bremner, Charlton, Hunter, Lorimer, Clarke, Jones, Giles, Madeley. Subs: Yorath, Faulkner, Jordan.

John Charles All Stars XI: Davies (Bournemouth), Thomas (Swindon Town), Nish (Leicester City), Godfrey (Bristol Rovers), Mackay (Swindon Town), Johnstone (Celtic), Haynes (ex-Fulham), Toshack (Liverpool), MacDougall (Bournemouth), Greaves (ex-Chelsea, Tottenham and West Ham – Reece, Sheffield United), Gibson (Cardiff City). Sub: Phillips (Cardiff City).

Ref: Clive Thomas (Treorchy) *Att:* 18,950

Jack Charlton

7 May 1973 v Celtic (h) 3–4 (1–1)

(Clarke 2, Bremner)

About 4,000 Celtic fans, including James Bond actor Sean Connery, boosted Big Jack's testimonial crowd to near 35,000 at Elland Road.

They were treated to a dazzling exhibition by both teams with Celtic, whose marksmen were Jimmy Johnstone (2), Bobby Lennox and Kenny Dalglish, earning a standing ovation for their display.

But the biggest cheers remained for Charlton, in his final game for Leeds, before taking up his managerial post with Middlesbrough. The battle-hardened veteran of a record 773 appearances for United admitted he had tears in his eyes as he went on a lap of honour after the match.

Leeds United: Sprake, Reaney, Madeley, Bremner, Charlton (McQueen), Hunter (Cherry), Lorimer, Clarke, Jones (Jordan), Giles (Bates), E. Gray (Yorath).

Celtic: Hunter, Hay, McGrain, Murdoch, McNeill, Connelly (McCluskey), Johnstone, Murray, Dalglish, Lennox, Callaghan.

Referee: Gordon Hill (Leicester) *Att:* 34,963

Billy Bremner

30 October 1973 v Stirling Albion (a) 3–2 (1–1)

Bates 2, Jones

This game launched Billy Bremner's testimonial season and provided the home club with one of its biggest attendances at Annfield Park for many years.

Mick Bates proved the star of the show with two fine goals, the winner coming in the 63rd minute, barely 60 seconds after Mick Jones had scored the equaliser.

Before the game Bremner presented a trophy to his former school, St Modan's, who had won a local five-a-side final.

Stirling Albion: Young, Jones, Hancock, Duffin, McAleer, Carr, McPhee, Clark (Christie), Steele, McMillan, Lawson (Murphy).

Leeds United: Harvey (Shaw), Reaney, Cherry, Bremner, McQueen, Hunter (Mann), Lorimer (Liddell), Jordan, Jones (F.T. Gray), Bates, Yorath.

Ref: A.F.J. Webster (Falkirk) *Att:* 9,000

6 May 1974 v Sunderland (h) 0–0 (0–0)

United were presented with the League Championship trophy from Football League president Len Shipman, who also handed the players their winners' medals, before the kick-off.

In typical combative fashion, Billy Bremner wanted Sunderland for his testimonial to avenge the previous season's FA Cup Final defeat. That didn't happen as their Second Division opponents matched the newly crowned champions in a competitive match.

If fact, Sunderland, still in the Second Division, almost repeated their Wembley triumph as Dennis Tueart's shot in the final minute beat David Harvey but came back off a post. Tueart and Mick Horswill, two of the Rokerites 1973 heroes were borrowed from Manchester City so Bob Stokoe could field as near as possible the team that won the FA Cup.

The attendance topped Jack Charlton's game the previous year by about 3,000 and saw Bremner bank between £35,000 and £40,000.

Leeds United: Harvey, Reaney, Cherry, Bremner, McQueen, Hunter, Lorimer, Clarke, Jordan, Yorath, Madeley.

Sunderland: Montgomery, Malone, Bolton, Horswill (Towers), Watson, Young, Kerr, Hughes, Belfitt, Porterfield, Tueart.

Ref: Gordon Hill (Leicester) *Att:* 37,708

Norman Hunter

5 May 1975 v Don Revie XI (h) 2–3 (0–0)

Bremner 2

This was the last home game before United flew to Paris for the European Cup Final against Bayern Munich and ensured a bumper crowd for Norman Hunter as Leeds fans gave their heroes a big send off.

There was also the unusual sight of Don Revie in the opposition dugout as his side of England stars edged it with goals from Mike Channon (2) and Malcolm Macdonald while Gary Sprake got some time between the posts as a replacement for Gordon Banks. Billy Bremner netted both United goals.

Much to the delight of the crowd the game's first foul came when Hunter up-ended Dennis Tueart on 14 minutes.

There was a six-a-side curtain-raiser between Leeds Superstars and a Rugby League team which saw Albert Johanneson score a hat-trick in a 5–1 Superstars win. United boss Jimmy Armfield and old midfield maestro Bobby Collins was also on target while the RL marksman was United junior Gary Felix.

Leeds United: Stewart, Reaney, Cherry, Bremner, McQueen (E. Gray), Hunter, Lorimer, Clarke (Liddell), Jordan, Yorath, F.T. Gray.

Don Revie XI: Banks (Stoke City – Gary Sprake, Birmingham City), Whitworth (Leicester City), Kennedy (Newcastle United), Francis (Birmingham City – Thomas, QPR), Jones (Bolton Wanderers), Bell (Manchester City), Ball (Arsenal – Osgood, Southampton), Channon (Southampton), Macdonald (Newcastle United), Tueart (Manchester City), Keegan (Liverpool).

Ref: Jack Taylor (Wolverhampton) *Att:* 36,118

Johnny Giles

22 October 1975 v West Bromwich Albion (a) 1–3

McKenzie

Irish ace Johnny Giles was blessed with the presence of World Cup winners Geoff Hurst, Bobby Charlton and Nobby Stiles (Giles' brother-in-law) for his testimonial at The Hawthorns.

United were the obvious opponents for the masterly midfielder who had left Leeds to become West Brom's player-manager.

Albion's goalscorers were Derek Dougan, just a few days after his own testimonial with Wolves, Paddy Mulligan and Alistair Brown. Duncan McKenzie wiped out The Doog's opener but the Baggies emerged victors.

Giles also had a testimonial in Dublin against a Don Revie XI, which was essentially an England trial squad, and included McKenzie, which was the nearest the mercurial forward got to winning a full cap.

West Bromwich Albion: Osbourne, Mulligan, Wilson, Cantello, Wile, Stiles, Dougan, Hurst, Charlton, Giles, Johnston. Subs: T. Brown, A. Brown, Martin, Robertson.

Leeds United: Harvey, Reaney, Cherry, Bremner, Parkinson, Hunter, Lorimer (Liddell), Clarke, McKenzie, Yorath, Bates. Subs: Letheran, Stevenson.

Att: 8,652

Paul Reaney

3 May 1976 v Newcastle United (h) 4–5 (2–2)

Lorimer 2 (1 pen), Clarke, Stevenson

Paul Reaney picked Newcastle United for his testimonial because they scored plenty of goals and the Magpies didn't disappoint.

Alan Gowling opened the scoring for the visitors in the first minute, Peter Lorimer and Allan Clarke had the Whites ahead after 12 minutes, but the Geordies levelled before the break through England man Malcolm Macdonald, who added a second shortly after the break. A Lorimer penalty made it 3–3, immediately followed by a Byron Stevenson strike, but Newcastle hit back through Micky Burns and Alan Kennedy to win.

Johnny Giles returned from West Brom to play for Leeds and fans were delighted to see Duncan McKenzie do his famous leap over a Mini on the side of the pitch. He'd done it in the club car park for the players before but this was the first time his party piece was seen in public.

Leeds United: Stewart (Letheran), Reaney, Cherry (Hampton), Bremner, Madeley, Hunter (Stevenson), Lorimer, Clarke, Yorath (McNiven), Giles, McKenzie.

Newcastle United: Mahoney (Jones), Nattrass, Kennedy, Hudson (Blackhall), McCaffrey, Oates, Burns, Cassidy, Macdonald, Gowling, Craig.

Ref: Bob Matthewson (Bolton) *Att:* 19,376

Paul Madeley

26 March 1977 v Johnny Giles Eire XI (h) 2–5 (1–4)

Harris, Jordan

Unusually for a testimonial match it was played on a Saturday as the First Division programme was virtually wiped out because of international games the following Wednesday.

Versatile Paul Madeley missed a great chance to net a rare goal when he had strode up to take a penalty but was denied from the spot by Bohemians goalkeeper Mick Smyth after 25 minutes as Johnny Giles' Eire XI ran out easy winners.

Madeley had scored quite a few goals earlier in his career but had not found the net since scoring the winner at Manchester City on Boxing Day 1975.

Ireland player-manager Giles and his team treated the game quite seriously as a warm-up for their World Cup qualifying game against France four days later, a game which they won 1–0.

Leeds United: Stewart (Letheran), Stevenson, Hampton, Lorimer, McQueen, Madeley, F.T. Gray, Clarke (McNiven), Jordan, Currie (McGhie), Harris.

Johnny Giles Eire XI: Smyth (Bohemians), Langan (Derby County), Macken (Derby County), Martin (West Brom), Mulligan (West Brom), Brady (Arsenal), Daly (Derby County), Treacy (West Brom), Conway (Manchester City), Giles (West Brom), Givens (QPR).

Ref: George Hartley (Wakefield) *Att:* 12,501

Peter Lorimer

9 November 1977 v Scottish Select XI (h) 5–2 (1–1)

Giles 2 (1 pen), Currie, Flynn, Thomas

Four days after scoring his 150th League goal for United, Peter Lorimer lined up for the Scots alongside familiar Elland Road faces David Stewart, Gordon McQueen, Frank Gray, Joe Jordan and Arthur Graham.

But Leeds, with Johnny Giles pulling the strings back on his old stamping ground, won comfortably.

Also appearing in the Scottish side were Jack Charlton, who played the last 40 minutes, and John Lukic, who replaced Stewart for the final quarter of an hour.

Leeds United: Harvey, Stevenson, Cooper, Bremner, B. Greenhoff, Madeley, Harris (Thomas 61), Flynn, Hankin, Currie, Giles.

Scottish Select XI: Stewart (Lukic), Forsyth, Blackley (Charlton), Lorimer, McQueen, Buchan, F.T. Gray, Craig, Jordan, Dalglish, Graham.
Ref: Terry Morris (Leeds) *Att:* 18,812

Eddie Gray

28 March 1979 v Super Leeds (h) 1–4 (0–1)
Stevenson (pen)
Peter Lorimer delayed his flight across the Atlantic to join Toronto Blizzard to make sure he played in this game for his fellow Scottish international Eddie Gray.

Lorimer went out with a bang, scoring twice for the classy Super Leeds side whose other goals came from Rod Belfitt and Johnny Giles.

The ever popular Gray, later to have two managerial spells at Elland Road, took a well deserved lap of honour at the end of the game to the strains of a Scots pipe band.
Leeds United: Lukic, Hird, Stevenson, Flynn, Hart, Cherry, Harris, Hankin, Hawley, Currie, Graham.
Super Leeds: Harvey, F.T. Gray, Cooper, Bremner, Charlton, Hunter, Lorimer, Galvin (Collins), Belfitt, Giles, E. Gray.
Ref: Keith Styles (Barnsley) *Att:* 19,079

David Harvey

5 March 1980 v Vancouver Whitecaps (h) 2–1 (1–0)
Graham, Parkinson
Only a few days after his testimonial, Harvey jetted off to Canada to join North American Soccer League champions Vancouver Whitecaps thus ending a 14-year association with United for the Scottish international who had lost his place to rising star John Lukic.

Harvey played for his new employers, but was upstaged by his opposite number, Henry Smith, who pulled off several fine saves, including a penalty from David Robb after a Gwyn Thomas handball. Smith didn't make the Leeds first team but had a long career at Hearts and played three times for Scotland.

United's team was a mixture of legends – Billy Bremner, Norman Hunter, Jack Charlton and Allan Clarke – and younger players including Smith, Duncan Reynard and Brendan Hawkins.
Leeds United: Smith, Reynard, Hawkins, Bremner, Parkinson, Hunter, Charlton, Thomas, Hankin (Balcombe), Clarke, Graham.
Vancouver Whitecaps: Harvey, Bolitho (Nelson), Lenarduzzi, Lewington, Kenyon, O'Leary, Valentine, Gray (Parsons), Whymark (Ingram), Robb (Dunlop), Johnston.
Ref: Terry Morris (Leeds) *Att:* 11,222

Trevor Cherry

14 October 1981 v Sheffield Wednesday (h) 3–3 (0–1)
Connor, Hird (pen), Cherry (pen)
Trevor Cherry was the Leeds skipper at the time of his testimonial, but a few days later Allan Clarke signed Kenny Burns from Nottingham Forest and handed his new signing the captaincy.

Leeds referee Terry Morris was officiating for the last time before taking up an appointment as assistant secretary to the Football League. He had a busy finale, awarding three penalties. Fittingly it was Cherry who netted from the spot six minutes from time to earn Leeds a draw.

The match was one of the few times the Leeds public got the chance to see youth team goalkeeper David Seaman in action after coming on after just over an hour. Unable to break into the Leeds first team, he joined Peterborough and later became one of the all-time greats with Arsenal and England.

Leeds United: Lukic (Seaman), Hird, E. Gray, Cherry, Hart (Parkinson), Stevenson (Sabella), Connor, Graham, McKenzie, Hamson, Barnes.

Sheffield Wednesday: Bolder, Blackhall, Williamson, Smith, Shirtliff (Pickering 68), Taylor, Megson, Mirocevic (Hornsby), Bannister, McCulloch (Pearson), Curran (Mellor).

Ref: Terry Morris (Leeds) *Att:* 9,331

Peter Lorimer

20 November 1985 v Manchester United (h) 2–2 (1–2)

McCluskey, Sheridan

Leeds played host to First Division leaders Manchester United in a 60-minute game which was preceded by a curtain-raiser between Old Leeds United and a Vintage All-Stars XI.

Don Revie returned to Elland Road to lead out the Old Leeds team, who won 1–0 with, inevitably, a Lorimer goal, converting after Rod Belfitt knocked down a Paul Reaney cross. The All Stars included a good smattering of former Leeds players.

The main event saw early goals for George McCluskey and Frank Stapleton, who netted from the penalty spot. Mark Hughes made it 2-1 to the Red Devils, but John Sheridan ensured an honourable draw just before the hour.

Leeds United: Day, Irwin, Phelan (Robinson), Snodin, McGregor, Hamson, Ritchie, Sheridan, McCluskey, Wright (Simmonds), Sellars.

Manchester United: Bailey, Robinson, Garton, Dempsey, McGrath, Moran, Russell, Olsen, Hughes (Hanrahan), Stapleton, Murphy.

Old Leeds United: Harvey, Reaney, Cherry, Hunter, Yorath, Giles, Bremner, Lorimer, E. Gray, Belfitt, Bates.

Vintage All Stars: Swinburne, Balcombe, Knowles, Smith, Lumsden, F.T. Gray, McKenzie, Bell, Worthington, Kidd, Tueart.

Referee: Trevor Simpson (Leeds) *Att:* 8,500

Bobby Collins and John Charles

12 April 1988 v Everton (h) 3–2

Rush 3

Four stars from world football turned out for United in a testimonial game for United legends John Charles and Bobby Collins against Collins' former club Everton. Charles was adored at his time with Juventus and the Italian giants had two of their players, Ian Rush and Gaetano Scirea, as well as the recently retired Michel Platini in the Leeds team, which also included Liverpool's Kenny Dalglish. The game was televised live in Turin with Rush, who was to join Leeds eight years later, scoring a first-half hat-trick.

Everton included Wayne Clarke, brother of Allan, and former United skipper Ian Snodin in their ranks.

United: Sinclair, Brockie, Snodin, Haddock (Grayson), Rennie, Scirea, Dalglish, Sheridan, Rush (Baird), Platini (Stiles), Batty (Speed).

Everton: Southall, Stevens, Van den Hauwe, Mountfield, Watson, Harper, Adams, Heath, Clarke, Snodin, Carberry.

Ref: Keith Hackett (Sheffield) *Att:* 13,671

Don Revie

11 May 1988 v Don Revie International XI (h) 2–1 (0–1)

Baird, Sheridan

After the shock revelation that former boss Don Revie was suffering from the incurable muscle-wasting motor neurone disease, a fund-raising game was held at Elland Road.

The proceeds, which amounted to £24,519, were split between motor neurone disease research, Leeds City Council children's charity Give For Life appeal and the ailing Revie. The wheelchair-bound Revie managed to attend at the start and most of the stars from his great squad were there for an emotional reunion on the pitch.

Leeds included Peter Shilton – a former Revie transfer target – in their line-up, while Norman Hunter came on in the second half for goalscorer Ian Baird. Revie's International XI included Eddie Gray, Kevin Keegan, Paul Gascoigne, who opened the scoring with a backheel, and Graeme Souness, making his final appearance before retiring as a player.

Leeds United: Shilton, Haddock, McDonald, Aizlewood, Swan, Rennie, Batty, Sheridan, Baird (Hunter), Taylor, Snodin.

Don Revie International XI: Woods (Rangers), Gidman (Manchester City), E. Gray (ex-Leeds United), Wilkins (Rangers), Wright (Derby County), Miller (Aberdeen), Keegan (ex-Liverpool and Newcastle – Williams (Arsenal) – Cooper, ex-Leeds United), Gascoigne (Newcastle United), Souness (Rangers), Nicholas (Aberdeen), Robertson (ex-Nottingham Forest).

Ref: Jim McAulay (Leeds) *Att:* 7,305

Mel Sterland

12 November 1990 v Sheffield Wednesday (h) 2–7 (1–1)

Pearson, Varadi

Mel Sterland's testimonial was originally to have been played at Sheffield Wednesday's ground at the end of the 1988–89 season, but the date was just weeks after the Hillsborough tragedy which claimed the lives of 96 people so did not go ahead.

Sheffield-born Sterland, forced to quit the full-time game in 1993 with a persistent ankle injury, was a title winner with Leeds but his game would probably have been better attended had it been staged at Hillsborough where he held super-hero status. Fittingly, the two Leeds goals were scored by former Owls players, John Pearson and Imre Varadi.

Aberdeen-born Ray Stephen, a former Dundee midfield player with French First Division outfit Nancy, who had been taken on a two-week trial by Leeds, started.

Eddie Gray, Peter Lorimer, Trevor Cherry and Vinnie Jones all began the game for Leeds who were no match for a younger Wednesday team, which featured Tony Currie and Frank

Worthington in their starting XI. Wednesday powered away in the second half with six goals in a 21-minute spell, including a hat-trick for Trevor Francis.

Leeds United: Day (Edwards), Sterland (Grayson), Kamara, Jones (Kerr), Fairclough (McClelland), Whyte (O'Donnell), Lorimer (Strachan), Cherry (Williams), Chapman (Pearson – Shutt), Stephen (Varadi), E. Gray (Snodin).

Sheffield Wedneday: Beresford, Fee, Shirtliff, Madden, King (Barwick), Harkes, Currie (Palmer), McCall, Francis, Worthington (Hirst), Williams (Mooney).

Ref: John Key (Sheffield) *Att:* 6,246

Maurice Lindley

31 July 1991 v Bradford City (a) 1–0 (1–0)

Fairclough

This West Riding Cup tie doubled as a testimonial for Maurice Lindley, who had been caretaker manager at Elland Road four times in a 20-year association with the club.

The game was settled by a header in the 31st minute by Chris Fairclough as Howard Wilkinson's expensively assembled side had their hands full keeping their near neighbours at bay.

The match generated receipts of about £15,000 for Lindley whose meticulous dossiers on the opposition were a key factor of the successful Revie era.

Bradford City: Tomlinson, Mitchell, Dowson, James, Oliver, Gardner, Babb, Duxbury, Torpey, Reid, McCarthy (Stuart).

Leeds United: Day, McClelland, Snodin, Wetherall, Fairclough, Speed, Strachan (Dorigo), Davison (Varadi), Chapman, McAllister, Wallace.

Ref: Stephen Bell (Bradford) *Att:* 3,650

Jim Beglin

11 August 1992 v Liverpool (h) 1–4 (0–2)

Batty

This match was played just three days after Leeds beat Liverpool 4-3 in the FA Charity Shield.

Jim Beglin's career was brought to a premature end by a persistent knee injury and he made a 17-minute appearance in the white of United against Liverpool with whom he had won the double.

The Reds gained revenge for their defeat at Wembley with a comprehensive win with goals from Ian Rush (2), Jamie Redknapp and Dean Saunders. David Rocastle and Gordon Strachan, who didn't start at Wembley, were the only Leeds players to complete 90 minutes.

Leeds boss Howard Wilkinson was away running the rule over future European Cup opponents Stuttgart in Germany and missed a rare David Batty goal from long range.

Leeds United: Lukic (Day), Newsome (Ray Wallace), Beglin (Speed), Hodge, Wetherall (Batty), Whyte (Rod Wallace), Strachan, Rocastle, Chapman (Shutt), Cantona (Varadi), Kerr (McAllister).

Liverpool: James, Tanner, Burrows, Marsh, Redknapp, Wright, Saunders, Stewart, Rush (Hutchison) Rosenthal, Walters

Ref: Stephen Lodge (Barnsley) *Att:* 8,492

John Buckley

31 January 1994 v Rotherham United (a) 2–4 (1–1)

Forrester, Whelan

Former United winger John Buckley was forced to quit football after suffering a fractured skull when playing for Rotherham against Plymouth in March.

Buckley, who later managed Doncaster Rovers Belles women's team, did come on for a token appearance for the final few minutes by which time the Millers were heading to victory after strikes by Shaun Goater, Des Hazel, Jonathan Howard and an own-goal by United trainee Gary O'Hara.

Scorers for United, who had John Lukic in goal for the first time in five months, were Jamie Forrester and Noel Whelan.

Among the playing substitutes were Mark Humphries, signed as a youngster from Aberdeen, and South African international trialist George Dearnaley, who was top scorer in his country with Amazulu in 1992. Neither player made the Leeds first team.

Rotherham United: Clarke (Wietcecha), Wilder (Pickering), Jacobs (Hurst), Williams, Brien, Marshall (Richardson), Hazel (Howard), Roberts (Marginson), Helliwell (Buckley – Wilder), Williamson (Goater), Dolby.

Leeds United: Lukic, Pemberton (Kelly), Dorigo (Humphries), Hodge (Ford), Fairclough (Tinkler), Wetherall (O'Hara), Strachan (Wallace), Forrester (Dearnaley), White, Whelan, Speed (Sharp – Couzens).

Ref: Alan Dawson (Jarrow) *Att:* 4,735

Peter Haddock

21 March 1994 v Bradford City (h) 3–2 (1–2)

Hoyle (og), Forrester, Wallace

The match raised £25,000 for the versatile Haddock whose career was cut short by a knee injury he sustained in a League Cup semi-final with Manchester United two years earlier.

Bradford led twice through Paul Jewell and Neil Tolson, but United, who included former players David Batty, Vinnie Jones, Chris Kamara and Bobby Davison in their first-half line-up hit back to win 3–2. David White was the only United player to feature in both halves after coming on for the injured Gordon Strachan after 26 minutes as 22 players got a run out for Leeds.

Leeds United: Lukic (Beeney), Kamara (Couzens), Dorigo (Sharp), Batty (Hodge), Newsome (Bowman), Fairclough (Wetherall), Strachan (White), Davison (Forrester), Deane (Wallace), Jones (Tinkler), Speed (Whelan).

Bradford City: P. Tomlinson, Williams, Heseltine (Lawford), Duxbury, Hoyle, Richards (G. Tomlinson), McHugh, Robson, Tolson (Stapleton), Jewell, Reid.

Ref: Robert Hart (Darlington) *Att:* 6,100

Mervyn Day

8 August 1994 v Carlisle United (a) 1–0 (0–0)

Wetherall

Carlisle boss Mervyn Day made 640 senior appearances in his career including nine seasons at Leeds with whom he won a Second Division Championship medal.

The Whites were his automatic choice as opposition for his testimonial at Brunton Park where he led out the Cumbrians and kept a clean sheet in his seven minutes between the posts before being replaced by Tony Caig.

Tony Elliott became Carlisle's third 'keeper of the night when he took over from Caig on 55 minutes and conceded the only goal of the game when he was beaten by David Wetherall's header just after an hour.

Day returned to Elland Road in July 2010 as chief scout.

Carlisle United: Day (Caig – Elliott), Joyce, Gallimore, Walling, Mountfield, Edmondson, Thomas (Thorpe), Currie (Pearson), Reeves, Davey, Peddish (Procas).

Leeds United: Lukic, Kelly, Dorigo, Palmer, Wetherall, Worthington (Fairclough), White, Wallace, Deane (Masinga), McAllister, Speed.

Ref: Iain Cruickshanks (Darlington) *Att:* 7,500

Mel Sterland

3 September 1995 v Boston United (a) **1–0** (1–0)

Whelan

Leeds boss Howard Wilkinson took a strong United side back to Boston where he strutted his stuff as a winger before getting his first break in management with the Pilgrims.

He was keen to salute Mel Sterland, who had played for him both at Elland Road and Sheffield Wednesday, before the right-back had to quit top class football in January 1994 with persistent ankle trouble.

Sterland was Boston's manager and his team was bolstered by Gordon Strachan and former England defender Des Walker while ex-Leeds striker Imre Varadi was also on Boston's books.

Noel Whelan thumped home the only goal from distance after 34 minutes to give victory to Leeds, whose substitutes included Matthew Smithard, a member of United's 1993 FA Youth Cup winning team, who didn't get a first team breakthrough.

Boston United: Bastock, James, Hardy, Sterland (Smith), Walker, Circuit (Gray), Strachan, Appleby (Melsom), Bright, Varadi, Brown.

Leeds United: Lukic (Beeney), Bowman (Forrester), Dorigo, Ford, Pemberton (Beesley), Wetherall, White (Sharp), Tinkler, Masinga (Smithard), Whelan, Couzens.

Ref: Uriah Rennie (Sheffield) *Att:* 3,165

John Lukic

31 August 1996 v Arsenal 1–2 (1–1)

Kewell

With the rapid rise in players' wages, fans facing ever more expensive season tickets and one-club men becoming increasingly scarce, testimonial games were falling out of favour by the time Leeds and Arsenal honoured goalkeeper John Lukic.

He made 430 appearances for United and a further 238 for the Gunners in two spells for each club, but the Elland Road attendance to salute one of the greatest uncapped net-minders was poor.

Local newspaper coverage of the match was also limited and since this game the emphasis has been on players' charity matches rather than testimonial games.

Lukic played the first half for Arsenal and the second period for Leeds, who trailed to an early Glenn Helder goal before Carlton Palmer went off injured after 12 minutes. Rising star Harry Kewell netted the equaliser but the Gunners came out on top with a goal by youngster Ross Taylor 12 minutes from time, although some sources give the winning goal to Paul Shaw.

Sixteen-year-old Stephen McPhail was among the substitutes who played in the second half. Former England striker Mark Hateley was on loan to United from QPR.

Arsenal: Lukic (Harper), Anderson (McGowan), Thomas, Robson, Hughes, Williams, Rocastle, Wright, Kiwomya (Clarke), Platt (Shaw), Helder.

Leeds United: Beeney (Lukic), Maybury, Beesley, Palmer, Jobson, Wetherall, Tinkler, Wallace, Couzens, Hateley, Kewell. Subs: Blunt, Boyle, Hackworth, Bowman, McPhail, Jackson, Foster.

Ref: Stephen Lodge (Barnsley) *Att:* 2,773

Brendan Ormsby

15 November 1998 v Garforth Town 4–0 (3–0)

Ritchie 3, Morley

The day after teenager Alan Smith burst on to the scene with his goalscoring debut in a 3–1 win at Liverpool, an older generation of Leeds stars paid tribute to former skipper Brendan Ormsby.

Veterans from United and the defender's first club, Aston Villa, teamed up for his testimonial at Garforth where he had been a player since 1995.

Ormsby, who had been forced to quit playing earlier in the season after suffering double vision, made a donation from the game's receipts to the Daniel Yorath Trust. The Trust was named after the 15-year-old United trainee son of Terry Yorath, who collapsed and died of a heart condition known as hypertrophic cardiomypathy in 1992.

Leeds United/Aston Villa XI from: Batty, Speed, Lorimer, Yorath, G. Snodin, I. Snodin, McLelland, Wright, Davison, Sheridan, Ritchie (all Leeds), Spink, Shaw, Mortimer, Cowans, Bremner, Morley, Deehan, Gibson (all Villa) and Ormsby and G. Williams, who both played for both clubs.

Garforth Town from: Baker, Holmes, Woodhead, Shaw, Sullivan, Allen, Ramsden, Abrams, Falk, Beddard, Watson, Firth, Haigh, Sullivan, Hamer.

Att: 1,014

Gary Kelly

7 May 2002 v Celtic (h) 1–4 (1–2)

Bowyer

Republic of Ireland full back Gary Kelly wanted all the money from his testimonial to go to charity – a wonderful gesture in an era when top players are often portrayed as being money-orientated.

All proceeds from the game were shared by the Teenage Cancer Society in Leeds and the Cancer Support Centre in Kelly's hometown of Drogheda. His sister, Mandy, had died of cancer four years earlier. The match generated nearly £1 million in receipts.

Celtic, three days after losing Scottish Cup Final, were the dominant force, scoring through Alan Thompson, who later had a spell with Leeds, the excellent Henrik Larsson, John Hartson and Sean Maloney. Lee Bowyer netted for United and Kelly, the only Leeds player to top the 500 appearance mark outside the Revie era, completed the full 90 minutes. Steve Guppy, briefly at Leeds, started for Celtic.

Leeds United: Robinson, Kelly, Duberry (Matteo), Ferdinand (Mills), Harte (Radebe), Johnson (Bakke), Dacourt (Batty), Bowyer (Burns), Wilcox (Bridges), Smith, Keane (McPhail).

Celtic: Douglas, Balde (Kennedy), Mjallby (Boyd), McNamara, Sylla (Wieghorst), Guppy (McPartland), Smith (Wallace), Thompson (Petrov), Healy, Hartson (Lynch), Larsson (Maloney).

Ref: Dermot Gallagher (Oxfordshire) *Att:* 26,440

Lucas Radebe

2 May 2005 v International World XI (h) 3–7 (1–2)

Lennon, Ward, Kilgallon

Elland Road's biggest crowd of the 2004–05 season paid homage to the man known as The Chief.

Appropriately, it was a fun occasion to mark the retirement of the popular Lucas Radebe, a man who always had a smile on his face despite often playing with a string of injuries.

Many Leeds greats from the past were rolled out to honour the South African who played 45 minutes for both sides, swapping with Matthew Kilgallon, and twice got on the scoresheet for his International squad, once from the penalty spot.

Bolton boss Sam Allardyce managed the International XI which included a couple of his players Ivan Campo and Jay-Jay Okocha and assistant manager Phil Brown as well as former Leeds notables Lee Sharpe, Olivier Dacourt, Eirik Bakke and Gunnar Halle, who scored one of the goals. Other International marksmen were Ally McCoist (2), John Carew and Mario Melchiot.

Leeds United Ladies player Lucy Ward came on, prompting a chorus of 'We've only got 10 men', and scored with virtually her first touch.

Money raised from the game was shared by a string of children's charities in Yorkshire and Africa.

Leeds United: Martyn (Sullivan), Kelly (Kamara), Wetherall, Radebe (Kilgallon), Halle (Johnson), Strachan (Jones), Batty, McAllister (Wijnhard), Speed (Ward), Masinga (Lennon), Hasselbaink (Yeboah – Richardson).

International World XI: Grobbelaar, Melchiot (Brown), Sharpe, Kilgallon (Radebe), Dacourt (Halle), Campo, Khumalo (McAllister), Bakke, Okocha, Wijinhard (McCoist), Carew.

Ref: Dermot Gallagher (Oxfordshire) *Att:* 37,886

FA Youth Cup

LEEDS United's youngsters have lifted the FA Youth Cup twice.

They won it for the first time in 1993 by beating Manchester United 4–1 on aggregate in the two-legged Final played out in front of more than 60,000 fans.

The boys from Manchester were hailed by their boss Alex Ferguson as the best batch of youngsters he had ever worked with, but they were eclipsed by the lads from Leeds.

Jamie Forrester caught the eye for Leeds in the early rounds, scoring hat-tricks against Stoke City and Queen's Park Rangers.

Leeds virtually booked a place in the Final with a 4–1 win at Norwich in the semi-final first leg, going through despite losing the home leg 2–0.

In the Final, 'Fergie's Fledglings' started as hot favourites but were stunned by a rampant Leeds in front of 30,562 at Old Trafford. The Whites got their noses in front when Rob Bowman flicked on a Matthew Smithard corner which Forrester knocked in from close range. On the hour Noel Whelan made it 2–0 with a shot from the edge of the box.

Anticipating silverware success, 31,037 fans flocked to Elland Road to see if the Leeds youngsters could finish the job.

It didn't take Leeds long to extend their aggregate lead with a stunning overhead kick from Forrester. Paul Scholes levelled on the night with a penalty, but within a minute a Smithard goal gave Leeds a 4–1 aggregate lead.

There were no more goals in the second half, so skipper Mark Ford hoisted the FA Youth Cup and led his jubilant players on a lap of honour. It was a great triumph for former Leeds star Paul Hart, who was in his first season as director of youth coaching at Elland Road.

Five of the Leeds players, Forrester, Whelan, Bowman, Kevin Sharp and Mark Tinkler were all in the England Under-18 squad which won the European Championship. Those five, plus Ford and Couzens all sampled first team football with Leeds.

The magnitude of the young Whites' victory is reflected in the talent at Ferguson's disposal – David Beckham, Paul Scholes, Nicky Butt, Phil and Gary Neville all became household names with England, Robbie Savage skippered Wales and Keith Gillespie and Colin Murdock represented Northern Ireland.

Final, first leg, 10 April 1993
Manchester United 0
Leeds United 2 *(Forrester, Whelan)*
Manchester United: Darren Whitmarsh, John O'Kane, Steven Riley, Chris Casper, Gary Neville, Keith Gillespie, Nicky Butt, David Beckham (Robbie Savage), Richard Irving (Colin Murdock), Paul Scholes, Ben Thornley.
Leeds United: Paul Pettinger, Andy Couzens, Kevin Sharp, Mark Tinkler, Kevin Daly, Rob Bowman, Matthew Smithard, Mark Ford, Noel Whelan, Simon Oliver, Jamie Forrester
Referee: Paul Durkin (Portland).
Att: 30,562

Final, second leg, 13 May 1993
Leeds United 2 *(Forrester, Smithard)*
Manchester United 1 *(Scholes pen)*
Leeds United: Paul Pettinger, Andy Couzens, Kevin Sharp, Mark Tinkler, Kevin Daly, Rob Bowman (Steve Tobin), Matthew Smithard, Mark Ford, Noel Whelan, Simon Oliver (Alex Byrne), Jamie Forrester.
Manchester United: Darren Whitmarsh, Phil Neville, Steven Riley, Chris Casper, Gary Neville, Keith Gillespie, Paul Scholes, David Beckham, Richard Irving (Colin Murdock), Robbie Savage, Ben Thornley.
Referee: Paul Durkin (Portland)
Att: 31,037
Leeds won 4–1 on aggregate

Paul Hart repeated his Youth Cup success four years later with one of the strongest Leeds United junior squads ever produced.

It was bristling with talent with six members going on to win full international honours – Paul Robinson and Jonathan Woodgate (England), Harry Kewell (Australia), Matthew Jones (Wales) and Republic of Ireland duo Stephen McPhail and Alan Maybury.

McPhail was sent off in the second half of a feisty first leg Final against Crystal Palace at Elland Road after the Whites had threatened to overwhelm their South London visitors.

Kewell's run and pass set up Wes Boyle for the opener after only four minutes and Jones' header doubled the lead just over 10 minutes later.

A more aggressive Palace came into it in the second half and pulled a goal back on 66 minutes through Jason Harris shortly before McPhail was ordered off for a second yellow.

McPhail was available for the return leg and set up the only goal for Lee Matthews at Selhurst Park 10 minutes from the end, Palace having already been reduced to 10 men after David Stevens elbowed Jonathan Woodgate on 70 minutes.

The Youth Cup triumph capped a superb season for Leeds' youngsters who had also won the Northern Intermediate League for the first time since 1966.

Final, first leg, 24 April 1997
Leeds United 2 *(Boyle, Jones)*
Crystal Palace 1 *(Harris)*
Leeds United: Paul Robinson, Alan Maybury, Harry Kewell, Kevin Dixon, Jonathan Woodgate, Damien Lynch, Stephen McPhail, Wes Boyle, Matthew Jones, Lee Matthews, Tommy Knarvik.
Crystal Palace: Gareth Ormshaw, James Hibbert, Haydn Mullins, David Woozley, Anthony Folan, Wayne Carlisle (Jason Harris), Richard Kennedy, David Stevens, Gareth Graham, Andrew Martin, Clinton Morrison (Paul Sears).
Referee: Graham Barber (Warwick)
Att: 6,649

Final, second leg, 25 May 1997
Crystal Palace 0
Leeds United 1 *(Matthews)*
Crystal Palace: Gareth Ormshaw, James Hibbert, Haydn Mullins, David Woozley, Anthony Folan, Wayne Carlisle (Jason Harris), Richard Kennedy, David Stevens, Gareth Graham, Andrew Martin, Clinton Morrison (Paul Sears).
Leeds United: Paul Robinson, Alan Maybury, Harry Kewell, Kevin Dixon, Jonathan Woodgate, Damien Lynch, Stephen McPhail, Wes Boyle, Matthew Jones (Andy Wright), Lee Matthews, Tommy Knarvik.
Referee: Graham Barber (Warwick)
Att: 4,759

Leeds United's record in the FA Youth Cup

1952–53
Round 1 v Manchester United (a) 0–4

1953–54
Round 1 v Blackburn Rovers (h) 1–0
Round 2 v Blackpool (h) 6–0
Round 3 v Bury (a) 3–1
Round 4 v Manchester City (h) 3–1
Round 5 v West Bromwich Albion (a) 1–3 aet

1954–55
Round 1 v Penrith (h) 7–1
Round 2 v Bradford City (a) 4–3
Round 3 v Newcastle United (a) 1–3

1955–56
Round 1 v Huddersfield Town (a) 0–0
Replay v Huddersfield Town (h) 1–0
Round 2 v Liverpool (h) 0–1

1956–57
Round 1 v Bradford City (h) 1–0
Round 2 v Blackpool (a) 3–4

1957–58
Round 1 v Manchester City (h) 2–0
Round 2 v Morecambe (a) 8–0
Round 3 v Manchester United (h) 1–4

1958–59
Round 1 v Everton (a) 0–3

1959–60
Qual v Burnley (a) 3–2
Round 1 v Blackpool (h) 1–1 aet
Replay v Blackpool (a) 2–3

1960–61
Qual v Hyde United (a) 3–4

1961–62
Qual v Manchester City (a) 1–3

1962–63
Round 1 v Bradford (h) 3–0
Round 2 v Burnley (a) 0–2

1963–64
Round 1 v Billingham Synthonia (a) 10–0
Round 2 v Barnsley (a) 5–0
Round 3 v Sheffield Wednesday (a) 1–0
Round 4 v Everton (a) 2–1
Round 5 v Manchester City (h) 3–4

1964–65
Round 1 Bye
Round 2 v Bradford City (a) 1–0
Round 3 v Bolton Wanderers (a) 2–0
Round 4 v Sunderland (a) 1–3

1965–66
Round 1 Bye
Round 2 v Mansfield Town (h) 8–1
Round 3 v Scunthorpe United (a) 0–0
Replay v Scunthorpe United (h) 2–0
Round 4 v Burnley (a) 1–1
Replay v Burnley (h) 4–0
Round 5 v Sunderland (a) 0–3

1966–67
Round 1 Bye
Round 2 v Bradford City (a) 8–0
Round 3 v Blackburn Rovers (h) 3–1
Round 4 v Scunthorpe United (a) 0–1

1967–68
Round 1 Bye
Round 2 v Bury (a) 1–2

1968–69
Round 1 v Darlington (a) 5–0
Round 2 v Sheffield United (a) 1–1
Replay v Sheffield United (h) 2–1
Round 3 v Rotherham United (a) 2–1
Round 4 v Sunderland (a) 0–0
Replay v Sunderland (h) 0–1

1969–70
Round 1 Bye
Round 2 v Sheffield Wednesday (h) 2–1
Round 3 v Liverpool (a) 0–0
Replay v Liverpool (h) 3–2
Round 4 v Sunderland (a) 2–0
Round 5 v Bristol City (a) 1–2

1970–71
Round 1 Bye
Round 2 v Middlesbrough (a) 1–2

1971–72
Round 1 Bye
Round 2 v North Kenton Juniors (h) 8–0
Round 3 v Oldham Athletic (a) 3–1
Round 4 v Bolton Wanderers (a) 0–1

1972–73
Round 1 Bye
Round 2 v Newcastle United (h) 0–1

1973–74
Round 1 Bye
Round 2 v Newcastle United (h) 1–0
Round 3 v Middlesbrough (h) 1–1
Replay v Middlesbrough (a) 1–2

1974–75
Round 1 Bye
Round 2 v Sheffield United (h) 2–0
Round 3 v Sunderland (a) 2–0
Round 4 v Huddersfield Town (h) 1–2

1975–76
Round 1 Bye
Round 2 v Hull City (a) 1–0
Round 3 v Sunderland (h) 1–1
Replay v Sunderland (a) 0–1

1976–77
Round 1 Bye
Round 2 v York City (a) 3–3
Replay v York City (h) 2–0
Round 3 v Sunderland (h) 1–2

1977–78
Round 1 Bye
Round 2 v Huddersfield Town (a) 3–0
Round 3 v Sunderland (h) 1–0
Round 4 v Crystal Palace (a) 0–0
Replay v Crystal Palace (h) 0–1

1978–79
Round 1 Bye
Round 2 v Yorkshire Amateurs (h) 2–0
Round 3 v Bolton Wanderers (a) 1–1
Replay v Bolton Wanderers (h) 3–1
Round 4 v Charlton Athletic (h) 1–3

1979–80
Round 1 Bye
Round 2 v Sunderland (a) 2–3

1980–81
Round 1 Bye
Round 2 v Blackpool (a) 3–0
Round 3 v Sunderland (h) 1–0
Round 4 v Shrewsbury Town (a) 3–0
Round 5 v Tottenham Hotspur (h) 1–3

1981–82
Round 1 Bye
Round 2 v Bolton Wanderers (a) 1–1
Replay v Bolton Wanderers (h) 2–0
Round 3 v Newcastle United (a) 2–2
Replay v Newcastle United (h) 3–2
Round 4 v Manchester United (h) 0–0
Replay v Manchester United (a) 0–1

1982–83
Round 1 Bye
Round 2 v Manchester City (h) 3–2
Round 3 v Tranmere Rovers (a) 1–0
Round 4 v Barnsley (a) 0–2

1983–84
Round 1 Bye
Round 2 v Wigan Athletic (h) 4–1
Round 3 v Newcastle United (a) 0–1

1984–85
Round 1 Bye
Round 2 v Manchester United (a) 3–2
Round 3 v Newcastle United (a) 0–1

1985–86
Round 1 Bye
Round 2 v Chester City (h) 0–5

1986–87
Round 1 Bye
Round 2 v Chester City (a) 2–0
Round 3 v Birmingham City (h) 2–0
Round 4 v Mansfield Town (a) 1–0
Round 5 v Manchester City (a) 0–3

1987–88
Round 1 Bye
Round 2 v Wigan Athletic (a) 1–2

1988–89
Round 1 Bye
Round 2 v Burnley (a) 2–1
Round 3 v Birmingham City (h) 0–0
Replay v Birmingham City (a) 1–1
2nd replay v Birmingham City 2–4

1989–90
Round l Bye
Round 2 v Carlisle United (h) 4–1
Round 3 v Wolverhampton Wanderers (a) 2–3

1990–91
Round 1 Bye
Round 2 v Blackburn Rovers (a) 1–1
Replay v Blackburn Rovers (h) 3–1
Round 3 v Doncaster Rovers (a) 3–0
Round 4 v Hull City (h) 1–2

1991–92
Round 1 Bye
Round 2 v Oldham Athletic (h) 3–3
Replay v Oldham Athletic (a) 2–3

1992–93
Round 1 Bye
Round 2 v Sheffield Wednesday (a) 2–1
Round 3 v Stoke City (a) 6–2
Round 4 v Queen's Park Rangers (h) 5–1
Round 5 v Sheffield United (a) 2–2
Replay v Sheffield United (h) 2–1
Semi-final 1st leg v Norwich City (a) 4–1
Semi-final 2nd leg v Norwich City (h) 0–2
Final 1st leg v Manchester United (a) 2–0
Final 2nd leg v Manchester United (h) 2–1

1993–94
Round 1 Bye
Round 2 v Burnley (a) 0–3

1994–95
Round 1 Bye
Round 2 v Aston Villa (a) 0–1

1995–96
Round 1 Bye
Round 2 v Barnsley (h) 3–1
Round 3 v Middlesbrough (h) 0–1

1996–97
Round 1 v Sheffield Wednesday (h) 2–2
Replay v Sheffield Wednesday (a) 4–0
Round 2 v Crewe Alexandra (h) 2–0
Round 3 v Manchester City (a) 2–1
Round 4 v Queen's Park Rangers (h) 2–0
Round 5 v Tranmere Rovers (h) 0–0
Replay v Tranmere Rovers (a) 1–0
Semi-final 1st leg v Luton Town (a) 2–1
Semi-final 2nd leg v Luton Town (h) 1–0
Final 1st leg v Crystal Palace (h) 2–1
Final 2nd leg v Crystal Palace (a) 1–0

1997–98
Round 1 Bye
Round 2 v Oldham Athletic (h) 3–2
Round 3 v Crystal Palace (h) 3–1
Round 4 v Middlesbrough (a) 0–0
Replay v Middlesbrough (h) 2–0
Round 5 v Arsenal (h) 1–0
Semi-final 1st leg v Everton (h) 0–1
Semi-final 2nd leg v Everton (a) 1–2

1998–99
Round 1 Bye
Round 2 Bye
Round 3 v Swindon Town (a) 2–2
Replay v Swindon Town (h) 0–1

1999–2000
Round 1 Bye
Round 2 Bye
Round 3 v Ipswich Town (a) 1–0
Round 4 v Colchester United (h) 0–0
Replay v Colchester United (a) 0–0 (Leeds won 4–3 on penalties)
Round 5 v Wimbledon (h) 1–0
Round 6 v Arsenal (a) 1–1
Replay v Arsenal (h) 2–5

2000–01
Round 1 Bye
Round 2 Bye
Round 3 v Millwall (a) 3–1
Round 4 v Southampton (h) 3–0
Round 5 v Aston Villa (a) 0–1

2001–02
Round 1 Bye
Round 2 Bye
Round 3 v Liverpool (h) 1–0
Round 4 v Middlesbrough (a) 1–1 (Leeds won 4–3 on penalties)
Round 5 v Tottenham Hotspur (h) 0–1

2002–03
Round 1 Bye
Round 2 Bye
Round 3 v Gillingham (h) 4–0
Round 4 v Cambridge United (a) 4–2
Round 5 v Blackburn Rovers (h) 3–2
Round 6 v Charlton Athletic (h) 0–1

2003–04
Round 1 Bye
Round 2 Bye
Round 3 v Ipswich Town (h) 1–2

2004–05
Round 1 Bye
Round 2 Bye
Round 3 Wigan Athletic (a) 2–1
Round 4 v Fulham (h) 0–0 (Fulham won 5–4 on penalties)

2005–06
Round 1 Bye
Round 2 Bye
Round 3 v Ipswich Town (h) 0–1

2006–07
Round 1 Bye
Round 2 Bye
Round 3 v Hull City (h) 2–2 (Hull City won 4–3 on penalties)

2007–08
Round 1 v Darlington (a) 1–0
Round 2 v Walsall (a) 2–1
Round 3 v Luton Town (a) 3–0
Round 4 v Bristol City (a) 1–2

2008–09
Round 1 v Chester City (a) 2–0
Round 2 v Oadby Town (a) 3–0
Round 3 v Liverpool (h) 1–2

2009–10
Round 1 v Crewe Alexandra (h) 0–1

2010–11
Round 1 Bye
Round 2 Bye
Round 3 v Scunthorpe United 3–0
Round 4 v Crewe Alexandra 0–0 (Leeds won 3–2 on penalties)
Round 5 v Aston Villa (h) 0–2

2011–12
Round 1 Bye
Round 2 Bye
Round 3 v Ipswich Town (a) 0–2

Best and Worst League Seasons

Victories

Most home wins	18	1968–69
Most away wins	12	1963–64, 1973–74, 2007–08*
Most wins	27	1968–69, 1970–71, 2007–08*
Fewest home wins	5	2003–04†
Fewest away wins	0	1946–47, 1992–93
Fewest wins	6	1946–47
Successive home wins	12	1968–69
Successive away wins	5	1931–32, 1973–74
Successive wins	9	1931–32

Draws

Most home draws	11	1981–82, 1982–83
Most away draws	11	1952–53, 1969–70
Most draws	21	1982–83
Fewest home draws	2	1927–28, 1929–30, 1962–63, 1970–71, 1999–2000†, 2008–09*
Fewest away draws	1	1926–27, 1936–37, 1946–47, 1981–82
Fewest draws	4	1936–37
Successive home draws	4	1926–27, 1958–59, 1974–75
Successive away draws	6	1998–99†
Successive draws	5	1961–62

Defeats

Most home defeats	11	2011-12*
Most away defeats	20	1946–47
Most defeats	30	1946–47
Fewest home defeats	0	1963–64, 1968–69, 1971–72
Fewest away defeats	2	1969–69, 1970–71
Fewest defeats	2	1968–69
Successive home defeats	5	2002–03*
Successive away defeats	12	1946–47
Successive defeats	6	1946–47, 1995–96*, 2003–4*

Goals Scored

Most home goals scored	63	1927–28
Most away goals scored	42	1931–32
Most goals scored	98	1927–28

Fewest home goals scored	15	1996–97
Fewest away goals scored	10	1920–21
Fewest goals scored	28	1996–97

Goals Conceded

Most home goals conceded	46	1959–60
Most away goals conceded	60	1936–37, 1946–47
Most goals conceded	92	1934–35, 1959–60
Fewest home goals conceded	9	1968–69, 1998–99
Fewest away goals conceded	13	1973–74
Fewest goals conceded	26	1968–69

Clean Sheets

Most at home	14	1923–24, 1980–81
Most away	13	1973–74
Most	24	1968–69, 1970–71
Fewest at home	2	2003–04*
Fewest away	0	1926–27, 1946–47
Fewest	3	1926–27, 1946–47, 2003–04*
Successive	9	1927–28

Failed to Score

Most at home	10	1996–97*
Most away	13	1920–21
Most	21	1996–97*
Fewest at home	0	1955–56, 1967–68
Fewest away	1	1927–28
Fewest	3	1927–28, 1962–63, 1963–64, 1969–70
Successive	6	1981–82

Points

Most at home (3 for a win)	54	1989–90
Most at home (2 for a win)	39	1968–69
Most away (3 for a win)	42	2007–08†
Most away (2 for a win)	30	1963–64, 1970–71
Most points (3 for a win)	85	1989–90‡
Most points (2 for a win)	67	1968–69
Fewest at home (3 for a win)	22	2003–04*
Fewest at home (2 for a win)	17	1946–47
Fewest away (3 for a win)	7	1992–93
Fewest away (2 for a win)	1	1946–47
Least points (3 for a win)	33	2003–04*
Least points (2 for a win)	18	1946–47

League Doubles in a Season

Most home and away wins	8	1927–28, 1963–64, 1964–65, 1968–69
Most home and away defeats	9	1946–47

*Indicates a 46 match season from the Championship & League One.
† Indicates a 38 match season from the Premiership.
All other Leeds United League seasons that are not annotated comprised of 42 games. Please note that only 1987–88 of 44 matches varied from all of the other seasons.
‡ It should be noted that in 2007–08 the club would have had 91 points from 46 games were it not for the 15-point deduction imposed by the Football League before the season commenced. The club actually won 91 points although that is not reflected in the League table as the positive total is only 76 points.

League

Without a defeat

Most at home	39	14 August 1968 to 28 February 1970
Most away	17	2 November 1968 to 26 August 1969
Most	34	26 October 1968 to 26 August 1969
Most from start of season	29	1973–74

Without a victory

Most at home	10	6 February 1982 to 12 May 1982
Most away	26	1 April 1939 to 27 August 1947 (not inc two games in 1939–40)
Most	17	1 February 1947 to 26 May 1947
Most from start of season	6	1935–36, 1951–52

Without a draw

Most at home	23	18 November 1977 to 25 November 1978
Most away	24	6 September 1926 to 1 October 1927
Most	19	2 January 1929 to 8 March 1930 and 17 December 1977 to 12 April 1978
Most from start of season	11	1947–48

FA Cup

Without a defeat

Most at home	15	6 January 1962 to 30 March 1968
Most away	14	5 February 1972 to 18 January 1979
Most	14	15 January 1972 to 7 April 1973

Without a victory

Most at home	7	23 February 1952 to 6 January 1962
Most away	14	7 January 1922 to 9 January 1932
Most	16	23 February 1952 to 10 January 1962

Without a draw

Most at home	13	16 January 1929 to 21 January 1939 and 8 April 1967 to 18 March 1972
Most away	14	10 January 1953 to 12 February 1966
Most	10	27 March 1975 to 18 January 1979

League Cup

Without a defeat

Most at home	10	13 September 1966 to 27 September 1971
Most away	4	8 September 1971 to 31 October 1972
Most	9	13 September 1967 to 25 September 1968

Without a victory

Most at home	8	24 January 1979 to 9 November 1983
Most away	8	6 October 1969 to 10 September 1974
Most	9	24 January 1979 to 27 October 1982

Without a draw

Most at home	18	13 September 1961 to 25 September 1968
Most away	21	10 October 1978 to 24 September 1991
Most	13	12 October 1966 to 3 September 1969 and 4 November 1987 to 24 September 1991

Europe

Without a defeat

Most at home	14	26 October 1966 to 18 December 1968
Most away	11	9 December 1970 to 7 November 1973
Most	16	6 September 1967 to 13 November 1968

Without a victory

Most at home	3	28 April 1971 to 29 September 1971 and 4 November 1992 to 17 October 1995
Most away	6	10 January 1968 to 27 November 1968
Most	4	18 October 2000 to 22 November 2000

Without a draw

Most at home	16	20 December 1967 to 10 March 1971
Most away	10	27 November 1968 to 9 December 1970
Most	22	23 October 1968 to 14 April 1971

(Regarding draws, scores level after 90 minutes are referred to as draws although Cup games may have had extra-time and penalties added.)

ATTENDANCES

Most at home

League	56,796	v Arsenal	27 December 1932
FA Cup	57,892	v Sunderland	15 March 1967
League Cup	43,222	v Nottingham Forest	8 February 1978
FM Cup	13,387	v Everton	19 March 1992

FL Trophy	20,128	v Bradford City	2 September 2008
Europe	50,498	v Rangers	9 April 1968

Most away

League	67,744	v Manchester United	21 February 2004
FA Cup	74,526	v Manchester United	3 January 2010
League Cup	46,185	v Aston Villa	4 October 1972
FM Cup	17,543	v Aston Villa	17 January 1990
FL Trophy	9,430	v Carlisle United	9 February 2010
Europe	136,505	v Celtic (Hampden Pk)	15 April 1970

Fewest home

League	3,950	v Sheffield Wednesday	9 April 1930
FA Cup	9,531	v Northampton Town	7 November 2008
League Cup	4,517	v Brentford	13 September 1961
FM Cup	2,274	v Sheffield United	16 October 1985
FL Trophy	8,429	v Darlington	6 October 2009
Europe	13,682	v Valletta	3 October 1979

Fewest away

League	3,492	v Wimbledon	7 December 1985
FA Cup	3,960	v Northampton Town	17 November 2008
League Cup	2,021	v Chesterfield	23 November 1960
FM Cup	4,029	v Manchester City	14 October 1985
FL Trophy	4,658	v Rotherham United	8 October 2008
Europe	2,500	v Spora Luxembourg	3 October 1967

(not including Preliminary Rounds of FA Cup in 1920–21)

Leeds City

Leeds United beat all the records established by Leeds City with the following exceptions:

Fewest home draws	2	1913–14
Fewest away draws	1	1914–15
Fewest draws	4	1914–15
Successive defeats	7	1908–09
Fewest away goals scored	8	1908–09
Fewest clean sheets	0	1911–12
Most games without a League draw	23	1914–15
Most games without an FA Cup draw	10	11 February 1909 to 30 January 1915
Fewest home League attendance	2,000	v Chesterfield 27 February 1906
	2,000	v Leicester Fosse 30 April 1910
Fewest away League attendance	1,000	on six occasions (three v Glossop)
Fewest home FA Cup attendance	7,000	v Oldham Athletic 11 January 1908

(not including FA Cup Preliminary Rounds)

All Leeds City seasons comprised of 38 matches apart from the truncated 1919–20 campaign of eight games which Port Vale took into their League record.

TRANSFER RECORDS

To Leeds United

£53,000	August 1962	John Charles	from Juventus
£53,000	February 1964	Alan Peacock	from Middlebrough
£100,000	October 1967	Mick Jones	from Sheffield United
£165,000	July 1969	Allan Clarke	from Leicester City
£250,000	August 1974	Duncan McKenzie	from Nottingham Forest
£300,000	March 1978	Paul Hart	from Blackpool
£357,000	February 1979	Kevin Hird	from Blackburn Rovers
£370,000	May 1979	Alan Curtis	from Swansea City
£930,000	August 1981	Peter Barnes	from Manchester City
£1,700,000	July 1991	Rod & Ray Wallace*	from Southampton
£2,000,000	July 1992	David Rocastle	from Arsenal
£2,700,000	July 1993	Brian Deane	from Sheffield United
£3,400,000	January 1995	Tony Yeboah	from Eintracht Frankfurt
£4,200,000	November 1995	Tomas Brolin	from Parma
£5,600,000	July 1999	Michael Bridges	from Sunderland
£18,000,000	November 2000	Rio Ferdinand	from West Ham United

(* Ray Wallace was valued at £100,000)

From Leeds United

£65,000	May 1957	John Charles	to Juventus
£80,000	September 1969	Mike O'Grady	to Wolverhampton W
£100,000	September 1973	Gary Sprake	to Birmingham City
£200,000	June 1976	Duncan McKenzie	to Anderlecht
£350,000	January 1978	Joe Jordan	to Manchester United
£495,000	February 1978	Gordon McQueen	to Manchester United
£500,000	July 1979	Frank Gray	to Nottingham Forest
£825,000	July 1987	Ian Snodin	to Everton
£1,200,000	November 1992	Eric Cantona	to Manchester United
£2,700,000	October 1993	David Batty	to Blackburn Rovers
£3,400,000	Jun 1996	Gary Speed	to Evertone
£12,000,000	July 1999	Jimmy Floyd Hasselbaink	to Atletico Madrid
£29,100,000	July 2002	Rio Ferdinand	to Manchester United

Players of the Year

Four Leeds United players have won the Footballer of the Year – Bobby Collins (1965), Jack Charlton (1967), Billy Bremner (1970) and Gordon Strachan (1991).

Four others who played for Leeds, but won the award at other clubs, are Don Revie (Manchester City) 1955, Kenny Burns (Nottingham Forest) 1978, Ian Rush (Liverpool) 1984 and Eric Cantona (Manchester United) 1996. United manager Jimmy Adamson won it as a Burnley player in 1962 and Syd Owen, who had a long association with Leeds as a coach, gained the award in 1959 when with Luton Town.

Although the award, run by the Football Writers' Association, has been running since 1948, it is surprising John Charles was never a winner, although he did finish third in 1956. It was only after he joined Juventus in Italy that his greatness was acknowledged, finishing third in the European Footballer of the Year award in 1959, having come equal fourth with Fiorentina and Sweden's Kurt Hamrin the previous year. The award, run by France Football is known as the Ballon d'or (Golden Ball), has been in existence since 1956.

Only one player has featured in the top 10 of the European award while at Leeds – Bremner in 1973 when he came fifth. Others to have a top 10 European rating who played for Leeds include Strachan (Aberdeen) 1983, Ian Rush (Liverpool) 1984, Eric Cantona (Manchester United) 1993 and Tomas Brolin (Parma) 1994.

Brolin also made the World Player top 10 in 1994, a year after Tony Yeboah was also

Footballer of the Year 1965 Bobby Collins

Footballer of the Year 1967 Jack Charlton

Footballer of the Year 1970 Billy Bremner

recognised in the top 10 for his scoring exploits with Ghana and in the Bundeslegia with Eintracht Frankfurt.

The Professional Footballers' Association in England launched their own awards in 1993–94 with votes cast by players. The first winner was Norman Hunter after United's second title success.

No other Leeds player has won it since, but those to have taken the honour with other clubs are Ian Rush (Liverpool) 1984 and Eric Cantona (Manchester United) 1994 while Leeds manager Peter Reid won the trophy in 1985 while at Everton.

Harry Kewell landed the PFA's Young Player of the Year Trophy in 2000 and former Leeds starlet James Milner won the same award 10 years later when with Aston Villa. Players who won the Young Player award before arriving at Elland Road include Mervyn Day (West Ham) 1975, Peter Barnes (Manchester City) 1976, Ian Rush (Liverpool) 1983, Lee Sharpe (Manchester United) 1991 and Robbie Fowler (Liverpool) 1995 and 1996.

The PFA have also voted for their divisional team of the year since 1973–74 when Leeds supplied five of the 11 top players.

1973–74 (Div 1):	Paul Madeley, Norman Hunter, Billy Bremner, Johnny Giles, Allan Clarke
1974–75 (Div 1):	Paul Madeley, Gordon McQueen, Duncan McKenzie
1975–76 (Div 1):	Paul Madeley, Duncan McKenzie
1978–79 (Div 1):	Tony Currie
1985–86 (Div 2):	John Sheridan, Mark Aizlewood
1986–87 (Div 2):	John Sheridan
1987–88 (Div 2):	John Sheridan
1988–89 (Div 2):	John Sheridan
1989–90 (Div 2):	Chris Fairclough, Gordon Strachan
1990–91 (Div 1):	Gordon Strachan
1991–92 (Prem):	Gary McAllister
1992–93 (Prem):	Tony Dorigo, Gary Speed
1993–94 (Prem):	Gary Kelly, Gary McAllister
1997–98 (Prem):	Nigel Martyn
1998–99 (Prem):	Nigel Martyn
1999–2000 (Prem):	Nigel Martyn, Gary Kelly, Ian Harte, Harry Kewell
2001–02 (Prem):	Rio Ferdinand
2005–06 (Champ):	Gary Kelly
2007–08 (League 1):	Jermaine Beckford

Footballer of the Year 1991 Gordon Strachan

2008–09 (League 1):	Fabian Delph
2009–10 (League 1):	Patrick Kisnorbo, Robert Snodgrass

The Football League launched its own awards in 2006 and Jermaine Beckford was named League One Player of the Year in 2008 and 2010.

Fabian Delph was the organisation's Young Player of the Year in 2009 while former United manager Jimmy Armfield received an award for his outstanding contribution to League football in 2008.

Leeds United first introduced their own club award in 1970–71 with Norman Hunter being the first recipient. Only three men have won it twice – Gordon McQueen, Lee Bowyer and Jermaine Beckford, the latter being the only one to win it in successive seasons.

The winners, season-by-season, are:

1970–71:	Norman Hunter	**1978–79:**	Brian Flynn
1971–72:	Peter Lorimer	**1979–80:**	John Lukic
1972–73:	Allan Clarke	**1980–81:**	Trevor Cherry
1973–74:	Mick Jones	**1981–82:**	Eddie Gray
1974–75:	Gordon McQueen	**1982–83:**	Kenny Burns
1975–76:	Paul Madeley	**1983–84:**	Tommy Wright
1976–77:	Gordon McQueen	**1984–85:**	Neil Aspin
1977–78:	Tony Currie	**1985–86:**	Ian Snodin

Club player of the year 1999 and 2001 Lee Bowyer
Picture: Ian Harber, *Morley Observer and Advertiser.*

1986–87:	John Sheridan
1987–88:	Peter Haddock
1988–89:	Ian Baird
1989–90:	Chris Fairclough
1990–91:	David Batty
1991–92:	Tony Dorigo
1992–93:	Gordon Strachan
1993–94:	Gary McAllister
1994–95:	Brian Deane
1995–96:	Tony Yeboah
1996–97:	Nigel Martyn
1997–98:	Lucas Radebe
1998–99:	Lee Bowyer
1999–2000:	Harry Kewell
2000–01:	Lee Bowyer
2001–02:	Rio Ferdinand
2002–03:	Paul Robinson
2003–04:	Alan Smith
2004–05:	Neil Sullivan
2005–06:	Gary Kelly

Club player of the year 2000 Harry Kewell
Picture: Ian Harber, *Morley Observer and Advertiser.*

Club player of the year Rio Ferdinand 2002
Picture: Ian Harber, *Morley Observer and Advertiser.*

Club player of the year 2004 Alan Smith
Picture: Ian Harber, *Morley Observer and Advertiser.*

2006–07:	Eddie Lewis
2007–08:	Jermaine Beckford
2008–09:	Jermaine Beckford
2009–10:	Patrick Kisnorbo
2010–11:	Max Gradel
2011–12:	Robert Snodgrass

Club player of the year 2011 Max Gradel
Picture: Ian Harber, *Morley Observer and Advertiser.*

Top Appearances and Goalscorers

Top Twenty League Appearances

1.	J. Charlton	629	11.	G.O. Kelly	419/11
2.	W.J. Bremner	586/1	12.	W. Edwards	417
3.	P. Reaney	549/7	13.	T.J. Cherry	393/33
4.	N. Hunter	540	14.	Jack Milburn	385
5.	P.E. Madeley	528/8	15.	M.J. Giles	380/3
6.	P.P. Lorimer	503/22	16.	G. Sprake	380
7.	E. Gray	440/13	17.	J. Lukic	355
8.	E.A. Hart.	446	18.	D. Harvey	350
9.	K.G.A. Hair	443	19.	E. Kerfoot	336
10.	J. Dunn	442	20.	F.T. Gray	328/6

Overall Top Twenty Appearances

Including League, League Play-offs, FA Cup, League Cup, Full Members Cup, Associate Members Cup, Charity Shield, Europe and Fairs Cup Play-off.

1.	J. Charlton.	773	11.	T.J. Cherry	477/8
2.	W.J. Bremner	772/1	12.	K.G.A. Hair	474
3.	P. Reaney	736/11	13.	E.A. Hart.	471
4.	N. Hunter	724/2	14.	D. Harvey	445/2
5.	P.E. Madeley	712/13	15.	W. Edwards	444
6.	P.P. Lorimer	677/28	16.	J. Dunn	443
7.	E. Gray	560/8	17.	J. Lukic	433
8.	M.J. Giles	523/4	18.	Jack Milburn	407
9.	G.O. Kelly	516/15	19.	F.T. Gray	397/10
10.	G. Sprake	505/2	20.	A.J. Clarke	361/5

Top Ten League Goalscorers

1	P.P. Lorimer	168	6.	W.J. Bremner.	90
2.	W.J. Charles	153	7.	M.J. Giles	88
3.	T.H.O. Jennings	112	8.	W.R. Wainscoat.	87
4.	A.J. Clarke	110	9.	M.D. Jones	77
5.	C.F. Keetley	108	10.	A. Hydes	74

Overall Top Ten Goalscorers

(As for appearances)

1.	P.P. Lorimer. 238	5.	M.J. Giles 115
2.	W.J. Charles 157	7.	M.D. Jones 111
3.	A.J. Clarke 151	8.	C.F. Keetley. 110
4.	T.H.O. Jennings 117	9.	J. Charlton 96
5.	W.J. Bremner 115	10.	W.R. Wainscoat 93

Hat-Trick Heroes

Leeds City

7 October 1905	4	Fred Hargraves	v Morley	(h)	FA Cup (Pre)
7 October 1905	4	Dickie Morris	v Morley	(h)	FA Cup (Pre)
3 March 1906	3	David Wilson	v Clapton Orient	(h)	Div 2
15 December 1906	3	John Lavery	v Stockport County	(h)	Div 2
12 December 1908	3	Jimmy Gemmell	v Wolverhampton W	(h)	Div 2
9 November 1912	3	Billy McLeod	v Glossop	(h)	Div 2
25 March 1913	3	Billy McLeod	v Bury	(h)	Div 2
29 November 1913	4	Billy McLeod	v Nottingham Forest	(h)	Div 2
14 February 1914	3	Billy McLeod	v Wolverhampton W	(h)	Div 2
14 March 1914	3	Billy McLeod	v Huddersfield Town	(h)	Div 2
12 December 1914	3	Arthur Price	v Leicester Fosse	(h)	Div 2
16 January 1915	5	Billy McLeod	v Hull City	(a)	Div 2
10 April 1915	3	Arthur Price	v Nottingham Forest	(h)	Div 2
4 October 1919	3	Billy McLeod	v Wolverhampton W	(a)	Div 2

Leeds United

11 September 1920	3	Eugene O'Doherty	v Boothtown	(h)	FA Cup (Q1)
25 September 1920	3	Walter Butler	v Leeds Steelworks	(h)	FA Cup (Q2)
11 December 1920	3	Bob Thompson	v Notts County	(h)	Div 2
20 February 1922	3	Billy Poyntz	v Leicester City	(h)	Div 2
25 March 1922	3	Jack Swan	v Coventry City	(h)	Div 2
4 November 1922	3	Percy Whipp	v West Ham United	(h)	Div 2
29 September 1923	3	Joe Richmond	v Hull City	(h)	Div 2
25 December 1924	3	Percy Whipp	v Aston Villa	(h)	Div 1
6 February 1926	3	Tom Jennings	v Arsenal	(h)	Div 1
25 September 1926	3	Tom Jennings	v Arsenal	(h)	Div 1
2 October 1926	4	Tom Jennings	v Liverpool	(a)	Div 1
9 October 1926	4	Tom Jennings	v Blackburn Rovers	(h)	Div 1
20 November 1926	3	Tom Jennings	v Bury	(h)	Div 1
30 April 1927	4	Russell Wainscoat	v West Ham United	(h)	Div 1

10 December 1927	4	Tom Jennings	v Chelsea	(h)	Div 2
28 January 1928	3	Charlie Keetley	v Bristol City	(h)	Div 2
17 March 1928	3	Charlie Keetley	v Notts County	(h)	Div 2
14 April 1928	3	Charlie Keetley	v Clapton Orient	(h)	Div 2
25 August 1928	3	Charlie Keetley	v Aston Villa	(h)	Div 1
20 October 1928	3	Jock White	v Manchester City	(h)	Div 1
5 January 1929	3	Charlie Kettley	v Leicester City	(h)	Div 1
9 March 1929	3	Charlie Keetley	v Everton	(h)	Div 1
11 January 1930	3	Russell Wainscoat	v Crystal Palace	(h)	FA Cup
9 April 1930	3	Charlie Keetley	v Sheffield Wed	(h)	Div 1
8 September 1930	3	Charlie Keetley	v Manchester City	(h)	Div 1
20 December 1930	3	Bobby Turnbull	v Manchester United	(h)	Div 1
3 October 1931	3	Charlie Keetley	v Oldham Athletic	(h)	Div 2
14 January 1933	3	Arthur Hydes	v Newcastle United	(a)	FA Cup
11 March 1933	3	Charlie Keetley	v Wolverhampton W	(a)	Div 1
28 August 1933	4	Arthur Hydes	v Middlesbrough	(h)	Div 1
30 December 1933	3	Arthur Hydes	v Blackburn Rovers	(h)	Div 1
5 January 1935	3	Arthur Hydes	v Blackburn Rovers	(h)	Div 1
9 November 1935	3	Harry Duggan	v Sheffield Wed	(h)	Div 1
4 December 1937	3	Eric Stephenson	v Sunderland	(h)	Div 1
26 February 1938	4	Gordon Hodgson	v Everton	(h)	Div 1
23 April 1938	3	Gordon Hodgson	v Brentford	(h)	Div 1
1 October 1938	5	Gordon Hodgson	v Leicester City	(h)	Div 1
5 October 1946	3	George Ainsley	v Huddersfield Town	(h)	Div 1
10 September 1947	3	Aubrey Powell	v Plymouth Argyle	(h)	Div 2
1 May 1948	3	Albert Wakefield	v Bury	(h)	Div 2
11 November 1950	3	Frank Dudley	v Leicester City	(a)	Div 2
13 January 1951	3	Len Browning	v Southampton	(h)	Div 2
1 November 1952	3	John Charles	v Hull City	(h)	Div 2
29 November 1952	3	John Charles	v Brentford	(h)	Div 2
17 January 1953	3	John Charles	v Rotherham United	(h)	Div 2
19 August 1953	4	John Charles	v Notts County	(h)	Div 2
22 August 1953	3	John Charles	v Rotherham United	(h)	Div 2
10 October 1953	3	Bobby Forrest	v Bristol Rovers	(h)	Div 2
7 November 1953	3	Albert Nightingale	v Doncaster Rovers	(h)	Div 2
14 November 1953	3	John Charles	v Bury	(a)	Div 2
19 December 1953	3	John Charles	v Rotherham United	(a)	Div 2
2 January 1954	3	Ray Iggleden	v Leicester City	(h)	Div 2
13 February 1954	3	John Charles	v Lincoln City	(h)	Div 2
11 September 1954	3	Albert Nightingale	v Swansea Town	(h)	Div 2
24 September 1955	3	Keith Ripley	v Rotherham United	(h)	Div 2
2 April 1956	3	John Charles	v Fulham	(h)	Div 2
18 August 1956	3	Harold Brook	v Everton	(h)	Div 1

10 November 1956	3	John Charles	v Sheffield Wed	(h)	Div 1
26 December 1956	3	Harold Brook	v Blackpool	(h)	Div 1
26 March 1957	3	John Charles	v Sheffield Wed	(a)	Div 1
22 November 1958	3	Alan Shackleton	v Blackburn Rovers	(a)	Div 1
22 April 1959	3	Alan Shackleton	v Nottingham Forest	(a)	Div 1
13 September 1961	4	John McCole	v Brentford	(h)	League Cup
17 November 1962	3	Jim Storrie	v Plymouth Argyle	(h)	Div 2
15 December 1962	3	Don Weston	v Stoke City	(h)	Div 2
27 April 1963	3	Jim Storrie	v Cardiff City	(h)	Div 2
22 January 1966	3	Peter Lorimer	v Bury	(h)	League Cup
26 October 1966	3	Albert Johanneson	v DWS Amsterdam	(h)	UEFA Cup
24 May 1967	3	Rod Belfitt	v Kilmarnock	(h)	UEFA Cup
13 September 1967	3	Peter Lorimer	v Luton Town	(h)	League Cup
3 October 1967	4	Peter Lorimer	v Spora Luxembourg	(a)	UEFA Cup
17 October 1967	3	Albert Johanneson	v Spora Luxembourg	(h)	UEFA Cup
6 January 1968	3	Jimmy Greenhoff	v Fulham	(a)	Div 1
17 September 1969	3	Mick Jones	v SK Lyn Oslo	(h)	Euro Cup
29 October 1969	3	Peter Lorimer	v Nottingham Forest	(h)	Div 1
24 January 1970	4	Allan Clarke	v Sutton United	(a)	FA Cup
23 January 1971	3	Mick Jones	v Swindon Town	(h)	FA Cup
3 April 1971	4	Allan Clarke	v Burnley	(h)	Div 1
19 February 1972	3	Mick Jones	v Manchester United	(h)	Div 1
4 March 1972	3	Peter Lorimer	v Southampton	(h)	Div 1
29 January 1973	3	Allan Clarke	v Norwich City	(n)	FA Cup
9 May 1973	3	Peter Lorimer	v Arsenal	(h)	Div 1
8 September 1973	3	Peter Lorimer	v Birmingham City	(h)	Div 1
14 January 1978	3	Arthur Graham	v Birmingham City	(h)	Div 1
28 March 1978	3	Eddie Gray	v Leicester City	(h)	Div 1
19 September 1979	3	Arthur Graham	v Valletta	(a)	UEFA Cup
5 September 1981	3	Arthur Graham	v Wolverhampton W	(h)	Div 1
29 September 1984	3	Andy Ritchie	v Oldham Athletic	(h)	Div 2
1 December 1984	3	Andy Ritchie	v Wimbledon	(h)	Div 2
19 January 1985	3	Tommy Wright	v Notts County	(h)	Div 2
28 March 1987	3	Ian Baird	v Plymouth Argyle	(h)	Div 2
19 March 1988	3	John Pearson	v Sheffield United	(h)	Div 2
1 April 1989	3	Carl Shutt	v Bournemouth	(h)	Div 2
23 September 1989	3	Gordon Strachan	v Swindon Town	(h)	Div 2
13 April 1991	3	Lee Chapman	v Liverpool	(h)	Div 1
12 January 1992	3	Lee Chapman	v Sheffield Wed	(a)	Div 1
14 March 1992	3	Lee Chapman	v Wimbledon	(h)	Div 1
8 August 1992	3	Eric Cantona	v Liverpool	(n)	Charity Sh
25 August 1992	3	Eric Cantona	v Tottenham Hotspur	(h)	Prem
10 April 1993	3	Gordon Strachan	v Coventry City	(h)	Prem

8 May 1993	3	Rod Wallace	v Coventry City	(a)	Prem
17 January 1995	3	Phil Masinga	v Walsall	(h)	FA Cup
5 April 1995	3	Tony Yeboah	v Ipswich Town	(h)	Prem
12 September 1995	3	Tony Yeboah	v AS Monaco	(a)	UEFA Cup
23 September 1995	3	Tony Yeboah	v Wimbledon	(a)	Prem
28 October 1995	3	Gary McAllister	v Coventry City	(h)	Prem
11 August 1999	3	Michael Bridges	v Southampton	(a)	Prem
4 November 2000	4	Mark Viduka	v Liverpool	(h)	Prem
9 October 2001	3	Robbie Keane	v Leicester City	(a)	League Cup
19 December 2001	3	Robbie Fowler	v Bolton Wanderers	(a)	Prem
14 November 2002	4	Alan Smith	v Hapoel Tel Aviv	(a)	UEFA Cup
5 April 2003	3	Mark Viduka	v Charlton Athletic	(a)	Prem
20 November 2004	4	Brian Deane	v Queen's Park Rangers	(h)	Champ
28 September 2005	3	Rob Hulse	v Derby County	(h)	Champ
12 August 2008	3	Jermaine Beckford	v Chester City	(a)	League Cup
17 November 2008	3	Jermaine Beckford	v Northampton Town	(a)	FA Cup
10 March 2009	3	Jermaine Beckford	v Yeovil Town	(h)	League 1
30 October 2010	3	Jonny Howson	v Scunthorpe United	(a)	Champ
13 November 2010	3	Luciano Becchio	v Bristol City	(h)	Champ

- United have scored 108 trebles against 57 different League sides in domestic competitions. They have additionally netted eight hat-tricks against seven European teams and three against non-League opposition in the FA Cup. City scored 12 trebles against nine League sides and two players each scored four times against non-League Morley in 1905.

- Clubs suffering most from Leeds sharpshooters over the years have been:

Leicester City	8
Sheffield Wednesday	5
Wolverhampton W	5 (including 3 by City)
Blackburn Rovers	4
Bury	4
Liverpool	4
Nottingham Forest	4 (including 2 by City)
Notts County	4
Rotherham United	4

- Top hat-trick aces have been:

John Charles	11
Charlie Keetley	10
Peter Lorimer	7
Billy McLeod (City)	7
Tom Jennings	6

- Highest number of goals in one game were recorded by:

Billy McLeod (City)	5	v Hull City	(a)	16 January 1915
Gordon Hodgson	5	v Leicester City	(h)	1 October 1938

- Hat-tricks were scored in thee consecutive League games by Tom Jennings in 1926–27 (a feat that has been equalled but not beaten): three on 25 September v Arsenal, four on 2 October v Liverpool and another four goals on 9 October v Blackburn Rovers.

- The hat-trick recorded by Billy Poyntz on 20 February 1922 was recorded on the afternoon of his wedding day!

- The hat-trick scored by Phil Masinga on 17 January 1995 was unique in that it was the first by a substitute and all three came in extra-time.

- Jermaine Beckford scored three hat-tricks in 2008–09 to become the first United player to register hat-tricks in the League, FA Cup and League Cup in the one season.

- The eight hat-tricks in 1953–54 represents the most registered by United in any season.

- There have been four instances of United scoring hat-tricks at home and away against the same opposition in the same season:

1953–54	Rotherham United	both netted by John Charles
1956–57	Sheffield Wednesday	both netted by John Charles
1967–68	Spora Luxembourg	the home hat-trick came from Albert Johanneson with Peter Lorimer scoring four times in the away tie.
1992–93	Coventry City	Gordon Strachan scored the home treble with Rod Wallace the away one.

- United's 119 hat-tricks to date have been netted in the following competitions (City's 14 hat-tricks in brackets):

	Home	**Away**	**Neutral**	**Total**
Premier Division	5	5		10
Division One	35	8		43
Division Two	35 (10)	3 (2)		38 (12)
Championship	3	1		4
League One	1	0		1
FA Cup	6 (2)	3	1	10 (2)
League Cup	2	2		4
Charity Cup	0	0	1	1
European Cup	1	0		1
UEFA/Fairs Cup	3	4		7
Totals	91 (12)	26 (2)	2	119 (14)

International Appearances

Appearances given here refer to caps won while with Leeds, including those on loan from other clubs. The number of caps won is shown in brackets after each player's name. The figures in brackets after results are goals scored by the player in that match.

Before 1924 there was only one Ireland team, then the Republic of Ireland began separate matches.

Attendances have been obtained from contemporary sources, newspapers, handbooks and various websites of countries' Football Associations and the RSSSF (Rec. Sport Soccer Statistics Foundation).

In the key to games, it should be noted that the current European Championship was called the European Nations Cup from 1958 to 1966 when a knockout format was used.

The details provided go up to the end of May 2009.

Key: AC= Asian Cup, ANF = African Cup Finals, ACQ = African Cup Qualifier, CAQ = Central American Qualifier, CC = Confederations Cup, CGC = Concacaf Gold Cup, CNC = Carling Nations Cup, ECC = England Challenge Cup, ECF = European Nations/European Championship Finals, ENQ = European Nations/European Championship Qualifier, F = Friendly, HC = Home Championship, IC = Independence Cup, KC= Kirin Cup, NMC = Nelson Mandela Challenge, OG = Olympic Games, TT= Toulon Tournament, WCF = World Cup Finals, WCQ = World Cup Qualifier, USBT = USA Bicentennial Tournament, USC = US Cup

Leeds United Full Internationals

ANGOLA

Rui Marques (16 + 4 apps)

1 March 2006	F	South Korea (sub)	Seoul	0–1	63,255
2 June 2006	WCF	Iran (sub)	Leipzig	1–1	38,000
16 June 2006	WCF	Mexico (sub)	Hanover	0–0	43,000
13 January 2008	F	Egypt (sub)	Alvercera	3–3	7,705
17 January 2008	F	Morocco	Rabat	1–2	25,000
23 January 2008	ANF	South Africa	Tamale	1–1	15,000
27 January 2008	ANF	Senegal	Tamale	3–1	10,000
31 January 2008	ANF	Tunisia	Tamale	0–0	10,000
4 February 2008	ANF	Egypt	Kumasi	2–1	40,000
1 June 2008	WCQ	Benin	Luanda	3–0	6,000
8 June 2008	WCQ	Niger	Niamey	2–1	23,000
14 June 2008	WCQ	Uganda	Kampala	1–3	20,000
23 June 2008	WCQ	Uganda	Luanda	0–0	16,000
11 February 2009	F	Mali	Paris	0–4	–
30 December 2009	F	Estonia	Vila Real de St Antonio	0–1	200

3 January 2010	F	Gambia	Vila Real de St Antonio	1–1	–
10 January 2010	ANF	Mali	Luanda	4–4	45,000
14 January 2010	ANF	Malawi	Luanda	2–0	48,500
18 January 2010	ANF	Algeria	Luanda	0–0	40,000
24 January 2010	ANF	Ghana	Luanda	0–1	50,000

AUSTRALIA

Jacob Burns (1+1 apps)

15 November 2000	F	Scotland (sub)	Hampden Park	2–0	30,985
28 February 2001	F	Colombia	Bogata	2–3	2,071

Harry Kewell (12+ 1 apps, 4gls)

24 April 1996	F	Chile	Antofagasta	0–3	30,000
9 October 1996	F	Saudi Arabia	Riyadh	0–0	–
1 October 1997	F	Tunisia (sub)	Tunis	3–0	20,000
22 November 1997	WCQ	Iran	Teheran	1–1 (1)	128,000
29 November 1997	WCQ	Iran	Melbourne	2–2 (1)	85,022
16 December 1997	CC	Saudi Arabia	Riyadh	0–1	20,000
19 December 1997	CC	Uruguay	Riyadh	1–0 (1)	22,000
21 December 1997	CC	Brazil	Riyadh	0–6	65,000
23 February 2000	F	Hungary	Budapest	3–0	14,000
11 November 2001	F	France	Melbourne	1–1	53,228
20 November 2001	WCQ	Uruguay	Melbourne	1–0	84,656
25 November 2001	WCQ	Uruguay	Montevideo	0–3	62,000
12 February 2003	F	England	Upton Park, London	3–1 (1)	34,590

Neil Kilkenny (1+5 apps)

22 June 2008	WCQ	China (sub)	Sydney	0–1	70,054
5 January 2011	F	United Arab Emirates	Al Ain, Abu Dhabi	0–0	–
18 January 2011	AC	Bahrain (sub)	Qatar	1–0	3,919
22 January 2011	AC	Iraq (sub)	Qatar	1–0 aet	7,889
25 January 2011	AC	Uzbekistan (sub)	Qatar	6–0	24,826
29 January 2011	AC	Japan (sub)	Qatar	0–1 aet	37,174

Patrick Kisnorbo (2+2 apps, 1gl)

12 August 2009	F	Republic of Ireland	Limerick	3–0	19,429
5 September 2009	F	South Korea	Seoul	1–3 (1)	30,000
10 October 2009	F	Holland (sub)	Sydney	0–0	40,537
18 November 2009	ACQ	Oman (sub)	Muscat	2–1	12,000

Paul Okon (2 apps)

12 February 2003	F	England	West Ham	3–1	34,590
19 August 2003	F	Republic of Ireland	Dublin	1–2	37,200

Mark Viduka (7 apps, 1gl)

11 November 2001	F	France	Melbourne	1–1	53,228
20 November 2001	WCQ	Uruguay	Melbourne	1–0	84,656
25 November 2001	WCQ	Uruguay	Montevideo	0–3	62,000
12 February 2003	F	England	Upton Park, London	3–1	34,590
19 August 2003	F	Republic of Ireland	Dublin	1–2 (1)	37,200
7 September 2003	F	Jamaica	Reading	2–1	8,050
30 March 2004	F	South Africa	Loftus Road, London	1–0	16,108

AUSTRIA

Martin Hiden (4+3 apps, 1gl)

25 March 1998	F	Hungary	Vienna	2–3	21,000
24 April 1998	F	USA	Vienna	0–3	17,000
27 May 1998	F	Tunisia (sub)	Vienna	2–1	12,000
19 August 1998	F	France (sub)	Vienna	2–2	44,000
5 September 1998	ECQ	Israel (sub)	Vienna	1–1	20,000
10 October 1998	ECQ	Cyprus	Larnaca	3–0	10,000
14 October 1998	ECQ	San Marino	Serravalle	4–1 (1)	1,218

BRAZIL

Roque Junior (3 apps)

12 October 2003	F	Jamaica	Leicester	1–0	32,000
16 November 2003	WCQ	Peru	Lima	1–1	80,000
19 November 2003	WCQ	Uruguay	Curitiba	3–3	30,000

On loan from AC Milan

BULGARIA

Radostin Kishishev (1 app)

28 March 2007	ECQ	Albania	Sofia	0–0	25,000

On loan from Leicester City

CAMEROON

Salomon Olembe (0+1 app)

3 February 2004	ANF	Egypt (sub)	Monastir	0–0	20,000

On loan from Marseille

DR CONGO

Tresor Kandol (1 app)

20 August 2008	F	Togo	Dreux	2–1	1,000

On loan at Millwall

ENGLAND

Peter Barnes (0+2 apps)

9 September 1981	WCQ	Norway (sub)	Oslo	1–2	22,000
25 May 1982	F	Holland (sub)	Wembley	2–0	69,000

David Batty (17+ 2 apps)

21 May 1991	ECC	USSR (sub)	Wembley	3–1	23,798
25 May 1991	ECC	Argentina	Wembley	2–2	44,497
1 June 1991	F	Australia	Sydney	1–0	36,827
3 June 1991	F	New Zealand	Auckland	1–0	17,500
12 June 1991	F	Malaysia	Kuala Lumpur	4–2	41,248
11 September 1991	F	Germany	Wembley	0–1	59,493
16 October 1991	ECQ	Turkey	Wembley	1–0	50,896
12 May 1992	F	Hungary (sub)	Budapest	1–0	12,500
14 June 1992	ECF	France	Malmo	0–0	26,535
17 June 1992	ECF	Sweden	Solna	1–2	30,126
14 October 1992	WCQ	Norway	Wembley	1–1	51,441
17 February 1993	WCQ	San Marino	Wembley	6–0	51,154

9 June 1993	WCQ	United States	Boston	0–2	37,652
13 June 1993	F	Brazil	Washington	1–1	54,118
28 April 1999	F	Hungary	Budapest	1–1	20,000
5 June 1999	ECQ	Sweden	Wembley	0–0	75,824
9 June 1999	ECQ	Bulgaria	Sofia	1–1	22,000
4 September 1999	ECQ	Luxembourg	Wembley	6–0	68,772
8 September 1999	ECQ	Poland	Warsaw	0–0	17,000
Lee Bowyer (1 app)					
7 September 2002	F	Portugal	Villa Park	1–1	40,058
Jack Charlton (34 apps, 6gls)					
10 April 1965	HC	Scotland	Wembley	2–2	98,199
5 May 1965	F	Hungary	Wembley	1–0	52,000
9 May 1965	F	Yugoslavia	Belgrade	1–1	60,000
12 May 1965	F	West Germany	Nuremburg	1–0	67,000
16 May 1965	F	Sweden	Gothenburg	2–1	18,000
2 October 1965	HC	Wales	Cardiff	0–0	30,000
20 October 1965	F	Austria	Wembley	2–3	65,000
10 November 1965	HC	Northern Ireland	Wembley	2–1	71,000
8 December 1965	F	Spain	Madrid	2–0	25,000
5 January 1966	F	Poland	Goodison Park	1–1	47,750
23 February 1966	F	West Germany	Wembley	1–0	75,000
2 April 1966	HC	Scotland	Hampden Park	4–3	133,000
4 May 1966	F	Yugoslavia	Wembley	2–0	54,000
26 June 1966	F	Finland	Helsinki	3–0 (1)	10,500
3 July 1966	F	Denmark	Copenhagen	2–0 (1)	32,000
5 July 1966	F	Poland	Chorzow	1–0	70,000
11 July 1966	WCF	Uruguay	Wembley	0–0	87,148
16 July 1966	WCF	Mexico	Wembley	2–0	92,570
20 July 1966	WCF	France	Wembley	2–0	98,270
23 July 1966	WCF	Argentina	Wembley	1–0	90,584
26 July 1966	WCF	Portugal	Wembley	2–1	94,493
30 July 1966	WCF	West Germany	Wembley	4–3 aet	96,924
22 October 1966	HC/ECQ	Northern Ireland	Belfast	2–0	45,000
2 November 1966	F	Czechoslvakia	Wembley	0–0	75,000
16 November 1966	HC/ECQ	Wales	Wembley	5–1 (1)	76,000
15 April 1967	HC/ECQ	Scotland	Wembley	2–3 (1)	99,063
21 October 1967	HC/ECQ	Wales	Cardiff	3–0	45,000
3 April 1968	ECF	Spain	Wembley	1–0	100,000
15 January 1969	F	Romania	Wembley	1–1 (1)	77,000
12 March 1969	F	France	Wembley	5–0	83,000
7 May 1969	HC	Wales	Wembley	2–1	72,000
5 November 1969	F	Holland	Amsterdam	1–0	40,000
10 December 1969	F	Portugal	Wembley	1–0 (1)	100,000
14 January 1970	F	Holland	Wembley	0–0	75,000
11 June 1970	WCF	Czechoslovakia	Guadalajara	1–0	49,000
Trevor Cherry (23 + 4 apps)					
24 March 1976	F	Wales	Wrexham	2–1	21,000
15 May 1976	HC	Scotland (sub)	Hampden Park	1–2	85,165
23 May 1976	USBT	Brazil	Los Angeles	1–0	32,495
13 June 1976	WCQ	Finland	Helskini	4–1	24,500

8 September 1976	F	Republic of Ireland	Wembley	1–1	51,000
17 November 1976	WCQ	Italy	Rome	0–2	70,750
30 March 1977	WCQ	Luxembourg	Wembley	5–0	78,000
28 May 1977	HC	Northern Ireland	Belfast	2–1	34,000
4 June 1977	HC	Scotland (sub)	Wembley	1–2	100,000
8 June 1977	F	Brazil	Rio de Janeiro	0–0	77,000
12 June 1977	F	Argentina	Buenos Aires	1–1	60,000
15 June 1977	F	Uruguay	Montevideo	0–0	36,000
7 September 1977	F	Switzerland	Wembley	0–0	43,000
12 October 1977	WCQ	Luxembourg	Luxembourg	2–0	9,250
16 November 1977	WCQ	Italy	Wembley	2–0	92,000
19 April 1978	F	Brazil	Wembley	1–1	92,000
13 May 1978	HC	Wales	Cardiff	3–1	17,750
29 November 1978	F	Czechoslovakia	Wembley	1–0	92,000
23 May 1979	HC	Wales	Wembley	0–0	70,250
10 June 1979	F	Sweden	Solna	0–0	35,691
6 February 1980	ECQ	Republic of Ireland	Wembley	2–0	90,250
13 May 1980	F	Argentina (sub)	Wembley	3–1	90,000
17 May 1980	HC	Wales	Wrexham	4–1	24,250
20 May 1980	HC	Northern Ireland	Wembley	1–1	32,000
24 May 1980	HC	Scotland	Hampden Park	2–0	85,000
31 May 1980	F	Australia	Sydney	2–1	26,750
18 June 1980	ECF	Spain (sub)	Naples	1–2	14,500
Allan Clarke (16+3 apps, 10gls)					
11 June 1970	WCF	Czechoslovakia	Guadalajara	1–0 (1p)	49,000
12 November 1970	F	East Germany	Wembley	3–1 (1)	93,000
12 May 1971	ECQ	Malta	Wembley	5–0 (1p)	36,000
15 May 1971	HC	Northern Ireland	Belfast	1–0 (1)	33,500
19 May 1971	HC	Wales (sub)	Wembley	0–0	70,000
22 May 1971	HC	Scotland (sub)	Wembley	3–1	91,469
14 February 1973	F	Scotland	Hampden Park	5–0 (2)	48,470
15 May 1973	HC	Wales	Wembley	3–0	39,000
19 May 1973	HC	Scotland	Wembley	1–0	95,950
27 May 1973	F	Czechoslavakia	Prague	1–1 (1)	25,000
6 June 1973	WCQ	Poland	Chorzow	0–2	118,000
10 June 1973	F	USSR	Moscow	2–1	85,000
14 June 1973	F	Italy	Turin	0–2	52,000
26 September 1973	F	Austria	Wembley	7–0 (2)	48,000
17 October 1973	WCQ	Poland	Wembley	1–1 (1p)	100,000
14 November 1973	F	Italy	Wembley	0–2	95,000
20 November 1974	ECQ	Portugal	Wembley	0–0	70,750
30 October 1975	ECQ	Czechoslovakia	Bratislava	1–2	45,000
19 November 1975	ECQ	Portugal (sub)	Lisbon	1–1	30,000
Terry Cooper (20 apps)					
12 March 1969	F	France	Wembley	5–0	83,000
7 May 1969	HC	Wales	Wembley	2–1	72,000
10 May 1969	HC	Scotland	Wembley	4–1	89,902
1 June 1969	F	Mexico	Mexico City	0–0	105,000
14 January 1970	F	Holland	Wembley	0–0	75,000
25 February 1970	F	Belgium	Brussels	3–1	20,500

21 May 1970	F	Colombia	Bogata	4–0	28,000
24 May 1970	F	Ecuador	Quito	2–0	22,250
2 June 1970	WCF	Romania	Guadalajara	1–0	50,000
7 June 1970	WCF	Brazil	Guadalajara	0–1	66,750
11 June 1970	WCF	Czechoslovakia	Guadalajara	1–0	49,000
14 June 1970	WCF	West Germany	Leon	2–3 aet	23,250
25 November 1970	F	East Germany	Wembley	3–1	93,000
12 May 1971	ECQ	Malta	Wembley	5–0	36,500
15 May 1971	HC	Northern Ireland	Belfast	1–0	33,500
19 May 1971	HC	Wales	Wembley	0–0	70,000
22 May 1971	HC	Scotland	Wembley	3–1	91,469
13 October 1971	ECQ	Switzerland	Basle	3–2	58,000
10 November 1971	ECQ	Switzerland	Wembley	1–1	98,000
20 November 1974	ECQ	Portugal	Wembley	0–0	70,750
Wilf Copping (7 apps)					
13 May 1933	F	Italy	Rome	1–1	50,000
20 May 1933	F	Switzerland	Berne	4–0	26,000
14 October 1933	HC	Ireland	Belfast	3–0	35,000
15 November 1933	HC	Wales	Newcastle	1–2	12,000
6 December 1933	F	France	Tottenham	4–1	17,097
14 April 1934	HC	Scotland	Wembley	3–0	92,963
24 May 1939	F	Romania	Bucharest	2–0	40,000
Tony Currie (8+2 apps, 2gls)					
19 April 1978	F	Brazil	Wembley	1–1	92,000
13 May 1978	HC	Wales (sub)	Cardiff	3–1 (1)	17,750
16 May 1978	HC	Northern Ireland	Wembley	1–0	48,000
20 May 1978	HC	Scotland	Hampden Park	0–1	90,000
24 May 1987	F	Hungary (sub)	Wembley	4–1 (1)	74,000
29 November 1978	F	Czechoslovakia	Wembley	1–0	92,000
7 February 1979	ECQ	Northern Ireland	Wembley	4–0	92,000
19 May 1979	HC	Northern Ireland	Belfast	2–0	34,000
23 May 1979	HC	Wales	Wembley	0–0	70,250
10 June 1979	F	Sweden	Solna	0–0	35,691
Tony Dorigo (8+1 apps)					
11 September 1991	F	Germany	Wembley	0–1	59,493
25 March 1992	F	Czechoslovakia (sub)	Prague	2–2	12,320
12 May 1992	F	Hungary	Budapest	1–0	12,500
17 May 1992	F	Brazil	Wembley	1–1	53,428
17 February 1993	WCQ	San Marino	Wembley	6–0	51,154
29 May 1993	WCQ	Poland	Katowice	1–1	60,000
9 June 1993	USC	USA	Boston	0–2	37,652
13 June 1993	USC	Brazil	Washington	1–1	54,118
13 October 1993	WCQ	Holland	Rotterdam	0–2	48,000
Willis Edwards (16 apps)					
1 March 1926	HC	Wales	Crystal Palace	3–1	23,000
17 April 1926	HC	Scotland	Old Trafford	0–1	49,429
20 October 1926	HC	Ireland	Anfield	3–3	20,000
14 February 1927	HC	Wales	Wrexham	3–3	16,910
2 April 1927	HC	Scotland	Hampden Park	2–1	111,214
11 May 1927	F	Belgium	Brussels	9–1	35,000

Willis Edwards, the first Leeds player to be picked for England.

21 May 1927	F	Luxembourg	Esch	5–2	5,000
26 May 1927	F	France	Colombes	6–0	25,000
31 March 1928	HC	Scotland	Wembley	1–5	80,868
17 May 1928	F	France	Colombes	5–1	40,000
19 May 1928	F	Belgium	Antwerp	3–1	25,000
22 October 1928	HC	Ireland	Goodison Park	2–1	34,000
17 November 1928	HC	Wales	Swansea	3–2	14,000
13 April 1929	HC	Scotland	Hampden Park	0–1	110,512
19 October 1929	HC	Ireland	Belfast	3–0	37,000
20 November 1929	HC	Wales	Stamford Bridge	6–0	32,945
Rio Ferdinand (17 apps)					
28 February 2001	F	Spain	Villa Park	3–0	42,129
24 March 2001	WCQ	Finland	Anfield	2–1	44,262
28 March 2001	WCQ	Albania	Tirana	3–1	18,000
25 May 2001	F	Mexico	Derby	4–0	33,597
6 June 2001	WCQ	Greece	Athens	2–0	46,000
1 September 2001	WCQ	Germany	Munich	5–1	63,000
5 September 2001	WCQ	Albania	Newcastle	2–0	51,046
6 October 2001	WCQ	Greece	Old Trafford	2–2	66,009
10 November 2001	F	Sweden	Old Trafford	1–1	64,413
13 February 2002	F	Holland	Amsterdam	1–1	48,500
21 May 2002	F	South Korea	Seoguipo	1–1	39,876
26 May 2002	F	Cameroon	Kobe	2–2	42,000
2 June 2002	WCF	Sweden	Saitama	1–1	52,271
7 June 2002	WCF	Argentina	Sappsoro	1–0	35,927
12 June 2002	WCF	Nigeria	Osaka	0–0	44,864
15 June 2002	WCF	Denmark	Niigata	3–0	40,582
21 June 2002	WCF	Brazil	Shizuoka	1–2	47,436
Robbie Fowler (0+4 apps, 2gls)					
27 March 2002	F	Italy (sub)	Leeds	1–2 (1)	36,635
17 April 2002	F	Paraguay (sub)	Anfield	4–0	42,713
26 May 2002	F	Cameroon (sub)	Kobe	2–2 (1)	42,000
15 June 2002	WCF	Denmark (as sub)	Niigata	3–0	40,582
Billy Furness (1 app)					
13 May 1933	F	Italy	Rome	1–1	50,000
Brian Greenhoff (0+1 app)					
31 May 1980	F	Australia (sub)	Sydney	2–1	26,750
Ernie Hart (8 apps)					
17 November 1928	HC	Wales	Swansea	3–2	14,000
19 October 1929	HC	Ireland	Belfast	3–0	37,000
20 November 1929	HC	Wales	Stamford Bridge	6–0	32,945
7 December 1932	F	Austria	Stamford Bridge	4–3	42,000
1 April 1933	HC	Scotland	Hampden Park	1–2	134,710
14 April 1933	HC	Scotland	Wembley	3–0	92,363
10 May 1934	F	Hungary	Budapest	1–2	40,000
16 May 1934	F	Czechoslovakia	Prague	1–2	40,000
Norman Hunter (24 + 4 apps, 2gls)					
8 December 1965	F	Spain (sub)	Madrid	2–0	25,000
23 February 1966	F	West Germany	Wembley	1–0	75,000
4 May 1966	F	Yugoslavia	Wembley	2–0	54,000

Robbie Fowler, the last Leeds player to score for England, receives the congratulations of Phil Neville after netting against Italy at Elland Road.

26 June 1966	F	Finland	Helsinki	3–0	10,500
27 May 1967	F	Austria	Vienna	1–0	85,000
8 May 1968	ECQ	Spain	Madrid	2–1 (1)	120,000
22 May 1968	F	Sweden	Wembley	3–1	72,500
1 June 1968	F	West Germany	Hanover	0–1	79,250
5 June 1968	ECF	Yugoslavia	Florence	0–1	40,000
8 June 1968	ECF	USSR	Rome	2–0	80,000
15 January 1969	F	Romania	Wembley	1–1	77,000

7 May 1979	HC	Wales	Wembley	2–1	72,000
14 January 1970	F	Holland	Wembley	0–0	75,000
14 June 1970	WCF	West Germany (sub)	Leon	2–3 aet	23,250
3 February 1971	ECQ	Malta	Ta'qali	1–0	20,000
29 April 1972	ECF	West Germany	Wembley	1–3	95,000
13 May 1972	ECF	West Germany	Berlin	0–0	75,000
20 May 1972	HC	Wales	Cardiff	3–0	33,000
23 May 1972	HC	Northern Ireland	Wembley	0–1	43,000
27 May 1972	HC	Scotland	Hampden Park	1–0	119,325
15 November 1972	WCQ	Wales	Cardiff	1–0	39,000
24 January 1973	WCQ	Wales	Wembley	1–1 (1)	73,000
10 June 1973	F	USSR (sub)	Moscow	2–1	85,000
26 September 1973	F	Austria	Wembley	7–0	48,000
17 October 1973	WCQ	Poland	Wembley	1–1	100,000
15 May 1974	HC	Northern Ireland (sub)	Wembley	1–0	47,000
18 May 1974	HC	Scotland	Hampden Park	0–2	94,487
30 October 1974	ECQ	Czechoslovakia	Wembley	3–0	85,000
Mick Jones (1 app)					
14 January 1970	F	Holland	Wembley	0–0	75,000
Paul Madeley (24 apps)					
15 May 1971	HC	Northern Ireland	Belfast	1–0	33,500
13 October 1971	ECQ	Switzerland	Basle	3–2	58,000
10 November 1971	ECQ	Switzerland	Wembley	1–1	98,000
1 December 1971	ECQ	Greece	Pireus	2–0	42,000
29 April 1972	ECF	West Germany	Wembley	2–3	95,000
13 May 1972	ECF	West Germany	Berlin	0–0	75,000
20 May 1972	HC	Wales	Cardiff	3–0	33,000
27 May 1972	HC	Scotland	Hampden Park	1–0	119,325
14 February 1973	F	Scotland	Hampden Park	5–0	48,470
27 May 1973	F	Czechoslovakia	Prague	1–1	25,000
6 June 1973	WCQ	Poland	Chorzow	0–2	118,000
10 June 1973	F	USSR	Moscow	2–1	85,000
14 June 1973	F	Italy	Turin	0–2	52,000
26 September 1973	F	Austria	Wembley	7–0	48,000
17 October 1973	WCQ	Poland	Wembley	1–1	100,000
14 November 1973	F	Italy	Wembley	0–1	95,000
30 October 1974	ENQ	Czechoslovakia	Wembley	3–0	85,000
20 November 1974	ENQ	Portugal	Wembley	0–0	70,750
16 April 1975	ENQ	Cyprus	Wembley	5–0	65,000
30 October 1975	ENQ	Czechoslovakia	Bratislava	1–2	30,000
19 November 1975	ENQ	Portugal	Lisbon	1–1	40,000
13 June 1976	ENQ	Finland	Helsinki	4–1	24,500
8 September 1976	F	Republic of Ireland	Wembley	1–1	51,000
9 February 1977	F	Holland	Wembley	0–2	90,000
Nigel Martyn (17+3 apps)					
24 May 1997	F	South Africa	Old Trafford	2–1	52,676
15 November 1997	F	Cameroon	Wembley	2–0	46,176
11 February 1998	F	Chile	Wembley	0–2	65,228
29 May 1998	F	Belgium	Casablanca	0–0	25,000
18 November 1998	F	Czech Republic	Wembley	2–0	38,535

10 February 1999	F	France (sub)	Wembley	0–2	74,111
4 September 1999	ECQ	Luxembourg	Wembley	6–0	68,772
8 September 1999	ECQ	Poland	Warsaw	0–0	17,000
10 October 1999	F	Belgium (sub)	Sunderland	2–1	40,897
31 May 2000	F	Ukraine	Wembley	2–0	55,975
20 June 2000	ECF	Romania	Charleroi	2–3	30,000
28 February 2001	F	Spain (sub)	Villa Park	3–0	42,129
25 May 2001	F	Mexico	Derby	4–0	33,597
15 August 2001	F	Holland	Tottenham	0–2	35,238
6 October 2001	WCQ	Greece	Old Trafford	1–1	66,009
10 November 2001	F	Sweden	Old Trafford	1–1	64,413
13 February 2002	F	Holland	Amsterdam	1–1	48,500
27 March 2002	F	Italy	Elland Road	1–2	36,635
21 May 2002	F	South Korea	Seoguipo	1–1	39,876
26 May 2002	F	Cameroon	Kobe	2–2	42,000
Danny Mills (11+8 apps)					
25 May 2001	F	Mexico (sub)	Derby	4–0	33,597
15 August 2001	F	Holland (sub)	Tottenham	0–2	35,238
10 November 2001	F	Sweden (sub)	Old Trafford	1–1	64,413
27 March 2002	F	Italy	Elland Road	1–2	36,635
17 April 2002	F	Paraguay (sub)	Anfield	4–0	42,713
21 May 2002	F	South Korea	Seoguipo	1–1	39,876
26 May 2002	F	Cameroon (sub)	Kobe	2–2	42,000
2 June 2003	WCF	Sweden	Saitana	1–1	52,271
7 June 2003	WCF	Argentina	S appsoro	1–0	35,927
12 June 2003	WCF	Nigeria	Osaka	0–0	44,864
15 June 2003	WCF	Denmark	Niigata	3–0	40,582
21 June 2003	WCF	Brazil	Shizuoka	1–2	47,436
7 September 2003	F	Portugal	Villa Park	1–1	40,058
12 February 2003	F	Australia (sub)	West Ham	1–3	34,590
22 May 2003	F	South Africa	Durban	2–1	48,000
3 June 2003	F	Serbia Montenegro	Leicester	2–1	30,900
11 June 2003	F	Slovakia	Middlesbrough	2–1	35,000
20 August 2003	F	Croatia (sub)	Ipswich	3–1	28,700
18 February 2003+	F	Portugal (sub)	Faro	1–1	27,000
+ On loan at Middlesbrough					
Mike O'Grady (1pp, 1gl)					
12 March 1969	F	France	Wembley	5–0 (1)	83,000
Alan Peacock (2 apps, 1gl)					
2 October 1965	HC	Wales	Cardiff	0–0	30,000
10 November 1965	HC	Northern Ireland	Wembley	2–1 (1)	71,000
Paul Reaney (2+1 apps)					
11 December 1968	F	Bulgaria (sub)	Wembley	1–1	80,000
10 December 1969	F	Portugal	Wembley	1–0	100,000
3 February 1971	ECQ	Malta	Ta'quali	1–0	20,000
Paul Robinson (0+4 apps)					
12 February 2003	F	Australia (sub)	West Ham	1–3	34,590
22 May 2003	F	South Africa (sub)	Durban	2–1	48,000
20 August 2003	F	Croatia (sub)	Ipswich	3–1	28,700
16 November 2003	F	Denmark (sub)	Old Trafford	2–3	64,159

Alan Smith (2+6 apps, 1gl)

25 May 2001	F	Mexico (sub)	Derby	4–0	33,597
6 June 2001	WCQ	Greece (sub)	Athens	2–0	46,000
15 August 2001	F	Holland (sub)	Tottenham	0–2	35,238
7 September 2002	F	Portugal	Villa Park	1–1 (1)	40,058
12 October 2002	ECQ	Slovakia (sub)	Bratislava	2–1	30,000
16 October 2002	ECQ	Macedonia	Southampton	2–2	32,095
18 February 2003	F	Portugal (sub)	Faro	1–1	27,000
31 March 2003	F	Sweden (sub)	Gothenburg	0–1	40,464

Bert Sproston (8 apps)

17 October 1936	HC	Wales	Cardiff	1–2	40,000
23 October 1937	HC	Ireland	Belfast	5–1	40,000
17 November 1937	HC	Wales	Middlesbrough	2–1	30,608
1 December 1937	F	Czechoslovakia	Tottenham	5–4	35,000
9 April 1938	HC	Scotland	Wembley	0–1	93,267
14 May 1938	F	Germany	Berlin	6–3	105,000
21 May 1938	F	Switzerland	Zurich	1–2	25,000
26 May 1938	F	France	Paris	4–2	55,000

Eric Stephenson (2 apps)

9 April 1938	HC	Scotland	Wembley	0–1	93,267
16 November 1938	HC	Ireland	Old Trafford	7–0	40,386

Russell Wainscoat (1 app)

13 April 1929	HC	Scotland	Hampden Park	0–1	110,512

Jason Wilcox (1 app)

23 February 2000	F	Argentina	Wembley	0–0	74,008

Jonathan Woodgate (3+ 1 apps)

9 June 1999	ECQ	Bulgaria	Sofia	1–1	22,000
7 September 2002	F	Portugal (sub)	Villa Park	1–1	40,058
12 October 2002	ECQ	Slovakia	Bratislava	2–1	30,000
16 October 2002	ECQ	Macedonia	Southampton	2–2	32,095

FINLAND

Mikael Forsell (3 apps)

7 October 2011	ECQ	Sweden	Helsinki	1–2	23,257
11 October 2011	ECQ	Hungary	Budapest	0–0	34,981
15 November 2011	F	Denmark (sub)	Esjberg	1–2	14,000

Mika Vayrynen (1 + 1 apps)

7 October 2011	ECQ	Sweden	Helsinki	1–2	23,257
11 October 2011	ECQ	Hungary (sub)	Budapest	0–0	34,981

FRANCE

Eric Cantona (9 apps, 2gls)

19 February 1992	F	England	Wembley	0–2	58,723
25 March 1992	F	Belgium	Paris	3–3	25,000
27 May 1992	F	Switzerland	Lausanne	2–1	21,000
5 June 1992	F	Holland	Lens	1–1	40,000
10 June 1992	ECF	Sweden	Stockholm	1–1	29,860
14 June 1992	ECF	England	Malmo	0–0	26,535
17 June 1992	ECF	Denmark	Malmo	1–2	25,763
14 October 1992	WCQ	Austria	Paris	2–0 (1)	39,186
14 November 1992	WCQ	Finland	Paris	2–1 (1)	30,000

Olivier Dacourt (2+3 apps)

30 May 2001	CC	South Korea (sub)	Taegu	5–0	61,500
1 June 2001	CC	Australia	Taegu	1–0	44,000
3 June 2001	CC	Mexico (sub)	Ulsan	4–0	28,000
16 October 2002	ECQ	Malta (sub)	Valletta	4–0	10,000
30 April 2003	F	Egypt	Paris	5–0	54,554

GHANA

Tony Yeboah (19 apps, 5gls)

23 April 1995*	ANQ	Niger	Accra	1–0 (1)	40,000
25 May 1995	F	Norway	Oslo	2–3	8,312
1 July 1995	F	Ivory Coast	Abidjan	0–2	–
30 July 1995	ANQ	Congo	Brazzaville	2–0	21,000
12 November 1995	F	Sierra Leone	Accra	2–0	–
14 December 1995	F	Egypt	Cairo	2–1	15,000
14 January 1995	ANQ	Ivory Coast	Port Elizabeth	2–0 (1)	8,000
5 January 1996	F	Saudi Arabia	Jeddah	1–1	20,000
9 January 1996	F	Zimbabwe	Harare	1–1	–
14 January 1996	ANF	Ivory Coast	Port Elizabeth	2–0 (1)	8,000
19 January 1996	ANF	Tunisia	Port Elizabeth	2–1	1,000
25 January 1996	ACF	Mozambique	Bloemfontein	2–0	3,500
28 January 1996	ACF	Zaire	Port Elizabeth	1–0 (1)	8,000
31 January 1996	ACF	South Africa	Johannesburg	0–3	80,000
27 March 1996	F	Brazil	Sao Joue de Rio Preto	2–8 (1)	20,000
6 January 1997	F	Togo	Lome	0–4	–
12 January 1997	WCQ	Morocco	Kumasi	2–2	45,000
26 January 1997	ANQ	Zimbabwe	Harare	0–0	45,000
5 April 1997	WCQ	Sierra Leone	Freetown	1–1	70,000

* This match was later annulled as Niger withdrew from the competition.

HOLLAND

Jimmy Floyd Hasselbaink (5 apps, 2gls)

27 May 1998	F	Cameroon	Arnhem	0–0	24,000
1 June 1998	F	Paraguay	Eindhoven	5–1 (1)	21,000
5 June 1998	F	Nigeria	Amsterdam	5–1 (1)	44,500
13 June 1998	WCF	Belgium	St Denis	0–0	75,000
25 June 1998	WCF	Mexico	St Etienne	2–2	35,000

HONDURAS

Ramon Nunez (5 + 7 apps, 2gls)

12 October 2010	F	Guatemala	Los Angeles	2–0	10,000
14 January 2011	CACQ	Costa Rica (sub)	Panama City	1–1 (1)	6,000
18 January 2011	CACQ	Guatemala	Panama City	3–1 (1)	500
23 January 2011	CACF	Costa Rica	Panama City	2–1	2,000
9 February 2011	F	Ecuador (sub)	La Ceiba	1–1	–
29 March 2011	F	China	Wuhan	0–3	–
29 May 2011	F	El Salvador	Houston	2–2	25,380
6 June 2011	CGC	Guatemala (sub)	Los Angeles	0–0	21,507
10 June 2011	CGC	Grenada (sub)	Miami	7–1	18,057

13 June 2011	CGC	Jamaica (sub)	New Jersey	0–1	25,000
18 June 2011	CGC	Costa Rica (sub)	New York	1–1 aet*	78,807
22 June 2011	CGC	Mexico (sub)	Houston	0–2 aet	70,627

* Honduras won 4–2 on penalties

ICELAND

Gylfi Einarsson (5 + 3 apps)

26 March 2005	WCQ	Croatia	Zagreb	0–4	17,912
30 March 2005	F	Italy	Padova	0–0	16,687
4 June 2005	WCQ	Hungary	Reykjavik	2–3	4,613
18 August 2005	F	South Africa (sub)	Reykjavik	4–1	3,302
3 September 2005	WCQ	Croatia	Reykjavik	1–3	5,520
7 October 2005	F	Poland	Warsaw	2–3	7,500
12 October 2005	WCQ	Sweden (sub)	Solna	1–3	33,000
28 February 2006	F	Trinidad & Tobago (sub)	Loftus Road	0–2	7,890

IVORY COAST

Max Gradel (1+1 apps)

5 June 2011	ANQ	Benin (sub)	Cotonou	6–2	–
10 August 2011	F	Israel	Geneva	4–3	–

NORTHERN IRELAND

Bobby Browne (6 apps)

19 October 1935	HC	England	Belfast	1–3	40,000
11 March 1936	HC	Wales	Belfast	3–2	20,000
23 October 1937	HC	England	Belfast	1–5	40,000
16 March 1938	HC	Wales	Belfast	1–0	15,000
8 October 1938	HC	Scotland	Belfast	0–2	40,000
16 November 1938	HC	England	Maine Road	0–7	40,386

David Cochrane (12 apps)

16 November 1938	HC	England	Maine Road	0–7	40,386
15 March 1939	HC	Wales	Wrexham	1–3	24,000
28 September 1946	HC	England	Belfast	2–7	57,000
27 November 1946	HC	Scotland	Hampden Park	0–0	98,776
16 April 1947	HC	Wales	Belfast	2–1	43,000
4 October 1947	HC	Scotland	Belfast	2–0	52,000
5 November 1947	HC	England	Goodison Park	2–2	68,000
10 March 1948	HC	Wales	Wrexham	0–2	33,160
17 November 1948	HC	Scotland	Hampden Park	2–3	100,000
9 March 1949	HC	Wales	Belfast	0–2	–
1 October 1949	HC	Scotland	Belfast	2–8	50,000
16 November 1949	HC	England	Maine Road	2–9	70,000

Wilbur Cush (15 apps, 5gls)

4 December 1957	F	Italy	Belfast	2–2 (2)	50,000
15 January 1958	WCQ	Italy	Belfast	2–1 (1)	60,000
16 April 1958	HC	Wales	Cardiff	1–1	38,000
8 June 1958	WCF	Czechoslovakia	Halmstad	1–0 (1)	10,647
11 June 1958	WCF	Argentina	Halmstad	1–3	14,174
15 June 1958	WCF	West Germany	Malmo	2–2	21,990

17 June 1958	WCF	Czechoslovakia	Malmo	2–1	6,196
19 June 1958	WCF	France	Norrkopping	0–4	11,800
4 October 1958	HC	England	Belfast	3–3 (1)	58,000
15 October 1958	F	Spain	Madrid	2–6	120,000
5 November 1958	HC	Scotland	Hampden Park	2–2	72,732
22 April 1959	HC	Wales	Belfast	4–1	35,000
3 October 1959	HC	Scotland	Belfast	0–4	56,000
18 November 1959	HC	England	Wembley	1–2	60,000
6 April 1960	HC	Wales	Wrexham	2–3	16,500
Harry Duggan (8 apps)					
19 October 1929	HC	England	Belfast	0–3	37,000
20 October 1930	HC	England	Bramall Lane	1–5	30,000
22 April 1931	HC	Wales	Wrexham	2–3	11,693
17 October 1932	HC	England	Blackpool	0–1	23,000
14 October 1933	HC	England	Belfast	0–3	35,000
20 October 1934	HC	Scotland	Belfast	2–1	39,752
27 March 1935	HC	Wales	Wrexham	1–3	17,000
13 November 1935	HC	Scotland	Tynecastle	1–2	30,000
David Healy (17 apps, 13gls)					
9 February 2005	F	Canada	Belfast	0–1	11,156
26 March 2005	WCQ	England	Old Trafford	0–4	65,239
30 March 2005	WCQ	Poland	Warsaw	0–1	25,000
4 June 2005	F	Germany	Belfast	1–4(1p)	14,000
17 August 2005	F	Malta	Valetta	1–1 (1)	1,850
3 September 2005	WCQ	Azerbajian	Belfast	2–0	11,909
7 September 2005	WCQ	England	Belfast	1–0 (1)	14,000
8 October 2005	WCQ	Wales	Belfast	2–3	14,000
12 October 2005	WCQ	Austria	Vienna	0–2	20,000
1 March 2006	F	Estonia	Belfast	1–0	14,000
16 August 2006	F	Finland	Helsinki	2–1 (1)	12,500
2 September 2006	ECQ	Iceland	Belfast	0–3	14,500
6 September 2006	ECQ	Spain	Belfast	3–2 (3)	14,500
7 October 2006	ECQ	Denmark	Copenhagen	0–0	41,482
11 October 2006	ECQ	Latvia	Belfast	1–0 (1)	14,500
24 March 2007	ECQ	Liechtenstein	Vaduz	4–1 (3)	4,340
28 March 2007	ECQ	Sweden	Belfast	2–1 (2)	14,500
Billy McAdams (1 app)					
9 May 1962	F	Holland	Rotterdam	0–4	30,000
Jim McCabe (6 apps)					
17 November 1948	HC	Scotland	Hampden Park	2–3	100,000
9 March 1949	HC	Wales	Belfast	0–2	–
16 November 1949	HC	England	Maine Road	2–9	70,000
7 March 1951	HC	Wales	Belfast	1–2	12,000
15 April 1953	HC	Wales	Belfast	2–3	45,000
3 October 1953	HC	Scotland	Belfast	2–0	58,248
John McClelland (1 app)					
27 March 1990	F	Norway	Belfast	2–3	3,500
Con Martin (3 apps)					
4 October 1947	HC	Scotland	Belfast	2–0	52,000

5 November 1947	HC	England	Goodison Park	2–2	68,000
10 March 1948	HC	Wales	Wrexham	0–2	33,160
Jim Twomey (2 apps)					
16 March 1938	HC	Wales	Belfast	1–0	15,000
16 November 1938	HC	England	Maine Road	0–7	40,386
Nigel Worthington (14 apps)					
7 September 1994	ECQ	Portugal	Belfast	1–2	6,000
12 October 1994	ECQ	Austria	Vienna	2–1	26,000
16 November 1994	ECQ	Republic of Ireland	Belfast	0–4	10,336
29 March 1995	ECQ	Republic of Ireland	Dublin	1–1	32,200
26 April 1995	ECQ	Latvia	Riga	1–0	1,560
22 May 1995	F	Canada	Edmondton	0–0	12,112
26 May 1995	F	Chile	Edmondton	1–2	6,124
7 June 1995	ECQ	Latvia	Belfast	1–2	6,000
3 September 1995	ECQ	Portugal	Porto	1–1	50,000
11 October 1995	ECQ	Liechtenstein	Eschen	4–0	1,100
15 November 1995	ECQ	Austria	Belfast	5–2	8,000
27 March 1996	F	Norway	Belfast	0–2	5,343
24 April 1996	F	Sweden	Belfast	1–2	5,666
29 May 1996	F	Germany	Belfast	1–1	11,770

NORWAY

Eirik Bakke (22 + 2 apps)					
23 February 1999	F	Turkey (sub)	Istanbul	2–0	7,000
27 February 2000	F	Slovakia	Oslo	2–0	16,518
3 June 2000	F	Italy	Oslo	1–0	25,248
13 June 2000	ECF	Spain	Rotterdam	1–0	50,000
18 June 2000	ECF	Yugoslavia	Liege	0–1	24,000
21 June 2000	ECF	Slovenia	Arnhem	0–0	22,000
7 October 2000	WCQ	Wales	Cardiff	1–1	55,000
11 October 2000	WCQ	Ukraine	Oslo	0–1	23,612
28 February 2001	F	Northern Ireland	Belfast	4–0	7,502
25 April 2001	F	Bulgaria	Oslo	2–1	6,211
2 June 2001	WCQ	Ukraine	Kiev	0–0	45,000
6 June 2001	WCQ	Belarus	Oslo	1–1	17,164
6 October 2001	WCQ	Armenia	Yerevan	4–1	12,000
17 April 2002	F	Sweden (sub)	Oslo	0–0	20.759
14 May 2002	F	Japan	Oslo	3–0	8,348
21 August 2002	F	Holland	Oslo	0–1	15,356
7 September 2002	ECQ	Denmark	Oslo	2–2	25,114
12 October 2002	ECQ	Romania	Bucharest	1–0	20,000
16 October 2002	ECQ	Bosnia-Herzegovina	Oslo	2–0	24,169
2 April 2003	ECQ	Luxembourg	Luxembourg	2–0	3,000
22 May 2003	F	Finland	Oslo	2–0	13,436
7 June 2003	ECQ	Denmark	Copenhagen	0–1	41,824
11 June 2003	ECQ	Romania	Oslo	1–1	24,890
Alf-Inge Haaland (7 + 3 apps)					
20 August 1997	WCQ	Finland (sub)	Helsinki	4–0	35,520
25 August 1997	F	France	Marseilles	3–3	55,000
10 September 1997	WCQ	Switzerland (sub)	Oslo	5–0	22,603

25 March 1998	F	Belgium (sub)	Brussels	2–2	13,371
27 May 1998	F	Saudi Arabia	Molde	6–0	13,114
10 October 1998	ECQ	Slovenia	Ljubljana	2–1	6,200
14 October 1998	ECQ	Albania	Oslo	2–2	17,770
18 November 1998	F	Egypt	Cairo	1–1	25,000
28 April 1998	ECQ	Georgia	Tbilisi	4–1	20,000
5 June 1998	ECQ	Albania	Tirana	2–1	6,211
Gunnar Halle (7 + 4 apps)					
30 April 1997	WCQ	Finland (sub)	Oslo	1–1	22,287
30 May 1997	F	Brazil (sub)	Oslo	4–2	21,799
20 July 1997	F	Iceland	Reykjavik	1–0	7,500
20 August 1997	WCQ	Finland	Helsinki	4–0	35,520
6 September 1997	WCQ	Azerbajdjan (sub)	Baku	1–0	10,000
10 September 1997	WCQ	Switzerland	Oslo	5–0	22,603
25 March 1998	F	Belgium	Brussels	2–2	13,371
20 May 1998	F	Mexico	Oslo	5–2	16,274
16 June 1998	WCF	Scotland	Bordeaux	1–1	30,236
27 March 1999	ECQ	Greece (sub)	Athens	2–0	50,000
20 May 1999	F	Jamaica	Oslo	6–0	9,630
Frank Strandli (2 apps, 1gl)					
15 January 1994	F	USA	Phoenix	1–0 (1)	20,000
20 April 1994	F	Portugal	Oslo	0–0	17,509

REPUBLIC OF IRELAND

Jeff Chandler (1 +1 apps)					
26 September 1979	F	Czechoslovakia (sub)	Prague	1–4	12,000
29 October 1979	F	USA	Dublin	3–2	17,000
Jonathan Douglas (2+ 3 apps)					
7 October 2006	ECQ	Cyprus (sub)	Nicosia	2–5	12,000
11 October 2006	ECQ	Czech Republic	Dublin	1–0	35,500
15 November 2006	ECQ	San Marino (sub)	Dublin	5–0	34,018
24 March 2007	ECQ	Wales	Dublin	1–0	72,539
8 September 2007	ECQ	Slovakia (sub)	Bratislava	2–2	12,360
Harry Duggan (4 apps)					
27 April 1927	F	Italy B	Dublin	1–2	20,000
11 May 1930	F	Belgium	Brussels	3–1	15,000
3 May 1936	F	Hungary	Budapest	3–3	20,000
9 May 1936	F	Luxembourg	Luxembourg	5–1	8,000
Peter Fitzgerald (3 apps, 2gls)					
28 September 1960	F	Wales	Dublin	2–3	20,000
6 November 1960	F	Norway	Dublin	3–1 (2)	26,000
7 May 1961	WCQ	Scotland	Dublin	0–3	36,000
Johnny Giles (32 apps, 2gls)					
23 September 1963	ECQ	Austria	Vienna	0–0	26,800
13 October 1963	ECQ	Austria	Dublin	3–2	40,000
11 March 1964	ECQ	Spain	Seville	1–5	27,200
8 April 1964	ECQ	Spain	Dublin	0–2	38,100
10 May 1964	F	Poland	Cracow	1–3	60,000
13 May 1964	F	Norway	Oslo	4–1 (1)	14,354

24 May 1964	F	England	Dublin	1–3	40,000
5 May 1965	WCQ	Spain	Dublin	1–0	40,772
27 October 1965	WCQ	Spain	Seville	1–4	29,452
10 November 1965	WCQ	Spain	Paris	0–1	35,731
22 May 1966	F	Austria	Vienna	0–1	33,000
25 May 1966	F	Belgium	Liege	3–2	3,000
23 October 1966	ECQ	Spain	Dublin	0–0	37,000
16 November 1966	ECQ	Turkey	Dublin	2–1	20,000
22 February 1967	ECQ	Turkey	Ankara	1–2	35,000
10 November 1968	F	Austria	Dublin	2–2	18,000
4 December 1968	WCQ	Denmark*	Dublin	1–1 (1p)	23,000
4 May 1969	WCQ	Czechoslovakia	Dublin	1–2	32,002
21 September 1969	F	Scotland	Dublin	1–1	27,000
6 May 1970	F	Poland	Poznan	1–2	35,000
9 May 1970	F	West Germany	Berlin	1–2	60,000
10 May 1971	ECQ	Italy	Dublin	1–2	25,000
15 November 1972	WCQ	France	Dublin	2–1	30,000
13 May 1973	WCQ	USSR	Moscow	0–1	70,000
5 May 1974	F	Brazil	Rio de Janiero	1–2	74,696
8 May 1974	F	Uruguay	Montevideo	0–2	40,000
12 May 1974	F	Chile	Santiago	2–1	16,000
30 October 1974	WCQ	USSR	Dublin	3–0	35,000
20 November 1974	ECQ	Turkey	Izmir	1–1	67,000
10 May 1975	ECQ	Switzerland	Dublin	2–1	50,000
18 May 1975	ECQ	USSR	Kiev	1–2	100,000
21 May 1975	ECQ	Switzerland	Berne	0–1	20,000

*Abandoned after 50 minutes because of fog. Caps were still awarded.

Ian Harte (48+8 apps, 9gls)

2 June 1996	F	Croatia (sub)	Dublin	2–2	29,100
4 June 1996	F	Holland	Rotterdam	1–3	15,002
9 June 1996	USC	Mexico	New Jersey	2–2	25,332
15 June 1996	USC	Bolivia	New Jersey	3–0 (1)	14,624
31 August 1996	WCQ	Liechtenstein	Eschen	5–0 (1)	4,000
9 October 1996	WCQ	Macedonia	Dublin	3–0	31,671
10 November 1996	WCQ	Iceland (sub)	Dublin	0–0	33,869
11 February 1997	F	Wales	Cardiff	0–0	7,000
2 April 1997	WCQ	Macedonia (sub)	Skopje	3–0	8,000
30 April 1997	WCQ	Romania	Bucharest	0–1	21,500
21 May 1997	WCQ	Liechtenstein	Dublin	5–0	28,575
20 August 1997	WCQ	Lithuania	Dublin	0–0	32,600
6 September 1997	WCQ	Iceland	Reykjavik	4–2	5,000
10 September 1997	WCQ	Lithuania	Vilnius	2–1	7,000
29 October 1997	WCQ	Belgium	Dublin	1–1	32,305
16 November 1997	WCQ	Belgium	Brussels	1–2	38,000
22 April 1998	F	Argentina	Dublin	0–2	38,000
23 May 1998	F	Mexico	Dublin	0–0	25,500
10 February 1999	F	Paraguay	Dublin	2–0 (1)	27,600
4 September 1999	ECQ	Croatia (sub)	Zagreb	0–1	25,000
8 September 1999	ECQ	Malta (sub)	Valletta	3–2	6,200
23 February 2000	F	Czech Republic	Dublin	3–2	30,543

2 September 2000	WCQ	Holland	Amsterdam	2–2	50,000
7 October 2000	WCQ	Portugal	Lisbon	1–1	65,000
11 October 2000	WCQ	Estonia	Dublin	2–0	34,562
15 November 2000	F	Finland	Dublin	3–0	22,368
24 March 2001	WCQ	Cyprus	Nicosia	4–0 (1)	13,000
28 March 2001	WCQ	Andorra	Barcelona	3–0 (1p)	5,000
25 Apr 2001	WCQ	Andorra	Dublin	3–1	30,000
2 June 2001	WCQ	Portugal	Dublin	1–1	34,000
6 June 2001	WCQ	Estonia	Tallin	2–0	9,000
15 August 2001	F	Croatia	Dublin	2–2	27,000
1 September 2001	WCQ	Holland	Dublin	1–0	49,000
6 October 2001	WCQ	Cyprus	Dublin	4–0 (1)	35,000
10 November 2001	WCQPO	Iran	Dublin	2–0 (1p)	35,000
15 November 2001	WCQPO	Iran	Teheran	0–1	110,000
13 February 2002	F	Russia	Dublin	2–0	44,000
27 March 2002	F	Denmark	Dublin	3–0 (1)	42,000
17 Apr 2002	F	United States	Dublin	2–1	39,000
16 May 2002	F	Nigeria	Dublin	1–2	42,652
1 June 2002	WCF	Cameroon	Niigata	1–1	33,679
5 June 2002	WCF	Germany	Ibaraki	1–1	35,854
11 June 2002	WCF	Saudi Arabia	Yokohama	3–0	65,320
16 June 2002	WCF	Spain	Suwon	1–1*	38,926
21 August 2002	F	Finland	Helsinki	3–0	12,225
7 September 2002	ECQ	Russia	Moscow	2–4	23,000
16 October 2002	ECQ	Switzerland	Dublin	1–2	40,000
12 February 2003	F	Scotland	Glasgow	2–0	33,337
20 April 2003	F	Norway	Dublin	1–0	32,643
19 August 2003	F	Australia (sub)	Dublin	2–1	37,200
6 September 2003	ECQ	Russia (sub)	Dublin	1–1	36,000
9 September 2003	F	Turkey	Dublin	2–2	27,000
11 October 2003	ECQ	Switzerland	Basle	0–2	31,006
18 November 2003	F	Canada (sub)	Dublin	3–0	23,253
31 March 2004	F	Czech Republic	Dublin	2–1 (1)	42,000
28 April 2004	F	Poland	Bydoszcz	0–0	18,000

*Spain won 3–2 on penalties

Robbie Keane (16 apps, 7gls)

24 March 2001+	WCQ	Cyprus	Nicosia	4–0	13,000
28 March 2001+	WCQ	Andorra	Barcelona	3–0	5,000
2 June 2001+	WCQ	Portugal	Dublin	1–1	34,000
15 August 2001	F	Croatia	Dublin	2–2	27,000
1 September 2001	WCQ	Holland	Dublin	1–0	49,000
10 November 2001	WCQPO	Iran	Dublin	2–0 (1)	35,000
15 November 2001	WCQPO	Iran	Teheran	0–1	110,000
13 February 2002	F	Russia	Dublin	2–0 (1)	44,000
27 March 2002	F	Denmark	Dublin	3–0 (1)	42,000
17 Apr 2002	F	United States	Dublin	2–1	39,000
16 May 2002	F	Nigeria	Dublin	1–2	42,652
1 June 2002	WCF	Cameroon	Niigata	1–1	33,679
5 June 2002	WCF	Germany	Ibaraki	1–1 (1)	35,854
11 June 2002	WCF	Saudi Arabia	Yokohama	3–0 (1)	65,320

16 June 2002	WCF	Spain	Suwon	1–1*(1p)	38,926
21 August 2002	F	Finland	Helsinki	3–0 (1)	12,225

+ On loan from Inter Milan
*Spain won 3–2 on penalties

Gary Kelly (43+8 apps, 2gls)

23 March 1994	F	Russia	Dublin	0–0	34,000
20 April 1994	F	Holland	Tilburg	1–0	30,000
24 May 1994	F	Bolivia (sub)	Dublin	1–0	32,500
29 May 1994	F	Germany (sub)	Hanover	2–0 (1)	50,000
5 June 1994	F	Czech Republic	Dublin	1–3	43,465
28 June 1994	WCF	Norway	New York	0–0	76,332
4 July 1994	WCF	Holland	Orlando	0–2	61,355
7 September 1994	ECQ	Latvia	Riga	3–0	2,200
12 October 1994	ECQ	Liechtenstein	Dublin	4–0	32,980
16 November 1994	ECQ	Northern Ireland	Belfast	4–0	10,336
29 March 1995	ECQ	Northern Ireland	Dublin	1–1	32,500
26 April 1995	ECQ	Portugal	Dublin	1–0	33,000
3 June 1995	ECQ	Liechtenstein	Eschen	0–0	4,500
11 June 1995	ECQ	Austria	Dublin	1–3	33,000
6 September 1995	ECQ	Austria	Vienna	1–3	24,000
11 October 1995	ECQ	Latvia	Dublin	2–1	33,000
15 November 1995	ECQ	Portugal	Lisbon	0–3	80,000
13 December 1995	ECQ	Holland	Anfield	0–2	40,000
19 February 1997	F	Wales (sub)	Cardiff	0–0	7,000
30 April 1997	WCQ	Romania	Bucharest	0–1	21,500
21 May 1997	WCQ	Liechtenstein	Dublin	5–0	28,575
6 September 1997	WCQ	Iceland	Reykjavik	4–2	5,500
10 September 1997	WCQ	Lithuania	Vilnius	2–1	7,000
29 October 1997	WCQPO	Belgium	Dublin	1–1	32,305
15 November 1997	WCQPO	Belgium	Brussels	1–2	38,000
25 March 1998	F	Czech Republic	Olomouc	1–2	9,405
22 April 1998	F	Argentina	Dublin	0–2	38,500
23 May 1998	F	Mexico	Dublin	0–0	8,500
4 September 1999	ECQ	Croatia	Zagreb	0–1	25,000
9 October 1999	ECQ	Macedonia	Skopje	1–1	4,500
23 February 2000	F	Czech Republic	Dublin	3–2	30,543
2 September 2000	WCQ	Holland (sub)	Amsterdam	2–2	50,000
15 November 2000	F	Finland	Dublin	3–0	22,368
24 March 2001	WCQ	Cyprus	Nicosia	4–0 (1)	13,000
28 March 2001	WCQ	Andorra	Barcelona	3–0	5,000
25 April 2001	WCQ	Andorra	Dublin	3–1	34,000
2 June 2001	WCQ	Portugal	Dublin	1–1	34,000
6 June 2001	WCQ	Estonia	Tallin	2–0	9.000
15 August 2001	F	Croatia	Dublin	2–2	27,000
1 September 2001	WCQ	Holland	Dublin	1–0	49,000
10 November 2001	WCQP	Iran (sub)	Dubin	2–0	35,000
15 November 2001	WCQP	Iran (sub)	Tehran	0–1	110,000
13 February 2002	F	Russia	Dublin	2–0	44,000
27 March 2002	F	Denmark	Dublin	3–0	42,000
17 April 2002	F	USA (sub)	Dublin	2–1	39,000

16 May 2002	F	Nigeria (sub)	Dublin	1–2	42,652
1 June 2002	WCF	Cameroon	Niigata	1–1	33,679
5 June 2002	WCF	Germany	Ibaraki	1–1	35,854
11 June 2002	WCF	Saudi Arabia	Yokohama	3–0	65,320
16 June 2002	WCF	Spain	Suwon	1–1 (aet)*	38,926
21 August 2002	F	Finland	Helsinki	3–0	12,225
16 October 2002	ECQ	Switzerland	Dublin	1–2	40,000

*Spain won 3–2 on penalties

Stephen McPhail (5+5 apps, 1gl)

30 May 2000	F	Scotland	Dublin	1–2	30,213
6 June 2000	NC	USA	Boston	1–1	16,319
11 June 2000	NC	South Africa	New Jersey	2–1 (1)	45,008
15 August 2001	F	Croatia (sub)	Dublin	2–2	27,000
6 October 2001	WCQ	Cyprus (sub)	Dublin	4–0	35,000
21 August 2002	F	Finland (sub)	Helsinki	3–0	12,225
20 November 2002	F	Greece	Athens	0–0	5,500
9 September 2003	F	Turkey (sub)	Dublin	2–2	27,000
18 November 2003	F	Canada (sub)	Dublin	3–0	23,253
29 May 2004	F	Nigeria	Charlton, London	0–3	7,438

Con Martin (3 apps)

2 March 1947	F	Spain	Dublin	3–2	42,102
23 May 1948	F	Portugal	Lisbon	0–2	50,000
30 May 1948	F	Spain	Barcelona	1–2	65,000

Alan Maybury (2 apps)

25 March 1998	F	Czech Republic	Olomouc	1–2	9,405
29 May 1999	F	Northern Ireland	Dublin	0–1	12,100

Liam Miller (0+1 app, 1gl)

1 March 2006	F	Sweden (sub)	Dublin	3–0 (1)	34,000

On loan from Manchester United

Darren O'Dea (2+1 apps)

10 August 2011	F	Croatia (sub)	Dublin	0–0	20,179
6 September 2011	ECQ	Russia	Moscow	0–0	48,717
7 October 2011	ECQ	Andorra	Aixovall	2–0	500
29 February 2012	F	Czech Republic	Dublin	1–1	37,741

On loan from Celtic

Noel Peyton (5 apps)

11 May 1960	F	West Germany	Dusseldorf	1–0	51,000
18 May 1960	F	Sweden	Malmo	1–4	31,339
28 September 1960	F	Wales	Dublin	2–3	20,000
2 September 1962	ECQ	Iceland	Reykjavik	1–1	9,100
9 June 1963	F	Scotland	Dublin	1–0	26,000

John Sheridan (4+1 apps, 1gl)

23 March 1988	F	Romania	Dublin	2–0	15,000
27 April 1988	F	Yugoslavia	Dublin	2–0	12,000
22 May 1988	F	Poland	Dublin	3–1 (1)	18,500
1 June 1988	F	Norway (sub)	Oslo	0–0	9,494
16 November 1988	WCQ	Spain	Seville	0–2	50,000

SCOTLAND

Barry Bannan (1+2 apps)

27 March 2011	F	Brazil (sub)	Emirates Stadium	0–2	53,087
25 May 2011	CNC	Wales (sub)	Dublin	3–1	6,036
29 May 2011	CNC	Republic of Ireland	Dublin	0–1	17,694

On loan from Aston Villa

Willie Bell (2 apps)

18 June 1966	F	Portugal	Hampden Park	0–1	24,000
25 June 1966	F	Brazil	Hampden Park	1–1	74,933

Billy Bremner (53+1 apps, 3gls)

8 May 1965	F	Spain	Hampden Park	0–0	60,146
13 October 1965	WCQ	Poland	Hampden Park	1–2	107,580
9 November 1965	WCQ	Italy	Hampden Park	1–0	100,393
7 December 1965	WCQ	Italy	Naples	0–3	79,000
2 April 1966	ENQ	England	Hampden Park	3–4	134,000
18 June 1966	F	Portugal	Hampden Park	0–1	24,000
25 June 1966	F	Brazil	Hampden Park	1–1	74,933
22 October 1966	ECQ	Wales	Cardiff	1–1	32,500
16 November 1966	HC	Northern Ireland	Hampden Park	2–1	45,281
15 April 1967	ECQ	England	Wembley	3–2	99,063
22 November 1967	HC	Wales	Hampden Park	3–2	57,472
24 February 1968	ECQ	England	Hampden Park	1–1	134,000
16 October 1968	F	Denmark	Copenhagen	1–0	12,000
6 Nov1968	WCQ	Austria	Hampden Park	2–1 (1)	80,856
11 Dec1968	WCQ	Cyprus	Nicosia	5–0	10,000
16 April 1969	WCQ	West Germany	Hampden Park	1–1	115,000
3 May 1969	HC	Wales	Wrexham	5–3 (1)	18,765
6 May 1969	HC	Northern Ireland	Hampden Park	1–1	7,483
10 May 1969	HC	England	Wembley	1–4	89,902
17 May 1969	WCQ	Cyprus	Hampden Park	8–0	39,095
21 September 1969	F	Republic of Ireland	Dublin	1–1	30,000
22 October 1969	WCQ	West Germany	Hamburg	2–3	72,000
5 Nov1970	WCQ	Austria	Vienna	0–2	11,000
15 May 1971	HC	Wales	Cardiff	0–0	19,068
22 May 1971	HC	England	Wembley	1–3	91,469
13 October 1971	ECQ	Portugal	Hampden Park	2–1	58,612
10 Nov1971	ECQ	Belgium	Aberdeen	1–0	36,500
1 December 1971	F	Holland	Amsterdam	1–2	18,000
20 May 1972	HC	Northern Ireland	Hampden Park	2–0	39,710
24 May 1972	HC	Wales	Hampden Park	1–0	21,332
27 May 1972	HC	England	Hampden Park	0–1	119,325
29 June 1972	IC	Yugoslavia	Belo Horizonte	2–2	4,000
2 July 1972	IC	Portugal	Porto Alegre	0–0	15,000
5 July 1972	IC	Brazil	Rio de Janeiro	0–1	130,000
18 October 1972	WCQ	Denmark	Copenhagen	4–1	31,000
15 November 1972	WCQ	Denmark	Hampden Park	2–0	47,109
14 February 1973	F	England	Hampden Park	0–5	48,470
16 May 1973	HC	Northern Ireland (sub)	Hampden Park	1–2	39,018
19 May 1973	HC	England	Wembley	0–1	95,950
22 June 1973	F	Switzerland	Berne	0–1	10,000

One of Billy Bremner's Scotland shirts in the Elland Road reception area.

30 June 1973	F	Brazil	Hampden Park	0–1	70,000
26 September 1973	WCQ	Czechoslovakia	Hampden Park	2–1	100,000
14 November 1973	F	West Germany	Hampden Park	1–1	58,235
11 May 1974	HC	Northern Ireland	Hampden Park	0–1	53,775
14 May 1974	HC	Wales	Hampden Park	2–0	41,969
18 May 1974	HC	England	Hampden Park	2–0	94,487
1 June 1974	F	Belgium	Bruges	1–2	12,000
6 June 1974	F	Norway	Oslo	2–1	18,432
14 June 1974	WCF	Zaire	Dortmund	2–0	30,000
18 June 1974	WCF	Brazil	Frankfurt	0–0	62,000
22 June 1974	WCF	Yugoslavia	Frankfurt	1–1	56,000
20 November 1974	ECQ	Spain	Hampden Park	1–2 (1)	92,100
5 February 1975	ECQ	Spain	Valencia	1–1	60,000
3 September 1975	ECQ	Denmark	Copenhagen	1–0	40,300

Stephen Caldwell (1+1 apps)					
18 February 2004	F	Wales	Cardiff	0–4	47,124
30 May 2004	F	Trinidad & Tobago (sub)	Edinburgh	4–1	16,187
On loan from Sunderland					
Bobby Collins (3 apps)					
10 April 1965	HC	England	Wembley	2–2	98,199
8 May 1965	F	Spain	Hampden Park	0–0	60,146
23 May 1965	WCQ	Poland	Chorzow	1–1	95,000
Arthur Graham (8+2 apps, 2gls)					
7 September 1977	F	East Germany (sub)	Berlin	0–1	50,000
20 September 1978	ECQ	Austria (as sub)	Vienna	2–3	71,500
25 October 1978	ECQ	Norway	Hampden Park	3–2	65,372
19 May 1979	HC	Wales	Cardiff	0–3	20,371
22 May 1979	HC	Northern Ireland	Hampden Park	1–0 (1)	28,524
26 May 1979	HC	England	Wembley	1–3	100,000
2 June 1979	F	Argentina	Hampden Park	1–3 (1)	61,918
7 June 1979	ECQ	Norway	Oslo	4–0	17,269
17 October 1979	ECQ	Austria	Hampden Park	1–1	72,700
16 May 1981	HC	Wales	Swansea	0–2	18,935
Eddie Gray (12 apps, 3gls)					
10 May 1969	HC	England	Wembley	1–4	89,902
17 May 1969	WCQ	Cyprus	Hampden Park	8–0 (1)	39,095
22 October 1969	WCQ	West Germany	Hamburg	2–3	72,000
5 November 1969	WCQ	Austria	Vienna	0–2	11,000
15 May 1971	HC	Wales	Cardiff	0–0	19,068
18 May 1971	HC	Northern Ireland	Hampden Park	0–1	31,643
10 November 1971	ECQ	Belgium	Aberdeen	1–0	36,500
1 December 1971	F	Holland	Amsterdam	1–2	18,000
6 May 1976	HC	Wales	Hampden Park	3–1 (1)	25,000
15 May 1976	HC	England	Hampden Park	2–1	85,165
8 September 1976	F	Finland	Hampden Park	6–0 (1)	16,338
17 November 1976	WCQ	Wales	Hampden Park	1–0	63,233
Frank Gray (17+1 apps, 1 gl)					
7 April 1976	F	Switzerland	Hampden Park	1–0	15,531
25 October 1978	ECQ	Norway	Hampden Park	3–2	65,372
29 November 1978	ECQ	Portugal	Lisbon	0–1	70,000
19 May 1979	HC	Wales	Cardiff	0–3	20,371
22 May 1979	HC	Northern Ireland	Hampden Park	1–0	28,524
26 May 1979	HC	England	Wembley	1–3	100,000
2 June 1979	F	Argentina (sub)	Hampden Park	1–3	61,918
19 May 1981	HC	Northern Ireland	Hampden Park	2–0	22,448
23 May 1981	HC	England	Wembley	1–0	90,000
9 September 1981	WCQ	Sweden	Hampden Park	2–0	81,511
18 November 1981	WCQ	Portugal	Lisbon	1–2	25,000
24 February 1982	F	Spain	Valencia	0–3	30,000
23 March 1982	F	Holland	Hampden Park	2–1 (1)	71,000
24 May 1982	HC	Wales	Hampden Park	1–0	25,284
15 June 1982	WCF	New Zealand	Malaga	5–2	20,000
18 June 1982	WCF	Brazil	Seville	1–4	47,379
22 June 1982	WCF	USSR	Malaga	2–2	45,000

13 October 1982	ECQ	East Germany	Hampden Park	2–0	40,355
17 November 1982	ECQ	Switzerland	Berne	0–2	26,000
15 December 1982	ECQ	Belgium	Brussels	2–3	48,877
30 March 1983	ECQ	Switzerland	Hampden Park	2–2	36,923
28 May 1984	HC	Wales	Cardiff	2–0	14,100
1 June 1983	HC	England	Wembley	0–2	84,000
12 June 1983	F	Canada	Vancouver	2–0	15,000
David Harvey (16 apps)					
15 November 1972	WCQ	Denmark	Hampden Park	2–0	47,109
26 September 1972	WCQ	Czechoslovakia	Bratislava	0–1	15,500
14 November 1973	F	West Germany	Hampden Park	1–1	58,235
11 May 1974	HC	Northern Ireland	Hampden Park	0–1	53,775
14 May 1974	HC	Wales	Hampden Park	2–0	41,969
18 May 1974	HC	England	Hampden Park	2–0	94,487
1 June 1974	F	Belgium	Bruges	1–2	12,000
14 June 1974	WCF	Zaire	Dortmund	2–0	30,000
18 June 1974	WCF	Brazil	Frankfurt	0–0	62,000
22 June 1974	WCF	Yugoslavia	Frankfurt	1–1	56,000
30 October 1974	F	East Germany	Hampden Park	3–0	39,445
20 November 1974	ECQ	Spain	Hampden Park	1–2	92,100
5 February 1975	ECQ	Spain	Valencia	1–1	60,000
3 September 1975	ECQ	Denmark	Copenhagen	1–0	40,300
29 October 1975	ECQ	Denmark	Hampden Park	3–1	48,021
8 September 1976	F	Finland	Hampden Park	6–0	16,338
David Hopkin (4+1 apps, 2gls)					
7 September 1997	WCQ	Belarus	Aberdeen	4–1 (2)	12,000
12 November 1997	F	France (sub)	St Etienne	1–2	19,514
31 March 1999	ECQ	Czech Republic	Glasgow	1–2	44,513
4 September 1999	ECQ	Bosnia	Sarajevo	1–2	26,000
5 October 1999	ECQ	Bosnia	Glasgow	1–0	30,574
Joe Jordan (23+4 apps, 5gls)					
19 May 1973	EC	England (sub)	Wembley	0–1	95,950
22 May 1973	F	Switzerland	Berne	0–1	10,000
30 June 1973	F	Brazil	Hampden Park	0–1	70,000
26 September 1973	WCQ	Czechoslovakia (sub)	Hampden Park	2–1 (1)	100,000
17 October 1973	WCQ	Czechoslovakia	Bratislava	0–1	15,000
14 November 1973	F	West Germany (sub)	Hampden Park	1–1	58,235
11 May 1974	HC	Northern Ireland (sub)	Hampden Park	0–1	53,775
14 May 1974	HC	Wales	Hampden Park	2–0	41,969
18 May 1974	HC	England	Hampden Park	2–0 (1)	94,487
1 June 1974	F	Belgium	Bruges	1–2	12,000
6 June 1974	F	Norway	Oslo	2–1	18,432
14 June 1974	WCF	Zaire	Dortmund	2–0 (1)	30,000
18 June 1974	WCF	Brazil	Frankfurt	0–0	62,000
22 June 1974	WCF	Yugoslavia	Frankfurt	1–1 (1)	56,000
30 October 1974	F	East Germany	Hampden Park	3–0	39,445
20 November 1974	ECQ	Spain	Hampden Park	1–2	92,100
5 February 1975	ECQ	Spain	Valencia	1–1 (1)	60,000
6 May 1976	HC	Wales	Hampden Park	3–1	25,000
8 May 1976	HC	Northern Ireland	Hampden Park	3–0	49,897

15 May 1976	HC	England	Hampden Park	2–1	85,165
13 October 1976	WCQ	Czechoslovakia	Prague	0–2	38,000
17 November 1976	WCQ	Wales	Hampden Park	1–0	63,233
1 June 1977	HC	Northern Ireland	Hampden Park	3–0	44,699
4 June 1977	HC	England	Wembley	2–1	98,108
7 September 1977	F	East Germany	Berlin	0–1	50,000
21 September 1977	WCQ	Czechoslovakia	Hampden Park	3–1	85,000
12 October 1977	WCQ	Wales	Anfield	2–0	50,800
Peter Lorimer (17+4 apps, 4gls)					
5 November 1969	WCQ	Austria (sub)	Vienna	0–2	11,000
15 May 1971	HC	Wales	Cardiff	0–0	19,068
18 May 1971	HC	Northern Ireland	Hampden Park	0–1	31,643
20 May 1972	HC	Northern Ireland (sub)	Hampden Park	2–0 (1)	39,710
24 May 1972	HC	Wales	Hampden Park	1–0 (1)	21,332
27 May 1972	HC	England	Hampden Park	0–1	119,325
18 October 1972	WCQ	Denmark	Copenhagen	4–1	31,000
15 November 1972	WCQ	Denmark	Hampden Park	2–0 (1)	47,109
14 February 1973	F	England	Hampden Park	0–5	48,470
19 May 1973	HC	England	Wembley	0–1	95,950
14 November 1973	F	West Germany (sub)	Hampden Park	1–1	58,235
18 May 1974	HC	England	Hampden Park	2–0	94,487
1 June 1974	F	Belgium	Bruges	1–2	12,000
6 June 1974	F	Norway	Oslo	2–1	18,432
14 June 1974	WCF	Zaire	Dortmund	2–0 (1)	30,000
18 June 1974	WCF	Brazil	Frankfurt	0–0	62,000
22 June 1974	WCF	Yugoslavia	Frankfurt	1–1	56,000
20 November 1974	ECQ	Spain (sub)	Hampden Park	1–2	92,100
3 September 1975	ECQ	Denmark	Copenhagen	1–0	40,300
29 October 1975	ECQ	Denmark	Hampden Park	3–1	48,021
17 December 1975	ECQ	Romania	Hampden Park	1–1	11,375
Dominic Matteo (6 apps)					
15 November 2000	F	Australia	Hampden Park	0–2	30,985
24 March 2001	WCQ	Belgium	Hampden Park	2–2	37,480
28 March 2001	WCQ	San Marino	Hampden Park	4–0	27,313
1 September 2001	WCQ	Croatia	Hampden Park	0–0	47,384
5 September 2001	WCQ	Belgium	Brussels	0–2	48,500
27 March 2002	F	France	Paris	0–4	80,000
Gary McAllister (37+4 apps, 4gls)					
12 September 1990	ECQ	Romania	Hampden Park	2–1	12,081
17 October 1990	ECQ	Switzerland	Hampden Park	2–1 (1)	20,740
14 November 1990	ECQ	Bulgaria	Sofia	1–1	40,000
6 February 1991	F	USSR (sub)	Hampden Park	0–1	20,763
1 May 1991	ECQ	San Marino	Serravalle	2–0	3,412
11 September 1991	ECQ	Switzerland (sub)	Berne	2–2	48,000
13 November 1991	ECQ	San Marino	Hampden Park	4–0	35,170
19 February 1992	F	Northern Ireland	Hampden Park	1–0	13,650
25 March 1992	F	Finland (sub)	Hampden Park	1–1	9,275
17 May 1992	F	USA	Denver	1–0	24,157
21 May 1992	F	Canada	Toronto	3–1 (2,1p)	10,872
3 June 1992	F	Norway	Oslo	0–0	8,786

12 June 1992	ECF	Holland	Gothenburg	0–1	35,720
15 June 1992	ECF	Germany	Norrkoping	0–2	17,638
18 June 1992	ECF	CIS	Norrkopping	3–0 (1p)	14,660
9 September 1992	WCQ	Switzerland	Berne	1–3	10,000
14 October 1992	WCQ	Portugal	Ibrox Park	0–0	22,583
18 Nov1992	WCQ	Italy	Ibrox Park	0–0	33,029
17 February 1993	WCQ	Malta	Ibrox Park	3–0	35,490
8 September 1993	WCQ	Switzerland	Aberdeen	1–1	24,000
13 October 1993	WCQ	Italy	Rome	1–3	61,178
17 November 1993	WCQ	Malta	TaQ'uali	2–0	8,000
23 March 1994	F	Holland	Hampden Park	0–1	36,809
20 April 1994	F	Austria	Vienna	2–1	35,000
27 May 1994	F	Holland	Utrecht	1–3	17,500
7 September 1994	ECQ	Finland	Helsinki	2–0	12,845
16 November 1994	ECQ	Russia	Hampden Park	1–1	31,254
18 December 1994	ECQ	Greece	Athens	0–1	20,310
29 March 1995	ECQ	Russia	Moscow	0–0	25,000
26 April 1995	ECQ	San Marino	Serraville	2–0	2,738
16 August 1995	ECQ	Greece	Hampden Park	1–0	34,910
6 September 1995	ECQ	Finland	Hampden Park	1–0	35,505
11 October 1995	F	Sweden	Stockholm	0–2	19,121
15 November 1995	ECQ	San Marino	Hampden Park	5–0	30,306
27 March 1996	F	Australia	Hampden Park	1–0	20,608
24 April 1996	F	Denmark	Copenhagen	0–2	23,031
26 May 1996	F	USA (sub)	New Britain	1–2	8,526
30 May 1996	F	Colombia	Miami	0–1	5,000
10 June 1996	ECF	Holland	Villa Park	0–0	34,363
15 June 1996	ECF	England	Wembley	0–2	76,864
18 June 1996	ECF	Switzerland	Holland	1–0	34,926
Ross McCormack (1+1 apps)					
25 May 2011	CNC	Wales	Dublin	3–1	6,036
29 May 2011	CNC	Republic of Ireland (sub)	Dublin	0–1	17,694
Gordon McQueen (17 apps, 3gls)					
1 June 1974	F	Belgium	Bruges	1–2	12,000
20 November 1974	ECQ	Spain	Hampden Park	3–0	39,445
5 February 1975	ENQ	Spain	Valencia	1–1	60,000
13 May 1975	F	Portugal	Hampden Park	1–0	34,307
17 May 1975	HC	Wales	Cardiff	2–2	23,509
20 May 1975	HC	Northern Ireland	Hampden Park	3–0	64,696
24 May 1975	HC	England	Wembley	1–5	98,241
1 June 1975	ENQ	Romania	Bucharest	1–1 (1)	80,000
3 September 1975	ENQ	Denmark	Copenhagen	1–0	40,300
13 October 1976	WCQ	Czechoslovakia	Prague	0–2	38,000
17 November 1976	WCQ	Wales	Hampden Park	1–0	62,233
28 May 1977	HC	Wales	Wrexham	0–0	14,468
1 June 1977	HC	Northern Ireland	Hampden Park	3–0 (1)	44,699
4 June 1977	HC	England	Wembley	2–1 (1)	98,103
7 September 1977	F	East Germany	Berlin	0–1	50,000
21 September 1977	WCQ	Czechoslovakia	Hampden Park	3–1	85,000
12 October 1977	WCQ	Wales	Anfield	2–0	50,800

Robert Snodgrass, right, celebrates his first goal for Scotland against Denmark in 2011.

Robert Snodgrass (2+3 apps, 1gl)

9 February 2011	CNC	Northern Ireland (sub)	Dublin	3–0	18,747
27 March 2011	F	Brazil (sub)	Emirates Stadium	0–2	53,087
10 August 2011	F	Denmark	Hampden Park	2–1 (1)	17,582
6 September 2011	ECQ	Lithuania	Hampden Park	1–0	34,071
29 February 2012	F	Slovenia (sub)	Koper	1–1	4,190

David Stewart (1 app)

7 September 1977	F	East Germany	Berlin	0–1	50,000

Gordon Strachan (8 apps, 1gl)

11 October 1989	WCQ	France	Paris	0–3	25,000
6 February 1991	F	USSR	Hampden Park	0–1	20,763
27 March 1991	ECQ	Bulgaria	Hampden Park	1–1	33,119
1 May 1991	ECQ	San Marino	Serravalle	2–0 (1p)	3,512
11 September 1991	ECQ	Switzerland	Berne	2–2	48,000
16 October 1991	ECQ	Romania	Bucharest	0–1	30,000
19 February 1992	F	Northern Ireland	Hampden Park	1–0	13,650
25 March 1992	F	Finland	Hampden Park	1–1	9,275

SENEGAL

Lamine Sakho (1+1 apps)

2 February 2004	ANF	Mali (sub)	Tunis	1–1	7,500
7 February 2004	ANF	Tunisia	Rades	0–1	57,000

On loan from Marseille

SLOVAKIA

Lubomir Michalik (0+1 app)

28 March 2007*	ECQ	Republic of Ireland (sub)	Dublin	0–1	71,297

On loan from Bolton Wanderers

SOUTH AFRICA

Phil Masinga (12 apps, 4gls)

4 September 1994	ANQ	Madagascar	Antananario	1–0 (1)	35,000
15 October 1994	ANQ	Mauritius	Mabopane	1–0 (1)	20,000
13 November 1994	ANQ	Zambia	Lusaka	1–1	40,000
13 May 1995	F	Argentina	Johannesburg	1–1	45,000
15 December 1995	F	Germany	Johannesburg	0–0	27,500
13 January 1996	ANF	Cameroon	Johannesburg	3–0 (1)	80,000
20 January 1996	ANF	Angola	Johannesburg	1–0	60,000
24 January 1996	ANF	Egypt	Johannesburg	0–1	40,000
27 January 1996	ANF	Algeria	Johannesburg	2–1	30,000
4 February 1996	ANF	Tunisia	Johannesburg	2–0	80,000
24 April 1996	F	Brazil	Johannesburg	2–3 (1)	80,000
1 June 1996	WCQ	Malawi	Blantyre	1–0	55,000

Lucas Radebe (58 apps, 2gls)

4 September 1994	ANQ	Madagascar	Antananario	1–0	35,000
15 October 1994	ANQ	Mauritius	Mabopane	1–0	20,000
13 November 1994	ANQ	Zambia	Lusaka	1–1	40,000
20 January 1996	ANF	Angola	Johannesburg	1–0	60,000
24 January 1996	ANF	Egypt	Johannesburg	0–1	40,000
27 January 1996	ANF	Algeria	Johannesburg	2–1	30,000
21 January 1996	ANF	Ghana	Johannesburg	3–0	70,000
3 February 1996	ANF	Tunisia	Johannesburg	2–0	80,000
24 April 1996	F	Brazil	Johannesburg	2–3	80,000
1 June 1996	WCQ	Malawi	Blantyre	1–0	55,000
15 June 1996	WCQ	Malawi	Johannesburg	3–0	30,000
9 November 1996	WCQ	Zaire	Johannesburg	1–0	55,000
11 January 1997	WCQ	Zambia	Lusaka	0–0	27,500
6 April 1997	WCQ	Congo	Pointe Noire	0–2	10,000
27 April 1997	WCQ	Zaire	Lome	2–1	7,000
24 May 1997	F	England	Manchester	1–2	52,676
4 June 1997	F	Holland	Johannesburg	0–2	35,000
8 June 1997	WCQ	Zambia	Johannesburg	3–0	73,000
16 August 1997	WCQ	Congo	Johannesburg	1–0	95,000
11 October 1997	F	France	Lens	1–2	29,677
17 November 1997	F	Germany	Dusseldorf	0–3	27,000
7 December 1997	F	Brazil	Johannesburg	1–2	40,000
17 December 1997	CC	Uruguay	Riyadh	3–4 (1)	15,000
8 February 1998	ANF	Angola	Bobo–Dioulasso	0–0	20,000
11 February 1998	ANF	Ivory Coast	Bobo–Dioulasso	1–1	10.000
16 February 1998	ANF	Namibia	Bobo–Dioulasso	4–1	500
22 February 1998	ANF	Morocco	Ouagadougou	2–1	20,000
25 February 1998	ANF	DR Congo	Ouagadougou	2–1	40,000
28 February 1998	ANF	Egypt	Ouagadougou	0–2	40,000
20 May 1998	F	Zambia	Johannesburg	1–1	25,000
25 May 1998	F	Argentina	Buenos Aires	0–2	40,000

6 June 1998	F	Iceland	Baiersbroon, Germany	1–1	1,500
12 June 1998	WCF	France	Marseilles	0–3	55,000
18 June 1998	WCF	Denmark	Toulouse	1–1	33,500
24 June 1998	WCF	Saudi Arabia	Bordeaux	2–2	31,800
3 October 1998	ANQ	Angola	Johannesburg	1–0	20,000
23 January 1999	ANQ	Mauritius	Curepipe	1–1	2,385
27 February 1999	ANQ	Gabon	Pretoria	4–1	50,000
10 April 1999	ANQ	Gabon	Libreville	0–1	40,000
28 April 1999	F	Denmark	Copenhagen	1–1	17,592
5 June 1999	ANQ	Mauritius	Durban	2–0	40,000
16 June 1999	F	Zimbabwe	Johannesburg	0–1	40,000
27 November 1999	F	Sweden	Pretoria	1–0	28,000
23 January 2000	ANF	Gabon	Kumasi, Ghana	3–1	20,000
27 January 2000	ANF	DR Congo	Kumasi, Ghana	1–0	3,500
2 February 2000	ANF	Algeria	Kumasi, Ghana	1–1	2,000
6 February 2000	ANF	Ghana	Kumasi, Ghana	0–1	50,000
10 February 2000	ANF	Nigeria	Lagos, Ghana	0–2	40,000
12 February 2000	ANF	Tunisia	Accra, Ghana	2–2*	3,000
13 January 2001	ANQ	Liberia	Johannesburg	2–1	10,000
27 January 2001	WCQ	Burkino Faso	Rustenburg	1–0	25,000
12 May 2002	F	Madagascar	Durban	1–0	35,000
20 May 2002	RC	Scotland	Hong Kong	2–0	5,000
22 May 2002	RC	Turkey	Hong Kong	2–0	10,000
2 June 2002	WCF	Paraguay	Busan, Korea	2–2	25,000
8 June 2002	WCF	Slovenia	Daegu, Korea	1–0	47,000
12 June 2002	WCF	Spain	Daejeon, Korea	2–3 (1)	31,000
22 May 2003	F	England	Durban	1–2	48,000

* After extra-time, South Africa won 4–3 on penalties

Davide Somma (2+1 apps, 1gl)

17 November 2010	NMC	USA	Cape Town	0–1	52,000
8 February 2011	F	Kenya	Rustenburg	2–0 (1)	22,500
5 June 2011	ANCQ	Egypt (sub)	Cairo	0–0	–

SPAIN

Raul Bravo (1 app)

2 April 2003	ECQ	Armenia	Amilivia	3–0	13,500

On loan from Real Madrid

SWEDEN

Teddy Lucic (3 apps)

20 November 2002	F	Czech Republic	Teplice	3–3	10,238
2 April 2003	ECQ	Hungary	Budapest	2–1	28,000
30 April 2003	F	Croatia	Stockholm	1–2	15,109

On loan from AIK Solna

WALES

Mark Aizlewood (6+3 apps)

18 February 1987	F	USSR	Swansea	0–0	17,617
1 April 1987	ECQ	Finland (sub)	Wrexham	4–0	7,696
9 September 1987	ECQ	Denmark (sub)	Cardiff	1–0	20,535
27 April 1988	F	Sweden	Stockholm	1–4	11,656
1 June 1988	F	Malta	Valletta	3–2	7,000

4 June 1988	F	Italy	Brescia	1–0	21,000
14 September 1988	WCQ	Holland	Amsterdam	0–1	58,000
26 April 1989	F	Sweden (sub)	Wrexham	0–2	8,000
31 May 1989	WCQ	West Germany	Cardiff	0–0	25,000
John Charles (24 apps, 12gls)					
8 March 1950	HC	Northern Ireland	Wrexham	0–0	33,000
16 May 1951	F	Switzerland	Wrexham	3–2	28,000
15 April 1953	HC	Northern Ireland	Belfast	3–2 (2)	45,000
14 May 1953	F	France	Paris	1–6	33,020
21 May 1953	F	Yugoslavia	Belgrade	2–5	55,000
10 October 1953	HC	England	Cardiff	1–4	61,000
4 November 1953	HC	Scotland	Hampden Park	3–3 (2)	71,378
21 March 1954	HC	Northern Ireland	Wrexham	1–2 (1)	32,187
9 May 1954	F	Austria	Vienna	0–2	58,000
22 September 1954	F	Yugoslavia	Cardiff	1–3	48,000
16 October 1954	HC	Scotland	Cardiff	0–1	60,000
10 November 1954	HC	England	Wembley	2–3 (2)	91,112
20 April 1955	HC	Northern Ireland	Belfast	3–2 (3)	30,000
22 October 1955	HC	England	Cardiff	2–1	60,000
9 November 1955	HC	Scotland	Hampden Park	0–2	53,887
23 November 1955	ECQ	Austria	Wrexham	1–2	23,000
11 April 1956	HC	Northern Ireland	Cardiff	1–1	45,000
20 October 1956	HC	Scotland	Cardiff	2–2	60,000
14 November 1956	HC	England	Wembley	1–3 (1)	93,796
10 April 1957	HC	Northern Ireland	Belfast	0–0	30,000
20 October 1962	HC	Scotland	Cardiff	2–3 (1)	50,000
Alan Curtis (6 apps, 2gls)					
23 May 1979	HC	England	Wembley	0–0	70,250
25 May 1979	HC	Wales	Belfast	1–1	6,500
2 June 1979	ECQ	Malta	Valetta	2–0	9,000
11 September 1979	F	Republic of Ireland	Swansea	2–1 (1)	6,825
17 October 1979	ECQ	West Germany	Cologne	1–5 (1)	60,000
21 November 1979	ECQ	Turkey	Izmir	0–1	50,000
Brian Flynn (31+ 1 apps, 5gls)					
16 November 1977	WCQ	Czechoslovakia	Prague	0–1	20,000
14 December 1977	F	West Germany	Dortmund	1–1	53,000
18 April 1978	F	Iran (sub)	Teheran	1–0	45,000
13 May 1978	HC	England	Cardiff	1–3	17,698
17 May 1978	HC	Scotland	Hampden Park	1–1	70,241
19 May 1978	HC	Northern Ireland	Wrexham	1–0	9,077
25 October 1978	ECQ	Malta	Wrexham	7–0 (1)	11,475
29 November 1978	ECQ	Turkey	Wrexham	1–0	11,800
19 May 1979	HC	Scotland	Cardiff	3–0	20,371
23 May 1979	HC	England	Wembley	0–0	75,000
25 May 1979	HC	Northern Ireland	Belfast	1–1	6,500
2 June 1979	ECQ	Malta	Valetta	2–0 (1)	9,000
11 September 1979	F	Republic of Ireland	Swansea	2–1	6,825
17 October 1979	ECQ	West Germany	Cologne	1–5 (1)	60,000
17 May 1980	HC	England	Wrexham	4–1	24,236
21 May 1980	HC	Scotland	Hampden Park	0–1	24,236

23 May 1980	HC	Northern Ireland	Cardiff	0–1	12,913
2 June 1980	WCQ	Iceland	Reykjavik	4–0 (1p)	10,254
15 October 1980	WCQ	Turkey	Cardiff	4–0 (1)	11,770
19 November 1980	WCQ	Czechoslovakia	Cardiff	1–0	20,175
24 February 1980	F	Republic of Ireland	Cardiff	3–1	15,000
25 March 1981	WCQ	Turkey	Ankara	1–0	35,000
16 May 1981	HC	Scotland	Swansea	2–0	18,985
20 May 1981	HC	England	Wembley	0–0	34,250
30 May 1981	WCQ	USSR	Wrexham	0–0	29,366
9 September 1981	WCQ	Czechoslovakia	Prague	0–2	41,500
18 November 1981	WCQ	USSR	Tibilisi	0–3	80,000
27 April 1982	HC	England	Cardiff	0–1	23,000
24 April 1982	HC	Scotland	Hampden Park	0–1	25,284
27 May 1982	HC	Northern Ireland	Wrexham	3–0	2,315
2 June 1982	F	France	Toulouse	1–0	35,000
22 September 1982	ECQ	Norway	Swansea	1–0	5,000
Carl Harris (20+4 apps, 2gls)					
24 March 1976	F	England	Wrexham	1–2	21,000
6 May 1976	HC	Scotland	Hampden Park	1–3	35,000
14 Dec1977	F	West Germany	Dortmund	1–1	53,000
18 April 1978	F	Iran (sub)	Teheran	1–0	45,000
13 May 1978	HC	England	Cardiff	1–3	17,698
17 May 1978	HC	Scotland	Hampden Park	1–1	70,241
19 May 1978	HC	Northern Ireland	Wrexham	1–0	9,077
25 October 1978	ECQ	Malta	Wrexham	7–0 (1)	11,475
29 Nov1978	ECQ	Turkey	Wrexham	1–0	11,800
2 May 1979	ECQ	West Germany	Wrexham	0–2	26,900
23 May 1979	HC	England	Wembley	0–0	70,250
2 June 1979	ECQ	Malta	Valetta	2–0	9,000
23 May 1980	HC	Northern Ireland (sub)	Cardiff	0–1	12,913
2 June 1980	WCQ	Iceland (sub)	Reykjavik	4–0	10,254
15 October 1980	WCQ	Turkey	Cardiff	4–0	11,770
19 November 1980	WCQ	Czechoslovakia (sub)	Cardiff	1–0	20,175
24 February 1980	F	Republic of Ireland	Cardiff	3–1	15,000
25 March 1981	WCQ	Turkey	Ankara	1–0 (1)	35,000
16 May 1981	HC	Scotland	Swansea	2–0	18,985
20 May 1981	HC	England	Wembley	0–0	34,250
30 May 1981	WCQ	USSR	Wrexham	0–0	29,366
9 September 1981	WCQ	Czechoslovakia	Prague	0–2	41,500
7 October 1981	WCQ	Iceland	Swansea	2–2	20,000
27 April 1982	HC	England	Cardiff	0–1	50,000
Matthew Jones (3+2 apps)					
9 October 1999	ECQ	Switzerland (sub)	Wrexham	0–2	5,064
23 February 2000	F	Qatar	Doha	1–0	2,000
23 May 2000	F	Brazil	Cardiff	0–3	72,500
2 June 2000	F	Portugal	Chaves	0–3	11,000
11 October 2000	WCQ	Poland (sub)	Warsaw	0–0	14,000
Aubrey Powell (5 apps)					
19 October 1946	HC	Scotland	Wrexham	3–1	29,568
13 November 1946	HC	England	Maine Road	0–3	59,250

Portrait of Aubrey Powell and a collection of his Welsh caps and an international shirt.

18 October 1947	HC	England	Cardiff	0–3	55,000
12 November 1947	HC	Scotland	Hampden Park	2–1	88,000
10 March 1948	HC	Northern Ireland	Wrexham	2–0	33,160
Gary Speed (27+8 apps, 2gls)					
20 May 1990	F	Costa Rica (sub)	Cardiff	1–0	5,977
11 September 1990	F	Denmark	Copenhagen	0–1	8,700

Gary Speed won the first of his 85 caps with Leeds.

14 November 1990	ECQ	Luxembourg (sub)	Luxembourg	1–0	6,800
6 February 1990	F	Republic of Ireland (sub)	Wrexham	0–3	9,168
1 May 1991	F	Iceland	Cardiff	1–0	3,656
5 June 1991	ECQ	Germany (sub)	Cardiff	1–0	38,000
11 September 1991	F	Brazil	Cardiff	1–0	20,000
16 October 1991	ECQ	Germany (sub)	Nuremburg	1–4	46,000
13 November 1991	ECQ	Luxembourg	Cardiff	1–0	20,000
19 February 1992	F	Republic of Ireland	Dublin	1–0	15,100
20 May 1992	WCQ	Romania	Bucharest	1–5	23,000
30 May 1992	F	Holland	Utrecht	0–4	20,000
3 June 1992	KC	Argentina	Tokyo	0–1	31,000
7 June 1992	KC	Japan	Matsuyama	1–0	30,000
9 September 1992	WCQ	Faeroes	Cardiff	6–0	6,000
14 October 1992	WCQ	Cyprus	Limassol	1–0	15,000
18 November 1992	WCQ	Belgium	Brussels	0–2	21,000
17 February 1993	F	Republic of Ireland	Dublin	1–2	9,500
31 March 1993	WCQ	Belgium	Cardiff	2–0	27,002
6 June 1993	WCQ	Faroe Islands (sub)	Toftir	3–0	4,209
8 September 1993	WCQ	RCS (sub)	Cardiff	2–2	37,558
13 October 1993	WCQ	Cyprus	Cardiff	2–0	10,000
17 November 1993	WCQ	Romania	Cardiff	1–2	40,000
9 March 1994	F	Norway	Cardiff	1–3	10,000
20 April 1994	F	Sweden	Wrexham	0–2	4,694
7 September 1994	ECQ	Albania	Cardiff	2–0	15,791
12 October 1994	ECQ	Moldova	Kishinev	2–3 (1)	12,000
16 November 1994	ECQ	Georgia	Tblisi	0–5	45,000
14 December 1994	ECQ	Bulgaria	Cardiff	0–3	20,000
29 March 1995	ECQ	Bulgaria	Sofia	1–3	60,000
26 April 1995	ECQ	Germany	Dussledorf	1–1	45,000
6 September 1995	ECQ	Moldova	Cardiff	1–0 (1)	5,000
1 October 1995	ECQ	Germany	Cardiff	1–2	25,000
15 November 1995	ECQ	Albania	Tirana	1–1	6,000
24 January 1996	F	Italy	Terni	0–3	20,000
24 April 1996	F	Switzerland (sub)	Lugano	0–2	8,000
Gary Sprake (32 apps)					
20 November 1963	HC	Scotland	Hampden Park	1–2	56,067
15 April 1964	HC	Northern Ireland	Swansea	2–3	10,434
3 October 1964	HC	Scotland	Cardiff	3–2	50,000
21 October 1964	WCQ	Denmark	Copenhagen	0–1	30,000
9 December 1964	WCQ	Greece	Athens	0–2	26,000
2 October 1965	HC	England	Cardiff	0–0	30,000
27 October 1965	WCQ	USSR	Cardiff	2–1	34,521
30 March 1966	HC	Northern Ireland	Cardiff	1–4	12,860
22 October 1966	HC	Scotland	Cardiff	1–1	32,500
21 October 1967	HC	England	Cardiff	0–3	45,000
22 November 1967	HC	Scotland	Hampden Park	2–3	57,472
26 March 1969	F	West Germany	Frankfurt	1–1	40,000
3 May 1969	HC	Scotland	Wrexham	3–5	18,765
7 May 1969	HC	England	Wembley	1–2	70,000
10 May 1969	HC	Northern Ireland	Belfast	0–0	12,500

Gary Sprake plucks the ball off the head of Leeds teammate Jack Charlton in a Home International encounter.

28 July 1969	F	Rest of UK	Cardiff	0–1	14,000
22 October 1969	WCQ	East Germany	Cardiff	1–3	22,409
4 November 1969	WCQ	Italy	Rome	1–4	90,000
11 November 1969	ECQ	Romania	Cardiff	0–0	29,000
15 May 1971	HC	Scotland	Cardiff	0–0	19,068
18 May 1971	HC	England	Wembley	0–0	85,000
22 May 1971	HC	Northern Ireland	Belfast	0–1	22,000
13 October 1971	ECQ	Finland	Swansea	3–0	10,301

20 May 1972	HC	England	Cardiff	0–3	34,000
24 May 1972	HC	Scotland	Hampden Park	0–1	21,332
27 May 1972	HC	Northern Ireland	Wrexham	0–0	15,647
15 November 1972	WCQ	England	Cardiff	0–1	36,384
24 January 1973	WCQ	England	Wembley	1–1	62,000
28 March 1973	WCQ	Poland	Cardiff	2–0	12,000
12 May 1973	HC	Scotland	Wrexham	0–2	17,765
19 May 1973	HC	Northern Ireland	Anfield	0–1	4,946
26 September 1973	WCQ	Poland	Anfield	0–3	120,000
Byron Stevenson (10+1 apps)					
19 May 1978	HC	Northern Ireland	Wrexham	1–0	9,077
25 October 1978	ECQ	Malta	Wrexham	7–0	11,475
29 November 1978	ECQ	Turkey	Wrexham	1–0	11,800
19 May 1979	HC	Scotland	Cardiff	3–0	20,371
23 May 1979	HC	England	Wembley	0–0	75,000
25 May 1979	HC	Northern Ireland	Belfast	1–1	6,500
2 June 1979	ECQ	Malta	Valetta	2–0	9,000
17 October 1979	ECQ	West Germany	Cologne	1–5	60,000
21 November 1979	ECQ	Turkey	Izmir	0–1	50,000
2 June 1980	WCQ	Iceland (sub)	Reykjavik	4–0	10,254
9 September 1981	WCQ	Czechoslovakia	Prague	0–2	41,500
Sam Vokes (0+1 app)					
14 November 2009	F	Scotland (sub)	Cardiff	3–0	13,844
On loan from Wolverhampton Wanderers					
Harold Williams (4 apps)					
8 March 1950	HC	Northern Ireland	Wrexham	0–0	33,000
21 October 1950	HC	Scotland	Cardiff	1–3	60,000
8 March 1950	HC	Northern Ireland	Wrexham	0–0	33,000
21 October 1950	HC	Scotland	Cardiff	1–3	60,000
Terry Yorath (28 apps, 1gl)					
4 November 1969	WCQ	Italy	Rome	1–4	90,000
15 May 1971	HC	Scotland	Cardiff	0–0	19,068
18 May 1971	HC	England	Wembley	0–0	85,000
22 May 1971	HC	Northern Ireland	Belfast	0–1	22,000
27 October 1971	ECQ	Czechoslovakia	Prague	0–1	32,000
20 May 1972	HC	England	Cardiff	0–3	34,000
24 May 1972	HC	Scotland	Hampden Park	0–1	21,332
27 May 1972	HC	Northern Ireland	Wrexham	0–0	15,647
24 January 1973	WCQ	England	Wembley	1–1	62,000
28 March 1973	WCQ	Poland	Cardiff	2–0	12,000
12 May 1973	HC	Scotland	Wrexham	0–2	17,765
26 September 1973	WCQ	Poland	Chorzow	0–3	120,000
11 May 1974	HC	England	Cardiff	0–2	26,000
14 May 1974	HC	Scotland	Hampden Park	0–2	41,969
18 May 1974	HC	Northern Ireland	Wrexham	1–0	9,311
14 September 1974	ECQ	Austria	Vienna	1–2	34,000
30 October 1974	ECQ	Hungary	Cardiff	2–0	8,445
20 November 1974	ECQ	Luxembourg	Swansea	5–0 (1)	10,530
16 April 1975	ECQ	Hungary	Budapest	2–1	30,000
1 May 1975	ECQ	Luxembourg	Luxembourg	3–1	5,000

17 May 1975	HC	Scotland	Cardiff	2–2	23,509
19 November 1975	ECQ	Austria	Wrexham	1–0	28,182
24 March 1976	F	England	Wrexham	1–2	20,987
24 April 1976	ECF	Yugoslavia	Zagreb	0–2	55,000
6 May 1976	HC	Scotland	Hampden Park	1–3	25,000
8 May 1976	HC	England	Cardiff	0–1	24,500
14 May 1976	HC	Northern Ireland	Swansea	1–0	10,000
22 May 1976	ECF	Yugoslavia	Cardiff	1–1	30,000

UNITED STATES OF AMERICA

Eric Lichaj (0+1 app)

29 March 2011	F	Paraguay (sub)	Nashville	0–1	29,059

On loan from Aston Villa

Eddie Lewis (7+1 apps)

17 August 2005	WCQ	Trinidad & Tobago	East Hartford	1–0	25,488
3 September 2005	WCQ	Mexico	Ohio	2–0	24,685
8 October 2005	WCQ	Costa Rica	San Jose	0–3	30,000
1 March 2006	F	Poland	Kaiserslautern	1–0	13,395
26 May 2006	F	Venezuela (sub)	Cleveland	2–0	29,745
28 May 2006	F	Latvia	East Hartford	1–0	24,636
12 June 2006	WCF	Czech Republic	Gelsenkirchen	0–3	52,000
22 June 2006	WCF	Ghana	Nuremburg	1–2	41,000

B INTERNATIONALS

AUSTRALIA

Harry Kewell (1 app)

12 June 1999	World Stars	Sydney	3–2	88,101

ENGLAND

David Batty (5 apps)

14 November 1989	Italy	Brighton	1–0	16,125
12 December 1989	Yugoslavia	Millwall	2–1	8,231
27 March 1990	Republic of Ireland	Cork	1–4	10,000
27 April 1991	Iceland	Watford	1–0	3,814
24 March 1992	Czechoslovakia	Budejovice	1–0	6,000

Lee Chapman (1 app)

27 April 1991	Iceland	Watford	1–0	3,814

Jack Charlton (2 apps)

20 May 1970	Colombia	Bogata	1–0	28,000
24 May 1970	Liga Deportiva Universidad	Quito	4–1	22,250

Allan Clarke (2 apps)

20 May 1970	Colombia	Bogata	1–0	28,000
24 May 1970	Liga Deportiva Universidad	Quito	4–1	22,250

Tony Dorigo (1+1 apps)

18 February 1992	France	Loftus Road	3–0	4,827
24 March 1992	Czechoslovakia (sub)	Budejovice	1–0	6,000

Norman Hunter (2 apps)

20 May 1970	Colombia	Bogata	1–0	28,000
24 May 1970	Liga Deportiva Universidad	Quito	4–1	22,250

John Lukic (1 app)

11 December 1990		Algeria (sub)	Algiers	0–0	1,000

Mel Sterland (1+1 apps)

12 December 1989		Yugoslavia (sub)	Millwall	2–1	8,231
11 December 1990		Algeria	Algiers	0–0	1,000

REPUBLIC OF IRELAND

Jim Beglin (1 app)

27 March 1990		England	Cork	4–1	10,000

Alan Maybury (1 app)

11 March 1998		Northern Ireland	Dublin	0–1	10,200

SCOTLAND

David Hopkin (1 app)

21 April 1998		Norway U23	Tynecastle	1–2	7,845

WALES

Matthew Jones (1 app)

24 March 1998		Scotland	Cumbernauld	0–4	5,989

UNDER-23 INTERNATIONALS

AUSTRALIA

Neil Kilkenny (3+3 apps)

27 June 2008		Chile (sub)	Darwin	3–4	1,404
29 June 2008		Chile	Darwin	1–1	1,780
20 July 2008		China	Changchung	0–1	10,000
24 July 2008		Japan (sub)	Kobe	1–2	17,185
31 July 2008		South Korea (sub)	Seoul	0–1	20,533
10 August 2008	OG	Argentina	Shanghai	0–1	38,182

ENGLAND

Chris Crowe (2 apps, 1gl)

11 November 1959		France	Sunderland	2–0 (1)	26,495
2 March 1960		Scotland	Hampden Park	4–4	25,000

Norman Hunter (3 apps)

4 November 1964		Wales	Wrexham	3–2	15,193
25 November 1964		Romania	Coventry	5–0	27,476
24 February 1965		Scotland	Aberdeen	0–0	25,000

Mike O'Grady (1 app)

3 November 1965		France	Norwich	3–0	20,203

Paul Reaney (4 apps)

8 April 1964		France	Rouen	2–2	15,000
24 February 1965		Scotland	Aberdeen	0–0	25,000
25 May 1965		West Germany	Frieburg	0–1	15,000
29 May 1965		Czechoslovakia	Liberec	0–0	6,000

REPUBLIC OF IRELAND

John Sheridan (1 app, 1gl)

11 April 1989		Northern Ireland	Dublin	3–0 (1p)	3,200

SCOTLAND

Billy Bremner (3 apps, 1gl)

24 May 1964		France	Nantes	2–0	1,000
2 December 1964		Wales	Kilmarnock	3–0 (1)	6,000
24 February 1965		England	Aberdeen	0–0	25,000

Eddie Gray (2 apps, 2gls)

30 November 1966		Wales	Wrexham	6–0 (2)	5,341
1 March 1967		England	Newcastle	3–1	22,097

Frank Gray (5 apps)

13 March 1974		England	Newcastle	0–2	4,511
2 September 1975	ECQ	Denmark	Frederikshavn	1–0	6,000
28 October 1975	ECQ	Denmark	Easter Road, Edinburgh	4–1	16,500
16 December 1975	ECQ	Romania	Falkirk	4–0	8,000
24 March 1975	ECQ	Holland	Easter Road, Edinburgh	2–0*	32,593

*After extra-time, Holland won 4–3 on penalties. The first leg finished 2–0 to Holland in Breda.

Joe Jordan (1 app)

24 March 1975	ECQ	Holland	Easter Road, Edinburgh	2–0*	32,593

*After extra time, Holland won 4–3 on penalties. The first leg finished 2–0 to Holland in Breda.

Peter Lorimer (2 apps, 2gls)

3 December 1969		France	Hampden Park	4–0 (2)	5,004
14 January 1970		Wales	Aberdeen	1–1	14,500

WALES

Carl Harris (1 app)

4 February 1976	Scotland	Wrexham	2–3	2,222

Denis Hawkins (5 apps)

30 November 1966	Scotland	Wrexham	0–6	5,341
22 February 1967	Northern Ireland	Belfast	1–2*	8,000
1 November 1967	England	Swansea	1–2	14,928
20 March 1968	Northern Ireland	Cardiff	0–1	2,669
2 October 1968	England	Wrexham	1–3	11,084

*Abandoned after 73 minutes, ground waterlogged

Glan Letheran (1 app)

4 February 1976	Scotland	Wrexham	2–3	2,222

Gary Sprake (5 apps)

13 November 1963	England	Ashton Gate, Bristol	1–1	16,841
4 December 1963	Scotland	Wrexham	3–1	10,716
5 February 1964	Northern Ireland	Belfast	3–3	18,000
4 November 1964	England	Wrexham	3–2	15,193
10 February 1965	Northern Ireland	Cardiff	2–2	6,000

Terry Yorath (7 apps)

2 October 1968	England	Wrexham	1–3	11,084
1 October 1969	England	Ashton Gate, Bristol	0–2	22,286
14 January 1970	Scotland	Aberdeen	1–1	14,500
2 December 1970	England	Wrexham	0–0	16,367
5 January 1972	England	Swindon	0–2	18,028
26 January 1972	Scotland	Aberdeen	0–2	15,000
29 November 1972	England	Swansea	0–3	6,414

UNDER-21 INTERNATIONALS
(1976 to date)

ENGLAND

David Batty (5+2 apps, 1gl)					
28 May 1988	F	Switzerland (sub)	Lausanne	1–1	1,000
7 February 1989	F	Greece (sub)	Patras	0–1	2,000
5 June 1989	TT	Bulgaria	Toulon	2–3	1,000
7 June 1989	TT	Senegal	Toulon	6–1 (1)	1,000
9 June 1989	TT	Republic of Ireland	Toulon	0–0	1,000
11 June 1989	TT	USA	Toulon	0–2	1,000
10 October 1989	ECQ	Poland	Jastrzbruj	3–1	5,000
Lee Bowyer (9 apps, 1gl)					
31 August 1996	ECQ	Moldova	Chisinau	2–0	850
12 February 1997	ECQ	Italy	Bristol	1–0	13,850
1 April 1997	F	Switzerland	Swindon	0–0	10,167
29 April 1997	ECQ	Georgia	Charlton	0–0	12,714
9 September 1997	ECQ	Moldova	Wycombe	1–0	5,534
9 February 1998	F	France	Derby	2–1	32,865
26 March 1998	EC	Poland	Southampton	5–0	15,202
8 October 1999	F	Denmark	Bradford	4–1 (1)	15,220
22 February 2000	F	Argentina	Fulham	1–0	15,748
Michael Bridges (1 app)					
8 October 1999	F	Denmark	Bradford	4–1	15,220
Scott Carson (8 apps)					
17 Feb 2004	F	Holland	Hull	3–2	25,280
30 March 2004	F	Sweden	Kristiansund	2–2	7,330
17 Aug 2004	F	Ukraine	Middlesbrough	3–1	5,658
3 Sept 2004	F	Austria	Krems	2–0	4,500
7 Sept 2004	ECQ	Poland	Rybnik	3–1	3,000
8 Oct 2004	ECQ	Wales	Blackburn	2–0	17,500
12 Oct 2004	ECQ	Azerbaijan	Baku	0–0	1,500
16 Nov 2004	F	Spain	Alcala	0–1	3,000
Andy Couzens (1+2 apps)					
8 June 1995	TT	Malaysia (sub)	Toulon	2–0	700
10 June 1995	TT	Angola	Toulon	1–0	250
12 June 1995	TT	France (sub)	Toulon	0–2	650
Fabian Delph (0+1 app)					
18 November 2008	F	Czech Republic (sub)	Bramall Lane	2–0	18,735
Mark Ford (2 apps)					
23 April 1996	F	Croatia	Sunderland	0–1	4,376
31 August 1996	ECQ	Moldova	Chisinau	2–0	850
Jonny Howson (0+1 app)					
6 February 2011	F	Italy (sub)	Empoli	0–1	3,700
Seth Johnson (1 app)					
16 April 2002	F	Portugal	Stoke	0–1	28,000
Matthew Kilgallon (2+3 apps)					
30 March 2004	F	Sweden (sub)	Kristiansand	2–2	7,320
17 August 2005	F	Ukraine	Middlesbrough	3–1	5,658

7 September 2005	ECQ	Poland (sub)	Rybnik	3–1	3,000
12 October 2005	ECQ	Azerbaijan (sub)	Baku	0–0	1,500
14 November 2006	F	Holland	Alkmaar	1–0	15,000
John Lukic (7 apps)					
9 September 1980	F	Norway	Southampton	3–0	6,973
14 October 1980	ECQ	Romania	Ploesti	0–4	10,000
25 February 1980	F	Republic of Ireland	Anfield	1–0	5,882
28 April 1981	ECQ	Romania	Swindon	3–0	8,739
31 May 1981	ECQ	Switzerland	Neuchatel	0–0	1,500
5 June 1981	ECQ	Hungary	Keszthely	2–1	8,000
17 November 1981	ECQ	Hungary	Nottingham	2–0	8,734
Danny Mills (7+1 apps, 3gls)					
3 September 1999	ECQ	Luxembourg	Reading	5–0	18,094
7 September 1999	ECQ	Poland	Plock	1–3 (1)	1,500
8 October 1999	F	Denmark	Bradford	4–1 (1)	15,220
22 February 2000	F	Argentina	Fulham	1–0	15,748
29 March 2000	ECQ	Yugoslavia (sub)	Barcelona	3–0	1,000
27 May 2000	ECF	Italy	Bratislava	0–2	1,000
29 May 2000	ECF	Turkey	Bratislava	6–0 (1)	250
1 June 2000	ECF	Slovenia	Bratislava	0–2	9,113
James Milner (0+1 sub)					
30 March 2004	F	Sweden (sub)	Kristiansand	2–2	7,320
Paul Robinson (11 apps)					
8 October 2000	F	Denmark	Bradford	4–1	15,220
31 August 2001	F	Georgia	Middlesbrough	6–1	5,103
6 October 2001	ECQ	Germany	Derby	1–1	30,155
10 October 2001	ECQ	Finland	Valkeakoski	2–2	1,426
27 February 2001	F	Spain	Birmingham	0–4	13,761
12 February 2002	F	Slovenia	Nova Gorica	1–0	350
26 March 2002	F	Italy	Bradford	1–1	21,642
16 April 2002	F	Portugal	Stoke	0–1	28,000
17 May 2002	ECF	Switzerland	Zurich	2–1	16,000
20 May 2002	ECF	Italy	Basle	1–2	12,980
22 May 2002	ECF	Portugal	Zurich	1–3	10,000
Alan Smith (9+1 apps, 2gls)					
8 October 1999	F	Denmark	Bradford	4–1 (1)	15,220
22 February 2000	F	Argentina (sub)	Fulham	1–0	15,748
6 October 2001	ECQ	Germany	Derby	1–1	30,155
10 October 2001	ECQ	Finland	Valkeaksoski	2–2 (1)	1,426
27 February 2001	F	Spain	Birmingham	0–4	17.176
26 March 2002	F	Italy	Bradford	1–1	21,642
16 April 2002	F	Portugal	Stoke	0–1	28,000
17 May 2002	ECF	Switzerland	Zurich	2–1	16,000
20 May 2002	ECF	Italy	Basle	1–2	12,980
22 May 2002	ECF	Portugal	Zurich	1–3	10,000
Rod Wallace (4app, 1g)					
27 May 1991	TT	Senegal	Arles	2–1	1,000
29 May 1991	TT	Mexico	Vitrolles	6–0 (1)	1,000
31 May 1991	TT	CIS	Aix-en-Provence	2–1	2,000
3 June 1991	TT	France	Toulon	1–0	6,000

Noel Whelan (1+1 apps, 1gl)

11 October 1994	F	Austria (sub)	Kapfenburg	3–1	2,800
15 November 1994	F	Republic of Ireland	Newcastle	1–0 (1)	25,863

Jonathan Woodgate (1 app)

22 February 2000	F	Argentina	Fulham	1–0	15,748

NORTHERN IRELAND

Wes Boyle (3+4 apps, 1gl)

21 April 1998	ECQ	Switzerland (sub)	Lurgan	2–1	300
20 May 1998	TT/ECQ	Scotland (sub)	Toulon	1–1	500
23 March 2001	ECQ	Czech Republic (sub)	Ballymena	0–2	1,411
27 March 2001	ECQ	Bulgaria	Vratsa	0–2	3,400
1 June 2001	ECQ	Bulgaria (sub)	Belfast	1–1	769
5 June 2001	ECQ	Czech Republic	Prague	0–4	–
5 October 2002	ECQ	Malta	Ta'Quali	2–2 (1)	–

Gary O'Hara (1 app)

22 March 1994	F	Romania	The Oval, Belfast	0–0	–

O'Hara did not play first-team football for Leeds United

NORWAY

Frank Strandli (5+1 apps, 2gls)

27 April 1993	ECQ	Turkey (sub)	Honefoss	5–2 (1)	4,000
1 June 1993	ECQ	England	Stavanger	1–1	6,840
8 June 1993	ECQ	Holland	Utrecht	1–2	1,500
21 September 1993	ECQ	Poland	Stavanger	3–1	2,395
12 October 1993	ECQ	Poland	Pitka	0–2	10,000
9 November 1993	ECQ	Turkey	Istanbul	1–3 (1)	–

REPUBLIC OF IRELAND

Len Curtis (2 apps)

24 March 1992	F	Switzerland	Dublin	1–1	1,500
25 May 1992	ECQ	Albania	Dublin	3–1	1,200

Curtis did not play first-team football for Leeds United

Ian Harte (2 apps)

23 March 1996	F	Russia	Drogheda	0–1	2,500
30 May 1996	F	Norway	Drogheda	1–1	500

Paul Keegan (5app)

19 Aug 2003	F	Poland	Gdansk	5–1	2,500
10 Oct 2003	ECQ	Switzerland	Neuchatel	2–0	2,500
23 Feb 2004	F	Portugal	Funchal	0–0	4,000
25 Feb 2004	F	Italy	Funchal	1–0	2,500
27 Feb 2004	F	Madeira Select	Funchal	4–0	4,000

Keegan did not play first-team football for Leeds United

Gary Kelly (4+1 apps)

17 November 1992	ECQ	Spain (sub)	Jerez	1–2	12,000
9 March 1993	ECQ	Germany	Dublin	0–1	–
23 March 1993	ECQ	Germany	Baunatal	0–8	6,000
26 May 1993	ECQ	Albania	Tirana	1–1	–
12 October 1993	ECQ	Spain	Drogheda	0–2	500

Stephen McPhail (5+2 apps)

13 October 1998	ENQ	Malta (sub)	Arklow	2–1	4,500
31 May 1999	F	Scotland	Elgin	0–1	3,816
2 June 1999	F	Northern Ireland (sub)	Inverness	1–0	605
8 June 1999	ENQ	Macedonia	Galway	0–0*	2,000
31 August 1999	ENQ	Yugoslavia	Dublin	0–2	740
3 September 1999	ENQ	Croatia	Zagreb	1–5	1,103
31 August 2001	ENQ	Holland	Waterford	1–0	–

* UEFA awarded the Republic of Ireland a 3–0 win as Macedonia fielded a suspended player

Alan Maybury (5+1 apps)

10 October 1998	ENQ	Romania	Drogheda	0–2	1,250
27 April 1999	ENQ	Sweden	Birr Town	0–3	1,800
31 May 1999	F	Scotland	Elgin	0–1	3,816
2 June 1999	F	Northern Ireland (sub)	Inverness	1–0	605
31 August 1999	ENQ	Yugoslavia	Dublin	0–2	740
7 September 1999	ENQ	Malta	Ta'Quali	3–1	1,158

Henry McStay (4app, 1g)

23 Feb 2004	F	Portugal (sub)	Funchal	0–0	4,000
17 Aug 2004	F	Bulgaria	Drogheda	3–2	-
3 Sept 2003	ECQ	Cyprus (sub)	Kilkenny	3–0	1,200
25 Mar 2005	ECQ	Israel	Tel Aviv	3–1 (1)	3,500

McStay did not play first-team football for Leeds United

Tony O'Dowd (2+1 apps)

30 May 1990	F	Malta (sub)	Valetta	1–1	–
16 October 1990	ECQ	Turkey	Dublin	3–2	3,500
13 November 1990	ECQ	England	Cork	0–3	3,000

O'Dowd did not play first-team football for Leeds United

John Sheridan (2 apps)

25 March 1985	F	England	Portsmouth	2–3	5,489
17 February 1987	ECQ	Scotland	Easter Road, Edinburgh	1–4	4,136

Aidan White (5 apps)

10 August 2011	F	Austria	Sligo	2–1	1,800
1 September 2011	ECQ	Hungary	Sligo	2–1	2,500
7 September 2011	ECQ	Turkey	Manisa	0–1	–
11 October 2011	ECQ	Liechtenstein	Eschen	4–1	293
14 November 2011	ECQ	Liechtenstein	Sligo	2–0 (1)	2,108

SCOTLAND

David McNiven (1+2 apps, 1gl)

12 October 1976	ECQ	Czechoslovakia	Pilsen	0–0	3,000
9 February 1977	F	Wales (sub)	Edinburgh	3–2 (1)	4,538
30 March 1978	ECQ	Switzerland (sub)	Berne	0–2	500

Alan Martin (12 apps)

18 November 2008*	F	Northern Ireland	Hamilton	1–3	2,149
28 March 2009*	ECQ	Albania	Elbasan	1–0	1,600
1 Apr 2009*	ECQ	Albania	Falkirk	5–2	3,000
5 September 2009+	ECQ	Austria	Maria Endersdorf	0–1	1,500
10 October 2009+	ECQ	Belarus	Paisley	1–0	4,017
14 November 2009+	ECQ	Azerbaijan	Baku	4–0	485
21 March 2010+	ECQ	Azerbaijan	Falkirk	2–2	2,793

11 August 2010	F	Sweden	Paisley	1–1	2,726
3 September 2010*	ECQ	Belarus	BorisovCity	1–1	4,500
7 September 2010*	ECQ	Austria	Aberdeen	2–1	2,064
7 October 2010*	ECPO	Iceland	Reykjavik	1–2	7,255
11 October 2010*	ECPO	Iceland	Easter Road, Edinburgh	1–2	12,330

Martin did not play first-team football for Leeds United

* On loan at Barrow

+ On loan at Accrington Stanley

WALES

Steve Balcombe (0+1 app)

24 February 1982	F	France (sub)	Troyes	0–0	4,811

Kevin Evans (1+1 apps)

4 June 1999	ENQ	Italy (sub)	Paolo Mazza	2–6	7,000
8 June 1999	ENQ	Denmark	Wrexham	1–2 (1)	881

Evans did not play first-team football for Leeds United

Glan Letheran (2 apps)

15 December 1976	F	England	Wolverhampton	0–0	4,389
9 February 1977	F	Scotland	Edinburgh	2–3	4,538

Matthew Jones (7 apps, 1gl)

10 October 1997	ENQ	Belgium	Mouscron	0–1	500
4 September 1998	ENQ	Italy	Wrexham	1–2	1,375
9 October 1998	ENQ	Denmark	Odense	2–2	947
13 October 1998	ENQ	Belarus	Barry	0–0	326
30 March 1999	ENQ	Switzerland	Winterthur	0–1	1,050
4 June 1999	ENQ	Italy	Paolo Mazza	2–6 (1)	7,000
8 October 1999	ENQ	Switzerland	Newtown	0–0	1,050

Gary Speed (3 apps, 2gls)

19 May 1990	F	Poland	Merthyr	2–0	1,785
5 December 1990	F	England	Tranmere	0–0	6,288
30 May 1991	F	Poland	Warsaw	2–0 (2)	–

Byron Stevenson (3 apps)

15 December 1976	F	England	Wolverhampton	0–0	4,389
9 February 1977	F	Scotland	Easter Road, Edinburgh	2–3	4,538
8 February 1978	F	Scotland	Chester	1–0	2,454

Gwyn Thomas (3 apps)

15 December 1976	F	England	Wolverhampton	0–0	4,389
6 February 1979	F	England	Swansea	0–1	5,642
20 September 1979	ECQ	Norway	Frederikstad	3–2	1,051

UNOFFICIAL INTERNATIONALS
(Including Wartime and Victory games)

ALL IRELAND

Johnny Giles

4 July 1973		Brazil	Dublin	3–4	34,000

This match, at Lansdowne Road, was regarded as a full international by the Brazilian FA, but not the Irish FA

ENGLAND

Jack Charlton

4 June 1969	Mexico XI	Guadalajara	4–0	45,000

This game was played as part of England's 1970 World Cup warm-up programme.

Trevor Cherry

31 May 1976	Team America	Philadelphia	3–1	16,231

This game was played as part of the United States Bicentennial Tournament.

Terry Cooper

17 May 1967	Young England	Highbury	1–4	20,077

Wilf Copping

13 April 1939	Wales	Wembley	0–1	40,000

Paul Reaney

17 May 1967	Young England	Highbury	1–4	20,077

FA OF IRELAND XI

Johnny Giles

5 January 1972	West German Olympic XI	Dublin	3–0	–

GREAT BRITAIN

John Charles

13 August 1955	Rest of Europe	Belfast	1–4	60,000

Played at Windsor Park to mark the 75th anniversary of the Irish FA.

IRELAND

David Cochrane

9 September 1944	Combined Services	Belfast	4–8	49,875

IRELAND/WALES

John Charles

14 May 1956	England/Scotland	Dublin	3–3	–

IRISH FREE STATE

Harry Duggan

6 May 1936	Rhineland	Cologne	1–4	–

The Irish international side were touring Germany and played a German international side which was chosen from players from the Rhineland only, so it has never been included by the Republic in official records.

REST OF UK

Billy Bremner, Jack Charlton and Terry Cooper all played for the Rest of the United Kingdom v Wales at Ninian Park on 28 July 1969 in a game to mark the investiture of Charles, the Prince of Wales. The Rest won 1–0 in front of 13,605 fans with money raised from the game going to the Aberfan Disaster Fund. Gary Sprake was in goal for Wales (see facing page).

SCOTLAND

Billy Bremner

24 February 1964	Scottish League	Ibrox Park, Glasgow	3–1	12,000

Peter Lorimer

27 January 1971	Celtic/Rangers XI	Hampden Park	2–1 (1)	81,405

This game was played to raise funds for the Ibrox Park Disaster.

WALES

Aubrey Powell

8 May 1943	England	Cardiff	1–1	25,000
25 September 1943	England	Wembley	3–8 (1)	80,000
20 October 1945	England	West Bromwich	1–0 (1)	56,000
4 May 1946	Northern Ireland	Cardiff	0–1	45,000

Gary Sprake

28 July 1969	Rest of UK	Cardiff	0–1	13,605

WORLD STARS

Lucas Radebe

12 June 1999	Australia	Sydney	2–3	88,101

YOUNG ENGLAND

Norman Hunter

17 May 1967	England	Highbury	4–1	20,077

Paul Reaney

13 May 1966	England	Stamford Bridge	4–1	18,274

Other International Matches

AUSTRALIAN OLYMPIC TEAM

Danny Milosevic

6 September 2000	F	Kuwait	Melbourne	3–0	x
8 September 2000	F	South Africa	Melbourne	1–0	–
13 September 2000	OG	Italy	Melbourne	0–1	93,252
16 September 2000	OG	Nigeria	Sydney	2–3	38,080
19 September 2000	OG	Honduras	Sydney	1–2	37,788

x Played behind closed doors

Mark Viduka

13 September 2000	OG	Italy	Melbourne	0–1	93,252
16 September 2000	OG	Nigeria	Sydney	2–3	38,080
19 September 2000	OG	Honduras	Sydney	1–2	37,788

International Trials Matches

ENGLAND

Matches involving Leeds players were England v The Rest, and Possibles v Probables

Wilf Copping

22 March 1933	England	Portsmouth	5–1	15,103
21 March 1934	The Rest	Sunderland	1–7	13,500

Willis Edwards

16 February 1926	The Rest	Newcastle	3–4	15,000
17 January 1927	The Rest	Stamford Bridge	7–3	11,473
7 February 1927	The Rest	Bolton	2–3	14,000
23 February 1928	The Rest	West Bromwich	5–1	10,355
8 Feb1928	The Rest	Middlesbrough	8–3	18,431
4 February 1929	The Rest	Hillsborough	4–3	17,400
11 March 1929	The Rest	Tottenham	1–2	16,000
12 March 1930	The Rest	Anfield	1–6	12,000

Billy Furness				
21 March 1934	The Rest	Sunderland	1–7	13,500
Ernie Hart				
4 February 1929	The Rest	Hillsborough	4–3	17,400
11 March 1929	The Rest	Tottenham	1–2	16,000
21 March 1934	The Rest	Sunderland	1–7	13,500
Bert Sproston				
13 October 1937	Possibles	Goodison Park	1–1	7,000
Russell Wainscoat				
4 February 1929	The Rest	Hillsborough	4–3	17,400

SCOTLAND

Anglo-Scots v Scots

Tom Jennings				
13 March 1928	Scots	Partick	1–1 (1)	6,000

Assorted Representative Matches

YORKSHIRE

Both Willis Edwards and Russell Wainscoat played for Yorkshire against Lancashire on 27 April 1925 at Turf Moor, Burnley, Yorkshire winning 4–3 in front of 6,000 fans. The match was a benefit game for the dependents of Jack Howarth, a Burnley player, and was used by the Football League to experiment with a new offside law.

FA XI

Jack Charlton				
18 October 1961	British Army	Sunderland	1–2	–
Willis Edwards				
10 October 1928	Lancashire	Bolton	5–6	8,000
Russell Wainscoat				
10 October 1928	Lancashire (sub)	Bolton	5–6	8,000

IRISH NATIONAL LOTTERY XI

Both Gordon Strachan and Gordon McAllister played for the Irish National Lottery XI against a Republic of Ireland XI at Dublin on 11 May 1994, the Republic winning 5–1 in front of 42,630 fans.

COMMON MARKET CELEBRATION MATCH

Johnny Giles, Norman Hunter and Peter Lorimer all played for The Three against The Six in a match at Wembley to mark the entry of the United Kingdom, Republic of Ireland and Denmark (The Three) to the existing Common Market (The Six) comprising players from Belgium, France, Holland, Italy, Luxembourg and West Germany. The Three won 2–0 in front of 36,500 fans.

FOOTBALL LEAGUE REPRESENTATIVES

Although not international games, Football League representative games were often used as trial matches ahead of international fixtures.

Jack Charlton				
9 October 1957	League of Ireland	Elland Road	3–1	13,000
17 March 1965	Scottish League	Hampden Park	2–2 (1)	38,409
27 October 1965	League of Ireland	Hull	5–0 (1)	28,283

16 March 1966	Scottish League	Newcastle	1–3	32,900
21 September 1966	Irish League	Plymouth	12–0	35,458
27 September 1966	Belgian League	Brussels	2–2	35,000
Trevor Cherry				
17 March 1976	Scottish League	Hampden Park	1–0 (1)	8,874
Wilf Copping				
4 October 1933	Irish League	Preston	4–0	14,400
10 February 1934	Scottish League	Hampden Park	2–2	59,000
Willis Edwards				
13 March 1926	Scottish League	Hampden Park	2–0	49,000
9 October 1926	Irish League	Belfast	6–1	14,000
19 March 1927	Scottish League	Leicester	2–2	26,000
21 September 1927	Irish League	Newcastle	9–1	1,122
10 March 1928	Scottish League	Hampden Park	6–2	60,000
22 September 1928	Irish League	Belfast	5–0	15,000
7 November 1928	Scottish League	Villa Park	2–1	25,000
25 September 1928	Irish League	Goodison Park	7–2	18,000
2 November 1929	Scottish League	Hampden Park	1–2	40,000
23 September 1931	Irish League	Blackpool	3–0	15,233
7 November 1931	Scottish League	Hampden Park	3–4	51,000
Ernie Hart				
7 November 1928	Scottish League	Villa Park	2–1	25,000
25 September 1928	Irish League	Goodison Park	7–2	18,000
2 November 1929	Scottish League	Hampden Park	1–2	40,000
Norman Hunter				
28 October 1964	Irish League	Belfast	4–0	20,000
17 March 1965	Scottish League	Hampden Park	2–2	38,409
27 October 1965	League of Ireland	Hull	5–0	28,283
16 March 1966	Scottish League	Newcastle	1–3	32,900
27 September 1967	Belgian League	Brussels	2–2	35,000
10 September 1969	League of Ireland	Barnsley	3–0	11,939
Paul Madeley				
10 September 1969	League of Ireland	Barnsley	3–0	11,939
Paul Reaney				
16 March 1966	Scottish League	Newcastle	1–3	32,900
10 September 1969	League of Ireland	Barnsley	3–0	11,939
17 March 1971	Scottish League	Hampden Park	1–0	17,657
Bert Sproston				
22 September 1937	Scottish League	Hampden Park	1–0	40,000
6 October 1937	Irish League	Blackpool	3–0	14,700

FA TOURS

George Ainsley				
1 July 1939	South Africa	Johannesburg	2–1	17,000
Ken Gadsby				
1 July 1939	South Africa	Johannesburg	2–1	17,000
Grenville Hair				
13 May 1961	Malaya	Kuala Lumpur	4–2	20,000
17 May 1961	Singapore	Singapore	9–0	14,294
21 May 1961	Hong Kong	Hong Kong	4–2	–

23 May 1961		Combined Chinese XI	Hong Kong	3–0	20,000
5 June 1961		New Zealand	Wellington	8–0	–
10 June 1961		New Zealand	Auckland	6–1	–

Also to Bermuda and West Indies 1955, Ghana and Nigeria 1958, Malaysia, Hong Kong

Ernie Hart

15 June 1929	South Africa	Durban	3–2 (1)	12,000
13 July 1929	South Africa	Johannesburg	2–1	–
17 July 1929	South Africa	Cape Town	3–2	–

Norman Hunter

3 June 1967	Leon (Mexico)	Montreal	3–0	–
9 June 1967	First Vienna (Austria)	Montreal	2–1	–
11 June 1967	Borussia Dortmund (Germany)	Montreal	3–2 (1)	22,467

Paul Madeley

3 June 1967	Leon (Mexico)	Montreal	3–0	–
9 June 1967	First Vienna (Austria)	Montreal	2–1	–
11 June 1967	Borussia Dortmund (Germany)	Montreal	3–2 (1)	22,467

Bobby Turnbull

13 July 1929	South Africa	Johannesburg	2–1	–
17 July 1929	South Africa	Cape Town	3–2	–

Russell Wainscoat

to Canada 1926

Ernie Hart played for the Professionals against Amateurs at Millwall on 7 October 1929. The Professionals won 3–0.

George Ainsley played for the English Professional Trainers against Norway in Oslo on 2 August 1946. The trainers, drawn from players who were coaching in Norway in summer 1946, won 1–0 in front of a 25,000 crowd.

LEEDS CITY Full Internationals

WALES

Dickie Morris (1 app)

3 March 1906	HC	Scotland	Tynecastle, Edinburgh	2–0	25,000

IRELAND

Joe Enright (1 app)

16 March 1912	HC	Scotland	Belfast	1–4	12,000

Joe Moran (1 app)

16 March 1912	HC	Scotland	Belfast	1–4	12,000

Billy Scott (3 apps)

18 January 1913	HC	Wales	Belfast	0–1	20,000
15 February 1913	HC	England	Belfast	2–1	20,000
15 March 1913	HC	Scotland	Dublin	1–2	12,000

Amateur Internationals

ENGLAND

Ivan Sharpe (5 apps, 4gls)

7 February 1914	F	Wales	Plymouth	9–1 (1)	–
24 February 1914	F	Belgium	Brussels	8–1 (2)	10,000

Dickie Morris of Wales, the first Leeds player to be capped.

5 June 1914	F	Denmark	Copenhagen	0–8	18,500
10 June 1914	F	Sweden	Stockholm	5–1 (1)	5,000
12 June 1914	F	Sweden	Stockholm	5–0	–

Amateur Representative Games

Ivan Sharpe

6 October 1913	for Amateurs v Professionals	Millwall	2–7	20,000

UNITED CAREER RECORDS 1920-2012

Below are the career records (League, FA Cup and League Cup) of every United first-team player since the club's first FA Cup match in 1920. The years given are the first years of seasons. Thus, 1946 means 1946–47. FA Premiership and Football League appearances are classified together under League. In the 'Others' list are all competitions not accounted for in the rest of the table. This contains figures for the Charity Shield, European Cup, European Cup-Winners' Cup, UEFA Cup, Inter-Cities Fairs' Cup (including the 1971 Play-off), Full Members' Cup, Football League Trophy and League Play-off games. Substitute appearances are given to the right of full appearances (eg 26/2).

		LEAGUE		FA CUP		FL CUP		OTHERS		TOTAL	
Player	**Played**	**App**	**Gls**	**App**	**Gls**	**App**	**Gls**	**App**	**Gls**	**App**	**Gls**
ABEL, C.R.	1934	1	0	0	0	0	0	0	0	1	0
ADAMS, M.R.	1986–88	72/1	2	6	1	4	0	6	0	88/1	3
ADDY, M.	1962	2	0	0	0	2	0	0	0	4	0
AGANA, F.A.O.	1991	1/1	0	0	0	0	0	0	0	1/1	0
AINSLEY, G.E.	1936–47	91	30	6	3	0	0	0	0	97	33
AIZLEWOOD, M.	1986–88	65/5	3	1	0	3	0	7	1	76/5	4
ALDERSON, T.	1930	4	2	0	0	0	0	0	0	4	2
ALLAN, J.	1925–27	70	0	4	0	0	0	0	0	74	0
ALLEN, J.W.A.	1923	2	0	0	0	0	0	0	0	2	0
AMEOBI, T.	2007	0	0	0	0	1	0	0/1	0	1/1	0
ANDREWS, I.E.	1988	1	0	0	0	0	0	0	0	1	0
ANDREWS, W.M.H.	2007	1	0	0	0	0	0	1	0	2	0
ANKERGREN, C.	2006–09	117/2	0	9	0	5	0	9	0	140/2	0
ARINS, A.F.	1981	0/1	0	0	0	0	0	0	0	0/1	0
ARMAND, J.E.	1922–28	74	23	5	1	0	0	0	0	79	24
ARMANDO de SA, M.C.	2006	6/5	0	0/1	0	0	0	0	0	6/6	0
ARMES, S.	1935–38	78	8	3	1	0	0	0	0	81	9
ARMITAGE, L.	1920–22	48	11	5	3	0	0	0	0	53	14
ASHALL, J.	1958–60	89	0	2	0	0	0	0	0	91	0
ASHURST, J.	1986–88	88/1	1	6	0	6	0	8	0	108/1	1
ASPIN, N.	1981–88	203/4	5	17	0	9	1	11	0	240/4	6
ASSOUMANI, M.	2008	1	0	0	0	0	0	0	0	1	0
ATKINSON, J.W.	1924–27	52	0	1	0	0	0	0	0	53	0
BAIRD, H.	1957–58	46	22	0	0	0	0	0	0	46	22

Player	Played	LEAGUE App	LEAGUE Gls	FA CUP App	FA CUP Gls	FL CUP App	FL CUP Gls	OTHERS App	OTHERS Gls	TOTAL App	TOTAL Gls
BAIRD, I.J.	1984–86/88–90	160/2	51	8	6	9	1	13	0	190/2	58
BAKER, A.	1927	2	0	0	0	0	0	0	0	2	0
BAKER, J.W.	1920–25	200	2	8	0	0	0	0	0	208	2
BAKER, L.H.	1923–24	10	0	0	0	0	0	0	0	10	0
BAKKE, E.	1999–2005	116/27	8	9/1	6	7	2	32/4	5	164/32	21
BALCOMBE, S.W.	1981	1	1	0	0	1	0	0	0	2	1
BANNAN, B.	2010	3/4	0	0	0	0	0	0	0	3/4	0
BANNISTER, E.	1946–49	44	1	0	0	0	0	0	0	44	1
BARMBY, N.J.	2002–03	17/8	4	0/2	0	1	0	3	1	21/10	5
BARNES, P.S.	1981–83	55/2	5	1	0	5	1	0	0	61/2	6
BARRITT, R.	1951	6	1	0	0	0	0	0	0	6	1
BATES, M.J.	1966–75	106/15	4	10/4	1	9/8	1	26/9	3	151/36	9
BATEY, N.R.	1946	8	0	0	0	0	0	0	0	8	0
BATTY, D.	1987–93/98–2003	280/21	4	16	0	21	0	33/2	0	350/23	4
BAYLY, R.	2006–07	1	0	0	0	0/1	0	0	0	1/1	0
BECCHIO, L.H.	2008–11	131/33	60	7/3	2	7/3	3	3/3	2	148/42	67
BECKFORD, J.P.	2006–09	111/15	71	9	8	5/4	4	7/1	1	132/20	84
BEENEY, M.R.	1992–98	38	0	4/1	0	3	0	0	0	45/1	0
BEESLEY, P.	1995–96	19/3	0	7	0	5/1	0	2/2	0	33/6	0
BEGLIN, J.M.	1989–90	18/1	0	0	0	0	0	2	0	20/1	0
BELFITT, R.M.	1964–71	57/19	17	6/1	3	17/2	5	24/3	8	104/25	33
BELL, A.	1923	1	0	0	0	0	0	0	0	1	0
BELL, T.G.	1922	1	0	0	0	0	0	0	0	1	0
BELL, W.J.	1960–67	205	15	24	1	15	1	17	1	261	18
BENNETT, I.M.	2005	4	0	0	0	0	0	0	0	4	0
BENNETT, W.	1931	10	4	1	0	0	0	0	0	11	4
BESSONE, F.L.	2010	6	0	0	0	2	0	0	0	8	0
BEST, J.	1920	11	1	0	0	0	0	0	0	11	1
BLAKE, N.A.	2004	2	0	0	0	0	0	0	0	2	0
BLAKE, N.L.G.	1988–89	51	4	0	0	4/1	0	4	0	59/1	4
BLAKE, R.J.	2005–06	59/19	20	3/1	0	3/2	1	0/2	0	65/24	21
BLUNT, J.J.	1995	2/2	0	0	0	0/1	0	0	0	2/3	0
BOARDMAN, W.	1920	4	0	0	0	0	0	0	0	4	0
BOWMAN, R.	1992–96	4/3	0	0	0	0/1	0	1	0	5/4	0
BOWYER, L.D.	1996–2002	196/7	38	16	3	7/1	1	38	13	257/8	55
BOYLE, W.S.	1996–2001	0/1	0	0	0	0	0	0	0	0/1	0
BRAVO, R.S.	2002	5	0	1	0	0	0	0	0	6	0
BREMNER, W.J.	1959–76	586/1	90	69	6	38	3	79	16	772/1	115
BRIDGES, M.	1999–2003	40/16	19	1/1	0	3/2	0	17/2	2	61/21	21
BROCK, J.R.E.	1920	6	0	0	0	0	0	0	0	6	0
BROCKIE, V.	1987	2	0	0	0	0	0	0	0	2	0

		LEAGUE		FA CUP		FL CUP		OTHERS		TOTAL	
Player	**Played**	**App**	**Gls**	**App**	**Gls**	**App**	**Gls**	**App**	**Gls**	**App**	**Gls**
BROLIN, T.	1995–97	17/2	4	1/1	0	2/2	0	0	0	20/5	4
BROMBY, L.D.	2009–11	46/8	1	6/2	0	1/1	0	2	0	55/11	1
BROOK, H.	1954–57	102	46	4	1	0	0	0	0	106	47
BROWN, A.J.	1982–84	24	1	0	0	0	0	0	0	24	1
BROWN, G.	1935–36	37	19	4	2	0	0	0	0	41	21
BROWN, J.R.	2010	3/1	0	0	0	0	0	0	0	3/1	0
BROWN M.R.	2011	21/1	1	0/1	0	1	0	0	0	22/2	1
BROWN, V.C.	1931	1	0	0	0	0	0	0	0	1	0
BROWNE, R.J.	1935–46	110	0	4	0	0	0	0	0	114	0
BROWNING, L.J.	1946–51	97	42	8	4	0	0	0	0	105	46
BRUCE, A.S.	2010–11	29	1	2	0	2	0	0	0	33	1
BUCK, E.	1928	8	0	0	0	0	0	0	0	8	0
BUCKLEY, A.	1936–39	83	20	3	2	0	0	0	0	86	22
BUCKLEY, J.W.	1986–87	6/4	1	0/1	0	0	0	1	0	7/5	1
BULLIONS, J.L.	1947–49	35	0	2	0	0	0	0	0	37	0
BURBANKS, W.E.	1953	13	1	0	0	0	0	0	0	13	1
BURDEN, T.D.	1948–54	243	13	16	0	0	0	0	0	259	13
BURGIN, E.	1958–60	58	0	0	0	1	0	0	0	59	0
BURNS, J.G.	2000–02	2/1	0	0	0	1	0	3/1	0	6/2	0
BURNS, K.	1981–83	54/2	2	3	0	7	2	0	0	64/2	4
BUTLER, P.J.	2004–06	99	4	2	0	4	0	1	0	106	4
BUTLER, W.J.	1920	1	0	2	3	0	0	0	0	3	3
BUTTERWORTH, A.J.	1981–83	54/10	15	6	1	4	1	0	0	64/10	17
BUTTERWORTH, F.C.	1945	0	0	2	0	0	0	0	0	2	0
CADAMARTERI, D.L.	2004	0	0	0	0	0/1	0	0	0	0/1	0
CAIRNS, A.	2011	0/1	0	0	0	0	0	0	0	0/1	0
CALDWELL, S.	2003	13	1	0	0	0	0	0	0	13	1
CALDWELL, T.	1959–60	20	0	0	0	2	0	0	0	22	0
CAMARA, Z.	2003	13	1	0	0	2	0	0	0	15	1
CAMERON, R.	1959–61	57	9	2	0	4	2	0	0	63	11
CANTONA, E.D.P.	1991–92	18/10	9	0	0	1	0	6	5	25/10	14
CAPALDI, A.C.	2009	3	0	1/1	0	0	0	0	0	4/1	0
CARLING, T.P.	1960–61	5	0	0	0	1	0	0	0	6	0
CARLISLE, C.J.	2004	29/6	4	0	0	3	0	0	0	32/6	4
CAROLE, S.	2006–07	24/21	3	2	0	3	0	1/1	0	30/22	3
CARR, J.P.	1935	2	0	0	0	0	0	0	0	2	0
CARSON, S.P.	2003–04	2/1	0	0	0	0	0	0	0	2/1	0
CASEY, T.D.	1961	3	0	0	0	1	0	0	0	4	0
CASEY, T.	1949	4	0	0	0	0	0	0	0	4	0
CASWELL, B.L.	1985	9	0	0	0	0	0	0	0	9	0
CHADWICK, W.	1925–26	16	3	0	0	0	0	0	0	16	3

		LEAGUE		FA CUP		FL CUP		OTHERS		TOTAL	
Player	Played	App	Gls	App	Gls	App	Gls	App	Gls	App	Gls
CHANDLER, J.G.	1979–80	21/5	2	1	0	1	0	0	0	23/5	2
CHAPMAN, L.R.	1989–92/1995	135/4	62	11	4	15	8	10	4	171/4	78
CHAPUIS, C.S.T.	2003	0/1	0	0	0	1/1	0	0	0	1/2	0
CHARLES, W.J.	1948–62	308	153	19	4	0	0	0	0	327	157
CHARLTON, J.	1952–72	629	70	52	8	35	7	57	11	773	96
CHERRY, T.J.	1972–82	393/6	24	28/1	1	35	4	21/1	3	477/8	32
CHISHOLM, K.M.	1947–48	40	17	0	0	0	0	0	0	40	17
CHRISTIE, M.N.	2008	1/3	1	1	0	0	0	0	0	2/3	1
CLAPHAM, J.R.	2007	12/1	0	0/1	0	0	0	0/1	0	12/3	0
CLARK, J.R.	1924	3	0	0	0	0	0	0	0	3	0
CLARK, W.	1921–22	13	0	0	0	0	0	0	0	13	0
CLARKE, A.J.	1969–77	270/3	110	43/2	25	13	2	35	14	361/5	151
CLARKE, J.H.	1946	14	1	0	0	0	0	0	0	14	1
CLAYTON, A.S.	2010–11	42/5	6	1	0	3	0	0	0	46/5	6
COATES, W.A.	1921–22	47	3	3	1	0	0	0	0	50	4
COCHRANE, D.A.	1937–50	176	28	10	4	0	0	0	0	186	32
COCHRANE, T.	1928–36	244	23	15	4	0	0	0	0	259	27
COLLINS, N.	2009–10	29/1	0	0	0	2	0	0	0	31/1	0
COLLINS, R.Y.	1962–66	149	24	13	0	2	1	3	0	167	25
CONNOLLY, P.	2010–11	54/4	0	2	0	4	0	0	0	60/4	0
CONNOR, T.F.	1979–82	83/13	19	6	2	4/2	1	0	0	93/15	22
CONSTANTINE, L.	2007	1/3	1	0/2	0	0	0	1	1	2/5	2
COOPE, D.	1920	0	0	2	0	0	0	0	0	2	0
COOPER, G.F.	1920	0	0	2	0	0	0	0	0	2	0
COOPER, T.	1963–74	240/10	7	30/1	0	21	2	49	2	340/11	11
COPPING, W.	1930–39	174	4	9	0	0	0	0	0	183	4
COUTTS, T.	1927	1	0	0	0	0	0	0	0	1	0
COUZENS, A.	1993–96	17/11	1	0	0	4/1	1	0/2	0	21/14	2
COYNE, C.	1945	0	0	2	0	0	0	0	0	2	0
CRAINEY, S.D.	2004–06	51/1	0	2	0	6	0	2	0	63/1	0
CRESSWELL, R.P.W.	2005–06	30/8	9	0/2	0	1/1	2	0/2	0	31/13	11
CROWE, C.	1956–59	97	27	3	0	0	0	0	0	100	27
CROWE, J.W.R.	2009	16/1	0	3/1	0	3	0	3	2	25/2	2
CURRIE, A.W.	1976–78	102	11	9	0	13	5	0	0	124	16
CURTIS, A.	1979–80	28	5	1	0	2	0	4	1	35	6
CUSH, W.	1957–59	89	9	3	0	0	0	0	0	92	9
DA COSTA, G.P.M.	2007	0/4	0	0/1	0	0	0	1/1	0	1/6	0
DACOURT, O.N.A.	2000–02	53/4	3	1	0	2	0	22	0	78/4	3
DANIELS, J.F.C.	1934	1	0	0	0	0	0	0	0	1	0
DANSKIN, R.	1930–31	5	1	1	0	0	0	0	0	6	1
DARK, A.J.	1922	3	0	0	0	0	0	0	0	3	0

		LEAGUE		FA CUP		FL CUP		OTHERS		TOTAL	
Player	Played	App	Gls	App	Gls	App	Gls	App	Gls	App	Gls
DAVEY, N.G.	1967–70	13/1	0	1	0	2	0	4/2	0	20/3	0
DAVIES, B.	1953	1	0	0	0	0	0	0	0	1	0
DAVISON, R.	1987–91	79/12	30	2/4	1	4	1	7/2	3	92/18	35
DAWSON, R.	1953	1	0	0	0	0	0	0	0	1	0
DAY, M.R.	1984–92	227	0	11	0	14	0	11	0	268	0
DE MANGE, K.J.P.P.	1987	14/1	1	0	0	3	0	2	0	19/1	1
DEANE, B.C.	1993–96/2004	154/15	38	13/3	4	9/4	3	3	0	179/22	45
DELPH, F.	2006–08/2011	45/4	6	2	0	3/2	0	2/1	0	52/7	6
DEPEAR, E.R.	1948	4	0	1	0	0	0	0	0	5	0
DERRY, S.P.	2003–07	71	3	1/1	0	0/2	0	3	0	78/3	3
DE VRIES, M.	2007	1/5	1	0	0	0	0	2	0	3/5	1
DICKINSON, C.M.	2008	7	0	0	0	0	0	0	0	7	0
DICKINSON, L.M.	2008	4/4	0	0	0	0	0	0	0	4/4	0
DICKINSON, M.J.	1979–85	100/3	2	6	0	10	0	0	0	116/3	2
DICKOV, P.	2009	1/3	0	0	0	0	0	0	0	1/3	0
DOIG, R.	1986–87	3/3	0	1	0	1/2	0	0	0	5/5	0
DOMI, D.	2003	9/3	0	0	0	0/2	0	0	0	9/5	0
DONNELLY, J.	1982–84	36/4	4	1	0	3	0	0	0	40/4	4
DORIGO, A.R.	1991–96	168/3	5	16	0	12/1	0	9	1	205/4	6
DOWN, W.	1920–24	96	0	5	0	0	0	0	0	101	0
DOUGLAS, J.	2005–08	130/12	10	6	0	8/2	1	5/1	0	149/15	11
DOYLE, M.P.	2009	42	0	6	0	3	0	1	0	52	0
DUBERRY, M.W.	1999–2004	54/4	4	4/2	0	0/4	0	9/1	0	67/11	4
DUDLEY, F.E.	1949–50	64	23	7	4	0	0	0	0	71	27
DUFFIELD, A.	1920–25	203	0	8	0	0	0	0	0	211	0
DUGGAN, H.A.	1926–36	187	45	9	4	0	0	0	0	196	49
DUNDERDALE, W.L.	1938–39	4	0	0	0	0	0	0	0	4	0
DUNN, J.	1947–58	422	1	21	0	0	0	0	0	443	1
DUTHOIT, J.	1945	0	0	2	0	0	0	0	0	2	0
DUXBURY, T.	1924	2	0	0	0	0	0	0	0	2	0
EDWARDS, K.	1986	28/10	6	2/3	1	2	0	2/4	2	34/17	9
EDWARDS, M.K.	1971	0/1	0	0	0	0	0	0	0	0/1	0
EDWARDS, N.R.	1989	0	0	0	0	0	0	1	0	1	0
EDWARDS, W.	1948	2	0	0	0	0	0	0	0	2	0
EDWARDS, W.	1924–39	417	6	27	0	0	0	0	0	444	6
EHIOGU, U.	2006	6	1	0	0	0	0	0	0	6	1
EINARSSON, G.	2004–06	12/9	1	0/1	0	3	0	0	0	15/10	1
ELDING, A.L.	2007	4/5	1	0	0	0	0	0	0	4/5	1
ELI, R.	1984–85	1/1	0	0	0	0	0	0	0	1/1	0
ELLAM, R.	1972–73	9/2	0	2	0	2	0	6	0	19/2	0
ELLIOTT, R.J.	2006	5/2	0	1	0	0	0	0	0	6/2	0

		LEAGUE		FA CUP		FL CUP		OTHERS		TOTAL	
Player	Played	App	Gls	App	Gls	App	Gls	App	Gls	App	Gls
ELLIOTT, T.J.	2006–07	0/3	0	0	0	1	0	0	0	1/3	0
ELLSON, M.F.	1920–21	37	8	0	0	0	0	0	0	37	8
ENTWISTLE, W.P.	1979	7/4	2	0/1	0	0	0	0	0	7/5	2
EPHRAIM, H.P.	2009	1/2	0	0	0	0	0	1	0	2/2	0
EVANS, G.J.	2000	0/1	0	0	0	0	0	0/1	0	0/2	0
FAIRCLOUGH, C.H.	1988–94	187/6	21	14/1	0	17/2	2	14	0	232/9	23
FAULKNER, J.G.	1969	2	0	0	0	0	0	2	0	4	0
FAYE, A.M.	2010	6/2	0	0	0	0	0	0	0	6/2	0
FEARNLEY, H.L.	1946–48	28	0	1	0	0	0	0	0	29	0
FELL, J.W.	1925–26	13	1	0	0	0	0	0	0	13	1
FERDINAND, R.G.	2000–01	54	2	3	0	2	0	14	1	73	3
FIDLER, F.	1951–52	22	8	1	0	0	0	0	0	23	8
FINLAY, J.	1951	1	0	0	0	0	0	0	0	1	0
FIRM, N.J.	1979–81	11/1	0	0	0	0	0	0	0	11/1	0
FIRTH, J.	1928–34	72	25	3	0	0	0	0	0	75	25
FITZGERALD, P.J.	1960	8	0	0	0	0	0	0	0	8	0
FLO, T.A.	2006–07	5/18	4	0/1	0	0	0	0	0	5/19	4
FLYNN, B.	1977–82	152/2	11	6/1	0	12/1	0	4	0	174/4	11
FLYNN, P.	1953	1	0	0	0	0	0	0	0	1	0
FORD, M.S.	1993–96	27/2	1	5	0	7	0	0/1	0	39/3	1
FORREST, J.R.	1952–58	119	36	2	1	0	0	0	0	121	37
FORRESTER, J.M.	1992–94	7/2	0	1	2	0	0	0	0	8/2	2
FORSSELL, M.K.	2011	1/14	0	0/1	0	0/1	0	0	0	1/16	0
FOWLER, A.	1932–33	15	8	0	0	0	0	0	0	15	8
FOWLER, R.B.	2001–02	24/6	14	1/1	0	0	0	0/1	0	25/8	14
FOXE, H.V.	2006	12/6	1	1	0	2	0	0	0	15/6	1
FRANCIS, C.T.	1937	1	0	0	0	0	0	0	0	1	0
FRANCIS, G.	1959–61	46	9	1	0	3	0	0	0	50	9
FREEDMAN, D.A.	2007	9/2	5	0	0	0	0	3	1	12/2	6
FREW, J.H.	1920–23	96	0	3	0	0	0	0	0	99	0
FROST, D.	1949–50	10	2	0	0	0	0	0	0	10	2
FULLAM, R.	1923	7	2	0	0	0	0	0	0	7	2
FURNESS, W.I.	1929–36	243	62	14	4	0	0	0	0	257	66
GADSBY, K.J.	1936–47	81	0	6	0	0	0	0	0	87	0
GALVIN, C.J.	1969–72	6/1	1	0/2	0	1	0	4/2	1	11/5	2
GARDNER, S.A.	2007	1	0	0	0	1	0	0	0	2	0
GASCOIGNE, T.C.	1921–23	20	0	0	0	0	0	0	0	20	0
GAVIN, M.W.	1982–84	20/10	3	0	0	4/1	1	0	0	24/11	4
GIBSON, A.	1954–59	165	5	5	0	0	0	0	0	170	5
GILES, M.J.	1963–74	380/3	88	61	15	19	1	63/1	11	523/4	115
GOLDBERG, L.	1938–46	33	0	0	0	0	0	0	0	33	0

		LEAGUE		FA CUP		FL CUP		OTHERS		TOTAL	
Player	**Played**	**App**	**Gls**	**App**	**Gls**	**App**	**Gls**	**App**	**Gls**	**App**	**Gls**
GOLDTHORPE, E.H.	1920	6	2	0	0	0	0	0	0	6	2
GOODWIN, F.	1959–63	107	2	4	0	9	0	0	0	120	2
GRADEL, M.A.	2009-11	53/24	25	2	0	1/1	0	2/1	0	58/26	25
GRAHAM, A.	1977–82	222/1	37	12	3	22	4	3	3	259/1	47
GRAHAM, D.A.W.	2005	1/2	0	0	0	0	0	0	0	1/2	0
GRAINGER, C.	1960	33	5	1	0	3	1	0	0	37	6
GRAINGER, D.	1945–47	37	5	3	1	0	0	0	0	40	6
GRANVILLE, D.P.	1998	7/2	0	3	0	1	0	0/1	0	11/3	0
GRAVER, F.	1924	3	0	0	0	0	0	0	0	3	0
GRAY, A.D.	1995–97	13/9	0	0/2	0	3/1	0	0	0	16/12	0
GRAY, E.	1965–83	440/13	52	46/1	5	33/2	6	41/2	6	560/18	69
GRAY, F.T.	1972–84	328/6	27	27/1	3	30/1	4	12/2	1	397/10	35
GRAY, M.	2005–06	16	0	0	0	0	0	0	0	16	0
GRAYSON, S.N.	1988–91	2	0	0	0	0	0	1/1	0	3/1	0
GREEN, H.	1930–33	19	4	0	0	0	0	0	0	19	4
GREENHOFF, B.	1979–81	68/4	1	1	0	5	0	0	0	74/4	1
GREENHOFF, J.	1962–68	88/6	21	10/1	2	12	4	18/1	6	128/8	33
GREGAN, S.M.	2004–06	63/1	0	1	0	6	0	3	0	73/1	0
GRELLA, M.	2008–10	3/26	1	1/3	3	2/2	0	3/2	1	9/33	5
GRIBBEN, W.H.	1928	3	0	0	0	0	0	0	0	3	0
GRIFFIT, L.	2004	0/1	0	0	0	0	0	0	0	0/1	0
GRIFFITHS, J.M.	2005	0/2	0	0	0	0	0	0	0	0/2	0
GUPPY, S.A.	2004	1/2	1	0	0	1	0	0	0	2/2	1
HAALAND, A.R.	1997–99	57/17	8	5/1	0	3	0	7/2	0	72/20	8
HACKWORTH, A.	1999–2000	0	0	0	0	0/1	0	0/2	0	0/3	0
HADDOCK, P.M.	1986–91	106/12	1	6/2	0	9/2	0	9/1	0	130/17	1
HAIR, K.G.A.	1950–63	443	1	21	1	10	0	0	0	474	2
HALLE, G.	1996–98	65/5	4	8/1	0	3/1	0	2	0	78/7	4
HALLETT, T.	1962	0	0	0	0	1	0	0	0	1	0
HAMPSON, T.	1938	2	0	0	0	0	0	0	0	2	0
HAMPTON, P.J.	1972–79	63/5	2	5	1	5/1	0	3/1	0	76/7	3
HAMSON, G.	1979–85	126/8	3	10/1	1	4	0	2/1	0	142/10	4
HANKIN, R.	1976–79	82/1	32	1	0	15	3	4	1	102/1	36
HARDING, D.A.	2005	20	0	0	0	1	0	0	0	21	0
HARGREAVES, J.	1935–39	46	10	2	1	0	0	0	0	48	11
HARLE, D.	1985	3	0	0	0	0	0	0	0	3	0
HARRIS, C.S.	1974–81	124/30	26	5	2	7/7	1	1/3	0	137/40	29
HARRIS, J.	1922–25	126	14	8	0	0	0	0	0	134	14
HARRISON, P.	1949–51	65	9	2	0	0	0	0	0	67	9
HARRISON, R.	1949	2	0	0	0	0	0	0	0	2	0
HART, E.A.	1920–35	446	14	25	1	0	0	0	0	471	15

		LEAGUE		FA CUP		FL CUP		OTHERS		TOTAL	
Player	Played	App	Gls	App	Gls	App	Gls	App	Gls	App	Gls
HART, P.A.	1977–82	191	16	11	1	17	1	4	2	223	20
HARTE, I.P.	1995–2003	199/14	28	16/2	3	10/2	2	45	6	270/18	39
HARVEY, D.	1965–84	350	0	31	0	38	0	26/3	0	445/3	0
HASSELBAINK, J.F.	1997–98	66/3	34	9	5	5	2	4	1	84/3	42
HASTIE, J.K.G.	1952	4	2	0	0	0	0	0	0	4	2
HATELEY, M.W.	1996	5/1	0	0	0	0	0	0	0	5/1	0
HAWKINS, D.R.	1966–67	2	0	0	0	2	0	0	0	4	0
HAWKSBY, J.F.	1960–62	36	2	1	0	7	0	0	0	44	2
HAWLEY, J.E.	1978–79	30/3	16	3	0	6	1	0	0	39/3	17
HAY, D.J.	1999–2001	2/2	0	0	0	1	0	0/1	0	3/3	0
HEALY, D.J.	2004–06	81/29	29	3/1	2	3/1	0	1/1	0	88/32	31
HEATH, M.P.	2006–07	51/1	4	3	0	2	0	1/1	0	57/2	4
HEATON, W.H.	1946–48	59	6	1	0	0	0	0	0	60	6
HENDERSON, J.S.P.	1954–55	15	4	0	0	0	0	0	0	15	4
HENDERSON, T.W.	1962–63	24	2	6	0	4	0	0	0	34	2
HENDRIE, J.G.	1989	22/5	5	1	0	1	0	2	0	26/5	5
HENRY, G.R.	1938–46	44	4	3	1	0	0	0	0	47	5
HIBBITT, T.A.	1965–70	32/15	9	1	0	5	0	8/2	2	46/17	11
HIDEN, M.	1997–99	25/1	0	1	0	1	0	4	0	31/1	0
HIGGS, S.P.	2009–10	25	0	0	0	4	0	0	0	29	0
HILAIRE, V.M.	1988–89	42/3	6	2	0	3	1	2	0	49/3	7
HILL, G.	1920	7	0	1	0	0	0	0	0	8	0
HILTON, J.	1949	1	0	0	0	0	0	0	0	1	0
HINDLE, T.	1945–48	45	2	3	0	0	0	0	0	48	2
HIRD, K.	1978–83	165/16	19	6/2	2	7/1	0	3	0	181/19	21
HODGE, S.B.	1991–93	28/26	10	2/1	0	4/3	0	0/3	0	34/33	10
HODGKINSON, E.S.	1946–47	3	0	0	0	0	0	0	0	3	0
HODGSON, G.	1936–39	82	51	4	2	0	0	0	0	86	53
HODGSON, J.P.	1945–47	19	0	2	0	0	0	0	0	21	0
HOLLEY, T.	1936–48	164	1	5	0	0	0	0	0	169	1
HOPKIN, D.	1997–99	64/9	6	6	0	7	0	6/1	0	83/10	6
HORNBY, C.F.	1930–35	88	5	1	0	0	0	0	0	89	5
HORSFIELD, G.M.	2006	11/3	2	0	0	1	0	0	0	12/3	2
HOWARTH, J.T.	1921	45	19	1	0	0	0	0	0	46	19
HOWSON, J.M.	2006–11	157/28	23	13/1	1	11/3	1	11	3	192/32	28
HUCKERBY, D.C.	1999–2000	11/29	2	1/2	0	1/1	2	1/10	2	14/42	6
HUDSON, W.A.	1951	4	0	0	0	0	0	0	0	4	0
HUGHES, A.J.	2007–10	93/23	1	8/1	0	5/2	0	5/2	0	111/28	1
HUGHES, C.	1950–51	21	2	2	0	0	0	0	0	23	2
HUGHES, P.A.	1983–84	6	0	1	0	0	0	0	0	7	0
HULSE, R.W.	2004–05	45/7	18	2	1	1/1	0	3	1	51/8	20

		LEAGUE		FA CUP		FL CUP		OTHERS		TOTAL	
Player	**Played**	**App**	**Gls**	**App**	**Gls**	**App**	**Gls**	**App**	**Gls**	**App**	**Gls**
HUMPHREYS, A.	1959–61	40	0	1	0	3	0	0	0	44	0
HUMPHRIES, W.M.	1958–59	25	2	1	0	0	0	0	0	26	2
HUNTER, N.	1962–76	540	18	65/1	1	39	1	80/1	1	724/2	21
HUNTINGTON, P.D.	2007–09	16/5	1	2	0	3	0	6	1	27/5	2
HUTCHINSON, G.H.	1955	11	5	0	0	0	0	0	0	11	5
HYDES, A.	1930–36	127	74	10	8	0	0	0	0	137	82
IGGLEDEN, H.	1948–54	169	47	12	3	0	0	0	0	181	50
INGHAM, A.	1947–49	3	0	0	0	0	0	0	0	3	0
IRWIN, D.J.	1983–85	72	1	3	0	5	0	2	0	82	1
JACKLIN, H.	1921	3	0	2	0	0	0	0	0	5	0
JACKSON, M.G.	1995–99	11/8	0	4	0	0	0	0	0	15/8	0
JACKSON, W.	1925–26	38	2	1	0	0	0	0	0	39	2
JENNINGS, T.H.O.	1924–30	167	112	7	5	0	0	0	0	174	117
JOACHIM, J.K.	2004	10/17	2	0/1	0	3	0	0	0	13/18	2
JOBSON, R.	1995–97	22	1	1	0	3	0	0	0	26	1
JOHANNESON, A.	1960–69	170/2	48	14	5	8	6	5/1	8	197/3	67
JOHNSON, A.	2006	4/1	0	0	0	0	0	0	0	4/1	0
JOHNSON, B.P.	2007–10	91/26	16	6	1	5/2	0	5/5	0	107/33	17
JOHNSON, J.P.	2006	3/2	0	0	0	0	0	0	0	3/2	0
JOHNSON, R.	1964–67	18/4	4	1	1	6/1	1	0	0	25/5	6
JOHNSON, S.A.M.	2001–04	43/11	4	3/1	0	1	0	0	0	47/12	4
JOHNSON, S.A.	2000–04	3/8	0	0	0	1	0	0	0	4/8	0
JOHNSON, W.	1923–27	72	0	1	0	0	0	0	0	73	0
JONES, A.	1960–61	25	0	1	0	3	0	0	0	29	0
JONES, M.G.	1997–2000	11/12	0	0/2	0	1/1	0	4/2	0	16/17	0
JONES, M.D.	1967–73	216/4	77	36	12	13/1	5	43	17	308/5	111
JONES, V.P.	1989	44/2	5	1	0	2	0	4	0	51/2	5
JORDAN, J.	1971–77	139/30	35	16/3	4	9/1	3	19/4	6	183/38	48
KAMARA, C.	1989–91	15/5	1	0	0	1/2	0	1	0	17/7	1
KANDOL, T.O.	2006–09	43/26	14	2/1	1	2	0	2/3	1	49/30	16
KANE, R.	1935–46	58	0	3	0	0	0	0	0	61	0
KEANE, R.D.	2000–01	28/18	13	2	0	2	3	6	3	38/18	19
KEETLEY, C.F.	1927–34	160	108	9	2	0	0	0	0	169	110
KELLY, D.	1937	4	0	0	0	0	0	0	0	4	0
KELLY, G.O.	1991–06	419/11	2	31/1	2	28/2	0	38/1	0	516/15	4
KELLY, J.	1934–37	59	17	5	1	0	0	0	0	64	18
KELLY, J. 'Mick'	1934–35	4	0	0	0	0	0	0	0	4	0
KEMP, J.	1958	1	0	0	0	0	0	0	0	1	0
KENNEDY, D.	1969	2	1	0	0	0	0	1	0	3	1
KENTON, D.E.	2007	16	0	0	0	0	0	0	0	16	0
KEOGH, A.D.	2003/2011	17/5	2	0	0	2/1	0	0	0	19/6	2

Player	Played	LEAGUE		FA CUP		FL CUP		OTHERS		TOTAL	
		App	Gls	App	Gls	App	Gls	App	Gls	App	Gls
KERFOOT, E.	1949–58	336	9	13	1	0	0	0	0	349	10
KERR, D.	1988–90	6/7	0	1	0	2	0	0/4	0	9/11	0
KERSLAKE, D.	1992	8	0	0	0	0	0	0	0	8	0
KEWELL, H.	1995–2002	169/12	45	16	6	8	4	34/3	8	227/15	63
KILFORD, J.D.	1958–61	21	0	0	0	2	0	0	0	23	0
KILGALLON, M.S.	2003–06	73/7	3	4	0	6/1	0	3/1	0	86/9	3
KILKENNY, N.M.	2007–10	96/22	8	6	0	5/3	1	11/1	2	118/26	11
KING, M.F.	2004	4/5	0	0	0	0	0	0	0	4/5	0
KIRBY, D.	1947	8	0	0	0	0	0	0	0	8	0
KIRK, R.	1950–51	34	1	5	3	0	0	0	0	39	4
KIRKPATRICK, J.M.	1925–26	10	0	0	0	0	0	0	0	10	0
KISHISHEV, R.P.	2006–07	15/2	0	0	0	0	0	0	0	15/2	0
KISNORBO, P.F.M.	2009–11	47/1	1	3	0	3/1	0	0/1	0	53/3	1
KNARVIK, T.	1997–99	0	0	0/1	0	0	0	0	0	0/1	0
KORSTEN, W.	1997–98	4/3	2	2/1	0	0	0	0	0	6/4	2
LAMBERT, J.	1923	1	0	0	0	0	0	0	0	1	0
LAMPH, T.	1920	6	0	0	0	0	0	0	0	6	0
LANGLEY, E.J.	1952	9	3	0	0	0	0	0	0	9	3
LAURENT, P.	1996–97	2/2	0	0	0	0	0	0	0	2/2	0
LAWSON, F.I.	1961–64	44	17	3	1	4	3	0	0	51	21
LEES, T.J.	2011	41/1	2	1	0	1/1	0	0	0	43/2	2
LENNON, A.J.	2003–04	19/19	1	1/1	0	1/2	0	0	0	21/22	1
LETHERAN, G.	1974	1	0	0	0	0	0	0/1	0	1/1	0
LEWIS, E.J.	2005–07	82/2	8	3	0	4/1	0	3	1	92/3	9
LICHAJ, E.J.	2010	16	0	0	0	0	0	0	0	16	0
LIDDELL, G.	1972–74	2/1	0	0	0	1	0	1/1	1	4/2	1
LILLEY, D.S.	1996–98	4/17	1	0/1	0	0/3	0	0/1	0	4/22	1
LINIGHAN, A.	1984–85	66	3	2	0	6	1	2	0	76	4
LIVERMORE, J.C.	2010	4/1	0	0	0	0	0	0	0	4/1	0
LOMAS, A.	1948	1	0,	0	0	0	0	0	0	1	0
LONGDEN, E.	1928–30	28	7	0	0	0	0	0	0	28	7
LONERGAN, A.M.	2011	35	0	1	0	2	0	0	0	38	0
LORIMER, P.P.	1962–85	503/22	168	56/3	20	41/1	19	77/2	31	677/28	238
LOWRY, S.T.	2009	11	0	0	0	0	0	1	0	12	0
LUCAS, D.A.	2007–08	16	0	2/1	0	1	0	4	0	23/1	0
LUCIC, T.	2002	16/1	1	2/1	0	1	0	0	0	19/2	1
LUKIC, J.	1978–82/90–95	355	0	28	0	30	0	18	0	431	0
LUMSDEN, J.	1966–69	3/1	0	0	0	0	0	0	0	3/1	0
LYDON, G.M.	1954	4	1	0	0	0	0	0	0	4	1
LYON, J.	1920	33	2	0	0	0	0	0	0	33	2
McADAM, D.F.	1948–49	24	0	0	0	0	0	0	0	24	0

		LEAGUE		FA CUP		FL CUP		OTHERS		TOTAL	
Player	Played	App	Gls	App	Gls	App	Gls	App	Gls	App	Gls
McADAMS, W.J.	1961	11	3	2	1	0	0	0	0	13	4
McALLISTER, G.	1990–95	230/1	31	24	6	26	4	14	4	294/1	45
McCABE, J.J.	1947–53	152	0	9	0	0	0	0	0	161	0
McCALL, A.	1952–54	62	8	2	0	0	0	0	0	64	8
McCARTHY A.S.	2011	6	0	0	0	0	0	0	0	6	0
McCARTNEY, G.	2010	32	0	0	0	0	0	0	0	32	0
McCLELLAND, J.	1988–89	22/2	0	2	0	2/1	0	0	0	26/3	0
McCLUSKEY, G.M.C.	1983–85	57/16	16	4	0	5/3	1	1	0	67/19	17
McCOLE, J.	1959–61	78	45	2	1	5	7	0	0	85	53
McCONNELL, P.	1958–61	49	4	2	0	3	1	0	0	54	5
McCORMACK, R.L.M.	2010–11	48/18	20	0/1	0	3	1	0	0	51/19	21
McDONALD, R.W.	1986–87	18	1	0	0	1	0	5	0	24	1
McDOUGALL, J.	1934–36	52	0	7	1	0	0	0	0	59	1
McGEE, J.	1920	0	0	1	0	0	0	0	0	1	0
McGHIE, W.L.	1976	2	1	0	0	0	0	0	0	2	1
McGINLEY, W.D.	1972	0/1	0	0	0	0	0	0/1	0	0/2	0
McGOLDRICK, J.	1983	7	0	3	0	2	0	0	0	12	0
McGOVERN, J.P.	1974	4	0	0	0	0	0	0	0	4	0
McGREGOR, J.R.	1985	5	0	0	0	0	0	0	0	5	0
McGUGAN, J.H.	1960	1	0	0	0	0	0	0	0	1	0
McINROY, A.	1935–36	67	0	4	0	0	0	0	0	71	0
McKENNA, F.	1956	6	4	0	0	0	0	0	0	6	4
McKENZIE, D.	1974–75	64/2	27	6/3	2	5	1	1/1	0	76/6	30
McMASTER, J.	1999–2004	0/11	0	0	0	1/1	0	0	0	1/12	0
McMORRAN, E.J.	1948–49	38	6	2	0	0	0	0	0	40	6
McNAB, N.	1982	5	0	1	0	0	0	0	0	6	0
McNEISH, S.	1950	1	0	0	0	0	0	0	0	1	0
McNESTRY, G.	1928	3	0	0	0	0	0	0	0	3	0
McNIVEN, D.S.	1975–77	15/7	6	0	0	1	0	0	0	16/7	6
McPHAIL, S.J.P.	1996–2003	52/26	3	3	0	2/4	0	15/4	0	72/34	3
McQUEEN, G.	1972–77	140	15	13	1	5	0	13/1	3	171/1	19
McSHEFFREY, G.	2009	9/1	1	0	0	0	0	1	0	10/1	1
MADDEN, S.	2007	0	0	0	0	0	0	1	0	1	0
MADELEY, P.E.	1963–80	528/8	25	64/3	2	49/1	3	71/1	4	712/13	34
MAGUIRE, P.J.	1987	2	0	0	0	0	0	0	0	2	0
MAHON, J.	1931–35	78	20	6	3	0	0	0	0	84	23
MAKINSON, J.	1935–39	68	0	2	0	0	0	0	0	70	0
MANGNALL, D.	1929	9	6	0	0	0	0	0	0	9	6
MANN, J.A.	1971–72	2	0	0	0	0/1	0	2	0	4/1	0
MARQUES, R.M.	2005–09	85/5	4	3	0	4	0	2	0	94/5	4
MARSDEN, J.	1952–58	71	0	4	0	0	0	0	0	75	0

Player	Played	LEAGUE App	LEAGUE Gls	FA CUP App	FA CUP Gls	FL CUP App	FL CUP Gls	OTHERS App	OTHERS Gls	TOTAL App	TOTAL Gls
MARSH, C.	1948	4	1	1	0	0	0	0	0	5	1
MARTIN, C.J.	1946–48	47	1	2	0	0	0	0	0	49	1
MARTIN, D.E.	2009	0	0	0	0	0	0	1	0	1	0
MARTIN, G.	1960	0	0	0	0	1	0	0	0	1	0
MARTIN, J.	1924	2	0	0	0	0	0	0	0	2	0
MARTYN, A.N.	1996–2002	207	0	18	0	12	0	36	0	273	0
MASINGA, P.R.	1994–95	20/11	5	3/2	4	3	2	0	0	26/13	11
MASON, C.E.	1961–62	31	0	0	0	2	0	0	0	33	0
MASON, G.	1920–22	65	6	1	0	0	0	0	0	66	6
MASON, R.	1923–24	16	0	0	0	0	0	0	0	16	0
MATTEO, D.	2000–03	115	2	7	0	2	0	23	2	147	4
MATTHEWS, L.J.	1995–97	0/3	0	0	0	0	0	0	0	0/3	0
MAYBURY, A.P.	1995–2001	10/4	0	2	0	1	0	1	0	14/4	0
MAYERS, D.	1961	20	5	2	0	2	0	0	0	24	5
MEARS, F.	1925–26	2	0	1	0	0	0	0	0	3	0
MEEK, G.	1952–59	196	19	4	0	0	0	0	0	200	19
MELROSE, J.M.	1987	3/1	0	0/1	0	0/1	0	0	0	3/3	0
MENZIES, W.J.	1923–31	248	1	10	1	0	0	0	0	258	2
MICHALIK, L.	2006–09	46/10	2	6/1	0	5	0	8	0	65/11	2
MILBURN, G.W.	1928–36	158	1	9	0	0	0	0	0	167	1
MILBURN, Jack	1929–38	385	28	22	2	0	0	0	0	407	30
MILBURN, Jim	1939–51	208	15	12	2	0,	0	0	0	220	17
MILLER, E.G.	1950–51	13	1	1	0	0	0	0	0	14	1
MILLER, L.W.M.	2005	26/2	1	2	0	0	0	3	0	31/2	1
MILLS, D.J.	1999–2003	96/5	3	6/1	0	4	1	27/2	0	133/8	4
MILLS, D.G.	1951–52	34	9	3	1	0	0	0	0	37	10
MILLS, F.	1934–38	67	2	3	0	0	0	0	0	70	2
MILNER, J.P.	2002–03	28/20	5	1/4	0	1	0	0	0	30/24	5
MITCHELL, R.G.	1958	4	0	0	0	0	0	0	0	4	0
MITCHELL, T.M.	1926–30	142	19	10	2	0	0	0	0	152	21
MOLENAAR, R.	1996–2000	47/4	5	5	1	4/1	0	4	0	60/5	6
MOLLATT, R.V.	1951–54	17	0	0	0	0	0	0	0	17	0
MOORE, I.R.	2004–06	21/39	2	1	0	3/3	3	0	0	25/42	5
MOORE, J.	1921	27	4	1	0	0	0	0	0	28	4
MOORE, S.	1931–34	78	0	5	0	0	0	0	0	83	0
MOORE, W.R.	1924	6	0	0	0	0	0	0	0	6	0
MORRIS, J.S.	2003	11/1	0	0	0	0	0	0	0	11/1	0
MORTON, N.	1947	1	0	0	0	0	0	0	0	1	0
MOSS, J.	1948–50	23	2	0	0	0	0	0	0	23	2
MUMBY, P.	1987–88	3/3	0	0	0	0/2	1	0	0	3/5	1
MURRAY, T.	1960	7	2	0	0	0	0	0	0	7	2

		LEAGUE		FA CUP		FL CUP		OTHERS		TOTAL	
Player	**Played**	**App**	**Gls**	**App**	**Gls**	**App**	**Gls**	**App**	**Gls**	**App**	**Gls**
MUSGROVE, R.	1920	36	2	0	0	0	0	0	0	36	2
NAYLOR, R.A.	2008–10	64/2	4	2	0	0	0	7	0	73/2	4
NEAL, T.W.	1931–35	20	0	3	0	0	0	0	0	23	0
NEWSOME, J.	1991–93	62/14	3	3/1	0	3	0	5	0	73/15	3
NICHOLLS, K.J.R.	2006	12/1	0	1	0	1	0	0	0	14/1	0
NIGHTINGALE, A.	1952–56	130	48	5	0	0	0	0	0	135	48
NIMMO, W.R.	1957	1	0	0	0	0	0	0	0	1	0
NOBLE, A.H.	1922–24	60	4	3	0	0	0	0	0	63	4
NOTEMAN, K.S.	1988–89	0/1	0	0	0	0	0	1	1	1/1	1
NUNEZ, R.F.	2010–11	6/12	1	1	0	2/1	4	0	0	9/13	5
O'BRIEN, A.J.	2010–11	32/2	2	2	0	2	0	0	0	36/2	2
O'BRIEN, G.	1956–58	43	6	0	0	0	0	0	0	43	6
O'DEA D.	2011	35	2	1	0	2	0	0	0	38	2
O'DOHERTY, E.F.J.	1920	0	0	2	4	0	0	0	0	2	4
O'DONNELL, C.	1989–90	0/1	0	0	0	0	0	0	0	0/1	0
O'GRADY, H.	1932	8	2	1	0	0	0	0	0	9	2
O'GRADY, M.	1965–69	90/1	12	5	1	5	0	20	3	120/1	16
O'HARE, J.	1974	6	1	0	0	1	0	0	0	7	1
OKON, P.M.	2002	15	0	5	0	0	0	1	0	21	0
O'LEARY, D.A.	1993–95	10	0	0	0	0	0	0	0	10	0
OLEMBE, S.R.	2003	8/4	0	0	0	2	0	0	0	10/4	0
O'NEILL, J.	1973	0	0	0	0	0/1	0	0/2	0	0/3	0
ORMEROD, B.R.	2004	6	0	0	0	0	0	0	0	6	0
ORMSBY, B.T.C.	1985–89	46	5	4	1	1	0	6	1	57	7
OSTER, J.M.	2004	8	1	0	0	0	0	0	0	8	1
OVERFIELD, J.	1955–59	159	20	4	0	0	0	0	0	163	20
PALMER, C.L.	1994–96	100/2	5	12	1	12	0	4	1	128/2	7
PARKER, B.B.C.	2007–11	32/7	0	6	1	5	0	5	0	48/7	1
PARKER, N.	1977	0/1	0	0	0	0	0	0	0	0/1	0
PARKINSON, K.J.	1977–80	25/6	0	1	0	4	0	2	0	32/6	0
PARLANE, D.J.	1979–82	45/5	10	2	0	1	0	0	0	48/5	10
PARRY, W.	1938	6	0	2	0	0	0	0	0	8	0
PAYNTER, W.P.	2010-11	10/17	3	1	0	0	0	0	0	11/17	3
PEACOCK, A.	1963–66	54	27	6	2	2	1	3	1	65	31
PEARSON, J.S.	1986–90	51/48	12	5/5	0	5/4	0	6/3	0	67/60	12
PEMBERTON, J.M.	1993–96	44/9	0	5/2	0	3/1	0	4	0	56/12	0
PENNANT, J.L.	2003–04	34/2	2	0	0	0	0	0	0	34/2	2
PETERSON, P.W.	1969	3/1	0	0	0	0	0	0	0	3/1	0
PEYTON, N.	1957–62	104	17	3	1	9	2	0	0	116	20
PHELAN, T.M.	1985	12/2	0	0	0	3	0	2	0	17/2	0
POTTS, J.F.	1925–32	247	0	15	0	0	0	0	0	262	0

		LEAGUE		FA CUP		FL CUP		OTHERS		TOTAL	
Player	**Played**	**App**	**Gls**	**App**	**Gls**	**App**	**Gls**	**App**	**Gls**	**App**	**Gls**
POTTS, J.	1921–22	10	0	0	0	0	0	0	0	10	0
POWELL, A.	1936–47	112	25	5	0	0	0	0	0	117	25
POWELL, S.	1920–24	28	7	0	0	0	0	0	0	28	7
POYNTZ, W.I.	1921–22	29	7	0	0	0	0	0	0	29	7
PRICE, A.	1945–46	6	0	1	0	0	0	0	0	7	0
PRUTTON, D.T.M.	2007–09	47/18	4	1	0	3	0	8/1	0	59/19	4
PUGH, D.A.	2004–05/11	65/19	7	1/1	0	6	1	0	0	72/20	8
RACHUBKA, P.S.	2011	5/1	0	0	0	0	0	0	0	5/1	0
RADEBE, L.V.	1994–2004	180/20	0	19/2	1	9/5	0	27	2	235/27	3
REANEY, P.	1962–77	549/7	6	72/1	3	39	0	76/3	0	736/11	9
REED, G.	1925–29	141	2	9	1	0	0	0	0	150	3
RENNIE, D.	1985–88	95/6	5	7	1	7	0	4	1	113/6	7
REVIE, D.G.	1958–61	77	11	1	0	3	1	0	0	81	12
RIBEIRO, B.M.F.	1997–99	35/7	4	4	1	3/1	1	1/1	0	43/9	6
RICHARDSON, F.	1999–2008	122/27	3	5	0	11	1	7/1	1	145/28	5
RICHMOND, J.	1922–24	56	19	4	0	0	0	0	0	60	19
RICKETTS, M.B.	2004–05	10/15	0	0	0	3/1	2	0	0	13/16	2
RILEY, V.	1926	0	0	1	0	0	0	0	0	1	0
RIPLEY, S.K.	1954–57	69	15	2	0	0	0	0	0	71	15
RITCHIE, A.T.	1982–86	127/9	40	9	1	11	3	2/1	0	149/10	44
ROBERTS, H.	1925–30	84	2	3	0	0	0	0	0	87	2
ROBERTSON, D.	1997–2000	24	0	1	0	4	0	0	0	29	0
ROBINSON,, A.M.	2008–09	20/18	2	2	1	3/1	2	3/3	2	28/22	7
ROBINSON, D.	1926–27	5	0	0	0	0	0	0	0,	5	0
ROBINSON, P.P.	2011	9/1	0	0	0	0	0	0	0	9/1	0
ROBINSON, P.W.	1997–2003	93/2	0	7	0	5	1	12	0	117/2	1
ROBINSON, R.	1985–86	27	0	0	0	0	0	0	0	27	0
ROBSON, C.	1924	17	4	0	0	0	0	0	0	17	4
ROBSON, W.	1921–22	10	0	1	0	0	0	0	0	11	0
ROCASTLE, D.C.	1992–93	17/8	2	0/3	0	0/3	0	2/1	0	19/15	2
RODGERSON, R.	1920–21	27	0	1	0	0	0	0	0	28	0
ROGERS, R.H.	2011	1/3	0	0	0	0	0	0	0	1/3	0
ROPER, H.	1932–34	18	3	0	0	0	0	0	0	18	3
ROQUE JUNIOR, J.V.	2003	5	0	0	0	2	2	0	0	7	2
ROSS, R.A.	1951	5	0	0	0	0	0	0	0	5	0
RUDD, J.J.	1948–49	18	1	0	0	0	0	0	0	18	1
RUSH, I.J.	1996	34/2	3	2/2	0	2	0	0	0	38/4	3
RUSSELL, D.P.	1924	9	0	0	0	0	0	0	0	9	0
SABELLA, A.	1980	22/1	2	2	0	2	0	0	0	26/1	2
SAKHO, L.	2003–04	9/8	1	0/1	0	1	0	0	0	10/9	1
SAM, L.E.	2010–11	10/25	2	0/1	0	3	1	0	0	13/26	3

Player	Played	LEAGUE App	LEAGUE Gls	FA CUP App	FA CUP Gls	FL CUP App	FL CUP Gls	OTHERS App	OTHERS Gls	TOTAL App	TOTAL Gls
SAVAGE, R.	1934–38	79	0	5	0	0	0	0	0	84	0
SCAIFE, G.	1938	9	0	0	0	0	0	0	0	9	0
SCHMEICHEL, K.P.	2010	37	0	2	0	1	0	0	0	40	0
SCOTT, J.A.	1950–54	110	0	3	0	0	0	0	0	113	0
SEARSON, H.V.	1948–51	104	0	12	0	0	0	0	0	116	0
SELLARS, S.	1982–85/92	78/5	12	4	0	5/1	1	3	1	90/6	14
SHACKLETON, A.	1958–59	30	16	1	1	0	0	0	0	31	17
SHARP, K.P.	1992–94	11/6	0	0	0	0	0	0/1	0	11/7	0
SHARPE, I.G.	1920	1	0	0	0	0	0	0	0	1	0
SHARPE, L.S.	1996–98	28/2	5	0/1	0	3	1	1/2	0	32/5	6
SHEEHAN, A.M.A.	2007–08	21	2	1	0	1	0	0/1	0	23/1	2
SHAW, J.	1971–73	0	0	0	0	0	0	2	0	2	0
SHEPHERD, P.D.	1996	1	0	0	0	0	0	0	0	1	0
SHERIDAN, J.J.	1982–88	225/5	47	11/1	1	14	3	11	1	261/6	52
SHERWIN, H.	1921–24	99	2	9	0	0	0	0	0	108	2
SHORT, J.D.	1946–48	60	18	3	1	0	0	0	0	63	19
SHOWUNMI, E.O.	2008–09	3/12	2	0/3	0	2/4	3	2/2	1	7/21	6
SHUTT, C.S.	1988–92	46/33	17	10	1	6/2	2	4/5	4	66/40	24
SIBBALD, R.L.	1966–67	1/1	0	0	0	0	0	0	0	1/1	0
SIMMONDS, R.L.	1984–86	6/3	3	0	0	0	0	1/1	0	7/4	3
SINCLAIR, R.M.	1985–88	8	0	0	0	1	0	0	0	9	0
SISSONS, A.E.	1925–27	30	1	1	0	0	0	0	0	31	1
SMELT, A.	1920	1	0	1	0	0	0	0	0	2	0
SMITH, A.	1998–2003	148/24	38	11/4	4	4/2	0	28/7	14	191/37	56
SMITH, A.J.	2011	3	0	0	0	0	0	0	0	3	0
SMITH, J.B.	1952	2	1	0	0	0	0	0	0	2	1
SMITH, J.E.	1960–62	65	3	3	0	4	0	0	0	72	3
SMITH, L.	1922–25	33	0	1	0	0	0	0	0	34	0
SNODGRASS, R	2008–11	141/25	35	9/1	1	7	4	8	1	165/26	41
SNODIN, G.	1987–91	83/11	10	5/2	0	9/1	3	5	0	102/14	13
SNODIN, I.	1985–86	51	6	1	0	3	2	0	0	55	8
SODJE, S.O.	2008	5	0	0	0	0	0	2	0	7	0
SOMMA, D.E.	2009–10	12/17	11	0/2	0	1	1	0/1	0	13/20	12
SPEAK, G.	1923–24	28	0	4	0	0	0	0	0	32	0
SPEED, G.A.	1988–95	231/17	39	21	5	25/1	11	14/3	2	291/21	57
SPRAKE, G.	1961–72	380	0	45	0	22	0	58/2	0	505/2	0
SPRING, M.J.	2004	4/9	1	0	0	2	0	0	0	6/9	1
SPROSTON, B.	1933–37	130	1	10	0	0	0	0	0	140	1
STACEY, A.	1927–33	51	0	0	0	0	0	0	0	51	0
STACK, G.C.	2006	12	0	0	0	0	0	0	0	12	0
STEPHENSON, J.E.	1934–39	111	21	4	1	0	0	0	0	115	22

		LEAGUE		FA CUP		FL CUP		OTHERS		TOTAL	
Player	Played	App	Gls	App	Gls	App	Gls	App	Gls	App	Gls
STERLAND, M.	1989–93	111/2	16	10	1	13	1	9	2	143/2	20
STEVENSON, E.	1950–51	16	5	0	0	0	0	0	0	16	5
STEVENSON, W.B.	1974–81	88/7	4	5	0	7/1	1	2	0	102/8	5
STEWART, D.S.	1973–78	55	0	8	0	6	0	5	0	74	0
STEWART, J.G.	1951–52	9	2	2	0	0	0	0	0	11	2
STILES, J.C.	1984–88	49/16	2	5	1	4/2	0	3/2	0	61/20	3
STONE, S.B.	2005–06	6/6	1	0	0	1	0	0/2	0	7/8	1
STORRIE, J.	1962–66	123/3	58	12	3	8	5	10	1	153/3	67
STRACHAN, G.D.	1988–94	188/9	37	14	2	18	3	14/1	3	234/10	45
STRANDLI, F.	1992–93	5/9	2	1	0	0/1	0	0	0	6/10	2
STUART, G.E.	1920	1	0	2	0	0	0	0	0	3	0
SULLIVAN, N.	2003–06	95	0	4	0	8	0	3	0	110	0
SUTHERLAND, H.R.	1938	3	1	0	0	0	0	0	0	3	1
SWAN, J.	1921–24	108	47	8	3	0	0	0	0	116	50
SWAN, P.H.	1985–88	43/6	11	3	0	3	2	1/2	0	50/8	13
SWEENEY, P.H.	2007	6/3	0	0	0	0	0	0	0	6/3	0
SWINBURNE, T.	1985	2	0	0	0	0	0	0	0	2	0
TAYLOR, C.J.	2011	2	0	0	0	0/2	0	0	0	2/2	0
TAYLOR, F.G.	1949	3	0	0	0	0	0	0	0	3	0
TAYLOR, J.B.	1951	11	0	0	0	0	0	0	0	11	0
TAYLOR, J.R.	1985–88	33/9	9	1	0	5/1	3	4/1	1	43/11	13
TELFER, P.N.	2008	14	0	2	0	2	0	0	0	18	0
THOM, J.	1924	7	3	0	0	0	0	0	0	7	3
THOMAS, D.G.	1979–83	79/11	3	4/1	0	9	0	0	0	92/12	3
THOMAS, M.R.	1989	3	0	0	0	0	0	0	0	3	0
THOMPSON, A.	2006–07	18/6	5	0	0	0	0	1	0	19/6	5
THOMPSON, N.D.	1983–86	6/1	0	0	0	2	0	1/1	0	9/2	0
THOMPSON, R.	1920	23	11	2	1	0	0	0	0	25	12
THOMPSON, Z.	2011	7/2	0	1	0	1	0	0	0	9/2	0
THOMSON, J.	1936–38	41	11	0	0	0	0	0	0	41	11
THORNTON, R.G.	1925	1	0	0	0	0	0	0	0	1	0
TILLOTSON, A.	1920	2	0	0	0	0	0	0	0	2	0
TINKLER, M.R.	1991–96	14/11	0	0	0	1	0	0/1	0	15/12	0
TONER, J.	1954	7	1	0	0	0	0	0	0	7	1
TOWNSEND, A.D.	2011	5/1	1	1	0	0	0	0	0	6/1	1
TOWNSLEY, T.	1925–30	159	2	8	0	0	0	0	0	167	2
TRAINOR, J.	1936	3	0	1	0	0	0	0	0	4	0
TRUNDLE, L.C.	2008	7/3	1	0	0	0	0	0	0	7/3	1
TURNBULL, R.	1925–31	204	45	11	1	0	0	0	0	215	46
TURNER, C.J.	1933–34	13	0	0	0	0	0	0	0	13	0
TURNER, C.R.	1989	2	0	0	0	0	0	0	0	2	0

		LEAGUE		FA CUP		FL CUP		OTHERS		TOTAL	
Player	Played	App	Gls	App	Gls	App	Gls	App	Gls	App	Gls
TURNER, J.K.	1935–37	14	0	0	0	0	0	0	0	14	0
TWOMEY, J.F.	1937–48	110	0	2	0	0	0	0	0	112	0
TYRER, A.S.	1951–53	39	4	3	0	0	0	0	0	42	4
UNDERWOOD, B.	1928–30	6	0	0	0	0	0	0	0	6	0
VARADI, I.	1989–92	21/5	5	0	0	1	0	1/1	1	23/6	6
VARYRYNEN, M.	2011	2/8	0	1	0	0/1	0	0	0	3/9	0
VICKERS, P.	1950–55	20	4	1	0	0	0	0	0	21	4
VIDUKA, M.A.	2000–03	126/4	59	8	5	3	1	25	7	162/4	72
VOKES, S.M.	2009	8	1	0	0	0	0	1/1	0	9/1	1
WAINSCOAT, W.R.	1925–31	215	87	11	6	0	0	0	0	226	93
WAKEFIELD, A.J.	1947–48	49	23	1	0	0	0	0	0	50	23
WALLACE, R.G.	1991–93	5/2	0	0	0	0	0	0	0	5/2	0
WALLACE, R.S.	1991–97	187/25	53	16/5	4	18/1	8	1/4	1	222/35	66
WALTON, J.	1920–22	69	4	2	0	0	0	0	0	71	4
WALTON, S.W.	2004–05	26/8	3	2	0	1/1	0	0	0	29/9	3
WARNER, A.R.	2006	13	0	0	0	1	0	0	0	14	0
WATERHOUSE, F.	1920	0	0	2	1	0	0	0	0	2	1
WATSON, A.	1983–84	37/1	7	1	0	4	0	0	0	42/1	7
WATT, H.O.S.	2009–10	10/18	1	2	0	1/1	0	0	0	13/19	1
WEBB, J.P.	2008	0	0	0/1	0	0	0	0	0	0/1	0
WEBB, R.	1953–54	3	0	0	0	0	0	0	0	3	0
WEBBER, D.V	2011	2/11	1	0	0	0	0	0	0	2/11	1
WESTLAKE, I.J.	2006–07	29/18	1	1	0	2/1	1	1	0	33/19	2
WESTON, C.J.	2007	1/6	1	1/1	0	0/1	0	1	0	3/8	1
WESTON, D.P.	1962–65	68	24	7	1	3	1	0	0	78	26
WETHERALL, D.	1991–98	188/14	12	21/3	4	19/1	2	4	0	232/18	18
WHALLEY, F.H.	1921–23	87	0	4	0	0	0	0	0	91	0
WHARTON, C.N.	1939	2	0	0	0	0	0	0	0	2	0
WHEATLEY, T.	1953	6	0	0	0	0	0	0	0	6	0
WHELAN, N.D.	1993–95	28/20	7	2	0	3/2	1	3	0	36/22	8
WHIPP, P.L.	1922–26	145	44	9	3	0	0	0	0	154	47
WHITE, A.P.	2008-11	45/6	0	2/5	0	3/2	0	3	0	53/13	0
WHITE, D.	1993–95	28/14	9	6	2	2	0	1/1	0	37/15	11
WHITE, J.	1926–29	102	36	6	2	0	0	0	0	108	38
WHITLOW, M.W.	1988–91	62/15	4	0/4	0	4/1	0	9	0	75/20	4
WHYTE, C.A.	1990–92	113	5	8	0	14/1	1	11	0	146/1	6
WHYTE, D.	1976	1/1	0	0	0	0	0	0	0	1/1	0
WIJNHARD, C.	1998	11/7	3	1/1	1	1	0	1/3	0	14/11	4
WILCOCKSON, E.S.	1934	4	0	0	0	0	0	0	0	4	0
WILCOX, J.M.	1999–2003	52/29	4	5/1	0	3	0	9/6	2	69/36	6
WILKINS, E.G.	1949	3	0	0	0	0	0	0	0	3	0

		LEAGUE		FA CUP		FL CUP		OTHERS		TOTAL	
Player	**Played**	**App**	**Gls**	**App**	**Gls**	**App**	**Gls**	**App**	**Gls**	**App**	**Gls**
WILKINSON, C.E.	1931	3	0	0	0	0	0	0	0	3	0
WILLIAMS, A.	1988–91	25/21	3	2	0	3/3	0	5/2	2	35/26	5
WILLIAMS, G.	1987–89	39	3	1/1	0	4	0	0	0	44/1	3
WILLIAMS, H.	1949–55	210	32	17	3	0	0	0	0	227	35
WILLIAMS, J.	1948	1	0	0	0	0	0	0	0	1	0
WILLIAMSON, B.W.	1962	5	0	1	0	2	0	0	0	8	0
WILLINGHAM, C.K.	1946	34	0	1	0	0	0	0	0	35	0
WILLIS, J.G.	1953	3	0	0	0	0	0	0	0	3	0
WILSON, G.M.	1928	3	0	0	0	0	0	0	0	3	0
WILSON, J.	1928	3	0	1	0	0	0	0	0	4	0
WINDLE, W.H.	1947	2	0	0	0	0	0	0	0	2	0
WOOD, B.	1920–21	56	2	0	0	0	0	0	0	56	2
WOOD, R.	1953–59	197	0	7	0	0	0	0	0	204	0
WOODGATE, J.S.	1997–2002	100/4	4	11	0	7	0	20	0	138/4	4
WOODS, M.P.	2002–03	0/1	0	0	0	0	0	0	0	0/1	0
WORSLEY, H.	1934	3	0	0	0	0	0	0	0	3	0
WORTHINGTON, F.S.	1981–82	32	14	0	0	3	1	0	0	35	15
WORTHINGTON, N.	1994–95	33/10	1	6/1	0	4/1	0	0	0	43/12	1
WRIGHT, A.G.	2006	1	0	0	0	0	0	0	0	1	0
WRIGHT, B.	1962–63	5	0	0	0	3	0	0	0	8	0
WRIGHT, J.M.	2004–05	36/2	3	1	0	1	0	0	0	38/2	3
WRIGHT, R.W.	1960	1	0	0	0	1	0	0	0	2	0
WRIGHT, T.E.	1982–86	73/8	24	4	3	3/3	1	0/1	0	80/12	28
YEBOAH, A.	1994–96	44/3	24	6/2	2	7	3	4	3	61/5	32
YORATH, T.C.	1967–76	121/20	10	14/3	1	10/1	0	20/7	1	165/31	12
YOUNGER, T.	1961–62	37	0	2	0	3	0	0	0	42	0
Own-Goal Totals			105		13		5		2		125
Totals		**39325/2376**	**5270**	**2684/174**	**394**	**1804/192**	**269**	**2101/218**	**307**	**45914/2960**	**6305**

Roll of Honour

Christopher Probert
Timothy Court
Bernard McNulty
Anthony Oates
Michael Garlick
Andrew Learmonth
Mr. John King
Terry Mosley
Trevor Wilks
David John Firth
Michael J. Wilkinson
James Bradley
Russell Vernon
Paul Bly
David Young
Andrew J. Marston
John Webster
Maurice Whitbread
Ryan Southwart
Stephen R. Thompson
Phillip Bell
Mrs. Yvonne M. Fearn
David Rock
David Hunter
Andrew Nettleton
John M. Rogers
Mick Townend Bramley
Mr. Ken Claybrough
Ian & Simon Ward (Thorner)
Pete Hill
Richard Bradley
Steve Dixon
W. L. Peel

Mathew Pounder
Andrew Potter
LeBron Edward Kemp
Aaron Taylor
Mr. Robert Scott Gray
Shirley Ellis
Harvey Briggs
Barrie Williamson
Christopher M. Child
Brian Victor Bentley
John C. Crossland
Keith Atkinson
Mr. Ian Taylor
Graham Brown
Alwyne Fisher
LUFC Talk
Örjan Hansson
Alan Benn
Martyn Jerome Phillips
Graeme Clive Brumwell
Tom Wilkinson-Pycock
Ray Harding
Andrew Hall
Michael Colledge
Andrew W. Green
Eric Drummond
Alan Swan
Niel Hudson
Ian Pickles
Lynn Stephens
John C. Hird
Andrew Scully
Gareth Jones
David Gatenby
Neil Metchette
Paul Anthony Holroyd
Andy Holmes
Shaun Matthew Wager

Roger B. Seaton
Frank Lister
Malcolm John Sharp
Kristian McMullan
Robert Sumner
Stephen Swalwell
Neil Hodgson
Chris Hodgson
Christopher Swales
Michael A. Tabor
Paul Christopher
Paul Martin
Terry Walls
Mark Sweeney
David F. Johnson
Adam B. Johnson
Anthony Thornton
David Ian Hallett
Oakley Cannonier
R. E. Rook
Paul James Gibbs
Lee Bland
Liam Binks
Raymond Arthur Probert
Timothy Johnson
Patrick Brady
Danilo "Dan" Ronzani (BO)
Billy Rae
Max Shellabear
E. D. & M. Froud
Steve Caron
James Caron
Matthew Caron
Daniel Caron
Mark Roberts
Brooke Roberts
Jude Roberts
Eva Roberts

Richard Michael Roberts
John McDermott
Sam Gibbard
David Paulger
Mari de-Laat
Simon Turnpenny
Kevin Pattison
Bob Dunning
Paul Willis